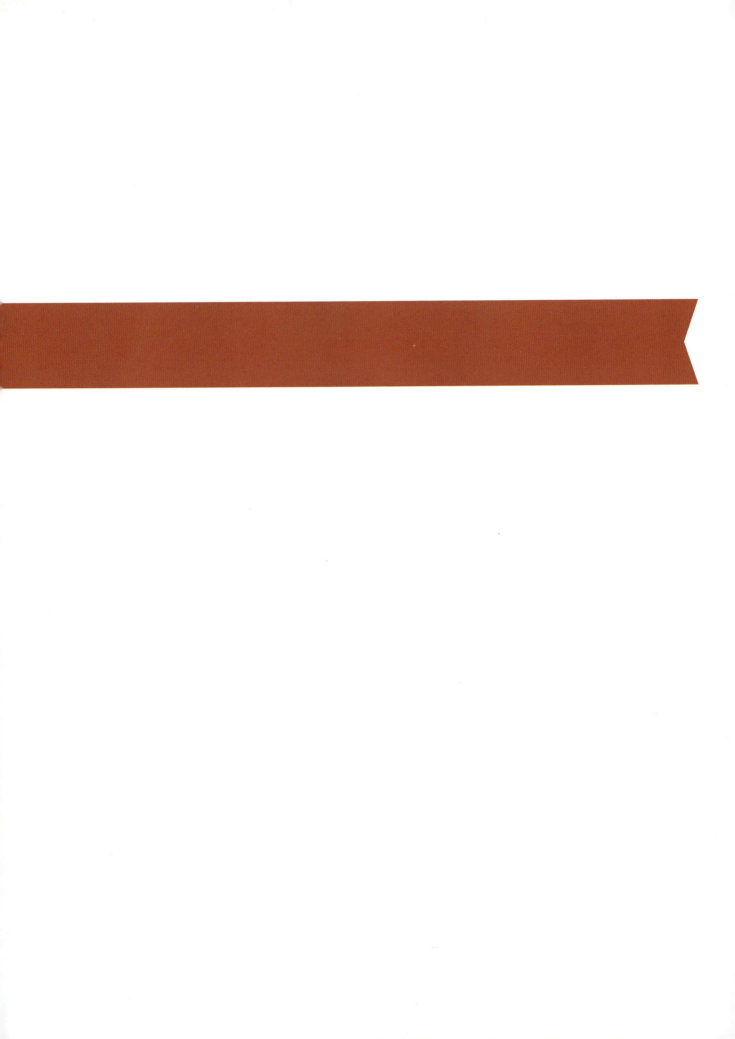

THE
CRIMINAL JUSTICE
SYSTEM

CRIME

REPORTED AND OBSERVED CRIME

UNRESOLVED CRIME OR NO ARREST

INVESTIGATION

RELEASED WITHOUT PROSECUTION

ARREST

CHARGES FILED

RELEASED WITHOUT PROSECUTION

INITIAL APPEARANCE

CHARGES DROPPED OR DISMISSED

BAIL OR DETENTION HEARING

CHARGES DROPPED OR DISMISSED

GATHER INFORMATION

FELONIES

MISDEMEANORS

REFUSAL TO INDICT

GRAND JURY

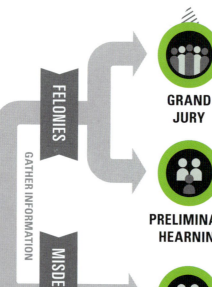

PRELIMINARY HEARING

PRELIMINARY HEARING

CHARGES DISMISSED

ARRAIGNMENT

REDUCTION OF CHARGE

CHARGES DISMISSED

ARRAIGNMENT

TRIAL

PLEA BARGAIN

TRIAL

PLEA BARGAIN

CONVICTION

APPEAL FILED

NEW TRIAL GRANTED

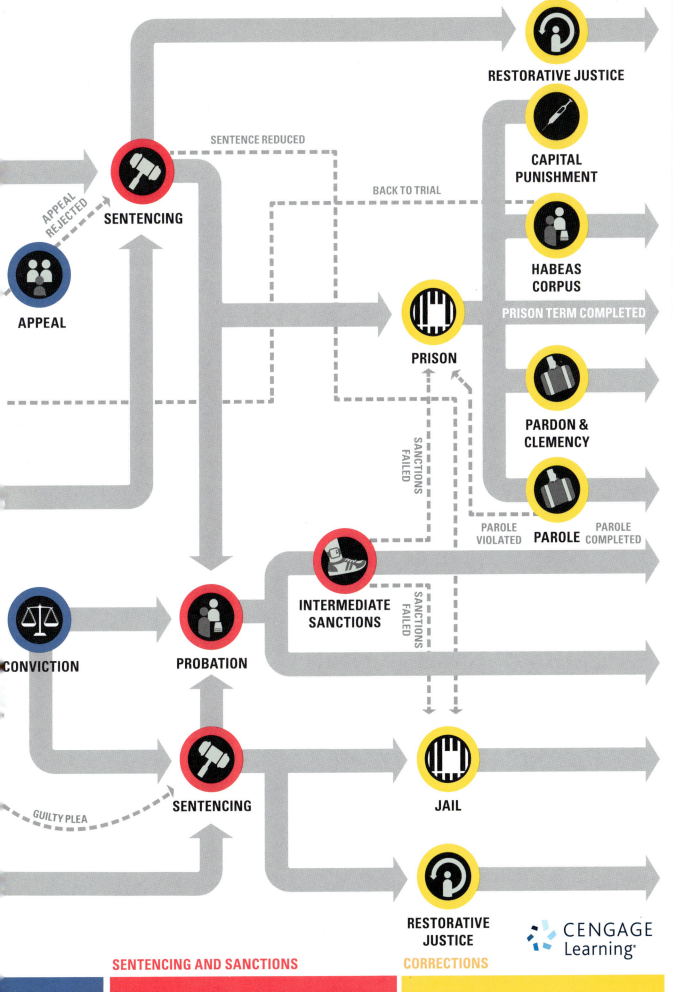

APPEAL

APPEAL REJECTED

SENTENCING

SENTENCE REDUCED

BACK TO TRIAL

RESTORATIVE JUSTICE

CAPITAL PUNISHMENT

HABEAS CORPUS

PRISON TERM COMPLETED

PRISON

PARDON & CLEMENCY

PAROLE

PAROLE VIOLATED

PAROLE COMPLETED

SANCTIONS FAILED

INTERMEDIATE SANCTIONS

SANCTIONS FAILED

CONVICTION

PROBATION

GUILTY PLEA

SENTENCING

JAIL

RESTORATIVE JUSTICE

SENTENCING AND SANCTIONS

CORRECTIONS

CENGAGE Learning

OUT OF SYSTEM

THE

CRIMINAL JUSTICE

SYSTEM

See inside for an illustration of

FIFTEENTH EDITION

Introduction to
CRIMINAL JUSTICE

Larry J. Siegel
University of Massachusetts, Lowell

John L. Worrall
University of Texas at Dallas

Australia • Brazil • Japan • Korea • Mexico • Singapore • Spain • United Kingdom • United States

Introduction to Criminal Justice,
Fifteenth Edition
Larry J. Siegel and John L. Worrall

Product Director: Marta Lee-Perriard

Senior Product Manager: Carolyn Henderson Meier

Senior Content Developer: Shelley Murphy

Product Assistant: Stephen Lagos

Media Developer: Ting Jian Yap

Senior Marketing Manager: Kara Kindstrom

Senior Content Project Manager: Christy Frame

Art Director: Brenda Carmichael, Lumina Datamatics

Senior Manufacturing Planner: Judy Inouye

Production Service: Integra

Photo Development: Kim Adams Fox

Photo Researcher: Sundar Ananthapadmanabhan, Lumina Datamatics

Text Researcher: Kavitha Balasundaram, Lumina Datamatics

Copy Editor: Lunaea Weatherstone

Text and Cover Designer: Brenda Carmichael, Lumina Datamatics

Cover Image: arguz/Shutterstock

Composition: Integra

Library of Congress Control Number: 2014950537

ISBN: 978-1-305-26104-4

Cengage Learning
20 Channel Center Street
Boston, MA 02210
USA

Cengage Learning is a leading provider of customized learning solutions with office locations around the globe, including Singapore, the United Kingdom, Australia, Mexico, Brazil, and Japan. Locate your local office at **www.cengage.com/global**.

Cengage Learning products are represented in Canada by Nelson Education, Ltd.

To learn more about Cengage Learning Solutions, visit **www.cengage.com**.

Purchase any of our products at your local college store or at our preferred online store **www.cengagebrain.com**.

Printed in the United States of America
Print Number: 01 Print Year: 2014

This book is dedicated to my children, Eric, Andrew, Julie,

and Rachel, and to my grandchildren, Jack, Kayla, and Brooke.

It is also dedicated to Jason Macy (thanks for marrying Rachel)

and Therese J. Libby (thanks for marrying me).

L. J. S.

This book is dedicated to my wife, Sabrina.

Thank you for your continued love and support.

J. L. W.

LARRY J. SIEGEL was born in the Bronx in 1947. While living on Jerome Avenue and attending City College of New York in the 1960s, he was swept up in the social and political currents of the time. He became intrigued with the influence contemporary culture had on individual behavior: Did people shape society or did society shape people? He applied his interest in social forces and human behavior to the study of crime and justice. After graduating CCNY, he attended the newly opened program in criminal justice at the State University of New York at Albany, earning both his M.A. and Ph.D. degrees there. After completing his graduate work, Dr. Siegel began his teaching career at Northeastern University, where he was a faculty member for nine years. After leaving Northeastern, he held teaching positions at the University of Nebraska–Omaha and Saint Anselm College in New Hampshire. He is currently a professor at the University of Massachusetts, Lowell. Dr. Siegel has written extensively in the area of crime and justice, including books on juvenile law, delinquency, criminology, criminal justice, and criminal procedure. He is a court-certified expert on police conduct and has testified in numerous legal cases. The father of four and grandfather of three, Larry Siegel and his wife, Terry, now reside in Bedford, New Hampshire, with their two dogs, Watson and Cody.

JOHN L. WORRALL is Professor of Criminology and Program Head at the University of Texas at Dallas. A Seattle native, he received a B.A., double majoring in psychology and law and justice, from Central Washington University in 1994. Both his M.A. (criminal justice) and Ph.D. (political science) were received from Washington State University, where he graduated in 1999. From 1999–2006, he was a member of the criminal justice faculty at California State University, San Bernardino. He joined UTD in Fall 2006.

Dr. Worrall has published articles and book chapters on a wide range of topics ranging from legal issues in policing to crime measurement. He is the author or coauthor of several books, including *Essentials of Criminal Justice* (with Larry Siegel, 9th edition, Cengage, 2015), *Crime Control in America: What Works?* (3rd edition, Pearson, 2015) and *Criminal Procedure: From First Contact to Appeal* (5th edition, Pearson, 2015). He also currently serves as editor of the journal *Police Quarterly*.

BRIEF CONTENTS

CONTENTS

CHAPTER 6
The Police: Organization, Role, and Function   202

CHAPTER 7
Issues in Policing   238

CHAPTER 8
Police and the Rule of Law   282

PART THREE
COURTS AND ADJUDICATION

CHAPTER 9
Court Structure and Personnel   328

CHAPTER 10
Pretrial and Trial Procedures   374

CHAPTER 14
Prison Life: Living in and Leaving Prison 526

PART FIVE
CONTEMPORARY CHALLENGES IN CRIMINAL JUSTICE 575

CHAPTER 15
Juvenile Justice 576

CHAPTER 16

Crime and Justice in the New Millennium   612

FEATURES

PREFACE

He was a famous athlete known as the Blade Runner because he ran on artificial limbs; she was a beautiful model with a reality TV show. They seemed to be living a golden life with a glorious future when on February 14, 2013 police, were called to the gated community in Oscar Pistorius's hometown of Pretoria, South Africa to find that his girlfriend, Reeva Steenkamp, had been shot to death. Police arrested Pistorius on suspicion of murder and a 9mm pistol was recovered from the scene. While at first there was talk that Pistorius mistook Steenkamp for an intruder, these rumors were quashed when it turned out that she had been shot four times through a bathroom door. There were also reports that Pistorius called his father at 3:20 A.M. and asked him to come to the house. When the family arrived, Pistorius was allegedly carrying a nightgown-clad Steenkamp down the stairs, her head and arms dangling. When the police inspected Pistorius's bedroom, they found her overnight bag and iPad on the floor. A holster for a 9mm pistol was found on Oscar's side of the bed. On March 3, 2014, one of the most celebrated trials of the century began. Six months later, Pistorius was found guilty of culpable homicide, a crime similar to involuntary manslaughter. The judge in the case was convinced Pistorius did not intend to kill Steenkamp.

While the Pistorius case occurred in South Africa, it made headlines around the world. Such incidents tell the general public that crime occurs everywhere, and can occur among the rich and powerful as well as the poor and downtrodden. Because crime is everywhere and all of us are potential victims, these highly reported incidents remind us why we rely on the criminal justice system. Empowered by case law and legislation, these agencies are designed to protect us from crimes ranging from a furious boyfriend with anger management issues to international drug cartels that use sophisticated technology to launder money in overseas capitals.

The justice system has become an enterprise costing more than $150 billion each year. It employs millions of people in law enforcement, courts, and correctional agencies. *Introduction to Criminal Justice* was written to help students interested in justice better understand this enormous and complex system and to aid their journey in introductory-level criminal justice courses. The text analyzes and describes the agencies of justice and the variety of procedures they use to apprehend, adjudicate, and treat criminal offenders. It covers what most experts believe are the critical issues in criminal justice and analyzes their impact on the justice system. The primary goals in writing this, the Fifteenth Edition, remain as they have been for previous editions:

- To provide students with a thorough knowledge of criminal justice agencies
- To be as thorough and up-to-date as possible
- To be objective and unbiased
- To challenge students to think critically about justice

Every attempt has been made to present the material in an interesting, balanced, and objective manner, making sure that no single political or theoretical position dominates the text. Instead, we present the many diverse views that shape the contemporary criminal justice system and characterize its interdisciplinary nature. Diversity of opinion is what the study of criminal justice is all about and is the central focus of the text. We have tried to provide a text that is scholarly and informative, comprehensive yet interesting, and well organized and objective while at the same time provocative and thought provoking.

ORGANIZATION OF THE TEXT

Part One gives the student a basic introduction to crime, law, and justice—from as far back as the American Revolution into the new millennium. The first chapter briefly describes the history of criminal justice, the agencies of justice, and the formal justice process, and it introduces students to the concept of the informal justice system, which involves discretion, deal making, and plea bargains. The chapter also describes the major perspectives on justice. Chapter 2 addresses such questions as: How is crime measured? Where and when does it occur? Who commits crime? Who are its victims? What social factors influence the crime rate? Chapter 3 covers crime patterns and theories of crime. Chapter 4 provides a discussion of the criminal law and its relationship to criminal justice.

Part Two provides an overview of the law enforcement field. Four chapters cover the history and development of law enforcement, the role, organization, and function of police in modern society, issues in policing, and police and the rule of law.

Part Three is devoted to the adjudication process, from pretrial indictment to the sentencing of criminal offenders. Chapters focus on organization of the court system, an analysis of the prosecution and defense functions, pretrial procedures, and the criminal trial. Topics included range from court structure to the processing of felony cases, indigent defense systems, attorney competence, legal ethics, pretrial services, and bail reform. Part Three wraps up with a chapter on punishment and sentencing.

Part Four focuses on the correctional system, including probation, intermediate sanctions, and restorative justice. The traditional correctional system of jails, prisons, community-based corrections, and parole are also discussed at length. Such issues as technocorrections and the problem of prisoner reentry are analyzed.

Part Five covers special topics in criminal justice. The juvenile justice system chapter contains information on preventive detention of youths, waiving youths to the adult court, and recent changes in the death penalty for children. Part Five also includes a chapter on criminal justice in the new millennium. It covers topics such as corporate enterprise crime, cybercrime, transnational organized crime, and terrorism. This final chapter reflects the challenges now facing the justice system in the new millennium.

NEW IN THIS EDITION

Because the study of criminal justice is a dynamic field of scientific inquiry and the concepts and processes of justice are constantly changing and evolving, the Fifteenth Edition has been thoroughly revised. In addition to revising and updating the text, we have added two new features. One of them, a marginal feature we call Fact Check, compares students' opinions to public opinion, then pits opinion against reality by illustrating how perceptions and the "real world" are often at odds with one another. A new Global Criminal Justice feature explores crime-related issues that are international in scope. This edition of *Introduction to Criminal Justice* also includes updated and expanded web content throughout, helping readers gain further insight into the topics covered.

Chapter-by-Chapter Changes

Chapter 1: The opening vignette features the latest fallout from the 2012 Trayvon Martin case, including George Zimmerman's acquittal in 2013. Numerous CourseMate web links have been added throughout the chapter, affording readers an opportunity to more thoroughly explore certain chapter topics. The latest criminal justice system size and cost estimates are included. The chapter wraps up with a new Ethical Challenges in Criminal Justice writing assignment concerning the use of red light cameras.

Chapter 2: A new chapter opening story features the infamous Newtown, Connecticut, mass school shooting. The Careers in Criminal Justice box now features the job of crime analyst, a more attainable position than statistician, which was highlighted in the previous edition. A new section on property crimes appears in the "What Are the Different Categories of Crime?" section. Chapter 2 also contains the first of several new Global Criminal Justice features, this one comparing crime rates in the United States to those of other countries around the world. The latest crime and victimization statistics also appear throughout the chapter.

Chapter 3: In addition to being updated with the latest research on crime causation, this chapter now begins with a story featuring the 2013 Washington Navy Yard shooting, plus updates on other recent mass shootings carried out in recent years. A new Criminal Justice and Technology box explores the feasibility of brain scans for detecting signs of antisocial behavior, and the ethics assignment at the end of the chapter challenges students to decide whether nature or nurture is most important in terms of explaining crime.

Chapter 4: The justification and excuse defense sections have been revised and reorganized. For clarity of presentation, the ignorance and mistake section was moved up in the chapter and away from the "Criminal Defenses" section. Chapter 4 also contains a new Analyzing Criminal Justice Issues box featuring the controversial Florida "stand-your-ground" law. The "Reforming the Criminal Law" section now contains the latest facts on marijuana legalization in Washington and Colorado. Finally, the Criminal Justice and Technology box features the latest developments in government searches of cell phone records and the NSA's controversial metadata collection program.

Chapter 5: A new chapter opening story features the use of robotic drones in domestic law enforcement. A new "Policing Since 2000" section has been added into the police history discussion. It features changes in policing due to 9/11, the evidence-based justice movement, and the great recession of 2008. The chapter also includes the latest facts and figures on federal, state, county, and municipal police departments. A new Global Criminal Justice box features the role of INTERPOL in modern law enforcement.

Chapter 6: Police budget cuts remain a consistent problem. While the economy is rebounding, many agencies are still reeling from the effects of the 2008 recession. The revised chapter opening story highlights several of the initiatives police departments have taken to "do more with less," including the controversial strategy of public safety consolidation. The Criminal Justice and Technology box now moves beyond in-car cameras and includes body-worn cameras. A new Careers in Criminal Justice box features the position of victim advocate.

Chapter 7: Chapter 7 begins with an examination of the FBI's recent probe into shootings by officers of the Albuquerque, New Mexico, Police Department. A new Criminal Justice and Technology box features the so-called "Dazer Laser," an alternative to the popular Taser. The Careers in Criminal Justice box now features the position of intelligence analyst. The chapter has also been updated with the latest facts and figures concerning police demographics, use of force incidents, and contemporary policing problems.

Chapter 8: The chapter begins with a new opening story on the Supreme Court's decision in *Missouri v. McNeely*. The case dealt with forced, warrantless blood draws in a drunk driving context. The chapter is also updated with the latest Supreme Court decisions relevant in the world of law enforcement. Finally, a new Analyzing Criminal Justice Issues box features the constitutional rules and cases dealing with police canine searches.

Chapter 9: This chapter begins with a new story featuring St. Louis Circuit Attorney Jennifer Joyce and her use of Facebook and Twitter. It also includes the latest facts and figures on court structure and workloads, the judiciary, prosecution, and the defense bar.

Chapter 10: The chapter opens with a story on Ariel Castro, who kidnapped three women in Ohio, holding them against their will for years until one escaped. Chapter 10 also includes the latest Supreme Court cases pertaining to pretrial and trial procedure.

Chapter 11: Chapter 11 web resources have been improved. The latest in sentencing statistics and cases are also included. The capital punishment section has been updated with the latest statistics. Fact Check boxes examine public support for the current number of prisoners locked up in America and capital punishment.

Chapter 12: The chapter leads off with a new opening story featuring recent celebrity convictions and their probation sentences. A new Evidence-Based Justice box features cognitive behavioral therapy for probationers. The chapter is also updated with all the latest facts and figures related to probation and intermediate sanctions. The "Intermediate Sanctions" section has been revised to more clearly distinguish among alternatives to imprisonment, intermediate sanctions, and probation.

Chapter 13: This chapter leads off with a story featuring California's recent prison realignment, which shifted responsibility for a large number of inmates from the state to the counties. A new Analyzing Criminal Justice Issues box addresses the problem of incarcerating elderly inmates. The latest statistics on prison and jail populations are also included.

Chapter 14: Chapter 14 starts off with a new story featuring Colorado inmate Scott Howard's harrowing prison experience. A new Criminal Justice and Technology box features the latest strategies for monitoring inmates and areas within prisons. Two new Analyzing Criminal Justice Issues boxes address the problems of postrelease recidivism and reentry success. The latest data on parole success are also included.

Chapter 15: The juvenile justice chapter has been updated with the latest statistics on delinquency cases, juvenile waiver, and other matters of relevance to young offenders. Web links have been expanded and a Fact Check feature explores opinions and reality concerning the treatment of juvenile offenders as adults.

Chapter 16: The chapter begins with a new story featuring Daniel Patrick Boyd, ringleader of a group of men accused of conspiring to commit terrorism. Chapter 16 is also updated to reflect the latest developments in corporate enterprise crime, cybercrime, transnational organized crime, and terrorism.

SPECIAL FEATURES

We have created a comprehensive, proven learning system designed to help students get the most out of their first course in criminal justice. In addition to the many changes already mentioned, we have included a wealth of new photographs to appeal to visual learners and make material more relevant and meaningful. Carefully updated tables and completely redrawn figures highlight key chapter concepts. Marginal definitions of key terms; concise, bulleted end-of-chapter summaries that align with chapter learning objectives; and a comprehensive end-of-book glossary all help students master the material. Web App links appearing in the text's margins let students explore topics further via the Internet.

Boxed Features

We have included a number of thematic boxes to introduce students to some of the field's most crucial programs, policies, and issues, providing them with an opportunity to analyze the material in greater depth.

- **Fact Check** These marginal boxes compare students' opinions on controversial criminal justice topics to the public's opinion. It then compares poll results to the reality surrounding the problem at hand. For example, the box in chapter 3 explores opinions concerning the best approach to dealing with crime, then compares those results to what we know about effective crime control policy.

- **Careers in Criminal Justice** We have updated this popular addition to the previous edition with the latest career paths in criminal justice. These boxes contain detailed information on salaries, educational requirements, and future prospects.

- **Global Criminal Justice** These boxes are aimed at helping students better understand the crime problems that know no geographical boundaries. They also offer comparative perspective. For example, the box in Chapter 2 compares U.S. crime rates to those of other countries around the world.

- **Criminal Justice and Technology** This feature focuses on some of the latest efforts to modernize the system using contemporary technological methods. For example, Chapter 8's Criminal Justice and Technology box discusses the use of GPS tagging in hot-pursuit cases.

- **Analyzing Criminal Justice Issues** This feature helps students to learn and think critically about current justice issues and practices. For example, an Analyzing Criminal Justice Issues box in Chapter 11 features efforts to reduce wrongful convictions.

- **Evidence-Based Justice** This feature summarizes the scientific evidence about the effectiveness of various criminal justice strategies and programs. For example, the Evidence-Based Justice box in Chapter 6 examines the research on the crime prevention effects of police work.

- **The Evolution of . . .** This feature summarizes the evolution of key Supreme Court decisions. For example, Chapter 8 discusses the evolution of *Carroll v. United States*, the key vehicle search case, and *Miranda v. Arizona*, which of course deals with confessions and interrogations. The feature summarizes nearly every subsequent Supreme Court case that builds on, expands, or restricts the original case.

- **The Victim Experience** This feature focuses on victims' role in the criminal justice system. We have chosen important elements of justice and engaged them through the lens of the victim rather than the criminal or agent of the justice system. The idea is to give students a feel for what it is like to be a crime victim and to promote classroom discussions of victimization. Topics covered include victim advocacy, victim services, and victims' rights.

Other Important Chapter Features

We have included numerous learning tools in every chapter to aid student mastery of the material. A few of the most valuable study aids we provide are the following.

- **Ethical Challenges in Criminal Justice: A Writing Assignment** Each chapter has a writing assignment that challenges students to solve an ethical dilemma they may someday confront while working within the justice system. The dilemma in Chapter 16, for example, focuses on whether it is ethical for government officials to engage in certain surveillance activities.

- **Web Apps** These are designed to guide students to websites that provide them with additional information if they want to conduct further research on the topics covered in the text.

- **Concept Summaries** Throughout the chapters, these tables or lists summarize the content of important concepts found in the chapter so students can compare and contrast ideas, views, cases, findings, and so on. For example, in Chapter 3 a Concept Summary reviews concepts and theories of criminology.

- **Significant Cases** Several chapters contain reference to multiple Supreme Court decisions. At the end of each of these chapters is a new Significant Cases in ... feature. For example, before the chapter summary at the end of Chapter 11 is a table summarizing significant cases in punishment and sentencing. Contents of the table include the name of the case, the year it was decided, the key issue at stake, and the Supreme Court's decision. While it was impossible to summarize every significant case, we believe readers will enjoy the comprehensiveness of the case selections we have included.

ANCILLARY MATERIALS

A number of supplements are provided by Cengage Learning to help instructors use *Introduction to Criminology* in their courses and to aid students in preparing for exams. Supplements are available to qualified adopters. Please consult your local sales representative for details.

To access additional course materials, please visit **www.cengagebrain.com**. At the CengageBrain.com home page, search for the ISBN of your title (from the back cover of your book), using the search box at the top of the page. This will take you to the product page where these resources can be found.

To get access, visit CengageBrain.com

MINDTAP CRIMINAL JUSTICE from Cengage Learning represents a new approach to a highly personalized, online learning platform. A fully online learning solution, MindTap combines all of a student's learning tools—readings, multimedia, activities, and assessments into a singular Learning Path that guides the student through the curriculum. Instructors personalize the experience by customizing the presentation of these learning tools for their students, allowing instructors to seamlessly introduce their own content into the Learning Path via "apps" that integrate into the MindTap platform. Additionally, MindTap provides interoperability with major Learning Management Systems (LMS) via support for open industry standards and fosters partnerships with third-party educational application providers to provide a highly collaborative, engaging, and personalized learning experience.

INSTRUCTOR'S RESOURCE MANUAL WITH LESSON PLANS AND TEST BANK revised for the 15th edition by Sameer Hinduja of Florida Atlantic University, includes learning objectives, key terms, a detailed chapter outline, a chapter summary, lesson plans, discussion topics, student activities, "What If" scenarios, media tools, and an expanded test bank with 30 percent more questions than the prior edition. The learning objectives are correlated with the discussion topics, student activities, and media tools.

Each chapter of the test bank contains questions in multiple-choice, true/false, completion, essay, and new critical thinking formats, with a full answer key. The test bank is coded to the learning objectives that appear in the main text, and includes the section in the main text where the answers can be found. Finally, each question in the test bank has been carefully reviewed by experienced criminal justice instructors for quality, accuracy, and content coverage so instructors can be sure they are working with an assessment and grading resource of the highest caliber.

CENGAGE LEARNING TESTING POWERED BY COGNERO This assessment software is a flexible, online system that allows you to import, edit, and manipulate test bank content from the *Introduction to Criminal Justice* test bank or elsewhere, including your own favorite test questions; create multiple test versions in an instant; and deliver tests from your LMS, your classroom, or wherever you want.

ONLINE POWERPOINT® LECTURES Helping you make your lectures more engaging while effectively reaching your visually oriented students, these handy Microsoft PowerPoint® slides revised for the 15th edition by Lisa Anne Zilney of Montclair State University outline the chapters of the main text in a classroom-ready presentation. The PowerPoint® slides are updated to reflect the content and organization of the new edition of the text, are tagged by chapter learning objective, and feature some additional examples and real-world cases for application and discussion.

ACKNOWLEDGMENTS

Desiré J.M. Anastasia, Metropolitan State University of Denver
Andre L. Barnes, City College of San Francisco
Robert Barnes, SUNY Westchester Community College
Curt Blakely, Truman State University
Kristen K. Bowen, Florida A & M University
Kenton J. Burns, South Plains College
Mark A. Byington, Jefferson College
Brian E. Cranny, Greenville Technical College
Barbara A. Crowson, Norwich University
Anthony Dangelantonio, Keene State College
Melchor C. De Guzman, The College at Brockport, SUNY
Peter Fenton, Kennesaw State University
Colin P. Gallagher, Wichita Area Technical College
Brian J. Gorman, Towson University
Michele Grillo, Monmouth University
Brittany Hayes, John Jay College
John E. Hertel, St Louis Community College
Carly Hilinski-Rosick, Grand Valley State University
Susan S. Hodge, University of North Carolina at Charlotte
Daniel L. Lawson, City College of San Francisco
John Mabry, University of Central Oklahoma
Tamara D. Madensen, University of Nevada, Las Vegas
Shana Mell, Virginia Commonwealth University
Eric Metchik, Salem State University

Nathan Moran, Midwestern State University
Barry "lynn" Parker, Palo Alto College
Rebecca Pfeffer, University of Houston-Downtown
Melissa L. Ricketts, Shippensburg University of Pennsylvania
Marny Rivera, University of Alaska, Anchorage
Martin D. Schwartz, George Washington University
Patrick L. Shade, Edison Community College
Susan Thomas, University of Tennessee Chattanooga
Suzanne Youngblood, Lancaster Campus, Harrisburg Area Community College

Many people helped make this book possible. Our marvelous product manager, Carolyn Henderson Meier, is always at our side and is an unofficial coauthor. A lot of credit for getting this book out must go to our wonderful, fantastic, patient, competent, and, did we mention, fabulous content developer, Shelley Murphy. Special thanks to our incredible content project manager Christy Frame; fantastic production editor Margaret McConnell; copy editor nonpareil, Lunaea Weatherstone; outstanding photo development editor Kim Adams; and our incredible marketing manager, Kara Kindstrom, all of whom do great and magnificent jobs.

To the reviewers of this edition as well as those for all previous editions, thank you.

Larry J. Siegel

John L. Worrall

THE NATURE OF CRIME, LAW, AND CRIMINAL JUSTICE

THE STUDY OF CRIMINAL JUSTICE should begin with a basic understanding of crime, law, and justice. There are differing views on what are the proper goals of this vast system. Some view the system as a treatment-dispensing institution designed to rehabilitate criminal offenders; others view it as an agency of social control that protects decent citizens from criminal predators. Some people who work in the system, like Daisy Mongeau, an investigator with the New Hampshire Public Defender's Office in Concord, are more concerned with providing people accused of crime with fair and equitable treatment before the law. She finds that a lot of her friends just can't understand why she works so hard to defend people who are guilty—even those who have confessed to the crime. "They don't seem to understand," she says, "that everyone is entitled to a criminal defense even if they actually committed the crime!"

When asked what is her greatest reward she says, "Getting the prosecutor to drop the case because of what a witness told me during an investigation." She finds that "clients are thrilled that someone actually believed them and helped them win the case. These are people not used to being given a helping hand."

The modern criminal justice system has evolved since ancient times. Some elements, such as courts and punishment, have been with us for thousands of years. Others, like police and corrections, are newer concepts, some developing in the United States in the nineteenth century. For example, probation and community treatment are relatively new concepts begun in 1841; today, probation officers supervise 4 million clients. One of them, Samantha J. O'Hara, is a U.S. probation officer for the U.S. District Court in the Southern District of Iowa, headquartered in Des Moines. O'Hara thoroughly enjoys her job. "I like learning of people's stories and how they became involved in their offenses. The contact with a variety of people, including offenders, their families, assistant U.S. attorneys, defense counsel, case agents, and the federal judges, makes for an extremely diverse mix. It is personally rewarding to me," she adds, "to see that the final product is helpful to the U.S. District court judges, later the Federal Bureau of Prisons, and eventually to my colleagues in the U.S. probation officer supervision units across the country." ■

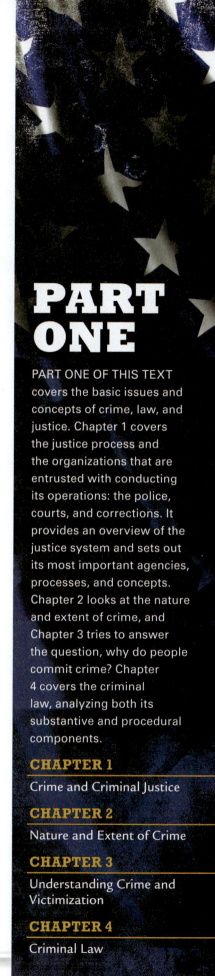

CHAPTER 1

Crime and Criminal Justice

Learning Objectives

L01 Define the concept of criminal justice.

L02 Summarize the long history of crime in America.

L03 Discuss the formation of the criminal justice system.

L04 Name the three basic component agencies of criminal justice.

L05 Describe the size and scope of the contemporary justice system.

L06 Describe the formal criminal justice process.

L07 Articulate what is meant by the term *criminal justice assembly line*.

L08 Discuss the wedding cake model of justice.

L09 Explain the various perspectives on criminal justice.

L010 Discuss the ethical issues that arise in criminal justice.

Chapter Outline

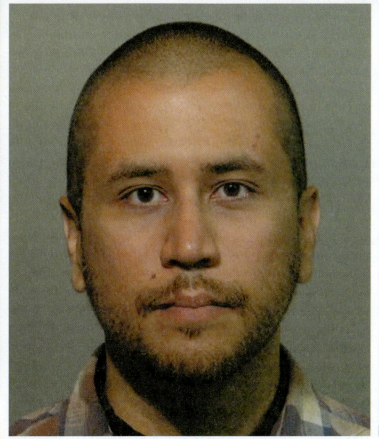

On the night of February 26, 2012, neighborhood watch captain George Zimmerman, 28, (above left photo) was driving his SUV though his Sanford, Florida, neighborhood when he called 911 to report "a real suspicious guy," a "black male" walking around. That was Trayvon Martin (above right photo), a teen who was heading back to the house where he was staying after a 7-Eleven run. Martin was wearing a hooded sweatshirt and carrying a can of iced tea, a bag of Skittles, and his cell phone. Zimmerman followed Martin, and the two eventually got involved in an argument. Things escalated and the altercation culminated in Zimmerman firing a fatal shot into Martin's chest. Zimmerman was brought to the police station, pleaded self-defense, and was released without charges being filed. In the aftermath of the incident, Trayvon Martin's parents, Tracy Martin and Sybrina Fulton, went public, calling for Zimmerman to be prosecuted. Under public pressure, police in Sanford eventually released the 911 calls made by Zimmerman in which he disregards the operator telling him not to chase after Martin. On April 12, 2012, after a great deal of media attention and public debate, including a famous statement by President Barack Obama saying that if he had a son he "would look like Trayvon Martin." George Zimmerman was tried for second-degree murder. On July 13, 2013, his trial ended in acquittal; Zimmerman was found not guilty.

The verdict gained national media attention and raised numerous legal and social questions. The main area of controversy is Florida's "stand your ground" gun law, which lets residents use deadly force against a threat when they feel their lives are in danger. It is widely assumed that Zimmerman invoked the Florida "stand your ground" law as part of his defense; the news media reported this on multiple occasions. In actuality, though, Zimmerman claimed self-defense, which is a traditional criminal law defense and distinct from "stand your ground." Even so, "stand your ground" was important in the case. Defending the verdict in an interview with CNN's Anderson Cooper, Juror B-37 reported that second-degree murder or manslaughter did not apply "… because of the heat of the moment and the 'stand your ground.' He had a right to defend himself. If he felt threatened that his life was going to be taken away from him or he was going to have bodily harm, he had a right."[1]

The case also raised concern about gun control. Should someone like Zimmerman be allowed to own a handgun? Should the "right to carry" be more carefully restricted and controlled? Or is the Second Amendment's right to bear arms inviolable and beyond government control? These questions came to light not just during Zimmerman's trial, but also after it when he became embroiled in additional legal troubles. On September 9, 2013, police responded to a 911 call by Zimmerman's estranged wife, who reported he threatened her and her father with a gun. No gun was found, however. Two months later, Zimmerman's girlfriend called police, claiming that after she asked Zimmerman to leave, he pointed a shotgun at her. She eventually withdrew her complaint and Zimmerman was not charged. ■

criminal justice system
The system of law enforcement, adjudication, and correction that is directly involved in the apprehension, prosecution, and control of those charged with criminal offenses.

High-profile cases such as this help focus interest on the criminal justice system. The public relies on the agencies of the **criminal justice system** for protection from elaborate schemes. This loosely organized collection of agencies is responsible for protecting the public, maintaining order, enforcing the law, identifying transgressors, bringing the guilty to justice, and treating criminal behavior. The public depends on this vast system, which employs more than 2 million people and costs taxpayers more than $200 billion per year, to protect them from criminals and to bring justice to their lives. The criminal justice system is now taking on new duties, including protecting the country from international and domestic terrorists, transnational organized crime syndicates, and cyber criminals, groups that were almost unknown a decade ago. Member agencies must cooperate to investigate complex criminal conspiracies and meet these new challenges.

This text serves as an introduction to the study of criminal justice. This chapter covers some basic issues and concepts, beginning with a discussion of the concept and study of criminal justice. The major processes of the criminal justice system are then examined to provide an overview of how the system functions. Because no single view exists of the underlying goals that help shape criminal justice, the varying perspectives on what criminal justice really is—or should be—are set out in some detail.

Is Crime a Recent Development?

 L01 Define the concept of criminal justice.

Due to the extensive media coverage of high-profile criminal events, people are routinely heard to say, "Crime is getting worse every day" and "I can remember when it was safe to walk the streets at night," but their memories may be colored by wishful thinking. Crime and violence have existed in the United States for more than 200 years and the crime rate was much higher 100 years ago than it is today.

Crime and violence have been common since the nation was first formed.[2] Guerilla activity was frequent before, during, and after the Revolutionary War. Bands supporting the British (Tories) and the American revolutionaries engaged in savage attacks on each other, using hit-and-run tactics, burning, and looting.

Crime in the Old West

After the Civil War, many former Union and Confederate soldiers headed west with the dream of finding gold or starting a cattle ranch. Some even resorted to murder, theft, and robbery. The notorious John Wesley Hardin (who is alleged to have killed 30 men) studied law in prison and became a practicing attorney before his death. Henry McCarty, better known as the infamous "Billy the Kid," participated in range wars and may have killed more than 20 people before being gunned down in 1881 by Sheriff Pat Garrett; Billy had just turned 22. Others formed outlaw bands that terrorized the western territories. There is no more storied bad man in the history of America than the outlaw Jesse James, who made his living robbing banks and trains. A folk hero, James remained an active

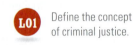
FACT CHECK ☑

YOUR OPINION: Is there more or less crime in the United States as there was last year?

PUBLIC OPINION:

MORE: ▬▬▬▬▬ 64%

LESS: ▬▬ 19%

REALITY: Violent crime rose from 19 victimizations per thousand people in 2010 to 26 in 2012. Crime dropped significantly, however, from the 1990s through 2010, so the recent uptick may or may not be the start of a new trend.

DISCUSSION: What fuels perceptions that crime is more of a problem than it really is?

Sources: Gallup, http://www.gallup.com/poll/165653/crime-americans-seem-noticed.aspx (accessed April 2014); J. Truman, L. Langton, and M. Planty, *Criminal Victimization, 2012* (Washington, DC: Bureau of Justice Statistics, 2013).

outlaw until April 3, 1882, when he was shot in the back by Bob Ford, a fellow gang member, who did the deed in order to claim a $5,000 reward. Folktales aside, James was in fact more of an impulsive killer than a latter-day Robin Hood. In September 1864, during the Civil War, Jesse, riding with the guerilla band led by Bloody Bill Anderson, held up a train in the town of Centralia, Missouri, and helped to kill 22 unarmed Union soldiers on board.[3]

Facing these outlaws was an equally colorful group of lawmen who developed reputations that have persisted for more than a century. Of these, none is more famous than Wyatt Earp. In 1876, he became chief deputy marshal of Dodge City, Kansas, a lawless frontier town, and he later moved on to Deadwood, in the Dakota Territory. In 1879, Earp and his brothers Morgan and Virgil journeyed to Tombstone, Arizona, where he eventually was appointed acting deputy U.S. marshal for the Arizona Territory. The Earps, along with their gunslinging dentist friend Doc Holliday, participated in the famous O.K. Corral gunfight in 1881, during which they killed several members of a rustler gang known as the Cowboys.

Crime in the Cities

The Old West was not the only area where gang activity flourished. In East Coast cities, gangs bearing colorful names such as the Hudson Dusters and the Shirt-tails battled rivals for control of the streets. In New York City, many gangs, including the Plug Uglies, the Swamp Angels, the Daybreak Boys, and the Bowery Boys, competed for dominance in the Five Point section of the lower East Side. Gang battles were extremely brutal, and men were killed with knives, hatchets, cleavers, and anything else that could puncture or slice flesh.

The Civil War also produced widespread business crime. The great robber barons bribed government officials and plotted to corner markets and obtain concessions for railroads, favorable land deals, and mining and mineral rights on government land. The administration of President Ulysses S. Grant was tainted by numerous corruption scandals.

From 1900 to 1935, the nation experienced a sustained increase in criminal activity. This period was dominated by Depression-era outlaws who later became mythic figures. Charles "Pretty Boy" Floyd was a folk hero among the sharecroppers of eastern Oklahoma, and the whole nation eagerly followed the exploits of its premier bank robber, John Dillinger, until he was killed in front of a Chicago movie house. The infamous "Ma" Barker and her sons Lloyd, Herman, Fred, and Arthur are believed responsible for killing more than 10 people, and Bonnie Parker and Clyde Barrow killed more than 13 before they were slain in a shoot-out with federal agents.

The crime problem, then, is not a recent phenomenon; it has been evolving along with the nation itself. Crime has provided a mechanism for the frustrated to vent their anger, for business leaders to maintain their position of wealth and power, and for those outside the economic mainstream to take a shortcut to the American dream. To protect itself from this ongoing assault, the public has supported the development of a wide array of government agencies whose stated purpose is to control and prevent crime; to identify, apprehend, and bring to those who violate the law; and to devise effective methods of criminal These agencies make up the criminal justice system.

Creating Criminal Justice

In 1829, the first police agency, the London Metropolitan Police, was created both to keep the peace and to identify and apprehend criminal suspects. A huge success in England, police agencies began to appear in the United States during the mid-nineteenth century. Another nineteenth-century innovation, the penitentiary (or prison) offered an alternative to physical punishments such as whipping, branding, or hanging.

 L02 Summarize the long history of crime in America.

As criminal justice developed over the next century, these fledgling agencies of justice rarely worked together in a systematic fashion. It was not until 1919—when the Chicago Crime Commission, a professional association funded by private contributions, was created—that the work of the criminal justice system began to be recognized.[4] The Chicago Crime Commission acted as a citizens advocate group and kept track of the activities of local justice agencies. The commission still carries out its work today and is active in administering anticrime programs.[5]

In 1931, President Herbert Hoover appointed the National Commission of Law Observance and Enforcement, which is commonly known as the Wickersham Commission. This national study group made a detailed analysis of the U.S. justice system, helped usher in the era of treatment and rehabilitation, and found that the existing system of justice was flawed by too many rules and regulations.[6]

The modern era of criminal justice can be traced to a series of research projects begun in the 1950s under the sponsorship of the American Bar Foundation (ABF).[7] The ABF project discovered that the justice system contained many procedures that had been kept hidden from the public view—investigation, arrest, prosecution, and plea negotiations—and that justice professionals had a great deal of latitude in decision making. For the first time, the term *criminal justice system* began to be used, reflecting a view that justice agencies could be connected in an intricate, yet often unobserved, network of decision-making processes.

Federal Involvement

 Discuss the formation of the criminal justice system.

In 1967, the President's Commission on Law Enforcement and Administration of Justice (the Crime Commission), which had been created by President Lyndon B. Johnson, published its final report, *The Challenge of Crime in a Free Society*.[8] Concomitantly, Congress passed the Safe Streets and Crime Control Act of 1968, providing for the expenditure of federal funds for state and local crime control efforts.[9] This act helped launch a massive campaign to restructure the justice system. It funded the National Institute of Law Enforcement and Criminal Justice, which encouraged research and development in criminal justice. Renamed the National Institute of Justice in 1979, it has remained a major source of funding for the implementation and evaluation of innovative experimental and demonstration projects in the criminal justice system.[10]

Law Enforcement Assistance Administration (LEAA)
Federal agency that provided technical assistance and hundreds of millions of dollars in aid to state and local justice agencies between 1969 and 1982.

The Safe Streets Act provided funding for the **Law Enforcement Assistance Administration (LEAA)**, which, throughout its 14-year history, granted hundreds of millions of dollars in federal aid to local and state justice agencies. On April 15, 1982, the program came to an end when Congress ceased funding it. Although the LEAA attracted its share of criticism, it supported many worthwhile programs, including the development of a vast number of criminal justice departments in colleges and universities and the use of technology in the criminal justice system.

Evidence-Based Justice: A Scientific Evolution

With continued funding from federal agencies such as the National Institute of Justice, the Office of Juvenile Justice and Delinquency Prevention, and the Bureau of Justice Statistics—as well as from private foundations such as the Pew and Annie E. Casey foundations—the study of criminal justice has embraced careful research analysis to support public policy initiatives. Whereas programs, policies, and procedures may have been shaped by political goals in the past, a mature justice system now relies more on the scientific collection of data to determine whether programs work and what policies should be adopted. According to this "What Works" movement,[11] empirical evidence, carefully gathered using scientific methods, must be collected and analyzed in order to determine whether criminal justice programs work and whether they actually reduce crime rates and offender recidivism. Programs must now undergo rigorous review to ensure that they achieve their stated goals and have a real and measurable effect on behavior. **Evidence-based justice** efforts have a few unifying principles:[12]

■ *Target audience.* Programs must be reaching the right audience. A drug treatment program that is used with groups of college students caught smoking pot may look successful, but can it work with hard-core substance abusers? It is important for programs to work with high-risk offenders who have the greatest probability of recidivating. Targeting low-risk offenders may make programs look good, but it really proves little because the client group might not have repeated their criminal offenses even if left untreated.

■ *Randomized experiments.* Whenever possible, random experiments are conducted. For example, two groups of drug users are randomly selected, the first group is placed in the special treatment program, and the other is treated in a traditional fashion, such as being put in prison. If the recidivism rates of the experimental group are superior, we have strong evidence that the novel treatment method really works. Although it is sometimes difficult to select subjects randomly, other methods (such as matching subjects on key characteristics such as age, race, gender, and prior record) can be substituted.

■ *Intervening factors.* Evidence-based programming must consider intervening factors that enhance or impede program success. A community-based crime prevention program that is used in a high-income neighborhood may be met with general approval and prove effective in reducing local problems, such as kids drinking at night in the local park. But will the program work in a high-crime area where well-armed gangs frighten residents? Conversely, a program that is deemed a failure with a group of at-risk kids living in an inner-city neighborhood may work quite well with at-risk youngsters living in a rural environment.

■ *Measurement of success.* Evidence-based programs must develop realistic measures of success. For example, a treatment may seem to work, but careful analysis might reveal that the effect quickly wears off; long-term measures of program effectiveness are needed. Program retention must also be considered. A program for teens may seem to work because those who complete the program are less likely to commit crime in the future. But before success is declared and the program is adopted on a national level, research must closely evaluate such issues as the dropout rate: Are potential failures removed before the program is completed in order to ensure overall success (and continued funding)? And what about selectivity? Is the program open to everyone, including repeat offenders, or is it limited to people who are considered to have the greatest potential for success?

■ *Cost-effectiveness.* Programs may work, but the cost may be too high. In an era of tight budgets, program effectiveness must be balanced with cost. It is not enough for a program to be effective; it must also prove to be efficient.

Scientific research is now being used to dispute commonly held beliefs that may be misleading and erroneous. For example, the track record of school-based drug education programs has proven to be spotty at best: the evidence shows that the best intentions do not necessarily result in the best practice.[13] Throughout the text, we will highlight programs that have passed careful, evidence-based evaluations *and* some that have failed to stand up to such scrutiny.

The Contemporary Criminal Justice System

The contemporary criminal justice system is society's instrument of **social control**. Some behaviors are considered so dangerous that they must be either strictly controlled or outlawed outright; some people are so destructive that they must be monitored or even confined. The agencies of justice seek to prevent

evidence-based justice
Determining through the use of the scientific method whether criminal justice programs actually reduce crime rates and offender recidivism.

 **Web App 1.1**
Visit http://www.crimesolutions.gov/ for an overview of the federal government's latest evidence-based justice initiative.

social control
A society's ability to control individual behavior in order to serve the best interests and welfare of the society as a whole.

 LO4 Name the three basic component agencies of criminal justice.

or reduce outlawed behavior by apprehending, adjudicating, and sanctioning lawbreakers. Society maintains other forms of informal social control, such as parental and school discipline, but these are designed to deal with moral—not legal—misbehavior. Only the criminal justice system has the power to control crime and punish outlawed behavior through the arm of the criminal law.

The contemporary criminal justice system can be divided into three main components: law enforcement agencies (see the accompanying Careers in Criminal Justice feature), which investigate crimes and apprehend suspects; the court system, which charges, indicts, tries, and sentences offenders; and the correctional system, which incapacitates convicted offenders and attempts to aid in their treatment and rehabilitation (see Figure 1.1).

Criminal justice agencies are political entities whose structure and function are lodged within the legislative, judicial, and executive branches of the government:

■ *Legislative.* Under our current justice system, the legislature defines the law by determining what conduct is prohibited and establishes criminal penalties for those who violate the law. The legislative branch of government helps shape justice policy by creating appropriations for criminal justice agencies and acting as a forum for the public expression of views on criminal justice issues.

■ *Judicial.* The judiciary interprets existing laws and determines whether they meet constitutional requirements. It also oversees criminal justice practices and has the power to determine whether existing operations fall within the bounds

Police	Courts	Corrections
Police departments are those public agencies created to maintain order, enforce the criminal law, provide emergency services, keep traffic on streets and highways moving freely, and develop a sense of community safety. Police officers work actively with the community to prevent criminal behavior; they help divert members of special needs populations, such as juveniles, alcoholics, and drug addicts, from the criminal justice system; they participate in specialized units such as a drug prevention task force or antirape unit; they cooperate with public prosecutors to initiate investigations into organized crime and drug trafficking; they resolve neighborhood and family conflicts; and they provide emergency services, such as preserving civil order during strikes and political demonstrations.	The criminal courthouse is the scene of the trial process. Here the criminal responsibility of defendants accused of violating the law is determined. Ideally, the court is expected to convict and sentence those found guilty of crimes while ensuring that the innocent are freed without any consequence or burden. The court system is formally required to seek the truth, to obtain justice for the individual brought before its tribunals, and to maintain the integrity of the government's rule of law. The main actors in the court process are the judge, whose responsibilities include overseeing the legality of the trial process, and the prosecutor and the defense attorney, who are the opponents in what is known as the adversary system. These two parties oppose each other in a hotly disputed contest—the criminal trial—in accordance with rules of law and procedure.	In the broadest sense, correctional agencies include community supervision or probation, various types of incarceration (including jails, houses of correction, and state prisons), and parole programs for both juvenile and adult offenders. These programs range from the lowest security, such as probation in the community with minimum supervision, to the highest security, such as 23-hour lockdown in an ultra-maximum-security prison. Corrections ordinarily represent the postadjudicatory care given to offenders when a sentence is imposed by the court and the offender is placed in the hands of the correctional agency.

FIGURE 1.1   Components of the Criminal Justice System

of the state constitution and, ultimately, the U.S. Constitution. The courts have the right to overturn or ban poli[...]onflict with constitutional rights.

■ **Executive.** The executive bran[...]rnment is responsible for the day-to-day operation of justice agenc[...]s not make or interpret the laws but is trusted with their enforcen[...]is capacity, it must create and oversee the agencies of justice, deter[...]budget, and guide their direction and objectives. Laws cannot be e[...]nless the executive supplies crime control agencies with sufficient [...]o support their efforts.

Web App 1.2

For extensive details on justice system expenditures, visit http://www.bjs.gov/index.cfm?ty=pbdetail&iid=4679.

Scope of the System

Because of its varied and comp[...]n, the contemporary criminal justice system in the [...]tates is monumental in size. It now costs federal, state, and local governments more than $260 billion per year for civil and criminal justice. One reason why the justice system is so expensive to run is that it employs more than 2 million people in thousands of independent law enforcement, court-related, and correctional agencies. The nation now has almost 18,000 law enforcement agencies, including more than 12,000 local police departments, 3,000 county sheriffs' offices, and 49 state police departments (every state has one except Hawaii).[14] In addition, there are 2,000 other specialized law enforcement agencies ranging from transit police in large cities to county constables.

These police and law enforcement agencies now employ more than a million people; more than 765,000 are sworn personnel with general arrest powers, and the rest are civilian employees. Of these, about 600,000 are in local agencies, 350,000 work in county sheriffs' offices, and 90,000 work for state police.[15] There are nearly 17,000 courts; more than 8,000 prosecutorial agencies employ around 80,000 people; and about 1,200 correctional institutions (such as jails, prisons, and detention centers) employ around half a million people. There are also thousands of community corrections agencies, including more than 3,500 probation and parole departments.

The system is massive because it must process, treat, and care for millions of people. Although the crime rate has declined substantially in the past several years, more than 12 million people are still being arrested each year, including 520,000 for violent crimes and 1,600,000 for property

FACT CHECK ✓

YOUR OPINION: Are we spending too much, too little, or about the right amount of money on the crime problem?

PUBLIC OPINION:

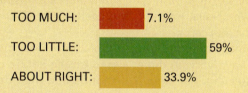

TOO MUCH: 7.1%

TOO LITTLE: 59%

ABOUT RIGHT: 33.9%

REALITY: Whether we should spend more on criminal justice boils down to personal preference. Criminal justice professionals often complain about shrinking budgets and being forced to do "more with less," yet there is evidence our priorities could be out of whack. For example, the vast majority of states spend more per inmate than they do per student. Some states spend five or more times as much on prisoners as they do students!

DISCUSSION: Why do a majority of Americans feel we do not spend enough tackling the crime problem?

Sources: T. W. Smith, *Trends in National Spending Priorities, 1973–2012: General Social Survey Trend Report* (Chicago: NORC, 2013), http://www.norc.org/PDFs/GSS%20Spending%20Priorities.pdf (accessed April 2014); CNN Money, *Education vs. Prison Costs*, http://www.money.cnn.com/infographic/economy/education-vs-prison-costs/ (accessed July 2014).

TABLE 1.1 **Justice Expenditure**

Activity	AMOUNT (THOUSANDS OF DOLLARS)			
	All governments	Federal government	State governments	Local governments
Total justice system	260,533,129	54,384,819	84,871,303	131,704,218
Police protection	124,191,060	31,525,685	13,828,055	83,106,216
Judicial and legal	56,100,520	14,352,695	22,493,697	22,074,259
Corrections	80,241,549	8,506,439	48,549,551	26,523,743

Source: Bureau of Justice Statistics, *Justice Expenditure and Employment Extracts* (Washington, DC: Bureau of Justice Statistics, July 1, 2013), http://www.bjs.gov/index.cfm?ty=pbdetail&iid=4679 (accessed April 2014).

CAREERS in criminal justice

POLICE OFFICER

DUTIES AND CHARACTERISTICS OF THE JOB

Police officers are responsible for enforcing the written laws and ordinances of their jurisdiction. Police officers patrol within their jurisdiction and respond to calls wherever police attention is needed. Duties can be routine, such as writing a speeding ticket, or more involved, such as responding to a domestic disturbance or investigating a robbery. Their nonpatrol duties include testifying in court and writing reports of their law enforcement actions. Some officers will choose or be chosen to work in specialized units such as the well-known special weapons and tactics (SWAT) teams or canine (K9) corps.

Police officers patrol jurisdictions of various sizes and have varying duties based on the nature of their jurisdiction. For example, sheriffs and their deputies enforce the laws within a county. State police primarily patrol state highways and respond to calls for backup from police units across their state. Institutions such as colleges and universities often have their own police forces as well, which enforce laws and rules in this specific area.

Police work can be an intense and stressful job; it sometimes entails encounters with hostile and potentially violent people. Police are asked to put their lives on the line to preserve order and safety. Their actions are watched closely and reflect upon their entire department. Because the places that police protect must be watched at all times, police work shifts may fall on

Boston Globe/Getty Images

CAMBRIDGE, MA - DECEMBER 16: A member of the Boston Police K-9 unit is seen on Harvard Yard near the Science Center during a bomb scare at Harvard University in Cambridge, Massachusetts December 16, 2013.

weekends and holidays. Quite often it is the younger police officers who take these less desirable shifts. Additionally, police officers often have to work overtime; 45-hour workweeks are common.

JOB OUTLOOK

Government spending ultimately determines how many officers a department has. Overall opportunities in local

L05 Describe the size and scope of the contemporary justice system.

crimes; in all more than 2 million arrests are now being made each year for serious felony offenses.[16] In addition, the juvenile courts handle about 1.5 million juveniles. Today, state and federal courts process, convict, and sentence over 1 million adults each year.[17] It is not surprising, considering these numbers, that today nearly 7 million people are under some form of correctional supervision, including 2.2 million men and women in the nation's jails and prisons and an additional 4.8 million adult men and women being supervised in the community while on probation or parole.[18] How can this trend be explained? The answer is that people are more likely to be convicted than in the past and, if sent to prison or jail, to serve more of their sentence. The cost of corrections is now about $80 billion per year, a cost of about $36,000 per inmate, reinforcing the old saying that "It costs more to put a person in the state pen than to send a student to Penn State."

police departments will be excellent for individuals who meet the stringent psychological, personal, and physical qualifications. Many openings are created by the need to replace workers who retire and those who leave local agencies for federal jobs or for employment in private-sector security.

Most police officers are employed at the local level, so this is where a majority of the jobs are found. There are generally more opportunities for employment in larger departments, such as those that serve large urban or suburban areas. Not surprisingly, most opportunities exist in areas with comparatively high crime rates or low salaries.

SALARY

The most recent data available indicate that the median salary (half are above, half below) for police and sheriffs' patrol officers is $56,980. Overtime pay and various incentives, such as a salary bump for college graduates, can quickly increase the base salary. However, smaller agencies in rural areas tend to pay considerably less than their urban counterparts.

OPPORTUNITIES

Police work is often appealing to many because of the good benefits and retirement policies. These factors may contribute to the fact that for the better-paying positions, such as state police, there may be more applicants than available positions. This competition means that those with qualifications such as a college education will have a better chance of being hired. After several years, those with the proper education who build a reputation for good work can rise in the ranks

of their department or be assigned to other desirable positions, such as detective or investigator.

QUALIFICATIONS

To be a police officer, you must be in good shape mentally and physically, as well as meet certain education requirements and pass written tests. New police officers undergo thorough, rigorous training and testing—normally by spending 12 to 14 weeks at a local police academy—before they go out on the streets. During training, new officers learn diverse skills that will be necessary for their job, such as knowledge of laws and individual rights, self-defense, and first aid. Applicants can also expect to be asked to pass lie detector and drug tests.

Because of the enormous responsibility associated with being a police officer, certain personal qualities are considered indispensable for future officers. These include responsibility, good communication skills, good judgment, and the ability to make quick decisions.

EDUCATION AND TRAINING

In most cases, one needs a high school diploma to be a police officer, but more and more jurisdictions are requiring at least some college education. Some college credits may be enough for an applicant to obtain a position on the police force, but more education, generally in the form of a bachelor's degree in a relevant field (especially criminal justice), is necessary for being promoted and moving up in rank.

Source: "Police and Detectives," *Occupational Outlook Handbook* (Bureau of Labor Statistics, U.S. Department of Labor), http://www.bls.gov/ooh/Protective-Service/Police-and-detectives.htm (accessed April 2014).

The Formal Criminal Justice Process

 **Web App 1.3**

For more information about data on the criminal justice system, visit http://www.bjs.gov/.

Another way of understanding criminal justice is to view it as a process that takes an offender through a series of decision points beginning with arrest and concluding with reentry into society. During this process, key decision makers resolve whether to maintain the offender in the system or to discharge the suspect without further action. This decision making is often a matter of individual discretion, based on a variety of factors and perceptions. Legal factors, including the seriousness of the charges, available evidence, and the suspect's prior record, are usually considered legitimate influences on decision making. Troubling is the fact that the suspect's race, gender, class, and age may also influence decision outcomes. Critics believe that such extralegal factors determine the direction a case will take, whereas supporters argue that the system is relatively fair and unbiased.[19]

In reality, few cases are actually processed through the entire formal justice system. Most are handled informally and with dispatch. The system of justice has been roundly criticized for its "backroom deals" and bargain justice. It is true that most criminal suspects are treated informally, but more important is the fact that every defendant charged with a serious crime is entitled to a full range of legal rights and constitutional protections.

Formal Procedures

The formal criminal process includes a complex series of steps, from initial contact to postrelease.

INITIAL CONTACT In most instances, an offender's initial contact with the criminal justice system takes place as a result of a police action:

- Patrol officers observe a person acting suspiciously, conclude the suspect is under the influence of drugs, and take her into custody.

- Police officers are contacted by a victim who reports a robbery; they respond by going to the scene of the crime and apprehending a suspect.

- An informer tells police about some ongoing criminal activity in order to receive favorable treatment.

- Responding to a request by the mayor or other political figure, the local department may initiate an investigation into an ongoing criminal enterprise such as gambling, prostitution, or drug trafficking.

- A person walks into the police station and confesses to committing a crime—for example, he killed his wife after an altercation.

- Initial contact can also be initiated by citizens when no crime is involved—for example, when a parent files a petition in juvenile court alleging that his child is beyond control and needs to be placed in a state detention facility.

L06 Describe the formal criminal justice process.

INVESTIGATION The purpose of the criminal investigation is to gather enough evidence to identify a suspect and support a legal arrest. An investigation can take just a few minutes, as when a police officer sees a crime in progress and apprehends the suspect quickly. Or it can take many years and involve hundreds of law enforcement agents. Dennis Rader, the notorious BTK (Bind, Torture, Kill) serial killer, began his murderous streak in 1974 and was finally apprehended in 2005 after an investigation that lasted more than 30 years.[20]

During the investigatory stage, police officers gather information in an effort to identify the perpetrator of a crime, understand the perpetrator's methods and motives, and determine whether the crime was an individual event or one of many similar crimes committed by a single individual. Gathering information means engaging in such activities as interviewing victims and witnesses at the crime scene, canvassing the neighborhood to locate additional witnesses, securing the crime scene, and then conducting a thorough search for physical evidence, such as weapons, fluids, and fingerprints.

Experienced officers recognize that all material gathered during a criminal investigation must be carefully collected, recorded, classified, processed, and stored. Because they may have to testify at trial under strict rules of evidence, they know that even early in the investigatory process, all evidence must be marked for identification and protectively packaged. If the police fail to follow proper procedures, the "chain of evidence" may be broken, tainting the evidence and making it inadmissible in court. Similarly, police must follow proper procedures while interviewing and/or searching suspects, being careful to uphold the constitutionally guaranteed right to privacy. If police overstep the boundaries set by the law to protect the rights of the accused, relevant information may later be excluded from trial.

ARREST An arrest is considered legal when all of the following conditions exist:

- The police officer believes there is sufficient evidence, referred to as "probable cause," that a crime is being or has been committed and that the suspect is the person who committed the illegal act.
- The officer deprives the individual of freedom.
- The suspect believes that he is now in the custody of the police and has lost his liberty. The police officer is not required to use the word "arrest" or any similar term to initiate an arrest, nor does the officer have to handcuff or restrain the suspect or bring him to the police station.

Justin Bieber appears briefly in front of Judge Joseph Farina, via video, clad in red jail-issued scrubs, at Miami-Dade Circuit Court in Florida. Bond was set at $2,500.

Under most circumstances, to make an arrest in a misdemeanor, the officer must have witnessed the crime personally, a principle known as the **in-presence requirement**. However, some jurisdictions have waived the in-presence requirement in specific classes of crimes, such as domestic violence offenses, enabling police officers to take formal action after the crime has been committed even if they were not present when it occurred. Arrests can also be made when a magistrate, presented with sufficient evidence by police and prosecutors, issues a warrant authorizing the arrest of the suspect.

CUSTODY After an arrest and while the suspect is being detained, the police may wish to search for evidence, conduct an interrogation, or even encourage a confession. Witnesses may be brought to view the suspect in a lineup or in a one-on-one confrontation. Because these procedures are so crucial and can have a great impact at trial, the U.S. Supreme Court has granted suspects in police custody protection from the unconstitutional abuse of police power, such as illegal searches and intimidating interrogations. If a suspect who is under arrest is to be questioned about her involvement in or knowledge of a crime, the police must advise her of her right to remain silent and inform her that she is under no obligation to answer questions. Furthermore, recognizing that the police can take advantage of or exploit the suspect's psychological distress, the Court has ordered interrogating officers to advise the suspect that she is entitled to have a lawyer present and that the state will provide one at no charge if she cannot afford legal services. This so-called ***Miranda* warning** must be given if the police intend to use the answers against the person in a criminal case. If the arrested person chooses to remain silent, the questioning must stop. (*Miranda* will be discussed further in Chapter 8.)

CHARGING If the arresting officers or their superiors believe that sufficient evidence exists to charge a person with a crime, the case will be turned over to the prosecutor's office. The prosecutor's decision whether to charge the suspect with a specific criminal act involves many factors, including evidence sufficiency, crime seriousness, case pressure, and political issues, as well as personal factors such as a prosecutor's own specific interests and biases.

in-presence requirement
The principle that in order to make an arrest in a misdemeanor, the arresting officer must have personally witnessed the crime being committed.

***Miranda* warning**
Miranda v. Arizona established that suspects under arrest must be advised that they have no obligation to answer questions and that they are entitled to have a lawyer present during questioning, if necessary, at no expense to themselves.

Charging is a critical decision in the justice process. Depending on the prosecutor's interpretation of the case, the suspect could be charged with a felony or a misdemeanor, and the subsequent differences between the charges can be vast. It is also possible that after conducting a preliminary investigation of its legal merits, prosecutors may decide to take no further action in a case; this is referred to as a ***nolle prosequi***.

PRELIMINARY HEARING/GRAND JURY Created in England in the twelfth century, the grand jury's original purpose was to act as a buffer between the king (and his prosecutors) and the common citizen. The practice was instituted in the colonies, and later the U.S. Constitution mandated that before a trial can take place, the government must first show probable cause to believe that the accused committed the crime for which he is being charged. In about half the states and in the federal system, this determination is made by a grand jury in a closed hearing. In its most classic form, the **grand jury** consists of 12 to 23 persons, who convene in private session to evaluate accusations against the accused and determine whether the evidence warrants further legal action. If the prosecution can present sufficient evidence, the grand jury will issue a **true bill of indictment**, which specifies the exact charges on which the accused must stand trial.

In some instances, and especially in the federal system, prosecutors have used the grand jury as an investigative instrument directed against ongoing criminal conspiracies, including racketeering and political corruption. In this capacity, the grand jury has wide, sweeping, and almost unrestricted power to subpoena witnesses, solicit their testimony, and hand down indictments. Because the power to use the grand jury in this way is virtually in complete control of the prosecutor, and thus its proper application depends on his or her good faith, critics have warned of abuse and potential "witch hunts."[21]

In most states (and ironically, in England, where the practice began), the grand jury system has been either replaced or supplemented by the preliminary hearing. In a preliminary hearing, the prosecution files a charging document (usually called an "information") before a lower trial court, which then conducts an open hearing on the merits of the case. During this procedure, which is often referred to as a "probable cause hearing," the defendant and the defendant's attorney may appear and dispute the prosecutor's charges. The suspect will be called to stand trial if the presiding magistrate or judge accepts the prosecutor's evidence as factual and sufficient.

Both the grand jury and the preliminary hearing are designed to protect citizens from malicious or false prosecutions that can damage their reputations and cause them both financial distress and psychological anguish.

ARRAIGNMENT Before the trial begins, the defendant will be arraigned, or brought before the court that will hear the case. At this time, formal charges are read; the defendant is informed of his constitutional rights (the right to be represented by legal counsel and to have the state provide one if he is indigent); an initial plea (not guilty or guilty) is entered in the case; a trial date is set; and bail issues are considered.

BAIL/DETENTION Bail is a money bond levied to ensure the return of a criminal defendant for trial, allowing the defendant to remain in the community prior to trial. Defendants who do not show up for trial forfeit their bail. Those people who cannot afford to put up bail or who cannot borrow sufficient funds for it remain in state custody prior to trial. In most instances, this means an extended stay in a county jail or house of correction. If they are stable members of the community and have committed nonviolent crimes,

---

nolle prosequi

The term used when a prosecutor decides to drop a case after a complaint has been formally made. Reasons for a *nolle prosequi* include evidence insufficiency, reluctance of witnesses to testify, police error, and office policy.

grand jury

A type of jury responsible for investigating alleged crimes, examining evidence, and issuing indictments.

true bill of indictment

A written statement charging a defendant with the commission of a crime, drawn up by a prosecuting attorney and considered by a grand jury. If the grand jury finds sufficient evidence to support the indictment, it will issue a true bill of indictment.

defendants may be released on their own recognizance (promise to the court), without bail.

PLEA BARGAINING After an arraignment, if not before, the defense and prosecution discuss a possible guilty plea in exchange for reducing or dropping some of the charges or agreeing to a request for a more lenient sentence or some other consideration, such as placement in a treatment facility rather than a maximum-security prison. It is generally accepted that almost 90 percent of all cases end in a plea bargain, rather than a criminal trial.

TRIAL/ADJUDICATION If an agreement cannot be reached or if the prosecution does not wish to arrange a negotiated settlement of the case, a criminal trial will be held before a judge (bench trial) or jury, who will decide whether the prosecution's evidence against the defendant is sufficient beyond a reasonable doubt to prove guilt. If a jury cannot reach a decision—that is, if it is deadlocked—the case is left unresolved, leaving the prosecution to decide whether it should be retried at a later date.

SENTENCING/DISPOSITION If after a criminal trial the accused has been found guilty as charged, he will be returned to court for sentencing. Possible dispositions may include a fine, probation, some form of community-based corrections, a period of incarceration in a penal institution, and, in rare instances, the death penalty.

APPEAL/POSTCONVICTION REMEDIES After conviction, the defense can ask the trial judge to set aside the jury's verdict because the jury has made a mistake of law, such as misinterpreting the judge's instructions or convicting on a charge that was not supported by the evidence. Failing that, the defendant may file an appeal if, after conviction, she believes that her constitutional rights were violated by errors in the trial process. Appellate courts review such issues as whether evidence was used properly, whether the judge conducted the trial in an approved fashion, whether jury selection was properly done, and whether the attorneys in the case acted appropriately. If the court finds that the appeal has merit, it can rule that the defendant be given a new trial or, in some instances, order her outright release.

CORRECTIONAL TREATMENT After sentencing, the offender is placed within the jurisdiction of state or federal correctional authorities. The offender may serve a probationary term, be placed in a community correctional facility, serve a term in a county jail, or be housed in a prison. During this stage of the criminal justice process, the offender may be asked to participate in rehabilitation programs designed to help her make a successful readjustment to society.

RELEASE Upon completion of the sentence and period of correction, the offender will be free to return to society. Most inmates do not serve the full term of their sentence but are freed through an early-release mechanism, such as parole or pardon, or by earning time off for good behavior. Offenders sentenced to community supervision simply finish their term and resume their lives in the community.

POSTRELEASE After termination of their correctional treatment, offenders may be asked to spend some time in a community correctional center, which acts as a bridge between a secure treatment facility and absolute freedom. Offenders may find that their conviction has cost them some personal privileges, such as the right to hold certain kinds of employment. These may be returned by court order once the offenders have proved their trustworthiness and willingness to abide by society's rules.

The Criminal Justice Assembly Line

L07 Articulate what is meant by the term *criminal justice assembly line.*

To justice expert Herbert Packer, the image that comes to mind from the criminal justice process is an assembly-line conveyor belt down which moves an endless stream of cases, never stopping, carrying them to workers who stand at fixed stations and who perform, on each case as it comes by, the same small but essential operation that brings it one step closer to being a finished product—or, to exchange the metaphor for the reality, a closed file.[22] Criminal justice is seen as a screening process in which each successive stage (prearrest investigation, arrest, postarrest investigation, preparation for trial or entry of plea, conviction, disposition) involves a series of routinized operations whose success is gauged primarily by their ability to pass the case along to a successful conclusion.[23]

According to this view, each of the stages is a decision point through which cases flow. At the investigatory stage, police must decide whether to pursue the case or to terminate involvement because insufficient evidence exists to identify a suspect, because the case is considered trivial, or because the victim decides not to press charges. At the bail stage, a decision must be made whether to set bail so high that the defendant remains in custody, to set a moderate bail, or to release the defendant on her own recognizance. Each of these decisions can have a critical effect on the defendant, the justice system, and society. If an error is made, an innocent person may suffer or, conversely, a dangerous individual may be released to continue to prey upon the community.

In practice, many suspects are released before trial because of a procedural error, evidence problems, or other reasons that result in a case dismissal by the prosecutor (*nolle prosequi*). Although most cases that go to trial wind up in a conviction, others are dismissed by the presiding judge because of a witness's or complainant's failure to appear or because of procedural irregularities. Thus the justice process can be viewed as a funnel that holds many cases at its mouth and relatively few at its stem end.

Theoretically, nearly every part of the process requires that individual cases be disposed of as quickly as possible. However, the criminal justice process is slowed by congestion, inadequate facilities, limited resources, inefficiency, and the nature of governmental bureaucracy. When defendants are not processed smoothly, often because of the large caseloads and inadequate facilities that exist in many urban jurisdictions, the procedure breaks down, and the ultimate goal of a fair and efficient justice system cannot be achieved.

Figure 1.2 illustrates the approximate number of offenders removed from the criminal justice system at each stage of the process. As the figure shows, most people who commit crime escape detection, and of those who do not, relatively few are bound over for trial, convicted, and eventually sentenced to prison. However, more than a million people are convicted on felony charges each year—about 30 percent of all people arrested on felony charges. About 70 percent of people convicted on felony charges are sentenced to a period of incarceration, either in state prison or in a local jail. Of the remainder, about 25 percent receive a probation sentence with no jail or prison time. The rest receive fines, restitution, treatment, community service, or some other penalty (for example, house arrest or periodic drug testing).[24] The average prison sentence is about five years; most imprisoned felons are able to get out early via parole, early release for good behavior, or both. Concept Summary 1.1 shows the interrelationship of the component agencies of the criminal justice system and the criminal justice process.

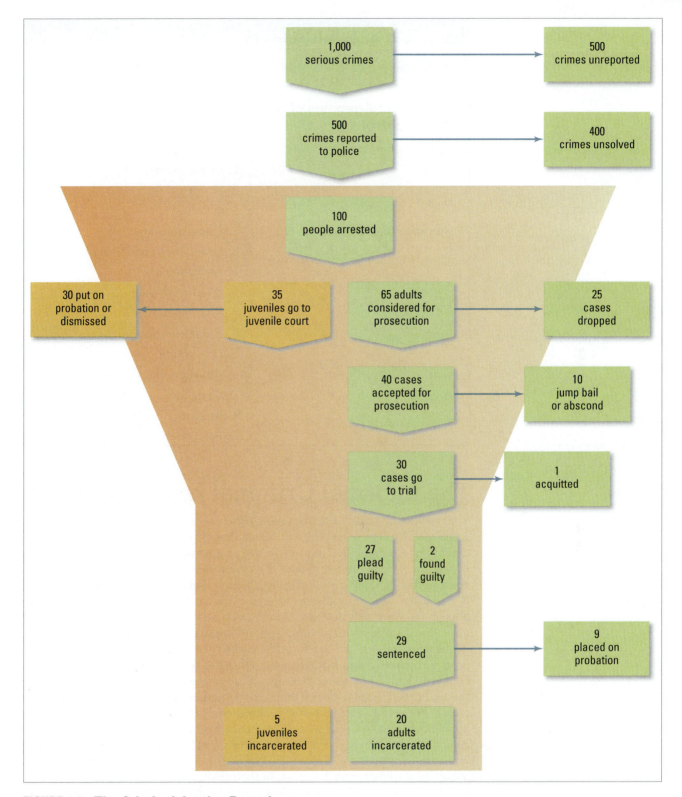

FIGURE 1.2 **The Criminal Justice Funnel**

Sources: Thomas H. Cohen and Tracey Kyckelhahn, *Felony Defendants in Large Urban Counties, 2006* (Washington, DC: Bureau of Justice Statistics, 2010); Matthew Durose, Donald Farole, and Sean Rosenmerkel, *Felony Sentences in State Courts, 2006* (Washington, DC: Bureau of Justice Statistics, 2009).

CONCEPT SUMMARY 1.1

The Interrelationship of the Criminal Justice System and the Criminal Justice Process

The System: Agencies of Crime Control	The Process
Police	1. Contact
	2. Investigation
	3. Arrest
	4. Custody
Prosecution and Defense	5. Complaint/charging
	6. Grand jury/preliminary hearing
	7. Arraignment
	8. Bail/detention
	9. Plea negotiations
Courts	10. Adjudication
	11. Disposition
	12. Appeal/postconviction remedies
Corrections	13. Correction
	14. Release
	15. Postrelease

The Informal Criminal Justice System

The traditional model of the criminal justice system depicts the legal process as a series of decision points through which cases flow. Each stage of the system is defined by time-honored administrative procedures and controlled by the rule of law. The public's perception of the system, fueled by the media, is that it is composed of daredevil, crime-fighting police officers who never ask for overtime or sick leave, crusading district attorneys who stop at nothing to send the mob boss up the river, wily defense attorneys who neither ask clients for up-front cash nor cut short office visits to play golf, no-nonsense judges who are never inept political appointees, and tough wardens who rule the yard with an iron hand. Yet it would be overly simplistic to assume that the system works this way for every case. Although a few cases illustrate all the rights and procedures that make up the traditional, formal model, many are settled in an informal pattern of cooperation between the major actors in the justice process. For example, police may be willing to make a deal with a suspect to gain his cooperation, and the prosecutor may bargain with the defense attorney to get a plea of guilty as charged in return for a promise of leniency. Law enforcement agents and court officers are allowed tremendous discretion in their decisions whether to make an arrest, to bring formal charges, to handle a case informally, to substitute charges, and so on. Crowded courts operate in a spirit of getting the matter settled quickly and cleanly, instead of engaging in long, drawn-out criminal proceedings with an uncertain outcome.

The recognition of the informal justice process has spurred development of two concepts—the courtroom work group and the wedding cake model—that help us better understand how U.S. justice really operates.

The Courtroom Work Group

Whereas the traditional model regards the justice process as an adversary proceeding in which the prosecution and defense are combatants, the majority of criminal cases are cooperative ventures in which all parties get together to work out a deal.

This **courtroom work group**, which is made up of the prosecutor, defense attorney, judge, and other court personnel, functions to streamline the process of justice through the extensive use of plea bargaining and other trial alternatives. Instead of looking to provide a spirited defense or prosecution, these legal agents (who have often attended the same schools, know one another, and have worked together for many years) try to work out a case to their own professional advantage. Their goal is to remove "unnecessary" delays and avoid formal trials at all costs. Because most defendants who have gotten this far in the system are assumed to be guilty, the goal is to process cases efficiently rather than to seek justice.

In most criminal cases, cooperation, not conflict, between prosecution and defense appears to be the norm. The adversarial process comes into play in only a few widely publicized criminal cases involving rape or murder. Consequently, more than 90 percent of all cases are settled without trial.

What has developed is a system in which criminal court experiences can be viewed as a training ground for young defense attorneys looking for seasoning and practice. It provides a means for newly established lawyers to receive government compensation for cases they take to get their practice going and an arena in which established firms can place their new associates for experience before they assign them to paying clients. Similarly, successful prosecutors often look forward to a political career or a highly paid partnership in a private firm. To further their career aspirations, prosecutors must develop and maintain a winning track record in criminal cases. Although the courtroom work group limits the constitutional rights of defendants, it may be essential for keeping the overburdened justice system afloat. Moreover, it is not clear that the informal justice system is inherently unfair to both the victim and the offender. Rather, evidence shows that the defendants who benefit the most from informal court procedures commit the least serious crimes, whereas most chronic offenders gain relatively little.[25]

The Wedding Cake Model of Justice

Samuel Walker, a justice historian and scholar, has come up with a dramatic way of describing the informal justice process. He compares it with a four-layer cake, as depicted in Figure 1.3.[26]

LEVEL I The first layer of Walker's model is made up of the celebrated cases involving famous people and those charged with committing particularly heinous crimes that capture national headlines. For example, there was an avalanche of media interest in the kidnapping of Elizabeth Smart from her Salt Lake City home on June 5, 2002, and her rescue nine months later. Media attention rebounded in 2010 when her abductors, Brian David Mitchell and Wanda Barzee, were tried and convicted of the crime, Barzee receiving a 15-year sentence and Mitchell life without the chance of parole.[27]

Cases in the first layer of the criminal justice wedding cake usually receive the full array of criminal justice procedures, including competent defense attorneys, expert witnesses, jury trials, and elaborate appeals. The media typically focus on Level I cases, and the TV-watching public gets the impression that most criminals are sober, intelligent people, and most victims are members of the upper classes—a patently false impression.

LEVEL II In the second layer are the serious felonies—rapes, robberies, and burglaries—that have become all too familiar in U.S. society. These are serious

Web App 1.4

Read more about how the courtroom work group functions in a specialized court by reading the article here: http://www.academia.edu/865168/New_Roles_in_the_Courtroom_Workgroup_Developing_Federal_Problem_Solving_Courts.

---

courtroom work group
A term used to imply that all parties in the justice process work together in a cooperative effort to settle cases efficiently rather than to engage in a true adversarial procedure.

L08 Discuss the wedding cake model of justice.

FIGURE 1.3 **The Criminal Justice Wedding Cake**

Source: Based on Samuel Walker's *Sense and Nonsense about Crime* (Monterey, CA: Brooks/Cole, 1983).

Michael Fee, defense attorney for former New England Patriots tight end Aaron Hernandez, speaks to the media outside Attleboro (Massachusetts) District Court after Hernandez was arraigned. Hernandez was charged with murdering Odin Lloyd, a 27-year-old semi-pro football player for the Boston Bandits, whose body was found in an industrial park. High-profile cases like this one occupy the top of the criminal justice wedding cake.

crimes committed by experienced offenders. Burglaries are included if the amount stolen is high and the techniques that were used indicate the suspect is a pro. Violent crimes, such as rape and assault, are vicious incidents against an innocent victim and may involve a weapon and extreme violence. Robberies involve large amounts of money and suspects who brandish handguns or other weapons and are considered career criminals. Police, prosecutors, and judges all agree that these cases demand the full attention of the justice system. Offenders in such Level II cases receive a full jury trial and, if convicted, can look forward to a prison sentence.

LEVEL III Although they can also be felonies, crimes that fall in the third layer of the wedding cake are less serious offenses committed by young or first-time offenders or involving people who knew each other or were otherwise related: An inebriated teenager committed a burglary and netted $50; the rape victim had gone on a few dates with her assailant before he attacked her; the robbery involved members of rival gangs and no weapons; the assault was the result of a personal dispute, and there is some question who hit whom first. Agents of the criminal justice system relegate these cases to the third level because they see them as less important and less deserving of attention. Level III crimes may be dealt with by an outright dismissal, a plea bargain, reduction in charges, or (most typically) a probationary sentence or intermediate sanction, such as victim restitution.

LEVEL IV The fourth layer of the cake is made up of the millions of misdemeanors, such as disorderly conduct, shoplifting, public drunkenness, and minor assault. The lower criminal courts handle these cases in assembly-line fashion. Few defendants insist on exercising their constitutional rights, because the delay would cost them valuable time and money. Because the typical penalty is a small fine, everyone wants to get the case over with.[28]

The wedding cake model of informal justice is an intriguing alternative to the traditional criminal justice flowchart. Criminal justice officials handle individual cases differently, yet there is a high degree of consistency in the way particular types or classes of cases are dealt with in every legal jurisdiction. The model is also useful because it shows that all too often public opinion about criminal justice is formed on the basis of what happened in an atypical case.

Perspectives on Justice

Since the 1960s, when the field of criminal justice began to be the subject of both serious academic study and attempts at unified policy formation, significant debate has continued over the meaning of the term *criminal justice* and how the problem of crime control should be approached. After decades of research and policy analysis, criminal justice is still far from a unified field. Practitioners, academics, and commentators alike have expressed irreconcilable differences concerning its goals, purpose, and direction. Some conservatives believe the solution to the crime problem is to increase the number of police, apprehend more criminals, and give them long sentences in maximum-security prisons. In contrast, liberals call for increased spending on social services and community organization. Others worry about giving the government too much power to regulate and control behavior and to interfere with individual liberty and freedom.

 LO9 Explain the various perspectives on criminal justice.

Given the multitude of problems facing the justice system, this lack of consensus is particularly vexing. The agencies of justice must try to eradicate such diverse social problems as substance abuse, gang violence, pornography, cyber crime, and terrorism, all the while respecting individual liberties and civil rights. The agencies of the justice system also need adequate resources to carry out their complex tasks effectively, but this hope often seems to be wishful thinking. Experts are still searching for the right combination of policies and actions that will significantly reduce crime and increase public safety, while upholding individual freedom and social justice.

Considering the complexity of criminal justice, it is not surprising that no single view, perspective, or philosophy dominates the field. What are the dominant views of the criminal justice system today? What is the role of the justice system, and how should it approach its tasks?

The Crime Control Perspective

According to the **crime control perspective** on criminal justice, the proper role of the justice system is to prevent crime through the judicious use of criminal sanctions. People want protection from dangerous criminals and expect the government to do what is necessary to make them feel secure; crime control is part of the democratic process.[29] Because the public is outraged by crime, it demands an efficient justice system that hands out tough sanctions to those who violate the law.[30]

> **crime control perspective**
> A model of criminal justice that emphasizes the control of dangerous offenders and the protection of society through harsh punishment as a deterrent to crime.

According to crime control philosophy, if the justice system operated in an effective manner, most potential criminals would be deterred from crime. The few who broke the law would be apprehended, tried, and punished so that they would never again risk committing crime. Effective law enforcement, strict mandatory punishment, and expanding the use of prison are the keys to reducing crime rates. Although crime control may be expensive, reducing the appeal of criminal activity is well worth the price.

EFFECTIVENESS AND EFFICIENCY According to the crime control perspective, the true goal of the justice system, protecting society, can be achieved through more effective police protection, tough criminal punishments, and the incapacitation of hardened criminals. If the system could be made more efficient, few would be tempted to break the law, and its effectiveness would improve.

Crime control advocates do not want legal technicalities to help the guilty go free and tie the hands of justice. They lobby for the abolition of legal restrictions on law enforcers.[31] The police may sometimes be forced to use tactics that abridge civil liberties for the sake of effectiveness, such as profiling people at an airport on the basis of their race or ethnic origin in an effort to identify and apprehend suspected terrorists. Civil libertarians are wary of racial profiling, but crime control advocates argue that we are in the midst of a national emergency and that the ends justify the means.

ABOLISHING LEGAL ROADBLOCKS One impediment to effective crime control is the legal roadblocks set up by the courts to protect the due process rights of criminal defendants. Several hundred thousand criminals go free every year in cases dropped because courts find that police have violated the suspects' *Miranda* rights.[32] Crime control advocates lobby for abolition of the exclusionary rule, which requires that illegally seized evidence be barred from criminal proceedings. Their voices have been heard: a more conservative Supreme Court has given police greater latitude to search for and seize evidence and has eased restrictions on how police operate. However, research shows that even in this permissive environment, police routinely violate suspects' rights when searching for evidence, and the majority of these incidents are never reviewed by the courts because the search was not followed up by arrest or citation.[33]

In recent years, the crime control model has emerged as the dominant vision of justice. Its proponents have helped shape public attitudes toward crime and its control. As a result, the American public seems quite punitive toward criminals, and about two-thirds approve availability of the death penalty.[34] The Victim Experience feature recounts a notorious incident stemming from the application of the crime control perspective to everyday life.

The Rehabilitation Perspective

rehabilitation perspective
A perspective on criminal justice that sees crime as an expression of frustration and anger created by social inequality that can be controlled by giving people the means to improve their lifestyles through conventional endeavors.

If the crime control perspective views the justice system in terms of protecting the public and controlling criminal elements, the **rehabilitation perspective** sees the justice system as a means of caring for and treating people who cannot manage themselves. Advocates of this perspective view crime as an expression of frustration and anger created by social inequality. Crime can be controlled by giving people the means to improve their lifestyle through conventional endeavors.

The rehabilitation concept assumes that people are at the mercy of social, economic, and interpersonal conditions and interactions. Criminals themselves are the victims of racism, poverty, strain, blocked opportunities, alienation, family disruption, and other social problems. They live in socially disorganized neighborhoods that are incapable of providing proper education, health care, or civil services. Society must help them compensate for their social problems.

the VICTIM experience

NEIGHBORHOOD WATCH

BACKGROUND The Trayvon Martin case drew attention to neighborhood watch programs. Originally designed as neighborhood surveillance programs or groups created so that concerned residents could patrol the streets in an attempt to prevent crime and reduce victimization, they are not a new phenomenon, having been around for more than 30 years. An early example began more than 20 years ago in Laurel Lake, New Jersey, where community residents working with law enforcement founded the Laurel Lake Community Crime Watch in response to an increase in property crime and drug activity in the rural community (population 2,800). Police calculated that 90 percent of the crimes in the area were property crimes committed by those involved in buying and selling drugs. As a consequence of the community watch group's efforts, there was no more graffiti nor any other acts of vandalism. In addition, when the town began enforcing local ordinances such as the late-night juvenile curfew, residents noticed fewer youth on the streets and in trouble.

THE BIG PICTURE While popular, do these programs really help people and reduce victimization? A recent study by Trevor Bennett, Katy Holloway, and David Farrington evaluated 19 carefully chosen studies of neighborhood watch program effectiveness. Their review included stand-alone schemes and those that included other programs such as property marking efforts. They found that about half of the studies indicated neighborhood watch is effective in reducing crime, while the other half found that it has little effect or may even increase crime. Taken together, the research found that in areas with neighborhood watch, crime rates decreased 16 percent more than those without watch programs. The authors find these results "encouraging."

Despite the negative publicity the neighborhood watch program has received over the Martin case, it needs further study to determine whether it can truly prevent people from becoming crime victims.

CLASSROOM EXERCISE Have class members contact neighborhood watch groups in the surrounding areas (if there aren't any, say in a rural area, find groups on the Internet). Ask them about their procedures, their success, and whether members routinely carry guns.

Source: Trevor Bennett, Katy Holloway, and David Farrington, "The Effectiveness of Neighborhood Watch," Campbell Systematic Reviews, 2008, http://www.crim.cam.ac.uk/people/academic_research/david_farrington/nw.pdf (accessed April 2014).

ALTERNATIVES TO CRIME Rehabilitation advocates believe that government programs can help reduce crime on both a societal (macro) and an individual (micro) level. On the macro, or societal, level, research shows that as the number of legitimate opportunities to succeed declines, people are more likely to turn to criminal behaviors, such as drug dealing, to survive. Increasing economic opportunities through job training, family counseling, educational services, and crisis intervention is a more effective crime reducer than prisons and jails. As legitimate opportunities increase, violence rates decline.[35]

Society has a choice: pay now, by funding treatment and educational programs, or pay later, when troubled youths enter costly correctional facilities over and over again. This view is certainly not lost on the public. Although the public may want to get tough on crime, many people are willing to make exceptions—for example, by advocating leniency for younger offenders.[36]

The Due Process Perspective

Advocates of the **due process perspective** argue that the greatest concern of the justice system should be treating all those accused of crime fairly.[37] This means providing impartial hearings, competent legal counsel, equitable treatment, and reasonable sanctions. The use of discretion within the justice system should be strictly monitored to ensure that no one suffers from racial, religious, or ethnic

due process perspective
A perspective on criminal justice that emphasizes individual rights and constitutional safeguards against arbitrary or unfair judicial or administrative proceedings.

discrimination. The system must be attuned to the civil rights afforded every citizen by the U.S. Constitution. Therefore, it is vexing to due process advocates when the Supreme Court extends the scope of law enforcement's reach, enabling police agencies to monitor and control citizens at the expense of their right to privacy.

Although many views exist of what the true goals of justice should be, the system undoubtedly must be expected to operate in a fair and unbiased manner. Those who advocate the due process orientation point out that the justice system remains an adversary process that pits the forces of an all-powerful state against those of a solitary individual accused of committing a crime. If concern for justice and fairness did not exist, the defendant who lacked resources could easily be overwhelmed.

Miscarriages of justice are common. Numerous criminal convictions have been overturned because newly developed DNA evidence later showed that the accused could not have committed the crimes. Many of those who were falsely convicted spent years in prison before their release.[38] Evidence also shows that many innocent people have been executed for crimes they did not commit.

Because such mistakes can happen, even the most apparently guilty offender deserves all the protection the justice system can offer. Having a competent attorney who mounts a spirited defense may mean the difference between life and death. When Talia Roitberg Harmon and William Lofquist studied the cases of people who had been falsely convicted of murder, they found that those who employed private counsel were much more likely to be exonerated than those who could not afford a private attorney.[39] Is it fair that a life-or-death outcome may rest on the ability to afford private counsel?

nonintervention perspective

A perspective on criminal justice that favors the least intrusive treatment possible: decarceration, diversion, and decriminalization.

Those who question the due process perspective claim that the legal privileges that are afforded to criminal suspects have gone too far and that the effort to protect individual rights now interferes with public safety. Is it fair, they argue, for evidence to be suppressed when it is obtained in violation of the constitutional right to be free from illegal search and seizure, even if it means that a guilty person goes free? Yet, many people who appear guilty may actually be victims of slipshod justice. Certainly, the danger of convicting an innocent person still remains a frightening possibility.

Due process advocates are concerned about errors in justice that may cause an innocent person permanent harm. Here, Andre Davis speaks with his mother as his father, Richard Davis, holds a cell phone to his ear outside the Tamms Correctional Center in Illinois, after being released on July 6, 2012. Davis, who spent the last 30 years in prison, was released after his conviction was overturned based on new DNA evidence.

The Nonintervention Perspective

Supporters of the **nonintervention perspective** believe that justice agencies should limit their involvement with criminal defendants. Regardless of whether intervention is designed to punish people or to treat them, the ultimate effect of any involvement is harmful. Whatever their goals or design, programs that bring people in contact with a social control agency—such as the police, a mental health department, the correctional system, or a criminal court—will have long-term negative effects. Once involved with such an agency, criminal defendants may be watched, people might consider them dangerous and untrustworthy, and they can develop a lasting record that has negative connotations. Bearing an official label disrupts their personal and family life and harms parent–child relationships. Eventually, they may even come to believe what their official record suggests; they may view themselves as bad, evil, outcasts, troublemakers, or crazy. Thus, official intervention promotes, rather than reduces, the tendency to engage in antisocial activities.[40]

Noninterventionists are concerned about the effect of the stigma that convicted criminals bear when they are branded "rapist" or "child abuser." As horrifying as these crimes are, such labels imply chronic criminality, and they will stick with the perpetrators forever. Noninterventionists point out that this may not be in the best interests of society. Once labeled, people may find it difficult to be accepted back into society, even after they have completed their sentence. It is not surprising, considering these effects of stigma and labeling, that recidivism rates are so high. When people are given less stigmatizing forms of punishment, such as probation, they are less likely to become repeat offenders.[41]

Fearing the harmful effects of stigma and labels, noninterventionists have tried to place limitations on the government's ability to control people's lives. They have called for the **decriminalization** (reduction of penalties) and legalization of nonserious victimless crimes, such as the possession of small amounts of marijuana, public drunkenness, and vagrancy.

Noninterventionists demand the removal of nonviolent offenders from the nation's correctional system, a policy referred to as **deinstitutionalization**. First offenders who commit minor crimes should instead be placed in informal, community-based treatment programs, a process referred to as pretrial diversion.

Sometimes the passage of new criminal laws can stigmatize offenders beyond the scope of their offense, a phenomenon referred to as widening the net of justice. For example, a person who purchases pornography on the Internet may be labeled a dangerous sex offender, or someone caught for a second time with marijuana may be considered a habitual drug abuser. Noninterventionists have fought implementation of community notification–type laws that require convicted sex offenders to register with state law enforcement officials and that allow officials to publicly disclose when a registrant moves into a community. Their efforts have resulted in rulings stating that these laws can be damaging to the reputation and future of offenders who have not been given an opportunity to defend themselves from the charge that they are chronic criminal sex offenders.[42] As a group, noninterventionist initiatives have been implemented to help people avoid the stigma associated with contact with the criminal justice system.

decriminalization
Reducing the penalty for a criminal act without legalizing it.

deinstitutionalization
The policy of removing from secure confinement as many first offenders of minor, nonviolent crimes as possible and treating them in the community.

AP Images/Brennan Linsley

Employees help customers at the crowded sales counter inside Medicine Man marijuana retail store, which opened as a legal recreational retail outlet in Denver on its opening day, January 1, 2014, a day some called "Green Wednesday." What perspective on justice explains marijuana legalization in Colorado?

The Equal Justice Perspective

equal justice perspective

A perspective on criminal justice based on the idea that all people should receive the same treatment under the law and should be evaluated on the basis of their current behavior, not on what they have done in the past.

racial animus model

The view that white America has developed a mental image of the typical offender as a young, inner-city black male who offends with little remorse.

The **equal justice perspective** asserts that all people should receive the same treatment under the law. The discretion routinely employed in criminal justice making has created a system of individualized justice that can be unfair, and that unfairness undermines the goals of the system. Frustration arises when two people commit the same crime but receive different sentences or punishments. The resulting anger and sense of unfairness will increase the likelihood of recidivism.

The equal justice model has legitimacy, according to its advocates, because there is still evidence that perceptions of race shape the contours of how Americans think about crime and its control. According to the **racial animus model**, white America has developed a mental image of the typical offender as a young, inner-city black male who offends with little remorse.[43] Criminal justice decision makers have responded to the general public's perceptions by endorsing mass imprisonment and the death penalty. Their views rest on the belief that the targets of these harsh crime control efforts are African American young men, a group already feared and loathed by the white majority. These feelings are supported by political pundits who constantly dwell on the failings of the court system and the "coddling of criminals." It is therefore important to ensure the equal treatment of all defendants, regardless of their race or class.[44]

To remedy this situation, each criminal act must be treated independently and punished proportionately. Punishment must not be based on race, class, or status, nor on past events for which people have already paid their debt to society. It is also critical not to base punishment on often erroneous guesses about what defendants may do in the future. The treatment of criminal offenders must be based solely on present behavior. Punishment must be equitably administered and based on the principle of "just deserts."

The equal justice perspective has had considerable influence in molding the nation's sentencing policy. An ongoing effort has been made to reduce discretion and guarantee that every offender convicted of a particular crime receives equal and precisely computed punishment. This change has been particularly welcome, given the charges of racial discrimination that have beset the sentencing process. A number of initiatives have been designed to achieve this result, including mandatory sentences, which require that all people convicted of a crime receive the same prison sentence. Truth-in-sentencing laws require offenders to serve a substantial portion of their prison sentence behind bars, thus limiting their eligibility for early release on parole.

The Restorative Justice Perspective

restorative justice perspective

A perspective on criminal justice that sees the main goal of the criminal justice system as making a systematic response to wrongdoing that emphasizes healing victims, offenders, and communities wounded by crime. It stresses peacemaking, not punishment.

According to the **restorative justice perspective**, the true purpose of the criminal justice system is to promote a peaceful and just society; the justice system should aim for peacemaking, not punishment.[45] The restorative justice perspective draws its inspiration from religious and philosophical teachings ranging from Quakerism to Zen. Advocates of restorative justice view the efforts of the state to punish and control as "crime encouraging" rather than "crime discouraging." The violent punishing acts of the state, they claim, are not unlike the violent acts of individuals.[46] Therefore, mutual aid, not coercive punishment, is the key to a harmonious society. Without the capacity to restore damaged social relations, society's response to crime has been almost exclusively punitive.

According to restorative justice, resolution of the conflict between criminal and victim should take place in the community in which that conflict originated, not in some far-off prison. The victim should be given a chance to voice his story, and the offender can directly communicate her need for social reintegration and treatment. The goal is to enable the offender to appreciate the damage she has caused, to make amends, and to be reintegrated into society.

Restorative justice programs are now being geared to these principles. Mediation and conflict-resolution programs are now common in efforts to resolve harmful human interactions ranging from domestic violence to hate crimes.[47] Police officers, as elements of community policing programs, are beginning to use mediation techniques to settle disputes instead of resorting to formal arrest.[48] Financial and community service restitution programs as an alternative to imprisonment have been in operation for more than two decades.

Perspectives in Perspective

The variety of tactics being used to combat crime today aptly illustrates the impact of the various perspectives on the operations of the criminal justice system. Advocates of each view have attempted to promote their vision of what justice is all about and how it should be applied. During the past decade, the crime control and equal justice models have dominated. Laws have been toughened and the rights of the accused curtailed, the prison population has grown, and the death penalty has been employed against convicted murderers. Because the crime rate has been dropping, these policies seem to be effective. They may be questioned if crime rates once again begin to rise. At the same time, efforts to rehabilitate offenders, to provide them with elements of due process, and to administer the least intrusive treatment have not been abandoned. Police, courts, and correctional agencies supply a wide range of treatment and rehabilitation programs to offenders in all stages of the criminal justice system. Whenever possible, those accused of a crime are treated informally in nonrestrictive, community-based programs, and the effects of stigma are guarded against.

Although the legal rights of offenders are being closely scrutinized by the courts, the basic constitutional rights of the accused remain inviolate. Guardians of the process have made sure that defendants are afforded the maximum protection possible under the law. For example, criminal defendants have been awarded the right to *competent* legal counsel at trial; merely having a lawyer to defend them is not considered sufficient legal protection.

AP Images/Jeff Roberson

Inmate James Burton Jr. waters the "Restorative Justice Gardens" at the Southeast Correctional Center in Charleston, Missouri, on September 5, 2007. Inmates have produced tens of thousands of pounds of fresh vegetables from a six-acre garden at the state prison complex, all of it donated to the Bootheel Food Bank in Sikeston, Missouri, which serves some of the poorest counties in the state. Should society attempt to restore law violators to the community, or should violators merely be punished for their misdeeds?

In sum, understanding the justice system today requires analyzing a variety of occupational roles, institutional processes, legal rules, and administrative doctrines. Each predominant view of criminal justice offers a vantage point for understanding and interpreting these complex issues. No single view is *the* right or correct one. Each individual must choose the perspective that best fits his or her ideas and judgment—or they can all be discarded and the individual's own view substituted. The various perspectives on justice and their key elements are set out in Concept Summary 1.2.

CONCEPT SUMMARY 1.2
Key Elements of the Perspectives on Justice

Perspective on Justice	Main Beliefs
Crime control perspective	■ The purpose of the justice system is to deter crime through the application of punishment. ■ The more efficient the system, the greater its effectiveness. ■ The role of the justice system is not to treat people but, rather, to investigate crimes, apprehend suspects, and punish the guilty.
Rehabilitation perspective	■ In the long run, it is better to treat than to punish. ■ Criminals are society's victims. ■ Helping others is part of the American culture.
Due process perspective	■ Every person deserves his or her full array of constitutional rights and privileges. ■ Preserving the democratic ideals of American society takes precedence over the need to punish the guilty. ■ Because of potential errors, decisions made within the justice system must be carefully scrutinized. ■ Steps must be taken to treat all defendants fairly, regardless of their socioeconomic status. ■ Illegally seized evidence should be suppressed even if it means that a guilty person will go free. ■ Despite the cost, the government should supply free legal counsel at every stage of the justice system to prevent abuse.
Nonintervention perspective	■ The justice process stigmatizes offenders. ■ Stigma locks people into a criminal way of life. ■ Less is better. Decriminalize, divert, and deinstitutionalize whenever possible.
Equal justice perspective	■ People should receive equal treatment for equal crimes. ■ Decision making in the justice system must be standardized and structured by rules and regulations. ■ Whenever possible, individual discretion must be reduced and controlled. ■ Inconsistent treatment undermines respect for the system.
Restorative justice perspective	■ Offenders should be reintegrated into society. ■ Coercive punishments are self-defeating. ■ The justice system must become more humane. ■ Crime is a community-level problem.

Ethics in Criminal Justice

Both the general public and criminal justice professionals are concerned with the application of ethics.[49] Both would like every police officer on the street, every district attorney in court, and every correctional administrator in prison to be able to discern what is right, proper, and moral; to be committed to ethical standards; and to apply equal and fair justice. These demands are difficult to meet, however, because justice system personnel are often forced to work in an environment in which moral ambiguity is the norm.

Should a police officer be forced to arrest, a prosecutor to charge, and a correctional official to punish a woman who for many years was the victim of domestic abuse and in desperation retaliated against her abusive spouse? Who is the victim here, and who is the aggressor? And what about the parent who attacks the man who has sexually abused her young child? Should she be prosecuted as a felon? And what happens if the parent mistakenly attacks and injures the wrong person? Can a clear line be drawn between righteous retribution and vigilante justice? As students of justice, we are concerned with identifying the behavioral standards that should govern everyone involved in the administration of justice. And if these standards can be identified, can we find ways to disseminate them to police departments, courts, and correctional agencies around the nation?

Ethics in criminal justice is an especially important topic today, considering the power granted to those who work in, operate, and control the justice system. We rely on the justice system to exert power over people's lives and to be society's instrument of social control, so we give the system and its agents the authority to deny people their personal liberty on a routine basis. A police officer's ability to arrest and use force, a judge's power to sentence, and a correctional administrator's authority to punish an inmate give them considerable personal power, which must be governed by ethical considerations. Without ethical decision making, individual civil rights may suffer, and personal liberties guaranteed by the U.S. Constitution may be trampled upon.

The need for an ethical criminal justice system is further enhanced by cyberage advances in record keeping and data recording. Agents of the criminal justice system now have immediate access to our most personal information, ranging from arrest record to medical history. Issues of privacy and confidentiality, which can have enormous economic, social, and political consequences, are now more critical than ever.

Take, for instance, the Megan's Law movement, which began in New Jersey in 1994, after 7-year-old Megan Kanka was murdered by a paroled child molester who had moved in across the street. The form of Megan's Laws differs from state to state, but most require law enforcement officials to maintain a registry of convicted sex offenders living in the area and make this registry available to the public. Although monitoring convicted sex offenders may seem like an effective crime deterrent, the American Civil Liberties Union has fought the effort around the nation because they consider such laws overreaching and dangerous. Monitoring of sex offenders has also been challenged on the grounds that it simply does not work, an issue discussed in the accompanying Evidence-Based Justice feature.

Ethical issues transcend all elements of the justice system. Yet specific issues shape the ethical standards in each branch.

Ethics and Law Enforcement

Ethical behavior is particularly important in law enforcement because police officers have the authority to deprive people of their liberty. And in carrying out their daily activities, they also have the right to use physical and even deadly force.

LO10 Discuss the ethical issues that arise in criminal justice.

EVIDENCE-based justice

DOES MONITORING SEX OFFENDERS REALLY WORK?

Keeping tabs on sex offenders remains a controversial issue. Do Internet-based sex offender registration lists violate the privacy of offenders who have served their time? After all, there is no arsonist, drug dealer, or murderer list, even though these offenders may present a danger to society. Should people who have served their time be left alone? Or are neighbors entitled to know when a former sex offender moves into the community?

There is no question that sex offender registration lists are legal. The Supreme Court, in *Connecticut Dept. of Public Safety v. Doe* (2003), upheld the legality of sex offender registration when it ruled that persons convicted of sexual offenses may be required to register with a state's Department of Public Safety and may then be listed on a sex offender registry that contains registrants' names, addresses, photographs, and descriptions and can be accessed on the Internet. In a 9–0 opinion upholding the plan, the Court reasoned that, because these defendants had been convicted of a sex offense, disclosing their names on the registry without a hearing did not violate their right to due process.

Thus sex offender registration laws have been ruled constitutional, are pervasive (they are used in all 50 states), appeal to politicians who may be swayed by media crusades against child molesters (such as "To Catch a Predator" on *Dateline NBC*), and appease the public's desire to "do something" about child predators. But do they actually work? Does registration deter offenders from committing further sex offenses and reduce the incidence of predatory acts against children?

To answer this question, criminologists Kristen Zgoba and Karen Bachar recently conducted an in-depth study of the effectiveness of the New Jersey registration law and found that, although it was maintained at great cost to the state, the system did not produce effective results. Sex offense rates in New Jersey were in steep decline before the system was installed, and the rate of decline actually slowed down after 1995 when the law took effect. The study showed that the greatest rate of decline in sex offending occurred prior to the passage and implementation of Megan's Law. Zgoba and Bachar also found that the passage and implementation of Megan's Law did not reduce the number of rearrests for sex offenses, nor did it have any demonstrable effect on the time between when sex offenders were released from prison and the time they were rearrested for any new offense, such as a drug offense, theft, or another sex offense.

Zgoba and Bachar's results can be used to rethink legal changes such as sex offender registration. Rather than deterring them from committing crime, such laws may merely cause sex offenders to be more cautious, while giving parents a false sense of security. For example, sex offenders may target victims in other states or in communities where they do not live and parents are less cautious.

Sources: *Connecticut Dept. of Public Safety v. Doe*, 538 U.S. 1 (2003); Kristen Zgoba and Karen Bachar, "Sex Offender Registration and Notification: Research Finds Limited Effects in New Jersey," National Institute of Justice, April 2009, http://www.ncjrs.gov/pdffiles1/nij/225402.pdf (accessed April 2014).

Depriving people of liberty and using force are not the only police behaviors that require ethical consideration. Police officers have considerable discretion in choosing whom to investigate, how far the investigation should go, and how much effort is required—does an investigation merit undercover work, listening devices, surveillance? While carrying out their duties, police officers must be responsive to the public's demand for protection and at the same time remain sensitive to the rights and liberties of those they must deter from committing crime and/or control. In this capacity, they serve as the interface between the power of the state and the citizens it governs. This duality creates many ethical dilemmas. Consider the following:

■ Should law enforcement agents target groups whom they suspect are heavily involved in crime and violence, or does this practice lead to racial/ethnic profiling? Is it unethical for a security agent to pay closer attention to a young Arab male getting on an airline flight than she pays to a clean-cut American

Andrew Burton/Getty Images News/Getty Images

Police officers eat a meal at Junior's restaurant, a staple of Brooklyn dining since the 1950s. Should officers patronize the same restaurants, even if they do not receive or are barred by policy from receiving discounted meals or free drinks?

soldier from upstate New York? Why suspect a blue-eyed, blonde soldier of being a terrorist when the 9/11 terrorists were of Arab descent? But don't forget that Tim McVeigh, who grew up in rural Pendleton, New York, and spent more than three years in the army, went on to become the Oklahoma City Bomber. How can police officers balance their need to protect public security with the ethical requirement that they protect citizens' legal rights?

■ Should police officers tell the truth even if it means that a guilty person will go free? Let's say that a police officer stops a car for a traffic violation and searches it illegally. In so doing, he finds a weapon that was used in a particularly heinous shooting in which three children were killed. Would it be ethical for the officer to lie on the witness stand and say he noticed the gun on the car seat in plain sight (and hence subject to legal and proper seizure)? Or should he tell the truth and risk having the charges against the suspect dismissed, leaving the offender free to kill again?

■ Should police officers be loyal to their peers even when they know that these officers have violated the law? A new officer soon becomes aware that his partner is taking gratuities from local gangsters in return for looking the other way and allowing their prostitution and bookmaking operations to flourish. Should the rookie file a complaint and turn in his partner? Will she be labeled a "rat" and lose the respect of her fellow officers? After all, gambling and prostitution are not violent crimes and do not really hurt anyone. Or do they?

■ Is it ethical for police agencies to profit financially from their law enforcement activities? Police departments have instituted a number of money-making schemes ranging from selling ads on the back of police cars to ticket-writing campaigns. In some instances, individual officers can benefit. For example, when contractors are required to have paid police officer details present at job sites, officers are paid two or three times the standard wage. Profiting from police services is controversial, and it can also have unexpected consequences.

How can law enforcement officers be aided in making ethical decisions? Various national organizations have produced model codes of conduct that can serve as behavioral guides. One well-known document created by the International Association of Chiefs of Police says,[50]

> As a Law Enforcement Officer my fundamental duty is to serve mankind; to safeguard lives and property; to protect the innocent against deception, the weak against oppression or intimidation, and the peaceful against violence or disorder; and to respect the Constitutional Rights of all men to liberty, equality and justice....

Ethics and the Court Process

Ethical concerns do not stop with an arrest. As an officer of the court and the "people's attorney," the prosecutor must seek justice for all parties in a criminal matter and should not merely be targeting a conviction. To be fair, prosecutors must share evidence with the defense, not use scare tactics or intimidation, and represent the public interest. It would be inexcusable and illegal for prosecutors to suppress critical evidence, a practice that might mean the guilty walk free and the innocent are convicted.

Prosecutorial ethics may be tested when the dual role of a prosecutor causes her to experience role conflict. On the one hand, she represents the people and has an obligation to present evidence, uphold the law, and obtain convictions as vigorously as possible. In the adversary system, it is the prosecutor who takes the side of the victims and on whom they depend for justice.

However, as a fair and impartial officer of the court, the prosecutor must oversee the investigation of crime and make sure that all aspects of the investigation meet constitutional standards. If during the investigation it appears that the police have violated the constitutional rights of suspects—for example, by extracting an illegal confession or conducting an illegal search—the prosecutor has an ethical obligation to take whatever action is necessary and appropriate to remedy legal or technical errors, even if that means rejecting a case in which the defendant's rights have been violated. Moreover, the canon of legal ethics in most states forbids the prosecutor from pursuing charges when there is no probable cause and mandates that all evidence that might mitigate guilt or reduce the punishment be turned over to the defense.

THE DEFENSE ATTORNEY As an officer of the court, along with the judge, prosecutors, and other trial participants, the defense attorney seeks to uncover the basic facts and elements of the criminal act. In this dual capacity of being both an advocate for defendants and an officer of the court, this attorney often experiences conflicting obligations to his client and his profession. Suppose a client confides that she is planning to commit a crime. What are the defense attorney's ethical responsibilities in this case? Obviously, the lawyer would have to counsel the client to obey the law; if the lawyer assisted the client in engaging in illegal behavior, he would be subject to charges of unprofessional conduct and even to criminal liability.

Ethics and Corrections

Ethical issues do not cease to arise when a defendant has been convicted. The ethical issues surrounding punishment are too vast to discuss here, but they include the following:

■ Is it fair and ethical to execute a criminal? Can capital punishment ever be considered a moral choice?

■ Should people be given different punishments for the same criminal law violation? Is it fair and just when some convicted murderers and rapists receive probation for their crimes, while others are sentenced to prison for the same offense?

■ Is it fair to grant leniency to criminals who agree to testify against their co-conspirators and therefore allow them to benefit from their perfidy, while others not given the opportunity to "squeal" are forced to bear the full brunt of the law?

 **Web App 1.5**

To read more about the ethical responsibilities of prosecutors, visit http://www.americanbar.org/groups/professional_responsibility/publications/model_rules_of_professional_conduct/rule_3_8_special_responsibilities_of_a_prosecutor.html.

■ Should some criminal inmates be granted early release because they can persuade the parole board that they have been rehabilitated, while others who are not so glib, convincing, or well spoken are forced to serve their entire sentence behind bars?

■ Should technology be used to monitor offenders in the community? Would it be ethical to track a probationer's movements with a GPS unit attached to an ankle bracelet she is required to wear at all times? Should her Internet use and computer downloads be monitored?

■ Should profit be an issue in correctional administration? There has been a trend to privatize aspects of corrections, ranging from outsourcing food and health services to running the prisons themselves. Is it ethical to turn the care and custody of incarcerated people over to corporations that may give profit higher priority than treatment?

Ethical standards are also challenged by the discretion afforded to correctional workers and administrators. Discretion is involved when a correctional officer decides to report an inmate for disorderly conduct, which might jeopardize his or her parole. And although the Supreme Court has issued many rulings related to prisoners' rights, implementing these mandates is left to others, who may or may not carry them out in an orderly way.

Correctional officers have significant coercive power over offenders. They are under a legal and professional obligation not to use unnecessary force or to take advantage of inmates' powerlessness. One example of abuse is an officer beating an inmate; another is a staff member coercing sex from an inmate. These abuses of power can occur because of the powerlessness of the offender relative to the correctional professional. One national survey uncovered evidence that this breach of ethics is significant: of the thousands of incidents of sexual violence in prison each year, more than 40 percent involved staff-on-inmate sexual misconduct, and more than 10 percent involved staff sexual harassment of inmates. In other words, staff members were involved in more cases of sexual violence and harassment in correctional facilities than were inmates![51]

Ethical considerations pervade all elements of the justice system. Making ethical decisions is an increasingly important task in a society that is becoming more diverse, pluralistic, and complex every day.

ETHICAL CHALLENGES in Criminal Justice

A WRITING ASSIGNMENT

Cities across the country have installed "red light cameras" that take snapshots of busy intersections, capturing the license plates of cars that are running the light, under the assumption that this use of technology would simultaneously save lives and generate millions of dollars in extra fines. However, researchers have started to challenge this assumption. Some studies have shown that while red light cameras may prevent accidents in intersections (so-called "right-angle crashes"), they are also responsible for a greater number of rear-end accidents, which occur after people slam on their brakes to avoid entering the intersection on a red light. A number of cities have started to remove red light cameras. Some states even prohibit them altogether. The critics claim that the cameras do little more than generate revenue.

Write about the ethics of red light cameras. In doing so, answer the following questions: Is it ethical to remove or reduce a crime/safety device that is effective but does not generate profits? Should financial concerns ever play a role in the justice system? If so, when and how? What other possible sources of revenue generation exist within the criminal justice system?

Summary

L01 **Define the concept of criminal justice.**

- The criminal justice system consists of the agencies that dispense justice and the process by which justice is carried out.

L02 **Summarize the long history of crime in America.**

- America has experienced crime throughout most of its history.
- In the Old West, justice was administered by legendary lawmen such as Wyatt Earp.
- Crime rates skyrocketed during the Depression and hit their peak in the 1930s.

L03 **Discuss the formation of the criminal justice system.**

- There was little in the way of a formal criminal justice system until the nineteenth century when the first police agencies were created.
- The term *criminal justice system* became prominent in the United States around 1967, when the President's Commission on Law Enforcement and the Administration of Justice began a nationwide study of the nation's crime problem.
- Criminal justice is a field that applies knowledge gleaned from various disciplines in an attempt to understand what causes people to commit crimes and how to deal with the crime problem.

L04 **Name the three basic component agencies of criminal justice.**

- The main function of law enforcement agencies is to investigate crimes and apprehend suspects.
- Agencies of the court system charge, indict, try, and sentence criminal offenders.
- The correctional system's role is to incapacitate convicted offenders and attempt to aid in their treatment and rehabilitation.

L05 **Describe the size and scope of the contemporary justice system.**

- The contemporary criminal justice system in the United States is monumental in size.

- It costs federal, state, and local governments more than $200 billion per year to maintain a criminal justice system that employs more than 2 million people.
- The system processes, treats, and cares for millions of people. More than 14 million people are being arrested each year; and there are more than 7 million people in the correctional system.

L06 **Describe the formal criminal justice process.**

- The process consists of the actual steps the offender takes from the initial investigation through trial, sentencing, and appeal.
- The justice process comprises 15 stages, each of which is a decision point through which cases flow.
- Each of these decisions can have a critical effect on the defendant, the justice system, and society.

L07 **Articulate what is meant by the term *criminal justice assembly line*.**

- Herbert Packer described the criminal justice process as an assembly-line conveyor belt down which moves an endless stream of cases.
- The system also acts as a funnel: most people who commit crime escape detection, and of those who do not, relatively few are bound over for trial, and even fewer are convicted and eventually sentenced to prison.
- The justice funnel holds many cases at its mouth and relatively few at its stem end.

L08 **Discuss the wedding cake model of justice.**

- In many instances, the criminal justice system works informally to expedite the disposal of cases.
- Criminal acts that are very serious or notorious may receive the full complement of criminal justice processes, from arrest to trial. However, less serious cases are often settled when a bargain is reached between the prosecution and the defense.

L09 **Explain the various perspectives on criminal justice.**

- The role of criminal justice can be interpreted in many ways.
- People who study the field or work in its agencies bring their own ideas and feelings to bear when they try to decide on the right course of action to take or recommend. Therefore, there are a number of different perspectives on criminal justice today.

- Perspectives range from the most conservative (crime control) to the most liberal (restorative justice).

 L010 **Discuss the ethical issues that arise in criminal justice.**

- The justice system must deal with many ethical issues.
- The challenge is to determine what is fair and just and to balance that with the need to protect the public.

Key Terms

criminal justice system, 4
Law Enforcement Assistance
    Administration (LEAA), 6
evidence-based justice, 7
social control, 7
in-presence requirement, 13
Miranda warning, 13

nolle prosequi, 14
grand jury, 14
true bill of indictment, 14
courtroom work group, 19
crime control perspective, 21
rehabilitation perspective, 22
due process perspective, 23

nonintervention perspective, 24
decriminalization, 25
deinstitutionalization, 25
equal justice perspective, 26
racial animus model, 26
restorative justice perspective, 26

Critical Thinking Questions

1. Can a single standard of ethics be applied to all criminal justice agencies? Or is the world too complex to legislate morality and ethics?
2. Describe the differences between the formal and informal justice systems. Is it fair to treat some offenders informally?
3. What are the layers of the criminal justice wedding cake model? Give an example of a crime for each layer.

4. What are the basic elements of each perspective on justice? Which perspective best represents your own point of view?
5. How would each perspective on criminal justice view the use of the death penalty as a sanction for first-degree murder?

Notes

1. http://transcripts.cnn.com/TRANSCRIPTS/1307/15/acd.01.html (accessed April 2014).
2. This section leans heavily on Ted Robert Gurr, "Historical Trends in Violent Crime: A Critical Review of the Evidence," in *Crime and Justice: An Annual Review of Research*, vol. 3, ed. Michael Tonry and Norval Morris (Chicago: University of Chicago Press, 1981); Richard Maxwell Brown, "Historical Patterns of American Violence," in *Violence in America: Historical and Comparative Perspectives*, ed. Hugh Davis Graham and Ted Robert Gurr (Beverly Hills, CA: Sage, 1979).
3. T. J. Stiles, *Jesse James, Last Rebel of the Civil War* (New York: Vintage, 2003); Ted Yeatman, *Frank & Jesse James: The Story Behind the Legend* (Nashville, TN: Cumberland House, 2003).
4. Samuel Walker, *Popular Justice* (New York: Oxford University Press, 1980).
5. Visit the commission's website, http://www.chicagocrimecommission.org (accessed April 2014).
6. Lexis/Nexis, "Records of the Wickersham Commission on Law Observance and Enforcement," http://www.lexisnexis.com/academic/upa_cis/group.asp?g=256 (accessed April 2014).
7. For an insightful analysis of this effort, see Samuel Walker, "Origins of the Contemporary Criminal Justice Paradigm: The American Bar Foundation Survey, 1953–1969," *Justice Quarterly* 9 (1992): 47–76.

8. President's Commission on Law Enforcement and the Administration of Justice, *The Challenge of Crime in a Free Society* (Washington, DC: U.S. Government Printing Office, 1967).

9. See Public Law 90–351, Title I—Omnibus Crime Control Safe Streets Act of 1968, 90th Congress, June 19, 1968.

10. For a review, see Kevin Wright, "Twenty-Two Years of Federal Investment in Criminal Justice Research: The National Institute of Justice, 1968–1989," *Journal of Criminal Justice* 22 (1994): 27–40.

11. Lawrence Sherman, Denise Gottfredson, Doris MacKenzie, John Eck, Peter Reuter, and Shawn Bushway, *Preventing Crime: What Works, What Doesn't, What's Promising* (Washington, DC: U.S. Department of Justice, Office of Justice Programs, 1997).

12. See, generally, Brandon Welsh and David Farrington, *Preventing Crime: What Works for Children, Offenders, Victims and Places* (London: Springer-Verlag, 2006).

13. Dennis Rosenbaum and Gordon Hanson, "Assessing the Effects of School-Based Drug Education: A Six-Year Multilevel Analysis of Project D.A.R.E.," *Journal of Research in Crime and Delinquency* 35 (1998): 381–412.

14. Brian A. Reaves, *Census of State and Local Law Enforcement Agencies, 2008* (Washington, DC: Bureau of Justice Statistics, 2011), http://bjs.ojp.usdoj.gov/content/pub/pdf/csllea08.pdf (accessed April 2014).

15. Ibid.

16. Federal Bureau of Investigation, *Crime in the United States, 2012* (Washington, DC: Federal Bureau of Investigation), Table 29, http://www.fbi.gov/about-us/cjis/ucr/crime-in-the-u.s/2012/crime-in-the-u.s.-2012/tables/29tabledatadecpdf (accessed April 2014).

17. Matthew R. Durose, Donald Farole, and Sean P. Rosenmerkel, *Felony Sentences in State Courts, 2006* (Washington, DC: Bureau of Justice Statistics, 2009), http://bjs.ojp.usdoj.gov/content/pub/pdf/fssc06st.pdf (accessed April 2014). These are the latest figures as of this writing.

18. Lauren E. Glaze and Erinn J. Herberman, *Correctional Populations in the United States, 2012* (Washington, DC: Bureau of Justice Statistics, 2013), http://www.bjs.gov/content/pub/pdf/cpus12.pdf (accessed April 2014).

19. For an analysis of this issue, see William Wilbanks, *The Myth of a Racist Criminal Justice System* (Monterey, CA: Brooks/Cole, 1987); Stephen Klein, Joan Petersilia, and Susan Turner, "Race and Imprisonment Decisions in California," *Science* 247 (1990): 812–816; Alfred Blumstein, "On the Racial Disproportionality of the United States Prison Population," *Journal of Criminal Law and Criminology* 73 (1982): 1259–1281; Darnell Hawkins, "Race, Crime Type, and Imprisonment," *Justice Quarterly* 3 (1986): 251–269.

20. Marilyn Bardsley, Rachael Bell, and David Lohr, *BTK—Birth of a Serial Killer*, truTV Crime Library, http://www.trutv.com/library/crime/serial_killers/unsolved/btk/index_1.html (accessed April 2014).

21. American Bar Association Grand Jury System, http://www.americanbar.org/news/abanews.html (accessed April 2014).

22. Herbert L. Packer, *The Limits of the Criminal Sanction* (Stanford, CA: Stanford University Press, 1975), p. 21.

23. Ibid.

24. Durose, Farole, and Rosenmerkel, *Felony Sentences in State Courts, 2006.*

25. Douglas Smith, "The Plea Bargaining Controversy," *Journal of Criminal Law and Criminology* 77 (1986): 949–967.

26. Samuel Walker, *Sense and Nonsense about Crime* (Belmont, CA: Wadsworth, 1985).

27. Charles Montaldo, "The Elizabeth Smart Case, Background and Latest Developments," About.com, http://crime.about.com/od/current/a/elizabeth_smart.htm (accessed April 2014).

28. Malcolm Feeley, *The Process Is the Punishment* (New York: Russell Sage, 1979).

29. Vanessa Barker, "The Politics of Punishing," *Punishment and Society* 8 (2006): 5–32.

30. John DiIulio, *No Escape: The Future of American Corrections* (New York: Basic Books, 1991).

31. Richard Timothy Coupe and Laurence Blake, "The Effects of Patrol Workloads and Response Strength on Arrests at Burglary Emergencies," *Journal of Criminal Justice* 33 (2005): 239–255.

32. Paul Cassell, "How Many Criminals Has *Miranda* Set Free?" *Wall Street Journal*, March 1, 1995, p. A15.

33. Jon Gould and Stephen Mastrofski, "Suspect Searches: Assessing Police Behavior Under the U.S. Constitution," *Criminology and Public Policy* 3 (2004): 315–362.

34. For detailed opinion data, see http://www.albany.edu/sourcebook/toc_2.html (accessed April 2014). For death penalty opinion data, see http://www.albany.edu/sourcebook/pdf/t2512013.pdf (accessed April 2014).

35. Karen Parker and Patricia McCall, "Structural Conditions and Racial Homicide Patterns: A Look at the Multiple Disadvantages in Urban Areas," *Criminology* 37 (1999): 447–448.

36. Jane Sprott, "Are Members of the Public Tough on Crime? The Dimensions of Public 'Punitiveness,'" *Journal of Criminal Justice* 27 (1999): 467–474.

37. Packer, *The Limits of the Criminal Sanction*, p. 175.

38. For details, see http://www.innocenceproject.org (accessed April 2014).

39. Talia Roitberg Harmon and William S. Lofquist, "Too Late for Luck: A Comparison of Post-Furman Exonerations and Executions of the Innocent," *Crime and Delinquency* 51 (2005): 498–520.

40. Eric Stewart, Ronald Simons, Rand Conger, and Laura Scaramella, "Beyond the Interactional Relationship Between Delinquency and Parenting Practices: The Contribution of Legal Sanctions," *Journal of Research in Crime and Delinquency* 39 (2002): 36–60.

41. Cassia Spohn and David Holleran, "The Effect of Imprisonment on Recidivism Rates of Felony Offenders: A Focus on Drug Offenders," *Criminology* 40 (2002): 329–359.

42. *Doe v. Pryor M.D.*, Ala, Civ. No. 99-T-730-N, J. Thompson, August 16, 1999.

43. James Unnever and Francis Cullen, "The Social Sources of Americans' Punitiveness: A Test of Three Competing Models," *Criminology* 48 (2010): 99–129.

44. Ibid.

45. Herbert Bianchi, *Justice as Sanctuary* (Bloomington: Indiana University Press, 1994); Nils Christie, "Conflicts as Property," *British Journal of Criminology* 17 (1977): 1–15; L. Hulsman, "Critical Criminology and the Concept of Crime," *Contemporary Crises* 10 (1986): 63–80.

46. Larry Tifft, Foreword, in Dennis Sullivan, *The Mask of Love* (Port Washington, NY: Kennikat Press, 1980), p. 6.

47. Robert Coates, Mark Umbreit, and Betty Vos, "Responding to Hate Crimes Through Restorative Justice Dialogue," *Contemporary Justice Review* 9 (2006): 7–21; Kathleen Daly

and Julie Stubbs, "Feminist Engagement with Restorative Justice," *Theoretical Criminology* 10 (2006): 9–28.

48. Christopher Cooper, "Patrol Police Officer Conflict Resolution Processes," *Journal of Criminal Justice* 25 (1997): 87–101.

49. This section leans heavily on Jocelyn M. Pollock, *Ethics in Crime and Justice, Dilemmas and Decisions*, 4th ed. (Belmont, CA: Wadsworth, 2004).

50. International Association of Chiefs of Police, "Law Enforcement Code of Ethics," http://www.theiacp.org (accessed April 2014).

51. Allen Beck and Timothy Hughes, *Prison Rape Elimination Act of 2003, Sexual Violence Reported by Correctional Authorities, 2004* (Washington, DC: Bureau of Justice Statistics, 2005).

CHAPTER 2

The Nature and Extent of Crime

Learning Objectives

LO1 Discuss how crime is defined.

LO2 Define and discuss some of the different types of crime.

LO3 Explain the methods used to measure crime.

LO4 Discuss the development of the NIBRS program.

LO5 Discuss the strengths and weaknesses of various measures of crime.

LO6 Recognize the trends in the crime rate.

LO7 Summarize the various crime patterns.

LO8 Explain the problem of chronic offending.

Chapter Outline

How Is Crime Defined?
Consensus View
Careers in Criminal Justice: Crime Analyst
Conflict View
Interactionist View

What Are the Different Categories of Crime?
Violent Crimes
Property Crimes
Public Order Crimes
Economic Crimes

Sources of Crime Data
The Uniform Crime Reports (UCR)
Evidence-Based Justice: Do Police Fudge Crime Statistics?
National Incident-Based Reporting System (NIBRS)
National Crime Victimization Survey (NCVS)
Self-Report Surveys
The Victim Experience: Jaycee Lee Dugard
Evaluating Sources of Crime Data

Crime Trends
Trends in Violent Crime and Property Crime
Trends in Victimization
Trends in Self-Reporting
Global Criminal Justice: Crime in Other Countries

What the Future Holds
Analyzing Criminal Justice Issues: Explaining Trends in Crime Rates

Crime Patterns
The Ecology of Crime
Evidence-Based Justice: Immigration and Crime
Social Class, Socioeconomic Conditions, and Crime
Age and Crime
Gender and Crime
Explaining Gender Differences in the Crime Rate
Race and Crime
Chronic Offending and Crime

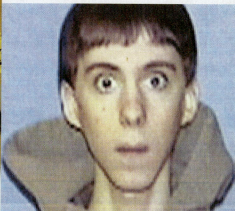

Who of us can ever forget the events of December 14, 2012, the day a young man named Adam Lanza walked into Sandy Hook Elementary School in Newtown, Connecticut, and, using high-powered weapons, methodically took the lives of 20 young children and 6 adults? Before he went on his murderous rampage, he shot his own mother in the home they shared.[1]

Former classmates and acquaintances of Lanza described him as an awkward loner who was deeply uncomfortable in social situations. He was described as someone who lived in their world but was not really part of it, a youth who would go through crises that would require his mother to come to school when he totally withdrew from whatever he was supposed to be doing, be it a class or just sitting and reading a book. When people approached Lanza in the hallways, he would press himself against the wall or walk in a different direction. No one really seemed to know him well, and those who did described him as someone who may have had serious psychological problems.

Tragically, school shootings have become all too common in the United States. Prior to Sandy Hook, the 1999 Columbine High School massacre resulted in 13 deaths. In 2007, 23-year-old Seung-Hui Cho methodically took the lives of 32 people—27 students and 5 professors—at Virginia Tech before taking his own life. Since the Newtown shooting, well over 40 school shootings have occurred (as of this writing).[2] They have resulted in 28 deaths and at least 37 injuries. Seventy percent of the shootings were committed by minors. In 16 of the cases, shootings were precipitated by school yard arguments. The most lethal school shooting since Newtown took place at Santa Monica College in California. Six people were killed, including the suspect. Four were injured. ■

The Lanza case illustrates how violent crime has become an ever-present part of American society. Americans are fascinated by highly publicized murder cases, particularly when they involve children. They are bombarded daily with stories of child abductions, gang killings, and drug busts. People hearing about these violent crimes demand that their legal representatives "do something about crime." How accurate is this vision? Is the crime rate truly skyrocketing or has intense media coverage given the public a false impression about crime in America?

Stories about such violent acts help convince most Americans that we live in a violent society. When people read headlines about a violent crime spree, they begin to fear crime and take steps to protect themselves, perhaps avoiding public places and staying at home in the evening.[3] Are Americans justified in their fear of crime? Should they barricade themselves behind armed guards? Are crime rates actually rising, or are they falling? And where do most crimes occur, and who commits them? To answer these and similar questions, crime experts have devised elaborate methods of crime data collection and analysis. Without accurate data on the nature and extent of crime, it would not be possible to formulate theories that explain the onset of antisocial behaviors or to devise criminal justice policies that facilitate their control or elimination.

Take the case of the death penalty. Many advocate its use to deter people from committing murder, but it would be impossible to know whether capital punishment is indeed an effective deterrent without a means of calculating murder rates and trends. Capital punishment might be justified if murder rates fell dramatically soon after the death penalty was imposed. If, however, imposition of the death penalty had little if any effect on murder rates, justifications for its use would be damaged. Because obtaining accurate crime data is so essential, there are many career opportunities for specially trained crime analysts in the criminal justice system (see the accompanying Careers in Criminal Justice feature). Accurate data collection is also critical for assessing the nature and extent of crime, tracking changes in the crime rate, and measuring the individual and social factors that may influence criminality.

In this chapter, we first define what is meant by the term *crime* and the various ways crime is viewed. We then review some major categories of criminal activity in America and around the world before we turn to the measurement of crime, how crime data are collected, and what this information tells us about crime patterns and trends. We also examine the concept of criminal careers and discover what available crime data can tell us about the onset, continuation, and termination of criminality.

How Is Crime Defined?

 Discuss how crime is defined.

The justice system focuses on crime and its control. While for most of us the concept of crime seems rather simple—a violation of criminal law—the question remains: why are some acts considered a violation of the law when other, seemingly more serious, acts are legal and noncriminal? There are actually three views of how and why some behaviors become illegal and are considered crimes while others remain noncriminal.

Consensus View

consensus view of crime
The view that the great majority of citizens agree that certain behaviors must be outlawed or controlled, and that criminal law is designed to protect citizens from social harm.

According to what is known as the **consensus view of crime**, behaviors that become crimes are those that (a) are essentially harmful to a majority of citizens in the society and therefore (b) have been controlled or prohibited by the existing criminal law. There is general agreement about which behaviors society needs to control by law and which should be beyond state regulation.

The criminal law, then, is a set of rules, codified by state authorities, that expresses the norms, goals, and values of *the vast majority of society*; it represents

CAREERS in criminal justice

CRIME ANALYST

DUTIES AND CHARACTERISTICS OF THE JOB

Crime analysts engage in a number of important law enforcement support functions. Foremost, they study patterns of criminal activity and profile suspects. They analyze crime data (calls for service, arrests made, etc.) and often use that information to forecast the days, times, and places those crimes are most likely to occur. They are called upon to provide information on demand, analyze long-term programs, and develop intelligence.

Crime analysts, sometimes called intelligence analysts, use three primary types of crime analysis. Tactical crime analysis is used to identify immediate crime threats, determine patterns (e.g., location, suspect descriptive), and disseminate that information to patrol officers and detectives. Strategic crime analysis involves gathering and interpreting crime data, then making recommendations as to where police resources are best concentrated. Finally, administrative crime analysis involves reporting to the chief, city council members, and other officials as required, making recommendations, sharing information with superiors and other stakeholders, and seeking additional resources, among other duties. A good crime analyst makes a police department look "good" to the public and local government officials.

JOB OUTLOOK

The job outlook for crime analysts is quite favorable. According to the International Association of Crime Analysts (IACA), the demand for qualified crime analysts has increased more than tenfold in the past 15 years. Law enforcement is always a top priority for local governments, so funding for crime analysts is not likely to wane. That said, their positions, like those of other government employees, hinge on funding. Also, some crime analysts are involved in grant writing and may earn part of their wages from "soft money," which can make the situation unpredictable for some of them. In general, though, crime analysts usually enjoy stable government jobs with good benefits.

SALARY

Specialized knowledge is required and, as such, crime analysts tend to do fairly well. An entry-level crime analyst can make as much as $60,000 per year. Experienced and well-educated crime analysts can make $80,000 per year or more. A supervising crime analyst in a large city like Los Angeles can make close to $100,000 per year, if not more.

OPPORTUNITIES

Most opportunities for crime analysts reside in large police departments. Less populous cities with few police officers generally do not require dedicated or full-time crime analysts. Opportunities also exist in certain task force offices. For example, federal High Intensity Drug Trafficking Area (HIDTA) offices, which are regional and often combine several states, employ crime intelligence analysts.

QUALIFICATIONS

Crime analysts are often civilian employees, which may prove desirable for those who do not want to become sworn peace officers. Crime analysts require knowledge of techniques and methods used in data collection, statistical analysis, report preparation, and research. Knowledge of numerous computer applications is also required, as is a full command of the English language for report writing and communications, familiarity with law enforcement operations, and the like.

EDUCATION AND TRAINING

Many positions require a four-year degree, often with a concentration in criminal justice, criminology, and/or policing. Some permit a combination of work experience and education short of a four-year degree. Positions may or may not require any particular licensing or certification, but either can make an applicant more competitive. For example, the International Association of Crime Analysts offers a certification program. According to IACA, graduates may be more marketable and/or earn more from their employing agencies as a result of the certification.

Sources: International Association of Crime Analysts, "What Crime Analysts Do," http://www.iaca.net/dc_analyst_role.asp (accessed April 2014); International Association of Crime Analysts, "Analyst Position Descriptions," http://www.iaca.net/dc_position_descriptions.asp (accessed April 2014).

the *consensus* of public opinion about right and wrong. In a democratic society no one is above the law; it applies evenly to everyone.

The consensus view rests on the assumption that criminal law has a social control function—restraining those whose behavior would otherwise endanger the social framework by taking advantage of others' weakness for their own personal gain. Criminal law works to control behaviors that are inherently destructive and dangerous in order to maintain the existing social fabric and ensure the peaceful functioning of society.

Conflict View

conflict view of crime
The view that criminal law is created and enforced by those who hold political and economic power and is a tool used by the ruling class to control dissatisfied have-not members of society.

The **conflict view of crime** holds that the ongoing class struggle between the rich and poor, the haves and have-nots, controls the content of criminal law and thereby shapes the definition of crime. According to this view, criminal law is created and enforced by the ruling class as a mechanism for controlling dissatisfied have-not members of society. The law is the instrument that enables the wealthy to maintain their position of power and control the behavior of those who oppose their ideas and values or who might rebel against the unequal distribution of wealth.[4] Laws defining property crimes, such as larceny and burglary, are created to protect the wealth of the affluent: people who steal from the wealthy are severely punished; the wealthy who manipulate the economic system for their personal gain are "above the law." Drug laws are developed to ensure that workers will be productive and sober. Laws defining violent crimes are created to keep the angry and frustrated lower classes under control. People who violate these laws are subject to severe punishments. In contrast, perpetrators of business and white-collar crimes receive relatively lenient punishments, considering the extent of the harm and damage they cause.

Interactionist View

interactionist view of crime
The view that criminal law reflects the preferences and opinions of people who hold social power in the society and use their influence to impose their own values and moral code on the rest of the population.

moral entrepreneurs
People who wage campaigns to control behaviors they view as immoral or wrong.

Falling between the consensus and conflict visions, the **interactionist view of crime** suggests that criminal law is structured to reflect the preferences and opinions of people who hold social power in a particular legal jurisdiction and use their influence to shape the legal process. These **moral entrepreneurs** wage campaigns (*moral crusades*) to control behaviors they view as immoral and wrong (e.g., abortion) or, conversely, to legalize behaviors they consider harmless social eccentricities (e.g., carrying a handgun for self-protection; smoking pot). Because drug use offends their moral sense, it is currently illegal to purchase marijuana and hashish, while liquor and cigarettes are sold openly, even though far more people die of alcoholism and smoking than from drug abuse each year.[5] Even the definition of serious violent offenses, such as rape and murder, depends on

According to the interactionist view of crime, acts are illegal because they are defined that way by law. A billboard erected on top of a liquor store in Denver promotes legalizing marijuana. The issue: should the state legalize marijuana for recreational use, regulating it like alcohol products? Why is smoking pot illegal and the consumption of alcohol legal? Are they really so different? Is it merely a matter of definition and labeling?

the prevailing moral values of those who shape the content of the criminal law. Fifty years ago a man could not be prosecuted for raping his wife; today, every state criminalizes marital rape. In sum, the definition of crime better reflects prevailing moral values than any objective standard of right and wrong.

The basics of these three views are set out in Concept Summary 2.1.

Although these views of crime differ, they generally agree (1) that criminal law defines crime, (2) that the definition of crime is constantly changing and evolving, (3) that social forces mold the definition of crimes, and (4) that criminal law has a social control function. Therefore, as used here, the term **crime** is defined as follows:

> Crime is a violation of social rules of conduct, interpreted and expressed by a written criminal code, created by people holding social and political power. Its content may be influenced by prevailing public sentiments, historically developed moral beliefs, and the need to protect public safety. Individuals who violate these rules may be subject to sanctions administered by state authority, which include social stigma and loss of status, freedom, and on occasion, their lives.

crime
A violation of social rules of conduct, interpreted and expressed by a written criminal code, created by people holding social and political power. Its content may be influenced by prevailing public sentiments, historically developed moral beliefs, and the need to protect public safety.

CONCEPT SUMMARY 2.1
Definition of Crime

Consensus View	Conflict View	Interactionist View
The will of the majority shapes the law and defines crimes.	The law is a tool of the ruling class.	Social crusaders and moral entrepreneurs define crime.
Agreement exists on right and wrong.	Crime is a politically defined concept.	The definition of crime is subjective, reflecting contemporary values and morals.
Laws apply to all citizens equally.	"Real crimes" are not outlawed. The law is used to control the underclass.	Criminal labels are life-transforming events.

What Are the Different Categories of Crime?

Millions of criminal acts occur each year, and their diversity and variety are staggering. Crimes range in seriousness from shoplifting to serial murder. Some crimes are violent and destructive; others target property; yet others are motivated by economic gain; and a fourth group, public order crimes, are made up of acts (such as prostitution and drug use) that threaten or violate the moral standards of society, or at least the segment of society that has the power to shape and control the law.

 L02 Define and discuss some of the different types of crime.

Violent Crimes

Americans are bombarded with television news stories and newspaper articles featuring grisly accounts of violent gangs, serial murder, child abuse, and rape. Although rates of violent crime have declined significantly over the past decade, most Americans still worry about becoming a victim of crime. Some criminal acts are **expressive violence**, acts that vent rage, anger, or frustration, and some are **instrumental violence**, acts designed to improve the financial or social position of the criminal—for example, through an armed robbery or murder for hire. What are the forms of violence that most people fear?

expressive violence
Violent behavior motivated by rage, anger, or frustration.

instrumental violence
Violent behavior that results from criminal activity designed to improve the financial status of the culprit, such as shooting someone during a bank robbery.

mass murderer
Type of multiple killer who kills many victims in a single violent outburst.

spree killers
Type of multiple killer who spreads the murderous outburst over a few days or weeks.

serial killer
Type of multiple killer who kills over a long period of time but typically assumes a "normal" identity between murders.

GANG VIOLENCE Whereas youth gangs once relied on group loyalty and emotional involvement with neighborhood turf to encourage membership, modern gangs seem more motivated by the quest for drug profits and street power. It is common for drug cliques to form within gangs and for established drug dealers to make use of gang members, also called "gang bangers," for protection and distribution services. As a consequence, gang-related killings have become so commonplace that the term "gang homicide" is now recognized as a separate and unique category of criminal behavior.[6]

Today, an estimated 29,900 gangs with about 783,000 gang members can be found in 3,300 jurisdictions in the United States.[7] The number of gangs has increased about 36 percent in the past decade, as has the number of gang members.[8] One reason for the increase: the emergence of gangs in rural and suburban areas.

MULTIPLE MURDER On July 22, 2011, in Oslo, Norway, Anders Behring Breivik, a right-wing extremist, began a murder spree that left 77 innocent people dead and many more wounded. After setting off a bomb, he dressed as a police officer and proceeded to a youth camp organized by the liberal Norwegian Labour Party on the island of Utøya, where he mercilessly gunned down 69 people, mostly young teens. After his capture, Breivik claimed that he was acting in self-defense. He told a Norwegian judge that his bombing and shooting rampage was aimed to save Europe from a Muslim takeover and that two more cells existed in his organization.[9] The United States is not immune to such horror: on July 20, 2012, James Holmes entered a movie theater in Aurora, Colorado, and shot into the audience with multiple firearms, killing 12 people and injuring 58 others.[10] These tragedies highlight the threat of mass killings by seemingly deranged gunmen.

There are three different types of multiple killers:

■ **Mass murderer** kill many victims in a single violent outburst.

■ **Spree killers** spread their murderous outburst over a few days or weeks.

■ **Serial killer** kill over a long period of time but typically assume a "normal" identity between murders.

Mass murderers, such as the Columbine High School killers Eric Harris and Dylan Klebold, serial killers, such as Jeffrey Dahmer of Milwaukee, and spree killers, such as John Allen Muhammad (the D.C. sniper), have become familiar to the American public.[11] The threat of the unknown, random, and deranged assailant has become a part of modern reality.

There is no single explanation for serial, spree, or mass murder. Such widely disparate factors as mental illness, sexual frustration, neurological damage, child abuse and neglect, smothering maternal relationships, and childhood anxiety have been suggested as possible causes. However, most experts view multiple murderers as sociopaths who from early childhood demonstrated bizarre behavior (such as torturing animals), enjoy killing, are impervious to their victims' suffering, and bask in the media limelight when caught.[12]

INTIMATE VIOLENCE Although violent attacks by strangers produce the most fear and create the most graphic headlines, Americans face greater physical danger from people with whom they are in close and intimate contact: spouses, other relatives, and dating partners.

One area of intimate violence that has received a great deal of media attention is child abuse, which is any physical or emotional trauma to a child for which no reasonable explanation, such as an accident or ordinary disciplinary practices, can be found. Child abuse can result from physical beatings administered by hands, feet, weapons, belts, or sticks, or from burning. The Department of Health and Human Services (DHHS) has been monitoring the extent of child maltreatment through its annual survey of child protective services (CPS).[13]

According to the latest data, there were 700,000 unique child victims in 2012, or 9.2 victims per 1,000 children in the population. Some of them were repeatedly victimized, totaling 3.8 million distinct victimizations. In about three-quarters of the cases, children suffered neglect, but in the remaining quarter, children suffered either physical abuse, sexual abuse, or both.

The effects of abuse can be devastating. Children who have experienced some form of maltreatment have a devalued sense of self, mistrust others, tend to assume others are hostile in situations where the intentions of others are ambiguous, tend to generate antagonistic solutions to social problems, and exhibit suspicion of close relationships.[14]

HATE CRIMES Violent acts directed toward a particular person or toward the members of a group merely because the targets share a discernible racial, ethnic, religious, or gender characteristic are known as **hate crimes** or **bias crimes**.[15] Hate crimes can include the desecration of a house of worship or cemetery, harassment of a minority-group family that has moved into a previously all-white neighborhood, or a racially motivated murder.

Hate crimes usually involve convenient, vulnerable targets who are incapable of fighting back. For example, there have been numerous reported incidents of teenagers attacking vagrants and the homeless in an effort to rid their town or neighborhood of people they consider undesirable.[16] Another group targeted for hate crimes is gay men and women: gay bashing has become common in U.S. cities.

In 2012, the most recent year for which data were available as of this writing, the FBI recorded more than 5,700 hate crime incidents—motivated by bias against a race, religion, disability, ethnicity, or sexual orientation—that involved almost 7,200 victims and 5,300 offenders.[17] Over 3,200 cases involved racial bias, with about two-thirds of those directed toward African Americans. Over 1,000 crimes were motivated by religious bias, and over 1,300 were motivated by sexual-orientation bias. And as incomprehensible as it seems, the FBI recorded over 100 hate crimes in 2012 directed against the physically handicapped or mentally ill.

hate crimes (bias crimes)
Criminal acts directed toward a particular person or members of a group because they share a discernible racial, ethnic, religious, or gender characteristic.

Property Crimes

Property crimes rarely draw as much attention as violent crimes, but they are far more common and, in many ways, more costly. According to the FBI, property crimes outnumber violent crimes by a margin of 7 to 1. They also cost America billions of dollars each year.

Property crimes fall into two broad categories: theft offenses and property damage/invasion. Theft offenses include, but are not limited to the following:

- Larceny (the legal term for theft, which we discuss further below)
- Receiving stolen property
- Extortion (also known as blackmail)
- Embezzlement (converting property to his/her own with intent to defraud the rightful owner)
- False pretenses (obtaining property through fraud/deception)
- Forgery (altering a document with intent to defraud)
- Uttering (passing a forged document, such as a check, with intent to fraud)

Property damage/invasion crimes include:

- Arson (intentionally setting fire to burn a structure or property)
- Criminal mischief (intentionally damaging or destroying another's property)
- Trespassing (physical entry onto the property of another without consent)
- Burglary (discussed further below)
- Certain cybercrimes (discussed in length in Chapter 16)

BURGLARY Burglary, like trespassing, involves property invasion. It is different from trespassing, though, in that it requires intent to commit a felony. Burglary is also a misunderstood property crime. It is often equated with robbery, but robbery is a crime of violence involving theft with the intent to harm. Someone who steals a purse at gunpoint commits robbery. In contrast, burglary is purely a property crime because the offender seeks to acquire someone else's property illegally.

Burglary is also much more common than robbery. There are approximately six burglaries to every one robbery. What's more, the odds of a burglar getting caught are not very good. We discuss the concept of "clearance rates" later in this chapter, but for now know that of the burglaries reported to police, approximately 13 percent are cleared by arrest. That is, in only 13 percent of reported burglaries is a suspect actually identified and arrested. Why? Because the vast majority of burglaries occur in unoccupied dwellings and the suspect is long gone before the property's owner even notices anything is missing.

Burglary inspires more fear than perhaps any other property crime (see the marginal Fact Check box later in this chapter for details). Public opinion polls routinely reveal that the prospect of having one's home broken into ranks highly on the list of people's fears. Companies that sell home security systems do not help the situation. Their television advertisements routinely depict ominous middle-of-the-night burglaries in which someone is suddenly awoken from sleep to the sound of a screaming siren. While these types of burglaries occur, they are the exception.

LARCENY Larceny, or theft, is the most common property crime. It makes up about 75 percent of all serious crimes reported to the police. The RAND Corporation estimated that each act of larceny costs, on average, $2,319.[18] If we multiply that by the number of larcenies reported in the United States during 2012, larceny costs society over $14 billion per year.

The law usually distinguishes between petty and grand larceny. The former generally refers to theft involving items worth less than $1,000. Grand larceny usually refers to theft of items valued in excess of that amount.

Larceny generally consists of three key elements: the *taking* and *carrying away* of another's *personal property*. Taking generally refers to removing property from another's possession. The carrying away component, or "asportation," is also important. You wouldn't be guilty of larceny if while shopping you kept merchandise you hadn't paid for with you. If, however, you left the store without paying for it, the carrying away component of larceny is satisfied. Finally, larceny occurs only with the property of another; you cannot steal your own property!

History is replete with examples of high-profile, costly incidents of theft. For example, in 2013, a staggering $53 million worth of diamonds and jewels were stolen from the Carlton Intercontinental Hotel in Cannes, France. The hotel was hosting a temporary jewelry exhibit for a wealthy Israeli billionaire, Lev Leviev. In the same year, a brazen heist in Belgium resulted in the theft of $50 million in precious stones from the global diamond center of Antwerp.

Public Order Crimes

Societies have long banned or limited behaviors that are believed to run contrary to social norms, customs, and values. These behaviors are commonly referred to as **public order crimes**, or victimless crimes, although the latter term can be misleading. Public order crimes involve acts that interfere with how society operates and functions. They are criminalized because those who shape the law believe that they conflict with social norms, prevailing moral rules, and current public opinion. They are considered a threat to society because they disrupt the "public order" and the ability of people to work and function efficiently. Included within this category are sex-related crimes such as prostitution and trafficking in pornography and the trafficking and sale of illegal substances.

PROSTITUTION A crime that typically involves engaging in sexual acts for money or compensation, prostitution is for good reason often referred to as "the world's oldest profession"; it was a common practice in ancient Greece and Babylon. Today fewer than 60,000 prostitution arrests are being made annually, with the gender ratio being about 2:1 female to male. The number of prostitution arrests has been trending downward for some time; about 100,000 arrests were made in 1995. It is possible that (a) fewer people are seeking the services of prostitutes, (b) police are reluctant to make arrests in prostitution cases, or (c) more sophisticated prostitutes using the Internet or other forms of technology to "make dates" are better able to avoid detection by police. Advertising on Internet sites, known as *ehooking*, may be responsible for a hidden and hard-to-measure resurgence in sex for hire, especially in times of economic turmoil.[19]

SUBSTANCE ABUSE Even though the United States has been waging a "war on drugs" for some time, millions of Americans still abuse substances on a routine basis. How widespread is the problem? A number of national surveys attempt to chart trends in drug abuse in the general population. Monitoring the Future, an annual national survey of drug abuse among high school students, indicates that drug use declined from a high point in the 1970s, when more than half of all high school seniors routinely used illegal substances, to a low point in 1992.[20] Use then increased until around 1997 and has remained more or less constant since then. Approximately 40 percent of high school seniors report having used an illicit drug within the past twelve months. Marijuana is the drug of choice; fewer than 20 percent of seniors report using other illicit drugs in the past twelve months.

Substance abuse is of much concern to criminal justice policy makers because there is unquestionably a link between substance abuse and criminal activities. Alcohol abuse, for example, is suspected of being involved in half of all U.S. murders, suicides, and accidental deaths.[21] Strong links also exist between alcohol consumption and certain types of homicide, especially those that occur during robberies and other criminal offenses.[22]

Although the association between substance abuse and crime is powerful, the true relationship between them is still uncertain,

public order crimes
Behaviors that are illegal because they run counter to existing moral standards. Obscenity and prostitution are considered public order crimes.

Alcohol, legal and easily obtained, is related to half of all U.S. murders, suicides, and accidental deaths. Alcohol-related deaths number 100,000 a year—far more than deaths related to all illegal drugs combined. Should pot be legalized and alcohol banned? Before you answer, remember they tried to do that once before.

Andrew Lichtenstein/The Image Works

because many users have had a history of criminal activity before the onset of their substance abuse. Here are some of the possible relationships:

- Chronic criminal offenders begin to abuse drugs and alcohol after they have engaged in crime—that is, crime causes drug abuse.
- Substance abusers turn to a life of crime to support their habits—that is, drug abuse causes crime.
- Drug use and crime co-occur in individuals—that is, both crime and drug abuse are caused by some other common factor, such as risk taking, for example (risk takers use drugs and also commit crime).[23]
- Drug users suffer social and personal problems—such as heavy drinking and mental instability—that are linked to crime.[24]

Economic Crimes

Millions of property- and theft-related crimes occur each year. Most are the work of amateur or occasional criminals whose decision to steal is spontaneous and whose acts are unskilled, unplanned, and haphazard. Many thefts, ranging in seriousness from shoplifting to burglary, are committed by school-age youths who are unlikely to enter into a criminal career.

Added to the pool of amateur thieves are the millions of adults whose behavior may occasionally violate the criminal law—shoplifters, pilferers, tax cheats—but whose primary income derives from conventional means and whose self-identity is noncriminal. Most of these property crimes occur when an immediate opportunity, or *situational inducement*, to commit crime arises.[25]

Professional thieves, in contrast, derive a significant portion of their income from crime. Professionals do not delude themselves that their acts are impulsive, one-time efforts. They also do not employ elaborate rationalizations to excuse the harmfulness of their action (e.g., "Shoplifting doesn't really hurt anyone"). Professionals pursue their craft with vigor, attempting to learn from older, experienced criminals the techniques that will garner them the most money with the least risk. Their numbers are relatively few, but professionals engage in crimes that produce greater losses to society and perhaps cause more significant social harm. Typical forms include pickpocketing, burglary, shoplifting, forgery and counterfeiting, extortion, and swindling.[26]

white-collar crime

White-collar crimes involve the violation of rules that control business enterprise. They include employee pilferage, bribery, commodities law violations, mail fraud, computer fraud, environmental law violations, embezzlement, Internet scams, extortion, forgery, insurance fraud, price fixing, and environmental pollution.

corporate crime

Crime committed by a corporation, or by individuals who control the corporation or other business entity, for such purposes as illegally increasing market share, avoiding taxes, or thwarting competition.

WHITE-COLLAR CRIME Some criminal activities involve people and institutions whose acknowledged purpose is profit through illegal business transactions. Included within the category of **white-collar crime** are such acts as income tax evasion, credit card fraud, and bank fraud. White-collar criminals also use their positions of trust in business or government to commit crimes. Their activities might include soliciting bribes or kickbacks, as well as embezzlement. Some white-collar criminals set up businesses for the sole purpose of victimizing the general public. They engage in land swindles, securities theft, medical fraud, and so on. And, in addition to acting as individuals, some white-collar criminals enter into conspiracies designed to improve the market share or profitability of corporations. This type of white-collar crime, which includes antitrust violations, price fixing, and false advertising, is known as **corporate crime**.

Estimating the extent of white-collar crime and its influence on victims is difficult because victimologists often ignore those who suffer the consequences of such crime. Some experts place its total monetary value in the hundreds of billions of dollars. Beyond their monetary cost, white-collar crimes often damage property and kill people. Violations of safety standards, pollution of the environment, and industrial accidents due to negligence can be classified as corporate violence. White-collar crime also destroys confidence, saps the integrity of commercial life, and has the potential to cause devastating destruction.

The topic of white-collar crime and the efforts of the justice system to affect its control will be discussed in Chapter 16.

ORGANIZED CRIME Organized crime involves the criminal activity of people and organizations whose acknowledged purpose is economic gain through illegal enterprise.[27] These criminal cartels provide outlawed goods and services demanded by the general public: prostitution, narcotics, gambling, loan sharking, pornography, and untaxed liquor and cigarettes. In addition, organized criminals infiltrate legitimate organizations, such as unions, to drain off their funds and profits for illegal purposes.

Federal and state agencies have been dedicated to wiping out organized crime, and some well-publicized arrests have resulted in the imprisonment of important leaders. The membership of the traditional Italian and Irish crime families has dropped an estimated 50 percent over a 20-year period. New groups—including Russian and eastern European, Hispanic, and African American gangs—have filled the vacuum created by federal prosecutors. Thousands of Russian immigrants are believed to be involved in criminal activity, primarily in Russian enclaves in New York City. Besides extortion from fellow eastern European immigrants, Russian organized crime groups have engaged in narcotics trafficking, fencing stolen property, money laundering, and other traditional organized crime schemes.[28]

AP Images/Juan Carlos Llorca

Organized crime is now a transnational phenomenon. Here, British and U.S. agents watch the search of a car that was seized with marijuana at the Paso del Norte Bridge, in El Paso, Texas. Three undercover agents from the U.K. Serious Organised Crime Agency visited the Immigration and Customs Enforcement–Homeland Security Investigations Office in El Paso to learn about techniques for fighting drug cartels.

The globalization of organized crime and the development of transnational organized crime groups will be covered in more detail in Chapter 16.

Beyond these criminal activities, the criminal justice system is now confronted by emerging forms of illegal behavior—transnational crimes, billion dollar business enterprise crimes, international sex trafficking, terrorism, and cybercrime. Because of their importance, these crimes will be discussed in greater detail in Chapter 16.

Sources of Crime Data

The primary sources of crime data routinely used to measure the nature and extent of crime are surveys and official records collected, compiled, and analyzed by government agencies such as the federal government's Bureau of Justice Statistics and the Federal Bureau of Investigation (FBI). Criminal justice data analysts use these techniques to measure the nature and extent of criminal behavior and the personality, attitudes, and background of criminal offenders. What are these sources of crime data, how are they collected, and how valid are their findings?

 L03 Explain the methods used to measure crime.

The Uniform Crime Reports (UCR)

The Federal Bureau of Investigation collects the most important crime record data from local law enforcement agencies and publishes it yearly in the bureau's

Uniform Crime Reports (UCR)

The official crime data collected by the FBI from local police departments.

Part I crimes

Those crimes used by the FBI to gauge fluctuations in the overall volume and rate of crime. The offenses included were the violent crimes of murder and nonnegligent manslaughter, forcible rape, robbery, and aggravated assault and the property crimes of burglary, larceny, motor vehicle theft, and arson.

Part II crimes

All other crimes reported to the FBI; these are less serious crimes and misdemeanors, excluding traffic violations.

Web App 2.1

The FBI's Uniform Crime Reports can be found in full here: http://www.fbi.gov/stats-services/crimestats.

Uniform Crime Reports (UCR). The UCR include crimes reported to local law enforcement departments and the number of arrests made by police agencies. The FBI receives and compiles records from more than 17,000 police departments serving a majority of the U.S. population. Its major unit of analysis involves **Part I crimes**: murder and nonnegligent manslaughter, forcible rape, robbery, aggravated assault, burglary, larceny, arson, and motor vehicle theft.

The FBI tallies and annually publishes the number of reported offenses by city, county, standard metropolitan statistical area, and geographical divisions of the United States. In addition to these statistics, the UCR shows the number and characteristics (age, race, and gender) of individuals who have been arrested for these and all other crimes, except traffic violations; these other crimes are referred to as **Part II crimes**.

COMPILING THE UNIFORM CRIME REPORTS The methods used to compile the UCR are quite complex. Each month, law enforcement agencies report the number of Part I crimes known to them. These data are collected from records of all crime complaints that victims, officers who discovered the infractions, or other sources reported to these agencies.

Whenever criminal complaints are revealed through investigation to be unfounded or false, they are eliminated from the actual count. However, the number of actual offenses known is reported to the FBI whether or not anyone is arrested for the crime, the stolen property is recovered, or prosecution ensues.

The UCR uses three methods to express crime data. First, the number of crimes reported to the police and arrests made is expressed as raw figures (e.g., "An estimated 14,827 persons were murdered nationwide in 2012"). Second, crime rates per 100,000 people are computed. That is, when the UCR indicates that the murder rate was 4.8 in 2012, it means that almost 5 people in every 100,000 were murdered between January 1 and December 31, 2012. This is the equation used:

$$\frac{\text{Number of Reported Crimes}}{\text{Total U.S. Population}} \times 100,000 = \text{Rate per } 100,000$$

cleared

An offense is cleared by arrest or solved when at least one person is arrested or charged with the commission of the offense and is turned over to the court for prosecution.

Third, the FBI computes changes in the rate of crime over time. This might be expressed as "The number of murders decreased 5.7 percent between 2013 and 2014." The FBI also computes a so-called "crime clock," which depicts the number of serious offenses committed every second.

CLEARANCE RATES In addition, each month law enforcement agencies report how many crimes were **cleared**. Crimes are cleared in two ways: (1) when at least

The FBI's crime clock offers a quick summary of how frequently seven index crimes occur. What are its limitations?

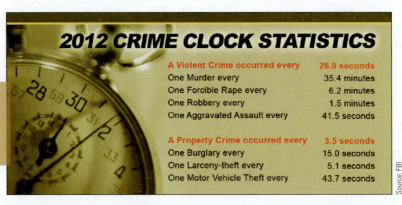

2012 CRIME CLOCK STATISTICS	
A Violent Crime occurred every	**26.0 seconds**
One Murder every	35.4 minutes
One Forcible Rape every	6.2 minutes
One Robbery every	1.5 minutes
One Aggravated Assault every	41.5 seconds
A Property Crime occurred every	**3.5 seconds**
One Burglary every	15.0 seconds
One Larceny-theft every	5.1 seconds
One Motor Vehicle Theft every	43.7 seconds

Source: FBI

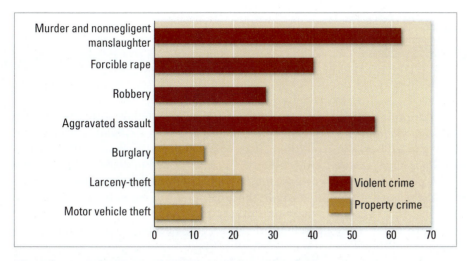

FIGURE 2.1   Percentage of Crimes Cleared by Arrest

Source: Federal Bureau of Investigation, *Crime in the United States, 2012,* http://www.fbi.gov/about-us/cjis/ucr/crime-in-the-u.s/2012/crime-in-the-u.s.-2012/offenses-known-to-law-enforcement/2012-clearance.gif (accessed May 2014).

one person is arrested, charged, and turned over to the court for prosecution; or (2) by exceptional means, when some element beyond police control precludes the physical arrest of an offender (e.g., the offender leaves the country). Data on the number of clearances involving the arrest of only juvenile offenders, data on the value of property stolen and recovered in connection with Part I offenses, and detailed information pertaining to criminal homicide are also reported.

Traditionally, slightly more than 20 percent of all reported Part I crimes are cleared by arrest each year. Not surprisingly, as Figure 2.1 shows, more serious crimes such as murder and rape are cleared at much higher rates than less serious property crimes such as larceny/theft. Factors contribute to this difference in clearance rate:

■ The media give more attention to serious violent crimes, and as a result, local and state police departments are more likely to devote time and spend more resources in their investigations.

■ There is more likely to be a prior association between victims of violent/serious crimes and their attackers, a fact that aids police investigations.

■ Even if they did not know one another beforehand, violent crime victims and offenders interact, which facilitates identification.

■ Serious violent crimes often produce physical evidence (blood, body fluids, fingerprints) that can be used to identify suspects.

VALIDITY OF THE UNIFORM CRIME REPORTS   Despite continued reliance on the UCR, its accuracy has been suspect. The three main areas of concern are reporting practices, law enforcement practices, and methodological problems.

■ *Reporting practices.* Many victims do not report these incidents to police; therefore, these crimes do not become part of the UCR. The reasons for not reporting vary. Some victims do not trust the police or have confidence in their ability to solve crimes. Others do not have property insurance and therefore believe reporting theft is useless. In other cases, victims fear reprisals from an offender's friends or family or, in the case of family violence, from their spouse or boyfriend or girlfriend.[29] According to surveys of crime victims, less than 40 percent of all criminal incidents are reported to the police. Some of these

EVIDENCE-based justice

DO POLICE FUDGE CRIME STATISTICS?

The FBI's Uniform Crime Reports (UCR) program, long considered the definitive source of official crime data and trends, tells us that crime rates have mostly been in decline over the past decade (there was a slight uptick between 2011 and 2012). Some find it perplexing that property rates have trended downward despite a struggling economy and high unemployment. This begs an important question: should the data be trusted?

A recent study of more than a hundred retired New York Police Department captains and higher-ranking officers has cast doubt on the accuracy of these data. According to a survey conducted by crime experts John Eterno and Eli Silverman, these former police commanders were under intense pressure to reduce crime. In order to placate hard-charging commissioners such as William Bratton, some local commanders manipulated crime statistics to suggest that their efforts at crime control were working. As a consequence of the need to lower crime rates, NYPD captains and above had lower perceptions of pressure for integrity in gathering crime statistics. One reason: managers' promotions are considerably more likely to be based on crime statistics, and those seeking advancement may have used any possible means to lower crime rates.

How did they cheat? One method was to check eBay and other websites to find prices for items that had been reported stolen that were actually lower than the value provided by the crime victim. They would then use the lower values to reduce felony grand larcenies, crimes that are in the UCR, to misdemeanor petit larcenies, which go unrecorded. Some commanders reported sending officers to crime scenes to persuade victims not to file complaints or altering crime details so they did not have to be reported to the FBI. For example, an attempted burglary must be reported, but not an illegal trespass.

Although it is possible that the New York police administrators were under more pressure to reduce crime than their counterparts around the country, the fact that members of the largest police department in the United States may have fudged UCR data suggests that the decade-long decline in crime may have been influenced by police reporting practices.

Sources: John Eterno and Eli B. Silverman, "The NYPD's Compstat: Compare Statistics or Compose Statistics?" *International Journal of Police Science and Management* 12 (2010): 1–23. See also John Eterno and Eli B. Silverman, *Unveiling Compstat: The Global Policing Revolution's Naked Truths* (London: CRC Press/Taylor and Francis Group, 2011).

victims justify nonreporting by stating that the incident was "a private matter," that "nothing could be done," or that the victimization was "not important enough." Changes in reporting can shape the crime trends reported in the UCR. When Eric Baumer and Janet Lauritsen examined data over several years, their findings showed that shifts in victim reporting can account for about half of the total yearly change in the official UCR crime rate.[30]

■ *Law enforcement practices.* The way police departments record and report criminal and delinquent activity also affects the validity of UCR statistics. Some police departments define crimes loosely—reporting a trespass as a burglary or an assault on a woman as an attempted rape—whereas others pay strict attention to FBI guidelines. These reporting practices may help explain interjurisdictional differences in crime.[31] Arson is seriously underreported because many fire departments do not report to the FBI and because those that do file such reports define many fires that may well have been set by arsonists as "accidental" or "spontaneous."[32]

Some local police departments make systematic errors in UCR reporting. They may count an arrest only after a formal booking procedure, even though the UCR requires arrests to be counted if the suspect is released without a formal charge. One survey of arrests found an error rate of about 10 percent in every Part I offense category.[33] More serious allegations claim that in some cases, police officials may deliberately alter reported crimes to improve their department's public image. Police administrators interested in lowering the crime rate may falsify crime reports by classifying a burglary as a nonreportable trespass.[34] See the accompanying Evidence-Based Justice feature for more on this issue.

Ironically, boosting police efficiency and professionalism may actually help increase crime rates: as people develop confidence in the police, they may be more motivated to report crime.[35] Higher crime rates may occur as departments adopt more sophisticated computer technology and hire better-educated, better-trained employees.[36]

■ *Methodological issues.* Several methodological issues contribute to skepticism about UCR validity:

- No federal crimes are reported.
- Reports are voluntary and vary in accuracy and completeness.
- Not all police departments submit reports.
- The FBI uses estimates in its total crime projections.
- If an offender commits multiple crimes, only the most serious is recorded. Thus, when a narcotics addict rapes, robs, and murders a victim, only the murder is recorded. Consequently, many lesser crimes go unreported.
- Each act is listed as a single offense for some crimes but not for others. When a man robs six people in a bar, the offense is listed as one robbery; but if he had assaulted or murdered them, his acts would have been listed as six assaults or six murders.
- Incomplete acts are lumped together with completed ones.
- Important differences exist between the FBI's definition of certain crimes and those used in a number of states.[37]

In addition to these issues, the complex scoring procedure used in the UCR program means that many serious crimes are not counted. If during an armed bank robbery, the robber strikes a teller with the butt of a handgun, runs from the bank, and steals an automobile at the curb, he has technically committed robbery, aggravated assault, and motor vehicle theft, which are three Part I offenses. However, the UCR records only the most serious crime, the robbery.[38]

National Incident-Based Reporting System (NIBRS)

Clearly there must be a more reliable source for crime statistics than the UCR as it stands today. Beginning in 1982, a five-year redesign effort was undertaken to provide more comprehensive and detailed crime statistics. The effort resulted in the **National Incident-Based Reporting System (NIBRS)**, a program that collects data on each reported crime incident. Instead of allowing local police agencies simply to indicate the kinds of crimes that individual citizens report to the police and to submit summary statements of resulting arrests, the new program requires them to provide at least a brief account of each incident and arrest, including the incident, victim, and offender information.

Under NIBRS, law enforcement authorities provide the FBI with information on each criminal incident that occurs in their jurisdiction and involves any of 46 specific offenses, including the eight Part I crimes; arrest information on the 46 offenses as well as 11 lesser offenses is also provided in the NIBRS. These expanded crime categories include numerous additional crimes, such as blackmail, embezzlement, drug offenses, and bribery. This allows a national database on the nature of crime, victims, and criminals to be developed. Other collected information includes statistics gathered by federal law enforcement agencies, as well as data on hate, or bias, crimes. When fully implemented, NIBRS will provide:

 L04 Discuss the development of the NIBRS program.

National Incident-Based Reporting System (NIBRS)
A form of crime data collection created by the FBI requiring local police agencies to provide at least a brief account of each incident and arrest within 22 crime patterns, including the incident, victim, and offender information.

Web App 2.2

For more information about NIBRS, visit http://www.bjs.gov/index.cfm?ty=dcdetail&iid=301.

- Expansion of the number of offense categories included
- Details on individual crime incidents (offenses, offenders, victims, property, and arrests)
- Links between arrests and crime clearances
- Inclusion of all offenses that occur in an incident, rather than only the most serious offense
- The ability to distinguish between attempted and completed crimes
- Links between offense, offender, victim, property, and arrestee variables, which permit examination of interrelationships[39]

Thus far, about half the states have implemented their NIBRS programs. When this program is fully implemented and adopted across the nation, it should bring about greater uniformity in cross-jurisdictional reporting and improve the accuracy of official crime data. Whether it can capture cases missing from the UCR remains to be seen.[40]

National Crime Victimization Survey (NCVS)

Because more than half of all victims do not report their experiences to the police, the UCR cannot measure all the annual criminal activity. To address the nonreporting issue, the federal government's Bureau of Justice Statistics sponsors the **National Crime Victimization Survey (NCVS)**, a comprehensive, nationwide survey of victimization in the United States. Begun in 1973, the NCVS provides a detailed picture of crime incidents, victims, and trends.[41]

National Crime Victimization Survey (NCVS)

The ongoing victimization study conducted jointly by the Justice Department and the U.S. Census Bureau that surveys victims about their experiences with law violation.

In the most recent survey as of this writing (2012), 92,390 households and 162,940 individuals age 12 or older were interviewed twice for the NCVS.[42] Households stay in the sample for three years. New households are rotated into the sample on an ongoing basis. The NCVS collects information on crimes suffered by individuals and households, whether or not those crimes were reported to law enforcement. It estimates the proportion of each crime type reported to law enforcement, and it summarizes the reasons that victims give for reporting or not reporting.

In 1993, the survey was redesigned to provide detailed information on the frequency and nature of the crimes of rape, sexual assault, personal robbery, aggravated and simple assault, household burglary, theft, and motor vehicle theft. In 2006, significant changes were made to the way the NCVS is collected so that victimization estimates are not totally comparable to previous years. The methodological changes included a new sampling method, a change in the method of handling first-time interviews with households, and a change in the method of interviewing. Some selected areas were dropped from the sample while others were added. Finally, computer-assisted personal interviewing (CAPI) replaced paper and pencil interviewing (PAPI). While these issues are critical, there is no substitute available that provides national information on crime and victimization with extensive detail on victims and the social context of the criminal event.

Web App 2.3

NCVS products and publications can be found here: http://www.bjs.gov/index.cfm?ty=pbse&sid=6

The survey provides information about victims (age, sex, race, ethnicity, marital status, income, and educational level), offenders (sex, race, approximate age, and victim–offender relationship), and crimes (time and place of occurrence, use of weapons, nature of injury, and economic consequences). Questions also cover the experiences of victims with the criminal justice system, self-protective measures used by victims, and possible substance abuse by offenders. Supplements are added periodically to the survey to obtain detailed information on topics such as school crime.

NCVS: ADVANTAGES AND PROBLEMS The greatest advantage of the NCVS over official data sources such as the UCR is that it can provide estimates of the total amount of annual crimes, not only those that are reported to police. Nonreporting is a significant issue: only about half of all violent victimizations and about one-third of all property crimes are reported to the police. As a result, the NCVS data provide a more nearly complete picture of the nation's crime problem.

Because some crimes are significantly underreported, the NCVS is an indispensable measure of their occurrence. Take the crimes of rape and sexual assault, relatively few of which are reported to police. The UCR reports that around 85,000 rapes or attempted rapes occur each year, compared to about 346,000 uncovered by the NCVS.[43] In other words, only about 25 percent of rapes are reported to the police.

The NCVS also helps us understand *why* crimes are not reported to police and whether the type and nature of the criminal event influences whether the police will ever know it occurred. With the crime of rape, research shows that victims are much more likely to report rape if it is accompanied by another crime, such as robbery, than they are if the rape is the only crime that occurred. Official data alone cannot provide that type of information.[44]

Although its utility and importance are unquestioned, the NCVS may also suffer from some methodological problems. As a result, its findings must be interpreted with caution. Among the potential problems:

■ Overreporting due to victims' misinterpretation of events. A lost wallet may be reported as stolen, or an open door may be viewed as a burglary attempt.

■ Underreporting due to the embarrassment of reporting crime to interviewers, fear of getting in trouble, or simply forgetting an incident.

■ Inability to record the personal criminal activity of those victims interviewed, such as drug use or gambling; murder is also not included, for obvious reasons.

■ Sampling errors, which may produce a group of respondents who do not represent the nation as a whole.

■ Inadequate question format that invalidates responses. Some groups, such as adolescents, may be particularly susceptible to reporting error because of faulty question format.[45]

The accompanying Victim Experience feature discusses a famous incidence of victimization.

Self-Report Surveys

Whereas the NCVS is designed to measure victimization directly and criminal activity indirectly, participants in **self-report survey** are asked to describe, in detail, their recent and lifetime participation in criminal activity. Self-reports are generally given anonymously in groups, so that the people being surveyed are assured that their responses will remain private and confidential. Secrecy and anonymity are essential to maintaining the honesty and validity of responses. Self-report survey questions might ask:

self-report survey
A research approach that questions large groups of subjects, such as high school students, about their own participation in delinquent or criminal acts.

■ How many times in the past year have you taken something worth more than $50?

■ How many times in the past year did you hurt someone so badly that they needed medical care?

■ How many times in the past year did you vandalize or damage school property?

■ How many times in the past year did you use marijuana?

Most self-report studies have focused on juvenile delinquency and youth crime, but they can also be used to examine the offense histories of select groups such as prison inmates, drug users, and even police officers.[46]

the VICTIM experience

JAYCEE LEE DUGARD

On August 24, 2009, parole officers monitoring Phillip Garrido, a long-time sex offender, became suspicious when he arrived for an interview with his wife Nancy, two children, and a young woman named Alyssa. After being separated from Garrido for a further interview, "Alyssa" told authorities that she was really Jaycee Lee Dugard, and the two young girls were children that she had borne Garrido, who along with his wife was placed under immediate arrest.

Jaycee Lee Dugard had been abducted on June 10, 1991, at a school bus stop within sight of her home in South Lake Tahoe, California. After being grabbed off the street by Garrido, the 11-year-old Jaycee was held captive for 18 years, living in a tent in a walled-off compound on land the Garridos owned in Antioch, California. Raped repeatedly, Dugard bore two daughters, in 1994 and 1998. On August 28, 2009, Philip and Nancy Garrido were indicted on charges including kidnapping, rape, and false imprisonment. After pleading guilty, Garrido was sentenced to 431 years in prison; Nancy received 36 years to life. In July 2010, the state of California approved a $20 million settlement with Jaycee Dugard to compensate her for "various lapses by the Corrections Department [which contributed to] Dugard's continued captivity, ongoing sexual assault and mental and/or physical abuse." Dugard has written a book about her experience in order to help other victims of abuse.

THE BIG PICTURE The Jaycee Dugard story shocked the nation and had a chilling effect on the general public. But while shocking, the case is not unique. On June 5, 2002, in another highly publicized case, Elizabeth Smart was abducted from her Salt Lake City, Utah, bedroom at the age of 14 and not found again until nine months later, even though she had been held only 18 miles from her home. Elizabeth's captors, Brian David Mitchell and Wanda Ileen Barzee, at first were both considered mentally incompetent and unfit to stand trial. However, after subsequent hearings, on May 25, 2011, Mitchell was sentenced to life in prison without parole for his crimes. Wanda Barzee received a 15-year sentence.

How common are child kidnappings by strangers? A national survey conducted by David Finkelhor and his associates found the following:

- During the study year, there were an estimated 115 *stereotypical kidnappings*, defined as abductions perpetrated by a stranger or slight acquaintance and involving a child who was transported 50 or more miles, detained overnight, held for ransom or with the intent to keep the child permanently, or killed. In 40 percent of stereotypical kidnappings, the child was killed, and in another 4 percent, the child was not recovered.

- There were an estimated 58,200 child victims of *nonfamily abduction*, defined more broadly to include all nonfamily perpetrators (friends and acquaintances as well as strangers) and crimes involving lesser amounts of forced movement or detention in addition to the more serious crimes entailed in stereotypical kidnappings.

According to these data, almost 30,000 children are taken and sexually assaulted by strangers each year. One result has been the implementation of America's Missing Broadcast Emergency Response, also known as the AMBER Alert, named after Amber Hagerman, a 9-year-old girl who was abducted while riding her bike near her home in Texas in 1996. So while cases involving long-term abduction and sexual exploitation, such as that of Jaycee Lee Dugard and Elizabeth Smart, are relatively rare, detention and rape of children is all too common.

CLASSROOM EXERCISE Have students contact local police in the area and find out if they employ the AMBER Alert protocol, how often it is used, and how successful has it been in recovering abducted kids.

Sources: BBC News, "Jaycee Dugard Kidnap: Victim Rues 'Stolen Life,'" June 2, 2011, http://www.bbc.co.uk/news/world-us-canada-13631641; David Finkelhor, Heather Hammer, and Andrea J. Sedlak, "Nonfamily Abducted Children: National Estimates and Characteristics," U.S. Department of Justice, 2002, http://www.missingkids.com/en_US/documents/nismart2_nonfamily.pdf; Sarah Netter and Sabina Ghebremedhin, "Jaycee Dugard Found After 18 Years, Kidnap Suspect Allegedly Fathered Her Kids," ABC News, August 27, 2009, http://abcnews.go.com/US/jaycee-lee-dugard-found-family-missing-girl-located/story?id=8426124 (all sites accessed May 2014).

In addition to crime-related items, most self-report surveys contain questions about attitudes, values, and behaviors. There may be questions about a participant's substance abuse history and his or her family relations, such as "Did your parents ever strike you with a stick or a belt?" Criminologists can then use statistical analysis of the responses to determine whether people who report being abused as children are also more likely to use drugs as adults. When psychologist Christiane Brems and her associates used this approach to collect data from 274 women and 556 men receiving drug detoxification services, they found that 20 percent of men and more than 50 percent of women reported childhood physical or sexual abuse. Individuals who report an abuse history also reported earlier age of onset of drinking, more problems associated with the use of alcohol/drugs, more severe psychopathology, and more lifetime arrests.[47]

MONITORING THE FUTURE One of the most important sources of self-report data is the Monitoring the Future (MTF) study, which researchers at the University of Michigan Institute for Social Research (ISR) have been conducting annually since 1978.[48] The MTF is considered the national standard for measuring substance abuse trends among American teens.

The MTF data indicate that the number of people who break the law is far greater than the number projected by official statistics. Almost everyone questioned is found to have violated a law at some time, including truancy, alcohol abuse, false ID use, shoplifting or larceny under $50, fighting, marijuana use, and damage to the property of others. Furthermore, self-reports dispute the notion that criminals and delinquents specialize in one type of crime or another; rather, offenders seem to engage in a mixed bag of crime and deviance.

VALIDITY OF SELF-REPORTS Critics of self-report studies frequently suggest that it is unreasonable to expect people to candidly admit illegal acts. This is especially true of those with official records, who may be engaging in the most criminality. At the same time, some people may exaggerate their criminal acts, forget some of them, or be confused about what is being asked. Some surveys contain an overabundance of trivial offenses, such as shoplifting small items or using false identification to obtain alcohol, often lumped together with serious crimes to form a total crime index. Consequently, comparisons between groups can be highly misleading.

The "missing cases" phenomenon is also a concern. Even if 90 percent of a school population voluntarily participate in a self-report study, researchers can never be sure whether the few who refuse to participate or are absent that day constitute a significant portion of the school's population of persistent high-rate offenders. Research indicates that offenders with the most extensive prior criminality are also the most likely "to be poor historians of their own crime commission rates."[49] And the most serious chronic offenders in the teenage population are the least likely to be willing to cooperate with criminologists administering self-report tests.[50] Institutionalized youths, who are not generally represented in the self-report surveys, are not only more delinquent than the general youth population, but are also considerably more misbehaving than the most delinquent youths identified in the typical self-report survey.[51] Consequently, self-reports may measure only nonserious, occasional delinquents, while ignoring hard-core chronic offenders.

There is also evidence that reporting accuracy differs among racial, ethnic, and gender groups. It is possible that some groups are more worried about image than others and less willing to report crime, deviance, and/or victimization for fear that it would make them or their group look bad.[52]

To address these criticisms, various techniques have been used to verify self-report data.[53] The "known group" method compares youths who are known to be offenders with those who are not to see whether the former report more

Web App 2.4

Data collected from the Monitoring the Future survey can be found here: http://www.monitoringthefuture.org/.

delinquency. Research shows that when kids are asked whether they have ever been arrested or sent to court, their responses accurately reflect their true-life experiences.[54]

Although these studies are supportive, self-report data must be interpreted with some caution. Asking subjects about their past behavior may capture more serious crimes but miss minor criminal acts. For example, people remember armed robberies and rapes better than minor assaults and altercations.[55] In addition, some classes of offenders, such as substance abusers, may have a tough time accounting for their prior misbehavior.[56]

Evaluating Sources of Crime Data

Discuss the strengths and weaknesses of various measures of crime.

The UCR, the NCVS, and self-reports are the standard sources of data used by criminologists to track trends and patterns in the crime rate. Each has its own strengths and weaknesses. The UCR contains information on the number and characteristics of people arrested—information that the other data sources lack. Some recent research indicates that for serious crimes, such as drug trafficking, arrest data can provide a meaningful measure of the level of criminal activity in a particular neighborhood environment, which other data sources cannot provide. It is also the source of information on particular crimes such as murder, which the other data sources cannot provide.[57] It remains the standard unit of analysis upon which most criminological research is based. However, UCR data omit many criminal incidents that victims choose not to report to police and are subject to the reporting caprices of individual police departments.

The NCVS includes unreported crime and important information on the personal characteristics of victims. However, the data consist of estimates made from relatively limited samples of the total U.S. population, so that even narrow fluctuations in the rates of some crimes can have a major impact on findings. It also relies on personal recollections, which may be inaccurate. The NCVS also does not include data on important crime patterns, including patterns in murder and drug abuse, that are critical issues for crime analysis.

CONCEPT SUMMARY 2.2
Data Collection Methods

Uniform Crime Reports (UCR)	■ Data are collected from records compiled by police departments across the nation, which include crimes reported to police and arrests. ■ Strengths of the UCR are that it measures homicides and arrests and that it is a consistent, national sample. ■ Weaknesses of the UCR are that it omits crimes not reported to police, omits most drug usage, and contains reporting errors.
National Crime Victimization Survey (NCVS)	■ Data are collected from a large national survey. ■ Strengths of the NCVS are that it includes crimes not reported to the police, uses careful sampling techniques, and is a yearly survey. ■ Weaknesses of the NCVS are that it relies on victims' memory and honesty and that it omits substance abuse.
Self-report surveys	■ Data are collected from local surveys. ■ Strengths of self-report surveys are that they include nonreported crimes and substance abuse and that offenders' personal information is included. ■ Weaknesses of self-report surveys are that they rely on the honesty of offenders and that they omit offenders who refuse to or are unable to participate and who may be the most deviant.

Self-report surveys can provide information on the personal characteristics of offenders—such as their attitudes, values, beliefs, and psychological profiles—that is unavailable from any other source. Yet at their core, self-reports rely on the honesty of criminal offenders and drug abusers, a population not generally known for accuracy and integrity.

Although their tallies of crimes are certainly not in sync, the crime patterns and trends recorded by the three methods are often quite similar (see Concept Summary 2.2).[58] All of the sources of crime data agree about the personal characteristics of serious criminals (such as age and gender) and about where and when crime occurs (such as urban areas, nighttime, and summer months). In addition, the problems inherent in each source are consistent over time. Therefore, even if the data sources do not provide an exact, precise, and valid count of crime at any given time, they are reliable indicators of changes and fluctuations in yearly crime rates.

In addition to the primary sources of crime data—UCR, NCVS, and self-report surveys—a number of other methods are routinely used to acquire data. These are discussed in Exhibit 2.1.

EXHIBIT 2.1 Alternative Crime Measures

COHORT RESEARCH DATA

Collecting cohort data involves observing over time a group of people who share certain characteristics. Researchers might select all girls born in Boston in 1970 and then follow their behavior patterns for 20 years. The research data might include their school experiences, arrests, and hospitalizations, along with information about their family life (marriages, divorces, and parental relations, for example). Data may also be collected directly from the subjects during interviews and meetings with family members. If the cohort is carefully drawn, it may be possible to accumulate a complex array of data that can be used to determine which life experiences are associated with criminal careers. Another approach is to take a contemporary cohort, such as men in prison in New York in 2009, and then look back into their past and collect data from educational, family, police, and hospital records—a format known as a retrospective cohort study. If criminologists wanted to identify childhood and adolescent risk factors for criminality, they might acquire the inmates' prior police and court records, school records, and so on.

EXPERIMENTAL DATA

Sometimes criminologists conduct controlled experiments to collect data on the cause of crime. To conduct experimental research, criminologists manipulate, or intervene in, the lives of their subjects to see the outcome or the effect of the intervention. True experiments usually have three elements: (1) random selection of subjects, (2) a control or comparison group, and (3) an experimental condition. For example, to determine whether viewing violent media content is a cause of aggression, a criminologist might randomly select one group of subjects and have them watch an extremely violent and gory film (such as *Evil Dead* or *Texas Chainsaw Massacre*) and then compare their behavior to that of a second randomly selected group who watch something mellow (such as a *Shrek* or *Toy Story* film). The behavior of both groups would be monitored; if the subjects who had watched the violent film were significantly more aggressive than those who had watched the nonviolent film, an association between media content and behavior would be supported. The fact that both groups were randomly selected would prevent some preexisting condition from invalidating the results of the experiment.

OBSERVATIONAL AND INTERVIEW RESEARCH

Sometimes criminologists focus their research on relatively few subjects, interviewing them in depth or observing them as they go about their activities. This research often results in the kind of in-depth data that large-scale surveys do not yield. In one such effort, Claire Sterk-Elifson focused on the lives of middle-class female drug

(continued)

EXHIBIT 2.1 *continued*

abusers. The 34 interviews she conducted provide insight into a group whose behavior might not be captured in a large-scale survey. Sterk-Elifson found that these women were introduced to cocaine at first "just for fun": "I do drugs," one 34-year-old lawyer told her, "because I like the feeling. I would never let drugs take over my life." Unfortunately, many of these subjects succumbed to the power of drugs and suffered both emotional and financial stress.

META-ANALYSIS AND SYSTEMATIC REVIEW

Meta-analysis involves gathering data from a number of previous studies. Compatible information and data are extracted and pooled together. When analyzed, the grouped data from several different studies provide a more powerful and valid indicator of relationships than the results of a single study. A systematic review is another widely accepted means of evaluating the effectiveness of public policy interventions. It involves collecting the findings from previously conducted scientific studies that address a particular problem, appraising and synthesizing the evidence, and using the collective evidence to address a particular scientific question.

DATA MINING

A relatively new criminological technique, data mining employs multiple advanced computational methods, including artificial intelligence (the use of computers to perform logical functions), to analyze large data sets that usually involve one or more data sources. The goal is to identify significant and recognizable patterns, trends, and relationships that are not easily detected through traditional analytical techniques. Data mining might be employed

to help a police department determine whether burglaries in its jurisdiction exhibit a particular pattern. To determine whether such a pattern exists, a criminologist might apply data-mining techniques with a variety of sources, including calls for service data, crime or incident reports, witness statements, suspect interviews, tip information, telephone toll analysis, and Internet activity. The data mining might uncover a strong relationship between the time of day and the place of occurrence. The police could use the findings to plan an effective burglary elimination strategy.

CRIME MAPPING

Crime mapping is a research technique that employs computerized crime maps and other graphical representations of crime data patterns. The simplest maps display crime locations or concentrations and can be used, for example, to help law enforcement agencies increase the effectiveness of their patrol efforts. More complex maps can be used to chart trends in criminal activity. For example, criminologists might be able to determine whether certain neighborhoods in a city have significantly higher crime rates than others—whether they are so-called hot spots of crime.

Sources: David Farrington, Lloyd Ohlin, and James Q. Wilson, *Understanding and Controlling Crime* (New York: Springer-Verlag, 1986), pp. 11–18; Claire Sterk-Elifson, "Just for Fun? Cocaine Use Among Middle-Class Women," *Journal of Drug Issues* 26 (1996): 63–76; William F. Whyte, *Street Corner Society* (Chicago: University of Chicago Press, 1955), p. 38; Herman Schwendinger and Julia Schwendinger, *Adolescent Subcultures and Delinquency* (New York: Praeger, 1985); David Farrington and Brandon Welsh, "Improved Street Lighting and Crime Prevention," *Justice Quarterly* 19 (2002): 313–343; Colleen McCue, Emily Stone, and Teresa Gooch, "Data Mining and Value-Added Analysis," *FBI Law Enforcement Bulletin* 72 (2003): 1–6; Jerry Ratcliffe, "Aoristic Signatures and the Spatio-Temporal Analysis of High Volume Crime Patterns," *Journal of Quantitative Criminology* 18 (2002): 23–43.

Crime Trends

L06 Recognize the trends in the crime rate.

Crime is not new to the last century.[59] Studies have indicated that a gradual increase in the crime rate, especially in violent crime, occurred from 1830 to 1860. Following the Civil War, this rate increased significantly for about 15 years. Then, from 1880 up to the time of World War I, with the possible exception of the years immediately preceding and following the war, the number of reported crimes decreased. After a period of readjustment, the crime rate steadily declined until the Depression (about 1930), when another crime wave was recorded. As measured by the UCR, crime rates increased gradually following the 1930s until the 1960s, when the growth rate became much greater. The homicide rate, which had actually declined from the 1930s to the 1960s, also began a sharp increase that continued for almost 30 years.

By 1991, police recorded about 14.6 million crimes. Since then, with a few exceptions, the number of crimes has been in decline. About 10 million crimes were reported in 2011—a drop of 4 million reported crimes since the 1991 peak, despite a boost of about 50 million in the general population. Are the crime trends and patterns experienced in the United States unique or do they occur in other countries as well? This issue is explored in the accompanying Global Criminal Justice feature.

Trends in Violent Crime and Property Crime

About 1.2 million violent crimes are now being reported to the police each year, a rate of around 394 per 100,000 Americans.[60] Of course, people are still disturbed by media reports of violent incidents, but in reality there are 1 million fewer violent crimes being reported today than in 1991, when almost 2 million incidents occurred, a violence rate of 758 per 100,000. This means that the violence rate has dropped about half from its peak. Violent crime did increase, however, about 0.7 percent between 2011 and 2012, so we will need to keep watching the numbers to get a sense of whether that is the start of a trend.

The property crime rate—including burglary, larceny, motor vehicle theft, and arson—has also been in decline, dropping more than 14 percent from 2003 to 2012. At its peak, in 1991, about 13 million property crimes were reported, a rate of almost 5,000 per 100,000 citizens. Currently, about 9 million property crimes are reported annually to police, a rate of about 2,900 per 100,000 population. Property crimes thus far outnumber violent crimes.

Trends in Victimization

According to the latest NCVS survey, U.S. residents age 12 or older experienced about 7.6 million violent and 19.7 million property victimizations.[61] The NCVS data show that criminal victimizations declined significantly between the 1990s and 2010, when the trend reversed. In 2012, for the second year, violent and property crime victimizations increased. Figure 2.2 shows trends in violent crime over the past several years. Note the recent uptick. Also note the discrepancy between total violent crime, crimes reported to police (those that appear in the UCR), and crimes not reported to police. The latter are what the NCVS seeks to uncover. The top line in Figure 2.2 shows the combined total of crimes reported and not reported and thus more closely approximates the "dark figure" of crime.

Trends in Self-Reporting

Self-report results appear to be more stable than the UCR. When the results of recent self-report surveys are compared with various studies conducted over a 20-year period, a uniform pattern emerges: The use of drugs and alcohol

---

FACT CHECK ✓

YOUR OPINION: How often do you worry about your home/residence being burglarized? Frequently, occasionally, rarely, or never?

PUBLIC OPINION:

| FREQUENTLY OR OCCASIONALLY: | 47% |
| RARELY OR NEVER: | 53% |

REALITY: It is disconcerting that nearly half of survey respondents fear having their residences burglarized. According to the FBI, the rate of burglary victimization in 2012 was 670.5 per 100,000 people. That translates into well under one burglary per 100 people. By relying only on perceptions and fear, one would develop an impression that burglary is far more common than it really is.

DISCUSSION: What are the limitations of the FBI's calculated burglary rate?

Sources: Federal Bureau of Investigation, *Crime in the United States 2012*, http://www.fbi.gov/about-us/cjis/ucr/crime-in-the-u.s/2012/crime-in-the-u.s.-2012/tables/16tabledatadecpdf/ table_16_rate_by_population_group_2012.xls (accessed May 2014); Sourcebook of Criminal Justice Statistics, http://www.albany.edu/sourcebook/pdf/t2392011.pdf (accessed May 2014).

Web App 2.5

To compare U.S. crime statistics to those of other nations around the world, visit the website of the United Nations Office on Drugs and Crime here: https://www.unodc.org/unodc/en/data-and-analysis/statistics/data.html.

GLOBAL criminal justice

CRIME IN OTHER COUNTRIES

Making international comparisons is often difficult because the legal definitions of crime vary from country to country. There are also differences in the way crime is measured. For example, in the United States, crime may be measured by counting criminal acts reported to the police or by using victim surveys, whereas in many European countries, the number of cases solved by the police is used as the measure of crime.

Despite these problems, simple comparisons can still be made about crime across different countries using a number of reliable data sources. The most comprehensive one-stop source is the United Nations Office on Drugs and Crime. What follows are a variety of crime statistics it collected in 2011. Not all countries reported, so readers should note that just because a country is not on the list does not mean it is any more or less safe. What do the data tell us?

HOMICIDE

Many nations, especially those experiencing social or economic upheaval, have murder rates much higher than the United States. The United States homicide rate in 2011 was around five per 100,000 people. It was vastly higher in other countries, however. The rates in Honduras, El Salvador, Ivory Coast, Venezuela, and Belize were 91.6, 69.2, 56.9, 45.1, and 41.4, respectively. Why are murder rates so high these other countries? Law enforcement officials link the upsurge in violence to drug trafficking, gang feuds, vigilantism, and disputes over trivial matters, in which young, unmarried, uneducated males are involved.

ROBBERY

The United States has a robbery rate around 113 per 100,000 people. France, however, has nearly 200 robberies per 100,000 people. The highest robbery rates are in Brazil, Mexico, Costa Rica, Spain, and Belgium.

ASSAULT

The United States reports around 240 assaults per 100,000 people. How does that figure compare with other nations? We fall somewhere in the middle. The five countries with the lowest assault rates are Egypt, Poland, São Tomé and Principe, Armenia, and Albania. The five countries with the highest assault rates are Finland, Botswana, the Bahamas, Sweden, and Saint Vincent and the Grenadines.

BURGLARY

The United States falls on the upper end of the burglary spectrum. There are roughly 700 burglaries per 100,000 people in the United States, compared to a high of over 1,600 in Denmark and a low of 3.2 in Egypt. Countries with higher burglary rates than the United States include Greece, Switzerland, Belgium, Australia, the Netherlands, Sweden, Austria, and New Zealand, among others.

THEFT

What countries have the greatest problems with theft? Again, the United States has one of the higher theft rates in the world, but several countries outpace it, including Australia, Germany, Norway, and Denmark. As of 2011, Sweden reported the largest theft rate of those countries that provided data.

Xinhua/eyevine/Redux

A soldier of the Mexican Army attends an operation to destroy seized weapons, in Ciudad Juarez, Mexico. Drug-related violence south of the border took approximately 60,000 lives between 2006 and 2012, the year in which this photo was taken.

DRUG CRIMES

Today there is an annual flow of about 450 tons of heroin into the global heroin market. Of that total, opium from Myanmar and the Lao People's Democratic Republic yields some 50 tons, while the rest, some 380 tons of heroin and morphine, is produced in Afghanistan. While approximately 5 tons are consumed and seized in Afghanistan, the remaining bulk of 375 tons is trafficked worldwide. The most common route is through Iran via Pakistan, Turkey, Greece, and Bulgaria, then across southeast Europe to the Western European market, with an annual market value of some $20 billion. The northern route runs mainly through Tajikistan and Kyrgyzstan (or Uzbekistan or Turkmenistan) to Kazakhstan and the Russian Federation. The size of that market is estimated to total $13 billion per year.

CRITICAL THINKING

1. Although risk factors at all levels of social and personal life contribute to youth violence, young people in all nations who experience change in societal-level factors—such as economic inequalities, rapid social change, and the availability of firearms, alcohol, and drugs—seem the most likely to get involved in violence. Can anything be done to help alleviate these social problems?

2. The United States is notorious for employing much tougher penal measures than European nations. Do you believe that our tougher measures would work abroad and should be adopted there as well? Is there a downside to putting lots of people in prison?

Sources: United Nations Office on Drugs and Crime, *Global Study on Homicide*, 2011, http://www.unodc.org/documents/data-and-analysis/statistics/Homicide/Globa_study_on_homicide_2011_web.pdf (accessed May 2014); United Nations Office on Drugs and Crime, https://www.unodc.org/unodc/en/data-and-analysis/statistics/data.html (accessed May 2014); United Nations Office on Drugs and Crime, *Drug Trafficking*, http://www.unodc.org/unodc/en/drug-trafficking/ (accessed May 2014).

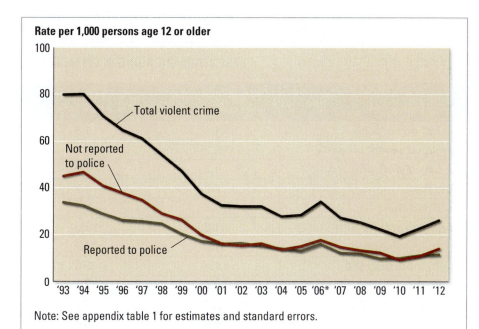

Rate per 1,000 persons age 12 or older

Total violent crime

Not reported to police

Reported to police

'93 '94 '95 '96 '97 '98 '99 '00 '01 '02 '03 '04 '05 '06* '07 '08 '09 '10 '11 '12

Note: See appendix table 1 for estimates and standard errors.

*Due to methodological changes in the 2006 NCVS, use caution when comparing 2006 criminal victimization estimates to other years. See *Criminal Victimization, 2007*, NCJ 224390, BJS web, December 2008, for more information.

Source: Bureau of Justice Statistics, National Crime Victimization Survey, 1993–2012.

FIGURE 2.2 Violent Victimization Reported and Not Reported to Police, 1993–2012

Source: Jennifer Truman, Lynn Langton, and Michael Planty, *Criminal Victimization, 2012* (Washington, DC: Bureau of Justice Statistics, 2013), p. 1.

increased markedly in the 1970s, leveled off in the 1980s, and then began to increase in the mid-1990s until 1997, when the use of most drugs began to decline. Theft, violence, and damage-related crimes seem more stable. Although a self-reported crime wave has not occurred, neither has there been any visible reduction in self-reported criminality. Table 2.1 contains data from the most recent Monitoring the Future survey. A surprising number of these "typical" teenagers reported involvement in serious criminal behavior. About 14 percent reported hurting someone badly enough that the victim needed medical care (7 percent said they did it more than once). About 27 percent reported stealing something worth less than $50, and another 11 percent stole something worth more than $50; 27 percent reported shoplifting one or more times; 10 percent damaged school property, half more than once.

If the MTF data are accurate, the crime problem is much greater than official statistics would lead us to believe. According to the U.S. Department of Education, there are about 15 million public school students in grades 9 through 12.[62] About 3 percent of high school students said they had used force to steal (which is the legal definition of a robbery). At this rate, high school students alone commit more than 450,000 million robberies per year. In comparison, the UCR now tallies about 350,000 robberies for all age groups yearly.[63] There is a huge discrepancy, then, between crimes reported to police and those disclosed in surveys such as Monitoring the Future.

TABLE 2.1   **Monitoring the Future Survey of Criminal Activity of High School Seniors**

PERCENTAGE ENGAGING IN OFFENSES

Type of Delinquency	Percent Committed at Least Once	Percent Committed More than Once
Set fire on purpose	1.4	1.5
Damaged school property	5.9	5.2
Damaged work property	1.7	2.0
Auto theft	2.2	1.7
Auto part theft	1.5	1.9
Break and enter	11.0	13.0
Theft, less than $50	11.0	14.3
Theft, more than $50	4.0	5.0
Shoplift	10.4	13.4
Gang or group fight	8.5	7.7
Hurt someone badly enough to require medical care	6.8	6.0
Used force or a weapon to steal	1.3	1.7
Hit teacher or supervisor	1.0	1.8
Participated in serious fight	6.7	4.6

Source: Lloyd D. Johnson, Jerald G. Bachman, and Patrick M. O'Malley, *Monitoring the Future, 2011* (Ann Arbor, MI: Institute for Social Research, 2013), pp. 115–17, http://www.monitoringthefuture.org/datavolumes/2011/2011dv.pdf (accessed May 2014).

What the Future Holds

Speculating about the future of crime trends is risky because current conditions can change rapidly, but some criminologists have tried to predict future patterns. There are approximately 50 million school-age children in the United States, and many are under age 10; this is a greater number than we have had for decades. Many come from stable homes, but some lack stable families and adequate supervision. These children will soon enter their prime crime years, and as a result, crime rates may increase in the future.[64] However, whereas kids increase crime rates, seniors depress them. Even if teens commit more crime in the future, their contribution may be offset by the aging of the population, which will produce a large number of senior citizens and elderly, a group with a relatively low crime rate.[65]

Although population trends are important, the economy, technological change, and social factors may shape the direction of the crime rate.[66] The narcissistic youth culture that stresses materialism is being replaced by more moralistic cultural values.[67] Positive social values have a "contagion effect"; that is, the values held by the baby boomers will influence the behavior of all citizens, even crime-prone teens. The result may be moderation in the potential growth of the crime rate. Such prognostication is reassuring, but there is, of course, no telling what changes are in store that may influence crime rates either up or down. Technological developments such as e-commerce on the Internet have created new classes of crime. Although crime rates have trended downward, it is too early to predict that this trend will continue into the foreseeable future. The Analyzing Criminal Justice Issues feature reviews the factors that influence crime rates and trends.

analyzing criminal justice ISSUES

EXPLAINING TRENDS IN CRIME RATES

Crime experts consider the explanation of crime trends one of their most important goals. Yet it is difficult to point to a single explanation for crime rate change. Let's look at a few of the most important social, ecological, and policy factors that are considered to be influences on the direction taken by crime rates.

AGE STRUCTURE OF THE POPULATION

The age composition of the population has a significant influence on crime trends. Teenagers have extremely high crime rates, whereas seniors rarely commit crime. The greater the proportion of teens in the population, the higher the crime rate and the greater the number of persistent offenders. When the "baby boomers" hit their teens in the mid-1960s, the crime rate skyrocketed. Because the number of senior citizens is expanding and the population is aging, crime rates may remain relatively low for some time.

IMMIGRATION

Immigration has become one of the most controversial issues in American society, and some people believe that immigrants should be prevented from entering the country because they have a disruptive effect on society. Research suggests the opposite, however, and some scholars, such as Harvard sociologist Robert Sampson, find that immigrants as a whole engage in criminal activities less than the general population. When Ramiro Martinez and his colleagues examined the association between drug crimes and immigration in Miami, Florida, and San Diego, California, they also found that immigration is *negatively* associated with homicides and with drug-related homicides specifically. This research indicates that as the number of immigrants in the population increases, the crime rate may actually decline; in other words, immigration has a suppressor effect on crime. Also see this chapter's

Evidence-Based Justice box for more on the relationship between immigration and crime.

ECONOMY/JOBS

Although it seems logical that high unemployment should increase crime rates and that a good economy should reduce criminal activity, especially theft-related crimes, there is actually significant debate over the association between the economy and crime rates.

- It is possible that *a poor economy actually helps lower crime rates* because unemployed parents are at home to supervise children and guard the family's possessions. Because there is less to spend, a poor economy reduces the number of valuables worth stealing. And it is unlikely that law-abiding, middle-aged workers will suddenly turn to a life of crime if they are laid off during an economic downturn.

- It is also possible that over the long haul, a *strong economy helps lower crime rates*, whereas long periods of sustained economic weakness and unemployment may eventually lead to increased rates: crime skyrocketed in the 1930s during the Great Depression.

One reason for this confusion is that short-term economic swings have different impacts on different segments of the population. When manufacturing moved overseas during the latter half of the twentieth century, it had a much greater impact on young minority men living in cities hit hardest by deindustrialization than on highly educated suburban dwellers who could get jobs in service and technology industries.

ABORTION

There is evidence that the recent drop in the crime rate can be attributed to the availability of legalized abortion. In 1973, *Roe v. Wade* legalized abortion nationwide, and the drop in crime rate began approximately 18 years later, in 1991. Crime rates began to decline when the first groups of potential offenders affected by the abortion decision began reaching the peak age of criminal activity. It is possible that the link between crime rates and abortion is the result of two mechanisms: (1) selective abortion on the part of women most likely to have children who would eventually engage in criminal activity, and (2) improved child rearing caused by better maternal, familial, and/or fetal care because women are having fewer children.

GUN AVAILABILITY

As the number of guns in the population increases, so do violent crime rates. There is evidence that more guns than ever before are finding their way into the hands of young people. Surveys of high school students indicate that up to 10 percent carry guns at least some of the time. As the number of gun-toting students increases, so does the seriousness of violent crime, as happens when a school yard fight turns into murder.

GANG MEMBERSHIP

According to government sources, there are now 800,000 gang members in the United States. Criminal gangs commit as much as 80 percent of the crime in many communities, including armed robbery, assault, auto theft, drug trafficking, extortion, fraud, home invasions, identity theft, murder, and weapons trafficking. Gang members are far more likely to possess guns than those not affiliated with gangs; criminal activity increases when kids join gangs. Drug-dealing gangs are heavily armed, a condition that persuades non–gang-affiliated kids to arm themselves for self-protection. The result is an arms race that generates an increasing spiral of violence.

DRUG USE

As drug use increases, crime rates increase. The surge in the violent crime rate between 1985 and 1993 has been tied directly to the crack cocaine epidemic that swept the nation's largest cities. Well-armed drug gangs did not hesitate to use violence to control territory, intimidate rivals, and increase market share. When crack use declined in urban areas after 1993, so did crime rates. A sudden increase in drug use may be a harbinger of future increases in the crime rate, especially if guns are easily obtained and the economy is weak.

MEDIA

The jury is still out, but some experts believe that violent media can influence the direction of crime rates. As the availability of media with a violent theme skyrocketed in the 1980s with the introduction of home video players, cable TV, and computer and video games, teen violence rates increased as well. Yet there is more violent video content than ever before and the violence rate has been dropping for the past decade.

MEDICAL TECHNOLOGY

Some crime experts believe that the presence and quality of health care can have a significant impact on murder rates. The big breakthrough occurred in the 1970s, when technology that was developed to treat injured soldiers in Vietnam was applied to trauma care in the nation's hospitals. Ever since then, fluctuations in the murder rate have been linked to the level and availability of emergency medical services.

LAW ENFORCEMENT PRACTICES

Reductions in crime rates may be attributed to adding large numbers of police officers and using them in aggressive police practices that target "quality of life" crimes, such as panhandling, graffiti, petty drug dealing, and loitering. By showing that even the smallest infractions will be dealt with seriously, police departments may be able to discourage potential criminals from committing more serious crimes. Cities that encourage focused police work may be able to lower homicide rates in the area.

INCARCERATION

It is also possible that tough laws imposing lengthy prison terms on drug dealers and repeat offenders can affect crime rates. The fear of punishment may inhibit some would-be criminals, and placing a significant number of potentially high-rate offenders behind bars seems to help lower crime rates. As the nation's prison population has expanded, the crime rate has fallen.

PRISONER REENTRY

Even though putting people in prison may have a short-term positive effect on crime rates, in the long run increasing punishments may backfire. The recidivism rate of paroled inmates is quite high, and about two-thirds of those released from state custody will eventually return to prison. Inmates reentering society may have a significant effect on local crime rates, and most reoffend shortly after being released.

CULTURAL CHANGE

In contemporary society, cultural change (such as increases in the number of single-parent families, high school dropout rates, racial conflict, and teen pregnancies) can affect crime rates. The number of teen pregnancies has declined in recent years and so too has the crime rate.

CRIMINAL OPPORTUNITY

As criminal opportunities increase, so do crime rates. The decline in the burglary rate over the past decade may be explained in part by the abundance, and subsequent decline in price, of commonly stolen merchandise such as smart phones and iPads. If the risk of getting caught outweighs the value of the goods, why bother? Improving home and commercial security devices may also discourage would-be burglars, convincing them to turn to other forms of crime, such as theft from motor vehicles. On the other hand, new targets may increase crime rates: subway crime increased in New York when thieves began targeting people carrying iPods and expensive cell phones.

Each of these factors may contribute to shifts in crime rate trends. They also have theoretical implications for social policy. For example, if crime is influenced by economic and justice-related factors, then criminals must be rational decision makers who will choose to commit crime if the need arises and the threat of punishment is limited. Effective crime control efforts might then be linked to convincing prospective offenders that crime does not pay and offering them alternative avenues to economic gain, such as job training and vocational education.

CRITICAL THINKING

While crime rates have been declining in the United States, they have been increasing around the world. Is it possible that factors that correlate with crime rate changes in the United States have little utility in predicting changes in other cultures? What other factors may increase or reduce crime rates?

Sources: Jeremy Staff, D. Wayne Osgood, John Schulenberg, Jerald Bachman, and Emily Messersmith, "Explaining the Relationship Between Employment and Juvenile Delinquency," *Criminology* 48 (2010): 1101–1131; Tim Wadsworth, "Is Immigration Responsible for the Crime Drop? An Assessment of the Influence of Immigration on Changes in Violent Crime Between 1990 and 2000," *Social Science Quarterly* 91 (2010): 531–553; Amy Anderson and Lorine Hughes, "Exposure to Situations Conducive to Delinquent Behavior: The Effects of Time Use, Income, and Transportation," *Journal of Research in Crime and Delinquency* 46 (2009): 5–34; Ramiro Martinez Jr. and Matthew Amie Nielsen, "Local Context and Determinants of Drug Violence in Miami and San Diego: Does Ethnicity and Immigration Matter?" *International Migration Review* 38 (2004): 131–157; Matthew Miller, David Hemenway, and Deborah Azrael, "State-Level Homicide Victimization Rates in the U.S. in Relation to Survey Measures of Household Firearm Ownership, 2001–2003," *Social Science and Medicine* 64 (2007): 656–664; Alfred Blumstein, "The Crime Drop in America: An Exploration of Some Recent Crime Trends," *Journal of Scandinavian Studies in Criminology and Crime Prevention* 7 (2006): 17–35; Thomas Arvanites and Robert Defina, "Business Cycles and Street Crime," *Criminology* 44 (2006): 139–164; Fahui Wang, "Job Access and Homicide Patterns in Chicago: An Analysis at Multiple Geographic Levels Based on Scale-Space Theory," *Journal of Quantitative Criminology* 21 (2005): 195–217; John J. Donohue and Steven D. Levitt, "The Impact of Legalized Abortion on Crime," *Quarterly Journal of Economics* 116 (2001): 379–420.

Crime Patterns

L07 Summarize the various crime patterns.

Criminologists look for stable crime rate patterns to gain insight into the nature of crime. The cause of crime may be better understood by examining the rate. If, for example, criminal statistics consistently show that crime rates are higher in poor neighborhoods in large urban areas, then the cause of crime may be related to poverty and neighborhood decline. If, in contrast, crime rates are spread evenly across society, and rates are equal in poor and affluent neighborhoods, this would suggest that crime has little economic basis. Instead, crime might be linked to socialization, personality, intelligence, or some other trait unrelated to class position or income. In this section we examine crime traits and patterns.

The Ecology of Crime

Patterns in the crime rate seem to be linked to temporal and ecological factors. Some of the most important of these are discussed here.

DAY, SEASON, AND CLIMATE Most reported crimes occur during the warm summer months of July and August. During the summer, teenagers, who usually have the highest crime levels, are out of school and have greater opportunity to commit crime. People spend more time outdoors during warm weather, making themselves easier targets. Similarly, homes are left vacant more often during the summer, making them more vulnerable to property crimes. Two exceptions to this trend are murders and robberies, which occur frequently in December and January (although rates are also high during the summer).

Crime rates may be higher on the first day of the month than at any other time. Government welfare and Social Security checks arrive at this time, and with them come increases in such activities as breaking into mailboxes and accosting recipients on the streets. Also, people may have more disposable income at this time, and the availability of extra money may be related to behaviors associated with crime, such as drinking, partying, gambling, and so on.[68]

Crime follows a number of patterns. Certain offenses occur more frequently during the day, when it is warmer outside, and in more temperate climates.

Izabela Habur/E+/Getty Images

EVIDENCE-based justice

IMMIGRATION AND CRIME

Some critics call for tough new laws limiting immigration and/or strictly enforcing laws because they believe that immigrants are prone to crime and represent a social threat. How true are their perceptions? Not very true, according to the Immigration Policy Center, whose research found that on the national level, U.S.-born men ages 18 to 39 are five times more likely to be incarcerated than are their foreign-born peers. Though the number of illegal immigrants in the country doubled between 1994 and 2004, violent crime declined by nearly 35 percent and property crimes by 25 percent over the same period. The declines also occurred in border cities where the immigration influx was largest.

In one of the most recent studies on the subject, Bianca Bersani and her colleagues found that first-generation immigrants (individuals born outside the United States) were less likely to commit serious crimes than their U.S.-born counterparts. They were also less likely to become chronic offenders. These findings stand in stark contrast to common perceptions that immigrants are disproportionately responsible for fluctuations in America's crime trends.

Also interesting is a finding from the study that second-generation immigrants (individuals born in the U.S. who have at least one foreign-born parent) offend at similar rates to the their native counterparts. What explains this phenomenon? According to Bersani and her colleagues, "...the finding that first-generation immigrants desist from crime at an earlier age compared to their peers may suggest that they are more easily deterred from further crime following criminal justice sanctions." In contrast, context, particularly neighborhood disadvantage, went a long way toward explaining delinquency in second-generation immigrants. In this way, second-generation immigrants were really no different than their native-born counterparts; faced with the same circumstances that predispose people toward breaking the law, both groups fared similarly.

Sources: Immigration Policy Center, "From Anecdotes to Evidence: Setting the Record Straight on Immigrants and Crime," http://www.immigrationpolicy.org/just-facts/anecdotes-evidence-setting-record-straight-immigrants-and-crime (accessed May 2014); Bianca E. Bersani, Thomas A. Loughran, and Alex R. Piquero, "Comparing Patterns and Predictors of Immigrant Offending Among a Sample of Adjudicated Youth," *Journal of Youth and Adolescence* 10 (2013).

Another reason for seasonal differences in the crime rate is that weather effects (such as temperature swings) may have an impact on violent crime. The association between temperature and crime is thought to resemble an inverted U-shaped curve: crime rates increase with rising temperatures and then begin to decline at some point (85 degrees) when it may be too hot for any physical exertion.[69] One way to protect yourself from violent crime: turn off your air conditioner.[70]

REGIONAL DIFFERENCES Large urban areas have by far the highest rates of violence, and rural areas have the lowest per capita crime rates. Exceptions to this trend are low-population resort areas with large transient or seasonal populations—such as Atlantic City, New Jersey. Typically, the western and southern states have had consistently higher crime rates than the Midwest and Northeast. This

YOUR OPINION: With respect to crime, are immigrants to the United States making the situation better, worse, or not having much of an effect?

PUBLIC OPINION:

BETTER: 4%

NOT MUCH EFFECT: 34%

WORSE: 58%

NO OPINION: 4%

REALITY: A growing body of literature suggests the immigration/crime connection is complicated and probably not what you think it is. The accompanying Evidence-Based Justice box compares crime among immigrants to crime by native-born persons. There is little evidence that first-generation immigrants (those born outside the U.S.) are having much of an effect on crime.

DISCUSSION: What are the means by which immigration and crime could be related?

Source: Christopher P. Muste, "The Dynamics of Immigration Opinion in the United States, 1992–2012," *Public Opinion Quarterly* 77 (2013): 398–416, at 406.

pattern has convinced some criminologists that regional cultural values influence crime rates; others believe that regional differences can be explained by economic differences.

One argument for higher crime rates in the West and South is related to the influx of immigrants into these areas. This issue is explored in the Evidence-Based Justice feature.

Social Class, Socioeconomic Conditions, and Crime

Official statistics indicate that crime rates in inner-city, high-poverty areas are generally higher than those in suburban or wealthier areas.[71] Surveys of known criminals consistently show that prisoners were members of the lower class and unemployed or underemployed in the years before their incarceration. Income inequality, poverty, and resource deprivation are all associated with the most serious violent crimes, including homicide and assault.[72] It is possible, as some research shows, that members of the lower classes are arrested more often and punished more harshly than their wealthier peers, creating the illusion that crime is a lower-class phenomenon.[73] However, the weight of recent evidence suggests that serious crime is more prevalent in socially disorganized lower-class areas, whereas less serious offenses are spread more evenly throughout the social structure.

EXPLAINING THE CLASS–CRIME RELATIONSHIP What is the connection between class and crime? It makes sense that crime is inherently a lower-class phenomenon. After all, people at the lowest rungs of the social structure have the greatest incentive to commit crimes, and those people who are undergoing financial difficulties are the ones most likely to become their targets.[74] It seems logical that people who are unable to obtain desired goods and services through conventional means may consequently resort to theft and other illegal activities—such as selling narcotics—to obtain them. These activities are referred to as instrumental crimes. Those living in poverty are also believed to engage in disproportionate amounts of expressive crimes, such as rape and assault, as a result of their rage, frustration, and anger against society. Alcohol and drug abuse, common in impoverished areas, help fuel violent episodes of rage, anger, or frustration.[75]

Members of the lower class are more likely to suffer psychological abnormality, including high rates of anxiety and conduct disorders, conditions that may promote criminality.[76] Community-level indicators of poverty and disorder—deteriorated neighborhoods, lack of informal social control, income inequality, presence of youth gangs, and resource deprivation—are all associated with the most serious violent crimes, including homicide and assault.[77]

Contemporary research also shows that the association between poverty and crime may be a community-level rather than an individual-level phenomenon. That is, even though a particular individual who is poor may not commit crime, groups of people living in communities that lack economic and social opportunities are influenced by their neighborhood disadvantage.[78] These community conditions also produce high levels of frustration: residents believe they are relatively more deprived than residents in more affluent areas and may then turn to criminal behavior to relieve their frustration.[79] Family life is disrupted, and law-violating youth groups thrive in a climate that undermines adult supervision.[80]

The class–crime association may become more acute as manufacturing moves overseas and less-educated, untrained young males are frozen out of the job market. These workers may find themselves competing in illegal markets: selling drugs may be more profitable than working in a fast-food restaurant.

Similarly, a young woman may find prostitution and/or sex work more lucrative relative to work in the legitimate market. When the economy turns, drug dealers do not suddenly quit the trade and get a job with GE or IBM. As criminologist Shawn Bushway points out, labor markets are the economic engine that shapes the crime rate and creates incentives for teens and adolescents to participate in illegal activities.[81]

Age and Crime

There is general agreement that age is inversely related to criminality.[82] Regardless of economic status, marital status, race, sex, and so on, younger people commit crime more often than their older peers. Official statistics tell us that young people are arrested at a rate disproportionate to their numbers in the population; victim surveys generate similar findings for crimes in which assailant age can be determined. Youth ages 14 through 17 make up about 6 percent of the total U.S. population, but account for about 15 percent of all arrests. In contrast, adults age 50 and older, who make up slightly less than a third of the population, account for only about 6 percent of all arrests. Even though the number of arrests has been in decline, the peak age for arrest remains the teen years.

As a general rule, the peak age for property crime is believed to be 16, and for violence, 18. In contrast, only 7 percent of arrests for serious crimes involve adults over 45. The elderly are particularly resistant to the temptations of crime; they make up more than 14 percent of the population and less than 1 percent of arrests. Elderly males 65 and over are predominantly arrested for alcohol-related matters (such as public drunkenness and drunk driving) and elderly females for larceny (such as shoplifting). The elderly crime rate has remained stable for the past 20 years.[83]

Research shows that on average, kids who are persistent offenders begin committing crime in their childhood, rapidly increase their offending activities in late adolescence, and then begin a slowdown in adulthood. Early starters tend to commit more crime and are more likely to continue to be involved in criminality over a longer period of time.[84]

Why are kids more involved in crime than adults? One view relies on the special status of youth in contemporary society. Adolescents are impatient, and because their future is uncertain, they are unwilling or unable to delay gratification. Deviance in adolescence is fueled by the need for money and sex and is reinforced by close relationships with peers who defy conventional morality. At the same time, teenagers are becoming independent from parents and other adults who enforce conventional standards of morality and behavior. They have a new sense of energy and strength and are involved with peers who are similarly vigorous and frustrated.

In adulthood, people become better able to delay gratification and forgo the immediate gains that law violations bring. They also start wanting to take responsibility for their behavior and to adhere to conventional mores, such as establishing long-term relationships and starting a family. Getting married, raising a family, and creating long-term family ties provide the stability that helps people desist from crime.[85]

Another view ties the association between age and crime to biological traits. Young people are simply stronger and more vigorous than adults and better equipped to deal with the rigors of crime. Young men also possess more abundant levels of testosterone, the principal male steroid hormone that has been linked to aggression and violence. Hormone levels decline during the life cycle, which may explain why violence rates diminish over time.[86]

Aging out of crime, then, may be a function of the natural history of the human life cycle rather than due to a change in social circumstances.[87]

Gender and Crime

Male crime rates are much higher than those of females. Victims report that their assailant was male in more than 80 percent of all violent personal crimes. The most recent Uniform Crime Report arrest statistics indicate that males account for more than 80 percent of all arrests for serious violent crimes and more than 60 percent of the arrests for serious property crimes.[88] Murder arrests are eight males to one female. Even though gender differences in the crime rate have persisted over time, there seems little question that females are now involved in more crime than ever before and that there are more similarities than differences between male and female offenders.[89] UCR arrest data show that over the past decade, while male arrest rates have declined by 10 percent, female arrest rates have increased by about 7 percent. Most notable have been increased female arrests for serious crimes such as robbery (up 29 percent) and burglary (up 30 percent). Thus, during a period of slowing overall growth in crime rates, women have increased their participation in crime. How can these differences be explained?

Explaining Gender Differences in the Crime Rate

Early criminologists pointed to emotional, physical, and psychological differences between males and females to explain the differences in crime rates: men are physically and emotionally stronger and better equipped to commit crimes. Another early view of female crime focused on the supposed dynamics of sexual relationships. Female criminals were viewed as either sexually controlling or sexually naive, either manipulating men for profit or being manipulated by them. The female's criminality was often masked because criminal justice authorities were reluctant to take action against a woman.[90] These early writings are no longer taken seriously, and today differences in the crime rate are explained by a number of different factors:

Robyn Ramsey, 25, is arrested after a police chase in Lancaster, California. Ramsey, detained in a car theft case, stole a sheriff's sport utility vehicle and led deputies on a two-hour pursuit through the Antelope Valley before being captured. Bonnie Ramsey, Robyn's mother, said her daughter had been addicted to methamphetamine but was trying to recover. Some experts say hormonal differences explain the gender gap in the crime rate, but when either males or females take drugs, their decision-making skills are impaired, and more crime ensues.

AP Images/Antelope Valley Press, Kelly Lacefield

TRAITS Some experts believe that gender-based traits are a key determinant of crime rate differences. Among the suspected differences are physical strength and hormonal influences. According to this view, male sex hormones (androgens) account for more aggressive male behavior, and gender-related hormonal differences explain the gender gap in the crime rate.[91]

SOCIALIZATION AND DEVELOPMENT Another view is that, unlike boys, a majority of young girls are socialized to avoid being violent and aggressive and are supervised more closely by parents.[92] The few female criminals are troubled individuals, alienated at home, who pursue crime as a means of compensating for their disrupted personal lives.[93] The streets are a second home to girls whose emotional adjustment was hampered by a strained home life marked by such conditions as absent fathers and overly competitive mothers.

Girls who are able to turn their lives around, some of whom become mothers themselves and take on the responsibility of child care, are able to forgo a life filled with delinquency and substance abuse.[94]

COGNITIVE DIFFERENCES Psychologists note significant cognitive differences between boys and girls that may affect their antisocial behaviors. Girls have been found to be superior to boys in verbal ability, while boys test higher in visual-spatial performance. Girls acquire language faster, learning to speak earlier and with better pronunciation. Their superior verbal skills may enable girls to talk rather than fight. When faced with conflict, women might be more likely to try negotiating rather than either responding passively or resisting physically, especially when they perceive an increased threat of harm or death.[95]

FEMINIST VIEWS In the 1970s, feminists focused attention on the social and economic role of women in society and its relationship to female crime rates.[96] **Liberal feminist theory** suggested that the traditionally lower crime rate for women could be explained by their second-class economic and social position. It was believed that as women's social roles changed and their lifestyles became more like those of males, the crime rates for the genders would converge.

Crime experts, responding to this research, began to refer to the "new female criminal." The rapid increase in the female crime rate during the 1960s and 1970s, especially in what had traditionally been male-oriented crimes (such as burglary and larceny), supported the feminist view. In addition, self-report studies seem to indicate that the pattern of female criminality, if not its frequency, is similar to that of male criminality and that the factors predisposing male criminals to crime have an equal impact on female criminals.[97] Crime experts began to assess the association among economic issues, gender roles, and criminality.

IS CONVERGENCE LIKELY? In sum, gender differences in the crime rate have been explained by such statements as these:

- Males are stronger and better able to commit violent crime.
- Hormonal differences make males more aggressive.
- Girls are socialized to be less aggressive than boys.[98]
- Girls have better verbal skills and use them to diffuse conflict.
- Boys are granted greater personal freedom; girls are subject to greater parental control.

Will the gender differences in the crime rate eventually dissolve? Some crime experts find that gender-based crime rate differences remain significant and argue that the emancipation of women has had relatively little influence on female crime rates.[99] They dispute the idea that increases in the female arrest rate reflect economic or social change brought about by the women's movement. For one thing, many female criminals come from the socioeconomic class least affected by the women's movement. Their crimes seem more a function of economic inequality than of women's rights. For another, the offense patterns of women are still quite different from those of men, who commit a disproportionate share of serious crimes, such as robbery, burglary, murder, and assault.[100] Police may be abandoning their traditional deference toward women in an effort to be "gender neutral." In addition, new laws such as dual arrest laws in domestic cases, which mandate that both parties be taken into custody, result in more women suffering arrest in domestic incidents.[101] Whether male and female crime rates will eventually converge remains to be seen.

Race and Crime

Official crime data indicate that minority group members are involved in a disproportionate share of criminal activity. African Americans make up about 13 percent of the general population, yet they account for 28 percent of persons arrested. It is possible that these data reflect true racial differences in the crime rate, but it is also likely that bias in the justice process plays a part.

We can evaluate this issue by comparing racial differences in self-report data with those found in official delinquency records. Charges of racial discrimination in the justice process would be substantiated if whites and blacks self-reported

liberal feminist theory
An ideology holding that women suffer oppression, discrimination, and disadvantage as a result of their sex and calling for gender equality in pay, opportunity, child care, and education.

equal numbers of crimes but minorities were arrested and prosecuted far more often. Self-report studies such as the MTF survey, for example, generally show similarity in offending differences between African American and European American youths for most crimes, but for some serious offenses, such as stealing more than $50 and using a weapon to steal, African American youths do in fact admit more offending than white youths, a finding that is reflective of the UCR arrest data.[102] How can the disproportionate number of African American youngsters arrested for serious crimes be explained?

SYSTEM BIAS Some critics charge that race-based differences in the crime rate can be explained by unequal treatment by the justice system. Minority group members are more likely to be formally stopped, searched, and arrested than European Americans. Research shows that police are more likely to single out young black men while treating older African Americans with greater deference. For example, police are much more likely to stop young black drivers than they are white or older black men. This creates a cycle of hostility: young black men see their experience with police as unfair or degrading; they approach future encounters with preexisting hostility. Police officers may take this as a sign that young black men pose a special danger; they respond with harsh treatment; a never-ending cycle of mutual mistrust is created.[103]

According to what is known as the **racial threat hypothesis**, as the percentage of minorities in the population increases, so does the amount of social control that police direct at minority group members.[104] Police are more likely to aggressively patrol minority neighborhoods; to suspect, search, and arrest minority group members; and to make arrests for minor infractions among members of these groups, thus helping to raise the minority crime rate.[105]

The "racial threat" effect does not end with the police, nor does system bias. As the percentage of minorities in a state jurisdiction increases, so does the use of draconian sentencing practices. As they are processed through the system, minority group members, especially those who are indigent or unemployed, continue to receive disparate treatment. Black and Latino adults are less likely than whites to be offered the opportunity to post bail in violent crime cases and consequently are more likely to be kept in detention pending trial.[106] They also receive longer prison sentences than whites who commit similar crimes and have similar criminal histories.

CULTURAL BIAS Another explanation of racial differences in the crime rate rests on the effects of the legacy of racial discrimination on personality and behavior.[107] The fact that U.S. culture influences African American crime rates is underscored by the fact that black violence rates are much lower in other nations—both those that are predominantly white, such as Canada, and those that are predominantly black, such as Nigeria.[108]

Some criminologists view black crime as a function of socialization in a society where the black family was torn apart and black culture destroyed in such a way that recovery has proved impossible. Early experiences, beginning with slavery, have left a wound that has been deepened by racism and lack of opportunity.[109] Children of the slave society were thrust into a system of forced dependency and ambivalence and antagonism toward one's self and one's group.

STRUCTURAL BIAS A third view is that racial differences in the crime rate are a function of disparity in the social and economic structure of society. William Julius Wilson, one of the nation's most prominent sociologists, provided a description of the plight of the lowest levels of the underclass, which he labeled the truly disadvantaged, most often minority group members who dwell in urban inner cities, occupy the bottom rung of the social ladder, and are the victims of discrimination. Now, because of the globalization of the economy, opportunities for

racial threat hypothesis
The view that young minority males are subject to greater police control—for example, formal arrest—when their numbers increase within the population.

economic advancement have evaporated. In the past, growth in the manufacturing sector fueled upward mobility. With manufacturing opportunities all but obsolete in the United States, service and retail establishments that depended on blue-collar spending have similarly disappeared, leaving behind an economy based on welfare and government supports. In less than 20 years, formerly active African American neighborhoods have become crime-infested inner-city ghettos.[110]

IS CONVERGENCE POSSIBLE? Considering these overwhelming social problems, is it possible that racial crime rates will soon converge? Race differences in family structure, economic status, education achievement, and other social factors persist. Does that mean that racial differences in the delinquency rate will persist, or is convergence possible? It is possible that when economic conditions improve in the minority community, differences in the delinquency rate will eventually disappear.[111] The trend toward residential integration, underway since 1980, may also help reduce crime rate differentials.[112] An important study (2010) by Gary LaFree and his associates tracked race-specific homicide arrest differences in 80 large U.S. cities from 1960 to 2000, and found substantial convergence in black/white homicide arrest rates over time.[113] If America's racial divide can be breached and overcome, so too will racial differences in the crime and delinquency rate.

Chronic Offending and Crime

Crime data show that most offenders commit a single criminal act and, upon arrest, discontinue their antisocial activity. Others commit a few less serious crimes. A small group of criminal offenders, however, account for a majority of all criminal offenses. These persistent offenders are referred to as **career criminals** or **chronic offenders**.

The concept of the chronic or career offender is most closely associated with the research efforts of Marvin Wolfgang, Robert Figlio, and Thorsten Sellin.[114] In their landmark 1972 study *Delinquency in a Birth Cohort*, they used official records to follow the criminal careers of a cohort of 9,945 boys born in Philadelphia in 1945 from the time of their birth until they reached 18 years of age in 1963. Official police records were used to identify delinquents. About one-third of the boys (3,475) had some police contact. The remaining two-thirds (6,470) had none. Each delinquent was given a seriousness weight score for every delinquent act.[115] The weighting of delinquent acts enabled the researchers to differentiate between a simple assault requiring no medical attention for the victim and serious battery in which the victim needed hospitalization.

The best-known discovery of Wolfgang and his associates was that of the so-called chronic offender. The cohort data indicated that 54 percent (1,862) of the sample's delinquent youths were repeat offenders, whereas the remaining 46 percent (1,613) were one-time offenders. The repeaters could be further categorized as nonchronic recidivists and chronic recidivists. The former consisted of 1,235 youths who had been arrested more than once but fewer than five times and who made up 35.6 percent of all delinquents. The latter were a group of 627 boys arrested five times or more, who accounted for 18 percent of the delinquents and 6 percent of the total sample of 9,945. (See Figure 2.3.)

The chronic offenders (known today as "the chronic 6 percent") were involved in the most dramatic amounts of delinquent behavior. They were responsible for 5,305 offenses, or 51.9 percent of all the offenses committed by the cohort. Even more striking was the involvement of chronic offenders in serious criminal acts. Of the entire sample, the chronic 6 percent committed 71 percent of the homicides, 73 percent of the rapes, 82 percent of the robberies, and 69 percent of the aggravated assaults.

L08 Explain the problem of chronic offending.

career criminals
Persistent repeat offenders who organize their lifestyle around criminality.

chronic offenders
As defined by Marvin Wolfgang, Robert Figlio, and Thorsten Sellin, delinquents arrested five or more times before the age of 18, who commit a disproportionate amount of all criminal offenses.

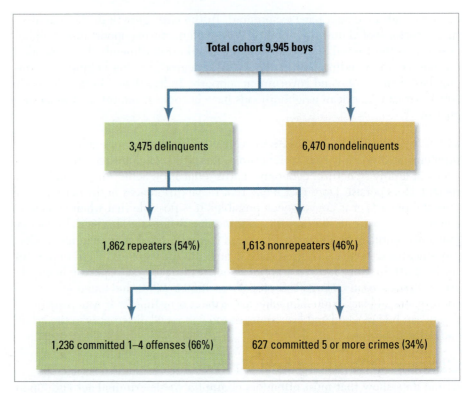

FIGURE 2.3   **Distribution of Offenses in the Philadelphia Cohort**

Source: From Marvin Wolfgang, Robert Figlio, and Thorsten *Sellin, Delinquency in a Birth Cohort.* Copyright © 1972 University of Chicago Press. Reprinted with permission.

Wolfgang and his associates found that arrests and court experience did little to deter the chronic offender. In fact, punishment was inversely related to chronic offending: The more stringent the sanction that chronic offenders received, the more likely they would be to engage in repeated criminal behavior.

In a second cohort study, Wolfgang and his associates selected a new, larger birth cohort, born in Philadelphia in 1958, which contained both male and female subjects.[116] Although the proportion of delinquent youths was about the same as that in the 1945 cohort, they again found a similar pattern of chronic offending. Chronic female delinquency was relatively rare—only 1 percent of the females in the survey were chronic offenders. Wolfgang's pioneering effort to identify the chronic career offender has been replicated by a number of other researchers in a variety of locations in the United States.[117] The chronic offender has also been found abroad.[118]

WHAT CAUSES CHRONICITY? As might be expected, kids who have been exposed to a variety of personal and social problems at an early age—a concept referred to as **early onset**—are the most at risk to repeat offending. One important study of delinquent offenders in Orange County, California, conducted by Michael Schumacher and Gwen Kurz, found several factors that characterized the chronic offender, including problems in the home and at school.[119] Other studies have found that involvement in criminal activity (getting arrested before age 15), relatively low intellectual development, and parental drug involvement were key predictive factors for chronicity.[120] Offenders who accumulate large debts, use drugs, and resort to violence are more likely to persist in crime.[121] In contrast, those who spend time in a juvenile facility and later in an adult prison are more likely to desist.[122]

early onset

The principle or fact that kids who have been exposed to a variety of personal and social problems at an early age are the most at risk to repeat offending.

three-strikes laws

Sentencing codes that require that an offender receive a life sentence after conviction for a third felony. Some states allow parole after a lengthy prison stay—for example, 25 years.

truth-in-sentencing laws

Laws requiring convicted felons to spend a significant portion of their sentence behind bars.

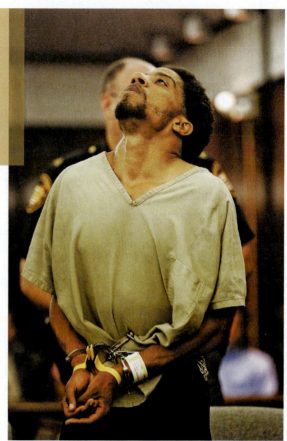

Career criminals are responsible for a significant portion of the total crime rate. Here, George Hyatte appears in a courtroom for an extradition hearing in Columbus, Ohio. George and his wife, Jennifer Hyatte, were arrested at the America's Best Value Inn in Columbus after a cab driver tipped off authorities that he had driven them there. Hyatte, a career-criminal inmate who was serving a 41-year sentence for robbery and related charges, killed a guard in the course of a daring escape attempt—a crime that brought him a sentence of life imprisonment without the possibility of parole.

AP Images/The Southern/Kiichiro Sato

POLICY IMPLICATIONS The chronic offender has become a central focus of crime control policy. Apprehension and punishment seem to have little effect on the offending behavior of chronic offenders, and most repeat their criminal acts after their release from a correctional facility.[123] Because chronic offenders rarely learn from their mistakes, sentencing policies designed to incapacitate chronic offenders for long periods of time, without hope of probation or parole, have been established. Incapacitation rather than rehabilitation is the goal. Among the policies spurred by the chronic offender concept are mandatory sentences for violent or drug-related crimes; **three-strikes laws**, which require people convicted of a third felony offense to serve a mandatory life sentence; and **truth-in-sentencing laws**, which require that convicted felons spend a significant portion of their sentence behind bars. Whether such policies can reduce crime rates or are merely get-tough measures designed to placate conservative voters remains to be seen.

ETHICAL CHALLENGES in Criminal Justice

A WRITING ASSIGNMENT

Critics complain that kids watch too much violent TV and that media violence is a cause of juvenile crime. They also argue that violent video games lead kids to commit despicable acts. Dylan Klebold, one of the infamous Columbine killers, was said to have enjoyed violent video games. People were quick to link his gaming habits to a mass school shooting.

Some people claim the connection between media violence and actual violence is tenuous. For one thing, the research is not completely clear about the linkages, if any. (We discuss media–violence research in an Analyzing Criminal Justice Issues box in Chapter 3.) As for video game violence, there is some evidence violent video games may contribute to aggressive tendencies (see, for example, the study discussed here: http://www .businessweek.com/articles/2014-04-15/violent-video-games-dont-make-you-aggressive-but-tetris-might), but results are far from conclusive. Then there are the constitutional issues at stake; attempts to limit or ban access to violent media or video games can run afoul of the First Amendment, which guarantees freedom of expression, including freedom of speech.

Write an essay on the ethical issues underlying this issue. How would you settle the dilemma? Can there be a proper balance between freedom of expression and the need for public safety? If so, what would it look like? What would be the implications if violence were banned from television? Hint: Would hockey games and boxing matches be banished from the airwaves? Would we want all media to be devoid of violence?

Summary

L01 **Discuss how crime is defined.**

- The consensus view holds that criminal behavior is defined by laws that reflect the values and morals of a majority of citizens.
- The conflict view states that criminal behavior is defined in such a way that economically powerful groups can retain their control over society.
- The interactionist view portrays criminal behavior as a relativistic, constantly changing concept that reflects society's current moral values.

L02 **Define and discuss some of the different types of crime.**

- Violent crimes involve acts ranging from mass murder to child abuse.
- Public order crimes involve acts that interfere with how society operates and functions, such as prostitution and drug use.
- Millions of property- and theft-related crimes occur each year, ranging from simple theft, such as larceny, to complex white-collar frauds and schemes.

L03 **Explain the methods used to measure crime.**

- The Uniform Crime Reports (UCR) are compiled by the FBI. This national survey compiles criminal acts reported to local police.
- The National Crime Victimization Survey (NCVS) surveys people about their experiences with crime.
- Self-report surveys ask offenders themselves to tell about their criminal behaviors.

L04 **Discuss the development of the NIBRS program.**

- The National Incident-Based Reporting System (NIBRS) collects data on each reported crime incident.
- This program requires local police agencies to provide at least a brief account of each incident and arrest, including the incident, victim, and offender information.
- Thus far, about 26 states have implemented their NIBRS programs.

L05 **Discuss the strengths and weaknesses of various measures of crime.**

- The validity of the UCR has been suspect because many people fail to report crime to police as a consequence of fear, apathy, or lack of respect for law enforcement.
- The NCVS can be used to measure unreported criminal incidents but relies on estimation from a small sample and the respondents' memory.
- Self-reports depend on the accuracy of respondents, many of whom are drug users or delinquent.

L06 **Recognize the trends in the crime rate.**

- Crime rates were high in the 1930s, declined afterward, and then began a rapid increase in the 1960s.
- Crime rates have been in a downward trend for about two decades.
- The number and rate of murders have declined significantly.

L07 **Summarize the various crime patterns.**

- Crime occurs more often in large cities in the South and West during the summer and at night.
- Arrest data indicate that males, minorities, the poor, and the young have relatively high rates of criminality.
- Victims of crime also tend to be poor, young, male, and members of a minority group.

L08 **Explain the problem of chronic offending.**

- Repeat career criminals are responsible for a significant amount of all law violations.
- Career criminals begin their careers early in life and, instead of aging out of crime, persist in their criminal behavior into adulthood.

Key Terms

consensus view of crime, 40
conflict view of crime, 42
interactionist view of crime, 42
moral entrepreneurs, 42
crime, 43
expressive violence, 43
instrumental violence, 43
mass murderer, 44
spree killer, 44
serial killer, 44

hate crimes (bias crimes), 46
public order crimes, 47
white-collar crime, 48
corporate crime, 48
Uniform Crime Reports (UCR), 50
Part I crimes, 50
Part II crimes, 50
cleared, 50
National Incident-Based Reporting
System (NIBRS), 53

National Crime Victimization
Survey (NCVS), 54
self-report survey, 58
liberal feminist theory, 73
racial threat hypothesis, 74
career criminals, 75
chronic offenders, 75
early onset, 76
three-strikes laws, 76
truth-in-sentencing laws, 76

Critical Thinking Questions

1. Would you answer honestly if a national crime survey asked you about your criminal behavior, including drinking and drug use? If not, why not? If you answered no, do you question the accuracy of self-report surveys?
2. How would you explain gender differences in the crime rate? Do you think males are more violent than females? Why?
3. Assuming that males are more violent than females, does this mean that crime has a biological rather than a social basis (because males and females share a similar environment)?

4. The UCR states that crime rates are higher in large cities than in small towns. What does that say about the effects of TV, films, and music on teenagers' behavior?
5. What social and environmental factors do you believe influence the crime rate? For example, do you think a national emergency such as the September 11, 2001, terrorist attacks would increase or decrease crime rates or have relatively little effect or influence?
6. If the characteristics of chronic offenders could be determined, should people with those traits be monitored from birth?

Notes

1. David M. Halbfinger, "A Gunman, Recalled as Intelligent and Shy, Who Left Few Footprints in Life," *New York Times*, December 14, 2012, http://www.nytimes.com/2012/12/15/nyregion/adam-lanza-an-enigma-who-is-now-identified-as-a-mass-killer.html (accessed April 2014).
2. Valerie Strauss, "At Least 44 School Shootings Since Newtown—New Analysis," *Washington Post*, February 13, 2014, http://www.washingtonpost.com/blogs/answer-sheet/wp/2014/02/13/at-least-44-school-shootings-since-newtown-new-analysis/ (accessed April 2014).
3. Mirka Smolej and Janne Kivivuori, "The Relation Between Crime News and Fear of Violence," *Journal of Scandinavian Studies in Criminology and Crime Prevention* 7 (2006): 211–227.
4. For a general discussion of Marxist thought on criminal law, see Michael Lynch, Raymond Michalowski, and W. Byron Groves, *The New Primer in Radical Criminology: Critical Perspectives on Crime, Power, and Identity*, 3rd ed. (Monsey, NY: Criminal Justice Press, 2000).

5. The National Council on Alcoholism and Drug Dependence, http://www.ncadd.org/ (accessed April 2014).
6. For more on this, go to the National Gang Center, http://www.nationalgangcenter.gov/ (accessed April 2014).
7. Arlen Egley Jr. and James C. Howell, *Highlights of the 2011 National Youth Gang Survey* (Washington, DC: Office of Juvenile Justice and Delinquency Prevention, 2013), http://www.ojjdp.gov/pubs/242884.pdf (accessed April 2014).
8. Ibid., p. 2.
9. Duncan Gardham, "Norway Killings: Breivik's Countdown to Mass Murder," *The Telegraph*, July 26, 2011, http://www.telegraph.co.uk/news/worldnews/europe/norway/8663758/Norway-killings-Breiviks-countdown-to-mass-murder.html (accessed April 2014).
10. Jennifer Brown, "12 Shot Dead, 58 Wounded in Aurora Movie Theater During Batman Premier," DenverPost.com, July 21, 2012, http://www.denverpost.com/news/ci_21124893/12-shot-dead-58-wounded-aurora-movie-theater (accessed April 2014).

11. James Alan Fox and Jack Levin, "Multiple Homicide: Patterns of Serial and Mass Murder," in *Crime and Justice: An Annual Edition*, vol. 23, ed. Michael Tonry (Chicago: University of Chicago Press, 1998), pp. 407–455.

12. Ibid.

13. Data in this section come from Department of Health and Human Services, *Child Maltreatment, 2012*, http://www.acf.hhs.gov/sites/default/files/cb/cm2012.pdf#page=11 (accessed April 2014).

14. Joseph Price and Kathy Glad, "Hostile Attributional Tendencies in Maltreated Children," *Journal of Abnormal Child Psychology* 31 (2003): 329–344.

15. James Garofalo, "Bias and Non-Bias Crimes in New York City: Preliminary Findings," paper presented at the annual meeting of the American Society of Criminology, Baltimore, November 1990.

16. "Boy Gets 18 Years in Fatal Park Beating of Transient," *Los Angeles Times*, December 24, 1987, p. 9B.

17. Federal Bureau of Investigation, *Hate Crime Statistics 2012*, http://www.fbi.gov/about-us/cjis/ucr/hate-crime/2012/topic-pages/incidents-and-offenses/incidentsandoffenses_final/ (accessed April 2014).

18. Paul Heaton, *Hidden in Plain Sight: What Cost-of-Crime Research Can Tell Us About Investing in Police* (Santa Monica, CA: RAND Corporation, 2010), p. 5.

19. Scott Shuger, "Hookers.com: How e-Commerce Is Transforming the Oldest Profession," *Slate Magazine*, http://www.slate.com/id/73797/ (accessed April 2014).

20. Lloyd D. Johnston, Patrick M. O'Malley, Richard A. Miech, Jerald G. Bachman, and John E. Schulenberg, *Monitoring the Future, 2013 Overview*, http://www.monitoringthefuture.org//pubs/monographs/mtf-overview2013.pdf (accessed April 2014).

21. Ruth Engs and David Hanson, "Boozing and Brawling on Campus: A National Study of Violent Problems Associated with Drinking over the Past Decade," *Journal of Criminal Justice* 22 (1994): 171–180.

22. Robert Nash Parker, "Bringing 'Booze' Back In: The Relationship Between Alcohol and Homicide," *Journal of Research in Crime and Delinquency* 32 (1993): 3–38.

23. Evelyn Wei, Rolf Loeber, and Helene White, "Teasing Apart the Developmental Associations Between Alcohol and Marijuana Use and Violence," *Journal of Contemporary Criminal Justice* 20 (2004): 166–183.

24. Susan Martin, Christopher Maxwell, Helene White, and Yan Zhang, "Trends in Alcohol Use, Cocaine Use, and Crime," *Journal of Drug Issues* 34 (2004): 333–360.

25. John Hepburn, "Occasional Criminals," in *Major Forms of Crime*, ed. Robert Meier (Beverly Hills: Sage, 1984), pp. 73–94.

26. James Inciardi, "Professional Crime," in *Major Forms of Crime*, ed. Robert Meier (Beverly Hills: Sage, 1984), p. 223.

27. See, generally, Jay Albanese, *Organized Crime in America*, 2nd ed. (Cincinnati: Anderson, 1989), p. 68.

28. James O. Finckenauer and Yuri A. Voronin, *The Threat of Russian Organized Crime* (Washington, DC: National Institute of Justice, 2001).

29. Richard Felson, Steven Messner, Anthony Hoskin, and Glenn Deane, "Reasons for Reporting and Not Reporting Domestic Violence to the Police," *Criminology* 40 (2002): 617–648.

30. Eric Baumer and Janet Lauritsen, "Reporting Crime to the Police, 1973–2005: A Multivariate Analysis of Long-Term Trends in the National Crime Survey (NCS) and National Crime Victimization Survey (NCVS)," *Criminology* 48 (2010): 131–186.

31. Duncan Chappell, Gilbert Geis, Stephen Schafer, and Larry Siegel, "Forcible Rape: A Comparative Study of Offenses Known to the Police in Boston and Los Angeles," in *Studies in the Sociology of Sex*, ed. James Henslin (New York: Appleton Century Crofts, 1971), pp. 169–193.

32. Patrick Jackson, "Assessing the Validity of Official Data on Arson," *Criminology* 26 (1988): 181–195.

33. Lawrence Sherman and Barry Glick, "The Quality of Arrest Statistics," *Police Foundation Reports* 2 (1984): 1–8.

34. David Seidman and Michael Couzens, "Getting the Crime Rate Down: Political Pressure and Crime Reporting," *Law and Society Review* 8 (1974): 457.

35. Robert Davis and Bruce Taylor, "A Proactive Response to Family Violence: The Results of a Randomized Experiment," *Criminology* 35 (1997): 307–333.

36. Robert O'Brien, "Police Productivity and Crime Rates: 1973–1992," *Criminology* 34 (1996): 183–207.

37. Leonard Savitz, "Official Statistics," in *Contemporary Criminology*, ed. Leonard Savitz and Norman Johnston (New York: Wiley, 1982), pp. 3–15.

38. FBI, *UCR Handbook* (Washington, DC: U.S. Government Printing Office, 1998), p. 33.

39. Bureau of Justice Statistics, *Data Collection: National Incident-Based Reporting System (NIBRS) Implementation Program*, http://www.bjs.gov/index.cfm?ty=dcdetail&iid=301 (accessed April 2014).

40. Lynn Addington, "The Effect of NIBRS Reporting on Item Missing Data in Murder Cases," *Homicide Studies* 8 (2004): 193–213.

41. Bureau of Justice Statistics, "The Nation's Two Crime Measures," http://bjs.ojp.usdoj.gov/content/pub/pdf/ntcm.pdf (accessed April 2014).

42. Jennifer Truman, Lynn Langton, and Michael Planty, *Criminal Victimization, 2012* (Washington, DC: Bureau of Justice Statistics, 2013), http://www.bjs.gov/content/pub/pdf/cv12.pdf (accessed April 2014).

43. 2012 data are reported. For the NCVS figures, see p. 2 here: http://www.bjs.gov/content/pub/pdf/cv12.pdf (accessed April 2014). For the FBI data, see http://www.fbi.gov/about-us/cjis/ucr/crime-in-the-u.s/2012/crime-in-the-u.s.-2012/violent-crime/rape (accessed April 2014).

44. Lynn Addington and Callie Marie Rennison, "Rape Co-occurrence: Do Additional Crimes Affect Victim Reporting and Police Clearance of Rape?" *Journal of Quantitative Criminology* 24 (2008): 205–226.

45. L. Edward Wells and Joseph Rankin, "Juvenile Victimization: Convergent Validation of Alternative Measurements," *Journal of Research in Crime and Delinquency* 32 (1995): 287–307.

46. Saul Kassin, Richard Leo, Christian Meissner, Kimberly Richman, Lori Colwell, Amy-May Leach, and Dana La Fon, "Police Interviewing and Interrogation: A Self-Report Survey of Police Practices and Beliefs," *Law and Human Behavior* 31 (2007): 381–400.

47. Christiane Brems, Mark Johnson, David Neal, and Melinda Freemon, "Childhood Abuse History and Substance Use Among Men and Women Receiving Detoxification Services," *American Journal of Drug and Alcohol Abuse* 30 (2004): 799–821.

48. Lloyd D. Johnson, Jerald G. Bachman, and Patrick M. O'Malley, *Monitoring the Future, 2011* (Ann Arbor, MI: Institute for Social Research, 2013), pp. 115–17, http://www.monitoringthefuture.org/datavolumes/2011/2011dv.pdf (accessed April 2014).

49. Leonore Simon, "Validity and Reliability of Violent Juveniles: A Comparison of Juvenile Self-Reports with Adult Self-Reports Incarcerated in Adult Prisons," paper presented at the annual meeting of the American Society of Criminology, Boston, November 1995, p. 26.

50. Stephen Cernkovich, Peggy Giordano, and Meredith Pugh, "Chronic Offenders: The Missing Cases in Self-Report Delinquency Research," *Journal of Criminal Law and Criminology* 76 (1985): 705–732.

51. Terence Thornberry, Beth Bjerregaard, and William Miles, "The Consequences of Respondent Attrition in Panel Studies: A Simulation Based on the Rochester Youth Development Study," *Journal of Quantitative Criminology* 9 (1993): 127–158.

52. Julia Yun Soo Kim, Michael Fendrich, and Joseph S. Wislar, "The Validity of Juvenile Arrestees' Drug Use Reporting: A Gender Comparison," *Journal of Research in Crime and Delinquency* 37 (2000): 419–432; Donald Tomaskovic-Devey, Cynthia Pfaff Wright, Ronald Czaja, and Kirk Miller, "Self-Reports of Police Speeding Stops by Race: Results from the North Carolina Reverse Record Check Survey," *Journal of Quantitative Criminology* 22 (2006): 279–297.

53. See Spencer Rathus and Larry Siegel, "Crime and Personality Revisited: Effects of MMPI Sets on Self-Report Studies," *Criminology* 18 (1980): 245–251; John Clark and Larry Tifft, "Polygraph and Interview Validation of Self-Reported Deviant Behavior," *American Sociological Review* 31 (1966): 516–523.

54. Mallie Paschall, Miriam Ornstein, and Robert Flewelling, "African-American Male Adolescents' Involvement in the Criminal Justice System: The Criterion Validity of Self-Report Measures in Prospective Study," *Journal of Research in Crime and Delinquency* 38 (2001): 174–187.

55. Jennifer Roberts, Edward Mulvey, Julie Horney, John Lewis, and Michael Arter, "A Test of Two Methods of Recall for Violent Events," *Journal of Quantitative Criminology* 21 (2005): 175–193.

56. Lila Kazemian and David Farrington, "Comparing the Validity of Prospective, Retrospective, and Official Onset for Different Offending Categories," *Journal of Quantitative Criminology* 21 (2005): 127–147.

57. Barbara Warner and Brandi Wilson Coomer, "Neighborhood Drug Arrest Rates: Are They a Meaningful Indicator of Drug Activity? A Research Note," *Journal of Research in Crime and Delinquency* 40 (2003): 123–139.

58. Alfred Blumstein, Jacqueline Cohen, and Richard Rosenfeld, "Trend and Deviation in Crime Rates: A Comparison of UCR and NCVS Data for Burglary and Robbery," *Criminology* 29 (1991): 237–248. See also Michael Hindelang, Travis Hirschi, and Joseph Weis, *Measuring Delinquency* (Beverly Hills: Sage, 1981).

59. Clarence Schrag, *Crime and Justice: American Style* (Washington, DC: U.S. Government Printing Office, 1971), p. 17.

60. Data in this section draw from the 2012 Uniform Crime Reports, http://www.fbi.gov/about-us/cjis/ucr/crime-in-the-u.s/2012/crime-in-the-u.s.-2012/cius_home/ (accessed April 2014).

61. Truman, Langton, and Planty, *Criminal Victimization, 2012*.

62. National Center for Education Statistics, *Fast Facts*, http://nces.ed.gov/fastfacts/display.asp?id=372 (accessed April 2014).

63. See http://www.fbi.gov/about-us/cjis/ucr/crime-in-the-u.s/2012/crime-in-the-u.s.-2012/violent-crime/robbery/ (accessed April 2014).

64. James A. Fox, *Trends in Juvenile Violence: A Report to the United States Attorney General on Current and Future Rates of Juvenile Offending* (Boston: Northeastern University, 1996).

65. Steven Levitt, "The Limited Role of Changing Age Structure in Explaining Aggregate Crime Rates," *Criminology* 37 (1999): 581–599.

66. Darrell Steffensmeier and Miles Harer, "Making Sense of Recent U.S. Crime Trends, 1980 to 1996/1998: Age Composition Effects and Other Explanations," *Journal of Research in Crime and Delinquency* 36 (1999): 235–274.

67. Ibid., p. 265.

68. Ellen Cohn, "The Effect of Weather and Temporal Variations on Calls for Police Service," *American Journal of Police* 15 (1996): 23–43.

69. R. A. Baron, "Aggression as a Function of Ambient Temperature and Prior Anger Arousal," *Journal of Personality and Social Psychology* 21 (1972): 183–189.

70. James Rotton and Ellen Cohn, "Outdoor Temperature, Climate Control, and Criminal Assault," *Environment and Behavior* 36 (2004): 276–306.

71. Victoria Brewer and M. Dwayne Smith, "Gender Inequality and Rates of Female Homicide Victimization Across U.S. Cities," *Journal of Research in Crime and Delinquency* 32 (1995): 175–190.

72. Chin-Chi Hsieh and M. D. Pugh, "Poverty, Income Inequality, and Violent Crime: A Meta-Analysis of Recent Aggregate Data Studies," *Criminal Justice Review* 18 (1993): 182–199.

73. Nancy Rodriguez, "Concentrated Disadvantage and the Incarceration of Youth: Examining How Context Affects Juvenile Justice," *Journal of Research in Crime and Delinquency*, first published online December 13, 2011.

74. Felipe Estrada and Anders Nilsson, "Segregation and Victimization: Neighbourhood Resources, Individual Risk Factors and Exposure to Property Crime," *European Journal of Criminology* 5 (2008): 193–216.

75. Parker, "Bringing 'Booze' Back In."

76. Richard Miech, Avshalom Caspi, Terrie Moffitt, Bradley Entner Wright, and Phil Silva, "Low Socioeconomic Status and Mental Disorders: A Longitudinal Study of Selection and Causation During Young Adulthood," *American Journal of Sociology* 104 (1999): 1096–1131; Marvin Krohn, Alan Lizotte, and Cynthia Perez, "The Interrelationship Between Substance Use and Precocious Transitions to Adult Sexuality," *Journal of Health and Social Behavior* 38 (1997): 87–103, at 88; Richard Jessor, "Risk Behavior in Adolescence: A Psychosocial Framework for Understanding and Action," in *Adolescents at Risk: Medical and Social Perspectives*, ed. D. E. Rogers and E. Ginzburg (Boulder, CO: Westview, 1992).

77. Robert J. Sampson, "Disparity and Diversity in the Contemporary City: Social (Dis)order Revisited," *British Journal of Sociology* 60 (2009): 1–31.

78. Ramiro Martinez, Jacob Stowell, and Jeffrey Cancino, "A Tale of Two Border Cities: Community Context, Ethnicity, and Homicide," *Social Science Quarterly* 89 (2008): 1–16.

79. Robert Agnew, "A General Strain Theory of Community Differences in Crime Rates," *Journal of Research in Crime and Delinquency* 36 (1999): 123–155.

80. Bonita Veysey and Steven Messner, "Further Testing of Social Disorganization Theory: An Elaboration of Sampson and Groves's Community Structure and Crime," *Journal of Research in Crime and Delinquency* 36 (1999): 156–174.

81. Shawn Bushway, "Economy and Crime," *The Criminologist* 35 (2010): 1–5.

82. Travis Hirschi and Michael Gottfredson, "Age and the Explanation of Crime," *American Journal of Sociology* 89 (1983): 552–584, at 581.

83. For a comprehensive review of crime and the elderly, see Kyle Kercher, "Causes and Correlates of Crime Committed by the Elderly," in *Critical Issues in Aging Policy*, ed. E. Borgatta and R. Montgomery (Beverly Hills: Sage, 1987), pp. 254–306; Darrell Steffensmeier, "The Invention of the 'New' Senior Citizen Criminal," *Research on Aging* 9 (1987): 281–311.

84. Misaki Natsuaki, Xiaojia Ge, and Ernst Wenk, "Continuity and Changes in the Developmental Trajectories of Criminal Careers: Examining the Roles of Timing of First Arrest and High School Graduation," *Journal of Youth and Adolescence* 37 (2008): 431–444.

85. Ryan King, Michael Massoglia, and Ross MacMillan, "The Context of Marriage and Crime: Gender, the Propensity to Marry, and Offending in Early Adulthood," *Criminology* 45 (2007): 33–65.

86. Walter Gove, "The Effect of Age and Gender on Deviant Behavior: A Biopsychosocial Perspective," in *Gender and the Life Course*, ed. A. S. Rossi (New York: Aldine, 1985), pp. 115–144.

87. James Q. Wilson and Richard Herrnstein, *Crime and Human Nature* (New York: Simon & Schuster, 1985), pp. 126–147.

88. See http://www.fbi.gov/about-us/cjis/ucr/crime-in-the-u.s/2012/crime-in-the-u.s.-2012/persons-arrested/persons-arrested/ (accessed March 4, 2014).

89. Paul Tracy, Kimberly Kempf-Leonard, and Stephanie Abramoske-James, "Gender Differences in Delinquency and Juvenile Justice Processing: Evidence from National Data," *Crime and Delinquency* 55 (2009): 171–215.

90. Otto Pollack, *The Criminality of Women* (Philadelphia: University of Pennsylvania, 1950).

91. Alan Booth and D. Wayne Osgood, "The Influence of Testosterone on Deviance in Adulthood: Assessing and Explaining the Relationship," *Criminology* 31 (1993): 93–118.

92. Daniel Mears, Matthew Ploeger, and Mark Warr, "Explaining the Gender Gap in Delinquency: Peer Influence and Moral Evaluations of Behavior," *Journal of Research in Crime and Delinquency* 35 (1998): 251–266.

93. Gisela Konopka, *The Adolescent Girl in Conflict* (Englewood Cliffs, NJ: Prentice Hall, 1966); Clyde Vedder and Dora Somerville, *The Delinquent Girl* (Springfield, IL: Charles C Thomas, 1970).

94. Derek Kraeger, Ross Matsueda, and Elena Erosheva, "Motherhood and Criminal Desistance in Advantaged Neighborhoods," *Criminology* 48 (2010): 221–258.

95. Debra Kaysen, Miranda Morris, Shireen Rizvi, and Patricia Resick, "Peritraumatic Responses and Their Relationship to Perceptions of Threat in Female Crime Victims," *Violence Against Women* 11 (2005): 1515–1535.

96. Freda Adler, *Sisters in Crime* (New York: McGraw-Hill, 1975); Rita James Simon, *The Contemporary Woman and Crime* (Washington, DC: Government Printing Office, 1975).

97. David Rowe, Alexander Vazsonyi, and Daniel Flannery, "Sex Differences in Crime: Do Mean and Within-Sex Variation Have Similar Causes?" *Journal of Research in Crime and Delinquency* 32 (1995): 84–100; Michael Hindelang, "Age, Sex, and the Versatility of Delinquency Involvements," *Social Forces* 14 (1971): 525–534; Martin Gold, *Delinquent Behavior in an American City* (Belmont, CA: Brooks/Cole, 1970); Gary Jensen and Raymond Eve, "Sex Differences in Delinquency: An Examination of Popular Sociological Explanations," *Criminology* 13 (1976): 427–448.

98. Mears, Ploeger, and Warr, "Explaining the Gender Gap in Delinquency."

99. Darrell Steffensmeier and Renee Hoffman Steffensmeier, "Trends in Female Delinquency," *Criminology* 18 (1980): 62–85. See also Darrell Steffensmeier and Renee Hoffman Steffensmeier, "Crime and the Contemporary Woman: An Analysis of Changing Levels of Female Property Crime, 1960–1975," *Social Forces* 57 (1978): 566–584; Joseph Weis, "Liberation and Crime: The Invention of the New Female Criminal," *Crime and Social Justice* 1 (1976): 17–27; Carol Smart, "The New Female Offender: Reality or Myth?" *British Journal of Criminology* 19 (1979): 50–59; Steven Box and Chris Hale, "Liberation/ Emancipation, Economic Marginalization or Less Chivalry," *Criminology* 22 (1984): 473–478.

100. Meda Chesney-Lind, "Female Offenders: Paternalism Reexamined," in *Women, the Courts and Equality*, ed. Laura Crites and Winifred Hepperle (Newbury Park, CA: Sage, 1987), pp. 114–139, at 115.

101. Susan Miller, Carol Gregory, and Leeann Iovanni, "One Size Fits All? A Gender-Neutral Approach to a Gender-Specific Problem: Contrasting Batterer Treatment Programs for Male and Female Offenders," *Criminal Justice Policy Review* 16 (2005): 336–359.

102. Johnston, O'Malley, and Bachman, *Monitoring the Future, 2011*.

103. Richard Rosenfeld, Jeff Rojek, and Scott Decker, "Age Matters: Race Differences in Police Searches of Young and Older Male Drivers," *Journal of Research in Crime and Delinquency* 49 (2011): 31–55.

104. Hubert Blalock Jr., *Toward a Theory of Minority-Group Relations* (New York: Capricorn Books, 1967).

105. Robin Shepard Engel and Jennifer Calnon, "Examining the Influence of Drivers' Characteristics During Traffic Stops with Police: Results from a National Survey," *Justice Quarterly* 21 (2004): 49–90.

106. Michael Leiber and Kristan Fox, "Race and the Impact of Detention on Juvenile Justice Decision Making," *Crime and Delinquency* 51 (2005): 470–497; Traci Schlesinger, "Racial and Ethnic Disparity in Pretrial Criminal Processing," *Justice Quarterly* 22 (2005): 170–192.

107. Barry Sample and Michael Philip, "Perspectives on Race and Crime in Research and Planning," in *The Criminal Justice System and Blacks*, ed. Daniel Georges-Abeyie (New York: Clark Boardman Callaghan, 1984), pp. 21–36.

108. Ruth Peterson, Lauren Krivo, and Mark Harris, "Disadvantage and Neighborhood Violent Crime: Do Local Institutions Matter?" *Journal of Research in Crime and Delinquency* 37 (2000): 31–63.

109. James Comer, "Black Violence and Public Policy," in *American Violence and Public Policy*, ed. Lynn Curtis (New Haven, CT: Yale University Press, 1985), pp. 63–86.

110. William Julius Wilson, *More than Just Race: Being Black and Poor in the Inner City* (New York: Norton, 2009); William Julius Wilson and Richard Taub, *There Goes the Neighborhood: Racial, Ethnic, and Class Tensions in Four Chicago Neighborhoods and Their Meaning for America* (New York: Knopf, 2006); William Julius Wilson, *The Truly Disadvantaged* (Chicago: University of Chicago Press, 1987); *When Work Disappears: The World of the Urban Poor* (New York: Knopf, 1996); *The Bridge over the Racial Divide: Rising Inequality and Coalition Politics*, Wildavsky Forum Series, 2 (Berkeley: University of California Press, 1999).

111. Roy Austin, "Progress Toward Racial Equality and Reduction of Black Criminal Violence," *Journal of Criminal Justice* 15 (1987): 437–459.

112. Reynolds Farley and William Frey, "Changes in the Segregation of Whites from Blacks During the 1980s: Small Steps Toward a More Integrated Society," *American Sociological Review* 59 (1994): 23–45.

113. Gary LaFree, Eric Baumer, and Robert O'Brien, "Still Separate and Unequal? A City-Level Analysis of the Black–White Gap in Homicide Arrests Since 1960," *American Sociological Review* 75 (2010): 75–100.

114. Marvin Wolfgang, Robert Figlio, and Thorsten Sellin, *Delinquency in a Birth Cohort* (Chicago: University of Chicago Press, 1972).

115. See Thorsten Sellin and Marvin Wolfgang, *The Measurement of Delinquency* (New York: Wiley, 1964), p. 120.

116. Paul Tracy and Robert Figlio, "Chronic Recidivism in the 1958 Birth Cohort," paper presented at the annual meeting of the American Society of Criminology, Toronto, October 1982; Marvin Wolfgang, "Delinquency in Two Birth Cohorts," in *Perspective Studies of Crime and Delinquency*, ed. Katherine Teilmann Van Dusen and Sarnoff Mednick (Boston: Kluwer-Nijhoff, 1983), pp. 7–17. The following sections rely heavily on these sources.

117. Lyle Shannon, *Criminal Career Opportunity* (New York: Human Sciences Press, 1988).

118. D. J. West and David P. Farrington, *The Delinquent Way of Life* (London: Hienemann, 1977).

119. Michael Schumacher and Gwen Kurz, *The 8% Solution: Preventing Serious Repeat Juvenile Crime* (Thousand Oaks, CA: Sage, 1999).

120. Peter Jones, Philip Harris, James Fader, and Lori Grubstein, "Identifying Chronic Juvenile Offenders," *Justice Quarterly* 18 (2001): 478–507.

121. Lila Kazemian and Marc LeBlanc, "Differential Cost Avoidance and Successful Criminal Careers," *Crime and Delinquency* 53 (2007): 38–63.

122. Rudy Haapanen, Lee Britton, and Tim Croisdale, "Persistent Criminality and Career Length," *Crime and Delinquency* 53 (2007): 133–155.

123. Michael Ezell and Amy D'Unger, "Offense Specialization Among Serious Youthful Offenders: A Longitudinal Analysis of a California Youth Authority Sample" (Durham, NC: Duke University, 1998, unpublished report).

CHAPTER 3

Understanding Crime and Victimization

Learning Objectives

 LO1 Ascertain why some experts believe that crime seems rational.

 LO2 Classify the strategies used to reduce crime by rational criminals.

 LO3 Identify the various biological traits linked to crime.

 LO4 Describe the various psychological views of the cause of crime.

 LO5 Identify the personality traits linked to crime.

 LO6 Compare and contrast the various social structure theories of crime.

 LO7 Distinguish among the three types of social process theories.

 LO8 Explain what is meant by critical criminology.

 LO9 Discuss the basics of developmental theory.

 LO10 Identify the various theories of victimization.

Chapter Outline

The Cause of Crime

Choice Theory
  Careers in Criminal Justice: Criminologist
  Rational Crimes
  Situational Crime Prevention
  General Deterrence
  Evidence-Based Justice: CCTV
  Specific Deterrence

Trait Theories
  Biochemical Factors
  Neurological Factors
  Criminal Justice and Technology: Child Exploitation Tracking System (CETS)
  Genetic Factors

Psychological Theories
  Psychodynamic Theory
  Analyzing Criminal Justice Issues: Does the Media Cause Violence?

  Behavioral Theory
  Cognitive Theory
  Personality and Crime
  IQ and Crime

Sociological Theories
  Social Structure Theory
  The Disorganized Neighborhood
  Social Process Theories

Critical Criminology
  State-Organized Crime
  Support for Critical Theory

Developmental Theories
  Criminal Careers
  Latent Trait Theory
  Life Course Theory
  Trajectory Theory

Theories of Victimization
  Victim Precipitation
  Lifestyle Theory
  Routine Activities Theory

On September 16, 2013, Aaron Alexis shot 12 people inside the Washington Navy Yard in Washington, DC. Two days before the shooting, Alexis, who worked as a subcontractor with Hewlett-Packard, visited a nearby small arms range and test fired an AR-15 semiautomatic rifle but did not buy it. He instead purchased a Remington tactical 12-gauge shotgun and two boxes of ammunition, after passing the usual federal background check. On the day of the shooting, Alexis disassembled the shotgun and was able to carry it past security (he already had security clearance to enter the building) in a bag on his shoulder. He assembled it in a bathroom in the building, then emerged with the gun and started shooting. Alexis was eventually shot and killed by a security guard, but not before taking 12 innocent lives. Eleven victims were killed at the scene and one more died later in the hospital.

On July 20, 2012, a man entered a movie theater in Aurora, Colorado, where the new Batman movie, The Dark Knight Rises, was showing and began methodically shooting patrons, killing 12 and injuring 58. James Holmes, 24, the alleged shooter, started building a sizeable arsenal—which included a Smith and Wesson assault rifle that was identified as the primary weapon used in

the shooting—two months prior to the massacre. He also bought 6,000 rounds of ammunition, all online. Holmes, a former graduate student, dropped out of the University of Colorado's neuroscience program on June 10. That was after he came to the attention of a university threat assessment team, which considered him a possible threat after Holmes's psychiatrist alerted the team to his increasingly disturbing behavior. Critics said his decision to drop out should have been a call to action. The University of Colorado said it did all it could. His trial is set to begin right around the time this book goes to press.

On August 5, 2012, Wade Michael Page, a former leader of a neo-Nazi music group called End Apathy, entered a Sikh temple in Oak Creek, Wisconsin, outside of Milwaukee, and began shooting. Six people were killed and four were wounded. Page, who had previously served in the army, legally purchased the 9-millimeter pistol used in the shooting less than 10 days prior. Page's motives were not entirely clear because he took his own life after being shot in the stomach by a responding officer, but authorities suspect the shooting may have been a hate crime because some Americans have confused Sikhism, the fifth-largest religion in the world, with Islam, in part because many male Sikhs wear full beards and turbans. And according to the Southern Poverty Law Center, which tracks hate groups, Page was a member of the Hammerskin Nation, one of the oldest and most violent skinhead groups in the United States.[1]

How can we understand why people commit these atrocious acts? Was there a predictable pattern of suspect behavior leading up to the shootings in each case? Did the killers manifest some underlying psychological or physiological trait that prompted their actions? Or was something external also responsible? Was easy access to guns to blame? Would stricter gun control have made a difference? These questions are not easy to answer, for a variety of reasons. Many people experience disappointments in life, whether it be loss of a job, frustration with the government, or the death of a close relative, but they do not resort to mass shootings. Likewise, scores of law-abiding gun owners never feel the urge to kill innocent people. What, then, is to blame? What is the driving force behind heinous acts like this? ■

The Cause of Crime

Despite years of study and research, crime experts are still not certain what drives people like Aaron Alexis and the shooters in Aurora and Oak Creek. Why do some people commit crime, while others who are part of the same family and live in the same community remain law abiding? To find an answer to this vexing question, **criminologists** study the nature, extent, cause, and control of criminal behavior. Criminologists study crime patterns in part to help agents of the criminal justice system plan and construct programs to reduce crime. At their core, all these different views of crime have a common theme: what causes people to behave the way they do? Why, given the same set of circumstances, is one person kind, caring, and law abiding, while another is selfish, covetous, and criminal?

criminologists
Social scientists who use the scientific method to study the nature, extent, cause, and control of criminal behavior.

If you are interested in becoming a criminologist, you may want to read the accompanying Careers in Criminal Justice feature.

In the following sections, we present the most important views of crime causation held by criminologists. We then look at the concept of victimization and discuss why some people are likely to be victimized while others tend not to be victimized by crime.

Choice Theory

According to choice theory, while most of us work hard to become successful, there are some greedy, immoral people who do not hesitate to use illegal means to get what they want. These rational criminals weigh the potential benefits and consequences of their acts, choosing to commit a crime if they believe that doing so will yield immediate benefits without the threat of long-term risks. Risk evaluations may cover a wide range of topics: What's the chance of getting caught? How difficult will it be to commit the crime? Is the profit worth the effort? Should I risk committing crime in my own neighborhood where I know the territory, or is it worth traveling to a strange place in order to increase my profits?[2]

People who decide to get involved in crime consider the chances of arrest (based on their past experiences), the subjective psychic rewards of crime (the excitement and social status crime brings), and perceived opportunities for easy gains. If the rewards are great, the perceived risk small, and the excitement high, the likelihood of their committing additional crimes increases.[3] Successful shoplifters say they will do it again in the future; past experience has taught them the rewards of illegal behavior.[4]

Drug trafficking fits this pattern. Before concluding a drug sale, experienced traffickers mentally balance the chances of making a large profit against the probability of being apprehended and punished for drug dealing. They know that most drug deals are not detected and that the potential for enormous, untaxed profits is great. They evaluate their lifestyle and determine how much cash they need to maintain their standard of living, which is usually extravagant. They may

CAREERS in criminal justice

CRIMINOLOGIST

DUTIES AND CHARACTERISTICS OF THE JOB

Criminologists are academics who analyze patterns in criminal activity and attempt to determine the causes of, future trends in, and potential solutions to crime in society. Criminologists are concerned with questions such as how to effectively deter crime, who will commit crime and why, and how to predict and prevent criminal behavior. Like statisticians, criminologists often design and carry out research projects to collect and analyze data with the intention of answering some aspect of these larger questions. Their ideas are written up into reports or articles for various agencies and publications and are used for academic, law enforcement, and policy purposes.

Criminologists often work with law enforcement at the local, state, or federal level. In these positions, they might do research on problems specific to the district they are working with, or they might examine case files and attend crime scenes to help determine whether a suspect's profile is accurate. Other criminologists seek positions at universities and colleges, where they conduct research, write books and articles, and teach courses about crime and criminal justice. In general, criminologists work normal 40-hour weeks in office settings.

JOB OUTLOOK

The demand for criminologists is expected to reflect the general demand for sociologists, which at present is expected to grow slowly at the government and law enforcement levels. There is much greater demand for criminologists working in the university setting, however. Those with more education can expect better job opportunities and higher salaries.

SALARY

Salaries will vary widely, depending on the employer. A doctorate-level criminologist working at a college or university can expect pay comparable to that of other faculty. Starting pay for an assistant professor ranges from around $45,000 to $70,000. A full professor may have an average annual salary of about $100,000 or more. Pay will vary with the institution and the individual's level of advancement.

OPPORTUNITIES

Those entering the field of criminology should be aware that they will face competition from other qualified candidates for a limited number of jobs, especially at the more financially rewarding positions with the federal government. However, the predicted increase in retirement in the near future will probably open up new positions. There is more opportunity in the university setting for criminologists than for psychologists or sociologists.

Many individuals who get a degree in criminology or work as criminologists can use their education and experience and successfully launch careers in related jobs, such as police officer, federal agent, or psychologist.

QUALIFICATIONS

Because of the academic nature of criminology, the primary requirement for a career in this field is proper academic training. Educational requirements usually include courses on human behavior and the criminal justice system, and they should involve developing skills in statistics and writing. Training should also include familiarity with computer programs used for statistical analysis, such as SAS or SPSS. Because criminology requires collecting and examining data, conducting research, and presenting these ideas to others, personal qualities such as intellectual curiosity and strong communicative and analytical skills are important. Those who want to be involved in law enforcement in a hands-on manner or who do not like math and writing reports may not be interested in this career.

Certain states require potential criminologists to pass a written test in order to become licensed before they can work. Additionally, those working with law enforcement agencies will have to pass background and security checks.

EDUCATION AND TRAINING

Although some criminologists enter the field with a bachelor's degree, a majority pursue postgraduate education. Typically, this means a master's degree in criminology and/or criminal justice. Other social science degrees can be acceptable. This is generally enough for those desiring work at law enforcement agencies. However, some positions—for example, teaching at the university level—will require a doctorate in one of the previously mentioned fields.

Sources: U.S. Bureau of Labor Statistics, "Sociologists," *Occupational Outlook Handbook*, 2013 edition (Washington, DC: Bureau of Labor Statistics, U.S. Department of Labor), http://www.bls.gov/oes/current/oes193041.htm (accessed May 2014); Comprehensive Career Profile List: Criminologist, http://careers .stateuniversity.com/pages/714/Criminologist.html (accessed May 2014).

POOL/Reuters/Landov

Actress Lindsay Lohan (left) sits in a Los Angeles court with her lawyer, Shawn Chapman Holley, during a compliance check to report her progress on 480 hours of community service for shoplifting a necklace from a Venice jeweler. Did Lindsay, who has had a long history of run-ins with the law, choose to commit a crime? If not, how else can we explain her behavior? A repentant Lindsay told an interviewer, "I've learned how to live my life in a way that I'm happy and can do the things I want to do," a statement that indicates a rational approach to decision making.

deterrent effect
The assumed ability of the threat of criminal sanctions to discourage crime before it occurs.

 L01 Ascertain why some experts believe that crime seems rational.

have borrowed to finance the drug deal, and their creditors are not usually reasonable if loans cannot be repaid promptly. They also realize that they could be the target of a sting operation by undercover agents and that if caught, they will get a long mandatory sentence in a forbidding federal penitentiary. If the greedy culprits conclude that the potential for profits is great enough, their need for cash urgent, and the chances of apprehension minimal, they will carry out the deal. Although the prevailing wisdom is that "crime does not pay," a small but significant subset of criminals earn a significant income from crime, and their success may help motivate other would-be offenders.[5] In this sense, rational choice is a function of a person's perception of conventional alternatives and opportunities.

If, however, they believe that the transaction will bring them only a small profit and entails a large risk of apprehension and punishment, they may forgo the deal. According to this view, crime is a matter of rational choice, involving a calculated decision made after a motivated offender weighs the potential costs and benefits of illegal activity. To deter the commission of crime, punishment must be sufficiently *strict, sure, and swift* to outweigh any benefits of law violation. A 30-year prison sentence should deter potential bank robbers, regardless of the amount of money in the bank's vault. However, no matter how severely the law punishes a criminal act, it will have negligible **deterrent effect** if potential law violators believe that they have little chance of being caught or that the wheels of justice are slow and inefficient.

Rational Crimes

That crime is rational can be observed in a wide variety of criminal events. White-collar and organized crime figures engage in elaborate and well-planned conspiracies, ranging from international drug deals to selling kiddie porn on the Web. But even predatory street criminals exhibit stealth and planning in their criminal acts. Burglars may try to determine which homes are easy targets by reading newspaper stories about weddings or social events that mean the attendees' homes will be unguarded. They choose houses that are easily accessible, are screened from public view, and offer good escape routes—for example, at the end of a cul-de-sac abutting a wooded area. They target high-value homes that do not have burglar alarms or other security devices.[6] Burglars seem to prefer working between 9 A.M. and 11 A.M. and in mid-afternoon, when parents are either working or dropping off or picking up children at school. Burglars appear to monitor car and pedestrian traffic and to avoid selecting targets on heavily traveled streets.[7]

Even violent criminals exhibit elements of rationality. Research shows that armed robbers choose targets close to their homes or in areas that they routinely travel. Familiarity with the area gives them knowledge of escape routes; this is referred to as their awareness space.[8] Robbers also report being wary of people who are watching the community for signs of trouble. Robbery levels are relatively low in neighborhoods where residents keep a watchful eye on their neighbors' property.[9] Robbers avoid freestanding buildings, where they can more easily be surrounded by police. Others select targets that are known to do a primarily cash business, such as bars, supermarkets, and restaurants.[10]

If crime is a rational choice, how can it be prevented or controlled? The following sections consider this possibility.

Situational Crime Prevention

Some advocates of rational choice theory argue that crime prevention can be achieved by reducing the opportunities people have to commit particular crimes, a technique known as *situational crime prevention*. This technique was first popularized in the United States in the early 1970s by Oscar Newman, who coined the term *defensible space*. The idea is that crime can be prevented or displaced through the use of residential architectural designs that reduce criminal opportunity, such as well-lit housing projects that maximize surveillance.[11] If criminals are rational planners, they will look elsewhere if homes are well monitored, goods kept under careful guard, and human targets willing and able to take precautions that protect them from attack.

Situational crime prevention can be achieved by creating a strategy to reduce specific crimes and then developing specific tactics to achieve those goals. Ronald Clarke has set out the main types of crime prevention tactics in use today[12]:

■ *Increase the effort needed to commit the crime*. Increasing the effort needed to commit crimes involves using target-hardening techniques and access control: placing steering locks on cars, putting unbreakable glass on storefronts, locking gates and fencing yards, having owners' photos on credit cards, and controlling the sale of spray paint (to reduce graffiti).

■ *Increase the risks of committing the crime*. It is also possible to increase the risks of committing a crime by improving surveillance lighting, creating neighborhood watch programs, controlling building entrances and exits, putting in burglar alarms and security systems, and increasing the number and effectiveness of private security officers and police patrols. Research shows that crime rates are reduced when police officers use aggressive crime reduction techniques and promote community safety by increasing lighting and cleaning up vacant lots.[13]

■ *Reduce the rewards for committing the crime*. Reward reduction strategies include making expensive goods valueless in the secondary market, cutting down on criminal profits. Marking or personalizing property so that it is more difficult to sell is one approach. Creating easily removable car audio systems, so they can be taken home at night, decreases the rewards of larcenies from automobiles.

■ *Induce shame or guilt*. Inducing guilt or shame might include such techniques as embarrassing offenders (e.g., publishing "john lists" in the newspaper to punish those arrested for soliciting prostitutes) and improving compliance by providing trash bins whose easy access might shame chronic litterers into using them.

■ *Reduce provocation*. Some crimes are the result of extreme provocation— for example, road rage. It might be possible to reduce provocation by creating programs that reduce conflict. An early closing time for local bars and pubs might limit assaults that result from late-night drinking. Posting guards outside schools at closing time might prevent childish taunts from escalating into full-blown brawls.

■ *Remove excuses*. Crime may be reduced by making it difficult for people to excuse their criminal behavior by saying things like "I didn't know that was illegal" or "I had no choice." To achieve this goal, municipalities have set up roadside displays that electronically flash a car's speed as it passes,

Web App 3.1

Read the report here for successful examples of situational crime prevention: http://www.popcenter.org/library/reading/PDFs/scp2_intro.pdf.

EVIDENCE-based justice

CCTV

Police departments in England and the United States, especially in Chicago and New York City, have installed thousands of closed-circuit TV (CCTV) surveillance

AP Images/Shizuo Kambayasi

One element of situational crime prevention is to make it difficult to commit crimes, thereby discouraging would-be criminals. This crime prevention principle is applied around the world. Here, a private security guard watches closed-circuit cameras to keep tabs on students and visitors at the Rikkyo Elementary School in Tokyo. At this school, small, gray plastic tags tucked inside students' backpacks beam a message to the computer, and the computer records the time students enter or leave. Rikkyo officials hope this radio frequency identification technology will serve as an early warning system for children who are missing or abducted.

cameras in areas that are at risk for crime. The idea is to have video surveillance of streets that are experiencing high crime rates. For example, the Chicago Police Department positioned remote-controlled and viewable cameras called Police Observation Devices—commonly referred to as PODs—to view and record crime in high-risk areas. Each POD was equipped with flashing blue lights on top to ensure that its highly visible presence would inform the public that the area was under police surveillance.

Do these measures really work? After a careful review of 41 studies conducted around the world, Brandon Welsh and David Farrington found that CCTV interventions (a) have a small but desirable effect on reducing area crime, (b) are most effective in reducing crime in parking lots, (c) are most effective in reducing vehicle crimes, and (d) are more effective in reducing crime in England, where there is a high level of public support for the use of CCTV cameras in public settings to prevent crime, than in the United States, where people are wary of the "Big Brother is watching you" implications of monitoring via surveillance technology. Thus, although American police agencies may be willing to spend millions on CCTV systems, these may be less effective than expected in reducing street crime.

Source: Brandon Welsh and David Farrington, *Making Public Places Safer: Surveillance and Crime Prevention* (New York: Oxford University Press, 2008).

---

eliminating the driver's excuse that she did not know how fast she was going when stopped by police. Litter boxes, brightly displayed, can eliminate the claim that "I just didn't know where to throw my trash."

LO2 Classify the strategies used to reduce crime by rational criminals.

The accompanying Evidence-Based Justice feature examines a crime prevention method that has become popular in a number of communities.

General Deterrence

general deterrence
A crime control policy that depends on the fear of criminal penalties.

If crime is a matter of choice, it follows that it can be controlled by convincing criminals that breaking the law is a bad or dangerous choice to make. If people believe that they are certain to be apprehended by the police, quickly tried, and severely penalized, they are more likely to dismiss any thought of breaking the law.[14] In other words, people will not choose crime if they fear legal punishment. The harsher the punishment, the more certain its application, and the speedier the judgment, the more effective it will be. This principle is referred to as **general deterrence**.

If the justice system could be made more effective, those who care little for the rights of others would be deterred by fear of the law's sanctioning power.[15]

People who fear punishment will be deterred from committing certain crimes.[16] Even the most committed offenders, such as gang members, will forego criminal activities if they fear legal punishments.[17] The prevailing wisdom is that the certainty of being punished is a greater deterrent to crime than its severity. If police can be more proactive, cracking down on crime, potential criminals will become wary and may choose not to commit crimes.[18] What happens to them after apprehension seems to have a lesser impact.[19]

Although certainty of punishment has some influence on crime, little hard evidence is yet available that fear of the law alone can be a general deterrent to crime.[20] Even the harshest punishment, the death penalty, appears to have very little effect on the murder rate.[21] The certainty of being punished may influence a few offenders, but has little effect on others.[22] The most significant deterrent effects can be achieved in minor crimes and offenses, whereas more serious crimes such as homicide are harder to discourage.[23]

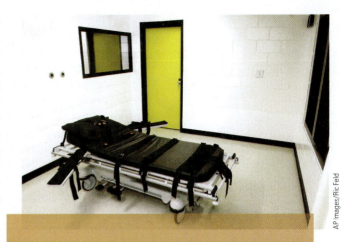

Several states have replaced the electric chair with a gurney on which lethal injection is administered. Shown here is the death chamber at the state prison in Jackson, Georgia. The yellow door goes to the holding cell, the two chrome encircled holes go to the control room behind the glass to the left, and the right windows allow a view from the witness room.

What factors inhibit the deterrent power of the criminal law? One is the lack of efficiency of the justice system. About 20 percent of serious reported crimes result in an arrest. Relatively few criminals are eventually tried, convicted, and sentenced to prison. Chronic offenders and career criminals may believe that the risk of apprehension and imprisonment is limited and conclude that the certainty of punishment—a key element in deterrence—is minimal. Even if they do fear punishment, their anxiety may be neutralized by the belief that a crime gives them a significant chance for large profit. Active burglars report that the fear of capture and punishment is usually neutralized by the hope of making a big score; greed overcomes fear.[24]

A majority of arrested criminals are under the influence of drugs or alcohol at the time of their arrest. Therefore, many offenders may be incapable of having the rational thought patterns upon which the concept of general deterrence rests. Relatively high rates of substance abuse may render even the harshest criminal penalties for violent crimes ineffective deterrents.[25]

In sum, the theory of rational choice views criminals as calculating individuals who can be deterred from crime by the threat of punishment. Yet research has so far failed to turn up clear and convincing evidence that the threat of punishment or its implementation can deter would-be criminals.

Specific Deterrence

Even if the threat of punishment cannot deter would-be criminals, actual punishment at the hands of the justice system should be sufficient to convince arrested offenders never to repeat their criminal acts. If punishment were severe enough, a convicted criminal would never dare repeat his or her offense. What rational person would? This view is called **specific deterrence**. Prior to the twentieth century, specific deterrence was a motive for the extreme tortures and physical punishments commonly inflicted on convicted criminals. By breaking the convicts physically, legal authorities hoped to control their spirit and behavior.[26] The more enlightened society in America today no longer uses such cruel and unusual punishments on its citizens. Instead, we rely on incarcerating criminals as the primary mode of punishment; more than one in 100 adults are now behind bars.[27]

specific deterrence
Punishment severe enough to convince convicted offenders never to repeat their criminal activity.

AP Images/Ric Feld

The theory of specific deterrence relies on the belief that experience will shape criminal choices. It assumes that those who have been caught and punished soon learn that "crime just does not pay." And there is evidence that people can learn from their mistakes; offenders who commit crime and suffer arrest will suffer greater perception of risk than someone who has escaped detection.[28] The less people perceive the benefits of crime, the more they may be willing to desist from a criminal career.[29]

While there is in fact some evidence that an increased perception of punishment risk reduces reoffending, the specific deterrent effect appears to have limits. For example, the more seasoned, experienced offender is less likely to be influenced by a current arrest than the novice.[30] The deterrent effect of an arrest becomes attenuated or, in some cases, lost altogether, as the number of arrests continue to mount.[31] In fact, a history of prior arrests, convictions, and punishments is the best predictor of recidivism.[32] As the extent of punishment increases, so too does the chance of recidivism.[33] Many offenders who are arrested soon repeat their criminal acts.[34] A majority of inmates repeat their criminal acts soon after returning to society, and most inmates have served time previously. Even those people imprisoned in super-maximum-security prisons, receiving the harshest treatment possible (solitary confinement 23 hours a day), are as likely to repeat their crimes upon release as those serving time in traditional institutions.[35]

Why have these draconian punishments failed as a specific deterrent?

■ Specific deterrence assumes a rational criminal, someone who learns from experience. Many offenders have impulsive personalities that interfere with their ability to learn from experience.

■ Being convicted and punished may expose people to more experienced offenders who encourage them to commit more crime and teach them criminal techniques.

■ A majority of criminal offenders have lifestyles marked by heavy substance abuse, lack of formal education, and disturbed home lives, which inhibit conventional behavior. Punishment does little to help an already troubled person readjust to society.

■ Punishment can produce a short-term specific deterrent effect, but because it also produces rage and anger, it fails to produce longer-term behavior change. People who are harshly treated may want to prove that they cannot be broken by the system.[36]

■ The stigma of having been in prison labels people and helps lock offenders into a criminal career instead of convincing them to avoid one.

■ Criminals who are punished may also believe that the likelihood of getting caught twice for the same type of crime is remote: "Lightning never strikes twice in the same spot," they may reason; no one is that unlucky.[37]

■ Experiencing the harshest punishments may cause severe psychological problems, while reducing the opportunities for interaction with law-abiding people.[38]

■ Punishment may produce defiance rather than deterrence. People who believe they have been unfairly punished and stigmatized may reoffend, especially if they do not feel ashamed about what they have done.[39]

■ If money can be made from criminal activity, there will always be someone to take the place of the incarcerated offender. New criminals will be recruited and trained, offsetting any benefit that can be attributed to incarceration.

While these issues remain, economics rather than effectiveness may control the use of specific deterrence strategies. As crime rates decline, as they have for almost two decades, the public may demand low-cost alternatives to

CONCEPT SUMMARY 3.1
Rational Choice Strategies

General deterrence strategies	■ Fear of the consequences of crime will deter potential criminals.
	■ The threat of punishment can convince rational criminals that crime does not pay.
	■ Techniques include the death penalty, mandatory sentences, and aggressive policing.
	■ Problems with these strategies are that criminals do not fear punishment, and the certainty of arrest and punishment is low.
Specific deterrence strategies	■ If punishment is severe enough, known criminals will never be tempted to repeat their offenses.
	■ If crime is rational, then painful punishment should reduce its future allure.
	■ Techniques include harsh prisons, long sentences, and stiff fines.
	■ Problems include defiance, stigma, and irrational offenders who are not deterred by punishment.
Situational crime prevention	■ Criminals will avoid specific targets if they are convinced that the targets are protected.
	■ Crime is reduced if motivated offenders are denied access to suitable targets.
	■ Emphasis is on the message that the potential reward is not worth the risk of apprehension.
	■ Techniques include security cameras, alarms, warning signs, and marking items.
	■ Problems with the strategy include extinction of the effect and the displacement of crime.

the "lock 'em up" policies that are the backbone of the specific deterrence concept.[40] Even if expensive specific deterrent strategies such as mass incarceration actually proved effective, they are expensive to maintain, especially in an era of declining crime rates.

The basic components of all three crime control strategies based on choice theory are set out in Concept Summary 3.1.

Trait Theories

As the nineteenth century came to a close, some criminologists began to suggest that crime was caused not so much by human choice but by inherited and uncontrollable biological and psychological traits: intelligence, body build, personality, biomedical makeup. The newly developed scientific method was applied to the study of social relations, including criminal behavior.

The origin of scientific criminology is usually traced to the research of Cesare Lombroso (1836–1909). Lombroso, an Italian army physician fascinated by human anatomy, became interested in finding out what motivated criminals to commit crimes. He physically examined hundreds of prison inmates and other criminals to discover any similarities among them. On the basis of his research, Lombroso proposed that criminals manifest *atavistic anomalies*: primitive, animal-like physical qualities such as an asymmetric face or excessive jaw, eye defects, large eyes, a receding forehead, prominent cheekbones, long arms, a twisted nose, and swollen lips.[41] Lombroso's views were discredited in the twentieth century, and biological explanations of crime were abandoned.

There has been a recent resurgence of interest in the biology of crime. Contemporary biological theory assumes that variation in human physical traits can explain behavior. Instead of being born equal and influenced by social and environmental conditions, each person possesses a unique biochemical, neurological, and genetic makeup. People may develop physical or mental traits at birth, or soon thereafter, that affect their social functioning over the life course and influence their behavior choices. So behavior has both biological and sociological elements, hence the term *sociobiological*, or *biosocial, theories*. It is possible, then, that while biochemical makeup influences behavior, social factors (such as nurturing parents and supportive environments) can mitigate its effects.[42] Biological and environmental factors have an interactive effect. Biosocial theory can be divided into four subareas: the biochemical, neurological, evolutionary, and genetic effects on behavior.

Biochemical Factors

Biocriminologists sometimes focus on the influence of biochemical factors on criminal behavior. It is believed that ingestion of or exposure to toxic substances or harmful chemicals, and poor diet in utero, at birth, and beyond, may affect people throughout their life course. Such factors can either trigger or make people susceptible to hostile or aggressive responses. Thus people who are exposed to toxic biochemical substances may be more likely than others to take hostile action when exposed to stressful events. What are suspected biochemical influences on behavior?

ENVIRONMENTAL CONTAMINANTS   Exposure to environmental contaminants such as the now-banned PCBs (polychlorinated biphenyls), a chemical that was once used in insulation materials, as well as to lead, mercury, and other metals, has been shown to influence brain functioning and intelligence levels.[43] Exposure to these contaminants may lead to cognitive and learning dysfunctions, factors associated with antisocial behaviors.[44]

FOOD PRODUCTS AND DIET   Some research efforts have linked antisocial behavior to vitamin and mineral deficiencies, food additives, and improper diet. Ingestion of common food additives such as calcium propionate, used to preserve bread, has been linked to problem behaviors.[45] The association may be direct: excessive amounts of harmful substances such as food dyes and artificial colors and flavors seem to provoke hostile, impulsive, and otherwise antisocial behaviors.[46] The association may also be indirect: attention deficit hyperactive disorder (ADHD) has long been linked to antisocial behavior, and there is evidence that ADHD is related to dietary intake. Substances linked to a higher rate of ADHD include fast foods, processed meats, red meat, high-fat dairy products, and candy.[47]

L03 Identify the various biological traits linked to crime.

HYPOGLYCEMIA   Another area of biological research focuses on hypoglycemia, a condition that occurs when blood glucose (sugar) falls below the levels necessary for normal and efficient brain functioning. Symptoms of hypoglycemia include irritability, anxiety, depression, crying spells, headaches, and confusion. Research shows that persistent abnormality in the way the brain metabolizes glucose is linked to substance abuse.[48]

HORMONES   One area of concern has been testosterone, the most abundant male hormone (androgen), which controls secondary sex characteristics such as facial hair and voice timbre. Excessive levels of testosterone have been linked to violence and aggression.[49] Children who have low levels of the stress hormone cortisol tend to be more violent and antisocial than those with normal levels.[50] A growing body of evidence suggests that hormonal changes are also related to mood and behavior and that adolescents experience more intense mood swings, anxiety, and restlessness than their elders; this may contribute to the high violence rates found among teenage males.[51]

In sum, biochemical studies suggest that criminal offenders have abnormal levels of certain organic or inorganic substances that influence their behavior and in some way make them prone to antisocial behavior.

Neurological Factors

Another area of interest to biosocial theorists is the relationship of brain activity to behavior.[52] Children who suffer from measurable neurological deficits at birth are believed also to later suffer from a number of antisocial traits ranging from habitual lying to antisocial violence.[53] Such damage can lead to reduction in executive functioning (EF), a condition that refers to impairment of the cognitive processes that facilitate the planning and regulation of goal-oriented behavior. Impairments in EF have been implicated in a range of developmental disorders, including attention deficit hyperactivity disorder (ADHD), conduct disorder (CD), autism, and Tourette syndrome. EF impairments also have been implicated in a range of neuropsychiatric and medical disorders, including schizophrenia, major depression, alcoholism, structural brain disease, diabetes mellitus, and normal aging.[54] These linkages can be important. For example, conduct disorder (CD) is considered a precursor to long-term chronic offending. Children with CD lie, steal, bully other children, get into fights frequently, and break schools' and parents' rules; many are callous and lack empathy and/or guilt.[55]

Studies conducted in the United States and other nations have indicated that the relationship between impairment in executive brain functions (such as abstract reasoning, problem-solving skills, and motor behavior skills) and aggressive behavior is significant.[56] Aggressive adolescents—most commonly boys—often misinterpret their surroundings, feel threatened, and act inappropriately aggressive. They tend to strike back when being teased, blame others when getting into a fight, and overreact to accidents.[57]

Some suspect that the cause of abnormal neurological function is impairment in **neurotransmitters**, which are chemical compounds that influence or activate brain functions. Neurotransmitters studied in relation to aggression include dopamine, serotonin, monoamine oxidase, and gamma aminobutyric acid. Evidence exists that abnormal levels of these chemicals are associated with aggression.[58] Studies of habitually violent criminals show that low serotonin levels are linked with poor impulse control, hyperactivity, increased irritability, and sensation seeking.[59]

ADHD People with an abnormal cerebral structure, referred to as minimal brain dysfunction, may experience periods of explosive rage. Brain dysfunction is sometimes manifested as attention deficit hyperactivity disorder (ADHD), another suspected cause of antisocial behavior. Several studies have shown that children with attention problems experience increased levels of antisocial behavior and aggression during childhood, adolescence, and adulthood.[60] Boys and girls who suffer from ADHD are impaired both academically and socially, factors that are related to long-term antisocial behaviors.[61]

The condition may cause poor school performance, bullying, stubbornness, and a lack of response to discipline. Although the origin of ADHD is still unknown, suspected causes include neurological damage, prenatal stress, and even food additives and chemical allergies. Research shows that youths with ADHD who grow up in a dysfunctional family are the most vulnerable to chronic delinquency that continues into their adulthood.[62]

neurotransmitters
Chemical substances that carry impulses from one nerve cell to another. Neurotransmitters are found in the space (synapse) that separates the transmitting neuron's terminal (axon) from the receiving neuron's terminal (dendrite).

Web App 3.2

For more information about the Attention Deficit Disorder Association, visit http://www.add.org/.

criminal justice and TECHNOLOGY

CAN BRAIN SCANS PREDICT CRIMINAL BEHAVIOR?

Scientists at the Mind Research Network (MRN), a non-profit association of scientists from several universities and laboratories around the country, use sophisticated imaging scans to understand, diagnose, prevent, and treat a variety of brain disorders. Recently, they have turned their attention to criminal activity, using MRI (magnetic resonance imaging) scans to explore the relationship between the brain and criminal activity.

Researchers have long known that certain youthful characteristics, such as impulsivity, can eventually lead to delinquency and crime if they persist into adulthood. So what do brain scans tell us that we don't already know? In a 2011 MRN study, researchers compared MRI results from incarcerated juveniles to those of a comparison group. They were looking specifically for connections between impulsive behavior and activity within certain

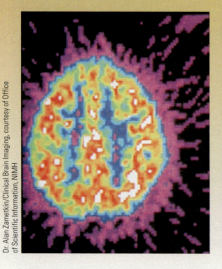

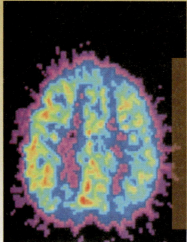

This scan compares a normal brain (left) and the brain of an individual with ADHD (right). The areas of orange and white demonstrate a higher rate of metabolism; the areas of blue and green represent an abnormally low metabolic rate. Why is ADHD so prevalent in the United States today? Some experts believe our immigrant forebears were risk-takers who impulsively left their homelands for a life in the new world. They may have brought with them a genetic predisposition to ADHD.

Dr. Alan Zametkin/Clinical Brain Imaging, courtesy of Office of Scientific Information, NIMH

Genetic Factors

Although the earliest biological studies of crime tried and failed to discover a genetic basis for criminality, modern biosocial theorists are still concerned with the role of heredity in producing crime-prone people. The relationship may be direct: (a) antisocial behavior is inherited, (b) the genetic makeup of parents is passed on to children, and (c) genetic abnormality is directly linked to a variety of antisocial behaviors.[63] For example, Ronald Simons and his associates recently found that adolescents who possess a particular genetic makeup are more likely to adopt an aggressive response to provocation.[64]

It is also possible that the association is indirect: genes are related to some personality or physical trait that is linked to antisocial behavior.[65] For example, genetic makeup may shape friendship patterns and orient people toward associating with either conventional or antisocial friends. Those who maintain deviant peers are more likely to become crime prone.[66] Similarly, attachment to parents may be influenced by a genetic component; adolescents whose attachment to their parents is weak and attenuated may be more likely to engage in delinquent acts.[67]

If inherited traits are related to criminality, twins should be more similar in their antisocial activities than other sibling pairs. However, because most twins brain regions. Interestingly, they found them, reporting that "in less-impulsive juveniles and normal controls, motor planning regions were correlated with brain networks associated with spatial attention and executive control. In more-impulsive juveniles, these same regions correlated with the default-mode network, a constellation of brain areas associated with spontaneous, unconstrained, self-referential cognition." In other words, the brain scans of impulsive study participants were different than those of the controls.

A similar study published in 2013 used MRI scans in an effort to predict antisocial behavior in adults. The researchers followed New Mexico prison inmates for a period of four years, first scanning and testing them, then tracking their postrelease activities. Subjects who had low activity in a certain brain region known as the anterior cingulated cortex were nearly twice as likely to commit another felony after being released from prison. What's more, the brain scans performed *better* at predicting future behavior than traditional risk assessment instruments. As one of the study's authors observed, "These findings have incredibly significant ramifications for the future of how our society deals with criminal justice and offenders.... Not only does this study give us a tool to predict which criminals may reoffend and which ones will not reoffend, it also provides a path forward for steering offenders into more effective targeted therapies to reduce the risk of future criminal activity."

The notion that technology can be used to predict crime generates plenty of debate. Supporters hail brain scans as a profound technological accomplishment that will change criminal justice as we know it. Critics raise privacy concerns and point out the science remains speculative and crude.

CRITICAL THINKING

What are the strengths and weaknesses of using brain scans to detect or predict criminal behavior? Assuming the technology is sound, *should* brain scans be introduced into the criminal process? Do we have a right to privacy to the thoughts within our own brains? The PBS program *Brains on Trial* explores both perspectives in more detail. More information plus the full episodes are available here: http://brainsontrial.com.

Sources: Benjamin J. Shannon, Marcus E. Raichle, Abraham Z. Snyder, Damien A. Fair, Kathryn L. Mills, Dongyang Zhang, Kevin Bache, Vince D. Calhoun, Joel T. Nigg, Bonnie J. Nagel, Alexander A. Stevens, and Kent A. Kiehl, "Premotor Functional Connectivity Predicts Impulsivity in Juvenile Offenders," *Proceedings of the National Academy of Sciences* 108 (2011): 11241–11245; Eyal Aharoni, Gina M. Vincent, Carla L. Harenski, Vince D. Calhoun, Walter Sinnott-Armstrong, Michael S. Gazzaniga, and Kent A. Kiehl, "Neuroprediction of Future Arrest," *Proceedings of the National Academy of Sciences*, 110 (2013): 6223–6228; Ashik Siddique, "Brain Scans Predict Crime Before It Happens: Can Neuroimaging Prevent Repeat Offenders?" *Medical Daily*, March 28, 2013, http://www.medicaldaily.com/brain-scans-predict-crime-it-happens-can-neuroimaging-prevent-repeat-offenders-244818 (accessed May 2014).

are brought up together, determining whether behavioral similarities are a function of environmental influences or genetics is difficult. To overcome this problem, biosocial theorists usually compare identical, or monozygotic (MZ), twins with fraternal, or dizygotic (DZ), twins of the same sex. MZ twins are genetically identical, so their behavior would be expected to be more similar than that of DZ twins. Preliminary studies have shown that this is true.[68] Some evidence exists that genetic makeup is a better predictor of criminality than either social or environmental variables.[69] If one MZ twin joins a gang, the other is sure to follow![70]

One famous study of twin behavior was the Minnesota Study of Twins Reared Apart. The research compared the behavior of MZ and DZ twin pairs who were raised together with others who were separated at birth and in some cases did not even know of the other's existence. The study revealed some striking similarities in behavior and ability for twin pairs raised apart. An MZ twin reared away from a co-twin had about as good a chance of being similar to the co-twin in terms of personality, interests, and attitudes as one who was reared with the co-twin.[71]

The various biosocial views of criminal behavior are summarized in Concept Summary 3.2.

CONCEPT SUMMARY 3.2
Biosocial Views of Crime Causation

View	Major Premise	Strengths	Research Focus
Biochemical	Crime, especially violence, is a function of diet, vitamin intake, hormonal imbalance, or food allergies.	Explains irrational violence; it shows how the environment interacts with personal traits to influence behavior.	Diet, hormones, enzymes, environmental contaminants, and lead intake.
Neurological	Criminals and delinquents often suffer brain impairment. Attention deficit hyperactivity disorder and other brain dysfunctions are related to antisocial behavior.	Explains irrational violence; it shows how brain activity influences behavior.	ADHD, learning disabilities, brain injuries, and brain chemistry.
Genetic	Criminal traits and predispositions are inherited.	Explains why a small percentage of youths in high-crime areas become chronic offenders.	Twin behavior, sibling behavior, and parent–child similarities.

Psychological Theories

L04 Describe the various psychological views of the cause of crime.

The view that criminals may be suffering from psychological abnormality or stress has also had a long history.

Psychodynamic Theory

Psychodynamic theory, the creation of Viennese physician Sigmund Freud (1856–1939), still holds a prominent position in psychological thought.[72] According to the psychodynamic view, some people encounter problems during their early development that cause an imbalance in their personality. Some have mood disorders and are extremely anxious, fearful, and impulsive. Patients with psychosis are people whose primitive impulses have broken through and actually control their personality; they may hear voices telling them what to do or see visions. One type of psychosis is schizophrenia, a condition marked by incoherent thought processes, a lack of insight, hallucinations, and feelings of persecution.

CRIME AND MENTAL ILLNESS Psychodynamic theorists believe that law violators have suffered damage to their personalities early in their development and that this damage renders them powerless to control their impulses. They may suffer delusions and feel persecuted, worthless, and alienated.[73] As a result, they seek immediate gratification of their needs without considering right and wrong or the needs of others. Mental illness dogs offenders across the life course: delinquent adolescents have higher rates of clinical mental disorders than adolescents in the general population.[74] As adult criminals, people who have been arrested for multiple crimes are more likely to suffer from a psychiatric disorder, particularly a psychotic disorder, than nonchronic offenders.[75]

What are some of the specific disorders that have been linked to antisocial youth?

oppositional defiant disorder (ODD)
A psychological condition whose symptoms include rebellious and aggressive behavior toward authority figures that seriously interferes with proper life functioning.

■ *Oppositional defiant disorder (ODD).* Victims of this disease experience an ongoing pattern of uncooperative, defiant, and hostile behavior toward authority figures that seriously interferes with day-to-day functioning. Symptoms of **oppositional defiant disorder (ODD)** may include frequent loss of temper, constant arguing with adults, defying adults or refusing adult requests or rules, deliberately annoying others, blaming others for mistakes or misbehavior, being angry and resentful, being spiteful or vindictive, swearing or using obscene language, or having a low opinion of themselves.[76]

■ *Conduct disorder (CD)*. People suffering from conduct disorder have great difficulty following rules and behaving in a socially acceptable way.[77] They are often viewed by other children, adults, and social agencies as severely antisocial. They are frequently involved in such activities as bullying, fighting, committing sexual assaults, and behaving cruelly toward animals. Adolescents with elevated levels of conduct disorder in childhood and adolescence have been found to be at risk for engaging in a pattern of delinquency that persists from adolescence into adulthood.[78]

■ *Clinical depression*. This psychiatric disorder is characterized by an inability to concentrate, insomnia, loss of appetite, and feelings of extreme sadness, guilt, helplessness, and hopelessness; there may be thoughts of death. Research shows that kids who are clinically depressed are more likely to engage in a wide variety of delinquent acts.[79]

■ *Alexithymia*. This deficit in emotional cognition that prevents people from being aware of their feelings or being able to understand or talk about their thoughts and emotions has been linked to antisocial behaviors.[80]

Despite this evidence, some doubt remains about whether the mentally ill commit more crime than the mentally sound. It is also possible that the link is caused by the treatment of the mentally ill: the police may be more likely to arrest the mentally ill, giving the illusion that the latter are crime prone.[81] However, even though some mental health problems increase the risk of arrest, others elicit more cautious or compassionate police responses that may result in treatment rather than arrest.[82] Further research is needed to clarify this important relationship.

Behavioral Theory

A second branch of psychological theory views behavior as learned through interactions with others. Behavior that is rewarded becomes habitual; behavior that is punished becomes extinguished. One subbranch of behavioral theory of particular relevance to criminology is **social learning theory**. According to social learning theorists, people act aggressively because, as children, they modeled their behavior after the violent acts of adults.[83] Later in life, antisocial behavioral patterns are reinforced by peers and other acquaintances.[84]

Social learning theorists conclude that the antisocial behavior of potentially violent people can be triggered by a number of different influences: verbal taunts and threats; the experience of direct pain; and perceptions of relative social disability, such as poverty and racial discrimination. Those who have learned violence and have seen it rewarded are more likely than others to react violently when subjected to these stimuli.

One area of particular interest to social learning theorists is whether the entertainment media can influence violence. This topic is discussed in the accompanying Analyzing Criminal Justice Issues feature.

Cognitive Theory

Cognitive psychologists are concerned with the way people perceive and mentally represent the world in which they live. Some researchers focus on how people process and store information, viewing the operation of human intellect as similar to the way computers analyze available information; the emphasis is

social learning theory
The view that human behavior is learned through observation of human social interactions, either directly from those in close proximity or indirectly from the media.

analyzing criminal justice ISSUES

DOES THE MEDIA CAUSE VIOLENCE?

Does the media influence behavior? Does broadcast violence cause aggressive behavior in viewers? This has become a hot topic because of the persistent theme of violence on television and in films. Critics have called for drastic measures, ranging from banning TV violence to putting warning labels on music albums with explicit lyrics that are thought to promote delinquency.

If there is in fact a TV–violence link, the problem is indeed alarming. Systematic viewing of TV begins at 2.5 years of age and continues at a high level during the preschool and early school years. Marketing research indicates that adolescents aged 11 to 14 view violent horror movies at a higher rate than any other age group. Children this age use older peers and siblings and apathetic parents to gain access to R-rated films.

A number of researchers have found that viewing media violence *contributes* to aggression. For example, developmental psychologist John Murray carefully reviewed existing research on the effect of TV violence on children and concluded that viewing media violence is related to both short- and long-term increases in aggressive attitudes, values, and behaviors. There is also evidence that kids who watch TV are more likely to persist in aggressive behavior as adults. Why does the effect persist?

There are several explanations for the effects of television and film violence on behavior:

- Media violence can provide aggressive "scripts" that children store in memory. Repeated exposure to these scripts can increase their retention and lead to changes in attitudes.

- Media violence increases the arousal levels of viewers and makes them more prone to act aggressively. Studies measuring the galvanic skin response of subjects—a physical indication of arousal based on the amount of electricity conducted across the palm of the hand—show that viewing violent media led to increased arousal levels in young children.

- Media violence promotes such negative attitudes as suspiciousness and the expectation that the viewer will become involved in violence. Frequent viewing of aggression and violence makes them seem common and socially acceptable behavior.

- Media violence allows aggressive youths to justify their behavior. It is possible that, instead of causing violence, media helps violent youths rationalize their behavior as a socially acceptable and common activity.

- Media violence may disinhibit aggressive behavior, which is normally controlled by other learning processes. Disinhibition takes place when adults

on information processing. Aggressive people may base their behavior on faulty information. They perceive other people as more aggressive than they really are. Consequently, they are more likely to be vigilant, on edge, or suspicious. When they attack victims, they may believe they are defending themselves, when they are simply misreading the situation.[85] The college student who rapes his date may have a cognitive problem rendering him incapable of distinguishing among behavioral cues. He misidentifies rejection as a come-on or as "playing hard to get."

Another area of cognitive psychology is moral development theory. According to this theory, people go through a series of stages beginning early in childhood and continuing through their adult years.[86] Each stage is marked by a different view of right and wrong. For example, a child may do what is right simply to avoid punishment and censure. Later in life, the same person will develop a sensitivity to others' needs and do what is right to avoid hurting others. Upon reaching a higher level of maturity, the same person may behave in are viewed as being rewarded for violence and when violence is seen as socially acceptable. This contradicts previous learning experiences in which violent behavior was viewed as wrong.

- Violent programming may actually alter brain activity. Functional magnetic resonance imaging (fMRI) used to test brain function finds that exposure to violent TV shows, movies, and video games desensitizes part of the brain—the lateral orbitofrontal cortex—to violence; those exposed to the highest levels of video violence at home showed the greatest desensitization.

IS THERE A MEDIA–VIOLENCE LINK?

The mere fact that kids who are exposed to violent media also engage in violent behaviors is not proof of a causal connection. It is also possible that kids who are already violent seek out violent media to enforce or justify their preexisting behaviors: What would we expect violent gang boys to watch on TV? *Phineas and Ferb* or *SpongeBob*? If violent TV shows did, indeed, cause interpersonal violence, then there should be few ecological and regional patterns in the crime rate, but there are many.

There is little evidence that areas that have high levels of violent TV viewing also have rates of violent crime that are above the norm. Millions of children watch violence yet fail to become violent criminals. And even if a violent behavior–TV link could be established, it would be difficult to show that antisocial

people develop aggressive traits merely from watching TV. Despite the inconclusive evidence, efforts are ongoing to reduce TV violence and the ability of children to access violent programming.

CRITICAL THINKING

1. Should the government control the content of TV shows and limit the amount of weekly violence? How could the national news be shown if violence were omitted? What about boxing matches and hockey games?

2. How can we explain the fact that millions of kids watch violent TV shows and remain nonviolent? If there is a TV–violence link, how can we explain the fact that violence rates may have been higher in the Old West than they are today? Do you think kids in violent gangs stay home and watch TV shows?

Sources: Ingrid Möller, Barbara Krahé, Robert Busching, and Christina Krause, "Efficacy of an Intervention to Reduce the Use of Media Violence and Aggression: An Experimental Evaluation with Adolescents in Germany," *Journal of Youth and Adolescence* 41 (2012): 105–120; Robert Morris and Matthew Johnson, "Sedentary Activities, Peer Behavior, and Delinquency Among American Youth," *Crime and Delinquency*, published online November 4, 2010; Maren Strenziok, Frank Krueger, Gopikrishna Deshpande, Rhoshel K. Lenroot, Elke van Der Meer, and Jordan Grafman, "Fronto-parietal Regulation of Media Violence Exposure in Adolescents: A Multi-method Study," *Social Cognitive and Affective Neuroscience*, published online October 7, 2010, http://scan.oxfordjournals.org/content/early/2010/10/18/scan.nsq079.full.pdf+html (accessed May 2014); George Comstock, "A Sociological Perspective on Television Violence and Aggression," *American Behavioral Scientist* 51 (2008): 1184–1211; John Murray, "Media Violence: The Effects Are Both Real and Strong," *American Behavioral Scientist* 51 (2008): 1212–1230.

---

accordance with his or her perception of universal principles of justice, equality, and fairness.

According to developmental psychologists, criminals may lack the ability to make moral judgments. Criminals report that their outlooks are characterized by self-interest and impaired moral development. They are unlikely to consider the rights of others, and they are not concerned with maintaining the rules of society.[87]

Personality and Crime

Some psychologists view criminal behavior as a function of a disturbed personality structure. Personality can be defined as the reasonably stable patterns of behavior, including thoughts and emotions, that distinguish one person from another.[88]

The terms *psychopath* and *sociopath* are commonly used to describe people who have an **antisocial personality**, defined as a pervasive pattern of disregard

antisocial personality
A personality characterized by a lack of warmth and feeling, inappropriate behavioral responses, and an inability to learn from experience (also called sociopath or psychopath).

 L05 Identify the personality traits linked to crime.

Although some research shows that people who act aggressively in social settings have lower IQ scores than their peers, other findings suggest that the association between intelligence and crime is insignificant. Should mentally challenged offenders be punished in the same manner as those who are not intellectually impaired? Here, Daryl Atkins walks into the York-Poquoson courtroom in York, Virginia. Atkins's 2002 case led the U.S. Supreme Court to bar execution of the mentally retarded as cruel and unusual—and hence unconstitutional. Ironically, upon rehearing the case in July 2005, a jury in Virginia decided that Atkins was intelligent enough to be executed and that the stimulation of the trial process had raised his IQ above 70, rendering him competent to be put to death under Virginia law. In January 2008, his sentence was commuted to life in prison as a consequence of prosecutorial misconduct in the original case.

for, and violation of, the rights of others that begins in childhood or early adolescence and continues into adulthood.[89]

Those suffering from this disease usually exhibit at least three of the following behaviors:

■ Failure to conform to social norms with respect to lawful behaviors, as indicated by repeatedly performing acts that are grounds for arrest

■ Deceitfulness, as indicated by repeatedly lying, using aliases, or conning others for personal profit or pleasure

■ Impulsivity or failure to plan ahead

■ Irritability and aggressiveness, as indicated by repeated physical fights or assaults

■ Reckless disregard for the safety of self or others

■ Consistent irresponsibility, as indicated by repeated failure to sustain consistent work behavior or to honor financial obligations

■ Lack of remorse, as indicated by being indifferent to or rationalizing having hurt, mistreated, or stolen from another[90]

People with an antisocial personality are believed to be dangerous and aggressive individuals who act in a callous manner. They neither learn from their mistakes nor are deterred by punishments.[91] Although they may appear charming and have at least average intelligence, they lack emotional depth, are incapable of caring for others, and maintain an abnormally low level of anxiety, traits that are linked to violence and other forms of criminality.[92]

IQ and Crime

One of the most enduring controversies in the psychology of crime is the relationship between intelligence, as measured by standardized intelligence quotient (IQ) tests, and violent or criminal behavior. Numerous studies link low IQ to violent and aggressive behavior and crime.[93] Some research examines samples of people to determine whether those with low IQ are also more aggressive in social settings. Evidence shows that people who act aggressively in social settings also have lower IQ scores than their peers.[94] Some studies have found a direct IQ–delinquency link among samples of adolescent boys.[95]

Although this evidence is persuasive, many experts dispute that an IQ–crime relationship exists. They offer the following reasons:

■ IQ tests are biased and reflect middle-class values. As a result, socially disadvantaged people do poorly on IQ tests, and members of that group are also the ones most likely to commit crime.

■ The measurement of intelligence is often varied and haphazard, and results may depend on the particular method used.[96]

■ People with low IQs are stigmatized and negatively labeled by middle-class decision makers such as police officers, teachers, and guidance counselors. It is stigma and labeling—not a low IQ—that causes criminal behavior. Because of their favorable treatment higher-IQ offenders avoid the stigma of criminal punishment, which helps reduce their chances of recidivism.

■ Having a low IQ may influence some criminal patterns, such as arson and sex crimes, but not others, further clouding the waters.[97]

Sociological Theories

Official, self-report, and victim data all indicate social patterns in the crime rate.[98] Some regions are more crime prone than others. Distinct differences are found in crime rates across states, cities, and neighborhoods. If crime rates are higher in Los Angeles, California, than in Woodstock, Vermont, it is probably not because Californians are more likely to suffer personality defects or eat more sugar than Vermonters. Crime rates are higher in large urban areas that house concentrations of the poor than they are in sparsely populated rural areas in which residents are relatively affluent. Prisons are filled with the poor and hopeless, not the rich and famous. Because crime patterns have a social orientation, sociological explanations of crime are common in criminology.

Sociological criminology is usually traced to the pioneering work of sociologist Émile Durkheim (1858–1917), who viewed crime as a social phenomenon.[99] In formulating his theory of anomie, Durkheim held that crime is an essential part of society and a function of its internal conflict. As he used the term, **anomie** means the absence or weakness of rules and social norms in any person or group; without these rules or norms, an individual may lose the ability to distinguish between right and wrong.

anomie
The absence or weakness of rules, norms, or guidelines on what is socially or morally acceptable.

As the field of sociological criminology emerged in the twentieth century, greater emphasis was placed on environmental conditions, whereas the relationship between crime and physical or mental traits (or both) was neglected. Equating the cause of criminal behavior with social factors, such as poverty and unemployment, was instrumental in the development of treatment-oriented crime prevention techniques. If criminals are made and not born—if they are forged in the crucible of societal action—then it logically follows that crime can be eradicated by eliminating the social elements responsible for crime. The focus of crime prevention shifted from punishing criminals to treatment and rehabilitation.

Social Structure Theory

At their core, **social structure** theories equate poverty and income inequality both in the United States and abroad with high crime rates.[100] This association is especially powerful in the United States, because we live in a stratified society. Social strata are created by the unequal distribution of wealth, power, and prestige. Social classes are segments of the population whose members share relatively similar attitudes, values, and norms and have an identifiable lifestyle. In U.S. society, it is common to identify people as members of the upper, middle, or lower socioeconomic class, with a broad range of economic variations existing within each group. The upper-upper class is made up of a small number of exceptionally well-to-do families who maintain enormous financial and social resources. Today more than 45 million Americans live in poverty, which is defined, for a family of four, as earnings of about $24,000 per year. Such families have scant, if any, resources and suffer socially and economically as a result. In contrast, the top

social structure
The stratifications, classes, institutions, and groups that characterize a society.

 L06 Compare and contrast the various social structure theories of crime.

1 percent have a household income of about $390,000, about 7.5 times the median household income; the affluent have an average net worth of about $8.4 million, or 69 times the median household's net holdings of $121,000.[101] This concentration of wealth is not unique to the United States; it is a worldwide phenomenon. According to the most recent World Wealth Report, there are about 12 million high-net-worth individuals in the world today (people with more than $1 million in assets, excluding their primary residence); they have a cumulative net worth of almost $43 trillion. The population of wealthy people in Asia is now at 3.7 million individuals, the second-largest in the world behind North America, and ahead of Europe for the first time.[102]

Millions of high school dropouts face dead-end jobs, unemployment, and social failure. Because of their meager economic resources, lower-class citizens are often forced to live with inadequate health care, poor educational opportunities, underemployment, and despair. They live in areas with deteriorated housing and abandoned buildings, which are magnets for crime, drug dealing, and prostitution.[103] Violence and crime have been found to spread in these areas in a pattern similar to an epidemic of a contagious disease.[104] When lower-class youths are exposed to a continual stream of violence, they are more likely to engage in violent acts themselves.[105] Living in poor areas magnifies the effect of personal, social, and economic problems. Kids whose families are poor *and* who reside in a poverty-stricken area are more likely to engage in antisocial behavior than kids from poor families growing up in more affluent areas. The combination of having a poor family and living in a disorganized area may be devastating.[106]

RACIAL DISPARITY The problems of lower-class culture are particularly acute for racial and ethnic minorities. The burdens of underclass life are often felt most acutely by minority group members. Whereas many urban European Americans use their economic, social, and political advantages to live in sheltered gated communities patrolled by security guards and police, most minorities do not have access to similar protections and privileges.[107]

Today, the average African American family median income is $33,321 in comparison to $57,009 for non-Hispanic white families. About 27 percent of African Americans in comparison to 10 percent of non-Hispanic whites are living at the poverty level. The current unemployment rate for blacks is twice the rate for non-Hispanic whites (13.1 percent and 6.5 percent, respectively). This pattern is consistent for both men and women.[108] These economic and social disparities continually haunt members of the minority underclass and their children. Even if they value education and other middle-class norms, their desperate life circumstances (including high unemployment and nontraditional family structures) may prevent them from developing the skills, habits, and aspirations that lead first to educational success and later to success in the workplace; these deficits have been linked to crime and drug abuse.[109]

If they do commit crime, minority youths are more likely to be officially processed to the juvenile court than Caucasian youths. This makes it more likely that they will develop an official record at an early age, an outcome that may increase the odds of their being incarcerated as adults.[110] According to a report by the Pew Foundation, the incarceration rate for white men was 678 inmates per 100,000. For black men, it was 4,347 per 100,000, meaning black men are incarcerated six times as much as white men.[111]

The crushing burden of urban poverty brings on the development of a **culture of poverty**.[112] This subculture is marked by apathy, cynicism, helplessness, and distrust. The culture is passed from one generation to the next, creating a permanent underclass referred to as the "truly disadvantaged."[113]

culture of poverty
The view that people in the lower class of society form a separate culture with its own values and norms that are in conflict with those of conventional society.

Considering the social disabilities and frustrations suffered by members of the lower class, it is not surprising that some turn to crime as a means of support and survival. The social forces operating in lower-class, inner-city areas produce high crime rates. What are these forces, and how do they produce crime?

The Disorganized Neighborhood

The effects of income inequality, poverty, racism, and despair are viewed by many crime experts as a key cause of youth crime and drug abuse. Kids who grow up poor and live in households that lack economic resources are much more likely to get involved in serious crime than their wealthier peers.[114] According to this view, crime is a natural outcome of life in neighborhoods characterized by physical deterioration and by conflicting values and social systems. Disorganized neighborhoods are undergoing the disintegration of their existing culture and services, the diffusion of cultural standards, and successive changes from purely residential to a mixture of commercial, industrial, transient, and residential populations. In these areas, the major sources of informal social control—family, school, neighborhood, and civil services—are broken and ineffective.

Impoverished urban areas are believed to be crime prone for a number of reasons:

- Long-term, unremitting poverty undermines a community and its residents. Crime rates are sensitive to the destructive social forces operating in lower-class urban neighborhoods.

- Residents develop a sense of hopelessness and mistrust of conventional society. Residents of such areas are frustrated by their inability to become part of the "American Dream."

- Kids growing up in these disadvantaged areas are at risk for criminality because they hear from adults that there is little chance of success in the conventional world.

- Poverty undermines the basic stabilizing forces of the community—family, school, peers, and neighbors—rendering them weakened, attenuated, and ineffective.

- The ability of the community to control its inhabitants—to assert informal social control—is damaged and frayed.

- The community has become socially disorganized, leaving its residents free to succumb to the lure of antisocial behaviors. Without social controls, kids are free to join gangs, violate the law, and engage in uncivil and destructive behaviors.

- Residents are constantly exposed to disruption, violence, and incivility—factors that increase the likelihood that they themselves will become involved in delinquency.[115]

- Because the poor and affluent often live in close proximity within large urban areas, actual or perceived income inequality creates a sense of relative deprivation that encourages people to commit crime.[116]

- People living in these disadvantaged areas are prone to psychological upheavals resulting in conduct problems that help to unsettle the neighborhood even further.[117]

As areas decline, residents flee to safer, more stable localities. Those who can move to more affluent neighborhoods find that their lifestyles and life chances improve immediately and continue to do so over their life span.[118] As the more affluent residents flee, leaving behind a neighborhood with nonexistent employment opportunities, inferior housing patterns, and unequal access to health care, poverty becomes concentrated in these areas.[119] Urban areas marked by concentrated poverty become isolated and insulated from the social mainstream and more prone to criminal activity, violence, and homicide.[120] Eventually the effect of concentrated poverty may abate for most crimes, reaching a saturation point perhaps, but by then the damage is done.[121]

Those who can't leave these areas because they cannot afford to live in more affluent communities face an increased risk of victimization. Because of racial differences in economic well-being, those "left behind" are all too often minority citizens.[122] Whites may feel threatened as the number of minorities in the population increases, generating competition for jobs and political power.[123] As racial prejudice increases, the call for "law and order" aimed at controlling the minority population grows louder.[124]

In contrast to areas plagued by poverty, cohesive communities with high levels of social control and social integration, where people know one another and develop interpersonal ties, may also develop **collective efficacy**: mutual trust, a willingness to intervene in the supervision of children, and the maintenance of public order.[125] It is the cohesion among neighborhood residents, combined with shared expectations for informal social control of public space, that promotes collective efficacy.[126] Residents in these areas are able to enjoy a better life because the fruits of cohesiveness can be better education, health care, and housing opportunities.[127] When neighborhood kids see that people care in the community, the presence of informal social controls help shapes their behavior. It provides them with expectations on how they should behave even when adults are not around to monitor their activities.[128]

The crime-producing influences of economic disadvantages are felt by all residents.[129] However, minority group members living in these areas suffer the added disadvantages of race-based income inequality and institutional racism.[130] The fact that significant numbers of African Americans are forced to live under these conditions can help explain the distinct racial patterns in the official crime statistics.

Unfortunately, the problems found in disorganized areas are stubborn and difficult to overcome. Even when an attempt is made to revitalize a neighborhood—for example, by creating institutional support programs such as community centers and better schools—the effort may be undermined by the chronic lack of economic and social resources.[131]

DEVIANT VALUES AND CULTURES People living in disorganized areas band together to form an independent lower-class subculture—a small reference group that provides members with a unique set of values, beliefs, and traditions distinct from those of conventional society. In this environment kids develop a jaundiced, pessimistic, and cynical view of life early in their adolescence. They learn to trust no one, take a dim view of their future, and figure out that the only way to get ahead in life is to break social rules. They see drug dealing rather than higher education as a roadway to success. They accept a unique cognitive framework that shapes not only the way they look at the world but also behavioral choices. As they try to cope with their environment, kids in lower-class culture begin to believe such things as "When people are friendly, they usually want something from you" and "Some people oppose you for no good reason." They want everything right away and are willing to take risks to get what they want. Persistent exposure to antagonistic social circumstances and lack of exposure to positive conditions increase the chances of someone developing a hostile view of relationships, a focus on immediate rewards, and cynicism regarding conventional conduct norms. Embracing these culturally

collective efficacy
A condition of mutual trust and cooperation that develops in neighborhoods that have a high level of formal and informal social control.

defined attitudes can lead to actions that are aggressive, opportunistic, and sometimes criminal.[132]

Residents in these communities often solve problems informally, without calling the police. Those who doubt that the agencies of justice can help them develop a degree of "legal cynicism"—they perceive the law as illegitimate, unresponsive, and ill equipped to ensure public safety.[133] The neighborhood culture codes support this type of problem solving, even if it leads to violence and death. In sum, in lower-class areas, social, cultural, and economic forces interact to produce a violent environment.[134]

STRAIN In lower-class neighborhoods, **strain**, or status frustration, occurs because legitimate avenues for success are all but closed. Frustrated and angry, with no acceptable means of achieving success, people may use deviant methods, such as theft or violence, to obtain their goals. Because they feel relatively deprived, the poor channel their anger and frustration into antisocial behaviors.[135]

The concept of strain can be traced to the pioneering work of famed sociologist Robert Merton, who recognized that members of the lower class experience anomie, or normlessness, when the means they have for achieving culturally defined goals—mainly wealth and financial success—are insufficient.[136] As a result, people begin to seek alternative solutions to meet their need for success; they may steal, sell drugs, or extort money. Merton referred to this method of adaptation as *innovation*—the use of innovative but illegal means to achieve success in the absence of legitimate means. Other youths, faced with the same dilemma, might reject conventional goals and choose to live as drug users, alcoholics, and wanderers; Merton referred to this as *retreatism*. Still others might join revolutionary political groups and work to change the system to one of their liking; Merton referred to this as *rebellion*.

Criminologist Robert Agnew has expanded anomie theory by recognizing other sources of strain in addition to failure to meet goals. These include both negative experiences, such as child abuse, and the loss of positive supports, such as the end of a stable romantic relationship (see Figure 3.1).[137] Some people, especially those with an explosive temperament, those with low tolerance for adversity, those with poor problem-solving skills, and those who are overly sensitive or emotional, are less likely to cope well with strain.[138] As their perceptions of strain increase, so does their involvement in antisocial behaviors.[139] In contrast,

strain
The emotional turmoil and conflict caused when people believe that they cannot achieve their desires and goals through legitimate means.

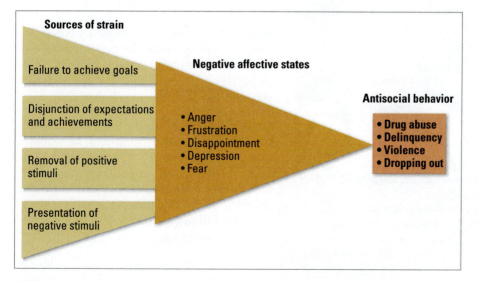

FIGURE 3.1 Agnew's Sources of Strain and Their Consequences

those people who can call on others for help and support from family, friends, and social institutions are better able to cope with strain.[140]

Social Process Theories

Not all social theorists agree that the root cause of crime can be found solely within the culture of poverty.[141] After all, self-report studies indicate that many middle- and upper-class youths take drugs and commit serious criminal acts. As adults, they commit white-collar and corporate crimes. Conversely, the majority of people living in the poorest areas hold conventional values and forgo criminal activity. Simply living in a violent neighborhood does not produce violent people. Research shows that family, peer, and individual characteristics play a large role in predicting violence.[142] These patterns indicate that forces must be operating in all strata of society to affect individual involvement in criminal activity.

If crime is spread throughout the social structure, then it follows that the factors that cause crime should be found within all social and economic groups. People commit crimes as a result of the experiences they have while they are being socialized by the various organizations, institutions, and processes of society. People are most strongly impelled toward criminal behavior by poor family relationships, destructive peer-group relations, educational failure, and labeling by agents of the justice system. Although lower-class citizens have the added burdens of poverty, strain, and blocked opportunities, middle- or upper-class citizens also may turn to crime if their socialization is poor or destructive.

FAMILY PROBLEMS Some social process theorists point to research efforts linking family problems to crime as evidence that socialization, not social structure, is the key to understanding the onset of criminality. Kids who experience family breakup and shifting family structures may be at risk for crime.[143] The effects of family dysfunction are felt well beyond childhood. Kids who experience high levels of family conflict grow up to have stressful adult lives, punctuated by periods of depression.[144] Children whose parents are harsh, angry, and irritable grow up to behave in the same way toward their own children, creating risk problems for their own offspring. Thus the seeds of adult dysfunction are planted early in childhood.

parental efficacy
Parents who are able to be supportive and who can therefore effectively control their children in a nonthreatening fashion.

In contrast, effective parenting may neutralize crime-producing forces in the environment. Parents who are supportive and who effectively control their children in a noncoercive fashion are more likely to raise children who refrain from delinquency; this is called **parental efficacy**.[145] Delinquency is reduced when parents provide the type of structure that integrates children into families, while giving them the ability to assert their individuality and regulate their own behavior.[146]

EDUCATION Studies show that chronic delinquents do poorly in school, lack educational motivation, and are frequently held back.[147] High school dropouts are more likely to become involved in crime than those who complete their education, especially if dropping out follows a history of school-related behavioral problems.[148]

PEERS Having prosocial friends who are committed to conventional success may help shield youths from crime-producing

AP Images/Garfield County Sheriff

Is crime learned? These booking photos show Patricia Marion Gray, 53, and her son Nathan Gray, 32, who were arrested near Rifle, Colorado, after a meeting with an undercover agent for a purported deal involving weapons, marijuana, and money. Did Nathan learn his criminal ways from his mom? Or can there be another explanation for their co-offending?

inducements in their environment.[149] Conversely, their less popular peers, who routinely suffer peer rejection, are more likely to display aggressive behavior and to disrupt group activities through bickering, bullying, or other antisocial behavior.[150] Deviant peers may then sustain or amplify antisocial behavior trends—for example, riding around, staying out late, and partying—and amplify delinquent careers.[151] Because delinquent friends tend to be "sticky" (once acquired, they are not easily lost), peer influence may continue through the life span.[152]

In sum, significant evidence exists that the direction and quality of interpersonal interactions and relationships influence behavior throughout the life span. However, disagreement arises over the direction this influence takes:

- *Social learning theory* suggests that people learn the techniques and attitudes of crime from close relationships with criminal peers. Crime is a learned behavior.

- *Social control theory* maintains that everyone has the potential to become a criminal but that most people are controlled by their bonds to society. Crime occurs when the forces that bind people to society are weakened or broken.

- *Social reaction (labeling) theory* says that people become criminals when significant members of society label them as such and they accept those labels as a personal identity.

SOCIAL LEARNING THEORY Those who advocate learning theories hold that people enter into a life of crime when, as adolescents, they are taught the attitudes, values, and behaviors that support a criminal career. They may learn the techniques of crime from a variety of intimates, including parents and family members.[153] Kids who are exposed to antisocial values will eventually incorporate them into personal attitudes and behaviors and act accordingly.[154]

The best-known example of the learning perspective is Edwin Sutherland's **differential association theory**.[155] Sutherland, considered by many to be the preeminent American criminologist, believed that the attitudes and behaviors that cause crime are learned in close and intimate relationships with significant others. People learn to commit crime in the same way they learn any other behavior. Some kids associate with criminal "mentors" who teach them how to be successful criminals and gain the greatest benefits from their criminal activities.[156] The more deviant an adolescent's social network and network of affiliations, including parents, peers, and romantic partners, the more likely that adolescent is to engage in antisocial behavior. It's likely that deviant affiliations provide attitudes ("definitions") toward delinquency.[157]

Adolescents who are exposed to an excess of definitions in support of deviant behavior will eventually view those behaviors as attractive, appropriate, and suitable, and then engage in a life of crime.[158] In other words, if one of your friends whom you look up to drinks and smokes, it is a lot easier for you to engage in those behaviors yourself and to believe they are appropriate.[159]

Because it is learned, crime is intergenerational. Deviant parents teach kids their pro-criminal attitudes and behavior; children learn crime from their parents.[160] They then teach their own children deviant values, in a never-ending cycle.[161]

SOCIAL CONTROL THEORY According to **social control theory**, all people may have the inclination to violate the law because crime is fun and profitable, but most of us are held in check due to the bond we have with conventional institutions and individuals, such as family, school, and peer group. When these relationships are strained or broken, people are free to engage in deviant acts that otherwise would be avoided. Crime occurs when the influence of official and informal sources of social control is weakened or absent.

L07 Distinguish among the three types of social process theories.

differential association theory
The view that criminal acts are related to a person's exposure to antisocial attitudes and values.

Web App 3.3
For more on intergenerational delinquency, read the article here: http://tinyurl.com/kp3wn6f.

social control theory
The view that most people do not violate the law because of their social bonds to family, peer group, school, and other institutions. If these bonds are weakened or absent, individuals are much more likely to commit crime.

Travis Hirschi's version of social control theory suggests that people whose bond to society is secure are unlikely to engage in criminal misconduct because they have a strong stake in society. Those who find their social bond weakened are much more likely to succumb to the temptations of criminal activity. After all, crime does have rewards, such as excitement, action, material goods, and pleasures. Hirschi does not give a definitive explanation of what causes a person's social bond to weaken, but there are probably two main sources: disrupted home life and poor school ability (leading to subsequent school failure and dislike of school).

Hirschi's theory is widely accepted, and there is a significant body of work that supports its key concepts. For example, research shows that both males and females who are detached from their parents and uninvolved in conventional activities are the ones most at risk for gang involvement and antisocial behavior.[162] Similarly, youths who are detached from the educational experience are at risk of turning to criminality; those who are committed to school are less likely to engage in delinquent acts.[163]

The most significant criticism of Hirschi's works is his contention that delinquents are detached loners whose bond to friends has been broken. It is commonly believed that delinquents are not "lone wolves" whose only personal relationships are exploitive; rather, their friendship patterns seem quite close to those of conventional youths.[164] Many join gangs and engage in group activities: they play sports, go to parties, and hang out with their peers. Some types of offenders, such as drug abusers, report having closer and more intimate relations with their peers than nonabusers.[165] Hirschi would counter that what appears to be a close friendship is really a relationship of convenience and that "birds of a feather flock together" only when it suits their criminal activities. Though co-offending is common, research shows that most juvenile offenses are committed by individuals acting alone and that group offending, when it does occur, is incidental rather than the norm.[166] Hirschi's version of social control theory is an enduring vision of the social processes that produce criminality.

social reaction (labeling) theory

The view that society produces criminals by stigmatizing certain individuals as deviants, a label that they come to accept as a personal identity.

SOCIAL REACTION THEORY   According to **social reaction (labeling) theory**, officially designating people as "troublemakers," and thus stigmatizing them with a permanent deviant label, leads them to criminality. People who commit undetected antisocial acts are called "secret deviants" or "primary deviants." Their illegal act has little influence or impact on their lifestyle or behavior. However, if another person commits the same act and his or her behavior is discovered by social control agents, the labeling process may be triggered. That person may be given a deviant label, such as "mentally ill" or "criminal." The deviant label transforms him or her into an outsider, shunned by the rest of society. In time, the stigmatized person may come to believe that the deviant label is valid and assume it as a personal identity. For example, the student placed in special education classes begins to view himself as "stupid" or "backward," the mental patient accepts society's view of her as "crazy," and the convicted criminal considers himself "dangerous" or "wicked."

Accompanying the deviant label are a variety of degrading social and physical restraints—handcuffs, trials, incarceration, bars, cells, and a criminal record—that leave an everlasting impression on the accused. These sanctions are designed to humiliate and are applied in what labeling experts call *degradation ceremonies*, in which the target is made to feel unworthy and despised.

Labels and sanctions work to define the whole person, meaning that a label evokes stereotypes that are used to forecast other aspects of the labeled person's character. A person labeled "mentally ill" is assumed to be dangerous, evil, cruel, or untrustworthy, even though he or she has exhibited none of these characteristics. Even among people who commit the same or similar crimes, those who are more harshly labeled or punished are more likely to repeat their criminal offenses than those who are spared harmful treatment and the resulting stigma.[167]

Faced with such condemnation, negatively labeled people may begin to adopt their new degraded identity. They may find no alternative but to seek others who are similarly stigmatized and form a deviant subculture. They are likely to make deviant friends and join gangs, associations that escalate their involvement in criminal activities.[168] Instead of deterring crime, labeling begins a deviance amplification process. If apprehended and subjected to even more severe negative labels, the offender may be transformed into a real deviant—one who views himself or herself as in direct opposition to conventional society. The deviant label may become a more comfortable and personally acceptable social status than any other. The individual whose original crime may have been relatively harmless is transformed by social action into a career deviant, a process referred to as *secondary deviance.* The entire labeling process is illustrated in Figure 3.2.

Labeling theorists also believe that the labeling process includes racial, gender, and economic discrimination. For example, judges may sympathize with white defendants and help them avoid criminal labels, especially if they seem to come from "good families," whereas minority youths are not afforded that luxury.[169] This may help explain racial and economic differences in the crime rate.

Critical Criminology

Critical criminology views the economic and political forces operating in society as the fundamental cause of criminality. The criminal law and criminal justice system are seen as vehicles for controlling the poor. The criminal justice system helps the powerful and rich impose their own morality and standards of good behavior on the entire society, while protecting their property and physical safety from the have-nots, even though the cost may be the legal rights of the lower class. Those in power control the content and direction of the law and the legal system. Crimes are defined in a way that meets the needs of the ruling classes. Thus, a poor person's theft of property worth five dollars can be punished much more severely than the misappropriation of millions by a large corporation. Those in the middle class are drawn into this pattern of control because they are led to believe that they, too, have a stake in maintaining the status quo and should support the views of the upper class; they are taught to fear the lower class.[170]

Critical criminologists often take a broad view of deviant behavior, and they most vigorously oppose racism, sexism, and genocide, rather than focusing on burglary, robbery, and rape.[171] They trace the history of criminal sanctions to show how those sanctions have been related to the needs of the wealthy. They attempt to show how police, courts, and correctional agencies have served as tools of the powerful members of society. Because of social and economic inequality, members of the lower class are forced to commit larceny and burglary, take part in robberies, and sell drugs as a means of social and economic survival. In some instances, the disenfranchised engage in rape, assault, and senseless homicides as a means of expressing their rage, frustration, and anger.

Initial criminal act
People commit crimes for a number of reasons.

Detection by the justice system
Arrest is influenced by racial, economic, and power relations.

Decision to label
Some are labeled "official" criminals by police and court authorities.

Creation of a new identity
Those labeled are known as troublemakers, criminals, and so on, and they are shunned by conventional society.

Acceptance of labels
Labeled people begin to see themselves as outsiders. Secondary deviance. Self-labeling.

Deviance amplification
Stigmatized offenders are locked into criminal careers.

FIGURE 3.2 **The Labeling Process**

Critical criminology
The view that crime results because the rich and powerful impose their own moral standards and economic interests on the rest of society.

 **Web App 3.4**

Visit the website of the American Society of Criminology's Critical Criminology section at http://critcrim.org/.

 L08 Explain what is meant by critical criminology.

State-Organized Crime

Critical theorists argue that mainstream criminologists often focus on the crimes of the poor and powerless, while ignoring the illegal acts of the rich and powerful.[172] They have identified **state-organized crime**—acts defined by law as criminal and committed by state officials, both elected and appointed, in pursuit of their jobs as government representatives. These antisocial behaviors arise from efforts either to maintain governmental power or to uphold the unfair advantages acquired by those who support the government.

state-organized crime
Criminal acts committed by state officials in pursuit of their jobs as government representatives.

State-organized crimes are manifested in a number of ways. Some individuals abuse their state authority or fail to exercise it when working with people and organizations in the private sector. These *state–corporate* crimes may occur when a state institution such as an environmental agency fails to enforce laws, resulting in the pollution of public waterways.[173] In an industrial society, some government officials, secretly on the payroll of large private corporations, do everything they can to protect the property rights of the wealthy, while opposing the real interests of the poor. They might even go to war to support the capitalist classes who covet the labor and natural resources of other nations.

State crimes may also involve violation of citizen trust through crimes such as soliciting bribes (usually money or some other economic benefit, such as a gift or service). Politicians, judges, police, and government regulators engage in corruption that damages public trust in the government. And unfortunately, when corruption is uncovered and the perpetrator brought to justice, it is difficult to determine whether a real criminal has been caught or a political opponent framed and punished.

To carry out state crimes, government agents may engage in a variety of illegal behaviors, ranging from listening in on telephone conversations to intercepting e-mails without proper approval in order to stifle dissent and monitor political opponents. In some rogue states, government agencies routinely deny citizens basic civil rights, holding them without trial and using "disappearances" and summary executions to rid themselves of political dissidents. Others may go as far as torturing opponents or employing death squads to eliminate any threat.[174]

Support for Critical Theory

A considerable body of research supports critical criminology. Criminologists routinely have found evidence that measures of social inequality, such as income level, deteriorated living conditions, and relative economic deprivation, are highly associated with crime rates, especially the felony murders that typically accompany robberies and burglaries.[175] The conclusion is that as people become economically marginalized, they will turn to violent crime for survival, producing an inevitable upswing in the number of street crimes and a corresponding spike in the murder rate.

Another area of critical research involves examining the criminal justice system to see whether it operates as an instrument of class oppression or as a fair, evenhanded social control agency. Research has found that jurisdictions with significant levels of economic disparity are also the most likely to have large numbers of people

SERGEI ILNITSKY/EPA /LANDOV

Ousted Ukrainian president Viktor Yanukovych, a pro-Russian leader who fled Ukraine for Russia in late February 2014 after three months of protests against his government, has been accused of corruption, human rights violations, and mass killings of protestors.

killed by police officers. Police may act more forcefully in areas where class conflict creates the perception that extreme forms of social control are needed to maintain order.[176] There is also evidence of racial discrimination. Police typically devote more resources to areas and neighborhoods that have large minority populations where there is fear that minorities are becoming more numerous and presenting a threat to the white majority.[177]

In one interesting study, Tammy Rinehart Kochel, David Wilson, and Stephen Mastrofski thoroughly reviewed the existing literature on police arrest practices, and found that minority suspects stopped by police are significantly more likely to be arrested than are white suspects. These findings may be used by critical criminologists as clear evidence of the racial bias they suspect is present in American policing.[178] Similarly, an analysis of national population trends and imprisonment rates shows that as the percentage of minority group members increases in a population, the imprisonment rate does likewise.[179]

Developmental Theories

Developmental theories seek to identify, describe, and understand the developmental factors that explain the onset and continuation of a criminal career. As a group, they do not ask the relatively simple question: Why do people commit crime? Instead, they focus on more complex issues: Why do some offenders persist in criminal careers, whereas others desist from or alter their criminal activity as they mature? Why do some people continually escalate their criminal involvement, whereas others turn their lives around? Do all criminals exhibit similar offending patterns, or are there different types of offenders and different paths to offending? Developmental theorists want to know not only why people enter a criminal way of life but also whether, once they do, they are able to alter the trajectory of their criminal involvement.

Criminal Careers

Rather than ask why people commit crime, developmental theories focus on the development and maintenance of criminal careers. Criminals start their journey at different times. Some are "precocious"—their criminal careers begin early and persist into adulthood—whereas others stay out of trouble in their early adolescence and do not violate the law until late in their teenage years.[180]

One important aspect of criminal career development is **early onset**: people who are antisocial during adolescence are the ones most likely to remain criminals throughout their life span.[181] The earlier the onset of criminality, the more frequent, varied, and sustained the criminal career.[182] Early rule breaking increases the probability of future rule breaking because it weakens inhibitions to crime and strengthens criminal motivation. In other words, once kids get a taste of antisocial behavior, they like it and want to continue down a deviant path.[183]

Early-onset criminals seem to get involved in such behaviors as truancy, cruelty to animals, lying, and theft; they also appear to be more violent than their less precocious peers.[184] In contrast, late starters are more likely to be involved in nonviolent crimes such as theft.[185] What causes some kids to begin offending at an early age? Among the suspected root causes are poor parental discipline and monitoring, inadequate emotional support, distant peer relationships, and psychological issues and problems.[186]

Why is early onset so important? Early delinquent behavior creates a downward spiral in a young person's life.[187] Thereafter, tension may begin to develop with parents and other family members, emotional bonds to conventional peers become weakened and frayed, and opportunities to pursue conventional activities such as sports dry up and wither away. Replacing them are closer attachment to

Developmental theories
A view of crime holding that as people travel through the life course, their experiences along the way influence their behavior patterns. Behavior changes at each stage of the human experience.

 LO9 Discuss the basics of developmental theory.

early onset
The beginning of antisocial behavior during early adolescence, after which criminal behavior is more likely to persist throughout the life span.

more deviant peers and involvement in a delinquent way of life.[188] Early starters are also the ones most likely to have troubled, disorganized lives. Not only are they more likely to commit crime as adults, but they are more likely to be "life failures"—experiencing high unemployment, living in substandard housing, and unable to maintain a stable romantic relationship.[189]

Developmental theories fall into three distinct groups: latent trait theory, life course theory, and trajectory theory.

Latent Trait Theory

Latent trait theories hold that human development is controlled by a master trait or **criminal propensity** present at birth or soon after. Some criminologists believe that this master trait remains stable and unchanging throughout a person's lifetime, whereas others suggest that it can be later altered or influenced by experience. In either event, as people travel through their life course this trait is always there, influencing decisions and directing their behavior. Because this master trait is enduring, the ebb and flow of criminal behavior are directed by the impact of external forces such as criminal opportunity and the reactions of others.[190] Suspected latent traits include defective intelligence, impulsive personality, and lack of attachment.[191]

GENERAL THEORY OF CRIME   The best-known latent trait theory is Michael Gottfredson and Travis Hirschi's General Theory of Crime.[192] In the general theory, Gottfredson and Hirschi argue that individual differences in the tendency to commit criminal acts can be found in a person's level of self-control. People with limited self-control tend to be impulsive, insensitive, physical (rather than mental), risk-taking, shortsighted, and nonverbal. They have a here-and-now orientation and refuse to work for distant goals. They lack diligence, tenacity, and persistence in a course of action. People lacking self-control tend to be adventuresome, active, physical, and self-centered. As they mature, they have unstable marriages, jobs, and friendships.

Criminal acts are attractive to such individuals because they provide easy and immediate gratification—or, as Gottfredson and Hirschi put it, "money without work, sex without courtship, revenge without court delays." Given the opportunity to commit crime, they will readily violate the law. Under the same set of circumstances, nonimpulsive people will refrain from antisocial behavior.

Criminal activity diminishes when the opportunity to commit crime is limited. People age out of crime because the opportunity to commit crimes diminishes with age. Teenagers simply have more opportunity to commit crimes than the elderly, regardless of their intelligence. Here the general theory integrates the concepts of latent traits and criminal opportunity: possessing a particular trait, plus having the opportunity to commit crime, results in the choice to commit crime.[193] Numerous tests have demonstrated that people who lack self-control are more likely to commit crime and that this association is independent of other factors, such as where they live and their social relationships.[194]

What causes people to have low self-control? Gottfredson and Hirschi believe that parents who refuse or are unable to monitor a child's behavior, to recognize deviant behavior when it occurs, and to punish that behavior will produce children who lack self-control. Children who are not attached to their parents, who are poorly supervised, and whose parents are criminal or deviant themselves are the most likely to develop poor self-control. Their belief is confirmed by research that suggests the root cause of poor self-control is inadequate child-rearing practices.[195]

Life Course Theory

In contrast to this view, **life course theories** view criminality as a dynamic process. They adopt a **state dependence** perspective, which means that behavior is influenced by a multitude of individual characteristics, traits, and social

---

latent trait theories
The view that human behavior is controlled by a master trait, present at birth or soon after, that influences and directs behavior.

criminal propensity
A natural inclination toward criminality, present at birth or soon after.

life course theories
The view that criminality is a dynamic process influenced by people's perceptions and experiences throughout their lives, which may change their behavior for the better or the worse.

state dependence
A process in which criminal behavior becomes embedded because antisocial behavior erodes social ties that encourage conformity and creates incentives to commit crime.

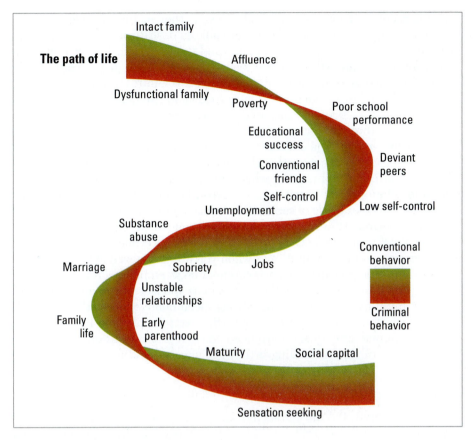

FIGURE 3.3 **Life Course Theory**

experiences, and that kids who manifest criminal behavior in childhood are more likely to become adult criminals because antisocial behavior erodes social ties and creates incentives to commit crime. As people travel through the life course, they are constantly bombarded by changing perceptions and experiences. As a result, their behavior may change direction, sometimes for the better and sometimes for the worse (see Figure 3.3).

Life course theorists dispute the existence of criminal propensity. Instead, they suggest that as people mature, the factors that influence their behavior also undergo change. At first, family relations may be most influential; in later adolescence, school and peer relations predominate; in adulthood, marital relations may be the most critical influence. Some antisocial youths who are in trouble throughout their adolescence may be able to find stable work and maintain intact marriages as adults. These life events help them desist from crime. In contrast, those who develop arrest records, get involved with the wrong crowd, and can find only menial jobs are at risk for criminal careers. Social forces that are critical at one stage of life may have little meaning or influence at another.

Life course theorists believe that social problems have a cumulative effect: the more risk factors a person suffers in childhood, the greater the likelihood that these will carry over into adulthood.[196] The psychic scars of childhood are hard to erase.[197]

AGE-GRADED THEORY Two of the leading life course theorists, criminologists Robert Sampson and John Laub, have formulated what they call *age-graded theory*.[198] According to Sampson and Laub, "turning points" in a criminal career are life events that enable people to "knife off" from a criminal career path into one of conventional and legitimate activities. As they mature, people who have had significant problems with the law are able to desist from crime if they can become attached to a spouse who supports and sustains them. They may encounter employers who are willing to give them a chance despite their record. People who cannot sustain secure marital relations or are failures in the labor market are less likely to desist from crime. Getting arrested can help sustain a criminal career because it reduces the chances of marriage, employment, and job stability, factors that are directly related to crime.

According to Sampson and Laub, these life events help people build **social capital**—positive relations with individuals and institutions that are life-sustaining. Building social capital, which includes acquiring personal connections and relationships, is critical if a person hopes to reach his or her life's objectives.[199] For example, a successful marriage creates social capital when it improves a person's stature, creates feelings of self-worth, and encourages people to give him a chance.[200] Getting a good job inhibits crime by creating a stake in conformity—why commit crimes when you are doing well at your job? The relationship is reciprocal: people who are chosen as employees return the favor by doing the best job possible; those chosen as spouses blossom into devoted partners. Building social capital and strong social bonds reduces the likelihood of long-term deviance. Research shows that even people who have long histories of criminal activity and have been convicted of serious offenses reduce the frequency of their offending if they get married and fall into a domestic lifestyle.[201]

> **social capital**
> Positive relations with individuals and institutions that foster self-worth and inhibit crime.

Trajectory Theory

Trajectory theory is the third branch of the developmental approach that combines elements of latent trait and life course theory. The basic premise is that there is more than one path to crime and more than one class of offender; there are different trajectories in a criminal career. According to this view, not all persistent offenders begin at an early age nor do they take the same path to crime. Some are precocious, beginning their offending careers early in adolescence and persisting into adulthood.[202] Others stay out of trouble and do not violate the law until their teenage years; they are "late bloomers."[203] Some offenders may peak at an early age and quickly desist, whereas others persist into adulthood. Some are high-rate offenders, whereas others offend at relatively low rates.[204] Some offenders are quite social and have a large peer group, while others are loners who make decisions on their own.[205] There may also be observed gender differences in criminal career trajectories.[206]

The trajectory view recognizes that people who commit violent crimes may be different from nonviolent property and drug offenders and maintain a unique set of personality traits and problem behaviors.[207] And even among violent offenders there may be distinct paths. Some are violent kids who eventually desist, while others are escalators whose severity of violence increases over time.[208]

ADOLESCENT-LIMITED AND LIFE-COURSE PERSISTENT OFFENDERS According to psychologist Terrie Moffitt, most young offenders follow one of two paths. **Adolescent-limited offenders** may be considered typical teenagers who get into minor scrapes and engage in what might be considered rebellious teenage behavior with their friends.[209] As they reach their mid-teens, adolescent-limited delinquents begin to mimic the antisocial behavior of more troubled teens, only to reduce the frequency of their offending as they mature to around age 18.[210]

The second path is the one taken by a small group of **life-course persisters** who begin their offending career at a very early age and continue to offend well into adulthood.[211] Moffitt finds that life-course persisters combine family

> **adolescent-limited offenders**
> Kids who get into minor scrapes as youths but whose misbehavior ends when they enter adulthood.
>
> **life-course persisters**
> Delinquents who begin their offending career at a very early age and continue to offend well into adulthood.

dysfunction with severe neurological problems that predispose them to antisocial behavior patterns. These afflictions can be the result of maternal drug abuse, poor nutrition, or exposure to toxic agents such as lead. It is not surprising then that life-course persisters display social and personal dysfunctions, including lower than average verbal ability, reasoning skills, learning ability, and school achievement.

Research shows that the persistence patterns predicted by Moffitt are valid and accurate.[212] Life-course persisters offend more frequently and engage in a greater variety of antisocial acts than other offenders; they also manifest significantly more mental health problems, including psychiatric pathologies, than adolescent-limited offenders.[213] Many have deviant friends who support their behavior choices.[214] The major views of crime causation are summarized in Concept Summary 3.3.

CONCEPT SUMMARY 3.3
Concepts and Theories of Criminology

Theory	Major Premise
Choice	People commit crime when they perceive that the benefits of law violation outweigh the threat and pain of punishment.
Biochemical	Crime, especially violence, is a function of diet, vitamin intake, hormonal imbalance, or food allergies.
Neurological	Criminals and delinquents often suffer brain impairment. Attention deficit hyperactivity disorder and minimum brain dysfunction are related to antisocial behavior.
Genetic	Delinquent traits and predispositions are inherited. The criminality of parents can predict the delinquency of children.
Psychodynamic	The development of personality early in childhood influences behavior for the rest of a person's life. Criminals have weak egos and damaged personalities. They lack attachment to others.
Social structure	The conflicts and problems of urban social life and communities control the crime rate. Crime is a product of transitional neighborhoods that manifest social disorganization and value conflict.
Strain	People who adopt the goals of society but lack the means to attain them seek alternatives, such as crime. Personal-level strain produces crime.
Social learning	People learn to commit crime from exposure to antisocial behaviors. Criminal behavior depends on the person's experiences with rewards for conventional behaviors and punishments for deviant ones. Being rewarded for deviance leads to crime.
Social control	A person's bond to society prevents him or her from violating social rules. If the bond weakens, the person is free to commit crime.
Self-control	People choose to commit crime when they lack self-control. People lacking self-control will seize criminal opportunities.
Critical	People commit crime when the law, controlled by the rich and powerful, defines their behavior as illegal. The immoral actions of the powerful go unpunished.
Developmental	Early in life, people begin relationships that determine their behavior through their life course. Life transitions control the probability of offending.

Theories of Victimization

For many years, criminological theory focused on the actions of the criminal offender. The role of the victim was virtually ignored. Then a number of scholars found that the victim is not a passive target in crime but someone whose behavior can influence his or her own fate. Hans Von Hentig portrayed the crime victim as someone who "shapes and molds the criminal."[215] The criminal may be a predator, but the victim may help the criminal by becoming a willing prey. Stephen Schafer extended this approach by focusing on the victim's responsibility in the "genesis of crime."[216] Schafer accused some victims of provoking or encouraging criminal behavior, a concept now referred to as **victim precipitation**. These early works helped focus attention on the role of the victim in the crime problem and led to the development of theories that try to explain why someone becomes a crime victim.

victim precipitation
The role of the victim in provoking or encouraging criminal behavior.

Victim Precipitation

The concept of victim precipitation was popularized by Marvin Wolfgang's 1958 study of criminal homicide. Wolfgang found that crime victims were often intimately involved in their demise and that as many as 25 percent of all homicides could be classified as victim-precipitated.[217]

There are two types of victim precipitation. *Active precipitation* occurs when victims act provocatively, use threats or fighting words, or even attack first.[218] For example, some experts have suggested that female rape victims contribute to their attacks by their manner of dress or by pursuing a relationship with the rapist.[219] Although this finding has been disputed, courts have continued to return not-guilty verdicts in rape cases if a victim's actions can in any way be construed as consenting to sexual intimacy.[220] A number of research efforts have found that both male and female victims score high on impulsivity scales, indicating that they have an impulsive personality that might render them abrasive and obnoxious—and thus might incite victimization.[221]

Passive precipitation occurs when the victim exhibits some personal characteristic that unintentionally either threatens or encourages the attacker. The crime may occur because of personal conflict. For example, a woman may become the target of intimate violence when she increases her job status and her success provokes jealousy in a spouse or partner.[222] Passive precipitation may also occur when the victim belongs to a group whose mere presence threatens the attacker's reputation, status, or economic well-being. For example, hate crime violence may be precipitated by immigrants arriving in the community and competing for jobs and housing.[223] Gender may play a role in the decision-making process: criminals may select female victims because they perceive them to be easier, less threatening targets.[224]

Lifestyle Theory

Some criminologists believe that people may become crime victims because their lifestyle increases their exposure to criminal offenders. Victimization risk is increased by such behaviors as associating with violent young men, going out in public places late at night, and living in an urban area. Research confirms that young women who engage in substance abuse and come into contact with men who are also substance abusers increase the likelihood that they will be sexual assault victims.[225]

Although we often think of criminals as victimizing others, people who engage in crime and gang activity actually have very high rates of victimization themselves.[226] Carrying a weapon is another surefire way to become a crime victim. Males who carry weapons are approximately three

times more likely to be victimized than those who go unarmed.[227] Kids who carry weapons to school are much more likely to become crime victims than those who avoid weapons. Carrying a weapon may embolden youths and encourage them to become involved in risk-taking behavior.[228]

One way for young males to avoid victimization: limit their male friends and hang out with girls! The greater the number of girls in their peer group, the lower their chances of victimization.[229] Those who have a history of engaging in serious delinquency, getting involved in gangs, carrying guns, and selling drugs have an increased chance of being shot and killed.[230]

Having a risky lifestyle increases victimization risk across the life course. College students who spend several nights each week partying and who take recreational drugs are much more likely to suffer violent crime than those who avoid such risky behavior.[231] As adults, those who commit crimes increase their chances of becoming the victims of homicide.[232]

Lifestyle theory suggests that a person can reduce her or his chances of victimization by reducing risk-taking behavior: by staying home at night, moving to a rural area, staying out of public places, earning more money, and getting married. Yet knowing the pitfalls, why do some people forgo safety and engage in a high-risk lifestyle? One reason may be that victims share personality traits commonly found in law violators—namely, impulsivity and low self-control. Perhaps their impetuous and reckless nature leads them to seek risky situations that put them in greater danger than they might have imagined.[233]

Routine Activities Theory

Routine activities theory holds that the incidence of criminal activity and victimization is related to the nature of normal, everyday patterns of human behavior. According to this view, predatory crime rates can be explained by three factors (see Figure 3.4): the supply of *motivated offenders* (such as large numbers of unemployed teenagers), *suitable targets* (goods that have value and can be easily transported, such as an iPad), and the absence of *capable guardians* (protections such as police and security forces or home security devices).[234]

The presence of these components increases the likelihood that a predatory crime will take place. For example, increasing the number of motivated offenders and placing them in close proximity to valuable goods will increase property victimizations. Even after-school programs, designed to reduce criminal activity, may produce higher crime rates because they lump together motivated offenders—teenage boys—with vulnerable victims—teenage boys.[235]

Similarly, the presence of valuable targets increases the likelihood of crime and victimization. As average family income increases because of an increase in the number of working mothers, and consequently the average family is able to afford more luxury goods such as laptop computers and iPhones, a comparable increase in the crime rate might be expected. Why? Because the number of suitable targets has expanded while the number of capable guardians left to protect the home has been reduced.[236] The absence of suitable targets has been shown to reduce the chances of victimization: crime rates go down during times of high unemployment because there is less to steal and more people are at home to guard their possessions.

Guardianship has also been found to be related to victimization. As people begin to buy more goods and services on the Internet, their chances of being victimized by fraudulent sellers and dealers increase; distance buying reduces the oversight of capable guardians.[237] Community crime rates have been found to decline as people begin to employ security devices, guard their homes, create neighborhood-level surveillance programs, and use other "target-hardening" methods.[238] Similarly, if victims fight back, their resistance can deter motivated

Routine activities theory
The view that crime is a product of three everyday factors: motivated offenders, suitable targets, and a lack of capable guardians.

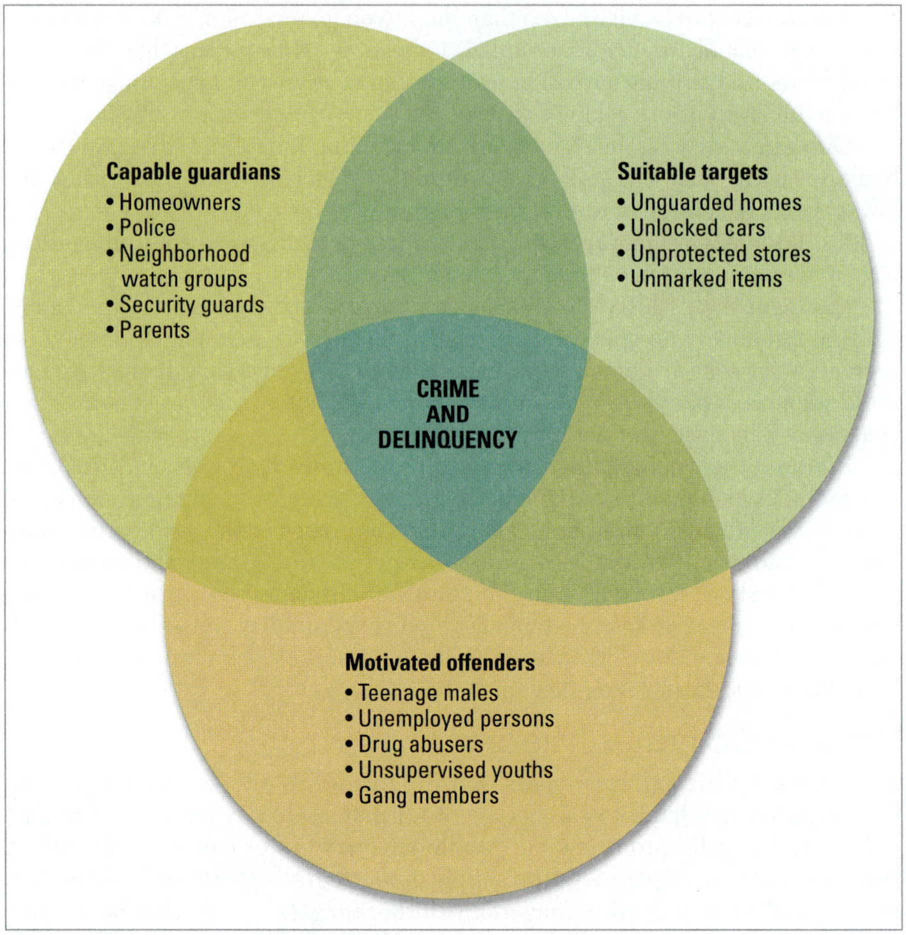

Capable guardians
- Homeowners
- Police
- Neighborhood watch groups
- Security guards
- Parents

Suitable targets
- Unguarded homes
- Unlocked cars
- Unprotected stores
- Unmarked items

CRIME AND DELINQUENCY

Motivated offenders
- Teenage males
- Unemployed persons
- Drug abusers
- Unsupervised youths
- Gang members

FIGURE 3.4   Routine Activities Theory

offenders: the effort needed to rob or attack an aggressive victim who is willing to defend his or her property may simply make the crime less attractive.[239] The routine activities approach is an important means of understanding crime and victimization patterns and predicting victim risk.

ETHICAL CHALLENGES in Criminal Justice

A WRITING ASSIGNMENT

There is an old saying that "people are a product of their environment," that nature is more important than nurture. If that is so, it would explain why there is so much crime in areas afflicted by poverty. Is it immoral and unethical to allow Americans to live in disorganized neighborhoods while we use tax money to send billions in foreign aid to such nations as Egypt, Pakistan, Israel, and Haiti, among many others? Write an essay addressing the association between poverty and crime and whether the government has a duty to conduct a "war on poverty" in our nation.

Recent research suggests that *nature*, not nurture, may go a long way toward explaining criminality. Research by J. C. Barnes and his colleagues (*Criminology* 49 (2011): 923–954) examined genetic and environmental influences on the criminal traits of 4,000 people and discovered a significant link between genes and criminality. If true, what are the ethical implications of such a finding? If genes are more important than the environment (or even if they enhance the relevance of certain environmental factors), what crime policies could or would flow from such thinking? Write an essay on the ethical issues surrounding the nature/nurture debate.

Summary

L01 **Ascertain why some experts believe that crime seems rational.**

- People choose to commit crime after weighing the potential benefits and consequences of their criminal act.
- People will commit a crime if they believe doing so will provide immediate benefits without much threat of long-term risks.
- If the rewards are great, the perceived risk small, and the excitement high, the likelihood of committing additional crimes increases.

L02 **Classify the strategies used to reduce crime by rational criminals.**

- General deterrence is designed to make potential criminals fear the consequences of crime.
- Specific deterrence strategies punish known criminals so severely that they will never be tempted to repeat their offenses.
- Situational crime prevention strategies are designed to convince would-be criminals to avoid specific targets.

L03 **Identify the various biological traits linked to crime.**

- Biochemical studies suggest that criminal offenders have abnormal levels of organic or inorganic substances that make them prone to antisocial behavior.
- The presence of brain abnormality causes irrational and destructive behaviors.
- Some criminal traits may be inherited.

L04 **Describe the various psychological views of the cause of crime.**

- According to the psychodynamic view, some people encounter problems during their early development that cause an imbalance in their personality.
- Behavior theory holds that human behavior is learned through interactions with others.
- Cognitive psychologists are concerned with the way people perceive and mentally represent the world in which they live.

L05 **Identify the personality traits linked to crime.**

- Psychologists have explored the link between personality and crime.
- The terms *psychopath* and *sociopath* are commonly used to describe people who have an antisocial personality.
- Some psychologists link IQ and criminality.

L06 **Compare and contrast the various social structure theories of crime.**

- Social disorganization theory suggests that the urban poor violate the law because they live in areas in which social control has broken down.
- Strain theories view crime as resulting from the anger people experience over their inability to achieve legitimate social and economic success.
- Cultural deviance theories hold that a unique crime-promoting value system develops in lower-class areas.

L07 **Distinguish among the three types of social process theories.**

- Social learning theory suggests that people learn the techniques and attitudes of crime from close relationships with criminal peers. Crime is a learned behavior.
- Social control theory maintains that everyone has the potential to become a criminal but that most people are controlled by their bonds to society. Crime occurs when the forces that bind people to society are weakened or broken.
- Social reaction (labeling) theory holds that people become criminals when significant members of society label them as such and they accept those labels as a personal identity.

L08 **Explain what is meant by critical criminology.**

- Critical theorists suggest that crime in any society is caused by class conflict. Laws are created by those in power to protect their rights and interests.
- One of the theory's most important premises is that the justice system is biased and designed to protect the wealthy.
- Critical criminology tries to explain how the workings of the capitalist system produce inequality and crime.

LO9 Discuss the basics of developmental theory.

- Life course theories argue that events that take place over the life course influence criminal choices.
- The cause of crime constantly changes as people mature. At first, the nuclear family influences behavior; during adolescence, the peer group dominates; in adulthood, marriage and career are critical.
- Latent trait theory suggests that a master trait guides people over the life course.

LO10 Identify the various theories of victimization.

- Victim precipitation theory looks at the victim's role in the criminal incident.
- Lifestyle theories suggest that victims put themselves in danger by engaging in high-risk activities, such as going out late at night, living in a high-crime area, and associating with high-risk peers.
- The routine activities theory maintains that a pool of motivated offenders exists and that these offenders will take advantage of suitable, unguarded targets.

Key Terms

criminologists, 86
deterrent effect, 88
general deterrence, 90
specific deterrence, 91
neurotransmitters, 95
oppositional defiant disorder (ODD), 98
social learning theory, 99
antisocial personality, 101
anomie, 103
social structure, 103

culture of poverty, 105
collective efficacy, 106
strain, 107
parental efficacy, 108
differential association theory, 109
social control theory, 109
social reaction (labeling) theory, 110
critical criminology, 111
state-organized crime, 112
developmental theories, 113
early onset, 113

latent trait theories, 114
criminal propensity, 114
life course theories, 114
state dependence, 114
social capital, 116
adolescent-limited offenders, 116
life-course persisters, 116
victim precipitation, 118
routine activities theory, 119

Critical Thinking Questions

1. What factors that are present in a disorganized urban area produce high crime rates?
2. If research could show that the tendency to commit crime is inherited, what should be done with the young children of violence-prone criminals?
3. How can psychological and biological theories be used to explain crime patterns and trends?
4. Are all criminals impulsive? How could impulsivity be used to explain white-collar and/or organized crime?
5. If crime is a routine activity, what steps should you take to avoid becoming a crime victim?

Notes

1. Ryan Lenz, "Neo-Nazi Killer Wade Page Was Member of Hammerskin Nation," http://www.splcenter.org/blog/2012/08/08/neo-nazi-killer-wade-page-was-member-of-hammerskin-nation/ (accessed May 2014).
2. Carlo Morselli and Marie-Noële Royer, "Criminal Mobility and Criminal Achievement," *Journal of Research in Crime and Delinquency* 45 (2008): 4–21.
3. Ross Matsueda, Derek Kreager, and David Huizinga, "Deterring Delinquents: A Rational Choice Model of Theft and Violence," *American Sociological Review* 71 (2006): 95–122.
4. Jeffrey Bouffard, "Predicting Differences in the Perceived Relevance of Crime's Costs and Benefits in a Test of Rational Choice Theory," *International Journal of Offender Therapy and Comparative Criminology* 51 (2007): 461–485.
5. Pierre Tremblay and Carlo Morselli, "Patterns in Criminal Achievement: Wilson and Abrahamse Revisited," *Criminology* 38 (2000): 633–660.
6. Andrew Buck, Simon Hakim, and George Rengert, "Burglar Alarms and the Choice Behavior of Burglars: A Suburban Phenomenon," *Journal of Criminal Justice* 21 (1993): 497–507;

Julia MacDonald and Robert Gifford, "Territorial Cues and Defensible Space Theory: The Burglar's Point of View," *Journal of Environmental Psychology* 9 (1989): 193–205; Paul Cromwell, James Olson, and D'Aunn Wester Avary, *Breaking and Entering: An Ethnographic Analysis of Burglary* (Newbury Park, CA: Sage, 1991), pp. 48–51.

7. Matthew Robinson, "Lifestyles, Routine Activities, and Residential Burglary Victimization," *Journal of Criminal Justice* 22 (1999): 27–52.

8. William Smith, Sharon Glave Frazee, and Elizabeth Davison, "Furthering the Integration of Routine Activity and Social Disorganization Theories: Small Units of Analysis and the Study of Street Robbery as a Diffusion Process," *Criminology* 38 (2000): 489–521.

9. Paul Bellair, "Informal Surveillance and Street Crime: A Complex Relationship," *Criminology* 38 (2000): 137–167.

10. John Gibbs and Peggy Shelly, "Life in the Fast Lane: A Retrospective View by Commercial Thieves," *Journal of Research in Crime and Delinquency* 19 (1982): 229–230.

11. Oscar Newman, *Defensible Space: Crime Prevention Through Urban Design* (New York: Macmillan, 1972).

12. Ronald Clarke, *Situational Crime Prevention* (Albany, NY: Harrow and Heston, 1992).

13. Anthony Braga, David Weisburd, Elin Waring, Lorraine Green Mazerolle, William Spelman, and Francis Gajewski, "Problem-Oriented Policing in Violent Crime Places: A Randomized Controlled Experiment," *Criminology* 37 (1999): 541–580.

14. James Q. Wilson, *Thinking About Crime* (New York: Basic Books, 1975); Ernest Van den Haag, *Punishing Criminals* (New York: Basic Books, 1975).

15. Herbert Packer, *The Limits of the Criminal Sanction* (Stanford, CA: Stanford University Press, 1968).

16. Steven Klepper and Daniel Nagin, "Tax Compliance and Perceptions of the Risks of Detection and Criminal Prosecution," *Law and Society Review* 23 (1989): 209–240.

17. Cheryl L. Maxson, Kristy N. Matsuda, and Karen Hennigan, "Deterrability Among Gang and Nongang Juvenile Offenders: Are Gang Members More (or Less) Deterrable than Other Juvenile Offenders?" *Crime and Delinquency* 57 (2011): 516–543.

18. Charis Kubrin, Steven Messner, Glenn Deane, Kelly McGeever, and Thomas D. Stucky, "Proactive Policing and Robbery Rates Across U.S. Cities," *Criminology* 48 (2010): 57–97.

19. Daniel Nagin and Greg Pogarsky, "An Experimental Investigation of Deterrence: Cheating, Self-Serving Bias, and Impulsivity," *Criminology* 41 (2003): 167–195.

20. Raymond Paternoster, "Decisions to Participate in and Desist from Four Types of Common Delinquency: Deterrence and the Rational Choice Perspective," *Law and Society Review* 23 (1989): 7–29.

21. Kenneth Land, Raymond Teske Jr., and Hui Zheng, "The Short-Term Effects of Executions on Homicides: Deterrence, Displacement, or Both?" *Criminology* 47 (2009): 1009–1043.

22. Shelley Keith Matthews and Robert Agnew, "Extending Deterrence Theory," *Journal of Research in Crime and Delinquency* 45 (2008): 91–118.

23. Dieter Dolling, Horst Entorf, Dieter Hermann, and Thomas Rupp, "Deterrence Effective? Results of a Meta-Analysis of Punishment," *European Journal on Criminal Policy and Research* 15 (2009): 201–224.

24. Alex Piquero and George Rengert, "Studying Deterrence with Active Residential Burglars," *Justice Quarterly* 16 (1999): 451–462.

25. Robert Nash Parker, "Bringing 'Booze' Back In: The Relationship Between Alcohol and Homicide," *Journal of Research in Crime and Delinquency* 32 (1993): 3–38.

26. Michel Foucault, *Discipline and Punishment* (New York: Random House, 1978).

27. Lauren E. Glaze and Erinn J. Herberman, *Correctional Populations in the United States*, 2012 (Washington, DC: Bureau of Justice Statistics), p. 2, Table 1.

28. Shamena Anwar and Thomas Loughran, "Testing a Bayesian Learning Theory of Deterrence Among Serious Juvenile Offenders," *Criminology* 49 (2011): 667–698.

29. Rudy Haapanen, Lee Britton, and Tim Croisdale, "Persistent Criminality and Career Length," *Crime and Delinquency* 53 (2007): 133–155.

30. Anwar and Loughran, "Testing a Bayesian Learning Theory of Deterrence Among Serious Juvenile Offenders."

31. Christina Dejong, "Survival Analysis and Specific Deterrence: Integrating Theoretical and Empirical Models of Recidivism," *Criminology* 35 (1997): 561–576.

32. Pamela Lattimore, Christy Visher, and Richard Linster, "Predicting Rearrest for Violence Among Serious Youthful Offenders," *Journal of Research in Crime and Delinquency* 32 (1995): 54–83.

33. Thomas Loughran, Edward Mulvey, Carol Schubert, Jeffrey Fagan, Alex Piquero, and Sandra Losoya, "Estimating a Dose-Response Relationship Between Length of Stay and Future Recidivism in Serious Juvenile Offenders," *Criminology* 47 (2009): 699–740.

34. Andrew Klein and Terri Tobin, "A Longitudinal Study of Arrested Batterers, 1995–2005: Career Criminals," *Violence Against Women* 14 (2008): 136–157.

35. Daniel Mears and William Bales, "Supermax Incarceration and Recidivism," *Criminology* 47 (2009): 1131–1166; David Lovell, L. Clark Johnson, and Kevin Cain, "Recidivism of Supermax Prisoners in Washington State," *Crime and Delinquency* 53 (2007): 633–656.

36. Klein and Tobin, "A Longitudinal Study of Arrested Batterers, 1995–2005."

37. Greg Pogarsky and Alex R. Piquero, "Can Punishment Encourage Offending? Investigating the 'Resetting' Effect," *Journal of Research in Crime and Delinquency* 40 (2003): 92–117.

38. Bruce Arrigo and Jennifer Bullock, "The Psychological Effects of Solitary Confinement on Prisoners in Supermax Units: Reviewing What We Know and Recommending What Should Change," *International Journal of Offender Therapy and Comparative Criminology* 52 (2008): 622–640.

39. Leana Bouffard and Nicole Leeper Piquero, "Defiance Theory and Life Course Explanations of Persistent Offending," *Crime and Delinquency* 56 (2010): 227–252; Lawrence Sherman, "Defiance, Deterrence, and Irrelevance: A Theory of the Criminal Sanction" *Journal of Research in Crime and Delinquency* 30 (1993): 445–473.

40. Michael Jacobson and Lynn Chancer, "From Left Realism to Mass Incarceration: The Need for Pragmatic Vision in Criminal Justice Policy," *Crime, Law and Social Change* 55 (2011): 187–196.

41. Cesare Lombroso, *Crime: Its Causes and Remedies* (Montclair, NJ: Patterson Smith, 1968).

42. Kevin Beaver, John Paul Wright, and Matt DeLisi, "Delinquent Peer Group Formation: Evidence of a Gene × Environment Correlation," *Journal of Genetic Psychology* 169 (2008): 227–244.

43. D. K. L. Cheuk and Virginia Wong, "Attention Deficit Hyperactivity Disorder and Blood Mercury Level: A Case-Control Study in Chinese Children," *Neuropediatrics* 37 (2006): 234–240; Jens Walkowiak, Jörg-A Wiener, Annemarie Fastabend, Birger Heinzow, Ursula Krämer, Eberhard Schmidt, Hans-J Steingürber, Sabine Wundram, and Gerhard Winneke, "Environmental Exposure to Polychlorinated Biphenyls and Quality of the Home Environment: Effects on Psychodevelopment in Early Childhood," *Lancet* 358 (2001): 92–93; Herbert Needleman, Christine McFarland, Roberta Ness, Stephen Fienberg, and Michael Tobin, "Bone Lead Levels in Adjudicated Delinquents: A Case Control Study," *Neurotoxicology and Teratology* 24 (2002): 711–717.

44. G. B. Ramirez, O. Pagulayan, H. Akagi, A. Francisco Rivera, L. V. Lee, A. Berroya, M. C. Vince Cruz, and D. Casintahan, "Tagum Study II: Follow-Up Study at Two Years of Age After Prenatal Exposure to Mercury," *Pediatrics* 111 (2003): 289–295.

45. S. Dengate and A. Ruben, "Controlled Trial of Cumulative Behavioural Effects of a Common Bread Preservative," *Journal of Pediatrics and Child Health* 38 (2002): 373–376.

46. Karen Lau, W. Graham McLean, Dominic P. Williams, and C. Vyvyan Howard, "Synergistic Interactions Between Commonly Used Food Additives in a Developmental Neurotoxicity Test," *Toxicological Science* 90 (2006): 178–187.

47. Wendy Oddy, Monique Robinson, Gina Ambrosini, Therese O'Sullivan, Nicholas de Klerk, Lawrence Beilin, Sven Silburn, Stephen Zubrick, and Fiona Stanley, "The Association Between Dietary Patterns and Mental Health in Early Adolescence," *Preventive Medicine* 49 (2009): 39–44.

48. Diana Fishbein, "Neuropsychological Function, Drug Abuse, and Violence: A Conceptual Framework," *Criminal Justice and Behavior* 27 (2000): 139–159.

49. Alan Booth and D. Wayne Osgood, "The Influence of Testosterone on Deviance in Adulthood," *Criminology* 31 (2006): 93–117.

50. Keith McBurnett et al., "Aggressive Symptoms and Salivary Cortisol in Clinic-Referred Boys with Conduct Disorder," *Annals of the New York Academy of Sciences* 794 (1996): 169–177.

51. Christy Miller Buchanan, Jacquelynne Eccles, and Jill Becker, "Are Adolescents the Victims of Raging Hormones? Evidence for Activational Effects of Hormones on Moods and Behavior at Adolescence," *Psychological Bulletin* 111 (1992): 62–107.

52. J. Arturo Silva, Gregory B. Leong, and Michelle M. Ferrari, "A Neuropsychiatric Developmental Model of Serial Homicidal Behavior," *Behavioral Sciences and the Law* 22 (2004): 787–799.

53. Yaling Yang, Adrian Raine, Todd Lencz, Susan Bihrle, Lori LaCasse, and Patrick Colletti, "Prefrontal White Matter in Pathological Liars," *British Journal of Psychiatry* 187 (2005): 320–325.

54. James Ogilvie, Anna Stewart, Raymond Chan, and David Shum, "Neuropsychological Measures of Executive Function and Antisocial Behavior: A Meta-Analysis," *Criminology* 49 (2011): 1063–1107.

55. Alice Jones, Kristin Laurens, Catherine Herba, Gareth Barker, and Essi Viding, "Amygdala Hypoactivity to Fearful Faces in Boys with Conduct Problems and Callous-Unemotional Traits," *American Journal of Psychiatry* 166 (2009): 95–102.

56. Jean Seguin, Robert Pihl, Philip Harden, Richard Tremblay, and Bernard Boulerice, "Cognitive and Neuropsychological Characteristics of Physically Aggressive Boys," *Journal of Abnormal Psychology* 104 (1995): 614–624; Deborah Denno, "Gender, Crime and the Criminal Law Defenses," *Journal of Criminal Law and Criminology* 85 (1994): 80–180.

57. Society for Neuroscience News Release, "Studies Identify Brain Areas and Chemicals Involved in Aggression; May Speed Development of Better Treatment," November 5, 2007, http://www.sfn.org/Press-Room/News-Release-Archives/2007/studies-identify-brain (accessed May 2014); Society for Neuroscience News Release, "New Research Sheds Light on Brain Differences in Adolescents, Understanding Their Impulsive Risk-Taking Behavior," November 6, 2007, http://www.sfn.org/Press-Room/News-Release-Archives/2007/new-research-sheds-light-on-brain-differences (accessedMay 2014).

58. Susan Young, Andrew Smolen, Robin Corley, Kenneth Krauter, John DeFries, Thomas Crowley, and John Hewitt, "Dopamine Transporter Polymorphism Associated with Externalizing Behavior Problems in Children," *American Journal of Medical Genetics* 114 (2002): 144–149.

59. Matti Virkkunen, David Goldman, and Markku Linnoila, "Serotonin in Alcoholic Violent Offenders," in *The Ciba Foundation Symposium: Genetics of Criminal and Antisocial Behavior* (Chichester, England: Wiley, 1995).

60. Rolf Loeber and Dale Hay, "Key Issues in the Development of Aggression and Violence from Childhood to Early Adulthood," *Annual Review of Psychology* 48 (1997): 371–410.

61. D. R. Blachman and S. P. Hinshaw, "Patterns of Friendship Among Girls with and without Attention-Deficit/Hyperactivity Disorder," *Journal of Abnormal Child Psychology* 30 (2002): 625–640.

62. Terrie Moffitt and Phil Silva, "Self-Reported Delinquency, Neuropsychological Deficit, and History of Attention Deficit Disorder," *Journal of Abnormal Child Psychology* 16 (1988): 553–569.

63. Anita Thapar, Kate Langley, Tom Fowler, Frances Rice, Darko Turic, Naureen Whittinger, John Aggleton, Marianne Van den Bree, Michael Owen, and Michael O'Donovan, "Catechol O-methyltransferase Gene Variant and Birth Weight Predict Early-Onset Antisocial Behavior in Children with Attention-Deficit/Hyperactivity Disorder," *Archives of General Psychiatry* 62 (2005): 1275–1278.

64. Ronald L. Simons, Man Kit Lei, Eric A. Stewart, Steven R. H. Beach, Gene H. Brody, Robert A. Philibert, and Frederick X. Gibbons, "Social Adversity, Genetic Variation, Street Code, and Aggression: A Genetically Informed Model of Violent Behavior," *Youth Violence and Juvenile Justice* 10 (2012): 3–24.

65. Kevin Beaver, John Paul Wright, and Matt DeLisi, "Delinquent Peer Group Formation: Evidence of a Gene X Environment Correlation," *Journal of Genetic Psychology* 169 (2008): 227–244.

66. Kevin M. Beaver, Chris L. Gibson, Michael G. Turner, Matt DeLisi, Michael G. Vaughn, and Ashleigh Holand, "Stability of Delinquent Peer Associations: A Biosocial Test of Warr's Sticky-Friends Hypothesis," *Crime and Delinquency* 57 (2011): 907–927.

67. Kevin M. Beaver, "The Effects of Genetics, the Environment, and Low Self-Control on Perceived Maternal and Paternal Socialization: Results from a Longitudinal Sample of Twins," *Journal of Quantitative Criminology* 27 (2011): 85–105.

68. See S. A. Mednick and Karl O. Christiansen, eds., *Biosocial Bases of Criminal Behavior* (New York: Gardner, 1977).

69. David Rowe and D. Wayne Osgood, "Heredity and Sociological Theories of Delinquency: A Reconsideration," *American Sociological Review* 49 (1984): 526–540.

70. John Paul Wright, Rebecca Schnupp, Kevin M. Beaver, Matt DeLisi, and Michael Vaughn, "Genes, Maternal Negativity, and Self-Control: Evidence of a Gene × Environment Interaction," *Youth Violence and Juvenile Justice* 10 (2012): 245–260.

71. Nancy L. Segal, *Born Together—Reared Apart* (Cambridge, MA: Harvard University Press, 2012).

72. For an analysis of Sigmund Freud, see Spencer Rathus, *Psychology* (New York: Holt, Rinehart, and Winston, 1990), pp. 412–420.

73. August Aichorn, *Wayward Youth* (New York: Viking, 1965).

74. Niranjan Karnik, Marie Soller, Allison Redlich, Melissa Silverman, Helena Kraemer, Rudy Haapanen, and Hans Steiner, "Prevalence of and Gender Differences in Psychiatric Disorders Among Juvenile Delinquents Incarcerated for Nine Months," *Psychiatric Services* 60 (2009): 838–841.

75. David Vinkers, Edwin de Beurs, and Marko Barendregt, "Psychiatric Disorders and Repeat Offending," *American Journal of Psychiatry* 166 (2009): 489.

76. Ellen Kjelsberg, "Gender and Disorder Specific Criminal Career Profiles in Former Adolescent Psychiatric In-Patients," *Journal of Youth and Adolescence* 33 (2004): 261–270.

77. Richard Rowe, Julie Messer, Robert Goodman, Robert Meltzer, and Howard Meltzer, "Conduct Disorder and Oppositional Defiant Disorder in a National Sample: Developmental

Epidemiology," *Journal of Child Psychology and Psychiatry and Allied Disciplines* 45 (2004): 609–621.

78. Amy Byrd, Rolf Loeber, and Dustin Pardini, "Understanding Desisting and Persisting Forms of Delinquency: The Unique Contributions of Disruptive Behavior Disorders and Interpersonal Callousness," *Journal of Child Psychology and Psychiatry* 53 (2012): 371–380.

79. Minna Ritakallio, Riittakerttu Kaltiala-Heino, Janne Kivivuori, Tiina Luukkaala, and Matti Rimpelä, "Delinquency and the Profile of Offences Among Depressed and Non-depressed Adolescents," *Criminal Behaviour and Mental Health* 16 (2006): 100–110.

80. Grégoire Zimmermann, "Delinquency in Male Adolescents: The Role of Alexithymia and Family Structure," *Journal of Adolescence* 29 (2006): 321–332.

81. Courtenay Sellers, Christopher Sullivan, Bonita Veysey, and Jon Shane, "Responding to Persons with Mental Illnesses: Police Perspectives on Specialized and Traditional Practices," *Behavioral Sciences and the Law* 23 (2005): 647–657.

82. Paul Hirschfield, Tina Maschi, Helene Raskin White, Leah Goldman Traub, and Rolf Loeber, "Mental Health and Juvenile Arrests: Criminality, Criminalization, or Compassion?" *Criminology* 44 (2006): 593–630.

83. This discussion is based on three works by Albert Bandura: *Aggression: A Social Learning Analysis* (Englewood Cliffs, NJ: Prentice Hall, 1973); *Social Learning Theory* (Englewood Cliffs, NJ: Prentice Hall, 1977); and "The Social Learning Perspective: Mechanisms of Aggression," in *The Psychology of Crime and Criminal Justice*, ed. H. Toch (New York: Holt, Rinehart, and Winston, 1979), pp. 198–226.

84. Mark Warr and Mark Stafford, "The Influence of Delinquent Peers: What They Think or What They Do?" *Criminology* 29 (1991): 851–866.

85. J. E. Lockman, "Self and Peer Perception and Attributional Biases of Aggressive and Nonaggressive Boys in Dyadic Interactions," *Journal of Consulting and Clinical Psychology* 55 (1987): 404–410.

86. Jean Piaget, *The Moral Judgement of the Child* (London: Kegan Paul, 1932).

87. Lawrence Kohlberg et al., *The Just Community Approach in Corrections: A Manual* (Niantic, CT: Connecticut Department of Corrections, 1973).

88. Walter Mischel, *Introduction to Personality*, 4th ed. (New York: Holt, Rinehart, and Winston, 1986), p. 1.

89. Essi Viding, James Blair, Terrie Moffitt, and Robert Plomin, "Evidence for Substantial Genetic Risk for Psychopathy in 7-Year-Olds," *Journal of Child Psychology and Psychiatry* 46 (2005): 592–597.

90. American Psychiatric Association, *Diagnostic and Statistical Manual of Mental Disorders*, 4th ed. (Washington, DC: American Psychiatric Association, 1994).

91. Albert Rabin, "The Antisocial Personality: Psychopathy and Sociopathy," in *The Psychology of Crime and Criminal Justice*, ed. H. Toch (New York: Holt, Rinehart, and Winston, 1979), pp. 236–251.

92. James Blair, Derek Mitchell, and Karina Blair, *The Psychopath: Emotion and the Brain* (New York: Blackwell Publishing, 2005).

93. Deborah Denno, "Sociological and Human Developmental Explanations of Crime: Conflict or Consensus?" *Criminology* 23 (1985): 711–741; Christine Ward and Richard McFall, "Further Validation of the Problem Inventory for Adolescent Girls: Comparing Caucasian and Black Delinquents and Nondelinquents," *Journal of Consulting and Clinical Psychology* 54 (1986): 732–733; L. Hubble and M. Groff, "Magnitude and Direction of WISC-R Verbal Performance IQ Discrepancies Among Adjudicated Male Delinquents," *Journal of Youth and Adolescence* 10 (1981): 179–183.

94. Peter R. Giancola and Amos Zeichner, "Intellectual Ability and Aggressive Behavior in Nonclinical-Nonforensic Males," *Journal of Psychopathology and Behavioral Assessment* 16 (1994): 20–32.

95. Donald Lynam, Terrie Moffitt, and Magda Stouthamer-Loeber, "Explaining the Relation Between IQ and Delinquency: Class, Race, Test Motivation, School Failure, or Self-Control?" *Journal of Abnormal Psychology* 102 (1993): 187–196; Alex Piquero, "Frequency, Specialization, and Violence in Offending Careers," *Journal of Research in Crime and Delinquency* 37 (2000): 392–418.

96. Murray Simpson, M. K. Simpson, and J. Hogg, "Patterns of Offending Among People with Intellectual Disability: A Systematic Review, Part I: Methodology and Prevalence Data," *Journal of Intellectual Disability Research* 45 (2001): 384–396.

97. Ibid.

98. Terance Miethe and Robert Meier, *Crime and Its Social Context: Toward an Integrated Theory of Offenders, Victims, and Situations* (Albany, NY: State University of New York Press, 1994).

99. Émile Durkheim, *The Division of Labor in Society* (New York: Free Press, 1964); Émile Durkheim, *Rules of the Sociological Method*, trans. S. A. Solvay and J. H. Mueller, ed. G. Catlin (New York: Free Press, 1966).

100. William Alex Pridemore, "A Methodological Addition to the Cross-National Empirical Literature on Social Structure and Homicide: A First Test of the Poverty-Homicide Thesis," *Criminology* 46 (2008): 133–154; John Hipp, "Income Inequality, Race, and Place: Does the Distribution of Race and Class Within Neighborhoods Affect Crime Rates?" *Criminology* 45 (2007): 665–697.

101. Robert Gebeloff and Shaila Dewan, "Measuring the Top 1% by Wealth, Not Income," *New York Times*, Jan 17, 2012, http://economix.blogs.nytimes.com/2012/01/17/measuring-the-top-1-by-wealth-not-income/ (accessed May 2014).

102. Capgemini and RBC Wealth Management, *World Wealth Report, 2013*, http://www.capgemini.com/resource-file-access/resource/pdf/wwr_2013_0.pdf (accessed May 2014).

103. William Spelman, "Abandoned Buildings: Magnets for Crime," *Journal of Criminal Justice* 21 (1993): 481–495.

104. Jeffrey Fagan and Garth Davies, "The Natural History of Neighborhood Violence," *Journal of Contemporary Criminal Justice* 20 (2004): 127–147.

105. Justin Patchin, Beth Huebner, John McCluskey, Sean Varano, and Timothy Bynum, "Exposure to Community Violence and Childhood Delinquency," *Crime and Delinquency* 2006 (52): 307–332.

106. Carter Hay, Edward Fortson, Dusten Hollist, Irshad Altheimer, and Lonnie Schaible, "Compounded Risk: The Implications for Delinquency of Coming from a Poor Family That Lives in a Poor Community," *Journal of Youth and Adolescence* 36 (2007): 593–605.

107. Maria Velez, Lauren Krivo, and Ruth Peterson, "Structural Inequality and Homicide: An Assessment of the Black–White Gap in Killings," *Criminology* 41 (2003): 645–672.

108. Bureau of Labor Statistics, *Labor Force Statistics from the Current Population Survey*, http://www.bls.gov/cps/demographics.htm#race (accessed May 2014).

109. James Ainsworth-Darnell and Douglas Downey, "Assessing the Oppositional Culture Explanation for Racial/Ethnic Differences in School Performances," *American Sociological Review* 63 (1998): 536–553.

110. Michael Leiber and Joseph Johnson, "Being Young and Black: What Are Their Effects on Juvenile Justice Decision Making?" *Crime and Delinquency* 54 (2008): 560–581.

111. Pew Research Center, *Incarceration Gap Widens Between Whites and Blacks*, http://www.pewresearch.org/fact-tank/2013/09/06/incarceration-gap-between-whites-and-blacks-widens (accessed May 2014).

112. Oscar Lewis, "The Culture of Poverty," *Scientific American* 215 (1966): 19–25.

113. William Julius Wilson, *The Truly Disadvantaged* (Chicago: University of Chicago Press, 1987).

114. David Bjerk, "Measuring the Relationship Between Youth Criminal Participation and Household Economic Resources," *Journal of Quantitative Criminology* 23 (2007): 23–39.

115. Hilary Byrnes, Chen Meng-Jinn, Brenda Miller, and Eugene Maguin, "The Relative Importance of Mothers' and Youths' Neighborhood Perceptions for Youth Alcohol Use and Delinquency," *Journal of Youth and Adolescence* 36 (2007): 649–659.

116. Paul Eberts and Kent P. Sehwirian, "Metropolitan Crime Rates and Relative Deprivation," *Criminology* 5 (1968): 43–52.

117. Jackson Goodnight, Benjamin Lahey, Carol Van Hulle, Joseph L. Rodgers, Paul Rathouz, Irwin Waldman, and Brian D'Onofrio, "A Quasi-experimental Analysis of the Influence of Neighborhood Disadvantage on Child and Adolescent Conduct Problems," *Journal of Abnormal Psychology* 121 (2012): 95–108.

118. John Hipp and Daniel Yates, "Ghettos, Thresholds, and Crime: Does Concentrated Poverty Really Have an Accelerating Increasing Effect on Crime?" *Criminology* 49 (2011): 955–990.

119. Paul Stretesky, Amie Schuck, and Michael Hogan, "Space Matters: An Analysis of Poverty, Poverty Clustering, and Violent Crime," *Justice Quarterly* 21 (2004): 817–841.

120. Gregory Squires and Charis Kubrin, "Privileged Places: Race, Uneven Development and the Geography of Opportunity in Urban America," *Urban Studies* 42 (2005): 47–68.

121. Charis E. Kubrin, "Structural Covariates of Homicide Rates: Does Type of Homicide Matter?" *Journal of Research in Crime and Delinquency* 40 (2003): 139–170.

122. Allen Liska and Paul Bellair, "Violent-Crime Rates and Racial Composition: Convergence over Time," *American Journal of Sociology* 101 (1995): 578–610.

123. Patricia McCall and Karen Parker, "A Dynamic Model of Racial Competition, Racial Inequality, and Interracial Violence," *Sociological Inquiry* 75 (2005): 273–294.

124. Steven Barkan and Steven Cohn, "Why Whites Favor Spending More Money to Fight Crime: The Role of Racial Prejudice," *Social Problems* 52 (2005): 300–314.

125. Jeffrey Michael Cancino, "The Utility of Social Capital and Collective Efficacy: Social Control Policy in Nonmetropolitan Settings," *Criminal Justice Policy Review* 16 (2005): 287–318; Chris Gibson, Jihong Zhao, Nicholas Lovrich, and Michael Gaffney, "Social Integration, Individual Perceptions of Collective Efficacy, and Fear of Crime in Three Cities," *Justice Quarterly* 19 (2002): 537–564; Felton Earls, *Linking Community Factors and Individual Development* (Washington, DC: National Institute of Justice, 1998).

126. Robert J. Sampson and Stephen W. Raudenbush, *Disorder in Urban Neighborhoods: Does It Lead to Crime?* (Washington, DC: National Institute of Justice, 2001).

127. Andrea Altschuler, Carol Somkin, and Nancy Adler, "Local Services and Amenities, Neighborhood Social Capital, and Health," *Social Science and Medicine* 59 (2004): 1219–1230.

128. David Maimon and Christopher R. Browning, "Unstructured Socializing, Collective Efficacy, and Violent Behavior Among Urban Youth," *Criminology* 48 (2010): 443–474.

129. Darrell Steffensmeier and Dana Haynie, "Gender, Structural Disadvantage, and Urban Crime," *Criminology* 38 (2000): 403–438.

130. Karen Parker and Matthew Pruitt, "Poverty, Poverty Concentration, and Homicide," *Social Science Quarterly* 81 (2000): 555–582.

131. Ruth Peterson, Lauren Krivo, and Mark Harris, "Disadvantage and Neighborhood Violent Crime: Do Local Institutions Matter?" *Journal of Research in Crime and Delinquency* 37 (2000): 31–63.

132. Ronald L. Simons and Callie Harbin Burt, "Learning to Be Bad: Adverse Social Conditions, Social Schemas, and Crime," *Criminology* 49 (2011): 553–598.

133. David Kirk and Andrew Papachristos, "Cultural Mechanisms and the Persistence of Neighborhood Violence," *American Journal of Sociology* 116 (2011): 1190–1233.

134. Charis Kubrin and Ronald Weitzer, "Retaliatory Homicide: Concentrated Disadvantage and Neighborhood Culture," *Social Problems* 50 (2003): 157–181.

135. Hipp, "Income Inequality, Race, and Place."

136. Robert Merton, "Social Structure and Anomie," *American Sociological Review* 3 (1938): 672–682.

137. Robert Agnew, "Foundation for a General Strain Theory of Crime and Delinquency," *Criminology* 30 (1992): 47–87; Robert Agnew, "Stability and Change in Crime over the Life Course: A Strain Theory Explanation," in *Advances in Criminological Theory*, Vol. 7, *Developmental Theories of Crime and Delinquency*, ed. Terence Thornberry (New Brunswick, NJ: Transaction, 1994).

138. Robert Agnew, Timothy Brezina, John Paul Wright, and Francis T. Cullen, "Strain, Personality Traits, and Delinquency: Extending General Strain Theory," *Criminology* 40 (2002): 43–71.

139. Lee Ann Slocum, Sally Simpson, and Douglas Smith, "Strained Lives and Crime: Examining Intra-Individual Variation in Strain and Offending in a Sample of Incarcerated Women," *Criminology* 43 (2005): 1067–1110.

140. Wan-Ning Bao, Ain Haas, and Yijun Pi, "Life Strain, Coping, and Delinquency in the People's Republic of China," *International Journal of Offender Therapy and Comparative Criminology* 51 (2007): 9–24.

141. Charles Tittle, Wayne Villemez, and Douglas Smith, "The Myth of Social Class and Criminality: An Empirical Assessment of the Evidence," *American Sociological Review* 43 (1978): 643–656.

142. Eric Stewart, Ronald Simons, and Rand Conger, "Assessing Neighborhood and Social Psychological Influences on Childhood Violence in an African American Sample," *Criminology* 40 (2002): 801–830.

143. Robert Apel and Catherine Kaukinen, "On the Relationship Between Family Structure and Antisocial Behavior: Parental Cohabitation and Blended Households," *Criminology* 46 (2008): 35–70.

144. Todd Herrenkohl, Rick Kosterman, David Hawkins, and Alex Mason, "Effects of Growth in Family Conflict in Adolescence on Adult Depressive Symptoms: Mediating and Moderating Effects of Stress and School Bonding, *Journal of Adolescent Health* 44 (2009): 146–152.

145. John Paul Wright and Francis Cullen, "Parental Efficacy and Delinquent Behavior: Do Control and Support Matter?" *Criminology* 39 (2001): 677–706.

146. Carter Hay, "Parenting, Self-Control, and Delinquency: A Test of Self-Control Theory," *Criminology* 39 (2001): 707–736.

147. Lyle Shannon, *Assessing the Relationship of Adult Criminal Careers to Juvenile Careers: A Summary* (Washington, DC: U.S. Government Printing Office, 1982); Donald J. West and David P. Farrington, *The Delinquent Way of Life* (London: Heineman, 1977); Marvin Wolfgang, Robert Figlio, and Thorsten Sellin, *Delinquency in a Birth Cohort* (Chicago: University of Chicago Press, 1972).

148. Gary Sweeten, Shawn D. Bushway, and Raymond Paternoster, "Does Dropping Out of School Mean Dropping into Delinquency?" *Criminology* 47 (2009): 47–91.

149. John Paul Wright and Francis Cullen, "Employment, Peers, and Life-Course Transitions," *Justice Quarterly* 21 (2004): 183–205.

150. Delbert Elliott, David Huizinga, and Suzanne Ageton, *Explaining Delinquency and Drug Use* (Beverly Hills, CA: Sage, 1985); Helene Raskin White, Robert Padina, and Randy La-Grange, "Longitudinal Predictors of Serious Substance Use and Delinquency," *Criminology* 6 (1987): 715–740.

151. Sylvie Mrug, Betsy Hoza, and William Bukowski, "Choosing or Being Chosen by Aggressive-Disruptive Peers: Do They Contribute to Children's Externalizing and Internalizing Problems?" *Journal of Abnormal Child Psychology* 32 (2004): 53–66; Terence Thornberry and Marvin Krohn, "Peers, Drug Use and Delinquency," in *Handbook of Antisocial Behavior*, ed. David Stoff, James Breiling, and Jack Maser (New York: Wiley, 1997), pp. 218–233.

152. Mark Warr, "Age, Peers, and Delinquency," *Criminology* 31 (1993): 17–40.

153. Denise Kandel and Mark Davies, "Friendship Networks, Intimacy, and Illicit Drug Use in Young Adulthood: A Comparison of Two Competing Theories," *Criminology* 29 (1991): 441–467.

154. Travis C. Pratt, Francis T. Cullen, Christine S. Sellers, L. Thomas Winfree Jr., Tamara D. Madensen, Leah E. Daigle, Noelle E. Fearn, and Jacinta M. Gau, "The Empirical Status of Social Learning Theory: A Meta-Analysis," *Justice Quarterly* 27 (2010): 765–802.

155. Edwin Sutherland and Donald Cressey, *Criminology* (Philadelphia: J. B. Lippincott, 1970), pp. 71–91.

156. Carlo Morselli, Pierre Tremblay, and Bill McCarthy, "Mentors and Criminal Achievement," *Criminology* 44 (2006): 17–43.

157. Robert Lonardo, Peggy Giordano, Monica Longmore, and Wendy Manning, "Parents, Friends, and Romantic Partners: Enmeshment in Deviant Networks and Adolescent Delinquency Involvement," *Journal of Youth and Adolescence* 38 (2009): 367–383.

158. Andy Hochstetler, Heith Copes, and Matt DeLisi, "Differential Association in Group and Solo Offending," *Journal of Criminal Justice* 30 (2002): 559–566.

159. Wesley Younts, "Status, Endorsement and the Legitimacy of Deviance," *Social Forces* 87 (2008): 561–590.

160. Terence Thornberry, Adrienne Freeman-Gallant, Alan Lizotte, Marvin Krohn, and Carolyn Smith, "Linked Lives: The Intergenerational Transmission of Antisocial Behavior," *Journal of Abnormal Child Psychology* 31 (2003): 171–184.

161. Terence P. Thornberry, "The Apple Doesn't Fall Far from the Tree (or Does It?): Intergenerational Patterns of Antisocial Behavior—The American Society of Criminology 2008 Sutherland Address," *Criminology* 47 (2009): 297–325; Thornberry et al., "Linked Lives: The Intergenerational Transmission of Antisocial Behavior."

162. Carl Maas, Charles Fleming, Todd Herrenkohl, and Richard Catalano, "Childhood Predictors of Teen Dating Violence Victimization," *Violence and Victims* 25 (2010): 131–149; Kerryn Bell, "Gender and Gangs: A Quantitative Comparison," *Crime and Delinquency* 55 (2009): 363–387; Tiffiney Barfield-Cottledge, "The Triangulation Effects of Family Structure and Attachment on Adolescent Substance Use" *Crime and Delinquency*, published online November 8, 2011; Sonia Cota-Robles and Wendy Gamble, "Parent-Adolescent Processes and Reduced Risk for Delinquency: The Effect of Gender for Mexican American Adolescents," *Youth and Society* 37 (2006): 375–392.

163. Allison Ann Payne, "A Multilevel Analysis of the Relationships Among Communal School Organization, Student Bonding, and Delinquency," *Journal of Research in Crime and Delinquency* 45 (2008): 429–455; Norman White and Rolf Loeber, "Bullying and Special Education as Predictors of Serious Delinquency," *Journal of Research in Crime and Delinquency* 45 (2008): 380–397.

164. Peggy Giordano, Stephen Cernkovich, and M. D. Pugh, "Friendships and Delinquency," *American Journal of Sociology* 91 (1986): 1170–1202.

165. Denise Kandel and Mark Davies, "Friendship Networks, Intimacy, and Illicit Drug Use in Young Adulthood: A Comparison of Two Competing Theories," *Criminology* 29 (1991): 441–467.

166. Lisa Stolzenberg and Stewart D'Alessio, "Co-Offending and the Age–Crime Curve," *Journal of Research in Crime and Delinquency* 45 (2008): 65–86.

167. Ted Chiricos, Kelle Barrick, William Bales, and Stephanie Bontrager, "The Labeling of Convicted Felons and Its Consequences for Recidivism," *Criminology* 45 (2007): 547–581.

168. Jón Gunnar Bernburg, Marvin Krohn, and Craig Rivera, "Official Labeling, Criminal Embeddedness, and Subsequent Delinquency: A Longitudinal Test of Labeling Theory," *Journal of Research in Crime and Delinquency* 43 (2006): 67–88.

169. Christina DeJong and Kenneth Jackson, "Putting Race into Context: Race, Juvenile Justice Processing, and Urbanization," *Justice Quarterly* 15 (1998): 487–504.

170. W. Byron Groves and Robert Sampson, "Critical Theory and Criminology," *Social Problems* 33 (1986): 58–80.

171. Andrew Woolford, "Making Genocide Unthinkable: Three Guidelines for a Critical Criminology of Genocide," *Critical Criminology* 14 (2006): 87–106.

172. Jeffrey Ian Ross, *The Dynamics of Political Crime* (Beverly Hills, CA: Sage, 2003).

173. Ibid.

174. Jessica Wolfendale, "Training Torturers: A Critique of the 'Ticking Bomb' Argument," *Social Theory and Practice* 31 (2006): 269–287; Vittorio Bufacchi and Jean Maria Arrigo, "Torture, Terrorism and the State: A Refutation of the Ticking-Bomb Argument," *Journal of Applied Philosophy* 23 (2006): 355–373.

175. Travis Pratt and Christopher Lowenkamp, "Conflict Theory, Economic Conditions, and Homicide: A Time-Series Analysis," *Homicide Studies* 6 (2002): 61–84.

176. David Jacobs and David Britt, "Inequality and Police Use of Deadly Force: An Empirical Assessment of a Conflict Hypothesis," *Social Problems* 26 (1979): 403–412.

177. Malcolm Holmes, Brad Smith, Adrienne Freng, and Ed Munoz, "Minority Threat, Crime Control, and Police Resource Allocation in the Southwestern United States," *Crime and Delinquency* 54 (2008): 128–153.

178. Tammy Rinehart Kochel, David Wilson, and Stephen Mastrofski, "Effect of Suspect Race on Officers' Arrest Decisions," *Criminology* 49 (2011): 473–512.

179. Thomas Arvanites, "Increasing Imprisonment: A Function of Crime or Socioeconomic Factors?" *American Journal of Criminal Justice* 17 (1992): 19–38.

180. Ick-Joong Chung, Karl G. Hill, J. David Hawkins, Lewayne Gilchrist, and Daniel Nagin, "Childhood Predictors of Offense Trajectories," *Journal of Research in Crime and Delinquency* 39 (2002): 60–91; Amy D'Unger, Kenneth Land, Patricia McCall, and Daniel Nagin, "How Many Latent Classes of Delinquent/-Criminal Careers? Results from Mixed Poisson Regression Analyses," *American Journal of Sociology* 103 (1998): 1593–1630.

181. Lila Kazemian, David Farrington, and Marc LeBlanc, "Can We Make Accurate Long-Term Predictions About Patterns of De-escalation in Offending Behavior?" *Journal of Youth and Adolescence* 38 (2009): 384–400.

182. David Nurco, Timothy Kinlock, and Mitchell Balter, "The Severity of Preaddiction Criminal Behavior Among Urban, Male Narcotic Addicts and Two Nonaddicted Control Groups," *Journal of Research in Crime and Delinquency* 30 (1993): 293–316.

183. Sarah Bacon, Raymond Paternoster, and Robert Brame, "Understanding the Relationship Between Onset Age and Subsequent Offending During Adolescence," *Journal of Youth and Adolescence* 38 (2009): 301–311.

184. W. Alex Mason, Rick Kosterman, J. David Hawkins, Todd Herrenkohl, Liliana Lengua, and Elizabeth McCauley, "Predicting Depression, Social Phobia, and Violence in Early Adulthood from Childhood Behavior Problems," *Journal of the American Academy of Child and Adolescent Psychiatry* 43 (2004): 307–315; Rolf Loeber and David Farrington, "Young Children Who Commit Crime: Epidemiology, Developmental Origins, Risk Factors, Early Interventions, and Policy Implications," *Development and Psychopathology* 12 (2000): 737–762; Patrick Lussier, Jean Proulx, and Marc LeBlanc, "Criminal Propensity, Deviant Sexual Interests and Criminal Activity of Sexual Aggressors Against Women: A Comparison of Explanatory Models," *Criminology* 43 (2005): 249–281.

185. Dawn Jeglum Bartusch, Donald Lynam, Terrie Moffitt, and Phil Silva, "Is Age Important? Testing a General versus a Developmental Theory of Antisocial Behavior," *Criminology* 35 (1997): 13–48.

186. Mary Campa, Catherine Bradshaw, John Eckenrode, and David Zielinski, "Patterns of Problem Behavior in Relation to Thriving and Precocious Behavior in Late Adolescence," *Journal of Youth and Adolescence* 37 (2008): 627–640.

187. W. Alex Mason, Rick Kosterman, J. David Hawkins, Todd Herrenkohl, Liliana Lengua, and Elizabeth McCauley, "Predicting Depression, Social Phobia, and Violence in Early Adulthood from Childhood Behavior Problems," *Journal of the American Academy of Child and Adolescent Psychiatry* 43 (2004): 307–315; Ronald Prinz and Suzanne Kerns, "Early Substance Use by Juvenile Offenders," *Child Psychiatry and Human Development* 33 (2003): 263–268.

188. Bacon, Paternoster, and Brame, "Understanding the Relationship Between Onset Age and Subsequent Offending During Adolescence."

189. Alex Piquero, David Farrington, Daniel Nagin, and Terrie Moffitt, "Trajectories of Offending and Their Relation to Life Failure in Late Middle Age: Findings from the Cambridge Study in Delinquent Development," *Journal of Research in Crime and Delinquency* 47 (2010): 151–173.

190. David Rowe, D. Wayne Osgood, and W. Alan Nicewander, "A Latent Trait Approach to Unifying Criminal Careers," *Criminology* 28 (1990): 237–270.

191. David Rowe and Daniel Flannery, "An Examination of Environmental and Trait Influences on Adolescent Delinquency," *Journal of Research in Crime and Delinquency* 31 (1994): 374–389.

192. Michael Gottfredson and Travis Hirschi, *A General Theory of Crime* (Stanford, CA: Stanford University Press, 1990).

193. Christian Seipel and Stefanie Eifler, "Opportunities, Rational Choice, and Self-Control: On the Interaction of Person and Situation in a General Theory of Crime," *Crime and Delinquency* 56 (2010): 167–197.

194. Michael Welch, Charles R. Tittle, Jennifer Yonkoski, Nicole Meidinger, and Harold G. Grasmick, "Social Integration, Self-Control, and Conformity," *Journal of Quantitative Criminology* 24 (2008): 73–92; Gregory Morris, Peter Wood, and Gregory Dunaway, "Self-Control, Native Traditionalism, and Native American Substance Use: Testing the Cultural Invariance of a General Theory of Crime," *Crime and Delinquency* 52 (2006): 572–598; Alexander Vazsonyi, Janice Clifford Wittekind, Lara Belliston, and Timothy Van Loh, "Extending the General Theory of Crime to 'The East': Low Self-Control in Japanese Late Adolescents," *Journal of Quantitative Criminology* 20 (2004): 189–216.

195. Chris Gibson, Christopher Sullivan, Shayne Jones, and Alex Piquero, "Does It Take a Village? Assessing Neighborhood Influences on Children's Self-Control," *Journal of Research in Crime and Delinquency* 47 (2010): 31–62.

196. Rolf Loeber, Dustin Pardini, D. Lynn Homish, Evelyn Wei, Anne Crawford, David Farrington, Magda Stouthamer-Loeber, Judith Creemers, Steven Koehler, and Richard Rosenfeld, "The Prediction of Violence and Homicide in Young Men," *Journal of Consulting and Clinical Psychology* 73 (2005): 1074–1088.

197. David Gadd and Stephen Farrall, "Criminal Careers, Desistance and Subjectivity: Interpreting Men's Narratives of Change," *Theoretical Criminology* 8 (2004): 123–156.

198. Robert Sampson and John Laub, *Crime in the Making: Pathways and Turning Points Through Life* (Cambridge, MA: Harvard University Press, 1993).

199. Nan Lin, *Social Capital: A Theory of Social Structure and Action* (Cambridge: Cambridge University Press, 2002).

200. Doris Layton MacKenzie and Spencer De Li, "The Impact of Formal and Informal Social Controls on the Criminal Activities of Probationers," *Journal of Research in Crime and Delinquency* 39 (2002): 243–278.

201. Alex Piquero, John MacDonald, and Karen Parker, "Race, Local Life Circumstances, and Criminal Activity over the Life Course," *Social Science Quarterly* 83 (2002): 654–671.

202. Chung et al., "Childhood Predictors of Offense Trajectories."

203. Ibid.

204. D'Unger et al., "How Many Latent Classes of Delinquent/ Criminal Careers?"

205. George E. Higgins, Melissa L. Ricketts, Catherine D. Marcum, and Margaret Mahoney, "Primary Socialization Theory: An Exploratory Study of Delinquent Trajectories," *Criminal Justice Studies* 23 (2010): 133–146.

206. Nicole Leeper Piquero and Terrie E. Moffitt, "Can Childhood Factors Predict Workplace Deviance?" *Justice Quarterly*, published online February 21, 2012.

207. Donald Lynam, Alex Piquero, and Terrie Moffitt, "Specialization and the Propensity to Violence: Support from Self-Reports but Not Official Records," *Journal of Contemporary Criminal Justice* 20 (2004): 215–228.

208. Jennifer Reingle, Wesley Jennings and Mildred Maldonado-Molina, "Risk and Protective Factors for Trajectories of Violent Delinquency Among a Nationally Representative Sample of Early Adolescents," *Youth Violence and Juvenile Justice*, published online February 16, 2012.

209. Alex Piquero and Timothy Brezina, "Testing Moffitt's Account of Adolescent-Limited Delinquency," *Criminology* 39 (2001): 353–370.

210. Terrie Moffitt, "Adolescence-Limited and Life-Course Persistent Antisocial Behavior: A Developmental Taxonomy," *Psychological Review* 100 (1993): 674–701.

211. Terrie Moffitt, "Natural Histories of Delinquency," in *Cross-National Longitudinal Research on Human Development and Criminal Behavior*, ed. Elmar Weitekamp and Hans-Jurgen Kerner (Dordrecht, Netherlands: Kluwer, 1994), pp. 3–65.

212. Andrea Donker, Wilma Smeenk, Peter van der Laan, and Frank Verhulst, "Individual Stability of Antisocial Behavior from Childhood to Adulthood: Testing the Stability Postulate of Moffitt's Developmental Theory," *Criminology* 41 (2003): 593–609.

213. Robert Vermeiren, "Psychopathology and Delinquency in Adolescents: A Descriptive and Developmental Perspective," *Clinical Psychology Review* 23 (2003): 277–318; Paul Mazerolle, Robert Brame, Ray Paternoster, Alex Piquero, and Charles Dean, "Onset Age, Persistence, and Offending Versatility: Comparisons across Sex," *Criminology* 38 (2000): 1143–1172.

214. Margit Wiesner, Deborah Capaldi, and Hyoun Kim, "General versus Specific Predictors of Male Arrest Trajectories: A Test

of the Moffitt and Patterson Theories," *Journal of Youth and Adolescence* 42 (2012): 217–228.

215. Hans Von Hentig, *The Criminal and His Victim: Studies in the Sociobiology of Crime* (New Haven, CT: Yale University Press, 1948), p. 384.

216. Stephen Schafer, *The Victim and His Criminal* (New York: Random House, 1968), p. 152.

217. Marvin Wolfgang, *Patterns of Criminal Homicide* (Philadelphia: University of Pennsylvania Press, 1958).

218. Ibid.

219. Menachem Amir, *Patterns in Forcible Rape* (Chicago: University of Chicago Press, 1971).

220. Susan Estrich, *Real Rape* (Cambridge, MA: Harvard University Press, 1987).

221. Pamela Wilcox, Marie Skubak Tillyer, and Bonnie S. Fisher, "Gendered Opportunity? School-Based Adolescent Victimization," *Journal of Research in Crime and Delinquency* 46 (2009): 245–269.

222. Edem Avakame, "Females' Labor Force Participation and Intimate Femicide: An Empirical Assessment of the Backlash Hypothesis," *Violence and Victims* 14 (1999): 277–283.

223. Rosemary Gartner and Bill McCarthy, "The Social Distribution of Femicide in Urban Canada, 1921–1988," *Law and Society Review* 25 (1991): 287–311.

224. Wilcox, Tillyer, and Fisher, "Gendered Opportunity?"

225. Elizabeth Reed, Hortensia Amaro, Atsushi Matsumoto, and Debra Kaysen, "The Relation Between Interpersonal Violence and Substance Use Among a Sample of University Students: Examination of the Role of Victim and Perpetrator Substance Use," *Addictive Behaviors* 34 (2009): 316–318.

226. Rolf Loeber, Mary DeLamatre, George Tita, Jacqueline Cohen, Magda Stouthamer-Loeber, and David Farrington, "Gun Injury and Mortality: The Delinquent Backgrounds of Juvenile Offenders," *Violence and Victims* 14 (1999): 339–351.

227. Rolf Loeber, Larry Kalb, and David Huizinga, *Juvenile Delinquency and Serious Injury Victimization* (Washington, DC: Office of Juvenile Justice and Delinquency Prevention, 2001).

228. Pamela Wilcox, David May, and Staci Roberts, "Student Weapon Possession and the 'Fear and Victimization Hypothesis': Unraveling the Temporal Order," *Justice Quarterly* 23 (2006): 502–529.

229. Dana Haynie and Alex Piquero, "Pubertal Development and Physical Victimization in Adolescence," *Journal of Research in Crime and Delinquency* 43 (2006): 3–35.

230. Loeber et al., "Gun Injury and Mortality."

231. Bonnie Fisher, John Sloan, Francis Cullen, and Chunmeng Lu, "Crime in the Ivory Tower: The Level and Sources of Student Victimization," *Criminology* 36 (1998): 671–710.

232. Adam Dobrin, "The Risk of Offending on Homicide Victimization: A Case Control Study," *Journal of Research in Crime and Delinquency* 38 (2001): 154–173.

233. Christopher Schreck, Eric Stewart, and Bonnie Fisher, "Self-Control, Victimization, and Their Influence on Risky Lifestyles: A Longitudinal Analysis Using Panel Data," *Journal of Quantitative Criminology* 22 (2006): 319–340.

234. Lawrence Cohen and Marcus Felson, "Social Change and Crime Rate Trends: A Routine Activities Approach," *American Sociological Review* 44 (1979): 588–608; Lawrence Cohen, Marcus Felson, and Kenneth Land, "Property Crime Rates in the United States: A Macrodynamic Analysis, 1947–1977, with Ex-Ante Forecasts for the Mid-1980s," *American Journal of Sociology* 86 (1980): 90–118; for a review, see James LeBeau and Thomas Castellano, "The Routine Activities Approach: An Inventory and Critique" (Carbondale: Center for the Studies of Crime, Delinquency, and Corrections, Southern Illinois University, 1987).

235. Denise Gottfredson and David Soulé, "The Timing of Property Crime, Violent Crime, and Substance Use Among Juveniles," *Journal of Research in Crime and Delinquency* 42 (2005): 110–120.

236. Cohen, Felson, and Land, "Property Crime Rates in the United States."

237. Kristy Holtfreter, Michael Reisig, and Travis Pratt, "Low Self-Control, Routine Activities, and Fraud Victimization," *Criminology* 46 (2008): 189–220.

238. Pamela Wilcox, Tamara Madensen, and Marie Skubak Tillyer, "Guardianship in Context: Implications for Burglary Victimization Risk and Prevention," *Criminology* 45 (2007): 771–803.

239. Rob Guerette and Shannon Santana, "Explaining Victim Self-Protective Behavior Effects on Crime Incident Outcomes: A Test of Opportunity Theory," *Crime and Delinquency* 56 (2010): 198–226.

CHAPTER 4

Criminal Law: Substance and Procedure

Learning Objectives

 LO1 List the similarities and differences between substantive and procedural criminal law and between civil law and public law.

 LO2 Discuss the concept of substantive criminal law and be familiar with its history.

 LO3 Discuss the sources of the criminal law.

 LO4 Describe how crimes are classified.

 LO5 Identify the elements of a crime.

 LO6 Define the term *strict liability*.

 LO7 Discuss excuse and justification defenses for crime.

 LO8 Discuss the concept of criminal procedure.

 LO9 Identify which amendments to the Constitution are the most important to the justice system.

 LO10 List the elements of due process of law.

Chapter Outline

The Development of Criminal Law
    Careers in Criminal Justice: Attorney
    The History of Criminal Law
    The Common Law

Sources of the Criminal Law
    The Victim Experience: Laci and Conner Peterson
    Constitutional Limits

Classifying Crimes
    Felonies and Misdemeanors
    The Legal Definition of a Crime

Criminal Defenses
    Excuse Defenses
    Justification Defenses
    Analyzing Criminal Justice Issues: Stand-Your-Ground Laws
    Changing Defenses

Reforming the Criminal Law
    Stalking Laws
    Prohibiting Assisted Suicide
    Registering Sex Offenders
    Clarifying Rape
    Controlling Technology
    Protecting the Environment
    Legalizing Marijuana
    Responding to Terrorism

The Law of Criminal Procedure
    Judicial Interpretation
    Criminal Justice and Technology: Criminal Procedure in the IT Era
    Due Process of Law

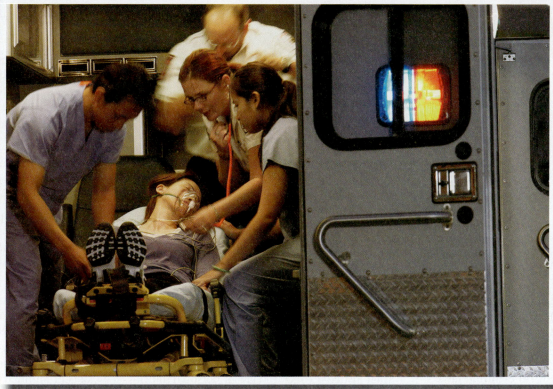

ERproductions Ltd/Blend Images/Getty Images

After her convictions for manslaughter in 2012, Jennifer Jorgensen, of Miller Place, New York, faced up to 15 years behind bars for a car crash that happened in 2008 when she was eight months pregnant. Jorgensen was driving without a seatbelt when she smashed head-on into a car driven by 74-year-old Robert Kelley. Both Kelley and his wife Mary died from their injuries.

Jorgensen was originally accused of drunken driving, but at her trial she claimed that the crash was a result of blacking out from pregnancy complications. She was acquitted of DWI and of charges related to the Kelleys' deaths, but was convicted of manslaughter in the death of her unborn child, which is legally permissible in New York. She was sentenced to three to nine years in prison.[1]

Under traditional law, a person could not be charged with murder if their victim was not "born and alive." However, changing social views in the United States have eroded that restriction. At the federal level, for example, the Unborn Victims and Violence Act of 2004 makes it a separate crime to harm a fetus during an assault on the mother.[2] If the attack causes death or bodily injury to a child who is in utero at the time the conduct takes place,

the penalty is the same as that for conduct had the injury or death occurred to the unborn child's mother.

More than two-thirds of the states have passed some form of legislation that criminalizes the killing of a fetus as murder even if the fetus is not "born and alive."[3] For example, a Tennessee law considers "a human embryo or fetus at any stage of gestation in utero" a potential victim of such offenses as murder, voluntary manslaughter, vehicular homicide, and reckless homicide. In a number of states, recent legislation has created a separate class of crime that increases criminal penalties when a person causes injury to a woman they know is pregnant and the injury results in miscarriage or stillbirth.

Legal changes like these have sparked heated debates. Those supporting penalizing the death of an unborn fetus claim that both the lives of the pregnant woman and her unborn should be explicitly protected. Those opposed believe that creating laws to protect the unborn could jeopardize a woman's right to choose an abortion and might create an adversarial relationship between the woman and her baby.

Fetal homicide laws were not on the founding fathers' radar when they wrote the U.S. Constitution and formulated the first written criminal code. Since the country's founding, however, new laws have been added and antiquated ones have been abandoned or replaced. The law must be flexible and able to react to shifting social priorities, rapidly advancing technological innovations, and other such changes. ■

L01 List the similarities and differences between substantive and procedural criminal law and between civil law and public law.

criminal law
The body of rules that define crimes, set out their punishments, and mandate the procedures for carrying out the criminal justice process.

substantive criminal law
A body of specific rules that declare what conduct is criminal and prescribe the punishment to be imposed for such conduct.

procedural criminal laws
The methods that must be followed in obtaining warrants, investigating offenses, effecting lawful arrests, conducting trials, introducing evidence, sentencing convicted offenders, and reviewing cases by appellate courts.

In modern U.S. society, the law governs nearly all phases of human enterprise, including commerce, family life, property transfer, and the regulation of interpersonal conflict. It contains elements that control personal relationships between individuals and public relationships between individuals and the government. The former is known as *civil law*, and the latter is called **criminal law**. The law, then, can generally be divided into four broad categories:

■ *Substantive criminal law.* The branch of the law that defines crimes and their punishment is known as **substantive criminal law**. It involves such issues as the mental and physical elements of crime, crime categories, and criminal defenses.

■ *Procedural criminal law.* Those laws that set out the basic rules of practice in the criminal justice system are **procedural criminal laws**. Some elements of the law of criminal procedure are the rules of evidence, the law of arrest, the law of search and seizure, and questions of appeal, jury selection, and the right to counsel.

■ *Civil law.* The set of rules governing relations between private parties, including both individuals and organizations (such as business enterprises and corporations), is known as **civil law**. The civil law is used to resolve, control, and shape such personal interactions as contracts, wills and trusts, property ownership, and commerce. The element of civil law that is most relevant to criminal justice is **torts**, the law of personal injuries (see Concept Summary 4.1).

■ *Public law.* The branch of law that deals with the government and its relationships with individuals or other governments. **Public law** governs the administration and regulation of city, county, state, and federal government agencies.

The four elements of the law can be interrelated: a crime victim may also sue the perpetrator for damages in a civil court; some crime victims may forgo

CONCEPT SUMMARY 4.1
Comparison of Criminal and Tort Law

Similarities	Differences
■ Goal of controlling behavior.	■ Crime is a public offense. Tort is a civil or private wrong.
■ Imposition of sanctions.	■ The sanction associated with tort law is monetary damages. Only a violation of criminal law can result in incarceration or even death.
■ Some common areas of legal action—for example, personal assault and control of white-collar offenses such as environmental pollution.	■ In criminal law, the right of enforcement belongs to the state. The individual brings the action in civil law.
■ The payment of damages to the victim in a tort case serves some of the same purposes as the payment of a fine in a criminal case.	■ In criminal law, monetary damages (fines) go to the state. In civil law, the individual receives damages as compensation for harm done.
■ Some acts, including rape, assault and battery, larceny, and corporate crimes, can be the basis for both criminal and civil actions.	

criminal action and choose to file a tort claim alone. It is also possible to seek civil damages from a perpetrator, even if he is found not guilty of crime (as in the case of the families of Nicole Brown and Ron Goldman, who successfully sued O. J. Simpson for damages), because the evidentiary standard in a tort action is less than that which evidence must meet for a criminal conviction. That is, in civil court defendants may be found guilty by a preponderance of the evidence, whereas in criminal court they must be found guilty beyond a reasonable doubt.

In some instances, the government has the option of either pursuing a legal matter through the criminal process or filing a tort action, or both. White-collar crimes, for example, often involve both criminal and civil penalties.

If you are interested in becoming an attorney, read the accompanying Careers in Criminal Justice feature.

The Development of Criminal Law

The criminal law is a living document that is constantly evolving to keep pace with society and its needs. The substantive criminal law defines crime and punishment in U.S. society. Each state government and the federal government has its own criminal code, developed over many generations and incorporating moral beliefs, social values, and political, economic, and other societal concerns. The goals of the substantive criminal law are set out in Exhibit 4.1.

civil law
All law that is not criminal, including tort, contract, personal property, maritime, and commercial law.

torts
The law of personal injuries.

public law
The branch of law that deals with the state or government agencies and controls their administrative relationships with individuals, corporations, or other branches of government.

EXHIBIT 4.1   Goals of the Substantive Criminal Law

- *Enforce social control.* The substantive criminal law is the main instrument of control at the disposal of an existing government. The criminal law can be used by those who hold political power to eliminate behaviors they believe pose a threat to society or challenge the government's authority. The law prevents actions that challenge the legitimacy of the government, such as planning its overthrow, collaborating with its enemies, committing terrorist acts, or engaging in espionage.

- *Distribute retribution.* By punishing people who infringe on the rights, property, and freedom of others, the law shifts the burden of revenge from the individual to the state. Although the thought of state-sponsored retribution may be offensive to some, it is greatly preferable to a system in which injured parties or their friends and relatives would seek to redress their injuries through personal vengeance or revenge.

- *Express public opinion and morality.* Criminal law reflects public opinions and moral values. Some crimes, such as murder and forcible rape, are almost universally prohibited, but others, such as substance abuse, prostitution, and gambling, reflect contemporary moral values and may undergo change according to social conditions and attitudes. The criminal law is used to codify changing social values and educate the public about what is expected of them and their behavior.

- *Deter criminal behavior.* Criminal law is designed through its application of punishment to control, restrain, and deter illegal acts before they actually occur. During the Middle Ages, public executions drove this point home; today, long prison sentences and an occasional execution are designed to achieve the same result.

- *Punish wrongdoing.* If the deterrent power of criminal law fails to prevent crime, the law gives the state the ability to sanction or punish offenders. Those who violate criminal law are subject to physical coercion and punishment.

- *Maintain social order.* All legal systems are designed to support and maintain the boundaries of the social system they serve. The free enterprise system is supported and sustained by criminal laws that protect property transfer and control market operations.

- *Provide restoration.* Victims deserve restitution or compensation for their pain and loss. The criminal law can be used to restore to victims what they have lost. Because we believe in equity and justice, it is only fair that the guilty help repair the harm they have caused others by their crimes. Punishments such as fines, forfeiture, and restitution are connected to this legal goal.

CAREERS in criminal justice

ATTORNEY

DUTIES AND CHARACTERISTICS OF THE JOB

Attorneys use their experience and extensive knowledge of the law and the legal system to defend the rights of their clients. They can fulfill this role by representing the best interests of their clients in a legal setting by defending them during a trial or settling their grievances in or out of court. However, lawyers also act as legal advisors and engage in such activities as drawing up and/or interpreting legal documents and contracts. They frequently act as advisors by informing their clients about changes in existing laws. Attorneys often choose a field of specialization, such as tax law or intellectual property rights.

Attorneys typically work in firms—organizations of lawyers who pool their resources on legal cases. Some attorneys gain experience within existing firms and then leave to start their own practice. Some work for the federal, state, or local government, and others take advantage of increasing opportunities for employment within businesses.

Attorneys generally work in offices and courtrooms, though at times they may have to travel to meet clients at their homes or even in prison. They often work long hours; especially if a case goes to trial, a 60-plus-hour workweek is not uncommon for an attorney.

JOB OUTLOOK

With the slowdown in the economy, competition for legal positions is considerable, especially at prestigious educational institutions and law firms. A good academic record from a major law school, as well as work experience, mobility, and additional education in a field of specialty, will be especially helpful. Jobs will be most available in urban areas, where there tend to be more law firms, big businesses, and government offices.

SALARY

Median annual earnings of all wage-and-salaried lawyers were recently $113,530. Partners in large national firms in Chicago or New York may have an annual salary in the millions. An attorney's salary depends on type of employer, experience, region, and type of law being practiced. For example, lawyers employed by the federal government tend to make more than state-employed lawyers. Extremely successful sole practitioners can win millions in tort actions.

The rules designed to implement the substantive law are known as procedural law. In contrast to the substantive law, the procedural law is concerned with the criminal process—the legal steps through which an offender passes—commencing with the initial criminal investigation and concluding with the release of the offender. Some elements of the law of criminal procedure (such as the rules of evidence, the right to notice of charges, questions of appeal, and the right to counsel) affect the substantive law. Many of the rights that have been extended to offenders over the past two decades lie within procedural law.

Because the law defines crime, punishment, and procedure, which are the basic concerns of the criminal justice system, it is essential for students to know something of the nature, purpose, and content of the substantive and procedural criminal law.

The History of Criminal Law

 LO2 Discuss the concept of substantive criminal law and be familiar with its history.

The roots of the criminal codes used in the United States can be traced back to such early legal charters as the Babylonian Code of Hammurabi (2000 BCE) and the Mosaic Code of the Israelites (1200 BCE). Another early code, the Roman Twelve Tables (451 BCE), was formulated by a special commission of 10 noble Roman men in response to pressure from the lower classes, who complained that the existing, unwritten legal code gave arbitrary and unlimited power to the wealthy classes. The original code was written on bronze plaques, which have been lost, but records of sections, which were memorized by every Roman male, survive. The remaining laws deal with debt, family relations, property, and other daily matters.

OPPORTUNITIES

Gaining entrance into law school can be challenging; there are many talented applicants applying for a limited number of spots. The competition for jobs with prestigious firms is fierce because there are more graduating lawyers than there are job openings. Making the law review at one's law school, publishing law review articles while in school, and obtaining prestigious internships can be helpful in securing coveted jobs.

Training and practice as a lawyer can be a personally and financially rewarding career in itself. However, many lawyers use their education and experience as a means of launching other careers. It is not uncommon for lawyers to have successful careers as business administrators, politicians, law professors, or judges.

QUALIFICATIONS

The primary qualification for a career as an attorney is a legal education. A bachelor's degree in a program that gives one strong analytical and writing skills is recommended for preparation for law school.

Becoming a successful lawyer can be challenging and requires personality traits such as discipline, commitment, and the ability to work hard. Additionally, those who like an intellectual challenge and communicate well are more likely to enjoy being an attorney and to be successful.

EDUCATION AND TRAINING

The primary requirements for a career as an attorney begin with proper educational training. Potential attorneys must have a bachelor's degree in order to gain entrance into an American Bar Association–accredited law school, which will prepare them for legal practice. After graduating from law school, attorneys must become certified before they can practice. Certification is obtained by passing a state bar exam. Completing these requirements can be challenging. Gaining admission to a law school requires not only hard work and discipline but also good grades and a desirable score on the Law School Admissions Test (LSAT).

Even after attorneys obtain a position, their education is not complete. Attorneys must stay informed of the latest developments in law and often attend conferences, and many states have continuing legal education (CLE) requirements that must be met. For certain positions, such as law school professor and specialties such as patent law, further experience and education are needed.

Source: "Lawyers," *Occupational Outlook Handbook*, "Lawyers" (Washington, DC: U.S. Department of Labor), http://www.bls.gov/ooh/Legal/Lawyers.htm (accessed May 2014).

Although the early formal legal codes were lost during the Dark Ages, German and Anglo-Saxon societies developed legal systems featuring monetary compensation, called *wergild* (*wer* means "worth" and refers to what the person, and therefore the crime, was worth), for criminal violations. Guilt was determined by two methods: *compurgation*, which involved having the accused person swear an oath of innocence while being backed up by a group of 12 to 25 oath helpers, who would attest to his or her character; and *claims of innocence and ordeal*, which were based on the principle that divine forces would not allow an innocent person to be harmed.

Determining guilt by ordeal involved such measures as having the accused place his or her hand in boiling water or hold a hot iron. If the wound healed, the person was found innocent; if the wound did not heal, the accused was deemed guilty. Trial by combat allowed the accused to challenge his accuser to a duel, with the outcome determining the legitimacy of the accusation. Punishments included public flogging, branding, beheading, and burning.

The Common Law

After the Norman Conquest of England in 1066, royal judges began to travel throughout the land, holding court in each county several times a year. When court was in session, the royal administrator, or judge, would summon a number of citizens who would, on their oath, tell of the crimes and serious breaches of the peace that had occurred since the judge's last visit. The royal judge would then

stare decisis

To stand by decided cases: the legal principle by which the decision or holding in an earlier case becomes the standard by which subsequent similar cases are judged.

decide what to do in each case, using local custom and rules of conduct as his guide—a system known as ***stare decisis*** (Latin for "to stand by decided cases"). Courts were bound to follow the law established in previous cases unless a higher authority, such as the king or the pope, overruled the law.

The present English system of law came into existence during the reign of Henry II (1154–1189), when royal judges began to publish their decisions in local cases. Judges began to use these written decisions as a basis for their decision making, and eventually a fixed body of legal rules and principles was produced. If the new rules were successfully applied in a number of different cases, they would become precedents, which would then be commonly applied in all similar cases—hence the term *common law*. Crimes such as murder, burglary, arson, and rape are common-law crimes whose elements were initially defined by judges. They are referred to as ***mala in se***, inherently evil and depraved. When the situation required it, the English Parliament enacted legislation to supplement the judge-made common law. These crimes were referred to as statutory or *mala prohibitum* crimes, which reflected existing social conditions. English common law evolved constantly to fit specific incidents that the judges encountered. For example, in the *Carriers* case (1473), an English court ruled that a merchant who had been hired to transport merchandise was guilty of larceny (theft) if he kept the goods for his own purposes.[4] Before the *Carriers* case, it was not considered a crime under the common law when people kept something that was voluntarily placed in their possession, even if the rightful owner had given them only temporary custody of the merchandise. Breaking with legal tradition, the court acknowledged that the commercial system could not be maintained unless the laws of theft were expanded. The definition of larceny was altered to meet the needs of a growing free enterprise economic system. The definition of theft was changed to include the taking of goods not only by force or stealth, but also by embezzlement and fraud.

mala in se

In common law, offenses that are by their own nature evil, immoral, and wrong; such offenses include murder, theft, and arson.

Before the American Revolution, the colonies, then under British rule, were subject to the common law. After the colonies won their independence, state legislatures standardized common-law crimes such as murder, burglary, arson, and rape by putting them into statutory form in criminal codes. As in England, whenever common law proved inadequate to deal with changing social and moral issues, the states and Congress supplemented it with legislative statutes. Similarly, statutes prohibiting such offenses as the sale and possession of narcotics or the pirating of DVDs have been passed to control human behavior unknown at the time the common law was formulated. Today, criminal behavior is defined primarily by statute. With few exceptions, crimes are removed, added, or modified by the legislature of a particular jurisdiction.

Sources of the Criminal Law

L03 Discuss the sources of the criminal law.

The contemporary U.S. legal system is codified by the state legislatures and the U.S. Congress. Each jurisdiction precisely defines "crime" in its legal code and sets out the appropriate punishments. However, like its English common-law roots, U.S. criminal law is not static and is constantly evolving. A state statute based on common law may define first-degree murder as the "unlawful killing, with malice and premeditation, of one human being by another." Over time, state court decisions might help explain the meaning of the term "malice" or clarify whether "human being" refers only to someone "born and alive" or can also refer to an unborn fetus. More than half the states have expanded their legal codes to include *feticide law*, which declares the killing of an unborn fetus to be murder. The Victim Experience feature discusses a famous case of feticide.

The content of the law may also be influenced by judicial decision making. A criminal statute may be no longer enforceable when an appellate judge rules

Web App 4.1

Visit Cornell University Law School's Legal Information Institute website on Constitutions, Statutes, and Codes for access to the U.S. Code and all 50 states' criminal codes: http://www.law.cornell.edu/statutes.html.

the VICTIM experience

LACI AND CONNER PETERSON

BACKGROUND A nationwide search began when eight-months-pregnant Laci Peterson, a 27-year-old substitute teacher in Modesto, California, disappeared on Christmas Eve of 2002. Her grieving husband Scott told her family and police that she had simply vanished from their home while he was on a fishing trip. She was going to take a walk in a nearby park, he said, and never came back. When the bodies of Laci and her unborn child Conner were found four months later, Scott was charged with two counts of murder.

The case made national headlines and dominated the media. Both Laci and Scott were attractive and engaging. How could this happen to such a nice middle-class couple? At first Scott received a great deal of public support and even Laci's parents and relatives could not believe that Scott Peterson could have harmed his wife. The tide turned when detectives found out that Scott was having an affair with a massage therapist named Amber Frey and had also taken a $250,000 life insurance policy out on Laci.

During the trial, the prosecution presented evidence of Scott's infidelity and suspicious activity: he was seen carrying a large wrapped object out of his house the night Laci disappeared; his "fishing trip" was in the vicinity of where her body was recovered. On November 12, 2004, the jury brought back a guilty verdict. Scott was convicted of first-degree murder in Laci's death and second-degree murder in the death of his unborn son, Conner. He was subsequently sentenced to death. Now he remains on death row in California and continues to appeal his conviction.

THE BIG PICTURE The jury's decision to convict Scott not just of Laci's death, but also Conner's reinforced the fact that it is legally permissible to be tried and convicted of killing a fetus; this is the crime of feticide, also discussed in the chapter opening vignette. Today, at least 38 states have fetal homicide laws. In a number of states, there also exists legislation creating a separate class of crime that increases criminal penalties when a person causes injury to a woman they know is pregnant, and the injury results in miscarriage or stillbirth.

There is still a great deal of state-to-state variation in feticide laws. Some make it a separate crime to kill a fetus or commit an act of violence against a pregnant woman. Others have a viability requirement: feticide can only occur if the unborn child could at the time have potentially lived outside the mother's body.

CLASSROOM EXERCISE Have the class conduct research on the state's feticide law and compare it to those in surrounding states. Research expert opinion on whether feticide should be a crime.

Source: National Conference of State Legislatures, *Fetal Homicide Laws*, February 2013, http://www.ncsl.org/research/health/fetal-homicide-state-laws.aspx (accessed May 2014).

that it is vague, deals with an act no longer of interest to the public, or is an unfair exercise of state control over an individual. Conversely, a judicial ruling may expand the scope of an existing criminal law, thereby allowing control over behaviors that heretofore were beyond its reach.

Constitutional Limits

Regardless of its source, all criminal law in the United States must conform to the rules and dictates of the U.S. Constitution.[5] Any criminal law that even appears to conflict with the various provisions and articles of the Constitution must reflect a compelling need to protect public safety or morals.[6]

Criminal laws have been interpreted as violating constitutional principles if they are too vague or too broad to give clear meaning of their intent. A law forbidding adults to engage in "immoral behavior" could not be enforced because it does not use clear and precise language or adequately explain which conduct is forbidden.[7]

The Constitution also prohibits laws that make a person's status a crime. Becoming or being a heroin addict is not a crime, although laws can forbid the sale, possession, and manufacture of heroin.

The Constitution also limits laws that are overly cruel and/or capricious. Whereas the use of the death penalty may be constitutionally approved, capital punishment would be forbidden if it were used for lesser crimes such as rape or employed in a random, haphazard fashion.[8] Cruel ways of executing criminals that cause excessive pain are likewise forbidden. One method used to avoid "cruelty" is lethal injection. In the 2008 case *Baze v. Rees*, the Court upheld the use of lethal injection unless there is a "substantial risk of serious harm" and suffering before death—for example, if it can be shown that the drugs will not work effectively.[9]

The Constitution also forbids *bills of attainder*: legislative acts that inflict punishment without a judicial trial. This device, used by the English kings to punish rebels and seize their property, was particularly troublesome to American colonials when it was used to seize the property of people considered disloyal to the Crown; hence, attainder is forbidden in the Constitution. Nor does the Constitution permit the government to pass any **ex post facto law**, examples of which include the following:

ex post facto law
A law that makes an act criminal after it was committed or retroactively increases the penalty for a crime; such laws are forbidden by the U.S. Constitution.

- A law that makes an action done before the passing of the law, and which was innocent when done, criminal and punishes such action
- A law that makes a crime more serious after the fact than it was when first committed
- A law that inflicts a greater punishment than was available when the crime was committed
- A law that makes convicting the offender easier than it was at the time the offender committed the crime[10]

Sometimes there is great debate over what the Constitution actually means, and no issue has inspired more debate than the Second Amendment's instruction: "A well-regulated militia, being necessary to the security of a free state, the right of the people to keep and bear arms, shall not be infringed." In the 2008 decision *District of Columbia v. Heller*, the Court ruled that the Second Amendment protects an individual's right to own weapons for self-defense—not merely a right related to membership in a "well-regulated militia"—and therefore a municipal government is prohibited from banning gun ownership.[11] Nonetheless, the Court allowed the registration and regulation of handguns. Because *Heller* applied only to the District of Columbia, which is under federal control, the Court took up the case of *McDonald v. Chicago*. On June 28, 2010, the Supreme Court ruled that the individual's Second Amendment right to bear arms must be recognized by the states, though it left open the door to regulation, such as limiting the right of ex-felons or mental patients to own guns.[12]

Classifying Crimes

LO4 Describe how crimes are classified.

The decision of how a crime should be classified rests with the individual jurisdiction. Each state has developed its own body of criminal law and consequently determines its own penalties for the various crimes. Thus the criminal law of a given state defines and grades offenses, sets levels of punishment, and classifies crimes into categories. Over the years, crimes have been generally grouped into (a) felonies, misdemeanors, and violations, and (b) other statutory classifications, such as juvenile delinquency, sex offender categories, and multiple- or first-offender classifications. In general terms, felonies are considered serious crimes, misdemeanors are seen as less serious crimes, and violations may be noncriminal offenses such as traffic offenses and public drunkenness. Some states consider violations to be civil matters, whereas others classify them as crimes.

Felonies and Misdemeanors

The most common classification in the United States is the division between felonies and misdemeanors.[13] This distinction is based primarily on the degree of seriousness of the crime. Distinguishing between a felony and a misdemeanor is sometimes difficult. *Black's Law Dictionary* defines the two terms as follows:

> A felony is a crime of a graver or more atrocious nature than those designated as misdemeanors. Generally it is an offense punishable by death or imprisonment in a penitentiary. A misdemeanor is lower than a felony and is generally punishable by fine or imprisonment otherwise than in a penitentiary.[14]

Each jurisdiction in the United States determines by statute what types of conduct constitute felonies or misdemeanors. The most common definition of a felony is a crime punishable in the statute by death or by imprisonment in a state or federal prison. Another way of determining what category an offense falls into is by providing, in the statute, that a felony is any crime punishable by imprisonment for more than one year. In the former method, the place of imprisonment is critical; in the latter, the length of the prison sentence distinguishes a felony from a misdemeanor.

In the United States today, felonies include serious crimes against the person, such as criminal homicide, robbery, and rape, as well as such crimes against property as burglary and larceny. Misdemeanors include petit (or petty) larceny, assault and battery, and the unlawful possession of marijuana. The least serious, or petty, offenses, which often involve criminal traffic violations, are called infractions or violations. The felony/misdemeanor classification has a direct effect on the offender charged with the crime. A person convicted of a felony may be barred from certain fields of employment or some professions, such as law and medicine. A felony offender's status as an alien in the United States might also be affected, or the offender might be denied the right to hold public office, vote, or serve on a jury.[15] These and other civil liabilities exist only when a person is convicted of a felony offense, not of a misdemeanor.

AP Images/Jose Luis Magana

Dick Heller, a licensed special police officer for the District of Columbia, carried a gun in federal office buildings, but was not allowed to have one in his home. Here, he signs an autograph outside the Supreme Court on June 26, 2008, after the Court ruled in the landmark case *District of Columbia v. Heller* that Americans have a constitutional right to keep guns in their homes for self-defense.

The Legal Definition of a Crime

Nearly all common-law crime contains both mental and physical elements. For example, in order to commit the crime of armed burglary, offenders must do the following things:

■ Willfully enter a dwelling

■ Be armed or arm themselves after entering the house, or commit an assault on a person who is lawfully in the house

■ Knowingly and intentionally commit the crime

L05 Identify the elements of a crime.

actus reus
An illegal act, or failure to act when legally required.

mens rea
A guilty mind: the intent to commit a criminal act.

To convict a person of the crime of armed burglary, the prosecution must prove that the accused (a) illegally entered a dwelling house (and that they were not invited in by the owner), (b) that they were armed when they arrived at the scene, (c) that their intentions were to take the owners' possessions, and that they did in fact do so.

In general, to fulfill the legal definition of a crime, all elements of the defining statute must be proved, including these:

■ The accused engaged in the guilty act (*actus reus*).

■ The accused had the intent to commit the act (*mens rea*).

■ Both the *actus reus* and the *mens rea* were concurrently present.

■ The defendant's actions were the proximate cause of the resulting injury.

■ Actual harm was caused. Thoughts of committing an act do not alone constitute a crime.

Each of these elements is discussed in greater detail next.

ACTUS REUS The *actus reus* is the criminal act, such as taking someone's money, burning a building, or shooting someone. The action must be voluntary for an act to be considered illegal. An accident or involuntary act would not be considered criminal. For example, if a person has a seizure while walking down the street, and as a result strikes another person in the face, he cannot be held criminally liable for assault. But if he knew beforehand that he could have a seizure and unreasonably put himself in a position where he was likely to harm others—for instance, by driving a car—he would be criminally liable for his behavior.

In addition, the failure or omission to act can be considered a crime on some occasions:

■ *Failure to perform a legally required duty that is based on relationship or status.* These relationships include parent and child and husband and wife. If a husband finds his wife unconscious because she took an overdose of sleeping pills, he is obligated to seek medical aid. If he fails to do so and she dies, he can be held responsible for her death. Parents are required to look after the welfare of their children; failure to provide adequate care can be a criminal offense.

■ *Imposition by statute.* Some states have passed laws that require a person who observes an automobile accident to stop and help the other parties involved.

■ *A contractual relationship.* These relationships include lifeguard and swimmer, doctor and patient, and babysitter or au pair and child. Because lifeguards have been hired to ensure the safety of swimmers, they have a legal duty to come to the aid of drowning persons. If a lifeguard knows a swimmer is in danger and does nothing about it and the swimmer drowns, the lifeguard is legally responsible for the swimmer's death.

The duty to act is a legal and not a moral duty. The obligation arises from the relationship between the parties or from explicit legal requirements. For example, a private citizen who sees a person drowning is under no legal obligation to save that person. Although it may be considered morally reprehensible, the private citizen could walk away and let the swimmer drown without facing legal sanctions.

MENS REA Under common law, for an act to constitute a crime, the actor must have criminal intent, or *mens rea*. To intend to commit a crime, the person must have clear knowledge of the consequences of his actions and must desire those consequences/outcomes to occur. A person who enters a store with a gun and shouts at the clerk to open the cash register is signaling his intent to commit a robbery. Criminal intent is implied if the results of an action, though originally unintended, are certain to occur. When Mohammed Atta and his terrorist band crashed airplanes into the World Trade Center on September 11, 2001, they did not intend to kill any particular person in the buildings. Yet the law would hold that anyone would be substantially certain that people in the buildings would be killed in the blast; therefore, the terrorists had the criminal intent to commit the crime of first-degree murder.

Mens rea is legally present when a person's reckless and/or negligent act produces social harm. Recklessness occurs when a person is or should be aware that his planned behavior is potentially harmful but goes ahead anyway, knowing his actions may expose someone to risk or suffering. Even though he may not desire to hurt the eventual victim, his act is considered intentional because he was willing to gamble with the safety of others rather than taking precautions to avoid injury. It would be considered reckless for a disgruntled student to set a fire in a dormitory supply closet to protest new restrictions on visitation rights. If some of her classmates were killed in the blaze, she might be charged with manslaughter even though she did not intend to cause injury. Her actions would be considered reckless because she went ahead with her plan despite the fact that she surely knew that a fire could spread and cause harm.

In contrast, **criminal negligence**, another form of *mens rea*, occurs when a person's careless and inattentive actions cause harm. If a student who stayed up for three days studying for a test and then drove home fell asleep at the wheel, thereby causing a fatal accident, his behavior might be considered negligent because driving while in a drowsy state creates a condition that a reasonable person can assume will lead to injury. Negligence differs from recklessness and is considered less serious because the person did not knowingly gamble with another's safety but simply failed to foresee possible dangers.

STRICT LIABILITY Certain statutory offenses exist in which *mens rea* is not essential. These offenses fall within a category known as a **public safety** or **strict liability crime**. A person can be held responsible for such a violation independent of the existence of intent to commit the offense. Strict liability criminal statutes generally include narcotics control laws, traffic laws, health and safety regulations, sanitation laws, and other regulatory statutes. A driver could not defend herself against a speeding ticket by claiming that she was unaware of how fast she was going and did not intend to speed, and a bartender could not claim that a juvenile to whom he sold liquor without checking an ID looked older than 21. No state of mind is generally required where a strict liability statute is violated.[16]

THE CONCURRENCE OF *MENS REA* AND *ACTUS REUS* The third element needed to prove that a crime was committed is the immediate relationship to or concurrence of the act with the criminal intent or result. The law requires that the offender's conduct be the proximate cause of any injury resulting from the criminal act. If, for example, a man chases a victim into the street intending to assault him, and the victim is struck and killed by a car, the accused could be convicted of murder if the court felt that his actions made him responsible for the victim's death. In other words, the victim would not have run into the street on his own accord and therefore would not have been killed. If, however, a victim dies from a completely unrelated illness after being assaulted, the court must determine whether the death was a probable consequence of the defendant's illegal conduct or would have resulted even if the assault had not occurred.

RESULTING HARM Most criminal acts must also result in harm, and it is the nature of the harm that ultimately determines what crime the person committed. For example, if someone trips another with the intent of making that person fall down and be embarrassed in public, he has committed the crime of battery. If by some chance the victim dies from the fall, the harm that was caused elevates the crime to manslaughter even if that was not the intended result. Or consider the crime of robbery. The *actus reus* is taking the property from the person or presence of another. In order to satisfy the harm requirement, the robber must

criminal negligence
Liability that can occur when a person's careless and inattentive actions cause harm.

public safety or strict liability crime
A criminal violation—usually one that endangers the public welfare—that is defined by the act itself, irrespective of intent.

 **LO6** Define the term *strict liability*.

acquire the victim's possessions, an act referred to as *asportation*. The legal definition of robbery is satisfied when possession of the property is transferred, even for a brief moment, to the robber. If a robber removes a victim's wallet from his pocket and immediately tosses it over a fence when he spies a police officer approaching, the robbery is complete because even the slightest change in possession of the property is sufficient to cause harm. Nor is the value of the property important: actual value is irrelevant so long as the property had some value to the victim.

Some crimes, however, do not require resulting harm. These are sometimes known as *conduct crimes*, or offenses which are completed simply by performing some act. Reckless driving is a good example. There is no requirement that harm occur to anyone (or anything) for reckless driving to occur.

IGNORANCE AND MISTAKE As a general rule, ignorance of the law is no excuse; the criminal law presumes people know what is and is not illegal. A mistake, however, might prevent someone from being convicted of a crime. How do we distinguish between ignorance and mistake? There are two common examples of ignorance: (1) a defendant does not know a law makes a particular action illegal and (2) a defendant who knows the act is illegal but is not sure whether the law applies in a particular circumstance. Ignorance of either variety almost never serves as a bar to criminal liability, but the latter form makes it easier for the defendant to argue that the crime was not *intended* (i.e., the *mens rea* component of the crime was not satisfied).

Mistake can also manifest in two forms: (1) a person knows a particular action is wrong but is not sure why, or (2) a person thinks what he or she is doing is legal but is not correct. The first of these is known as a mistake of law. The second is known as a mistake of fact. An example of mistake of law is this: Bob refuses to pay an auto mechanic because he thinks the mechanic overcharged him. The mechanic keeps Bob's keys, but Bob goes home, grabs a second set of keys, returns to the mechanic's shop, and takes his car. Bob knows this is probably not acceptable behavior, but he does not know a lien law permits the mechanic to keep the car until the customer pays. Alternatively, someone who accidentally leaves a store without paying for an item (assume, for example, it was on the bottom of the shopping cart and the clerk missed it, plus the customer forgot about it) commits a mistake of fact. Both examples also undermine the *mens rea* element of criminal liability.

Criminal Defenses

In 1884, two British sailors, desperate after being shipwrecked for days, made the decision to kill and eat a suffering cabin boy. Four days later, they were rescued by a passing ship and returned to England. In the case of *Regina v. Dudley and Stephens*, English authorities, wanting to end the practice of shipwreck cannibalism, tried the two men for murder and convicted them. Clemency was considered, and a reluctant Queen Victoria commuted the death sentences to six months behind bars.[17] Were the seamen justified in killing a shipmate to save their lives? If they had not done so, they probably would have died. Can there ever be a good reason to take a life? Can the killing of another ever be justified?

When people defend themselves against criminal charges, they must refute one or more of the elements of the crime of which they have been accused. Defendants may deny the *actus reus* by arguing that they were falsely accused and the real culprit has yet to be identified. Defendants may also claim that although they did engage in the criminal act they are accused of, they lacked the *mens rea*, or mental intent, needed to be found guilty of the crime. If a person whose mental state is impaired commits a criminal act, the person may seek to be excused of his or her criminal actions by claiming that he or she lacked the capacity to form sufficient intent to be held criminally responsible. Duress, insanity, intoxication, age, and entrapment are among the types of **excuse defenses**.

Another type of defense is **justification**. Here, the individual usually admits committing the criminal act but maintains that the act was justified under the circumstances and that he or she, therefore, should not be held criminally liable. Among the justification defenses are consent, self-defense, necessity, and law enforcement. Persons standing trial for criminal offenses may defend themselves by claiming either that their actions were justified under the circumstances or that their behavior should be excused by their lack of *mens rea*. If either the physical or the mental elements of a crime cannot be proved, then the defendant cannot be convicted.

Excuse Defenses

In these defenses, the accused claim they lacked *mens rea* when they engaged in criminal acts.

DURESS A duress (also called compulsion or coercion) defense may be used when the defendant claims he was forced to commit a crime as the only means of preventing death or serious harm to himself or others. For example, a bank employee might be excused from taking bank funds if she can prove that her family was being threatened and that consequently she was acting under duress. But widespread general agreement exists that duress is no defense for an intentional killing.

INSANITY Insanity is a defense to criminal prosecution in which the defendant's state of mind negates his or her criminal responsibility. A successful insanity defense results in a verdict of "not guilty by reason of insanity." Insanity, in this case, is a legal category. As used in U.S. courts, it does not mean that everyone who suffers from a form of mental illness can be excused from legal responsibility. Many people who are depressed, suffer mood disorders, or have a psychopathic personality can be found legally sane. Instead, insanity means that the defendant's state of mind at the time the crime was committed made it impossible for her to have the necessary *mens rea* to satisfy the legal definition of a crime. Thus,

excuse defenses
A defense in which a person states that his or her mental state was so impaired that he or she lacked the capacity to form sufficient intent to be held criminally responsible.

justification
A defense for a criminal act claiming that the criminal act was reasonable or necessary under the circumstances.

 L07 Discuss excuse and justification defenses for crime.

Amy Bishop is led away after her plea hearing in Huntsville, Alabama, on September 22, 2011. Bishop pleaded not guilty by reason of insanity in the shootings that killed three colleagues and wounded three others during a February 2010 faculty meeting. Before the murders, Bishop exhibited a long history of strange and bizarre behavior, including the fatal shooting of her brother and an attack on a woman in a local restaurant. Is it possible that extremely violent people like Bishop and Colorado shooter James Holmes are normal or are their actions clear evidence of mental illness?

AP Images/The Huntsville Times/Glenn Baeske

a person can be undergoing treatment for a psychological disorder but still be judged legally sane if it can be proved that, at the time she committed the crime, she had the capacity to understand the wrongfulness of her actions.

If a defendant uses the insanity plea, it is usually left to psychiatric testimony to prove that this defendant understood the wrongfulness of her or his actions and was therefore legally sane or, conversely, was mentally incapable of forming intent. The jury must then weigh the evidence in light of the test for sanity currently used in the jurisdiction. These tests vary throughout the United States. The standards most commonly used are listed in Exhibit 4.2.

INTOXICATION As a general rule, intoxication, which may include drunkenness or being under the influence of drugs, is not considered a defense. However, a defendant who becomes involuntarily intoxicated may be excused for crimes committed. Involuntary intoxication may also lessen the degree of the crime. For example, a judgment may be decreased from first- to second-degree murder because the defendant uses intoxication to prove the lack of the critical element of *mens rea*, or mental intent. Thus, the effect of intoxication on criminal liability depends on whether the defendant uses alcohol or drugs voluntarily. For example, a defendant who enters a bar for a few drinks, becomes intoxicated, and strikes someone can be convicted of assault and battery. If, however, the defendant ordered a nonalcoholic drink that was subsequently spiked by someone else, the defendant may have a legitimate legal defense.

EXHIBIT 4.2   Various Insanity Defense Standards

The *M'Naghten* Rule

The *M'Naghten* rule, first formulated in England in 1843, defines a person as insane if at the time she committed the act she stands accused of, she was laboring under such a defect of reason, arising from a disease of the mind, that she could not tell or know the nature and quality of the act or, if she did know it, that she did not know what she was doing was wrong. In other words, she could not tell "right from wrong." The *M'Naghten* rule is used in the majority of the states.

The Irresistible Impulse

The irresistible impulse test was formulated in Ohio in 1834. It is used quite often in conjunction with *M'Naghten* and defines a person as insane if he should or did know that his actions were illegal, but, because of a mental impairment, he couldn't control his behavior. His act was a result of an uncontrollable or irresistible impulse. A person who commits a crime during a "fit of passion" would be considered insane under this test. The most famous use of this defense occurred in 1994, when Lorena Bobbitt successfully defended herself against charges that she cut off the penis of her husband, John, after suffering abuse at his hands.

The *Durham* Rule

The *Durham* rule or "product test" was set forth by the United States Court of Appeals for the District of Columbia Circuit in 1954 and states that "an accused is not criminally responsible if his unlawful act was the product of mental disease or defect." It was used for some time in the state of New Hampshire.

The Insanity Defense Reform Act

The Insanity Defense Reform Act, Title 18, U.S. Code, Section 17, was enacted by Congress in 1984 and states that a person accused of a crime can be judged not guilty by reason of insanity if "the defendant, as a result of a severe mental disease or defect, was unable to appreciate the nature and quality or the wrongfulness of his acts."

The Substantial Capacity Test

The substantial capacity test was defined by the American Law Institute in its Model Penal Code. This argues that insanity should be defined as a lack of substantial capacity to control one's behavior. Substantial capacity is defined as "the mental capacity needed to understand the wrongfulness of act, or to conform ... behavior to the ... law." This rule combines elements of the *M'Naghten* rule with the concept of "irresistible impulse."

Because of the frequency of crime-related offenses involving drugs and alcohol, the impact of intoxication on criminal liability is a persistent issue in the criminal justice system. The connection among drug use, alcoholism, and violent street crime has been well documented. Although those in law enforcement and the judiciary tend to emphasize the use of the penal process in dealing with problems of chronic alcoholism and drug use, others in corrections and crime prevention favor approaches that depend more on behavioral theories and the social sciences. For example, in the case of *Robinson v. California*, the U.S. Supreme Court struck down a California statute making addiction to narcotics a crime, on the ground that it violated the defendant's rights under the Eighth and Fourteenth Amendments to the Constitution.[18] However, the landmark decision in *Powell v. Texas* placed severe limitations on the behavioral science approach in *Robinson* when it rejected the defense of chronic alcoholism of a defendant charged with the crime of public drunkenness.[19]

AGE The law holds that a child is not criminally responsible for actions committed at an age that precludes a full realization of the gravity of certain types of behavior. Under common law, there is generally a conclusive presumption of incapacity for a child under age 7, a reliable presumption for a child between the ages of 7 and 14, and no presumption for a child over the age of 14. This generally means that a child under age 7 who commits a crime will not be held criminally responsible for these actions and that a child between the ages of 7 and 14 may be held responsible. These common-law rules have been changed by statute in most jurisdictions. Today, the maximum age of criminal responsibility for children ranges from 14 to 17 or 18, whereas the minimum age may be set by statute at age 7 or under age 14.[20] In addition, every jurisdiction has established a juvenile court system to deal with juvenile offenders and children in need of court and societal supervision. Thus, the mandate of the juvenile justice system is to provide for the care and protection of children under a given age, established by state statute. In certain situations, a juvenile court may transfer a more serious chronic youthful offender to the adult criminal court.

ENTRAPMENT Under the rule of law, a defendant may be excused from criminal liability if he can convince the jury that law enforcement agents used traps, decoys, and deception to induce criminal action. Law enforcement officers can legitimately set traps for criminals by getting information about crimes from informers, undercover agents, and codefendants. Police officers are allowed to use ordinary opportunities for defendants to commit crime and to create these opportunities without excessive inducement. However, when the police instigate the crime, implant criminal ideas, and coerce individuals into bringing about crime, defendants can claim to have been entrapped.

Entrapment then must be viewed within the context of the defendant's predisposition to commit a crime. A defendant with a criminal record would have a tougher time using this defense successfully than one who had never been in trouble. However, in one of the most important entrapment cases, *Jacobson v. United States* (1992), the Supreme Court ruled that a defendant with a past history of child pornography had been entrapped by the government into purchasing more. Keith Jacobson had ordered *Bare Boys* magazines depicting nude children. When his name came up in their *Bare Boys* files, government agents sent him mailings for more than two and a half years in an effort to get him to purchase more kiddie porn. Such purchases are a violation of the Child Protection Act of 1984. Jacobson was arrested after he gave in to the inducements and ordered a magazine showing young boys engaged in sexual activities. A search of his house revealed no materials other than those sent by the government (and the original *Bare Boys* magazines). On appeal, the Court held that Jacobson was entrapped because the state could not prove a predisposition to break the law, and the purchase of the sexually charged magazines was the result of government coaxing.[21]

Justification Defenses

Criminal defenses may be based on the concept of justification. In these instances, defendants normally acknowledge that they committed the act but claim that they cannot be prosecuted because they were justified in doing so. Major types of criminal defenses involving justification are consent, self-defense, necessity, and law enforcement.

CONSENT As a general rule, the victim's consent to a crime does not automatically excuse the defendant who commits the action. The type of crime involved generally determines the validity of consent as an appropriate legal defense. Such crimes as common-law rape and larceny require lack of consent on the part of the victim. In other words, a rape does not occur if the victim consents to sexual relations. In the same way, a larceny cannot occur if the owner voluntarily consents to the taking of property. Consequently, in such crimes, consent is an essential element of the crime, and it is a valid defense where it can be proved or shown that it existed at the time the crime was committed. But in other crimes, such as sexual relations with a minor child, consent cannot be a defense because the state presumes that children are not capable of providing adequate or mature consent. Nor can consent be used to justify the crime of incest or bigamy.

SELF-DEFENSE A criminal defendant can claim to be not guilty because he or she acted in self-defense. To establish self-defense, the defendant must prove he acted with a reasonable belief that he was in imminent danger of death or harm and had no reasonable means of escape from the assailant.

As a general legal rule, a person defending herself may use only such force as is reasonably necessary to prevent personal harm. A person who is assaulted by another with no weapon is ordinarily not justified in hitting the assailant with a baseball bat. A person verbally threatened by another is not justified in striking the other party with his fists. If a woman hits a larger man, the man would not generally be justified in striking the woman and causing her physical harm. In other words, for the self-defense privilege to be legally exercised, the danger to the defendant must be immediate. Some states have enacted self-defense laws that give people a good bit of latitude in using deadly force to defend themselves. The accompanying Analyzing Criminal Justice Issues box features Florida's controversial stand-your-ground law.

In some instances, a person may kill his or her mate after years of abuse; this defense is known as *battered-wife syndrome* (or in cases involving child abuse, *battered-child syndrome*). Although a history of battering can be used to mitigate the seriousness of the crime, a finding of not guilty most often requires the presence of imminent danger and the inability of the accused to escape from the assailant.

FACT CHECK ✓

YOUR OPINION: If you own a gun, what are some reasons why you own it?

PUBLIC OPINION:

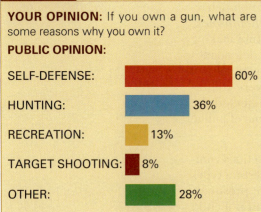

SELF-DEFENSE: 60%

HUNTING: 36%

RECREATION: 13%

TARGET SHOOTING: 8%

OTHER: 28%

REALITY: Clearly a majority of gun owners believe self-defense is an important reason to keep a firearm handy, yet defensive gun use is exceptionally rare. While the National Rifle Association has claimed that people use guns in self-defense as much as 2.5 million times each year, the National Crime Victimization Survey reports that crime victims threaten or attack perpetrators with a firearm in only 0.8 percent of violent victimizations—and only 0.1 percent of the time in property victimizations. It is also interesting to note that very few criminals are shot by law-abiding individuals; they are more often shot by other criminals. In fairness, however, research does show that *when* guns are used in self-defense, they are more effective than other alternatives.

DISCUSSION: Why do so many people cite self-defense as a reason for owning a gun when defensive gun use is exceptionally rare? Whose statistics about defense gun use should be believed and why?

NOTE: Poll percentages sum up to more than 100 percent because multiple responses were permissible in the poll.

Sources: Gallup, http://www.gallup.com/poll/165605/personal-safety-top-reason-americans-own-guns-today.aspx (accessed May 2014); David Hemenway, *Private Guns, Public Health* (Ann Arbor, MI: University of Michigan Press, 2004); Michael Planty and Jennifer L. Truman, *Firearm Violence, 1993–2011* (Washington, DC: Bureau of Justice Statistics, 2013), p. 12; John P. May, David Hemenway, Roger Oen, and Khalid R. Pitts, "Medical Care Solicitation by Criminals with Gunshot Wound Injuries: A Survey of Washington DC Jail Detainees," *Journal of Trauma* 48 (2000): 130–132; Jongyeon Tark and Gary Kleck, "Resisting Crime: The Effects of Victim Action on the Outcomes of Crime," *Criminology* 42 (2004): 861–910.

analyzing criminal justice ISSUES

STAND-YOUR-GROUND LAWS

Most self-defense statutes require a duty to retreat before reacting to a threat with physical violence. An exception is one's own home. According to the "castle exception" (from the old saying "A man's home is his castle"), a person is not obligated to retreat within his or her residence before fighting back. Some states, most notably Florida, now have "stand-your-ground" laws, which allow people to use force in a wide variety of circumstances and eliminate or curtail the need to retreat.

The traditional "castle doctrine" allowed people to use deadly force only when they reasonably believed that their lives were in danger. The new law allows average citizens to use deadly force when they reasonably believe that their homes or vehicles have been illegally invaded. Deadly force is allowed in these circumstances because, as the law states, the victim can assume that the unlawful entry will eventually involve the use of force or violence, so they can take preemptive measures to prevent being harmed.

FLORIDA'S CONTROVERSIAL LAW

Florida's law, made famous in the Trayvon Martin case, allows the use of deadly force when a person reasonably believes it necessary to prevent the commission of a "forcible felony," including carjacking, robbery, and assault. It also authorizes the use of defensive force by anyone "who is not engaged in an unlawful activity and who is attacked in any other place where he or she has a right to be." Furthermore, under the law, such a person has no duty to retreat and can stand his or her ground and meet force with force. Key provisions of Florida's law read as follows:

(1) A person is presumed to have held a reasonable fear of imminent peril of death or great bodily harm to himself or herself or another when using defensive force that is intended or likely to cause death or great bodily harm to another if:

(a) The person against whom the defensive force was used was in the process of unlawfully and forcefully entering, or

had unlawfully and forcibly entered, a dwelling, residence, or occupied vehicle, or if that person had removed or was attempting to remove another against that person's will from the dwelling, residence, or occupied vehicle; and

(b) The person who uses defensive force knew or had reason to believe that an unlawful and forcible entry or unlawful and forcible act was occurring or had occurred....

(3) A person who is not engaged in an unlawful activity and who is attacked in any other place where he or she has a right to be has no duty to retreat and has the right to stand his or her ground and meet force with force, including deadly force if he or she reasonably believes it is necessary to do so to prevent death or great bodily harm to himself or herself or another or to prevent the commission of a forcible felony....

(4) A person who unlawfully and by force enters or attempts to enter a person's dwelling, residence, or occupied vehicle is presumed to be doing so with the intent to commit an unlawful act involving force or violence.

CRITICAL THINKING

1. Revisit the facts surrounding the Trayvon Martin case (featured in depth in Chapter 1's opening story). Also brush up on the case timeline reported in detail here: http://www.cnn.com/2013/06/05/us/trayvon-martin-shooting-fast-facts/ (accessed May 2014). Did Zimmerman invoke the stand-your-ground law or a different defense? Why is this relevant?

2. Distinguish between stand-your-ground and ordinary self-defense (compare the Florida statute with the self-defense discussion in this chapter).

3. Should you be allowed to use deadly force to protect your property? The Texas stand-your-ground law permits just this (see Box Source Notes at the end of the chapter).

Sources: Florida Statutes, Title XLVI (Crimes), Chapter 776 (Justifiable Use of Force), http://www.leg.state.fl.us/statutes/ (accessed May 2014); Texas Penal Code, Title 2, Chapter 9, Section 9.42, http://www.statutes.legis.state.tx.us/Docs/PE/htm/PE.9.htm (accessed May 2014).

NECESSITY The defense of necessity is used when a crime was committed under extreme circumstances and could not be avoided. Unlike the duress defense, which involves threats made by another person, people act out of necessity according to their own judgment. Typically, to prove necessity, the burden is on the defendant to show that he acted to prevent imminent harm and that

Web App 4.2

Read more about the distinctions between stand-your-ground and so-called "castle doctrine" laws here: http://criminal.findlaw.com/criminal-law-basics/states-that-have-stand-your-ground-laws.html. The site also contains links to each type of state law.

there were no legal alternatives to violating the law. Using these criteria, a successful necessity defense could be launched if a woman in labor, fearing that she was about to give birth, stole a car in order to get to the hospital for an emergency delivery. It might also be considered necessity if a hunter shot an animal of an endangered species that was about to attack his child. However, defendants must prove that their actions were "the lesser of two evils." Unlike the case of the pregnant woman above, a defendant could not claim necessity for stealing a car because he was late for a soccer game.

LAW ENFORCEMENT Police officers, firefighters, and other first responders can use their occupation in defense of an alleged law violation committed while in the line of duty. For example, a police officer who shoots a suspect he or she believes is drawing a weapon cannot be charged with murder, even if it turns out that the suspect was unarmed. However, there are a number of exceptions to this rule. First, the action must be contained within the scope of their duties. A police officer who uses physical force while buying marijuana from a dealer would be just as criminally liable as any citizen. Second, protection from criminal liability would be limited in cases of gross negligence or malicious intent. For example, police officers could be charged with criminal assault if they used a weapon to batter a suspect they were interrogating. Police officers who drove at excessive speeds while not on emergency calls have been charged with manslaughter for causing the death of motorists.[22]

Immunity enjoyed by government agents can also sometimes spill over to private citizens who come to the aid of police or other civil servants. For example, a third party who sees a police officer grappling with a suspect and comes to the officer's aid cannot be prosecuted for assault if it later turns out that the suspect was innocent of crime. Many states have passed "Good Samaritan" laws that provide immunity from both civil and criminal actions to private citizens who, in good faith, cause injury while attempting to help someone in distress, including both private citizens and government officials.

Changing Defenses

Criminal defenses are undergoing rapid change. As society becomes more aware of existing social problems that may contribute to crime, it has become commonplace for defense counsels to defend their clients by raising a variety of new defenses based on preexisting conditions or syndromes with which their clients were afflicted. Examples include "battered-woman syndrome," "Gulf War Syndrome," "child sexual abuse syndrome," "Holocaust survivor syndrome," and "adopted-child syndrome."

Web App 4.3

Read about some unusual and creative criminal defenses here: http://www.oddee.com/item_97028.aspx.

In using these defenses, attorneys are asking judges either to recognize a new excuse for crime or to fit these conditions into preexisting defenses. For example, a person who used lethal violence in self-defense may argue that the trauma of serving in Iraq or Afghanistan caused him to overreact to provocation. Or a victim of child abuse may use her experiences to mitigate her culpability in a crime, asking a jury to consider her background when making a death penalty decision. In some instances, exotic criminal defenses have been gender specific. Attorneys have argued that their female clients' behavior was a result of their premenstrual syndrome (PMS) and that male clients were aggressive because of an imbalance in their testosterone levels. These defenses have achieved relatively little success in the United States.[23]

Although criminal law reform may be guided by good intentions, it is sometimes difficult to put the changes into operation. Law reform may necessitate creating new enforcement agencies or severely tax existing ones. As a result, the system becomes strained, and cases are backlogged.

Reforming the Criminal Law

In recent years, many states and the federal government have been examining their substantive criminal law. Because the law, in part, reflects public opinion and morality regarding various forms of behavior, what was considered criminal 40 years ago may not be considered so today. In some cases, states have reassessed their laws and reduced the penalties on some common practices such as public intoxication; this reduction of penalties is referred to as *decriminalization*. Such crimes, which in the past might have resulted in a prison sentence, may now be punished with a fine. In other instances, what was once considered a criminal act may be declared noncriminal or legalized. Sexual activity between consenting same-sex adults was punished as a serious felony under sodomy statutes in a number of states until the U.S. Supreme Court ruled such statutes illegal in 2003.[24]

Stalking Laws

More than 25 states have enacted **stalking** statutes, which prohibit and punish acts described typically as "the willful, malicious, and repeated following and harassing of another person."[25] Stalking laws were originally formulated to protect women terrorized by former husbands and boyfriends, although celebrities are often plagued by stalkers as well. In celebrity cases, these laws often apply to stalkers who are strangers or casual acquaintances of their victims.

stalking
The willful, malicious, and repeated following, harassing, or contacting of another person. Such behavior becomes a criminal act when it causes the victim to feel fear for his or her safety or the safety of others.

Prohibiting Assisted Suicide

Some laws are created when public opinion turns against a previously legal practice. Physician-assisted suicide became the subject of a national debate when Dr. Jack Kevorkian began practicing what he called **obitiatry**, helping people take their own lives.[26] In an attempt to stop Kevorkian, Michigan passed a statutory ban on assisted suicide, reflecting what lawmakers believed to be prevailing public opinion.[27] Convicted and imprisoned, Kevorkian was released on June 1, 2007, and gave lectures on college campuses until he passed away in 2011. Forty-six states, including Michigan, and the District of Columbia now disallow assisted suicide either by statute or by common law.[28]

obitiatry
Helping people take their own lives: assisted suicide.

Registering Sex Offenders

Some legal changes have been prompted by public outrage over a particularly heinous crime. One of the most well known is Megan's Law, named after 7-year-old Megan Kanka of Hamilton Township, New Jersey, who was killed in 1994. Charged with the crime was a convicted sex offender, who, unbeknownst to the Kankas, lived across the street. On May 17, 1996, President Bill Clinton signed Megan's Law, which contained two components:

■ *Sex offender registration*. A revision of the 1994 Jacob Wetterling Act, which had required the states to register individuals convicted of sex crimes against children, also established a community notification system.

■ *Community notification*. States were compelled to make private and personal information on registered sex offenders available to the public.

Variations of Megan's Law have been adopted by most state jurisdictions. Although civil libertarians have expressed concern that notification laws may interfere with an offender's post-release privacy rights, recent research indicates that registered offenders find value in Megan's Law because it helps deter future abuse. And when DNA collection is included in the law, it helps reduce false accusations and convictions.[29]

Clarifying Rape

Sometimes laws are changed to clarify the definition of crime and to quell public debate over the boundaries of the law. When does bad behavior cross the line into criminality, and when does it remain merely bad behavior? An example of the former can be found in changes to the law of rape. In several states, including California and Maryland, it is now considered rape if (a) the woman consents to sex, (b) the sex act begins, (c) she changes her mind during the act and tells her partner to stop, and (d) he refuses and continues. Before the legal change, such a circumstance was not considered rape but merely aggressive sex.[30]

Controlling Technology

Changing technology and the ever-increasing role of technology in people's daily lives will require modifications of the criminal law. Such technologies as automatic teller machines and cellular phones have already spawned a new generation of criminal acts involving theft of access numbers and software piracy. For example, a modification to Virginia's Computer Crimes Act that took effect in 2005 makes *phishing*—sending out bulk e-mail messages designed to trick consumers into revealing bank account passwords, Social Security numbers, and other personal information—a felony. Those convicted of selling the data or using the data to commit another crime, such as identity theft, now face twice as much prison time as before.

Protecting the Environment

In response to the concerns of environmentalists, the federal government has passed numerous acts designed to protect the nation's well-being. The Environmental Protection Agency has successfully prosecuted significant violations of these and other new laws, including data fraud cases (such as private laboratories submitting false environmental data to state and federal environmental agencies); indiscriminate hazardous waste dumping that resulted in serious injuries and death; industry-wide ocean dumping by cruise ships; oil spills that caused significant damage to waterways, wetlands, and beaches; and illegal handling of hazardous substances such as pesticides and asbestos that exposed children, the poor, and other especially vulnerable groups to potentially serious illness.[31]

Legalizing Marijuana

Some 20 states have legalized marijuana for medical purposes.[32] However, on November 6, 2012, Washington and Colorado voted to legalize possession of marijuana, up to a certain quantity. On December 5, one day before Washington's Initiative 502 went into effect, the Seattle Police Department's "SPD Blotter" website informed city residents that people were now free to consume marijuana in the privacy of their own homes. The site also noted that for the time being officers would only issue warnings to those caught smoking weed in public. The site went on to say:

> Does this mean you should flagrantly roll up a mega-spliff and light up in the middle of the street? No. If you're smoking pot in public, officers will be giving helpful reminders to folks about the rules and regulations under I-502 (like not

A woman smokes marijuana on the "420 Weed Tour" in Denver, Colorado. Since recreational marijuana was legalized in 2014, several companies have begun to offer tours (even multi-day tours) to dispensaries and growing operations throughout the state. Others now offer classes on how to "cook with cannabis."

smoking pot in public). But the police department believes that, under state law, you may responsibly get baked, order some pizzas, and enjoy a *Lord of the Rings* marathon in the privacy of your own home, if you want to.[33]

Colorado was first to actually implement legalization. Residents and nonresidents alike (they must be at least 21 years old) can now buy modest quantities of marijuana from licensed stores, possess the drug within Colorado, and consume it, as long as the consumption does not occur in public. Residents can purchase up to an ounce in a single transaction; nonresidents are limited to a quarter-ounce, again in a single transaction. Residents can even grow a certain number of marijuana plants in the privacy of their own homes.

The Washington and Colorado laws seem straightforward enough, right? Perhaps, but there is one major complication: marijuana remains illegal under federal law. What's more, Washington's and Colorado's neighboring states continue to criminalize marijuana. What happens, for example, if a Utah resident drives into Colorado and legally purchases an ounce of marijuana, drives back home, and gets caught with the drug? The easy answer is that the person will be prosecuted under Utah law. But will a prosecution actually occur? Utah, like other states neighboring Washington and Colorado, have plenty of other problems. Will so-called "marijuana tourists" create new headaches for officials in the states where marijuana is still illegal? How will police—and particularly prosecutors—adjust to the possible increase in their workload? "It would be like a place people go to get cheap beer. We're not talking about medical marijuana. We're talking about people who just want to get high," said a district attorney in Oregon.[34]

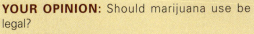

YOUR OPINION: Should marijuana use be legal?

PUBLIC OPINION:

YES:	58%
NO:	39%

REALITY: Public opinion concerning marijuana legalization has shifted markedly in recent years. In 1969, 84 percent of Americans felt the drug should be illegal. Legal changes in Colorado and Washington are likely responsible for the recent shift.

DISCUSSION: What are the possible consequences of legalizing marijuana? What problems have Colorado and Washington encountered? Is there an upside to legalization besides tax revenue generation? If so, what is it?

Source: Gallup, http://www.gallup.com/poll/165539/first-time-americans-favor-legalizing-marijuana.aspx (accessed May 2014).

Responding to Terrorism

Soon after the September 11 terrorist attacks, the U.S. government enacted several laws focused on preventing further acts of violence against the United States and creating greater flexibility in the fight to control terror activity. Most importantly, Congress passed the USA Patriot Act (USAPA) on October 26, 2001. The bill is over 342 pages long, creates new laws, and makes changes to more than 15 different existing statutes. Its aim is to give sweeping new powers to domestic law enforcement and international intelligence agencies in an effort to fight terrorism, to expand the definition of terrorist activities, and to alter sanctions for violent terrorism. On March 2, 2006, Congress passed a reauthorization bill that left most of the act intact, and on March 9, then-President George W. Bush signed it into law.

While it is impossible to discuss every provision of this sweeping legislation here, a few of its more important elements will be examined.

Web App 4.4

Read about marijuana laws in your state here: http://norml.org/laws/

THE USA PATRIOT ACT The USAPA expands all four traditional tools of surveillance—wiretaps, search warrants, pen/trap orders (installing devices that record phone calls), and subpoenas. The Foreign Intelligence Surveillance Act (FISA) that allows domestic operations by intelligence agencies is also expanded. The Patriot Act gives greater power to the FBI to check and monitor phone, Internet, and computer records without first needing to demonstrate that they were being used by a suspect or target of a court order.

The government may now serve a single wiretap, or pen/trap order, on any person regardless of whether that person or entity is named in a court order. Prior to this act, telephone companies could be ordered to install pen/trap devices on their networks that would monitor calls coming to a surveillance target and to whom the surveillance target made calls; the USAPA extends this monitoring to the Internet. Law enforcement agencies may now also obtain the e-mail addresses and websites visited by a target, and e-mails of the people with whom they communicate. It is possible to require that an Internet service provider install a device that records e-mail and other electronic communications on its servers, looking for communications initiated or received by the target of an investigation. Under USAPA, the government does not need to show a court that the information or communication is relevant to a criminal investigation, nor does it have to report where it served the order or what information it received.

The act also allows enforcement agencies to monitor cable operators and obtain access to their records and systems. Before the act, a cable company had to give prior notice to the customer, even if that person was a target of an investigation. Information can now be obtained on people with whom the cable subscriber communicates, the content of the person's communications, and the person's subscription records; prior notice is still required if law enforcement agencies want to learn what television programming a subscriber purchases.

The act also expands the definition of *terrorism* and enables the government to monitor more closely those people suspected of "harboring" and giving "material support" to terrorists (sections 803, 805). It increases the authority of the U.S. attorney general to detain and deport noncitizens with little or no judicial review. The attorney general may certify that he has "reasonable grounds to believe" that a noncitizen endangers national security and is therefore eligible for deportation. The attorney general and secretary of state are also given the authority to designate domestic groups as terrorist organizations and deport any noncitizen who is a member.

Though many critics have called for its repeal, the Patriot Act was reauthorized in 2006 with a slew of provisions ensuring that the act did not violate civil rights by limiting its surveillance and wiretap authorizations.[35] More recently, President Obama extended three controversial provisions that were set to expire:

■   *Lone wolf*. The government can track individuals who are not connected to a foreign power but who are thought to be affiliated with a terrorist group. This applies only to noncitizens.

■   *Business records*. The government can force third parties, such as travel and telephone companies, to provide access to a suspect's records without his or her knowledge.

■   *Roving wiretaps*. The government can monitor phone lines and Internet accounts that a terrorist suspect may be using, but it must first get approval from the Foreign Intelligence Surveillance Act court.[36]

The Patriot Act continues to come under scrutiny, most recently in the wake of the NSA's collection of cell phone records (more on this in the Criminal Justice and Technology box later in this chapter).

L08 Discuss the concept of criminal procedure.

The Law of Criminal Procedure

Whereas substantive criminal law primarily defines crimes, the law of criminal procedure consists of the rules and procedures that govern the processing of criminal suspects and the conduct of criminal trials. The right to remain silent, the right to an attorney, and the right to a speedy and fair trial are all critical elements of criminal procedure.

The main source of the procedural law is the ten amendments added to the U.S. Constitution on December 15, 1791, which are collectively known as the Bill of Rights. These amendments were added to the Constitution to quell fears among some of the founding fathers (such as George Mason) that, as drafted, the Constitution did not offer protections from the tyrannical exercise of power by an all-powerful central government.[37] The British violation of the colonists' civil rights before and during the Revolution was still fresh in their minds when they demanded a "bill of rights" that would spell out the rights and privileges of individual citizens. On September 25, 1789, the First Congress of the United States therefore proposed, to the state legislatures, twelve amendments to the Constitution that answered the arguments most frequently advanced against it. The first two proposed amendments, which concerned the number of constituents for each representative and the compensation of members of Congress, were not ratified. Articles 3 to 12, however, were ratified by three-fourths of the state legislatures, and they constitute the Bill of Rights.[38]

Judicial Interpretation

The purpose of these amendments was to prevent the government from usurping the personal freedoms of citizens. The U.S. Supreme Court's interpretation of these amendments has served as the basis for the creation of legal rights of the accused.

When the Supreme Court justices are conservative, they are less likely to create new rights and privileges and more likely to restrict civil liberties. Take what is known as the **exclusionary rule**: According to judicial doctrine, evidence seized by police in violation of the rights and privileges presented by the Constitution cannot be used in a court of law; it is as if the incriminating evidence did not exist. Thus, if police make an illegal arrest and find illegal substances hidden on the suspect's body, the contraband cannot be presented as evidence at a trial. Although that much is clear, it is up to judicial interpretation to define a citizen's constitutional rights and privileges and then determine when they are violated. There are countless cases defining what the police can and cannot do and when their actions trigger the exclusionary rule.

Take for instance the 2009 case of *Herring v. U.S.*[39] Bennie Dean Herring had been searched after the police were informed that there was an outstanding warrant against him on a felony charge. The search turned up methamphetamine and a pistol. Soon after, it was discovered that the warrant had actually been withdrawn five months earlier and had been left in the computer system by mistake. Should the evidence be discarded because the police made an error? Or should the evidence be allowed at trial because the police acted in good faith based on a mistaken belief that there was a warrant out for Herring? After all, the warrant *was* in the computer, so relying on it was an honest mistake. But if that mistake were excused, what would stop police from putting tainted warrants in their computer, leaving them there, and claiming they made many "honest mistakes"? The majority of the Supreme Court settled this conundrum when it ruled that "When police mistakes leading to an unlawful search are the result of isolated negligence attenuated from the search, rather than systemic error or reckless disregard of constitutional requirements, the exclusionary rule does not apply." The court ruled that the errors in the *Herring* case did not amount to deliberate police misconduct that should trigger the exclusionary rule, and the conviction of Bennie Herring was allowed to stand. We will revisit the exclusionary rule and its control over police conduct in Chapter 8.

Of primary concern in the law of criminal procedure are the Fourth, Fifth, Sixth, and Eighth Amendments, which limit and control the manner in which the federal government operates the justice system. In addition, the due process clause of the Fourteenth Amendment has been interpreted as imposing limits on government action at the state and local levels.

■ The Fourth Amendment bars illegal "searches and seizures," a right especially important for the criminal justice system because it means that police officers cannot indiscriminately use their authority to investigate a possible crime or arrest a suspect. Stopping, questioning, or searching an individual without legal justification represents a serious violation of the Fourth Amendment right to personal privacy. The concept of privacy is changing in our high-tech world, a topic covered in the Criminal Justice and Technology feature.

exclusionary rule
The principle that illegally obtained evidence cannot be used in a court of law.

 Identify which amendments to the Constitution are the most important to the justice system.

criminal justice and TECHNOLOGY

CRIMINAL PROCEDURE IN THE IT ERA

As technology plays a bigger role in law enforcement, there is a need to define the boundary between personal privacy and public security. For example, in *Kyllo v. United States*, the Supreme Court ruled that the use of technology to "see" into a suspect's home to seize information should be limited. The Court ruled that it was unconstitutional breach of privacy for police officers to use a thermal imaging (infrared) scanner to look into Danny Kyllo's home for evidence of high-intensity lamps used to grow marijuana indoors.

Another area of concern is the use of electronic tracking devices to keep tabs on suspects. In a recent case, *United States v. Jones*, the Court placed curbs on the use of a GPS responder placed on a suspect's car (*Jones* is discussed in greater detail in Chapter 8).

While the courts have placed limits on law enforcement use of *some* technologies, the federal government and most states have not enacted statutes to regulate how law enforcement can access the tracking data kept in more than 326 million smartphones and cellular phones in the United States. That data, when analyzed, can provide a great deal of information that people might want to keep private—trips to a psychiatrist, a strip club, or a boyfriend or girlfriend's home. Does this tracking violate a person's right to privacy? Does such tracking mean that many innocent Americans can never be confident that they will be free from round-the-clock surveillance by law enforcement of their activities?

NSA METADATA COLLECTION

In 2014, the National Security Agency (NSA) came under fire for the collection of so-called "metadata," records about when, where, and to whom people make calls, for all U.S. telephone communications. When looked at together, these data can reveal interesting details about a person's calling habits, which could then help authorities in their investigations.

Since the NSA program came to light, federal judges have issued conflicting opinions as to whether the program is unconstitutional. For example, U.S. District Court Judge Richard Leon held in 2014, "I cannot imagine a more 'indiscriminate' and 'arbitrary invasion' than this systematic and high-tech collection and retention of personal data on virtually every single citizen...." In supporting the practice, Judge William H. Pauley III, of the U.S. District Court for the Southern District of New York, concluded: "There is no evidence that the Government has used any of the . . . metadata it collected for any purpose other than investigating and disrupting terrorist attacks." This is an area of ongoing legal wrangling.

CELL PHONE TRACKING AND RECORDS

There is no evidence that metadata are or were shared with local law enforcement. Nevertheless, police can also track phones by analyzing signals from towers that connect cell phone calls or, in some cases, through GPS

■ The Fifth Amendment limits the admissibility of confessions that have been obtained unfairly. In 1966, in the landmark case of *Miranda v. Arizona*, the Supreme Court held that a person accused of a crime has the right to refuse to answer questions when placed in police custody.[40] The Fifth Amendment also guarantees defendants the right to a grand jury hearing and the right not to be tried twice for the same crime—that is, they are protected from double jeopardy. Its due process clause guarantees defendants the right to fundamental fairness and the expectation of fair trials, fair hearings, and similar procedural safeguards.

■ The Sixth Amendment guarantees the defendant the right to a speedy and public trial by an impartial jury, the right to be informed of the nature of the charges, and the right to confront any prosecution witnesses. It also contains the right of a defendant to be represented by an attorney, a privilege that has been extended to numerous stages of the criminal justice process, including pretrial custody, identification and lineup procedures, preliminary hearing, submission of a guilty plea, trial, sentencing, and postconviction appeal.

satellites. The precision varies. Data from a single tower in a rural area may only locate a phone within 10 miles. But combining signals from multiple towers in an urban area can locate a phone within 50 yards.

Tracking is becoming more precise as wireless companies install more towers. CTIA–The Wireless Association, a trade group, says there are now more than 300,000 cell phone sites in the United States, up from 139,000 just 10 years ago. GPS is more precise, but the signal doesn't work indoors and not all phones use GPS. As a result, the use of cell phone tracking has skyrocketed.

As the frequency of tracking has increased, more judges have raised the need for search warrants. Indeed, the U.S. Supreme Court decided that the search of an arrestee's cell phone required a search warrant and could not be conducted incident to arrest. In *Riley v. California*, prosecutors linked the defendant to the crime partly due to a photograph on his cell phone showing him posing next to a car similar to one at the crime scene. In an accompanying case, officers searched the record of calls made, which led them to another man's house, where drugs, cash, and a gun were found.

EMERGING ISSUES AND UNANSWERED QUESTIONS

Law enforcement agents are now worried about increasing restrictions on their ability to monitor suspects. Take for instance the case where police receive an anonymous call giving the identity of two gang members alleged to be involved in a murder. Detectives get information about the gang members' phones from previous arrests, and then are able to get geolocation data that show the men were in the same place at the same time where and when the murder took place. While this information alone is not enough to make an arrest or gain a conviction, it would be a powerful element in building a case. If a search warrant backed by probable cause becomes legally required to access historical cell phone records, this vital information would not be obtainable. Is this type of electronic tracking any different from such routine surveillance as following a suspect in an unmarked police car on city streets? There are instances where phone records have actually been essential to rescue abducted children, identify sexual predators, and apprehend suspected terrorists.

CRITICAL THINKING

Is placing a tracking device on your car an invasion of your privacy? Would you care if someone knew where you went each day if you were not involved in crime, drug deals, or terror plots? Is it worth giving up a little of your privacy if society could be protected from really dangerous people? What is your opinion of the NSA metadata collection program?

Sources: *Kyllo v. United States*, 533 U.S. 27 (2001); *United States v. Jones*, 565 U.S. ____ (2012); CTIA: The Wireless Association, *Wireless Quick Facts*, http://www.ctia.org/your-wireless-life/how-wireless-works/wireless-quick-facts (accessed May 2014); Marjorie Cohn, "NSA Metadata Collection: Fourth Amendment Violation," http://www.huffingtonpost.com/marjorie-cohn/nsa-metadata-collection-f_b_4611211.html (accessed May 2014); *Riley v. California*, 573 U.S. ____ (2014).

■ According to the Eighth Amendment, "Excessive bail shall not be required, nor excessive fines imposed, nor cruel and unusual punishments inflicted." Bail is a money bond put up by the accused to attain freedom between arrest and trial. Bail is meant to ensure a trial appearance, because the bail money is forfeited if the defendant misses the trial date. The Eighth Amendment does not guarantee a constitutional right to bail but instead prohibits the use of excessive bail, which is typically defined as an amount far greater than that imposed on similar defendants who are accused of committing similar crimes. The Eighth Amendment also forbids the use of cruel and unusual punishment. This prohibition protects both the accused and convicted offenders from actions regarded as unacceptable by a civilized society, including corporal punishment and torture.

The Fourteenth Amendment is the vehicle used to ensure that the protections enumerated in the Bill of Rights are applied by the states. It affirms that no state shall "deprive any person of life, liberty, or property, without due process of law." In essence, the same general constitutional restrictions previously applicable to the federal government can be imposed on the states.

AP Images/Liz Mineo

Maria Ines Peniche poses for a portrait on the campus of Pine Manor College in Newton, Massachusetts. She was arrested with other activists after attempting to cross the border from Mexico into the United States in protest of American immigration policy. She was released from federal custody in Arizona after the Homeland Security Department tentatively approved her asylum request. What legal challenges have been raised against U.S. immigration policy?

 **LO10** List the elements of due process of law.

Due Process of Law

The concept of due process, found in both the Fifth and Fourteenth Amendments, has been used to evaluate the constitutionality of legal statutes and to set standards and guidelines for fair procedures in the criminal justice system. In seeking to define the meaning of the term, most legal experts conclude that it refers to the essential elements of fairness under law.[41] This definition basically refers to the legal system's need for rules and regulations that protect individual rights.

Due process can be divided into two distinct categories: substantive and procedural. *Substantive due process* refers to the citizen's right to be protected from criminal laws that may be biased, discriminatory, or otherwise unfair. These laws may be vague or may apply unfairly to one group over another. For example, in an important 2003 case, *Lawrence v. Texas*, the U.S. Supreme Court declared that laws banning sodomy were unconstitutional in that they violated the due process rights of citizens because of their sexual orientation. A neighbor in 1998 had reported a "weapons disturbance" at the home of John G. Lawrence, and when police arrived they found Lawrence and another man, Tyron Garner, having sex. The two were held overnight in jail and later fined $200 each for violating the state's homosexual conduct law. In its decision, the Court said the following:

> Although the laws involved . . . here . . . do not do more than prohibit a particular sexual act, their penalties and purposes have more far-reaching consequences, touching upon the most private human conduct, sexual behavior, and in the most private of places, the home. They seek to control a personal relationship that, whether or not entitled to formal recognition in the law, is within the liberty of persons to choose without being punished as criminals. The liberty protected by the Constitution allows homosexual persons the right to choose to enter upon relationships in the confines of their homes and their own private lives and still retain their dignity as free persons.[42]

As a result of the decision, laws banning same-sex relations are now unconstitutional and unenforceable, a decision that paved the way for the legalization of gay marriage.

In contrast, *procedural due process* seeks to ensure that no person will be deprived of life, liberty, or property without proper and legal criminal process. Basically, procedural due process is intended to guarantee that fundamental fairness exists in each individual case. Specific due process procedures include the following:

■ Prompt notice of charges

■ A formal hearing

■ The right to counsel or some other representation

■ The opportunity to respond to charges

■ The opportunity to confront and cross-examine witnesses and accusers

■ The privilege to be free from self-incrimination

■ The opportunity to present one's own witnesses

■ A decision made on the basis of substantial evidence and facts produced at the hearing

■ A written statement of the reasons for the decision

■ An appellate review procedure

ETHICAL CHALLENGES in Criminal Justice

A WRITING ASSIGNMENT

You are chief prosecutor in a rural county. A man takes his 6-year-old daughter to a dude ranch run by a trusted friend. When his daughter goes missing he frantically searches the property. Some kids say that they saw the friend take the girl into the woods. He follows and finds his "trusted" friend assaulting the young girl. In a rage, he picks up a piece of wood lying nearby and strikes the man repeatedly around the head and neck, resulting in his death.

Write an essay answering this question: Would it be legally ethical to dismiss the charges considering the circumstances or would you charge the dad with murder since he used a weapon to kill? As you formulate your answer, bear these facts in mind: First, the legal penalty for child abuse and rape cannot be death; that is, capital punishment is not an option for people who commit such crimes. On the other hand, some state self-defense laws permit people to use deadly force in to protect another person (see, for example, Section 9.32 of the Texas Penal Code here: http://www.statutes.legis.state.tx.us/Docs/PE/htm/PE.9.htm). Also answer this question: Is it ethical to allow citizens to take the law into their own hands, no matter what the provocation?

Summary

 L01 **List the similarities and differences between substantive and procedural criminal law and between civil law and public law.**

- Substantive law defines crimes and their punishment.
- Procedural law sets out the basic rules of practice in the criminal justice system.
- Civil law governs relations between private parties.
- Public law regulates the activities of governmental agencies.

L02 **Discuss the concept of substantive criminal law and be familiar with its history.**

- The substantive criminal law defines crimes and their punishments.
- The underlying goal of the substantive criminal law is to enforce social control, distribute retribution, express public opinion and morality, deter criminal behavior, punish wrongdoing, maintain social order, and provide restoration.

L03 **Discuss the sources of the criminal law.**

- The roots of the criminal codes used in the United States can be traced back to early legal charters.
- In England, judges used local custom and rules of conduct as their guide in a system known as *stare decisis* (Latin for "to stand by decided cases").
- Eventually this system evolved into a common law of the country that incorporated local custom and practice into a national code.
- Based on the English common law, the contemporary American legal system has been codified by state and federal legislatures.

L04 **Describe how crimes are classified.**

- Felonies are considered serious crimes. Felonies include crimes against the person, such as criminal homicide, robbery, and rape, as well as such crimes against property as burglary and larceny.
- Misdemeanors are seen as less serious crimes. They include petit (or petty) larceny, assault and battery, and the unlawful possession of marijuana.
- Violations include public nuisance offenses such as traffic violations and public drunkenness.

L05 **Identify the elements of a crime.**

- For an act to constitute a crime, it must be a voluntary and deliberate illegal act, or *actus reus*, such as taking someone's money, burning a building, or shooting someone.

- For an act to constitute a crime, it must be done with deliberate purpose or criminal intent, or *mens rea*.
- For an action to constitute a crime, the law requires that a connection be made between the *mens rea* and *actus reus*, thereby showing that the offender's conduct was the proximate cause of the injury resulting.

LO6 **Define the term *strict liability*.**

- Certain statutory offenses exist in which *mens rea* is not essential. These offenses fall in a category known as public safety or strict liability crimes.
- Traffic crimes, public safety, and business crimes are typically strict liability crimes.

LO7 **Discuss excuse and justification defenses for crime.**

- Defendants may claim that even though they did engage in the criminal act they are accused of, they should be excused because they lacked *mens rea*: "I did not know what I was doing."
- Another type of defense is justification, such as self-defense, which involves maintaining that the act was justified under the circumstances: "Given the circumstances, anyone would have done what I did."

LO8 **Discuss the concept of criminal procedure.**

- The law of criminal procedure consists of the rules and procedures that govern the pretrial processing of criminal suspects and the conduct of criminal trials.
- The main source of the procedural law is the body of the Constitution and the first 10 amendments added to the U.S. Constitution. These are collectively known as the Bill of Rights.

LO9 **Identify which amendments to the Constitution are the most important to the justice system.**

- Of primary concern are the Fourth, Fifth, Sixth, and Eighth Amendments, which limit and control the manner in which the federal government operates the justice system.
- The Fourteenth Amendment applies these rights to the state and local governments.

LO10 **List the elements of due process of law.**

- Due process has been used to evaluate the constitutionality of legal statutes and to set standards and guidelines for fair procedures in the criminal justice system.
- Substantive due process refers to the citizen's right to be protected from criminal laws that may be biased, discriminatory, or otherwise unfair.

Key Terms

criminal law, 132
substantive criminal law, 132
procedural criminal laws, 132
civil law, 133
torts, 133
public law, 133
stare decisis, 136

mala in se, 136
ex post facto law, 138
actus reus, 140
mens rea, 140
criminal negligence, 141
public safety or strict liability
　crime, 141

excuse defense, 143
justification, 143
stalking, 149
obitiatry, 149
exclusionary rule, 153

Critical Thinking Questions

1. What are the specific aims and purposes of the criminal law? To what extent does the criminal law control behavior?
2. How would you cast your vote on an amendment legalizing recreational drugs? Why?
3. What is a criminal act? What is a criminal state of mind? When are individuals criminally liable for their actions?
4. Discuss the various kinds of crime classifications. To what extent or degree are they distinguishable?
5. Numerous states are revising their penal codes. Which major categories of substantive crimes—for example, laws banning prostitution—do you think should be revised?
6. Entrapment is a defense used when the defendant was lured into committing the crime. To what extent should law enforcement personnel induce the commission of an offense?

Notes

1. Long Island Newsday, "Mom Gets 3 to 9 Years in Baby's Death," http://www.newsday.com/long-island/suffolk/mom-gets-3-to-9-years-in-baby-s-death-1.3799074 (accessed May 2014).
2. Public Law 108–212.
3. National Conference of State Legislatures, *Fetal Homicide Laws*, http://www.ncsl.org/research/health/fetal-homicide-state-laws.aspx (accessed May 2014).
4. *Carriers* case, 13 Edward IV 9.pL.5 (1473).
5. See John Weaver, *Warren—The Man, the Court, the Era* (Boston: Little, Brown, 1967); see also "We the People," *Time*, July 6, 1987, p. 6.
6. *Kansas v. Hendricks*, 117 S.Ct. 2072 (1997); *Chicago v. Morales*, 119 S.Ct. 246 (1999).
7. *City of Chicago v. Morales et al.*, 527 U.S. 41 (1999).
8. Daniel Suleiman, "The Capital Punishment Exception: A Case for Constitutionalizing the Substantive Criminal Law," *Columbia Law Review* 104 (2004): 426–458.
9. *Baze v. Rees*, 553 U.S. 35 (2008).
10. *Calder v. Bull*, 3 U.S. 386 (1798).
11. *District of Columbia v. Heller*, 554 U.S. 570 (2008).
12. *McDonald v. Chicago*, 561 U.S. ____ (2010).
13. See American Law Institute, Model Penal Code, Sec. 104.
14. Henry Black, *Black's Law Dictionary*, rev. 5th ed. (St. Paul, MN: West, 1979), pp. 744, 1150.
15. Sheldon Krantz, *Law of Corrections and Prisoners' Rights, Cases, and Materials*, 3rd ed. (St. Paul, MN: West, 1986), p. 702; Barbara Knight and Stephen Early Jr., *Prisoners' Rights in America* (Chicago: Nelson-Hall, 1986), Ch. 1; see also Fred Cohen, "The Law of Prisoners' Rights—An Overview," *Criminal Law Bulletin* 24 (1988): 321–349.
16. See *United States v. Balint*, 258 U.S. 250 (1922); see also *Morissette v.United States*, 342 U.S. 246 (1952).
17. *Regina v. Dudley and Stephens*, 14 Q.B.D. 273 (1884).
18. *Robinson v. California*, 370 U.S. 660 (1962).
19. *Powell v. Texas*, 392 U.S. 514 (1968).
20. Samuel M. Davis, *Rights of Juveniles: The Juvenile Justice System* (New York: Boardman, 1974; updated 1993), Ch. 2; Larry Siegel and Joseph Senna, *Juvenile Delinquency: Theory, Practice, and Law* (St. Paul, MN: West, 1996).
21. *Jacobson v. United States*, 503 U.S. 540 (1992).
22. AOL News, "Cop in Fatal Crash Was Driving 94 MPH," November 18, 2009.
23. Rick Callahan, "Prosecutor Expects Others to Try Executed Vet's Gulf Illness Defense," Associated Press, March 18, 2003, http://www.texnews.com/1998/2003/texas/texas_Prosecuto318.html (accessed May 2014); Deborah W. Denno, "Gender, Crime, and the Criminal Law Defenses," *Journal of Criminal Law and Criminology* 85 (Summer 1994): 80–180.
24. *Lawrence v. Texas*, 539 U.S. 558 (2003).
25. National Institute of Justice, *Project to Develop a Model Anti-Stalking Statute* (Washington, DC: National Institute of Justice, 1994).
26. Marvin Zalman, John Strate, Denis Hunter, and James Sellars, "Michigan Assisted Suicide Three Ring Circus: The Intersection of Law and Politics," *Ohio Northern Law Review* 23 (1997): 863–903.
27. 1992 P.A. 270, as amended by 1993 P.A. 3, M.C. L. ss. 752.1021 to 752.1027.
28. For details, see http://euthanasia.procon.org/view.resource.php?resourceID=000132 (accessed May 2014).
29. Sarah Welchans, "Megan's Law: Evaluations of Sexual Offender Registries," *Criminal Justice Policy Review* 16 (2005): 123–140.
30. Matthew Lyon, "No Means No? Withdrawal of Consent During Intercourse and the Continuing Evolution of the Definition of Rape," *Journal of Criminal Law and Criminology* 95 (2004): 277–314.
31. Environmental Protection Agency, Criminal Enforcement Division, http://www2.epa.gov/enforcement/criminal-enforcement (accessed May 2014).
32. For a full list of such states and their laws, visit http://medicalmarijuana.procon.org/view.resource.php?resourceID=000881 (accessed May 2014).
33. Seattle Police Department, http://spdblotter.seattle.gov/2012/12/05/officers-shall-not-take-any-enforcement-action-other-than-to-issue-a-verbal-warning-for-a-violation-of-i-502 (accessed May 2014).
34. Terrence Petty, Associated Press, "Washington Could Become Pot Source for Neighbors," December 8, 2012, http://bigstory.ap.org/article/washington-could-become-pot-source-neighbors (accessed May 2014).
35. "President Signs USA PATRIOT Improvement and Reauthorization Act," http://georgewbush-whitehouse.archives.gov/infocus/patriotact/ (accessed May 2014).
36. John Stanton and David M. Drucker, "PATRIOT Act Reauthorization Makes Deadline," *Roll Call*, http://www.rollcall.com/news/house_clears_patriot_act_reauthorization-206012-1.html (accessed May 2014).
37. National Archives, http://www.archives.gov/exhibits/charters/charters.html (May 2014).
38. Ibid.
39. *Herring v. United States*, no. 07-513 (2008).
40. *Miranda v. Arizona*, 384 U.S. 436 (1966).
41. James MacGregor Burns and Steward Burns, *The Pursuit of Rights in America* (New York: Knopf, 1991).
42. *Lawrence et al. v. Texas*, 539 U.S. 558 (2003).

THE POLICE AND LAW ENFORCEMENT

THE POLICE ARE THE GATEKEEPERS of the criminal justice process. They initiate contact with law violators and decide whether to formally arrest them and start their journey through the criminal justice system, settle the issue in an informal way (such as by issuing a warning), or simply take no action at all. The strategic position of police officers, their visibility and contact with the public, and their use of weapons and arrest power have kept them in the forefront of public thought about law enforcement.

Policing is not easy, and it is not always glamorous work, but many who choose this important career wouldn't have it any other way. Steve Bishop, a sergeant with the Dallas Police Department, finds his job particularly rewarding: "I've come across some truly violent, vicious people that should never be out in society. I have worked many bloody and violent murders and sexual assaults, and putting those people in jail (particularly after assisting the prosecution in getting a conviction) gives me a huge sense of accomplishment and pride." Steve also enjoys being a role model for his four kids. These positives tend to outweigh the difficulties that can go along with constantly being in the spotlight and interacting with a public that doesn't always understand the nuances of the job.

Large cities like Dallas are the exception; most officers work in smaller agencies with relatively few officers. And while smaller towns may not see as much "action" as big cities, many of the same rules apply. For example, Larry Napolitano, a patrolman in Shrewsbury, Massachusetts, a town of 32,000 people, feels police officers must guard against complacency. They must always remain vigilant and prepared during any encounter, otherwise they may not be ready for the danger that could take place. "When you stop a motor vehicle, you really have no knowledge of who that person is, what kind of day they had, or what they are capable of. You obviously stopped them for a reason, whether it be motor vehicle–related or for another reason, but you really don't know what lies ahead. If you get complacent and treat every stop the same way, it could get you seriously hurt or killed." ■

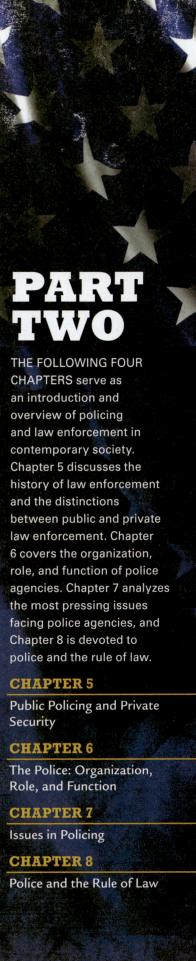

CHAPTER 5

Public Policing and Private Security

Learning Objectives

LO1 Recount the early development of the police in England.

LO2 Recount the development of the police in colonial America.

LO3 Discuss the emergence of police professionalism.

LO4 Identify the main events in policing between 1960 and the present.

LO5 Identify the four levels of law enforcement in America.

LO6 Identify the most prominent federal law enforcement agencies.

LO7 Discuss the differences among local, county, state, and federal law enforcement agencies.

LO8 Discuss the differences between public and private policing.

LO9 Identify various technologies currently used in law enforcement.

Chapter Outline

The History of Police
Private Police and Thief Takers
The London Metropolitan Police
Law Enforcement in Colonial America
Early Police Agencies
Twentieth-Century Reform
The Emergence of Professionalism

Policing from the 1960s to Present
Policing in the 1960s
Policing in the 1970s
Policing in the 1980s
Policing in the 1990s
Policing Since 2000

The Agencies of Law Enforcement
The U.S. Justice Department
Global Criminal Justice:
INTERPOL
The Department of Homeland Security (DHS)
State Law Enforcement Agencies
County Law Enforcement Agencies
Metropolitan Law Enforcement Agencies

Private Policing
Reasons for Private Policing
Careers in Criminal Justice:
Loss Prevention Specialist
Private and Public Police Compared
Types of Private Policing
Criticisms of Private Policing
The Victim Experience: From Vigilantism to United Victims

Technology and Law Enforcement
Identifying Criminals
Locating Criminals
Crime Scene Investigation
Criminal Justice and Technology: Gunshot Locators
Crime Mapping
Biometrics
Automated Fingerprint Identification Systems
DNA Testing
Social Media and Networking

Police departments across the country have purchased small unmanned surveillance drones, not unlike the drones used to track terrorists in Iraq and Afghanistan, for the purpose of tracking drug dealers and other persons of interest. Historically, the Federal Aviation Administration (FAA) made it very difficult for law enforcement agencies to secure approval for conducting drone patrols. In February 2012, however, President Obama signed a law requiring the FAA to write rules on how it would license police and other public safety agencies to fly drones at low altitudes, making it likely that small aircraft containing high definition cameras, sensors, and recording equipment would soon be flying over many more American cities. Later that year, the FAA released its first list of agencies that were authorized to fly drones. That list has since expanded.[1]

Hundreds of law enforcement agencies are now authorized to fly drones, but it is not clear that many of them are doing so. In addition, the FAA generally places limitations on drones' use, such as by limiting them to a defined block of airspace and/or daytime hours.[2]

Supporters of drone use in domestic law enforcement see the technology as a valuable tool necessary for apprehending law breakers. The police cannot be everywhere, they claim, so an extra set of "eyes" in the sky could prove helpful in fighting crime. Supporters also argue that gun detectors, security cameras, tracking devices, and other technologies are already in use, so drones are just one more tool that can be added to the law enforcement arsenal. Drones are also affordable compared to new helicopters and airplanes. Critics, however, claim that drone use, though perhaps useful for catching criminals, will also let "Big Brother" peer into the private lives of law-abiding citizens.

This chapter, the first of four on policing and law enforcement, begins with a history of policing, then provides an overview of the various governmental organizations that perform law enforcement functions. It also explores the role of technology in improving police operations.

The evolution of policing has been dramatic and somewhat cyclical. Many years ago, during tribal times, the people appointed villagers to protect them from outside marauders who wanted to destroy their lives. Then the government assumed responsibility for policing, and law enforcement became a public function. Now private security professionals and civilian volunteers are performing many of the same functions as government police. Does this represent a return to early policing? ■

The History of Police

The origin of U.S. police agencies, like that of criminal law, can be traced to early English society.[3] England had no regular police force before the Norman Conquest. Every person living in the villages scattered throughout the countryside was responsible for aiding neighbors and protecting the settlement from thieves and marauders. This was known as the pledge system. People were grouped in collectives of 10 families, called **tythings** (or **tithings**), and were entrusted with policing their own minor problems such as dealing with disturbances, fire, wild animals, or other threats. The leader was called the *tythingman*. When trouble occurred, he was expected to make a **hue and cry** to assemble his helpers and warn the village. Ten tythings were grouped into a **hundred**, whose affairs were supervised by a *hundredman* appointed by the local nobleman. The hundredman (later to be called the parish constable) might be considered the first real police officer, and he dealt with more serious breaches of the law.[4]

Shires, which resembled the counties of today, were controlled by the **shire reeve**, who was appointed by the Crown or local landowner to supervise the territory and ensure that order would be kept. The shire reeve, a forerunner of today's **sheriff**, soon began to pursue and apprehend law violators as part of his duties.

In the thirteenth century, the **watch system** was created to help protect property in England's larger cities and towns. Watchmen patrolled at night and helped protect against robberies, fires, and disturbances. They reported to the area **constable**, who became the primary metropolitan law enforcement agent. In larger cities, such as London, the watchmen were organized within church parishes and were usually members of the parish they protected.

In 1326, the office of **justice of the peace** was created to assist the shire reeve in controlling the county. Eventually, these justices took on judicial functions in addition to their primary role as peacekeeper. The local constable became the operational assistant to the justice of the peace, supervising the night watchmen, investigating offenses, serving summonses, executing warrants, and securing prisoners. This system helped delineate the relationship between police and the judiciary, which has continued for more than 600 years.

Private Police and Thief Takers

As the eighteenth century began, rising crime rates in the cities encouraged a new form of private, monied police, who were able to profit both legally and criminally from the lack of formal police departments. These private police agents, referred to as *thief takers*, were universally corrupt, taking profits not only from catching and informing on criminals but also from theft, receiving stolen property, intimidation, perjury, and blackmail. They often relieved their prisoners of money and stolen goods and made more income by accepting hush money, giving perjured evidence, swearing false oaths, and operating extortion rackets. Petty debtors were especially easy targets for those who combined thief taking with the keeping of alehouses and taverns. While prisoners were incarcerated, their health and safety were entirely at the whim of the keepers, who were virtually free to charge what they wanted for board and other necessities. Court bailiffs who also acted as thief takers were the most passionately detested legal profiteers. They seized debtors and held them in small lockups, where they forced their victims to pay exorbitant prices for food and lodging.

The thief takers' use of violence was notorious. They went armed and were prepared to maim or kill in order to gain their objectives. Before he was hanged in 1725, Jack Wild, the most notorious thief taker, "had two fractures in his skull and his bald head was covered with silver plates. He had seventeen wounds in various parts of his body from swords, daggers, and gunshots, [and] ... his throat had been cut in the course of his duties."[5]

---

tythings (tithings)

In medieval England, a collective group of 10 families that pledged to help one another and provide mutual aid.

hue and cry

In medieval England, a call for mutual aid against trouble or danger.

hundred

In medieval England, a group of 100 families responsible for maintaining order and trying minor offenses.

shire reeve

In early England, the chief law enforcement official in a county, forerunner of today's sheriff.

sheriff

The chief law enforcement officer in a county.

watch system

In medieval England, groups of men who organized in church parishes to guard at night against disturbances and breaches of the peace under the direction of the local constable.

constable

In early English towns, an appointed peacekeeper who organized citizens for protection and supervised the night watch.

justice of the peace

Official appointed to act as the judicial officer in a county.

 L01 Recount the early development of the police in England.

Henry Fielding, famed author of *Tom Jones*, along with Saunders Welch and Sir John Fielding (Henry's brother), sought to clean up the thief-taking system. Appointed a city magistrate in 1748, Fielding operated his own group of monied police out of Bow Street in London, directing and deploying them throughout the city and its environs, deciding which cases to investigate and what streets to protect. His agents were carefully instructed on their legitimate powers and duties. Fielding's Bow Street Runners were a marked improvement over the earlier monied police because they actually had an administrative structure that improved record-keeping and investigative procedures.

Although an improvement, Fielding's forces were not adequate, and by the nineteenth century, state police officers were needed. Ironically, almost 200 years later, private policing is now considered essential. Private police forces are a rapidly growing entity, and in many instances local police forces work closely with private security firms and similar entities. In some gated communities and special tax assessment districts, property owners pay a special levy, in addition to their tax dollars, to hire additional private police, who may work in partnership with local law enforcement to investigate criminal activities.[6]

The London Metropolitan Police

In 1829, Sir Robert Peel, England's home secretary, guided through Parliament an "Act for Improving the Police in and near the Metropolis." The legislation came to be known as the **Metropolitan Police Act**. Peel was also among the first influential figures in policing history to call for more than just a crime fighter role for officers. He identified nine principles that he felt should characterize police forces.[7] These appear in Exhibit 5.1.

Peel's Metropolitan Police Act established the first organized police force in London. Composed of more than 1,000 men, the London police force was structured along military lines. Its members would be known from then on as *bobbies*, after their creator. They wore a distinctive uniform and were led by two magistrates, who were later given the title of commissioner. However, the ultimate responsibility for the police fell to the home secretary and, consequently, Parliament.

Metropolitan Police Act
Sir Robert Peel's legislation that established the first organized police force in London.

EXHIBIT 5.1 Sir Robert Peel's Nine Principles of Policing

1. The basic mission for which the police exist is to prevent crime and disorder.

2. The ability of the police to perform their duties is dependent upon public approval of police actions.

3. Police must secure the willing co-operation of the public in voluntary observance of the law to be able to secure and maintain the respect of the public.

4. The degree of co-operation of the public that can be secured diminishes proportionately to the necessity of the use of physical force.

5. Police seek and preserve public favour not by catering to public opinion but by constantly demonstrating absolute impartial service to the law.

6. Police use physical force to the extent necessary to secure observance of the law or to restore order only when the exercise of persuasion, advice and warning is found to be insufficient.

7. Police, at all times, should maintain a relationship with the public that gives reality to the historic tradition that the police are the public and the public are the police; the police being only members of the public who are paid to give full-time attention to duties which are incumbent on every citizen in the interests of community welfare and existence.

8. Police should always direct their action strictly towards their functions and never appear to usurp the powers of the judiciary.

9. The test of police efficiency is the absence of crime and disorder, not the visible evidence of police action in dealing with it.

Source: Sir Robert Peel, http://www.nwpolice.org/inside-new-westminster-police-department/history/ (accessed May 2014).

Sir Robert Peel (1788–1850) was home secretary from 1822 to 1830 and prime minister of Great Britain twice in the 1830s and 1840s. He was also responsible for forming the Metropolitan Police, the first organized police force in London.

 LO2 Recount the development of the police in colonial America.

 **Web App 5.1**

To read about Sir Robert Peel's life and political career, visit http://www.victorianweb.org/history/pms/peel/peel10.html.

vigilantes
In the Old West, members of a vigilance committee or posse called upon to capture cattle thieves or other felons.

The early bobbies suffered many problems. Not only were many of them corrupt, but they were unsuccessful at stopping crime and they were influenced by the wealthy. Owners of houses of ill repute who in the past had guaranteed their undisturbed operations by bribing watchmen now turned their attention to the bobbies. Metropolitan Police administrators fought constantly to terminate cowardly, corrupt, and alcoholic officers, dismissing in the beginning about one-third of the bobbies each year.

Despite its recognized shortcomings, the London experiment proved a vast improvement over what had come before. It was considered so successful that the Metropolitan Police soon began providing law enforcement assistance to outlying areas that requested it. Another act of Parliament allowed justices of the peace to establish local police forces, and by 1856 every borough and county in England was required to form its own police force.

Law Enforcement in Colonial America

Law enforcement in colonial America paralleled the British model. In the colonies, the county sheriff became the most important law enforcement agent. In addition to keeping the peace and fighting crime, sheriffs collected taxes, supervised elections, and handled a great deal of other legal business.

The colonial sheriff did not patrol or seek out crime. Instead, he reacted to citizens' complaints and investigated crimes that had occurred. His salary, related to his effectiveness, was paid on a fee system. Sheriffs received a fixed amount for every arrest made. Unfortunately, their tax-collecting chores were more lucrative than fighting crime, so law enforcement was not one of their primary concerns.

In the cities, law enforcement was the province of the town marshal, who was aided, often unwillingly, by a variety of constables, night watchmen, police justices, and city council members. However, local governments had little power of administration, and enforcement of the criminal law was largely an individual or community responsibility. After the American Revolution, larger cities relied on elected or appointed officials to serve warrants and recover stolen property, sometimes in cooperation with the thieves themselves. Night watchmen, referred to as *leatherheads* because of the leather helmets they wore, patrolled the streets calling the hour while equipped with a rattle to summon help and a nightstick to ward off lawbreakers. Watchmen were not widely respected. Rowdy young men enjoyed tipping over watch houses with a leatherhead inside, and a favorite saying in New York was "While the city sleeps the watchmen do too."[8]

In rural areas in the South, "slave patrols" charged with recapturing escaped slaves were an early, if loathsome, form of law enforcement.[9] In the western territories, individual initiative was encouraged by the practice of offering rewards for the capture of felons. If trouble arose, the town vigilance committee might form a posse to chase offenders. These **vigilantes** were called on to use force or intimidation to eradicate such social problems as theft of livestock. For example, the San Francisco Vigilance Committee actively pursued criminals in the mid-nineteenth century.

As cities grew, it became exceedingly difficult for local leaders to organize ad hoc citizen vigilante groups. Moreover, the early nineteenth century was an era of widespread urban unrest and mob violence. Local leaders began to realize that a more structured police function was needed to control demonstrators and keep the peace.

Early Police Agencies

The modern police department was born out of the urban mob violence that wracked the nation's cities in the nineteenth century. Boston created the first formal U.S. police department in 1838. New York formed its police department in 1844; Philadelphia did so in 1854. The new police departments replaced the night watch system and relegated constables and sheriffs to serving court orders and running jails.

At first, the urban police departments inherited the functions of the institutions they replaced. For example, Boston police were charged with maintaining public health until 1853, and in New York, the police were responsible for street sweeping until 1881. Politics dominated the departments and determined the recruitment of new officers and the promotion of supervisors. An individual with the right connections could be hired despite a lack of qualifications. Early police agencies were corrupt, brutal, and inefficient.[10]

In the late nineteenth century, police work was highly desirable because it paid more than most other blue-collar jobs. By 1880, the average factory worker earned $450 per year, while a metropolitan police officer made double that amount. For immigrant groups, having enough political clout to be appointed to the police department was an important step up the social ladder.[11] However, job security was uncertain because it depended on the local political machine staying in power.

Police work itself was primitive. Few of even the simplest technological innovations common today, such as call boxes or centralized record keeping, were in place. Most officers patrolled on foot, without backup or the ability to call for help. Officers were commonly taunted by local toughs and responded with force and brutality. The long-standing conflict between police and the public was born in the difficulty that untrained, unprofessional officers had in patrolling the streets of nineteenth-century U.S. cities and in breaking up and controlling labor disputes. Police were not crime fighters as they are known today. Their major role was maintaining order, and their power was almost unchecked. The average officer had little training, no education in the law, and a minimum of supervision, yet the police became virtual judges of law and fact, with the ability to exercise unlimited discretion.[12]

At mid-nineteenth century, the detective bureau was set up as part of the Boston police. Until then, thief taking had been the province of amateur bounty hunters who hired themselves out to victims for a price. When professional police departments replaced bounty hunters, the close working relationships that developed between police detectives and their underworld informants produced many scandals and, consequently, high personnel turnover.

Police during the nineteenth century were regarded as incompetent and corrupt, and they were disliked by the people whom they served. The police role was only minimally directed at law enforcement. Its primary function was serving as the enforcement arm of the reigning political power, protecting private property, and keeping control of the ever-rising numbers of foreign immigrants.

Police agencies evolved slowly in the second half of the nineteenth century. Uniforms were introduced in 1853 in New York. The first technological breakthroughs in police operations came in the area of communications. The linking of precincts to central headquarters by telegraph began in the 1850s. In 1867, the first telegraph police boxes were installed. An officer could turn a key in a box, and his location and number would automatically register at headquarters. Additional technological advances were made in transportation. The Detroit Police Department outfitted some of its patrol officers with bicycles in 1897. By 1913, the motorcycle was being used by departments in the eastern part of the nation. The first police car was used in Akron, Ohio, in 1910, and the police wagon became popular in Cincinnati in 1912.[13] Nonpolice functions, such as care of the streets, began to be abandoned after the Civil War.

Big-city police were still disrespected by the public, unsuccessful in their role as crime stoppers, and uninvolved in progressive activities. The control of police departments by local politicians impeded effective law enforcement and fostered an atmosphere of graft and corruption.

Twentieth-Century Reform

In an effort to reduce police corruption, civic leaders in a number of jurisdictions created police administrative boards to lessen local officials' control over the police. These boards were responsible for appointing police administrators and controlling police affairs. In many instances, these measures failed because the private citizens appointed to the review boards lacked expertise in the intricacies of police work.

Another reform movement was the takeover of some big-city police agencies by state legislators. Although police budgets were financed through local taxes, control of police was usurped by rural politicians in the state capitals. New York City temporarily lost authority over its police force in 1857. It was not until the first decades of the twentieth century that cities regained control of their police forces.

The Boston police strike of 1919 heightened interest in police reform. The strike came about basically because police officers were dissatisfied with their status in society. Other professions were unionizing and increasing their standards of living, but police salaries lagged behind. The Boston police officers' organization, the Boston Social Club, voted to become a union affiliated with the American Federation of Labor. The police officers went on strike on September 9, 1919. Rioting and looting broke out, resulting in Governor Calvin Coolidge's mobilization of the state militia to take over the city. Public support turned against the police, and the strike was broken. Eventually, all the striking officers were fired and replaced by new recruits. The Boston police strike ended police unionism for decades and solidified power in the hands of reactionary, autocratic police administrators. In the aftermath of the strike, various local, state, and federal crime commissions began to investigate the extent of crime and the ability of the justice system to deal with it and made recommendations to improve police effectiveness.[14] However, with the onset of the Great Depression, justice reform became a less important issue than economic revival, and for many years, little changed in policing.

The Emergence of Professionalism

L03 Discuss the emergence of police professionalism.

Web App 5.2

Interested in police labor relations? Visit the International Union of Police Associations at http://www.iupa.org.

Around the turn of the twentieth century, a number of nationally recognized leaders called for measures to help improve and professionalize the police. In 1893, the International Association of Chiefs of Police (IACP), a professional society, was formed. Under the direction of its first president (District of Columbia Chief of Police Richard Sylvester), the IACP became the leading voice for police reform during the first two decades of the twentieth century. The IACP called for creating a civil service police force and for removing political influence and control. It also advocated centralized organizational structure and record keeping to curb the power of politically aligned precinct captains. Still another professional reform the IACP fostered was the creation of specialized units, such as delinquency control squads.

Great precaution is taken to guard police headquarters in Pemberton Square during the Boston police strike of 1919. Here, the cavalrymen of the state guard ride horses previously used by the mounted policemen who went on strike.

AP Images/Boston Public Library

In 1929, President Herbert Hoover created the National Commission on Law Observance and Enforcement, otherwise known as the **Wickersham Commission** (for George W. Wickersham, its chair), to study the U.S. criminal justice system and make recommendations for improvement. In 1931, it issued the so-called *Wickersham Commission Report*. Two volumes of the report dealt specifically with police. Volume 2, called *Lawlessness in Law Enforcement*, portrayed the police in an unfavorable light, calling them inept, inefficient, racist, brutal, and even criminal. Volume 14, called *The Police*, was authored mostly by August Vollmer, one of the most famous police reformers of the time. In it, he discussed methods that could be used to professionalize the police, several of which he had already used in his own law enforcement career.

While serving as police chief of Berkeley, California, Vollmer instituted university training for young officers. He also helped develop the School of Criminology at the University of California at Berkeley, which became the model for justice-related programs around the United States. Vollmer's protégés included O. W. Wilson, who pioneered the use of advanced training for officers when he took over and reformed the Wichita (Kansas) Police Department in 1928. Wilson was also instrumental in applying modern management and administrative techniques to policing. His text, *Police Administration*, became the single most influential work on the subject.[15]

Wickersham Commission
Formally known as the National Commission on Law Observance and Enforcement, a commission created in 1929 by President Herbert Hoover to study the U.S. criminal justice system, including the police.

Policing from the 1960s to the Present

The modern era of policing can be traced from the 1960s to the present. Several major events occurred during this important period of police history.

Policing in the 1960s

Turmoil and crisis were the hallmarks of policing during the 1960s. Throughout this decade, the U.S. Supreme Court handed down a number of decisions designed to control police operations and procedures. Police officers were now required to obey strict legal guidelines when questioning suspects, conducting searches, and wiretapping. As the civil rights of suspects were significantly expanded, police complained that they were being "handcuffed by the courts."

Also during this time, civil unrest produced a growing tension between police and the public. African Americans, who were battling for increased rights and freedoms in the civil rights movement, found themselves confronting police lines. When riots broke out in New York, Detroit, Los Angeles, and other cities between 1964 and 1968, the spark that ignited conflict often involved the police. When students across the nation began marching in anti–Vietnam War demonstrations, local police departments were called on to keep order. Police forces were ill equipped and poorly trained to deal with these social problems. Not surprisingly, the 1960s were marked by a number of bloody confrontations between the police and the public.

Compounding these problems was a rapidly growing crime rate. The number of violent and property crimes increased dramatically. Drug addiction and abuse, common in all social classes, grew to be national concerns. Urban police departments could not control the crime rate, and police officers resented the demands placed on them by dissatisfied citizens.

Policing in the 1970s

Identify the main events in policing between 1960 and the present.

The 1970s witnessed many structural changes in police agencies themselves. The end of the Vietnam War significantly reduced tensions between students and police. However, the relationship between police and minorities was still rocky. Local fears and distrust, combined with conservative federal policies, encouraged police departments to control what was perceived as an emerging minority group "threat."[16]

Increased federal government support for criminal justice greatly influenced police operations.[17] During the decade, the Law Enforcement Assistance Administration (LEAA) devoted a significant portion of its funds to police agencies. Although a number of police departments used this money to purchase little-used hardware, such as anti-riot gear, most of it went to supporting innovative research on police work and advanced training of police officers. Perhaps most significant, LEAA's Law Enforcement Education Program helped thousands of officers further their college education. Hundreds of criminal justice programs were developed on college campuses around the country, providing a pool of highly educated police recruits. LEAA funds were also used to import or transfer technology originally developed in other fields into law enforcement. Technological innovations involving computers transformed the way police kept records, investigated crimes, and communicated with one another. State training academies improved the way police learned to deal with such issues as job stress, community conflict, and interpersonal relations.

More women and minorities were recruited to police work. Affirmative action programs helped alter, albeit slowly, the ethnic, racial, and gender composition of U.S. policing.

Policing in the 1980s

As the 1980s began, the police role seemed to be changing significantly. A number of experts acknowledged that the police were not simply crime fighters

The 1960s were a time of social ferment. Here, Chicago policemen with nightsticks in hand confront a demonstrator on the ground in Grant Park, Chicago, on August 26, 1968. The police force converged at Grant Park when protesters opposing the Vietnam War climbed on the statue of Civil War general John Logan. Conflicts such as this between police and the public inspired the creation of university-based criminal justice programs.

AP Images/Anonymous

and called for police to develop a greater awareness of community issues, which resulted in the emergence of the community policing concept.[18]

Police unions, which began to grow in the late 1960s, continued to have a great impact on departmental administration in the 1980s. Unions fought for and won increased salaries and benefits for their members. In many instances, unions eroded the power of the police chief to make unquestioned policy and personnel decisions. During the decade, chiefs of police commonly consulted with union leaders before making major decisions concerning departmental operations.

Although police operations improved markedly during this time, police departments were also beset by problems that impeded their effectiveness. State and local budgets were cut back during the Reagan administration, and federal support for innovative police programs was severely curtailed with the demise of the LEAA.

Police–community relations continued to be a major problem. Riots and incidents of urban conflict occurred in some of the nation's largest cities.[19] They triggered continual concern about what the police role should be, especially in inner-city neighborhoods.

Policing in the 1990s

The 1990s began on a sour note and ended with an air of optimism. The incident that helped change the face of U.S. policing occurred on March 3, 1991, when two African American men, Rodney King and Bryant Allen, were driving in Los Angeles. They refused to stop when signaled by a police car, instead increasing their speed. King, who was driving, was apparently drunk or on drugs. When police finally stopped the car, they delivered 56 baton blows and 6 kicks to King in a period of two minutes, producing 11 skull fractures, brain damage, and kidney damage. They did not realize that their actions were being videotaped by an observer, who later gave the tape to the media. The officers involved were tried and acquitted in a suburban court by an all-white jury. The acquittal set off six days of rioting in South Central Los Angeles, and the California National Guard was called in to restore order. In total, 54 people were killed, 2,383 were known to have been injured, and 13,212 people were arrested.[20] The police officers involved in the beatings were later tried and convicted in federal court.

The King case prompted an era of reform. Several police experts decreed that the nation's police forces should be evaluated not on their crime-fighting ability but on their courteousness, behavior, and helpfulness. Interest renewed in reviving an earlier style of police work featuring foot patrols and increased citizen contact. Police departments began to embrace new forms of policing that stressed cooperation with the community and problem solving; this is referred to as the **community policing** model. Ironically, urban police departments began to shift their focus to working closely with community members at a time when technological improvements made it easier to fight crime from a distance.

An ongoing effort was made to bring diversity to police departments, and African Americans began to be hired as chiefs of police, particularly in Los Angeles. As a result of the reform efforts, the intellectual caliber of the police rose dramatically, and they became smarter, better informed, and more sophisticated than ever before. Management skills improved, and senior police managers began to implement information technology systems. As a result, policing became intellectually more demanding,

community policing

A law enforcement program that seeks to integrate officers into the local community to reduce crime and gain good community relations. It typically involves personalized service and decentralized policing, citizen empowerment, and an effort to reduce community fear of crime, disorder, and decay.

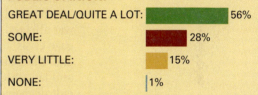

FACT CHECK ✓

YOUR OPINION: How much confidence do you have in the police? A great deal/quite a lot, some, very little, or none?

PUBLIC OPINION:

GREAT DEAL/QUITE A LOT:	56%
SOME:	28%
VERY LITTLE:	15%
NONE:	1%

REALITY: The majority of Americans are quite confident in the police year in and year out. That majority is not a large one, however. What's more, a number of factors can quickly shape public opinion for the better or worse. High-profile scandals weaken support for the police; crime control success stories strengthen it. Support for the police is sharply divided along demographic lines, as well. At the end of the day, questions about public confidence in the police are complicated and may not yield a lot of useful information, for at least two reasons. First, measuring success in policing is complicated, as crime prevention/control is only part of their job. Second, the police presence is spread rather thinly, so to the extent the police are faulted for not being everywhere people want them to be, it is not so much a policing problem as a funding problem.

DISCUSSION: What factors drive public support for the police? How might support for and confidence in the police vary by sex, race, age, and education level? What about income level? Region of the country? Political beliefs?

Source: Sourcebook of Criminal Justice Statistics, University at Albany, http://www.albany.edu/sourcebook/pdf/t2122012.pdf (accessed May 2014).

requiring specialized knowledge about technology, forensic analysis, and crime. Although a few notorious cases of police corruption and violence made headlines, by and large the police began to treat the public more fairly and more equitably than ever before.[21]

Policing Since 2000

The events of September 11, 2001, made an indelible mark on policing as we know it today. Federal agencies were reorganized in response to the terrorist attacks. State and local agencies shifted resources to terrorism prevention. Intelligence-gathering became important, and so did interagency cooperation. Joint anti-terrorism task forces began to pop up all around the country. To this day, a wealth of law enforcement activity, especially in large urban areas, is devoted to the prevention of another 9/11.

Since 2000, policing, along with other components of the criminal justice system, have entered into an evidence-based era. There is increasing pressure to "do more with less," so agencies are striving to identify best practices that most capably control and prevent crime. Not too long ago, most crime policy was akin to taking shots in the dark; little research was performed, and it was mainly political beliefs that drove police practice. Nowadays, through the efforts of criminal justice researchers and the government's crimesolutions.gov website, among others, police departments can draw on a growing body of scientific evidence to inform their decisions.

When the economy spiraled downward in 2008, the whole world economy was affected. The European sovereign debt crisis, the U.S.-based subprime mortgage crisis, high levels of household debt, trade imbalances, high unemployment, and other factors affected everyone, including the police. Tax revenues slipped and law enforcement agencies around the country were forced to make difficult decisions. Many put hiring freezes into effect; others went so far as to lay off officers. Some entire police departments closed up shop permanently. By all accounts, the economy has made something of a turn for the better (as of this writing, anyway), but police departments across the country are still reeling from the "Great Recession."

The Agencies of Law Enforcement

LO5 Identify the four levels of law enforcement in America.

Law enforcement agencies of today are organized into four broad categories: federal, state, county, and local policing agencies (and many subcategories within). The federal government has a number of law enforcement agencies designed to protect the rights and privileges of U.S. citizens. No single agency has unlimited jurisdiction. Each has been created to enforce specific laws and cope with particular situations. Federal police agencies have no particular rank order or hierarchy of command or responsibility, and each reports to a specific department or bureau.

The U.S. Justice Department

The U.S. Department of Justice is the legal arm of the federal government. Headed by the attorney general, it is empowered to enforce all federal laws, represent the United States when it is party to court action, and conduct independent investigations through its law enforcement services.

The Department of Justice maintains several separate divisions that are responsible for enforcing federal laws and protecting U.S. citizens. The Civil Rights Division proceeds legally against violations of federal civil rights laws that protect citizens from discrimination on the basis of their race, creed, ethnic background, age, or sex. Areas of greatest concern include discrimination in education, housing, and employment, including affirmative action cases. The

GLOBAL criminal justice

INTERPOL

INTERPOL (officially the International Criminal Police Organization) is the world's largest international police organization—with members from 190 countries. Its mission consists of "preventing and fighting crime through enhanced cooperation and innovation on police and security matters."

INTERPOL is not a law enforcement organization with arrest powers and all the other hallmarks of modern policing. Rather, its job is to provide technical and operational support to police organizations the world over. It is mostly an intelligence-gathering entity that helps member countries fight complicated international crime problems.

The idea of INTERPOL was born back in 1914 at the first International Criminal Police Congress. Representatives from 24 countries met in Monaco to find ways to solve crime, centralize record-keeping, and develop arrest and extradition policies. INTERPOL was officially created in 1923 and has since seen its membership grow markedly (only five formally recognized countries are not members). Today the organization is headquartered in Lyon, France. Each member country maintains a National Central Bureau, or NCB. The United States' NCB is housed within the U.S. Department of Justice.

ACTIVITIES

Amidst an increasingly complex international criminal landscape, INTERPOL helps law enforcement agencies combat problems such as corruption, organized crime, international drug trafficking, financial crime, high-tech crime, terrorism, and human trafficking. To assist in this regard, INTERPOL manages a variety of databases with information on wanted criminals, including fingerprints and DNA profiles.

INTERPOL also disseminates information through several types of international notices. A Red Notice seeks "the location and arrest of wanted persons with a view to extradition or similar lawful action." A Blue Notice seeks "to collect additional information about a person's identity, location or activities in relation to a crime." A Green Notice provides "warnings and intelligence about persons who have committed criminal offenses and are likely to repeat these crimes in other countries." Several other types of notices also exist, all with the intent of sharing information and/or gathering additional information on groups and persons suspected of involvement in criminal activity.

LIMITATIONS

INTERPOL's focus is on common criminals. Article 3 of its constitution states, "It is strictly forbidden for the Organization to undertake any intervention or activities of a political, military, religious, or racial character."

SUCCESS STORIES

In 2013, INTERPOL Buenos Aires sought (via a Red Notice) assistance from the United States in order to locate Rodolfo Adolfo Gimenez, a man accused of committing various war crimes in Argentina during that country's "dirty war" in the 1970s. In early 2014, U.S. officials were able to locate Gimenez, who was hiding in a safe house in Miami, arrest him, and extradite him to Argentina for prosecution. He faces life in prison if convicted.

In another case, INTERPOL led to the apprehension and prosecution of six Columbian nationals who were suspected of murdering DEA Special Agent James Terry Watson. The men were allegedly part of a kidnapping and robbery conspiracy that used taxi cabs in Bogota, Columbia, to commit their crimes. Once an intended victim entered a cab, the driver would signal other conspirators to commence the robbery. While working in Columbia, Agent Watson entered one of the cabs and was robbed, shocked with a stun gun, and stabbed.

CRITICAL THINKING

1. INTERPOL is not a law enforcement organization per se. It does not employ sworn officers who have arrest powers and can use force. Is this a strength or a limitation?

2. There is no requirement of INTERPOL members that they observe democratic principles or even the rule of law. Is this a problem? If so, how?

Sources: INTERPOL, *Strategic Framework, 2014–2016*, http://www.interpol.int/About-INTERPOL/Priorities (accessed May 2014); INTERPOL Washington, http://www.justice.gov/interpol-washington/ (accessed May 2014).

Tax Division brings legal actions against tax violators. The Criminal Division prosecutes violations of the Federal Criminal Code. Its responsibility includes enforcing statutes relating to bank robbery (because bank deposits are federally insured), kidnapping, mail fraud, interstate transportation of stolen vehicles, drug trafficking, and other offenses.

L06 Identify the most prominent federal law enforcement agencies.

Federal Bureau of Investigation (FBI)

The arm of the Justice Department that investigates violations of federal law, gathers crime statistics, runs a comprehensive crime laboratory, and helps train local law enforcement officers.

THE FEDERAL BUREAU OF INVESTIGATION The Justice Department first became involved in law enforcement when the attorney general hired investigators to enforce the Mann Act (forbidding the transportation of women between states for immoral purposes). These investigators were formalized in 1908 into a distinct branch of the government, the Bureau of Investigation. The agency was later reorganized into the **Federal Bureau of Investigation (FBI)**, under the direction of J. Edgar Hoover from 1924 until his death in 1972.

Today's FBI is not a police agency but an investigative agency with jurisdiction over all law enforcement matters in which the United States is or may be an interested party. However, its jurisdiction is limited to federal laws, including all federal statutes not specifically assigned to other agencies. Areas covered by these laws include espionage, sabotage, treason, civil rights violations, murder and assault of federal officers, mail fraud, robbery and burglary of federally insured banks, kidnapping, and interstate transportation of stolen vehicles and property. The FBI headquarters in Washington, D.C., oversees more than 50 field offices, approximately 400 satellite offices known as resident agencies, 4 specialized field installations, and more than 60 foreign liaison posts. The foreign liaison offices, each of which is headed by a legal attaché or legal liaison officer, work abroad with U.S. and local authorities on criminal matters within FBI jurisdiction. In all, the FBI has approximately 33,000 employees, including approximately 13,000 special agents and 20,000 support personnel, who perform professional, administrative, technical, clerical, craft, trade, or maintenance operations.[22]

The FBI offers a number of important services to local law enforcement agencies. Its identification division, established in 1924, collects and maintains a vast fingerprint file that can be used by local police agencies. Its sophisticated crime laboratory, established in 1932, aids local police in testing and identifying such evidence as hairs, fibers, blood, tire tracks, and drugs. The Uniform Crime Report (UCR) is another service of the FBI. The UCR is an annual compilation of crimes reported to local police agencies, arrests, police killed or wounded in action, and other information. Finally, the FBI's National Crime Information Center is a computerized network linked to local police departments that provides ready information on stolen vehicles, wanted persons, stolen guns, and so on.

The FBI mission has been evolving to keep pace with world events (see Exhibit 5.2). It is now charged with coordinating intelligence collection with the Border Patrol, the Secret Service, the CIA, and other law enforcement agencies. At the center of this initiative, the Counterterrorism Division of the FBI collects, analyzes, and shares critical information and intelligence on (a) international terrorism operations both within the United States and in support of extraterritorial investigations, (b) domestic terrorism operations, and (c) counterterrorism related to both international and domestic terrorism. Based in Washington, D.C., the Counterterrorism Division has the following responsibilities:

■ Manage a team of analysts who work to put together information gathered by the field offices.

■ Operate a national threat-warning system that enables the FBI to instantly distribute important terrorism alert bulletins to law enforcement agencies and public safety departments.

■ Send out "flying squads" of specially trained officers to provide counterterrorism knowledge and experience, language capabilities, and analytical support, as needed, to FBI field offices.

■ Maintain the Joint Terrorism Task Force (JTTF), which includes representatives from the Department of Defense, Department of Energy, Federal Emergency Management Agency, Central Intelligence Agency,

EXHIBIT 5.2   What the FBI Investigates

National Security Priorities

Terrorism
- International terrorism
- Domestic terrorism
- Weapons of mass destruction

Counterintelligence
- Counterespionage
- Counterproliferation
- Economic espionage

Cyber Crime
- Computer intrusions
- Internet fraud
- Identity theft

Criminal Priorities

Public Corruption
- Government fraud
- Election fraud
- Foreign corrupt practices

Civil Rights
- Hate crime
- Human trafficking
- Color of law
- Freedom of access to clinics

Organized Crime
- Italian Mafia/La Cosa Nostra
- Eurasian
- Balkan
- Middle Eastern

- Asian
- African
- Sports bribery

White-Collar Crime
- Antitrust
- Bankruptcy fraud
- Corporate fraud
- Financial institution fraud and failures
- Health care fraud
- Insurance fraud
- Mass marketing fraud
- Money laundering
- Mortgage fraud
- Piracy/intellectual property theft
- Securities and commodities fraud
- More white-collar frauds

Violent Crime and Major Thefts
- Art theft
- Bank robbery
- Cargo theft
- Gangs
- Indian country crime
- Jewelry and gem theft
- Online predators
- Retail theft
- Vehicle theft
- Violent crimes against children

Source: Federal Bureau of Investigation, http://www.fbi.gov/about-us/investigate/what_we_investigate (accessed May 2014).

Customs Service, Secret Service, and Immigration and Naturalization Service. Additionally, there are 66 local joint terrorism task forces in which representatives from federal agencies, state and local law enforcement personnel, and first responders work together to track down terrorists and prevent acts of terrorism in the United States.[23]

To carry out its newly formulated mission, the FBI is expanding its force of agents. In addition to recruiting candidates with the traditional backgrounds in law enforcement, law, and accounting, the bureau also concentrates on hiring agents with scientific and technological skills as well as foreign-language proficiency in priority areas such as Arabic, Farsi, Pashtun, Urdu, all dialects of Chinese, Japanese, Korean, Russian, Spanish, and Vietnamese, and with

Agents from several federal agencies, including the FBI and ATF, arrive on scene after explosions near the finish line of the Boston Marathon on April 15, 2013.

other priority backgrounds such as foreign counterintelligence, counterterrorism, and military intelligence.

BUREAU OF ALCOHOL, TOBACCO, FIREARMS AND EXPLOSIVES (ATF) The ATF helps control sales of untaxed liquor and cigarettes, and, through the Gun Control Act of 1968 and the Organized Crime Control Act of 1970, has jurisdiction over the illegal sale, importation, and criminal misuse of firearms and explosives. On January 24, 2003, ATF's law enforcement functions were transferred to the Department of Justice (DOJ), and ATF became the Bureau of Alcohol, Tobacco, Firearms and Explosives.

U.S. MARSHALS The Marshals Service is the nation's oldest federal law enforcement agency. Among its duties are the following:[24]

■ *Judicial security*. Protection of federal judicial officials, which includes judges, attorneys, and jurors. The Marshals Service also oversees each aspect of courthouse construction, from design through completion, to ensure the safety of federal judges, court personnel, and the public.

■ *Fugitive investigations*. Working with law enforcement authorities at federal, state, local, and international levels, the Marshals Service apprehends thousands of dangerous felons each year. The Marshals Service is the primary agency responsible for tracking and extraditing fugitives who are apprehended in foreign countries and wanted for prosecution in the United States.

■ *Witness security*. The Marshals Service Witness Security Program ensures the safety of witnesses who risk their lives testifying for the government in cases involving organized crime and other significant criminal activity. Since 1970, the Marshals Service has protected, relocated, and given new identities to more than 8,000 witnesses.

■ *Prisoner services*. The Marshals Service houses more than 55,000 federal unsentenced prisoners each day in federal, state, and local jails.

■ *Justice Prisoner and Alien Transportation System (JPATS)*. In 1995, the air fleets of the Marshals Service and the Immigration and Naturalization Service merged to form a more efficient and effective system for transporting prisoners and criminal aliens.

■ *Asset Forfeiture Program*. The Marshals Service is responsible for managing and disposing of seized and forfeited properties acquired by criminals through illegal activities.

The Department of Homeland Security (DHS)

Following the September 11, 2001, attacks, a new cabinet-level agency called the Department of Homeland Security (DHS) received congressional approval and was assigned the mission of preventing terrorist attacks within the United States, reducing America's vulnerability to terrorism, and minimizing the damage and aiding the recovery from attacks that do occur. DHS is the third-largest cabinet department in the federal government, after the Department of Defense and the Department of Veterans Affairs. It has approximately 180,000 employees. The Department of Homeland Security has a number of independent branches and

Neal Hamberg/Reuters/Landov

bureaus.[25] Of them, three are well-known law enforcement agencies: Customs and Border Protection, Immigration and Customs Enforcement, and the U.S. Secret Service.

CUSTOMS AND BORDER PROTECTION (CBP) This agency is responsible for protecting our nation's borders in order to prevent terrorism, human and drug smuggling, illegal immigration, and agricultural pests from entering the United States, while improving the flow of legitimate trade and travel.

Customs and Border Protection employs nearly 60,000 personnel, among them approximately 22,000 Border Patrol agents and CBP Air and Marine agents who patrol the country's borders and points of entry. CBP also partners with other countries through its Container Security Initiative and the Customs-Trade Partnership Against Terrorism program. The goal of each is to help ensure that goods destined for the United States are screened before they are shipped.[26]

IMMIGRATION AND CUSTOMS ENFORCEMENT (ICE) As the largest investigative arm of the Department of Homeland Security, ICE is responsible for identifying and shutting down vulnerabilities in the nation's border, and for economic, transportation, and infrastructure security. There are four main components of ICE:

■ The *Office of Investigations* investigates a wide range of domestic and international activities arising from the movement of people and goods that violate immigration and customs laws and threaten national security.

■ The *Office of Detention and Removal Operations* is responsible for public safety and national security by ensuring the departure from the United States of all removable aliens through the fair enforcement of the nation's immigration laws.

■ The *Office of Intelligence* is responsible for the collection, analysis, and dissemination of strategic and tactical intelligence data for use by ICE and DHS.

■ The *Office of International Affairs (OIA)* conducts and coordinates international investigations involving transnational criminal organizations responsible for the illegal movement of people, goods, and technology into and out of the United States.[27]

THE SECRET SERVICE The U.S. Secret Service has two significant missions. The first is to protect the president and vice president, their families, heads of state, and other high-level officials. Part of this function involves investigating threats against protected officials and protecting the White House, the vice president's residence, and other buildings within Washington, D.C.

The second mission is to investigate counterfeiting and other financial

Stringer/Mexico/Reuters/Landov

Law enforcement officials have discovered a number of cross-border drug tunnels running to California from Mexico. This particular tunnel linked warehouses in an industrial park south of San Diego and the Mexican border city of Tijuana, the U.S. Immigration and Customs Enforcement agency said in a news release. Much of the discussion over border security focuses on a fence or a wall between the United States and Mexico. What, if anything, could be done to prevent tunneling of this nature?

crimes, including financial institution fraud, identity theft, computer fraud, and computer-based attacks on our nation's financial, banking, and telecommunications infrastructure. Criminal investigations cover a range of conduct:

> … counterfeiting of U.S. currency (to include coins); counterfeiting of foreign currency (occurring domestically); identity crimes such as access device fraud, identity theft, false identification fraud, bank fraud and check fraud; telemarketing fraud; telecommunications fraud (cellular and hard wire); computer fraud; fraud targeting automated payment systems and teller machines; direct deposit fraud; investigations of forgery, uttering, alterations, false impersonations or false claims involving U.S. Treasury Checks, U.S. Saving Bonds, U.S. Treasury Notes, Bonds and Bills; electronic funds transfer (EFT) including Treasury disbursements and fraud within the Treasury payment systems; Federal Deposit Insurance Corporation investigations; Farm Credit Administration violations; and fictitious or fraudulent commercial instruments and foreign securities.[28]

State Law Enforcement Agencies

LO7 Discuss the differences among local, county, state, and federal law enforcement agencies.

Unlike municipal police departments, state police were legislatively created to deal with the growing incidence of crime in nonurban areas, a consequence of the increase in population mobility and the advent of personalized mass transportation in the form of the automobile. County sheriffs—elected officials with occasionally corrupt or questionable motives—had proven to be ineffective in dealing with the wide-ranging criminal activities that developed during the latter half of the nineteenth century. In addition, most local police agencies were unable to effectively protect against highly mobile lawbreakers who randomly struck at cities and towns throughout a state. In response to citizens' demands for effective and efficient law enforcement, state governors began to develop plans for police agencies that would be responsible to the state, instead of being tied to local politics and possible corruption.

The Texas Rangers, created in 1835, was one of the first state police agencies formed. Though the Texas Rangers still operate today (see Exhibit 5.3), at the time it was mainly a military outfit that patrolled the Mexican border. It was followed by the Massachusetts State constables in 1865 and the Arizona Rangers in 1901. Pennsylvania formed the first truly modern state police in 1905.[29]

Today, about 23 state police agencies have the same general police powers as municipal police and are territorially limited in their exercise of law enforcement regulations only by the state's boundaries. The remaining state police agencies are primarily responsible for highway patrol and traffic law enforcement. Some state police, such as those in California, direct most of their attention to the enforcement of traffic laws. Most state police organizations are restricted by legislation from becoming involved in the enforcement of certain areas of the law. For example, in some jurisdictions, state police are prohibited from becoming involved in strikes or other labor disputes, unless violence erupts.

The nation's 80,000 state police employees (55,000 officers and 25,000 civilians) are not only involved in law enforcement and highway safety but also carry out a variety of functions, including maintaining a training academy and providing emergency medical services. State police crime laboratories aid local departments in investigating crime scenes and analyzing evidence. State police also provide special services and technical expertise in such areas as bomb-site analysis and homicide investigation. Other state police departments, such as California's, are involved in highly sophisticated traffic and highway safety programs that include using helicopters for patrol and rescue, testing safety devices for cars, and conducting postmortem examinations to determine the causes of fatal accidents.

EXHIBIT 5.3 Texas Rangers' Job Duties

According to the Texas Department of Justice, Texas Rangers' job duties are as follows:

- The activities of the Texas Ranger Division consist primarily of making criminal and special investigations; apprehending wanted felons; suppressing major disturbances; the protection of life and property; and rendering assistance to local law enforcement officials in suppressing crime and violence.

- The Texas Ranger Division will, through investigation and close personal contact with all federal, state, county, and city law enforcement agencies, be responsible for the gathering and dissemination of criminal intelligence pertaining to all facets of organized crime. The Texas Ranger Division joins with all other enforcement agencies in the suppression of the same.

- Under orders of the Director, suppress all criminal activity in any given area, when it is apparent that the local officials are unwilling or unable to maintain law and order.

- Upon the request or order of a judge of a court of record, serve as officers of the court and assist in the maintenance of decorum, the protection of life, and the preservation of property during any judicial proceeding.

- When called upon, provide protection for elected officials at public functions and at any other time or place when directed to do so by a superior officer. Establish direct personal contact and maintain close liaison with all agencies, or branches thereof, concerned with the investigation and suppression of criminal activities. These contacts are not to be limited to the state but shall be nationwide. Every effort will be exerted to maintain a full and free flow of information on active offenders and offenses between all interested agencies.

- Participate in educational training programs and provide specialized instruction to local, state, and federal law enforcement representatives.

- With the approval of the Director, conduct investigations of any alleged misconduct on the part of other Department personnel.

- Be the primary Department investigator when a Department member is killed or suffers serious bodily injury, attributable to an intentional act.

- Provide forensic hypnotists for use as an investigative tool in gathering additional information.

- Provide forensic artwork for use as an investigative or procedural tool in major criminal cases.

- Assist the Governor's Protective Detail in providing security for the Texas Governor during his official travel throughout the state, as well as other dignitaries.

Source: The Texas Ranger Job Duties, http://www.txdps.state.tx.us/TexasRangers/rangerresponsibilities.htm (accessed May 2014).

STATE LAW ENFORCEMENT EFFORTS TO COMBAT TERRORISM In the wake of the 9/11 attacks, a number of states have beefed up their intelligence-gathering capabilities and aimed them directly at homeland security. For example, Arizona maintains the Arizona Counter Terrorism Information Center (ACTIC), a statewide intelligence system designed to combat terrorism.[30] It consists of two divisions. One is unclassified and draws together personnel from various public safety agencies. The other operates in a secretive manner and is made up of personnel from the FBI's Joint Terrorism Task Force. According to its website:

ACTIC provides a higher level of preparedness by disseminating focused, relevant incident alerts. The Fusion Center is responsible for sharing early, reliable and consistent incident information about situations that might affect jurisdictions. Situational Readiness is enhanced when agencies are enabled to be more aware of events surrounding their facilities. The Fusion Center leverages thousands of diverse informational sources to provide early warning of incidents at the local, regional, and state levels.[31]

ACTIC also has an outreach program known as the Community Liaison Program (CLP). Community partners, including religious groups, businesses, and community crime watches, provide intelligence information to ACTIC personnel as the need arises.

County Law Enforcement Agencies

The county sheriff's role has evolved from that of the early English shire reeve, whose primary duty was to assist the royal judges in trying prisoners and enforcing sentences. From the time of the westward expansion in the United States until municipal departments were developed, the sheriff was often the sole legal authority over vast territories.

Today, more than 3,000 sheriff's offices operate nationwide, employing more than 350,000 full-time staff, including about 183,000 sworn personnel.[32] Nearly all sheriff's offices provide basic law enforcement services such as routine patrol (97%), responding to citizen calls for service (95%), and investigating crimes (92%).[33] Typically, a sheriff's department's law enforcement functions are restricted to unincorporated areas within a county, unless a city or town police department requests its help.

The duties of a county sheriff's department vary according to the size and degree of development of the county. The standard tasks of a typical sheriff's department are serving civil process (summons and court orders), providing court security, operating the county jail, and investigating crimes. Less commonly, sheriff's departments may serve as coroners, tax collectors, overseers of highways and bridges, custodians of the county treasury, and providers of fire, animal control, and emergency medical services. In years past, sheriff's offices also conducted executions.

Some sheriff's departments are exclusively law enforcement oriented; some carry out only court-related duties; some are involved solely in correctional and judicial matters and not in law enforcement. However, a majority are full-service programs that carry out judicial, correctional, and law enforcement activities. As a rule, agencies serving large population areas (more than one million people) are devoted to maintaining county correctional facilities, whereas those in smaller population areas focus on law enforcement.

In the past, sheriffs' salaries were almost always based on the fees they received for the performance of official acts. They received fees for every summons, warrant, subpoena, writ, or other process they served. They were also compensated for summoning juries or locking prisoners in cells. Today, sheriffs are salaried to avoid conflict of interest.

COUNTY LAW ENFORCEMENT EFFORTS TO COMBAT TERRORISM

Some counties are now engaging in anti-terror and homeland security activities. For example, the Harris County, Texas, Office of Homeland Security & Emergency Management (OHSEM) is responsible for an emergency management plan that prepares for public recovery in the event of natural disasters

Madison County sheriff's deputies investigate the scene of a fatal shooting just outside Huntsville, Alabama. A 73-year-old man was shot in his driveway. How are sheriff and municipal police departments similar? How are they different?

Eric Schultz/AL.COM /Landov

or human-caused catastrophes or attacks. It works in conjunction with state, federal, and local authorities, including the city of Houston and other municipalities in the surrounding Harris County area when required. If needed, the OHSEM activates an emergency operations center to facilitate coordination of all support agencies to provide continuity of services to the public. OHSEM is responsible for advisement, notification, and assembly of services that are in the best interest of the citizens of Harris County. It prepares and distributes information and procedures governing the same.[34] Similarly, in Montgomery County, Maryland, the Homeland Security Department plans, prevents, prepares, and protects against major threats that may harm, disrupt, or destroy the community, its commerce, and institutions. Its mission is to effectively manage and coordinate the county's unified response, mitigation, and recovery from the consequences of such disasters or events, should they occur. It also serves to educate the public on emergency preparedness for all hazards and conducts outreach to diverse and special populations to protect, secure, and sustain critical infrastructures and ensure the continuity of essential services.[35]

Metropolitan Law Enforcement Agencies

Local police make up the majority of the nation's authorized law enforcement personnel. Metropolitan police departments range in size from the New York City Police Department, with almost 40,000 full-time officers and 10,000 civilian employees, to rural police departments, which may have only a single part-time officer. Today, local police departments have more than 450,000 sworn personnel.[36] In addition to sworn personnel, many police agencies hire civilian employees who bring special skills to the department. In this computer age, departments often employ information resource managers, who are charged with improving data processing, integrating the department's computer information database with others in the state, operating computer-based fingerprint identification systems and other high-tech investigative devices, and linking with national computer systems such as the FBI's national crime information system, which holds the records of millions of criminal offenders. To carry out these tasks, local departments employ an additional 130,000 civilians, bringing the entire number to more than 580,000 people.

Most individual metropolitan police departments perform a standard set of functions and tasks and provide similar services to the community. These include the following:

- Traffic enforcement
- Crime prevention
- Narcotics and vice control
- Property and violent crime investigation
- Accident investigation
- Fingerprint processing
- Radio communications
- Death investigation
- Patrol and peacekeeping
- Search and rescue

The police role is expanding, so procedures must be developed to aid special-needs populations, including AIDS-infected suspects, the homeless, and victims of domestic and child abuse. For a summary of the key enforcement-related differences between federal, state, county, and metropolitan law enforcement agencies, see Concept Summary 5.1.

CONCEPT SUMMARY 5.1

Differences Between Federal, State, County, and Metropolitan Law Enforcement

Agency	Jurisdiction	Crimes Most Often Targeted
Federal agencies (FBI, Secret Service)	Entire United States	Violations of federal law
State patrol	State	Traffic violations on highways
State police	State	Violations of state law
County sheriff	County, mostly unincorporated areas thereof	Violations of state law and county ordinances
Metropolitan police	City limits	Violations of state laws and city ordinances

These are only a few examples of the multiplicity of roles and duties assumed today in some of the larger urban police agencies around the nation. Smaller agencies can have trouble carrying out these tasks effectively. The hundreds of small police agencies in each state often provide duplicate services. Whether unifying smaller police agencies into superagencies would improve services is often debated among police experts. Smaller municipal agencies can provide important specialized services that might have to be relinquished if they were combined and incorporated into larger departments. Another approach has been to maintain smaller departments but to link them via computerized information-sharing and resource-management networks.[37]

POLICING IN SMALL CITIES Most TV police shows feature the work of big-city police officers, but an overwhelming number of departments have fewer than 50 officers and serve a population of less than 25,000. About 70 law enforcement agencies employ 1,000 or more full-time sworn personnel, including 48 local police departments with 1,000 or more officers. These agencies account for about one-third of all local police officers. In contrast, nearly 800 departments employ just one officer.[38]

While our attention is drawn to big-city police, it is important to think about policing in small towns. The officers who work in these locations rarely face the same problems as their big-city counterparts. Crime rates are lower, citizens know each other better, and the types of problems tend to differ from those of big cities. Researchers have found, in fact, that rural policing relies heavily on informal mechanisms, rather than arrest, for dealing with unwanted behaviors.[39] They have also found that officers engage citizens more informally and personably in such towns.[40] These findings are important because if the typical police officer works in a small town, then he affords some insight into what police work is really like. It is not necessarily about big busts, high-profile crimes, and rampant lawlessness.

LOCAL LAW ENFORCEMENT EFFORTS TO COMBAT TERRORISM Federal law enforcement agencies are not alone in responding to the threat of terrorism. And, of course, nowhere is the threat of terrorism being taken more seriously than in New York City—one of the main targets of the 9/11 attacks—which has established a Counterterrorism Bureau.[41] Teams within the bureau have been trained to examine potential targets in the city and are attempting to insulate those targets from possible attack. Viewed as prime targets are the city's bridges, the Empire State Building, Rockefeller Center, and the United Nations. Bureau detectives are assigned overseas to work with the police in several foreign cities, including cities in Canada and Israel. Detectives have been assigned as liaisons with the FBI and with INTERPOL in Lyon, France. The city is recruiting detectives with language skills ranging from Pashtun and Urdu to Arabic, Hokkien, and other tongues. The existing New York City Police Intelligence Division has been revamped, and agents are examining foreign newspapers and monitoring Internet sites.

The Counterterrorism Bureau has assigned more than 100 city police detectives to work with FBI agents as part of a Joint Terrorist Task Force. In addition, the Intelligence Division's 700 investigators now devote 35 to 40 percent of their resources to counterterrorism—up from about 2 percent before January 2002. The department is also drawing on the expertise of other institutions around the city. For example, medical specialists have been enlisted to monitor daily developments in the city's hospitals to detect any suspicious outbreaks of illness that might reflect a biological attack. And the police are conducting joint drills with the New York Fire Department to avoid the problems in communication and coordination that marked the emergency response on September 11.

Private Policing

Supplementing local police forces is a burgeoning private security industry. Private security service, or **private policing**, has become a multibillion-dollar industry with well in excess of 10,000 firms and more than 2 million employees.[42] Even some federal police services have been privatized to cut expenses. Private police and security officials outnumber public/governmental police by a factor of three to one.[43]

Some private security firms have become billion-dollar companies. For example, G4S Security Solutions is one of the world's largest providers of security services. Among its clients are a number of Fortune 500 companies. It has several subsidiaries that work for the federal government. It has also been a contractor for NASA and the U.S. Army, and it has provided security and emergency response services to local governments—helping them guard their public transport systems, among other services. G4S has helped the U.S. government protect nuclear reactors, guards the Trans-Alaska Pipeline System, and maintains security in closed government facilities. It also maintains a Custom Protection Officer Division, made up of highly trained uniformed security officers assigned to critical or complex facilities or situations requiring special skills in such places as government buildings, banks, and other special situations. (The Careers in Criminal Justice feature discusses a career in the private security area.)

Reasons for Private Policing

Why is private policing so popular? There are three answers to this question:

- A preference for nongovernmental provision of important services, particularly crime control. Many people feel the private sector can do a more effective job than traditional government-led policing.

- The growth of mass private property, particularly large shopping malls and other properties that attract large numbers of consumers and have little other police protection.

- A belief that government police are not capable of providing the level of service and presence that the public desires.[44]

private policing
Crime prevention, detection, and the apprehension of criminals carried out by private organizations or individuals for commercial purposes.

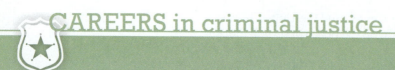

CAREERS in criminal justice

LOSS PREVENTION SPECIALIST

DUTIES AND CHARACTERISTICS OF THE JOB

The primary responsibility of a loss prevention specialist is to protect the merchandise in large retail establishments, such as Walmart or Target. Loss prevention specialists engage in surveillance and, as appropriate, detain suspected shoplifters. They may spend some of their time watching security camera displays. They also spend time "on the floor," moving throughout the store.

Loss prevention specialists are also tasked with protecting the company from theft by employees. They may also perform regularly inventory or "shrink" assessments, manage alarm systems, and control access to warehousing, distribution centers, and even manufacturing facilities. Loss prevention also extends beyond the retail setting. Shippers, wholesalers, and any other company engaged in commerce and concerned with loss and/or theft of its product may employ loss prevention specialists.

JOB OUTLOOK

Loss prevention is part of a multibillion-dollar security industry. According to ASIS International, the largest organization for security professionals, "Security is one of the fastest-growing professional careers worldwide." Opportunities exist at all levels within the security industry, and all businesses, no matter their size, need qualified personnel to address their security concerns, prevent theft, deter workplace violence, and otherwise protect themselves to ensure normal business operations. The Bureau of Labor Statistics estimates that employment of loss prevention specialists and other security/surveillance officers will grow by 18 percent over the next decade.

SALARY

Entry-level positions in retail loss prevention are among the lowest paying security jobs, but the pay prospects improve as one ascends to a management position. Loss prevention managers make between $27,000 and

---

L08 Discuss the differences between public and private policing.

Private and Public Police Compared

Private policing is different from public policing. Private policing is largely "client-driven," meaning that it serves the needs of those who pay the bills. And while the public police are driven by a public mandate, their primary focus is enforcement of the criminal law. Private police, in contrast, may do almost anything on behalf of their clients, some of which may have little to do with the criminal law itself. Private police are *directly* employed by a client. In contrast, public police are *indirectly* employed by taxpayers. Four additional factors distinguish private police from public police.[45]

FOCUS ON LOSS INSTEAD OF CRIME Much of private policing is concerned with loss prevention. Loss prevention includes most notably protection from theft. Major retailers employ loss prevention specialists (see accompanying Careers in Criminal Justice box) to protect their goods from being stolen. However, goods may also be "lost" through error, unethical practices, accidents, and so on. Such behaviors do not fall within the scope of the criminal law that the public police are tasked with enforcing.

The focus on loss also removes private police from the moral dimension of the criminal law. Instead of focusing on what is right and wrong, private police are concerned solely with what their *clients* view as priorities. As Elizabeth Joh notes, "When sanctions are imposed, there may be little or no emphasis on condemning the individual wrongdoer and 'making an example' out of him or her. A bank may require an embezzler to sign a loan guarantee to pay back stolen funds, for example, rather than choose public prosecution."[46]

$61,000 per year. Moving into other industries, such as banking and financial services, entry-level and mid-level management positions carry a salary range of $35,000 to $100,000.

OPPORTUNITIES

There are many opportunities for careers in loss prevention. While such careers are available in almost every area of human endeavor, including banking and financial services, commercial real estate, cultural properties (e.g., museums), educational institutions, and gaming/wagering facilities, most positions exist within the retail setting. The larger the retailer, the better the breadth of positions available. The upward mobility prospects will be better, too.

QUALIFICATIONS

The qualifications for an entry-level loss prevention position are minimal. Usually just a high school diploma is required, but employees will, at a minimum, be expected to pass routine drug tests, have strong interpersonal and administrative skills, and be comfortable around computers. Qualifications may be stricter and increase depending upon the individual's position in the corporate hierarchy or level of risk and responsibility associated with the position.

EDUCATION AND TRAINING

Managerial positions may require an associate or bachelor's degree in criminal justice or a related discipline, sometimes combined with a certain amount of real-world experience. Some colleges and universities also offer dedicated security education degrees. ASIS also offers three certifications for security professionals, including those of the Certified Protection Professional (CPP), the Professional Certified Investigator (PCI), and the Physical Security Professional (PSP). These certifications require that certain knowledge and skills be demonstrated, but they also help differentiate applicants from one another, and they improve an applicant's professional credibility and earnings potential.

Sources: ASIS International, *Career Opportunities in Security* (Alexandria, VA: ASIS International, 2005), https://www.asisonline.org/About-ASIS/FAQs/Documents/careers.pdf (accessed May 2014); Bureau of Labor Statistics, *Security Guards and Gaming Surveillance Officers*, http://www.bls.gov/ooh/Protective-Service/Security-guards.htm (accessed May 2014).

PREVENTIVE METHODS Private police are concerned almost solely with prevention. Public police also work to prevent crime, but the usual public policing method of addressing crime is reactionary; of necessity, the police usually wait for calls for service before responding. *Surveillance* is paramount in the private policing context, whereas public policing relies more heavily on detection of criminal acts and apprehension of suspects.

Surveillance includes the use of obvious technologies like closed-circuit television and security cameras, but private police also employ other "embedded" techniques to guard against loss and ensure compliance with expected norms of behavior. Clifford Shearing and Philip Stenning cite the example of Disneyland.[47] Every employee—and indeed, every feature, whether it be the costumed characters or the guardrails and ropes promoting a smooth flow of patrons—is there to entertain but also subtly enforce compliance with what Disney considers appropriate behavior. People who do not comply face expulsion.

PRIVATE JUSTICE Not surprisingly, private policing often employs private justice. For example, a "card counter" may be permanently banned from a casino. Another example is termination for an employee who steals from his or her employer.

Private companies often have an incentive to keep matters involving loss shielded from the public eye. High-profile incidents can result in negative publicity, which can in turn affect the bottom line. Similarly, cooperation with the police in an investigation takes time away from business activity, possibly eroding profits further. Interestingly, one study found that the Macy's department store in

New York City reported just over half of shoplifting incidents to the police, which again underscores the reality that private companies' priorities are often different than those of the public police.[48]

PRIVATE PROPERTY The public police focus their efforts on both public and private property. Whether it be burglary from a residence, assault at a bar, or vandalism on a highway overpass, the public police make few distinctions between the types of property where the crimes occur. Private property is of course protected (for example, by the U.S. Constitution's Fourth Amendment), but the point is that public police are able to enforce and focus on crime regardless of where it occurs. In contrast, private police are concerned almost exclusively with private property.

Types of Private Policing

There are four primary types of private policing.[49] They are protective policing, intelligence policing, publicly contracted policing, and corporate policing.

PROTECTIVE POLICING Protective private policing is concerned with guarding private property from theft, trespass, and damage. Preventive surveillance efforts are used to protect property, as are reactive efforts, such as going after shoplifters. A classic example of protective private policing is the armored transit service. Armored transit companies, which are private, transport cash and valuables for their clients and go to great lengths to protect the property from theft.

INTELLIGENCE POLICING Intelligence policing is private detection. Private detectives' and investigators' work comes in a variety of forms, but they primarily collect information for a client. Most often this will involve interviewing individuals, conducting surveillance, and conducting searches for information. Private investigators often specialize in a certain type of case, such as corporate, financial, or legal investigation. The kinds of cases that private investigators take on might include locating missing persons, investigating computer-based crimes, uncovering fraud, or conducting background checks. Because their work often involves legal issues, private detectives and investigators may be asked to prepare materials for a trial by producing evidence or writing reports, aiding attorneys, or testifying in court.

Another example of intelligence policing is found in the work of the National Insurance Crime Bureau (NICB).[50] On behalf of its clients, which consist mainly of insurance companies, NICB investigates cases of potential fraud. Its "questionable claims triage system," for example, investigates auto insurance claims that clients believe are suspect. The organization also provides intelligence for its members, business owners, and the general public in the area of crime prevention. It publishes a number of brochures, reports, and fact sheets aimed at helping people guard against such crimes as vehicle and identity theft.

PUBLICLY CONTRACTED POLICING With publicly contracted policing, a private company is paid by the government to perform policing-related functions. This approach is not particularly common, as it raises a number of legal issues. For example, if private police officers replace public police, what happens when it is necessary to use force? Can private police use deadly force? Answers to these questions are not immediately apparent.[51]

Several local governments have throughout the years contracted with private organizations to essentially replace their police forces. The first was Kalamazoo, Michigan.[52] In the 1950s, employees of a private security firm were sworn in as deputy sheriffs and took over law enforcement activities for the city. Litigation ensued and the contracting ceased after only three years. A number of other cities have experimented with privatization over the years.[53]

One of the more visible and controversial publicly contracted security companies is Blackwater USA. It is a private military company founded in 1987 and is one of the largest private security contractors for the U.S. State Department. Blackwater employees primarily provide diplomatic security in Iraq and other locations around the world where the U.S. has a military/political presence. Blackwater has also been contracted by numerous foreign governments to perform similar functions.

CORPORATE POLICING Corporations, especially large ones, often employ their own private police forces. Corporate police engage in many of the duties already discussed, but they may go further, such as by protecting key personnel who work for their companies. Corporate police often work within security departments or similarly described entities. The pharmaceutical industry, for example, maintains its own private security apparatus, concerned primarily with protecting the supply chain, from manufacturing to patient delivery.

A security guard questions a driver entering an office complex near Stamford, Connecticut. Corporate policing of this sort is essential in a world where the police presence is spread thin.

Criticisms of Private Policing

Private policing is controversial for a number of reasons. First, there is some concern that privatization puts the profit motive ahead of more lofty concerns like protection of public safety. Another concern is that private police could eventually replace government, or public, police. Fortunately, this looks unlikely. As one expert observed, "Private policing poses no risk of supplanting public law enforcement entirely, at least not in our lifetime, and it is far from clear to what extent the growing numbers of private security employees are actually performing functions previously carried out by public officers."[54]

There will also be more legal scrutiny as the private security business blossoms. A number of questions remain to be answered. One important issue is whether security guards are subject to the same search and seizure standards as police officers. The U.S. Supreme Court has repeatedly stated that purely private search activities do not violate the Fourth Amendment's prohibitions. Similar questions arise when ordinary citizens engage in their own private policing initiatives, as discussed further in The Victim Experience box.

Might security guards be subject to Fourth Amendment requirements if they are performing services that are traditionally reserved for the police? The Supreme Court answered this question with a yes in the 1964 case of *Griffin v. Maryland*.[55] In that case, an amusement park security guard was "deputized" by the county sheriff. He subsequently arrested five black men and charged them with criminal trespass for violating the privately owned park's racial segregation policy, which permitted only whites to enter the premises. The Court ruled not only that the arrest was inappropriate, but that it amounted to "state action." This decision, and some others since,[56] suggest that when

YOUR OPINION: Would children be safer if they attended schools with armed security guards?

PUBLIC OPINION:

YES:	62%
NO:	24%
NOT SURE:	15%

REALITY: High-profile school shootings, such as the one in 2012 at Sandy Hook Elementary in Newtown, Connecticut, engender a great deal of fear and paranoia. Schools are indeed vulnerable places and steps ought to be taken to secure them, but what is the *reality* of school victimizations of this sort? The Centers for Disease Control and Prevention (CDC) has been collecting data on what it calls "school-associated violent deaths" since 1992. According to the CDC, between 14 and 34 school-age children are killed either at school or on their way to/from school each year. Roughly 50 million children are enrolled in K-12 schools, public and private, each year. So while school homicides are tragic and deplorable events, they are exceptionally rare.

DISCUSSION: What are the advantages and disadvantages of having armed guards in our nation's schools? What about police officers or school resource officers (SROs)?

Sources: Rasmussen Reports, http://www.rasmussenreports.com/public_content/politics/current_events/gun_control/62_would_feel_safer_if_their_child_attended_a_school_with_an_armed_guard (accessed May 2014); Centers for Disease Control and Prevention, "School-Associated Violent Death Study," http://www.cdc.gov/violenceprevention/youthviolence/schoolviolence/savd.html (accessed May 2014).

the VICTIM experience

FROM VIGILANTISM TO UNITED VICTIMS

BACKGROUND Upset by a rash of vandalism, residents of a northeast Philadelphia neighborhood whose cars were damaged on multiple occasions banded together and installed security cameras in an effort to capture the people responsible. In one of the incidents, 17 cars were sprayed with an acidic chemical substance that caused significant paint damage. Police worked closely with the residents and stepped up patrols in the neighborhood, but they could not capture the perpetrators. The installation of security cameras was a last resort. At their wits' end, victims took matters into their own hands.

THE BIG PICTURE When offenders remain at large, crime victims often become frustrated, wondering why their cases are rarely at the top of the police priority list. Their frustration is understandable, but the police cannot be in all places at all times. With approximately one sworn police officer per 1,000 residents, most municipalities can only do so much to keep crime at bay. Also, when confronted with serious crime, the police cannot give vandalism the attention it might otherwise deserve.

Sometimes victims band together to simultaneously protect themselves *and* assist the police. Other times they work alone, independently of the police, by becoming vigilantes. The 1984 Bernhard Goetz case is perhaps the most famous. After being attacked in a subway, Goetz started to carry a gun, even though New York City denied him a permit to legally carry one. Twice, he scared off would-be muggers with the gun. On the third occasion, Goetz shot four teenagers, one of whom was severely injured. After nine days as a fugitive, he gave himself up to police. A jury later found him guilty of criminal possession of a weapon in the third degree, but it acquitted him on attempted murder charges.

Victims also unite through a number of more innocuous and less newsworthy means. One example is Crime Victims United of California. The organization uses "education, legislative advocacy and political action to enhance public safety, promote effective crime-reduction measures and strengthen the rights of crime victims." Its legislative advocacy arm works to strengthen victims' rights laws and otherwise improve the victim experience. Its political advocacy arm endorses and backs pro-victim candidates for elected office.

Other victims groups unite around specific causes, an example being Scam Victims United. According to the organization's website, it "offers support and resources to victims through message groups and networking with other victims. This provides for a safe environment in which they can share their stories with others who have been through the same experience without worry of blame or judgment."

CLASSROOM EXERCISE Divide the class into two groups. Propose a law that could be construed as beneficial to crime victims. Have one side argue in favor of the law and the other side argue against the law. For a brief overview of legislative priorities, visit the website of the National Center for Victims of Crime and examine their policy agenda: http://www.victimsofcrime.org/about-us/our-work.

Sources: Shelley Laurence and Rosemary Connors, "Vandalism Victims Set Up Cameras," NBC10 Philadelphia, March 28, 2012, http://www.nbcphiladelphia .com/news/local/Vandalism-Victims-Set-Up-Cameras-144741325.html; George P. Fletcher, *A Crime of Self-Defense: Bernhard Goetz and the Law on Trial* (Chicago: University of Chicago Press, 1990); Crime Victims United of California, http://www.crimevictimsunited.com; Scam Victims United, http://www .scamvictimsunited.com (all sites accessed May 2014).

private police are sworn or act as *de facto* public police, they are bound by the same constitutional constraints as any police officer.

States, on the other hand, have given private police much more latitude, exempting them from the Fourth Amendment,[57] the *Miranda* rule[58] (see Chapter 8), and the exclusionary rule[59] (also see Chapter 8). This does not mean, though, that private police have unbridled authority. In most instances, they have no more authority than the typical private citizen. As one expert put it, "Many private security guards … possess no greater legal capabilities than do ordinary citizens to forcibly detain persons who are suspected of or have in fact committed a crime."[60] But as time goes on and the private policing industry continues to grow, it will be interesting to see how the courts weigh in.

Technology and Law Enforcement

Budget realities demand that police leaders make the most effective use of their forces, and technology seems to be one method of increasing productivity at a relatively low cost. The introduction of technology has already been explosive. In 1964, only one city, St. Louis, had a police computer system; by 1968, 10 states and 50 cities had state-level criminal justice information systems. Today, nearly every law enforcement organization relies on computer technology.[61]

Law enforcement technology extends beyond computers, of course. It falls into two broad categories: hard technology and soft technology.[62] Hard technology includes new materials and equipment that police use to catch criminals and prevent crime. Soft technology primarily consists of software and information systems. Innovations in this area include new programs, crime classification techniques, system integration, and data sharing. Additional examples of hard and soft technology appear in Exhibit 5.4. In the following subsections, we explore in more detail several of the key technological innovations that have improved law enforcement capabilities in recent years.

L09 Identify various technologies currently used in law enforcement.

Identifying Criminals

Police are becoming more sophisticated in their use of computer software to identify and convict criminals. One of the most important computer-aided tasks is the identification of criminal suspects. Computers now link neighboring agencies so they can share information on cases, suspects, and warrants. On a broader

Web App 5.3

For news about police technology, visit http://www.policeone.com/police-products/police-technology.

EXHIBIT 5.4 The Application of Hard and Soft Technology to Crime Prevention and Police

	Hard Technology	Soft Technology
Crime Prevention	• CCTV • Street lighting • Citizen protection devices (e.g., mace, tasers) • Metal detectors • Ignition interlock systems (drunk drivers)	• Threat assessment instruments • Risk assessment instruments • Bullying ID protocol • Sex offender registration • Risk assessment prior to involuntary civil commitment • Profiling potential offenders • Facial recognition software used in conjunction with CCTV
Police	• Improved police protection devices (helmets, vests, cars, buildings) • Improved/new weapons • Less than lethal force (mobile/riot control) • Computers in squad cars • Hands-free patrol car control (Project 54) • Offender and citizen IDs via biometrics/fingerprints • Mobile data centers • Video in patrol cars	• Crime mapping (hot spots) • Crime analysis (e.g., CompStat) • Criminal history data systems enhancement • Info sharing in CJS and private sector • New technologies to monitor communications (phone, mail, Internet) to/from targeted individuals • AMBER alerts • Creation of watch lists of potential violent offenders • Gunshot location devices

Source: James Byrne and Gary Marx, "Technological Innovations in Crime Prevention and Policing: A Review of the Research on Implementation and Impact," *Cahiers Politiestudies Jaargang* 20 (2011): 17–40, at 20.

Web App 5.4

To read more about the National Crime Information Center, visit http://www.fbi.gov/about-us/cjis/ncic.

data mining

Using sophisticated computer software to conduct analysis of behavior patterns in an effort to identify crime patterns and link them to suspects.

jurisdictional level, the FBI implemented the National Crime Information Center in 1967. This system provides rapid collection and retrieval of data about persons wanted for crimes anywhere in the 50 states.

Some police departments are using computerized imaging systems to replace mug books. Photos or sketches are stored in computer memory and are easily retrieved for viewing. Several software companies have developed identification programs that help witnesses create a composite picture of the perpetrator. A vast library of photographed or drawn facial features can be stored in computer files and accessed on a terminal screen. Witnesses can scan thousands of noses, eyes, and lips until they find those that match the suspect's. Eyeglasses, mustaches, and beards can be added; skin tones can be altered. When the composite is created, an attached camera prints a hard copy for distribution.

In an effort to identify crime patterns and link them to suspects, many departments use computer software to conduct analysis of behavior patterns, a process called **data mining**.[63] By discovering patterns in crimes such as burglary, especially those involving multiple offenders, computer programs can be programmed to recognize a particular way of working a crime and thereby identify suspects most likely to fit the profile.

Locating Criminals

Many technologies have also been developed for the purpose of locating criminals. Given that there are relatively few police in relation to the number of citizens, officers cannot be everywhere at the same time. Nor can they readily identify or locate certain criminals who do not wish to be found. Several technological advances assist them in this regard.

The accompanying Criminal Justice and Technology feature describes the recent advent of gun detector technology. Cities can purchase devices that literally "listen" for gunfire so that officers can quickly be directed to the place where guns were recently fired. Companies have also developed gun detectors that officers can use to determine who is carrying an illegally concealed weapon. Millivision, one of the leaders in this area, has developed a portable gun detection device that officers can use from a distance. It does not reveal any anatomical information, only the outline of a gun.[64] Police departments even use closed-circuit television cameras to monitor certain urban areas from a distance.[65]

Another company has developed a device that can "listen" for a person hidden in the trunk of a vehicle. This is useful in the traffic stop context, when police officers are vulnerable to attack. The so-called Enclosed Space Detection System (ESDS) has been developed for police to ascertain whether one or more persons are hidden in a vehicle. It works by detecting the motion of the vehicle caused by the shock wave produced by a beating heart.[66]

More popular are so-called **thermal imagers**. These devices, which can be mounted on aircraft or handheld, use infrared technology to detect heat signals. Also known as "night vision," thermal imaging helps law enforcement officials detect everything from marijuana-growing operations to suspects hiding from officers in foot pursuits.

thermal imagers

A device that detects radiation in the infrared range of the electromagnetic spectrum, used in law enforcement to detect variations in temperature (warm images stand out against cool backgrounds).

Crime Scene Investigation

Traditionally, to investigate and evaluate a crime scene, detectives relied on photographic evidence and two-dimensional drawings. However, it can be difficult to visualize the positional relationships of evidence with two-dimensional tools. Now, through a combination of laser and computer technology, high-definition surveying (HDS) creates a virtual crime scene that allows investigators to maneuver every piece of evidence.

High-definition surveying gives law enforcement a complete picture of a crime scene. HDS reflects a laser light off objects in the crime scene and back

Web App 5.5

Interested in learning more about thermal imagers? Visit the Police Thermal Imaging site by going to http://www.policeone.com/police-products/police-technology/thermal-imaging.

criminal justice and TECHNOLOGY

GUNSHOT LOCATORS

Faced with a surge in the number of shootings, the city of Gary, Indiana, installed the ShotSpotter gunshot location system (GLS). The device uses a network of weatherproof acoustic sensors that locate and record gunshots. Most gunshots emit sound waves for a distance of up to two miles. The GLS sensors determine the direction from which the sound came. When several sensors are used in conjunction with one another, they can triangulate and determine the exact location where the gunshots were fired. Using this technology, the Gary Police Department seized 27 semiautomatic handguns in a single night. It happened over New Year's Eve because the department knew from previous experience that many guns were fired into the air near midnight.

TECHNOLOGY

ShotSpotter, the leading manufacturer of gunshot location systems, bases its product on the same technology that geologists use to pinpoint an earthquake's epicenter. In fact, the original concept was conceived by a U.S. Geological Survey seismologist. With at least three sensors, the system ties into a geographic information system (GIS) and maps the gunshot's location with a dot on a city map. Gunshots show up as red dots; different colors are used for other loud noises. The map then shows a dispatcher the gunshot's location, information which is then used to send the nearest officer to the scene.

An added feature of GLS technology is that it can be integrated with surveillance cameras so that both gunshots *and* shooters can be detected. ShotSpotter also markets the Rapid Deployment System, a portable version of its gunshot detector that can be used by SWAT teams and other first responders.

A few other companies have developed similar gunshot detection technologies. These include the SECURES Gunshot Detection and Localization System and the Safety Dynamics SENTRI. The Safety Dynamics product is especially adept at distinguishing gunshots from other noises in loud areas. Chicago used SENTRI in its "Operation Disruption," a crackdown on gun violence.

ADVANTAGES

The obvious advantage of gunshot location technology is rapid response by police. With real-time information on gunshot locations, police officers can be rapidly

dispatched to the scene and given a realistic opportunity to apprehend the shooter. A related advantage is an improved ability to provide medical treatment for gunshot victims. In one unfortunate example, 35-year-old landscaper Jose Villatory was fatally shot as he was mowing a yard outside a Washington, D.C., apartment complex. Neighbors reported hearing the shot, but they did not call police because gunshots were so common in the area. Perhaps ShotSpotter or a similar device could have saved his life. Gunshot location systems have also given police a better chance of locating forensic evidence at crime scenes. This occurred in a Washington, D.C.–area sniper case, where a man was shooting people from a freeway overpass. He was turned in by someone, but a gunshot locator the FBI installed assisted agents in locating spent shell casings.

LIMITATIONS

While gunshot locators clearly help authorities identify the whereabouts of shooters, it is unclear whether the technology deters criminals. Gunshot locators have been credited for significant reductions in gunfire in several cities, but whether the devices themselves are responsible cannot be known for sure. Another concern is that despite built-in mechanisms to prevent false positives, the devices sometimes alert authorities to a gunshot when in fact none occurred. Finally, gunshot locators are prohibitively expensive for many cities. The cost to cover one square mile is approximately $150,000, followed by an additional $100,000 to $120,000 for every other square mile covered. If cameras are added to the technology, the cost can add up to millions of dollars to cover a relatively small area within a single city.

CRITICAL THINKING

1. **Can gunshot locators help the police catch criminals? Are they worth the cost?**

2. **Can gunshot locators deter criminals? If not, what needs to be done to deter gun crime?**

Sources: SST, Inc., http://www.shotspotter.com (accessed May 2014); Bill Siuru, "Gunshot Location Systems," *Law and Order* 55 (2007): 10, 12, 15–17; Lorraine G. Mazerolle, James Frank, Dennis Rogan, and Cory Watkins, *Field Evaluation of the ShotSpotter Gunshot Location System: Final Report on the Redwood City Trial* (Washington, DC: National Institute of Justice, 2000); Fernicia Patrik and Tod W. Burke, "Gunshot Sensor Technology: Can You Hear Me Now?" *Police and Security News* 23 (2007): 1–3.

to a digital sensor, creating three-dimensional spatial coordinates that are calculated and stored using algebraic equations. An HDS device projects light in the form of a laser in a 360-degree horizontal circumference, measuring millions of points and creating a "point cloud." The data points are bounced back to the receiver, collected, converted, and used to create a virtual image of any location. A personal computer can now take the data file and project that site onto any screen.

Not only does HDS technology allow the crime scene to be preserved exactly, but the perspective can also be manipulated to provide additional clues. For instance, if the crime scene is the front room of an apartment, the three-dimensional image allows the investigator to move around and examine different points of view. Or if a victim was found seated, an investigator can see and show a jury what the victim might have seen just before the crime occurred. If witnesses outside said that they looked in a living room window, an investigator can zoom around and view what the witnesses could or could not have seen through that window.

HDS technology can also limit crime scene contamination. Investigators may inadvertently touch an object at a crime scene, leaving their fingerprints, or they may move or take evidence from the scene, perhaps by picking up fibers on their shoes. Evidence is compromised if moved or disturbed from its resting place, which may contaminate the scene and undermine the case. HDS technology is a "stand-off" device, allowing investigators to approach the scene in stages by scanning from the outer perimeter and moving inward, reducing the chances of contamination. The investigative and prosecutorial value of virtual crime scenes is evident. If an HDS device is used at the scene, detectives, prosecutors, and juries can return to a crime scene in its preserved state. Showing a jury exactly what a witness could or could not have seen can be very valuable.

Crime Mapping

It is now recognized that there are geographic "hot spots" where a majority of predatory crimes are concentrated.[67] Computer mapping programs that can translate addresses into map coordinates allow departments to identify problem areas for particular crimes, such as drug dealing. Computer maps allow police to identify the location, time of day, and linkage among criminal events and to concentrate their forces accordingly. Figure 5.1 illustrates a typical crime map that is now being used in Providence, Rhode Island.

Crime maps offer police administrators graphic representations of where crimes are occurring in their jurisdiction. Computerized crime mapping gives the police the power to analyze and correlate a wide array of data to create immediate, detailed visuals of crime patterns. The simplest maps display crime locations or concentrations and can be used to help direct patrols to the places they are most needed. More complex maps can be used to chart trends in criminal activity, and some have even proven valuable in solving individual criminal cases. For example, a serial rapist may be caught by observing and understanding the patterns of his crime so that detectives may predict where he will strike next and stake out the area with police decoys.

Crime mapping makes use of new computer technology. Instead of antiquated pin maps, computerized crime mappings let the police detect crime patterns and pathologies of related problems. It enables them to work with multiple layers of information and scenarios, and thus identify emerging hot spots of criminal activity far more successfully and target resources accordingly.

Most law enforcement agencies throughout the United States now use mapping techniques. The New York City Police Department's CompStat process relies on computerized crime mapping to identify crime hot spots.[68] The Chicago Police Department has developed the popular CLEARMAP Crime Incident web application. By visiting the department's web page, anyone can search a database

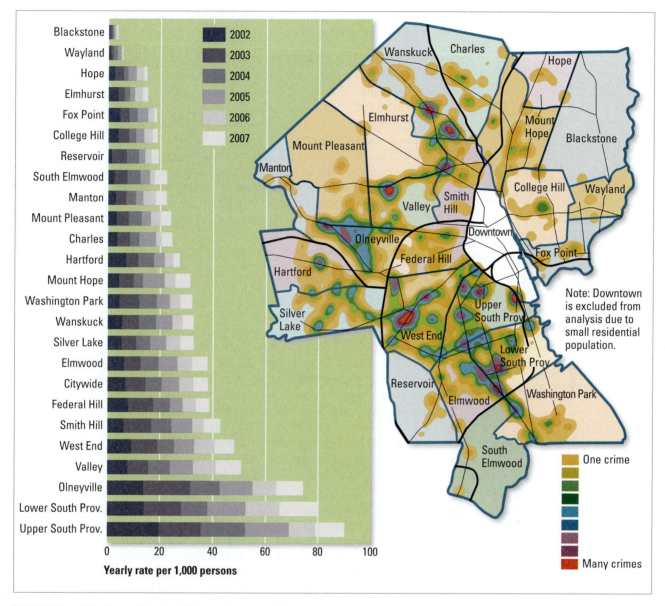

FIGURE 5.1 **Violent Crime in Providence, Rhode Island**

of reported crime within the city and map incident locations.[69] The system was awarded a prestigious Harvard Innovations in American Government award.

Some mapping efforts cross jurisdictional boundaries.[70] Examples of this approach have included the Regional Crime Analysis System in the greater Baltimore–Washington area and the multijurisdictional efforts of the Greater Atlanta PACT Data Center. The Charlotte–Mecklenburg Police Department (North Carolina) has used data collected by other city and county agencies in its crime mapping efforts. By coordinating the departments of tax assessor, public works, planning, and sanitation, police department analysts have made links between disorder and crime that have been instrumental in supporting the department's community policing philosophy.

Crime maps alone may not be a panacea for significantly improving police effectiveness. Many officers are uncertain about how to read maps and assess their data. To maximize the potential of this new technique, police agencies need to invest in training and infrastructure before crime mapping can have an impact on their service efficiency.

ALTERNATIVE MAPPING INITIATIVES Mapping serves other purposes besides just resource allocation. Law enforcement officials in the state of Washington have developed a new Internet-based mapping system that will provide critical information about public infrastructures to help them handle terrorist or emergency situations. The initiative, known as the Critical Incident Planning and Mapping System,[71] provides access to tactical response plans, satellite imagery, photos, floor plans, and hazardous chemical locations.

In West Virginia, local and state government entities are working with private firms to develop an emergency 911 system that can pinpoint the location of callers if they are unable to speak English, if they are unconscious, or even if they hang up. The West Virginia Statewide Addressing and Mapping Board is using geospatial information technology to produce maps that show a caller's exact location by a given number and street name. The project is designed to reduce emergency response times and improve disaster recovery planning, floodplain mapping, security, evacuation routing, counterterrorism efforts, crime analysis, and more.[72]

Mapping technology has recently been combined with GPS (global positioning system), a network of orbiting satellites that transmit signals to a portable device that tracks the precise whereabouts of a person or thing. Officers in one gruesome case found various parts of a man's badly decomposed body in Lake Powell, in Utah's Bryce Canyon National Park. They used a digital camera equipped with GPS technology to snap pictures of the exact locations where body parts and related evidence were found. The officers were then able to view all the photo locations on a map, which helped them determine that the body broke apart over time due to wave action, not because of foul play.[73] GPS technology is also used for a wide range of other applications, such as keeping track of the exact locations of officers' patrol cars.[74]

Biometrics

biometrics
Automated methods of recognizing a person based on a physiological or behavioral characteristic.

Biometrics is defined as automated methods of recognizing a person based on a physiological or behavioral characteristic.[75] Some biometric measures, such as fingerprint identification, have been used for years by law enforcement to identify criminals. However, recent improvements in computer technology have expanded the different types of measures that can be used for identification. Biometrics is now used to identify individuals based on voice, retina, facial features, and handwriting identification, just to name a few.

The field of biometrics can be used by all levels of government, including the military and law enforcement, and is also helpful in private businesses. Financial institutions, retail shopping, and health and social fields can all use biometrics as a way to limit access to financial information or to secure Internet sites.

As opposed to current personal identification methods, such as personal identification numbers (PINs) used for bank machines and Internet transactions, biometric authenticators are unique to the user and as a result cannot be stolen and used without that individual's knowledge.

The process of recording biometric data occurs in four steps. First, the raw biometric data are captured or recorded by a video camera or a fingerprint reading device. Second, the distinguishing characteristics of the raw data are used to create a biometric template. Third, the template is changed into a mathematical representation of the biometric sample and is stored in a database. Finally, a verification process will occur when an individual attempts to gain access to a restricted site. The individual will have to present his or her fingerprint or retina to be read and then matched to the biometric sample on record. Once verification is made, the individual will have access to restricted areas. Currently, a number of programs are in effect. Immigration and Customs Enforcement has been using hand geometry systems at major U.S. airports to check frequent international travelers. Casinos around the country have started to implement facial recognition software into their buildings so that security is notified when a known cheater enters their premises.

Automated Fingerprint Identification Systems

The use of computerized automated fingerprint identification systems (AFIS) is growing in the United States. Using mathematical models, AFIS can classify fingerprints and identify up to 250 characteristics (minutiae) of the print. These automated systems use high-speed silicon chips to plot each point of minutiae and count the number of ridge lines between that point and its four nearest neighbors, which substantially improves their speed and accuracy over earlier systems.

Some police departments report that computerized fingerprint systems are allowing them to make over 100 identifications per month from fingerprints taken at crime scenes. AFIS files have been regionalized. The Western Identification Network (WIN), for example, consists of eight central site members (Alaska, Idaho, Montana, Nevada, Oregon, Utah, Wyoming, and Portland Police Bureau), two interface members (California and Washington), multiple local members, and six federal members (Drug Enforcement Administration, Federal Bureau of Investigation, Immigration and Naturalization Service, Internal Revenue Service, Postal Inspection Service, and Secret Service).[76] When it began, the system had a centralized automated database of 900,000 fingerprint records; today, with the addition of new jurisdictions (Alaska, California, and Washington), the system's number of searchable fingerprint records has increased to more than 14 million. Technology is constantly improving the effectiveness and reliability of the AFIS system, making it easier to use and more efficient in identifying suspects.[77]

DNA Testing

DNA profiling, a procedure that gained national attention during the O. J. Simpson trial, allows suspects to be identified on the basis of the genetic material found in hair, blood, and other bodily tissues and fluids. When DNA is used as evidence in a rape trial, DNA segments are taken from the victim, the suspect, and blood and semen found on the victim. A DNA match indicates a four-billion-to-one likelihood that the suspect is the offender.

Every U.S. state and nearly every industrialized country now maintain DNA databases of convicted offenders.[78] These databases allow comparison of crime scene DNA to samples taken at other crime scenes and to known offenders. The United States has more than 3 million samples of offenders/arrestees in its state and federal DNA databases. The United States is not alone in gathering this material: Great Britain requires that almost any violation of law enforcement result in the collection of DNA of the violator.[79]

Leading the way in the development of the most advanced forensic techniques is the Forensic Science Research and Training Center, operated by the FBI in Washington, D.C., and Quantico, Virginia. The lab provides information and services to hundreds of crime labs throughout the United States. The National Institute of Justice is also sponsoring research to identify a wider variety of DNA segments for testing and is involved in developing a PCR-based DNA-profiling examination using fluorescent detection that will reduce the time required for DNA profiling.

The FBI is now operating the Combined DNA Index System (CODIS), which has assisted in nearly 50,000 investigations. CODIS is a computerized database that allows DNA taken at a crime scene to be searched electronically to find matches against samples taken from convicted offenders and from other crime scenes. Early on, the system linked evidence taken from crime scenes in

Web App 5.6

To read about the FBI's Integrated Automated Fingerprint Identification System, visit http://www.fbi.gov/about-us/cjis/fingerprints_biometrics/iafis/iafis.

DNA profiling
The identification of criminal suspects by matching DNA samples taken from their person with specimens found at the crime scene.

Web App 5.7

To read more about the U.S. government's DNA initiative, visit http://www.dna.gov.

Web App 5.8

If you want to read more about the science of DNA testing, visit http://www.scientific.org/tutorials/articles/riley/riley.html.

Saginaw, Michigan, Police Detective Sgt. Reggie Williams displays the Saginaw Police Department Facebook page on a smartphone, iPod, and desktop. He uses social media to communicate with the public and to receive tips and information on crimes. What social media other than Facebook can be used to assist the police?

Jacksonville, Florida, to ones in Washington, D.C., thereby tying nine crimes to a single offender.[80] When Timothy Spence was executed in Virginia on April 27, 1994, he was the first person convicted and executed almost entirely on the basis of DNA evidence.[81] More recently, CODIS has been expanded to include a wealth of information, including profiles of individuals convicted of crimes—and even of arrestees, if state law permits.[82] Critics of this information gathering cite concerns that some arrestees are innocent and that retaining data from innocent persons could be improperly used and constitute a violation of privacy and civil liberties.[83]

DNA evidence—and the forensic sciences in general—are not without some problems, however. A recent study reported that although there is widespread knowledge about the utility of forensic evidence, it is not being adequately used by law enforcement agencies.[84] The authors found that a significant number of unsolved homicides and rapes with forensic evidence had not been submitted to laboratories for analysis. And when cases with DNA evidence make it to trial, jurors are sometimes confused by the complexities involved.[85]

Social Media and Networking

Police departments have for several years used the Internet and particularly their websites to communicate with the public. More recently, they have jumped on the social media and social networking bandwagon. People voluntarily reveal intimate details of their lives on sites such as Facebook and MySpace, something that has proven quite useful for the police. People also follow police departments on Twitter and Nixle, the latter of which is a dedicated police local alert system to which anyone can sign up for free.

The Baltimore Police Department has used Facebook and Twitter since 2009.[86] They used Facebook to post information on wanted criminals and news updates. Individual officers also have their *own* Facebook pages, permitting citizens to interact with them directly online. The department uses Twitter to inform the public on important developments.

Baltimore does not rely on Twitter for crime tips, citing security concerns (anyone can see the postings). In contrast, the Boston Police Department, which has over 41,000 Twitter followers, relies on the social networking site heavily for the receipt of crime-fighting tips.[87] The department also maintains a "text-a-tip" program, allowing residents to send anonymous texts to the Crime Stoppers Unit.[88] Texters then receive an automatic reply: "Thx. We'll ask u a few questions." Special software then blocks the person's phone number as officers exchange information back and forth with them.

Facebook has proven particularly useful. For example, the Hartselle, Alabama, police department sees its Facebook page as providing an extra 1,300 sets of eyes in the community. The department, which has around 1,300 likes, recently used the site to identify a couple who ran up over $1,500 worth of charges on a stolen credit card.[89] After the department posted surveillance photos from a local Walmart on its Facebook page, the couple was identified by a member of the community. Other departments around the country have used Facebook to capture crooks, and not just thieves. Police in one Louisiana department successfully used Facebook as part of their effort to apprehend a suspected cop-killer.[90]

ETHICAL CHALLENGES in Criminal Justice

A WRITING ASSIGNMENT

The FBI's Combined DNA Index System (CODIS) helps law enforcement develop investigative leads in cases where biological evidence is secured from a crime scene. Biological samples are matched against DNA profiles of people in the database, including convicted criminals and arrestees. State and local law enforcement officials have access to the system and can possibly link several similar crimes to a single perpetrator.

Write an essay on the ethics of using this system. In doing so, answer these questions: Should every arrestee have a DNA sample taken? Does CODIS amount to an undesirable invasion of individual privacy, or does it represent a positive advance in police investigations that generates benefits for society? What other technological advances in law enforcement raise ethical questions? Why do they raise ethical questions? Refer to this chapter's "Technology and Law Enforcement" section for some guidance.

Summary

 Recount the early development of the police in England.

- Early in English history, law enforcement was a personal matter.

- Under the pledge system, people were grouped into tythings and hundreds. The leader of a tything was called a tythingman. The leader of a hundred was called the hundredman and later came to be called the constable. This rudimentary beginning was the seed of today's police departments.

- Shires, which resembled today's counties, were controlled by the shire reeve, the forerunner of the sheriff.

- Under the thirteenth-century watch system, watchmen patrolled at night and helped protect against robberies, fires, and disturbances.

- Early in the eighteenth century, paid private police called thief takers patrolled the streets.

- The Metropolitan Police Act established the first organized police force in London.

LO2 **Recount the development of the police in colonial America.**

- Law enforcement in colonial America resembled the British model.

- The county sheriff became the most important law enforcement official.

- Urban police departments were born out of urban mob violence.

- Boston created America's first urban police department in 1838.

LO3 **Discuss the emergence of police professionalism.**

- In the early years of the twentieth century, various reforms were undertaken with the intent of limiting local officials' control over the police.

- The Boston police strike of 1919 fueled interest in police reform.

- Nationally recognized leaders called for professionalization of the police. The International Association of Chiefs of Police, a key professional society, was formed.

LO4 **Identify the main events in policing between 1960 and the present.**

- Police professionalism was interpreted to mean tough, rule-oriented police work featuring advanced technology and hardware. However, the view that these measures would quickly reduce crime proved incorrect.

- During the 1970s, federal support for local law enforcement benefited police departments considerably. Criminal justice programs began to be formed in colleges and universities throughout the United States.

- Between 1960 and the 1990s, police were beset by many problems, including questions about their treatment of minorities and why they were not more effective. This paved the way for a radical change in policing and the development of community policing.

L05 Identify the four levels of law enforcement in America.

- There are four main levels of law enforcement in the United States: federal, state, county, and local.
- Most law enforcement is performed at the local level.
- The typical local police department employs fewer than 50 officers.

L06 Identify the most prominent federal law enforcement agencies.

- The most prominent federal law enforcement agencies within the Justice Department are the Federal Bureau of Investigation (FBI), the Bureau of Alcohol, Tobacco, Firearms and Explosives (ATF), and the U.S. Marshals Service.
- The most prominent federal law enforcement agencies within the Department of Homeland Security are Customs and Border Protection (CBP), Immigration and Customs Enforcement (ICE), and the Secret Service.

L07 Discuss the differences among local, county, state, and federal law enforcement agencies.

- Federal law enforcement agencies primarily enforce federal law.
- State law enforcement agencies come in two main varieties. State police generally enforce state law and have broad police power. State patrols and highway patrols focus mainly on traffic enforcement on state highways and interstates.
- County law enforcement officials enforce state laws and county ordinances. Most of their enforcement work occurs in unincorporated areas. Some sheriff's departments are mainly law enforcement oriented. Some also take on correctional responsibilities, such as running county jails.

- City and metropolitan police are the most common type of law enforcement official. They have broad authority to enforce state and local laws.

L08 Discuss the differences between public and private policing.

- Private police outnumber public police (those employed by the federal, state, or local government) by roughly three to one.
- Private police have emerged in response to (a) the desire for nongovernmental service provision, (b) growth in mass private property, such as shopping malls, and (c) a belief that the private sector can do a better job than the public sector (government) of preventing and controlling crime.
- Private policing is controversial due to concerns that (a) the profit motive will take precedence over crime control, (b) private police may replace public police, and (c) there are few constitutional constraints on private police.

L09 Identify various technologies currently used in law enforcement.

- Today, most police departments rely on advanced computer-based technology to identify suspects and collate evidence.
- Various technologies, such as gun detectors, have been developed to aid the police in locating the whereabouts of criminals.
- Many law enforcement agencies use mapping software to identify geographic "hot spots" of crime and to track their progress in crime control and prevention.
- Automated fingerprint systems and computerized identification systems have become widespread. Some believe that technology may make police overly intrusive and interfere with civil liberties.
- DNA testing, combined with DNA databases, helps law enforcement officials identify criminals.
- Police are increasingly relying on social media and social networking, particularly for the purpose of catching suspected criminals.

Key Terms

tything (tithing), 164
hue and cry, 164
hundred, 164
shire reeve, 164
sheriff, 164
watch system, 164
constable, 164

justice of the peace, 164
Metropolitan Police Act, 165
vigilantes, 166
Wickersham Commission, 169
community policing, 171
Federal Bureau of Investigation
  (FBI), 174

private policing, 183
data mining, 190
thermal imagers, 190
biometrics, 194
DNA profiling, 195

Critical Thinking Questions

1. List the problems faced by today's police departments that were also present during the early days of policing.
2. There is concern that history may be repeating itself in policing due to increased reliance on civilian volunteers and privatization. Is this cause for concern?
3. Distinguish among the duties of the state police, sheriff's departments, and local police departments.

4. What is the Department of Homeland Security? What are its component law enforcement agencies?
5. Private police outnumber public by a factor of three to one. Is this beneficial or harmful?
6. What are some of the technological advances that should help the police solve more crimes? What are the dangers of these advances?

Notes

1. Huffington Post, "Drone List Released by FAA Shows Which Police Departments Want to Fly Unmanned Aerial Vehicles," http://www.huffingtonpost.com/2013/02/08/drone-list-domestic-police-law-enforcement-surveillance_n_2647530.html (accessed May 2014). See http://tinyurl.com/b8nvtsr for a list of agencies currently authorized to fly drones (accessed May 2014).
2. Federal Aviation Administration, *Fact Sheet—Unmanned Aircraft Systems (UAS)*, http://www.faa.gov/news/fact_sheets/news_story.cfm?newsId=14153 (accessed May 2014).
3. This section relies heavily on such sources as Malcolm Sparrow, Mark Moore, and David Kennedy, *Beyond 911: A New Era for Policing* (New York: Basic Books, 1990); Daniel Devlin, *Police Procedure, Administration, and Organization* (London: Butterworth, 1966); Robert Fogelson, *Big-City Police* (Cambridge, MA: Harvard University Press, 1977); Roger Lane, *Policing the City, Boston 1822–1885* (Cambridge, MA: Harvard University Press, 1967); J. J. Tobias, *Crime and Industrial Society in the Nineteenth Century* (New York: Schocken, 1967); Samuel Walker, *A Critical History of Police Reform: The Emergence of Professionalism* (Lexington, MA: Lexington Books, 1977); Samuel Walker, *Popular Justice* (New York: Oxford University Press, 1980); John McMullan, "The New Improved Monied Police: Reform Crime Control and Commodification of Policing in London," *British Journal of Criminology* 36 (1996): 85–108.
4. Devlin, *Police Procedure, Administration, and Organization*, p. 3.
5. McMullan, "The New Improved Monied Police," at 92; Elizabeth Joh, "The Paradox of Private Policing," *Journal of Criminal Law and Criminology* 95 (2004): 49–131.
6. Edward J. Blakely and Mary G. Snyder, *Fortress America: Gated Communities in the United States* (Washington, DC: Brookings Institution Press, 1997).
7. Not everyone agrees there are only nine principles. There are also several variations on the nine principles. Those we have reprinted appear in several sources, but see Susan A. Lentz and Robert H. Chaires, "The Invention of Peels' Principles: A Study of Policing 'Textbook' History," *Journal of Criminal Justice* 35 (2007): 69–79.
8. Wilbur Miller, "The Good, the Bad, and the Ugly: Policing America," *History Today* 50 (2000): 29–32.
9. Phillip Reichel, "Southern Slave Patrols as a Transitional Type," *American Journal of Police* 7 (1988): 51–78.
10. Walker, *Popular Justice*, p. 61.
11. Ibid., p. 8.
12. Dennis Rousey, "Cops and Guns: Police Use of Deadly Force in Nineteenth-Century New Orleans," *American Journal of Legal History* 28 (1984): 41–66.
13. Law Enforcement Assistance Administration, *Two Hundred Years of American Criminal Justice* (Washington, DC: Government Printing Office, 1976).
14. National Commission on Law Observance and Enforcement, *Report on the Police* (Washington, DC: Government Printing Office, 1931), pp. 5–7.
15. Orlando W. Wilson, *Police Administration*, 4th ed. (New York: McGraw-Hill, 1977).
16. Pamela Irving Jackson, *Minority Group Threat, Crime, and Policing* (New York: Praeger, 1989).

17. For an overview of early federal support for local law enforcement, see John L. Worrall, "The Effects of Local Law Enforcement Block Grants on Serious Crime," *Criminology and Public Policy* 7 (2008): 325–350.

18. James Q. Wilson and George Kelling, "Broken Windows," *Atlantic Monthly* (March 1982): 29–38.

19. Frank Tippett, "It Looks Just Like a War Zone," *Time*, May 27, 1985, pp. 16–22; "San Francisco, New York Police Troubled by Series of Scandals," *Criminal Justice Newsletter* 16 (1985): 2–4; Karen Polk, "New York Police: Caught in the Middle and Losing Faith," *Boston Globe*, December 28, 1988, p. 3.

20. The Staff of the *Los Angeles Times, Understanding the Riots: Los Angeles Before and After the Rodney King Case* (Los Angeles: Times Syndicate Books, 1992).

21. David H. Bayley, "Policing in America," *Society* 36 (December 1998): 16–20.

22. Federal Bureau of Investigation, http://www.fbi.gov/about-us/quick-facts/quickfacts (accessed May 2014).

23. Federal Bureau of Investigation, *Protecting America Against Terrorist Attack: A Closer Look at the FBI's Joint Terrorism Task Forces*, http://www.fbi.gov/about-us/investigate/terrorism/terrorism_jttfs (accessed May 2014).

24. United States Marshals Service, http://www.usmarshals.gov/duties/factsheets/overview-2014.pdf (accessed May 2014).

25. Department of Homeland Security, http://www.dhs.gov/history (accessed May 2014).

26. Customs and Border Protection, http://www.cbp.gov/sites/default/files/documents/CBP%20Snapshot%20UPDATE%20013114%20-%20FINAL_1.pdf (accessed May 2014).

27. Immigration and Customs Enforcement, http://www.ice.gov/about/overview/ (accessed May 2014).

28. U.S. Secret Service, http://www.secretservice.gov/criminal.shtml (accessed May 2014).

29. Bruce Smith, *Police Systems in the United States* (New York: Harper and Row, 1960).

30. Arizona Department of Public Safety, "Arizona Fusion Center," http://www.azdps.gov/about/Task_Forces/Fusion/. Also see http://www.azactic.gov. (Sites accessed May 2014).

31. Arizona Counter Terrorism Information Center, http://www.azactic.gov/About/Operation/ (accessed May 2014).

32. The most recent data as of this writing are from 2008. See Brian Reaves, *Census of State and Local Law Enforcement Agencies, 2008* (Washington, DC: Bureau of Justice Statistics, 2011).

33. The most recent data as of this writing are from 2007. See Brian Reaves, *Local Police Departments, 2007* (Washington, DC: Bureau of Justice Statistics, 2010).

34. Harris County Homeland Security & Emergency Management, http://www.hcoem.org (accessed May 2014).

35. Montgomery County, Maryland, Homeland Security, http://www.montgomerycountymd.gov/oemhs/ (accessed May 2014).

36. Reaves, *Local Police Departments, 2007.*

37. See, for example, Robert Keppel and Joseph Weis, *Improving the Investigation of Violent Crime: The Homicide Investigation and Tracking System* (Washington, DC: National Institute of Justice, 1993).

38. Reaves, *Local Police Departments, 2007.*

39. Brian K. Payne, Bruce L. Berg, and Ivan Y. Sun, "Policing in Small Town America: Dogs, Drunks, Disorder, and Dysfunction," *Journal of Criminal Justice* 33 (2005): 31–41.

40. John Liederbach and James Frank, "Policing the Big Beat: An Observational Study of County Level Patrol and Comparisons to Local Small Town and Rural Officers," *Journal of Crime and Justice* 29 (2006): 21–44.

41. William K. Rashbaum, "Terror Makes All the World a Beat for New York Police," *New York Times,* July 15, 2002, p. B1; Al Baker, "Leader Sees New York Police in Vanguard of Terror Fight," *New*

York Times, August 6, 2002, p. A2; Stephen Flynn, "America the Vulnerable," *Foreign Affairs* 81 (January–February 2002): 60.

42. William C. Cunningham and John J. Strauchs, "Security Industry Trends: 1993 and Beyond," *Security Management* 36 (1992): 27–30, 32, 34–36.

43. Joh, "The Paradox of Private Policing."

44. David A. Sklansky, "The Private Police," *UCLA Law Review* 46 (1999): 1165–1287.

45. Elizabeth Joh, "Conceptualizing the Private Police," *Utah Law Review* (2005): 573–617, pp. 588–593.

46. Ibid.

47. Clifford Shearing and Philip Stenning, "Say 'Cheese'?: The Disney Order that Is Not So Mickey Mouse," in *Private Policing* (Thousand Oaks, CA: Sage, 1987).

48. Andrea Elliott, "In Stores, Private Handcuffs for Sticky Fingers," *New York Times,* June 17, 2003, A1.

49. Joh, "Conceptualizing the Private Police," pp. 610–615.

50. See National Insurance Crime Bureau, http://www.nicb.org (accessed May 2014).

51. See, for example, M. Rhead Enion, "Constitutional Limits on Private Policing and the State's Allocation of Force," *Duke Law Journal* 59 (2009): 519–553, Section IV.

52. Joh, "Conceptualizing the Private Police," p. 614.

53. Ibid., n. 230.

54. Sklansky, "The Private Police," p. 1168.

55. *Griffin v. Maryland*, 378 U.S. 130 (1964).

56. See, e.g., *Williams v. United States*, 341 U.S. 97 (1951).

57. See, e.g., *Wade v. Byles*, 83 F.3d 902 (7th Cir. 1996); *Gallagher v. "Neil Young Freedom Concert,"* 49 F.3d 1442 (10th Cir. 1995); *United States v. Francoeur*, 547 F.2d 891 (5th Cir. 1977); *People v. Taylor*, 271 Cal. Rptr. 785 (Ct. App. 1990); *United States v. Lima*, 424 A.2d 113 (D.C. 1980) (en banc); *People v. Toliver*, 377 N.E.2d 207 (Ill. App. Ct. 1978); *People v. Holloway*, 267 N.W.2d 454 (Mich. Ct. App. 1978); *State v. Buswell*, 460 N.W.2d 614 (Minn. 1990).

58. See, e.g., *United States v. Antonelli*, 434 F.2d 335 (2d Cir. 1970); *City of Grand Rapids v. Impens*, 327 N.W.2d 278 (Mich. 1982).

59. See, e.g., *United States v. Cruz*, 783 F.2d 1470, 1473 (9th Cir. 1986); *State v. Garcia*, 528 So. 2d 76 (Fla. Dist. Ct. App. 1988); *Perez v. State*, 517 So. 2d 106 (Fla. Dist. Ct. App. 1987); *People v. Gorski*, 494 N.E.2d 246 (Ill. App. Ct. 1986); *State v. Farmer*, 510 P.2d 180 (Kan. 1973); *Commonwealth v. Lindenmuth*, 554 A.2d 62 (Pa. Super. Ct. 1989).

60. Joh, "The Paradox of Private Policing," p. 64.

61. Lois Pliant, "Information Management," *Police Chief* 61 (1994): 31–35.

62. James Byrne and Gary Marx, "Technological Innovations in Crime Prevention and Policing: A Review of the Research on Implementation and Impact," *Cahiers Politiestudies Jaargang* 20 (2011): 17–40, at 20.

63. Rebecca Kanable, "Dig into Data Mining," *Law Enforcement Technology* 34 (2007): 62, 64–68, 70.

64. Millivision, http://www.millivision.com/technology.html (accessed May 2014).

65. Rebecca Kanable, "Setting Up Surveillance Downtown," *Law Enforcement Technology* (February 2008), http://www.officer.com/article/10249122/setting-up-surveillance-downtown (accessed May 2014).

66. Oak Ridge National Laboratory, http://infohouse.p2ric.org/ref/16/15985.htm (accessed May 2014).

67. This section is based on Derek Paulsen, "To Map or Not to Map: Assessing the Impact of Crime Maps on Police Officer Perceptions of Crime," *International Journal of Police Science and Management* 6 (2004): 234–246; William W. Bratton and Peter Knobler, *Turnaround: How America's Top Cop Reversed the Crime Epidemic* (New York: Random House, 1998), p. 289; Jeremy Travis, "Computerized Crime Mapping," *NIJ News*, January 1999.

68. James J. Willis, Stephen D. Mastrofski, and David Weisburd, "Making Sense of COMPSTAT: A Theory-Based Analysis of Organizational Change in Three Police Departments," *Law and Society Review* 41 (2007): 147–188.

69. Chicago Police Department, http://gis.chicagopolice.org/ (accessed May 2014).

70. Nancy G. La Vigne and Julie Wartell, *Mapping Across Boundaries: Regional Crime Analysis* (Washington, DC: Police Executive Research Forum, 2001).

71. http://www.youtube.com/watch?v=9JNqPsh7kmU (accessed May 2014).

72. West Virginia Statewide Addressing and Mapping Board, http://www.dhsem.wv.gov/gis/Pages/default.aspx (accessed May 2014).

73. Kevin Corbley, "GPS Photo Mapping in Law Enforcement," *Law Enforcement Technology* 35 (2008): 96, 98–101.

74. Geoffrey Gluckman, "Eye in the Sky: GPS Has Changed the Way Law Enforcement Does Fleet Management," *Law Enforcement Technology* 33 (2006): 68, 70–75.

75. "Introduction to Biometrics," http://www.biometrics.org/introduction.php (accessed May 2014); Fernando L. Podio, "Biometrics—Technologies for Highly Secure Personal Authentication," *ITL Bulletin* (National Institute of Standards and Technology).

76. Western Identification Network, http://www.winid.org/winid/ (accessed May 2014).

77. Weipeng Zhang, Yan Yuan Tang, and Xinge You, "Fingerprint Enhancement Using Wavelet Transform Combined with Gabor Filter," *International Journal of Pattern Recognition and Artificial Intelligence* 18 (2004): 1391–1406.

78. Ibid.

79. Frederick Bieber, Charles Brenner, and David Lazer, "Finding Criminals Through DNA of Their Relatives," *Science* 312 (2006): 1315–1316.

80. "FBI's DNA Profile Clearinghouse Announces First 'Cold Hit,'" *Criminal Justice Newsletter* 16 (1999): 5.

81. "South Side Strangler's Execution Cited as DNA Evidence Landmark," *Criminal Justice Newsletter* 2 (1994): 3.

82. Federal Bureau of Investigation, "CODIS: Combined DNA Index System," http://www.fbi.gov/about-us/lab/biometric-analysis/codis (accessed May 2014).

83. Karen Norrgard, "Forensics, DNA Fingerprinting, and CODIS," *Nature Education* 1 (2008): 1.

84. Kevin. J. Strom and Matthew J. Hickman, "Unanalyzed Evidence in Law-Enforcement Agencies: A National Examination of Forensic Processing in Police Departments," *Criminology and Public Policy* 9 (2010): 381–404.

85. Valerie Hans, David Kay, Michael Dann, Erin Farley, and Stephanie Albertson, "Science in the Jury Box: Jurors' Comprehension of Mitochondrial DNA Evidence," *Law and Human Behavior* 35 (2011): 60–71.

86. National Law Enforcement and Corrections Technology Center, *Social Networking for Law Enforcement* (Rockville, MD: NLECTC, 2010), http://www.justnet.org/pdf/SocialNetworking.pdf (accessed May 2014).

87. Martine Powers, "A Social Media Tip Line for Police," *Boston Globe*, April 6, 2012, http://www.boston.com/news/local/massachusetts/articles/2012/04/06/twitter_text_messaging_yield_crime_solving_tips_for_boston_police_department/ (accessed May 2014).

88. Ibid.

89. Shumuriel Ratliff, "Hartselle Police Use Social Networking to Catch Crooks," http://www.waff.com/story/17316642/hartselle-police-use-social-networking-to-crack-down-on-crooks (accessed May 2014).

90. See http://www.facebook.com/note.php?note_id=10150225332920329 (accessed May 2014).

CHAPTER 6

The Police: Organization, Role, and Function

Learning Objectives

 LO1 Explain the organization of police departments.

 LO2 Differentiate between the patrol function and the investigation function.

 LO3 Discuss various efforts to improve patrol.

 LO4 Discuss key issues associated with the investigative function.

 LO5 Explain the concept of community policing.

 LO6 List several challenges associated with community policing.

 LO7 Discuss the concept of problem-oriented policing.

 LO8 Define intelligence-led policing and explain ways in which it occurs.

 LO9 Explain the various police support functions.

 LO10 Identify some of the cost-saving measures that may be employed to improve police productivity.

Chapter Outline

The Police Organization

The Police Role

The Patrol Function
　Evidence-Based Justice: The Police Presence and Deterrence
　Patrol Activities
　Improving Patrol
　Criminal Justice and Technology: In-Car and Body-Worn Cameras

The Investigation Function
　How Do Detectives Detect?
　Sting Operations
　Undercover Work
　Analyzing Criminal Justice Issues: Forensics Under the Microscope
　Evaluating Investigations
　Improving Investigations Using Technology
　The Victim Experience: Secondary Victimization and Victim Cooperation

Community Policing
　Implementing Community Policing
　The Challenges of Community Policing
　Overcoming Obstacles

Problem-Oriented Policing (POP)
　Criminal Acts, Criminal Places
　Analyzing Criminal Justice Issues: The Displacement Problem

Intelligence-Led Policing (ILP)
　Intelligence and the Intelligence Process

Fusion Centers

Police Support Functions
　Careers in Criminal Justice: Victim Advocate

Improving Police Productivity

In recent years, cities all across the country have been forced to do more with less. Services have being curtailed, employees have been furloughed, and capital improvements have been delayed—if not cancelled altogether. Throughout history, police department spending has rarely landed on the chopping block, but these days no public agency is immune. The economy has rebounded markedly since 2008, and a number of criminal justice agencies have resumed hiring and are once again expanding, but shrinking—or at least stagnant—budgets remain a real issue.

Police departments across the country have adopted a range of creative—and controversial—strategies to respond to mandates that they limit spending. Some have placed limits on overtime, putting caps on the amount of extra work officers can put in.[1] Other cities have left hundreds of positions unfilled.[2] Still others have offered senior officers early retirement. The list goes on.

One of the most interesting policing trends in this new era of austerity is "consolidation." Consolidation refers to merging historically separate functions and sharing responsibilities.[3] For example, merging two police departments together reduces staffing needs. So does merging police and fire services into a single agency. As another example, sharing SWAT responsibilities among several agencies in a given jurisdiction helps reduce the costs of training and maintaining several separate teams. Even charging for certain services, such as responding to excessive false security system alarms can fall under the consolidation umbrella, as doing so spreads out the costs of crime control.

A few agencies have been fortunate enough to buck the budget cut trend. Some, including the Dallas Police Department, continue to hire year in and year out. But the Dallas experience is not the norm. Spending limits and budget cuts seem to prevail more than growth and expansion. This trend raises interesting questions for public safety. Do cuts in hiring affect crime? Do other restrictions limit police effectiveness? Will consolidation help or hurt law enforcement? What form of consolidation, if any, is most desirable? ■

YOUR OPINION: Do you agree or disagree with this statement? "Merging a city's police, fire, and emergency medical services into a single agency would reduce quality."

PUBLIC OPINION:

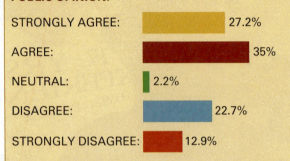

STRONGLY AGREE: 27.2%

AGREE: 35%

NEUTRAL: 2.2%

DISAGREE: 22.7%

STRONGLY DISAGREE: 12.9%

REALITY: In 2012, researchers at Michigan State University surveyed state residents about their perceptions of such consolidation. A sizeable majority of respondents expressed concern that consolidation will hurt service quality. Nearly two-thirds of respondents agreed or strongly agreed that service would suffer with consolidation.

Despite what people think about consolidation, the practice has been around for some time. It is not a thought exercise. For example, Sunnyvale, California, was one of the first cities to merge police, fire, and emergency medical services. All the way back in 1950, the city created a single "Department of Public Safety," and to this day, all new hires get police, fire, *and* medical training. In fairness, though, some formerly consolidated agencies have since abandoned the approach. For example, Eugene, Oregon, abandoned consolidation because doing so created another layer of administration between city management and the police and fire chiefs.

DISCUSSION: What are the possible consequences of public safety consolidation? How should a fully consolidated public safety department be organized? What forms could consolidation take?

Sources: Justin Heinonen and Jeremy M. Wilson, *Resident Perceptions of Public-Safety Consolidation* (East Lansing, MI: Michigan State University, 2013), http://policeconsolidation.msu.edu/sites/default/files/Perceptions%20of%20Public%20Safety%20Consolidation_Brief.pdf (accessed June 2014); Jeremy M. Wilson, Alexander Weiss, and Clifford Grammich, *Public Safety Consolidation: What Is It? How Does It Work?* (Washington, DC: Office of Community-Oriented Policing Services, 2012), http://a-capp.msu.edu/sites/default/files/files/Consolidation_BOLO_august2012.pdf (accessed June 2014).

L01 Understand the organization of police departments.

The Police Organization

Although many police agencies are today in the process of rethinking their organization and goals, the majority are still organized in a hierarchical manner, as illustrated in Figure 6.1. Within this organizational model, each element of the department normally has its own chain of command and rank system. New York City ranks include the following, from lowest to highest:

■ Police officer
■ Detective specialist
■ Detective investigator
■ Sergeant (symbol of rank: 3 chevrons)
■ Lieutenant (symbol of rank: 1 gold bar)
■ Captain (symbol of rank: 2 gold bars)
■ Deputy inspector (symbol of rank: gold oak leaf)
■ Inspector (symbol of rank: gold eagle)
■ Deputy chief (symbol of rank: 1 gold star)
■ Assistant chief (symbol of rank: 2 gold stars)
■ Bureau chief (symbol of rank: 3 gold stars)
■ Chief of department (symbol of rank: 4 gold stars)
■ Deputy commissioner (symbol of rank: 3 gold stars)
■ First deputy commissioner (symbol of rank: 4 gold stars)
■ Police commissioner (symbol of rank: 5 gold stars)

In a large municipal department, there may be a number of independent units headed by a bureau chief who serves as the senior administrator, a captain who oversees regional or precinct units and acts as liaison with other police agencies, a lieutenant who manages daily activities, and sergeants and patrol officers who carry out fieldwork. Smaller departments may have a captain or lieutenant as a unit head. At the head of the organization is the police chief, who sets policy and has general administrative control over all the department's various operating branches.

Problems regarding a police department's organizational structure are not uncommon, nor are they unique to policing agencies, as anyone who has ever dealt with any governmental bureaucracy is aware. Most often they are attributable to personnel changes (due to retirements, promotions, transfers, or resignations) or simply to a periodic internal reorganization. As a result, citizens may sometimes have difficulty determining who is responsible for a particular police function or operational policy, or two divisions may unknowingly compete with each other over jurisdiction on a particular case. The large number of operating divisions and the lack of any clear relationship among them almost guarantee that the decision-making practices of one branch will be unknown to another. These are common management problems that are not insurmountable, and they are typically resolved over time.

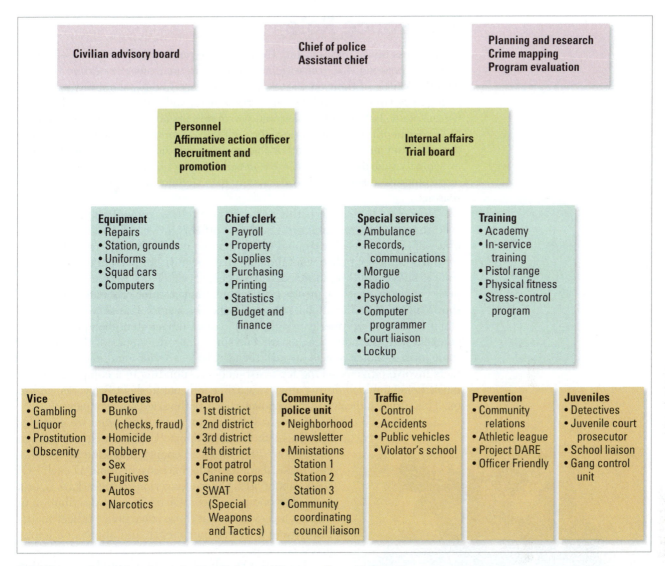

FIGURE 6.1 **Organization of a Traditional Metropolitan Police Department**

In promoting personnel, most departments also follow a system called the **time-in-rank system**. This means that before moving up the administrative ladder, an officer must spend a certain amount of time in the next lowest rank. Thus a sergeant cannot become a captain without serving an appropriate amount of time as a lieutenant. In New York City, for example, promotions from police officer to sergeant, from sergeant to lieutenant, and from lieutenant to captain all occur via a civil service formula that involves such criteria as performance on a civil service written examination, length of service, citations awarded, and optional physical fitness test (for extra points). Promotion beyond the rank of captain is discretionary. Unlike the private sector, where people can be hired away from another company and given an immediate promotion and boost in pay, the time-in-rank system prohibits departments from allowing officers to skip ranks and sometimes prevents them from hiring an officer from another department and awarding her a higher rank. Although this system is designed to promote fairness and stability in police agencies and to limit favoritism, it may restrict administrative flexibility.

 **Web App 6.1**

For more information about the New York City Police Department, visit http://www.nyc.gov/html/nypd/.

time-in-rank system

The promotion system in which a police officer can advance in rank only after spending a prescribed amount of time in the preceding rank.

The Police Role

In countless books, movies, and TV shows, the public has been presented with a view of policing that romanticizes police officers as fearless crime fighters who think little of their own safety as they engage in daily shootouts with Uzi-toting drug runners, psychopathic serial killers, and organized crime hit men. Occasionally, but not often, fictional patrol officers and detectives seem aware of departmental rules, legal decisions, citizens' groups, civil suits, or physical danger. They are rarely faced with the economic necessity of moonlighting as security guards, taking on extra details, caring about an annual pay raise, or griping when someone less deserving gets a choice assignment for political reasons.

How close to real life is this portrayal of a selfless crime fighter? Not very, according to most research efforts. Police officers are asked to deal with hundreds of incidents each year, and crime fighting is only a small part of the daily routine. Studies of police work indicate that a significant portion of an officer's time is spent handling minor disturbances, service calls, and administrative duties. Police work, then, involves much more than catching criminals. Figure 6.2 shows the results of a national survey of police behavior.[4] This survey found that about 17 percent of Americans aged 16 and older (about 40 million people) have contacts with the police each year. The single largest number of these involve some form of motor vehicle or traffic-related issues. About 5 million annual contacts involve citizens asking for assistance—responding to a complaint about music being too loud during a party, warning kids not to shoot fireworks, and so on. This survey indicates that the police role is both varied and complex.

These results are not surprising when we consider the Uniform Crime Report (UCR) arrest data. Each year, about 700,000 local, county, and state police officers make about 12 million arrests, or about 17 each.[5] Of these, about 500,000 are for serious crimes (Part I), or a little over one per officer. Given an even distribution of arrests, it is evident that the average police officer makes fewer than 2 arrests per month and about one felony arrest per year.

These figures should be interpreted with caution because not all police officers are engaged in activities that allow them to make arrests, such as patrol or detective work, and many work in rural and suburban departments in areas with very low crime rates. About one-third of all sworn officers in the nation's largest police departments are in such units as communications, antiterrorism, administration, and personnel. Even if the number of arrests per officer were adjusted by one-third, it would still amount to about four serious crime arrests per officer per year, and these figures include such crimes as shoplifting and other minor larcenies. So although police handle thousands of calls each year, relatively few result in an arrest for a serious crime such as a robbery or burglary; in suburban and rural areas, years may go by before a police officer makes a felony arrest.

The evidence, then, shows that unlike TV and film portrayals, the police role involves many non-crime-related activities. Although the media depict police officers busting criminals and engaging in high-speed chases, the true police role is much more complex. Police officers function in a variety of roles, ranging from dispensers of

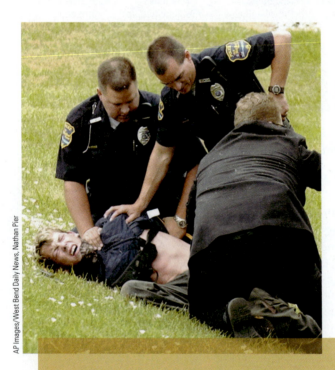

AP Images/West Bend Daily News, Nathan Pier

The role of the police involves activities ranging from emergency medical care to traffic control, but law enforcement and crime control are critical (and often misunderstood) elements of policing. Here, a bank robbery suspect is being subdued. The suspect was able to make it only across the street from the bank before being apprehended.

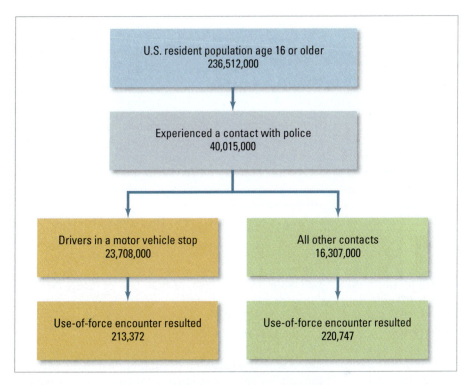

FIGURE 6.2 **Police Encounters with Citizens Each Year**

Source: Christine Eith and Matthew R. Durose, *Contacts Between the Police and the Public, 2008* (Washington, DC: Bureau of Justice Statistics, 2011).

beats
Designated police patrol areas.

 Differentiate between the patrol function and the investigation function.

emergency medical care to keepers of the peace on school grounds. Although officers in large urban departments may be called on to handle more felony cases than those in small towns, they too will probably find that most of their daily activities are not related to crime. What are some of the most important functions of police?

The Patrol Function

Regardless of style of policing, uniformed patrol officers are the backbone of the police department, usually accounting for about two-thirds of a department's personnel.[6] Patrol officers are the most highly visible members of the entire criminal justice system. They are charged with supervising specific areas of their jurisdiction, called **beats**, whether in a patrol car, or by motorcycle, horse, helicopter, or boat, or even on foot in some departments. Each beat, or patrol area, is covered 24 hours a day by different shifts. The major purposes of patrol are to:

- Deter crime by maintaining a visible police presence
- Maintain public order (peacekeeping) within the patrol area

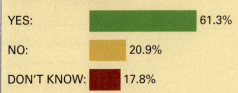

YOUR OPINION: If you have ever requested and received a police response for any perceived problem, did the police improve the situation?

PUBLIC OPINION:

YES: 61.3%

NO: 20.9%

DON'T KNOW: 17.8%

REALITY: According to the Bureau of Justice Statistics, only about one in eight U.S. residents request support from police during any given year. The vast majority of those who do request police assistance report that officer acted properly during the encounter (93 percent). Whether having an officer respond improved the situation, however, is something of a different story. But importantly, if police failed to improve the situation, it may be through no fault of their own! For example, if someone wakes up in the morning to find their car was broken into overnight, reporting the crime to the police may come a little too late; it is difficult to catch burglars when the trail has gone cold. These results also mask important details. According to the BJS, the police receive much higher marks for their responses to noncrime emergencies (70 percent yes) than reports of problems such as neighborhood disturbances (58 percent yes).

DISCUSSION: Why do you think the police receive higher marks for noncrime emergencies? In contrast, why do they receive lower marks for their responses to neighborhood emergencies?

Source: Matthew Durose and Lynn Langton, *Requests for Police Assistance, 2011* (Washington, DC: Bureau of Justice Statistics, 2013), p. 4, Table 6.

EVIDENCE-based justice

THE POLICE PRESENCE AND DETERRENCE

For many years, preventive police patrol was considered one of the greatest deterrents to criminal behavior. The visible presence of patrol cars on the street and the rapid deployment of police officers to the scene of the crime were viewed as particularly effective law enforcement techniques. However, research efforts have questioned the basic assumptions of patrol. The most widely heralded attempt at measuring patrol effectiveness was undertaken during the early 1970s in Kansas City, Missouri, under sponsorship of the Police Foundation, a private institute that studies police behavior. To evaluate the effectiveness of patrol, the researchers divided 15 police districts into three groups: one group retained normal patrol, the second (proactive) set of districts were supplied with two to three times the normal amount of patrol forces, and the third (reactive) group had their preventive patrols eliminated, with police officers responding only when summoned by citizens to the scene of a particular crime. Data from the Kansas City study indicated that these variations in patrol techniques had little effect on the crime patterns in the 15 districts. The presence or absence of patrol did not seem to affect residential or business burglaries, motor vehicle thefts, larcenies involving auto accessories, robberies, vandalism, or other criminal behavior. Moreover, variations in patrol techniques appeared to have little influence on citizens' attitudes toward police, their satisfaction with police, or their fear of future criminal behavior.

The Kansas City experiment gave the impression that there is little the police can do to reduce crime, but it is important to note that there were limitations associated with the research design. For example, officers sometimes entered reactive beats in order to respond promptly to calls for service. There are several other

- Enable the police department to respond quickly to law violations or other emergencies
- Identify and apprehend law violators
- Aid individuals and care for those who cannot help themselves
- Facilitate the movement of traffic and people
- Create a feeling of security in the community[7]

Patrol officers' responsibilities are immense. They may suddenly be faced with an angry mob, an armed felon, or a suicidal teenager and be forced to make split-second decisions on what action to take. At the same time, they must be sensitive to the needs of citizens who are often of diverse racial and ethnic backgrounds. When police are present and visible, a sense of security is created in a neighborhood, and residents' opinions of the police improve.[8] But does patrol deter crime? This question is explored in the Evidence-Based Justice box.

Patrol Activities

order maintenance (peacekeeping)
Maintaining order and authority without the need for formal arrest ("handling the situation")—keeping things under control by means of threats, persuasion, and understanding.

Most experts agree that the bulk of patrol effort is devoted to what has been described as **order maintenance**, or **peacekeeping**: maintaining order and civility within the officer's assigned jurisdiction.[9] Order-maintenance policing generally targets behavior that falls somewhere between criminal and noncriminal. The patrol officer's discretion often determines whether a noisy neighborhood dispute involves the crime of disturbing the peace or whether it can be controlled with street-corner diplomacy and the combatants sent on their way. Similarly, teenagers milling around in the shopping center parking lot can be brought in and turned over to the juvenile authorities or handled in a less formal and often more efficient manner.

reasons why we shouldn't put too much faith in the Kansas City experiment:

- Dozens of studies are almost evenly divided on whether patrol and crime go hand in hand. Almost as many researchers have found less crime in areas with a higher police presence as have found less crime in areas with a lower police presence.

- Some studies from other countries have shown that when the police go on strike (they are usually prohibited by law from doing so in the United States), crime rates surge. This suggests that patrol certainly does something to reduce crime.

- Recent federal funding for the hiring of additional police officers has been linked to significant reductions in crime rates in cities across the country.

- When the Department of Homeland Security increases the terror threat alert level, more police are put on patrol. Researchers have found that these surges in the police presence have led to less crime.

- Increasing the size of the local police force may have other benefits for the overall effectiveness of the justice system. Adding police and bolstering resources can increase prosecution and conviction rates. Inadequate resources make it difficult to gather sufficient evidence to ensure a conviction, and prosecutors are likely to drop these cases. Adding police resources helps increase prosecutorial effectiveness.

Sources: George Kelling, Tony Pate, Duane Dieckman, and Charles Brown, *The Kansas City Preventive Patrol Experiment: A Summary Report* (Washington, DC: Police Foundation, 1974); Richard C. Larson, "What Happened to Patrol Operations in Kansas City? A Review of the Kansas City Preventive Patrol Experiment," *Journal of Criminal Justice* 3 (1975): 267–297; Thomas B. Marvell and Carlisle E. Moody, "Specification Problems, Police Levels, and Crime Rates," *Criminology* 24 (1996): 609–646; Tuija Makinen and Hannu Takala, "The 1976 Police Strike in Finland," *Scandinavian Studies in Criminology* 7 (1980): 87–106; William N. Evans and Emily Owens, "COPS and Crime," *Journal of Public Economics* 91 (2007): 181–201; Government Accountability Office, *Community Policing Grants: COPS Grants Were a Modest Contributor to Declines in Crime in the 1990s* (Washington, DC: Government Accountability Office, 2005); Jonathan Klick and Alexander Tabarrok, "Using Terror Alert Levels to Estimate the Effect of Police on Crime," *Journal of Law and Economics* 48 (2005): 267–279; Joan Petersilia, Allan Abrahamse, and James Q. Wilson, "A Summary of RAND's Research on Police Performance, Community Characteristics, and Case Attrition," *Journal of Police Science and Administration* 17 (1990): 219–229.

Police encounter many troubling incidents that need some sort of fixing.[10] Enforcing the law might be one tool a patrol officer uses; threats, coercion, sympathy, understanding, and apathy might be others. SWAT teams often handle the most difficult situations, but most important is keeping things under control so that no complaints arise. The real police role, then, may be that of a community problem solver.

Police officers practice a policy of selective enforcement, concentrating on some crimes but handling the majority in an informal manner. A police officer is supposed to know when to take action and when not to, whom to arrest and whom to deal with by issuing a warning or taking some other informal action. If a mistake is made, the officer can come under fire from his peers and superiors, as well as from the general public. Consequently, the patrol officer's job is extremely demanding and often unrewarding and unappreciated. The attitudes of police officers toward the public, not surprisingly, are sometimes characterized as being ambivalent and cynical.[11]

Improving Patrol

In response to the aforementioned issues, police departments have initiated a number of programs and policies to try to improve patrol effectiveness. Some have proved more effective than others. Some are also more controversial than others.

 L03 Discuss various efforts to improve patrol.

AGGRESSIVE PATROL The Kansas City study greatly influenced the way police experts viewed the effectiveness of patrol. Its lukewarm findings set the stage for community- and problem-oriented policing models, which stress social service over crime deterrence. However, it may be too soon to dismiss police patrol as a crime-fighting technique. Although the mere presence of police may not be sufficient to deter crime, the manner in which they approach their task may make a difference.

Police departments that use **proactive policing**, or an aggressive law enforcement style, may also help reduce crime rates. Proactive policing can include increased targeting of specific offenses, more arrests or citations for specific offenses or infractions, or a combination of each. For example, jurisdictions that encourage patrol officers to stop motor vehicles to issue citations and to aggressively arrest and detain suspicious persons also experience lower crime rates than jurisdictions that do not follow such proactive policies.[12] Aggressive traffic enforcement can also have the added benefit of reducing more serious crimes.[13] Likewise, research has shown that a concentrated focus on drug sales can be successful,[14] as can a focus on gun-related offenses.[15]

BROKEN WINDOWS POLICING   The order maintenance function has become all the more important in light of George Kelling and James Q. Wilson's popular **broken windows model** of policing.[16] Their highly influential article made three key points:

- *Neighborhood disorder creates fear.* Urban areas filled with street people, youth gangs, prostitutes, and the mentally disturbed are the ones most likely to maintain a high degree of crime.

- *Neighborhoods give out crime-promoting signals.* A neighborhood filled with deteriorated housing, unrepaired broken windows, and disorderly behavior gives out crime-promoting signals. Honest citizens live in fear in these areas, and predatory criminals are attracted to them.

- *Police need to aggressively target low-level "quality of life" crimes.* If they are to successfully reduce fear and prevent more serious crime from coming into neighborhoods, they must first address the minor problems that invite more serious ones.[17]

Broken windows policing is controversial because some people perceive it as harassment.[18] Why focus on low-level petty crimes when there are more serious problems? Others feel that broken windows policing is remarkably effective. Researchers have claimed it was responsible for the drastic reductions in crime that took place in New York City during the 1990s.[19] Other researchers have put broken windows policing to the test and found that, indeed, it can be an effective approach.[20] The downturn in the New York City violent crime rate during the 1990s has been attributed to aggressive police work aimed at lifestyle crimes: vandalism, panhandling, and graffiti.[21]

RAPID RESPONSE   It is widely assumed that criminals can be caught if the police can simply get to the scene of a crime quickly. As one researcher put it,

> ... the shorter the police travel time from assignment to arrival at a crime scene, the more likely it is that police can arrest offenders before they flee. This claim is then extended to rapid response, producing three crime prevention effects. One is a reduction in harm from crimes interrupted in progress by police intervention. Another, more general benefit of rapid response time is a greater deterrent effect.... The third hypothesized prevention effect comes from the incapacitation through imprisonment of offenders....[22]

But does the research support this view? Does rapid response really increase the chances of police catching lawbreakers? Unfortunately, the jury is still out, but some researchers have found that a quick response can be beneficial.[23]

PROCEDURAL JUSTICE   Patrol can be made more effective when police pay attention to how they treat citizens. For example, researchers have found that when officers treat citizens with dignity and respect, the citizens are more likely

---

proactive policing
An aggressive law enforcement style in which patrol officers take the initiative against crime instead of waiting for criminal acts to occur. For example, they stop motor vehicles to issue citations and aggressively arrest and detain suspicious persons.

broken windows model
The role of the police as maintainers of community order and safety.

to be satisfied with the experience, to accept police decisions,[24] and even to participate in crime prevention programs.[25] Research also indicates that precinct-level efforts to ensure that officers are respectful of citizens can help lower the number of complaints and improve community relations.[26] In other words, the police must pay attention to **procedural justice**, a concern with making decisions that are arrived at through procedures viewed as fair.[27] If people view procedures as unfair, they will be less likely to support police in their crime-fighting efforts.[28]

USE OF TECHNOLOGY Police departments have also relied on technology to help guide patrol efforts. One of the best-known programs, CompStat, was begun in New York City as a means of directing police efforts in a more productive fashion.[29] William Bratton, Commissioner of the NYPD, wanted to revitalize the department and break through its antiquated bureaucratic structures. He installed a computerized system that gave local precinct commanders up-to-date information about where and when crime was occurring in their jurisdictions. Part of this CompStat program, twice-weekly "crime-control strategy meetings," brought precinct commanders together with the department's top administrators, who asked them to report on crime problems in their precincts and tell what they were doing to turn things around. Those involved in the strategy sessions had both detailed data and electronic pin maps that showed how crime clustered geographically in the precinct and how patrol officers were being deployed. The CompStat program required local commanders to demonstrate their intimate knowledge of crime trends and to develop strategies to address them effectively. When the assembled police administrators presented their ideas, the local commander was required to demonstrate, in follow-up sessions, how he had incorporated the new strategies in the local patrol plan. CompStat proved extremely successful and made a major contribution to the dramatic decline in New York City's crime rate during the past decade. CompStat-like programs have since been implemented in other jurisdictions around the country.[30] Concept Summary 6.1 summarizes efforts to improve patrol effectiveness.

Lt. Travis St. Pierre of the New Orleans Police Department displays a body-worn camera during a press conference. What are the advantages and disadvantages of body-worn cameras?

Brett Duke/The Times-Picayune/Landov

procedural justice
A concern with making decisions that are arrived at through procedures viewed as fair.

CONCEPT SUMMARY 6.1
Improving Patrol

Strategy	Tactic	Goal
Aggressive patrol	Enforce law vigorously	Give message that crime will not be tolerated
Broken windows policing	Target low-level offenses and incivilities	Prevent serious crime
Rapid response	Respond to 911 calls quickly	Increase odds of catching lawbreakers
Procedural justice	Treat citizens with dignity and respect	Increase chances of citizens helping police fight crime, such as by calling officers
Use of technology	Employ latest communication and mapping technologies	Identify criminals and target crimes efficiently

criminal justice and TECHNOLOGY

IN-CAR AND BODY-WORN CAMERAS

During the 1990s, lawsuits alleging racial bias in police traffic stops began to be filed. This, coupled with some questionable shootings and other police–suspect encounters, prompted many agencies to install cameras in their patrol cars. Between 2000 and 2004, the Office of Community-Oriented Policing Services in the U.S. Justice Department awarded over $20 million in grants to local police departments so they could purchase and install in-car camera systems. Before the funding program, 11 percent of state police and highway patrol vehicles were equipped with cameras. A few years later, nearly 75 percent of these agencies were able to equip their police cars with cameras.

More recently, a number of police departments around the country have begun equipping their officers with body-worn cameras. As of this writing, the Phoenix Police Department is having several of its officers carry body-worn cameras. Researchers at Arizona State University are exploring whether the cameras deter unprofessional conduct on the part of the officers, but also help disprove false allegations and discourage suspects from resisting arrest or assaulting officers. Other goals are to improve perceptions of police legitimacy, plus reduce complaints and lawsuits.

REASONS FOR CAMERAS

In-car and body-worn cameras offer several advantages. The International Association of Chiefs of Police (IACP) came up with several reasons why this technology is desirable:

- *Officer safety*. Perhaps the single most beneficial feature of an in-car camera is the positive effect it can have on officer safety. Having a recording of, say, traffic stops enables the officers to view it and critique their actions after the fact.

- *Professionalism and performance*. Officers report altering their behavior to some extent when in front of the camera. The IACP found that many officers reported performing to the best of their ability, knowing their actions were being recorded. Other officers argue that a camera's recordings are useful for preparing courtroom testimony; there is less need to rely on memory, which bolsters an officer's credibility when he or she is testifying.

- *Defense against complaints*. A recording of a police–citizen contact helps protect the officer and the department for which he or she works from meritless complaints or lawsuits. The IACP study revealed that roughly half of citizen complaints are withdrawn once complainants are made aware that a camera recorded the alleged incident.

- *Leadership benefits*. Police administrators regard in-car cameras as desirable because they aid in investigations of misconduct and promote accountability of officers working in the field. Years of research on public perceptions of police have revealed that professionalism and courtesy promote citizen satisfaction and support. Cameras help further this.

Untold numbers of other technological innovations have assisted the police in their crime control and prevention efforts. Some have helped them detect and apprehend criminals more quickly. Others have been developed in response to community concerns, making departments more accessible to the communities they serve. Still others have been put in police cars to protect officers from allegations of impropriety. One such technology, the in-car camera (or the body-worn camera), is featured in the accompanying Criminal Justice and Technology box.

The Investigation Function

Since the first independent detective bureau was established by the London Metropolitan Police in 1841, criminal investigators have been romantic figures vividly portrayed in novels, movies, and TV shows. The fictional police detective is usually depicted as a loner who is willing to break departmental rules, perhaps

- *Training.* Just as individual officers may review the recordings from their in-car cameras, so can training personnel use the recordings to arm trainees with the knowledge they need and stories of "what not to do."

CRITICISMS

Cameras are not supported by all concerned. To this day, some agencies have yet to install cameras because of resistance on the part of line officers and their collective bargaining units. In Montgomery, Alabama, officials agreed to install in-car cameras in the city's police cruisers years ago, mainly in response to one officer's shooting of an unarmed suspect, but union officials say the cameras threaten officer privacy. Critics make these points about in-car cameras:

- *Distraction from the job.* If cameras encourage officers to be on their best behavior, then some of them may obsess over the camera so much that their actions amount to performing for the camera rather than focusing on the task at hand. A small number of officers in the IACP study reported that the cameras distracted them from violators. Sometimes the officers would even worry more about positioning the camera for optimal viewing than about guarding their own safety.

- *Too much reliance on the camera.* Some officers also reported relying more on recordings of their stops than on their own memory. This could be detrimental from a court testimony standpoint (see above), and some officers reported that their note-taking skills suffered as a consequence of heavy reliance on technology.

- *Too much information.* There is a concern that the cameras reveal too much information. Union challenges, such as those in Montgomery, Alabama, underscore the controversy associated with requiring that officers always be on their toes because a camera is recording their every move. Is this desirable? Many agencies compromise by setting the cameras to turn on only when the vehicle's flashing lights and/or siren are turned on.

- *Stress and job performance.* The IACP study found that some officers reported increased stress levels associated with the cameras. A small percentage reported reduced job satisfaction. Some officers even reported making fewer traffic stops because of the presence of a camera.

CRITICAL THINKING

1. **What do you feel is the most important reason for in-car and body-worn cameras? Is it a good reason?**

2. **Do in-car and body-worn cameras make the police more effective or less effective? Why?**

Sources: Ernesto Londono, "Police Car Camera Plan Stalls in Union Dispute," *Washington Post*, March 22, 2008, p. B01; International Association of Chiefs of Police, *The Impact of Video Evidence on Modern Policing: Research and Best Practices from the IACP Study on In-Car Cameras* (Alexandria, VA: International Association of Chiefs of Police, 2002); Lonnie J. Westphal, "The In-Car Camera: Value and Impact," *Police Chief* 71 (2004): 59–60, 62, 65; Charles M. Katz, *Evaluating the Impact of Officer Worn Body Cameras in the Phoenix Police Department* (Washington, DC: Bureau of Justice Statistics, 2012), http://www.smartpolicinginitiative.com/sites/all/files/ASC_SPI_Phoenix.pdf (accessed June 2014).

even violate the law, to capture the suspect. The average fictional detective views departmental policies and U.S. Supreme Court decisions as unfortunate roadblocks to police efficiency. Civil rights are either ignored or actively scorned.[31]

Although every police department probably has a few aggressive detectives who may take matters into their own hands at the expense of citizens' rights, modern criminal investigators are likely to be experienced civil servants, trained in investigatory techniques, knowledgeable about legal rules of evidence and procedure, and at least somewhat cautious about the legal and administrative consequences of their actions.[32]

Investigative services can be organized in a variety of ways. In New York City, each borough or district has its own detective division that supervises investigators assigned to neighborhood police precincts (stations). Local squad detectives work closely with patrol officers to provide an immediate investigative response to crimes and incidents. New York City also maintains specialized borough squads—homicide, robbery, and special victims—to aid local squads and help identify suspects whose crimes may have occurred in multiple locations. There are also specialty squads that help in areas such as forensics. Other departments maintain special divisions with prime responsibility for addressing specific types of crimes.

Some jurisdictions maintain **vice squads**, which are usually staffed by plainclothes officers or detectives specializing in victimless crimes, such as prostitution or gambling. Vice squad officers may set themselves up as customers for illicit activities to make arrests. For example, male undercover detectives may frequent public men's rooms and make advances toward other men. Those who respond are arrested for homosexual soliciting. In other instances, female police officers may pose as prostitutes. These covert police activities have often been criticized as violating the personal rights of citizens, and their appropriateness and fairness have been questioned.

> **vice squads**
> Police units assigned to enforce morality-based laws, such as those addressing prostitution, gambling, and pornography.

How Do Detectives Detect?

Detectives investigate the causes of crime and attempt to identify the individuals or groups responsible for committing particular offenses. They may enter a case after patrol officers have made the initial contact, such as when a patrol car interrupts a crime in progress and the offenders flee before they can be apprehended. Detectives can investigate a case entirely on their own, sometimes by following up on leads provided by informants. Sometimes detectives go undercover in order to investigate crime: a lone agent can infiltrate a criminal group or organization to gather information on future criminal activity. Undercover officers can also pose as victims to capture predatory criminals who have been conducting street robberies and muggings.[33]

In a study of investigation techniques, Martin Innes found that police detectives rely heavily on interviews and forensic evidence to reconstruct or manufacture a narrative of the crime, creating in a sense the "story" that sets out how, where, and why the incident took place.[34] To create their story, contemporary detectives typically use a three-pronged approach:[35]

■ *Specific focus*. Detectives interview witnesses, gather evidence, record events, and collect facts that are available at the immediate crime scene.

■ *General coverage*. This process involves detectives who (a) canvass the neighborhood and make observations; (b) conduct interviews with friends, families, and associates; (c) contact coworkers or employers for information regarding victims and suspects; and (d) construct victim/suspect timelines to outline their whereabouts before the incident.

■ *Informative data gathering*. Detectives use modern technology to collect records of cell phones and pagers, computer hard drives (tablets, laptops, notebooks, desktops, and servers), diaries, notes, and documents. Information includes data used by persons of interest in the investigation that tell about their lives, interactions with others, and geographical connections (see Exhibit 6.1).

EXHIBIT 6.1 Investigative Functions

Specific	General Coverage	Informative Data Gathering
Specific witnesses	Neighborhood canvass	Cell phone records
Specific evidence	Friends, family, and associates	Computer hard drives
Specific events	Coworkers	Other records
Specific facts	Victim/suspect time lines	Private papers

Source: John B. Edwards, "Homicide Investigative Strategies," *FBI Law Enforcement Bulletin* 74 (2005): 11–21.

Detectives may successfully identify a criminal suspect if these methods pan out. But that is only the beginning of building an airtight case. Next, the detectives attempt to gain as much information as possible from their suspect, perhaps even getting him to confess.

An undercover Palm Beach County (Florida) Sheriff's deputy posing as a prostitute is approached by a man during a sting that was one of several recent sting operations designed to catch "johns" in the act. The man was not arrested and did not hire the decoy for sexual acts.

Sting Operations

Another approach to detective work, commonly referred to as a **sting operation**, involves organized groups of detectives who deceive criminals into openly committing illegal acts or conspiring to engage in criminal activity.[36] Numerous sting operations have been aimed at capturing various types of criminals, ranging from professional thieves to sex offenders. To catch professional thieves, undercover detectives often pose as fences, set up ongoing fencing operations, and encourage thieves interested in selling stolen merchandise. Transactions are videotaped to provide prosecutors with strong cases. A similar approach is sometimes used to catch sex offenders.

Sting operations have drawbacks. By its very nature, a sting involves deceit by police agents that often borders on entrapment.[37] Covert police activities have been criticized as violating the personal rights of citizens while forcing officers into demeaning roles, such as having female officers act like prostitutes. (Ironically, research by Mary Dodge and her associates found that rather than considering it demeaning, female officers found their sting work as make-believe prostitutes exciting and considered it a stepping-stone toward promotion.[38])

Sting operations may encourage criminals to commit new crimes because they have a new source for fencing stolen goods. Innocent people may hurt their reputations by buying merchandise from a sting operation when they had no idea that the items had been stolen. By putting the government in the fencing business, such operations blur the line between law enforcement and criminal activity.

sting operation
Organized groups of detectives who deceive criminals into openly committing illegal acts or conspiring to engage in criminal activity.

Undercover Work

Sometimes detectives go undercover to investigate crime.[39] Undercover work can take a number of forms. A lone agent can infiltrate a criminal group or organization to gather information on future criminal activity. Or a Drug Enforcement Administration agent may go undercover to gather intelligence on drug smugglers. Undercover officers can also pose as victims to capture predatory criminals who have been conducting street robberies and muggings.

Undercover work is considered a necessary element of police work, although it can prove dangerous for the agent. Police officers may be forced to engage in illegal or immoral behavior to maintain their cover. They also face significant physical danger in playing the role of a criminal and dealing with mobsters, terrorists, and drug dealers. In far too many cases, undercover officers are mistaken for real criminals and injured by other law enforcement officers or private citizens trying to stop a crime. Arrest situations involving undercover officers may also provoke violence when suspects do not realize they are in the presence of police and therefore violently resist arrest.

Undercover officers may also experience psychological problems. Being away from home, keeping late hours, and always worrying that their identity

 L04 Discuss key issues associated with the investigative function.

analyzing criminal justice ISSUES

FORENSICS UNDER THE MICROSCOPE

The *Chicago Tribune's* "Forensics Under the Microscope" series suggests that all is not well in the world of forensic sciences. Such concerns were echoed in a more recent National Academy of Sciences (NAS) report entitled *Strengthening Forensic Science in the United States: A Path Forward*. The authors of the report highlighted a series of problems with the forensic sciences, many of which are not well known to people on the outside—and particularly not to those who owe their knowledge of forensics and investigations to fictional television programs. Here are some of those problems.

● *Case backlog*. The NAS called attention to another report in which it was learned that federal, state, and local laboratories reported a backlog of nearly 500,000 requests for forensic analysis. This backlog has been made even more serious by requests for quick test results. Labs are having a difficult time keeping up.

● *DNA demands*. The ascendancy of DNA evidence and the opportunities to use it during investigations has further burdened crime labs. And even though the NAS, along with other experts and commissions, has heralded the advent of DNA testing

as valuable for criminal investigation, there is only so much it can do. According to the NAS report, "DNA evidence comprises only about 10 percent of case work and is not always relevant to a particular case. Even if DNA evidence is available, it will assist in solving a crime only if it supports an evidential hypothesis that makes guilt or innocence more likely. For example, the fact that DNA evidence of a victim's husband is found in the house in which the couple lived and where the murder took place proves nothing. The fact that the husband's DNA is found under the fingernails of the victim who put up a struggle may have very different significance."

● *Questionable evidence*. Now that DNA evidence is regarded as a gold standard in criminal investigations, this has started to cast doubt on convictions secured through other, more traditional types of evidence. According to the report, "The fact is that many forensic tests—such as those used to infer the source of tool marks or bite marks—have never been exposed to stringent scientific scrutiny.... Even fingerprint analysis has been called into question."

will be uncovered can create enormous stress. Officers have experienced post-undercover strain, resulting in trouble at work and, in many instances, ruined marriages and botched prosecutions. Hanging around with criminals for a long time, making friends with them, and earning their trust can also have a damaging psychological impact.

Evaluating Investigations

Serious criticism has been leveled at the nation's detective forces for getting bogged down in paperwork and being relatively inefficient in clearing cases. One famous study of 153 detective bureaus found that a great deal of a detective's time was spent in nonproductive work and that investigative expertise did little to solve cases. Half of all detectives could be replaced without negatively influencing crime clearance rates.[40]

Although some question remains about the effectiveness of investigations (see the Analyzing Criminal Justice Issues box), police detectives do make a valuable contribution to police work because their skilled interrogation and case-processing techniques are essential to eventual criminal conviction.[41] Nonetheless, in a majority of cases that are solved, the perpetrator is identified at the scene of the crime by patrol officers. Research by the Police Executive

- *Errors.* The NAS also called attention to several disturbing examples of errors and fraud in the forensic sciences. In one case, a state-mandated examination of the West Virginia State Police laboratory revealed that the convictions of more than 100 people were in doubt. Another scandal involving the Houston Crime Laboratory came to light in 2003. An investigation revealed "routine failure to run essential scientific controls, failure to take adequate measures to prevent contamination of samples, failure to adequately document work performed and results obtained, and routine failure to follow correct procedures for computing statistical frequencies."

- *Incompatible fingerprint identification systems.* Law enforcement agencies around the country have developed and put in place automated fingerprint identification systems in an effort to solve crimes. The problem, according to the NAS, is that there is inadequate integration of these systems.

- *Lack of preparation for mass disasters.* According to the NAS, "Threats to food and transportation, concerns about nuclear and cyber security, and the need to develop rapid responses to chemical, nuclear, radiological, and biological threats underlie the need to ensure that there is a sufficient supply of adequately trained forensic specialists...[but] public crime laboratories are insufficiently prepared to handle mass disasters."

- *The CSI effect.* The so-called "CSI effect," named for the popular television programs, is concerned with the real-world implications of Hollywood's fictional spin on the forensic sciences and criminal investigations. The NAS found that some prosecutors believe they must make their in-court presentations as visually appealing as possible in an effort to please jurors who think they understand forensic work from having watched their favorite television programs. Attempts to satisfy such unrealistic expectations may possibly compromise the pursuit of justice.

CRITICAL THINKING

1. To what extent has the recent attention paid to wrongful convictions fueled calls for improvement, such as those in the NAS report?

2. At the other extreme, what improvements have been made in recent years?

Sources: *Chicago Tribune*, "Forensics Under the Microscope," http://www.chicagotribune.com/news/watchdog/chi-forensics-specialpackage,0,7787855.special (accessed June 2014); National Academy of Sciences, National Research Council, *Strengthening Forensic Science in the United States: A Path Forward* (Washington, DC: The National Academies Press), pp. 1–13, www.nap.edu/catalog.php?record_id=12589 (accessed June 2014).

Research Forum shows that if a crime is reported while in progress, the police have about a 33 percent chance of making an arrest; the arrest probability declines to about 10 percent if the crime is reported 1 minute later, and to 5 percent if more than 15 minutes elapse. As the time between the crime and the arrest grows, the chances of a conviction are also reduced, probably because the ability to recover evidence is lost. To put it another way, the longer the gap between completion of the crime and the placing of the investigation into the hands of detectives, the lower the odds that the perpetrator will be identified and arrested.[42]

Improving Investigations

A number of efforts have been made to revamp and improve investigation procedures. One practice has been to give patrol officers greater responsibility for conducting preliminary investigations at the scene of the crime. In addition, specialized units, such as homicide or burglary squads, now operate over larger areas and can bring specific expertise to bear. Technological advances in DNA and fingerprint identification have also boosted investigation effectiveness. Investigations also improve with cooperative victims, as discussed in The Victim Experience box.

One reason for investigation ineffectiveness is that detectives often lack sufficient resources to carry out a lengthy ongoing probe of any but the most serious cases. Research shows the following:[43]

■ *Unsolved cases*. Almost 50 percent of burglary cases are screened out by supervisors before assignment to a detective for a follow-up investigation. Of those assigned, 75 percent are dropped after the first day of the follow-up investigation. Although robbery cases are more likely to be assigned to detectives, 75 percent of them are also dropped after one day of investigation.

■ *Length of investigation*. The vast majority of cases are investigated for no more than 4 hours stretching over 3 days. An average of 11 days elapse between the initial report of a crime and the suspension of the investigation.

■ *Sources of information*. Early in an investigation, the focus is on the victim; as the investigation is pursued, emphasis shifts to the suspect. The most critical information for determining case outcome is the name and description of the suspect and related crime information. Victims are most often the source of information. Unfortunately, witnesses, informants, and members of the police department are consulted far less often. However, when these sources are tapped, they are likely to produce useful information.

■ *Effectiveness*. Preliminary investigations by patrol officers are critical. In situations in which the suspect's identity is not known immediately after the crime is committed, detectives make an arrest in less than 10 percent of all cases.

Given these findings, detective work may be improved if greater emphasis is placed on collecting physical evidence at the scene of the crime, identifying witnesses, checking departmental records, and using informants. The probability of successfully settling a case is improved if patrol officers gather evidence at the scene of a crime and effectively communicate it to detectives working the case. Also recommended is the use of targeted investigations that direct attention at a few individuals, such as career criminals, who are known to have engaged in the behavior under investigation.

Using Technology

Police departments are now employing advanced technology in all facets of their operations, from assigning patrol routes to gathering evidence. Similarly, investigators are starting to use advanced technology to streamline and enhance the investigation process. Gathering evidence at a crime scene and linking clues to a list of suspects can be a tedious job for many investigators. Yet linkage is critical if suspects are to be quickly apprehended before they are able to leave the jurisdiction, intimidate witnesses, or cover up any clues they may have left behind.

One innovative use of technology enables investigators to compare evidence found at the crime scene with material collected from similar crimes by other police agencies. Police agencies are using a program called Coplink to help with this time-consuming task. Coplink integrates information from different jurisdictions into a single database that detectives can access when working investigations.[44] The Coplink program allows investigators to search the entire database of past criminal records and compile a list of possible suspects even when only partial data are available, such as first or last name, partial license plate numbers, vehicle type, vehicle color, location of crime, or weapon used. The Coplink program enables police to access data from other police agencies in minutes, a process that otherwise could take days or weeks. The Coplink system allows for easy information sharing between law enforcement agencies, a task that has been problematic in the past. It is one of the new breed of computer-aided investigation techniques that are beginning to have a significant impact on capture ratios in the nation's police departments.

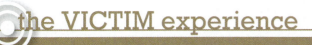

the VICTIM experience

SECONDARY VICTIMIZATION AND VICTIM COOPERATION

BACKGROUND Research suggests that some crime victims are traumatized during the criminal justice process, a phenomenon dubbed *secondary victimization*. Rape victims in particular often relive certain aspects of the initial incident, perhaps when testifying at trial or while interacting with investigators soon after calling police. Shana Maier conducted interviews with a number of rape victim advocates, one of whom reported:

> … a lot of police don't have training on sexual assault. And if you have just been raped by a man and you have a man coming in who is talking down to you in a way or making it feel like it is your fault, asking questions like, "Well, did you go with him to his room? Were you alone with him in his room?" Things like that, it tends to make you feel like it was your fault.

This is not to suggest that the police are uniformly insensitive to the plight of sexual assault victims. Much has changed in the past few decades. Much attention is now being paid to the victim experience, especially in sensitive cases involving sexual assault. Serious strides have been made in the criminal justice system and beyond to ensure victims are not forgotten, and the police are often trained in how to deal appropriately with crimes in which the secondary victimization potential looms large.

THE BIG PICTURE Moving in to other areas of criminal activity, some domestic violence victims have reported unpleasant experiences in the investigative process. Others believe that the system did not take their case seriously enough. Additional research published by the National Institute of Justice confirms as much. Domestic violence victims who felt the police did not handle the initial incident effectively were less likely to report subsequent incidents, which of course makes it more difficult to identify and apprehend the perpetrator. This line of research thus suggests that the police need to take great care in investigating such cases, not just to make victims "feel good," but to make sure offenders are held accountable.

Homicide is a special case. Obviously the immediate victim cannot be "revictimized," but surviving family members, other close relatives, and friends sometimes are. These "co-victims" often suffer post-traumatic stress disorder (PTSD) symptoms, stress, physical illness, loss of trust, intense grief, and a host of other ailments. And they, too, occasionally report unpleasant interactions with criminal justice officials. For example, a study by Paul Stretesky and his colleagues found that the vast majority of homicide co-victims were dissatisfied with their level of communication with investigators, especially in so-called "cold cases," those in which the offender has successfully eluded authorities for a long time. Co-victims reported frustration with a dwindling level of communication over time, staff turnover, and a general lack of updates concerning the status of the case. Their experiences are not particularly surprising, though; investigators have a lot on their plates and it is difficult to pour slim resources into the pursuit of perpetrators who may never be found. Even so, steps should be taken to encourage victim involvement, communication, and cooperation for as long as possible during the investigative process.

CLASSROOM EXERCISE Organize the class into groups representing a variety of different victims, such as victims of sexual assault, domestic violence, human trafficking, burglary, drunk driving crashes, and homicide co-victims (the preferred number of students in each group and the size of the class will dictate the variety of offenses). Have each group come up with a bulleted list of recommendations they would give to first responders in order to facilitate positive interaction with the victims and minimize the chances of secondary victimization. A helpful starting point for gathering information is the website of the Office for Victims of Crime at http://www.ovc.gov.

Sources: Shana L. Maier, "'I Have Heard Horrible Stories . . . .': Rape Victim Advocates' Perceptions of the Revictimization of Rape Victims by the Police and Medical System," *Violence Against Women* 14 (2008): 786–808; Gerald T. Hotaling and Eve S. Buzawa, *Forgoing Criminal Justice Assistance: The Non-Reporting of New Incidents of Abuse in a Court Sample of Domestic Violence Victims* (Washington, DC: National Institute of Justice, 2003); Paul B. Stretesky, Tara O'Connor Shelley, Michael J. Hogan, and N. Prabha Unnithan, "Sense-Making and Secondary Victimization Among Unsolved Homicide Co-Victims," *Journal of Criminal Justice* 38 (2010): 880–888.

Community Policing

L05 Explain the concept of community policing.

Web App 6.2

Read more about community policing at the website of the Michigan Regional Community Policing Institute. You can access it here: http://cj.msu.edu/programs/ regional-community-policing-institute/.

For generations, police agencies have been trying to gain the cooperation and respect of the communities they serve. At first, efforts at improving the relationships between police departments and the public involved programs with the general title of police–community relations (PCR). Developed at the station house and departmental levels, these initial PCR programs were designed to make citizens more aware of police activities, alert them to methods of self-protection, and improve general attitudes toward policing.

Although PCR efforts showed a willingness of police agencies to cooperate with the public, some experts believed that law enforcement agencies needed to undergo a significant transformation to create meaningful partnerships with the public. In their view, community relations and crime control effectiveness cannot be the province of a few specialized units housed within a traditional police department. Instead, the core police role must be altered if community involvement is to be won and maintained. To accomplish this goal, police departments should return to an earlier style of policing, in which officers on the beat had intimate contact with the people they served. Modern police departments generally rely on motorized patrol to cover wide areas, to maintain a visible police presence, and to ensure rapid response time. Although effective and economical, the patrol car removes officers from the mainstream of the community, alienating people who might otherwise be potential sources of information and help to the police.

community-oriented policing (COP)
Programs designed to bring police and public closer together and create a more cooperative environment between them.

In response to the limitations of earlier approaches to policing, **community-oriented policing (COP)** programs have been implemented in large cities, suburban areas, and rural communities.[45] Also described as simply "community policing," such programs promote interaction between officers and citizens and give officers the time to meet with local residents to talk about crime in the neighborhood and to use personal initiative to solve problems. Although not all programs work (police–community newsletters and cleanup campaigns do not seem to do much good), the overall impression has been that patrol officers can reduce the level of fear in the community. Some studies have also shown that community policing programs reduce crime.[46] Exhibit 6.2 elaborates on the elements of community-oriented policing.

One method of implementing community policing is to improve the bonds between officers and the residents who live in the neighborhoods they serve. Here, police officer Patrick Ecelberger, one of several District of Columbia officers assigned to a walking beat, chats with two neighborhood residents.

The Washington Post/Getty Images

EXHIBIT 6.2   Three Key Components of Community-Oriented Policing

Community Partnerships

Collaborative partnerships between the law enforcement agency and the individuals and organizations they serve to develop solutions to problems and increase trust in police.

- Other government agencies
- Community members/groups
- Nonprofits/service providers
- Private businesses
- Media

Organizational Transformation

The alignment of organizational management, structure, personnel, and information systems to support community partnerships and proactive problem solving.

Agency Management
- Climate and culture
- Leadership
- Labor relations
- Decision making
- Strategic planning
- Policies
- Organizational evaluations
- Transparency
- Organizational structure

Geographical Assignment of Officers
- Despecialization
- Resources and finances

Personnel
- Recruitment, hiring, and selection
- Personnel supervision/evaluations
- Training

Information Systems (Technology)
- Communication/access to data
- Quality and accuracy of data

Problem Solving

The process of engaging in the proactive and systematic examination of identified problems to develop and rigorously evaluate effective responses.

- Scanning: Identifying and prioritizing problems
- Analysis: Researching what is known about the problem
- Response: Developing solutions to bring about lasting reductions in the number and extent of problems
- Assessment: Evaluating the success of the responses
- Using the crime triangle to focus on immediate conditions (victim/offender/location)

Source: Office of Community Oriented Policing Services, http://www.cops.usdoj.gov/ (accessed June 2014).

Implementing Community Policing

The community policing concept was originally implemented through a number of innovative demonstration projects.[47] Among the most publicized were experiments in **foot patrol**, which took officers out of cars and had them walking beats in the neighborhood. Foot patrol efforts were aimed at forming a bond with community residents by acquainting them with the individual officers who patrolled their neighborhood, letting them know that police were caring and available. The first foot patrol experiments were conducted in cities in Michigan and New Jersey. An evaluation of foot patrol indicated that although it did not bring down the crime rate, residents in areas where foot patrol was added perceived greater safety and were less afraid of crime.[48]

Since the advent of these programs, the federal government has encouraged the growth of community policing by providing millions of dollars to hire and train officers.[49] The U.S. Justice Department's Office of Community Oriented Policing Services is the go-to source for community policing funding.[50] Hundreds of communities have adopted innovative forms of decentralized, neighborhood-based community policing models. Recent surveys indicate that a significant

Web App 6.3

For more information about the Office of Community Oriented Policing Services, visit http://www.cops.usdoj.gov.

foot patrol

Police patrol that takes officers out of cars and puts them on a walking beat to strengthen ties with the community.

increase is evident in community policing activities in recent years and that certain core programs such as crime prevention activities have become embedded in the police role.[51]

The Challenges of Community Policing

 L06 List several challenges associated with community policing.

The core concepts of police work are changing as administrators recognize the limitations and realities of police work in modern society. If they are to be successful, community policing strategies must be able to react effectively to some significant administrative problems:

■ *Defining community*. Police administrators must be able to define the concept of community as an ecological area characterized by common norms, shared values, and interpersonal bonds.[52] After all, the main focus of community policing is to activate the community norms that make neighborhoods more crime resistant. If, in contrast, community policing projects cross the boundaries of many different neighborhoods, any hope of learning and accessing community norms, strengths, and standards will be lost.[53]

■ *Defining roles*. Police administrators must also establish the exact role of community police agents. How should they integrate their activities with those of regular patrol forces? For example, should foot patrols have primary responsibility for policing in an area, or should they coordinate their activities with officers assigned to patrol cars?

■ *Changing supervisor attitudes*. Some supervisors are wary of community policing because it supports a decentralized command structure. This would mean fewer supervisors and, consequently, less chance for promotion and a potential loss of authority.[54] Those supervisors who learn to actively embrace community policing concepts are the ones best able to encourage patrol officers to engage in self-initiated activities, including community policing and problem solving.[55]

■ *Reorienting police values*. Research shows that police officers who have a traditional crime control orientation are less satisfied with community policing efforts than those who are public service oriented.[56] In some instances, officers holding traditional values may go as far as looking down on their own comrades assigned to community policing, who as a result feel "stigmatized" and penalized by lack of agency support.[57]

■ *Revising training*. Community policing requires that police departments alter their training requirements, especially during field training.[58] Future officers must develop community-organizing and problem-solving skills, along with traditional police skills. Their training must prepare them to succeed less on their ability to make arrests or issue citations and more on their ability to solve problems, prevent crime effectively, and deal with neighborhood diversity and cultural values.[59]

■ *Reorienting recruitment*. To make community policing successful, mid-level managers who are receptive to and can implement community-change strategies must be recruited and trained.[60] The selection of new recruits must be guided by a desire to find individuals with attitudes that support community policing. They must be open to the fact that community policing will help them gain knowledge of the community, give them opportunities to gain skill and experience, and help them engage in proactive problem solving.[61]

■ *Reaching out to every community*. Because each neighborhood has its own particular needs, community policing must become flexible and adaptive. In neighborhoods undergoing change in racial composition, special initiatives to reduce tensions may be required.[62] Some neighborhoods are cohesive and highly organized, and residents work together to solve problems. In other neighborhoods, it takes more work for community policing to succeed.

Overcoming Obstacles

Although there are formidable obstacles to overcome, growing evidence suggests that community- and problem-oriented policing can work and fit well with traditional forms of policing.[63] Many police experts and administrators have embraced these concepts as revolutionary revisions of the basic police role. Community policing efforts have been credited with helping reduce crime rates in large cities such as New York and Boston. The most professional and highly motivated officers are the ones most likely to support community policing efforts.[64]

These results are encouraging, but there is no clear-cut evidence that community policing is highly successful at reducing crime or changing the traditional values and attitudes of police officers involved in the programs.[65] Some research does show that the arrest rate actually increases after COP programs have been implemented.[66] However, crime rate reductions in cities that have used COP may be the result of an overall downturn in the nation's crime rate, rather than a result of community policing efforts.

Despite these professional obstacles, community policing has become a common part of municipal police departments. The concept is also being exported around the world, with varying degrees of success; some nations do not seem to have the stability necessary to support community policing.[67] Where it is used, citizens seem to like community policing initiatives, and those who volunteer and get involved in community crime prevention programs report higher confidence in the police force and its ability to create a secure environment.[68] They also tend to be more likely to report crime.[69]

Web App 6.4

For more information about training, advice, and discussion on community policing, visit http://www.policing.com.

Problem-Oriented Policing (POP)

Closely associated with, yet independent from, the community policing concept are **problem-oriented policing (POP)** strategies. Traditional police models focus on responding to calls for help in the least possible time, dealing with the situation, and then getting on the street again as soon as possible.[70] In contrast, the core of problem-oriented policing is a proactive orientation.

Problem-oriented policing strategies require police agencies to identify particular long-term community problems—street-level drug dealers, prostitution rings, gang hangouts—and to develop strategies to eliminate them.[71] Like community policing, being problem solvers requires that police departments rely on local residents and private resources. This means that police managers must learn how to develop community resources, design efficient and cost-effective solutions to problems, and become advocates as well as agents of reform.[72] A significant portion of police departments are using special units to confront specific social problems. For example, departments may employ special units devoted to youth issues ranging from child abuse to gangs.

Problem-oriented policing models are supported by the fact that a great deal of urban crime is concentrated in a few hot spots.[73] A large number of all police calls in metropolitan areas typically radiate from a relatively few locations: bars, malls, the bus depot, hotels, and certain apartment buildings.[74] By implication, concentrating police resources on these **hot spots of crime** could appreciably reduce crime.[75]

L07 Discuss the concept of problem-oriented policing.

problem-oriented policing (POP)
A style of police management that stresses proactive problem solving instead of reactive crime fighting.

hot spots of crime
The relatively few locations—bars, malls, the bus depot, hotels, and certain apartment buildings—from which a significant portion of police calls typically originate in metropolitan areas.

Criminal Acts, Criminal Places

Problem-oriented strategies are being developed that focus on specific criminal problem areas, specific criminal acts, or both. They have proved so popular and effective[76] that an organization has emerged whose mission is to share information between police agencies concerning best practices. The Center for Problem-Oriented Policing makes available an extensive collection of problem-specific

Web App 6.5

For more information about the Center for Problem-Oriented Policing, visit http://www.popcenter.org.

guides that police officers around the country can access, read, and apply to situations in their respective jurisdictions.[77] Examples of problem-solving efforts include combating auto theft and violence.

COMBATING AUTO THEFT Because of problem-oriented approaches (combined with advanced technology), car thieves in many jurisdictions are no longer able to steal cars with as much ease as before. To reduce the high number of car thefts occurring each year, some police departments have invested in bait cars, which are parked in high-theft areas and are equipped with technology that alerts law enforcement personnel when someone has stolen a vehicle. A signal goes off when either a door is opened or the engine starts. Then, through the use of global positioning satellite (GPS) technology, police officers can watch the movement of the car. Some cars are also equipped with microscopic video and audio recorders, which enable officers to see and hear the suspect(s) within the car, and with remote engine and door locks, which can trap the thief inside. The technology has been used in conjunction with an advertising campaign to warn potential car thieves about the program. The system has been instituted in several cities, with impressive results. Motor vehicle theft dropped over 40 percent in Minneapolis over a three-year period in which bait cars were used and dropped 30 percent in Vancouver within six months of the time the program was begun. In addition to cutting down on auto theft, the system (which costs roughly $3,500 per car) tends to reduce the danger of high-speed pursuits because police officers can put obstacles on the road to stop the car.[78]

REDUCING VIOLENCE A number of efforts have been made to reduce violence by using problem-oriented community policing techniques. Perhaps the best-known program, Operation Ceasefire, was a problem-oriented policing intervention aimed at reducing youth homicide and youth firearms violence in Boston. Evaluations of the program found that Ceasefire produced significant reductions in youth homicide victimization and gun assault incidents in Boston—reductions that were not experienced in other communities in New England or elsewhere in the nation.[79]

The Jersey City, New Jersey, police recently applied a variety of aggressive crime-reducing techniques in some of the city's gang-ridden areas. Evaluations of the program show that crime rates were reduced when police officers used aggressive problem solving (e.g., drug enforcement) and community improvement techniques (e.g., increased lighting and cleaned vacant lots) in high-crime areas.[80] Recent research on efforts to reduce gun violence suggest that a strategy of "pulling levers" can be quite effective. This approach focuses on communicating penalties to criminals and using every get-tough strategy available when laws are violated.[81]

Although programs such as these seem successful, the effectiveness of any street-level problem-solving efforts must be interpreted with caution.[82] Criminals could merely be dispersing to other, safer areas of the city and planning to return shortly after the program has been declared a success and the additional police forces have been pulled from the area.[83] Nonetheless, evidence shows that simply saturating an area with police may not deter crime but that focusing efforts at a particular problem may have a crime-reducing effect.

Gauging the effectiveness of problem-oriented policing is difficult. On the one hand, it may have a deterrent effect: hot-spots policing increases the community perception that police arrest many criminals and that most violators get caught. On the other hand, there is the possibility of **displacement**: criminals move from an area targeted for increased police presence to another that is less well protected.[84] When the police leave, the criminals return to business as usual. The displacement issue is discussed further in the Analyzing Criminal Justice Issues feature.

displacement
An effect that occurs when criminals move from an area targeted for increased police presence to another that is less well protected.

analyzing criminal justice ISSUES

THE DISPLACEMENT PROBLEM

One of the most common criticisms of problem-oriented policing is that it simply pushes crime into surrounding areas. In other words, the criminal element follows the path of least resistance. This can be both a blessing and curse. On the one hand, a city mayor who is responsible to those in the city he or she serves may not care if a successful intervention pushed crime into a neighboring city; the people in the neighboring city don't elect the mayor! On the other hand, when crime moves elsewhere, it doesn't go away. This means that some problem-oriented strategies help one community (or neighborhood) but hurt the next.

Unfortunately, few efforts to investigate the effectiveness of problem-oriented policing consider the issue of displacement. Few take a hard look at whether crime went up in surrounding areas—or at other aspects of displacement. Researchers have identified five types of displacement:

- *Temporal.* Offenders change the times at which they offend.
- *Spatial.* Offenders offend in different locations.
- *Target.* Offenders choose different targets.
- *Tactical.* Offenders use different methods to accomplish their objectives.
- *Offense.* Offenders switch to different crime types.

Note that four of these varieties of displacement do not require that offenders move to a different area. This complicates matters, because it means the police need to be cognizant of more than just spatial displacement. They have to look for unanticipated consequences. If, for example, a city sees a surge in car thefts from mall parking lots, the police may launch an initiative to aggressively patrol the areas to catch and deter criminals. Their work is not done, however, if they succeed. They also need to ensure that offenders didn't opt for different targets, such as residences—or cars parked in private driveways. This is difficult to do.

What factors influence whether displacement will occur? A recent study by the Center for Problem-Oriented Policing identifies three factors:

- *Offender motivation.* What drives offenders to break the law is likely to influence displacement.

Drug-addicted offenders, for example, may substitute one type of theft for another in order to generate cash to sustain their habits.

- *Offender familiarity.* A large body of literature confirms that offenders, like people in general, don't like to step out of their comfort zone. More often than not, if displacement is going to occur, it will occur close to the same location and offenders will opt for familiar targets and tactics.
- *Crime opportunity.* When there are opportunities to offend, motivated offenders will do so. A community-wide initiative that puts all residents on high alert may do wonders to "harden" targets and make it difficult for offenders simply to move up the street to the next suitable target. Alternatively, if one specific location is targeted, but others are not, then those other areas may become attractive for motivated offenders.

Many problem-oriented policing initiatives do not result in displacement. In fact, some produce positive spillover effects, a phenomenon known as *diffusion.* Diffusion involves the reduction of crime (or similar benefits) in areas other than the one initially targeted. Many studies have shown evidence of diffusion, so it is important for evaluators to be aware that there can be additional benefits associated with problem-oriented policing programs. But they can be just as difficult to detect as displacement.

CRITICAL THINKING

1. Why may displacement not occur?
2. What are the ideal boundaries for detecting displacement?
3. How exactly could displacement be measured?

Sources: Rob T. Guerette, *Analyzing Crime Displacement and Diffusion* (Washington, DC: Office of Community-Oriented Policing Services, Center for Problem-Oriented Policing, 2009); Robert Barr and Ken Pease, "Crime Placement, Displacement and Deflection," in *Crime and Justice: A Review of Research*, Vol. 12, ed. Michael Tonry and N. Morris (Chicago: University of Chicago Press, 1990); Rob T. Guerette and Kate J. Bowers, "Assessing the Extent of Crime Displacement and Diffusion of Benefits: A Review of Situational Crime Prevention Evaluations," *Criminology* 47 (2009): 7–18.

Intelligence-Led Policing (ILP)

Since 9/11, policing has experienced a fundamental philosophical change. It has combined a homeland security focus with the many advances made in the realms of community- and problem-oriented policing.[85] An outgrowth of this combination is **intelligence-led policing (ILP)**: "the collection and analysis of information to produce an intelligence end product designed to inform police decision making at both the tactical and strategic levels."[86] More simply, ILP is intended to further shift the emphasis in police work away from reactive responses and individual case investigations. It instead emphasizes information sharing, collaboration, and strategic solutions to crime problems at various levels. It relies heavily on:

intelligence-led policing (ILP)

The collection and analysis of information to generate an "intelligence end product" designed to inform police decision making at both the tactical and the strategic level.

- Confidential informants
- Offender interviews
- Careful analysis of crime reports and calls for service
- Suspect surveillance
- Community sources of information[87]

 L08 Define intelligence-led policing and explain ways in which it occurs.

The British have a long history of sophisticated intelligence gathering and analysis. All 43 British constabularies, as well as the London Metropolitan Police, have had intelligence units for some time, to deal with problems ranging from drugs to organized crime.[88] The UK's National Drugs Intelligence Unit, created in the 1980s, gathers intelligence to aid in the enforcement of laws against drug trafficking. In 1992, the National Criminal Intelligence Service (NCIS) was formed, mainly to deal with the problem of organized crime. One of its responsibilities is to work with the chemical industry in the UK to identify and disrupt the production of synthetic drugs.

In contrast, American law enforcement agencies have, until recently, had little intelligence-gathering capacity. If it occurred at all, intelligence gathering was mostly reserved for large police agencies. According to David Carter, one of the leading experts on ILP, "Early law enforcement initiatives typically had no analysis and essentially consisted of dossiers kept on individuals who were suspicious or were deemed to be threats of some sort, often based on intuitive, rather than empirical, threat criteria."[89] Current ILP initiatives attempt to compensate for this shortcoming.

Intelligence-led policing bears a great deal of similarity to problem-oriented policing. The two are somewhat different, however. Problem-oriented policing puts problem identification and solution in the hands of individual street-level officers. In contrast, ILP emphasizes a top-down managerial approach by which administrators set priorities for crime prevention and enforcement and then pass these priorities down through the agency.[90] ILP is also similar to community policing in that it relies on residents as part of the intelligence-gathering process. But it is different, too, because whereas community policing emphasizes the desires of the community, intelligence-led policing relies on problem identification through careful analysis of the criminal environment as a whole. Intelligence-led policing has even been likened to CompStat, which is discussed earlier in this chapter. See Exhibit 6.3 for a summary of the differences and commonalities between CompStat and intelligence-led policing.

To gain a more concrete grasp of the concept of intelligence-led policing, consider these examples:

- A county sheriff's office identifies narcotics control as its top priority and develops strategies accordingly. The office targets known offenders and groups, shuts down open-air drug markets and crack houses, and participates in school-based drug awareness programs to help prevent drug use.

EXHIBIT 6.3 Comparison of CompStat and Intelligence-Led Policing

CompStat	Commonalities	Intelligence-Led Policing
Single jurisdiction	Both have a goal of prevention	Multiple jurisdictions
Incident-driven	Both require:	Threat-driven
	• Organizational flexibility	
	• Consistent information input	
	• A significant analytic component	
Street crime and burglary		Criminal enterprises and terrorism
Crime mapping		Commodity flow; trafficking and transiting logistics
Time-sensitive (24-hour feedback and response)		Strategic
Disrupt crime series (e.g., burglary ring)		Disrupt enterprises
Drives operations:		Drives operations:
• Patrol		• Joint terrorism task forces
• Tactical unit		• Organized crime investigations
• Investigators		• Task forces
Analysis of offender MO (modus operandi)		Analysis of enterprise MO (modus operandi)

Source: Office of Community-Oriented Policing Services, *Intelligence-Led Policing: The Integration of Community Policing and Law Enforcement Intelligence,* *Part 4* (Washington, DC: COPS Office, n.d.), p. 43, http://www.cops.usdoj.gov/pdf/e09042536_Chapter_04.pdf (accessed June 2014).

■ A statewide agency identifies vehicle insurance fraud as a top area for enforcement. The agency targets those involved in staged accidents, identifies communities in which insurance fraud is prevalent, exposes ongoing fraudulent activity, and mounts a public education campaign.

■ A police agency in a small city makes safe streets a priority. The agency focuses on directed enforcement in identified hot spots. It also targets career criminals whose apprehension will significantly reduce the number of crimes being committed. Preventive measures include enhanced patrols, improved street lighting, and crime watch programs.[91]

Intelligence and the Intelligence Process

Because intelligence-led policing emphasizes policing based on intelligence, it is only fitting that we devote more attention to the concept of intelligence. Basically, there are two types of intelligence. **Tactical intelligence** "includes gaining or developing information related to threats of terrorism or crime and using this information to apprehend offenders, harden targets, and use strategies that will eliminate or mitigate the threat."[92] It consists of information that can be used immediately. An example of tactical intelligence is knowing that a wanted fugitive is at a particular location. This is information that can be used immediately for the purpose of making an arrest. **Strategic intelligence** provides information to decision makers about the changing nature of certain problems and threats for the purpose of "developing response strategies and reallocating resources."[93] It

tactical intelligence
Gaining or developing information related to threats of terrorism or crime and using this information to apprehend offenders, harden targets, and use strategies that will eliminate or mitigate the threat.

strategic intelligence
Information about the changing nature of certain problems and threats for the purpose of developing response strategies and reallocating resources.

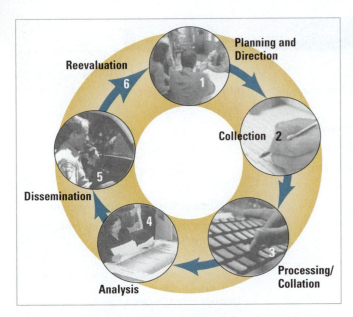

FIGURE 6.3 **The Intelligence Process**

Source: Office of Justice Programs, *National Criminal Intelligence Sharing Plan* (Washington, DC: U.S. Department of Justice, 2003), p. 6.

is more general and is used to direct operations. An example of strategic intelligence is awareness that a particular gang traffics in a particular type of drug. With this information, pressure can be brought to bear on the gang as a whole, even though law enforcement officials may not have the tactical intelligence necessary to make an arrest.

Intelligence gathering follows a six-step process (see Figure 6.3). The first step, planning and direction, involves deciding what it is that officials want to know and what data to collect to that end. The next step, collection, consists of gathering the data that will be used for making decisions. Step three, processing and collation, involves evaluating the reliability and validity of the data collected. Officials need to sift through the data and decide what information will be useful. Fourth comes analysis. This includes crime analysis (such as detecting patterns of certain types of crimes) and investigative analysis (such as examining bank records). The fifth step, dissemination, involves getting the information to the decision makers who need it. Finally, reevaluation entails getting feedback on the products generated by the intelligence function. Note that the process is cyclical and continues on indefinitely. Figure 6.3 emphasizes that intelligence is fluid and constantly subject to change.

Fusion Centers

In the spring of 2002, law enforcement executives from around the country met at a Criminal Intelligence Sharing Summit. Summit participants called for the development of a national intelligence plan, one that could be used to prevent future terrorist attacks like the ones that occurred on 9/11. After this meeting, the Global Justice Information Sharing Initiative and the Intelligence Working Group were formed. These groups eventually developed the **National Criminal Intelligence Sharing Plan (NCISP)**.[94] The report outlined a number of "action steps" that could be taken to improve intelligence gathering and sharing among law enforcement agencies across the country. The NCISP sought to communicate:

National Criminal Intelligence Sharing Plan (NCISP)
A formal intelligence-sharing initiative that identifies the security and intelligence-sharing needs recognized in the wake of the 9/11 terrorist attacks.

■ A model intelligence-sharing plan

■ A mechanism to promote intelligence-led policing

■ A blueprint for law enforcement administrators to follow when enhancing or building an intelligence system

■ A model for intelligence process principles and policies

■ A plan that respects and protects individuals' privacy and civil rights

■ A technology architecture to provide secure, seamless sharing of information among systems

■ A national model for intelligence training

■ An outreach plan to promote timely and credible intelligence sharing

■ A plan that leverages existing systems and networks, yet allows flexibility for technology and process enhancements

fusion centers
A mechanism to exchange information and intelligence, maximize resources, streamline operations, and improve the ability to fight crime and terrorism by analyzing data from a variety of sources.

As part of this process, many states and large cities have formed **fusion centers**. According to the National Fusion Center Guidelines, a fusion center is "an effective and efficient mechanism to exchange information and intelligence, maximize resources, streamline operations, and improve the ability to fight crime and terrorism by analyzing data from a variety of sources."[95] Often located in police departments, these centers are set up for the purpose of sharing information and intelligence within specific jurisdictions and across levels of government. Fusion centers often emphasize terrorism prevention and crime fighting with extensive use of technology. They frequently resemble a department's technological "nerve center" and are usually housed in a central location where information is collected and then shared with decision makers. There are four main goals for fusion centers:

■ Provide support for a range of law enforcement activities, including anticrime operations and terrorism prevention

■ Provide help for major incident operations and support for units charged with interdiction and criminal investigations

■ Provide the means for community input, often through tip lines

■ Provide assistance to law enforcement executives so they can make informed decisions about departmental priorities[96]

The Palm Beach Regional Fusion Center (PBRFC)—operated by the Homeland Security Bureau of the Palm Beach County (Florida) Sheriff's Office in conjunction with other public agencies, federal authorities, and private sector representatives—is responsible for the management of real-time situational awareness and the monitoring of criminal activity. The PBRFC works to detect, deter, and prevent terrorist acts and other criminal activity, as well as prepare for and respond to natural or manmade disasters.

Fusion centers are intended to provide a mechanism through which government agencies, law enforcement, and the private sector can work together for the common purpose of protecting the homeland and preserving public safety. They are based on a model of collaboration. Collaboration between agencies and across levels of government has been lacking throughout history, but the events of 9/11 affirmed a need for change. The concept of fusion centers will continue to catch on, and more will probably be developed as law enforcement becomes increasingly aware of the benefits they can yield.

Police Support Functions

As the model of a typical police department indicates (see Figure 6.1 near the beginning of the chapter), not all members of a department engage in what the general public regards as real police work—patrol, detection, and traffic control. Even in departments that are embracing community- and problem-oriented policing, a great deal of police resources are devoted to support and administrative functions.

Many police departments maintain their own personnel service, which carries out such functions as recruiting new police officers, creating exams to determine the most qualified applicants, and handling promotions and transfers. Innovative selection techniques are constantly being developed and tested. For example, the Behavioral-Personnel Assessment Device (B-PAD) requires police applicants to view videotaped scenarios and respond as though they were officers handling the situation. Reviews indicate that this procedure may be a reliable and unbiased method of choosing new recruits.[97]

Larger police departments often maintain an **internal affairs** branch, which is charged with policing the police. The internal affairs division processes citizen

L09 Explain the various police support functions.

internal affairs
The police unit that investigates allegations of police misconduct.

complaints of police corruption, investigates allegations of unnecessary use of force by police officers, and even probes allegations of police participation in criminal activity, such as burglaries or narcotics violations. In addition, the internal affairs division may assist police managers when disciplinary action is brought against individual officers. Internal affairs is a controversial function because investigators are feared and distrusted by fellow police officers. Nonetheless, rigorous self-scrutiny is the only way that police departments can earn citizens' respect. Some type of citizen oversight of police practices and civilian review boards with the power to listen to complaints and conduct investigations have become commonplace in police departments.

Most police departments are responsible for the administration and control of their own budgets. This task includes administering payroll, purchasing equipment and services, planning budgets for future expenditures, and auditing departmental financial records.

Police departments maintain separate units charged with recording and disseminating information on wanted offenders, stolen merchandise, traffic violators, and so on. Modern data-management systems enable police to use their records in a highly sophisticated way. For example, officers in a patrol car who spot a suspicious-looking vehicle can instantly receive a computerized rundown on whether it has been stolen. And when property is recovered during an arrest, police using this sort of system can determine who reported the loss of the merchandise and arrange for its return.

Another important function of police communication is the effective and efficient dispatching of patrol cars. Again, modern computer technologies have been used to make the most of available resources.[98]

In many departments, training is continuous throughout an officer's career. Training usually begins at a police academy, which may be run exclusively for larger departments or be part of a regional training center that services smaller and varied governmental units. More than 90 percent of all police departments require preservice training, including nearly all departments in larger cities (population over 100,000). The average officer receives almost 1,000 hours of preservice training, including 600 in the academy and the rest in field training. Police in large cities receive more than 1,700 hours of instruction.[99] Among the topics usually covered are law and civil rights, firearms handling, emergency medical care, and restraint techniques.[100]

After assuming their police duties, new recruits are assigned to field-training officers who "break them in" on the job. However, training does not stop here. On-the-job training is a continuous process in the modern police department and covers such areas as weapons skills, first aid, crowd control, and community relations. Some departments use roll-call training, in which superior officers or outside experts address police officers at the beginning of the workday. Other departments allow police officers time off to attend annual training sessions to sharpen their skills and learn new policing techniques.

Police departments provide emergency aid to the ill, counsel youngsters, speak to school and community agencies on safety and drug abuse, and provide countless other services designed to improve citizen–police interactions (see the accompanying Careers in Criminal Justice feature for more detail on one such service—that of the victim advocate).

Larger police departments maintain specialized units that help citizens protect themselves from criminal activity. For example, they advise citizens on effective home security techniques or conduct Project ID campaigns—engraving valuables with an identifying number so they can be returned if recovered after a burglary. Police also work in schools, some by patrolling them and others by teaching youths how to avoid drug use.[101] Police agencies maintain (or have

CAREERS in criminal justice

VICTIM ADVOCATE

DUTIES AND CHARACTERISTICS OF THE JOB

Victim advocates (sometimes called victim service providers, victim/witness coordinators, or victim/witness specialists) are professionals trained to assist victims of crime. They offer information to crime victims, provide emotional support, and help victims access a variety of services. Advocates sometimes go to court with victims and also serve as liaisons between victims and other criminal justice organizations. They may even staff crisis hotlines, run support groups, and provide counseling. Victim advocates may be employed by cities or counties and they may work in a variety of criminal justice agencies, including police departments. A number of victim advocate jobs correspond to the usual government calendar and, so, are ideal from a scheduling standpoint. Some advocates, however, must be available on call and/or able to assist victims of crime at unusual hours and on weekends.

JOB OUTLOOK

Victim advocate careers are of the civilian variety. With an increasing push toward civilianization in a large number of criminal justice agencies, employment prospects look quite favorable over the years to come.

SALARY

Victim advocates, who fall under the Bureau of Labor Statistics "social worker" banner, typically earn between $40,000 and $45,000 per year. The pay varies depending on experience and the size of the jurisdiction. A number of jurisdictions also offer part time and hourly positions.

OPPORTUNITIES

Opportunities for careers as a victim advocate exist across the criminal justice spectrum. Most are employed by police departments, prosecutors' offices, and courts, but positions also exist in certain nonprofit organizations.

QUALIFICATIONS

Victim advocates who work for government agencies must first survive the formal government hiring process. This can take several months and also involve a background investigation. Applicants must also possess a driver's license and meet other minimum entrance criteria, such as being proficient with standard office equipment and able to work in a collaborative, group-based setting.

EDUCATION AND TRAINING

Most victim advocate positions require at least a bachelor's degree, perhaps with some relevant experience. The most common degrees earned by victim advocates are those in criminal justice, psychology, and social work. Advanced degrees can be beneficial in terms of pay and promotion prospects. Bilingual skills are also advantageous. It can also prove helpful to work as an intern and/or a volunteer before formally applying for a position as a victim advocate.

The National Organization for Victim Awareness offers a variety of credentialing programs for victim advocates. Its entry-level certification requires a minimum of 40 hours of preservice training. Some colleges and universities also offer certification programs for aspiring victim advocates.

Sources: National Center for Victims of Crime, *What Is a Victim Advocate?*, http://www.victimsofcrime.org/help-for-crime-victims/get-help-bulletins-for-crime-victims/what-is-a-victim-advocate- (accessed June 2014); Bureau of Labor Statistics, *Social Workers*, http://www.bls.gov/ooh/community-and-social-service/social-workers.htm (accessed June 2014).

access to) forensic laboratories that enable them to identify substances to be used as evidence and to classify fingerprints.

Planning and research functions include designing programs to increase police efficiency and strategies to test program effectiveness. Dedicated crime analysts often assist in this regard. Police planners monitor recent technological developments and institute programs to adapt them to police services. Many small agencies do not have the luxury of extensive support divisions. The larger the agency, the more likely there will be several distinct support divisions and functions.

Improving Police Productivity

Identify some of the cost-saving measures that may be employed to improve police productivity.

police productivity
The amount of order maintenance, crime control, and other law enforcement activities provided by individual police officers and concomitantly by police departments as a whole.

Police administrators have sought to increase the productivity of their line, support, and administrative staff. As used today, the term **police productivity** refers to the amount of order, maintenance, crime control, and other law enforcement activities provided by individual police officers and concomitantly by police departments as a whole. By improving police productivity, a department can keep the peace, deter crime, apprehend criminals, and provide useful public services without necessarily increasing its costs. This goal is accomplished by having each police officer operate with greater efficiency, thus using fewer resources to achieve greater effectiveness. Cost-saving productivity measures include, but are not limited to, consolidation, informal arrangements, sharing, pooling, contracting, service districts, civilian employees, multiple tasking, special assignment programs, and differential police responses.[102]

- *Consolidation.* One way to increase police efficiency, as discussed in the chapter's opening story, is to consolidate police services.[103] This means combining small departments (usually with fewer than 10 employees) in adjoining areas into a superagency that serves the previously fragmented jurisdictions. Consolidation has the benefit of creating departments large enough to use expanded services (such as crime labs, training centers, communications centers, and emergency units) that are not cost-effective in smaller departments.

- *Informal arrangements.* Unwritten cooperative agreements may be made between localities to perform collectively a task that would be mutually beneficial (such as monitoring neighboring radio frequencies so that needed backup can be provided).

- *Sharing.* Services that aid in the execution of a law enforcement function can be shared (such as the sharing of a communications system by several local agencies). Some agencies form mutual-aid pacts so that they can share infrequently used services, such as emergency response teams.[104] Some states have gone as far as setting up centralized data services that connect most local police agencies into a statewide information net.[105] Information sharing is becoming increasingly popular.

- *Pooling.* Some police agencies combine the resources of two or more agencies to perform a specified function under a predetermined, often formalized arrangement with direct involvement by all parties. One example is the use of a city–county law enforcement building or training academy; another is the establishment of a crime task force.

- *Contracting.* Another productivity measure is a limited and voluntary approach in which one government enters into a formal binding agreement to provide all or certain specified law enforcement services (such as communications or patrol service) to another government for an established fee. This often occurs in small cities located within a county that has a large established law enforcement agency. It is often cost-prohibitive for a small city to have its own full-service police agency, so contracting with a sheriff's department, for example, can be helpful.[106]

- *Service districts.* Some jurisdictions have set aside areas, usually within an individual county, where a special level of service is provided and financed through a special tax or assessment. In California, residents of an unincorporated portion of a county may petition to form such a district to provide more intensive patrol coverage than is available through existing systems. Such service may be provided by a sheriff, another police department, or a private person or agency.

- *Civilian employees.* One common cost-saving method is to use civilians in administrative support or even in some line activities. Civilians' duties have included operating communications gear, performing clerical work, planning and doing research, and staffing traffic control (meter monitors). Using civilian employees can be a real savings to taxpayers, because civilian salaries are considerably lower than those of regular police officers. In addition, trained, experienced officers are then able to spend more time on direct crime control and enforcement activities.

■ *Multiple tasking*. Some police officers are trained to carry out other functions of municipal government. For example, in a number of smaller departments, the roles of firefighters and police officers have been merged into a job called a public safety officer. The idea is to increase the number of people trained in both areas in order to be able to put more police at the scene of a crime, or more firefighters at a blaze, than was possible when the two tasks were separated. The system provides greater coverage at far less cost.

■ *Special assignments*. Some departments train officers for special assignments that are required only occasionally, such as radar operation, crowd control, and security.

■ *Differential police responses*. These strategies maximize resources by differentiating among police requests for services in terms of the form that the police response takes. Some calls will result in the dispatching of a sworn officer, others in the dispatching of a less highly trained civilian. Calls considered low in priority are handled by asking citizens to walk in or to mail in their requests.[107]

In sum, police departments are now implementing a variety of administrative models designed to stretch resources while still providing effective police services.

Debbie Isabell-Nelson, with the volunteer citizens patrol in the Morgan Park neighborhood in Duluth, Minnesota, checks in on neighbor Chris Parenteau during rounds. What authority should citizen patrol personnel be given?

AP Images/Duluth News Tribune/Bob King

Web App 6.6

For more information about civilian employment opportunities within law enforcement organizations, visit http://discoverpolicing.org/whats_like/?fa=civilian_alternatives.

ETHICAL CHALLENGES in Criminal Justice

A WRITING ASSIGNMENT

You are chief of the Middle City Police Department. Your city has seen a surge in violent crime in a popular downtown tourist area. Having learned of the value of "broken windows" policing, you have ordered the officers patrolling the area to be on the lookout for low-level offenses in hopes that cleaning up the streets will send a message that serious crime won't be tolerated. Two weeks later, you begin to hear complaints from some residents that patrol officers are harassing them. They argue that officers target even the most minor infractions, making it very unpleasant for people who frequent the area. Now the mayor is pressuring you to adopt a different strategy. You are aware of broken windows success stories in surrounding cities, and you are also aware of the research on its effectiveness, but you are increasingly being called upon to defend your actions.

Write an essay on the ethics of broken windows policing. In doing so, answer these questions: Should minor offenses be prioritized over more serious crimes? What are the possible drawbacks of this approach? What points would you raise to defend broken windows policing? If you opt to abandon the broken windows strategy, what other approaches might you take to make policing in your city more effective? What ethical dilemmas, if any, do those strategies pose? For help and further insights into these issues, refer to the "Improving Patrol" section earlier in this chapter.

Summary

LO1 **Explain the organization of police departments.**

- Today's police departments operate in a military-like fashion.
- Policy generally emanates from the top of the hierarchy.
- The time-in-rank system requires that before moving up the administrative ladder, an officer must spend a certain amount of time in the next lowest rank.

LO2 **Differentiate between the patrol function and the investigation function.**

- The bulk of the patrol effort is devoted to order maintenance and peacekeeping. Patrol serves a deterrent function and is intended to promote a sense of security in the community.
- Investigative work is less visible than patrol and is necessary when it is not certain who the offender is and/or when the offender eludes police.

LO3 **Discuss various efforts to improve patrol.**

- Police departments have taken several steps to improve patrol, including aggressive patrol, proactive policing, adopting a broken windows policing strategy, responding to 911 calls quickly, paying attention to procedural justice, and using technology.
- Some efforts to improve patrol have proved more effective than others. For example, it may be more effective to target specific types of crimes than to be concerned solely with rapid response.

LO4 **Discuss key issues associated with the investigative function.**

- Contemporary detectives typically use a three-pronged approach. This consists of specific, general, and informative (data collection) elements.
- Sting operations occur when organized groups of detectives deceive criminals into openly committing illegal acts or conspiring to engage in criminal activity.
- Detectives frequently work undercover. Undercover work is considered a necessary element of police work, although it can be dangerous for the agent.

LO5 **Explain the concept of community policing.**

- Community policing consists of a return to an earlier style of policing, in which officers on the beat had intimate contact with the people they served.
- Community policing gives officers the time to meet with local residents to talk about crime in the neighborhood and to use personal initiative to solve problems.

LO6 **List several challenges associated with community policing.**

- Implementing community policing can be challenging because of difficulties in defining community, choosing appropriate roles for officers, changing supervisor attitudes, reorienting police values, revising training, and recruiting different types of officers.
- One of the most significant obstacles associated with community policing is reaching out to citizens.

LO7 **Discuss the concept of problem-oriented policing.**

- Problem-oriented policing strategies require police agencies to identify particular long-term community problems and to develop strategies to eliminate them.
- Concentrating police resources on so-called hot spots of crime could appreciably reduce crime.

LO8 **Define intelligence-led policing and explain ways in which it occurs.**

- ILP consists of the collection and analysis of information to produce an "intelligence end product" designed to inform police decision making at both the tactical and strategic levels.
- ILP emphasizes problem solving but from the top down. It relies on community input, but priorities are set at the department level, not identified by residents.

LO9 **Explain the various police support functions.**

- Other organizations or divisions that support patrol, investigations, and traffic include personnel, internal affairs, administration, records, dispatch, training, planning, and research.
- The larger the police department, the more extensive its support divisions.

LO10 Identify some of the cost-saving measures that may be employed to improve police productivity.

- Police departments have sought to improve their productivity by consolidating, adopting informal arrangements, sharing, pooling, contracting, assigning service districts, hiring civilians, multiple tasking, using special assignments, and trying differential response.

Key Terms

Critical Thinking Questions

1. Should the primary police role be law enforcement or community service? Explain.
2. Should a police chief be permitted to promote an officer with special skills to a supervisory position, or should all officers be forced to spend time in rank? Why or why not?
3. Do the advantages of proactive policing outweigh the disadvantages? Explain.
4. Can the police and the community ever form a partnership to fight crime? Why or why not? Does the community policing model remind you of early forms of policing? Explain.
5. What are the relationships among community policing, problem-oriented policing, and intelligence-led policing? Are they similar or fundamentally different?

Notes

1. Jeff Horseman, "Temecula to Plug Budget Gap with Overtime Limits," *Press-Enterprise*, February 23, 2010, p. A4.
2. Carrie Johnson, "Double Blow for Police: Less Cash, More Crime," *Washington Post*, February 28, 2009, http://www.washingtonpost.com/wp-dyn/content/article/2009/02/07/AR2009020701157.html (accessed June 2014).
3. For more on consolidation trends, see http://policeconsolidation.msu.edu/ (accessed June 2014).
4. Christine Eith and Matthew R. Durose, *Contacts Between the Police and the Public, 2008* (Washington, DC: Bureau of Justice Statistics, 2011).
5. FBI, "Uniform Crime Reports," http://www.fbi.gov/about-us/cjis/ucr/crime-in-the-u.s/2012/crime-in-the-u.s.-2012/persons-arrested/persons-arrested (accessed June 2014).
6. Brian A. Reaves, *Local Police Departments, 2007* (Washington, DC: Bureau of Justice Statistics, 2010), p. 15.
7. American Bar Association, *Standards Relating to Urban Police Function* (New York: Institute of Judicial Administration, 1974), Standard 2.2.
8. James Hawdon and John Ryan, "Police-Resident Interactions and Satisfaction with Police: An Empirical Test of Community Policing Assertions," *Criminal Justice Policy Review* 14 (2003): 55–74.
9. Albert J. Reiss, *The Police and the Public* (New Haven, CT: Yale University Press, 1971), p. 19.
10. James Q. Wilson, *Varieties of Police Behavior: The Management of Law and Order in Eight Communities* (Cambridge, MA: Harvard University Press, 1968).
11. See Harlan Hahn, "A Profile of Urban Police," in *The Ambivalent Force*, ed. A. Niederhoffer and A. Blumberg (Hinsdale, IL: Dryden, 1976), p. 59.
12. James Q. Wilson and Barbara Boland, "The Effect of Police on Crime," *Law and Society Review* 12 (1978): 367–384.
13. Alexander Weiss and Sally Freels, "The Effects of Aggressive Policing: The Dayton Traffic Enforcement Experiment," *American Journal of Police* 15 (1996): 45–64.
14. Jennifer B. Robinson, "Measuring the Impact of a Targeted Law Enforcement Initiative on Drug Sales," *Journal of Criminal Justice* 36 (2008): 90–101.
15. Lawrence Sherman, James Shaw, and Dennis Rogan, *The Kansas City Gun Experiment* (Washington, DC: National Institute of Justice, 1994).
16. George Kelling and James Q. Wilson, "Broken Windows: The Police and Neighborhood Safety," *Atlantic Monthly* 249 (March 1982): 29–38.
17. Ibid.

18. Robert Panzarella, "Bratton Reinvents Harassment Model of Policing," *Law Enforcement News* 24 (1998): 14–15.

19. Eli Silverman, *NYPD Battles Crime: Innovative Strategies in Policing* (Boston: Northeastern University Press, 1999).

20. Barbara Brown, Douglas D. Perkins, and Graham Brown, "Crime, New Housing, and Housing Incivilities in a First-Ring Suburb: Multilevel Relationships Across Time," *Housing Policy Debate* 15 (2004): 301–345.

21. Richard Rosenfeld, Robert Fornango, and Andres F. Rengifo, "The Impact of Order-Maintenance Policing on New York City Homicide and Robbery Rates: 1988–2001," *Criminology* 45 (2007): 355–384; Steven F. Messner, Sandro Galea, Kenneth J. Tardiff, and Melissa Tracy, "Policing, Drugs, and the Homicide Decline in New York City in the 1990s," *Criminology* 45 (2007): 385–414.

22. Lawrence W. Sherman, "Policing for Crime Prevention," in *Preventing Crime: What Works, What Doesn't, What's Promising*, ed. Lawrence W. Sherman, Denise C. Gottfredson, Doris L. MacKenzie, John Eck, Peter Reuter, and Shawn W. Bushway (Washington, DC: National Institute of Justice, 1998), Ch. 8.

23. John L. Worrall, *Crime Control in America: What Works?* 2nd ed. (Boston: Allyn & Bacon, 2008), pp. 53–54.

24. Tom Tyler and Jeffrey Fagan, "Legitimacy and Cooperation: Why Do People Help the Police Fight Crime in Their Communities?" *Public Law and Legal Theory Working Paper Group* (Paper Number 06-99) (New York: Columbia Law School).

25. Mike D. Reisig, "Procedural Justice and Community Policing: What Shapes Residents' Willingness to Participate in Crime Prevention Programs?" *Policing: A Journal of Policy and Practice* 1 (2007): 359–369.

26. Robert Davis, Pedro Mateu-Gelabert, and Joel Miller, "Can Effective Policing Also Be Respectful? Two Examples in the South Bronx," *Police Quarterly* 8 (2005): 229–247.

27. Tom Tyler, "Procedural Justice, Legitimacy, and the Effective Rule of Law," in *Crime and Justice: A Review of Research*, ed. M. H. Tonry (Chicago: University of Chicago Press, 2003), pp. 283–357.

28. Jacinta M. Gau and Rod K. Brunson, "Procedural Justice and Order Maintenance Policing: A Study of Inner-City Young Men's Perceptions of Police Legitimacy," *Justice Quarterly* 27 (2010): 255–279; Patrick J. Carr, Laura Napolitano, and Jessica Keating, "We Never Call the Cops and Here Is Why: A Qualitative Examination of Legal Cynicism in Three Philadelphia Neighborhoods," *Criminology* 45 (2007): 445–480.

29. William Bratton, *Turnaround: How America's Top Cop Reversed the Crime Epidemic* (New York: Random House, 1998).

30. James J. Willis, Stephen D. Mastrofski, and David Weisburd, "CompStat and Bureaucracy: A Case Study of Challenges and Opportunities for Change," *Justice Quarterly* 21 (2004): 463–496.

31. See, for example, James Q. Wilson, "Movie Cops—Romantic vs. Real," *New York Magazine*, August 19, 1968, pp. 38–41.

32. For a view of the modern detective, see William Sanders, *Detective Work: A Study of Criminal Investigations* (New York: Free Press, 1977).

33. Mark Pogrebin and Eric Poole, "Vice Isn't Nice: A Look at the Effects of Working Undercover," *Journal of Criminal Justice* 21 (1993): 385–396; Gary Marx, *Undercover: Police Surveillance in America* (Berkeley: University of California Press, 1988).

34. Martin Innes, *Investigating Murder: Detective Work and the Police Response to Criminal Homicide* (Clarendon Studies in Criminology) (London: Oxford University Press, 2003).

35. John B. Edwards, "Homicide Investigative Strategies," *FBI Law Enforcement Bulletin* 74 (2005): 11–21.

36. Graeme R. Newman, *Sting Operations* (Washington, DC: Center for Problem-Oriented Policing, 2007).

37. Robert Langworthy, "Do Stings Control Crime? An Evaluation of a Police Fencing Operation," *Justice Quarterly* 6 (1989): 27–45.

38. Mary Dodge, Donna Starr-Gimeno, and Thomas Williams, "Puttin' on the Sting: Women Police Officers' Perspectives on Reverse Prostitution Assignments," *Policing: An International Journal of Police Strategies and Management* 7 (2005): 71–85.

39. Pogrebin and Poole, "Vice Isn't Nice"; Marx, *Undercover: Police Surveillance in America*.

40. Peter Greenwood and Joan Petersilia, *The Criminal Investigation Process: Summary and Policy Implications*, ed. Peter Greenwood et al. (Santa Monica, CA: RAND Corporation, 1975).

41. Mark Willman and John Snortum, "Detective Work: The Criminal Investigation Process in a Medium-Size Police Department," *Criminal Justice Review* 9 (1984): 33–39.

42. Police Executive Research Forum, *Calling the Police: Citizen Reporting of Serious Crime* (Washington, DC: Police Executive Research Forum, 1981).

43. John Eck, *Solving Crimes: The Investigation of Burglary and Robbery* (Washington, DC: Police Executive Research Forum, 1984).

44. Alan D. Fischer, "Coplink Nabs Criminals Faster," *Arizona Daily Star*, January 7, 2001, p. 1; Alexandra Robbins, "A. I. Cop on the Beat," *PC Magazine* 22 (2002); M. Sink, "An Electronic Cop that Plays Hunches," *New York Times*, November 2, 2002, p. B1; also see IBM, http://www-03.ibm.com/software/products/en/coplink (accessed June 2014).

45. Albert Cardarelli, Jack McDevitt, and Katrina Baum, "The Rhetoric and Reality of Community Policing in Small and Medium-Sized Cities and Towns," *Policing* 21 (1998): 397–415.

46. Nadine M. Connell, Kristen Miggans, and Jean Marie McGloin, "Can a Community Policing Initiative Reduce Serious Crime?" *Police Quarterly* 11 (2008): 127–150.

47. For a general review, see Robert Trojanowicz and Bonnie Bucqueroux, *Community Policing: A Contemporary Perspective* (Cincinnati: Anderson, 1990).

48. Police Foundation, *The Newark Foot Patrol Experiment* (Washington, DC: Police Foundation, 1981).

49. John L. Worrall and Jihong Zhao, "The Role of the COPS Office in Community Policing," *Policing* 26 (2003): 64–87.

50. Office of Community Oriented Policing Services, http://www.cops.usdoj.gov (accessed June 2014).

51. Jihong Zhao, Nicholas Lovrich, and Quint Thurman, "The Status of Community Policing in American Cities," *Policing* 22 (1999): 74–92.

52. Jack R. Greene, "The Effects of Community Policing on American Law Enforcement: A Look at the Evidence," paper presented at the International Congress on Criminology, Hamburg, Germany, September 1988, p. 19.

53. Roger Dunham and Geoffrey Alpert, "Neighborhood Differences in Attitudes Toward Policing: Evidence for a Mixed-Strategy Model of Policing in a Multi-Ethnic Setting," *Journal of Criminal Law and Criminology* 79 (1988): 504–522.

54. Scott Lewis, Helen Rosenberg, and Robert Sigler, "Acceptance of Community Policing Among Police Officers and Police Administrators," *Policing* 22 (1999): 567–588.

55. Robin Shepard Engel, *How Police Supervisory Styles Influence Patrol Officer Behavior* (Washington, DC: National Institute of Justice, 2003).

56. Amy Halsted, Max Bromley, and John Cochran, "The Effects of Work Orientations on Job Satisfaction Among Sheriffs' Deputies Practicing Community-Oriented Policing," *Policing* 23 (2000): 82–104.

57. Venessa Garcia, "Constructing the 'Other' Within Police Culture: An Analysis of a Deviant Unit Within the Police Organization," *Police Practice and Research* 6 (2005): 65–80.

58. Allison T. Chappell, "Community Policing: Is Field Training the Missing Link?" *Policing* 30 (2007): 498–517.

59. Michael Palmiotto, Michael Birzer, and N. Prabha Unnithan, "Training in Community Policing: A Suggested Curriculum," *Policing* 23 (2000): 8–21.

60. Lisa Riechers and Roy Roberg, "Community Policing: A Critical Review of Underlying Assumptions," *Journal of Police Science and Administration* 17 (1990): 112–113.

61. John Riley, "Community-Policing: Utilizing the Knowledge of Organizational Personnel," *Policing* 22 (1999): 618–633.

62. Donald Green, Dara Strolovitch, and Janelle Wong, "Defended Neighborhoods: Integration and Racially Motivated Crime," *American Journal of Sociology* 104 (1998): 372–403.

63. David Kessler, "Integrating Calls for Service with Community- and Problem-Oriented Policing: A Case Study," *Crime and Delinquency* 39 (1993): 485–508.

64. L. Thomas Winfree, Gregory Bartku, and George Seibel, "Support for Community Policing versus Traditional Policing Among Nonmetropolitan Police Officers: A Survey of Four New Mexico Police Departments," *American Journal of Police* 15 (1996): 23–47.

65. Jihong Zhao, Ni He, and Nicholas Lovrich, "Value Change Among Police Officers at a Time of Organizational Reform: A Follow-Up Study of Rokeach Values," *Policing* 22 (1999): 152–170.

66. Jihong Zhao, Matthew Scheider, and Quint Thurman, "A National Evaluation of the Effect of COPs Grants on Police Productivity (Arrests) 1995–1999," *Police Quarterly* 6 (2003): 387–410.

67. Mike Brogden, "'Horses for Courses' and 'Thin Blue Lines': Community Policing in Transitional Society," *Police Quarterly* 8 (2005): 64–99.

68. Ling Ren, Liqun Cao, Nicholas Lovrich, and Michael Gaffney, "Linking Confidence in the Police with the Performance of the Police: Community Policing Can Make a Difference," *Journal of Criminal Justice* 33 (2005): 55–66.

69. Stephen M. Schnebly, "The Influence of Community-Oriented Policing on Crime-Reporting Behavior," *Justice Quarterly* 25 (2008): 223–251.

70. Walter Baranyk, "Making a Difference in a Public Housing Project," *Police Chief* 61 (1994): 31–35.

71. Herman Goldstein, "Improving Policing: A Problem-Oriented Approach," *Crime and Delinquency* 25 (1979): 236–258.

72. Jerome Skolnick and David Bayley, *Community Policing: Issues and Practices Around the World* (Washington, DC: National Institute of Justice, 1988), p. 12.

73. Lawrence Sherman, Patrick Gartin, and Michael Buerger, "Hot Spots of Predatory Crime: Routine Activities and the Criminology of Place," *Criminology* 27 (1989): 27–55.

74. Ibid. p. 45.

75. Dennis Roncek and Pamela Maier, "Bars, Blocks, and Crimes Revisited: Linking the Theory of Routine Activities to the Empiricism of 'Hot Spots,'" *Criminology* 29 (1991): 725–753.

76. David Weisburd, Cody W. Telep, Joshua C. Hinkle, and John E. Eck, "Is Problem-Oriented Policing Effective in Reducing Crime and Disorder? Findings from a Campbell Systematic Review," *Criminology and Public Policy* 9 (2010): 139–172.

77. Center for Problem-Oriented Policing, http://www.popcenter.org (accessed June 2014).

78. C. Jewett, "Police Use Bait Cars to Reduce Theft," *Knight Ridder/Tribune Business News*, March 3, 2003, p. 1.

79. Anthony Braga, David Kennedy, Elin Waring, and Anne Morrison Piehl, "Problem-Oriented Policing, Deterrence, and Youth Violence: An Evaluation of Boston's Operation Ceasefire," *Journal of Research in Crime and Delinquency* 38 (2001): 195–225.

80. Anthony Braga, David Weisburd, Elin Waring, Lorraine Green Mazerolle, William Spelman, and Francis Gajewski, "Problem-Oriented Policing in Violent Crime Places: A Randomized Controlled Experiment," *Criminology* 37 (1999): 541–580.

81. Anthony A. Braga, Glenn L. Pierce, Jack McDevitt, Brenda J. Bond, and Shea Cronin, "The Strategic Prevention of Gun Violence Among Gang-Involved Offenders," *Justice Quarterly* 25 (2008): 132–162.

82. Bureau of Justice Assistance, *Problem-Oriented Drug Enforcement: A Community-Based Approach for Effective Policing* (Washington, DC: National Institute of Justice, 1993).

83. Ibid., pp. 64–65.

84. Brian A. Lawton, Ralph B. Taylor, and Anthony J. Luongo, "Police Officers on Drug Corners in Philadelphia, Drug Crime, and Violent Crime: Intended, Diffusion, and Displacement Impacts," *Justice Quarterly* 22 (2005): 427–451.

85. David L. Carter and Jeremy G. Carter, "Intelligence-Led Policing: Conceptual and Functional Considerations for Public Police," *Criminal Justice Policy Review* 20 (2009): 310–325, at 310.

86. Global Intelligence Working Group, *National Criminal Intelligence Sharing Plan* (Washington, DC: Office of Justice Programs, 2003), p. 6.

87. Jerry Ratcliffe, *Intelligence-Led Policing* (Cullompton, UK: Willan, 2008).

88. Carter and Carter, p. 310.

89. Carter and Carter, p. 312.

90. Ratcliffe, *Intelligence-Led Policing.*

91. Marilyn B. Peterson, "Toward a Model for Intelligence-Led Policing in the United States," in *Turnkey Intelligence: Unlocking Your Agency's Intelligence Capability* (Lawrenceville, NJ: International Association of Law Enforcement Intelligence Analysts, Law Enforcement Intelligence Unit, and National White Collar Crime Center, 2002), p. 5.

92. David L. Carter, *Law Enforcement Intelligence: A Guide for State, Local, and Tribal Law Enforcement Agencies* (Washington, DC: U.S. Department of Justice, 2004), p. 8.

93. Ibid., p. 8.

94. *National Criminal Intelligence Sharing Plan*, https://it.ojp.gov/ documents/National_Criminal_Intelligence_Sharing_Plan.pdf (accessed June 2014).

95. *Fusion Center Guidelines: Developing and Sharing Information and Intelligence in a New Era*, http://www.it.ojp.gov/documents/ fusion_center_guidelines.pdf (accessed June 2014).

96. Charles R. Swanson, Leonard Territo, and Robert W. Taylor, *Police Administration: Structures, Processes, and Behavior*, 7th ed. (Upper Saddle River, NJ: Prentice Hall, 2008), pp. 77–78.

97. William Boerner and Terry Nowell, "The Reliability of the Behavioral Personnel Assessment Device (B-PAD) in Selecting Police Recruits," *Policing* 22 (1999): 343–352.

98. See, for example, Richard Larson, *Urban Police Patrol Analysis* (Cambridge, MA: MIT Press, 1972).

99. Brian A. Reaves, *Local Police Departments, 2007* (Washington, DC: Bureau of Justice Statistics, 2010), p. 12.

100. Philip Ash, Karen Slora, and Cynthia Britton, "Police Agency Officer Selection Practices," *Journal of Police Science and Administration* 17 (1990): 258–269.

101. Dennis Rosenbaum, Robert Flewelling, Susan Bailey, Chris Ringwalt, and Deanna Wilkinson, "Cops in the Classroom: A Longitudinal Evaluation of Drug Abuse Resistance Education (DARE)," *Journal of Research in Crime and Delinquency* 31 (1994): 3–31.

102. Adapted from Terry Koepsell and Charles Gerard, *Small Police Agency Consolidation: Suggested Approaches* (Washington, DC: Government Printing Office, 1979).

103. International Association of Chiefs of Police, *Consolidating Police Services: An IACP Planning Approach* (Alexandria, VA: International Association of Chiefs of Police, 2003).

104. Mike D'Alessandro and Charles Hoffman, "Mutual Aid Pacts," *Law and Order* 43 (1995): 90–93.

105. Leonard Sipes Jr., "Maryland's High-Tech Approach to Crime Fighting," *Police Chief* 61 (1994): 18–20.

106. See, for example, Peter J. Nelligan and William Bourns, "Municipal Contracting with County Sheriffs for Police Services in California: Comparison of Cost and Effectiveness," *Police Quarterly* 14 (2011): 70–85.

107. Robert Worden, "Toward Equity and Efficiency in Law Enforcement: Differential Police Response," *American Journal of Police* 12 (1993): 1–24.

CHAPTER 7

Issues in Policing

Every year, approximately 400 people are justifiably killed by police officers. In a country of about 300,000,000 people, that number seems exceptionally low. But police critics think it is too high. Any time a person is fatally shot by the police, whether justified or otherwise, the event is closely scrutinized. The agency for which the officer works typically performs an in-depth investigation. The local prosecutor's office usually investigates in order to rule out the possibility of criminal behavior. Sometimes federal agencies launch their own probes, as has recently occurred in Albuquerque, New Mexico.

On March 16, 2014, James Boyd, a homeless man who was camping in the Sandia foothills outside of Albuquerque, was shot following a lengthy and tense standoff with police. Boyd, armed with two small knives, initially threatened to kill police and did not back down when he was ordered to discard his weapon. In their efforts to subdue Boyd, officers fired stun guns, bean bags, and ultimately six live rounds. Boyd was killed.

Real-time helmet cam footage was made available by the Albuquerque Police Department and, as of this writing, is available on YouTube.[1] Was the shooting justifiable? Albuquerque Police Chief Gordon Eden said yes. Critics, however, said no. You can watch the video and decide for yourself.

So controversial was the shooting, the Federal Bureau of Investigation launched a criminal probe promptly afterward. The agency was concerned not just with what happened in the Boyd case, but also with what it felt was an unusually high rate of police shootings in Albuquerque. At the time the probe was launched, 37 people had been shot by Albuquerque police since 2010. In 23 of the shootings the suspect was killed, giving Albuquerque the dubious distinction of having one of the highest rates of police shootings in the country.[2] But in a city of roughly 550,000 people, some would say 23 deaths is not many. Which perspective is correct? Unfortunately, there are no easy answers. ■

The police have always been put in a difficult spot when it comes to enforcing the law and, at the same time, preventing unnecessary loss of life. Many people feel the police should control and prevent crime, even if doing so requires a no-nonsense, heavy-handed approach. Supporters of "get-tough" law enforcement feel that if the greater good is served, then occasional injuries and deaths go with the territory. On the other hand, police do not work in a vacuum. They work in a very visible, politically contentious, media-driven world. Anything that even *possibly* results in unnecessary injury or death places the police in the hot seat, forcing them to defend their public image.

The problem of police shootings (even the justified ones!) raises important questions about the problems that departments face while interacting with the society they are entrusted with supervising: Are police officers too forceful and brutal, and do they discriminate in their use of deadly force? When officers need to use force, what options are available to them? Which option should they pursue and under what circumstances? Are police too quick to resort to force? How many officers are deviant and to what extent can deviance be controlled? This chapter focuses on these and other questions facing police officers in contemporary society. First, we begin with a discussion of the makeup of the police and the police profession.

Who Are the Police?

The composition of the nation's police forces is changing. Traditionally, police agencies were composed of white males with a high school education who viewed policing as a secure position that brought them the respect of family and friends and a step up the social ladder. It was not uncommon to see police families in which one member of each new generation would enter the force. This picture has been changing and will continue to change. As criminal justice programs turn out thousands of graduates every year, an increasing number of police officers have at least some college education. In addition, affirmative action programs have helped slowly change the racial and gender composition of police departments to reflect community makeup.

Police and Education

In recent years, many police experts have argued that police recruits should have a college education. This development is not unexpected, considering that higher education for police officers has been recommended by national commissions since 1931.[3]

L01 Recognize the benefits likely to accrue from higher education for police.

Although most law enforcement agencies still do not require recruits to have an advanced degree, the number requiring some higher education in the hiring and promotion process is growing. Today, nearly all local police departments (98 percent) have an education requirement for new officer recruits:

- About 16 percent of departments have some type of college requirement.
- About 9 percent require a two-year degree.
- Only 1 percent of local police departments require a four-year degree.
- When asked, most departments express a preference for criminal justice majors, usually because of their enhanced knowledge of the entire criminal justice system and issues in policing.[4]

Another promising trend is that, although they do not require college credits for promotion, most police departments recognize that college education is an important element in promotion decisions. The United States is not alone in this regard; police departments around the world are now encouraging recruits and in-service officers to earn college credits.[5]

What are the benefits of higher education for police officers? Better communication with the public, especially minority and ethnic groups, is believed to be one benefit. Educated officers write better and more clearly and are more likely to be promoted. Police administrators believe that education enables officers to perform more effectively, generate fewer citizen complaints, show more initiative in performing police tasks, and generally behave more professionally.[6] In addition, educated officers are less likely to have disciplinary problems, are viewed as better decision makers,[7] and are less inclined to use force.[8] Research indicates that educated officers are more likely to rate themselves higher on most performance indicators, indicating that higher education is associated with greater self-confidence and assurance.[9]

Although education has its benefits, little conclusive evidence has been found that educated officers are more effective crime fighters.[10] The diversity of the police role, the need for split-second decision making, and the often boring and mundane tasks that police are required to do are all considered reasons why formal education may not improve performance on the street.[11] Nonetheless, because police administrators value educated officers, and citizens find them to be exceptional in the use of good judgment and problem solving, the trend toward a better-educated police force is likely to continue.[12]

Minorities in Policing

For some time, U.S. police departments have made a concerted effort to attract minority police officers, and there have been some impressive gains. As might be expected, cities with large minority populations have a higher proportion of minority officers in their police departments.[13]

The reasons for this effort are varied. African Americans generally have less confidence in the police than whites and are skeptical of their ability to protect citizens from harm.[14] African Americans also seem more likely to have been victimized when well-publicized incidents of police misconduct occur.[15] African American juveniles seem particularly suspicious of police, even when they deny having had negative encounters with them.[16] A heterogeneous police force can thus be instrumental in gaining the confidence of the minority community by helping dispel the view that police departments are generally bigoted or biased organizations. Furthermore, minority police officers possess special qualities that can serve to improve police performance. Spanish-speaking officers can help with investigations in Hispanic neighborhoods, and Asian American officers are essential for undercover or surveillance work with Asian gangs and drug importers.

THE AFRICAN AMERICAN EXPERIENCE The earliest known date when an African American was hired as a police officer was 1861 in Washington, D.C.; Chicago hired its first African American officer in 1872.[17] At first, African American officers suffered a great deal of discrimination. Their work assignments were restricted, as were their chances for promotion. They were often assigned solely to the patrol of African American neighborhoods, and in some cities they were required to call a white officer to make an arrest. White officers held highly prejudicial attitudes, and as late as the 1950s some refused to ride with African Americans in patrol cars.[18]

The experience of African American police officers has not been an easy one. In his classic book *Black in Blue*, written more than 40 years ago, Nicholas Alex pointed out that African American officers of the time suffered from what he called **double marginality**.[19] On the one hand, African American officers had to deal with the expectation that they would give members of their own race a break. On the other hand, they often experienced overt racism from their police colleagues. Alex found that African American officers' adaptation to these pressures ranged from denying that African American suspects should be treated

L02 Describe how the role of women and minorities in local police agencies has evolved over time.

double marginality
According to Nicholas Alex, the social burden that African American police officers carry by being both minority group members and law enforcement officers.

differently from whites to treating African American offenders more harshly than white offenders (to prove their lack of bias). Alex offered several reasons why some African American officers were tougher on African American offenders: They desired acceptance from their white colleagues, they were particularly sensitive to any disrespect shown them by African American teenagers, and they viewed themselves as protectors of the African American community. Ironically, minority citizens may be more likely to accuse a minority officer of misconduct than a white officer—a circumstance that underscores the difficult position of the minority officer in contemporary society.[20]

MINORITY REPRESENTATION TODAY Table 7.1, which contains the most up-to-date data as of this writing, illustrates the increasing diversity in America's police departments. Approximately 25 percent of local police officers are African American, Hispanic, or other minority races.

The increased representation of minorities in police department ranks has fueled a number of changes. Minority police officers now seem more aggressive, more self-assured, and less willing to accept any discriminatory practices by the police department.[21] Researchers have found that they are more willing than white officers to use their authority to take official action. For example, the higher the percentage of black officers on the force, the higher the arrest rate for crimes such as assault.[22] Nor do black officers hesitate to use their arrest powers on African American suspects. Using observational data on police–citizen encounters in Cincinnati, Robert Brown and James Frank found that although white officers were more likely to arrest suspects than black officers were, black suspects were more likely to be arrested when the decision maker was a black officer.[23]

Yet as their numbers increase, minority officers appear to be experiencing some of the same problems and issues encountered by white officers.[24] They report feeling similar rates of job-related stress and strain, stemming from the same types of stressors, such as family conflict.[25] Minority officers do report more stress when they consider themselves "tokens," marginalized within the department.[26] They may also deal with stress in a somewhat different fashion: they are more likely to seek aid from fellow minority officers, whereas white officers are more likely to try to express their feelings to others, form social bonds, and try to get others to like them more.[27]

TABLE 7.1 **Race and Ethnicity of Full-Time Sworn Personnel in Local Police Departments, by Size of Population Served**

Population served	White	Black/African American	Hispanic/Latino	Asian/Pacific Islander	American Indian/Alaska Native	Multi-race
All sizes	74.7%	11.9%	10.3%	2.0%	0.7%	0.3%
1,000,000 or more	56.0%	17.6%	22.9%	3.2%	0.3%	0.0%
500,000–999,999	60.6	24.1	9.3	4.1	0.4	1.6
250,000–499,999	69.5	16.5	11.2	2.0	0.6	0.1
100,000–249,999	73.7	13.4	9.1	2.6	0.9	0.3
50,000–99,999	83.6	7.0	7.5	1.4	0.3	0.3
25,000–49,999	88.2	5.0	5.1	0.9	0.6	0.2
10,000–24,999	87.5	5.6	5.1	0.6	1.0	0.2
2,500–9,999	87.9	5.1	4.4	0.6	1.8	0.1
Under 2,500	88.3	5.8	3.0	0.1	2.3	0.5

Source: Brian Reaves, *Local Police Departments, 2007* (Washington, DC: Bureau of Justice Statistics, 2007), p. 14.

When affirmative action was first instituted, white police officers viewed it as a threat to their job security.[28] As more minorities have joined U.S. police forces, their situation seems to have changed. Caucasian officers are more likely to appreciate the contribution of minority officers. When Charles Katz examined the formation of a police gang unit in a midwestern city, he found that commanders chose minority officers so the unit could be representative of the community they served.[29] As one Hispanic officer told Katz, "When you talk to Hispanics, you have to know and be familiar with their culture … [For example, you] always talk to the man of the house, never presenting your position to the kid or to the mother."[30] These benefits are not lost on citizens either, and research shows that the general public cares little about the racial or ethnic makeup of the police officers in their neighborhood and more about their effectiveness.[31]

Despite the many advances minority police officers have made, clear differences exist between white and, in particular, black police officers. A recent study by Peter Moskos, a professor at the John Jay College of New York, revealed that there are "two shades of blue."[32] That is, "[b]lack and white police officers have different attitudes towards the role of police in society, police department politics, and the minority community." Detailed findings from his research, which was based on several months of participant observation (he once worked as an officer in the city he studied) and interviewing, appear in Exhibit 7.1.

EXHIBIT 7.1 Summary of White and Black Police Attitudes

Attitudes Shared

Subject	(No significant racial differences)
The ghetto	Violent, bad, dirty
Departmental discipline	Department will sacrifice an officer for political reasons
Social ideology	Conservative
Victims who know their assailants	Deserve what they get
Lower-class whites	Fat, wife-beating, inbred, no teeth, cop-fighting, redneck drunks
Lower-class blacks	Baby-making, welfare-dependent, drug-using, cop-hating drunks

Attitudes Not Shared

Subject	(Significant racial differences)	
	Black police	**White police**
Residents of the ghetto	Good and bad people live in ghetto	All bad
Departmental discipline	Biased against blacks because an "old-boys' network" protects whites	Biased against whites because department is politically afraid to punish blacks
Hiring process	Process is tougher for blacks	Standards are lowered for blacks
Black police identity	Cop identity more important than race identity	Many are black before blue
White police identity	Too many racist redneck crackers	More "professional"
Self-identity as police	Strong, but just a job	Strong
Political ideology	Independent, conservative, or liberal	Independent or conservative
Role of police	Peacekeepers	Crime fighters
The city	Bad, but problems are everywhere	Bad, where trouble comes from

Source: Peter C. Moskos, "Two Shades of Blue: Black and White in the Blue Brotherhood," *Law Enforcement Executive Forum* 8 (2008): 57–86.

Women in Policing

In 1910, in Los Angeles, Alice Stebbins Wells became the first woman to hold the title of police officer and to have arrest powers.[33] As Figure 7.1 shows, about 15 percent of all sworn officers in larger cities (over 250,000) are women; women are more underrepresented in smaller cities and counties.[34] And unfortunately, recent research suggests that the increase in female representation among sworn officers may be leveling off.[35]

The road to success in police work has not been easy for women. For more than half a century, female officers endured separate criteria for selection, were given menial tasks, and were denied the opportunity for advancement.[36] Some relief was gained with the passage of the 1964 Civil Rights Act and its subsequent amendments. Courts have consistently supported the addition of women to police forces by striking down entrance requirements that eliminated almost all female candidates but that could not be proved to predict job performance (such as height and upper-body strength).[37] Women do not perform as well as men on strength tests and are much more likely to fail the entrance physical than male recruits. Critics contend that many of these tests do not reflect the actual tasks that police do on the job.[38] Nonetheless, the role of women in police work is still restricted by social and administrative barriers that have been difficult to remove.

Studies of policewomen indicate that they are still struggling for acceptance, believe that they do not receive equal credit for their job performance, and report that it is common for them to be sexually harassed by their coworkers.[39] One reason may be that many male police officers tend to view policing as an overtly masculine profession not appropriate for women. For example, officers in the Los Angeles Police Department make an important distinction between two models of officers—"hard chargers" and "station queens." The former display such characteristics as courage and aggressiveness; they are willing to place themselves in danger and handle the most hazardous calls.[40] The latter like to work in the

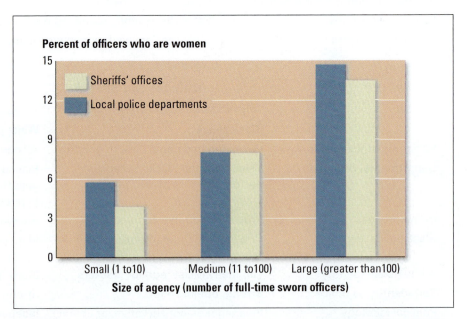

FIGURE 7.1 Percent of Full-Time Sworn Law Enforcement Officers Who Are Women Among Local Police Departments and Sheriffs' Offices

Source: Lynn Langton, *Women in Law Enforcement, 1987–2008* (Washington, DC: Bureau of Justice Statistics, 2010), p. 2.

Stephanie Sinclair/VII/Corbis News/Corbis

District of Columbia Police Chief Cathy L. Lanier converses with another police officer while on patrol in Washington, D.C. Lanier rose to her position from humble beginnings: she was a high school dropout after ninth grade and an unwed mother at the age of 15. Despite a rough start, she later earned advanced academic degrees from Johns Hopkins University and the Naval Postgraduate School in Monterey, California, where she completed a master's in security studies. Lanier also attended the John F. Kennedy School of Government at Harvard University and is a graduate of the FBI Academy and the University of the District of Columbia. She has been on the force for 24 years.

station house doing paperwork or other administrative tasks. The term "queen" is designed as a pejorative to indicate that these officers are overly feminine.[41]

Female police officers may also be targeted for more disciplinary actions by administrators and, if cited, are more likely to receive harsher punishments than male officers.[42] Considering the sometimes hostile reception they get from male colleagues and supervisors, it is not surprising that female officers report significantly higher levels of job-related stress than male officers.[43] Women have also faced considerable obstacles to promotion within the ranks, although recently this issue has become rather clouded and complex. For example, Carol Archbold and Dorothy Schulz found that female officers were frequently encouraged by their male supervisors to seek promotion, but this dissuaded many of the women from seeking promotion for fear that they would be promoted because of their status as a woman rather than their competencies.[44]

JOB PERFORMANCE Research indicates that female officers are highly successful police officers.[45] In an important study of recruits in the Metropolitan Police Department of Washington, D.C., policewomen were found to display extremely satisfactory work performances.[46] Compared with male officers, women were found to respond to similar types of calls, and the arrests they made were as likely to result in conviction. Women were more likely than their male colleagues to receive support from the community and were less likely to be charged with improper conduct. On the other hand, there is evidence that female officers are more likely to be assaulted during domestic violence incidents.[47]

GENDER CONFLICTS Despite the overwhelming evidence supporting their performance, policewomen have not always been fully accepted by their male peers or the general public.[48] In a recent survey, nearly three-quarters of female officers reported that policing is male-dominated and not very woman friendly.[49] This form of bias is not unique to the United States. Research shows that policewomen working in northern England report being excluded from full membership in the force, based on gender inequality. Although policewomen in England are enthusiastic about crime-related work, their aspirations are frequently frustrated in favor of male officers.[50]

Female officers are frequently caught in a classic Catch-22 dilemma: if they are physically weak, male partners view them as a risk in street confrontations; if they are more powerful and aggressive than their male partners, they are regarded as an affront to a male officer's manhood. Ironically, to adapt to this paternalistic culture, they may develop values and attitudes that support traditional concepts of police work instead of the new community policing models, which are viewed as taking a more humanistic, people-oriented approach.[51] The Catch-22 dilemma can also lead to stress and burnout, but recent studies suggest that female officers may have achieved a measure of equality with their male colleagues when it comes to reporting these conditions.[52]

MINORITY FEMALE OFFICERS   In a study of African American policewomen serving in five large municipal departments, Susan Martin found that they perceive significantly more racial discrimination than both other female officers and African American male officers.[53] However, white policewomen were significantly more likely to perceive sexual discrimination than African American policewomen were. Martin also found that when they were on patrol, African American policewomen were treated differently by male officers than white policewomen were. Neither group of women was viewed as equals.

African American women also reported having difficult relationships with African American male officers. Their relationships were strained by tensions and dilemmas "associated with sexuality and competition for desirable assignments and promotions."[54] Surprisingly, little unity was found among the female officers. As Martin concluded, "The idealized image of the representative of the forces of 'law and order' and protector who maintains 'the thin blue line' between 'them' and 'us' remains white and male."[55]

Despite these problems, the future of women in policing grows continually brighter.[56] Female officers want to remain in policing because it pays a good salary, offers job security, and is a challenging and exciting occupation.[57] These factors should continue to bring women to policing for years to come.

The Police Profession

All professions have unique characteristics that distinguish them from other occupations and institutions. Policing is no exception. Police experts have long sought to understand the unique nature of the police experience and to determine how the challenges of police work shape the profession and its employees.

Police Culture

Police experts have found that the experience of becoming a police officer and the nature of the job itself cause most officers to band together in a police subculture characterized by cynicism, clannishness, secrecy, and insulation from others in society—the so-called **blue curtain**. Police officers tend to socialize together and believe that their occupation cuts them off from relationships with civilians. Officers perceive their working environment to be laden with danger or the risk of danger, and they become preoccupied with the personal risks and violence that surround them, always anticipating both.[58] Perceptions of danger have a unifying effect on officers and work to separate them from the public and help create the boundaries of a police subculture. Joining the police subculture means always having to stick up for fellow officers against outsiders; maintaining a tough, macho exterior personality; and distrusting the motives and behavior of outsiders.[59] Six core beliefs are viewed as being at the heart of the police culture:

- *Police are the only real crime fighters.* The public wants the police officer to fight crime; other agencies, both public and private, only play at crime fighting.

Web App 7.1

For more information on law enforcement research, visit http://www.policefoundation.org/.

blue curtain
The secretive, insulated police culture that isolates officers from the rest of society.

- *No one else understands the real nature of police work.* Lawyers, academics, politicians, and the public in general have little concept of what it means to be a police officer.

- *Loyalty to colleagues counts above everything else.* Police officers have to stick together because everyone is out to get the police and make the job more difficult.

- *The war against crime cannot be won without bending the rules.* Courts have awarded criminal defendants too many civil rights.

- *Members of the public are basically unsupportive and unreasonably demanding.* People are quick to criticize police unless they need police help themselves.

- *Patrol work is the pits.* Detective work is glamorous and exciting.[60]

The forces that support a police culture are generally believed to develop out of on-the-job experiences. Most officers originally join the police force because they want to help people, fight crime, and have an interesting, exciting, prestigious career with a high degree of job security.[61] Recruits often find that the social reality of police work does not mesh with their original career goals. They are unprepared for the emotional turmoil and conflict that accompany police work today.

 L03 Explain the concept of a police culture.

Membership in the police culture helps recruits adjust to the rigors of police work and provides the emotional support needed for survival.[62] The culture encourages decisiveness in the face of uncertainty and the ability to make split-second judgments that may later be subject to extreme criticism. The police sub-culture also encourages its members to draw a sharp distinction between good and evil. Officers, more than mere enforcers of the law, are warriors in the age-old battle between right and wrong.[63] Also, criminals are referred to as "terrorists" and "predators," terms that convey the view that they are evil individuals ready to prey upon the poor and vulnerable. Because the predators represent a real danger, the police culture demands that its members be both competent and concerned with the safety of their peers and partners.

In sum, the police culture has developed in response to the insulated, dangerous lifestyle of police officers. Policing is a hazardous occupation, and the availability of the unquestioned support and loyalty of their peers is not something officers could readily do without.[64] Nonetheless, some experts fear that the police culture will divide officers from the people they serve and create an "us against the world" mentality.[65]

Police Personality

Along with an independent police culture, some experts believe that police officers develop a unique set of personality traits that distinguish them from the average citizen.[66] To some commentators, the typical police personality can be described as dogmatic, authoritarian, and suspicious.[67] **Cynicism** has been found at all levels of policing, including chiefs of police, and throughout all stages of a police career.[68] Maintenance of these negative values and attitudes is believed to cause police officers to be secretive and isolated from the rest of society, producing the blue curtain.[69]

cynicism
The belief that most people's actions are motivated solely by personal needs and selfishness.

The police officer's working personality is shaped by constant exposure to danger and the need to use force and authority to reduce and control threatening situations.[70] Police feel suspicious of the public they serve and defensive about the actions of their fellow officers. There are two opposing viewpoints on the cause of this phenomenon. One position holds that police departments attract recruits who are by nature cynical, authoritarian, and secretive.[71] Other experts maintain that socialization and experience on the police force itself cause these character traits to develop.

 L04 Describe the reasons why experts believe police have a unique personality.

Since the first research measuring police personality was published, numerous efforts have been made to determine whether the typical police recruit possesses a unique personality that sets her apart from the average citizen. The results have been mixed.[72] Although some research concludes that police values are different from those of the general adult population, other efforts reach an opposing conclusion. Some have found that police officers are more psychologically healthy than the general population, less depressed and anxious, and more social and assertive.[73] Still other research on police personality has found that police officers highly value such personality traits as warmth, flexibility, and emotion. These traits are far removed from rigidity and cynicism.[74] Thus no one position dominates on the issue of how the police personality develops—or even whether one exists.

In his classic study of police personality, *Behind the Shield* (1967), Arthur Neiderhoffer examined the assumption that most police officers develop into cynics as a function of their daily duties.[75] Among his most important findings were that police cynicism increased with length of service and that military-like police academy training caused new recruits to quickly become cynical about themselves.[76]

Police Style

L05 Recognize the different types of police officer styles.

Policing encompasses a multitude of diverse tasks, including peacekeeping, criminal investigation, traffic control, and providing emergency medical service. Part of the socialization of a police officer is developing a working attitude, or style, through which he approaches policing. For example, some police officers may view their job as a well-paid civil service position that stresses careful compliance with written departmental rules and procedures. Other officers may see themselves as part of the "thin blue line" that protects the public from wrongdoers. They will use any means to get the culprit, even if it involves such cheating as planting evidence on an obviously guilty person who so far has escaped arrest. Should the police bend the rules to protect the public? This has been referred to as the "Dirty Harry problem," after the popular Clint Eastwood film character who routinely (and successfully) violated all known standards of police work.[77]

police styles
The working personalities adopted by police officers that can range from being a social worker in blue to being a hard-charging crime fighter.

Several studies have attempted to define and classify **police styles** into behavioral clusters. These classifications, called typologies, attempt to categorize law enforcement agents by groups, each of which has a unique approach to police work. The purpose of such classifications is to demonstrate that the police are not a cohesive, homogeneous group, as many believe, but individuals with differing approaches to their work.[78] The approach that police take to their task and their attitude toward the police role, as well as toward their peers and superior officers, have been shown to affect their work.[79]

An examination of the literature suggests that four styles of police work seem to fit the current behavior patterns of most police agents: the crime fighter, the social agent, the law enforcer, and the watchman. These four styles are described in Exhibit 7.2.

CURRENT VIEWS ON POLICE CULTURE, PERSONALITY, AND STYLES Although some experts have found that a unique police personality and culture do exist, others have challenged that assumption.[80] No clear-cut agreement has been reached on the matter. In either event, changes in contemporary police agencies will soon have a significant impact on police culture and personality, if they have not done so already. Police departments have become diverse, attracting women and minorities in growing numbers. Police are becoming more educated and technologically sophisticated. The vision of a monolithic department whose employees share similar and uniform values, culture, and personality traits seems somewhat naive in the presence of such diversity.

Furthermore, today's police officer is unlikely to be able to choose to embrace a particular style of policing while excluding others. Although some police officers

EXHIBIT 7.2 The Four Basic Styles of Policing

The Crime Fighter

To crime fighters, the most important aspect of police work is investigating serious crimes and apprehending criminals. Their focus is on the victim, and they view effective police work as the only force that can keep society's "dangerous classes" in check. They are the "thin blue line" protecting society from murderers and rapists. They consider property crimes less significant, and they believe that misdemeanors, traffic control, and social service functions would be better handled by other agencies of government. The ability to investigate criminal behavior that poses a serious threat to life and safety, combined with the power to arrest criminals, separates a police department from other municipal agencies. The crime fighters see diluting these functions with minor social service and nonenforcement duties as harmful to police efforts to create a secure society.

The Social Agent

Social agents believe that police should be involved in a wide range of activities without regard for their connection to law enforcement. Instead of viewing themselves as criminal catchers, the social agents consider themselves community problem solvers. They are troubleshooters who patch the holes that appear where the social fabric wears thin. They are happy to work with special-needs populations, such as the homeless, school kids, and those who require emergency services. Social agents fit well within a community policing unit.

The Law Enforcer

According to this view, duty is clearly set out in law, and law enforcers stress playing it "by the book." Because the police are specifically charged with apprehending all types of lawbreakers, they see themselves as generalized law enforcement agents. Although law enforcers may prefer working on serious crimes—which are more intriguing and rewarding in terms of achievement, prestige, and status—they see the police role as one of enforcing all statutes and ordinances. They perceive themselves as neither community social workers nor vengeance-seeking vigilantes. Simply put, they are professional law enforcement officers who perform the functions of detecting violations, identifying culprits, and taking the lawbreakers before a court. Law enforcers are devoted to the profession of police work and are the officers most likely to aspire to command rank.

The Watchman

The watchman style is characterized by an emphasis on the maintenance of public order as the police goal, not on law enforcement or general service. Watchmen ignore many infractions and requests for service unless they believe that the social or political order is jeopardized. They expect juveniles to misbehave and believe such mischief is best ignored or treated informally. Motorists will often be left alone if their driving does not endanger or annoy others. Vice and gambling are problems only when the currently accepted standards of public order are violated. Like the watchmen of old, these officers take action only if and when a problem arises. Watchmen are the most passive officers, more concerned with retirement benefits than crime rates.

Sources: William Muir, *Police: Streetcorner Politicians* (Chicago: University of Chicago Press, 1977); James Q. Wilson, *Varieties of Police Behavior* (Cambridge, MA: Harvard University Press, 1968).

---

may emphasize one area of law enforcement over another, their daily activities are likely to require them to engage in a wide variety of duties. A contemporary police officer can seldom choose to concentrate on crime fighting and ignore his other duties. Police departments are seeking public support through community police models and are reorienting the police role toward community outreach.[81]

Police Discretion

A critical aspect of a police officer's professional responsibility is the personal discretion each officer has in carrying out his daily activities. **Discretion** can involve the selective enforcement of the law, as when a vice-squad plainclothes officer decides not to take action against a tavern that is serving drinks after hours. Patrol officers use discretion when they decide to arrest one suspect for

discretion
The use of personal decision making and choice in carrying out operations in the criminal justice system.

CAREERS in criminal justice

INTELLIGENCE ANALYST

DUTIES AND CHARACTERISTICS OF THE JOB

Intelligence analysts (sometimes called investigative analysts) work primarily to piece together bits of information to form integrated views on subjects of interest to their employing agencies. For example, FBI intelligence analysts:

- Use language and with cultural and historical knowledge of specific areas or regions to discover threats
- Leverage local and national intelligence databases (e.g., INTERPOL) to develop fact-based reports and conclusions for the purpose of guiding investigations
- Shape intelligence policies through networks of contacts at all levels of government and internationally

In the case of federal law enforcement agencies, there are usually three career paths for intelligence analysts. Some are embedded with investigative squads and special agents in the field and provide support on active cases. Others work behind the scenes collecting data and reporting on their findings. Still others conduct research to identify trends and threats to security and public safety.

JOB OUTLOOK

Intelligence analyst positions are not as common as, say, those for municipal police officers, but there is an ongoing and growing need for competent analysts. In an era of global crime and interagency cooperation (across levels of government and between nations), intelligence analysts perform a valuable function.

SALARY

At the federal level, intelligence analyst salaries vary by the level of the position. In the FBI, for example, entry-level analysts start out at the GS-7 level, which as of this writing is around $35,000 per year. Experienced hires will often enter service at GS-11 or above. As of this writing, GS-11 pay starts at $50,790. Various opportunities for advancement and overtime exist, so these salaries should be interpreted as bare minimums. Pay is similar in state and local government, where other positions are often available.

OPPORTUNITIES

Opportunities for intelligence analysts exist in federal law enforcement agencies and large urban police

---

disorderly conduct but escort another home. Because police have the ability to deprive people of their liberty, arrest them, take them away in handcuffs, and even use deadly force to subdue them, their use of discretion is a vital concern.

The majority of police officers use a high degree of personal discretion in carrying out daily tasks, sometimes referred to in criminal justice as **low-visibility decision making**.[82] This terminology suggests that, unlike members of almost every other criminal justice agency, police are neither regulated in their daily procedures by administrative scrutiny nor subject to judicial review (except when their behavior clearly violates an offender's constitutional rights). As a result, the exercise of discretion by police may sometimes deteriorate into discrimination, violence, and other abusive practices. Nonetheless, the public recognizes the right of police to exercise their discretion, even if it means using force to control an unruly suspect while treating a more respectful one with deference and respect.[83]

> **low-visibility decision making**
> Decision making by police officers that is not subject to administrative review—for example, a decision not to arrest someone or not to stop a speeding vehicle.

Factors Influencing Discretion

A number of factors influence police discretion.[84] Some are expected; others are more controversial.

 Identify the factors that influence police discretion.

CRIME FACTORS Police discretion is related to the severity of the offense. There is relatively little, if any, discretion used for the most serious crimes such as murder and aggravated assault.[85] Far more personal discretion is available when police confront a suspect in a minor case involving a simple assault or trespass. Related to offense seriousness is the issue of who brings it to the attention of departments. At the federal level, the FBI, the DEA, and ATF are among the law enforcement agencies that employ a cadre of intelligence analysts. Police departments in high-crime urban areas also need intelligence analysts. For example, the Phoenix Police Department employs intelligence analysts to "conduct research and perform analysis of criminal information received by investigation units ... relating to criminal activities and relationships." According to the department, "work involves extensive reading, report writing, data analyses and development of hypothetical links between criminals and crime groups."

QUALIFICATIONS

In most cases, intelligence analysts are part of an agency's professional staff. The positions are nonsworn. For those drawn to careers in law enforcement but who do not necessarily want to work on the "front lines," such civilian positions may be desirable.

Because of the sensitive nature of the information intelligence analysts work with, securing a position can be something of an arduous process. The first stop is an application. The candidate must also meet various criteria, including but not limited to being a U.S. citizen, passing a drug test, and not having a criminal background. Assuming the applicant passes through this first stage, then a testing/interview phase usually begins. Various

computer-based tests and writing assignments will be conducted and evaluated. Interviews will gauge applicants' oral communication skills, interpersonal skills, organization, and thinking styles. Candidates who pass through the testing phase must also pass a background check.

Applicants for intelligence analysts positions, especially with federal agencies, must be willing to accept assignments in various places. FBI analysts often start at headquarters in Washington, D.C., but may also be assigned at any number of field offices around the country—and perhaps abroad.

EDUCATION AND TRAINING

Education and training requirements generally depend on the nature and level of the position. Law enforcement agencies often hire intelligence specialists not so much because of their formal education, but because of their special skills. Experience with certain foreign languages, an understanding of distant cultures, and familiarity with complex crime problems are often valuable assets.

Sources: Federal Bureau of Investigation, *Intelligence Analysts*, https://www.fbijobs.gov/121.asp (accessed June 2014); Phoenix Police Department, *Criminal Intelligence Analyst*, http://phoenix.gov/employment/descrip/code/62550.html (accessed June 2014).

police. If, for example, a police officer stumbles upon an altercation or break-in, the discretionary response may be different from a situation in which the officer is summoned by police radio.[86]

VICTIM FACTORS The relationship between the parties involved influences decision making and discretion. An altercation between two friends or relatives may be handled differently than an assault on a stranger. A case in point is policing domestic violence cases. Research indicates that police are reluctant to even respond to these kinds of cases because they are a constant source of frustration and futility.[87] Police sometimes intentionally delay responding to domestic disputes, hoping that by the time they get there the problem will be settled.[88] Victims, they believe, often fail to get help or change their abusive situation.[89]

ENVIRONMENTAL FACTORS The degree of discretion that an officer will exercise is at least partially defined by the living and working environment.[90] An officer who lives in the community she serves probably shares a large part of the community's beliefs and values and is likely to be sensitive to and respect the wishes of neighbors, friends, and relatives. However, conflict may arise when the police officer commutes to an assigned area of jurisdiction, as is often the case in inner-city precincts. The officer who holds personal values that are at odds with those of the community can exercise discretion in ways that conflict with the community's values and result in ineffective law enforcement.[91]

AP Images/Tracy Gitnick

Whether a police officer makes an arrest may depend on how the individual officer views offense severity. Here, officer Deon Joseph waits for a squad car to transport Marco Rodriguez to a detox center in the skid row area of downtown Los Angeles, rather than to jail.

overload hypothesis
The theory that police workload influences discretion so that as workload increases, less time and attention can be devoted to new cases, especially petty crimes.

According to the **overload hypothesis**, community crime rates may shape officer discretion. As local crime rates increase, police resources become strained to the breaking point; officers are forced to give less time and attention to each new case. The amount of attention they can devote to less serious crimes decreases, and they begin to treat petty offenders more leniently than officers in less crime-ridden neighborhoods might have done.[92]

DEPARTMENTAL FACTORS The policies, practices, and customs of the local police department are another influence on discretion. These conditions vary from department to department and strongly depend on the judgment of the chief and others in the organizational hierarchy.[93] Efforts by the administration to limit or shape the behavior of the officer on patrol may prompt it to issue directives aimed at influencing police conduct. For example, in an effort to crack down on a particular crime—such as adolescent drug abuse—the department can create a strict arrest and referral policy for those engaging in that crime.

A patrol officer's supervisor can influence discretion. The ratio of supervisory personnel to subordinates may also influence discretion. Departments with a high ratio of sergeants to patrol officers may experience fewer officer-initiated actions than ones in which fewer eyes are observing the action in the streets. Supervisory style may also affect how police use discretion. Robin Shepard Engel found that patrol officers supervised by sergeants who are take-charge types and like to participate in high levels of activity in the field themselves spend significantly more time per shift engaging in self-initiated and community policing or problem-solving activities than in administrative activities. In contrast, officers with supervisors whose style involves spending time mentoring and coaching subordinates are more likely to devote significantly more attention to engaging in administrative tasks.[94]

PEER FACTORS Police discretion is subject to peer pressure.[95] Police officers suffer a degree of social isolation because the job involves strange working conditions and hours, including being on 24-hour call, and their authority and responsibility to enforce the law may cause embarrassment during social encounters. At the same time, officers must handle irregular and emotionally demanding encounters involving the most personal and private aspects of people's lives. As a result, police officers turn to their peers for both on-the-job advice and off-the-job companionship, essentially forming a subculture that provides a source of status, prestige, and reward.

The peer group affects how police officers exercise discretion on two distinct levels. First, in an obvious, direct manner, other police officers dictate acceptable responses to street-level problems by displaying or withholding approval in office discussions. Second, the officer who takes the job seriously and desires the respect and friendship of others will take their advice, abide by their norms, and seek out the most experienced and most influential patrol officers on the force and follow their behavioral models.

demeanor
The way a person outwardly manifests his or her personality.

SUSPECT BEHAVIOR AND CHARACTERISTICS Researchers have also found that suspect behavior and characteristics weigh heavily in the use of discretionary powers.[96] Suspect **demeanor** (the attitude and appearance of the offender) is one of the most important influences. If an offender is surly, talks back, or otherwise challenges the officer's authority, formal action is more likely to be taken.[97] According to this view, a negative demeanor will result in formal police action.[98] Suspects who behave in a civil manner, accept responsibility for their offense, and admit their guilt are less likely to be sanctioned than those who display a less courteous demeanor.[99]

What if a suspect acts out physically or resists? Suspects who physically resist are much more likely to receive some form of physical coercion in return, but those who offer verbal disrespect are not likely to be physically coerced.[100] Therefore, police officers' response to a suspect's challenge to their authority is dependent on the way the challenge is delivered. Verbal challenges are met with verbal responses, and physical with physical.[101]

It is not particularly surprising that suspects' attitudes and behavior influence police officers' decisions. But what about the way a suspect *looks*? Should gender, age, or race matter? Ideally, the answer is no, but reality tells a different story. We look at the controversial issue of racial profiling in the accompanying Analyzing Criminal Justice Issues feature, but one finding is fairly clear: Race matters. It either influences officers' behavior directly or affects the level of suspicion officers display toward minority versus white suspects.[102] Gender is also important. One study found that women are less likely to be arrested than men.[103] And as for age, researchers have found that young people tend to be arrested more often or dealt with more harshly than their older counterparts.[104]

OFFICER CHARACTERISTICS The characteristics of police officers themselves are also important predictors of discretionary decision making. It is possible that officer education and experience are important, but researchers have yet to reach any consensus on this.[105] As for gender, researchers have found that female officers are less likely to use force than male officers.[106] Because female officers seem to have the ability to avoid violent encounters with citizens and to deescalate potentially violent arrest situations, they are typically the target of fewer citizen complaints.[107] Finally, there is some evidence that police officers' career aspirations affect their decision making. One study found that those officers who desired promotion tended to make the most arrests.[108]

Police discretion is one of the most often debated issues in criminal justice (see Concept Summary 7.1). On its face, the unequal enforcement of the law smacks of unfairness and violates the Constitution's doctrines of due process and equal protection. Yet if some discretion were not exercised, police would be forced to function as robots merely following the book. Administrators have sought to control discretion so that its exercise may be both beneficial to citizens and nondiscriminatory.[109]

CONCEPT SUMMARY 7.1
Factors that Influence Police Discretion

Category	Elements
Crime factors	Offense severity, officer's perceptions of offense severity, and reasons for the call
Victim factors	Victim–offender relationship
Environmental factors	Community culture and values
Departmental factors	Policies and orders, supervisory style and control
Peer factors	Friendships, norms, subculture
Suspect behavior and characteristics	Suspect demeanor, resistance, race, gender, and age
Officer characteristics	Officer's education, experience, gender, and career aspirations

analyzing criminal justice ISSUES

RACIAL PROFILING

The term *racial profiling* has been coined to describe the racial influence over police discretion. A number of empirical studies have found that state and local police officers routinely stop and/or search African American motorists at a rate far greater than their representation in the driving pool:

- Brian Withrow looked at police practices in Wichita, Kansas, and found that African American citizens are stopped at disproportionately higher rates than non–African American citizens and that African American and Hispanic citizens are more likely to be searched and arrested than non–African American and non-Hispanic citizens. Another of his studies, this one from San Jose, California, revealed that Hispanics made up 31 percent of the city's population but accounted for 43 percent of the people stopped.

- Researchers at Northeastern University in Boston used four statistical tests to analyze 1.6 million traffic citations issued between April 1, 2001, and June 30, 2003, in towns across Massachusetts and found the following: ticketing resident minorities disproportionately more than whites, ticketing all minorities disproportionately more than whites, searching minorities more often than whites, and issuing warnings to whites more often than to minorities. According to the study, 15 police departments failed all four tests, 42 failed three tests, 87 failed two tests, and 105 failed one.

- Richard Lundman's analysis of citizen encounters with police indicates that (a) minority citizens are more likely to be stopped than whites, but (b) searches of minority-driven vehicles are no more likely to yield drugs or contraband than searches of vehicles driven by whites.

- Michael Smith and Geoffrey Alpert found that once blacks and Hispanics are stopped, they are more likely than whites to be searched and arrested. Similar findings were reported by the New Jersey attorney general's office, which found that nearly 80 percent of people searched during traffic stops were black or Hispanic.

DOES RACE MATTER?

Some experts question whether profiling and racial discrimination are as widespread as currently feared. One approach has been to measure the attitudes that

AP Images/Ross D. Franklin

Amaria Lopez, of Phoenix, protests at the Arizona Capitol. She and other activists called for the repeal of a law that required Arizona police officers to question people about their immigration status if there was reasonable suspicion that they were in the United States illegally. In 2012, the U.S. Supreme Court invalidated portions of the law, a clear victory for its opponents.

minority citizens hold toward police. When Ronald Weitzer surveyed residents in three Washington, D.C., neighborhoods, he found that African Americans value racially integrated police services and welcome the presence of both white and African American police officers, a finding that would seem improbable if most white officers were racially biased. The African American community is generally supportive of the local police, especially when officers respond quickly to calls for service. It is unlikely that African Americans would appreciate rapid responses from racist police.

Another approach is to directly measure whether police treat minority and majority citizens differently—that is, use racial profiling in making decisions. Some studies show little evidence that police use racial profiling:

- David Eitle, Lisa Stolzenberg, and Stewart J. D'Alessio found that whites are more likely to be arrested for assaults than African Americans.

- Matt DeLisi and Bob Regoli found that whites are nine times more likely to experience DWI arrests than African Americans, a finding that would be unlikely if racial profiling were routine.

- Jon Gould and Stephen Mastrofski studied illegal police searches and found that race has little influence on police conduct. Although police may routinely conduct illegal searches, the suspect's race does not influence their tactics.

- Joseph Schafer, David Carter, and Andra Katz-Bannister found that although race plays some role in traffic stops, age and gender actually have a greater influence on police decision making.

- James Lange, Mark Johnson, and Robert Voas surveyed drivers on the New Jersey Turnpike and found that the proportion of speeding drivers who were identified as African American coincided with the proportion of African American drivers stopped by police. Their findings suggest that police are less likely to engage in racial profiling today and that efforts to control profiling have been successful.

- Geoffrey Alpert, Roger Dunham, and Michael Smith investigated racial profiling by the Miami-Dade Police Department and found that there was no pattern of discriminatory activity toward minority citizens during traffic stops, but there was some evidence of unequal treatment after the stop.

- Some studies show that searches of white suspects yield more contraband than black suspects, but this may be due to what Geoffrey Alpert has called the "carrying rate differential"—the likelihood that blacks rarely carry contraband for fear of getting caught. One young black male made this observation in his study: "We expect to be stopped and we know we're going to be searched—we're not stupid enough to carry."

- Tammy Rinehart Kochel and her colleagues found that, once stopped, minority suspects are more likely to be arrested than white suspects.

- In another interesting study, Robert Worden compared police stops between daylight and nighttime hours, finding that African Americans were no more likely to be stopped during the daylight hours than the nighttime hours, which suggests an absence of racial profiling. Presumably it would be easier for officers to detect a driver's race during the daylight hours compared to the nighttime hours.

CAN RACIAL PROFILING BE JUSTIFIED?

Whereas most experts condemn any form of racial profiling, two Harvard scholars, Mathias Risse and Richard Zeckhauser, have argued that profiling may have utility as a crime control tactic. First, they suggest that there is a significant correlation between membership in certain racial groups and the propensity to commit certain crimes. This explains why profiling takes place. Second, they suggest that given such a propensity, stopping, searching, or investigating members of such groups differentially will help curb crime. That is, racial profiling has utility because it can eliminate more crime than other law enforcement practices for equivalent expenditures of resources and disruption. If these assumptions are true, then racial profiling is morally justified in a broad range of cases, including many cases that tend to be controversial. Some people consider profiling abusive, but Risse and Zeckhauser believe that police abuse is a separate issue and should not be considered an aspect of profiling.

A key element of Risse and Zeckhauser's position is that racial profiling is not as harmful as crime and therefore is not too high a price to pay in order to achieve reductions in crime rates. Most stops are not abusive, and police try to act as civilly as possible under the circumstances. But as legal scholars Samuel Gross and Katherine Barnes point out, the assumption that a stop-and-search is intrinsically a minor inconvenience is questionable. Its effect can be corrosive:

> As the level of the police officer's interest increases, the cost to the innocent citizen escalates rapidly. It's one thing to get a speeding ticket and an annoying lecture … it's quite another to be told to step out of the car and to be questioned. … The questions may seem intrusive and out of line, but you can hardly refuse to answer an armed cop. At some point you realize you are not just another law-abiding citizen who's being checked out … like everyone else. You've been targeted. The trooper is not going through a

routine so he can let you go … he wants to find drugs on you. … Those of us who have not been through this sort of experience probably underestimate its impact. To be treated as a criminal is a basic insult to a person's self-image and his position in society. It cannot easily be shrugged off.

In other words, although some may argue that profiling can reduce some forms of criminal behavior, such as drug trafficking, the social costs it brings are too high a price to pay for modest crime reductions.

Most researchers have looked at traffic stops and resulting searches in their efforts to determine whether racial profiling is a problem. Recently, economists have called for a different approach: focusing only on successful searches. A successful search is one that turns up evidence of contraband. Nicola Persico and Petra Todd have argued that an unbiased officer will focus his or her efforts on people who, if searched, are mostly likely to possess contraband. In contrast, a biased officer will take pleasure from searching people because they are minorities. This is known as the "outcome test," and it calls for looking past who is stopped and focusing on what the end result of a stop is. In other words, just because one group may be stopped more than another does not necessarily mean profiling is occurring. It could just be good police work! Robin Engel has been critical of this argument, claiming that it makes too many assumptions about how policing is really done.

CRITICAL THINKING

1. What, if anything, can be done to reduce racial bias on the part of police? Would adding minority officers help? Would it be a form of racism to assign minority officers to minority neighborhoods?

2. Would research showing that police are more likely to make arrests in interracial incidents than in intraracial incidents constitute evidence of racism?

3. Police spot three men of Middle Eastern descent carrying a large, heavy box into a crowded building. Should they stop and question them and demand to look into the carton? Is this racial profiling?

Sources: Brian Withrow, "Race-Based Policing: A Descriptive Analysis of the Wichita Stop Study," *Police Practice and Research* 5 (2004): 223–240; Brian Withrow, "A Comparative Analysis of Commonly Used Benchmarks in Racial Profiling: A Research Note," *Justice Research and Policy* 6 (2004): 71–92; Amy Farrell, Jack McDevitt, Lisa Bailey, Carsten Andresen, and Erica Pierce, "Massachusetts Racial and Gender Profiling Final Report" (Boston: Northeastern University, 2004), http://iris .lib.neu.edu/cgi/viewcontent.cgi?article=1001&context=race_justice_pubs (accessed June 2014); Richard Lundman, "Driver Race, Ethnicity, and Gender and Citizen Reports of Vehicle Searches by Police and Vehicle Search Hits," *Journal of Criminal Law and Criminology* 94 (2004): 309–350; Michael Smith and Geoffrey Alpert, "Explaining Police Bias: A Theory of Social Conditioning and Illusory Correlation," *Criminal Justice and Behavior* 34 (2007): 1262–1283; *Interim Report of the State Police Review Team Regarding Allegations of Racial Profiling* (Trenton, NJ: Office of the Attorney General, 1999); Ronald Weitzer, "White, Black, or Blue Cops? Race and Citizen Assessments of Police Officers," *Journal of Criminal Justice* 28 (2000): 313–324; David Eitle, Lisa Stolzenberg, and Stewart J. D'Alessio, "Police Organizational Factors, the Racial Composition of the Police, and the Probability of Arrest," *Justice Quarterly* 22 (2005): 30–57; Matt DeLisi and Robert Regoli, "Race, Conventional Crime, and Criminal Justice: The Declining Importance of Skin Color," *Journal of Criminal Justice* 27 (1999): 549–557; Jon Gould and Stephen Mastrofski, "Suspect Searches: Assessing Police Behavior Under the U.S. Constitution," *Criminology and Public Policy* 3 (2004): 315–362; Joseph Schafer, David Carter, and Andra Katz-Bannister, "Studying Traffic Stop Encounters," *Journal of Criminal Justice* 32 (2004): 159–170; James Lange, Mark Johnson, and Robert Voas, "Testing the Racial Profiling Hypothesis for Seemingly Disparate Traffic Stops on the New Jersey Turnpike," *Justice Quarterly* 22 (2005): 193–223; Geoffrey P. Alpert, Roger G. Dunham, and Michael R. Smith, "Investigating Racial Profiling by the Miami-Dade Police Department: A Multimethod Approach," *Criminology and Public Policy* 6 (2007): 25–56; Geoffrey P. Alpert, "Eliminate Race as the Only Reason for Police-Citizen Encounters," *Criminology and Public Policy* 6 (2007): 671–678; Tammy Rinehart Kochel, David Wilson, and Stephen Mastrofski, "The Effect of Suspect Race on Officers' Arrest Decisions," *Criminology* 49 (2011): 473–512; Robert Worden, Sarah McLean, and Andrew Wheeler, "Testing for Racial Profiling with the Veil-of-Darkness Method," *Police Quarterly* 15 (2012): 92–111; Mathias Risse and Richard Zeckhauser, "Racial Profiling," *Philosophy and Public Affairs* 32 (2004): 131–170; Samuel Gross and Katherine Barnes, "Road Work: Racial Profiling and Drug Interdiction on the Highway," *Michigan Law Review* 101 (2003): 651–754, at 745–746; Nicola Persico and Petra E. Todd, "The Hit Rates Test for Racial Bias in Motor-Vehicle Searches," *Justice Quarterly* 25 (2008): 37–53; Robin S. Engel, "A Critique of the 'Outcome Test' in Racial Profiling Research," *Justice Quarterly* 25 (2008): 1–36.

Problems of Policing

Law enforcement is not an easy job. The role ambiguity, social isolation, and threat of danger present in working the streets are the police officer's constant companions. What effects do these strains have on police? The most significant problems are job stress, fatigue, violence and brutality, and corruption.

Job Stress

The complexity of their role, the need to exercise prudent discretion, the threat of using violence and having violence used against them, and isolation from the rest of society all take a toll on law enforcement officers. Police officer stress leads to negative attitudes, burnout, loss of enthusiasm and commitment (cynicism), increased apathy, substance abuse problems, divorce, health problems, and many other social, personal, and job-related problematic behaviors.[110] Evidence suggests that police officers are often involved in marital disputes and even incidents of domestic violence, which may be linked to stress.[111] Stress may not be constant, but at some time during their career (usually the middle years), most officers will feel its effects.[112]

CAUSES OF STRESS A number of factors have been associated with job stress. Some are related to the difficulties that police officers have in maintaining social and family relationships, considering their schedule and workload.[113] Police suffer stress in their personal lives when they bring the job home or when their work hours are shifted, causing family disruptions.[114] Those who perceive themselves as alienated from family and friends at home are more likely to feel stress on the job.[115]

Some stressors are job related. The pressure of being on duty 24 hours per day leads to stress and emotional detachment from both work and public needs. Policing is a dangerous profession, and officers are at risk of many forms of job-related injury. Every year, several officers are killed. On the other hand, law enforcement officers contemplating retirement also report high stress levels. So although the job may be dangerous, many officers are reluctant to leave it.[116]

Stress has been related to internal conflict with administrative policies that deny officers support and a meaningful role in decision making.[117] Stress may result when officers are forced to adapt to a department's new methods of policing, such as community-oriented policing, and they are skeptical about the change in policy.[118] Other stressors include poor training, substandard equipment, inadequate pay, lack of opportunity, job dissatisfaction, role conflict, exposure to brutality, and fears about competence, success, and safety.[119] Some officers may feel stress because they believe that the court system favors the rights of the criminal and handcuffs the police; others might be sensitive to a perceived lack of support from governmental officials and the general public.[120] Still others believe that their superiors care little about their welfare.[121] And stress levels are far from constant. Researchers who have monitored officers' heart rates during the course of their shifts have found that, indeed, stress levels fluctuate depending on the situations an officer encounters.[122]

Police psychologists have divided these stressors into four distinct categories:

- External stressors, such as verbal abuse from the public, justice system inefficiency, and liberal court decisions that favor the criminal. What are perceived to be antipolice judicial decisions may alienate police and reduce their perceptions of their own competence.[123]

- Organizational stressors, such as low pay, excessive paperwork, arbitrary rules, and limited opportunity for advancement.

- Duty stressors, such as rotating shifts, work overload, boredom, fear, and danger.

- Individual stressors, such as discrimination, marital difficulties, and personality problems.[124]

The effects of stress can be shocking. Police work has been related to both physical and psychological ailments. Police have a significantly high rate of premature death caused by such conditions as heart disease and diabetes. They also experience a disproportionate number of divorces and other marital problems. Research indicates that police officers in some departments, but not all, have higher suicide rates than the general public. (Recent research shows that New York City police have suicide rates equal to or lower than the general public, and some researchers have found a lower than average police suicide rate in other areas of the country.[125]) Alcohol and drug abuse have been linked to stress, as well.[126] Police who feel stress may not be open to adopting new ideas and programs such as community policing.[127]

COMBATING STRESS   The more support police officers get in the workplace, the lower their feelings of stress and anxiety.[128] Consequently, departments have attempted to fight job-related stress by training officers to cope with its effects. Today, stress training includes diet information, biofeedback, relaxation and meditation, and exercise. Many departments include stress management as part of an overall wellness program that is also designed to promote physical and mental health, fitness, and good nutrition.[129] Some programs have included family members: they may be better able to help the officer cope if they have more knowledge about the difficulties of police work. Research also shows that because police perceive many benefits from their job and enjoy the quality of life it provides, stress-reduction programs might help officers focus on the positive aspects of police work.[130]

Stress is a critically important aspect of police work. Further research is needed to create valid methods of identifying police officers who are under considerable stress and to devise effective stress-reduction programs.[131]

Fatigue

L07   Recognize the consequences of stress and fatigue.

Nearly everyone has been tired at work from time to time. While on-the-job sleepiness is inconsequential for many workers, it can lead to disaster for others. No one wants airline pilots to fall asleep, and the prospect of a truck driver sleeping behind the wheel is equally disturbing. What about a police officer? A police officer who is overly tired may be at higher risk of acting inappropriately or being injured on the job.

The problem of "tired cops"[132] has largely been overlooked, but it should not be.[133] Police officers often work lengthy shifts with unpredictable hours. The *Boston Globe* investigated one agency and found that 16 officers worked more than 80 hours in a week.[134] One even worked 130 hours! While it is difficult to fault anyone for seeking overtime pay, too much work can lead to disaster. Here are some examples:

- A Michigan police officer working nearly 24 hours straight crashes his cruiser while chasing a fleeing motorist. He is critically injured.

- In California, a sheriff's deputy working alone drifts off a deserted highway and is killed instantly when his patrol car crashes into a tree.

- An officer in Florida who has had trouble staying awake runs a red light in her patrol car and crashes into a van driven by a deputy sheriff, injuring him severely.

- A police officer driving home from working in Ohio nods off at the wheel, begins swerving in and out of traffic, and runs off the road, striking and killing a man jogging down the sidewalk.[135]

CONTROLLING POLICE FATIGUE   What can be done to control police fatigue? One option is for administrators to pay special attention to scheduling so that officers do not work too much overtime. Another is for administrators to adopt policies that place limitations on second jobs. Many officers moonlight as security guards, which may affect their on-the-job performance. A recent government report offered several other recommendations for limiting fatigue. Administrators should:

- Review the policies, procedures, and practices that affect shift scheduling and rotation, overtime, moonlighting, the number of consecutive hours allowed, and the way in which the department deals with overly tired employees.

- Assess how much of a voice officers are given in work-hour and shift-scheduling decisions. The number of hours that officers work and the time of day they are assigned to work affect their personal, social, family, and professional lives. Excluding officers from decisions affecting this arena increases stress, which in turn reduces their ability to deal with fatigue and tends to diminish their job performance and ability to deal with stress.

- Assess the level of fatigue that officers experience, the quality of their sleep, and how tired they are while on the job, as well as their attitudes toward fatigue and work-hour issues.

- Review recruit and in-service training programs to determine whether officers are receiving adequate information about the importance of good sleep habits, the hazards associated with fatigue and shift work, and strategies for managing them. Are officers taught to view fatigue as a safety issue? Are they trained to recognize drowsiness as a factor in vehicle crashes?[136]

Violence and Brutality

Police officers are empowered to use force and violence in pursuit of their daily tasks. Some scholars argue that the use of violent measures is the core of the police role.[137] Even so, since their creation, U.S. police departments have wrestled with the charge that they are brutal, physically violent organizations. Early police officers resorted to violence and intimidation to gain the respect that was not freely given by citizens. In the 1920s, the Wickersham Commission detailed numerous instances of **police brutality**, including the use of the "third degree" to extract confessions.

Today, police brutality continues to be a concern, especially when police use excessive violence against members of the minority community. The nation looked on in disgust when a videotape was aired on network newscasts showing members of the Los Angeles Police Department beating, kicking, and using electric stun guns on Rodney King. Other incidents reported in both national and local media over the years also illustrate the persistent problems that police departments have in regulating violent contacts with citizens.

WHO ARE THE PROBLEM COPS? Evidence shows that only a small proportion of officers are continually involved in problem behavior.[138] What kind of police officer gets involved in problem behavior? Aggressive cops may be ones who overreact to the stress of police work while at the same time feeling socially isolated. They believe that the true sources of their frustration—such as corrupt politicians or liberal judges—are shielded from their anger, so they take their frustrations out on readily available targets: vulnerable people in their immediate environment.[139]

Some officers are chronic offenders. Research conducted in a southeastern city by Kim Michelle Lersch and Tom Mieczkowski found that a few officers (7 percent) were chronic offenders who accounted for a significant portion of all citizen complaints (33 percent). Those officers receiving the bulk of the complaints tended to be younger and less experienced, and they had been accused of harassment or violence after a proactive encounter that they had initiated. Although repeat offenders were more likely to be accused of misconduct by minority citizens, there was little evidence that attacks were racially motivated.[140]

police brutality
Actions such as using abusive language, making threats, using force or coercion unnecessarily, prodding with nightsticks, and stopping and searching people to harass them.

L08 Distinguish between brutality and corruption.

YOUR OPINION: Is police brutality a problem near where you live?

PUBLIC OPINION:

YES: 31%

NO: 65%

REALITY: According to a Gallup poll, roughly one-third of survey respondents feel police brutality is a problem. This implies that roughly one in three police officers acts violently toward citizens. Like fear of crime, the reality of the underlying problem is much less of a problem than people think it is. There are some "bad apples" who act with unjustifiable force toward criminal suspects, but outright police brutality is quite low. Indeed, statistics from the U.S. Justice Department show that among persons who had contact with the police in one year, only 1.4 percent of them reported having force used or threatened against them. Clearly the perceptions of police brutality fail to line up with the reality.

DISCUSSION: Why do so many people seem to feel police brutality is a problem? What exactly is police brutality? How should it be measured? Who should conduct the measurements? Why do you feel that way?

Sources: Sourcebook of Criminal Justice Statistics, *Respondents' Perceptions of Police Brutality in Their Area*, http://www.albany.edu/sourcebook/pdf/t200022005.pdf (accessed June 2014); Christine Eith and Matthew R. Durose, *Contacts Between Police and the Public, 2008* (Washington, DC: Bureau of Justice Statistics, 2008), p. 1.

Stanley Wrice, center, convicted of rape and sentenced to 100 years in prison in 1982, speaks to the media with his lawyer, Heidi Linn Lambros, left, and his daughter, Gail Lewis, while leaving the Pontiac Correctional Center in Illinois. Wrice was released after serving more than 30 years in prison. He claimed for decades he was beaten and coerced into confessing to the rape by Chicago police detectives who worked for disgraced former Chicago police lieutenant Jon Burge, who is now in federal prison after being convicted of perjury related to torture allegations.

Efforts to deal with these problem cops are now being undertaken in police departments around the nation. A number of departments have instituted early-warning systems to change the behavior of individual officers who have been identified as having performance problems. The basic intervention strategy involves a combination of deterrence and education. According to the deterrence strategy, officers who are subject to intervention will presumably change their behavior in response to a perceived threat of punishment. Early-warning systems operate on the assumption that training, as part of the intervention, can help officers improve their performance. Evaluations show that early-warning systems appear to have a dramatic effect on reducing citizen complaints and other indicators of problematic police performance among those officers subject to intervention.[141]

DEALING WITH PROBLEM COPS

Detailed rules of engagement that limit the use of force are common in major cities. However, the creation of departmental rules limiting behavior is often haphazard and is usually a reaction to a crisis situation (for example, a citizen is seriously injured) instead of part of a systematic effort to improve police–citizen interactions.[142] Some departments have developed administrative policies that stress limiting the use of force and containing armed offenders until specially trained backup teams are sent to take charge of the situation. Administrative policies have been found to be an effective control on deadly force, and their influence can be enhanced if the chief of police gives them the proper support.[143]

The most significant factors in controlling police brutality may be the threat of civil judgments against individual officers who use excessive force, police chiefs who ignore or condone violent behavior, and the cities and towns in which they are employed. Civilians routinely file civil actions against police departments when they believe that officers have violated their civil rights. Police may be sued when a victim believes that excessive force was used during his or her arrest or custody. Civilians may collect damages if they can show that the force used was unreasonable, considering all the circumstances known to the officer at the time he or she acted. Excessive-force suits commonly occur when police use a weapon, such as a gun or baton, to subdue an unarmed person who is protesting his or her treatment. The U.S. Supreme Court in 1978 (*Monell v. Department of Social Services*) ruled that local agencies could be held liable under the federal Civil Rights Act (42 U.S.C. 1983) for actions of their employees if such actions were part of an official custom or practice.[144]

The few "bad apples" who ruin it for the rest of the police force can have harmful effects on a department's public image. In response, many urban police departments have implemented neighborhood and community policing models to improve relations with the public. Improved trust in police may lead to a perception that brutality is not a problem.[145]

Corruption

Police departments have almost always wrestled with the problem of controlling illegal and unprofessional behavior by their officers. **Corruption** pervaded the U.S. police when the early departments were first formed. In the nineteenth century, police officers systematically ignored violations of laws related to drinking, gambling, and prostitution in return for regular payoffs. Some entered into relationships with professional criminals, especially pickpockets. Illegal behavior was tolerated in return for goods or information. Police officers helped politicians gain office by allowing electoral fraud to flourish. Some senior officers sold promotions to higher ranks within the police department.[146]

Since the early nineteenth century, scandals involving police abuse of power have occurred in many urban cities, and elaborate methods have been devised to control or eliminate the problem. Although most police officers are not corrupt, the few who are dishonest bring discredit to the entire profession. And corruption is often hard to combat because the police code of silence demands that officers never turn in their peers, even if they engage in corrupt or illegal practices.[147] Fortunately, however, recent studies reveal that corruption is quite rare and that career-ending misconduct is the exception.[148]

VARIETIES OF CORRUPTION Police corruption can include a number of activities. In a general sense, it involves misuse of authority by police officers in a manner designed to produce personal gain for themselves or others.[149] However, debate continues over whether a desire for personal gain is an essential part of corruption. Some experts argue that the unnecessary use of force, unreasonable searches, and an immoral personal life also constitute police misconduct and should be considered as serious as corruption devoted to economic gain.

Scholars have attempted to create typologies categorizing the forms that the abuse of police powers can take. For example, the **Knapp Commission**, a public body set up to investigate the New York City police in the 1970s, classified abusers into two groups: **meat eaters** and **grass eaters**.[150] Meat eaters aggressively misuse police power for personal gain by demanding bribes, threatening legal action, or cooperating with criminals. Across the country, police officers have been accused, indicted, and convicted of shaking down club owners and other businesspeople.[151] In contrast, grass eaters accept payoffs when their everyday duties place them in a position to be solicited by the public. For example, police officers have been investigated for taking bribes to look the other way while neighborhood bookmakers ply their trade.[152] The Knapp Commission concluded that the vast majority of police officers on the take are grass eaters, although the few meat eaters who are caught capture all the headlines. In 1993, another police scandal prompted the formation of the **Mollen Commission**, which found that some New York cops were actively involved in violence and drug dealing.

Other police experts have attempted to create models to better understand police corruption. Several types of corruption have been identified:[153]

- *Internal corruption.* This corruption takes place among police officers themselves, involving both the bending of departmental rules and the outright performance of illegal acts. For example, Chicago police officers conspired to sell relatively new police cars to other officers at cut-rate prices, forcing the department to purchase new cars unnecessarily. A major scandal hit the Boston Police Department when a captain was indicted in an exam tampering and selling scheme. Numerous officers bought promotion exams from the captain, and others had him lower the scores of rivals who were competing for the same job.[154]

- *Selective enforcement or nonenforcement.* This form occurs when police officers abuse or exploit their discretion. If an officer frees a drug dealer in

corruption
Exercising legitimate discretion for improper reasons or using illegal means to achieve approved goals.

Knapp Commission
A public body that conducted an investigation into police corruption in New York City in the early 1970s and uncovered a widespread network of payoffs and bribes.

meat eater
A term used to describe a police officer who actively solicits bribes and vigorously engages in corrupt practices.

grass eater
A term used to describe a police officer who accepts payoffs when everyday duties place him or her in a position to be solicited by the public.

Mollen Commission
An investigative unit set up to inquire into police corruption in New York City in the 1990s.

return for valuable information, that is considered a legitimate use of discretion; if the officer does so for money, that is an abuse of police power.

■ *Active criminality.* This is participation by police in serious criminal behavior. Police may use their positions of trust and power to commit the very crimes they are entrusted with controlling. The case of New York police detectives Louis Eppolito and Stephen Caracappa is perhaps the most shocking example of police criminality in recent history. Eppolito and Caracappa sold police files on key witnesses to the mob and were convicted on charges linking them to 11 mob hits.[155]

■ *Bribery and extortion.* This includes practices in which law enforcement roles are exploited specifically to raise money. Bribery is initiated by the citizen; extortion is initiated by the officer. Bribery or extortion can be a one-shot transaction, as when a traffic violator offers a police officer $500 to forget about issuing a summons. Or the relationship can be an ongoing one, in which the officer solicits (or is offered) regular payoffs to ignore criminal activities, such as gambling or narcotics dealing. This is known as "being on the pad." Sometimes police officers accept routine bribes and engage in petty extortion without considering themselves corrupt. They consider these payments as unofficial fringe benefits of police work. For example, *mooching* involves receiving free gifts of coffee, cigarettes, meals, and so on in exchange for possible future acts of favoritism. *Chiseling* occurs when officers demand admission to entertainment events or price discounts. And *shopping* involves taking small items, such as cigarettes, from a store whose door was accidentally left unlocked after business hours.[156]

THE CAUSES OF CORRUPTION No single explanation satisfactorily accounts for the various forms that the abuse of power takes:

■ *Police personality.* One view puts the blame on the type of person who becomes a police officer. This position holds that policing tends to attract lower-class individuals who do not have the financial means to maintain a coveted middle-class lifestyle. As they develop the cynical, authoritarian police personality, accepting graft seems an all-too-easy method of achieving financial security.

■ *Institutions and practices.* A second view is that the wide discretion that police enjoy, coupled with the low visibility they maintain with the public and their own supervisors, makes them likely candidates for corruption. In addition, the code of secrecy maintained by the police subculture helps insulate corrupt officers from the law. Similarly, police managers, most of whom have risen through the ranks, are reluctant to investigate corruption or punish wrongdoers. Thus, corruption may also be viewed as a function of police institutions and practices.[157]

■ *Moral ambivalence.* A third position holds that corruption is a function of society's ambivalence toward many forms of vice-related criminal behavior that police officers are sworn to control. Unenforceable laws governing moral standards promote corruption because they create large groups with an interest in undermining law enforcement. These include consumers—people who gamble, wish to drink after the legal closing hour, or patronize a prostitute—who do not want to be deprived of their chosen form of recreation. Even though the consumers may not actively corrupt police officers, their existence creates a climate that tolerates active corruption by others.[158] Because vice cannot be controlled and the public apparently wants it to continue, the officer may have little resistance to inducements for monetary gain offered by law violators.

■ *Environmental conditions.* A fourth position is that corruption may be linked to specific environmental and social conditions that enhance the likelihood that police officers may become involved in misconduct. For example, in some areas a rapid increase in the minority residential population may be viewed as a threat to dominant group interests. Police in these areas may become overly aggressive and routinely use coercive strategies. The conflict produced by these outcomes may lead to antagonism between the police and the minority public, and to eventual police misconduct of all types. One recent study, in which social/ecological conditions in New York City police precincts and divisions were associated with patterns of police misconduct from 1975 to 1996, found that misconduct cases involving bribery, extortion, excessive force, and other abuses of police authority were linked to trends in neighborhood structural disadvantage, increasing population mobility, and increases in the Latino population.[159]

■ *Corrupt departments.* It has also been suggested that police corruption is generated at the departmental level and that conditions within the department produce and nurture deviance.[160] In some departments, corrupt officers band together and form what is called a "rotten pocket."[161] Rotten pockets help institutionalize corruption because their members expect newcomers to conform to their illegal practices and to a code of secrecy.

■ *Officer characteristics.* A study of police misconduct in the New York City Police Department revealed that factors such as officer race, prior criminal history, and problems in prior jobs were associated with on-the-job misconduct. The authors argued that "[b]y screening out those with prior arrests and prior employment problems, departments can significantly reduce the likelihood of hiring future 'bad cops.'"[162]

CONTROLLING CORRUPTION How can police misconduct be controlled? One approach is to strengthen the internal administrative review process within police departments. A strong and well-supported internal affairs division has been linked to lowered corruption rates.[163] However, asking police to police themselves is not a simple task. Officers are often reluctant to discipline their peers. One review of disciplinary files of New York City police officers found that many miscreants escaped punishment when their cases were summarily dismissed by the police department without anyone ever interviewing victims or witnesses or making any other efforts to examine the evidence.[164] One reason may be the blue curtain mentality that inhibits police from taking action against their fellow officers. Surveys indicate that police officers are more reluctant than ordinary citizens to report unethical behavior on the part of their colleagues.[165] Engaging in illegal brutality or bending the rules of procedure falls under the code of silence.[166]

Another approach, instituted by then–New York Commissioner Patrick Murphy in the wake of the Knapp Commission, is the **accountability system**. This holds that supervisors at each level are directly accountable for the illegal behaviors of the officers under them. Consequently, a commander can be demoted or forced to resign if one of her command officers is found guilty of corruption.[167] However, close scrutiny by a department can lower officer morale and create the suspicion that the officers' own supervisors distrust them.

Police departments have also organized outside review boards or special prosecutors to investigate reported incidents of corruption. However, outside investigators and special prosecutors are often limited by their lack of intimate knowledge of day-to-day operations. As a result, they depend on the testimony of a few officers who are willing to cooperate, either to save themselves from prosecution or because they have a compelling moral commitment. Outside evaluators

Web App 7.2

For more information about police attitudes toward abuse of authority, read the document here: https://www.ncjrs.gov/pdffiles1/nij/181312.pdf.

accountability system

A system that makes police supervisors responsible for the behavior of the officers in their command.

also face the problem of the blue curtain, which is quickly closed when police officers feel that their department is under scrutiny.

A more realistic solution to corruption, albeit a difficult one, might be to change the social context of policing. Police operations must be made more visible, and the public must be given freer access to police operations. All too often, the public finds out about police problems only when a scandal hits the newspaper. Another option is that some of the vice-related crimes the police now deal with might be decriminalized or referred to other agencies. Although decriminalization of vice cannot in itself end the problem, it could lower the pressure placed on individual police officers and help eliminate their moral dilemmas.

Use of Force

Despite some highly publicized incidents that get a lot of media attention, data show that the use of force is not a very common event. A national survey on police contacts with civilians sponsored by the federal government found that in a single year, of the 40 million people who had one or more police contacts, about 1.4 percent (574,000 persons) reported that an officer used or threatened to use force.[168] African Americans (3.4 percent) and Hispanics (1.6 percent) were more likely than whites (1.2 percent) to experience police threat or use of force during the contact; young people (ages 16 to 29) were almost three times more likely to experience force than people over 29. When force was applied, it was most likely to be pushing or grabbing (approximately 53 percent of cases). In about 25 percent of the 574,000 force incidents, a police officer pointed a gun at the individual. These data indicate that police use of force may not be as common as previously believed, but it still remains a central part of the police role.

Race and Force

The routine use of force may be diminishing, but there is still debate over whether police are more likely to get rough with minority suspects. The national survey on police contacts with civilians found that African Americans and Hispanics were more likely than whites to experience police threat or use of force as a consequence of police contact. Cities with large African American populations also experience the highest amount of lethal violence by police.[169]

Considering this evidence, it is not surprising that surveys of minority group members show they are more likely to disapprove of the police view of force than majority group members.[170] Minority citizens are much more likely to claim that police "hassle them" by stopping them or watching them closely when they have done nothing wrong.[171]

Race may be a factor that determines the outcome of police–citizen encounters, but it is certainly not the only one. Joel Garner's study of police encounters with citizens, using a wide variety of samples taken in different locales, found that race actually played an insignificant role in the decision to use force.[172] The suspect's behavior is a much more powerful determinant of police response than age or race. William Terrill studied 3,544 police–suspect encounters and found that situational factors often influence the extent to which force is applied. Use of force seems to escalate when a police officer gives a suspect a second chance (such as "Dump the beer out of your car, and I'll let you go"), but the suspect hesitates or defies the order.[173] People who resist police orders or actually grapple with officers are much more likely to be the target of force than those who are respectful, passive, and noncombative.

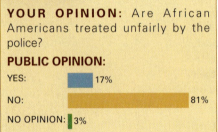

FACT CHECK ☑

YOUR OPINION: Are African Americans treated unfairly by the police?

PUBLIC OPINION:

YES: 17%

NO: 81%

NO OPINION: 3%

REALITY: Gallup surveyed African Americans in 2013 and asked, "Can you think of any occasion in the last thirty days when you felt you were treated unfairly in … dealings with the police …?" Almost one in five respondents answered with a yes. Limiting responses to males under the age of 35, the percentage answering yes went up to approximately one in four. That is, 25 percent of African Americans under the age of 35 reported they were treated unfairly by the police. However, African American females were considerably less likely than male African Americans to claim unfair treatment by the police. Unfortunately, there is a wealth of research showing uneven treatment across various races throughout the criminal justice process.

DISCUSSION: Does reality match up with perceptions in this case? If so, why are African Americans treated differently by police? Police departments themselves have become more racially diverse over the years. Has this helped or hurt the situation?

Sources: Gallup, *In U.S., 24% of Young Black Men Say Police Dealings Unfair*, http://www.gallup.com/poll/163523/one-four-young-black-men-say-police-dealings-unfair.aspx (accessed June 2014); Samuel Walker, Cassia Spohn, and Miriam DeLone, *The Color of Justice: Race, Ethnicity, and Crime in America*, 5th ed. (Belmont, CA: Cengage, 2012).

The general public seems to understand the situational use of force: Even people who condemn police violence—such as racial minorities—are more supportive of its use if the officer is in danger or a suspect is confrontational.[174] So the evidence suggests that whether African American or white, suspect behavior may be a more important determinant of force than race or ethnicity.

Deadly Force

Deadly force is force that is likely to cause death or significant bodily harm. The FBI defines it as "the intentional use of a firearm or other instrument resulting in a high probability of death."[175] The justification for the use of deadly force can be traced to English common law, in which almost every criminal offense was a felony and bore the death penalty. The use of deadly force in the course of arresting a felon was considered expedient, saving the state the burden of trial (the "fleeing felon" rule).[176]

Although the media depict hero cops in a constant stream of deadly shoot-outs in which scores of bad guys are killed, the number of people killed by the police each year is somewhere around 400.[177] Although these data are encouraging, some researchers believe that the actual number of police shootings is far greater and may be hidden or masked by a number of factors. For example, coroners may be intentionally or accidentally underreporting police homicides by almost half.[178]

FACTORS RELATED TO POLICE SHOOTINGS Is police use of deadly force a random occurrence, or are there social, legal, and environmental factors associated with its use? The following seven patterns have been related to police shootings:

■ *Local and national violence levels.* The higher the levels of violence in a community, the more likely police in the area will use deadly force.[179] A number of studies have found that fatal police shootings were closely related to reported national violent crime rates and criminal homicide rates. Police officers kill civilians at a higher rate in years when the general level of violence in the nation is higher. The perception of danger may contribute to the use of violent means for self-protection.[180]

■ *Exposure to violence.* Police officers may be exposed to violence when they are forced to confront the emotionally disturbed. Some distraught people attack police as a form of suicide.[181] This tragic event has become so common

deadly force
The intentional use of a firearm or other instrument, resulting in a high probability of death.

L09 Explain the difference between deadly and nondeadly force.

The possible use of deadly force is an integral part of police work. Here, an officer aims his gun at a suspect in a home invasion case. What steps have been taken to control police use of deadly force?

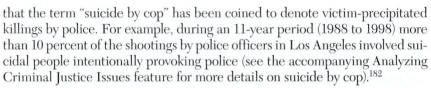

that the term "suicide by cop" has been coined to denote victim-precipitated killings by police. For example, during an 11-year period (1988 to 1998) more than 10 percent of the shootings by police officers in Los Angeles involved suicidal people intentionally provoking police (see the accompanying Analyzing Criminal Justice Issues feature for more details on suicide by cop).[182]

■ *Workload.* A relationship exists among police violence and the number of police on the street, the number of calls for service, the number and nature of police dispatches, the number of arrests made in a given jurisdiction, and police exposure to stressful situations.

■ *Firearms availability.* Cities that experience a large number of crimes committed with firearms are also likely to have high police violence rates. A strong association has been found between police use of force and gun density (the proportion of suicides and murders committed with a gun).[183]

■ *Social conflict.* According to the threat hypothesis, more police are killed in cities with a large underclass.[184] The greatest number of police shootings occur in areas that have significant disparities in economic opportunity and high levels of income inequality.[185] Economic disadvantage within the minority community, coupled with political alienation, leads to a climate in which police–citizen conflict is sharpened. Politically excluded groups may turn to violence to gain ends that those not excluded can acquire with conventional tactics. One conflict-reduction approach is to add minority police officers. However, recent research by Brad Smith shows that the mere addition of minority officers to a department is not sufficient to reduce levels of police violence.[186] The presence of an African American mayor has also been linked with reductions in the likelihood of police–citizen violence.[187] Such a mayor may help reduce feelings of powerlessness in the minority community, which in turn reduces anger against the state, of which the police are the most visible officials.

■ *Administrative policies.* The philosophy, policies, and practices of individual police chiefs and departments significantly influence the police use of deadly force.[188] Departments that stress restrictions on the use of force generally have lower shooting rates than those that favor tough law enforcement and encourage officers to shoot when necessary. Poorly written or ambivalent policies encourage shootings because they allow the officer at the scene to decide when deadly force is warranted, often under conditions of high stress and tension.

■ *Race.* No other issue is as important to the study of the police use of deadly force as racial discrimination. A number of critics have claimed that police are more likely to shoot and kill minority offenders than they are whites. In a famous statement, sociologist Paul Takagi charged that police have "one trigger finger for whites and another for African-Americans."[189] Takagi's complaint was supported by a number of research studies that showed that a disproportionate number of police killings involved minority citizens— almost 80 percent in some of the cities surveyed.[190]

Do these findings alone indicate that police discriminate in the use of deadly force? Some pioneering research by James Fyfe helps provide an answer to this question. In his study of New York City shootings over a five-year period, Fyfe found that police officers were most likely to shoot suspects who were armed and with whom they became involved in violent confrontations. Once such factors as being armed with a weapon, being involved in a violent crime, and attacking an officer were considered, the racial differences in the police use of force ceased to be significant. Fyfe found that African American officers were almost twice as likely as white officers to have shot citizens. He attributed this finding to the

analyzing criminal justice ISSUES

SUICIDE BY COP

As strange as it sounds, some individuals shot by the police actually *want* to be shot. The problem of "suicide by cop" occurs when an individual who is intent on ending his or her life engages in behavior that makes it likely that police will use deadly force.

An example is the case of John T. Garczynski Jr., a Florida Power and Light Company employee, separated from his wife and despondent over the breakup of his marriage and their financial situation. One night after their breakup, Garczynski met his wife at a bowling alley and gave her a packet containing a suicide note, an obituary, and a eulogy that he wanted read at his funeral. After Garczynski left the bowling alley and his wife discovered what was in the package, she called the police, who were then able to track down Garczynski with the help of his cellular phone company. When officers confronted him, he pointed a gun at them, so the officers fired. Garczynski died in a hail of 26 bullets.

Cases like Garczynski's can be difficult for police officers. As Rebecca Stincelli, author of the book *Suicide by Cop: Victims from Both Sides of the Badge*, has noted, "In the past, people have used rope, a gun, gas, [or] jumped off a building. A police officer is just another method ... They say it's nothing personal, [but] they are wrong. It's very personal." The FBI has raised a similar point, noting that "Suicide-by-cop incidents are painful and damaging experiences for the surviving families, the communities, and all law enforcement professionals."

How common is suicide by cop? One study of fatal shootings by Los Angeles police officers found that more than 10 percent could be classified as suicide by cop! Researchers have since placed such killings into three categories. The first is a "direct confrontation," where the suicidal party initiates a confrontation with police for the purpose of dying. The second is a "disturbed intervention," in which a suicidal subject takes advantage of the police presence to further his or her suicide attempt. The third is a "criminal intervention," where a criminal suspect would rather die than be apprehended.

CRITICAL THINKING

1. What can police officers do to avoid potential suicide-by-cop situations? If they are forced into one, what options are available?

2. To what extent can police officers infer, in a potential suicide-by-cop situation, that a person is intent on dying? Are other options available?

Sources: Stephanie Slater, "Suicidal Man Killed by Police Fusillade," *Palm Beach Post*, March 11, 2005, p. 1A; Rebecca Stincelli, *Suicide by Cop: Victims from Both Sides of the Badge* (Folsom, CA: Interviews and Interrogations Institute, 2004); Vivian Lord and Michael Sloop, "Suicide by Cop: Police Shooting as a Method of Self-Harming," *Journal of Criminal Justice* 38 (2010): 889–895; Anthony J. Pinizzotto, Edward F. Davis, and Charles E. Miller III, "Suicide by Cop: Defining a Devastating Dilemma," *FBI Law Enforcement Bulletin* 74 (2005): 15; "Ten Percent of Police Shootings Found to Be 'Suicide by Cop,'" *Criminal Justice Newsletter*, September 1, 1998, pp. 1–2; Robert J. Homant and Daniel B. Kennedy, "Suicide by Police: A Proposed Typology of Law Enforcement Officer–Assisted Suicide," *Policing: An International Journal of Police Strategies and Management* 23 (2000): 339–355.

fact that African American officers work and live in high-crime, high-violence areas where shootings are more common and that African American officers hold proportionately more line positions and fewer administrative posts than white officers, which would place them more often on the street and less often behind a desk.[191]

CONTROLLING DEADLY FORCE Since police use of deadly force is such a serious problem, ongoing efforts have been made to control it. One of the most difficult problems that undermined its control was the continued use of the fleeing-felon rule in a number of states. However, in 1985 the U.S. Supreme Court outlawed the indiscriminate use of deadly force with its decision in the case of *Tennessee v. Garner*. In this case, the Court ruled that the use of deadly force against apparently unarmed and nondangerous fleeing felons is an illegal seizure of their person under the Fourth Amendment. Deadly force may not be used unless it is necessary to prevent escape and the officer has probable cause to believe that the suspect poses a significant threat of death or serious injury to the officer or others. The majority opinion stated that when the suspect poses no immediate threat to the officer and no threat to others, the harm resulting from failing to apprehend the suspect does not justify the use of deadly force to do so: "A police officer may not seize an unarmed, nondangerous suspect by shooting him dead."[192]

Individual state jurisdictions still control police shooting policy. Some states have adopted statutory policies that restrict the police use of violence. Others have adopted use-of-force continuums like the one illustrated in Figure 7.2, to teach officers the proper method to escalate force in response to the threat they face. As the figure shows, resistance ranges from compliant and cooperative to assaultive with the threat of serious bodily harm or death. Officers are taught via lecture, demonstration, computer-based instruction, and training scenarios to assess a suspect's behavior and apply an appropriate and corresponding amount of force.[193]

Another method of controlling police shootings is through internal review and policy making by police administrative review boards and other top-level officials.[194] Since 1972, the New York City Police Department has conducted an internal investigation any time an officer's weapon is discharged (with the exception of training situations). The process works as follows:

■ NYPD policy requires an officer to provide immediate notification to his or her supervisor of any firearm discharge.

■ The department dispatches a "firearm-discharge investigative team" (also called a "shooting team") to the scene. The team investigates the scene, gives the shooting officer a breath-alcohol test, and prepares a detailed incident report pursuant to the department's *Firearm Discharges Investigation Manual.*

■ If the incident involved shooting of a person, the commissioner is briefed the next day.

■ The district attorney is notified of the shooting.

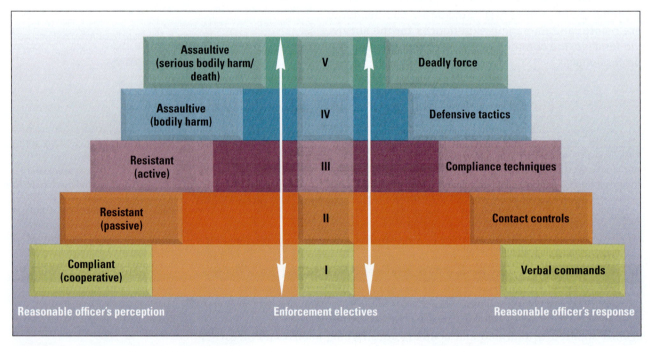

FIGURE 7.2 A Use-of-Force Continuum

Source: Franklin Graves and Gregory Connor, Federal Law Enforcement Training Center, Glynco, Georgia.

■ The shooting team's final report is due 90 days after the incident, at which point it is examined by the patrol borough's Firearms Discharge Review Board (FDRB), the patrol borough commander, the department's FDRB, and ultimately the department chief. Accidental discharges and other shootings not of people do not receive full review.[195]

The review board approach is controversial because it can mean that the department recommends that one of its own officers be turned over for criminal prosecution.

There is evidence that police officers involved in shootings often suffer from "perceptual distortions."[196] That is, they sometimes perceive reality as different than it is. In the heat of the moment, they may lose track of time, hear things that didn't occur, and even see things that were not there. Knowing that these distortions can occur is important, because it suggests some latitude be given to officers who discharge their weapons; their actions should not always be judged with the benefit of 20/20 hindsight but rather with an understanding of what was going through their heads at the time. Realizing this, according to experts, "may help concerned members of the public to appreciate the realities of what officers experience when they face decisions about whether to fire their weapons and to make more informed judgments about whether a given officer acted reasonably when he or she fired his or her weapon."[197]

Nondeadly Force

Nondeadly force is force that is unlikely to cause death or significant bodily harm. Nondeadly force can range from the use of handcuffs and suspect compliance techniques to rubber bullets and stun guns. Officers resort to nondeadly force in a number of circumstances. They may begin with verbal commands and then escalate the force used when confronted with a resistant suspect. Researchers have found that the crime in question is strongly linked to the type of nondeadly force used and that officers are also influenced by past experience, the presence of other officers, and the presence and behavior of bystanders.[198] And even though nondeadly force is used more often than deadly force, it is still relatively rare—and at the lower end of the severity scale (e.g., grabbed by officer instead of hit). Researchers have estimated that police use or threaten to use nondeadly force in only 1.7 percent of all contacts and 20 percent of all arrests.[199]

Although nondeadly force is unlikely to cause death, it sometimes does. For example, medical examiners have attributed some Taser deaths (we discuss Tasers in more detail shortly) to a condition known as excited delirium, a supposed overdose of adrenaline that can occur in heated confrontations with the police. Not everyone agrees that **excited delirium** is an actual medical condition, but it has been listed as the cause of death in some situations, particularly when the suspect was found to be under the influence of stimulants.[200]

CONTROLLING NONDEADLY FORCE In *Graham v. Connor*, the Supreme Court created a reasonableness standard for the use of nondeadly force. The Court held that force is excessive when, considering all the circumstances known to the officer at the time he acted, the force used was unreasonable.[201] For example, an officer is approached in a threatening manner by someone wielding a knife. The assailant fails to stop when warned and is killed by the officer. The officer would not be held liable if it turns out that the shooting victim was deaf and could not hear the officer's command and if the officer at the time of the incident had no way of knowing about the person's disability.

LESS-LETHAL WEAPONS In the last few years, about 1,000 local police forces have started using some sort of less-lethal weapons designed to subdue suspects. The term *less-lethal* is the preferred description because even though these weapons fall into the nondeadly force category, some have been linked to

nondeadly force
Force that is unlikely to cause death or significant bodily harm.

excited delirium
An overdose of adrenaline that can occur in heated confrontations with the police.

LO10 Recall the leading types of less-lethal weapons.

impact munitions

Less-lethal weapons that are used to stun or otherwise incapacitate uncooperative suspects so they can be subdued. Examples include rubber bullets and beanbag projectiles.

Taser

A nonlethal conducted energy device that administers a shock to an uncooperative suspect by way of an electrified dart.

deaths. Despite this, experts have heralded less-lethal weapons as helpful additions to the law enforcement arsenal.[202]

Among the most widely used nonlethal weapons are so-called **impact munitions**, including rubber bullets. At short distances, officers use pepper spray and Tasers, which deliver electric shocks from long wire tentacles, producing intense muscle spasms. Other technologies include guns that shoot giant nets, guns that squirt sticky glue, and lights that can temporarily blind a suspect.[203] All such technologies can reduce the risk of injury and death to both police officers and suspects during difficult encounters.[204]

Impact munitions include foam rubber bullets, wooden dowels, beanbags, and other projectiles that are usually fired from 12-gauge shotguns or 37/40-millimeter gas grenade launchers.[205] An example of one such device is Combined Tactical Systems' (CTS) 12-gauge launching cap. It can fire a large rubber projectile from a distance of 75 to 100 meters. Beanbags can also be fired from these types of devices. "Area rounds" are 12-gauge shotgun shells full of rubber pellets that deliver strong blows to people without penetrating the skin. Sponge point grenades, fired from grenade launchers, also help police subdue unruly individuals. Even rubber pellet–filled hand grenades have been used, as have flash grenades and flash-bang stun hand grenades.[206] Impact munitions are often used as an alternative to deadly force, but it is possible for their use to result in loss of life. When some of these devices are fired from distances of less than 30 feet, serious injury and death can result. A National Institute of Justice study of 373 incidents revealed that eight individuals died as a result of injuries sustained from impact munitions.[207] At least one suspect died as a result of being hit in the neck with a beanbag round. The rest died as a result of having broken ribs pierce their heart or lungs.

A conducted energy device (CED) administers a nonlethal shock to an uncooperative suspect. The most well-known CED is the popular **Taser**, manufactured by Taser International.[208] The efficacy of such devices is discussed further in the accompanying Evidence-Based Justice feature. More recently, companies have developed lasers that interrupt suspects' vision. One such device, the so-called "Dazer Laser," is featured in the accompanying Criminal Justice and Technology box.

Another less-lethal weapon being used by law enforcement personnel is oleoresin capsicum, also known as pepper spray. This product, which is made from peppers, is so strong that when suspects are sprayed, their eyes automatically shut and they experience shortness of breath. Pepper spray is used in a variety of scenarios, from subduing an agitated individual to subduing groups that are uncooperative and causing problems.

Some law enforcement agencies have adopted more high-powered pepper spray models, including the PepperBall system, which is a semiautomatic high-pressure launcher that fires projectiles that contain the strongest form of oleoresin capsicum and burst on impact. The launcher is accurate up to 30 feet and can saturate an area up to 100 feet across, which allows police officers to safely stand back while incapacitating suspects.

Pepper spray is appropriately considered a less-lethal weapon because some people have died as a result of its use.[209] Researchers at the University of Texas Southwestern Medical Center identified 63 cases of death where pepper spray was thought to be the culprit. On closer examination, they found that only two of the deaths were linked to pepper spray, and those suspects were asthmatics whose conditions were aggravated by the use of pepper spray.[210]

Police as Victims

Police use of force continues to be an important issue, but control measures seem to be working. Fewer people are being killed by police, and fewer officers are being killed in the line of duty than ever before—about 50 each year. The number

EVIDENCE-based justice

ARE TASERS EFFECTIVE?

As Tasers have found their way into mainstream law enforcement use, researchers have been drawn to the question of whether they present an effective alternative to conventional use-of-force measures. This research has yielded a wide range of conclusions, ranging from very supportive to very critical. Staunch advocates of Tasers include the manufacturer and much of the law enforcement community. Critics include most notably Amnesty International, the human rights organization. It has been especially critical of Taser deaths. Most research findings fall somewhere between these extremes.

For example, research has shown that Tasers are more effective at incapacitating suspects than pepper spray. And as Eugene Paoline and his colleagues found, Taser use reduces officer injury compared to other force measures. Dozens of studies have also concluded that Tasers pose minimal risk of death or serious injury, but much of the research has been conducted in laboratory settings on animals and healthy human volunteers. In response to this limitation, Michael White and Justin Ready compared news reports of fatal and nonfatal Taser incidents. They found that suspect drug use, mental illness, and continued resistance were associated with Taser deaths, but they concluded that more research is necessary if we are ever to know for sure. In the meantime, they suggest the development of model policy guidelines for Taser use, because the hope is that policy guidance for police can minimize any unfortunate consequences associated with Taser use. Indeed, the Police Executive Research Forum has come up with several guiding principles for the proper use of Tasers and related CEDs:

1. ECWs [electronic control weapons] should be considered less-lethal weapons.

2. ECWs should be used as a weapon of need, not a tool of convenience.

3. Officers should not over-rely on ECWs in situations where more effective and less risky alternatives are available.

4. ECWs are just one of a number of tools that police have available to do their jobs, and they should be considered one part of an agency's overall use-of-force policy.

5. In agencies that deploy ECWs, officers should receive comprehensive training on when and how to use ECWs.

6. Agencies should monitor their own use of ECWs and should conduct periodic analyses of practices and trends.

7. Agencies should consider the expectations of their community when developing an overall strategy for using ECWs.

A recent National Institute of Justice report on the safety of conducted energy devices concluded that use of the devices against healthy adults poses minimal risk of death or bodily injury. The report, which contained findings from a panel of experts, concluded:

> There is no conclusive medical evidence in the current body of research literature that indicates a high risk of serious injury or death to humans from the direct or indirect cardiovascular or metabolic effects of short-term CED exposure in healthy, normal, nonstressed, nonintoxicated persons. Field experience with CED use indicates that short-term exposure is safe in the vast majority of cases. The risk of death in a CED-related use-of-force incident is less than 0.25 percent, and it is reasonable to conclude that CEDs do not cause or contribute to death in the large majority of those cases.

Sources: Taser International, http://www.taser.com/research-and-safety/field-use-and-statistics (accessed June 2014); Amnesty International, "Stricter Limits Urged as Deaths Following Police Taser Use Reach 500," February 15, 2012, http://www.amnesty.org/en/news/usa-stricter-limits-urged-deaths-following-police-taser-use-reach-500-2012-02-15 (accessed June 2014); Taser International, *Advanced Taser M26 Field Report Analysis* (Scottsdale, AZ: Taser International, 2002); Robert J. Kaminski, "Research on Conducted Energy Devices: Findings, Methods, and Possible Alternatives," *Criminology and Public Policy* 8 (2009): 903–913; Eugene Paoline, William Terrill, and Jason Ingram, "Police Use of Force and Officer Injuries: Comparing Conducted Energy Devices (CEDs) to Hands- and Weapons-Based Tactics," *Police Quarterly* 15 (2012): 115–136; Michael D. White and Justin Ready, "Examining Fatal and Nonfatal Incidents Involving the Taser," *Criminology and Public Policy* 8 (2009): 865–891; Police Executive Research Forum, *2011 Electronic Control Weapon Guidelines* (Washington, DC: Police Executive Research Forum, 2011), p. 11, http://cops.usdoj.gov/Publications/e021111339-PERF-ECWGb.pdf (accessed June 2014); National Institute of Justice, *Study of Deaths Following Electro-Muscular Disruption* (Washington, DC: National Institute of Justice, 2011), p. viii, http://www.ncjrs.gov/pdffiles1/nij/233432.pdf (accessed June 2014); Douglas Zipes, "Sudden Cardiac Arrest and Death Associated with Application of Shocks from a TASER Electronic Control Device," *Circulation*, April 30, 2012 (published online ahead of print).

criminal justice and TECHNOLOGY

THE DAZER LASER

The Taser is by far the most popular less-lethal weapon in the modern law enforcement arsenal. Its key limitation, however, is that the officer must be in fairly close proximity to the suspect, usually a maximum of 35 feet. Also, the Taser has come under fire for contributing to deaths in certain cases (very rarely) or for being used too often relative to other force alternatives. In response to these concerns, Laser Energetics has developed the "Dazer Laser," a nonlethal optical distractor that can be used to incapacitate suspects. The range of engagement can stretch to as much as 2,400 feet, meaning the operator can engage the target at a safe distance. Similar devices have been developed and put in use by the military for some time. Only now are they finding their way into domestic law enforcement.

How does the Dazer Laser work? It uses directional optical energy, basically a bright green light, that overwhelms a target's visual response. Why the color green? According to Laser Energetics, it is because the human eye sees the color better than any other. The bright green light temporarily eliminates the target's ability to see, making it easy for law enforcement to apprehend the suspect. The laser is effective even if the target's eyelids are closed, and it produces nauseating effects that last for up to four hours. While unpleasant, it does not cause any lasting vision damage.

Of course, the Dazer Laser is not without its faults. While it blinds the target, it does not incapacitate like a Taser does. The target could still thrash around while officers attempt to effect an arrest. Also, using the laser is similar to shining a flashlight in someone's eyes, so if the person is faced the other way and/or running away quickly, it is doubtful optical distraction technology can effectively stop all suspects. Even so, the Dazer Laser provides an interesting and contemporary alternative to the popular Taser and other less-lethal weapons.

CRITICAL THINKING

1. Watch the Dazer Laser video demonstration here: https://www.youtube.com/watch?v=xASD_eNE4VU. What is your impression of the technology? Can the Dazer Laser become as popular as the Taser?

2. What are the strengths and limitations of less-lethal weapons?

3. If less-lethal weapons are readily available and highly unlikely to kill a suspect, could they be used more often than they should? If so, what steps should be taken to limit less-lethal weapon use?

Source: Laser Energetics, http://www.laserenergetics.com (accessed June 2014).

---

rose dramatically in 2001 because 23 officers were killed in the September 11 terrorist attacks, along with 343 firefighters. Before the 2001 spike, the number of officers slain in the line of duty had been trending downward for the previous decade.[211] In 2012, the last year for which data were available as of this writing, 48 law enforcement officers were feloniously killed. What were the circumstances surrounding their deaths? Of the 48 officers slain, 12 were killed in arrest situations, 8 were killed while handling traffic stops or during vehicle pursuits, 8 died while investigating suspicious places or persons, and 6 died in ambush situations. The remaining officers were killed during tactical operations, disturbance calls, investigative activities, and prisoner transport.[212] Many more officers are assaulted than killed. Figure 7.3, which includes all officers killed between 2003 and 2012, makes this clear. Roughly 1,000 officers are assaulted for every officer who is killed.

One long-cherished myth is that police officers who answer domestic violence calls are at risk for violent victimization. The scenario goes that, when they are confronted, one of the two battling parties turns on the outsider who dares interfere in a private matter. However, research conducted in Charlotte, North Carolina, indicates that domestic violence calls may be no more dangerous than many other routine police interactions.[213] So although police officers should be

Web App 7.3

For more information about the concerns of police survivors, visit http://nationalcops.org/.

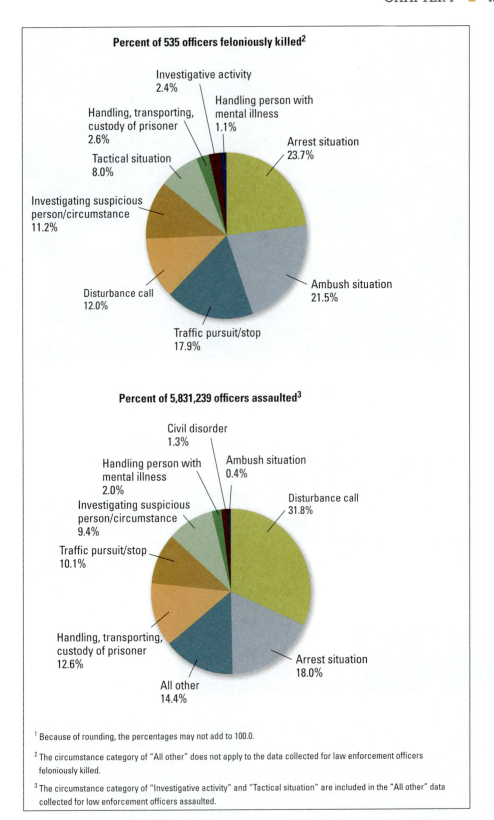

FIGURE 7.3 Law Enforcement Officers Feloniously Killed or Assaulted
Percent Distribution[1] by Circumstances at Scene of Incident, 2003–2012

Source: Federal Bureau of Investigation, *Law Enforcement Officers Killed and Assaulted, 2012* (Washington, DC: Federal Bureau of Investigation, 2012, http://www.fbi.gov/about-us/cjis/ucr/leoka/2012/2012-figures/figure-4 (accessed June 2014).

Tina Crouse, the wife of slain Officer Derek W. Crouse, a Virginia Tech police officer who was killed during a traffic stop, cries as she is escorted by Virginia Tech Police Department officers Kendrah Cline, left, and Milford Palmer to the section of the National Law Enforcement Officers Memorial where her husband's name was unveiled on April 26, 2012, in Washington, D.C.

Barbara L. Salisbury/*The Washington Times*/Landov

on their guard when investigating a call for assistance from an abused spouse, the risk of violence against them may be no greater than when they answer a call for a burglary or car theft.

National Law Enforcement Officers Memorial

The nation's monument to police officers who have died in the line of duty.

MEMORIALIZING LOST OFFICERS The **National Law Enforcement Officers Memorial** is the nation's monument to police officers who have died in the line of duty. Located in Washington, D.C., the monument consists of two curving marble walls that display the names of over 19,000 men and women who lost their lives while serving on duty as police officers. Only those who died as a direct result of a personal injury sustained in the line of duty have their names featured on the wall. Also included are law enforcement officers who, in an off-duty capacity, died while responding to law violations or who died en route to or from an emergency or call for assistance. Officers who were killed traveling en route to or from work may also have their names displayed on the memorial.[214]

ETHICAL CHALLENGES in Criminal Justice

A WRITING ASSIGNMENT

You work for a police department that is seriously understaffed and relies heavily on officer overtime to pick up the slack. At least two of your colleagues worked over 100 overtime hours last month. You also worked plenty of overtime and have come to enjoy the extra income, but you are also becoming deeply concerned the amount of time you work is compromising your ability to be an effective police officer. One of your fellow officers crashed his car on the way home the other night and you are convinced it would not have happened but for his fatigue. Your chief is supportive of the overtime and essentially requires it, but you feel something needs to be done.

Write an essay on the ethics of working excess hours when evidence suggests prolonged fatigue threatens one's judgment and alertness. In doing so, answer these questions: How much of a threat to effective police work is fatigue? How much overtime is too much? Why? What could be done to address the situation depicted in the scenario? If the chief is supportive of the overtime policy and you as the officer are not, what can you do? Should you go above the chief's head? Why or why not? In the event you did, what potential fallout could result?

Summary

L01 **Recognize the benefits likely to accrue from higher education for police.**

- It is believed that a well-educated officer can communicate better with the public.
- Police administrators believe well-educated officers perform more effectively.
- Research shows that educated officers are less likely to have disciplinary problems.

L02 **Describe how the role of women and minorities in local police agencies has evolved over time.**

- A heterogeneous police force can be instrumental in gaining the confidence of the minority community.
- In some larger departments, the percentage of minorities on police forces now reflects their representation in the general population.
- Today about 16 percent of all sworn officers in larger cities (population over 250,000) are women. African American women account for less than 5 percent of police officers.

L03 **Explain the concept of a police culture.**

- There is an independent and unique police culture, which insulates police officers from the rest of society. This culture has distinct rules and loyalties.
- Police culture is characterized by cynicism, clannishness, secrecy, and insulation from others in society. Together, these elements of police culture have been called the "blue curtain."
- Police culture is largely developed from on-the-job experiences.

L04 **Describe the reasons why experts believe police have a unique personality.**

- Experts believe the police personality is shaped by constant exposure to danger and the need to use force and authority to defuse and control threatening situations.
- Some experts believe that policing attracts recruits who are by nature cynical, authoritarian, and secretive. Others maintain that socialization and experience on the police force itself cause these character traits to develop.

L05 **Recognize the different types of police officer styles.**

- Police officers may develop a unique working style. Four distinct police styles have been identified: the crime fighter, the social agent, the law enforcer, and the watchman.
- Some experts have challenged the argument that there are distinct officer styles.

L06 **Identify the factors that influence police discretion.**

- Discretion is the use of personal decision making and choice in carrying out operations in the criminal justice system.
- A number of factors influence police discretion: the crime in question, victim factors, environmental factors, departmental factors, peer factors, suspect behavior and characteristics, and officer characteristics.

L07 **Recognize the consequences of stress and fatigue.**

- Stress leads to negative attitudes, burnout, loss of enthusiasm and commitment (cynicism), increased apathy, substance abuse problems, divorce, health problems, and many other social, personal, and job-related problematic behaviors.
- A police officer who is fatigued may be at higher risk of acting inappropriately or being injured on the job.

L08 **Distinguish between brutality and corruption.**

- Brutality refers to actions such as using abusive language, making threats, using force or coercion unnecessarily, prodding with nightsticks, and stopping and searching people to harass them.
- Corruption consists of exercising legitimate discretion for improper reasons or using illegal means to achieve approved goals.

L09 **Explain the difference between deadly and nondeadly force.**

- Deadly force is force that is likely to cause death or significant bodily harm.
- Nondeadly force is force that is *unlikely* to cause death or significant bodily harm.

L010 **Recall the leading types of less-lethal weapons.**

- The term *less-lethal* comes from the fact that such weapons are less lethal than guns, but it is still possible for death to result in exceptional cases.
- Popular less-lethal weapons include impact munitions, conducted energy devices (such as Tasers), and pepper spray.

Key Terms

Critical Thinking Questions

1. Should male and female officers have exactly the same duties in a police department? If not, why not?

2. Do you think that working the street will eventually lead an officer to develop a cynical personality and distrust for civilians? Explain.

3. How can education help police officers?

4. Should a police officer who accepts a free meal from a restaurant owner be dismissed from the force? Why or why not?

5. A police officer orders an unarmed person running away from a burglary to stop. The suspect keeps running and is shot and killed by the officer. Has the officer committed a crime? Explain.

6. Would you like to live in a society that abolished police discretion and followed a full-enforcement policy? Why or why not?

Notes

1. "APD James Boyd Shooting Albuquerque," https://www.youtube.com/watch?v=uAPb04HGwYA (accessed June 2014).

2. Patrik Jonsson, "Feds Probe Albuquerque Camper Shooting as Police Rethink Use of Force," *Christian Science Monitor*, March 29, 2014, http://www.csmonitor.com/USA/Justice/2014/0329/Feds-probe-Albuquerque-camper-shooting-as-police-rethink-use-of-force-video (accessed June 2014).

3. See Larry Hoover, *Police Educational Characteristics and Curricula* (Washington, DC: U.S. Government Printing Office, 1975).

4. Brian Reaves, *Local Police Departments, 2007* (Washington, DC: Bureau of Justice Statistics, 2010).

5. Maggy Lee and Maurice Punch, "Policing by Degrees: Police Officers' Experience of University Education," *Policing and Society* 14 (2004): 233–249.

6. Bruce Berg, "Who Should Teach Police? A Typology and Assessment of Police Academy Instructors," *American Journal of Police* 9 (1990): 79–100.

7. David Carter and Allen Sapp, *The State of Police Education: Critical Findings* (Washington, DC: Police Executive Research Forum, 1988), p. 6.

8. Jason Rydberg and William Terrill, "The Effect of Higher Education on Police Behavior," *Police Quarterly* 13 (2010): 92–120.

9. John Krimmel, "The Performance of College-Educated Police: A Study of Self-Rated Police Performance Measures," *American Journal of Police* 15 (1996): 85–95.

10. Robert Worden, "A Badge and a Baccalaureate: Policies, Hypotheses, and Further Evidence," *Justice Quarterly* 7 (1990): 565–592.

11. See Lawrence Sherman and Warren Bennis, "Higher Education for Police Officers: The Central Issues," *Police Chief* 44 (1977): 32.

12. Worden, "A Badge and a Baccalaureate," 587–589.

13. Jihong Zhao and Nicholas Lovrich, "Determinants of Minority Employment in American Municipal Police Agencies: The Representation of African American Officers," *Journal of Criminal Justice* 26 (1998): 267–278.

14. David Murphy and John Worrall, "Residency Requirements and Public Perceptions of the Police in Large Municipalities," *Policing* 22 (1999): 327–342.

15. Steven Tuch and Ronald Weitzer, "The Polls: Trends, Racial Differences in Attitudes Toward the Police," *Public Opinion Quarterly* 61 (1997): 662; Sutham Cheurprakobkit, "Police–Citizen Contact and Police Performance: Attitudinal Differences Between Hispanics and Non-Hispanics," *Journal of Criminal Justice* 28 (2000): 325–336.

16. Yolander G. Hurst, James Frank, and Sandra Lee Browning, "The Attitudes of Juveniles Toward the Police: A Comparison of African-American and White Youth," *Policing* 23 (2000): 37–53.

17. Jack Kuykendall and David Burns, "The African-American Police Officer: An Historical Perspective," *Journal of Contemporary Criminal Justice* 1 (1980): 4–13.

18. Ibid.

19. Nicholas Alex, *Black in Blue: A Study of the Negro Policeman* (New York: Appleton-Century-Crofts, 1969).

20. Kim Michelle Lersch, "Predicting Citizen Race in Allegations of Misconduct Against the Police," *Journal of Criminal Justice* 26 (1998): 87–99.

21. Nicholas Alex, *New York Cops Talk Back* (New York: Wiley, 1976).

22. David Eitle, Lisa Stolzenberg, and Stewart J. D'Alessio, "Police Organizational Factors, the Racial Composition of the Police, and the Probability of Arrest," *Justice Quarterly* 22 (2005): 30–57.

23. Robert Brown and James Frank, "Race and Officer Decision Making: Examining Differences in Arrest Outcomes Between Black and White Officers," *Justice Quarterly* 23 (2006): 96–126.

24. Stephen Leinen, *African-American Police, White Society* (New York: New York University Press, 1984).

25. Ni He, Jihong Zhao, and Ling Ren, "Do Race and Gender Matter in Police Stress? A Preliminary Assessment of the Interactive Effects," *Journal of Criminal Justice* 33 (2005): 535–547; Merry Morash, Robin Haarr, and Dae-Hoon Kwak, "Multilevel Influences on Police Stress," *Journal of Contemporary Criminal Justice* 22 (2006): 26–43.

26. Joseph L. Gustafson, "Tokenism in Policing: An Empirical Test of Kanter's Hypothesis," *Journal of Criminal Justice* 36 (2008): 1–10; Meghan Stroshine and Steven Brandl, "Race, Gender, and Tokenism in Policing: An Empirical Elaboration," *Police Quarterly* 14 (2011): 344–365.

27. Robin Haarr and Merry Morash, "Gender, Race, and Strategies of Coping with Occupational Stress in Policing," *Justice Quarterly* 16 (1999): 303–336.

28. James Jacobs and Jay Cohen, "The Impact of Racial Integration on the Police," *Journal of Police Science and Administration* 6 (1978): 182.

29. Charles Katz, "The Establishment of a Police Gang Unit: An Examination of Organizational and Environmental Factors," *Criminology* 39 (2001): 37–73.

30. Ibid., p. 61.

31. Ronald Weitzer, "White, Black, or Blue Cops?" *Journal of Criminal Justice* 28 (2000): 313–324.

32. Peter C. Moskos, "Two Shades of Blue: Black and White in the Blue Brotherhood," *Law Enforcement Executive Forum* 8 (2008): 57–86.

33. For a review of the history of women in policing, see Dorothy Moses Schulz, "From Policewoman to Police Officer: An Unfinished Revolution," *Police Studies* 16 (1993): 90–99; Cathryn House, "The Changing Role of Women in Law Enforcement," *Police Chief* 60 (1993): 139–144.

34. Lynn Langton, *Women in Law Enforcement, 1987–2008* (Washington, DC: Bureau of Justice Statistics, 2010).

35. Gary Cordner and AnnMarie Cordner, "Stuck on a Plateau? Obstacles to the Recruitment, Selection, and Retention of Women Police," *Police Quarterly* 14 (2011): 207–226.

36. Susan Martin, "Female Officers on the Move? A Status Report on Women in Policing," in *Critical Issues in Policing*, ed. Roger Dunham and Geoffrey Alpert (Grove Park, IL: Waveland, 1988), pp. 312–331.

37. *Le Bouef v. Ramsey*, 26 FEP Cases 884 (September 16, 1980).

38. Michael Birzer and Delores Craig, "Gender Differences in Police Physical Ability Test Performance," *American Journal of Police* 15 (1996): 93–106.

39. James Daum and Cindy Johns, "Police Work from a Woman's Perspective," *Police Chief* 61 (1994): 46–49.

40. Steve Herbert, "'Hard Charger' or 'Station Queen'? Policing and the Masculinist State," *Gender, Place and Culture: A Journal of Feminist Geography* 8 (2001): 55–72.

41. Ibid., p. 58.

42. Matthew Hickman, Alex Piquero, and Jack Greene, "Discretion and Gender Disproportionality in Police Disciplinary Systems," *Policing* 23 (2000): 105–116.

43. Robin Haarr and Merry Morash, "Gender, Race, and Strategies of Coping with Occupational Stress in Policing," *Justice Quarterly* 16 (1999): 303–336.

44. Carol A. Archbold and Dorothy M. Schulz, "The Lingering Effects of Tokenism on Female Police Officers' Promotion Aspirations," *Police Quarterly* 11 (2008): 50–73.

45. Merry Morash and Jack Greene, "Evaluating Women on Patrol: A Critique of Contemporary Wisdom," *Evaluation Review* 10 (1986): 230–255.

46. Peter Bloch and Deborah Anderson, *Policewomen on Patrol: Final Report* (Washington, DC: Police Foundation, 1974).

47. Cara E. Rabe-Hemp and Amie M. Schuck, "Violence Against Police Officers: Are Female Officers at Greater Risk?" *Police Quarterly* 10 (2007): 411–428.

48. Daum and Johns, "Police Work from a Woman's Perspective."

49. Cordner and Cordner, "Stuck on a Plateau? Obstacles to the Recruitment, Selection, and Retention of Women Police."

50. Simon Holdaway and Sharon K. Parker, "Policing Women Police: Uniform Patrol, Promotion, and Representation in the CID," *British Journal of Criminology* 38 (1998): 40–48.

51. Michael Birzer and Robert Nolan, "Learning Strategies of Selected Urban Police Related to Community Policing," *Policing* 25 (2002): 242–255.

52. William P. McCarty, Jihong "Solomon" Zhao, and Brett E. Garland, "Occupational Stress and Burnout Between Male and Female Police Officers: Are There Any Gender Differences?" *Policing* 30 (2007): 672–691.

53. Susan Martin, "Outsider Within the Station House: The Impact of Race and Gender on African-American Woman Police," *Social Problems* 41 (1994): 383–400, at 387.

54. Ibid., p. 394.

55. Ibid., p. 397.

56. Ibid.

57. Eric Poole and Mark Pogrebin, "Factors Affecting the Decision to Remain in Policing: A Study of Women Officers," *Journal of Police Science and Administration* 16 (1988): 49–55.

58. Eugene Paoline, "Taking Stock: Toward a Richer Understanding of Police Culture," *Journal of Criminal Justice* 31 (2003): 199–214.

59. See, for example, Richard Harris, *The Police Academy: An Inside View* (New York: Wiley, 1973); John Van Maanen, "Observations on the Making of a Policeman," in *Order Under Law*, ed. R. Culbertson and M. Tezak (Prospect Heights, IL: Waveland, 1981), pp. 111–126; Jonathan Rubenstein, *City Police* (New York: Ballantine, 1973); John Broderick, *Police in a Time of Change* (Morristown, NJ: General Learning Press, 1977).

60. Malcolm Sparrow, Mark Moore, and David Kennedy, *Beyond 911: A New Era for Policing* (New York: Basic Books, 1990), p. 51.

61. M. Steven Meagher and Nancy Yentes, "Choosing a Career in Policing: A Comparison of Male and Female Perceptions," *Journal of Police Science and Administration* 16 (1986): 320–327.

62. Michael K. Brown, *Working the Street* (New York: Russell Sage, 1981), p. 82.

63. Anthony Bouza, *The Police Mystique: An Insider's Look at Cops, Crime, and the Criminal Justice System* (New York: Plenum Press, 1990), p. 17.

64. Egon Bittner, *The Functions of Police in Modern Society* (Cambridge, MA: Oelgeschlager, Gunn, and Hain, 1980), p. 63.

65. Venessa Garcia, "Constructing the 'Other' Within Police Culture: An Analysis of a Deviant Unit Within the Police Organization," *Police Practice and Research* 6 (2005): 65–80.

66. Wallace Graves, "Police Cynicism: Causes and Cures," *FBI Law Enforcement Bulletin* 65 (1996): 16–21.

67. Richard Lundman, *Police and Policing* (New York: Holt, Rinehart, and Winston, 1980). See also Jerome Skolnick, *Justice Without Trial* (New York: Wiley, 1966).

68. Micael Bjork, "Fighting Cynicism," *Police Quarterly* 11 (2008): 88–101.

69. William Westly, *Violence and the Police: A Sociological Study of Law, Custom, and Morality* (Cambridge, MA: MIT Press, 1970).

70. Skolnick, *Justice Without Trial*, pp. 42–68.

71. Milton Rokeach, Martin Miller, and John Snyder, "The Value Gap Between Police and Policed," *Journal of Social Issues* 27 (1971): 155–171.

72. Bruce Carpenter and Susan Raza, "Personality Characteristics of Police Applicants: Comparisons Across Subgroups and with Other Populations," *Journal of Police Science and Administration* 15 (1987): 10–17.

73. Larry Tifft, "The 'Cop Personality' Reconsidered," *Journal of Police Science and Administration* 2 (1974): 268; David Bayley and Harold Mendelsohn, *Minorities and the Police* (New York: Free Press, 1969); Robert Balch, "The Police Personality: Fact or Fiction?" *Journal of Criminal Law, Criminology, and Police Science* 63 (1972): 117.

74. Lowell Storms, Nolan Penn, and James Tenzell, "Policemen's Perception of Real and Ideal Policemen," *Journal of Police Science and Administration* 17 (1990): 40–43.

75. Arthur Niederhoffer, *Behind the Shield: The Police in Urban Society* (Garden City, NY: Doubleday, 1967).

76. Ibid., pp. 216–220.

77. Carl Klockars, "The Dirty Harry Problem," *Annals* 452 (1980): 33–47.

78. Jack Kuykendall and Roy Roberg, "Police Manager's Perceptions of Employee Types: A Conceptual Model," *Journal of Criminal Justice* 16 (1988): 131–135.

79. Stephen Matrofski, R. Richard Ritti, and Jeffrey Snipes, "Expectancy Theory and Police Productivity in DUI Enforcement," *Law and Society Review* 28 (1994): 113–138.

80. John P. Crank, *Understanding Police Culture* (Cincinnati, Ohio: Anderson, 1998).

81. Paoline, "Taking Stock."

82. Skolnick, *Justice Without Trial*.

83. Carroll Seron, Joseph Pereira, and Jean Kovath, "Judging Police Misconduct: 'Street-Level' versus Professional Policing," *Law and Society Review* 38 (2004): 665–710.

84. William Terrill and Eugene A. Paoline III, "Nonarrest Decision Making in Police–Citizen Encounters," *Police Quarterly* 10 (2007): 308–331.

85. Kenneth Litwin, "A Multilevel Multivariate Analysis of Factors Affecting Homicide Clearances," *Journal of Research in Crime and Delinquency* 41 (2004): 327–351.

86. Lawrence W. Sherman, "Causes of Police Behavior: The Current State of Quantitative Research," in *The Ambivalent Force*, ed. A. S. Blumberg and E. Niederhoffer, 3rd ed. (New York: Holt, Rinehart, and Wilson, 1985), pp. 183–195, at p. 187.

87. Helen Eigenberg, Kathryn Scarborough, and Victor Kappeler, "Contributory Factors Affecting Arrest in Domestic and Nondomestic Assaults," *American Journal of Police* 15 (1996): 27–51.

88. Leonore Simon, "A Therapeutic Jurisprudence Approach to the Legal Processing of Domestic Violence Cases," *Psychology, Public Policy, and Law* 1 (1995): 43–79.

89. Peter Sinden and B. Joyce Stephens, "Police Perceptions of Domestic Violence: The Nexus of Victim, Perpetrator, Event, Self and Law," *Policing* 22 (1999): 313–326.

90. Gregory Howard Williams, *The Law and Politics of Police Discretion* (Westport, CT: Greenwood, 1984).

91. Douglas Smith and Jody Klein, "Police Control of Interpersonal Disputes," *Social Problems* 31 (1984): 468–481.

92. David Klinger, "Negotiating Order in Patrol Work: An Ecological Theory of Police Response to Deviance," *Criminology* 35 (1997): 277–306.

93. Allison Chappell, John Macdonald, and Patrick Manz, "The Organizational Determinants of Police Arrest Decisions," *Crime and Delinquency* 52 (2006): 287–306.

94. Robin Shepard Engel, "Patrol Officer Supervision in the Community Policing Era," *Journal of Criminal Justice* 30 (2002): 51–64.

95. Westly, *Violence and the Police*.

96. John McCluskey, William Terrill, and Eugene Paoline III, "Peer Group Aggressiveness and the Use of Coercion in Police–Suspect Encounters," *Police Practice and Research* 6 (2005): 19–37.

97. Nathan Goldman, *The Differential Selection of Juvenile Offenders for Court Appearance* (New York: National Council on Crime and Delinquency, 1963).

98. Joseph Schafer, "Negotiating Order in the Policing of Youth Drinking," *Policing* 28 (2005): 279–300; Richard Lundman, "Demeanor or Crime? The Midwest City Police–Citizen Encounters Study," *Criminology* 32 (1994): 631–653.

99. Joseph Schafer and Stephen Mastrofski, "Police Leniency in Traffic Enforcement Encounters: Exploratory Findings from Observations and Interviews," *Journal of Criminal Justice* 33 (2005): 225–238.

100. William Terrill and Stephen Mastrofski, "Situational and Officer-Based Determinants of Police Coercion," *Justice Quarterly* 19 (2002): 215–248.

101. William Terrill, *Police Coercion: Application of the Force Continuum* (New York: LFB Scholarly Publishing, 2001).

102. Geoffrey P. Alpert, John M. Macdonald, and Roger G. Dunham, "Police Suspicion and Discretionary Decision Making During Citizen Stops," *Criminology* 43 (2005): 407–434.

103. Christy A. Visher, "Gender, Police Arrest Decisions, and Notions of Chivalry," *Criminology* 21 (1983): 5–28.

104. Kenneth J. Novak, James Frank, Brad W. Smith, Robin Shepard Engel, "Revisiting the Decision to Arrest: Comparing Beat and Community Officers," *Crime and Delinquency* 48 (2002): 70–98.

105. Roy Roberg, Kenneth Novak, and Gary Cordner, *Police and Society*, 3rd ed. (Los Angeles: Roxbury, 2005), p. 292.

106. Joel Garner, Christopher Maxwell, and Cederick Heraux, "Characteristics Associated with the Prevalence and Severity of Force Used by the Police," *Justice Quarterly* 19 (2002): 705–747.

107. Steven Brandl, Meghan Stroshine, and James Frank, "Who Are the Complaint-Prone Officers? An Examination of the Relationship Between Police Officers' Attributes, Arrest Activity, Assignment, and Citizens' Complaints About Excessive Force," *Journal of Criminal Justice* 29 (2001): 521–529.

108. William F. Walsh, "Police Officer Arrest Rates," *Justice Quarterly* 3 (1986): 271–290.

109. Brown, *Working the Street*, p. 290.

110. Judith A. Waters and William Ussery, "Police Stress: History, Contributing Factors, Symptoms, and Interventions," *Policing* 30 (2007): 169–188.

111. Karen Kruger and Nicholas Valltos, "Dealing with Domestic Violence in Law Enforcement Relationships," *FBI Law Enforcement Bulletin* 71 (2002): 1–7.

112. Donald Yates and Vijayan Pillai, "Frustration and Strain Among Fort Worth Police Officers," *Sociology and Social Research* 76 (1992): 145–149.

113. Ni He, Jihong Zhao, and Carol Archbold, "Gender and Police Stress: The Convergent and Divergent Impact of Work Environment, Work–Family Conflict, and Stress Coping Mechanisms of Female and Male Police Officers," *Policing* 25 (2002): 687–709.

114. Francis Cullen, Terrence Lemming, Bruce Link, and John Wozniak, "The Impact of Social Supports on Police Stress," *Criminology* 23 (1985): 503–522.

115. Morash, Haarr, and Kwak, "Multilevel Influences on Police Stress."

116. Deborah Wilkins Newman and LeeAnne Rucker-Reed, "Police Stress, State-Trait Anxiety, and Stressors Among U.S. Marshals," *Journal of Criminal Justice* 32 (2004): 631–641.

117. Jihong Zhao, Ni He, and Nicholas Lovrich, "Predicting Five Dimensions of Police Officer Stress: Looking More Deeply into Organizational Settings for Sources of Police Stress," *Police Quarterly* 5 (2002): 43–63.

118. Lawrence Travis III and Craig Winston, "Dissension in the Ranks: Officer Resistance to Community Policing and Support for the Organization," *Journal of Crime and Justice* 21 (1998): 139–155.

119. R. E. Farmer, "Clinical and Managerial Implications of Stress Research on the Police," *Journal of Police Science and Administration* 17 (1990): 205–218; Nancy Norvell, Dale Belles, and Holly Hills, "Perceived Stress Levels and Physical Symptoms in Supervisory Law Enforcement Personnel," *Journal of Police Science and Administration* 16 (1988): 75–79.

120. Donald Yates and Vijayan Pillai, "Attitudes Toward Community Policing: A Causal Analysis," *Social Science Journal* 33 (1996): 193–209.

121. Harvey McMurray, "Attitudes of Assaulted Police Officers and Their Policy Implications," *Journal of Police Science and Administration* 17 (1990): 44–48.

122. Matthew J. Hickman, Jennifer Fricas, Kevin J. Strom, and Mark W. Pope, "Mapping Police Stress," *Police Quarterly* 14 (2011): 227–250.

123. Robert Ankony and Thomas Kelly, "The Impact of Perceived Alienation of Police Officers' Sense of Mastery and Subsequent Motivation for Proactive Enforcement," *Policing* 22 (1999): 120–132.

124. John Blackmore, "Police Stress," in *Policing Society*, ed. Clinton Terry (New York: Wiley, 1985), p. 395.

125. Stephen Curran, "Separating Fact from Fiction About Police Stress," *Behavioral Health Management* 23 (2003): 38–40; Peter Marzuk, Matthew Nock, Andrew Leon, Laura Portera, and Kenneth Tardiff, "Suicide Among New York City Police Officers, 1977–1996," *American Journal of Psychiatry* 159 (2002): 2069–2072; Rose Lee Josephson and Martin Reiser, "Officer Suicide in the Los Angeles Police Department: A Twelve-Year Follow-Up," *Journal of Police Science and Administration* 17 (1990): 227–230.

126. Vicki Lindsay, "Police Officers and Their Alcohol Consumption," *Police Quarterly* 11 (2008): 74–87.

127. Yates and Pillai, "Attitudes Toward Community Policing," 205–206.

128. Ibid.

129. Rosanna Church and Naomi Robertson, "How State Police Agencies Are Addressing the Issue of Wellness," *Policing* 22 (1999): 304–312; Farmer, "Clinical and Managerial Implications of Stress Research on the Police," p. 215.

130. Peter Hart, Alexander Wearing, and Bruce Headey, "Assessing Police Work Experiences: Development of the Police Daily Hassles and Uplifts Scales," *Journal of Criminal Justice* 21 (1993): 553–573.

131. Vivian Lord, Denis Gray, and Samuel Pond, "The Police Stress Inventory: Does It Measure Stress?" *Journal of Criminal Justice* 19 (1991): 139–149.

132. Bryan Vila and Dennis J. Kenney, "Tired Cops: The Prevalence and Potential Consequences of Police Fatigue," *NIJ Journal* 248 (2002): 16–21.

133. Luenda E. Charles, Cecil M. Burchfiel, Desta Fekedulegn, Bryan Vila, Tara A. Hartley, James Slaven, Anna Mnatsakanova, and John M. Violanti, "Shift Work and Sleep: The Buffalo Police Health Study," *Policing* 30 (2007): 215–227.

134. Vila and Kenney, "Tired Cops: The Prevalence and Potential Consequences of Police Fatigue," p. 18.

135. Ibid., p. 17.

136. Ibid., pp. 19–20.

137. Bittner, *The Functions of Police in Modern Society*, p. 46.

138. Frank Hughes and Lisa B. Andre, "Problem Officer Variables and Early-Warning Systems," *Police Chief* 74 (2007): 164, 166, 168, 172.

139. Sean Griffin and Thomas Bernard, "Angry Aggression Among Police Officers," *Police Quarterly* 6 (2003): 3–21.

140. Kim Michelle Lersch and Tom Mieczkowski, "Who Are the Problem-Prone Officers? An Analysis of Citizen Complaints," *American Journal of Police* 15 (1996): 23–42.

141. Samuel Walker, Geoffrey P. Alpert, and Dennis J. Kenney, *Early Warning Systems: Responding to the Problem Police Officer, Research in Brief* (Washington, DC: National Institute of Justice, 2001).

142. Samuel Walker, "The Rule Revolution: Reflections on the Transformation of American Criminal Justice, 1950–1988," *Working Papers, Series 3* (Madison: University of Wisconsin Law School, Institute for Legal Studies, December 1988).

143. Michael D. White, "Controlling Police Decisions to Use Deadly Force: Reexamining the Importance of Administrative Policy," *Crime and Delinquency* 47 (2001): 131.

144. Victor Kappeler, Stephen Kappeler, and Rolando Del Carmen, "A Content Analysis of Police Civil Liability Cases: Decisions of the Federal District Courts, 1978–1990," *Journal of Criminal Justice* 21 (1993): 325–337.

145. See, for example, Ronald Weitzer, "Citizen Perceptions of Police Misconduct: Race and Neighborhood Context," *Justice Quarterly* 16 (1999): 819–846.

146. Samuel Walker, *Popular Justice* (New York: Oxford University Press, 1980), p. 64.

147. Louise Westmarland, "Police Ethics and Integrity: Breaking the Blue Code of Silence," *Policing and Society* 15 (2005): 145–165.

148. Robert J. Kane and Michael D. White, "A Study of Career-Ending Misconduct Among New York City Police Officers," *Criminology and Public Policy* 8 (2009): 737–769.

149. Herman Goldstein, *Police Corruption* (Washington, DC: Police Foundation, 1975), p. 3.

150. Knapp Commission, Report on Police Corruption (New York: Braziller, 1973), pp. 1–34.

151. Elizabeth Neuffer, "Seven Additional Detectives Linked to Extortion Scheme," *Boston Globe*, October 25, 1988, p. 60.

152. Kevin Cullen, "U.S. Probe Eyes Bookie Protection," *Boston Globe*, October 25, 1988, p. 1.

153. Michael Johnston, *Political Corruption and Public Policy in America* (Monterey, CA: Brooks/Cole, 1982), p. 75.

154. William Doherty, "Ex-Sergeant Says He Aided Bid to Sell Exam," *Boston Globe*, February 26, 1987, p. 61.

155. Alan Feuer and William K. Rashbaum, "Blood Ties: 2 Officers' Long Path to Mob Murder Indictments," *New York Times*, March 12, 2005; Lisa Stein, "Cops Gone Wild," *U.S. News and World Report*, March 21, 2005, p. 14.

156. Ellwyn Stoddard, "Blue Coat Crime," in *Thinking about Police*, ed. Carl Klockars (New York: McGraw-Hill, 1983), pp. 338–349.

157. Lawrence Sherman, *Police Corruption: A Sociological Perspective* (Garden City, NY: Doubleday, 1974), pp. 40–41.

158. Samuel Walker, *Police in Society* (New York: McGraw-Hill, 1983), p. 181.

159. Robert Kane, "The Social Ecology of Police Misconduct," *Criminology* 40 (2002): 867–897.

160. Sherman, *Police Corruption*.

161. Robert Daley, *Prince of the City* (New York: Houghton Mifflin, 1978).

162. Kane and White, "A Study of Career-Ending Misconduct," p. 763.

163. Sherman, *Police Corruption*, p. 194.

164. Kevin Flynn, "Police Dept. Routinely Drops Cases of Officer Misconduct, Report Says," *New York Times*, September 15, 1999, p. 1.

165. Gary R. Rothwell and J. Norman Baldwin, "Whistle-Blowing and the Code of Silence in Police Agencies," *Crime and Delinquency* 53 (2007): 605–632.

166. Westmarland, "Police Ethics and Integrity."

167. Barbara Gelb, *Tarnished Brass: The Decade After Serpico* (New York: Putnam, 1983); Candace McCoy, "Lawsuits Against Police: What Impact Do They Have?" *Criminal Law Bulletin* 20 (1984): 49–56.

168. Christine Eith and Matthew Durose, *Contacts Between Police and the Public, 2008* (Washington, DC: Bureau of Justice Statistics, 2011).

169. Brad Smith, "The Impact of Police Officer Diversity on Police-Caused Homicides," *Policy Studies Journal* 31 (2003): 147–162.

170. Brian Thompson and James Daniel Lee, "Who Cares If Police Become Violent? Explaining Approval of Police Use of Force Using a National Sample," *Sociological Inquiry* 74 (2004): 381–410.

171. Sandra Lee Browning, Francis Cullen, Liqun Cao, Renee Kopache, and Thomas Stevenson, "Race and Getting Hassled by the Police: A Research Note," *Police Studies* 17 (1994): 1–11.

172. Joel Garner, Christopher Maxwell, and Cederick Heraux, "Characteristics Associated with the Prevalence and Severity of Force Used by the Police," *Justice Quarterly* 19 (2002): 705–747.

173. William Terrill, "Police Use of Force: A Transactional Approach," *Justice Quarterly* 22 (2005): 107–138.

174. Thompson and Lee, "Who Cares If Police Become Violent?"

175. Sam W. Lathrop, "Reviewing Use of Force: A Systematic Approach," *FBI Law Enforcement Bulletin* 69 (2000): 16–20.

176. Ibid.

177. Alexia Cooper and Erica L. Smith, *Homicide Trends in the United States, 1980–2008* (Washington, DC: Bureau of Justice Statistics, 2011), p. 32, Figure 51, http://www.bjs.gov/content/pub/pdf/htus8008.pdf (accessed June 2014).

178. Lawrence W. Sherman and Robert H. Langworthy, "Measuring Homicide by Police Officers," *Journal of Criminal Law and Criminology* 70 (1979): 546–560.

179. Brad Smith, "The Impact of Police Officer Diversity on Police-Caused Violence," *Policy Studies Journal* 31 (2003): 147–163.

180. John MacDonald, Geoffrey Alpert, and Abraham Tennenbaum, "Justifiable Homicide by Police and Criminal Homicide: A Research Note," *Journal of Crime and Justice* 22 (1999): 153–164.

181. Richard Parent and Simon Verdun-Jones, "Victim-Precipitated Homicide: Police Use of Deadly Force in British Columbia," *Policing* 21 (1998): 432–449.

182. "10% of Police Shootings Found to Be 'Suicide by Cop,'" *Criminal Justice Newsletter* 29 (1998): 1.

183. Sherman and Langworthy, "Measuring Homicide by Police Officers."

184. Brad Smith, "Structural and Organizational Predictors of Homicide by Police," *Policing* 27 (2004): 539–557.

185. Jonathan Sorenson, James Marquart, and Deon Brock, "Factors Related to Killings of Felons by Police Officers: A Test of the Community Violence and Conflict Hypotheses," *Justice Quarterly* 10 (1993): 417–440; David Jacobs and David Britt, "Inequality

and Police Use of Deadly Force: An Empirical Assessment of a Conflict Hypothesis," *Social Problems* 26 (1979): 403–412.

186. Smith, "The Impact of Police Officer Diversity on Police-Caused Violence."

187. David Jacobs and Jason Carmichael, "Subordination and Violence Against State Control Agents: Testing Political Explanations for Lethal Assaults Against the Police," *Social Forces* 80 (2002): 1223–1252.

188. James Fyfe, "Police Use of Deadly Force: Research and Reform," *Justice Quarterly* 5 (1988): 165–205.

189. Paul Takagi, "A Garrison State in a 'Democratic' Society," *Crime and Social Justice* 5 (1974): 34–43.

190. Mark Blumberg, "Race and Police Shootings: An Analysis in Two Cities," in *Contemporary Issues in Law Enforcement*, ed. James Fyfe (Beverly Hills, CA: Sage, 1981), pp. 152–166.

191. James Fyfe, "Shots Fired," Ph.D. dissertation, State University of New York, Albany, 1978.

192. *Tennessee v. Garner*, 471 U.S. 1 (1985).

193. Franklin Graves and Gregory Connor, "The FLETC Use-of-Force Model," *Police Chief* 59 (1992): 56–58.

194. Gregory B. Morrison, "Deadly Force Programs Among Larger U.S. Police Departments," *Police Quarterly* 9 (2006): 331–360.

195. Bernard D. Rostker, Lawrence M. Hanser, William M. Hix, Carl Jensen, Andrew R. Morral, Greg Ridgeway, and Terry. L. Schell, *Evaluation of the New York City Police Department Firearm Training and Firearm-Discharge Review Process* (Santa Monica, CA: RAND Corporation, 2008), pp. 41–46.

196. David A. Klinger and Rod. K. Brunson, "Police Officers' Perceptual Distortions During Lethal Force Situations: Informing the Reasonableness Standard," *Criminology and Public Policy* 8 (2009): 117–140.

197. Ibid., pp. 136–137.

198. Brian A. Lawton, "Levels of Nonlethal Force: An Examination of Individual, Situational, and Contextual Factors," *Journal of Research in Crime and Delinquency* 44 (2007): 163–184.

199. Matthew J. Hickman, Alex R. Piquero, and Joel H. Garner, "Toward a National Estimate of Police Use of Nonlethal Force," *Criminology and Public Policy* 7 (2008): 563–604.

200. Theresa G. DiMaio and Vincent J. M. DiMaio, *Excited Delirium Syndrome: Cause of Death and Prevention* (Boca Raton, FL: CRC Press, 2005).

201. *Graham v. Connor*, 490 U.S. 386 (1989).

202. Gary M. Vilke and Theodore C. Chan, "Less Lethal Technology: Medical Issues," *Policing* 30 (2007): 341–357.

203. Warren Cohen, "When Lethal Force Won't Do," *U.S. News and World Report*, June 23, 1997, p. 12.

204. Michael R. Smith, Robert J. Kaminski, Jeffrey Rojek, Geoffrey P. Alpert, and Jason Mathis, "The Impact of Conducted Energy Devices and Other Types of Force and Resistance on Officer and Suspect Injuries," *Policing* 30 (2007): 423–446.

205. David Klinger, "Impact Munitions: A Discussion of Key Information," *Policing* 30 (2007): 385–397.

206. National Institute of Justice, *Department of Defense Nonlethal Weapons and Equipment Review: A Research Guide for Civil Law Enforcement and Corrections* (Washington, DC: National Institute of Justice, 2004).

207. National Institute of Justice, *Impact Munitions Use: Types, Targets, Effects* (Washington, DC: National Institute of Justice, 2004), p. 3.

208. Michael D. White and Justin Ready, "The TASER as a Less Lethal Force Alternative," *Police Quarterly* 10 (2007): 170–191.

209. For some research in this area, see R. J. Kaminski, S. M. Edwards, and J. W. Johnson, "Assessing the Incapacitative Effects of Pepper Spray During Resistive Encounters with Police," *Policing* 22

(1999): 7–29; R. J. Kaminski, S. M. Edwards, and J. W. Johnson, "The Deterrent Effects of Oleoresin Capsicum on Assaults Against Police: Testing the Velcro-Effect Hypothesis," *Police Quarterly* 1 (1998): 1–20.

210. National Institute of Justice, *The Effectiveness and Safety of Pepper Spray, Research for Practice* (Washington, DC: National Institute of Justice, 2003), http://www.ncjrs.gov/pdffiles1/nij/195739.pdf (accessed June 2014).

211. Federal Bureau of Investigation, "Law Enforcement Officers Killed and Assaulted, 2000," press release, November 26, 2001.

212. Federal Bureau of Investigation, "Law Enforcement Officers Killed and Assaulted, 2012," http://www.fbi.gov/about-us/cjis/ucr/leoka/2012/officers-feloniously-killed/felonious_topic_page_-2012 (accessed June 2014).

213. J. David Hirschel, Charles Dean, and Richard Lumb, "The Relative Contribution of Domestic Violence to Assault and Injury of Police Officers," *Justice Quarterly* 11 (1994): 99–118.

214. National Law Enforcement Officers Memorial Fund, http://www.nleomf.org/memorial/names/ (accessed June 2014).

CHAPTER 8

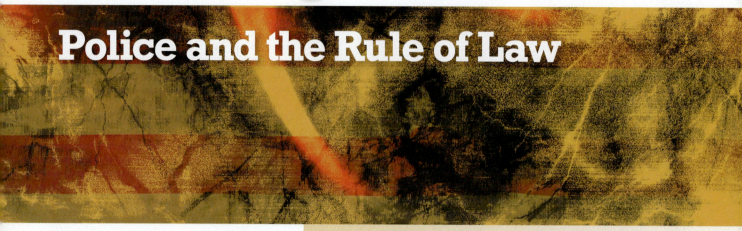

Police and the Rule of Law

Learning Objectives

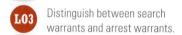

L01 Describe how the Fourth Amendment controls law enforcement officials.

L02 Define search and arrest.

L03 Distinguish between search warrants and arrest warrants.

L04 Explain when warrants are required.

L05 Recognize that there are three requirements that must be met before a warrant can be secured.

L06 Explain the rules for serving warrants.

L07 Discuss several types of warrantless searches and arrests.

L08 Explain the *Miranda v. Arizona* decision.

L09 Identify what purpose a lineup serves.

L010 Discuss the exclusionary rule, including its extensions and exceptions.

Chapter Outline

While on patrol at 2 A.M., a Missouri police officer stopped Tyler McNeely's truck for speeding and repeatedly crossing the centerline. On approaching the vehicle, the officer noticed several signs that McNeely was intoxicated. He had bloodshot eyes, slurred his speech, and smelled of alcohol. McNeely acknowledged he had indeed drunk "a couple beers" before getting in his truck. The officer then ordered McNeely out of the truck and performed a field sobriety test. McNeely performed poorly, whereupon the officer asked him to submit to a breathalyzer test. McNeely refused and was arrested and taken to a nearby hospital for a blood test. The officer never attempted to secure a warrant. McNeely refused to consent to the blood test, but a hospital technician performed it anyway. Results revealed that McNeely had be driving while intoxicated.

McNeely sought to have the results of the blood test excluded as evidence on the grounds that the forced blood draw was a violation of his Fourth Amendment right to protection from unreasonable searches and seizures. The case eventually arrived at the U.S. Supreme Court, where it was decided in *Missouri v. McNeely*[1] that "the metabolization of alcohol in the bloodstream and the ensuing loss of evidence are among the factors that must be considered in deciding whether a warrant is required." In other words, the officer's actions were justified in this specific case. The Court did not, however, rule that all such blood draws are constitutional. Instead, "when officers in drunk-driving investigations can reasonably obtain a warrant before having a blood sample drawn without significantly undermining the efficacy of the search, the Fourth Amendment mandates that they do so."[2] ■

The *McNeely* case highlights the complex legal landscape within which the police work on a daily basis. Influential court cases from all levels of government are routinely decided, and officers need to stay abreast of these changes. What's more, a court decision today could overrule another court decision from yesterday. Officers need to be aware of not just new rules handed down by the courts, but also *changes* in long-standing rules.

Although police want a free hand to search homes and cars for evidence, the Constitution's Fourth Amendment restricts police activities by requiring that they obtain a warrant before conducting a search. When police want to vigorously interrogate a suspect, they must also honor the Fifth Amendment's prohibition against forcing people to incriminate themselves.

Police and the Courts

Once a crime has been committed and an investigation begun, the police may use various means to collect the evidence needed for criminal prosecution. A number of critical decisions must take place:

■ Should surveillance techniques be employed to secure information?

■ How can information be gathered to support a request for a search warrant?

■ If the suspect is driving a vehicle, can the car be searched without a warrant?

■ Can a suspect's phone be tapped or her conversations recorded?

■ Is there reasonable suspicion to justify stopping and frisking a suspect?

■ Can a legal arrest be made?

■ If a suspect has been detained, what constitutes an appropriate interrogation?

■ Can witnesses be brought in to identify the suspect?

The U.S. Supreme Court has taken an active role in answering these questions. Its primary concern has been to balance the law enforcement agent's need for a free hand to investigate crimes with the citizen's constitutional right to be free from illegal searches and interrogations. In some instances, the Supreme Court has expanded police power—for example, by increasing the occasions when police can search without a warrant. In other cases, the Supreme Court has restricted police operations—for example, by ruling that every criminal suspect has a right to an attorney when being interrogated by police. Changes in the law often reflect such factors as the justices' legal philosophy and their concern about the ability of police to control crime, their views on the need to maintain public safety versus their commitment to the civil liberties of criminal defendants, and recent events such as the September 11, 2001, terrorist attacks.

What are the key areas of court involvement with police activities, and how have they been shaped by legal authority? We answer these questions throughout this chapter.

Search and Seizure

L01 Describe how the Fourth Amendment controls law enforcement officials.

Some of the key elements of police investigation are the search for incriminating evidence, the seizure of that evidence, and its use during a criminal trial. The Fourth Amendment protects criminal suspects against unreasonable searches and seizures by placing limitations on what the police can do in their efforts to catch lawbreakers and collect evidence.

A "search" occurs when a government actor infringes on a person's reasonable expectation of privacy. Pictured here are a New York City Police Department surveillance helicopter's cameras, including one for infrared photography. The chopper's arsenal of sophisticated surveillance and tracking equipment is powerful enough to stealthily read license plates, pedestrians' faces, and heat signatures from high above. Should authorities be allowed to use such devices at will? Would doing so raise any Fourth Amendment concerns?

The Fourth Amendment states:

The right of the people to be secure in their persons, houses, papers, and effects, against unreasonable searches and seizures, shall not be violated, and no warrants shall issue, but upon probable cause, supported by oath or affirmation, and particularly describing the place to be searched, and the persons or things to be seized.

There are two important parts of the Fourth Amendment, called the "reasonable clause" and the "warrants clause." The reasonable clause stops at "shall not be violated." It simply states that searches and seizures must be reasonable. The warrant clause starts at "and no warrants shall issue ..." This part of the Fourth Amendment lists warrant requirements. These two Fourth Amendment parts are not necessarily connected. A search can be reasonable without a warrant, but if a warrant is required, it must meet specific requirements.

Defining a Search

The dictionary definition of "search" is straightforward—namely, to look for something. In the search and seizure context, however, "search" has a very distinct meaning. A Fourth Amendment **search** occurs only when a government actor infringes on a person's reasonable expectation of privacy.[3]

A government actor is most often a police officer, in contrast to a private citizen. As a private citizen, a person could enter someone else's property and search for contraband without triggering the Fourth Amendment prohibitions. This person may commit the offense of criminal trespass, but the Fourth Amendment would not be triggered. Police officers' actions almost always trigger the Fourth Amendment.

Assuming a police officer is the one looking for evidence, then what has to happen for the officer to infringe on someone's reasonable expectation of privacy? The officer must be looking in a place where a person could reasonably expect privacy. Usually this includes private property, such as cars, houses, and personal effects (the reality is often quite complicated, however, as the accompanying Analyzing Criminal Justice Issues box about drug dog searches attests). So if an officer looks for contraband in a person's private home, the officer is

 LO2 Define search and arrest.

search
A government actor's infringement on a person's reasonable expectation of privacy.

CONCEPT SUMMARY 8.1

Distinguishing Between Open Fields and Curtilage

Open Fields	Curtilage
Park	Yard surrounding house
Public street	Fenced in and secure portion of private property (such as with "No Trespassing" signs)
Remote, unprotected area on private property	Secured outbuildings, such as a detached workshop

conducting a search. In contrast, if the officer looks for evidence in a public park, a search has not occurred because the park is public and does not belong to any one individual. Following are three key examples of actions that are *not* considered searches.

ABANDONED PROPERTY If a person abandons his or her property, such as by placing trash at the side of the road for pickup, that person cannot continue to assert privacy in the property. In *California v. Greenwood* (1988),[4] investigators found incriminating information in a person's garbage that was set to be picked up. The Supreme Court ruled that this action did not amount to a search. The officers were authorized to seize the evidence.

open field
Any unoccupied or undeveloped real property outside the curtilage of a home.

curtilage
Grounds or fields attached to a house.

OPEN FIELDS In *Oliver v. United States* (1984),[5] the U.S. Supreme Court distinguished between the privacy granted persons in their own home or its adjacent grounds and fields (curtilage) and the lack of expectation of privacy in open fields. The Court ruled that when the police look for evidence in an **open field**, defined as any unoccupied or undeveloped real property outside the curtilage of a home, a search does not occur. What, then, is **curtilage**? It is defined as the grounds or fields attached to and in close proximity to the house. Concept Summary 8.1 distinguishes between open fields and curtilage in more detail.

Jellico, Tennessee, police officers remove marijuana plants seized from a remote area of Campbell County. The find was one of the largest ever in Tennessee. Officers used a helicopter to transport the marijuana to a nearby state park for destruction in a controlled burn.

© Wade Payne/Knoxville News Sentinel

FLY-OVERS In *California v. Ciraola* (1986), the police received a tip that marijuana was growing in the defendant's backyard.[6] The yard was surrounded by fences, one of which was 10 feet high. The officers flew over the yard in a private plane at an altitude of 1,000 feet to ascertain whether it contained marijuana plants. On the basis of this information, a search warrant was obtained and executed, and with the evidence against him, the defendant was convicted on drug charges. On appeal, the Supreme Court found that his privacy had not been violated—that a search did not occur. This holding was later expanded in *Florida v. Riley* (1989), when the Court ruled that police do not need a search warrant to conduct even low-altitude helicopter searches of private property.[7] The Court allowed Florida prosecutors to use evidence obtained by a police helicopter that flew 400 feet over a greenhouse in which defendants were growing marijuana plants. The Court said the search was constitutionally permissible because the flight was within airspace legally available to helicopters under federal regulations.

Defining an Arrest

The Fourth Amendment does not mention arrests, but it does mention seizures. Arrest is one of the most common types of seizures. Some other actions, such as field interrogations, are also considered seizures. Here our concern is with arrest.

The arrest power of the police involves taking a person into custody in accordance with lawful authority and holding that person to answer for a violation of the criminal law. Police officers have complete law enforcement responsibility and unrestricted powers of arrest in their jurisdictions. Private citizens also have the right to make an arrest, generally when a crime is committed in their presence.

An **arrest** occurs when a police officer takes a person into custody or deprives a person of freedom for having allegedly committed a criminal offense. The police stop unlimited numbers of people each day for a variety of reasons, so the time when an arrest occurs may be hard to pinpoint. Some persons are stopped for short periods of questioning, others are informally detained and released, and still others are formally placed under arrest. However, a legal arrest occurs when the following conditions exist:

- The police officer believes that sufficient legal evidence—that is, probable cause—exists that a crime is being or has been committed and intends to restrain the suspect.
- The police officer deprives the individual of freedom.
- The suspect believes that he is in the custody of the police officer and cannot voluntarily leave. He has lost his liberty.

AP Images/Tony Dejak

Investigators dig in the backyard of Anthony Sowell's home in Cleveland, Ohio. Sowell, a registered sex offender, was arrested as a suspect in the murder of 11 women whose bodies were discovered at his Cleveland duplex. Investigators, along with the city police and buildings department, the FBI, and the coroner's office, had search warrants to dig by hand in areas of interest identified via FBI thermal-imaging and radar scans. Sowell was subsequently found guilty of the murders and is now on death row.

arrest
Occurs when a police officer takes a person into custody or deprives a person of freedom for having allegedly committed a criminal offense.

 L03 Distinguish between search warrants and arrest warrants.

analyzing criminal justice ISSUES

POLICE CANINE SEARCHES

Law enforcement officials rely extensively on dogs' keen sense of smell to help them in their duties. Trained police dogs can locate everything from bombs and drugs to fleeing suspects and crash survivors. They can also be sent into situations that are too dangerous for humans or into confined spaces their handlers cannot go. And they are of course faster on their feet than humans, which often proves helpful during foot pursuits. So valuable are police dogs that in most states they are considered full-fledged officers and are sometimes even given badges.

Police dogs are a fixture in modern law enforcement, but for various reasons their activities have come into question. Animal rights activists often object to using dogs in place of humans, claiming it violates dogs' right to be free. Others claim criminals are more apt to attack police dogs than a police officer attempting to do the same job. And still others have claimed that the use of police dogs in certain contexts (especially for locating drugs and explosives) is unconstitutional. Here we briefly summarize the four leading Supreme Court cases that have addressed the subject of police canine searches.

UNITED STATES v. PLACE (1983)

A traveler aroused the suspicion of police officers as he waited in line at the Miami International Airport. The officers confronted the suspect and noticed some discrepancies on the bag tags tied to his luggage. They summoned Drug Enforcement Administration agents who asked the suspect for consent to search the bags. He declined, at which point the agents took the luggage to a different airport and subjected it to a dog sniff. The dog alerted to one of the suitcases. With that

information, the agents secured a search warrant for the suitcase and opened it, finding cocaine inside. The man was arrested and charged with narcotics violations. He sought suppression of the evidence and the case eventually arrived at the Supreme Court. It held that "under the circumstances, the seizure of [the man's] luggage violated the Fourth Amendment ... [and that] the evidence obtained from the subsequent search of the luggage was inadmissible." Why? One reason was the luggage was held for over 90 minutes. Also, the "Fourth Amendment violation was exacerbated by the DEA agents' failure to inform [the man] accurately of the place to which they were transporting his luggage, of the length of time he might be dispossessed, and of what arrangements would be made for return of the luggage if the investigation dispelled the suspicion." The Court also noted, however, that ordinarily a dog sniff of a person's luggage does not constitute a search. The kicker in this case was, again, the lengthy detention of the luggage at a different location.

ILLINOIS v. CABALLES (2005)

An Illinois state trooper stopped a vehicle for speeding. During the 10-minute stop, while the trooper was in the process of issuing a citation, another trooper arrived and allowed his canine to sniff the driver's vehicle. It alerted to the trunk, so a search was conducted. Marijuana was found, and the driver was arrested. The Supreme Court upheld the dog sniff, citing three factors: (1) the legality of the stop; (2) its short duration; and (3) no one can claim legal ownership to—and thereby assert a privacy interest in—contraband. In the Court's words, "A dog sniff conducted during a concededly lawful traffic stop that reveals no information other than the location of a

---

search warrant
An order, issued by a judge, directing officers to conduct a search of specified premises for specified objects.

arrest warrant
An order, issued by a judge, directing officers to arrest a particular individual.

Search Warrants and Arrest Warrants

There are two varieties of warrants: **search warrants** and **arrest warrants**. A search warrant is an order, issued by a judge, directing officers to conduct a search of specified premises for specified objects. An arrest warrant is an order, issued by a judge, directing officers to arrest a particular individual. Examples of search and arrest warrants appear in Figures 8.1 and 8.2.

The Fourth Amendment does not necessitate warrants for all searches and arrests. In some situations, however, warrants are necessary. These situations include:

substance that no individual has any right to possess does not violate the Fourth Amendment."

FLORIDA v. HARRIS (2013)

Officer Wheetley stopped respondent Harris for an expired license plate. On approaching Harris's vehicle, Wheetley noticed that Harris was "visibly nervous" and unable to stop shaking. He also observed an open beer can in a cup holder. Wheetley asked for permission to search Harris's vehicle. Harris refused. Wheetley then went back to his cruiser and retrieved Aldo, a trained narcotics detection dog, and walked him around Harris's vehicle on a "free air sniff." Aldo alerted to the driver's side door handle. Harris then searched the truck, finding various items used in the manufacture of methamphetamine, but not the drug itself. Harris moved to suppress the items, claiming that Aldo's "false positive" did not give Wheetley probable cause to search. In a hearing on the subject, Wheetley testified to Aldo's training record and training performance. On cross-examination, Harris's attorney focused not on Aldo's training, but on the dog's certification and performance in the field. Wheetley acknowledged that Aldo's certification had expired before he stopped Harris and also that he did not keep complete records on Aldo's field performance. The Supreme Court was confronted with the question of whether the state must supply evidence of a drug dog's performance history in order to determine whether probable cause to search existed. It decided no such performance history must be kept and that the totality of circumstances must be considered in determining whether probable cause to search exists.

FLORIDA v. JARDINES (2013)

Detective William Pedraja of the Miami-Dade Police Department received a tip that marijuana was being grown in the home of Joelis Jardines. After surveilling the property for a time, Pedraja and another detective, Bartelt, a trained canine handler, approached the front porch. After sniffing the base of the door, the dog sat down, which he was trained to do on detecting the odor's strongest point. The detectives left and applied for a search warrant based on the dog's positive alert. A search warrant was granted later that day. The search revealed marijuana plants and Jardines was charged with trafficking in cannabis. Jardines moved to suppress the marijuana on the grounds that the canine investigation constituted an unreasonable search in violation of the Fourth Amendment. The question before the Supreme Court: Does use of a drug dog to sniff a person's front porch constitute a search within the meaning of the Fourth Amendment? The answer, according to the Court, was yes. It held that a person's porch is a constitutionally protected area and is part of the curtilage of a home.

CRITICAL THINKING

1. Do these decisions provide sufficient guidance for the proper execution of police canine searches?

2. What additional limitations, if any, should be placed on police canine searches?

3. Do you agree with the Supreme Court's decision in each case? Defend your answer.

Sources: *United States v. Place*, 462 U.S. 696 (1983); *Illinois v. Caballes*, 543 U.S. 405 (2005); *Florida v. Harris*, 568 U.S. ___ (2013); *Florida v. Jardines*, 569 U.S. ___ (2013).

- *Arrests and searches in private homes or on specific types of private property.* Subject to some limited exceptions (see the section "Warrantless Searches and Arrests"), warrants are always required for searches and arrests in private homes.[8]

- *Arrests for minor offenses committed out of view of the arresting officer.* There is no clear definition of "minor offense," but generally this includes misdemeanors. Limiting arrests in this fashion is known as the **in-presence requirement**; a misdemeanor needs to occur in the officer's presence for the arrest to be valid.[9]

in-presence requirement
A police officer cannot arrest someone for a misdemeanor unless the officer sees the crime occur. To make an arrest for a crime the officer did not witness, an arrest warrant must be obtained.

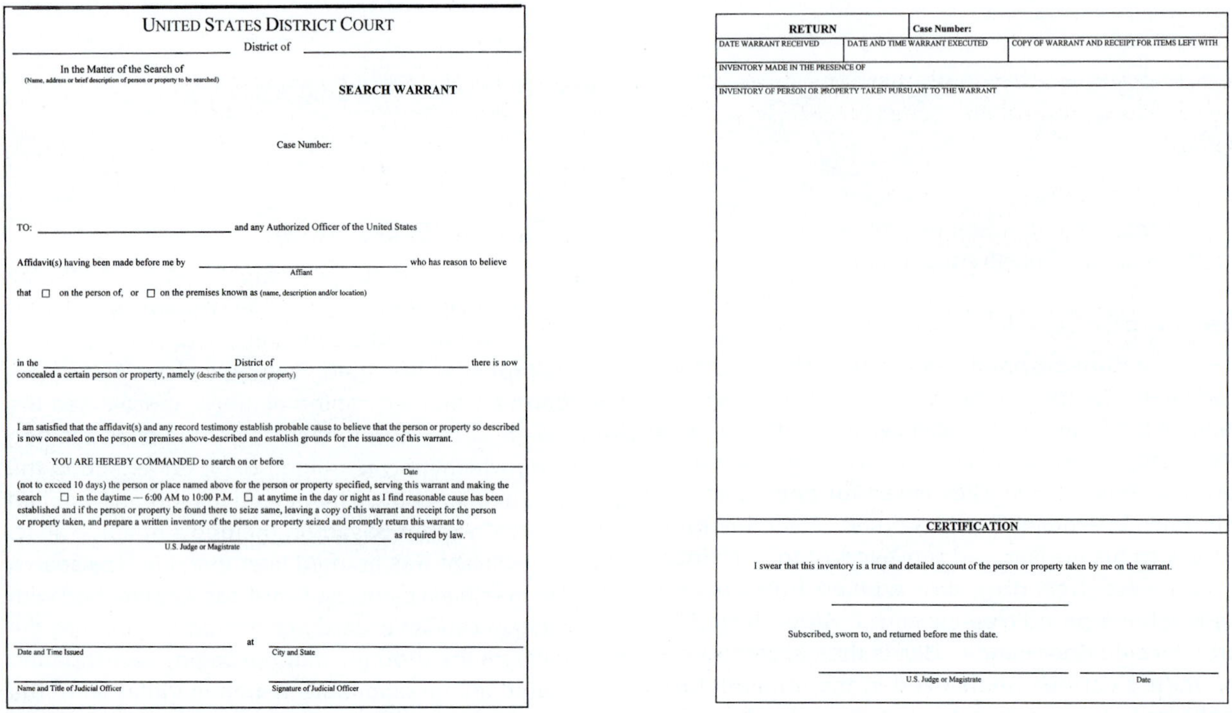

UNITED STATES DISTRICT COURT

District of

In the Matter of the Search of
(Name, address or brief description of person or property to be searched)

SEARCH WARRANT

Case Number:

TO: and any Authorized Officer of the United States

Affidavit(s) having been made before me by (Affiant) who has reason to believe

that ☐ on the person of, or ☐ on the premises known as (name, description and/or location)

in the District of there is now concealed a certain person or property, namely (describe the person or property)

I am satisfied that the affidavit(s) and any record testimony establish probable cause to believe that the person or property so described is now concealed on the person or premises above-described and establish grounds for the issuance of this warrant.

YOU ARE HEREBY COMMANDED to search on or before (Date)

(not to exceed 10 days) the person or place named above for the person or property specified, serving this warrant and making the search ☐ in the daytime — 6:00 AM to 10:00 P.M. ☐ at anytime in the day or night as I find reasonable cause has been established and if the person or property be found there to seize same, leaving a copy of this warrant and receipt for the person or property taken, and prepare a written inventory of the person or property seized and promptly return this warrant to (U.S. Judge or Magistrate) as required by law.

Date and Time Issued — at — City and State

Name and Title of Judicial Officer — Signature of Judicial Officer

RETURN		Case Number:
DATE WARRANT RECEIVED	DATE AND TIME WARRANT EXECUTED	COPY OF WARRANT AND RECEIPT FOR ITEMS LEFT WITH

INVENTORY MADE IN THE PRESENCE OF

INVENTORY OF PERSON OR PROPERTY TAKEN PURSUANT TO THE WARRANT

CERTIFICATION

I swear that this inventory is a true and detailed account of the person or property taken by me on the warrant.

Subscribed, sworn to, and returned before me this date.

U.S. Judge or Magistrate — Date

FIGURE 8.1 A Typical Search Warrant Form

Source: John N. Ferdico, Henry F. Fradella, and Christopher D. Totten, *Criminal Procedure for the Criminal Justice Professional*, 10th ed. (Belmont, CA: Cengage Learning, 2008).

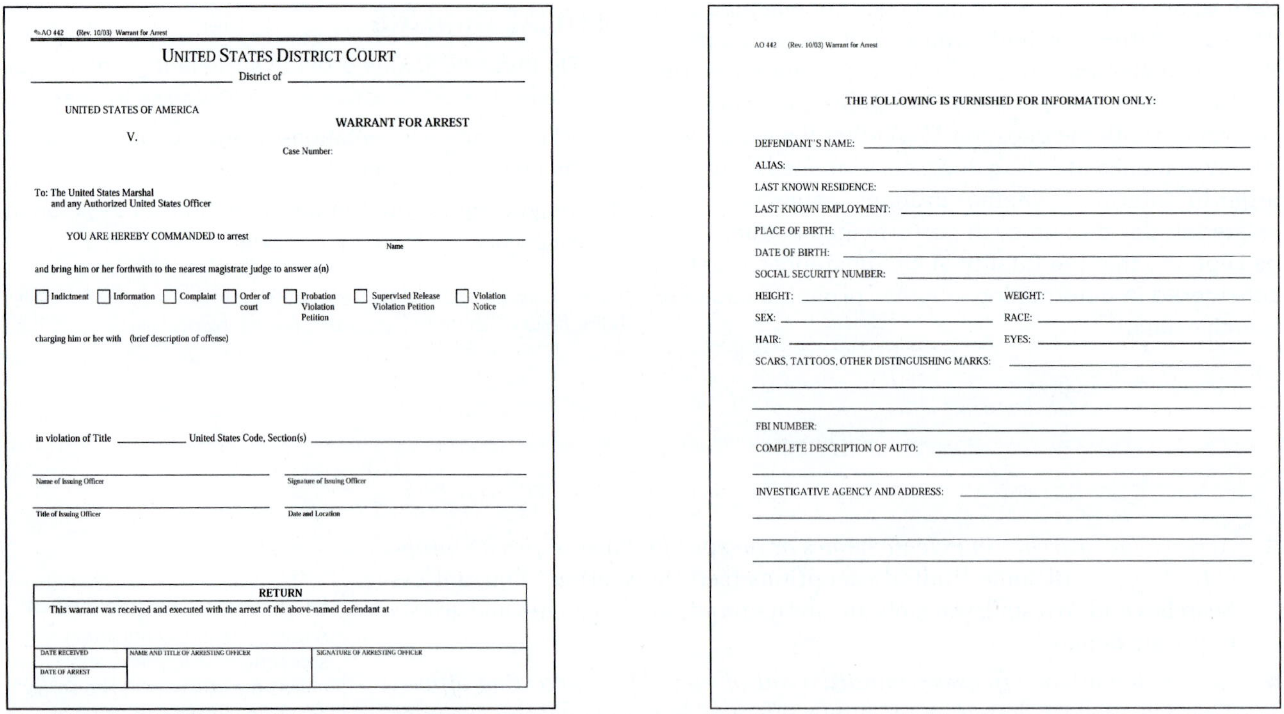

AO 442 (Rev. 10/03) Warrant for Arrest

UNITED STATES DISTRICT COURT

District of

UNITED STATES OF AMERICA

V.

WARRANT FOR ARREST

Case Number:

To: The United States Marshal
and any Authorized United States Officer

YOU ARE HEREBY COMMANDED to arrest (Name)

and bring him or her forthwith to the nearest magistrate judge to answer a(n)

☐ Indictment ☐ Information ☐ Complaint ☐ Order of court ☐ Probation Violation Petition ☐ Supervised Release Violation Petition ☐ Violation Notice

charging him or her with (brief description of offense)

in violation of Title United States Code, Section(s)

Name of Issuing Officer — Signature of Issuing Officer

Title of Issuing Officer — Date and Location

RETURN

This warrant was received and executed with the arrest of the above-named defendant at

DATE RECEIVED	NAME AND TITLE OF ARRESTING OFFICER	SIGNATURE OF ARRESTING OFFICER
DATE OF ARREST		

AO 442 (Rev. 10/03) Warrant for Arrest

THE FOLLOWING IS FURNISHED FOR INFORMATION ONLY:

DEFENDANT'S NAME:
ALIAS:
LAST KNOWN RESIDENCE:
LAST KNOWN EMPLOYMENT:
PLACE OF BIRTH:
DATE OF BIRTH:
SOCIAL SECURITY NUMBER:
HEIGHT: WEIGHT:
SEX: RACE:
HAIR: EYES:
SCARS, TATTOOS, OTHER DISTINGUISHING MARKS:
FBI NUMBER:
COMPLETE DESCRIPTION OF AUTO:
INVESTIGATIVE AGENCY AND ADDRESS:

FIGURE 8.2 A Typical Arrest Warrant Form

Source: John N. Ferdico, Henry F. Fradella, and Christopher D. Totten, *Criminal Procedure for the Criminal Justice Professional*, 10th ed. (Belmont, CA: Cengage Learning, 2008).

Warrant Requirements

There are three requirements that must be satisfied before a warrant can be issued. They are probable cause, a neutral and detached magistrate, and particularity.

 L04 Explain when warrants are required.

Probable Cause

A warrant cannot be issued unless it is based on **probable cause**, which is typically defined as a reasonable belief, based on fact, that a crime has been committed and that the person, place, or object to be searched and/or seized is linked to the crime with a reasonable degree of certainty.

Under normal circumstances, a search warrant cannot be obtained unless the request for it is supported by facts, supplied under oath by a law enforcement officer, that are sufficient to convince the court that a crime has been or is being committed.

To establish probable cause, the police must provide the judge or magistrate with information in the form of written affidavits, which report either their own observations or those of private citizens or police undercover informants. If the magistrate believes that the information is sufficient to establish probable cause to conduct a search, he or she will issue a warrant. Although the suspect is not present when the warrant is issued and therefore cannot contest its issuance, he can later challenge the validity of the warrant before trial.

The Fourth Amendment does not explicitly define probable cause, and its precise meaning still remains unclear. However, police officers have to provide factual evidence to define and identify suspicious activities; they may not simply offer their beliefs or suspicions. In addition, the officers must show how they obtained the information and provide evidence of its reliability. There are several sources of information that officers can use to show probable cause, including firsthand knowledge, informants' statements, anonymous tips, and telephone tips (also see Exhibit 8.1).

FIRSTHAND KNOWLEDGE Police can obtain a warrant if their investigation turns up sufficient evidence to convince a judge that a crime probably has been committed and that the person or place the police wish to search is probably involved materially in that crime. The ideal source of information is the officer's firsthand knowledge. If the officer witnesses a crime being committed, the warrant requirement can often be disposed of altogether and the officer will make a warrantless arrest (we look at warrantless searches and seizures later). If the officer cannot make a particular arrest or engage in a particular search without a warrant, but he or she nevertheless has information that could establish probable cause, then the officer's knowledge will be weighted heavily. For example, if during a drug sting operation an officer buys drugs from a suspect on several occasions, this officer's firsthand information will be important in getting a warrant to search the suspect's property.

L05 Recognize that there are three requirements that must be met before a warrant can be secured.

probable cause
The evidentiary criterion necessary to sustain an arrest or the issuance of an arrest or search warrant: a set of facts, information, circumstances, or conditions that would lead a reasonable person to believe that an offense was committed and that the accused committed that offense.

EXHIBIT 8.1   Sources of Information for Probable Cause

- A police informant whose reliability has been established because he has provided information in the past
- Someone who has firsthand knowledge of illegal activities
- A co-conspirator who implicates herself as well as the suspect
- An informant whose information can be partially verified by the police
- A victim of a crime who offers information
- A witness to the crime related to the search
- A fellow law enforcement officer

Web App 8.1

For more information about the use of informants, visit http://www.snitching.org/.

INFORMANTS   Police often rely on informants. Informants can include victims, witnesses, accomplices, and people familiar with the crime or suspects in question. Unfortunately, many informants often act out of self-interest instead of civic duty, and the reliability of the evidence they provide may be questionable. Moreover, their statements reflect only what they have seen and heard and are not substantiated by hard evidence.

The U.S. Supreme Court has been concerned about the reliability of evidence obtained from informants. The Court has determined that hearsay evidence must be corroborated to serve as a basis for probable cause and thereby justify the issuance of a warrant. In the case of *Aguilar v. Texas* (1964), the Court articulated a two-part test for issuing a warrant on the word of an informant. The police had to show (1) why they believed the informant and (2) how the informant acquired personal knowledge of the crime.[10] This ruling restricted informant testimony to people who were in direct contact with police and whose information could be verified.

ANONYMOUS TIPS   Because the *Aguilar* case required that an informant be known and that his or her information be likely to be reliable, it all but ruled out using anonymous tips to secure a search warrant. This was changed in a critical 1983 ruling, *Illinois v. Gates*, in which the Court eased the process of obtaining search warrants by developing a totality-of-the-circumstances test to determine probable cause for issuing a search warrant. In *Gates*, the police received a knowledgeable and detailed anonymous letter describing the drug-dealing activities of Lance and Sue Gates. On the basis of that tip, the police began surveillance and eventually obtained a warrant to search their home. The search was later challenged on the grounds that it would be impossible to determine the accuracy of information provided by an anonymous letter, a condition required by the *Aguilar* case. However, the Court ruled that to obtain a warrant, the police must prove to a judge that, considering the totality of the circumstances, an informant has relevant and factual knowledge that a fair probability exists that evidence of a crime will be found in a certain place.[11] The anonymous letter, rich in details, satisfied that demand.

TELEPHONE TIPS   Can the police conduct a search based on an anonymous tip, such as one that is given via telephone? In *Alabama v. White* (1990), the police received an anonymous tip that a woman was carrying cocaine.[12] Only after police observation showed that the tip had accurately predicted the woman's movements did it become reasonable to believe the tipster had inside knowledge about the suspect and was truthful in his assertion about the cocaine. The Supreme Court ruled that the search based on the tip was legal because it was corroborated by independent police work. In its ruling, the Court stated the following:

> Standing alone, the tip here is completely lacking in the necessary indicia of reliability, since it provides virtually nothing from which one might conclude that the caller is honest or his information reliable and gives no indication of the basis for his predictions regarding [Vanessa] White's criminal activities. However, although it is a close question, the totality of the circumstances demonstrates that significant aspects of the informant's story were sufficiently corroborated by the police to furnish reasonable suspicion. ... Thus, there was reason to believe that the caller was honest and well informed, and to impart some degree of reliability to his allegation that White was engaged in criminal activity.[13]

The *White* case seemed to give police powers to search someone after corroborating an anonymous tip. However, in *Florida v. J. L.*, the Court narrowed that right. In *J. L.*, an anonymous caller reported to the Miami-Dade police that a young black male standing at a particular bus stop, wearing a plaid shirt, was carrying a gun.[14] The tip was not recorded, and nothing was known about the caller. Two officers went to the bus stop and spotted three black males. One of them, the 15-year-old J. L., was wearing a plaid shirt. Apart from the anonymous tip, the officers had no reason to suspect that any of the males were involved in any criminal activity. The officers did not see a firearm, and J. L. made no threatening or unusual movements. One officer approached J. L., frisked him, and seized a gun from his pocket. The Court disallowed the search, ruling that a police officer must have reasonable suspicion that criminal activity is being conducted prior to stopping a person. Because anonymous tips are generally considered less reliable than tips from known informants, they can be used to search only if they include specific information that shows they are reliable. Unlike the *White* case, the police in *J. L.* failed to provide independent corroboration of the tipster's information.

Neutral and Detached Magistrate

Warrants can be issued only by neutral and detached magistrates. Any judge is considered a neutral and detached magistrate. Requiring that a judge "sign off" on a warrant brings an element of objectivity to the criminal process. It serves as a check on police officers' decisions concerning who should be arrested and/or searched. The Supreme Court echoed this point over 60 years ago in the important case of *Johnson v. United States* (1948):

> The point of the Fourth Amendment … is not that it denies law enforcement the support of the usual inferences reasonable men draw from evidence. Its protection consists in requiring that those inferences be drawn by a neutral and detached magistrate instead of being judged by the officer engaged in the often competitive enterprise of ferreting out crime.[15]

Before a warrant will be issued, a police officer must offer sworn testimony that the facts on which the request for the search warrant is made are trustworthy and true. If the judge issues the warrant, it will authorize police officers to search for particular objects, at a specific location, at a certain time. A warrant may authorize the search of "the premises at 221 Third Avenue, Apt. 6B, between the hours of 8 A.M. and 6 P.M." and direct the police to search for and seize "substances, contraband, paraphernalia, scales, and other items used in connection with the sale of illegal substances." Generally, warrants allow the seizure of a variety of types of evidence, as described in Exhibit 8.2.

Particularity

Recall that the Fourth Amendment states, in part, that warrants must *particularly* describe "the place to be searched, and the persons or things to be seized." This **particularity** requirement was included in the Fourth Amendment to counteract the use of general warrants by government agents. This was a device used against the colonists by the English crown. British officials had obtained

particularity
The requirement that a search warrant state precisely where the search is to take place and what items are to be seized.

EXHIBIT 8.2   Categories of Evidence

Warrants are typically issued to search for and seize a variety of evidence:

- Property that represents evidence of the commission of a criminal offense—for example, a bloody glove or shirt

- Contraband, the fruits of crime, smuggled goods, illegal material, or anything else that is of a criminal nature

- Property intended for use or which has been used as the means of committing a criminal offense—for example, burglary tools, safecracking equipment, and drug paraphernalia

- People may be seized when there is probable cause for their arrest

- Conversation involving criminal conspiracy and other illegalities can be seized via tape recordings and wiretaps

CONCEPT SUMMARY 8.2
Warrant Requirements

■ *Probable cause.* Probable cause is determined by whether a police officer has objective, reasonable, and reliable information, based on fact, that the person under investigation has committed or was committing an offense.

■ *Neutral and detached magistrate.* Neither a search warrant nor an arrest warrant can be issued without the signature of a neutral and detached magistrate. Judges are considered neutral and detached.

■ *Particularity.* A search warrant must set forth and precisely specify the places to be searched and the items to be seized so that it can provide reasonable guidance to the police officers and prevent them from having unregulated and unrestricted discretion to search for evidence. An arrest warrant must specify the name of the person to be arrested or provide a sufficiently specific description of the individual.

general warrants empowering them to search any suspected places for smuggled goods, placing the liberty of every man in the hands of government officials.[16]

The particularity requirement is also designed to curtail potential abuse that may result from an officer being allowed to conduct a search with unbridled discretion. If a warrant is issued in violation of the particularity clause, the ensuing search is invalid even if the officers actually exercise proper restraint in executing their search. What and who are to be searched must be clearly spelled out. The police cannot search the basement of a house if the warrant specifies the attic; they cannot look in a desk drawer if the warrant specifies a search for a missing piano. However, this does not mean that police officers can seize only those items listed in the warrant. If, during the course of their search, police officers come across contraband or evidence of a crime that is not listed in the warrant, they can lawfully seize the unlisted items. This is referred to as the plain view exception (see the section "Warrantless Searches and Arrests" for more on plain view). But they cannot look in places that are off-limits within the scope of the warrant.

The particularity requirement applies to arrest warrants, as well. To satisfy this requirement, the police must clearly specify the name of the individual who is to be arrested. If no name is available, they must provide a sufficiently specific description of the individual. Concept Summary 8.2 sums up this and the other two requirements for obtaining a warrant.

Web App 8.2

For more information about U.S. Supreme Court decisions on criminal procedure, visit http://www.law.cornell.edu/supremecourt/text/.

Serving the Warrant

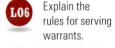

LO6 Explain the rules for serving warrants.

Once a warrant is secured, it needs to be served. There are important procedural steps that must be followed when a warrant is served. The steps are mostly the same for each type of warrant. They include:

1. *Knock and announce.* In general, when a warrant is served, officers must knock on the door and announce their presence.[17] Officers must announce their authority and their intentions.[18] When it is likely that an announcement would threaten officer safety, the knock-and-announce rule can be waived. To protect themselves, officers often secure so-called "no-knock" warrants that authorize them in advance to make entry without knocking and announcing. The knock-and-announce rule was dealt a blow in the case of *Hudson v. Michigan*, where the Supreme Court held that evidence seized following a violation of the rule does not have to be excluded from trial.[19]

2. *Keep property damage to a minimum.* It may be necessary for officers to forcibly enter the premises if the door is locked or barricaded. Likewise, it could be necessary to damage a person's property when searching for items

named in a warrant. In either case, the standard is "shocks the conscience." If the property damage shocks the conscience, officers may be held liable for the damages they inflict.[20]

3. *Use appropriate force.* It may be necessary for officers to use force during service of either an arrest warrant or a search warrant. An arrestee may resist, or the person whose property is searched could decide to attack the police. In both instances, the standards governing deadly and nondeadly force apply. We discussed these in the previous chapter.

4. *Pay attention to time constraints with search warrants.* Most search warrants require daytime service.[21] The warrant may also limit the amount of time officers can take to search for the evidence they seek. In most jurisdictions, these requirements can be avoided if officers obtain warrants that permit night service or contain other special instructions.

5. *Limit the scope and manner of searches.* The scope and manner of the search must be reasonable in light of what is sought. For example, if a search warrant authorizes police to look for stolen jewelry, then they can look almost anywhere. In contrast, if the warrant names stolen big-screen televisions, then the police cannot look in drawers, cabinets, and other small places where such items could not be stored.[22]

6. *No reporters allowed.* The Supreme Court has held that the police cannot bring members of the media along on the service of search warrants unless they are there to serve a legitimate law enforcement function, such as videotaping the execution of the warrant for training purposes.[23]

Warrantless Searches and Arrests

Under normal circumstances, the police must obtain a warrant to conduct a search. However, over the years the Supreme Court has carved out some significant exceptions to the warrant requirement of the Fourth Amendment. These include:

- Exigent (emergency) circumstances
- Stop and frisk
- Searches incident to lawful arrest
- Automobile searches
- Consent searches
- Searches based on plain view
- Crimes committed in an officer's presence

A warrantless search or arrest must be reasonable. For example, a search would be considered unreasonable if it was conducted simply because of an offender's prior behavior or status. Police officers cannot stop and search a vehicle driven by a known drug dealer unless some other factors support the search. Unless there was something discernible to a police officer that indicated a crime was then being committed, the suspect's past history would not justify an officer's stopping and searching the vehicle. Nor would it be considered reasonable if police decided to search someone simply because he was seen engaging in a pattern of behavior that seemed similar or comparable to the activity of known criminals. A person could not be searched because he was seen driving a flashy new car and making routine stops at the same places each day merely because that is a pattern of behavior typical of drug dealing.

Also, the mere fact that a warrantless arrest is permissible does not mean the officer has complete autonomy to determine whether probable cause is in place. Every person who is subject to warrantless arrest must be brought before a judge, usually within 48 hours, for a **probable cause hearing**.[24]

L07 Discuss several types of warrantless searches and arrests.

probable cause hearing
If a person is subjected to a warrantless arrest, a hearing is held to determine whether probable cause exists that he committed the crime.

Exigent Circumstances

exigent circumstances

Emergency or urgent circumstances.

The Supreme Court has identified a number of **exigent circumstances** in which a search warrant might normally have been required, but, because of some immediate emergency, police officers can search suspects and places without benefit of a warrant. These include hot pursuit, danger of escape, threats to evidence, and threats to others. In each situation, officers must have probable cause.

The definition of exigent circumstances is not written in stone, and situations that a police officer considers exigent may be later disputed in the courts. In *Kirk v. Louisiana* (2002), police officers observed a suspect engaging in what they believed to be drug deals. Without a warrant, they entered his home, arrested him, frisked him, found a drug vial in his underwear, and seized contraband that was in plain view in the apartment. Only after these actions did the officers obtain a warrant. The Supreme Court ruled that police officers need either a warrant or probable cause plus exigent circumstances to make a lawful entry into a home. Although the Court left unclear the factors that define exigent circumstances, the facts of the *Kirk* case indicate that merely observing a suspect committing what appears to be a nonviolent crime is not enough to justify a warrantless entry of a person's home.[25]

HOT PURSUIT   Let's say that police officers become involved in a shoot-out with three suspects who then run into a house. The police would be allowed to enter the premises without a warrant in order to find and arrest the suspects. The warrantless search would be allowed because the police were in **hot pursuit** of the suspects and because failure to search could put citizens in danger, a condition that courts typically view as exigent.[26]

hot pursuit

A legal doctrine that allows police to perform a warrantless search of premises where they suspect a crime has been committed when delay would endanger their lives or the lives of others and lead to the escape of the alleged perpetrator.

In order to justify a warrantless search by claiming hot pursuit, there are five important requirements that must all be met:

- The police must have probable cause that the suspect is on the premises to be searched.
- The police must have reason to believe that an immediate apprehension is necessary.
- Hot pursuit must be commenced from a lawful vantage point. For example, if officers wrongfully entered private property and commenced a pursuit from there, they could not claim hot pursuit.
- The offense in question must be serious, usually a felony.

Ryan Stone, 29, runs from a stolen car after causing a crash in Lone Tree, Colorado. Suspected of stealing an SUV with a 4-year-old boy inside, carjacking two other vehicles, and seriously injuring a state trooper, Stone was arrested after police tracked him around the Denver area during morning rush hour.

■ The pursuit must occur prior to or close to apprehension of the suspect. For example, officers cannot justify a search based on hot pursuit if they already have the suspect in custody.[27]

Sometimes hot pursuits end badly, perhaps with an injury to the suspect or an innocent bystander. And sometimes officers are sued for their decisions to pursue, even by the offenders who flee! The Supreme Court decided such a case in *Scott v. Harris*. In that case, the driver of a fleeing vehicle crashed and became a quadriplegic. He sued the police, claiming that the force that officers used to bring him to a halt was excessive (an officer rammed Harris's vehicle). The Court held that because Harris posed such a danger to others as

criminal justice and TECHNOLOGY

GPS TAGGING IN HOT-PURSUIT CASES

It seems there is an enduring fascination with watching criminals run for their lives. High-speed police pursuits are staples on the evening news. Popular programs such as *World's Wildest Police Chases* quench viewers' thirst for witnessing desperate suspects try to escape law enforcement's clutches. All told, some 100,000 high-speed pursuits are recorded each year. Some of the chases end peacefully, others in fiery blazes.

Although most fleeing suspects get caught, there is nothing easy about making the decision to give chase. On the one hand, when a pursuit begins, there is the risk that innocent pedestrians or motorists could be hurt. Officers need to guard against this possibility, especially when the chase could go through a residential neighborhood. On the other hand, if officers gave too much weight to the possibility that others could be hurt and did not give chase, criminals would learn quickly that they can run and avoid apprehension.

Most police departments have policies that guide officers in their decision whether or not to pursue. Some permit pursuit only in cases involving violent felonies. Others are more "generous" and allow officers to commence a pursuit in virtually any situation where a suspect decides to flee. These pursuit policies have been based not just on individual departments' experiences but also on scientific study. Researchers have examined the relationships between various types of pursuit policies and resulting injuries. Others have tried to identify the factors most often associated with injury to innocent third parties and fleeing suspects. In spite of all these efforts, the solution to the pursuit problem has remained elusive—until now. Police officers in several cities are now using GPS-based technology to tag and track fleeing suspects' vehicles.

The pioneer in this area is a company by the name of StarChase. Its Pursuit Management System, reminiscent of a James Bond–like car-mounted rocket launcher, consists of a compressed air launcher affixed to a police cruiser's bumper that fires GPS tagging darts at fleeing vehicles. The darts attach to the fleeing vehicle and send a signal that can be tracked. A dispatcher views the location and movements of the vehicle in real time via a secure Internet connection and relays the information to officers on the ground, who then easily locate the suspect.

LAPD Chief William Bratton has said this about the technology, which *Time* magazine labeled one of the "best innovations of the year":

> Instead of us pushing them doing 70 or 80 miles an hour … this device allows us not to have to pursue after the car. … It allows us to start vectoring where the car is. Even if they bail out of the car, we'll have pretty much instantaneous information where they are.

The Arizona Department of Public Safety was the first state law enforcement agency to adopt the technology.

CRITICAL THINKING

1. **Is GPS tagging likely to solve the problems that can result from police pursuits? Why or why not?**

2. **What other options do officers have available for dealing with fleeing motorists? Are they more or less effective than tagging?**

Sources: Geoffrey P. Alpert, *Police Pursuit: Policies and Training* (Washington, DC: National Institute of Justice, 1997); StarChase, http://www.starchase.com (accessed June 2014); Laurie Sullivan, "L.A. Cops Fight Car Chases with GPS Devices," http://www.informationweek.com/news/178601965 (accessed June 2014); Arizona Department of Public Safety, http://www.azdps.gov/Media/News/View/?p=115 (accessed June 2014).

he was fleeing, the officer was justified in using force to bring Harris's vehicle to a stop.[28] The Court reached a similar decision in 2014; in *Plumhoff v. Rickard*, the justices unanimously sided with six police officers who shot and killed a driver and his passenger during a chaotic pursuit in the city of West Memphis.[29] In response to this and other high-profile pursuit incidents, police departments have adopted policies and acquired technologies intended to help reduce loss of life and injury. See the accompanying Criminal Justice and Technology box for more on this.

DANGER OF ESCAPE   If there is a possibility that a suspect will escape if the police have to take time to secure a warrant, they may be able to dispense with the warrant requirement. For example, if the police learn through an informant that a dangerous robbery suspect just entered an apartment complex, they may be able to enter the premises to find the suspect if they cannot secure the property or obtain a warrant in time.[30]

THREATS TO EVIDENCE   If the police have probable cause to believe that an individual is about to destroy critical evidence, such as flushing drugs down the toilet, they can enter private property and seize the evidence without first obtaining a warrant.[31] The Supreme Court has also sanctioned the seizure of blood (via a needle) from a man's arm to prove he had been drinking—a practice that continues in some jurisdictions, especially around the holidays.[32]

The case on which this decision was based, *Breithaupt v. Abram* (1957), predated Breathalyzers, so we are unlikely to see additional cases where needles are used to obtain evidence of intoxication. Regardless of the technique used, the key to the case was that the evidence would have disappeared had the police not obtained it quickly. The suspect would have metabolized the alcohol.

THREATS TO OTHERS   If a suspect poses a risk to others, this also can be considered an exigent circumstance. For example, in a hostage situation, the police can usually dispense with the warrant requirement and storm the property (if it is safe) in order to protect the lives of innocent persons held within. In one recent case, the Supreme Court sanctioned the actions of some officers who, without a warrant, entered a house where a loud party was going on because they observed a fight taking place.[33] The Court stated that "Police may enter a home without a warrant when they have an objectively reasonable basis for believing that an occupant is seriously injured or imminently threatened with such injury."[34]

The same applies, it seems, even if it is not clear whether any one person is being threatened. In *Michigan v. Fisher*,[35] officers arrived at a house and saw Jeremy Fisher, who was screaming and throwing objects, through a window. The officers knocked, but Fisher did not answer. They noticed his hand was bleeding and asked whether he needed medical attention. He ignored the officers' questions and told them to get a warrant. One officer then forced open the door. Fisher drew a gun but was subdued and charged with assault with a dangerous weapon. Fisher sought suppression of the gun at trial, but the Supreme Court decided that his Fourth Amendment rights were not violated.

Field Interrogation: Stop and Frisk

stop-and-frisk
The situation in which police officers who are suspicious of an individual run their hands lightly over the suspect's outer garments to determine whether the person is carrying a concealed weapon; also called a threshold inquiry or pat-down.

One important exception to the rule requiring a search warrant is the **stop-and-frisk** procedure. This type of search typically occurs when a police officer encounters a suspicious person on the street and frisks or pats down his outer garments to determine whether he is in possession of a concealed weapon. The police officer need not have probable cause to arrest the suspect but simply must be reasonably suspicious based on the circumstances of the case (that is, time and

Tens of thousands of New Yorkers participate in a silent march to protest NYPD racial profiling, including the department's controversial stop-and-frisk program, which critics allege disproportionally targeted minority groups.

Tony Savino/Corbis News/Corbis

place) and her experience as a police officer. The stop-and-frisk search consists of two distinct components:

1. The stop, in which a police officer wishes to briefly detain a suspicious person in an effort to effect crime prevention and detection.
2. The frisk, in which an officer pats down, or frisks, a person who is stopped, in order to check for weapons. The purpose of the frisk is protection of the officer making the stop.

The stop and the frisk are separate actions, and each requires its own factual basis. Stopping a suspect allows for brief questioning, and frisking affords the officer an opportunity to avoid the possibility of attack. For instance, a police officer patrolling a high-crime area observes two young men loitering outside a liquor store after dark. The two men confer several times and stop to talk to a third person who pulls up alongside the curb in an automobile. From this observation, the officer may conclude that the men are casing the store for a possible burglary. He can then stop the suspects and ask them for some identification and an explanation of their conduct. However, the facts that support a stop do not automatically allow a frisk. The officer must have reason to believe that the suspect is armed or dangerous. In this instance, if the three men identify themselves as security guards and produce identification, a frisk would not be justified. If they seem nervous and secretive and the officer concludes that they are planning a crime, the suspicion would be enough to justify a pat-down.

The landmark case of *Terry v. Ohio* (1968) shaped the contours of the stop and frisk.[36] In *Terry*, a police officer found a gun in the coat pocket of one of three men he frisked when their suspicious behavior convinced him that they were planning a robbery. At trial, the defendants futilely moved to suppress the gun on the grounds that it was the product of an illegal search. On appeal,

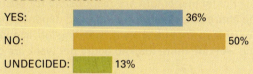

YOUR OPINION: New York City allows police to stop and frisk anyone on the street whom they consider suspicious. Do you favor or oppose having a stop-and-frisk law where you live?

PUBLIC OPINION:

YES:	36%
NO:	50%
UNDECIDED:	13%

REALITY: Regardless of what a city law permits, the Supreme Court has permitted stop and frisk, as long as police have reasonable suspicion that criminal activity is afoot. This was the decision in *Terry v. Ohio*, a case discussed in this chapter. The question above, asked of likely voters by Rasmussen Reports, is interesting, but incomplete. For example, it does not discuss specifics about the law in question. Nevertheless, it seems at least half of respondents have a problem with stop and frisk, even though the Supreme Court permits it!

DISCUSSION: How likely is it that innocent people will be inconvenienced by stop and frisk? Is there a racial component to the stop-and-frisk decision? If so, explain. New York City has recently come under fire for its stop-and-frisk policies. Read about and offer your opinion on the lawsuit that has been filed against the City of New York (see http://ccrjustice.org/floyd).

Source: Rasmussen Reports, 36% *Favor a Stop and Frisk Law Where They Live*, http://www.rasmussenreports.com/public_content/politics/general_politics/november_2013/36_favor_a_stop_and_frisk_law_where_they_live (accessed June 2014).

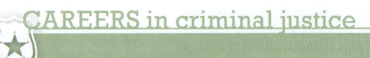

CAREERS in criminal justice

POSTAL INSPECTOR

DUTIES AND CHARACTERISTICS OF THE JOB

The Postal Inspection Service is a law enforcement body of the U.S. government. Postal inspectors investigate crimes that break postal laws, and they ensure the security of the U.S. Postal Service. The duties of postal inspectors include general law enforcement tasks such as executing warrants, arresting offenders, and testifying in court. However, a large part of a postal inspector's job is investigating crimes perpetrated through the mail, such as mail theft, mail fraud, drug trafficking, child pornography, and identity theft. Postal inspectors conduct investigations using a combination of advanced technology and forensic skills. They investigate harassment and threats against postal employees and the postal service itself. Postal inspectors are also responsible for investigating any threat that involves the mail as a medium. For example, postal inspectors were involved in the 2001 investigation into the envelopes containing anthrax that were mailed to government and news offices.

Postal inspectors are responsible for ensuring that the entire postal service is safe and dependable. Being a postal inspector can be a demanding job; irregular hours and working more than 40 hours per week are common.

JOB OUTLOOK

Unfortunately, opportunities for employment as a postal inspector open at irregular intervals. However, when the postal service is hiring, a diversity of skills and backgrounds is desirable in potential postal inspectors.

SALARY

As with other federal employees, salaries for postal inspectors are determined by the General Pay Scale, and various factors, such as employment qualifications, are used to determine position on the scale. Postal inspectors are exempt from the Fair Labor Standards Act and so cannot earn overtime pay. Entry-level salaries range from $41,563 to $78,355 (not including locality pay, which includes a cost-of-living adjustment in the upward direction). A candidate's qualifications and current pay are considered when the initial salary is set.

OPPORTUNITIES

Because of the good pay, benefits, prestige, and opportunities that these positions offer, applicants should expect competition. Accounting experience,

the Supreme Court ruled that if a reasonably prudent police officer believes that her safety or that of others is endangered, she may make a reasonable search for weapons on the person, regardless of whether she has probable cause to arrest that individual for a crime or is absolutely certain that the individual is armed. The *Terry* case illustrates the principle that although the police officer must, whenever possible, secure a warrant to make a search and seizure, still, when swift action is called for based upon on-the-spot observations, the need for the warrant is removed.

What kind of behavior can trigger a *Terry* search? How suspicious does a person have to look before the police can legally stop him and pat him down? In *Illinois v. Wardlow* (2000), the defendant was walking on the street in an area known for narcotics trafficking. When he made eye contact with a police officer riding in a marked police car, he ran away. The officer caught up with the defendant on the street, stopped him, and conducted a protective pat-down search for weapons. A handgun was discovered in the frisk, and the defendant was convicted of unlawful use of a weapon by a felon. The Illinois Supreme Court ruled that the frisk violated *Terry v. Ohio* because flight may simply be an exercise of the right to "go on one's way" and does not constitute reasonable suspicion. However, on appeal, the U.S. Supreme Court reversed the state court ruling that computer skills, and a law degree are helpful when applying for a position. Law enforcement experience as a detective or even a patrol officer will also be helpful. Finally, good students who earned a bachelor's or an advanced degree with a 3.0 or higher average can qualify for the academic achievement track with or without full-time job experience.

QUALIFICATIONS

Candidates must be U.S. citizens 21 or over, but younger than 36½, and they must have a four-year degree, no felony or domestic violence convictions, and a driver's license. A candidate must also be in sound mental and physical health and must pass a hearing test. Qualities such as good communications skills (written and oral), sound decision-making skills, and the ability to follow instructions are also highly valued. Once having satisfied the general requirements, a candidate must qualify for training under one of several tracks offered: language skills, postal experience, specialized nonpostal experience (includes those with law degrees, certification in auditing or computer systems, law enforcement experience, and others), or academic achievement.

Additionally, applicants must undergo a background check, pass a polygraph, and be interviewed. After completing the proper training, a postal inspector may be relocated, so a willingness to move is also necessary.

EDUCATION AND TRAINING

In order to even apply for a position, a potential candidate must have a four-year degree. After successfully moving through the application process and being hired, new employees will be sent to Basic Inspector Training in Potomac, Maryland, where they will learn about the responsibilities of their organization, investigative techniques, firearms proficiency, and physical defense. Those with no postal experience will then be on a six-month probation period before becoming full-time employees.

Sources: U.S. Postal Inspection Service Employment, https://postalinspectors .uspis.gov/employment/eligibility.aspx (accessed June 2014); U.S. Office of Personnel Management, http://www.opm.gov/policy-data-oversight/pay-leave/salaries-wages/#url=2014 (accessed June 2014).

a person's presence in a "high crime area," in and of itself, is not enough to support a reasonable, particularized suspicion of criminal activity.[37] It held that a location's characteristics are sufficiently suspicious to warrant further investigation and that, in this case, the additional factor of the defendant's unprovoked flight added up to reasonable suspicion. The officers found that the defendant possessed a handgun, and as a result of the pat-down and search, they had probable cause to arrest him for violation of a state law. The frisk and arrest were thus proper under *Terry v. Ohio*.

The Supreme Court's recent decision in *Arizona v. Johnson*[38] combined the issue of stop and frisk with a vehicle stop. In that case, police officers serving on a gang task force stopped a vehicle for an infraction, but they did not suspect criminal activity. One officer confronted the driver; another questioned one of the passengers, Johnson. After the officer learned that Johnson had a criminal record, he was asked to exit the vehicle, which he did. The officer then frisked Johnson and found a gun. He was arrested, charged, and convicted of illegally carrying a weapon. The Supreme Court sanctioned the search, reinforcing the *Terry* decision's language that police may need to "act instantly if they have reasonable cause to suspect that the persons temporarily detained are armed and dangerous."[39]

Search Incident to a Lawful Arrest

Traditionally, a search without a warrant is permissible if it is made incident to a lawful arrest. *Incident* means close in time to an arrest, usually right after the arrest. The police officer who searches a suspect incident to a lawful arrest must generally observe two rules: (1) the search must be conducted at the time of or immediately following the arrest, and (2) the police may search only the suspect and the area within the suspect's immediate control. The search may not legally go beyond the area where the person can reach for a weapon or destroy any evidence. For example, if shortly after the armed robbery of a grocery store, officers arrest a suspect hiding in the basement with a briefcase, a search of the suspect's person and of the briefcase would be a proper **search incident to a lawful arrest** without a warrant.

**search incident to a
lawful arrest**

An exception to the search warrant
rule, limited to the immediate
surrounding area.

The legality of this type of search depends almost entirely on the lawfulness of the arrest. The arrest will be upheld if the police officer observed the crime being committed or had probable cause to believe that the suspect committed the offense. If the arrest is found to have been invalid, then any warrantless search made incident to the arrest would be considered illegal, and the evidence obtained from the search would be excluded from trial.

The U.S. Supreme Court defined the permissible scope of a search incident to a lawful arrest in *Chimel v. California* (1969).[40] According to the *Chimel* doctrine, the police can search a suspect without a warrant after a lawful arrest to protect themselves from danger and to secure evidence. But a search of his home is illegal even if the police find contraband or evidence during the course of that search and if the police would otherwise be forced to obtain a warrant to search the premises. Likewise, police cannot search certain effects obtained during the course of a lawful arrest. In the 2014 landmark decision of *Riley v. California*, the Supreme Court unanimously decided that it is a Fourth Amendment violation to search the cell phone of an arrestee without a warrant.[41] The decision will likely have sweeping implications for other technologies.

Automobile Searches

The U.S. Supreme Court has also established that certain situations justify the warrantless search of an automobile on a public street or highway. Evidence can be seized from an automobile when a suspect is taken into custody in a lawful arrest. In *Carroll v. United States*, which was decided in 1925, the Supreme Court ruled that distinctions should be made among searches of automobiles, persons, and homes. The Court also concluded that a warrantless search of an automobile is valid if the police have probable cause to believe that the car contains evidence they are seeking.[42] This same rule is in effect today. The accompanying feature "Evolution of *Carroll v. United States*" summarizes several of the Court's important vehicle search decisions in the wake of *Carroll*, which are discussed further throughout this section.

Because police are now confronting such significant social problems as drug trafficking and terrorist activity, the Supreme Court has given them some additional leeway in terms of making stops. For example, in the 2002 case *United States v. Arvizu*, the Court allowed a stop (and eventual search) of a vehicle based on a pattern of suspicious behavior:

■   A vehicle registration check showing that the vehicle was registered to an address in an area notorious for alien and narcotics smuggling

■   The patrol officer's personal experience and his knowledge that the suspect had taken a route frequently used by drug smugglers

■   The driver's route having been designed to pass through the area during a border patrol shift change

Although each fact alone was insufficient to justify the stop, together they supported the officer's decision to stop the vehicle.[43]

Evolution of *Carroll v. United States*

Carroll v. United States (1925)	An automobile can be searched without a warrant if the police have probable cause.[44]
United States v. Lee (1927)	An automobile is any conveyance being used for transportation, including even a motor home.[45]
Cardwell v. Lewis (1974)	People enjoy a lesser expectation of privacy in their vehicles than in their homes and offices.[46]
Pennsylvania v. Mimms (1977)	During routine traffic stops, officers can order drivers out of their cars and frisk them.[47]
United States v. Ross (1982)	With probable cause, police can search an automobile without a warrant, including any containers within.[48]
Michigan v. Long (1983)	Police can frisk a driver and search the passenger compartment of a vehicle following a valid stop, provided they have reasonable suspicion that the driver poses a danger.[49]
Michigan Dept. of State Police v. Sitz (1990)	Suspicionless seizures of motorists are permissible for purposes of detecting drunk driving.[50]
Whren v. United States (1996)	The constitutional reasonableness of a traffic stop does not depend on an officer's initial motivation. It depends only on whether there was justification to stop the vehicle.[51]
Maryland v. Wilson (1997)	During a routine traffic stop, the officer can order a passenger out of the vehicle and frisk him or her.[52]
City of Indianapolis v. Edmund (2000)	The police cannot operate roadblocks for the purpose of detecting illegal drugs.[53]
Illinois v. Lidster (2004)	Police are constitutionally authorized to conduct suspicionless vehicle checkpoints for the purpose of gaining information about a crime recently committed in the area.[54]
Brendlin v. California (2007)	Passengers, like drivers, are considered "seized" during traffic stops, meaning they enjoy Fourth Amendment protection from unreasonable searches and seizures.[55]
Arizona v. Gant (2009)	If a motorist is arrested, police may search the vehicle only if it is reasonable to assume the arrestee could access the vehicle *or* the vehicle contains evidence of the offense of arrest.[56]
Davis v. United States (2011)	The post-arrest seizure of evidence not connected with the offense of arrest is constitutionally permissible if based on objectively reasonable reliance on appropriate appellate precedent.[57] *Gant* would have invalidated the seizure in this case, but it had not been decided at the time the seizure took place.

SCOPE OF THE AUTOMOBILE SEARCH The legality of searching automobiles without a warrant has always been a trouble spot for police and the courts. Should the search be limited to the interior of the car, or can the police search the trunk? What about a suitcase in the trunk? What about the glove compartment? Does a traffic citation give the police the right to search an automobile? These questions have produced significant litigation over the years. To clear up the matter, the Supreme Court has focused on two types of situations: "pure" vehicle searches and vehicle searches following driver arrests and/or detentions.

A "pure" vehicle search is one in which the police seek to search a vehicle without regard to whether the vehicle is being driven by a person. In other words, these are searches of the vehicle that do not concern the passenger.

In *United States v. Ross* in 1982,[58] the Supreme Court held that if probable cause exists to believe that an automobile contains criminal evidence, a warrantless search by the police is permissible, including a search of closed containers in the vehicle. Probable cause is the all-important requirement. In the absence of probable cause, the search will run afoul of the Fourth Amendment, and any resulting evidence will be inadmissible in court. With probable cause, however, the car may be stopped and searched, contraband can be seized, and the occupant can be arrested, all without violating the Fourth Amendment.

What if, however, a driver is stopped for speeding and the officer has no intent—in advance—to search the vehicle? In *Michigan v. Long*,[59] police officers observed a vehicle swerve into a ditch. When officers approached the vehicle, they noticed that the driver was intoxicated and that there was a large hunting knife on the passenger seat. The officers arrested the driver and searched the passenger compartment of the vehicle. Both actions were sanctioned by the Supreme Court. The search was justified on the grounds that it was necessary to protect officer safety.

More recently, in *Arizona v. Gant*,[60] the Supreme Court held that a full vehicle search following the driver's arrest is permissible only if it is reasonable to assume the arrestee could access the vehicle *or* the vehicle contains evidence of the offense of arrest. Concerning the latter requirement, if the person was stopped for trafficking in illegal weapons, then with probable cause the police would be authorized to search the vehicle for weapons, even if the driver was arrested, handcuffed, and locked in the back seat of a police car. It is important to note that the *Gant* decision did not overturn *Michigan v. Long*; officers can still search a vehicle's passenger compartment when they have reasonable suspicion that the driver, whether or not he or she is arrested, might gain access to it and obtain a weapon.

SEARCHING DRIVERS AND PASSENGERS Can police officers search drivers and passengers during routine traffic stops? In 1977, the Supreme Court ruled in *Pennsylvania v. Mimms* that officers could order drivers out of their cars and frisk them during routine traffic stops. Officers' safety outweighed the intrusion on individual rights.[61] In 1997, the Court held in *Maryland v. Wilson* that the police had the same authority with respect to passengers.[62] In the *Wilson* case, a state patrol officer lawfully stopped a vehicle for speeding. While the driver was producing his license, the front-seat passenger, Jerry Lee Wilson, was ordered out of the vehicle. As he exited, crack cocaine dropped to the ground. Wilson was arrested and convicted of drug possession. His attorney moved to suppress the evidence, but the U.S. Supreme Court disagreed and extended the *Mimms* rule to passengers. The Court noted that lawful traffic stops had become progressively more dangerous to police officers and that thousands of officers were assaulted and even killed during such stops. The decision means that passengers must comply when ordered out of a lawfully stopped vehicle.

In 2007, the Supreme Court decided another vehicle search case, this one dealing with searches of passengers. In *Brendlin v. California*,[63] a car was stopped to check its registration. After stopping the vehicle, the officers learned that a passenger, Brendlin, was a parole violator. The officers arrested him, searched him, and found an orange syringe cap on his person. A pat-down search of the driver also revealed contraband. She was also arrested. Then the car was searched incident to the driver's arrest, and methamphetamine paraphernalia was discovered. Brendlin challenged the search, seeking to have the evidence excluded, but the California Supreme Court held that Brendlin was not "seized" in the traffic stop. This meant he could not even challenge his arrest and subsequent search. Not surprisingly, the U.S. Supreme Court disagreed, holding that Brendlin *was* seized. This case was important because the Court held that anyone detained in a traffic stop, not just the driver, is "seized." This means such persons can challenge the police action on constitutional grounds.

PRETEXT STOPS A pretext stop is one in which police officers stop a car because they suspect the driver is involved in a crime such as drug trafficking, but, lacking probable cause, they use a pretext such as a minor traffic violation to stop the car and search its interior. The legality of pretext stops was challenged in *Whren v. United States* (1996).[64] Two defendants claimed that plainclothes police officers used relatively minor traffic violations as an excuse, or pretext, to stop their vehicle because the officers lacked objective evidence that they were drug couriers. However, the Supreme Court ruled that if probable cause exists to stop a person for a traffic violation, then the actual motivation of the officers is irrelevant; therefore, the search was legal. This point was reiterated in *Arkansas v. Sullivan*, in which the Court ruled that if an officer has a legal basis for making a custodial arrest for a particular crime, it does not matter whether he has suspicions that the suspect is involved in any other criminal activity.[65] Thus, as long as there is a legal basis for making an arrest, officers may do so, even in cases in which they are motivated by a desire to gather evidence of other suspected crimes.

ROADBLOCK SEARCHES Police departments often wish to set up roadblocks to check driver's licenses or the condition of drivers. Is such a stop an illegal search and seizure? In *Delaware v. Prouse* (1979), the Supreme Court forbade the practice of random stops in the absence of any reasonable suspicion that some traffic or motor vehicle law has been violated.[66] Unless there is at least reasonable belief that a motorist is unlicensed, that an automobile is not registered, or that the occupant is subject to seizure for violation of the law, stopping and detaining a driver to check his or her license violates the Fourth Amendment. In *City of Indianapolis v. Edmond* (2000), the Court ruled that the police may not routinely stop all motorists in the hope of finding a few drug criminals.[67] The general rule is that any seizure must be accompanied by individualized suspicion; the random stopping of cars to search for drugs is illegal.

Although random stops are forbidden, a police department can set up a roadblock to stop cars in some systematic fashion to ensure public safety. As long as the police can demonstrate that the checkpoints are conducted in a uniform manner and that the operating procedures have been determined by someone other than the officer at the scene, roadblocks can be used to uncover violators of even minor traffic regulations. In *Michigan Dept. of State Police v. Sitz* (1990), the Court held that brief, suspicionless seizures at highway checkpoints for the purposes of combating drunk driving were constitutional.[68] Police can stop a predetermined number of cars at a checkpoint and can request each motorist to produce his or her license, registration, and insurance card. While doing so, they can check for outward signs of intoxication. The Court has sanctioned similar stops for purposes of assisting police in a criminal investigation. In *Illinois v. Lidster*, officers briefly detained motorists to ask whether they witnessed a hit-and-run accident that occurred earlier in the same location.[69]

Pennsylvania State Police block a road in an attempt to catch a robbery suspect. Does this kind of road block comply with constitutional requirements?

Bill Adams/Express-Times / Landov

Consent Searches

Police officers may also undertake warrantless searches when the person in control of the area or object consents to the search. Those who consent to a search essentially waive their constitutional rights under the Fourth Amendment. Ordinarily, courts are reluctant to accept such waivers and require the state to prove that the consent was voluntarily given. In addition, the consent must be given intelligently, and in some jurisdictions, consent searches are valid only after the suspect is informed of the option to refuse consent.

VOLUNTARINESS The major legal issue in most consent searches is whether the police can prove that consent was given voluntarily. In general, consent cannot be the result of "duress or coercion, express or implied."[70] For example, in the case of *Bumper v. North Carolina* (1968), police officers searched the home of an elderly woman after informing her that they possessed a search warrant.[71] At the trial, the prosecutor informed the court that the search was valid because the woman had given her consent. When the government was unable to produce the warrant, the court decided that the search was invalid because the woman's consent was not given voluntarily. On appeal, the U.S. Supreme Court upheld the lower court's finding that the consent had been illegally obtained by the false claim that the police had a search warrant.

In most consent searches, however, voluntariness is a question of fact to be determined from all the circumstances of the case. In *Schneckloth v. Bustamonte* (1973), the defendant helped the police by opening the trunk and glove compartment of the car. The Court said this action demonstrated that the consent was voluntarily given.[72] Furthermore, the police are usually under no obligation to inform a suspect of the right to refuse consent.[73] Failure to tell a suspect of this right does not make the search illegal, but it may be a factor used by the courts to decide whether the suspect gave consent voluntarily.

THIRD-PARTY CONSENT Can a person give consent for someone else? In *United States v. Matlock* (1974), the Court ruled that it is permissible for one co-occupant of an apartment to give consent to the police to search the premises in the absence of the other occupant, as long as the person giving consent shares common authority over the property and no present co-tenant objects.[74] What happens if one party gives consent to a search while another interested party refuses? This is what happened in the 2006 case of *Georgia v. Randolph*. Police were called to Scott Randolph's home because of a domestic dispute. His wife told police that Randolph had been using a lot of cocaine and that drugs were on the premises. One officer asked Randolph whether he could conduct a search of the home, and Randolph said no. Another officer asked his wife for permission, and she not only said yes but also led the officer upstairs to a bedroom where he allegedly found cocaine residue. The Supreme Court held that because Randolph was present when the police came to his home, they were required by the Fourth Amendment to heed his objection to the search; the seizure of the drugs was ruled illegal.[75]

BUS SWEEPS Today, consent searches have additional significance because of their use in drug control programs. On June 20, 1991, the U.S. Supreme Court, in *Florida v. Bostick*, upheld the drug interdiction technique known as the **bus sweep**, in which police board buses and, without suspicion of illegal activity, question passengers, ask for identification, and request permission to search luggage.[76] Police in the *Bostick* case boarded a bus bound from Miami to Atlanta during a stopover in Fort Lauderdale. Without suspicion, the officers picked out the defendant and asked to inspect his ticket and identification. After identifying themselves as narcotics officers looking for illegal drugs, they asked to inspect the defendant's luggage. Although there was some uncertainty about

bus sweep
Police investigation technique in which officers board a bus or train without suspicion of illegal activity and question passengers, asking for identification and seeking permission to search their baggage.

whether the defendant consented to the search in which contraband was found, and about whether he was informed of his right to refuse consent, the defendant was convicted.

The Supreme Court was faced with deciding whether consent was freely given or the nature of the bus sweep negated the defendant's consent. The Court concluded that drug enforcement officers, after obtaining consent, may search luggage on a crowded bus without meeting the Fourth Amendment requirements for a search warrant or probable cause.

This case raises fundamental questions about the legality of techniques used to discourage drug trafficking. Are they inherently coercive? In *Bostick*, when the officers entered the bus, the driver exited and closed the door, leaving the defendant and other passengers alone with two officers. Furthermore, Terrance Bostick was seated in the rear of the bus, and officers blocked him from exiting. Finally, one of the officers was clearly holding his handgun in full view. In light of these circumstances, was this a consensual or a coercive search? The Supreme Court ruled, despite the coercive circumstances, that the search was appropriate because consent had been given voluntarily.

"FREE TO GO" What if a police officer stops a motorist and asks for consent to search the vehicle? Must the officer inform the driver that he or she is "free to go" before asking consent to search the vehicle? In *Ohio v. Robinette* (1996), the Court concluded that no such warning is needed to make consent to a search reasonable. Robert D. Robinette was stopped for speeding. After checking his license, the officer asked whether Robinette was carrying any illegal contraband in the car. When the defendant answered in the negative, the officer asked for and received permission to search the car. The search turned up illegal drugs. The Supreme Court ruled that police officers do not have to inform a driver that he is "free to go" before asking whether they can search the car. According to the Court, the touchstone of the Fourth Amendment is reasonableness, which is assessed by examining the totality of the circumstances.[77] In this case, the search was ruled a reasonable exercise of discretion.

Plain View

The Supreme Court has also ruled that police can search for and seize evidence without benefit of a warrant if it is in plain view.[78] For example, if a police officer is conducting an investigation and notices, while questioning some individuals, that one has drugs in her pocket, the officer can seize the evidence and arrest the suspect. Or if the police are conducting a search under a warrant authorizing them to look for narcotics in a person's home, and they come upon a gun, the police can seize the gun, even though it is not mentioned in the warrant. The 1986 case of *New York v. Class* illustrates the **plain view doctrine**.[79] A police officer stopped a car for a traffic violation. Wishing to check the vehicle identification number (VIN) on the dashboard, he reached into the car to clear away material that was obstructing his view. While clearing the dash, he noticed a gun under the seat—in plain view. The U.S. Supreme Court upheld the seizure of the gun as evidence because the police officer had the right to check the VIN; therefore, the sighting of the gun was legal.

The doctrine of plain view was applied and further developed in *Arizona v. Hicks* (1987).[80] In that case, the Court held that moving a stereo component in plain view a few inches to record the serial number constituted a search under the Fourth Amendment. When a check with police headquarters revealed that the item had been stolen, the equipment was seized and offered as evidence at James Hicks's trial. The Court held that a plain view search and seizure could be justified only by probable cause, not reasonable suspicion, and suppressed the evidence against the defendant. In this case, the Court decided to take a firm

plain view doctrine
The principle that evidence in plain view of police officers may be seized without a search warrant.

stance on protecting Fourth Amendment rights. The *Hicks* decision is uncharacteristic in an era when most decisions have tended to expand the exceptions to the search warrant requirement.

PLAIN TOUCH If the police touch contraband, can they seize it legally? Is "plain touch" like plain view? In the 1993 case of *Minnesota v. Dickerson*, two Minneapolis police officers noticed the defendant acting suspiciously after leaving an apartment building they believed to be a crack house. The officers briefly stopped Timothy Dickerson to question him and conducted a pat-down search for weapons. The search revealed no weapons, but one officer felt a small lump in the pocket of Dickerson's nylon jacket. The lump turned out to be one-fifth of a gram of crack cocaine, and Dickerson was arrested and charged with drug possession. In its decision, the Court added to its plain view doctrine a plain touch or plain feel corollary. However, the pat-down must be limited to a search for weapons, and the officer may not extend the "feel" beyond that necessary to determine whether what is felt is a weapon.[81]

Although *Dickerson* created the plain feel doctrine, the Supreme Court limited its scope in *Bond v. United States*.[82] In that case, a federal border patrol agent boarded a bus near the Texas–Mexico border to check the immigration status of the passengers. As he was leaving the bus, he squeezed the soft luggage that passengers had placed in the overhead storage space. When he squeezed a canvas bag belonging to the defendant, he noticed that it contained a "brick-like" object. The defendant consented to a search of the bag, the agent discovered a "brick" of methamphetamine, and the defendant was charged with and convicted of possession. The court of appeals ruled that the agent's manipulation of the bag was not a search under the Fourth Amendment. On appeal, however, the Supreme Court held that the agent's manipulation of the bag violated the Fourth Amendment's rule against unreasonable searches. Personal luggage, according to the Court, is protected under the Fourth Amendment. The defendant had a privacy interest in his bag, and his right to privacy was violated by the police search.

Crimes Committed in an Officer's Presence

The decision to arrest is often made by the police officer during contact with the suspect and does not rely on a warrant being used. In the case of a felony, most jurisdictions provide that a police officer may arrest a suspect without a warrant when probable cause exists, even though the officer was not present when the offense was committed.

As a general rule, if the police make an arrest without a warrant, the arrestee must be promptly brought before a magistrate for a probable cause hearing. The U.S. Supreme Court dealt with the meaning of "promptly" in the 1991 case of *Riverside County v. McLaughlin*.[83] The Court said that the police may detain an individual arrested without a warrant for up to 48 hours without a court hearing to determine whether the arrest was justified.

NONCRIMINAL ACTS Can police arrest someone for a noncriminal act such as a traffic violation? This issue was decided in the case of *Atwater et al. v. City of Lago Vista*.[84] Gail Atwater was stopped for failing to wear a seat belt as she drove her two children home from soccer practice in Lago Vista, near Austin, Texas. She unbuckled for just a moment, she said, to look for a toy that had fallen from the pickup truck onto the street. The Lago Vista patrolman pulled her over, berated her, and arrested her. Under Texas law, she had committed a misdemeanor. Atwater subsequently was found to be driving without a license and to lack proof of insurance.

The standard for determining whether a police action was reasonable under the circumstances in this case is difficult. Some might argue that Atwater's traffic violation was not a breach of the peace, but others might suggest that Atwater's arrest was legal because she had violated a state statute. Whatever your opinion

CONCEPT SUMMARY 8.3

Warrantless Searches

Action	Scope of Search
Exigent circumstances	Limitless if exigency exists.
Stop and frisk	Pat-down of a suspect's outer garments.
Search incident to arrest	Full body search after a legal arrest.
Automobile search	If probable cause exists, full search of car including driver, passengers, and closed containers found in trunk. Search must be reasonable.
Consent search	Warrantless search of person or place is justified if the suspect knowingly and voluntarily consents to a search.
Plain view	Suspicious objects seen in plain view can be seized without a warrant.
Crime committed in an officer's presence	Arrest followed by search incident to arrest.

is, in April 2001 the U.S. Supreme Court upheld the right to arrest a suspect for a traffic violation.

In a twist on the *Atwater* case, the Supreme Court recently decided a case where officers in Virginia stopped a motorist for driving with a suspended license. In *Virginia v. Moore*,[85] state law required that the officer issue a citation to the driver, but instead they arrested him. The driver sought to suppress contraband that was seized during a search of the vehicle, arguing that this search violated the Fourth Amendment, but the Court held that police did not violate the Fourth Amendment because the search was based on probable cause. This case raises a really interesting question: is it fair to allow states to have restrictive laws governing searches but then essentially abandon such laws in favor of a looser standard when it suits the police? This is exactly what happened in the present case. The state of Virginia argued that although the officers' actions violated state law, they did not violate the U.S. Constitution. Is this fair and reasonable?

For a summary of the discussion on warrantless searches, see Concept Summary 8.3.

Electronic Surveillance

The use of wiretapping to intercept conversations between parties has significantly affected police investigative procedures. Electronic devices enable people to listen to and record the private conversations of other people over telephones, through walls and windows, and even over long-distance phone lines. Using these devices, police are able to intercept communications secretly and obtain information related to criminal activity.

The oldest and most widely used form of electronic surveillance is wiretapping. With approval from the court

Transportation engineer associate Abeer Kliefe works at the Los Angeles Department of Transportation's Automated Traffic Surveillance and Control Center in downtown Los Angeles. Advocates of increased surveillance believe more electronic eyes on the streets will help law enforcement catch more criminals.

AP Images/Reed Saxon

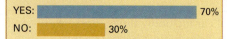
and a search warrant, law enforcement officers place listening devices on telephones to overhear oral communications of suspects. Such devices are also often placed in homes and automobiles. The evidence collected is admissible and can be used in the defendant's trial.

Many citizens believe that electronic eavesdropping through hidden microphones, radio transmitters, telephone taps, and bugs represents a grave threat to personal privacy.[86] Although the use of such devices is controversial, the police are generally convinced of their value in investigating criminal activity. However, opponents believe that these techniques are often used beyond their lawful intent to monitor political figures, harass suspects, or investigate cases involving questionable issues of "national security."

In response to concerns about invasions of privacy, the U.S. Supreme Court has increasingly limited the use of electronic eavesdropping in the criminal justice system. In *Katz v. United States* (1967), the Court ruled that when federal agents eavesdropped on a phone conversation using a listening device that could penetrate the walls of a phone booth, they had conducted an illegal search and seizure.[87] The *Katz* doctrine is usually interpreted to mean that the government must obtain a court order if it wishes to listen in on conversations in which the parties have a reasonable expectation of privacy, such as in their own homes or on the telephone. Meanwhile, public utterances or actions are fair game. *Katz* concluded that electronic eavesdropping is a search, even though there is no actual trespass. Therefore, it is unreasonable, and a warrant is needed.

Surveillance Law

It can be relatively painless to secure a warrant for an ordinary search, but the police have to jump through many more hoops when it comes to electronic surveillance. There are two key laws that restrict government wiretap authority. The first, the Federal Wiretap Act (more formally called Title III of the Omnibus Crime Control and Safe Streets Act), was adopted in 1968 and revised in 1986.[88] It requires court approval of all real-time eavesdropping on electronic communications, including voice, e-mail, fax, Internet, and those connected with criminal investigations. More recently, this authority has been used to support eavesdropping on communications between suspected terrorists. The Patriot Act, the controversial antiterrorism legislation enacted after 9/11, has expanded the number of criminal statutes for which such wiretaps can be authorized.

The second key statute controlling wiretaps and eavesdropping is the Foreign Intelligence Surveillance Act (FISA) of 1978.[89] It authorizes wiretapping of any alien the government believes is a member of a foreign terrorist group or is an agent of a foreign power. In the case of U.S. citizens, there must be probable cause that the person targeted for a wiretap is involved in criminal activity; otherwise, there is no such requirement for aliens. FISA warrants are authorized by the secret Foreign Intelligence Surveillance Court, which meets in a heavily secured room within the U.S. Justice Department. The court is staffed by 11 judges, appointed by the chief justice of the U.S. Supreme Court, who serve seven-year terms.

Just as the Patriot Act altered the Federal Wiretap Act, it also altered FISA. It did so by allowing prosecutors to gather evidence in cases involving national security crimes. In 2007, President Bush signed into law the controversial Protect America Act. It removed the warrant requirement for surveillance of foreign intelligence targets that the government "reasonably believes" are operating outside the United States. The law was especially controversial because it permitted electronic surveillance of all communications, including some domestic ones that involved foreign targets. Because of a sunset clause, the law expired in early 2008, but portions of it were replaced by the FISA Amendments Act of 2008. This area of law continues to change.

Technologies for Local Law Enforcement

The Federal Wiretap Act and FISA have limited applicability to local law enforcement. Most terrorism investigations and related surveillance activity tend to be federal affairs. For example, most FISA warrants are sought by the FBI. Yet there are plenty of technological advances that have benefited local law enforcement officials. Gone are the days of crude wiretaps outside phone booths and other antiquated devices. Now the police can avail themselves of several technological advances to help them keep tabs on the criminal element. Some devices even permit listening to and looking in on the activities of *everyone*, not just criminals. These devices are controversial because there is no warrant requirement. Examples include surveillance cameras and GPS tracking devices.

SURVEILLANCE CAMERAS Many large cities (including Baltimore, Chicago, Los Angeles, Dallas, Washington, and New York) have installed, in public locations, security cameras that can be monitored by officers from a distance. Since 2006, Washington, D.C., has installed dozens of cameras across the city. Initially they were used as investigative tools, so that officers could go back through recorded video and find evidence of crimes committed in the cameras' view. They were eventually monitored on a regular basis.[90] The cameras have proved helpful on more than one occasion, but critics claim that these "prying eyes" violate people's privacy.

GPS TRACKING DEVICES In *United States v. Jones*,[91] the Supreme Court decided on the constitutionality of GPS tracking of criminal suspects. Without a warrant, police installed a GPS tracking device on Antoine Jones's vehicle and tracked his movements for a month. They were able to use the evidence obtained from the tracking device to successfully build a drug trafficking case against Jones, who was ultimately sentenced to life in prison. Interestingly, the Supreme Court sided with Jones and reversed his conviction, concluding that the use of the GPS tracking device constituted a search and needed to be supported by probable cause and a warrant.

On its face, the *Jones* case seems somewhat at odds with former Supreme Court cases involving tracking devices. In one case, *United States v. Knotts*, the Court held that it was constitutional for police to use a "beeper," a less sophisticated tracking device, to monitor a suspect's movements.[92] The difference in *Knotts*, however, was that the beeper was placed in a container with the consent of its owner who then passed it off to Knotts. In other words, Knotts was not the victim of any sort of government trespass. Moreover, the government tracked Knotts's movements only in public areas. A similar decision was reached in *United States v. Karo*, another case in which the tracking device was inserted into a container *before* it came into the possession of the individual whose movements were tracked.[93] *Jones* is distinguished from these cases because, according to the Court, the police trespassorily attached the tracking device to Jones's vehicle.

Interrogation

After a suspect is taken into custody, it is routine to question him about his involvement in the crime. The police may hope to find out about co-conspirators or even whether the suspect was involved in similar crimes. This is a particularly unsettling time, and the arrestee may feel disoriented, alone, and afraid. Consequently, he may give police harmful information that can be used against him in a court of law. Exacerbating the situation is the fact that the interrogating

LO8 Explain the *Miranda v. Arizona* decision.

Web App 8.3

To see Chief Justice Earl Warren's handwritten notes on the *Miranda* case, go to http://www.loc.gov/exhibits/treasures/images/uc005076x.jpg.

officers sometimes use extreme pressure to get suspects to talk or to name their accomplices. Because of these concerns, the Supreme Court has issued rulings that protect criminal suspects from police intimidation, the most important of which was set down in the 1966 case of *Miranda v. Arizona*.[94]

The *Miranda* Warning

In the landmark case of *Miranda v. Arizona* (1966), the Supreme Court held that suspects in custody must be told that they have the following rights if they are subjected to interrogation:

- They have the right to remain silent.
- If they decide to make a statement, the statement can and will be used against them in a court of law.
- They have the right to have an attorney present at the time of the interrogation, or they will have an opportunity to consult with an attorney.
- If they cannot afford an attorney, one will be appointed for them by the state.

Miranda **warning**

The requirement that when a person is custodially interrogated, police inform the individual of the right to remain silent, the consequences of failing to remain silent, and the constitutional right to counsel.

The police must give this information—collectively known as the ***Miranda warning***—to a person in custody before questioning begins.

Some suspects choose to remain silent. However, simply remaining silent is not the same as invoking *Miranda* protection. As the Supreme Court recently decided, if a suspect does not assert his or her *Miranda* rights and makes a self-incriminating voluntary statement in response to police questioning, that statement can be used in court.[95] To enjoy the benefits of *Miranda*, then, the suspect must state that he or she intends to remain silent. Also, the suspect can insist on having counsel present.

A suspect's constitutional rights under *Miranda* can be given up (waived). A suspect can choose to talk to the police or sign a confession. However, for the waiver to be effective, the state must first show that it was voluntary and that the defendant was aware of all of his *Miranda* rights. People who cannot understand the *Miranda* warning because of their age, mental handicaps, or language problems may not be legally questioned without an attorney present. If they can understand their rights, they may be questioned.[96]

Once the suspect asks for an attorney, all questioning must stop until the attorney is present. And if the criminal suspect has invoked his or her *Miranda* rights, police officials cannot reinitiate interrogation in the absence of counsel even if the accused has consulted with an attorney in the meantime.[97] This rule was recently modified to some extent; it doesn't apply if the suspect has been released from custody for at least two weeks.[98]

Even if the suspect has invoked his *Miranda* rights and demanded an attorney, the police can question the offender about another, separate crime (as long as they give the *Miranda* warning for the second crime as well). For example, say a person is arrested on burglary charges and requests an attorney. The next day, police question him about a murder after reading the suspect his *Miranda* rights. He decides to waive his rights and confesses to the murder without a lawyer being present. The murder confession would be legal even though the suspect had requested an attorney in the burglary case, because they are two separate legal matters.[99]

The *Miranda* Rule Today

The Supreme Court has used case law to define the boundaries of the *Miranda* warning since its inception. Although statements made by a suspect who was not given the *Miranda* warning or received it improperly cannot be used against him in a court of law, it is possible to use illegally gained statements and the evidence they produce in some well-defined instances:

- If a defendant perjures himself, evidence obtained in violation of the *Miranda* warning can be used by the government to impeach his testimony during trial.[100]

- At trial, the testimony of a witness is permissible even though her identity was revealed by the defendant in violation of the *Miranda* rule.[101]

Initial errors by police in getting statements do not make subsequent statements inadmissible. A subsequent *Miranda* warning that is properly given can cure the condition that made the initial statements inadmissible.[102] However, if police intentionally mislead suspects by questioning them before giving them a *Miranda* warning, their statements made after the warning is given are inadmissible in court. The "*Miranda* rule would be frustrated were the police permitted to undermine its meaning and effect."[103]

Over the years, the Supreme Court has decided a number of cases that have both limited and expanded the reach of *Miranda*. Indeed, a new *Miranda* decision is handed down nearly every term. See the accompanying "Evolution of *Miranda v. Arizona*" feature for a summary of several of these important decisions.

The Impact of *Miranda*

After *Miranda* was decided, law enforcement officials became concerned that the Supreme Court had gone too far in providing defendants with procedural protections. Subsequent research indicates that the decision has had little effect on the number of confessions obtained by the police and that it has not affected the rate of convictions.[104] It now seems apparent that the police formerly relied too heavily on confessions to prove a defendant's guilt. Other forms of evidence, such as witness statements, physical evidence, and expert testimony, have generally proved adequate to win the prosecution's case. Blaming *Miranda* for increased crime rates in the 1970s and 1980s now seems problematic, given that rates are down and *Miranda* is still the law.[105]

Critics have called the *Miranda* decision incomprehensible and difficult to administer. How can one tell whether a confession is truly voluntary or has been elicited by pressure and coercion? Aren't all police interrogations essentially coercive?[106] These criticisms aside, the Supreme Court is unlikely ever to reverse course. In the 2003 case of *Dickerson v. United States*, for example, the Court made it clear that the *Miranda* ruling is here to stay and has become enmeshed in the prevailing legal system.[107] In that case, the Court invalidated a federal

Web App 8.4

For more information about *Miranda v. Arizona*, visit http://www.law.cornell.edu/supremecourt/text/384/436.

public safety doctrine
The principle that a suspect can be questioned in the field without a *Miranda* warning if the information the police seek is needed to protect public safety.

Evolution of *Miranda v. Arizona*

Miranda v. Arizona (1966)	Any person subjected to custodial interrogation must be advised of his or her Fifth Amendment right to be free from compelled self-incrimination and to have the assistance of counsel.[108]
Fare v. Michael C. (1978)	The *Miranda* warning applies only to the right to have an attorney present. The suspect cannot demand to speak to a priest, a probation officer, or any other official.[109]
New York v. Quarles (1984)	A suspect can be questioned in the field without a *Miranda* warning if the information the police seek is needed to protect public safety. For example, in an emergency, suspects can be asked where they hid their weapons.[110] This is known as the **public safety doctrine**.
Oregon v. Elstad (1985)	Admissions made in the absence of *Miranda* warnings are not admissible at trial, but post-*Miranda* voluntary statements are admissible. A post-*Miranda* voluntary statement is admissible even if an initial incriminating statement was made in the absence of *Miranda* warnings.[111]

(continued)

Evolution of *Miranda v. Arizona* (continued)

***Colorado v. Connelly* (1986)**	The admissions of mentally impaired defendants can be admitted in evidence as long as the police acted properly and there is a preponderance of the evidence that the defendants understood the meaning of *Miranda*.[112]
***Moran v. Burbine* (1986)**	An attorney's request to see the defendant does not affect the validity of the defendant's waiver of the right to counsel. Police misinformation to an attorney does not affect waiver of *Miranda* rights.[113] For example, a suspect's statements may be used if they are given voluntarily, even though his family has hired an attorney and the statements were made before the attorney arrived. Only the suspect can request an attorney, not his friends or family.
***Colorado v. Spring* (1987)**	Suspects need not be aware of all the possible outcomes of waiving their rights for the *Miranda* warning to be considered properly given.[114]
***Minnick v. Mississippi* (1990)**	When counsel is requested, interrogation must cease and cannot be resumed until an attorney is present.[115]
***Arizona v. Fulminante* (1991)**	The erroneous admission of a coerced confession at trial can be ruled a harmless error that would not automatically result in overturning a conviction.[116]
***Davis v. United States* (1994)**	A suspect who makes an ambiguous reference to an attorney during questioning, such as "Maybe I should talk to an attorney," is not protected under *Miranda*. The police may continue their questioning.[117]
***Chavez v. Martinez* (2003)**	Failure to give a suspect a *Miranda* warning is not illegal unless the case becomes a criminal issue.[118]
***United States v. Patane* (2004)**	A voluntary statement given in the absence of a *Miranda* warning can be used to obtain evidence that can be used at trial. Failure to give the warning does not make seizure of evidence illegal per se.[119]
***Missouri v. Seibert* (2004)**	Miranda warnings must be given before interrogation begins. The accused in this case was interrogated and confessed in the absence of *Miranda* warnings. *Miranda* rights were then read, at which point the accused "re-confessed." The pre-*Miranda* questioning was improper.[120]
***Maryland v. Shatzer* (2010)**	*Miranda* protections do not apply if a suspect is released from police custody for at least 14 days and then questioned. However, if the suspect is rearrested, then *Miranda* warnings must be read.[121]
***Florida v. Powell* (2010)**	The *Miranda* warnings do not require that the suspect be advised that he or she has the right to have an attorney present during questioning. It is sufficient to advise the suspect that he or she has the right to talk with a lawyer before questioning and to consult a lawyer at any time during questioning.[122]
***Berghuis v. Thompkins* (2010)**	Unless a suspect asserts his or her *Miranda* rights, any subsequent voluntary statements given after the warnings are admissible in court. Simply remaining silent does not imply that a suspect has invoked *Miranda* protection.[123]
***J.D.B. v. North Carolina* (2011)**	Children may be more prone to confessing to crimes they did not commit, and this needs to be taken into consideration in deciding whether a police interrogation is also custodial. In other words, the suspect's age factors into the *Miranda* custody analysis.[124]
***Bobby v. Dixon* (2011)**	Murder confession is admissible because it was voluntary and *Miranda* rights were both read by police and waived by the suspect—this despite the fact that *Miranda* rights were *not* read in a previous interrogation of the suspect arising out of the same criminal act.[125]

statute enacted shortly after the *Miranda* decision that said any confession could be used against a suspect if it was voluntarily obtained.

Not surprisingly, police administrators who in the past might have been wary of the restrictions imposed by *Miranda* now favor its use.[126] One survey found that nearly 60 percent of police chiefs believe that the *Miranda* warning should be retained, and the same number report that abolishing *Miranda* would change the way that the police function.[127] To ensure that *Miranda* rules are being followed, many departments now routinely videotape interrogations, although research shows that this procedure is not a sure cure for police intimidation.[128]

With the ongoing war on terrorism, law enforcement officers may find themselves in unique situations involving national security and forced to make an immediate decision about whether the *Miranda* rule applies. It is also important to note that *Miranda* is an American creation. *Miranda*-like warnings are not always required in other countries, as discussed in the Global Criminal Justice feature.

GLOBAL criminal justice

INTERROGATION LAW IN THREE OTHER COUNTRIES

The Fifth Amendment ensures that those suspected of criminal activity cannot be forced to incriminate themselves and that they have the right to counsel. The Supreme Court's *Miranda* decision requires the police to advise certain criminal suspects of these important protections. In no other area of criminal procedure are the police required to advise suspects of their rights.

Miranda and the Fifth Amendment's self-incrimination clause are controversial. On the one hand, they help protect the innocent from being forced to confess. On the other hand, is justice served when the one person who may know most about a particular crime is under no obligation to talk?

To gain an appreciation for the significance of the right to counsel in the United States—and for the *Miranda* decision—it is helpful to take a look at interrogation laws in some other countries. Neither *Miranda*-like warnings nor the right to counsel are uniquely American creations. Several other countries have similar procedures but to varying degrees. Here we look at three of them: the United Kingdom, France, and China.

THE UNITED KINGDOM

The United Kingdom has no single constitutional document as the United States does. Police interrogation is instead governed by the Police and Criminal Evidence Act and the Code of Practice for the Detention, Treatment, and Questioning of Persons by Police Officers.

In the United Kingdom, if a suspect is taken into custody and the police intend to question the suspect, they are required to advise him or her that there is no obligation to talk. The British approach is somewhat stricter than that employed in the United States, because police are required to advise the suspect of the right to silence as soon as there are reasonable grounds to believe he or she has committed an offense. The *Miranda* rule applies only when there is custody and interrogation.

There is also a right to counsel in the United Kingdom, but the suspect generally receives assistance only when he or she asks for it. If a suspect exercises his or her rights and refuses to answer police questions, the court is later permitted to draw adverse inferences from this action. For example, the prosecutor can comment at trial that the suspect failed to answer questions. This can work against him or her at trial. In the United States, the prosecutor *cannot* comment on a defendant's pretrial silence.

FRANCE

In contrast to the United States and the United Kingdom, France is known for long having put society's interest in crime control ahead of individual rights and liberties. France's interrogation law provides evidence of this. First, there is no clear requirement that a suspect be advised that he or she is not required to answer police questions. Second, the right to counsel is limited. Suspects do not have the right to counsel immediately following their detention; the right does not apply until 20 hours after the person has been detained for ordinary offenses. For more serious cases, such as those involving drug rings or terrorism, the right to counsel does not attach for up to 72 hours from the detention. Finally, the accused has the right to consult with counsel only for a limited time; there is no right to have counsel present during police interrogations.

CHINA

In its earlier days, the People's Republic operated without much regard for individual rights. To this day there are criticisms that its government curtails citizens' freedoms, but legal reforms have brought China's criminal justice system somewhat in line with that of other modernized nations. The 1979 Criminal Procedure Law (CPL), which was significantly amended in 1996, has led to considerable progress in terms of protections afforded to those accused of criminal activity.

The CPL requires that before an interrogation, the police must give the suspect an opportunity to make a statement about his or her involvement (or lack of involvement) in the crime. This presumably protects the suspect from having the police proceed under the assumption that he or she is guilty. Critics have argued that the police routinely ignore this requirement and

use psychological pressures to extract confessions. In any case, there is no recognized right to freedom from self-incrimination in China. The CPL prohibits the use of torture, but this does not protect a suspect from incriminating himself or herself. There *is* a right to counsel, but it attaches only after the police have completed their first interrogation.

CRITICAL THINKING

1. Which country—the United States, the United Kingdom, France, or China—is least concerned with the rights of those who are interrogated? Why?

2. Could the United States improve its interrogation laws vis-à-vis those of other countries? Is there something to be learned from the United Kingdom, France, or China—or from all three?

Sources: Yue Ma, "A Comparative View of the Law of Interrogation," *International Criminal Justice Review* 17 (2007): 5–26; Craig M. Bradley, ed., *Criminal Procedure: A Worldwide Study* (Durham, NC: Carolina Academic Press, 1999); Stephen C. Thaman, "*Miranda* in Comparative Law," *Saint Louis University Law Journal* 45 (2001): 581–624.

Pretrial Identification

L09   Identify what purpose a lineup serves.

booking

The administrative record of an arrest, listing the offender's name, address, physical description, date of birth, employer, time of arrest, offense, and name of arresting officer; it also includes photographing and fingerprinting of the offender.

lineup

Placing a suspect in a group for the purpose of being viewed and identified by a witness.

After the accused is arrested, he or she is ordinarily brought to the police station, where the police list the possible criminal charges. At the same time, they obtain other information, such as a description of the offender and the circumstances of the offense, for booking purposes. The **booking** process is a police administrative procedure in which the date and time of the arrest are recorded; arrangements are made for bail, detention, or removal to court; and any other information needed for identification is obtained. The defendant may be fingerprinted, photographed, and required to participate in a lineup.

In a **lineup**, a suspect is placed in a group for the purpose of being viewed and identified by a witness. Lineups are one of the primary means that the police have of identifying suspects. Others are show-ups, which occur at the crime scene, and photo displays or mug shots of possible suspects. In accordance with the U.S. Supreme Court decisions in *United States v. Wade* (1967) and *Kirby v. Illinois* (1972), the accused has the right to have counsel present at the post-indictment lineup or in a show-up.[129] There is no right to counsel associated with photographic identification.

In the *Wade* case, the Supreme Court held that a defendant has a right to counsel if the lineup takes place after the suspect has been formally charged with a crime. This decision was based on the Court's belief that the post-indictment lineup procedure is a critical stage of the criminal justice process. In contrast, the suspect does not have a comparable right to counsel at a pretrial lineup when a complaint or indictment has not been issued. Right to counsel does not apply until judicial proceedings have begun and the defendant is formally charged with a crime. When the right to counsel is violated, the evidence of any pretrial identification must be excluded from the trial.

One of the most difficult legal issues in this area is determining whether the identification procedure is suggestive and consequently in violation of the due process clauses of the Fifth and Fourteenth Amendments.[130] In *Simmons v. United States* (1968), the Supreme Court said that "The primary evil to be avoided is a very substantial likelihood of irreparable misidentification."[131] In its decision in *Neil v. Biggers* (1972), the Court established the following general criteria by which to judge the suggestiveness of a pretrial identification procedure:

- The opportunity of the witness to view the criminal at the time of the crime
- The degree of attention by the witness and the accuracy of the prior description by the witness
- The level of certainty demonstrated by the witness
- The length of time between the crime and the confrontation[132]

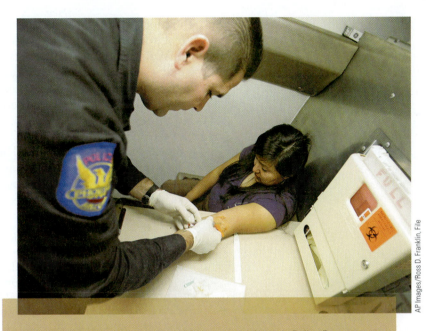

After reading the rights to an alleged DUI suspect, Phoenix Police Department Officer James Lawler administers a blood test as he works out of a mobile DUI processing van in Phoenix. The Arizona Supreme Court ruled that police must get search warrant to take a blood sample from a DUI suspect unless the person clearly consents to providing a sample.

Weighing all these factors, the court determines the substantial likelihood of misidentification.

The Exclusionary Rule

No review of the legal aspects of policing would be complete without a discussion of the **exclusionary rule**, the principal means used to restrain police conduct. The Fourth Amendment guarantees individuals the right to be secure in their persons, homes, papers, and effects against unreasonable searches and seizures. The exclusionary rule provides that all evidence obtained by illegal searches and seizures is inadmissible in criminal trials. Similarly, it excludes the use of illegal confessions under Fifth Amendment prohibitions.

For many years, evidence obtained by unreasonable searches and seizures that consequently should have been considered illegal was admitted by state and federal governments in criminal trials. The only criteria for admissibility were whether the evidence was incriminating and whether it would assist the judge or jury in ascertaining the innocence or guilt of the defendant. How the evidence was obtained was unimportant; its admissibility was determined by its relevance to the criminal case.

In 1914, however, the rules on the admissibility of evidence underwent a change of direction when the Supreme Court decided the case of *Weeks v. United States*.[133] The defendant, Fremont Weeks, was accused by federal law enforcement authorities of using the mail for illegal purposes. After his arrest, the home in which Weeks was staying was searched without a valid search warrant. Evidence in the form of letters and other materials was found in his room and admitted at the trial. Weeks was then convicted of the federal offense based on the incriminating evidence. On appeal, the Supreme Court held that evidence obtained by unreasonable search and seizure must be excluded in a federal criminal trial.

exclusionary rule
The principle that prohibits using illegally obtained evidence in a trial.

 Discuss the exclusionary rule, including its extensions and exceptions.

AP Images/Ross D. Franklin, File

Web App 8.5

For more information about *Mapp v. Ohio,* visit http://www.law.cornell.edu/supremecourt/text/367/643.

fruit of the poisonous tree
Secondary evidence obtained from a search that violates the exclusionary rule.

good faith exception
The principle that evidence may be used in a criminal trial even though the search warrant used to obtain it was technically faulty, as long as the police acted in good faith when they sought the warrant from a judge.

Thus, for the first time, the Court held that the Fourth Amendment barred the use of evidence obtained through illegal search and seizure in a federal prosecution. With this ruling, the Court established the exclusionary rule. The rule was based not on legislation but on judicial decision making. Can the criminal go free because the constable blunders? That became the question.

In 1961, the Supreme Court made the exclusionary rule applicable to the state courts in the landmark decision of *Mapp v. Ohio.* In *Mapp,* police officers forcibly searched a home while using a fake warrant. The Court held that although the search had turned up contraband, it violated the Fourth Amendment's prohibition against unreasonable searches and seizures, so the illegally seized evidence could not be used in court. Justice Tom Clark, delivering the majority opinion of the Court, made clear the importance of this constitutional right in the administration of criminal justice:

> There are those who say, as did Justice [then Judge Benjamin] Cardozo, that under our constitutional exclusionary doctrine "[t]he criminal is to go free because the constable has blundered." In some cases this will undoubtedly be the result. But ... there is another consideration—the imperative of judicial integrity. ... The criminal goes free, if he must, but it is the law that sets him free. Nothing can destroy a government more quickly than its failure to observe its own laws, or worse, its disregard of the charter of its own existence.[134]

The exclusionary rule has also been extended to include derivative, or secondary, evidence, which is also called **fruit of the poisonous tree**.[135] This doctrine applies not only to evidence obtained directly from a violation of the Fourth Amendment but also to evidence indirectly obtained from such a violation. For example, if the police, without probable cause and a warrant, searched a private home and found a key to a locker at a nearby bus station, a subsequent search of the locker would be considered fruit of the poisonous tree.

Current Status of the Exclusionary Rule

In the 1980s, a more conservative U.S. Supreme Court gradually began to limit the scope of the exclusionary rule. It created three major exceptions:

■ *Independent source exception.* This rule allows admission of evidence that has been discovered by means wholly independent of any constitutional violation. So if police enter a drug dealer's home with an arrest warrant and, while arresting him, illegally search for and seize evidence such as drug paraphernalia, the illegally seized material may be allowed in court if, independently, a warrant had been issued to search the apartment for the same evidence but had not yet arrived at the scene.[136]

■ *Good faith exception.* In *United States v. Leon* (1984), the Court ruled that evidence seized by police relying on a warrant issued by a detached and neutral magistrate can be used in a court proceeding, even if the judge who issued the warrant erred in drawing up the document.[137] In this case, the Court articulated a **good faith exception** to the exclusionary rule: evidence obtained with a less than adequate search warrant may be admissible in court if the police officers acted in good faith when obtaining court approval for their search. However, deliberately misleading a judge or using a warrant that the police know is unreasonably deficient would be grounds to invoke the exclusionary rule. In a subsequent case, *Arizona v. Evans,* the Court ruled that the exclusionary rule was designed as a means of deterring police misconduct, not to punish police for honest mistakes; it does not apply when they have acted in objectively reasonable reliance on an apparently valid warrant but later find out it was technically faulty.[138] In 2009, the Supreme Court decided *Herring v. United States,*[139] another good faith case. Officers searched Herring based on a warrant listed in a neighboring county's database. Unbeknownst to them, the warrant had been recalled months earlier. The Supreme Court sanctioned the search and further noted that the exclusionary rule will be violated only when there is "systemic error or reckless disregard of constitutional requirements."[140]

■ *Inevitable discovery rule.* This rule holds that evidence obtained through an unlawful search or seizure is admissible in court if it can be established, to a very high degree of probability, that police investigation would be expected to lead to the discovery of the evidence. In the case that established the rule, *Nix v. Williams* (1984), police illegally interrogated a suspect and found the location of his victim's body. The evidence obtained was allowed at trial when the Court ruled that because the body was lying in plain sight and many police officers were searching for the body, it would have been obtained anyway, even without the information provided by the illegal interrogation; this is now referred to as the **inevitable discovery rule.**[141]

In these and other cases, the Supreme Court has made it easier for the police to conduct searches of criminal suspects and their possessions and then use the seized evidence in court proceedings. The Court has indicated that, as a general rule, the protection afforded the individual by the Fourth Amendment may take a back seat to concerns about public safety if criminal actions pose a clear threat to society.

The Future of the Exclusionary Rule

Should the exclusionary rule be retained? Those who favor retention of the exclusionary rule believe it is justified because it deters illegal searches and seizures. However, the rule appears to result in relatively few case dismissals.

Yet the public wants to be protected from overzealous police officers and is concerned with reports that police routinely violate suspects' rights when searching for evidence. Jon Gould and Stephen Mastrofski made direct observations of police searches in a medium-sized U.S. city and found that nearly one-third of searches performed were unconstitutional and that almost none of these illegal searches were recognized as such by the courts. Surprisingly, the majority of illegal searches were made by a relatively small number of otherwise conscientious officers who may have become overzealous in their attempts to enforce the municipality's crackdown on drug offenders.[142]

Supporters believe the rule is fundamentally sound and can be justified on the basis of such legal principles as checks and balances and separation of power. When agents of the executive branch (the police) disregard or sidestep the terms of court-issued search warrants, the judicial branch can respond by overruling the misbehavior. Judges can also react when executive branch prosecutors attempt to introduce illegally seized evidence in court.[143] This power is especially important for warrantless searches, because the judge is not on the scene when a search takes place and becomes aware of the circumstances surrounding the search only when prosecutors are in court seeking to present the evidence that the police acquired. The rule gives the judge the opportunity to correct executive branch excesses before they can influence the outcome of the proceedings.[144]

How can the rule be improved? Suggested approaches to dealing with violations of the exclusionary rule include criminal prosecution of police officers who violate constitutional rights, internal police control, civil lawsuits against state or municipal police officers, and federal lawsuits against the government under the Federal Tort Claims Act.

Law professor Donald Dripps has derived a novel approach for modifying the exclusionary rule.[145] The contingent exclusionary rule would apply when a judge who finds police testimony questionable concludes that the release of the guilty would be unpleasant and unwarranted. Instead of excluding the evidence, she could request that the prosecution or police pay a fee, similar in form to a fine, to

inevitable discovery rule
The principle that evidence can be used in court even though the information that led to its discovery was obtained in violation of the *Miranda* rule if a judge finds it would have been discovered anyway by other means or sources.

Web App 8.6

For more information about the exclusionary rule, visit http://www.law.cornell.edu/wex/exclusionary_rule.

use the evidence in court. Exclusion of the evidence would be contingent on the failure of the police department to pay the damages set by the court. Thereby, the judge could uphold the Constitution without freeing the guilty. The contingent exclusionary rule would force the prosecution to decide whether obtaining justice was worth the damages.

The United States is the only nation that applies an exclusionary rule to protect individuals from illegal searches and seizures. Whether the U.S. Supreme Court or legislative bodies adopt any further significant changes to the rule remains to be seen. However, like the *Miranda* warning, the exclusionary rule has been incorporated in modern police procedure and seems to be a permanent fixture.

Significant Cases in Policing

Case	Issue	Decision
Aguilar v. Texas (1964)	Informants	If police use informants to develop probable cause to obtain a warrant, they must show why the informant should be believed and how the informant obtained his or her knowledge.
Alabama v. White (1990)	Anonymous tips	An anonymous phone tip can help formulate probable cause for a warrant, provided the tip is corroborated by independent police work.
Breithaupt v. Abram (1957)	Drawing blood from suspects	Police can seize a blood sample from a suspect without a warrant, provided they have probable cause to do so.
Brigham v. Stuart (2006)	Warrantless search, threats to occupants	If police have an objectively reasonable basis to believe the occupant of a dwelling is seriously injured or threatened with injury, they may enter without a warrant.
California v. Greenwood (1988)	Abandoned property	Abandoned property does not enjoy Fourth Amendment protection.
Carroll v. United States (1925)	Automobile searches	The police may search an automobile without a warrant, provided they have probable cause to do so. Also see the "Evolution of *Carroll v. United States*" feature earlier in this chapter for details on post-*Carroll* decisions.
Chimel v. California (1969)	Search incident to arrest	The police may search a suspect after a lawful arrest.
Coolidge v. New Hampshire (1971)	Plain view	The police can search for and seize evidence without benefit of a warrant if it is in plain view.
Florida v. Bostick (1991)	Consent to search on a bus	Drug enforcement officers, after obtaining consent, may search luggage on a crowded bus without meeting the Fourth Amendment requirements for a search warrant or probable cause.
Harris v. United States (1947)	Scope of a search based on a search warrant	The scope of a search should be limited to the items named in the search warrant.
Hudson v. Michigan (2006)	Knock and announce	Evidence need not be excluded because police failed to announce their presence when serving a warrant.
Katz v. United States (1967)	Definition of a search	A search occurs when a government actor infringes on a person's reasonable expectation of privacy.

(continued)

Case	Issue	Decision
Kirby v. Illinois (1972)	Right to counsel in lineups	The accused has no right to have counsel present at a pre-indictment lineup.
Mapp v. Ohio (1961)	Exclusionary rule, states	Evidence obtained in violation of the Fourth Amendment is not admissible in a state criminal trial (the exclusionary rule applies to the states).
Minnesota v. Olson (1990)	Warrantless search, suspect escape	In the absence of hot pursuit, if there is danger that the suspect will escape, police can enter private property and arrest the suspect without a warrant.
Miranda v. Arizona (1966)	Custodial interrogation	Suspects subjected to custodial interrogation must be advised of their Fifth Amendment privilege against self-incrimination. Also see the "Evolution of *Miranda v. Arizona*" feature in this chapter for details on post-*Miranda* decisions.
Nix v. Williams (1984)	Exclusionary rule, inevitable discovery	Evidence obtained through an unlawful search or seizure is admissible in court if it can be established, to a very high degree of probability, that police investigation would be expected to lead to the discovery of the evidence.
Oliver v. United States (1984)	Search of an open field	Open fields do not enjoy Fourth Amendment protection.
Payton v. New York (1980)	Search warrant requirement	The Fourth Amendment prohibits warrantless, nonconsensual entry into private property for the purpose of making an arrest.
Riley v. California (2014)	Search incident to arrest	Police cannot search a cell phone incident to arrest without a warrant.
Schneckloth v. Bustamonte (1973)	Consent	If a suspect consents to a search, the officer does not need a warrant or probable cause, but such consent must not be the result of duress or coercion.
Segura v. United States (1984)	Exclusionary rule, independent source	Evidence that has been discovered by means wholly independent of any constitutional violation will be admissible.
Silverthorne Lumber Co. v. United States (1920)	Fruit of the poisonous tree	The exclusionary rule extends to "fruit of the poisonous tree," or derivative evidence.
Terry v. Ohio (1968)	Stop and frisk	An officer may stop and frisk a person if he or she has reasonable suspicion that criminal activity is afoot.
United States v. Leon (1984)	Exclusionary rule, good faith	Evidence obtained with a less than adequate search warrant may be admissible in court if the police officers acted in good faith when obtaining court approval for their search.
United States v. Matlock (1974)	Co-occupant consent	It is permissible for one co-occupant of a dwelling to give consent to the police to search the premises in the absence of the other occupant, as long as the person giving consent shares "common authority" over the property and no present co-occupant objects.

(continued)

Significant Cases in Policing (*continued*)

Case	Issue	Decision
United States v. Wade (1967)	Right to counsel in lineups	The accused has the right to have counsel present at a post-indictment lineup.
Warden v. Hayden (1967)	Hot pursuit	Hot pursuit authorizes the police to dispense with the Fourth Amendment warrant requirement.
Weeks v. United States (1914)	Exclusionary rule, federal court	Evidence obtained in violation of the Fourth Amendment is not admissible in a federal criminal trial (the exclusionary rule is created).

ETHICAL CHALLENGES in Criminal Justice

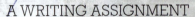

A WRITING ASSIGNMENT

Officer Rodriguez stopped Susan Smart for speeding. After approaching Smart's vehicle to ask for her license and registration, he asked whether he could search her vehicle. She asked, "Why do you want to search my car?" He said, "We have seen an increase in drug trafficking along this stretch of freeway." She said, "I don't know why you think I would be transporting drugs, and I'm not sure whether this is legal, but okay, go ahead and search." Officer Rodriguez searched Smart's car and found nothing incriminating. He issued her a citation for speeding and sent her on her way.

   Write an essay on the ethics of the behavior presented in this hypothetical situation. Assuming Smart was actually speeding, Officer Rodriguez was authorized to ask consent to search her vehicle. What's more, he was under no obligation to tell her she could refuse consent. Even so, Smart seemed a bit apprehensive and uncertain whether she should grant consent. Should Officer Rodriguez have explained the law to her? Why or why not? If a police officer benefits from someone's ignorance of the law, is it just good policing—or is it deviant? See this chapter's "Consent Searches" section for additional information. In what other areas besides consent may law enforcement benefit from citizens' lack of understanding of the law? Answers to this question can be found throughout the chapter.

Summary

 L01   **Describe how the Fourth Amendment controls law enforcement officials.**

- The Fourth Amendment controls searches and seizures.
- The Fourth Amendment contains two parts: the reasonableness clause and the warrants clause. Each clause is independent because

a search can be reasonable without a warrant, but if a warrant is required, certain steps must be taken.

 L02   **Define search and arrest.**

- A search occurs when a government actor infringes on a person's reasonable expectation of privacy.

- When police look through abandoned property, look in open fields, or use aerial surveillance, they do not "search."
- An arrest occurs when a police officer takes a person into custody or deprives a person of freedom for having allegedly committed a criminal offense.

LO3 **Distinguish between search warrants and arrest warrants.**

- A search warrant is an order, issued by a judge, directing officers to conduct a search of specified premises for specified objects.
- An arrest warrant is an order, issued by a judge, directing officers to arrest a particular individual.

LO4 **Explain when warrants are required.**

- Warrants are required in two key situations:
  - Arrests and searches in private homes or on specific types of private property.
  - Arrests for minor offenses committed out of view of the arresting officer.

LO5 **Recognize that there are three requirements that must be met before a warrant can be secured.**

- There are three requirements that must be met before a warrant can be secured: probable cause, neutral and detached magistrate, and particularity.
- Probable cause is usually defined as a reasonable belief, based on fact, that a crime has been committed and that the person, place, or object to be searched and/or seized is linked to the crime with a reasonable degree of certainty.
- Judges are considered to be neutral and detached.
- Particularity is concerned with specifically naming the items to be seized pursuant to a search or specifically naming the individual to be arrested pursuant to an arrest warrant.

LO6 **Explain the rules for serving warrants.**

- There are six general rules governing the service of warrants: Officers should (1) knock and announce their presence, subject to certain exceptions; (2) keep property damage to a minimum; (3) use appropriate force if needed; (4) pay attention to time constraints when serving search warrants; (5) limit the scope and manner of their search to the items named in the search warrant; and (6) not bring reporters along when warrants are served.

LO7 **Discuss several types of warrantless searches and arrests.**

- The seven types of warrantless searches and arrests are (1) searches based on exigent circumstances; (2) stop and frisk; (3) searches incident to lawful arrest; (4) automobile searches; (5) consent searches; (6) plain view seizures; and (7) arrests committed in an officer's presence.
- Exigent circumstances include hot pursuit, danger of escape, threats to evidence, and threats to others.
- Stop and frisk are two separate acts. Each requires that an officer have reasonable suspicion.
- For a search incident to lawful arrest, the search must be conducted at the time of or immediately following the arrest. Also, the police may search only the suspect and the area within the suspect's immediate control.
- Automobiles can be searched without a warrant, so long as there is probable cause to search.
- Consent searches do not require warrants or probable cause, because the consenting party effectively waives his or her Fourth Amendment rights.
- If an officer is engaged in a lawful search and has probable cause that an item in plain view is subject to seizure, the item can be seized.
- If a person commits a crime in an officer's presence, no warrant is necessary before an arrest is made.

LO8 **Explain the *Miranda v. Arizona* decision.**

- *Miranda v. Arizona* requires that police officers advise people who are both in custody and interrogated of their constitutional right (from the Fifth Amendment) not to incriminate themselves.
- Suspects who are advised of their *Miranda* rights are told: (1) they have the right to remain silent; (2) if they decide to make a statement, the statement can and will be used against them in a court of law; (3) they have the right to have an attorney present at the time of the interrogation, or they will have an opportunity to consult with an attorney; and (4) if they cannot afford an attorney, one will be appointed for them by the state.

- The Supreme Court has modified the *Miranda* rule to some extent over the years. Mostly, its decisions have relaxed the *Miranda* rule.

- The impact of *Miranda* on law enforcement, such as through lost convictions, has been fairly minimal.

L09 **Identify what purpose a lineup serves.**

- In a lineup, a suspect is placed in a group for the purpose of being viewed and identified by a witness.

- Lineups are one of the primary means that the police have of identifying suspects.

- The accused has the right to have counsel present at a post-indictment lineup. This is also true for a show-up, which occurs at the crime scene. There is no right to counsel for photographic identifications.

L010 **Discuss the exclusionary rule, including its extensions and exceptions.**

- The exclusionary rule provides that all evidence obtained by illegal searches and seizures is inadmissible in criminal trials.

- The exclusionary rule has been extended to include "fruit of the poisonous tree," or indirect evidence.

- Exceptions to the exclusionary rule include independent source, good faith, and inevitable discovery.

Key terms

search, 285
open field, 286
curtilage, 286
arrest, 287
search warrant, 288
arrest warrant, 288
in-presence requirement, 289
probable cause, 291

particularity, 293
probable cause hearing, 295
exigent circumstances, 296
hot pursuit, 296
stop and frisk, 298
search incident to a lawful arrest, 302
bus sweep, 306
plain view doctrine, 307

Miranda warning, 312
public safety doctrine, 313
booking, 316
lineup, 316
exclusionary rule, 317
fruit of the poisonous tree, 318
good faith exception, 318
inevitable discovery rule, 319

Critical Thinking Questions

1. Can a search and seizure be reasonable if it is not authorized by a warrant?
2. Should illegally seized evidence be excluded from trial, even though it is conclusive proof of a person's criminal acts?
3. What is a pretext traffic stop? Does it violate a citizen's civil rights?
4. Should a person be put in a lineup without the benefit of counsel?
5. What is the purpose of the *Miranda* warning?
6. Should obviously guilty persons go free because police originally arrested them with less than probable cause?
7. Have criminals been given too many rights? Should courts be more concerned with the rights of the victims or the rights of offenders?

Notes

1. *Missouri v. McNeely*, 569 U.S. ___ (2013).
2. Ibid.
3. *Katz v. United States*, 389 U.S. 347 (1967).
4. *California v. Greenwood*, 486 U.S. 35 (1988).
5. *Oliver v. United States*, 466 U.S. 170 (1984).
6. *California v. Ciraola*, 476 U.S. 207 (1986).
7. *Florida v. Riley*, 488 U.S. 445 (1989).
8. *Payton v. New York*, 445 U.S. 573 (1980).
9. *Welsh v. Wisconsin*, 466 U.S. 740 (1984).
10. *Aguilar v. Texas*, 378 U.S. 108 (1964).
11. *Illinois v. Gates*, 462 U.S. 213 (1983).
12. *Alabama v. White*, 496 U.S. 325 (1990).
13. Ibid., at 325, 326.
14. *Florida v. J. L.*, No. 98-1993 (2000).

15. *Johnson v. United States*, 333 U.S. 10 (1948), pp. 13–14.
16. Mark I. Koffsky, "Choppy Waters in the Surveillance Data Stream: The Clipper Scheme and the Particularity Clause," *Berkeley Technology Law Journal* 9 (1994), p. 131.
17. *Ker v. California*, 374 U.S. 23 (1963); *Wilson v. Arkansas*, 514 U.S. 927 (1995).
18. *Miller v. United States*, 357 U.S. 301 (1958).
19. *Hudson v. Michigan*, 547 U.S. 586 (2006).
20. *County of Sacramento v. Lewis*, 523 U.S. 833 (1998).
21. *Gooding v. United States*, 416 U.S. 430 (1974).
22. *Harris v. United States*, 331 U.S. 145 (1947).
23. *Wilson v. Layne*, 526 U.S. 603 (1999).
24. *Gerstein v. Pugh*, 420 U.S. 103 (1975); *Riverside County v. McLaughlin*, 500 U.S. 44 (1991).
25. *Kirk v. Louisiana*, 565 U.S. 635 (2002).
26. *Warden v. Hayden*, 387 U.S. 294 (1967).
27. John L. Worrall, *Criminal Procedure: From First Contact to Appeal*, 2nd ed. (Boston: Allyn & Bacon, 2007), pp. 143–144.
28. *Scott v. Harris*, 550 U.S. 372 (2007).
29. *Plumhoff v. Rickard*, 572 U.S. ___ (2014).
30. *Minnesota v. Olson*, 495 U.S. 91 (1990).
31. *Kentucky v. King*, 563 U.S. ___ (2011).
32. *Breithaupt v. Abram*, 352 U.S. 432 (1957); also see the chapter opening story.
33. *Brigham City v. Utah*, 547 U.S. 398 (2006).
34. Ibid.
35. *Michigan v. Fisher*, 558 U.S. ___ (2009).
36. *Terry v. Ohio*, 392 U.S. 1 (1968).
37. *Illinois v. Wardlow*, 120 S.Ct. 673 (2000).
38. *Arizona v. Johnson*, 555 U.S. 323 (2009).
39. *Terry v. Ohio*, p. 24.
40. *Chimel v. California*, 395 U.S. 752 (1969).
41. *Riley v. California*, 573 U.S. ___ (2014).
42. *Carroll v. United States*, 267 U.S. 132 (1925). See also James Rodgers, "Poisoned Fruit: Quest for Consistent Rule on Traffic Stop Searches," *American Bar Association Journal* 81 (1995): 50–51.
43. *Carroll v. United States*, 267 U.S. 132 (1925).
44. *United States v. Lee*, 274 U.S. 559 (1927).
45. *Cardwell v. Lewis*, 417 U.S. 583 (1974).
46. *Pennsylvania v. Mimms*, 434 U.S. 106 (1997).
47. *United States v. Ross*, 456 U.S. 798 (1982).
48. *Michigan v. Long*, 463 U.S. 1032 (1983).
49. *Michigan Dept. of State Police v. Sitz*, 496 U.S. 444 (1990).
50. *Whren v. United States*, 517 U.S. 806 (1996).
51. *Maryland v. Wilson*, 519 U.S. 408 (1997).
52. *City of Indianapolis v. Edmond*, 531 U.S. 32 (2000).
53. *Illinois v. Lidster*, 540 U.S. 419 (2004).
54. *Brendlin v. California*, 551 U.S. 249 (2007).
55. *Arizona v. Gant*, 556 U.S. 332 (2009).
56. *Davis v. United States*, 564 U.S. ___ (2011). 556 U.S. 332.
57. *United States v. Arvizu*, 534 U.S. 266 (2002).
58. *United States v. Ross*, 456 U.S. 798 (1982). See also Barry Latzer, "Searching Cars and Their Contents: *U.S. v. Ross*," *Criminal Law Bulletin* 6 (1982): 220; Joseph Grano, "Rethinking the Fourth Amendment Warrant Requirements," *Criminal Law Review* 19 (1982): 603.
59. *Michigan v. Long*, 463 U.S. 1032 (1983).
60. *Arizona v. Gant*, 556 U.S. 332 (2009); also see *New York v. Belton*, 453 U.S. 454 (1981) and *Thornton v. United States*, 541 U.S. 615 (2004).
61. *Pennsylvania v. Mimms*, 434 U.S. 106 (1977).
62. *Maryland v. Wilson*, 65 U.S.L.W. 4124 (1997).
63. *Brendlin v. California*, 551 U.S. 249 (2007).
64. *Whren v. United States*, 116 S.Ct. 1769 (1996); Mark Hansen, "Rousting Miss Daisy?" *American Bar Association Journal* 83 (1997): 22; *Wyoming v. Houghton*, 526 U.S. 295 (1999).
65. *Arkansas v. Sullivan*, 121 S.Ct. 1876 (2001).
66. *Delaware v. Prouse*, 440 U.S. 648 (1979). See also Lance Rogers, "The Drunk-Driving Roadblock: Random Seizure or Minimal Intrusion?" *Criminal Law Bulletin* 21 (1985): 197–217.
67. *City of Indianapolis v. Edmond*, 531 U.S. 32 (2000).
68. *Michigan v. Sitz*, 496 U.S. 444 (1990).
69. *Illinois v. Lidster*, 540 U.S. 419 (2004).
70. *Schneckloth v. Bustamonte*, 412 U.S. 218 (1973).
71. *Bumper v. North Carolina*, 391 U.S. 543 (1968).
72. *Schneckloth v. Bustamonte*, 412 U.S. 218 (1973).
73. *Ohio v. Robinette*, 519 U.S. 33 (1966).
74. *United States v. Matlock*, 415 U.S. 164 (1974).
75. *Georgia v. Randolph*, 547 U.S. 103 (2006).
76. *Florida v. Bostick*, 501 U.S. 429 (1991).
77. *Ohio v. Robinette*, 519 U.S. 33 (1996).
78. *Coolidge v. New Hampshire*, 403 U.S. 443 (1971).
79. *New York v. Class*, 475 U.S. 106 (1986).
80. *Arizona v. Hicks*, 480 U.S. 321 (1987).
81. *Minnesota v. Dickerson*, 508 U.S. 366 (1993).
82. *Bond v. United States*, 120 S.Ct. 1462 (2000).
83. *Riverside County v. McLaughlin*, 500 U.S. 44 (1991).
84. *Atwater et al. v. City of Lago Vista*, 532 U.S. 318 (2001).
85. *Virginia v. Moore*, 553 U.S. 164 (2008).
86. Gary T. Marx, *Undercover: Police Surveillance in America* (Berkeley: University of California Press, 1988).
87. *Katz v. United States*.
88. 18 U.S.C. §§ 2510–20.
89. 50 U.S.C. §§1801–11, 1821–29, 1841–46, and 1861–62.
90. Allison Keith, "Police Go Live Monitoring D.C. Crime Cameras," *Washington Post*, February 11, 2008, A1.
91. *United States v. Jones*, 565 U.S. ___ (2012).
92. *United States v. Knotts*, 460 U.S. 276 (1983).
93. *United States v. Karo*, 468 U.S. 705 (1984).
94. *Miranda v. Arizona*, 384 U.S. 436 (1966).
95. *Berghuis v. Thompkins*, 560 U.S. (2010).
96. *Colorado v. Connelly*, 479 U.S. 157 (1986).
97. *Minnick v. Mississippi*, 498 U.S. 46 (1990).
98. *Maryland v. Shatzer*, 559 U.S. (2010).
99. *Texas v. Cobb*, 532 U.S. 162 (2001).
100. *Harris v. New York*, 401 U.S. 222 (1971).
101. *Michigan v. Tucker*, 417 U.S. 433 (1974).
102. *Oregon v. Elstad*, 470 U.S. 298 (1985).
103. *Missouri v. Seibert*, 542 U.S. 600 (2004).
104. *Miranda v. Arizona*, 384 U.S. 436 (1966).
105. *Fare v. Michael C*, 439 U.S. 1310 (1978).
106. *New York v. Quarles*, 467 U.S. 649 (1984).
107. *Oregon v. Elstad*, 470 U.S. 298 (1985).
108. *Colorado v. Connelly*, 479 U.S. 157 (1986).
109. *Moran v. Burbine*, 475 U.S. 412 (1986).
110. *Colorado v. Spring*, 479 U.S. 564 (1987).
111. *Minnick v. Mississippi*, 498 U.S. 146 (1990).
112. *Arizona v. Fulminante*, 499 U.S. 279 (1991).
113. *Davis v. United States*, 512 U.S. 452 (1994).
114. *Chavez v. Martinez*, 538 U.S. 760 (2003).
115. *United States v. Patane*, 542 U.S. 630 (2004).
116. *Missouri v. Seibert*, 542 U.S. 600 (2004).
117. *Maryland v. Shatzer*, 559 U.S. 98 (2010).
118. *Florida v. Powell*, 559 U.S. ___ (2010).
119. *Berghuis v. Thompkins*, 560 U.S. 370 (2010).
120. *J.D.B. v. North Carolina*, 564 U.S. ___ (2011).
121. Michael Wald and others, "Interrogations in New Haven: The Impact of *Miranda*," *Yale Law Journal* 76 (1967): 1519. See also Walter Lippman, "*Miranda v. Arizona*—Twenty Years Later," *Criminal Justice Journal* 9 (1987): 241; Stephen J. Schulhofer, "Reconsidering *Miranda*," *University of Chicago Law Review* 54 (1987): 435–461; Paul Cassell, "How Many Criminals

Has *Miranda* Set Free?" *Wall Street Journal*, March 1, 1995, p. A12.

122. "Don't Blame *Miranda*," *Washington Post*, December 2, 1988, p. A26. See also Scott Lewis, "*Miranda* Today: Death of a Talisman," *Prosecutor* 28 (1994): 18–25; Richard Leo, "The Impact of *Miranda* Revisited," *Journal of Criminal Law and Criminology* 86 (1996): 621–648.

123. Ronald Allen, "*Miranda's* Hollow Core," *Northwestern University Law Review* 100 (2006): 71–85.

124. *Dickerson v. United States*, 530 U.S. 428 (2000).

125. *Bobby v. Dixon*, 565 U.S. ___ (2011).

126. Marvin Zalman and Brad Smith, "The Attitudes of Police Executives Toward *Miranda* and Interrogation Policies," *Journal of Criminal Law and Criminology* 97 (2007): 873–942.

127. Victoria Time and Brian Payne, "Police Chiefs' Perceptions About *Miranda*: An Analysis of Survey Data," *Journal of Criminal Justice* 30 (2002): 77–86.

128. G. Daniel Lassiter, Jennifer Ratcliff, Lezlee Ware, and Clinton Irvin, "Videotaped Confessions: Panacea or Pandora's Box?" *Law and Policy* 28 (2006): 192–210.

129. *United States v. Wade*, 388 U.S. 218 (1967); *Kirby v. Illinois*, 406 U.S. 682 (1972).

130. Marvin Zalman and Larry Siegel, *Key Cases and Comments on Criminal Procedure* (St. Paul, MN: West, 1994).

131. *Simmons v. United States*, 390 U.S. 377 (1968).

132. *Neil v. Biggers*, 409 U.S. 188 (1972).

133. *Weeks v. United States*, 232 U.S. 383 (1914).

134. *Mapp v. Ohio*, 367 U.S. 643 (1961).

135. *Silverthorne Lumber Co. v. United States*, 251 U.S. 385 (1920).

136. *Segura v. United States*, 468 U.S. 796 (1984).

137. *United States v. Leon*, 468 U.S. 897 (1984).

138. *Arizona v. Evans*, 514 U.S. 260 (1995).

139. *Herring v. United States*, 555 U.S. 135 (2009).

140. Ibid., p. 11.

141. *Nix v. Williams*, 467 U.S. 431 (1984).

142. Jon Gould and Stephen Mastrofski, "Suspect Searches: Assessing Police Behavior Under the U.S. Constitution," *Criminology and Public Policy* 3 (2004): 315–362.

143. Timothy Lynch, *In Defense of the Exclusionary Rule* (Washington, DC: Cato Institute, Center for Constitutional Studies, 1998).

144. Ibid.

145. Donald Dripps, "The Case for the Contingent Exclusionary Rule," *American Criminal Law Review* 38 (2001): 1–47.

COURTS AND ADJUDICATION

THE ADJUDICATION PHASE OF THE CRIMINAL PROCESS is intended to ensure that every person charged with a crime is treated according to the applicable rules of legal procedure in an atmosphere of fair play and objectivity. If this process is compromised, the case may be taken to a higher, appellate court, where the trial court proceedings are reexamined. If the defendant's rights have been violated, the appellate court may deem the findings of the original trial improper and either order a new hearing or hold that some other remedy be provided.

Many people work to ensure the court process works as intended, but judges are especially important figures. Judges, as you will see in Chapter 9, preside over trials and ensure that the rules are followed. Becoming a judge is a significant achievement, but the job is not easy. Ruben Andres Martino, presiding justice of the Harlem Community Justice Center, understands the tremendous responsibility judges have as they make decisions that directly affect people's lives. But, he says, "we make these decisions with all of our human limitations. Often, we only have part of the information and hear conflicting versions of the situation. However, we try to do our best to make sure that justice is done and the integrity of our judicial system is upheld."

Judges often rely on the contributions of court reporters, the officials whose job it is to keep an accurate record (or transcript) of the proceedings. Carlos Martinez, an official court reporter who works for the Sonoma County (California) Superior Courts, is but one of many court reporters who are tasked with making a verbatim record of everything that is said in a hearing—trials included. The greatest technical challenges that Carlos faces in a typical day are dealing with rapid speakers and technical jargon. He sometimes has to interrupt the proceedings and ask rapid speakers to slow down so the record can reflect their statements accurately. Also, he finds that he has to read back the record and ask many questions of expert witnesses in order to ensure that no mistakes are made. On a more personal level, Carlos finds some cases, especially those involving murders, molestations, rapes, and abuse, difficult to listen to. "You never get used to it and you never really forget," he says. "You just learn to live with it." Even so, he finds his career especially rewarding and feels he is an integral part of the adjudication process. ■

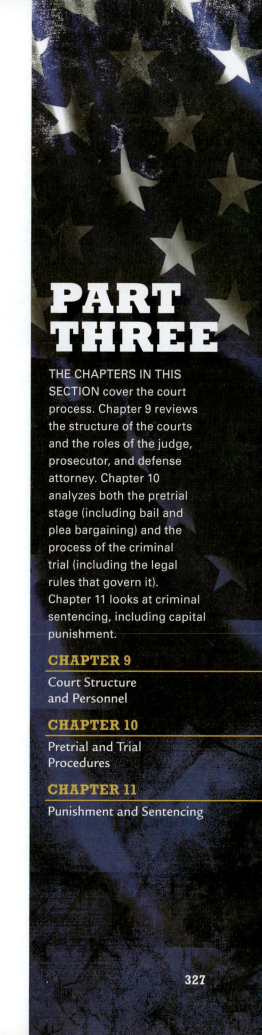

PART THREE

THE CHAPTERS IN THIS SECTION cover the court process. Chapter 9 reviews the structure of the courts and the roles of the judge, prosecutor, and defense attorney. Chapter 10 analyzes both the pretrial stage (including bail and plea bargaining) and the process of the criminal trial (including the legal rules that govern it). Chapter 11 looks at criminal sentencing, including capital punishment.

CHAPTER 9

Court Structure and Personnel

Learning Objectives

 **L01** Describe state court structure.

 **L02** Describe federal court structure.

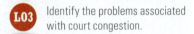 **L03** Identify the problems associated with court congestion.

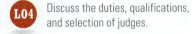 **L04** Discuss the duties, qualifications, and selection of judges.

L05 Explain the different types of judicial alternatives.

L06 Identify factors associated with judicial decision making.

L07 Characterize the role of the prosecutor.

L08 Recognize the role of prosecutorial discretion in the criminal justice system.

L09 Identify the role of the defense attorney.

L010 Explain the right to counsel.

Chapter Outline

The Criminal Court Process

State Court Systems
Courts of Limited Jurisdiction
Courts of General Jurisdiction
Analyzing Criminal Justice Issues: Specialized Courts
Model State Court Structure

Federal Courts
District Courts
Federal Appeals Courts
The U.S. Supreme Court

Court Congestion

The Judiciary
Other Judicial Functions
Judicial Qualifications
Selecting Judges
Judicial Alternatives
Judicial Decision Making

The Prosecutor
Careers in Criminal Justice: Prosecutor
Types of Prosecutors
The Prosecutor Within Society
Prosecutorial Discretion
Evidence-Based Justice: No-Drop Prosecution
Overzealous Prosecution

The Defense Attorney
The Role of the Criminal Defense Attorney
Ethical Issues

Defending the Accused
Legal Services for the Indigent
The Private Bar
Public versus Private Attorneys
Problems of the Criminal Bar

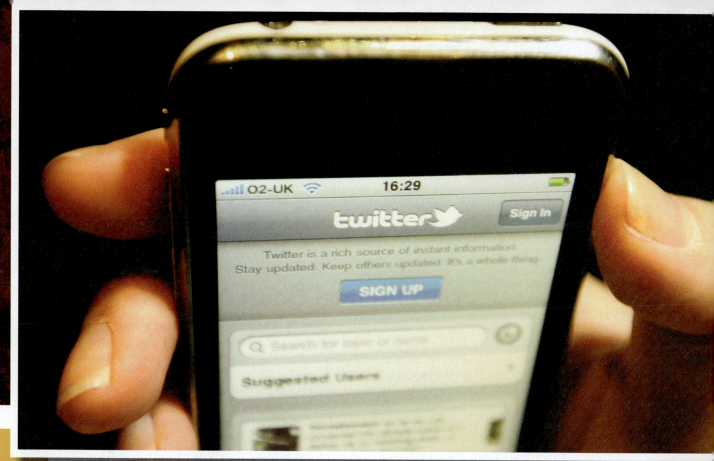

St. Louis Circuit Attorney Jennifer Joyce is a force to be reckoned with on Twitter and Facebook. Unlike many of her predecessors who chose to stick to the confines of the courthouse, she has chosen to have a particularly vocal presence in social media. Some of her tweets include:

- "Bad guys take heed: Lafayette Park folks WILL catch you & they WILL go to court to get your bond raised. Saw this today!"
- "Carl Barnes and David Townes came to City to steal dumpsters. Both now charged with felony stealing. Stay out of our town!"
- "Stanley Bailey assaulted an 80 yr old lady & stole her purse. He now has 20 yrs to ask himself why he's a jerk."
- "Don't threaten police with a weapon, unless you want to be shot AND charged with a felony (unlawful use of a weapon), like Carl Evans was today."

Some would say Joyce's comments are a breath of fresh air, making it clear to all who follow her how her office will treat those who break the law. Other prosecutors take a more measured stance, refusing to publicly discuss specific offenders and/or cases. Is there an ethical dilemma here? For example, can publicity of this sort contaminate the jury pool? Could tweets and Facebook status posts come back to later haunt the officials who post them? Indeed, a Florida defense attorney was fired and a mistrial was declared after she posted on Facebook a picture of her client's leopard-print underwear, apparently mocking him.[1] Another post questioned her client's innocence.[2] Arguably she went too far in that particular case, but where do we draw the line between proper and improper use of social media in the court context? ■

The court is a complex and *necessary* social agency with many independent but interrelated subsystems—clerk, prosecutor, defense attorney, judge, and probation department—each playing a role in the adjudicatory process. Ideally, the entire process, from filing the initial complaint to final sentencing of the defendant, is governed by precise rules of law designed to ensure fairness, without regard to financial considerations. Unfortunately, though, in today's crowded and underfunded court system, such abstract goals are often impossible to achieve.

The dual curses of overcrowding and underfunding have become standard features of the court system. These constraints have a significant impact on the way that courts do justice. The U.S. court system is often the scene of accommodation and "working things out," instead of an arena for a vigorous criminal defense. **Plea negotiations/plea bargaining** and other nonjudicial alternatives, such as diversion, are far more common than the formal trial process.

The Criminal Court Process

The U.S. court system has evolved over the years into an intricately balanced legal process that has recently come under siege because of the sheer numbers of cases it must consider and the ways in which it is forced to handle such overcrowding.

Overloaded court dockets have given rise to charges of "assembly-line justice," in which a majority of defendants are induced to plead guilty, jury trials are rare, and the speedy trial is highly desired but unattainable. Overcrowding causes the poor to languish in detention while the wealthier go free on bail. An innocent person can be frightened into pleading guilty; conversely, a guilty person can be released because a trial has been delayed too long.[3] Whether providing more judges or new or enlarged courts will solve the problem of overcrowding remains to be seen. Trial alternatives such as mediation, diversion, and bail reform offer other avenues of possible relief. Making court management and administration more efficient is also seen as a step that might ease the congestion of the courts. The introduction of professional trial court managers—administrators, clerks, and judges with management skills—has had a significant influence on court efficiency.

State Court Systems

To house this complex process, each state maintains its own state court organization and structure. There are 50 state trial and appellate systems, with separate courts for the District of Columbia, Puerto Rico, and other U.S. territories. Usually three (or more) separate court systems exist within each state jurisdiction. States are free to create as many courts as they wish, to name courts what they like (in New York, felony courts are known as supreme courts!), and to establish specialized courts that handle a single legal matter, such as drug courts and/or domestic courts. Consequently, there is a great deal of diversity in court organization from one state to the next. State courts handle a wide variety of cases and regulate numerous personal behaviors, ranging from homicide to property maintenance. The various state court systems are described below.

Courts of Limited Jurisdiction

Depending on the jurisdiction in which they are located, state **courts of limited jurisdiction** are known by a variety of names, such as municipal courts, county courts, district courts, and metropolitan courts. The term derives from the fact

**plea negotiations/
plea bargaining**
Discussions between defense counsel and prosecution in which the accused agrees to plead guilty in exchange for certain considerations, such as reduced charges or a lenient sentence.

**court of limited
jurisdiction**
A court that has jurisdiction over misdemeanors and conducts preliminary investigations of felony charges.

Describe state court structure.

that the jurisdiction of these courts is limited to minor or less serious civil and criminal cases.

Courts of limited jurisdiction are restricted in the types of cases they may hear. Usually, they will handle misdemeanor criminal infractions, violations of municipal ordinances, traffic violations, and civil suits where the damages involve less than a certain amount of money (usually $1,000). In criminal matters, they hear misdemeanors such as shoplifting, disorderly conduct, or simple assault. Their sanctioning power is also limited. In criminal matters, punishments may be limited to fines, community sentencing, or incarceration in the county jail for up to a year. In addition to their trial work, limited-jurisdiction courts conduct arraignments, preliminary hearings, and bail hearings in felony cases (before they are transferred to superior courts).

Some states separate limited courts into those that handle civil cases only and those that settle criminal cases. Included in the category of courts of limited jurisdiction are special courts, such as juvenile, family, and probate (divorce, estate issues, and custody) courts. State lawmakers may respond to a particular social problem, such as drug use, by creating **specialized courts** that focus on treatment and care for these special-needs offenders. One of the most common is the family or juvenile court, which handles custody cases, delinquency, and other issues involving children (juvenile courts will be discussed further in Chapter 15). Some recent types of specialized courts are discussed in the Analyzing Criminal Justice Issues feature.

The nation's approximately 13,500 limited jurisdiction courts make up 90 percent of all state courts.[4] They are the courts most often accused of providing assembly-line justice. Because the matters they decide involve minor personal confrontations and conflicts—family disputes, divorces, landlord–tenant conflicts, barroom brawls—the rule of the day is "handling the situation" and resolving the dispute.

Courts of General Jurisdiction

Approximately 2,000 **courts of general jurisdiction** exist in the United States, variously called felony, superior, supreme, county, and circuit courts. Courts of general jurisdiction handle the more serious felony cases (e.g., murder, rape, robbery) and civil cases where damages are over a specified amount, such as $10,000. Courts of general jurisdiction may also be responsible for reviewing cases on appeal from courts of limited jurisdiction. In some instances they base their decision on a review of the transcript of the case, whereas in others they can actually grant a new trial; this latter procedure is known as the *trial de novo process*. Changes in the courts of general jurisdiction, such as increases in felony filing rates, are watched closely because serious crime is of great public concern.

Courts of general jurisdiction are typically organized in judicial districts or circuits, based on a political division such as a county or a group of counties (such as Superior Court for the Southern Tier). They then receive cases from the various limited courts located within the county/jurisdiction. Some general courts separate criminal and civil cases so that some specialize in civil matters, whereas others maintain a caseload that is exclusively criminal. In 10 states, Washington, D.C., and Puerto Rico, general and limited courts have consolidated their jurisdictions, creating a unified court system.

State criminal appeals are heard in the **appellate courts** in the 50 states and the District of Columbia. Each state has at least one court of last resort, usually called a state supreme court, which reviews issues of law and fact appealed from the trial courts. A few states have two high courts, one for civil appeals and the other for criminal cases. In addition, many states have established intermediate

Web App 9.1

For information about the National Center for State Courts (NCSC), visit http://www.ncsc.org/.

---

specialized court
A court that has primary jurisdiction over specific types of offenses and that operates differently than a traditional criminal court, such as with a concern over outcomes and extensive judicial monitoring.

---

court of general jurisdiction
A state or federal court that has jurisdiction over felony offenses—serious crimes that carry a penalty of incarceration in a state or federal prison for one year or more.

---

appellate court
A court to which appeals are made on points of law resulting from the judgment of a lower court; the appellate court may be asked to evaluate the impact of new evidence but more typically decides whether the state or federal constitution was improperly interpreted during a case.

analyzing criminal justice ISSUES

SPECIALIZED COURTS

A growing phenomenon in the United States is the creation of specialized courts that focus on one type of criminal act—for example, drug abuse or domestic violence. All cases within the jurisdiction that involve this particular type of crime are funneled to the specialized court, where presumably they will get prompt resolution.

WHAT MAKES SPECIALIZED COURTS DIFFERENT?

Specialized courts differ from traditional courts in several key respects. According to the Center for Court Innovation, specialized courts have these six features:

- *Outcomes are elevated above process.* The main concern is reducing recidivism.

- *Judicial monitoring is critical.* Judges closely monitor offenders.

- *Informed decision making is necessary.* Judges hand down sentences with more information about offenders' backgrounds than may be available in traditional sentencing contexts.

- *Collaboration.* Specialized courts typically collaborate with other public and private agencies, many of which are often housed in the courthouse.

- *Nontraditional roles.* Specialized court personnel often assume different roles. For example, prosecutors in specialized courts are more interested in helping defendants than in seeing that they are convicted or punished.

- *Systemic change.* Specialized courts try to change the way the criminal justice system works.

DRUG COURTS

The drug court movement began in Florida to address the growing problem of prison overcrowding due in large part to an influx of drug-involved offenders. Drug courts were created to have primary jurisdiction over cases involving substance abuse and drug trafficking. The aim is to place nonviolent first offenders into intensive treatment programs rather than in jail or prison. Today, there are nearly 3,000 drug courts across the United States. Drug courts address the overlap between the public health threats of drug abuse and crime: crimes are often drug-related, and drug abusers are frequently involved with the criminal justice system. Drug courts provide an ideal setting to address these problems by

Leon Castillas inspects a toaster that was dropped off as a donation at the Goodwill Donation Center in Evansville, Indiana. Castillas, a veteran of the U.S. Army, was one of the first participants to complete the Vanderburgh County's Veterans Treatment Court.

linking the justice system with health services and drug treatment providers, while easing the burden on the already overtaxed correctional system.

MENTAL HEALTH COURTS

Based largely on the organization of drug courts, mental health courts focus their attention on mental health treatment to help people with emotional problems reduce their chances of reoffending. By focusing on the need for treatment, along with providing supervision and support from the community, mental health courts provide a venue for those dealing with mental health issues to avoid the trauma of jail or prison, where they will have little if any access to treatment.

Although mental health courts tend to vary in their approach, most share a few basic operating procedures:

- Most demand active participation by the defendant.

- The participant must be diagnosed with a mental illness, and a direct link must be established between the illness and the crime committed.

- Intervention must occur quickly; individuals must be screened and referred to the program either immediately after arrest or within three weeks.

- Once in the program, participants are closely monitored by case managers.

- Most provide voluntary outpatient or inpatient mental health treatment, in the least restrictive manner appropriate as determined by the court, that carries with it the possibility of dismissal of charges or reduced sentencing on successful completion of treatment.

- Centralized case management involves the consolidation of cases that include mentally ill or mentally disabled defendants (including probation violators) and the coordination of mental health treatment plans and social services, including life skills training, placement, health care, and relapse prevention for each participant who requires such services.

- Supervision of treatment plan compliance continues for a term not to exceed the maximum allowable sentence or probation for the charged or relevant offense, and to the extent practicable, psychiatric care continues at the end of the supervised period.

The mental health court concept seems beneficial, but it has encountered a few operational difficulties. It is hard to get community support for programs and institutions treating mentally ill offenders. Most programs accept only the nonviolent mentally ill; those who are violence prone are still lost in the correctional system without receiving the proper treatment. It is also difficult to assess the benefits of having specialized mental health courts. With other specialized courts, measuring offender improvement is relatively easy. For example, people sent to drug court programs must simply prove they can remain drug free. However, those involved with mental health court programs suffer from complex mental issues, and case managers must ensure that these individuals have gained control over their illness, which can be difficult to determine.

COMMUNITY COURTS

Community courts are also becoming popular. Rather than targeting specific types of problems such as drugs or mental health, these courts take a more generalized focus. The main concern with community courts is providing "accessible justice" for residents who cannot easily get to downtown courthouses and focusing on quality-of-life offenses that may not be seen as top priority in traditional criminal courts. Community courts often have several on-site services available, as well. The first community court was Manhattan's Midtown Community Court.

DOMESTIC VIOLENCE COURTS

Several jurisdictions across the country have created their own domestic violence courts. Brian Ostrom described domestic violence courts in this way: They "seek to coordinate with medical, social service, and treatment providers and establish special procedures and alternative sentencing options to promote effective outcomes. Success necessitates systemwide collaboration and the ongoing commitment of judges, health care professionals, the police, prosecution, and citizens who witness violent acts." Today, there are some 300 domestic violence courts in operation nationwide. Given how new they are, however, not many of them have been evaluated.

GUN COURTS

Rhode Island created the nation's first gun court in 1994. Unlike some of the other specialized courts, this gun court was concerned mainly with minimizing delay and ensuring that gun offenders received the toughest penalties the law allows. Other gun courts emphasize educating defendants about gun violence and safety. Many such courts have focused their efforts on juvenile gun offenders. According to David Sheppard and Patricia Kelly, common features of juvenile gun courts include:

- Early intervention—in many jurisdictions, before resolution of the court proceedings

- Short-term (often a single two- to four-hour session), intensive programming

- An intensive educational focus, using knowledgeable, concerned adults from the community to show youths the harm that can come from unlawful gun use, the choices they can make about carrying and/or using guns versus nonviolent alternatives for resolving conflicts, and the immediate response by adults in positions of authority that will result when youths are involved with guns

- The inclusion of a wide range of court personnel and law enforcement officials—judges, probation officers, prosecutors, defense counsel, and police—working together with community members

OTHER SPECIALIZED COURTS

There are specialized courts for many different types of crime and social problems. In addition to targeting the above crimes, specialized courts have been formed to deal with everything from homelessness and sex offenses to parole reentry and teen bullying. We have moved well beyond the world of the traditional limited jurisdiction court. Limited jurisdiction courts still exist, but these are often being supplanted by courts whose jurisdiction is not only limited but also very narrow.

CRITICAL THINKING

1. Do you believe that specialized courts are needed for other types of crimes, such as sex offenses?

2. Should a judge preside over a specialized court, or should it be administered by treatment personnel?

Sources: Greg Berman and John Feinblatt, *Problem-Solving Courts: A Brief Primer* (New York: Center for Court Innovation, 2001); U.S. Department of Justice, *Drug Courts* (Washington, DC: U.S. Department of Justice, 2012), http://www.ncjrs.gov/pdffiles1/nij/238527.pdf (accessed July 2014); Shelli Rossman et al., *Criminal Justice Interventions for Offenders with Mental Illness: Evaluation of Mental Health Courts in Bronx and Brooklyn, New York* (Washington, DC: U.S. Department of Justice, National Institute of Justice, 2012); Brian J. Ostrom, "Domestic Violence Courts: Editorial Introduction," *Criminology and Public Policy* 3 (2003): 105–108; Office of Juvenile Justice and Delinquency Prevention, *Gun Court—Providence, RI, Profile No. 37* (Washington, DC: U.S. Department of Justice, Office of Juvenile Justice and Delinquency Prevention, n.d.), http://www.ojjdp.gov/pubs/gun_violence/profile37.html (accessed July 2014); David Sheppard and Patricia Kelly, *Juvenile Gun Courts: Promoting Accountability and Providing Treatment* (Washington, DC: U.S. Department of Justice, Office of Juvenile Justice and Delinquency Prevention, 2002), p. 2; Greg Berman, John Feinblatt, and Sarah Glazer, *Good Courts: The Case for Problem-Solving Justice* (New York: New Press, 2005).

appellate courts (IACs) to review decisions by trial courts and administrative agencies before they reach the supreme court stage. Currently, 40 states have at least one permanent IAC.[5] Appeals from criminal cases are the most common types of appeals, with the others arising primarily from civil judgments and administrative agency decisions.[6]

State courts have witnessed a fairly steady and high caseload in recent years.[7] In the meantime, the number of judges and support staff has not kept pace. The resulting imbalance has led to the increased use of intermediate courts to screen cases.

In sum, most states have at least two trial courts and two appellate courts, but they differ about where jurisdiction over such matters as juvenile cases and felony versus misdemeanor offenses is found. Such matters vary from state to state and between the state courts and the federal system.

Model State Court Structure

Figure 9.1 illustrates the interrelationship of appellate and trial courts in a typical state court structure. Each state's court organization varies from this standard pattern. Every state has a tiered court organization (lower, upper, and appellate courts), but states differ in the way they have delegated responsibility to a particular court system. For example, the court organizations of Texas and New York are complex in comparison with the model court structure (see Figures 9.2 and 9.3). Texas separates its highest appellate divisions into civil and criminal courts. The Texas Supreme Court hears civil, administrative, and juvenile cases, and an independent court of criminal appeals has the final say on criminal matters. New York's unique structure features two separate intermediate appellate courts with different geographic jurisdictions and an independent family court, which handles both domestic relations (such as guardianship and custody, neglect, and abuse) and juvenile delinquency. Surrogate court handles adoptions and settles disagreements over estate transfers. The court of claims handles civil matters in which the state is a party. In contrast to New York, which has ten independent courts, six states (Idaho, Illinois, Iowa, Massachusetts, Minnesota, and South Dakota) have unified their trial courts into a single system.

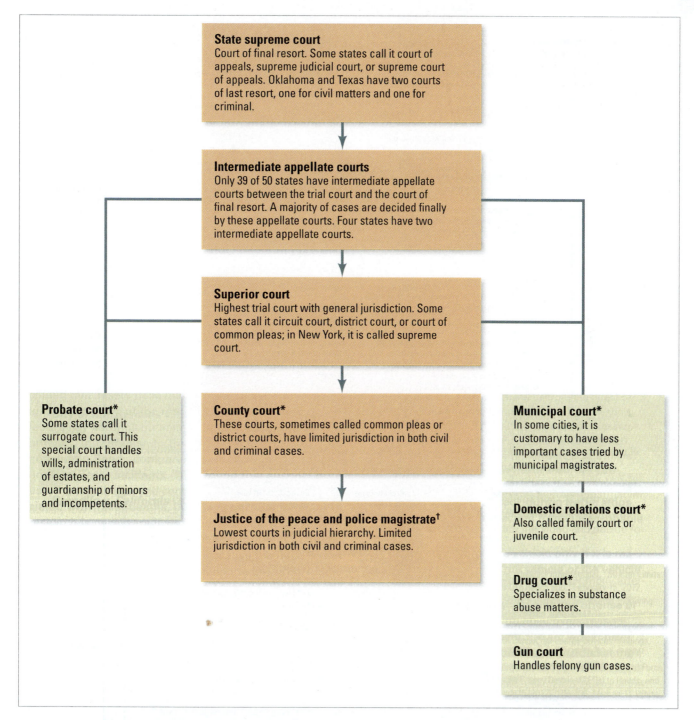

State supreme court
Court of final resort. Some states call it court of appeals, supreme judicial court, or supreme court of appeals. Oklahoma and Texas have two courts of last resort, one for civil matters and one for criminal.

Intermediate appellate courts
Only 39 of 50 states have intermediate appellate courts between the trial court and the court of final resort. A majority of cases are decided finally by these appellate courts. Four states have two intermediate appellate courts.

Superior court
Highest trial court with general jurisdiction. Some states call it circuit court, district court, or court of common pleas; in New York, it is called supreme court.

Probate court*
Some states call it surrogate court. This special court handles wills, administration of estates, and guardianship of minors and incompetents.

County court*
These courts, sometimes called common pleas or district courts, have limited jurisdiction in both civil and criminal cases.

Municipal court*
In some cities, it is customary to have less important cases tried by municipal magistrates.

Justice of the peace and police magistrate[†]
Lowest courts in judicial hierarchy. Limited jurisdiction in both civil and criminal cases.

Domestic relations court*
Also called family court or juvenile court.

Drug court*
Specializes in substance abuse matters.

Gun court
Handles felony gun cases.

FIGURE 9.1   A Model of a State Judicial System

Source: David B. Rottman and Shauna M. Strickland, *State Court Organization, 2004* (Arlington, VA: National Center for State Courts, 2006), p. 9.

* Courts of special jurisdictions, such as probate, family, or juvenile courts, and the so-called inferior courts, such as common pleas or municipal courts, may be separate courts or part of the trial court of general jurisdiction.

† Justices of the peace do not exist in all states. Where they do exist, their jurisdictions vary greatly from state to state.

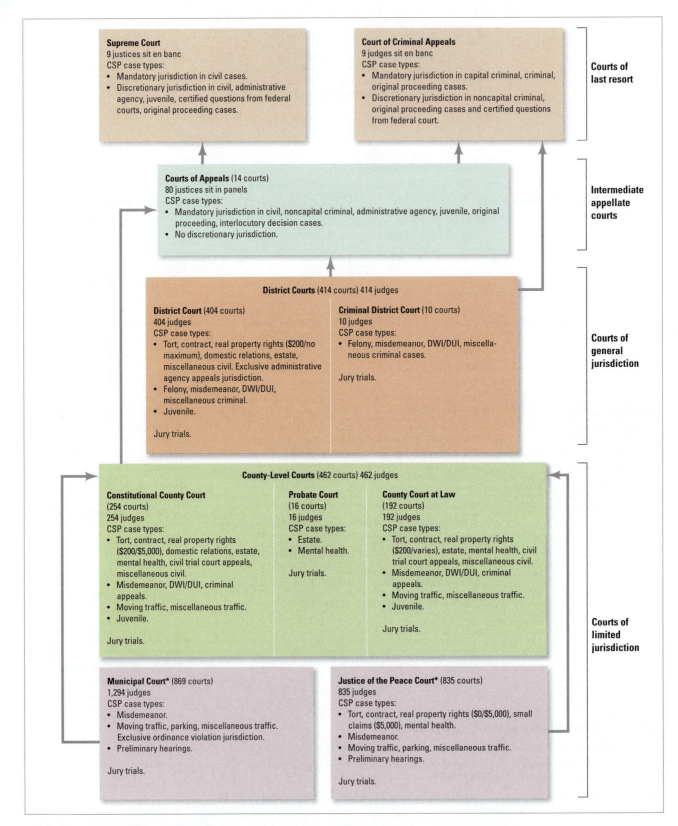

FIGURE 9.2 Texas Court Structure

Source: National Center for State Courts, www.ncsconline.org/D_Research/Ct_Struct/state_inc.asp?STATE=TX (accessed June 2014).

Note: CSP = Court Statistics Project. DWI/DUI = driving while intoxicated/driving under the influence.

* Some municipal and justice of the peace courts may appeal to the district court.

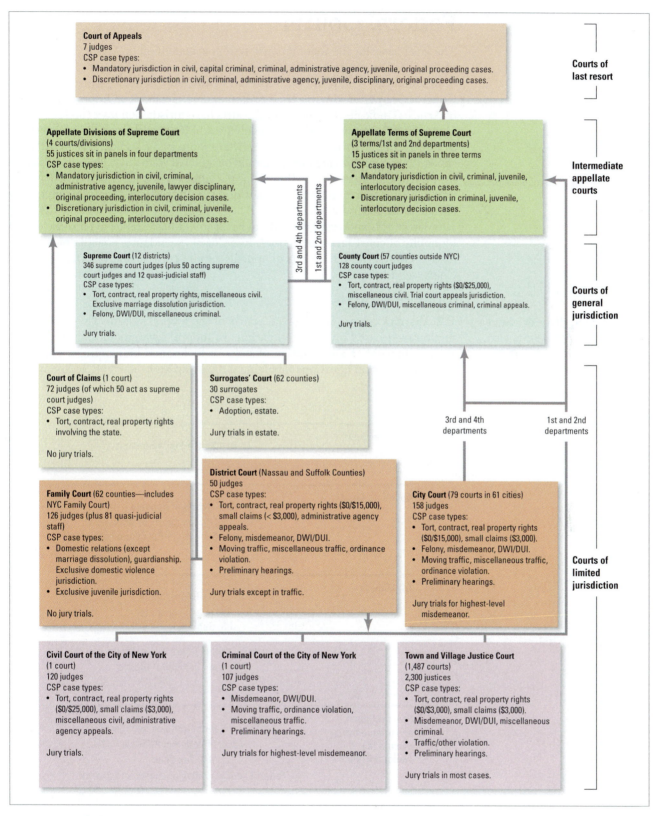

FIGURE 9.3 **New York Court Structure**

Source: National Center for State Courts, www.ncsconline.org/D_Research/Ct_Struct/state_inc.asp?STATE=NY (accessed June 2014).

Note: Unless otherwise noted, numbers reflect statutory authorization. Many judges sit in more than one court so the number of judgeships indicated in this chart does not reflect the actual number of judges in the system. Fifty county court judges also serve surrogate court and six county court judges also serve family court. CSP = Court Statistics Project. DWI/DUI = driving while intoxicated/driving under the influence.

Federal Courts

The legal basis for the federal court system is contained in Article 3, Section 1, of the U.S. Constitution, which provides that "the judicial power of the United States shall be vested in one Supreme Court, and in such inferior courts as Congress may from time to time ordain and establish." The important clauses in Article 3 indicate that the federal courts have jurisdiction over the laws of the United States, treaties, and cases involving admiralty and maritime jurisdiction, as well as over controversies between two or more states and citizens of different states.[8] This complex language generally means that state courts have jurisdiction over all legal matters, unless they involve a violation of a federal criminal statute or a civil suit between citizens of different states or between a citizen and an agency of the federal government.

 Describe federal court structure.

Within this authority, the federal government has established a three-tiered hierarchy of court jurisdiction that, in order of ascendancy, consists of the U.S. district courts, the U.S. courts of appeals (circuit courts), and the U.S. Supreme Court (see Figure 9.4).

District Courts

U.S. district court
A trial court in the federal court system.

U.S. district courts are the trial courts of the federal system. They have jurisdiction over cases involving violations of federal laws, including civil rights abuses, interstate transportation of stolen vehicles, and kidnappings. They may also hear cases on questions involving citizenship and the rights of aliens. The

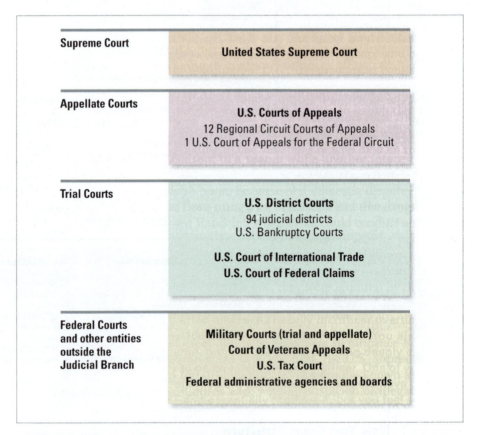

FIGURE 9.4   The Federal Judicial System

Source: Administrative Office of the U.S. Courts, *The United States Federal Courts*, www.uscourts.gov/EducationalResources/FederalCourtBasics/CourtStructure/StructureOfFederalCourts.aspx (accessed June 2014).

jurisdiction of the U.S. district court will occasionally overlap that of state courts. For example, citizens who reside in separate states and are involved in litigation of an amount in excess of $10,000 may choose to have their cases heard in either of the states or in the federal court. Finally, federal district courts hear cases in which one state sues a resident (or firm) in another state, where one state sues another, or where the federal government is a party in a suit. A single judge ordinarily presides over criminal trials; a defendant may also request a jury trial.

Federal district courts were organized by Congress in the Judicial Act of 1789, and today 94 independent courts are in operation. Originally, each state was allowed one court. As the population grew, however, so did the need for courts. Now each state has from one to four district courts, and the District of Columbia has one for itself.

Federal Appeals Courts

There are 13 **U.S. courts of appeals**, sometimes referred to as U.S. circuit courts. This name is derived from the historical practice of having judges ride the circuit and regularly hear cases in the judicial seats of their various jurisdictions. Today, appellate judges are not required to travel (although some may sit in more than one court), and each federal appellate court jurisdiction contains a number of associate justices who share the caseload. Circuit court offices are usually located in major cities, such as San Francisco and New York, and cases to be heard must be brought to these locations by attorneys.

The circuit court is empowered to review federal and state appellate court cases on substantive and procedural issues involving rights guaranteed by the Constitution. Circuit courts neither retry cases nor determine whether the facts brought out during trial support conviction or dismissal. Instead, they analyze judicial interpretations of the law, such as the charge (or instructions) to the jury, and reflect on the constitutional issues involved in each case they hear.

Although federal court criminal cases make up only a small percentage of appellate cases, they are still of concern to the judiciary. Steps have been taken to make the appeal process more difficult. For example, the U.S. Supreme Court has tried to limit the number of appeals being filed by prison inmates, which often represent a significant number of cases appealed in the federal criminal justice system. For a map of the federal appeals courts (and the districts within them), see Figure 9.5.

The U.S. Supreme Court

The **U.S. Supreme Court** is the nation's highest appellate body and the **court of last resort** for all cases tried in the various federal and state courts. The Supreme Court is composed of nine members appointed for lifetime terms by the president, with the approval of Congress. (The size of the Court is set by statute.) The Court has discretion over most of the cases it will consider and may choose to hear only those it deems important, appropriate, and worthy of its attention. The Court chooses around 300 of the 5,000 cases that are appealed each year; fewer than half of these typically receive full opinions.

The Supreme Court is unique in several ways. First, it is the only court established by constitutional mandate instead of federal legislation. Second, it decides basic social and political issues of grave consequence and importance to the nation. Third, the justices shape the future meaning of the U.S. Constitution. Their decisions identify the rights and liberties of citizens throughout the United States.

Web App 9.2
For more information about the federal courts, visit http://www.uscourts.gov/.

U.S. courts of appeals
An appellate court in the federal court system.

U.S. Supreme Court
The highest appellate court in the United States.

court of last resort
A court that handles the final appeal on a matter—in the federal system, the U.S. Supreme Court.

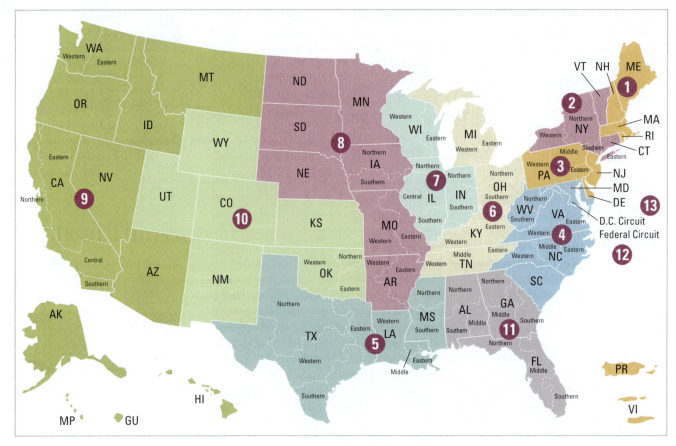

FIGURE 9.5   U.S. Circuit Map

Source: Administrative Office of the U.S. Courts, www.uscourts.gov/court_locator.aspx (accessed June 2014).

When the Supreme Court rules on a case, usually by majority decision (at least five votes), the outcome becomes a precedent that must be honored by all lower courts. For example, if the Court grants a particular litigant the right to counsel at a police lineup, all similarly situated clients must be given the same right. This type of ruling is usually referred to as a *landmark decision*. The use of precedent in the legal system gives the Supreme Court power to influence and mold the everyday operating procedures of the police, trial courts, and corrections agencies. This influence became particularly pronounced during the tenure of Chief Justices Earl Warren (1953–1969) and Warren Burger (1969–1986), who greatly amplified and extended the power of the Court to influence criminal justice policies. Under William H. Rehnquist, who was elevated to chief justice in 1986, the Court continued to influence criminal justice matters, ranging from the investigation of crimes to the execution of criminals. The newest chief justice, John Roberts, has also had an influence on the criminal justice system through several recent decisions. The personal legal philosophies of the justices and their orientation toward the civil and personal rights of victims and criminals significantly affect the daily operations of the justice system.

Web App 9.3

For more information about the Supreme Court, visit http://www.supremecourt.gov/,

HOW A CASE GETS TO THE SUPREME COURT   When the nation was first established, the Supreme Court did not review state court decisions involving issues of federal law. Even though Congress had given the Supreme Court jurisdiction to review state decisions, much resistance and controversy surrounded the relationship between the states and the federal government. However, in a famous decision, *Martin v. Hunter's Lessee* (1816), the Court reaffirmed the legitimacy of its jurisdiction over state court decisions when such courts handled issues of federal or constitutional law.[9] This decision allowed the Court to actively review actions by states and their courts and reinforced the Court's power to make the supreme law of the land. Since that time, a defendant who indicates that governmental action— whether state or federal—violates a constitutional law is in a position to have the Court review such action. Today, most cases that come before the Supreme Court involve significant federal questions, usually of a constitutional nature.

To carry out its responsibilities, the Supreme Court had to develop a method for dealing with the large volume of cases coming from the state and federal courts for final review. In the early years of its history, the Court sought to review every case brought before it. Since the middle of the twentieth century, however, the Court has used the **writ of certiorari** to decide what cases it should hear (*certiorari* is a Latin term meaning to bring the record of a case from a lower court up to a higher court for immediate review). Today, more than 90 percent of the cases heard by the Court are brought by petition for a writ of certiorari.[10] Under this procedure, the justices have discretion to select the cases they will review for a decision. For a writ to be granted, ordinarily four justices must agree to hear the case. This is known as the **rule of four**. However, the Court is required to hear cases in a few instances, such as decisions from a three-judge federal district court on reapportionment and cases involving the Voting Rights Act.

After the Supreme Court decides to hear a case, it reviews written and oral arguments. The written materials are referred to as legal briefs, and oral arguments are normally presented to the justices at the Court in Washington, D.C.

After the material is reviewed and the oral arguments heard, the justices normally meet in what is known as a case conference. At this case conference, they discuss the case and vote to reach a decision. The cases voted on by the Court generally come from the judicial systems of the various states or the U.S. courts of appeals, and they represent the entire spectrum of law.

In reaching a decision, the Supreme Court reevaluates and reinterprets state statutes, the U.S. Constitution, and previous case decisions. Based on a review of the case, the Court either affirms or reverses the decision of the lower court. When the justices reach a decision, the chief justice of the Court assigns someone of the majority group to write the opinion. Another justice normally writes a dissenting, or minority, opinion. When the case is finished, it is submitted to the public and becomes the law of the land. The decision represents the legal precedents that add to the existing body of law on a given subject, change it, and guide its future development. Figure 9.6 shows the course a case takes as it progresses from a federal or state court to the Supreme Court.

In the area of criminal justice, the decisions of the U.S. Supreme Court have had the broadest impact on the reform of the system. The Court's action is the final step in settling constitutional criminal disputes throughout the nation. By discretionary review through a petition for certiorari, the Court requires state courts to

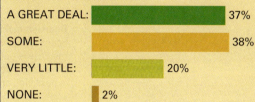

FACT CHECK ✓

YOUR OPINION: How much confidence do you have in the U.S. Supreme Court? A great deal, some, very little, or none?

PUBLIC OPINION:

A GREAT DEAL: 37%

SOME: 38%

VERY LITTLE: 20%

NONE: 2%

REALITY: The vast majority of Americans have at least some confidence in the U.S. Supreme Court. These perceptions have also remained fairly stable over time. How do these rankings measure up to the rankings of other institutions? Among the consistently lowest rated are the executive branch of the government, Congress, Wall Street, television news, large corporations, and law firms. Confidence in the Supreme Courts is approximately double that of any of these other institutions.

DISCUSSION: Public opinion polls are popular and commonplace. They are used to gauge people's beliefs on a wide range of topics for an equally wide range of reasons. Should opinion polls matter in the case of the Supreme Court, whose justices are appointed to their posts for life? Should the Supreme Court consider public opinion in its deliberations?

Sources: Sourcebook of Criminal Justice Statistics, http://www.albany.edu/sourcebook/pdf/t2142012.pdf and http://www.albany.edu/sourcebook/pdf/t29.pdf (accessed July 2014).

writ of certiorari
An order of a superior court requesting that a record of an inferior court (or administrative body) be brought forward for review or inspection.

rule of four
The convention that four justices must agree to hear a case before a writ of certiorari is granted.

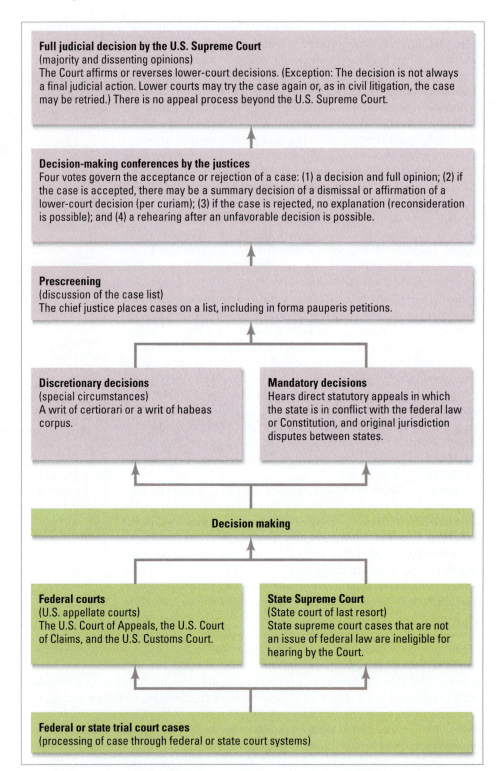

Full judicial decision by the U.S. Supreme Court
(majority and dissenting opinions)
The Court affirms or reverses lower-court decisions. (Exception: The decision is not always a final judicial action. Lower courts may try the case again or, as in civil litigation, the case may be retried.) There is no appeal process beyond the U.S. Supreme Court.

Decision-making conferences by the justices
Four votes govern the acceptance or rejection of a case: (1) a decision and full opinion; (2) if the case is accepted, there may be a summary decision of a dismissal or affirmation of a lower-court decision (per curiam); (3) if the case is rejected, no explanation (reconsideration is possible); and (4) a rehearing after an unfavorable decision is possible.

Prescreening
(discussion of the case list)
The chief justice places cases on a list, including in forma pauperis petitions.

Discretionary decisions
(special circumstances)
A writ of certiorari or a writ of habeas corpus.

Mandatory decisions
Hears direct statutory appeals in which the state is in conflict with the federal law or Constitution, and original jurisdiction disputes between states.

Decision making

Federal courts
(U.S. appellate courts)
The U.S. Court of Appeals, the U.S. Court of Claims, and the U.S. Customs Court.

State Supreme Court
(State court of last resort)
State supreme court cases that are not an issue of federal law are ineligible for hearing by the Court.

Federal or state trial court cases
(processing of case through federal or state court systems)

FIGURE 9.6   **Tracing the Course of a Case to the U.S. Supreme Court**

accept its interpretation of the Constitution. In doing so, the Court has changed the day-by-day operations of the criminal justice system.

Court Congestion

The vast U.S. court system has been overloaded by the millions of cases that are brought each year. State court systems now handle about 100 million new cases annually. Here is how the cases break down:

- Civil cases: 18 percent
- Domestic violence cases: 6 percent
- Criminal cases: 20 percent
- Juvenile cases: 2 percent
- Traffic and ordinance violation cases: 54 percent[11]

The number of cases in all state courts, especially limited jurisdiction courts, has been increasing at a steady pace for more than a decade. Two-thirds of all cases at the state level are processed in limited jurisdiction courts, compared to just one-third in general jurisdiction courts.[12]

Although they are fewer in number, federal courts are equally burdened: approximately 100,000 criminal cases receive dispositions in the district courts each year.[13] The U.S. courts of appeals decide approximately 57,000 criminal appeals each year.[14]

Congestion is undesirable for various reasons. First, it makes people wait too long for resolution. Second, it costs money. For example, it is costly to jail dangerous criminal defendants in the time leading up to their court date. Third, too much delay can violate the Sixth Amendment's provisions concerning the right to a speedy trial.

Why has the court system become so congested? Numerous factors produce trial delay and court congestion:[15]

- Rapidly increasing populations in some states, such as Nevada, have outpaced growth in the court system.

AP Images

Serial killer Tommy Lynn Sells, pictured here, was executed in Texas in 2014 following his conviction in the stabbing death of a 13-year-old girl. Sells claimed he killed as many as 70 people in various states as a drifter and carnival worker. The death penalty is reserved for the worst of the worst, but does it live up to those expectations?

L03 Identify the problems associated with court congestion.

AP Images/*Miami Herald*, Cammy Clark

On March 3, 2010, Lonnie Helms, who has been arrested in Monroe County (Florida) 15 times since 2004, tells Key West police officers he's doing nothing wrong. In the two previous months, Key West police arrested more than 70 vagrants for "quality of life" offenses: aggressive panhandling, trespassing, fighting, public intoxication, defecating on public property, and using residents' outdoor showers and electricity. Such arrests invariably lead to congestion in the courts, and many such offenders are promptly released.

Inmates file out of the prison bakery after working the morning shift at the Rikers Island jail in New York. Prosecutors want state legislation that would automatically turn a certain number of misdemeanor convictions into a felony, thus calling for prison time. Critics say ramping up prison time for repeat offenders committing low-level crimes could unintentionally increase courtroom backlogs. Who is correct?

AP Images/Bebeto Matthews

■ Some communities have attempted to control crime by aggressively prosecuting petty offenses and nuisance crimes such as panhandling and vagrancy.

■ As the law becomes more complex, and involves such technological issues as intellectual property rights concerning computer programs, the need for a more involved court process has escalated.

■ Ironically, efforts being made to reform the criminal law may also be helping to overload the courts. The increase of mandatory prison sentences for some crimes may reduce the use of plea bargaining and increase the number of jury trials because defendants fear that a conviction will lead to incarceration and thus must be avoided at all costs.

■ Civil litigation has increased as people have come to view the court process as a means of redressing all kinds of personal wrongs. This can result in *frivolous lawsuits*—for example, when overweight people file suit against manufacturers, distributors, or sellers of food products, charging these parties with responsibility for their obesity.[16] Increased civil litigation can add to the backlog because most courts handle both criminal and civil matters.

If relief is to be found, it will probably be in the form of better administrative and management techniques that improve the use of existing resources.[17] Another possible method of creating a more efficient court system is to unify existing state courts into a single administrative structure using modern management principles. This has happened already in several states, such as California. In the late 1990s, voters in that state voted to change the state constitution so that municipal and superior courts were unified into a single type of court.

The Judiciary

judge
The senior officer in a court of law, who is authorized to hear and decide cases.

The **judge** is the senior officer in a court of law who is authorized to hear and decide cases. A judge's duties are varied and far more extensive than might be expected. During trials, the judge rules on the appropriateness of conduct, settles questions of evidence and procedure, and guides the questioning of witnesses. In a jury trial, the judge must instruct jurors on which evidence is proper to examine and which should be ignored. The judge also formally charges the jury by instructing its members on what points of law and evidence they must consider to

reach a verdict of either guilty or not guilty. When a jury trial is waived, the judge must decide whether to hold for the complainant or for the defendant. Finally, if a defendant is found guilty, the judge must decide on the sentence (in some cases, this is legislatively determined), which includes choosing the type of sentence and its length, as well as the conditions under which probation may be revoked.

While carrying out her duties, the judge must be wary of the legal controls placed on the trial process by the appellate court system. If an error is made, the judge's decision may be reversed, causing, at the very least, personal embarrassment. Although some experts believe that fear of reversal shapes judicial decision making, recent research by David Klein and Robert Hume indicates that judges may be more independent than previously believed, especially if they can use their judicial power as a policymaking tool to influence important social policies such as affirmative action or privacy.[18]

Web App 9.4

For information about the American Judges Association, visit http://aja.ncsc.dni.us/.

Other Judicial Functions

Beyond these stated duties, the trial judge has extensive control and influence over the other agencies of the court: probation, the court clerk, court reporters, the public defender, and the district attorney's office (see Exhibit 9.1). Probation and the clerk may be under the judge's explicit control. In some courts, the operations, philosophy, and procedures of these agencies are within the magistrate's administrative domain. In others—for example, where a state agency controls the probation department—the attitudes of the county or district court judge greatly influence the way a probation department is run and how its decisions are made. Judges often consult with probation staff on treatment decisions, and many judges are interested in providing the most innovative and up-to-date care possible.

EXHIBIT 9.1 Court Staff

The most visible courtroom personnel include the judge, the prosecutor, and the defense attorney. But there are many other important court personnel and staff persons. The typical large jurisdiction probably has a mix of the following personnel working in the courtroom or courthouse at any given time.

Clerk

Court clerks are responsible for a wide range of duties. Their main responsibilities include maintaining court records; receiving, processing, and maintaining judgments; issuing process, such as summonses, subpoenas, and wage garnishments; preserving the court seal; swearing in witnesses, jurors, and grand jurors; collecting fees and fines; handling inquiries from attorneys and other parties; and printing and distributing opinions of the court.

Court Administrator

There are two general types of court administrators. The first is a state employee. In each state, these individuals are part of the state administrative office of the court, which is usually under the direction of the state supreme court. Court administrators help develop and implement policies and services for the judicial branch throughout the state. They also conduct research and determine whether judicial needs are identified and incorporated into long-term plans. They establish priorities for the courts, address financial problems and budgeting issues, and manage the use of technology within a state's judicial branch.

The second type of court administrator is a local court administrator. These individuals manage the daily operations of the court, usually under the direction of the presiding judge. They provide administrative support for court programs, help the court establish new programs and evaluate them, and manage purchasing and accounts payable, among other responsibilities.

Court Security

The marshal or bailiff for the court is responsible for courthouse security. In some states, such as California, court security is provided by sheriffs' deputies who screen people entering the building, provide security during trials, and transport suspects to court from jail. Depending on the

(continued)

EXHIBIT 9.1 Court Staff *(continued)*

jurisdiction, court security personnel may take on additional responsibilities, including some investigation, bond supervising, community service monitoring, and making arrests as needed.

Legal Staff

The larger and more powerful the court, the more likely it will have a variety of legal staff. These personnel can include legal counsel (prosecutors and defense attorneys), staff attorneys, research attorneys, and law clerks. Law clerks are not to be confused with court clerks. Unlike court clerks, law clerks are often recent law school graduates who assist judges with researching issues before the courts and writing opinions. U.S. Supreme Court law clerks are the cream of the crop, having graduated from many of the nation's top law schools.

Judicial Support Staff

A judge's support staff may include executive assistants, administrative assistants, secretaries, or a mix of all three. Support staff edit and type judicial opinions, create and arrange files, coordinate meetings, coordinate travel arrangements, answer telephone and e-mail inquiries, mail correspondence, and serve as an intermediary between the judge and other outside parties.

Court Reporter

The court reporter records judicial proceedings word for word. Court reporters create the official transcripts of legal proceedings such as trials and depositions. These transcripts include all the dialogue as well as other important details such as emotional reactions. The court reporter records these events as they occur in real time. Although the court reporter's primary purpose is to record courtroom legal proceedings and depositions, at times a court reporter may do more than just transcription. For example, when a request is made to review the transcript, the court reporter will provide the information from the official record. Court reporters may also advise lawyers on legal procedure when necessary.

Jury Staff

Many courts have dedicated jury personnel who maintain and review lists of prospective jurors. They may also determine who is eligible to serve, determine the number of jurors needed, issue summonses for jury service, and handle requests by jurors for dismissal, exemption, or disqualification. These individuals may also meet with prospective jurors to explain the process, tell them where to go, and dismiss them from service at the end of the day.

Other Officers

Many courts have representatives on site from other criminal justice agencies. There may be juvenile officers who are vested with the authority to take charge of children who come under the jurisdiction of the juvenile or family court. Representatives from probation may assist judges by performing presentence investigations that can be used during sentencing. In some states, the probation department is part of the judiciary and is thus more closely connected with the court than probation departments in other states.

Police and prosecutors are also directly influenced by the judge, whose sentencing discretion affects the arrest and charging processes. For example, if a judge usually chooses minimal sentences—such as a fine for a particular offense—the police may be reluctant to arrest offenders for that crime, knowing that doing so will basically be a waste of time. Similarly, if a judge is known to have an open attitude toward police discretion, the local department may be more inclined to engage in practices that border on entrapment or to pursue cases through easily obtained wiretaps. However, a magistrate oriented toward strict use of due process guarantees would stifle such activities by dismissing all cases involving apparent police abuses of personal freedoms. The district attorney's office may also be sensitive to judicial attitudes. The district attorney might forgo indictments in cases that the presiding magistrate expressly considers trivial or quasi-criminal and in which the judge has been known to take only token action, such as the prosecution of pornographers.

Finally, the judge considers requests by police and prosecutors for leniency (or severity) in sentencing. The judge's reaction to these requests is important

LO4 Discuss the duties, qualifications, and selection of judges.

if the police and the district attorney are to honor the bargains they may have made with defendants to secure information, cooperation, or guilty pleas. For example, when police tell informers that they will try to convince the judge to go easy on them to secure required information, they will often discuss the terms of the promised leniency with representatives of the court. If a judge ignores police demands, the department's bargaining power is severely diminished, and communication within the criminal justice system is impaired.

There is always concern that judges will discriminate against defendants on the basis of their gender, race, or class. Although this issue is of great social concern, most research efforts have failed to find consistent bias in judicial decision making. Judges tend to dismiss cases that they consider weak and less serious.[19]

Judicial Qualifications

The qualifications for appointment to one of the existing 30,000 judgeships vary from state to state and court to court. Typically, the potential judge must be a resident of the state, licensed to practice law, a member of the state bar association, and at least 25 and less than 70 years of age. However, a significant degree of diversity exists in the basic qualifications, depending on the level of court jurisdiction. Although almost every state requires judges to have a law degree if they are to serve on appellate courts or courts of general jurisdiction, it is not uncommon for municipal or town court judges to lack a legal background, even though they have the power to incarcerate criminal defendants.

Judges are held in high esteem, but they must sacrifice many financial benefits if they shift careers from lucrative private practices to low-paid government positions. Table 9.1 shows the average and median salaries of different kinds of judges (and court administrators) in state courts. Although an average of $160,435 for the chief of the highest court seems substantial, it is relatively modest when compared to corporate salaries and to what partners in top law firms earn. The *starting pay* in some high-powered New York City law firms (e.g., Goodwin Proctor) is now more than what the chief justice of the state's highest court makes!

A great deal of concern has been raised about the qualifications of judges. In most states, people appointed to the bench have had little or no training in how to be a judge. Others may have held administrative posts and may not have appeared before a court in years. The relatively low level of judicial salaries may make it difficult to attract the most competent attorneys to the bench.

A number of agencies have been created to improve the quality of the judiciary. For example, the National Conference of State Court Judges, part of the Judicial Division of the American Bar Association,[20] operates judicial training seminars and publishes manuals and guides on state-of-the-art judicial technologies. Its efforts are designed to improve the quality of the nation's judges.

TABLE 9.1 Judicial Salaries at a Glance

	Mean	Median	Range
Chief, highest court	$160,435	$156,727	$122,686 to 228,856
Associate justice, court of last resort	155,143	150,000	119,476 to 218,237
Judge, intermediate appellate courts	148,834	140,732	114,994 to 204,599
Judge, general jurisdiction trial courts	139,166	134,943	111,631 to 182,429
State court administrators	138,500	133,450	89,960 to 211,272

Source: National Center for State Courts, *Survey of Judicial Salaries*, Vol. 38, No. 1, January 1, 2013, http://www.ncsc.org/~/media/Microsites/Files/Judicial%20 Salaries/jud_2012.ashx (accessed July 2014).

Selecting Judges

Many methods are used to select judges.[21] In some jurisdictions, the governor appoints judges. It is common for the governor's recommendations to be confirmed by the state senate, the governor's council, a special confirmation committee, an executive council elected by the state assembly, or an elected review board. Some states employ a judicial nominating commission that submits names to the governor for approval.

Another form of judicial selection is popular election. In some jurisdictions, judges run as members of the Republican, Democratic, or other parties; in others, they run without party affiliation. In some states, partisan elections are used for selecting all general jurisdiction court judges. In other states, nonpartisan elections are used. A number of other states hold retention elections for judges who are appointed, usually a year or two after appointment. In some of these elections, judges run uncontested.[22] Altogether, about 90 percent of state trial judges face elections of some type and at some time during their tenure on the bench. Elections are less common in the higher-level state courts. Only a handful of states have partisan elections for intermediate appellate court judges and supreme court justices.

Judicial elections are troubling to some because they involve partisan politics in a process to select people who must be nonpolitical and objective. The process itself has been tainted by charges of scandal—for example, when political parties insist that judicial candidates hire favored people or firms to run their campaigns or have them make contributions to the party to obtain an endorsement.[23]

To avoid this problem, a number of states have adopted some form of what is known as the **Missouri Plan** (a form of what has been called "merit selection") to select appellate court judges. This plan consists of three parts: (1) a judicial nominating commission to nominate candidates for the bench, (2) an elected official (usually from the executive branch) to make appointments from the list submitted by the commission, and (3) subsequent nonpartisan and noncompetitive elections in which incumbent judges run on their records and voters can choose either to retain or to dismiss them.[24]

The quality of the judiciary is a concern. Although merit plans, screening committees, and popular elections are designed to ensure a competent judiciary, it has often been charged that many judicial appointments are made to pay off political debts or to reward cronies and loyal friends. Also not uncommon are charges that those desiring to be nominated for judgeships are required to make significant political contributions. For a review of judicial selection, see Concept Summary 9.1.

Judicial Alternatives

Increased judicial caseloads have prompted the use of alternatives to the traditional judge. For example, to expedite matters in civil cases, it has become common for both parties to agree to hire a retired judge or other neutral party and abide by his or her decision.

Other jurisdictions have created new quasi-judicial officers, such as referees or magistrates, to relieve the traditional judge of time-consuming responsibilities. The

Web App 9.5

For more information about judicial selection, visit http://www.judicialselection.com/.

Missouri Plan

A method of judicial selection that combines a judicial nominating commission, executive appointment, and nonpartisan confirmation elections.

CONCEPT SUMMARY 9.1

Judicial Selection

Type	Process
Appointment	Governor selects a candidate, who is confirmed by state senate or other official body.
Election	Potential judge runs as partisan or nonpartisan politician during regular election.
Missouri Plan	Bar committee searches for qualified candidates, governor chooses among them, and the judge runs for reappointment in a nonpartisan election.

Magistrate Act of 1968 created a new type of judicial officer in the federal district court system to handle pretrial duties.[25] Federal magistrates also handle civil trials if both parties agree to the arrangement.[26]

Some jurisdictions use part-time judges. Many of these are attorneys who carry out their duties *pro bono*—for no or limited compensation. These judicial adjuncts assist the courts on a temporary basis while maintaining an active law practice.[27] Federal judges who are close to retirement age enjoy "senior status" and also work part-time, thus easing the caseload burden on full-time judges.[28]

ALTERNATIVE DISPUTE RESOLUTION

Every state now has a means of settling disputes with alternatives to litigation. This court-connected **alternative dispute resolution** (ADR) has spread rapidly as court delays remain and legal expenses have increased. There is no single definition of ADR, but it typically refers to any means of settling disputes outside the courtroom.[29]

There are two common forms of ADR: arbitration and mediation.[30] **Arbitration** is a simplified version of a trial. There is no discovery and the rules of evidence are simplified. Either both sides select an arbitrator (other than a judge) or each selects one arbitrator and the two select a third to make up a panel of arbitrators. Arbitration hearings are relatively short, unlike trials, and the opinions are not made available to the public. Arbitration is often binding, which means that each side must abide by the arbitrator's decision.

Arbitration is governed by law at both the federal and state levels. Title 9 of the U.S. Code contains federal arbitration law. Nearly every state has adopted its own version of the 1956 Uniform Arbitration Act. The Act was revised in 2000 and adopted by 12 states. These laws generally make arbitration agreements and arbitrators' decisions enforceable by law. In 1970, the United States joined the United Nations Convention on the Recognition and Enforcement of Foreign Arbitral Awards, affirming this country's commitment to the process.

Arbitration can essentially amount to a mini-trial. Such mini-trials have been described as follows:

1. The parties negotiate a set of procedural ground rules (a protocol) that will govern the nonbinding mini-trial.
2. The time for preparation is relatively short—between six weeks and three months—and the amount of discovery is relatively limited.
3. The hearing itself is sharply abbreviated—usually no more than two days.
4. The hearing is often conducted by a third-party neutral, typically called the "neutral adviser."
5. The case is presented to representatives of the parties with authority to settle; there is no judge or jury.
6. The lawyers present their "best" case; they do not have time to delve into side issues.
7. Immediately after the hearing, the party representatives meet privately to negotiate a settlement.
8. If they cannot reach a settlement, the neutral adviser may render an advisory opinion on how he thinks a judge would rule if the case were to go to court.
9. The proceedings are confidential: the parties generally commit themselves to refrain from disclosing details of the proceedings to any outsider.[31]

Roy Moore, Chief Justice of the Alabama Supreme Court, speaks to guests at his election victory party in Montgomery. Known for fighting to display the Ten Commandments in a judicial building, Moore had also written to all 50 governors urging them to support a federal constitutional amendment defining marriage as between only a man and a woman. Should elected candidates for judicial office be permitted to run on partisan platforms?

AP Images/David Bundy

 L05 Explain the different types of judicial alternatives.

alternative dispute resolution
A means of settling disputes outside the courtroom.

arbitration
A process of dispute resolution in which a neutral third party (arbitrator) renders a decision after a hearing at which both parties agree to be heard.

mediation
An informal dispute resolution process in which a neutral third party (mediator) helps disputing parties reach an agreement.

Mediation is an even less formal process than arbitration. Mediators are trained to help disputing parties come together to reach an agreement that is satisfactory to both. Unlike an arbitrator, the mediator has no power to impose a decision on the parties. For this reason, mediation is often used before arbitration. If an agreement cannot be reached, the parties may elect to pursue arbitration.

Still other forms of alternative dispute resolution have emerged. One, advocated by a U.S. district court judge, is a summary jury trial. In this type of trial, people from a real jury pool are selected and asked to decide a matter following a one-day trial. The jurors do not know until after their verdicts are rendered that they are not binding. The verdict gives the parties an impression of what would happen at a real trial, thus giving them an incentive to settle their differences with something less than a full trial. This technique has been used with some regularity at the federal level.

These approaches are more common in the civil context than in the criminal context. For example, many real estate purchase contracts require mediation before the parties can go forward with litigation. In contrast, the preferred (or at least the most common) method of resolving criminal matters is via the formal criminal process. Arbitration and mediation can be—and are—used to settle some criminal disputes, as an alternative to the criminal process.

Judicial Decision Making

In an ideal world, judges would base their decisions only on the law and not let personal biases and preferences creep in. Unfortunately, the law is but one factor that appears to influence judges' decisions. Researchers have long found that judges' decisions are influenced by factors such as their ideology, their attitudes toward certain individuals, whether they face reelection, public opinion, and basic demographic characteristics, such as the judge's race or sex.[32] Much of the research has been focused on high-level judges, such as those in appellate and supreme courts.

ATTITUDES, IDEOLOGY, AND OPINIONS Judges' decisions are influenced by the attitudes and ideology they bring to the bench. This is especially true of U.S. Supreme Court justices. The authors of one important study found that Supreme Court justices' ideology and beliefs were almost perfectly correlated with their decisions.[33] Judges' attitudes and ideology also appear to be shaped by public opinion. One study revealed that Supreme Court decisions aligned with public opinion polls about two-thirds of the time.[34] Other researchers have found strong correlations between people's attitudes on controversial subjects and related Supreme Court decisions.[35]

LO6 Identify factors associated with judicial decision making.

DEMOGRAPHIC CHARACTERISTICS Judges' sex and race may influence their decisions as well. For example, one study of state supreme court justices revealed that female justices voted in a more liberal direction.[36] Indeed, the very presence of a female on a state supreme court appears to influence the probability that male justices will decide liberally.[37] What about race? It is not clear that race is as influential as sex, but it matters to some extent.[38]

REELECTION If a judge is facing reelection, to what extent should this factor into his or her decision making? Research shows that election considerations do shape judicial decision making.[39] For example, judges hand down decisions that draw less attention to themselves during election time.[40] The author of another study found that during election time, "a justice will either vote with the majority or will mask his or her disagreement in a concurrence rather than a dissent."[41] Another team of researchers found that "all judges, even the most punitive, increase their sentences as reelection nears."[42] It appears, then, that judges' decisions are based on a multitude of factors. The law may be only one of them.[43]

The Prosecutor

The prosecutor is one of the two adversaries who face each other every day in the criminal trial process: the **prosecutor**, who represents the state's interest and serves as the "people's attorney," and the defense attorney, who represents the accused. Although the judge manages the trial process, ensuring that the rules of evidence are obeyed, the prosecution and defense attorneys control the substance of the criminal process. They share the goal and burden of protecting the civil rights of the criminal defendant while they conduct the trial process in a fair and even-handed manner, a difficult task in the current era of vast media coverage and national fascination with high-profile cases.

Depending on the level of government and the jurisdiction in which the prosecutor functions, he or she may be known as a district attorney, a county attorney, a state's attorney, or a U.S. attorney. Whatever the title, the prosecutor is ordinarily a member of the practicing bar who has been appointed or elected to be a public prosecutor responsible for bringing the state's case against the accused. He focuses the power of the state on those who disobey the law by charging them with a crime and eventually bringing them to trial or, conversely, releasing them after deciding that the evidence at hand does not constitute proof of a crime (see the Careers in Criminal Justice box for more details on a career as a prosecutor).

Although the prosecutor's primary duty is to enforce the criminal law, his fundamental obligation as an attorney is to seek justice as well as convict those who are guilty. If, for example, the prosecutor discovers facts suggesting that the accused is innocent, he must bring this information to the attention of the court.[44] The American Bar Association's Model Code of Professional Responsibility requires that prosecutors never bring false or unsupported charges and that they disclose all relevant evidence to the defense (a full list of prosecutorial duties appears in Exhibit 9.2).

The senior prosecutor must make policy decisions on the exercise of prosecutorial enforcement powers in a wide range of cases in criminal law, consumer protection, housing, and other areas. In so doing, the prosecutor determines and ultimately shapes the manner in which justice is exercised in society.[45] Although these decisions should be rendered in a fair and objective manner, the prosecutor remains a political figure who has a party affiliation, a constituency of voters and supporters, and a need to respond to community pressures and interest groups.

The political nature of the prosecutor's office can heavily influence decision making. When deciding whether, when, and how to handle a case, the prosecutor cannot forget that he may be up for election soon and may have to answer to an electorate that will scrutinize those decisions. In a murder trial involving a highly charged issue such as child killing, the prosecutor's decision to ask for the death penalty may hinge on his perception of the public's will. Individual prosecutors

prosecutor
An appointed or elected member of the practicing bar who is responsible for bringing the state's case against the accused.

 L07 Characterize the role of the prosecutor.

 **Web App 9.6**

For more information about the ABA's Model Code of Professional Responsibility, visit http://www.americanbar.org/content/dam/aba/migrated/cpr/mrpc/mcpr.authcheckdam.pdf.

EXHIBIT 9.2 Prosecutorial Duties

- Investigating possible violations of the law
- Cooperating with police in investigating a crime
- Determining what the charge will be
- Interviewing witnesses in criminal cases
- Reviewing applications for arrest warrants and search warrants
- Subpoenaing witnesses
- Representing the government in pretrial hearings and in motion procedures
- Entering into plea-bargaining negotiations
- Trying criminal cases
- Recommending sentences to courts upon conviction
- Representing the government in appeals

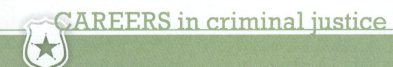

CAREERS in criminal justice

PROSECUTOR

DUTIES AND CHARACTERISTICS OF THE JOB

Prosecutors represent the public in criminal trials and are responsible for proving in court that the accused is guilty of the charges brought against him. Prosecutors work at municipal, state, and federal levels of government. During a trial, a prosecutor is opposed by a defense attorney, who is trying to maintain the innocence of the accused offender. In order to convince the judge or jury of the defendant's guilt, the prosecutor questions witnesses and gives statements using evidence collected during the investigative phase of the case. Prosecutors also decide which cases to bring to trial and have the authority to settle cases out of court. Even though they represent the people, prosecutors often meet with victims of crime and present the case from that point of view when in court.

This job comes with many responsibilities and pressures. Prosecutors must be mindful of their actions and words as representatives of the government body for which they work. Victims of crime and their families, community members, and law enforcement are depending on the prosecutor to prove the guilt of an alleged offender to a jury or judge and gain a conviction. Prosecutors may work long hours, especially during trials. In general, prosecutors may tend to be paid less than their counterparts in private practice; however, many report high personal satisfaction from seeing that justice is served.

JOB OUTLOOK

Crime rates and budgets will dictate the number of job openings. However, job opportunities open up on a regular basis because the position has a high turnover rate. Positions should be more readily available in smaller communities and at lower levels of government.

SALARY

Prosecutors working in federal and state offices tend to earn more than those working at the county and

---

are often caught between being compelled by their supervisors to do everything possible to obtain a guilty verdict and acting as a concerned public official to ensure that justice is done.

There are more than 2,300 state court prosecutors' offices employing more than 79,000 attorneys, investigators, and support staff.[46] This represents a 39 percent increase from 1992 and a 13 percent increase from 1996. Most of these offices are relatively small. Half employ nine or fewer people and have a budget of about $300,000 or less.

Types of Prosecutors

In the federal system, **United States attorneys** serve as the nation's principal litigators and are appointed by the president. Their subordinates, assistant United States attorneys, are tasked with, among other duties, prosecuting criminal defendants in federal district court. The appointed United States attorney is usually an administrator, whereas assistants normally handle the preparation and trial work. Federal prosecutors are professional civil service employees with reasonable salaries and job security.

At the state and county levels, the **attorney general** and the **district attorney**, respectively, are the chief prosecutorial officers. Again, the bulk of the criminal prosecution and staff work is performed by scores of full-time and part-time attorneys, police investigators, and clerical personnel. Most attorneys who work for prosecutors on the state and county levels are political appointees who earn low salaries, handle many cases, and in some jurisdictions maintain private law practices. Many young lawyers take these staff positions to gain the trial

United States attorneys
The nation's principal (federal) litigators, appointed by the president. Assistant United States attorneys are tasked with, among other duties, prosecuting criminal defendants in federal court.

attorney general
The chief legal officer and prosecutor of each state and of the United States.

district attorney
The county prosecutor who is charged with bringing offenders to justice and enforcing the criminal laws of the state.

municipal levels. Pay is also higher in larger cities. Entering prosecutors earn an average of approximately $50,000. Senior prosecutors often earn in excess of $100,000 per year.

OPPORTUNITIES

There are opportunities for advancement in larger offices, especially in urban areas. A state prosecutor may also wish to seek a position as a federal prosecutor. A position as a prosecutor is quite often used as a stepping-stone to other prestigious government and law careers. After leaving their position, former prosecutors might open up their own private practice, possibly with the intent of running a lucrative defense attorney business. Prosecutors can also seek appointments to prestigious and well-paying judge positions or choose to leave law practice for a political career.

QUALIFICATIONS

The basic qualifications for becoming a prosecutor are the same as those for any successful career as an attorney. This means that in addition to the demanding educational requirements of college and law school, a future lawyer will need to pass the bar exam of the state in which he or she wants to work.

Like other lawyers, prosecutors need to be comfortable and practiced at public speaking, and they need well-developed analytical skills. There is also a political aspect to being a prosecutor, because in some areas one must be elected or appointed to this position.

EDUCATION AND TRAINING

A bachelor's degree with an emphasis on building writing, analytical, and research skills is necessary. In addition to a four-year degree, taking the standardized Law School Admission Test (LSAT) is necessary in order to gain entry into a law school. Entry into law school is very competitive, and the educational requirements are challenging.

Sources: Bureau of Labor Statistics, "Lawyer," http://www.bls.gov/ooh/Legal/Lawyers.htm; PayScale, "District Attorney Salary," http://www.payscale.com/research/US/Job=District_Attorney/Salary; The Princeton Review, "Career: Attorney," http://www.princetonreview.com/careers.aspx?cid=16 (sites accessed July 2014).

experience that will qualify them for better opportunities. In most state, county, and municipal jurisdictions, however, the attorneys working within the office of the prosecutor can be described as having the proper standards of professional skill and personal integrity.

In urban jurisdictions, the structure of the district attorney's office is often specialized, with separate divisions for felonies, misdemeanors, and trial and appeal assignments. In rural offices, chief prosecutors handle many of the criminal cases themselves. When assistant prosecutors are employed in such areas, they often work part-time, have limited professional opportunities, and depend on the political patronage of chief prosecutors for their positions. See Figure 9.7 for an organizational chart of a county district attorney's office.

The Prosecutor Within Society

Prosecutors are routinely criticized for bargaining justice away, for using their positions as a stepping-stone to higher political office, and for failing to investigate (or simply dismissing) criminal cases. In response to these criticisms, during the past decade local, state, and federal prosecutors have become extremely aggressive in attacking particular crime problems. Federal prosecutors have made extraordinary progress in the war against insider trading and securities fraud on Wall Street, using information, wiretaps, and the federal racketeering laws. Some commentators now argue that the government may be going overboard in its efforts to punish white-collar criminals, especially for crimes that are the result of negligent business practices, not intentional criminal conspiracy.[47] Both fines and penalties have been increasing. And even such notorious white-collar

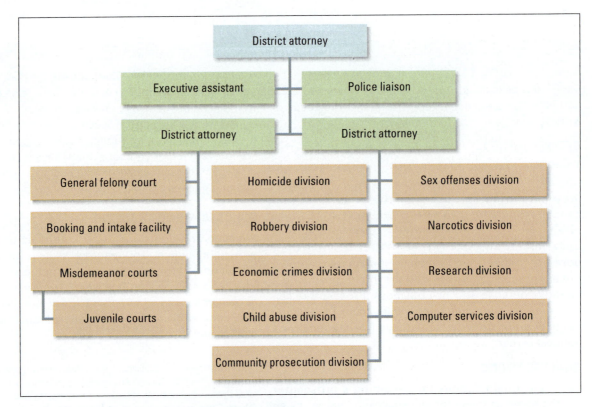

FIGURE 9.7   **County District Attorney's Office**

criminals as Tyco's Dennis Kozlowski (8 to 25 years in prison) and WorldCom's Bernie Ebbers (a 25-year sentence) have received sympathy because of the severity of their criminal sentences.[48]

In addition, prosecutors are now sharpening their working relationships with both the law enforcement community and the general public. These relationships are key to greater prosecutorial effectiveness.

PROSECUTORS AND LAW ENFORCEMENT
One of the most important of the prosecutor's many functions involves the relationship between the prosecutor and law enforcement agents. When it comes to processing everyday offenses and minor crimes, the prosecutor often relies on law enforcement officers to provide and initiate the formal complaint. With more serious offenses, such as some felonies, the prosecutor's office may become directly involved in the criminal investigation. Some district attorneys' offices carry out special investigations of organized crime, corruption of public officials, and corporate and white-collar crime, as well as vice and drug offenses. Much of the investigative work is handled by police personnel directly assigned to the prosecutor.

Police and prosecutorial relationships vary from one jurisdiction to another and often

Tony Rackauckas, Orange County California's elected district attorney, simulates in court what he believed were blows to Kelly Thomas's head with a taser by Fullerton police officer Jay Cicinelli. Thomas, a mentally ill homeless man, was beaten by Fullerton police and died from his injuries. Cicinelli and his partner, Manuel Ramos, were acquitted on all charges.

depend on whether the police agency is supplying the charge or the district attorney is investigating the matter. In either case, the prosecutor is required to maintain regular contact with the police department to develop the criminal prosecution properly. Some of the areas in which the police officer and the prosecutor work together include the following:

- *The police investigation report.* This report is one of the most important documents in the prosecutor's file. It is basically a statement by the police of the details of the crime, including all the evidence needed to support each element of the offense. It is a critical first step in developing the government's case against a suspect.

- *Providing legal advice.* Often the prosecutor advises the police officer about the legal issues in a given case. The prosecutor may also assist the officer by limiting unnecessary court appearances, informing the officer of the disposition of the case, and preparing the officer for pretrial appearances. As an officer of the court, the prosecutor enjoys civil immunity when assisting the police in criminal cases. This means that she is not liable to a criminal defendant in a civil suit.

- *Training police personnel.* In many jurisdictions, prosecutors help train police officers in securing warrants, making legal arrests, interrogating persons in custody, and conducting legal lineups. Some police departments have police legal advisers who work with the prosecutor in training new and experienced police personnel in legal matters.[49]

THE PROSECUTOR AND THE COMMUNITY Today, many prosecutors' offices are improving their working relationship with the community.[50] The concept of **community prosecution** recognizes that crime reduction is built on community partnerships.[51] It is not just a program, but also a new strategy for prosecutors to do their job. Just as police officers no longer simply make arrests, prosecutors need to do more than try cases. They become problem solvers looking to improve the overall safety and well-being of the communities over which they have jurisdiction.[52]

The traditional prosecutorial model is case-oriented and reactive to crime, not problem-oriented and proactive. Prosecutors are centrally located and assigned to teams focusing on specific types of crimes (homicide, narcotics, sex offenses, misdemeanors, and so on), with the most senior prosecutors handling the most serious felonies. Most prosecutions are arrest-generated. There is not much direct interaction among prosecutors, police, and members of the community outside of specific cases.

The lack of direct involvement by prosecutors in the community, when combined with an arrest-generated, case-oriented approach, often leads to an inefficient allocation of criminal justice resources. Frequently, no effort is made to allocate resources on a geographical basis or to assign prosecutors where they are needed. To align resources with community needs, some prosecutors must be in the community daily. In this way, the prosecutors can gauge the seriousness of the crime problem and play a positive role in its solution, along with other law enforcement and community groups. Community prosecution requires that field prosecutors work directly with the police to improve public safety in a particular district.

The main components of such a program include placing prosecutors in selected communities to work at police stations; increasing communication with police and with community groups, schools, and other organizations so prosecutors can be made aware of which cases and problems need the most attention; and using prosecutorial resources to solve community problems, not just to prosecute individual cases.

community prosecution
A prosecutorial philosophy that emphasizes community support and cooperation with other agencies in preventing crime, as well as a less centralized and more proactive role for local prosecutors.

Web App 9.7
For more information about community prosecution, visit http://www.courtinnovation.org/topic/community-prosecution.

What is the role of community prosecutors? They meet with the police daily to discuss law enforcement problems, strategize about the methods used to approach criminal behaviors, attend community meetings to learn about criminal incidents ranging from nuisances to felonies, and screen citizen complaints by diverting those cases that should not be in the criminal justice system. In short, field prosecutors build partnerships with the police, citizen groups, schools, and businesses to ensure public safety for the community.

Community prosecution programs have been started in many jurisdictions, with notable accomplishments. For example, prosecutors working with police and business leaders reduced the incidence of robberies near a local theater by implementing measures to make the area less attractive to criminals (better lighting, stricter enforcement of trespass laws, and increased police surveillance). In another example, community prosecutors, police, and housing inspectors closed and condemned a drug house where illegal drug activities were consistently taking place.[53]

Establishing partnerships with the community and law enforcement, as well as strong working relationships with other public and private agencies, is the key to a successful community prosecution approach. Community prosecution is not a new program, but rather an important new philosophy. It is the result of efforts, similar to those involved in community policing, to provide better criminal justice service to the community.

Finally, one of the greatest challenges facing community prosecution is the task of evaluating its effectiveness. What is the best measure of success for a prosecutor? Is it the number of prosecutions? What about the percentage of cases won in court? Is it how many offenders are given prison time? Or is it whether crime is reduced in the community? Each of these factors provides a useful measure for determining the success or failure of community prosecution efforts.

Prosecutorial Discretion

One might expect that after the police make an arrest and bring a suspect to court, the entire criminal court process would be mobilized. This is often not the case, however. For a variety of reasons, a substantial percentage of defendants are never brought to trial. The prosecutor decides whether to bring a case to trial or to dismiss it outright. This is known as **prosecutorial discretion**. Even if the prosecutor decides to pursue a case, the charges may later be dropped, in a process called *nolle prosequi*, if conditions are not favorable for a conviction.

Even in felony cases, the prosecutor ordinarily exercises considerable discretion in deciding whether to charge the accused with a crime.[54] After a police investigation, the prosecutor may be asked to review the sufficiency of the evidence to determine whether a criminal complaint should be filed. In some jurisdictions, this may involve presenting the evidence at a preliminary hearing. In other cases, the prosecutor may decide to seek a criminal complaint through a **grand jury** or other information procedure. These procedures, representing the formal methods of charging the accused with a felony offense, are discussed in Chapter 10.

Prosecutors exercise a great deal of discretion in even the most serious cases. In a classic study of prosecutorial discretion in three counties, Barbara Boland found that prosecutors used their discretion to dismiss a high percentage of the cases before trial.[55] However, when cases were forwarded for trial, few defendants were acquitted, indicating that prosecutorial discretion was exercised to screen out the weakest cases. The reasons why some cases are rejected or dismissed are summarized in Concept Summary 9.2. Evidence problems are the most common reason for rejecting cases; many other cases are dropped because defendants plead guilty to lesser crimes. And sometimes victims are noncooperative, which has forced prosecutors to abandon charges in domestic violence cases. But see the Evidence-Based Justice box for one approach to getting around this problem in domestic violence cases.

prosecutorial discretion
The prosecutor's authority to decide whether to bring a case to trial or to dismiss it outright.

nolle prosequi
The decision by a prosecutor to drop a case after a complaint has been made because of, for example, insufficient evidence, witness reluctance to testify, police error, or office policy.

grand jury
A group of citizens chosen to hear charges against persons accused of crime and to determine whether there is sufficient evidence to bring those persons to trial.

L08 Recognize the role of prosecutorial discretion in the criminal justice system.

CONCEPT SUMMARY 9.2

Common Reasons for Rejection or Dismissal of a Criminal Case

■ *Insufficient evidence.* A failure to find sufficient physical evidence linking the defendant to the offense.

■ *Witness problems.* For example, when a witness fails to appear, gives unclear or inconsistent statements, is reluctant to testify, or is unsure of the identity of the offender, or when a prior relationship exists between the victim or witness and the offender.

■ *The interests of justice.* Deciding not to prosecute certain types of offenses, particularly those that violate the letter but not the spirit of the law (for example, offenses involving insignificant amounts of property damage).

■ *Due process problems.* Violations of the constitutional requirements for seizing evidence and for questioning the accused.

■ *A plea on another case.* For example, when the accused is charged in several cases and the prosecutor agrees to drop one or more of the cases in exchange for a plea of guilty in another case.

■ *Pretrial diversion.* Agreeing to drop charges when the accused successfully meets the conditions for diversion, such as completion of a treatment program.

■ *Referral for other prosecution.* When there are other offenses, perhaps of a more serious nature, in a different jurisdiction, or deferring to a federal prosecution.

EVIDENCE-based justice

NO-DROP PROSECUTION

Throughout the 1980s and 1990s, prosecutors were faced with a high rate of dismissals in domestic violence cases. The key problem was that victims often refused to participate in the process and testify against their abusers. It sometimes proved difficult for prosecutors to secure convictions without the testimony from victims. In response to this problem, some jurisdictions enacted so-called "no-drop prosecution" policies, which are also referred to as "evidence-based" prosecution. These policies *require* prosecutors to bring charges against domestic abusers regardless of whether the victim participates. Calling them evidence-based means that if there is enough evidence (such as police reports and accounts of witnesses), then the prosecutor will bring charges even without the victim's testimony. No-drop prosecution policies have since caught on, but do they work? Unfortunately, the evidence is not encouraging.

In a recent evaluation, researchers compared the rearrest rates of abusers in two different jurisdictions in New York: the Bronx and Brooklyn. In the Bronx, domestic violence cases are usually not pursued if the victim does not wish to participate. In Brooklyn, the opposite is true; if there is an arrest, charges are filed, regardless of the victim's wishes. After following defendants for six months, the researchers found basically no difference in rearrest rates. They cautiously concluded that no-drop prosecution does not lead to dramatic reductions in arrest patterns among offenders, and it is important to note that there is not much research in this area because the strategy is relatively new. The researchers did find that victims offered some support for evidence-based prosecution because it put the onus for taking a case forward on the prosecutor, not the victim: "Many of those who preferred that their cases not be prosecuted would not have minded if the prosecution proceeded without them; they wanted to avoid confronting the abusers in court and were wary of assuming the responsibility for ensuring that the abusers experienced penalties for their crimes."

Sources: Robert C. Davis, Chris S. O'Sullivan, Donald J. Farole Jr., and Michael Rempel, "A Comparison of Two Prosecution Policies in Cases of Intimate Partner Violence: Mandatory Case Filing versus Following the Victim's Lead," *Criminology and Public Policy* 7 (2008): 633–662, quote from p. 658; see also John L. Worrall, *Crime Control in America: What Works?* 2nd ed. (Boston: Allyn & Bacon, 2008), pp. 110–111.

THE EXERCISE OF DISCRETION The power to institute or discontinue formal charges against the defendant is the key to the prosecutorial function, representing the control and power that the prosecutor has over an individual's liberty. The prosecutor has broad discretion in the exercise of his or her duties. This discretion is subject to few limitations and often puts the prosecutor in the position of making difficult decisions without appropriate policies and guidelines. Prosecutorial discretion is rarely reviewed by the courts, unless the prosecutor specifically violates a defendant's constitutional rights.[56] As the U.S. Supreme Court stated in *United States v. Armstrong*,

> The Attorney General and the United States Attorneys retain "broad discretion" to enforce the Nation's criminal laws. They have this latitude because they are designated by statute as the President's delegates to help him discharge his constitutional responsibility to "take Care that the Laws be faithfully executed."[57]

Deciding whether to charge a person with a crime is not easy—nor is determining the appropriate charge. Should a 16-year-old boy be charged with burglary or handled as a juvenile offender in the juvenile court? Would it be more appropriate to reduce a drug charge from the sale of marijuana to mere possession? Should an offense be considered mayhem, battery, or simply assault? A host of factors influence the prosecutor's charging decision. These are briefly summarized in Concept Summary 9.3.

In determining which cases should be eliminated from the criminal process and which should be brought to trial, the prosecutor has the opportunity to select alternative actions if they are more appropriate. Some offenders may be alcoholics or narcotic addicts, they may be mentally ill, or they may have been led into crime by their family situation or their inability to get a job. If they are not helped, they

CONCEPT SUMMARY 9.3
Factors Linked to Prosecutorial Decision Making

System factors	■ Cost of trial
	■ Court backlog
	■ Serious crime prioritized over less serious crime
Case factors	■ Strength of evidence
	■ Victim–offender relationship
	■ Victim and/or offender background
	■ Victim injury
	■ Victim attitude and/or cooperation
	■ Concern with possible harm to the suspect (perhaps resulting from a prison sentence)
	■ Availability of alternative procedures
	■ Suspect cooperation
	■ Presence and/or use of a weapon
Disposition factors	■ Preference for diversion
	■ Preference for treatment or rehabilitation program
Political factors	■ Elected prosecutor pressuring subordinates or being pressured himself or herself
	■ Public outrage
	■ Media scrutiny
	■ Lobbying efforts

may return to crime. In many cases, only minimal intrusions on defendants' liberty seem necessary. Often it will be enough simply to refer offenders to the appropriate agency in the community and hope that they will take advantage of the help offered. The prosecutor might, for example, be willing to drop charges if a man goes to an employment agency and makes a bona fide effort to get a job, seeks help from a social service agency, or resumes his education. The prosecutor retains legal power to file a charge until the period of limitations has expired, but as a practical matter, unless the offense is repeated, reviewing the initial charge would be unusual.

Dealing with the accused in such a way has come to be known as pretrial **diversion**. In this process, the prosecutor postpones or eliminates criminal prosecution in exchange for the alleged offender's participation in a rehabilitation program.[58] In recent years, the reduced cost and general utility of such programs have made them an important factor in prosecutorial discretion and a major part of the criminal justice system. A more detailed discussion of pretrial diversion is found in Chapter 10.

> **diversion**
> The use of an alternative to trial, such as referral to treatment or employment programs.

The proper exercise of prosecutorial discretion can improve the criminal justice process, preventing unnecessarily rigid implementation of the criminal law. Discretion enables the prosecutor to consider alternative decisions and humanize the operation of the criminal justice system. If prosecutors had little or no discretion, they would be forced to prosecute all cases brought to their attention. According to Judge Charles Breitel, "If every policeman, every prosecutor, every court, and every postsentence agency performed his or its responsibility in strict accordance with the rules of law, precisely and narrowly laid down, the criminal law would be ordered but intolerable."[59]

On the other hand, too much discretion can lead to abuses that result in the abandonment of law. Prosecutors are political creatures. They are charged with serving the people, but they must also be mindful of their reputations. Losing too many high-profile cases might jeopardize their chances of reelection. Therefore, they may be unwilling to prosecute cases in which the odds of conviction are low. They are worried about convictability.[60]

Overzealous Prosecution

Unfortunately, prosecutors sometimes go "too far" in their efforts to secure convictions against criminals. For example, a prosecutor may engage in selective or unfair prosecution, such as by targeting one person for personal reasons rather than making a decision based on the evidence. In *Yick Wo v. Hopkins* (1886), the Supreme Court highlighted this problem:

> Though the law itself be fair on its face and impartial in appearance, yet, if it is applied and administered by public authority with an evil eye and an unequal hand, so as practically to make unjust and illegal discriminations between persons in similar circumstances, material to their rights, the denial of equal justice is still within the prohibition of the Constitution.[61]

Prosecutors have also been known to engage in what is known as pretextual prosecution. This occurs when a prosecutor who lacks evidence to charge a particular person with one crime instead charges the individual with a lesser, unrelated offense. The key here is "unrelated." If, for example, a prosecutor lacks evidence to charge someone with first-degree murder and instead pursues second-degree murder charges, such a decision is perfectly acceptable. In contrast, if a prosecutor lacks evidence to charge a person with racketeering and instead charges the individual with a violation of the Federal Meat Inspection Act, this is a pretextual prosecution.[62]

PUNISHING OVERZEALOUS PROSECUTORS In extreme cases, prosecutors have been known to fabricate evidence, use false statements at trial, withhold potentially favorable evidence from the defense (a violation of due process), influence witnesses, renege on plea agreements, and so on. What can be done? On the one hand, prosecutors cannot be sued for their decisions on whether to press charges or for how they act. Even in the most egregious of cases of flagrant misconduct, a prosecutor cannot be held liable for his or her actions during the judicial stage of a case.[63] This is known as absolute immunity. On the other hand, although prosecutors cannot be sued for misconduct, they can be punished by their superiors and state bar association disciplinary boards. Punishments vary depending on the misconduct in question, but they can include:

- Private admonition or reprimand
- Public reprimand
- Suspension from law practice for a designated time period
- Permanent disbarment (that is, losing the authority to practice law)

How often are punishments such as these imposed? The Center for Public Integrity investigated more than 11,000 cases of alleged prosecutorial misconduct that took place over more than three decades.[64] In more than 2,000 of the cases, appellate judges reduced sentences, reversed convictions, or dismissed charges, which suggests there were many cases of serious misconduct. Of 44 cases the Center identified where prosecutors were disciplined, only two were disbarred. The most common sanctions were reprimand and censure. Appellate courts generally uphold convictions when misconduct is not considered serious, so wayward prosecutors are rarely penalized for their behavior.

The Defense Attorney

The **defense attorney** is the counterpart of the prosecuting attorney in the criminal process. The accused has a constitutional right to counsel. If the defendant cannot afford an attorney, the state must provide one.

defense attorney
Legal counsel for the defendant in a criminal case, representing the accused person from arrest to final appeal.

For many years, much of the legal community looked down on the criminal defense attorney and the practice of criminal law. This attitude stemmed from the kinds of legal work a defense attorney was forced to do—working with shady characters, negotiating for the release of known thugs and hoodlums, and often overzealously defending alleged criminals in criminal trials. Lawyers were reluctant to specialize in criminal law because they received comparatively low pay and often provided services without compensation. In addition, law schools in the past seldom offered more than one or two courses in criminal law and trial practice.

In recent years, however, with the implementation of constitutional requirements regarding the right to counsel, interest in criminal law has grown. Almost all law schools today have clinical programs that employ students as voluntary defense attorneys. They also offer courses in trial tactics, brief writing, and appellate procedures. In addition, legal organizations such as the American Bar Association, the National Legal Aid and Defenders Association, and the National Association of Criminal Defense Lawyers have assisted in recruiting able lawyers to do criminal defense work. As the American Bar Association has noted, "An almost indispensable condition to

Pool/Reuters/Landov

Former U.S. Marine Itzcoatl Ocampo, 23, an Iraq war veteran, speaks with his defense attorney Randall Longwith during his arraignment on charges of four counts of first-degree murder in Santa Ana, California, February 6, 2012. Ocampo, who pleaded not guilty, was accused of several killings, including those of four homeless men.

fundamental improvement of American criminal justice is the active and knowledgeable support of the bar as a whole."[65]

The Role of the Criminal Defense Attorney

The defense attorney, like the prosecutor, is an officer of the court. As an attorney, the defense attorney is obligated to uphold the integrity of the legal profession and to observe the requirements of the Model Rules of Professional Conduct in the defense of a client. The defense attorney performs many functions while representing the accused in the criminal process. Exhibit 9.3 lists some of the major duties of a defense attorney, whether privately employed by the accused, appointed by the court, or serving as a public defender.

Because of the way the U.S. system of justice operates, criminal defense attorneys face many role conflicts. They are viewed as the prime movers in what is essentially an adversary process. The prosecution and the defense engage in conflict over the facts of the case, with the prosecutor arguing the case for the state and the defense attorney using all the means at her disposal to aid the client. This system can be compared to a sporting event, in which the government and the accused are the players, and the judge and the jury are the referees.

Ethical Issues

As an officer of the court, along with the judge, prosecutors, and other trial participants, the defense attorney seeks to uncover the basic facts and elements of the criminal act. In this dual capacity as both a defense advocate and an officer of the court, the attorney is often confronted with conflicting obligations to his or her client and profession. In a famous work, Monroe Freedman identified three of the most difficult problems involving the professional responsibility of the criminal defense lawyer:

- Is it proper to cross-examine for the purpose of discrediting the reliability or credibility of an adverse witness whom you know to be telling the truth?

- Is it proper to put a witness on the stand when you know he will commit perjury?

- Is it proper to give your client legal advice when you have reason to believe that the knowledge you give him will tempt him to commit perjury?[66]

Other equally important issues confound a lawyer's ethical responsibilities. Lawyers are required to keep their clients' statements confidential—that is, to honor the attorney–client privilege. Suppose a client confides that he is planning to commit a crime. What are the defense attorney's ethical responsibilities? The lawyer would have to counsel the client to obey the law. If the lawyer assisted the client in engaging in illegal behavior, the lawyer would be subject to charges of unprofessional conduct and criminal liability. If the lawyer believed that the

LO9 Identify the role of the defense attorney.

Web App 9.8

For information about the National Legal Aid and Defenders Association (NLADA), visit http://www.nlada100years.org/.

EXHIBIT 9.3 Functions of the Defense Attorney

- Investigating the incident
- Interviewing the client, police, and witnesses
- Discussing the matter with the prosecutor
- Representing the defendant at the various pretrial procedures, such as arrest, interrogation, lineup, and arraignment
- Entering into plea negotiations

- Preparing the case for trial, including developing tactics and strategy
- Filing and arguing legal motions with the court
- Representing the defendant at trial
- Providing assistance at sentencing
- Determining the appropriate basis for appeal

danger was imminent, he would have to alert the police. The criminal lawyer needs to be aware of these troublesome situations to properly balance the duties of being an attorney with those of being an officer of the court and a moral person. These decisions are often difficult to make.

What should an attorney do when her client reveals that he committed a murder and that an innocent person has been convicted of the crime and is going to be executed? Should the attorney do the moral thing and reveal the information before a terrible miscarriage of justice occurs? Or should the attorney do the professional thing and maintain her client's confidence? In general, there is no obligation on the defense attorney's part to disclose client confessions—or guilt in the absence of a confession.[67] However, defense attorneys are prohibited from knowingly allowing their clients to take the stand and offer perjured (false) testimony. For example, if a defense attorney knows her client committed the crime, she cannot have the defendant take the witness stand and testify that he was not involved.

Because the defense attorney and the prosecutor have different roles, their ethical dilemmas may also differ. The defense attorney must maintain confidentiality and advise his or her client of the constitutional requirements of counsel, the privilege against self-incrimination, and the right to trial. The prosecutor represents the public and is not required to abide by such restrictions in the same way. In some cases, the defense attorney may be justified in withholding evidence by keeping the defendant from testifying at the trial. In addition, whereas prosecutors are prohibited from expressing a personal opinion on the defendant's guilt during summation of the case, defense attorneys are not barred from expressing their belief about a client's innocence.

As a practical matter, therefore, ethical rules may differ because the state is bringing the action against the defendant and must prove the case beyond a reasonable doubt. This is also why a defendant who is found guilty can appeal, whereas a prosecutor must live with an acquittal, and it is why defense lawyers generally have more latitude in performing their duties on behalf of their clients.

Neither side should encourage unethical practices.[68] For example, it would be considered unethical for a prosecutor to withhold exculpatory evidence from the defense or for a defense lawyer to condone perjury by his client during cross-examination.

Defending the Accused

The Sixth Amendment right to counsel and the Fifth and Fourteenth Amendments' guarantees of due process of law have been judicially interpreted together to require counsel in all types of criminal proceedings (see Chapter 10 for more on the right to counsel at trial). The right to counsel begins at the earliest stages of the justice system, usually when a criminal suspect is interrogated while in police custody. *Miranda v. Arizona* (1966), a case we looked at closely in Chapter 8, held that any statements made by the accused when in custody are inadmissible at trial unless the accused has been informed of the right to counsel and the right, if indigent, to have an attorney appointed by the state.[69]

The Supreme Court also has extended the right to counsel to postconviction and other collateral proceedings, such as probation and parole revocation and appeal. When, for example, the court intends to revoke a defendant's probation and impose a sentence, the probationer has a right to counsel at the deferred sentence hearing.[70] When the state provides for an appellate review of the criminal conviction, the defendant is entitled to the assistance of counsel for this initial appeal.[71] The Supreme Court has also required states to provide counsel in other proceedings that involve the loss of personal liberty, such as juvenile delinquency hearings and mental health commitments.[72]

Areas still remain in the criminal justice system where the courts have not required assistance of counsel for the accused. These include preindictment lineups; booking procedures, including the taking of fingerprints and other forms of identification; grand jury investigations; appeals beyond the first review; disciplinary proceedings in correctional institutions; and postrelease revocation hearings. Nevertheless, the general rule is that persons cannot be deprived of freedom without representation by counsel if there is a chance that they will lose their liberty and be incarcerated in a correctional institution.

LO10 Explain the right to counsel.

Legal Services for the Indigent

One of the most critical issues in the justice system has been whether an **indigent defendant** has the right to counsel. Can an accused person who is poor and cannot afford an attorney have a fair trial without the assistance of counsel? Is counsel required at preliminary hearings? Should the convicted indigent offender be given counsel at state expense in appeals of the case? Questions such as these have arisen constantly in recent years. And they are important questions, because as many as 90 percent of criminal defendants are considered indigent.[73]

As far back as 1942, Justice Hugo Black, one of the greatest Supreme Court justices of the twentieth century, acknowledged the need for public defenders when he wrote, "A fair trial is impossible if an indigent is not provided with a free attorney."[74] In 1963, the U.S. Supreme Court took the first major step on the issue of right to counsel by holding that state courts must provide counsel to indigent defendants in felony prosecutions.[75] Nine years later, it extended the obligation to provide counsel to all criminal cases in which the penalty includes imprisonment—regardless of whether the offense is a felony or a misdemeanor.[76]

To satisfy the constitutional requirement that indigent defendants be provided with the assistance of counsel at various stages of the criminal process, the federal government and the states have had to evaluate and expand criminal defense services. Prior to 1963, public defense services were provided mainly by local private attorneys appointed and paid for by the court and called **assigned counsel**, or by limited **public defender** programs. In 1961, for example, public defender services existed in only 3 percent of the counties in the United States, serving only about one-quarter of the country's population.[77]

Over time, the criminal justice system has been forced to increase public defender services. Today, about 3,000 state and local agencies are providing indigent legal services in the United States.

Providing legal services for indigent offenders is a huge undertaking. Millions of offenders are given free legal services annually. And although most states have a formal set of rules for determining who is indigent, and many require repayment to the state for at least part of their legal services (known as **recoupment**), indigent legal services still cost billions of dollars annually.

Programs providing assistance of counsel to indigent defendants can be divided into three major categories: public defender systems, assigned counsel systems, and contract systems. Other approaches to the delivery of legal services include mixed systems, such as representation by both public defenders and the private bar; law school clinical programs; and prepaid legal services. Of the three major approaches, assigned counsel systems are the most common; a majority of U.S. courts use this method. However, public

indigent defendant
A defendant who lacks the funds to hire a private attorney and is therefore entitled to free counsel.

assigned counsel
A private attorney appointed by the court to represent a criminal defendant who cannot afford to pay for a lawyer.

public defender
An attorney employed by the government to represent criminal defendants who cannot afford to pay for a lawyer.

recoupment
Process by which the state later recovers some or all of the cost of providing free legal counsel to an indigent defendant.

Frazier Glenn Miller, 73, is taken into custody for allegedly killing three people outside of Jewish sites near Kansas City in 2014. A former white supremacist leader, Miller had a long criminal record, having previously served time in prison for weapons violations and violating a court order barring him from participation in paramilitary activities. As of this writing, prosecutors are deciding whether to pursue the death penalty.

AP Images

defender programs seem to be on the increase, and many jurisdictions use a combination of programs statewide.

PUBLIC DEFENDERS The first public defender program in the United States opened in 1913 in Los Angeles. Over the years, primarily as a result of efforts by judicial leaders and bar groups, the public defender program became the model for the delivery of legal services to indigent defendants in criminal cases throughout the country.

Most public defender offices can be thought of as law firms whose only clients are criminal offenders. However, they are generally administered at one of two government levels: state or county. About one-third of the states have a statewide public defender's office, headed by a chief public defender who administers the system. In some of these states, the chief defender establishes offices in all counties around the state; in others, the chief defender relies on part-time private attorneys to provide indigent legal services in rural counties. Statewide public defenders may be organized as part of the judicial branch, as part of the executive branch, as an independent state agency, or as a private nonprofit organization.

ASSIGNED COUNSEL SYSTEM In contrast to the public defender system, the assigned counsel system involves the use of private attorneys appointed by the court to represent indigent defendants. The private attorney is selected from a list of attorneys maintained by the court and is reimbursed by the state for any legal services rendered to the client. Assigned counsels are generally used in rural areas, which do not have sufficient caseloads to justify a full-time public defender staff.

There are two main types of assigned counsel systems. In an *ad hoc* assigned counsel system, the presiding judge appoints attorneys on a case-by-case basis. In a *coordinated* assigned counsel system, an administrator oversees the appointment of counsel and sets up guidelines for the administration of indigent legal services. The fees awarded to assigned counsels can vary widely and they tend to be much lower than what a lawyer would charge a non-indigent defendant for legal representation.

The assigned counsel system, unless organized properly, suffers from such problems as unequal assignments, inadequate legal fees, and the lack of supportive or supervisory services. Other disadvantages are the frequent use of inexperienced attorneys and the tendency to use the guilty plea too quickly. Some judicial experts believe that the assigned counsel system is still no more than an ad hoc approach that raises serious questions about the quality of representation. However, the assigned counsel system is simple to operate. It also offers the private bar an important role in providing indigent legal services, because most public defender systems cannot represent all needy criminal defendants. Thus, the appointed counsel system gives attorneys the opportunity to do criminal defense work.

CONTRACT SYSTEM The **contract system** is a relative newcomer in providing legal services to the indigent. It is being used in a small percentage of counties around the United States. In this system, a block grant is given to a lawyer or law firm to handle indigent defense cases. In some instances, the attorney is given a set amount of money and is required to handle all cases assigned. In other jurisdictions, contract lawyers agree to provide legal representation for a set number of cases at a fixed fee. A third system involves representation at an estimated cost per case until the dollar amount of the contract is reached. At that point, the contract may be renegotiated, but the lawyers are not obligated to take new cases.

The contract system is often used in counties that also have public defenders. Such counties may need independent counsel when a conflict of interest arises or

contract system
Provision of legal services to indigent defendants by private attorneys under contract to the state or county.

when there is a constant overflow of cases. It is also used in sparsely populated states that cannot justify the structure and costs of full-time public defender programs. Experts have found that contract attorneys are at least as effective as assigned counsel and are cost-effective.[78]

The per-case cost in any jurisdiction for indigent defense services is determined largely by the type of program offered. In most public defender programs, funds are obtained through annual appropriations. Assigned counsel costs relate to legal charges for the appointed counsel, and contract programs negotiate a fee for the entire service. No research currently available indicates which is the most effective way to represent the indigent on a cost-per-case basis. However, Lawrence Spears reports that some jurisdictions have adopted the contract model with much success. Advantages include the provision of comprehensive legal services, controlled costs, and improved coordination in counsel programs.[79]

MIXED SYSTEMS A mixed system uses both public defenders and private attorneys in an attempt to draw on the strengths of each. In this approach, the public defender system operates simultaneously with the assigned counsel system or contract system to offer total coverage to the indigent defendant. This need occurs when the caseload increases beyond the capacity of the public defender's office. In addition, many counties supply independent counsel to all codefendants in a single case to prevent a conflict of interest. In most others, separate counsel is provided if a codefendant requests it or if the judge or the public defender perceives a conflict of interest.

Other methods of providing counsel to the indigent include the use of law school students and prepaid legal service programs (similar to comprehensive medical insurance). Most jurisdictions have a student practice rule of procedure. Third-year law school students in clinical programs provide supervised counsel to defendants in nonserious offenses. In *Argersinger v. Hamlin*, Supreme Court Justice William Brennan suggested that law students are an important resource in fulfilling constitutional defense requirements.[80]

The Private Bar

The lawyer whose practice involves a substantial proportion of criminal cases is often considered a specialist in the field. And there is little question that having a preeminent private attorney can help clients prove their innocence. Private defense attorneys can give their full attention to the defendant, whereas public defenders often represent many different clients.

Although a lucky few defendants are able to afford the services of skilled and experienced private counsel, most criminal defendants are represented by lawyers who often accept many cases for minor fees. These lawyers may belong to small law firms or work alone, but a sizable portion of their practice involves representing those accused of crime. Other private practitioners occasionally take on criminal matters as part of their general practice. Criminal lawyers often work on the fringe of the legal business, and they may receive little respect from colleagues or the community as a whole.

All but the most eminent criminal lawyers are bound to spend much of their working lives in overcrowded, physically unpleasant courts, dealing with people who have committed questionable acts, and attempting to put the best possible construction on those acts. It is not the sort of working environment that most people choose. Sometimes a criminal lawyer is identified unjustifiably in the public eye with the client she represents. "How could someone represent a child killer and try to get him off?" is a question that many people may ask.

Another problem associated with the private practice of criminal law is that the fee system can create a conflict of interest. Private attorneys are usually paid in advance and do not expect additional funds whether their client is convicted or acquitted. Many are aware of the guilt of their client before the trial begins, and they earn the greatest profit if they get the case settled as quickly as possible. This usually means bargaining with the prosecutor instead of going to trial. Even if attorneys win the case at trial, they may lose personally because they have only the gratitude of their client to compensate them for the time they have spent. And many criminal defendants cannot afford even a modest legal fee and therefore cannot avail themselves of the services of a private attorney. For these reasons, an elaborate, publicly funded legal system has developed.

Public versus Private Attorneys

Do criminal defendants who hire their own private lawyers do better in court than those who depend on legal representatives provided by the state? Although having private counsel offers some advantages, national surveys indicate that state-appointed attorneys do well in court. According to data compiled by the federal government:

■ Conviction rates for indigent defendants and those with their own lawyers were about the same in federal and state courts. About 90 percent of the federal defendants and 75 percent of the defendants in the most populous counties were found guilty regardless of what type of attorney represented them.

■ Of defendants found guilty, however, those represented by publicly financed attorneys were incarcerated at a higher rate than those defendants who paid for their own legal representation: 88 percent compared with 77 percent in federal courts, and 71 percent compared with 54 percent in the most populous counties.

■ On average, sentence lengths for defendants sent to jail or prison were shorter for those with publicly financed attorneys than for those who hired counsel. In federal district court, those with publicly financed attorneys were given just under five years on average, and those with private attorneys were given just over five years. In large state courts, those with publicly financed attorneys were sentenced to an average of two and a half years and those with private attorneys to three years.[81]

The data indicate that private counsel may have a slightly better track record in some areas (such as death penalty cases) but that court-appointed lawyers do quite well. This finding was echoed in a study by Talia Roitberg Harmon and William Lofquist, who found that having a competent private attorney who puts on a rigorous defense is the single most important factor separating those who are exonerated in murder cases from those who are executed.[82] The authors of another study examined the outcomes of all felony cases filed in Denver, Colorado, in 2002 and

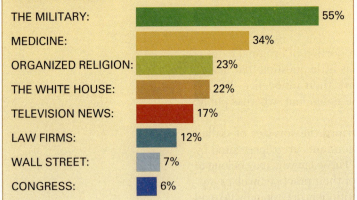

FACT CHECK ☑

YOUR OPINION: Consider this list of different institutions in American society: (1) the military, (2) medicine, (3) organized religion, (4) the White House, (5) television news, (6) law firms, (7) Wall Street, (8) Congress. Which do you have a great deal of confidence in?

PUBLIC OPINION:

THE MILITARY: 55%
MEDICINE: 34%
ORGANIZED RELIGION: 23%
THE WHITE HOUSE: 22%
TELEVISION NEWS: 17%
LAW FIRMS: 12%
WALL STREET: 7%
CONGRESS: 6%

REALITY: Americans are a skeptical lot! Only the military received a strong vote of confidence from respondents in the 2012 poll on which these findings are based. Law firms, which includes the private defense bar, scored somewhere between television news and Wall Street—not exactly a favorable ranking!

DISCUSSION: Why are Americans so distrustful of most major institutions? Why do law firms receive such low rankings relative to other institutions?

Source: Harris Interactive, *Confidence in Congress Stays at Lowest Point in Almost Fifty Years*, http://www.prnewswire.com/news-releases/confidence-in-congress-stays-at-lowest-point-in-almost-fifty-years-152253655.html (accessed July 2014).

found that, on average, public defenders achieved poorer sentencing outcomes for their clients relative to privately retained attorneys.[83]

Problems of the Criminal Bar

The problems of the criminal bar are numerous. Attorneys who specialize in criminal work base their reputation on their power and influence. A good reputation is based on the ability to get obviously guilty offenders acquitted on legal technicalities, to arrange the best deal for clients who cannot hope to evade punishment, and to protect criminals whose illegal activities are shocking to many citizens. Private attorneys are often accused of sacrificing their clients' interests for pursuit of profit. Many have a bad reputation in the legal community because of their unsavory clientele and their reputation as shysters who hang out in court hoping for referrals. Consequently, the private criminal attorney is not often held in high esteem by his or her colleagues.

Public defenders are often young attorneys who are seeking trial practice before going on to high-paying jobs in established law firms. They are in the unenviable position of being paid by the government yet acting in the role of the government's adversary. Generally, they find themselves at the bottom of the legal profession's hierarchy because, for limited wages, they represent clients without social prestige. Forced to work under bureaucratic conditions, public defenders can do only routine processing of their cases. Large caseloads prevent them from establishing more than a perfunctory relationship with their clients. To keep their caseload under control, they may push for the quickest and easiest solution to a case—a plea bargain.

Assigned counsel and contract attorneys may also be young lawyers just starting out and hoping to build their practice by taking on indigent cases. Because their livelihood depends on getting referrals from the court, public defender's office, or other government bodies, they risk the problem of conflict of interest. If they pursue too rigorous a defense or handle cases in a way not approved by the presiding judge or other authorities, they may be removed from the assigned counsel lists.

Very often, large firms contribute the services of their newest members for legal aid to indigents; these assignments are referred to as ***pro bono*** work. Although such efforts may be made in good spirit, they mean that inexperienced lawyers are handling legal cases in which a person's life may be at stake.

THE INFORMAL JUSTICE SYSTEM What has emerged is a system in which plea bargaining predominates because little time and insufficient resources are available to give criminal defendants a full-scale defense. Moreover, because prosecutors are under pressure to win their cases, they are often more willing to work out a deal than to pursue a case trial. After all, half a loaf is better than none. Defense attorneys also often find it easier to encourage their clients to plead guilty and secure a reduced sentence or probation instead of seeking an acquittal and risking a long prison term.

These conflicts have helped erode the formal justice process, which is based on the adversary system. Prosecutors and defense attorneys meet in the arena of the courtroom to do battle over the merits of the case. Through the give-and-take of the trial process, the truth of the matter becomes known. Guilty defendants are punished, and the innocent go free. Yet the U.S. legal system seldom works that way. Because of the pressures faced by defense attorneys and prosecutors, the defense and the prosecution more often work together in a spirit of cooperation to get the case over with rather than fighting it out, wasting each other's time, and risking an outright loss. In the process of this working relationship, the personnel in the courtroom—judge, prosecutor, defense attorney—form

pro bono
The practice by private attorneys of taking the cases of indigent offenders without fee as a service to the profession and the community.

Defense attorney Mark O'Mara, left, and prosecutor Bernie de la Rionda arrive in Seminole circuit court for the George Zimmerman trial in Sanford, Florida. Though they are adversaries in court, prosecutors and defense attorneys are not necessarily mortal enemies. They often work together behind the scenes, for example, to reach plea agreements.

subpoena
A court order requiring a witness to appear in court at a specified time and place.

working groups that leave the defendant on the outside. Criminal defendants may find that everyone they encounter in the courtroom seems to be saying "plead guilty," "take the deal," "let's get it over with."

The informal justice system revolves around the common interest of its members to move the case along and settle matters. In today's criminal justice system, defense attorneys share a common history, goals, values, and beliefs with their colleagues in prosecution. They are alienated by class and social background from the clients they defend. Considering the reality of who commits crime, who are its victims, and who defends, prosecutes, and tries the case, it should not be surprising that the adversary system has suffered.

RELATIONS BETWEEN PROSECUTOR AND DEFENSE ATTORNEY In the final analysis, the competence of the prosecutor and the defense attorney depends on their willingness to work together in the interest of the client, the criminal justice system, and the rest of society. However, serious adversarial conflicts have arisen between them in recent years.

The prosecutor, for instance, should exercise discretion in seeking to **subpoena** other lawyers to testify about any relationship with their clients. Although not all communication between a lawyer and his or her client is privileged, confidential information entrusted to a lawyer is ordinarily not available for prosecutorial investigation. Often, however, overzealous prosecutors try to use their subpoena power against lawyers whose clients are involved in drug cases or organized crime cases to obtain as much evidence as possible. Prosecutors interested in confidential information about defendants have subpoenaed lawyers to testify against them. Court approval should be needed before a lawyer is forced to give information about a client. Otherwise, the defendant is not receiving effective legal counsel under the Sixth Amendment. In addition, prosecutors should refrain from using their grand jury subpoena power to obtain information from private investigators employed by the defense attorney. Judicial remedies for violations of these rules often include suppression of subpoenaed evidence and dismissal of a criminal indictment.

By the same token, some criminal defense lawyers ignore situations in which a client informs them of his or her intention to commit perjury. The purpose of the defense attorney's investigation is to learn the truth from the client. The defense attorney also has a professional responsibility to persuade the defendant not to commit perjury, which is a crime.

It is the duty of the prosecutor to seek justice and not merely to obtain a conviction; this goal also applies to the criminal defense attorney. As legal scholar David G. Bress so aptly put it, "A defense attorney does not promote the attainment of justice when he secures his client's freedom through illegal and improper means."[84]

Often, the public image of prosecutors and defense attorneys is shaped by television programs, movies, and newspaper stories. You may hear of a prosecutor who takes a campaign donation and ignores a politician's crime. A defense attorney may use improper influence in representing a client. Unfortunately, corruption is still a fact of life in the justice system. Doing everything possible to deter such behavior is an important aspect of a fair justice system.

ETHICAL CHALLENGES in Criminal Justice

A WRITING ASSIGNMENT

Judge Eli Sampson, a Republican, has run unopposed—in a largely conservative county—during several past elections. Now he is facing stiff competition from a popular and vocal Democratic rival who seems to have come out of nowhere. In an effort to appeal to his conservative base, Sampson's new campaign slogan is "Tougher than Tough on Crime." His election signs and banners carry the phrase prominently. During debates with his opponent, he repeatedly announces his intentions to "get tough" with criminals.

Write an essay on the ethics of Sampson's approach. In doing so, answer these questions: Is it ethical for judicial candidates to run on partisan political platforms? It is most certainly legal in certain jurisdictions, but should it be allowed? What are the possible problems associated with allowing judicial candidates to align themselves with specific political parties? Could party affiliations influence the decision making of these who end up getting elected to the bench? See this chapter's "Selecting Judges" and "Judicial Decision Making" sections for guidance.

Summary

 Describe state court structure.

- Each state court system is different.

- Common state courts include limited jurisdiction courts, general jurisdiction courts, and appellate courts.

- Each state has at least one court of last resort, usually called a state supreme court.

- Many states have implemented specialized limited jurisdiction courts, including drug courts, domestic violence courts, mental health courts, and others.

- Limited jurisdiction courts have jurisdiction over minor or less serious civil and criminal cases.

- General jurisdiction courts handle the more serious felony cases (e.g., murder, rape, robbery) and civil cases where damages are over a specified amount, such as $10,000.

 Describe federal court structure.

- There are three levels of courts in the federal system: U.S. district courts, U.S. courts of appeals, and the U.S. Supreme Court.

- The U.S. district courts are the trial courts of the federal system.

- The 12 U.S. courts of appeals, sometimes referred to as U.S. circuit courts, are empowered to review federal and state appellate court cases on substantive and procedural issues involving rights guaranteed by the Constitution.

- The U.S. Supreme Court is the nation's highest appellate body and the court of last resort for all cases tried in the various federal and state courts.

- Most cases that come before the Supreme Court involve significant federal questions, usually of a constitutional nature.

- When the Supreme Court decides to hear a case, it grants a writ of certiorari, requesting a transcript of the proceedings of the case for review.

- For a writ to be granted, ordinarily four justices must agree to hear the case. This is known as the rule of four.

LO3 Identify the problems associated with court congestion.

- State court systems now handle about 100 million new cases annually. This has led to significant delay and congestion in the courts.

- Congestion is time-consuming and costly, and delay can threaten the Sixth Amendment right to a speedy trial.

Discuss the duties, qualifications, and selection of judges.

- During trials, the judge rules on the appropriateness of conduct, settles questions of evidence and procedure, and guides the questioning of witnesses.
- In a jury trial, the judge must instruct jurors on which evidence is proper to examine and which should be ignored.
- If a defendant is found guilty, the judge must decide on the sentence.
- Typically, a judge must be a resident of the state, licensed to practice law, a member of the state bar association, and at least 25 and less than 70 years of age at the time of appointment.
- Almost every state requires judges to have a law degree if they are to serve on appellate courts or courts of general jurisdiction.
- Some municipal or town court judges do not need law degrees.
- In some jurisdictions, the governor appoints judges.
- Another form of judicial selection is popular election.
- The Missouri Plan, another means of selecting judges, consists of three parts: (1) a judicial nominating commission nominates candidates for the bench, (2) an elected official makes the appointment, and (3) retention elections are held.

 Explain the different types of judicial alternatives.

- Alternative dispute resolution (ADR) is a judicial alternative.
- Arbitration, a type of ADR, is a process of dispute resolution in which a neutral third party (arbitrator) renders a decision following a hearing at which both parties agree to be heard.
- Mediation, another type of ADR, is an informal dispute resolution process in which a neutral third party (mediator) helps disputing parties reach an agreement.
- Mediation usually comes before arbitration.
- Arbitration is usually binding; mediation is not.

 Identify factors associated with judicial decision making.

- Researchers have found that in addition to legal considerations, judges base their decisions on ideology, their attitudes toward certain individuals, whether they face reelection, public attitudes, and basic demographic characteristics, such as the judge's race or sex.

Characterize the role of the prosecutor.

- The prosecutor is an appointed or elected member of the practicing bar who is responsible for bringing the state's case against the accused.
- The prosecutor is the chief law enforcement officer of a particular jurisdiction.
- Although the prosecutor's primary duty is to enforce the criminal law, his or her fundamental obligations are to seek justice and convict those who are guilty.
- In the federal system, prosecutors are known as U.S. attorneys and are appointed by the president.
- At the state and county levels, the attorney general and the district attorney, respectively, are the chief prosecutorial officers.
- Most prosecutions take place at the local level.

 Recognize the role of prosecutorial discretion in the criminal justice system.

- The prosecutor, who is the people's attorney, has discretion to decide the criminal charge and disposition.
- The prosecutor retains a great deal of discretion in processing cases.
- System, case, disposition, and political factors all shape a prosecutor's charging decisions.

Identify the role of the defense attorney.

- The defense attorney is the counterpart of the prosecuting attorney in the criminal process.
- Defense attorneys perform several functions while representing the accused. These tasks include investigating the incident; interviewing the client, police, and witnesses; discussing the matter with the prosecutor; representing the defendant at the various pretrial procedures, such as arrest, interrogation, lineup, and arraignment; entering into plea negotiations; preparing

the case for trial, including developing tactics and strategy; filing and arguing legal motions with the court; representing the defendant at trial; providing assistance at sentencing; and determining the appropriate basis for appeal.

- Defense attorneys face many ethical issues, such as whether they should keep their clients' statements confidential even though they know the clients are lying and whether they should defend criminals whom they know are guilty.

LO10 **Explain the right to counsel.**

- Under landmark decisions of the U.S. Supreme Court, particularly *Gideon v. Wainwright* and *Argersinger v. Hamlin*, all defendants who can face imprisonment for any offense must be afforded counsel at trial.

- Methods of providing counsel include assigned counsel systems, in which an attorney is selected by the court to represent the accused; public defender programs, in which public employees provide legal services; contract systems, in which legal services to indigent defendants are provided by private attorneys under contract with the state or county; and mixed systems, in which both public defendants and private attorneys are used.

- Plea bargaining is commonplace because little time and insufficient resources are available to give criminal defendants a full-scale defense.

- The prosecutor and the defense attorney have to work together, despite the presence of adversarial conflicts between the two.

Key Terms

plea negotiations/plea bargaining, 330
court of limited jurisdiction, 330
specialized court, 331
court of general jurisdiction, 331
appellate court, 331
U.S. district court, 338
U.S. courts of appeals, 339
U.S. Supreme Court, 339
court of last resort, 339
writ of certiorari, 341
rule of four, 341

judge, 344
Missouri Plan, 348
alternative dispute resolution, 349
arbitration, 349
mediation, 350
prosecutor, 351
United States attorneys, 352
attorney general, 352
district attorney, 352
community prosecution, 355
prosecutorial discretion, 356

nolle prosequi, 356
grand jury, 356
diversion, 359
defense attorney, 360
indigent defendant, 363
assigned counsel, 363
public defender, 363
recoupment, 363
contract system, 364
pro bono, 367
subpoena, 368

Critical Thinking Questions

1. What are the benefits and drawbacks of selecting judges through popular elections? Can a judge who considers herself or himself a Republican or a Democrat render fair and impartial justice?
2. Should more specialized courts be created and, if so, for what?
3. Should all judges be trained as attorneys? If not, what other professions are suitable for consideration?
4. What is the Missouri Plan? Do you consider it an ideal way to select judges?
5. Should attorneys disclose information given them by their clients concerning participation in earlier unsolved crimes?
6. Should defense attorneys cooperate with prosecutors if it means that their clients will go to jail?
7. Should prosecutors have absolute discretion over which cases to proceed on and which to drop? Do you believe prosecutors should have a great deal of discretion? Why?
8. Should potential clients have access to their attorney's track record in court?
9. Does the assigned counsel system present an inherent conflict of interest because attorneys are hired and paid by the institution they are to oppose?
10. Which kinds of cases do you think are most likely to be handled informally?
11. Explain the following: "It is the duty of the prosecutor to seek justice, not merely a conviction."

Notes

1. ABC News, "Florida Lawyer Fired for Posting Client's Leopard-Print Underwear," http://abcnews.go.com/blogs/headlines/2012/09/florida-lawyer-fired-for-posting-clients-leopard-print-underwear/ (accessed July 2014).
2. Ibid.
3. Thomas Henderson, *The Significance of Judicial Structure: The Effect of Unification on Trial Court Operations* (Washington, DC: National Institute of Justice, 1984).
4. Michael J. Friedman, *Outline of the U.S. Legal System* (Washington, DC: U.S. State Department, 2004).
5. Ron Malega and Thomas H. Cohen, *State Court Organization, 2011* (Washington, DC: Bureau of Justice Statistics, 2013), p. 3.
6. Robert C. LaFountain, Richard Y. Schauffler, Shauna M. Strickland, and Kathryn A. Holt, *Examining the Work of State Courts: An Analysis of 2010 State Court Caseloads* (Williamsburg, VA: National Center for State Courts, 2012), p. 46.
7. Ibid., p. 38.
8. U.S. Constitution, Article 3, Sections 1 and 2.
9. 1 Wharton 304, 4 L.Ed. 97 (1816).
10. Frank R. Baumgartner and Bryan D. Jones, *Policy Dynamics* (Chicago: University of Chicago Press, 2002), p. 272.
11. LaFountain, Schauffler, Strickland, and Holt, *Examining the Work of State Courts: An Analysis of 2010 State Court Caseloads*.
12. Ibid.
13. Administrative Office of the United States Courts, *Judicial Business of the United States Courts* (Washington, DC: Administrative Office of the United States Courts, 2012), http://www.uscourts.gov/Statistics/JudicialBusiness/2012.aspx (accessed July 2014).
14. Ibid.
15. Hans Zeisel, Harry Kalven Jr., and Bernard Buckholz, *Delay in the Court* (Boston: Little, Brown, 1959); for more recent information, see the National Center for State Court's Caseflow Management Resource Guide, http://www.ncsc.org/Topics/Court-Management/Caseflow-Management/Resource-Guide.aspx (accessed July 2014).
16. Jason Perez-Dormitzer, "Bill Safeguards Restaurants in Obesity-Related Lawsuits," *Providence Business News*, March 22, 2004, pp. 5–7.
17. Maureen Solomon and Douglas Somerlot, *Caseflow Management in the Trial Court: Now and for the Future* (Chicago: American Bar Association, 1987); Pamela Casey, "Defining Optimal Court Performance: The Trial Court Performance Standards," *Court Review* (Winter 1998): 24–33.
18. David Klein and Robert Hume, "Fear of Reversal as an Explanation of Lower Court Compliance," *Law and Society Review* 37 (2003): 579–607.
19. Huey-Tsyh Chen, "Dropping In and Dropping Out: Judicial Decisionmaking in the Disposition of Felony Arrests," *Journal of Criminal Justice* 19 (1991): 1–17.
20. American Bar Association, *Fact Sheet on Judicial Selection Methods in the States*, http://www.americanbar.org/content/dam/aba/migrated/leadership/fact_sheet.authcheckdam.pdf (accessed July 2014).
21. Ibid.
22. Ibid.
23. Daniel Wise, "Making a Criminal Case over Selection of Judges in Brooklyn," *New York Law Journal* (July 23, 2003): 1.
24. Sari Escovitz with Fred Kurland and Nan Gold, *Judicial Selection and Tenure* (Chicago: American Judicature Society, 1974), pp. 3–16.
25. Public Law 90-578, Title I, Sec. 101, 82 Stat. 1113 (1968), amended; Public Law 94-577, Sec. 1, Stat. 2729 (1976); Public Law 96-82, Sec. 2, 93 Stat. 643 (1979).
26. See, generally, Carroll Seron, "The Professional Project of Parajudges: The Case of U.S. Magistrates," *Law and Society Review* 22 (1988): 557–575.
27. Alex Aikman, "Volunteer Lawyer–Judges Bolster Court Resources," *NIJ Report* (January 1986): 2–6.
28. David C. Nixon and J. David Haskin, "Judicial Retirement Strategies," *American Politics Research* 28 (2000): 458–489.
29. Legal Information Institute, http://www.law.cornell.edu/wex/alternative_dispute_resolution (accessed July 2014).
30. Elena Nosyreva, "Alternative Dispute Resolution in the United States and Russia: A Comparative Evaluation," *Annual Survey of International and Comparative Law* 7 (2001): 7–19.
31. Jethro K. Lieberman and James F. Henry, "Lessons from the Alternative Dispute Resolution Movement," *University of Chicago Law Review* 53 (1986): 424–439.
32. Lawrence Baum, *The Puzzle of Judicial Behavior* (Ann Arbor: University of Michigan Press, 1998).
33. Jeffrey Segal and Albert Cover, "Ideological Values and the Votes of U.S. Supreme Court Justices," *American Political Science Review* 83 (1989): 557–565.
34. Thomas R. Marshall, *Public Opinion and the Supreme Court* (Boston: Unwin Hyman, 1989).
35. William Mishler and Reginald Sheehan, "The Supreme Court as a Counter-Majoritarian Institution? The Impact of Public Opinion on Supreme Court Decisions," *American Journal of Political Science* 41 (1997): 122–149.
36. Donald R. Songer and Kelley A. Crews-Meyer, "Does Judge Gender Matter? Decision Making in State Supreme Courts," *Social Science Inquiry* 81 (2000): 750–762.
37. Ibid.
38. Cassia Spohn, "Sentencing Decisions of Black and White Judges: Expected and Unexpected Similarities," *Law and Society Review* 24 (1990): 1197–1216.
39. Adam Liptak, "Rendering Justice, with One Eye on Re-election," *New York Times*, May 25, 2008, http://www.nytimes.com/2008/05/25/us/25exception.html (accessed July 2014).
40. Melinda G. Hall, "Electoral Politics and Strategic Voting in State Supreme Courts," *Journal of Politics* 52 (1992): 427–446.
41. Melinda G. Hall, "Constituent Influence in State Supreme Courts: Conceptual Notes and a Case Study," *Journal of Politics* 49 (1987): 1117–1124, at 1119.
42. Gregory A. Huber and Sanford C. Gordon, "Accountability and Coercion: Is Justice Blind When It Runs for Office?" *American Journal of Political Science* 48 (2004): 247–263, at 258.
43. Howard Gillman, "What's Law Got to Do with It? Judicial Behavioralists Test the 'Legal Model' of Judicial Decision Making," *Law and Social Inquiry* 26 (2001): 465–504.
44. See, for example, *United States v. Ruiz*, 536 U.S. 622 (2002).
45. *Berger v. United States*, 295 U.S. 78 (1935).
46. Steven W. Perry and Duren Banks, *Prosecutors in State Courts, 2007* (Washington, DC: Bureau of Justice Statistics, 2011).
47. Mark Cohen, "Environmental Crime and Punishment: Legal/Economic Theory and Empirical Evidence on Enforcement of Federal Environmental Statutes," *Journal of Criminal Law and Criminology* 82 (1992): 1054–1109.
48. Grace Wong, "Kozlowski Gets Up to 25 Years," http://money.cnn.com/2005/09/19/news/newsmakers/kozlowski_sentence/ (accessed July 2014).
49. American Bar Association, *Standards for Criminal Justice: Prosecution Function and Defense Function*, 3rd ed. (Washington, DC: 1993). See also American Bar Association, *Standards for Criminal Justice: Providing Defense Sources*, 3rd ed. (Washington, DC: 1993).

50. John L. Worrall and M. Elaine Nugent-Borakove, eds., *The Changing Role of the American Prosecutor* (Albany, NY: SUNY Press, 2008).

51. Eric Holden, "Community Prosecution," *Prosecutor* 34 (2000): 31.

52. William Scott Cunningham, Brian C. Renauer, and Christy Khalifa, "Sharing the Keys to the Courthouse: Adoption of Community Prosecution by State Court Prosecutors," *Journal of Contemporary Criminal Justice* 22 (2006): 202–219.

53. Douglas Gansler, "Implementing Community Prosecution in Montgomery County, Maryland," *Prosecutor* 34 (2000): 30.

54. Kenneth C. Davis, *Discretionary Justice* (Baton Rouge: Louisiana State University Press, 1969), p. 180. See also James B. Stewart, *The Prosecutor* (New York: Simon and Schuster, 1987).

55. Barbara Boland, *The Prosecution of Felony Arrests* (Washington, DC: Government Printing Office, 1983).

56. Leslie Griffin, "The Prudent Prosecutor," *Georgetown Journal of Legal Ethics* 14 (2001): 259–308.

57. *United States v. Armstrong*, 517 U.S. 456 at 464 (1996).

58. Michael Tonry and Richard Frase, *Sentencing and Sanctions in Western Countries* (London: Oxford University Press, 2001).

59. Charles D. Breitel, "Control in Criminal Law Enforcement," *University of Chicago Law Review* 27 (1960): 427.

60. Cassia Spohn, Dawn Beichner, and Erika Davis-Frenzel, "Prosecutorial Justifications for Sexual Assault Case Rejection: Guarding the 'Gateway to Justice,'" *Social Problems* 48 (2001): 206–235.

61. *Yick Wo v. Hopkins*, 118 U.S. 356 (1886).

62. *United States v. Cammisano*, 413 F.Supp. 886 (1976).

63. *Imbler v. Pachtman*, 424 U.S. 409 (1976); also see *Burns v. Reed*, 500 U.S. 478 (1991) and *Kalina v. Fletcher*, 522 U.S. 118 (1997).

64. Center for Public Integrity, *Harmful Error: Investigative America's Local Prosecutors*, http://www.publicintegrity.org/accountability/harmful-error (accessed July 2014).

65. American Bar Association, *Report of Standing Committee on Legal Aid and Indigent Defendants* (Chicago: ABA, 1991).

66. Monroe H. Freedman, "Professional Responsibility of the Criminal Defense Lawyer: The Three Hardest Questions," *Michigan Law Review* 64 (1966): 1468.

67. Michael Asimow and Richard Weisberg, "When the Lawyer Knows the Client Is Guilty: Client Confessions in Legal Ethics, Popular Culture, and Literature," *Southern California Interdisciplinary Law Journal* 18 (2009): 229–258.

68. Bennett Brummer, *Ethics Resource Guide for Public Defenders* (Chicago: American Bar Association, February 1992).

69. *Miranda v. Arizona*, 384 U.S. 436 (1966).

70. *Mempa v. Rhay*, 389 U.S. 128 (1967).

71. *Douglas v. California*, 372 U.S. 353 (1963).

72. *In re Gault*, 387 U.S. 1 (1967); *Specht v. Patterson*, 386 U.S. 605 (1967).

73. National Center for State Courts, *Indigent Defense Resource Guide*, http://www.ncsc.org/Topics/Access-and-Fairness/Indigent-Defense/Resource-Guide.aspx (accessed July 2014).

74. See *Betts v. Brady*, 316 U.S. 455 (1942). Justice Black subsequently wrote the majority opinion in *Gideon v. Wainwright*, guaranteeing defendants' right to counsel and overruling the *Betts* case.

75. *Gideon v. Wainwright*, 372 U.S. 335 (1963).

76. *Argersinger v. Hamlin*, 407 U.S. 25 (1972).

77. See F. Brownell, *Legal Aid in the United States* (Chicago: National Legal Aid Defender Association, 1961). For an interesting study of the Cook County, Illinois, Office of Public Defenders, see Lisa McIntyre, *Public Defenders: Practice of Law in Shadows of Dispute* (Chicago: University of Chicago Press, 1987).

78. Pauline Houlden and Steven Balkin, "Quality and Cost Comparisons of Private Bar Indigent Defense Systems: Contract vs. Ordered Assigned Counsel," *Journal of Criminal Law and Criminology* 76 (1985): 176–200. See also John Arrango, "Defense Services for the Poor," *American Bar Association Journal on Criminal Justice* 12 (1998): 35.

79. Lawrence Spears, "Contract Counsel: A Different Way to Defend the Poor—How It's Working in North Dakota," *American Bar Association Journal on Criminal Justice* 6 (1991): 24–31.

80. *Argersinger v. Hamlin*.

81. Caroline Wolf Harlow, *Defense Counsel in Criminal Cases* (Washington, DC: Bureau of Justice Statistics, 2000).

82. Talia Roitberg Harmon and William Lofquist, "Too Late for Luck: A Comparison of Post-Furman Exonerations and Executions of the Innocent," *Crime and Delinquency* 51 (2005): 498–520.

83. Morris B. Hoffman, Paul H. Rubin, and Joanna M. Shepherd, "An Empirical Study of Public Defender Effectiveness: Self-Selection by the 'Marginally Indigent,'" *Ohio State Journal of Criminal Law* 3 (2005): 223–251, at 225.

84. David G. Bress, "Professional Ethics in Criminal Trials," *Michigan Law Review* 64 (1966): 1493; John Mitchell, "The Ethics of the Criminal Defense Attorney," *Stanford Law Review* 32 (1980): 325.

CHAPTER 10

Pretrial and Trial Procedures

Learning Objectives

LO1 Discuss the procedures following arrest.

LO2 List a variety of bail systems.

LO3 Describe the history of bail reform.

LO4 Define pretrial services.

LO5 List the differences between the indictment process and the information process.

LO6 Discuss the purpose of arraignment.

LO7 Discuss the pros and cons of plea bargaining.

LO8 Explain the role of the prosecutor, defense attorney, judge, and victim in the plea negotiation.

LO9 Explain the legal rights of the accused at trial.

LO10 Summarize the trial process.

Chapter Outline

Between 2002 and 2004, Ariel Castro kidnapped three women, Michelle Knight, Amanda Berry, and Gina DeJesus, and held them prisoner in his Cleveland, Ohio, home. Each of the women, who ranged in age from 14 to 21 at the time of their abduction, had accepted a ride from Castro. He had driven them to his home, lured them inside, and then took them to the basement and restrained them. Castro's house was only three miles from the scene of each abduction.

On December 25, 2006, Amanda Berry gave birth to a daughter in the house where she and the other women were held against their will. DNA evidence later revealed that Castro was the father. Six years later, Berry managed to escape and contact the police. Her abduction, along with Gina DeJesus's, had been featured years earlier on *America's Most Wanted*, *The Montel Williams Show*, and even *The Oprah Winfrey Show*, but until her escape, authorities had all but given up on their search for the women.

Castro was arrested on May 6, 2013, and was soon charged with four counts of kidnapping and three counts of rape. Bail was set at $8 million. On May 14, Castro's defense attorneys said he would plead not guilty if

charged with kidnapping and rape. Three weeks later, a grand jury returned an indictment against Castro, setting out 329 different counts, including aggravated murder for Castro's alleged role in terminating one of the women's pregnancy. True to his word, Castro pleaded not guilty and was found competent to stand trial on June 3, 2013. He was subsequently charged with more crimes and, pursuant to a plea bargain, admitted to 937 of the 977 total charges against him. Castro was sentenced to life plus 1,000 years. At the sentencing hearing, Michelle Knight made this emotional statement:

> You took 11 years of my life away. I spent 11 years in hell, now your hell is just beginning. I will overcome all this that has happened, but you will face hell for eternity. I will live on, you will die a little every day as you think of the 11 years of atrocities that you inflicted on us. . . . I can forgive you, but I will never forget.[1]

One month into his prison term, Castro hanged himself with a bed sheet in his cell. He was not on suicide watch at the time of his death, but guards had checked on him every 30 minutes because of his notoriety. ■

This chapter reviews the pretrial and trial process, beginning with the pretrial procedures. **Pretrial procedures** are important components of the justice process because the vast majority of all criminal cases are resolved informally at this stage and never come before the courts. Although the media like to focus on the elaborate jury trial with its dramatic elements and impressive setting, formal criminal trials are relatively infrequent. Consequently, understanding the events that take place during the pretrial period is essential in grasping the reality of criminal justice policy.

Procedures Following Arrest

L01   Discuss the procedures following arrest.

After arrest, the accused is ordinarily taken to the police station, where the police list the possible criminal charges against him and obtain other information for the booking process. This may include recording a description of the suspect and the circumstances of the offense. The suspect may then be fingerprinted, photographed, and required to participate in a lineup.

The arrestee is usually detained by the police until it is decided whether a criminal complaint will be filed. The **complaint** is the formal written document identifying the criminal charge, the date and place where the crime occurred, and the circumstances of the arrest. The complaint is sworn to and signed under oath by the complainant, usually a police officer. The complaint will request that the defendant be present at an initial hearing held soon after the arrest is made. In some jurisdictions, this may be referred to by other names, such as arraignment. During **arraignment**, the judge informs the defendant of the charge, ensures that the accused is properly represented by counsel, and determines whether he should be released on bail or some other form of release pending a hearing or trial.

The defendant may plead guilty at the initial hearing, and the case may be disposed of immediately. A defendant who pleads not guilty to a minor offense has been informed of the formal charge, provided with counsel if he is unable to afford a private attorney, and asked to plead guilty or not guilty as charged. A date in the near future is set for trial, and the defendant is generally released on bail or on his own recognizance to await trial. When a felony or a more serious crime is involved, there is usually another step before a person can be tried. This involves proving to an objective body that there is probable cause to believe that a crime has taken place and that the accused should be tried on the matter. This step of the formal charging process is ordinarily an indictment from a grand jury or a charging document known as an information issued by a lower court.

In addition to these steps in the pretrial phase, the defendant is also considered for bail so that he may remain in the community to prepare his criminal defense. Even at this early stage, some may enter court-based treatment programs.

Bail

Bail is a form of security, usually a sum of money, that is put up or exchanged to secure the release of an arrested person before the trial begins. The bail amount serves as a bond, ensuring that the released criminal defendant will return for trial. Failure to appear results in the forfeiting of the bail.

Whether a defendant can be expected to appear at the next stage of the criminal proceedings is a key issue in determining bail.[2] Bail cannot be used to punish an accused, and it cannot be denied or revoked at the indulgence of the court. Bail is a critical stage in the justice process and a key ingredient of a fair and equitable adjudication process: it enables people charged with a crime to be free in the community in order to prepare a defense to the state's criminal charges. It also prevents an innocent person from spending months, if not years, behind bars awaiting trial, only to be freed after a not-guilty verdict is rendered.

The Legal Right to Bail

Bail is not a new practice. Under English common law, criminal defendants were eligible to be released before trial. Up through the thirteenth century, however, the county shire reeve (sheriff) controlled the release of defendants awaiting trial. The sheriffs were given discretion to determine who would be held and who released and how much bail was required. Because sheriffs sometimes exploited their power, Parliament issued the Statute of Westminster in 1275; it set out the offenses that were bailable and those that were not. Under the new law, the sheriff still retained the authority to determine the amount of bail.

English bail practices were continued in the original colonies. After the revolution, Congress passed the Judiciary Act of 1789, which set out conditions for bail and limited judicial discretion in setting bail amounts. As the Judiciary Act states, "Upon all arrests in criminal cases, bail shall be admitted, except where punishment may be by death, in which cases it shall not be admitted but by the supreme or a circuit court, or by a justice of the supreme court, or a judge of a district court, who shall exercise their discretion therein."[3]

Bail was also incorporated into the Eighth Amendment of the U.S. Constitution, but only insofar as it prohibits "excessive bail." There is no constitutional right to bail. The Eighth Amendment's excessive bail clause may be interpreted to mean that the sole purpose of bail is to ensure that the defendant returns for trial; bail may not be used as a form of punishment or to coerce or threaten a defendant. In most cases, a defendant has the right to be released on reasonable bail. Many jurisdictions also require a bail review hearing by a higher court in cases in which the initial judge set what might be considered excessive bail.

The U.S. Supreme Court's interpretation of the Eighth Amendment's provisions on bail was set out in the 1951 case of *Stack v. Boyle*.[4] In that case, the Court found bail to be a traditional right to freedom before trial that permits unhampered preparation of a defense and prevents the criminal defendant from being punished prior to conviction. The Court held that bail is excessive when it exceeds an amount reasonably calculated to ensure that the defendant will return for trial. The Court indicated that bail should be in the amount that is generally set for similar offenses. Higher bail can be imposed when evidence supporting the increase is presented at a hearing in which the defendant's constitutional

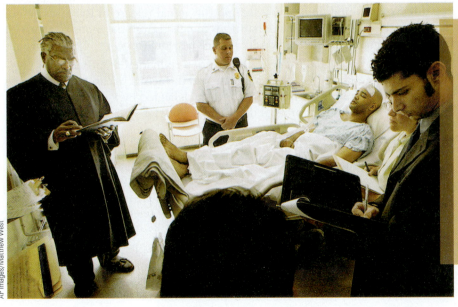

AP Images/Matthew West

Bail hearings are generally held in court, but there are always exceptions. At his bail hearing, carjacking suspect John Powell, 30, hospitalized with a gunshot wound to the head, lies on his bed at Boston Medical Center after his arraignment. Judge Edward Redd (left) arraigned Powell in private before opening the room to the media. At center is court officer Michael McCusker. At right are defense attorney Beth Eisenberg and intern Jason Benzahn, from the Roxbury Defenders League.

rights can be protected. Although *Stack* did not establish an absolute right to bail, it did set guidelines for state courts to follow: if a crime is bailable, the amount set should not be frivolous, unusual, or beyond a person's ability to pay.

Making Bail

A majority of criminal defendants are released prior to trial.[5] The most recent surveys of pretrial release practices show that about two-thirds of felony defendants are released prior to the final disposition of their case. As might be expected, defendants charged with the most serious violent offenses are less likely to be released than those charged with less serious public order or drug offenses. Defendants charged with murder are the least likely to be released prior to case disposition. In contrast, defendants charged with misdemeanors and nonviolent felonies are routinely granted bail. All else equal, the less serious the charge, the more likely it is that bail will be granted.

When and how are bail decisions made? Bail is typically considered at a court hearing conducted shortly after a person has been taken into custody. At the hearing, such issues as crime type, flight risk, and dangerousness are considered before a bail amount is set. Victim input is sometimes taken into account, too. This is discussed further in the Victim Experience box. In jurisdictions with pretrial release programs, program staff often interview arrestees detained at the jail prior to the first hearing, verify the background information, and present recommendations to the court at arraignment. Prior record is an important factor: fewer than half of defendants with an active criminal justice status, such as parole or probation, at the time of arrest are released, compared to 67 percent of these with no active status. Some jurisdictions have developed bail schedules to make amounts uniform based on the crime and the defendant's criminal history.

Alternative Bail Release Mechanisms

Although bail is typically granted during a court hearing, there are other stages in the system in which bail may be granted:

- *Police field citation release.* An arresting officer releases the arrestee on a written promise to appear in court made at or near the actual time and location of the arrest. This procedure is commonly used for misdemeanor charges and is similar to issuing a traffic ticket.

- *Police station house citation release.* The determination of an arrestee's eligibility and suitability for release and the actual release of the arrestee are deferred until after he or she has been removed from the scene of an arrest and brought to the station house or police headquarters.

- *Police/pretrial jail citation release.* The determination of an arrestee's eligibility and suitability for citation release and the actual release of the arrestee are deferred until after he or she has been delivered by the arresting department to a jail or other pretrial detention facility for screening, booking, and admission.

- *Pretrial/court direct release by pretrial bail program.* To streamline release processes and reduce the length of stay in detention, pretrial program courts may authorize pretrial programs to release defendants without direct judicial involvement. When court rules delegate such authority, the practice is generally limited to misdemeanor charges, but felony release authority has been granted in some jurisdictions.

- *Police/court bail schedule.* An arrestee can post bail at the station house or jail according to amounts specified in a bail schedule. The schedule is a list of all bailable charges and a corresponding dollar amount for each. Schedules may vary widely from jurisdiction to jurisdiction.

the VICTIM experience

INPUT INTO THE BAIL DECISION

BACKGROUND Joseph H. Gardner pleaded not guilty to raping the 3-year-old daughter of a woman he was dating. At the time of his arrest, he was out on bail, having pleaded not guilty to breaking into a distant relative's house and raping a 6-year-old girl. At his arraignment on the second charge, the mother of the 3-year-old victim was in attendance and strongly objected to his release. "I don't understand why he is still out," she said. "I think the courts should make sure he goes away and is not allowed to be around kids."

Twenty-seven-year-old Jose Alfredo Dominguez was charged with capital murder in the death of Ercile Rae Johnson, who was found stabbed to death in his apartment. As if the crime was not disturbing enough, Dominguez was actually out on bail at the time, having recently posted $50,000 bail for another murder charge in which he was accused of beating and choking to death 34-year-old Ever Gomez. Gomez's body was found behind a warehouse in the Houston area.

THE BIG PICTURE Judges are often tasked with making difficult bail decisions, and they get them right the vast majority of the time. A minority of defendants who are released on bail commit new crimes, but the percentages are of some concern, especially in the case of motor vehicle theft (see Figures 10.2 and 10.3 later in this chapter). And victims get particularly outraged when released defendants commit more crime, as was clear in the Joseph Gardner case. Fortunately, a number of states have extended a number of victims' rights to the bail stage. For example, Alaska gives crime victims a number of rights with respect to bail. They include:

- Notice of hearings at which the accused's release is considered.

- Input into the bail release decision. The court must consider the victim's comments.

- Being entitled to receive a copy of the release conditions, if bail is granted.

- Automated notification of a change in status of the offender.

Victim safety must also be taken into account as part of the release decision, and state law specifies that "victims should receive protection from harm and threats of harm arising out of cooperation with law enforcement and prosecution efforts and be provided with information regarding the protection available."

Similar rights are granted to victims in other states. Many states permit victims to attend and/or receive notice of hearings involving the offender. Others take it a step further. For example, Missouri permits victims to confer with the prosecutor concerning all key decisions, including bail, pleas, defenses, and even in sentencing and probation revocation hearings. Other states, such as Virginia, merely provide notification of the defendant's release on bail.

CLASSROOM EXERCISE Have students break into groups and search through news articles to find and report on a high-profile crime allegedly committed by a person who was out on bail. Try to identify reasons for the individual's release. Also make recommendations such that similar incidents can be avoided in the future. Finally, locate pertinent state statutes pertaining to victim rights and determine whether the incident took place in a state that grants crime victims rights specific to the bail determination process.

Sources: John R. Ellement and Jonathan Saltzman, "Suspect in Rape Was Out on Bail," *Boston Globe*, December 15, 2009, http://www.boston.com/news/local/massachusetts/articles/2009/12/15/kingston_man_out_on_bail_accused_of_2d_child_rape/; Anita Hassan, "Slaying Suspect Was Out on Bail in 2008 Murder Charge," *Houston Chronicle*, April 3, 2012, http://www.chron.com/news/houston-texas/article/Slaying-suspect-was-out-on-bail-in-2008-murder-3456450.php; Alaska Office of Victims' Rights, https://ovr.akleg.gov/; Missouri Attorney General's Office, *Crime Victim's Rights*, http://ago.mo.gov/publications/crimevictimsrights.pdf (sites accessed July 2014).

Types of Bail

There are a variety of ways or mechanisms to secure bail, depending on the jurisdiction, the crime, and the defendant:

- *Full cash bail.* The defendant pays the full bail amount out of pocket. In some jurisdictions, property can be pledged instead of cash.

■ *Deposit bail.* The defendant deposits a percentage of the bail amount, typically 10 percent, with the court. When the defendant appears in court, the deposit is returned, sometimes minus an administrative fee. If the defendant fails to appear, he or she is liable for the full amount of the bail.

■ *Surety bail.* The defendant pays a percentage of the bond, usually 10 percent, to a bonding agent, who posts the full bail. The fee paid to the bonding agent is not returned to the defendant if he or she appears in court. The bonding agent is liable for the full amount of the bond should the defendant fail to appear. Bail bonding agents hire bounty hunters to find defendants who fail to appear for their court dates.

■ *Conditional bail.* The defendant is released after promising to abide by some specified conditions in lieu of cash. For example, she promises to attend a treatment program prior to trial.

■ *Unsecured bond.* The defendant is released with no immediate requirement of payment. However, if the defendant fails to appear, he is liable for the full amount.

■ *Release on recognizance.* Eligible defendants are released without bail upon their promise to return for trial.

LO2 List a variety of bail systems.

Web App 10.2

For more information about surety bail, visit http://www.pbus.com/.

pretrial detainees
People who either are denied bail or cannot afford to post bail before trial and are kept in secure confinement.

As Figure 10.1 shows, surety bond is now the most common type of bail form used with felony defendants, followed by release on recognizance and conditional bail. Relatively few defendants pay full cash bail out of pocket.

Pretrial Detention

The criminal defendant who is not eligible for bail or release on recognizance is subject to pretrial detention in the local county jail. Unfortunately, the jail has long been a trouble spot for the criminal justice system. Conditions tend to be poor and rehabilitation nonexistent.

In terms of the number of persons affected each year, pretrial custody accounts for more U.S. incarceration than does imprisonment after sentencing. On any given day in the United States, nearly 800,000 people are held in more than 3,500 local jails.[6] Over the course of a year, many times that number pass through the jailhouse door. More than 50 percent of those held in local jails have been accused of crimes but not convicted; they are **pretrial detainees**. In the United States, people are detained at a rate twice that of neighboring Canada and three times that of Great Britain. Hundreds of jails are overcrowded, and many are under court orders to reduce their populations and improve conditions. The national jail-crowding crisis has worsened over the years.

Jails are often considered the weakest link in the criminal justice process. They are frequently dangerous, harmful, decrepit, and filled with the poor and friendless. The costs of holding a person in jail range up to more than $100 per day, or $36,000 per year.[7] In addition, detainees are often confined with those convicted of crimes and those who have been transferred from other institutions because of overcrowding. Many felons are transferred to jails from state prisons to ease crowding. It is possible to have in close quarters a convicted

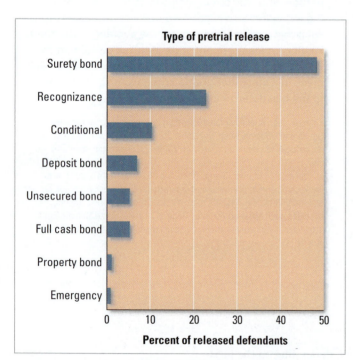

FIGURE 10.1   Type of Pretrial Release for Felony Defendants in the 75 Largest Counties

Source: Brian A. Reeves, *Felony Defendants in Large Urban Counties, 2009* (Washington, DC: Bureau of Justice Statistics, 2013), p. 18.

rapist, a father jailed for nonpayment of child support, and a person awaiting trial for a crime that he did not commit. This mix of inmates can lead to violence, brutality, and suicide.

What happens to those who find themselves jailed because they cannot afford to put up bail money? Traditionally, they are more likely to be convicted and get longer prison sentences than those who commit similar crimes but are released on bail. A federally sponsored study of case processing in the nation's largest counties found that about 59 percent of all defendants released prior to their trial were convicted; in contrast, 78 percent of detainees were convicted.[8] Detainees are also more likely than releasees to be convicted of a felony offense and, therefore, are eligible for a long prison sentence instead of the much shorter term of incarceration given misdemeanants. People being held in jails are in a less attractive bargaining position than those released on bail, and prosecutors, knowing their predicament, may be less generous in their negotiations. It is for these reasons that bail reform advocates have tried so hard to eliminate, whenever possible, the detention of nondangerous criminal defendants.

Bail Reform

Bail has been heavily criticized as one of the most unacceptable aspects of the criminal justice system. Some view it as discriminatory because it works against the poor, who have a much tougher time making bail. Others argue that it is costly because the government must pay to detain those offenders who are unable to make bail but who would otherwise remain in the community. Another problem is the legal effect of detention.

 L03 Describe the history of bail reform.

Most states place no precise limit on the amount of bail that a judge may impose. People charged with the most serious crimes usually receive the highest amount of bail. As Table 10.1 shows, for example, median bail for violent offenders is more than double of that for property offenders.

These data trouble experts who believe that the bail system is discriminatory because defendants who are financially well off can make bail, whereas indigent defendants languish in pretrial detention in the county jail. In addition, keeping a person in jail imposes serious financial burdens on local and state governments—and, in turn, on taxpayers, who must pay for the cost of confinement. These factors have given rise to bail reform programs that depend on the defendant's

Jails can be overcrowded and dangerous. Sometimes it takes a court order to improve conditions. Prisoners at Marion County Lockup in Indianapolis sleep on the floor. Many state prison systems have been using some form of early release to reduce the number of inmates. Despite early releases, crowding at the Marion County Lockup is still under scrutiny as its population continues to soar.

AP Images/*Indianapolis Star*/Mike Fender

TABLE 10.1   Median Bail Amount Set for Felony Defendants

Most Serious Arrest Charge	Total	Released	Detained
All offenses	$10,000	$6,000	$25,000
Violent offenses	25,000	10,000	50,000
Murder	1,000,000	125,000	1,000,000
Rape	50,000	25,000	100,000
Robbery	50,000	15,000	60,000
Assault	15,000	10,000	50,000
Other violent	25,000	10,000	50,000
Property offenses	$7,500	$5,000	$19,000
Burglary	15,000	10,000	25,000
Larceny/theft	5,000	3,500	15,000
Motor vehicle theft	9,000	3,500	15,000
Forgery	5,000	4,000	7,500
Fraud	5,000	5,000	25,000
Other property	5,000	4,000	20,000
Drug offenses	$10,000	$7,500	$20,000
Trafficking	20,000	10,000	30,000
Other drug	7,500	5,000	15,000
Public-order offenses	$10,000	$5,000	$20,000
Weapons	11,100	7,950	35,000
Driving-related	5,000	5,000	10,000
Other public-order	10,000	5,000	15,000

Note: Data on bail amounts were available for 96.9 percent of all defendants for whom a bail amount was set. Bail amounts have been rounded to the nearest hundred dollars. Table excludes defendants given nonfinancial release.

Source: Brian A. Reaves, *Felony Defendants in Large Urban Counties, 2009* (Washington, DC: Bureau of Justice Statistics, 2013), p. 19.

personal promise to appear in court for trial, instead of on financial ability to meet bail. These reforms have enabled many deserving but indigent offenders to go free, but another trend has been to deny people bail on the grounds that they are a danger to themselves or to others in the community.

RELEASE ON RECOGNIZANCE Efforts have been made to reform and even eliminate money bail and reduce the importance of bonding agents. Until the early 1960s, the justice system relied primarily on money bonds as the principal form of pretrial release. Many states now allow defendants to be released without any money bail. This is known as **release on recognizance (ROR)**. ROR programs were popular in the 1960s[9] and resulted in bail reforms that culminated in the enactment of the federal Bail Reform Act of 1966, the first change in federal bail laws since 1789.[10] This legislation sought to ensure that release would be granted in all noncapital cases in which sufficient reason existed to believe that the defendant would return to court. The law clearly established the presumption of ROR that must be overcome before money bail is required, authorized 10 percent deposit bail, introduced the concept of conditional release, and stressed the philosophy that release should be under the least restrictive method adequate to ensure court appearance.

During the 1970s and early 1980s, the pretrial release movement was hampered by public pressure over pretrial increases in crime. As a result, more recent

release on recognizance (ROR)

A pretrial release in which a defendant with ties to the community is not required to post bail but promises to appear at all subsequent proceedings.

federal legislation, the Bail Reform Act of 1984, mandated that no defendants shall be kept in pretrial detention simply because they cannot afford money bail, established the presumption for ROR in all cases in which a person is bailable, and formalized restrictive preventive detention provisions. The 1984 act required that community safety, as well as the risk of flight, be considered in the release decision. Consequently, such criminal justice factors as the seriousness of the charged offense, the weight of the evidence, the sentence that may be imposed upon conviction, court appearance history, and prior convictions are likely to influence the release decisions of the federal court.

PREVENTIVE DETENTION Whereas bail reform efforts are typically aimed at liberalizing bail, there are also efforts to tighten bail restrictions on the most dangerous offenders. The reason is the fear that serious criminals may reoffend while in the community. These fears are not unfounded. Figure 10.2 shows which arrestees are most likely to engage in misconduct while released on bail. For example, 41 percent of suspects arrested for motor vehicle theft committed misconduct (failed to show up for their scheduled court dates, violated release conditions, were rearrested for a new offense, etc.) while out on bail.

Figure 10.3 looks strictly at rearrests for felonies. Nearly 10 percent of those released prior to the trials on violent offense charges were rearrested on felony charges. For property offenses, the felony rearrest rate was 8 percent. Burglary and motor vehicle theft defendants were the most likely to be rearrested for a felony while out on bail. We call these people **avertable recidivists**—their crimes could have been prevented if they had not been given discretionary release and instead had been kept behind bars. Those rearrested tend to be on bail longer, to have a serious prior record, to abuse drugs, and to have a poor work record, and they are disproportionately young, male, and members of minority groups.

One response to the alleged failure of the bail system to protect citizens is the adoption of **preventive detention** statutes. These laws require that certain dangerous defendants be confined before trial for their own protection and that of the community. Preventive detention is an important manifestation of the crime control perspective on justice because it favors the use of incapacitation to control the future behavior of suspected criminals. Often, the key question is whether preventive detention is punishment before trial.

The most striking use of preventive detention can be found in the federal Bail Reform Act of 1984, which contrasted sharply with previous laws.[11] Although the act does contain provisions for ROR, it allows judges to order preventive detention if they determine "that no condition or combination of conditions will reasonably assure the appearance of the person as required and the safety of any other person and the community."[12]

A number of state jurisdictions have incorporated elements of preventive detention into their bail systems. Although most of the restrictions do not

Web App 10.3

For more information about the Bail Reform Act of 1984, visit http://www.fjc.gov/public/pdf.nsf/lookup/bailref.pdf/$file/bailref.pdf.

avertable recidivist
A person whose crime would have been prevented if he or she had not been given discretionary release and instead had been kept behind bars.

preventive detention
The statutory authorization to deny bail to a particular individual who is considered dangerous or a flight risk.

Most serious arrest charge	Released felony defendants committing misconduct in the 75 largest counties, by most serious arrest charge, 2009	
	Number	Percent with any pretrial misconduct
All offenses	32,824	29%
Violent offenses	7,275	23%
Murder	46	15
Rape	229	19
Robbery	1,623	31
Assault	3,853	23
Other violent	1,524	17
Property offenses	9,812	31%
Burglary	2,391	35
Larceny/theft	3,091	27
Motor vehicle theft	718	41
Forgery	963	29
Fraud	1,377	26
Other property	1,272	33
Drug offenses	11,190	32%
Trafficking	5,141	33
Other drug	6,049	32
Public-order offenses	4,547	28%
Weapons	1,234	27
Driving-related	1,545	26
Other public-order	1,768	31

FIGURE 10.2   Released Felony Defendants Committing Misconduct in the 75 Largest Counties

Source: Brian A. Reeves, *Felony Defendants in Large Urban Counties, 2009* (Washington, DC: Bureau of Justice Statistics, 2013), p. 20.

Note: Data on Misconduct were available for 96.4% of all cases. Types of misconduct included failure to appear in court, nearest for a new offense, or a technical violation of release conditions that resulted in the revocation of pretrial release. Data were collected for up to one year.

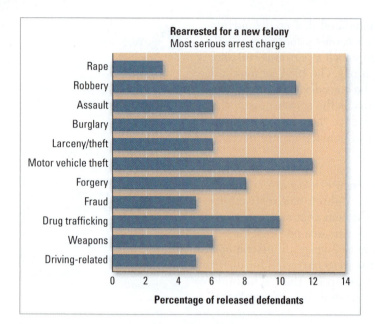

Rearrested for a new felony
Most serious arrest charge

Percentage of released defendants

FIGURE 10.3   Percentage of People Out on Bail Who Are Rearrested for a Felony, by Charge and Arrest Type

Source: Brian A. Reeves, *Felony Defendants in Large Urban Counties, 2009* (Washington, DC: Bureau of Justice Statistics, 2013), p. 21.

constitute outright preventive detention, they serve to narrow the scope of bail eligibility. These provisions include exclusion of certain crimes from bail eligibility, definition of bail to include appearance in court and community safety, and limitations on right to bail for those previously convicted.

Preventive detention has also been a source of concern for civil libertarians who believe it violates the due process clause of the Constitution, because it means that a person will be held in custody before proven guilty. In two important cases, the Supreme Court disagreed with this analysis. In *Schall v. Martin*, the Court upheld the application of preventive detention statutes to juvenile defendants on the grounds that such detention is useful to protect the welfare of the minor and society as a whole.[13] In 1987, the Court upheld the Bail Reform Act's provision on preventive detention for adults in the case of *United States v. Salerno*, when it ruled that the Bail Reform Act's denial of bail to dangerous defendants did not violate the Eighth Amendment.[14]

Pretrial Services

In our overburdened court system, it is critical to determine which defendants can safely be released on bail pending trial.[15] In many jurisdictions, specialized pretrial services help courts deal with this problem. Hundreds of pretrial programs have been established in rural, suburban, and urban jurisdictions; they are typically administered by probation departments, court offices, and local jails or handled by independent county contractors. These programs provide a number of critical services, including the following:

■   Gathering and verifying information about arrestees, including criminal history, current status in the criminal justice system, address, employment, and history of drug and alcohol use, which judicial officers can then take into account in making release/detention decisions.

■   Assessing each arrestee's likelihood of failure to appear and chances of being rearrested.

■   Providing supervision for defendants conditionally released and notifying the court of any failure to comply with release conditions.

L04   Define pretrial services.

Virtually all larger jurisdictions in the United States have pretrial release services in one form or another. Court-administered programs make up the greatest percentage of pretrial programs, although most newer programs are located within probation departments. The general criteria used to assess eligibility for release include the defendant's community ties and prior criminal justice involvement. Many jurisdictions have conditional and supervised release and third-party custody release, in addition to release on a person's own recognizance.

Some pretrial service programs are now being aimed at special needs. One type focuses on defendants suffering from mental illness; almost three-quarters of pretrial service programs now inquire about mental health status and treatment as a regular part of their interview, and about one-quarter report having implemented special supervision procedures for defendants with mental illness.

Another area of concern is domestic violence; about one-quarter of all pretrial programs have developed special risk-assessment procedures for defendants charged with domestic violence offenses, and about one-third have implemented special procedures to supervise such defendants.

Charging the Defendant

Charging a defendant with a crime is a critical stage in the pretrial process. The charge is selected by the prosecutor, who takes into consideration the facts of the case, strength of the evidence, availability of witnesses, and so on. The process varies depending on whether it occurs via a grand jury or a preliminary hearing.

The Indictment Process: The Grand Jury

The grand jury was an early development of English common law. Under the Magna Carta (1215), no "freeman" could be seized and imprisoned unless he had been judged by his peers. To determine fairly who was to be tried, a group of freemen from the district where a crime was committed would be brought together to examine the facts of the case and determine whether the charges had merit. Thus, the grand jury was created as a check against arbitrary prosecution by a judge who might be a puppet of the government.

The concept of the grand jury was brought to the American colonies by early settlers and later incorporated into the Fifth Amendment, which states that "no person shall be held to answer for a capital, or otherwise infamous crime, unless on a presentment or indictment of a grand jury." Today, the use of the grand jury is diminishing. Relatively few states require a grand jury indictment to begin all felony proceedings; most allow the prosecutor the option of calling a grand jury or proceeding with a preliminary hearing. The federal government employs both the grand jury and the preliminary hearing systems.

The grand jury today has two roles. First, it has the power to act as an independent investigating body. In this capacity, it examines the possibility of criminal activity within its jurisdiction. These investigative efforts are directed toward general, not individual, criminal conduct. After completing its investigation, the grand jury issues a report called a **presentment**, which contains its findings and (usually) a recommendation of indictment. An **indictment** is a written accusation charging a person with a crime. It is drawn up by a prosecutor and submitted to a grand jury, which—after considering the evidence presented by the prosecutor—votes to endorse or deny the indictment.

The grand jury's second and better-known role is accusatory in nature. In this capacity, the grand jury acts as the community's conscience in determining whether an accusation by the state (the prosecution) justifies a trial. The grand jury relies on the testimony of witnesses called by the prosecution through its subpoena power. After examining the evidence and the testimony of witnesses, the grand jury decides whether probable cause exists for prosecution. If it does, an indictment, or **true bill**, is affirmed. If the grand jury fails to find probable cause, a **no bill** (meaning that the indictment is ignored) is passed. In some states, a prosecutor can present evidence to a different grand jury if a no bill is returned; in other states, this action is prohibited by statute.

A grand jury is ordinarily made up of 16 to 23 individuals, depending on the requirements of the jurisdiction. This group theoretically represents a county. Selection of members varies from state to state, but for the most part, they are chosen at random (for example, from voting lists). To qualify to serve on a grand jury, an individual must be at least 18 years of age, must be a U.S. citizen, must have been a resident of the jurisdiction for one year or more, and must possess sufficient English-speaking skills for communication.

L05 List the differences between the indictment process and the information process.

presentment
The report of a grand jury investigation, which usually includes a recommendation of indictment.

indictment
A written accusation returned by a grand jury, charging an individual with a specified crime after determination of probable cause.

true bill
The action by a grand jury when it votes to indict an accused suspect.

no bill
The action by a grand jury when it votes not to indict an accused suspect.

AP Images/Kathy Willens

Former Texas Governor Rick Perry speaks to the media while a grand jury investigated whether he abused his power while in office. Perry would soon be indicted on charges that he withheld money from an Austin prosecutor's office because its elected Democratic district attorney refused to resign after pleading guilty to drunk driving. Grand juries are often useful in high-profile cases such as these because of their broad investigative authority.

Web App 10.4

For more information about grand juries, visit http://campus.udayton.edu/~grandjur/.

The grand jury usually meets at the request of the prosecution. Hearings are closed and secret. The prosecuting attorney presents the charges and calls witnesses who testify under oath to support the indictment. Usually, the accused individuals are not allowed to attend the hearing unless they are asked to testify by the prosecutor or the grand jury.

REFORMING THE GRAND JURY? The defense attorney, defendant, and general public are not allowed to attend grand jury proceedings. The prosecuting attorney presents the charges and calls witnesses who testify under oath to support the indictment. This process has been criticized as being a rubber stamp for the prosecution because the presentation of the evidence is shaped by the district attorney, who is not required by law to reveal information that might exonerate the accused.[16]

In the case of *United States v. Williams* (1992), the Supreme Court ruled that no supervisory power in the federal courts requires presentation to a grand jury of **exculpatory evidence** (evidence that can clear a defendant from blame or fault).[17] Some legal scholars find that the *Williams* decision conflicted with the grand jury's historical purpose of shielding criminal defendants from unwarranted and unfair prosecution and overrode the mandate that it be both informed and independent. An alternative might be to change the rule of criminal procedure so that prosecutors would be obliged to present exculpatory evidence to the grand jury, even if it might result in the issuance of no indictment.[18] Another alternative put forth by defense lawyers is to open the grand jury room to the defense and to hold the government to the same types of constitutional safeguards required to protect defendants that are now used at trial.[19]

The Information Process: The Preliminary Hearing

The purpose of the **preliminary hearing** is to require the prosecutor to present the case so that the judge can determine whether the defendant should be held to answer the charge against him or her in court. Preliminary hearings are used in about half the states as an alternative to the grand jury. Although the purpose of preliminary hearings and grand jury hearings is the same—to establish whether probable cause is sufficient to merit a trial—the procedures differ significantly.

The preliminary hearing is conducted before a magistrate or lower court judge and, unlike the grand jury hearing, is open to the public unless the defendant requests otherwise. Present at the preliminary hearing are the prosecuting attorney, the defendant, and the defendant's counsel, if already retained. The prosecution presents its evidence and witnesses to the judge. The defendant or the defense counsel then has the right to cross-examine witnesses and to challenge the prosecutor's evidence.

After hearing the evidence, the judge decides whether there is sufficient probable cause to believe that the defendant committed the alleged crime. If so, the defendant is bound over for trial, and the prosecuting attorney's information is filed with the trial court, usually within two weeks. The **information** is the charging document that is brought before a lower court judge in the preliminary hearing. If the judge does not find sufficient probable cause, the charges are dismissed, and the defendant is released from custody.

WAIVING THE PRELIMINARY HEARING A unique aspect of the preliminary hearing is the defendant's right to waive the proceeding. In most states, the

exculpatory evidence
All information that is material and favorable to the accused defendant because it casts doubt on the defendant's guilt or on the evidence the government intends to use at trial.

preliminary hearing
Hearing before a magistrate to determine whether the government has sufficient evidence to show probable cause that the defendant committed the crime.

information
A formal charging document, similar to an indictment, based on probable cause as determined at a preliminary hearing.

prosecutor and the judge must agree to this waiver. A waiver has advantages and disadvantages for both the prosecutor and the defendant. In most situations, a prosecutor will agree to a waiver because it avoids the need to reveal evidence to the defense before trial. However, if the state believes it is necessary to obtain a record of witness testimony because of the possibility that a witness or witnesses may be unavailable for the trial or unable to remember the facts clearly, the prosecutor might override the waiver. In this situation, the record of the preliminary hearing can be used at the trial.

The defendant may want to waive the preliminary hearing for one of three reasons: (a) he has already decided to plead guilty, (b) he wants to speed up the criminal justice process, or (c) he hopes to avoid the negative publicity that might result from the hearing. However, the preliminary hearing is of obvious advantage to the defendant who believes that it will result in a dismissal of the charges. In addition, the preliminary hearing gives the defense the opportunity to learn what evidence the prosecution has. Figure 10.4 outlines the significant differences between the grand jury and the preliminary hearing processes.

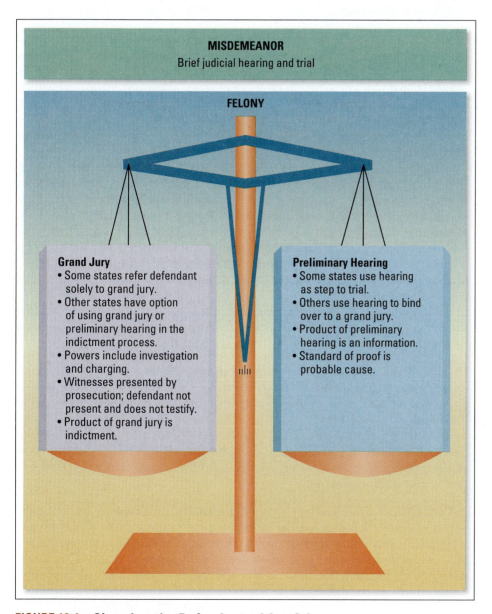

MISDEMEANOR
Brief judicial hearing and trial

FELONY

Grand Jury
- Some states refer defendant solely to grand jury.
- Other states have option of using grand jury or preliminary hearing in the indictment process.
- Powers include investigation and charging.
- Witnesses presented by prosecution; defendant not present and does not testify.
- Product of grand jury is indictment.

Preliminary Hearing
- Some states use hearing as step to trial.
- Others use hearing to bind over to a grand jury.
- Product of preliminary hearing is an information.
- Standard of proof is probable cause.

FIGURE 10.4   Charging the Defendant with a Crime

Arraignment

After an indictment or information is filed following a grand jury or preliminary hearing, an arraignment takes place before the court that will try the case. At the arraignment, the judge informs the defendant of the charges against him or her and appoints counsel if one has not yet been retained. According to the Sixth Amendment, the accused has the right to be informed of the nature and cause of the accusation. Thus, the judge at the arraignment must make sure that the defendant clearly understands the charges.

After the charges are read and explained, the defendant is asked to enter a plea. If a plea of not guilty or not guilty by reason of insanity is entered, a trial date is set. When the defendant pleads guilty or *nolo contendere* (see below), a date for sentencing is arranged. The magistrate then either sets bail or releases the defendant on personal recognizance.

 **LO6** Discuss the purpose of arraignment.

The Plea

Ordinarily, a defendant in a criminal trial will enter one of three pleas: guilty, not guilty, or *nolo contendere*.

GUILTY More than 90 percent of defendants appearing before the courts plead guilty prior to the trial stage. A guilty plea has several consequences. It functions not only as an admission of guilt but also as a surrender of the entire array of constitutional rights designed to protect a criminal defendant against unjustified conviction, including the right to remain silent, the right to confront witnesses against him or her, the right to a trial by jury, and the right to be proved guilty by proof beyond a reasonable doubt. For a guilty plea to be valid, however, it must be both understood[20] and voluntary.[21]

The judge must follow certain procedures when accepting a plea of guilty. First, the judge must clearly state to the defendant the constitutional guarantees automatically waived by this plea. Second, the judge must believe that the facts of the case establish a basis for the plea and that the plea is made voluntarily. Third, the defendant must be informed of the right to counsel during the pleading process. The defendant may be required to allocute or admit in open court to having committed the crime. Finally, the judge must inform the defendant of the possible sentencing outcomes, including the maximum sentence that can be imposed.

After a guilty plea has been entered, a sentencing date is arranged. In a majority of states, a guilty plea may be withdrawn and replaced with a not-guilty plea at any time prior to sentencing if good cause is shown.

NOT GUILTY At the arraignment or before the trial, a not-guilty plea is entered in two ways: (a) it is orally stated by the defendant or the defense counsel, or (b) it is entered for the defendant by the court when the defendant stands mute before the bench.

Once a plea of not guilty is recorded, a trial date is set. In misdemeanor cases, trials take place in the lower court system, whereas felony cases are normally transferred to the superior court. At this time, a continuance or issuance of bail is once again considered.

nolo contendere
A plea of "no contest"—the defendant submits to sentencing without any formal admission of guilt that could be used against him or her in a subsequent civil suit.

NOLO CONTENDERE The plea **nolo contendere** ("no contest") is essentially a plea of guilty. This plea has the same consequences as a guilty plea, with one exception: it may not be held against the defendant as proof in a subsequent civil matter because technically no admission of guilt has been made. This plea is accepted at the discretion of the trial court and must be voluntarily and intelligently made by the defendant.

Plea Bargaining

Plea bargaining is a relatively recent development that took hold late in the nineteenth century. During the first 150 years after the nation's birth, the trial by jury was viewed as the fairest and most reliable method of determining the truth in a criminal matter. Not surprisingly, the Constitution does not mention plea bargaining, nor does the Bill of Rights address the issue. However, by the middle of the nineteenth century, plea negotiations steadily became the dominant method of case disposition in the United States. Today, plea bargaining is one of the most common practices in the criminal justice system and a cornerstone of the informal justice system.[22] Even the Supreme Court has called it an "essential component of the administration of justice."[23]

During this period, criminal case processing came to be seen not primarily as a dispute between two parties that could be resolved through a trial but as a conflict between the state and an individual, controlled by police involvement and prosecutorial discretion. As this change evolved, the court process switched from dispensing individual, carefully considered justice via trials to dispensing mass justice through guilty pleas.[24] At first, judges were reluctant to accept pleas, preferring trials to sharing their power with prosecutors (who make the deal). However, plea bargaining became more attractive at the turn of the twentieth century, when the mechanization of manufacture and transportation prompted a flood of complex civil cases, which persuaded judges that criminal cases had to be settled quickly lest the court system break down.[25] Today, it is estimated that more than 90 percent of criminal convictions result from negotiated pleas of guilty. And, as Table 10.2 shows, most defendants are likely to plead guilty in even the most serious felony cases.

The data show that plea bargains benefit both the prosecution, which is assured of a conviction, and the defendant, who is rewarded with a lenient sentence.[26] For example, people who plead guilty to murder are much less likely to get the death penalty or a life sentence than those who are convicted at trial.

The Nature of the Bargain

Plea bargaining is the exchange of prosecutorial and judicial concessions for pleas of guilty (see Exhibit 10.1). Normally, a bargain can be made between the prosecutor and the defense attorney in four ways: (a) the initial charges may be reduced to those of a lesser offense, thus automatically reducing the sentence imposed; (b) in cases in which many counts are charged, the prosecutor may reduce the number of counts; (c) the prosecutor may promise to recommend a lenient sentence, such as probation; and (d) when the charge imposed has a negative label attached (for example, child molestation), the prosecutor may alter the charge to a more socially acceptable one (such as assault) in exchange for a plea of guilty (see the accompanying Analyzing Criminal Justice Issues box for some interesting exceptions). In a jurisdiction where sentencing disparities exist among judges, the prosecutor may even agree to arrange for a defendant to appear before a lenient judge in exchange for a plea; this practice is known as judge shopping.

Bargains are rarely a one-shot deal and may be negotiated many times as evidence becomes known and the case unfolds.[27] They are negotiated until the defense believes that it has gotten the best deal for its client and the prosecutor believes that, considering the totality of the circumstances, it has been able to dispense a fair amount of punishment. The defense attorney conducts the bargain as a form of negotiation, putting forth information that will convince the prosecutor that the case is very strong and the chances of an acquittal are quite high. If the defense attorney can magnify the strength of her case, the chances of a favorable plea outcome increase.

TABLE 10.2   Adjudication Outcome for Felony Defendants in the 75 Largest Counties, by Most Serious Arrest Charge

Most serious arrest charge	Number of defendants	Total convicted	CONVICTED FELONY			CONVICTED MISDEMEANOR			NOT CONVICTED			
			Total	Plea	Trial	Total	Plea	Trial	Total	Dismissed	Acquitted	Other outcome*
All offenses	48,939	66%	54%	53%	2%	12%	11%	—%	26%	25%	1%	9%
Violent offenses	11,601	61%	49%	46%	3%	13%	12%	1%	33%	31%	2%	6%
Murder	217	70	70	51	18	0	0	0	28	17	12	2
Rape	412	68	57	50	7	11	10	1	27	24	3	5
Robbery	3,217	66	59	57	2	7	7	—	29	28	1	5
Assault	5,484	56	39	37	2	16	15	1	37	35	2	7
Other violent	2,271	67	54	51	3	13	13	—	28	27	1	5
Property offenses	14,314	67%	55%	53%	2%	12%	12%	—%	24%	23%	—%	9%
Burglary	4,325	68	60	59	1	9	8	—	23	22	1	9
Larceny/theft	4,088	66	51	49	2	15	15	—	25	24	—	10
Motor vehicle theft	1,324	67	62	60	2	6	5	—	26	25	0	7
Forgery	1,281	71	57	55	1	15	14	—	20	19	1	10
Fraud	1,587	64	53	51	1	13	12	—	21	20	—	14
Other property	1,709	67	47	45	2	20	20	0	29	29	0	3
Drug offenses	16,456	66%	56%	56%	1%	9%	9%	—%	24%	23%	—%	11%
Trafficking	7,232	73	62	61	1	11	10	1	19	18	—	8
Other drug	9,224	60	52	51	—	8	8	—	27	27	—	13
Public-order offenses	6,568	73%	58%	57%	2%	14%	14%	—%	22%	21%	1%	6%
Weapons	1,798	67	57	57	1	9	9	—	27	26	1	6
Driving-related	2,063	84	69	67	2	15	15	0	10	10	0	6
Other public-order	2,708	68	51	49	2	17	16	—	27	27	—	5

Note: Table excludes cases that were still pending adjudication at the end of the one-year study period. Data on adjudication outcome were available for 99.9 percent of cases that had been adjudicated. Detail may not sum to total due to rounding.

—Less than 0.5%.

*Includes diversion and deferred adjudication. Murder cases were tracked for up to 2 years.

Source: Brian A. Reeves, *Felony Defendants in Large Urban Counties, 2009* (Washington, DC: Bureau of Justice Statistics, 2013), p. 24.

EXHIBIT 10.1   To Plea or Not to Plea?

Although nearly all cases are settled with a plea, a few proceed to a full-blown trial. What factors influence the decision "to plea or not to plea"?

- Court-appointed lawyers may want to gain trial experience. They convince their clients not to accept favorable bargains, fearing that the case will be settled out of court and they will lose the opportunity to try the case.

- Both the prosecution and the defense may be overly optimistic about their skills.

- The lawyers' overconfidence in their abilities may cloud their judgment, causing them either to refuse to offer a bargain (in the case of the prosecution) or to refuse to accept (in the case of the defense).

- Some defendants falsely assume that they are so charismatic and appealing that a jury will never reach a conviction.

Source: Stephanos Bibas, "Plea Bargaining Outside the Shadow of Trial," *Harvard Law Review* 117 (2004): 2464–2543.

analyzing criminal justice ISSUES

STRANGE PLEA AGREEMENTS

The typical plea agreement results in a reduced charge or a favorable sentencing recommendation by the prosecutor, but some agreements can only be described as strange, or at least outside the box. What follows are some examples identified by law professor and former judge Joseph Colquitt. In exchange for leniency, the defendant agrees to

- Make a charitable contribution
- Relinquish property ownership
- Surrender a professional license
- Undergo sterilization
- Undergo surgical castration
- Enter the military
- Not pursue appeals
- Undertake a shaming punishment, such as carrying a sign that says "I stole from this store"
- Seal the records of a case
- Surrender profits from crime, such as from books written about the crime
- Be banished to another location

These are examples of what Colquitt calls "ad hoc plea bargaining." In his view, ad hoc plea bargaining takes these forms:

(1) the court may impose an extraordinary condition of probation following a guilty plea, (2) the defendant may offer or be required to perform some act as a quid pro quo for a dismissal or more lenient sentence, (3) the court may impose an unauthorized form of punishment as a substitute for a statutorily established method of punishment, (4) the state may offer some unauthorized benefit in return for a plea of guilty, or (5) the defendant may be permitted to plead guilty to an unauthorized offense, such as a "hypothetical" or nonexistent charge, a nonapplicable lesser-included offense, or a nonrelated charge.

Ad hoc plea bargaining is controversial not just because it is unusual. In some cases it can border on unethical. In one case, the prosecutor offered leniency to a drug defendant if he would surrender several thousand dollars in cash that was found during a search of his property. In another case, a defendant was afforded leniency for agreeing to forfeit interest in his vehicle.

CRITICAL THINKING

1. Are ad hoc plea bargains reasonable? Are they fair?

2. What if the tables were turned and, say, a speeding motorist offered $100 to the officer who stopped her in exchange for leniency? What would happen then?

Sources: Joseph A. Colquitt, "Ad Hoc Plea Bargaining," *Tulane Law Review* 75 (2001): 695–776; Timothy Lynch, *The Case Against Plea Bargaining*, http://www.cato.org/pubs/regulation/regv26n3/v26n3-7.pdf (accessed July 2014).

Pros and Cons of Plea Bargaining

Because of excessive criminal court caseloads and the personal and professional needs of the prosecution and the defense (to reach disposition of the case in the least possible time), plea bargaining has become an essential yet controversial part of the administration of justice. Proponents contend that plea bargaining actually benefits both the state and the defendant in the following ways:

- The overall costs of the criminal prosecution are reduced.
- The administrative efficiency of the courts is greatly improved.
- The prosecution can devote more time to more serious cases.
- The defendant avoids possible detention and an extended trial and may receive a reduced sentence.
- Resources can be devoted more efficiently to cases that need greater attention.[28]

LO7 Discuss the pros and cons of plea bargaining.

Those who favor plea bargaining believe it is appropriate to enter into plea discussions when the interests of the state in the effective administration of justice will be served.

Opponents of the plea bargaining process believe that the negotiated plea should be eliminated for the following reasons:

- It encourages defendants to waive their constitutional right to trial.
- Plea bargains allow dangerous offenders to receive lenient sentences. Jesse Timmendequas, a previously convicted sex offender, was given a 10-year plea-bargained sentence for child rape. Upon his release, he raped and killed 7-year-old Megan Kanka in one of the nation's most notorious crimes.[29]
- Plea bargaining also raises the danger that an innocent person will be convicted of a crime if he or she is convinced that the lighter treatment ensured by a guilty plea is preferable to the risk of conviction and a harsher sentence following a formal trial.
- Prosecutors are given a free hand to induce or compel defendants to plea bargain, thus circumventing law.[30]
- It is possible that innocent persons will admit guilt if they believe that the system is biased and that they have little chance of being acquitted.
- A guilty-plea culture has developed among defense lawyers. Elements of this attitude include the belief that most of their clients are dishonest people who committed the crime with which they have been charged and that getting a "sentence discount" for them is the best and only way to go.[31]

Despite these issues, it is unlikely that plea negotiations will be eliminated or severely curtailed in the near future. Supporters of the total abolition of plea bargaining are in the minority. As a result of abuses, however, efforts are being made to improve plea bargaining operations. Such reforms include development of uniform plea practices, representation of counsel during plea negotiations, and establishment of time limits on plea negotiations.

The Problem of False Confessions

It is certainly not desirable to have an otherwise innocent offender plead guilty to a crime he or she did not commit, simply to avoid the possibility of being found guilty at trial. Unfortunately, some defendants conclude they will be better off by just admitting to the crime, even if they had nothing at all to do with it. Why take the chance of spending, say, 20 years in prison when they could be home in four? This is the problem of false confessions. How big a problem is it? Researchers have recently found that in approximately 25 percent of the cases where DNA testing resulted in a conviction being overturned, false confessions were given.[32] The testing is providing a window into the world of false confessions, revealing that the problem is perhaps more serious than anyone ever thought.

Why do innocent people confess? According to the Innocence Project, there are several reasons, including:

- Duress
- Coercion
- Intoxication
- Diminished capacity
- Mental impairment
- Ignorance of the law
- Fear of violence
- The actual infliction of harm
- The threat of a harsh sentence
- Misunderstanding the situation[33]

Chicago Tribune/Getty Images

Donny McGee is welcomed home by his children in Bourbonnais, Illinois, following a successful civil lawsuit against the Chicago Police Department. McGee was arrested for murder in 2001 after a police officer and a detective fabricated a polygraph result and false confession and spent three years in prison before being acquitted in a jury trial in 2004. The jury in McGee's civil case awarded him $1.3 million.

Legal Issues in Plea Bargaining

The U.S. Supreme Court has reviewed the propriety of plea bargaining in several decisions and, while imposing limits on the practice, has upheld its continued use. The Court has ruled in several key cases that:

- Defendants are entitled to the effective assistance of counsel to protect them from pressure and influence.[34]

- Pleas must be made voluntarily and without pressure. However, a prosecutor can tell defendants that they may be facing the death penalty if they go to trial.[35]

- Any promise made by the prosecutor during the plea negotiations must be kept after the defendant admits guilt in open court. A prosecutor who promises leniency in private negotiations must stick to that position in court.[36]

- Defendants must also keep their side of the bargain to receive the promised offer of leniency.[37] If they agree to testify against a co-defendant, they must give evidence at trial or forfeit the bargain.

- A defendant's due process rights are not violated when a prosecutor threatens to reindict the accused on more serious charges—for example, as a habitual offender—if the defendant does not plead guilty to a lesser offense.[38]

- Accepting a guilty plea from a defendant who maintains his or her innocence is valid.[39]

- Statements made during a plea bargain may be used under some circumstances at trial if the negotiations break down. Statements made during a plea negotiation can be used if the defendant (a) admits to a crime during the bargaining process but later testifies in open court that he or she (b) did not do the act and (c) is innocent of the charges.[40]

- Flawed advice from a defense attorney that leads to rejection of a plea deal can form the basis of an ineffective assistance of counsel claim.[41]

- Defense counsel must inform the defendant of any and all plea offers that contain favorable terms and conditions.[42]

The Role of the Prosecutor in Plea Bargaining

The prosecutor in the U.S. system of criminal justice has broad discretion in the exercise of his responsibilities. Such discretion includes deciding whether to initiate a criminal prosecution, determining the nature and number of the criminal charges, and choosing whether to plea bargain a case and under what conditions. Plea bargaining is one of the major tools the prosecutor uses to control and influence the criminal justice system (the other two are the decision to initiate a charge and the ability to take the case to trial).

Few states have placed limits on the discretion of prosecutors in plea bargaining situations. Instead, in making a plea bargaining decision, the prosecutor is generally free to weigh competing alternatives and factors, such as the seriousness of the crime, the attitude of the victim, the police report of the incident, and applicable sentencing provisions. Such factors as the offense, the defendant's prior record and age, and the type, strength, and admissibility of evidence are considered important in the plea bargaining decision.[43] The attitude of the complainant is also an important factor in the decision-making process. For example, in victimless cases, such as heroin possession, the police attitude is most often considered, whereas in victim-related crimes, such as rape, the attitude of the victim is a primary concern. Prosecutors in low-population or rural jurisdictions not only use more information when making their decisions but also seem more likely than their urban counterparts to accept plea bargains, a finding that suggests that case pressure alone is not the incentive for most plea bargains.[44]

Plea bargaining frequently occurs in cases in which the government believes the evidence is weak, such as when a key witness seems unreliable or unwilling to testify. Bargaining permits a compromise settlement in a weak case when the outcome of a criminal trial is in doubt.

Some jurisdictions have established guidelines to provide consistency in plea bargaining cases. They may require the district attorney to define the kinds and types of cases and offenders that may be suitable for plea bargaining. In other jurisdictions, approval to plea bargain may be required. Other controls might include procedures for internally reviewing decisions by the chief prosecutor and the use of written memoranda to document the need for and acceptability of a plea bargain in a given case. In some cases, pleas may be offered on a "take it or leave it" basis. In each case, a special prosecutor, whose job it is to screen cases, sets the bargaining terms. If the defense counsel cannot accept the agreement, there is no negotiation, and the case must go to trial. Only if complications arise in the case, such as witnesses changing their testimony, can negotiations be reopened.[45]

The Role of the Defense Counsel in Plea Bargaining

Both the U.S. Supreme Court and such organizations as the American Bar Association have established guidelines for the court receiving a guilty plea and for the defense counsel representing the accused in plea negotiations.[46] No court should accept a guilty plea unless the defendant has been properly advised by counsel and the court has determined that the plea is voluntary and has a factual basis. The court has the discretion to reject a plea if it is inappropriately offered.

The defense counsel—a public defender or a private attorney—is required to play an advisory role in plea negotiations. The defendant's counsel is expected to be aware of the facts of the case and of the law and to advise the defendant of the available alternatives. The defense attorney is basically responsible for making certain that the accused understands the nature of the plea bargaining process and the guilty plea. This means that the defense counsel should explain to the defendant that, by pleading guilty, she is waiving certain rights that would be available if the case went to trial. In addition, the defense attorney has the duty to keep the defendant informed of developments and discussions with the prosecutor regarding plea bargaining. While doing so, the attorney for the accused cannot misrepresent evidence or mislead the client into making a detrimental agreement. The defense counsel is not only ethically but also constitutionally required to communicate all plea bargaining offers to a client, even if counsel believes the offers to be unacceptable.[47]

In reality, most plea negotiations occur in the chambers of the judge, in the prosecutor's office, or in the courthouse hallway. Under these conditions, it is often difficult to assess the actual roles played by the prosecutor and the defense attorney. Even so, it is fundamental that a defendant not be required to plead guilty until advised by counsel and that a guilty plea should not be made unless it is done with the consent of the accused.

L08 Explain the role of the prosecutor, defense attorney, judge, and victim in the plea negotiation.

The Role of the Judge in Plea Bargaining

One of the most confusing issues in the plea bargaining process has been the proper role of the judge. Should the judge act only in a supervisory capacity or actually enter into the negotiation process? The leading national legal organization, the American Bar Association (ABA), is opposed to judicial participation in plea negotiations.[48] According to ABA standards, judges should not be a party to arrangements for the determination of a sentence, whether as a result of a guilty plea or a finding of guilty based on proof. The perception is that judicial participation in plea negotiations (a) creates the impression in the mind of defendants that they cannot receive a fair trial, (b) lessens the ability of the judge to make an objective determination of the voluntary nature of the plea, (c) is inconsistent with the theory behind the use of presentence investigation reports, and (d) may induce innocent defendants to plead guilty because they are afraid to reject the disposition desired by the judge.[49] To avoid these potential problems, judges generally limit their role to approval or disapproval of the plea agreement.

The Victim and Plea Bargaining

What role should victims play in plea bargaining? Crime victims are not empowered at the pretrial stage of the criminal process and thus do not play a role in the plea negotiations. Statutes do not require that the prosecutor defer to the victim's wishes, and there are no legal consequences for ignoring the victim in a plea bargaining decision. Even the ABA's *Model Uniform Victims of Crime Act* suggests only that the prosecutor "confer" with the victim.[50] Nonetheless, many prosecutors do confer with crime victims, and some supporters of the victims' rights movements have called for more extensive victim involvement in plea bargaining.[51] Some critics, however, have suggested that the system today is *too* victim-driven—that is, in too many cases prosecutors seek approval for the plea from a victim or family member.

Plea Bargaining Reform

In recent years, efforts have been made to convert plea bargaining into a more visible, understandable, and fair dispositional process. Many jurisdictions have developed safeguards and guidelines to prevent violations of due process and to ensure that innocent defendants do not plead guilty under coercion. Such safeguards include the following:

1. The judge questions the defendant about the facts of the guilty plea before accepting the plea.
2. The defense counsel is present and can advise the defendant of her rights.
3. The prosecutor and the defense attorney openly discuss the plea.
4. Full and frank information about the defendant and the offenses is made available at this stage of the process. In addition, judicial supervision ensures that plea bargaining is conducted in a fair manner.

What would happen if plea bargaining were banned outright, as its critics advocate? Numerous jurisdictions throughout the United States have experimented with bans on plea bargaining. In 1975, Alaska eliminated the practice. Honolulu, Hawaii, has also attempted to abolish plea bargaining. Other jurisdictions, including Arizona, Delaware, the District of Columbia, and Iowa, have sought to limit the use of plea bargaining.[52] In theory, eliminating plea bargains means that prosecutors in these jurisdictions give no consideration or concessions to a defendant in exchange for a guilty plea.

In reality, however, in these and most jurisdictions, sentence-related concessions, charge-reduction concessions, and alternative methods for prosecution continue to be used in one fashion or another.[53] When plea bargaining is limited or abolished, the number of trials may increase, the sentence severity may change, and more questions regarding the right to a speedy trial may arise. Discretion may also be shifted further up the system. Instead of spending countless hours preparing for and conducting a trial, prosecutors may dismiss more cases outright or decide not to prosecute them after initial action has been taken. Candace McCoy's study of plea reform in California investigated legislative efforts to eliminate the state's plea bargaining process. Instead of achieving a ban on plea bargaining, the process shifted from the superior to the municipal courts. McCoy found that the majority of defendants pleaded guilty after some negotiations and that the new law accelerated the guilty-plea process. McCoy suggests an alternative model of plea bargaining reform that includes emphasizing public scrutiny of plea bargaining, adhering to standards of professionalism, and making a greater commitment to due process procedures.[54] Other researchers have found that plea bargaining can be influenced by state sentencing arrangements. There tends to be less bargaining in states that limit judges' sentencing discretion.[55]

Pretrial Diversion

Another important feature of the early court process is placing offenders into noncriminal diversion programs before their formal trial or conviction. Pretrial diversion programs were first established in the late 1960s and early 1970s, when it became apparent that a viable alternative to the highly stigmatized criminal sentence was needed. In diversion programs, formal criminal proceedings against an accused are suspended while that person participates in a community treatment program under court supervision. Diversion helps the offender avoid the stigma of a criminal conviction and enables the justice system to reduce costs and alleviate prison overcrowding.

Many diversion programs exist throughout the United States. These programs vary in size and emphasis but generally pursue the same goal: to constructively bypass criminal prosecution by providing a reasonable alternative in the form of treatment, counseling, or employment programs.

The prosecutor often plays the central role in the diversion process. Decisions about nondispositional alternatives are based on the nature of the crime, special characteristics of the offender, whether the defendant is a first-time offender, whether the defendant will cooperate with a diversion program, the impact of diversion on the community, and consideration for the opinion of the victim.[56]

Some diversion programs are separate, independent agencies that were originally set up with federal funds but are now being continued with county or state assistance. Others are organized as part of a police, prosecutor, or probation department's internal structure. Still others are a joint venture between the county government and a private, nonprofit organization that carries out the treatment process.

First viewed as a panacea that could reduce court congestion and help treat minor offenders, diversion programs have come under fire for their alleged

Drug courts are often active in the diversion process. In Austin, Texas, a judge presides over the weekly meeting of the Drug Diversion Court, a yearlong program for defendants who have been arrested for felony possession of a controlled substance. The program relies on frequent drug screening, offers classes and treatment referrals, and can result in dismissal of charges if the defendant completes the program successfully.

failures. Some national evaluations have concluded that diversion programs are no more successful at avoiding stigma and reducing recidivism than traditional justice processing.[57] The most prominent criticism is that they help *widen the net* of the justice system. By this, critics mean that the people placed in diversion programs are the ones most likely to have otherwise been dismissed after a brief hearing with a warning or small fine.[58] Instead of limiting contact with the system, the diversion programs increase it. Not all justice experts agree with this charge, and some have championed diversion as a worthwhile exercise of the criminal justice system's rehabilitation responsibility. Although diversion may not be a cure-all for criminal behavior, it is an important effort that continues to be made in most jurisdictions across the United States. Even if diversion programs were no more successful than traditional court processing, they are certainly less expensive to operate and help reduce court crowding and trial delays.[59]

The Trial

The criminal trial is an open and public hearing designed to examine the facts of the case brought by the state against the accused. Criminal trials are relatively rare events (most cases are settled by a plea bargain during the pretrial stage), but they are an important and enduring fixture in the criminal justice system. By its very nature, the criminal trial is a symbol of the moral authority of the state. It symbolizes the administration of objective and impartial justice. Regardless of the issues involved, the defendant's presence in a courtroom is designed to guarantee that she will have a hearing conducted under rules of procedure in an atmosphere of fair play and objectivity and that the outcome of the hearing will be clear and definitive. If the defendant believes that her constitutional rights and privileges have been violated, she may appeal the case to a higher court, where the procedures of the original trial will be examined. If, after examining the trial transcript, the appellate court rules that the original trial employed improper and unconstitutional procedures, it may order that a new hearing be held or even that the charges against the defendant be dismissed.

Most formal trials are heard by a jury, although some defendants waive their constitutional right to a jury trial and request a **bench trial**, in which the judge

bench trial
The trial of a criminal matter by a judge only. The accused waives any constitutional right to a jury trial.

verdict

The finding of a jury or a judge on questions of fact at a trial.

adjudication

The determination of guilt or innocence—a judgment concerning criminal charges.

 LO9   Explain the legal rights of the accused at trial.

alone renders a **verdict**. In this situation, which occurs daily in the lower criminal courts, the judge may initiate a number of formal or informal dispositions, including dismissing the case, finding the defendant not guilty, finding the defendant guilty and imposing a sentence, or even continuing the case indefinitely. The decision the judge makes often depends on the seriousness of the offense, the background and previous record of the defendant, and the judgment of the court about whether the case can be properly dealt with in the criminal process. The judge may simply continue the case without a finding, in which case the verdict is withheld without a finding of guilt to induce the accused to improve her behavior in the community; if the defendant's behavior does improve, the case is ordinarily closed within a specific amount of time.

This section reviews some of the institutions and processes involved in **adjudication** and trial. We begin with a discussion of the legal rights that structure the trial process.

Legal Rights During Trial

Underlying every trial are constitutional principles, complex legal procedures, rules of court, and interpretations of statutes—all designed to ensure that the accused will receive a fair trial.

THE RIGHT TO AN IMPARTIAL JUDGE Even though the Constitution does not say so, every criminal defendant enjoys the right to a trial by an impartial judge. The Supreme Court ruled as much way back in the 1927 case of *Tumey v. Ohio*.[60] In that case, a municipal court judge was also the mayor, an executive official. What's more, he received fines and fees that he ordered against defendants who were convicted in his courtroom. The Supreme Court held that it is a violation of due process when a judge "has a direct, personal, substantial pecuniary interest in reaching a conclusion against [a defendant] in his case."[61]

What if a judge is not impartial? How can such a judge be removed? Generally, the judge will excuse himself or herself if there is a conflict of interest. Judicial codes of ethics provide the guidelines judges need to make such decisions. Some jurisdictions, however, permit peremptory removal of judges.[62] These are like the peremptory challenges used in jury selection (covered later in this chapter). When this occurs, one of the attorneys can move to have the judge removed, and another judge will come on board. Usually the peremptory removal can occur only once.

THE RIGHT TO BE COMPETENT AT TRIAL To stand trial, a criminal defendant must be considered mentally competent to understand the nature and extent of the legal proceedings. If a defendant is considered mentally incompetent, his trial must be postponed until treatment renders him capable of participating in his own defense.

Can state authorities force a mentally unfit defendant to be treated so that he can be tried? In *Riggins v. Nevada* (1992), the U.S. Supreme Court ruled that forced treatment does not violate a defendant's due process rights if it is medically appropriate and, considering less intrusive alternatives, is essential for the defendant's own safety or the safety of others.[63]

THE RIGHT TO CONFRONT WITNESSES The Sixth Amendment states that "In all criminal prosecutions, the accused shall enjoy the right ... to be confronted with the witnesses against him." The accused enjoys this right not just by being able to confront witnesses in person but also by being allowed to participate in his or her trial. That is, trials cannot be conducted without the accused being afforded the right to appear in person.

The right to confrontation is also violated if out-of-court testimony is used to convict the accused. In *Crawford v. Washington*,[64] the Supreme Court held that it was unconstitutional for a trial court to introduce the defendant's wife's prerecorded statement to police about the stabbing the defendant was accused of. Why? Because he could not cross-examine a video. The Court recently extended this decision to state forensic analyst laboratory reports; such reports are now considered testimonial, meaning the defendant should be allowed to confront and question the analyst at trial.[65] This was a very significant decision because, according to the dissenters, it dispensed with a long-standing rule that scientific evidence could be admitted at trial without the need to require the testimony of the analyst who produced it.

This right can be waived or forfeited through misconduct. The accused may choose not to show up,[66] which is constitutionally permissible, and he or she may forfeit the right to appear by causing significant disruption or distraction in the courtroom.[67] There are also some exceptions, such as in child abuse cases, where it is felt that child victims would suffer irreparable harm by being forced to appear before their abusers.[68] Recently, the Supreme Court decided that if a witness is made unavailable because of the defendant (if, for example, the defendant killed the witness), the confrontation clause will not be violated if that witness cannot appear at trial.[69]

The **confrontation clause** is essential to a fair criminal trial because it restricts and controls the admissibility of **hearsay evidence**. Hearsay evidence is akin to secondhand evidence; rather than being told firsthand, it consists of information related by a second party (it is what one person hears and then says—hence the term "hearsay"). The framers of the Constitution envisioned face-to-face accusations in which the defendant has a right to see and cross-examine all witnesses. The idea that it is always more difficult to tell lies about people to their face than behind their back is the foundation of the confrontation clause.

THE RIGHT TO COMPULSORY PROCESS The Sixth Amendment says, in part, that the accused shall "have compulsory process for obtaining witnesses in his favor." **Compulsory process** means to compel the production of witnesses via a subpoena. A subpoena is an order requiring a witness to appear in court at a specified time and place. The Supreme Court decided that compulsory process is a fundamental right in the case of *Washington v. Texas* (1967).[70]

THE RIGHT TO AN IMPARTIAL JURY It is no accident that of all the rights guaranteed to the people by the Constitution, only the right to a jury trial in criminal cases appears in both the original Constitution (Article III, Section 2) and the Bill of Rights (the Sixth Amendment). Although they may have disagreed on many points, the framers did not question the wisdom of the jury trial.

Today, the criminal defendant has the right to choose whether the trial will be before a judge or a jury. Although the Sixth Amendment guarantees the defendant the right to a jury trial, the defendant can and often does waive this right. A substantial proportion of defendants, particularly those charged with misdemeanors, are tried before the court without a jury.

The major legal issue surrounding jury trial has been whether all defendants—those accused of misdemeanors as well as those accused of felonies—have an absolute right to a jury trial. Although the Constitution says that the right to a jury trial exists in "*all criminal prosecutions*," the U.S. Supreme Court has restricted this right. In *Baldwin v. New York* (1970), the Supreme Court decided that a defendant has a constitutional right to a jury trial when facing a possible prison sentence of six months or more, regardless of whether the crime committed was a felony or a misdemeanor.[71] When the possible sentence is six months or less, the accused is not entitled to a jury trial unless it is authorized by state statute. In most jurisdictions, the more serious the charge, the greater likelihood of trial—and of a trial by jury.

confrontation clause
The constitutional right of a criminal defendant to see and cross-examine all the witnesses against him or her.

hearsay evidence
Testimony that is not firsthand but, rather, relates information told by a second party.

compulsory process
Compelling the production of a witness or evidence via a subpoena.

THE RIGHT TO COUNSEL AT TRIAL The right to counsel applies all throughout the criminal process. We said in Chapter 8's discussion of *Miranda v. Arizona* that criminal suspects enjoy the right to counsel during custodial interrogations. The Supreme Court has recently decided that a defendant's very first appearance before a judge also triggers the right to counsel.[72] Our focus in this section, however, is on the right to counsel at trial.

In 1932, the Supreme Court decided in *Powell v. Alabama* that indigent defendants enjoy the right to counsel.[73] The Court limited its decision, however, to "capital case[s], where the defendant is unable to employ counsel, and is incapable adequately of making his own defense because of ignorance, feeble-mindedness, illiteracy, or the like."[74] *In Johnson v. Zerbst*,[75] decided a few years later, the Supreme Court extended the right to counsel to all federal prosecutions. Then, in the 1963 case *Gideon v. Wainwright*,[76] the Court applied the Sixth Amendment right to counsel to the states, meaning that all criminal defendants in felony cases (even the indigent) benefit from it.

Today, state courts must provide counsel at trial to indigent defendants who face even the possibility of incarceration—and who are charged with any type of crime, not just a felony.[91] The threat of incarceration need not be immediate. Even if the defendant might be sentenced to probation in which a prison or jail term is suspended, or might receive any other type of sentence containing a threat of future incarceration, he is afforded the right to counsel at trial.[92] For a detailed treatment of exactly how and when the right to counsel applies, see the accompanying "Evolution of *Gideon v. Wainwright*" feature. It traces the evolution of right-to-counsel cases since 1963.

What if a defendant wants to serve as his or her own attorney? As a result of a 1975 Supreme Court decision, defendants are now permitted to proceed *pro se*, or for themselves.[93] When defendants ask to be permitted to represent

The Evolution of *Gideon v. Wainwright*

***Gideon v. Wainwright* (1963)** Indigent felony defendants enjoy the Sixth Amendment right to counsel. The Sixth Amendment right to counsel is fundamental, meaning the states must recognize it.[77]

***Douglas v. California* (1963)** The Fourteenth Amendment guarantees the defendant the right to counsel during his or her first mandatory appeal.[78]

***In re Gault* (1967)** Juveniles enjoy the right to counsel in adjudicatory hearings.[79]

***Coleman v. Alabama* (1970)** The preliminary hearing is a "critical stage," meaning that the defendant enjoys the right to counsel at it.[80]

***Argersinger v. Hamlin* (1972)** The Sixth Amendment right to counsel extends to those accused of committing misdemeanors.[81]

***Morrissey v. Brewer* (1972)** There is no right to counsel in parole revocation hearings.[82]

***Gagnon v. Scarpelli* (1973)** There is no right to counsel in probation revocation hearings.[83]

***Ross v. Moffitt* (1974)** There is no right to counsel provided for the second, discretionary appeal.[84]

***Scott v. Illinois* (1979)** If there is no possibility of confinement, the Sixth Amendment right to counsel does not apply.[85]

***Morris v. Slappy* (1983)** The Sixth Amendment does not require a "meaningful" relationship between the defendant and his or her attorney.[86]

***Wheat v. United States* (1988)** A trial court can deny the defendant's choice of counsel if the attorney's representation carries with it the strong possibility of a conflict of interest.[87]

***United States v. Monsanto* (1989)** It is not unconstitutional for a court to seize a defendant's assets such that it forces him or her to rely on a public defender.[88]

***United States v. Gonzalez-Lopez* (2006)** A convicted defendant has the automatic right to a new trial when a trial judge mistakenly refuses to allow the defendant's paid attorney to represent him.[89]

***Rothgery v. Gillespie County* (2008)** The right to counsel attaches at the initial appearance, shortly after arrest.[90]

themselves, the court normally approves their requests. However, these defendants are nearly always cautioned by the court against self-representation. When *pro se* defendants' actions are disorderly and disruptive, the court can terminate their right to represent themselves. Also, the state can require representation for those defendants who cannot, because of mental incompetency, effectively represent themselves.[94]

THE RIGHT TO A SPEEDY TRIAL The tactics employed by wary defense attorneys (pretrial motions, complex plea negotiations, delay tactics during trial), along with inefficiencies in the court process (such as the frequent granting of continuances, poor scheduling procedures, and the abuse of time by court personnel), have made delay in criminal cases a serious and constitutional issue. As the American Bar Association states in the *Standards Relating to Speedy Trial*, "Congestion in the trial courts of this country, particularly in urban centers, is currently one of the major problems of judicial administration."[95] Delays in the trial process conflict with the Sixth Amendment's guarantee of a right to a speedy trial.[96]

The Supreme Court has called the right to a speedy trial "as fundamental as any of the rights secured by the Sixth Amendment."[97] Its primary purposes are to:

■ Improve the credibility of the trial by having witnesses available for testimony as early as possible

■ Help criminal defendants avoid lengthy pretrial detention

■ Avoid extensive pretrial publicity and questionable conduct of public officials that may influence the defendant's right to a fair trial

■ Avoid any delay that could affect the defendant's ability to defend himself or herself against charges

There is no set time that defines a speedy trial. In *Doggett v. United States*, the Court found that a delay of eight and a half years between indictment and arrest was prejudicial to the defendant and required dismissal of the charges against the defendant.[98] But this is an extreme case. Typically, when a defendant invokes the speedy-trial clause, the appellate court will evaluate the length of delay, the reason for the delay, when the defendant made the claim, and what damage the delay caused. If the prosecution deliberately slows the case down, that may have a greater effect on the appeal process than if the case was delayed because a witness could not be located. And if the defendant agreed to the delay or caused the delay, the speedy-trial right may be lost.

THE RIGHT TO A PUBLIC TRIAL The Sixth Amendment refers to a "public trial." This simply means that all trials must be open to the public. The right to a public trial is generally unrestricted. Anyone who wants to see a criminal trial can do so.

Sometimes having a trial open to the public can cause problems. In the 1966 case of *Sheppard v. Maxwell*, the courtroom was packed with people, including members of the media, for all nine weeks of the trial. Reporters handled evidence and took pictures throughout the trial. The Supreme Court eventually reversed the defendant's conviction, citing the "carnival atmosphere."[99] The case did not lead to the exclusion of cameras from the courtroom, but some judges require that they be kept out. This is why one sometimes sees sketches of a case instead of actual photos.

Adverse pretrial publicity can prevent a defendant from getting a fair trial. The release of premature evidence by the prosecutor, extensive and critical reporting by the news media, and vivid and uncalled-for details in indictments can all prejudice a defendant's case. Press coverage can begin early in a criminal

Judge Susan Criss of the Texas District Court in Galveston discovered on Facebook that a lawyer who had requested a trial delay because of a death was drinking, not grieving, after the funeral.

Scott Dalton/*New York Times*/Redux

case and can even affect the outcome. Judges involved in newsworthy criminal cases have attempted to place restraints on pretrial media coverage to preserve the defendant's right to a fair trial. The Supreme Court has shaped pretrial publicity in several significant cases.[100]

As a general rule, pretrial publicity and reporting cannot be controlled. However, judges may bar the press from some pretrial legal proceedings and hearings, such as preliminary hearings, when police officers make an arrest, or when a warrant is being served, if their presence will infringe on the defendant's right to a fair trial.[101] Other steps can be taken as well. These include changes of venue (moving the trial to another jurisdiction, where there is less press coverage and hence less contamination of the pool of potential jurors) and gag orders (restrictions on what the parties or the media can report), among others.

What about press coverage *during* trial? In the landmark case *Richmond Newspapers, Inc. v. Virginia* (1980), the Supreme Court clearly established that criminal trials must remain open to the press.[102] The Court extended the right of the press to attend trials involving even highly sensitive, sexually related matters in which the victim is under 18 years of age.[103]

More recently, the issue of press coverage has focused on bringing TV cameras into the courtroom. Because of the public interest in high-profile criminal cases, whether jury trials should be televised is one of the most controversial questions in the criminal justice system. The legal community is divided over the use of TV cameras in the courtroom. Today, many state courts permit such coverage, often at the judge's discretion, but federal courts prohibit TV coverage altogether. In 1981, the U.S. Supreme Court in *Chandler v. Florida* removed any constitutional obstacles to the use of electronic media coverage and still photography of public criminal proceedings, over the objections of a criminal defendant.[104] Certainly, the defendant has a constitutional right to a public trial, but it is equally imperative that the media be allowed to exercise their **First Amendment** rights, which include making that public trial truly public.

THE RIGHT TO BE CONVICTED BY PROOF BEYOND A REASONABLE DOUBT The standard required to convict a defendant charged with a crime at the adjudicatory stage of the criminal process is **proof beyond a reasonable doubt**. This requirement dates back to early American history and over the years

First Amendment
The amendment to the U.S. Constitution that guarantees freedom of speech, religion, press, and assembly, and the right of the people to petition the government for redress of grievances.

proof beyond a reasonable doubt
The standard of proof needed to convict in a criminal case. The evidence offered in court does not have to amount to absolute certainty, but it should leave no reasonable doubt that the defendant committed the alleged crime.

has become the accepted measure of persuasion by which the prosecutor must convince the judge or jury of the defendant's guilt. Many twentieth-century U.S. Supreme Court decisions have reinforced this standard by making "beyond a reasonable doubt a due process and constitutional requirement."[105]

The reasonable-doubt standard is an essential ingredient of the criminal justice process. It is the prime instrument for reducing the risk of convictions based on factual errors.[106] The underlying premise of this standard is that it is better to release a guilty person than to convict someone who is innocent. Because the defendant is presumed innocent until proved guilty, this standard forces the prosecution to overcome this presumption with the highest standard of proof. Unlike the civil law, where a mere **preponderance of the evidence** is the standard, the criminal process requires proof beyond a reasonable doubt for each element of the offense.[107] The various evidentiary standards of proof are analyzed and compared in Exhibit 10.2.

preponderance of the evidence
The level of proof in civil cases; more than half the evidence supports the allegations of one side.

The Trial Process

The trial of a criminal case is a formal process conducted in a specific and orderly fashion in accordance with rules of criminal law, procedure, and evidence. Unlike what transpires in popular TV programs involving lawyers—where witnesses are often asked leading and prejudicial questions and where judges go far beyond their supervisory role—the modern criminal trial is a complicated and often time-consuming, technical affair. It is a structured adversary proceeding in which both prosecution and defense follow specific procedures and argue the

 Summarize the trial process.

EXHIBIT 10.2	Evidentiary Standards of Proof: Degrees of Certainty	
Standard	**Definition**	**Ruling**
Absolute certainty	No possibility of error, 100% certainty	Not used in civil or criminal law
Beyond reasonable doubt; moral certainty	Conclusive and complete proof, without leaving any reasonable doubt about the innocence or guilt of the defendant; allows the defendant the benefit of any possibility of innocence	Criminal trial
Clear and convincing	Prevailing and persuasive to the trier of fact	Civil commitments, insanity defense evidence
Preponderance of the evidence	Greater weight of evidence in terms of credibility; more convincing than an opposite point of view	Civil trial
Probable cause	U.S. constitutional standard for arrest and search warrants, requiring existence of facts sufficient to warrant that a crime has been committed	Arrest, preliminary hearing, motions
Sufficient evidence	Adequate evidence to reverse a trial court	Appellate review
Reasonable suspicion	Rational, reasonable belief that facts warrant investigation of a crime on less than probable cause	Police investigations
Less than probable cause	Mere suspicion; less than reasonable belief to conclude criminal activity exists	Prudent police investigation where safety of an officer or others is endangered

merits of their cases before the judge and jury. Each side seeks to present its case in the most favorable light. When possible, the prosecutor and the defense attorney object to evidence they consider damaging to their positions. The prosecutor uses direct testimony, physical evidence, and a confession, if available, to convince the jury that the accused is guilty beyond a reasonable doubt. The defense attorney rebuts the government's case with her own evidence, makes certain that the rights of the criminal defendant under the federal and state constitutions are considered during all phases of the trial, and determines whether an appeal is appropriate if the client is found guilty.

Although each jurisdiction in the United States has its own trial procedures, all jurisdictions conduct criminal trials in a generally similar fashion. The basic steps of the criminal trial, which proceed in an established order, are described in this section and outlined in Figure 10.5.

JURY SELECTION   In both civil and criminal cases, jurors are selected randomly from licensing or voter registration lists within each court's jurisdiction. Few states impose qualifications on those called for jury service, although most mandate a residency requirement.[108] There is also little uniformity in the amount of time served by jurors; the term ranges from one day to months, depending on the nature of the trial. In addition, most jurisdictions prohibit convicted felons from serving on juries, as well as others exempted by statute, such as public officials, physicians, and attorneys.

venire
The group called for jury duty from which jury panels are selected.

The initial list of persons chosen, which is called a **venire**, or jury array, provides the state with a group of potentially capable citizens able to serve on a jury. Many states, by rule of law, review the venire to eliminate unqualified persons and to exempt those who, by reason of their professions, are not allowed to be jurors. The actual jury selection process begins with those remaining on the list.

The court clerk, who handles the administrative affairs of the court—including the processing of the complaint and other documents—randomly selects what he believes will be enough names to fill the required number of places on the jury. After reporting to a courtroom, the prospective jurors are first required to swear that they will truthfully answer all questions asked about their qualifications to serve. A group of 12 will be asked to sit in the jury box while the remaining group stands by.

voir dire
The process in which a potential jury panel is questioned by the prosecution and the defense in order to select jurors who are unbiased and objective.

challenge for cause
Dismissal of a prospective juror by either the prosecution or the defense because he or she is biased, because he or she has prior knowledge about a case, or for other reasons that demonstrate the individual's inability to render a fair and impartial judgment.

peremptory challenges
Dismissal of a prospective juror by either the prosecution or the defense for unexplained, discretionary reasons.

Once prospective jurors are chosen, the lengthy process of **voir dire** (from the Old French for "to tell the truth") starts. To determine their appropriateness to sit on the jury, prospective jurors are examined under oath by the government, the defense, and sometimes the judge about their backgrounds, occupations, residences, and possible knowledge of or interest in the case. A juror who acknowledges any bias for or prejudice against the defendant—if the defendant is a friend or relative, or if the juror has already formed an opinion about the case—may be removed by either the prosecution or the defense with a **challenge for cause** asking the judge to dismiss the biased juror. If the judge accepts the challenge, the juror is removed for cause and replaced with another juror from the remaining panel. Because normally no limit is placed on the number of challenges for cause that can be exercised, it often takes considerable time to select a jury, especially for controversial and highly publicized criminal cases.

Besides challenges for cause, both the prosecution and the defense are allowed **peremptory challenges**, which enable the attorneys to excuse jurors for no particular reason or for undisclosed reasons. A prosecutor might not want a bartender as a juror in a drunk-driving case, believing that a person in that occupation would be sympathetic to the accused. Or the defense attorney might excuse a male prospective juror because the attorney prefers to have a predominantly female jury. The number of peremptory challenges accorded to the prosecution and defense is limited by state statute and often varies by case and jurisdiction.

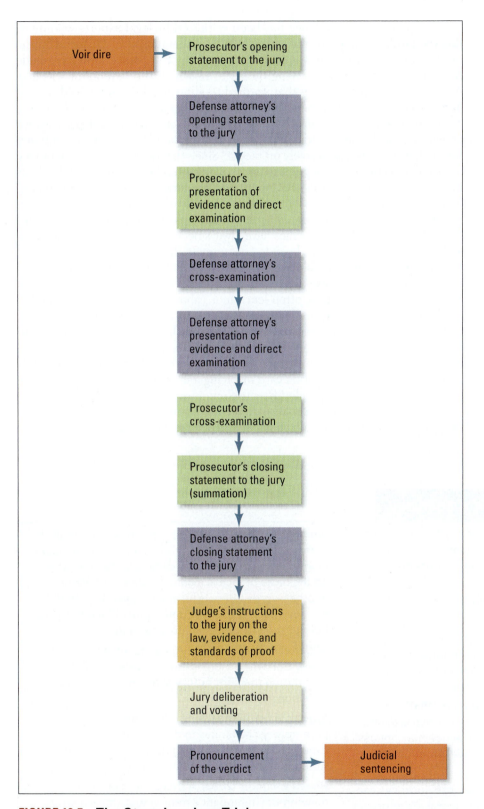

FIGURE 10.5 **The Steps in a Jury Trial**

Source: Marvin Zalman and Larry Siegel, *Criminal Procedure: Constitution and Society* (St. Paul, MN: West Publishing, 1991), p. 655.

The peremptory challenge has been criticized by legal experts who question the fairness and propriety with which it has been used.[109] Historically, the most significant criticism was that it was used by the prosecution to exclude African Americans from serving on juries in which the defendant was also African American—a policy that seemed to allow legally condoned discrimination against minority group members. In the landmark 1986 case *Batson v. Kentucky*, the Supreme Court held that the use of peremptory challenges against potential jurors by prosecutors in criminal cases violated the U.S. Constitution if the challenges were based solely on race.[110] Since that decision, the issue of race discrimination in the use of peremptory challenges has been raised by defendants in numerous cases. See the accompanying "Evolution of *Batson v. Kentucky*" feature for a summary of cases decided in the wake of *Batson*.

It is becoming increasingly difficult to find impartial jurors, especially in this technological age. Heinous crimes have always been broadcast all over the news, and the result has sometimes been to contaminate the pool of prospective jurors. Jurors nowadays are also able to turn to their BlackBerrys and iPhones to seek information about *any* case. By searching the Internet and sharing information (such as on Facebook), they often learn more about cases than is presented in court, which they are expressly forbidden to do. As one article recently noted, this practice is "wreaking havoc on trials around the country, upending deliberations and infuriating judges."[121] Although there is no official tally of the number of cases compromised by jurors' Internet research, the number is certainly growing. For example, a Florida case involving a man accused of illegally selling prescription drugs was upended because one juror researched the case on her own and was able to discover information not presented at trial. After her actions came to light, the judge had no choice but to declare a mistrial.

The Evolution of *Batson v. Kentucky*

***Batson v. Kentucky* (1986)** Prosecutors are barred, under the Fourteenth Amendment, from using peremptory challenges to remove jurors on the basis of race.[111]

***Hernandez v. New York* (1991)** The *Batson* rule extends to Hispanic jurors.[112]

***Powers v. Ohio* (1991)** Defendants can challenge race-based exclusions of jurors through peremptory challenges even if the defendant and the excluded jurors do not share the same race.[113]

***Edmonson v. Leesville Concrete Co.* (1991)** The *Batson* ruling applies to attorneys in civil lawsuits (that is, a private party in a civil action may not use peremptory challenges to exclude jurors on the basis of race).[114]

***Georgia v. McCollum* (1992)** Defense attorneys cannot use peremptory challenges to exclude jurors on the basis of race.[115]

***J.E.B. v. Alabama* (1994)** Peremptory challenges cannot be used to excuse jurors on the basis of their gender.[116]

***Johnson v. California* (2005)** California's "more likely than not" standard for proving that peremptory challenges are being used to exclude prospective jurors on the basis of race is incompatible with *Batson*.[117] In other words, there is no specific test that should be required to prove that peremptory challenges are being used in a discriminatory fashion.

***Miller-El v. Dretke* (2005)** A defendant is entitled to a new trial when there is strong evidence of racial bias during the peremptory challenge phase of jury selection.[118]

***Snyder v. Louisiana* (2008)** The state's use of peremptory challenges to dismiss all African American potential jurors violates the Fourteenth Amendment's equal protection clause.[119]

***Rivera v. Illinois* (2009)** A trial court's error in denying the defendant's motion to dismiss a juror (the court wrongfully concluded the dismissal was based on race) does not require automatic reversal of the defendant's conviction.[120]

OPENING STATEMENTS Once the jury has been selected and the criminal complaint has been read to the jurors by the court clerk, the prosecutor and the defense attorney may each make an opening statement about the case. The purpose of the prosecutor's statement is to acquaint the judge and jury with the particular criminal charges, to outline the facts, and to describe how the government will prove the defendant guilty beyond a reasonable doubt. The defense attorney reviews the case and indicates how the defense intends to show that the accused is not guilty.

Typically, the prosecutor is entitled to offer an opening statement, which is followed by the defense's opening statement. Both sides use the statement to give the jury a concise overview of the evidence that is to follow. Neither attorney is allowed to make prejudicial remarks or inflammatory statements or to mention irrelevant facts. Both are free, however, to identify what they will eventually prove by way of evidence, which includes witnesses, physical evidence, and the use of expert testimony. The opening statements are important because they give both sides an opportunity to sway the jury before the trial begins.

THE PROSECUTION'S CASE Following the opening statements, the government begins its case by presenting evidence to the court through its witnesses. Numerous types of evidence are presented at trial (see Exhibit 10.3). Those called as witnesses—such as police officers, victims, or experts—provide testimony via **direct examination**. During direct examination, the prosecutor questions the witness to reveal the facts believed pertinent to the government's case. Testimony involves what the witness actually saw, heard, or touched; it does not include opinions. However, a witness's opinion can be given in certain situations, such as when describing the motion of a vehicle or indicating whether a defendant appeared to act intoxicated or insane. Witnesses may also qualify to give opinions because they are experts on a particular subject relevant to the case. For example, a psychiatrist may testify about a defendant's mental capacity at the time of the crime.

Upon completion of the prosecutor's questioning, the defense usually conducts a **cross-examination** of the witness. During this exchange, the defense attorney may challenge elements of the testimony, such as the witness's accuracy in reporting what was seen or heard. The right to cross-examine witnesses is an

direct examination
The initial questioning of one's own (prosecution or defense) witness during a trial.

cross-examination
The questioning of a prosecution witness by the defense, or of a defense witness by the prosecution.

EXHIBIT 10.3   Types of Evidence Presented at Trial

In general, the primary test for the admissibility of evidence in a criminal proceeding is its relevance. In a prosecution for bribery, for example, photos of the defendant receiving a package from a co-conspirator would clearly be found relevant to the case. There are four main types of evidence:

- *Testimonial evidence.* Given by police officers, citizens, and experts, this is the most basic form of evidence. The witness must state, under oath, what he or she heard, saw, or experienced.

- *Real evidence.* Exhibits that can be taken into the jury room for review by the jury constitute real evidence. A revolver that may have been in the defendant's control at the time of a murder, tools in the possession of a suspect charged with a burglary, and a bottle allegedly holding narcotics are examples of real, or physical, evidence. Photographs, maps, diagrams, and crime scene displays are other types for real evidence.

- *Documentary evidence.* This type of evidence includes writings, government reports, public records, business or hospital records, fingerprint identification, and DNA profiling.

- *Circumstantial evidence.* In trial proceedings, circumstantial (indirect) evidence is often inferred or indirectly used to prove a fact in question. For example, in a murder case, evidence that carpet fibers found on the body match the carpet in the defendant's home may be used at trial to link the two, even though they do not provide direct evidence that the suspect actually killed the victim.

CAREERS in criminal justice

PARALEGAL

DUTIES AND CHARACTERISTICS OF THE JOB

Paralegals assist lawyers by conducting much of the preparation for trials. A paralegal's exact duties vary according to the needs of the office for which he or she works. However, a paralegal's work typically includes assisting with or carrying out client interviews, drafting legal documents, reviewing pertinent case law, summarizing legal proceedings, and doing some standard office work. Although a paralegal's work may at first be relatively simple, after some experience paralegals are usually given more responsibilities and more complex tasks. Paralegals working outside the law office setting have similar duties but also additional ones that reflect the specialty of their employer.

Paralegals do much of the same work as a lawyer, but there are definite limits on what they can do. For example, paralegals cannot advise on legal issues. Although most paralegals have general legal knowledge, it is becoming more common, especially for long-term or career paralegals, to choose a field of specialization.

A clear majority of paralegals work for law firms, but some find positions with the government, with corporations, or in community service. These paralegals can expect a normal 40-hour workweek, but a paralegal working in a law firm is expected to put in many hours of overtime during busy periods. Increasingly, paralegals are choosing the option of self-employment and working freelance.

JOB OUTLOOK

The paralegal profession is expected to grow rapidly in the near future for several reasons, most prominently the fact that some organizations need legal expertise but do not want the extra expense of hiring a lawyer.

SALARY

The median (half earn above the amount, half earn below it) annual salary for paralegals ranges is $46,990. The average is slightly higher. Paralegals who work for private firms often receive bonuses for good work.

---

essential part of a trial, and unless extremely unusual circumstances exist (such as a person's being hospitalized), witness statements will not be considered unless they are made in court and are open for question. If desired, the prosecutor may seek a second direct examination after the defense attorney has completed cross-examination; this allows the prosecutor to ask additional questions about information brought out during cross-examination. Finally, the defense attorney may then question, or re-cross-examine, the witness once again. All witnesses for the trial are sworn in and questioned in the same basic manner.

THE CRIMINAL DEFENSE   Once the prosecutor has provided all the government's evidence against a defendant, he informs the court that he rests the people's case. The defense attorney at this point may enter a motion for a **directed verdict**. This is a procedural device in which the defense attorney asks the judge to order the jury to return a verdict of not guilty. Depending on the weight of the prosecution's case, the judge may either sustain or overrule this motion. In essence, the defense attorney argues in the directed verdict that the prosecutor's case against the defendant is insufficient to support the legal elements needed to prove the defendant guilty beyond a reasonable doubt. If the court sustains the motion, the trial is terminated. If it rejects the motion, the defense begins to legally rebut the prosecution's case.

The defense attorney has the option of presenting many, some, or no witnesses on behalf of the defendant. The burden of proving guilt is on the prosecution,

directed verdict
A judge's order directing a jury to acquit a defendant because the state has not proved the elements of the crime or otherwise has not established guilt according to law.

OPPORTUNITIES

The number of people entering the profession has been steadily increasing, so those entering the paralegal field should expect competition for desirable jobs. Opportunities for advancement within the field come mainly in the form of supervisory positions, which entail more responsibilities and higher pay. Ultimately, many paralegals use their knowledge and skills to earn a law degree and become a lawyer or judge. They can also move on to better-paying careers where legal experience is useful, such as insurance claims adjuster.

QUALIFICATIONS

Much of a paralegal's work is focused on conducting legal research, so skills that aid this process are critical. Because much of this research can now be done using computer programs, databases, and the Internet, up-to-date computer skills confer a distinct advantage. Those with knowledge and experience in a specialized legal field are also in demand, especially for government and corporate positions. Real-world work experience and internship experience can also increase the chances of employment.

Relevant educational experience and certification are useful for gaining employment. Although one can work as a paralegal without certification, it provides a hiring advantage. Various groups such as the National Association of Legal Assistants provide certification if the applicant can pass rigorous exams.

EDUCATION AND TRAINING

There are many ways of entering the field. Most paralegals enter their profession with training from a two-year paralegal program approved by the American Bar Association. However, it is possible for people with a liberal arts degree to enter the field by working in legal offices and learning skills on the job. Others with bachelor's degrees enter certification programs or complete a combination bachelor's/paralegal degree. The entrance requirements for these programs vary. Classes in political science may provide useful knowledge for future paralegals. Finally, paralegals must always keep up to date on changes in the law in their area of specialization.

Sources: Bureau of Labor Statistics, *Paralegal*, http://www.bls.gov/ooh/Legal/Paralegals-and-legal-assistants.htm (accessed July 2014); *Princeton Review*, "Career: Paralegal," http://www.princetonreview.com/careers.aspx?cid=105 (accessed July 2014).

and if the defense team believes that the burden has not been met, it may feel there is no need to present witnesses of its own. In addition, the defense attorney must decide whether the defendant should take the stand and testify in his own behalf. In a criminal trial, the defendant is protected by the Fifth Amendment right to be free from self-incrimination, which means that a person cannot be forced by the state to testify against himself. However, defendants who choose to tell their side of the story can be subject to cross-examination by the prosecutor.

The defense attorney is charged with putting on a vigorous defense in the adversary system of justice. She presents her own witnesses and introduces evidence to refute the prosecution's allegations. After the defense concludes its case, the government may then present rebuttal evidence. If the judge grants permission, this involves bringing forward evidence to refute, counteract, or disprove evidence introduced by the defense. A prosecutor may not go into new matters or present evidence that further supports or reinforces his own case. At the end of rebuttal, the defense may be allowed so-called surrebuttal—presenting witnesses to respond to issues that were raised for the first time in the prosecutor's rebuttal case. The defense cannot restate its case or introduce new issues during surrebuttal.

CLOSING ARGUMENTS In closing arguments the attorneys review the facts and evidence of the case in a manner favorable to their respective positions. At this stage of the trial, both prosecution and defense are permitted to draw reasonable inferences and to show how the facts prove or refute the defendant's guilt. Often both attorneys have a free hand in arguing about the facts, issues, and evidence, including the applicable law. They cannot comment on matters not in evidence, however, or on the defendant's failure to testify in a criminal case. Normally, the prosecutor makes a closing statement first, followed by the defense, and many jurisdictions allow the prosecution an opportunity for rebuttal. Either party can elect to forgo the right to make a final summation to the jury.

INSTRUCTIONS TO THE JURY   In a criminal trial, the judge will instruct, or charge, the jury members on the principles of law that ought to guide and control their decision on the defendant's innocence or guilt. Included in the charge will be information about the elements of the alleged offense, the type of evidence needed to prove each element, and the burden of proof that must be met to obtain a guilty verdict. Although the judge commonly provides this instruction, he or she may ask the prosecutor and the defense attorney to submit instructions for consideration; the judge will then exercise discretion in determining whether to use any of their instructions. The instructions that cover the law applicable to the case are extremely important because they may serve as the basis for a subsequent appeal.

DELIBERATION AND VERDICT   Once the charge is given to the jury members, they retire to deliberate on a verdict. In highly publicized and celebrated cases, the judge may sequester the jury, preventing them from having contact with the outside world. This process is discretionary, and most judges believe that sequestering or "locking up" a jury is needed only in sensational cases.

A review of the case by the jury may take hours or even days. The jurors always meet privately during their deliberations, and in certain lengthy and highly publicized cases, they are kept overnight in a hotel until the verdict is reached. In less sensational cases, the jurors may be allowed to go home, but they are cautioned not to discuss the case with anyone.

If a verdict cannot be reached, the trial may result in a hung jury, after which the prosecutor must bring the defendant to trial again if the prosecution desires a conviction. If found not guilty, the defendant is released from the criminal process. If the defendant is convicted, the judge will normally order a presentence investigation by the probation department before imposing a sentence. Before sentencing, the defense attorney will probably submit a motion for a new trial, alleging that legal errors occurred in the trial proceedings. The judge may deny the motion and impose a sentence immediately—a practice quite common in most misdemeanor offenses. In felony cases, however, the judge will set a date for sentencing, and the defendant will either be placed on bail or be held in custody until that time.

Although jurors are required by law to base their decision on the facts of the case and on the judge's legal instructions, they are sometimes asked by the defense to ignore both and render decisions based on emotion and personal preference.[122] This strategy, called **jury nullification**, has been in practice since 1735 when John Peter Zenger, editor of the

---

jury nullification
A jury's refusal to render a verdict according to the law and fact regardless of the evidence presented.

FACT CHECK ✓

YOUR OPINION: Do the courts in your area deal too harshly or not harshly enough with criminals?

PUBLIC OPINION:

TOO HARSH: 11.9%

NOT HARSH ENOUGH: 64.2%

ABOUT RIGHT: 16.6%

DON'T KNOW: 6.7%

REALITY: Almost two-third of American's feel the courts are not harsh enough with criminals. Are they correct? The Bureau of Justice Statistics (BJS) periodically reports on sentencing practices throughout the United States. The most recent report reveals, among other things, that 75 percent of convicted felony defendants are sentenced to prison or jail. The mean prison sentence length was 52 months; the median was 30 months. The longest sentences were for murder (median: 360 months), rape (median: 120 months), and robbery (median: 60 months).

DISCUSSION: Does the BJS sentencing data match up with public opinion? Why do almost two in three Americans feel the courts are soft on crime?

Sources: General Social Survey, 2010, http://www.thearda.com/archive/files/Codebooks/GSS10PAN_CB.asp (accessed July 2014); Brian A. Reaves, *Felony Defendants in Large Urban Counties, 2009* (Washington, DC: Bureau of Justice Statistics, 2013).

New York Weekly Journal, was charged with printing libelous statements about the governor of the Colony of New York, William Cosby. Despite the fact that Zenger clearly printed the alleged libels and the trial judge gave the jury clear instructions for a finding of guilt, the jury found Zenger not guilty on all charges. The Zenger case remains one of the most famous examples of jury nullification in the nation's history.

Supporters of jury nullification argue that it is an important safeguard against government oppression and that the function of the jury is to serve as a safety valve against the unjust application of the law. Critics, however, see jury nullification as an abuse of power. Would it be fair if jurors, motivated by racial bias, found a person accused of a hate crime not guilty despite overwhelming evidence of guilt?[123]

There is also some question about what jurors expect when they hear the arguments made by the prosecution and defense and then go into deliberations. According to some critics, popular television programs such as *CSI: Crime Scene Investigation* (and its spinoffs) have caused jurors to have unrealistic expectations concerning what evidence is typically found at crime scenes and introduced at trial.

THE SENTENCE Imposing the criminal sentence is normally the responsibility of the trial judge. In some jurisdictions, the jury may determine the sentence or make recommendations involving leniency for certain offenses. Often, the sentencing decision is based on information and recommendations given to the court by the probation department after a presentence investigation of the defendant. The sentence itself is determined by the statutory requirements for the particular crime as established by the legislature; in addition, the judge ordinarily has a great deal of discretion in reaching a sentencing decision. The different criminal sanctions available include fines, probation, imprisonment, and even commitment to a state hospital. The sentence may be a combination of all these. The most critical trial stages are reviewed in Concept Summary 10.1.

James Leynse/Corbis

Julian P. Heicklen, 78, an advocate for jury nullification, stands outside his home in New Jersey. He believes that juries can come to a verdict in spite of the evidence or instructions of a judge. Heicklen, who has been handing out pamphlets outside courthouses, has been indicted for jury tampering. Is jury nullification appropriate in certain cases?

APPEALS Once a verdict has been rendered and a defendant found guilty, the defense may petition an appellate court to review the procedures used during trial. Defendants have two main avenues to challenge such procedures: appeals and *habeas corpus.* These both give the convicted person an opportunity to appeal to a higher state or federal court on the basis of an error that affected the conviction in the trial court. Extraordinary trial court errors, such as denial of the right to counsel or inability to provide a fair trial, are subject to the plain-error rule of the federal courts.[124] Harmless errors, such as the use of innocuous identification procedures or the denial of counsel at a noncritical stage of the proceeding, would not necessarily result in the overturning of a criminal conviction.

A postconviction **appeal** is a request for an appellate court to examine a lower court's decision in order to determine whether proper procedures were followed. It is important to note that appeals do not give the convicted an opportunity to try the case a second time, only to challenge procedural matters (such as a judge's decision to exclude a witness's testimony). Most defendants benefit from at least one so-called *direct appeal.* Direct appeals are guaranteed by law; the result is that most defendants get to appeal at least once, even if they cannot afford it.[125] *Discretionary appeals* are also possible. It is up to the appellate court to decide whether it will hear a discretionary appeal. There is no restriction on the number of discretionary appeals that can be filed.

Web App 10.5

For additional information about sentencing, visit http://www.sentencingproject.org/.

appeal
A request for an appellate court to examine a lower court's decision in order to determine whether proper procedures were followed.

CONCEPT SUMMARY 10.1
Stages of the Jury Trial

Stage 1 **Jury selection**	The judge and attorneys question potential jurors until a panel of 12 is agreed upon by all sides. The voir dire process is designed to excuse jurors who might have difficulty in rendering a fair and impartial verdict in that particular case.
Stage 2 **Opening statements**	Brief statements are made by prosecution and defense that outline their view of the facts of the case and what they hope to prove. The prosecutor in a criminal case gives the first statement and the defense attorney follows.
Stage 3 **Presentation of evidence**	Witnesses for the prosecution in a criminal case testify first, witnesses for the defense testify next, and any rebuttal witnesses testify last. The attorney who calls the witness asks questions in direct examination. The attorney for the opposing side then questions the witness in cross-examination.
Stage 4 **Closing arguments**	The prosecutor in a criminal case first attempts to convince the jury to decide in favor of her side of the case. The defense attorney follows with his argument, attempting to do the same. The prosecutor has the opportunity to present a rebuttal to the defense attorney's argument.
Stage 5 **Jury deliberations**	After the judge instructs the jury on the law they must apply in the particular case, they retire from the courtroom to deliberate in secret. When the jurors reach a verdict, they return to the courtroom and the verdict is read aloud to the parties.
Stage 6 **Sentencing**	If a guilty verdict is reached, the judge will impose a sentence, choosing the most appropriate sanction from those legislatively available.

writ of *habeas corpus*
A judicial order requesting that a person who detains another person produce the body of the prisoner and give reasons for his or her capture and detention. *Habeas corpus* is a legal device used to request that a judicial body review the reasons for a person's confinement and the conditions of confinement. *Habeas corpus* is known as "the great writ."

Through objections made at the pretrial and trial stages of the criminal process, the defense counsel reserves specific legal issues on the record as the basis for appeal. A copy of the transcript of these proceedings serves as the basis on which the appellate court will review any errors that may have occurred during the lower-court proceedings.

A **writ of *habeas corpus*** is the primary means by which state prisoners have their convictions or sentences reviewed in the federal court. A writ of *habeas corpus* (which means "you have the body") seeks to determine the validity of a detention by asking the court to release the person or give legal reasons for his or her the incarceration.

Significant Cases in the Trial Process

Case	Issue	Decision
Baldwin v. New York (1970)	Right to a jury trial	The defendant has the constitutional right to a jury trial when facing a possible prison sentence of six months or more, regardless of whether the crime committed was a felony or a misdemeanor.
Batson v. Kentucky (1986)	Peremptory challenges	The use of peremptory challenges based solely on race is unconstitutional. Also see the "Evolution of *Batson v. Kentucky*" feature earlier in this chapter for details on post-*Batson* decisions.

(continued)

Crawford v. Washington (2004)	Confrontation	The admission at trial of a prerecorded out-of-court statement violates the confrontation clause.
Faretta v. California (1975)	Waiver of the right to counsel	The defendant can waive the right to counsel and represent himself or herself (that is, proceed with a *pro se* defense).
Gideon v. Wainwright (1963)	Right to counsel	The Sixth Amendment right to counsel applies to the states, meaning all criminal defendants benefit from the right to counsel, even if they cannot afford it. Also see the "Evolution of *Gideon v. Wainwright*" feature earlier in this chapter for details on post-*Gideon* decisions.
Illinois v. Allen (1970)	Confrontation	The defendant can forfeit his or her right to confrontation at trial because of inappropriate conduct (such as being disruptive).
Johnson v. Zerbst (1938)	Right to counsel	All federal defendants enjoy the Sixth Amendment right to counsel.
Klopfer v. North Carolina (1967)	Right to a speedy trial	The Sixth Amendment right to a speedy trial is a fundamental right, meaning the states must recognize it.
Melendez-Diaz v. Massachusetts (2009)	Confrontation	State forensic analyst laboratory reports are considered testimonial evidence and thus require that the defendant be permitted to question the preparer of the report at trial.
Montejo v. Louisiana (2009)	Right to counsel	Police may approach and question, outside the presence of counsel, a defendant who has been charged with a crime.
Powell v. Alabama (1932)	Right to counsel	Indigent defendants enjoy the right to counsel, but only in capital cases.
Richmond Newspapers, Inc. v. Virginia (1980)	Right to a public trial	Criminal trials must remain open to the press.
Riggins v. Nevada (1992)	Competency at trial	The defendant can be forcibly administered antipsychotic drugs if the procedure is medically appropriate, no alternative is available, and it is necessary for the defendant's safety or the safety of others.
Sheppard v. Maxwell (1966)	Right to a public trial	A trial can be closed to the public if allowing access to people and/or the press results in a "carnival atmosphere."
Stack v. Boyle (1951)	Bail	In setting bail, judges should consider the nature and circumstances of the offense charged, the weight of the evidence against the accused, and the accused's ability to pay.
Tumey v. Ohio (1927)	Impartial judge	A violation of due process occurs when a judge has a personal and/or financial interest in the outcome of a case over which he or she presides.
United States v. Williams (1992)	Grand juries	The failure to present exculpatory evidence to a grand jury does not make the resulting indictment invalid.
Washington v. Texas (1967)	Compulsory process	Every defendant enjoys the Sixth Amendment right to compel the production of witnesses and evidence to assist in putting on his or her defense.

ETHICAL CHALLENGES in Criminal Justice

A WRITING ASSIGNMENT

Shantel is an unemployed former crack addict with an extensive criminal record. When she was actively using, she gave birth to six children, each of whom was taken away by Child Protective Services. She has since put her life back on track, secured a job, stopped using drugs, and given birth to her seventh child, Keisha, who lives with her. When Keisha was 2 years old, Shantel moved back in with her estranged boyfriend, Deshaun, whom she thought had also stopped using. Unbeknownst to Shantel, although Deshaun had stopped using crack, he had become hooked on OxyContin and was using the drug on a regular basis. Not long after they moved in together, the police served a search warrant on their property and found a stash of the drug. Both Shantel and Deshaun were charged with drug possession. Shantel's extensive criminal record would probably result in a long-term prison sentence, not to mention the possible loss of Keisha, if she were found guilty at a trial. Surprisingly, during Shantel's pretrial negotiations, the district attorney offered a plea bargain to give Shantel three years *or* probation and no jail time if she agreed to sterilization. Shantel did not want to take the chance of going to trial and getting a long-term prison sentence. She knew she would not have any chance of getting Keisha back if she got a long-term prison sentence. She felt her only option was to agree to the plea negotiation of probation and sterilization.

Write an essay on the ethical issues raised in this plea bargaining scenario. In doing so, answer these questions: Should Shantel plead guilty to a crime she did not commit? Should she subject herself to sterilization for a crime she did not commit? How many other defendants plead guilty to crimes they have not committed? Is it even possible to know? One of the main criticisms of plea bargaining is just this; a guilty plea does not always mean the offender is guilty. What other criticisms of plea bargaining have been raised? Consult this chapter's "Plea Bargaining" section as you answer the questions.

Summary

L01 Discuss the procedures following arrest.
- Many important decisions about what happens to a defendant are made prior to trial.
- Hearings, such as before the grand jury and the preliminary hearing, are held to determine whether probable cause exists to charge the accused with a crime. If so, the defendant is arraigned, enters a plea, is informed of his constitutional rights (particularly the right to the assistance of counsel), and is considered for pretrial diversion.

L02 List a variety of bail systems.
- Bail is a form of security, usually a sum of money, that is put up or exchanged to secure the release of an arrested person before the trial begins.
- There are several types of bail systems, including full cash bail, deposit bail, surety bail, conditional bail, unsecured bonds, and release on recognizance.

L03 Describe the history of bail reform.
- Bail has been heavily criticized as one of the most unacceptable aspects of the criminal justice system.
- Bail reform has resulted in the use of release on recognizance to replace money bail for nondangerous offenders.
- Whereas release on recognizance is a liberal bail reform, some reform efforts have included preventive detention.

L04 Define pretrial services.
- Pretrial service programs provide a number of services to those released into the community prior to their trial dates, including (a) gathering and verifying information about arrestees, (b) assessing each arrestee's likelihood of failure to appear and chances of being rearrested, and (c) providing supervision for defendants conditionally released and notifying the court of any failure to comply with release conditions.

LO5 **List the differences between the indictment process and the information process.**

- There are two primary charging mechanisms in the United States: a grand jury's indictment and a prosecutor's information.
- Grand juries perform two main functions: investigation and accusation.
- The grand jury usually meets, in secret, at the request of the prosecution and decides whether to charge a criminal suspect (that is, to issue an indictment).
- If the prosecutor proceeds by information, then a preliminary hearing is held to determine whether there is enough cause to believe that the defendant committed the crime to warrant a trial.
- Grand jury indictments and preliminary hearings are usually limited to serious offenses. Trials for misdemeanors often occur without either proceeding.

LO6 **Discuss the purpose of arraignment.**

- At the arraignment, the judge informs the defendant of the charges against her and appoints counsel if one has not yet been retained.
- The accused enters one of three pleas at arraignment: guilty, not guilty, or *nolo contendere*.

LO7 **Discuss the pros and cons of plea bargaining.**

- Research indicates that most cases never go to trial but, instead, are bargained out of the system.
- Bargains can be made for a plea of guilty in exchange for a reduced sentence, dropping charges, lowering the charge, or substituting a more socially acceptable charge for one with negative connotations.
- People who plead guilty generally get lighter sentences than those who go to trial.
- Critics of plea bargaining claim that it results in cynicism and disrespect for the judicial system.

LO8 **Explain the role of the prosecutor, defense attorney, judge, and victim in the plea negotiation.**

- The U.S. Supreme Court has shaped the legal contours of the plea system. For example, it has ruled that bargains must be kept on both sides.
- Plea bargains must be accepted and approved by the judge.

- The prosecutor must uphold his or her end of the bargain, but only after the judge accepts the bargain.
- A court will not accept a guilty plea unless the defendant has been properly advised by counsel and the court has determined that the plea is voluntary and has a factual basis.
- Victims have little to no involvement in the plea bargaining process, but some authorities would like to see this change.

LO9 **Explain the legal rights of the accused at trial.**

- Legal rights at trial include the right to an impartial judge, the right to be competent at trial, the right to confront witnesses, the right to compulsory process, the right to an impartial jury, the right to counsel, the right to a speedy trial, the right to a public trial, and the right to be convicted by proof beyond a reasonable doubt.

LO10 **Summarize the trial process.**

- The trial of a criminal case is a formal process conducted in a specific and orderly fashion in accordance with rules of criminal law, procedure, and evidence.
- In both civil and criminal cases, jurors are selected randomly from licensing or voter registration lists within each court's jurisdiction.
- Once prospective jurors are chosen, the lengthy process of voir dire (from the Old French for "to tell the truth") starts.
- During voir dire, a juror who acknowledges any bias in favor of or prejudice against the defendant may be removed by either the prosecution or the defense with a challenge for cause.
- During voir dire, both the prosecution and the defense are allowed peremptory challenges, which enables them to excuse jurors for no particular reason or for undisclosed reasons.
- Once the jury has been selected, the prosecutor and the defense attorney may each make an opening statement about the case.
- Following the opening statements, the government begins its case by presenting evidence to the court through its witnesses.
- The central purpose of the direct examination process is to introduce evidence upon which the jury can decide the case.
- Once the prosecution has provided all the government's evidence against a defendant,

it informs the court that it rests the people's case. The defense attorney at this point may enter a motion for a directed verdict.

- Closing arguments are used by the attorneys to review the facts and evidence of the case in a manner favorable to their respective positions.

- In a criminal trial, the judge instructs, or charges, the jury members on the principles of law that ought to guide and control their

decision on the defendant's innocence or guilt.

- Once the charge is given to the jury members, they retire to deliberate on a verdict.

- Imposing the criminal sentence is normally the responsibility of the trial judge.

- Once a verdict has been rendered and a defendant found guilty, that individual may petition an appellate court to review the procedures used during trial.

Key Terms

pretrial procedures, 376
complaint, 376
arraignment, 376
bail, 376
pretrial detainees, 380
release on recognizance (ROR), 382
avertable recidivist, 383
preventive detention, 383
presentment, 385
indictment, 385
true bill, 385
no bill, 385

exculpatory evidence, 386
preliminary hearing, 386
information, 386
nolo contendere, 388
bench trial, 397
verdict, 398
adjudication, 398
confrontation clause, 399
hearsay evidence, 399
compulsory process, 399
First Amendment, 402
proof beyond a reasonable doubt, 402

preponderance of the evidence, 403
venire, 404
voir dire, 404
challenge for cause, 404
peremptory challenge, 404
direct examination, 407
cross-examination, 407
directed verdict, 408
jury nullification, 410
appeal, 411
writ of *habeas corpus*, 412

Critical Thinking Questions

1. Should criminal defendants be allowed to bargain for a reduced sentence in exchange for a guilty plea? Should the victim always be included in the plea bargaining process?

2. Should those accused of violent acts be subjected to preventive detention instead of bail, even though they have not been convicted of a crime? Is it fair to the victim to have his alleged attacker running around loose?

3. What purpose does a grand jury or preliminary hearing serve in adjudicating felony offenses? Should one of these methods be abandoned? If so, which one?

4. Why should pretrial services be provided for defendants?

5. What are the pros and cons of a jury trial versus a bench trial?

6. Do defendants enjoy too many rights? Why or why not?

Notes

1. "Judge Sends Ariel Castro to Prison for Abduction, Rape of Amanda Berry, Gina DeJesus, and Michelle Knight," *Plain Dealer*, August 1, 2013, http://www.cleveland.com/metro/index.ssf/2013/08/judge_sends_ariel_castro_to_pr.html (accessed July 2014).

2. Christopher Stephens, "Bail," *Georgetown Law Journal* 90 (2002): 1395–1416.

3. The Judiciary Act of 1789, http://www.constitution.org/uslaw/judiciary_1789.htm (accessed July 2014).

4. *Stack v. Boyle*, 342 U.S. 1 (1951).

5. Data in this section come from Brian A. Reaves, *Felony Defendants in Large Urban Counties, 2009* (Washington, DC: Bureau of Justice Statistics, 2013).

6. Todd D. Minton, *Jail Inmates at Midyear 2012* (Washington, DC: Bureau of Justice Statistics, 2013).

7. James J. Stephan, *State Prison Expenditures, 2001* (Washington, DC: Bureau of Justice Statistics, 2004).

8. Reaves, *Felony Defendants in Large Urban Counties, 2009* (Figure 17).

9. *Vera Institute of Justice, 1961–1971: Programs in Criminal Justice* (New York: Vera Institute of Justice, 1972).

10. Public Law 89-465, 18 U.S.C., Sec. 3146 (1966).

11. 18 U.S.C, Sec. 3142 (1984).

12. Fred Cohen, "The New Federal Crime Control Act," *Criminal Law Bulletin* 21 (1985): 330–337.

13. *Schall v. Martin*, 467 U.S. 253 (1984).

14. *United States v. Salerno*, 481 U.S. 739 (1987).

15. This section leans on John Clark and D. Alan Henry, *Pretrial Services Programming at the Start of the 21st Century: A Survey* (Washington, DC: Bureau of Justice Assistance, 2003).

16. Ric Simmons, "Reexamining the Grand Jury: Is There Room for Democracy in the Criminal Justice System?" *Boston University Law Review* 82 (2002): 1–76, at 25; also see *United States v. Williams*, 504 U.S. 36 (1992).

17. *United States v. Williams*, 504 U.S. 36 (1992).

18. Suzanne Roe Neely, "Preserving Justice and Preventing Prejudice: Requiring Disclosure of Substantial Exculpatory Evidence to the Grand Jury," *American Criminal Law Review* 39 (2002): 171–200.

19. John Gibeaut, "Indictment of a System," *ABA Journal* 87 (2001): 34.

20. *Henderson v. Morgan*, 426 U.S. 637 (1976).

21. Federal Rules of Criminal Procedure, Rule 11[d].

22. F. Andrew Hessick and Reshma Saujani, "Plea Bargaining and Convicting the Innocent: The Role of the Prosecutor, the Defense Counsel, and the Judge," *BYU Journal of Public Law* 16 (2002): 189–243.

23. *Brady v. United States*, 397 U.S. 742 (1970).

24. Mike McConville and Chester Mirsky, *Jury Trials and Plea Bargaining: A True History* (Oxford, England: Hart, 2005).

25. George Fisher, "Plea Bargaining's Triumph," *Yale Law Journal* 109 (2000): 857–1058.

26. Reaves, *Felony Defendants in Large Urban Counties, 2009.*

27. Debra Emmelman, "Trial by Plea Bargain: Case Settlement as a Product of Recursive Decisionmaking," *Law and Society Review* 30 (1996): 335–361.

28. Fred Zacharis, "Justice in Plea Bargaining," *William and Mary Law Review* 39 (1998): 1121–1189.

29. Nathaniel J. Pallone, "Without Plea-Bargaining, Megan Kanka Would Be Alive Today," *Criminology and Public Policy* 3 (2003): 83–96.

30. William Stuntz, "Plea Bargaining and Criminal Law's Harvard Law Review Disappearing Shadow," 117 (2004): 2548–2569.

31. Mike McConville, "Plea Bargaining: Ethics and Politics," *Journal of Law and Society* 25 (1998): 526–555.

32. The Innocence Project, *False Confessions*, http://www .innocenceproject.org/understand/False-Confessions.php (accessed July 2014).

33. Ibid.

34. *Hill v. Lockhart*, 474 U.S. 52 (1985).

35. *Boykin v. Alabama*, 395 U.S. 238 (1969); *Brady v. United States*, 397 U.S. 742 (1970).

36. *Santobello v. New York*, 404 U.S. 257 (1971).

37. *Ricketts v. Adamson*, 483 U.S. 1 (1987).

38. *Bordenkircher v. Hayes*, 434 U.S. 357 (1978).

39. *North Carolina v. Alford*, 400 U.S. 25 (1970).

40. *United States v. Mezzanatto*, 513 U.S. 196 (1995).

41. *Lafler v. Cooper*, 566 U.S. ___ (2012).

42. *Missouri v. Frye*, 566 U.S. ___ (2012).

43. Jeremy D. Ball, "Is It a Prosecutor's World? Determinants of Court Bargaining Decisions," *Journal of Contemporary Criminal Justice* 22 (2006): 241–260.

44. Stephen P. Lagoy, Joseph J. Senna, and Larry J. Siegel, "An Empirical Study on Information Usage for Prosecutorial Decision Making in Plea Negotiations," *American Criminal Law Review* 13 (1976): 435–471, at 462.

45. Barbara Boland and Brian Forst, *The Prevalence of Guilty Pleas* (Washington, DC: Bureau of Justice Statistics, 1984), p. 3. See also

46. Gary Hengstler, "The Troubled Justice System," *American Bar Association Journal* 80 (1994): 44.

47. See American Bar Association, *Standards Relating to Pleas of Guilty*, 2nd ed. (Chicago: ABA, 1988). See also *North Carolina v. Alford*, 400 U.S. 25 (1970).

48. Keith Bystrom, "Communicating Plea Offers to the Client," in *Ethical Problems Facing the Criminal Defense Lawyer*, ed. Rodney Uphoff (Chicago: American Bar Association, Section on Criminal Justice, 1995), p. 84.

49. American Bar Association, Standards Relating to Pleas of Guilty, standard 3.3; *National Advisory Commission on Criminal Justice Standards and Goals, Task Force Report on Courts* (Washington, DC: U.S. Government Printing Office, 1973), p. 42.

50. American Bar Association, *Standards Relating to Pleas of Guilty*, p. 73; see also Alan Alschuler, "The Trial Judge's Role in Plea Bargaining," *Columbia Law Review* 76 (1976): 1059.

51. American Bar Association, *Model Uniform Victims of Crime Act* (Chicago: ABA, 1992).

52. Michael M. O'Hear, "Plea Bargaining and Victims: From Consultation to Guidelines," *Marquette Law Review* 91 (2007), http://scholarship.law.marquette.edu/mulr/vol91/iss1/14 (accessed July 2014).

53. National Institute of Law Enforcement and Criminal Justice, *Plea Bargaining in the United States*, pp. 37–40.

54. Gary Blankenship, "Debating the Pros and Cons of Plea Bargaining," *Florida Bar News* 30 (July 15, 2003): 6–7.

55. Candace McCoy, *Politics and Plea Bargaining: Victims' Rights in California* (Philadelphia: University of Pennsylvania Press, 1993).

56. Anne Morrison Piehl and Shawn D. Bushway, "Measuring and Explaining Charge Bargaining," *Journal of Quantitative Criminology* 23 (2007): 105–125.

57. National District Attorneys Association, *National Prosecution Standards*, 2nd ed. (Alexandria, VA: 1991), p. 130.

58. Franklyn Dunford, D. Wayne Osgood, and Hart Weichselbaum, *National Evaluation of Diversion Programs* (Washington, DC: Government Printing Office, 1982).

59. Sharla Rausch and Charles Logan, "Diversion from Juvenile Court: Panacea or Pandora's Box?" in *Evaluating Juvenile Justice*, ed. James Kleugel (Beverly Hills, CA: Sage, 1983), pp. 19–30.

60. See Malcolm Feeley, *Court Reform on Trial* (New York: Basic Books, 1983).

61. *Tumey v. Ohio*, 273 U.S. 510 (1927).

62. Ibid.

63. See, for example, Minn. R. Crim. P. 26.03, subd. 13(4).

64. *Riggins v. Nevada*, 504 U.S. 127 (1992).

65. *Crawford v. Washington*, 541 U.S. 36 (2004).

66. *Melendez-Diaz v. Massachusetts*, 557 U.S. 305 (2009).

67. *Diaz v. United States*, 223 U.S. 442 (1912); *Taylor v. Illinois*, 484 U.S. 400 (1988).

68. *Illinois v. Allen*, 397 U.S. 337 (1970).

69. *Maryland v. Craig*, 497 U.S. 836 (1990).

70. *Giles v. California*, 554 U.S. 353 (2008).

71. *Washington v. Texas*, 388 U.S. 14 (1967).

72. *Baldwin v. New York*, 399 U.S. 66 (1970).

73. *Rothgery v. Gillespie County*, 554 U.S. 191 (2008).

74. *Powell v. Alabama*, 287 U.S. 45 (1932).

75. Ibid., p. 71.

76. *Johnson v. Zerbst*, 304 U.S. 458 (1938).

77. *Gideon v. Wainwright*, 372 U.S. 335 (1963).

78. *Scott v. Illinois*, 440 U.S. 367 (1979).

79. *Shelton v. Alabama*, 122 U.S. 1764 (2002).

80. *Gideon v. Wainwright*, 372 U.S. 335 (1963).

81. *Douglas v. California*, 372 U.S. 353 (1963).

82. *In re Gault*, 387 U.S. 1 (1967).

83. *Coleman v. Alabama*, 399 U.S. 1 (1970).

84. *Argersinger v. Hamlin*, 407 U.S. 25 (1972).

84. *Morrissey v. Brewer*, 408 U.S. 471 (1972).

85. *Gagnon v. Scarpelli*, 411 U.S. 778 (1973).

86. *Ross v. Moffitt*, 417 U.S. 600 (1974).

87. *Scott v. Illinois*, 440 U.S. 367 (1979).

88. *Morris v. Slappy*, 461 U.S. 1 (1983).

89. *Wheat v. United States*, 486 U.S. 153 (1988).

90. *United States v. Monsanto*, 491 U.S. 600 (1989).

91. *United States v. Gonzalez-Lopez*, 548 U.S. 140 (2006).

92. *Rothgery v. Gillespie County*, 554 U.S. 191 (2008).

93. *Faretta v. California*, 422 U.S. 806 (1975).

94. *Indiana v. Edwards*, 554 U.S. 164 (2008).

95. See American Bar Association, *Standards Relating to Speedy Trial* (Chicago: ABA, 1995).

96. *Klopfer v. North Carolina*, 386 U.S. 213 (1967).

97. Ibid., p. 223.

98. *Doggett v. United States*, 505 U.S. 162 (1992).

99. *Sheppard v. Maxwell*, 384 U.S. 333 (1966).

100. *Nebraska Press Association v. Stuart*, 427 U.S. 539 (1976); *Gannett Co. v. DePasquale*, 443 U.S. 368 (1979); *Press Enterprise Co. v. Superior Court*, 464 U.S. 501 (1986).

101. *Wilson v. Layne*, 526 U.S. 603 (1999).

102. *Richmond Newspapers, Inc. v. Virginia*, 448 U.S. 555 (1980).

103. *Globe Newspaper Co. v. Superior Court for County of Norfolk*, 457 U.S. 596 (1982).

104. *Chandler v. Florida*, 449 U.S. 560 (1981); see also American Bar Association, *Criminal Justice Standards, Fair Trial, and Free Press* (Washington, DC: ABA, 1992).

105. See *Brinegar v. United States*, 338 U.S. 160 (1949); *In re Winship*, 397 U.S. 358, 90 (1970).

106. See *In re Winship*, p. 397.

107. Ibid., p. 371.

108. Brian Kalt, "The Exclusion of Felons from Jury Service," *American University Law Review* 53 (2003): 65–189.

109. George Hayden, Joseph Senna, and Larry Siegel, "Prosecutorial Discretion in Peremptory Challenges: An Empirical Investigation of Information Use in the Massachusetts Jury Selection Process," *New England Law Review* 13 (1978): 768.

110. *Batson v. Kentucky*, 476 U.S. 79 (1986); see also Alan Alschuler and Randall Kennedy, "Equal Justice—Would Color-Conscious Jury Selection Help?" *American Bar Association Journal* 81 (1995): 36–37.

111. *Batson v. Kentucky*, 476 U.S. 79 (1986).

112. *Hernandez v. New York*, 500 U.S. 352 (1991).

113. *Powers v. Ohio*, 499 U.S. 400 (1991).

114. *Edmonson v. Leesvile Concrete Co.*, 500 U.S. 614 (1991).

115. *Georgia v. McCollum*, 505 U.S. 42 (1992).

116. *J.E.B. v. Alabama*, 511 U.S. 127 (1994).

117. *Johnson v. California*, 542 U.S. 162 (2005).

118. *Miller-El v. Dretke*, 545 U.S. 231 (2005). This interpretation is a bit of a simplification. Readers are encouraged to read the narrative of the case and also this case: *Miller-El v. Cockrell*, 537 U.S. 322 (2003).

119. *Synder v. Louisiana*, 552 U.S. 472 (2008).

120. *Rivera v. Illinois*, 556 U.S. ___ (2009).

121. John Schwartz, "As Jurors Turn to Web, Mistrials Are Popping Up," *New York Times*, March 17, 2009, http://www.nytimes.com/2009/03/18/us/18juries.html (accessed July 2014).

122. Arie Rubenstein, "Verdicts of Conscience: Nullification and the Modern Jury Trial," *Columbia Law Review* 106 (2006): 959–993.

123. David Pepper, "Nullifying History: Modern-Day Misuse of the Right to Decide the Law," *Case Western Reserve Law Review* 50 (2000): 599–643.

124. *Chapman v. California*, 386 U.S. 18 (1967).

125. *Douglas v. California*, 372 U.S. 353 (1963).

CHAPTER 11

Punishment and Sentencing

Learning Objectives

LO1 Describe the historical development of punishment.

LO2 List the major goals of contemporary sentencing.

LO3 Distinguish among general and specific deterrence, incapacitation, and retribution.

LO4 Compare rehabilitation with just desert.

LO5 Explain how sentences are imposed.

LO6 Classify the various types of sentencing structures.

LO7 Discuss how people are sentenced today.

LO8 Describe the nature of capital punishment in the United States and abroad.

LO9 Articulate the arguments for and against capital punishment.

LO10 Discuss the legality of the death penalty.

Chapter Outline

At a speech to the American Bar Association, Supreme Court Justice Anthony Kennedy once stated, "Our resources are misspent, our punishments too severe, our sentences too long."[1] Yet many supporters of tough-on-crime policies think we should do even more to incarcerate criminals. Some feel judges are soft on crime; others complain that crafty defense attorneys help guilty criminals escape conviction through any number of justice system loopholes. Where does the truth lie? There is no easy answer. The debate over whether Americans incarcerate too many or too few criminals won't be resolved anytime soon, nor will the debate over how long we should put lawbreakers behind bars. But turning our attention outward beyond our borders helps put matters in perspective. How, then, does the U.S. sentence compared to other modern nations? A report authored by professors at the University of San Francisco School of Law offers some answers.[2] The following are some of the report's key findings:

- The United States has the highest incarceration rate in the world: 730 inmates per 100,000 population.
- U.S. prisoners account for a quarter of the world's prison population.
- One out of ten state prisoners in the United States is serving a life term.
- Another 11 percent of inmates are in prison for terms of more than 20 years.
- Between 1984 and 2008, the number of prisoners serving life terms in the United States increased from 34,000 to more than 140,000.
- The United States is one of a handful of countries that utilizes "life without parole" sentences. Even the International Criminal Court, which tries war criminals, cannot sentence convicts to life without parole.
- Only one in five countries, among them the United States, require mandatory (as opposed to based on judicial discretion) increased punishment for offenders who have prior convictions.
- Only 22 of 140 countries examined in the report permit the courts to try and sentence juveniles as adults. The United States is one of them.
- Only one in five countries, the United States included, permit uncapped consecutive sentences, meaning that the penalty for each additional count is added on to the penalty for the first count, with no upper limit. ■

Is punishment in the United States too harsh? Or are other countries not tough enough on crime? What can be learned by comparative research of this nature? Many other tough questions can be asked about incarceration length and the number of prisoners behind bars in America. Are we spending too much on prisons? Is society safer as a result of harsh imprisonment policies? Is sentencing discriminatory? If so, in what way? What matters most, race, gender, or social class? Or is there some other important consideration or set of considerations that affect sentencing decisions? How often are mistakes made? And what should be done with the most depraved of criminals, those whom everyone agrees should never be released? These are but a few of the most significant questions in the realm of punishment and sentencing.

This chapter first examines the history of punishment and then focuses on incarceration and capital punishment, the two most traditional and punitive forms of criminal sanctions used today. Chapter 12 reviews alternative sentences that have been developed to reduce the strain on the overburdened correctional system; these sentences provide intermediate sanctions designed to control people whose behavior and personality make incarceration unnecessary. Such sanctions include probation and other forms of community correction.

The History of Punishment

The punishment and correction of criminals has changed considerably through the ages, reflecting custom, economic conditions, and religious and political ideals.[3]

From Exile to Fines, Torture to Forfeiture

In early Greece and Rome, the most common state-administered punishment was banishment or exile. Only slaves were commonly subjected to harsh physical punishment for their misdeeds. Interpersonal violence, even attacks that resulted in death, was viewed as a private matter. These ancient peoples typically used economic punishments, such as fines, for such crimes as assault on a slave, arson, or housebreaking.

 Describe the historical development of punishment.

During the Middle Ages (the fifth to fifteenth centuries), there was little law or governmental control. Offenses were settled by blood feuds carried out by the families of the injured parties. When possible, the Roman custom of settling disputes by fine or an exchange of property was adopted as a means of resolving interpersonal conflicts with a minimum of bloodshed. After the

In earlier times, punishment was quite severe. Brutal public punishments, which included beheading and burning, were designed to teach the value of obedience to authority. Even kings, such as Charles I of England, were not immune from execution. Following his conviction on charges of treason during the English Civil War of 1642–1648, Charles was beheaded on January 30, 1649.

Dea Picture Library/Getty Images

eleventh century, during the feudal period, forfeiture of land and property was common punishment for persons who violated law and custom or who failed to fulfill their feudal obligations to their lord. The word "felony" has its origins in the twelfth century, when the term "felonia" referred to a breach of faith with one's feudal lord.

During this period the main emphasis of criminal law and punishment was on maintaining public order. If in the heat of passion or while intoxicated a person severely injured or killed his neighbor, freemen in the area would gather to pronounce a judgment and make the culprit do penance or pay compensation, called wergild. The purpose of the fine was to pacify the injured party and ensure that the conflict would not develop into a blood feud and anarchy. The inability of the peasantry to pay fines led to the use of corporal punishment, such as whipping or branding, as a substitute penalty.

The development of the common law in the eleventh century brought some standardization to penal practices. However, corrections remained an amalgam of fines and brutal physical punishments. The criminal wealthy could buy their way out of punishment and into exile, but capital and corporal punishments were used to control the criminal poor, who were executed or mutilated at ever-increasing rates. Execution, banishment, mutilation, branding, and flogging were used on a whole range of offenders, from murderers and robbers to vagrants and Gypsies. Punishments became unmatched in their cruelty, featuring a gruesome variety of physical tortures, often part of a public spectacle, presumably so that the sadistic sanctions would act as deterrents. But the variety and imagination of the tortures inflicted on even minor criminals before their death suggest that retribution, sadism, and spectacle were more important than any presumed deterrent effect.

Public Work and Transportation to the Colonies

By the end of the sixteenth century, the rise of the city and overseas colonization provided tremendous markets for manufactured goods and spurred the need for labor. Punishment of criminals changed to meet the demands created by these social conditions. Instead of being tortured or executed, many offenders were made to do hard labor for their crimes. "Poor laws," developed at the end of the sixteenth century, required that the poor, vagrants, and vagabonds be put to work in public or private enterprises. Houses of correction were developed to make it convenient to assign petty law violators to work details. In London, a workhouse was developed at Brideswell in 1557; its use became so popular that by 1576 Parliament ordered a Brideswell-type workhouse to be built in every county in England. Many convicted offenders were pressed into sea duty as galley slaves. Galley slavery was considered a fate so loathsome that many convicts mutilated themselves rather than submit to servitude on the high seas.

The constant shortage of labor in the European colonies also prompted authorities to transport convicts overseas. In England, an Order in Council of 1617 granted a reprieve and stay of execution to people convicted of robbery and other felonies who were strong enough to be employed overseas. Similar measures were used in France and Italy to recruit galley slaves and workers.

Transporting convicts to the colonies became popular: It supplied labor, cost little, and was actually profitable for the government, since manufacturers and plantation owners paid for the convicts' services. The Old Bailey Court in London supplied at least 10,000 convicts between 1717 and 1775. Convicts would serve a period as workers and then become free again.

The American Revolution ended the transportation of felons to North America, but it continued in Australia and New Zealand. Between 1787 and 1875, when the practice was finally abandoned, over 135,000 felons were transported to Australia.

Web App 11.1

For more information about crimes and punishment methods in colonial America, visit http://www.history.org/Foundation/journal/spring03/branks.cfm.

Although transportation in lieu of a death sentence may at first glance seem advantageous, transported prisoners endured enormous hardships. Those who were sent to Australia suffered incredible physical abuse, including severe whippings and mutilation. Many of the British prison officials placed in charge of the Australian penal colonies could best be described as sociopaths or sadists.

The Rise of the Prison

Between the American Revolution in 1776 and the first decades of the nineteenth century, the European and U.S. populations increased rapidly. Transportation of convicts to North America was no longer an option. The increased use of machinery made industry capital intensive, not labor intensive. As a result, there was less need for unskilled laborers in England, and many workers could not find suitable employment.

The gulf between poor workers and wealthy landowners and merchants widened. The crime rate rose significantly, prompting a return to physical punishment and increased use of the death penalty. During the latter part of the eighteenth century, 350 types of crime in England were punishable by death. Although many people sentenced to death for trivial offenses were spared the gallows, the use of capital punishment was common in England during the mid-eighteenth century. Prompted by the excessive use of physical and capital punishment, legal philosophers argued that physical punishment should be replaced by periods of confinement and incapacitation. Jails and workhouses were thus used to hold petty offenders, vagabonds, the homeless, and debtors. However, these institutions were not meant for hard-core criminals. One solution to imprisoning a growing criminal population was to keep prisoners in abandoned ships anchored in rivers and harbors throughout England. In 1777, the degradation under which prisoners lived in these ships inspired John Howard, the sheriff of Bedfordshire, to write *The State of the Prisons in England and Wales*, which led to Parliament's passage of legislation mandating the construction of secure and sanitary structures to house prisoners.

By 1820, long periods of incarceration in walled institutions called reformatories or **penitentiaries** began to replace physical punishment in England and the United States. These institutions were considered liberal reforms during a time when harsh physical punishment and incarceration in filthy holding facilities were the norm. The history of correctional institutions will be discussed further in Chapter 13. Incarceration has remained the primary mode of punishment for serious offenses in the United States since it was introduced in the early nineteenth century. Ironically, in our high-tech society, some of the institutions developed soon after the Revolutionary War are still in use today. In contemporary society, prison as a method of punishment has been supplemented by a sentence to community supervision for less serious offenders, and the death penalty is reserved for those considered to be the most serious and dangerous.

penitentiary
A state or federal correctional institution for incarceration of felony offenders for terms of one year or more.

FACT CHECK ✓

YOUR OPINION: Are there too many people in prison, too few, or about the right amount?

PUBLIC OPINION:

TOO MANY: 45%

TOO FEW: 13%

ABOUT THE RIGHT AMOUNT: 28%

DON'T KNOW: 14%

REALITY: There is no "acceptable" number of people in prison. Some people clearly feel there are too many people in prison; others think Americans have embarked on an imprisonment binge that drastically needs reversing. According to the International Centre for Prison Studies, the U.S. prison population rate (which adjusts for a country's population size) leads the rest of the world, particularly other prosperous and developed nations, by a wide margin.

DISCUSSION: Does the U.S. incarcerate too many people relative to other nations?

Sources: Public Opinion Strategies/The Mellan Group, *Public Opinion on Sentencing and Corrections Policy in America*, March 2012, https://www.prisonlegalnews.org/media/publications/pew_center_public_opinion_on_sentencing_and_corrections_policy_in_us_2012.pdf (accessed July 2014); International Centre for Prison Studies, *World Prison Brief*, http://www.prisonstudies.org/world-prison-brief (accessed July 2014).

The Goals of Punishment

When we hear about a notorious criminal receiving a long prison sentence or the death penalty for a particularly heinous crime, each of us has a distinct reaction. Some of us are gratified that a truly evil person "got just what he deserved." Many people feel safer because a dangerous person is now "where he can't harm any other innocent victims." Others hope the punishment serves as a warning to potential criminals that "everyone gets caught in the end." Some may actually feel sorry for the defendant—"he got a raw deal, he needs help, not punishment"—and still others hope that "when he gets out, he'll have learned his lesson." And when an offender is forced to pay a large fine, we say, "What goes around comes around."

Any of these sentiments may be at work when criminal sentences are formulated. After all, punishments are devised and implemented by judges, many of whom are elected officials and share the general public's sentiments and fears. The objectives of criminal sentencing today can usually be grouped into six distinct areas: general deterrence, incapacitation, specific deterrence, retribution/just desert, rehabilitation, and equity/restitution.

 LO2 List the major goals of contemporary sentencing.

General Deterrence

According to the concept of **general deterrence**, people should be punished to set an example for others. If someone is punished severely, others will be too afraid to break the law, knowing that they will face similar treatment. If the state can convince potential criminals that the punishment they face is certain, swift, and severe, they will be too afraid to even contemplate committing criminal offenses. However, punishment cannot be so harsh that it seems disproportionate and unfair. If it did, people would believe they have nothing to lose, and their crimes might escalate in frequency and severity. Thus, if the crime of rape were punished by death, rapists might be encouraged to kill their victims to dispose of the one person who could identify them at trial. Since they would already be facing the death penalty for rape, they would have nothing more to lose.

general deterrence
A crime control policy that depends on the fear of criminal penalties. General deterrence measures, such as long prison sentences for violent crimes, are aimed at convincing the potential law violator that the pains associated with the crime outweigh the benefits.

Some justice experts believe that the recent decline in the crime rate is a result of increasing criminal penalties. Once arrested, people have a greater chance of being convicted today than they did in the past. This phenomenon is referred to as "expected punishment," defined as the number of days in prison a typical criminal can expect to serve per crime.[4] Expected punishment rates are actually still quite low because (a) crime clearance rates remain well under 50 percent, (b) many cases are dropped at the pretrial and trial stages (*nolle prosequi*), and (c) about one-third of convicted felons are given probationary rather than prison sentences.

Take for instance the crime of burglary. About 2 million burglaries are reported to the police each year, about 300,000 burglars are arrested, 100,000 are convicted, and about 40,000 are sent to prison. Therefore, for every 50 reported burglaries, only one burglar is incarcerated. (Keep in mind that some burglars commit many crimes per year, so we are not talking about 2 million individual burglars but 2 million burglaries.) Such inefficiency limits the deterrent effect of punishment.

The story is more complicated if we look at time sentenced and time served. The average prison sentence received by violent felony offenders in state courts decreased from nearly seven years in 1992 to about five years, according to the most recent data available.[5] The actual time served per sentence, however, has increased somewhat during this period, meaning that inmates are spending more of their sentence behind bars before they are released.[6] On the one hand, deterrence advocates would argue that if prison sentences continue to decline, expected punishments will drop, and as a result crime rates may increase. On the other hand, if the actual time served continues to increase, crime rates may eventually drop because the "cost" of crime (the ratio of punishment to crime) has risen.

Incapacitation

incapacitation

The policy of keeping dangerous criminals in confinement to eliminate the risk of their repeating their offense in society.

Because criminals will not be able to repeat their criminal acts while they are under state control, **incapacitation** of criminals is another goal of sentencing. For some offenders, this means a period in a high-security state prison where behavior is closely monitored. If dangerous criminals are kept behind bars, they will not be able to repeat their illegal activities.

Does incapacitating criminals help reduce the crime rate? The evidence is mixed. Between 1990 and 2012, the prison population doubled (from 700,000 to more than 1.5 million[7]) and the crime rate dropped significantly during the same time, indicating a significant incarceration effect. However, there have also been periods, such as between 1980 and 1990, when the prison population increased and so did the crime rate. This indicates that incarceration trends may influence crime rates but that crime rates may be more closely related to other factors, such as population makeup, police effectiveness, drug use, and the economy.[8]

L03 Distinguish among general and specific deterrence, incapacitation, and retribution.

It is also possible that incarceration can have a short-term effect of reducing crime while the person is behind bars but that this effect quickly ends once the prisoner is released into the community. The prison experience may actually increase the likelihood of reoffending. Many inmates have not engaged in any correctional rehabilitation, and others are exposed to highly dangerous, experienced offenders. This produces a criminogenic effect, increasing the likelihood of their offending once released back into the community.[9]

specific deterrence

A crime control policy suggesting that punishment should be severe enough to convince convicted offenders never to repeat their criminal activity.

Even if an incarceration policy were effective, its benefits would diminish as more and more people were put in prison. Think of it this way: If the country had only a single prison cell and only one person could be locked up at a time, chances are that person would be the nation's most dangerous, violent chronic offender. The crime reduction benefit of locking up just that single person would be significant. If we could only incarcerate two, the second inmate would be slightly less dangerous. Each time a person is added to the prison population, the crime reduction benefit is somewhat less than that of jailing the inmate who came before. We now have more than 1.5 million people behind prison bars. The millionth-plus inmate is far less dangerous than the first, and the incarceration benefits of locking him or her up are significantly less, yet the *cost* of incarcerating each new inmate remains the same as the first![10] Thus, by definition, using incapacitation to reduce crime rates always brings diminishing returns.[11]

Nancy Stone/MCT/Landov

Shortly after being released from prison, Reynolds Wintersmith carries a box of donated clothes into a halfway house in Chicago where he will live for the next couple of months. Wintersmith was sentenced to life without parole when he was 17 for a nonviolent drug charge, but he was given clemency by President Obama and released from federal custody in 2014. It is unclear whether life sentences serve as general deterrents, but they clearly serve a specific deterrent function, preventing offenders from threatening the public.

Specific Deterrence

Another goal of punishment is to convince offenders that the pains of punishment are greater than the benefits of crime, so they will not repeat their criminal offending; the experience of suffering punishment should inhibit future law violations.

Does a **specific deterrence** strategy reduce crime rates? A few research efforts have found that experiencing punishment can have a significant specific deterrence effect on future criminality, but these findings are balanced by research that has failed to find specific deterrence effects. For example, some studies have found that punishment reduces the likelihood that spousal abusers will reoffend, but others have failed to get the same positive results.[12]

Claims for a specific deterrent effect are further weakened by data showing that most inmates (more than 80 percent) who are released from prison have had prior convictions, and the great majority (68 percent) will reoffend soon after their release.[13]

In some instances, rather than reducing the frequency of crime, severe punishments may actually increase reoffending rates.[14] Some states are now employing high-security "supermax" prisons, which use a bare minimum of treatment and 23-hour-a-day lockdown. Certainly such a harsh regimen should deter future criminality. But a recent study in the state of Washington that matched on a one-to-one basis supermax prisoners with inmates from more traditional prisons showed that upon release, supermax prisoners had significantly higher felony recidivism rates than similar inmates who did their time in less secure institutions.[15]

How is it possible that harsh sentences actually increase the likelihood of future crime?

- Punishment may bring defiance rather than deterrence. People who are harshly treated may want to show that they cannot be broken by the system.

- The stigma of harsh treatment labels people and helps lock offenders into a criminal career instead of convincing them to avoid one.

- Criminals who are punished may also believe that the likelihood of getting caught twice for the same type of crime is remote: "Lightning never strikes twice in the same spot," they may reason; no one is that unlucky.[16]

Despite these sketchy results, the goal of specific deterrence remains a fundamental part of sentencing. Some judges and policy makers maintain that a "taste of the bars" should reduce the desire for repeat offending.[17]

Retribution/Just Desert

According to the retributive goal of sentencing, the essential purpose of the criminal process is to punish offenders—fairly and justly—in a manner that is proportionate to the gravity of their crimes.[18] Offenders are punished simply and solely because they *deserve* to be disciplined for what they have done: "the punishment should fit the crime."[19] It would be wrong to punish people to set an example for others or to deter would-be criminals, as the general deterrence goal demands. Punishment should be no more or less than the offender's actions deserve; it must be based on how blameworthy the person is. This is referred to as the concept of **just desert**.[20]

According to this view, punishments must be equally and fairly distributed to all people who commit similar illegal acts. However, determining just punishments can be difficult because there is generally little consensus about the treatment of criminals, the seriousness of crimes, and the proper response to criminal acts. Consequently, there has been an ongoing effort to calculate fair and just sentences and to apply them in an equitable way.

Rehabilitation

Some sentences are based on the need to treat and/or rehabilitate criminal offenders. Because society has failed them, many offenders have been forced to grow up in disorganized neighborhoods, have been the target of biased police officers, and are disadvantaged at home, at school, and in the job market. To compensate for these deprivations, the justice system is obligated to help these unfortunate people and not

L04 Compare rehabilitation with just desert.

just desert
The philosophy of justice asserting that those who violate the rights of others deserve to be punished. The severity of punishment should be commensurate with the seriousness of the crime.

simply punish them for their misdeeds.[21] Rehabilitation advocates believe that if the proper treatment is applied, an offender will present no further threat to society.[22] It is not surprising, then, that the general public supports the treatment goal of sentencing and prefers it over policies based on punishment and incarceration.[23]

Diversion

In some instances, the court process is aimed at sparing nondangerous offenders from the stigma and labeling of a criminal conviction and further involvement with the justice process. Instead of being convicted and sentenced to traditional forms of correction, such as a stay in a county jail, the judge may allow them to be diverted into a community correctional program for treatment. As part of a diversionary sentence, the convicted offender might be asked to make restitution payments to the crime victim or participate in a community-based program that features counseling and/or drug monitoring.

Equity/Restitution

equity
The action or practice of awarding each person his or her just due. Sanctions based on equity seek to compensate individual victims and the general society for their losses due to crime.

Because criminals gain from their misdeeds, it seems both fair and just to demand that they reimburse society for its loss caused by their crimes. In the early common law, wergild and fines represented the concept of creating an equitable solution to crime by requiring the convicted offender to make restitution to both the victim and the state. The **equity** goal of punishment means that convicted criminals must pay back their victims for their loss, the justice system for the costs of processing their case, and society for any disruption they may have caused. In a so-called victimless crime such as drug trafficking, the social costs might include the expense of drug enforcement efforts, drug treatment centers, and care for infants born to drug-addicted mothers. In predatory crimes, the costs might include the services of emergency room doctors, lost workdays and productivity, and treatment for long-term psychological problems. To help defray these costs, convicted offenders might be required to pay a fine, forfeit the property they acquired through illegal gain, do community service work, make financial restitution to their victim, and reimburse the state for the costs of the criminal process. Because the criminals' actions helped expand their personal gains, rights, and privileges at society's expense, justice demands that they lose rights and privileges to restore the social balance.

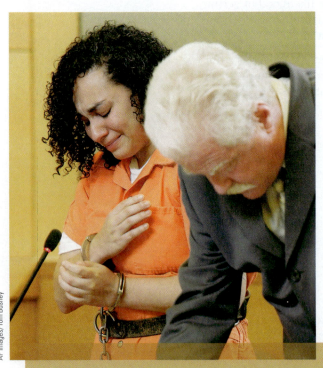

AP Images/Tom Bushey

Jessica Vega cries during her sentencing as her attorney Jeremiah Flaherty listens. Vega, who faked having cancer so donors would pay for her wedding and Caribbean honeymoon, was sentenced to the nearly two months she has already served in jail. She was also ordered to perform 300 hours of community service and pay back more than $13,000 to victims in the scam.

Restoration

Defendants may be asked to confront their behavior, the damage they caused the victim, and the shame they brought to their family, friends, and community. A restoration sentence might require that the convicted recognize that he or she caused injury to personal and social relations, along with a determination and acceptance of responsibility, accompanied by a statement of remorse. Restoration involves turning the justice system into a "healing" process rather a distributor of retribution and revenge. The intended result of the sentence is to repair injuries suffered by the victim and the community, while ensuring reintegration of the offender. Among the techniques used are programs that encourage reconciling the conflicts between offenders

CONCEPT SUMMARY 11.1
Goals of Criminal Sentencing

Sentencing Goal	Sentencing Purpose
General deterrence	By punishing the known offender for his or her misdeeds, society hopes to convince would-be offenders that the pains of punishment outweigh the potential benefits of criminal behavior. Punishment is based on its effect on others.
Specific deterrence	Experiencing harsh criminal punishments should convince convicted offenders that crime does not pay. The suffering caused by punishment should inhibit future law violations.
Incapacitation	By incapacitating a convicted offender in a secure facility, such as a prison or jail, the state seeks to reduce or eliminate his or her opportunity to commit future crimes. Offenders are confined not for what they have done but for what it is feared they might do in the future.
Rehabilitation	Sentencing is aimed at reducing future criminality by treating and eliminating the underlying causes of crime.
Diversion	Sentencing is aimed at sparing nondangerous offenders from the stigma and labeling of a criminal conviction and involvement with the justice process.
Retribution/just desert	Because criminals benefit from their misdeeds, they deserve to be punished for their criminal acts. It is only fair that criminals who have committed the most serious crime, murder, receive the most severe penalty, death.
Equity/restitution	Because criminals gain from their misdeeds, it seems both fair and just to demand that they reimburse society for the loss(es) it has sustained as a consequence of their crimes. The equity goal of punishment means that convicted criminals must pay back their victims for their loss, the justice system for the costs of processing their case, and society for any disruption they may have caused.
Restoration	Defendants may be asked to confront their behavior, the damage they caused the victim, and the shame they brought to their family, friends, and community. The goal is to satisfy everyone's needs and restore the wrongdoer to good standing in society.

and victims via victim advocacy, mediation programs, and sentencing circles, in which crime victims and their families are brought together with offenders and their families in an effort to formulate a sanction that addresses the needs of each party. Victims are given a chance to voice their stories, and offenders can help compensate them financially or provide some service (for example, fixing damaged property).[24] The goal is to enable offenders to appreciate the damage they have caused, to make amends, and to be reintegrated into society.

The goals of sentencing are summarized in Concept Summary 11.1.

Imposing the Sentence

In most felony cases, except where the law provides for mandatory prison terms, sentencing is usually based on a variety of information available to the judge. Some jurisdictions allow victims to make impact statements that are considered at sentencing hearings. Most judges also consider a presentence investigation report by the probation department in making a sentencing decision. This report is a social and personal history, as well as an evaluation of the defendant's chances for rehabilitation within the community.

Example: In state X
1. Rape is punishable by 10 years in prison
2. Possession of a handgun by 3 years
3. Possession of heroin by 4 years

Consecutive sentence
Rape + possession of a handgun + possession of heroin
10 + 3 + 4 = 17 years
(each sentence served individually)

Concurrent sentence
Rape + possession of a handgun + possession of heroin
10 years
(all sentences served simultaneously)

FIGURE 11.1   Consecutive vs. Concurrent Sentences

Explain how sentences are imposed.

concurrent sentences
Prison sentences for two or more criminal acts, served simultaneously and run together.

consecutive sentence
Prison sentences for two or more criminal acts, served one after the other.

Concurrent versus Consecutive Sentences

In some instances, when an accused is convicted of two or more charges, the judge must decide whether to impose consecutive or **concurrent sentences**. If the sentences are concurrent, they begin the same day and are completed when the longest term has been served. For example, a defendant is convicted of burglarizing an apartment and assaulting its occupant; he is sentenced to 3 years on a charge of assault and 10 years for burglary, with the sentences to be served concurrently. After 10 years in prison, the sentences would be completed.

In contrast, receiving a **consecutive sentence** means that on completion of the sentence for one crime, the offender begins serving time for the second of multiple crimes. If the defendant in the previous example had been sentenced consecutively, he would serve 3 years on the assault charge and then 10 years for the burglary. Therefore, the total term on the two charges would be 13 years. Concurrent sentences are the norm; consecutive sentences are requested for the most serious criminals and for those who are unwilling to cooperate with authorities. Figure 11.1 shows the difference between a consecutive and concurrent sentence.

The Effect of Good Time

When judges impose an incarceration sentence, they know and take into account the fact that the amount of time spent in prison is reduced by the implementation of "time off for good behavior." This concept was first used in 1817 in New York, and it was quickly adopted in most other jurisdictions. Good time is still in use today; state inmates can accrue standard good time at a rate ranging from 10 to 15 days per month. Federal inmates can get almost 50 days taken off the end of their sentence each year. In addition, some correctional authorities grant earned sentence reductions to inmates who participate in treatment programs, such as educational and vocational training, or who volunteer for experimental medical testing programs. In some jurisdictions, more than half of a determinate sentence (see the following section) can be erased by accumulating both standard and earned good time.

Good-time laws allow inmates to calculate their release date at the time they enter prison by subtracting the expected good time from their sentence. However, good time can be lost if inmates break prison rules, get into fights, or disobey correctional officers. In some jurisdictions, former inmates can be returned to prison to serve the balance of their unexpired sentence when their good time is revoked for failing to conform to conditions set down for their release (for example, not reporting to a postrelease supervisor or abusing drugs).

Sentencing Models

When a convicted offender is sentenced to prison, the statutes of the jurisdiction in which the crime was committed determine the penalties that may be imposed by the court. Over the years, a variety of sentencing structures have been used in the United States. They include indeterminate sentences, determinate sentences, and mandatory sentences.

Indeterminate Sentences

In the 1870s, prison reformers Enoch Wines and Zebulon Brockway and others called for creation of **indeterminate sentences** tailored to fit individual needs. Offenders, the argument went, should be confined only until they are rehabilitated and then released on parole. Criminals were believed to be "sick" rather than bad; they could be successfully treated in prison. Rather than holding that "the punishment should fit the crime," reformers believed "the treatment should fit the offender."

The indeterminate sentence is still the most widely used type of sentence in the United States. Convicted offenders are typically given a "light" minimum sentence that must be served and a lengthy maximum sentence that is the outer boundary of the time that can be served. For example, the legislature might set a sentence of a minimum of 2 years and a maximum of 20 years for burglary; the convicted offender must be sentenced to no less than 2 years but to no more than 20 years in prison. Under this scheme, the actual length of time served by the offender is controlled by both the judge and the correctional agency. A judge could sentence a burglar to 5 to 15 years; the inmate then would be paroled from confinement soon after serving the minimum sentence if the correctional authorities believe that she is ready to live in the community. If the inmate accumulates good time, she could be released in as little as 30 months; a troublesome inmate would be forced to do all 15 years.

Most jurisdictions that use indeterminate sentences employ statutes that specify minimum and maximum terms but allow judicial discretion to fix the actual sentence within those limits. The typical minimum sentence is at least one year; a few state jurisdictions require at least a two-year minimum sentence for felons.[25]

Determinate Sentences

Dissatisfaction with the disparity and uncertainty of indeterminate sentencing has prompted some states and the federal government to abandon it in favor of determinate sentencing models, or structured sentencing models aimed at curbing judicial discretion (discussed in the next section).

Determinate sentences offer a fixed term of years, the maximum set in law by the legislature, to be served by the offender sentenced to prison for a particular crime. If the law provides for a sentence of up to 20 years for robbery, the judge might sentence a repeat offender to a 15-year term; another, less-experienced felon might receive a more lenient sentence of 5 years.

SENTENCING GUIDELINES In order to regulate the length of determinate sentences and curb judicial discretion, most jurisdictions that employ them have developed methods to structure and control the sentencing process and make it more rational. To accomplish this task, **sentencing guidelines** have been implemented by determinate sentencing states and the federal government. Guidelines give judges a recommended sentence based on the seriousness of a crime and the background of an offender: the more serious the crime and the more extensive the offender's criminal background, the longer the prison term recommended by the guidelines. For example, guidelines might recommend a sentence of five years for robbery if the offender had no prior offense record and did not use excessive force or violence. For a second offense, the recommended sentence would increase to seven years; those who used force and had a prior record will have three years added to their sentence, and so on. By eliminating judicial discretion, guidelines are designed to reduce racial and gender disparity.[26]

Guidelines were created by appointed sentencing commissions whose members attempted to formulate what an "ideal" sentence would be for a particular crime and offender. In some instances, their decisions were based on empirical

indeterminate sentence
A term of incarceration with a stated minimum and maximum length, such as a sentence to prison for a period of from 3 to 10 years. The prisoner is eligible for parole after the minimum sentence has been served. Based on the belief that sentences should fit the criminal, indeterminate sentences allow individualized sentences and provide for sentencing flexibility. Judges can set a high minimum to override the purpose of the indeterminate sentence.

 L06 Classify the various types of sentencing structures.

determinate sentence
A fixed term of incarceration, such as three years' imprisonment. Determinate sentences are felt by many to be too restrictive for rehabilitative purposes; the advantage is that offenders know how much time they have to serve—that is, when they will be released.

sentencing guidelines
A set of standards that defines parameters for trial judges to follow in their sentencing decisions.

Web App 11.2

For more information about the federal sentencing guidelines, visit http://www.ussc.gov/.

analysis of existing sentencing practices; in other instances, sentences were based on the beliefs of the commissioners. Regardless of the formulation, there is a great deal of variation within guidelines. Some coexist with parole release, and some do not. Some deal with all crimes and others only with felonies. Some set narrow sentencing ranges, and some set broad ones. Some address sentences of all types, and some address only state prison sentences.[27] Some states employ what is known as a "comprehensive structured sentencing system," which sets sentencing standards for felonies and misdemeanors, and for prison, jail, intermediate, and community punishments. They also include mechanisms for tying sentencing policy to correctional capacity and for distributing state funds to stimulate and support local corrections programs.

THE SENTENCING GRID   One method of guideline creation is to create a grid with prior record and current offense as the two coordinates and set out specific punishments. Figure 11.2 shows Minnesota's guidelines. Note that as prior record and offense severity increase, so does recommended sentence length. After a certain point, probation is no longer an option, and the defendant must do prison time. A burglar with no prior convictions can expect to receive probation for a house break-in; an experienced burglar with six or more prior convictions can get up to 57 months for the same crime. Although it is expected that the guidelines will be followed, they are only recommendations based on typical circumstances. If a case is not typical, the judge can depart from the recommended sentence. If the court does depart, the judge must state the reasons for departure, and either the prosecution or the defense may appeal the pronounced sentence.

LEGAL CHALLENGES AND THEIR IMPACT   Several Supreme Court cases have changed how guidelines can be used. Examples include:

- *Apprendi v. New Jersey.* Apprendi pleaded guilty to second-degree possession of a firearm, a charge that carried a prison sentence of between 5 and 10 years. Prosecutors asked the court to impose the state's hate crime law sentencing enhancement provision, which would increase his sentence to between 10 and 20 years. The judge considered the evidence and found it met the hate crime standard. The enhanced prison sentence based on the hate crime statute exceeded the statutory maximum sentence for the underlying offense of weapon possession. The Supreme Court ruled that any factor other than a prior conviction that increases the penalty for the crime beyond the statutory maximum must be submitted to a jury and proved beyond a reasonable doubt.[28]

- *Blakely v. Washington.* Here the Court found that the state of Washington's sentencing guidelines were a violation of a defendant's Sixth Amendment rights because they allowed a judge to consider aggravating factors that would enhance the sentence.[29] The Court ruled that this amounts to a finding of fact without the benefit of a jury trial or personal admission. In *Blakely*, the sentencing judge, acting alone, decided that the offense involved "deliberate cruelty" and enhanced Blakely's sentence. Proving a state of mind such as "deliberate cruelty" must be determined by a jury beyond a reasonable doubt, not by a judge applying guidelines. Here the Court is saying that the right to a jury trial means that a defendant has the right to have a jury, not a judge, make all the factual findings required to impose a sentence in excess of the presumptive sentence guideline, unless the defendant formally admits some or all of the factors or formally waives that right.

- *United States v. Booker.* In *Booker*, the Court ruled that the federal guidelines were unconstitutional, allowing that judges should consider the guideline ranges but must also be permitted to alter sentences in consideration of

4.A. Sentencing Guidelines Grid

Presumptive sentence lengths are in months. Italicized numbers within the grid denote the discretionary range within which a court may sentence without the sentence being deemed a departure. Offenders with stayed felony sentences may be subject to local confinement.

CRIMINAL HISTORY SCORE

SEVERITY LEVEL OF CONVICTION OFFENSE (Example offenses listed in italics)		0	1	2	3	4	5	6 or more
Murder, 2nd Degree (intentional murder; drive-by-shootings)	11	306 *261–367*	326 *278–391*	346 *295–415*	366 *312–439*	386 *329–463*	406 *346–480[2]*	426 *363–480[2]*
Murder, 3rd Degree Murder, 2nd Degree (unintentional murder)	10	150 *128–180*	165 *141–198*	180 *153–216*	195 *166–234*	210 *179–252*	225 *192–270*	240 *204–288*
Assault, 1st Degree Controlled Substance Crime, 1st Degree	9	86 *74–103*	98 *84–117*	110 *94–132*	122 *104–146*	134 *114–160*	146 *125–175*	158 *135–189*
Aggravated Robbery, 1st Degree Controlled Substance Crime, 2nd Degree	8	48 *41–57*	58 *50–69*	68 *58–81*	78 *67–93*	88 *75–105*	98 *84–117*	108 *92–129*
Felony DWI	7	36	42	48	54 *46–64*	60 *51–72*	66 *57–79*	72 *62–84[2]*
Controlled Substance Crime, 3rd Degree	6	21	27	33	39 *34–46*	45 *39–54*	51 *44–61*	57 *49–68*
Residential Burglary Simple Robbery	5	18	23	28	33 *29–39*	38 *33–45*	43 *37–51*	48 *41–57*
Nonresidential Burglary	4	12[1]	15	18	21	24 *21–28*	27 *23–32*	30 *26–36*
Theft Crimes (over $5,000)	3	12[1]	13	15	17	19 *17–22*	21 *18–25*	23 *20–27*
Theft Crimes ($5,000 or less) Check Forgery ($251–$2,500)	2	12[1]	12[1]	13	15	17	19	21 *18–25*
Sale of Simulated Controlled Substance	1	12[1]	12[1]	12[1]	13	15	17	19 *17–22*

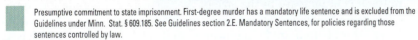 Presumptive commitment to state imprisonment. First-degree murder has a mandatory life sentence and is excluded from the Guidelines under Minn. Stat. § 609.185. See Guidelines section 2.E. Mandatory Sentences, for policies regarding those sentences controlled by law.

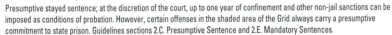 Presumptive stayed sentence; at the discretion of the court, up to one year of confinement and other non-jail sanctions can be imposed as conditions of probation. However, certain offenses in the shaded area of the Grid always carry a presumptive commitment to state prison. Guidelines sections 2.C. Presumptive Sentence and 2.E. Mandatory Sentences.

[1]12[1] = One year and one day

[2]Minn. Stat. § 244.09 requires that the Guidelines provide a range for sentences that are presumptive commitment to state imprisonment of 15% lower and 20% higher than the fixed duration displayed, provided that the minimum sentence is not less than one year and one day and the maximum sentence is not more than the statutory maximum. Guidelines section 2.C.1–2. Presumptive Sentence.

FIGURE 11.2 **Minnesota Sentencing Guidelines Grid**

other factors; sentences could then be subject to appellate review if they were unreasonable.[30] This case may be interpreted as suggesting that guidelines must be used in an advisory capacity alone.

These cases did not outlaw guidelines but, rather, ruled that changes are needed in the way they are administered. For example, the federal guidelines have been heavily criticized for their disparity in the punishment for possessing crack versus powdered cocaine. This differential was a source of irritation to critics who believed that the disparity reflected racism (that is, African Americans were more likely to use crack, while Caucasians favored powdered cocaine). In 2007, the Federal Sentencing Commission revised the guidelines and retroactively considered reducing sentences for people convicted of crack possession.[31] This was partly prompted by the Supreme Court's decision in *Kimbrough v. United States*, in which it was decided that the federal cocaine sentencing guidelines, like other federal sentencing guidelines, are advisory.[32]

The practical result of these decisions is this: If a sentence departs markedly from the guidelines, it is not necessarily problematic. On the other hand, as a consequence of the Court's decision in *Rita v. United States*, any sentence that falls within the federal sentencing guidelines is presumptively reasonable (meaning that as far as the Court is concerned, the sentence is reasonable).[33]

In a recent and rather ironic twist on all this, the U.S. Sentencing Commission found significant evidence that minorities are being treated *more harshly*, not less harshly, in the wake of the *Booker* decision.[34] Recall that *Booker* made the federal sentencing guidelines advisory. It was hoped that we would see *reduced* sentencing disparities in the years since 2006, when the decision was handed down. Yet the Sentencing Commission found that "black male offenders received longer sentences than white male offenders ... [and that] ... the differences in sentence length have increased steadily since *Booker*."

Mandatory Sentences

mandatory sentence
A statutory requirement that a certain penalty shall be set and carried out in all cases upon conviction for a specified offense or series of offenses.

Another effort to limit judicial discretion and at the same time get tough on crime has been the development of the **mandatory sentence**. Some states have passed legislation prohibiting people convicted of certain offenses, such as violent crimes or drug trafficking, from being placed on probation; they must serve at least some time in prison. Other statutes are aimed at chronic recidivists. Mandatory sentencing legislation may impose minimum and maximum terms, but usually it requires a fixed prison sentence.

Mandatory sentencing generally limits the judge's discretionary power to impose any disposition but that authorized by the legislature; as a result, it limits individualized sentencing and restricts sentencing disparity. More than 35 states have already replaced discretionary sentencing with fixed-term mandatory sentences for such crimes as the sale of hard drugs, kidnapping, gun possession, and arson. The results have been mixed. Mandatory sentences have contributed to the recent increase in the size of the correctional population to record levels. Because of mandatory sentences, many offenders who in the past might have received probation are being incarcerated. The Supreme Court has sanctioned certain mandatory sentences, holding that they do not violate the Eighth Amendment's prohibition against cruel and unusual punishment.[35]

THREE-STRIKES LAWS Three-strikes (and you're out) laws provide lengthy terms for any person convicted of three felony offenses, even if the third crime is relatively trivial. The law is applied differently in different state jurisdictions. Some require all three felony convictions to be for violent crimes in order for the mandatory sentence to be pronounced, whereas others provide enhanced sentencing for any third felony conviction as long as the first two felonies were deemed to be either violent or serious, or both.

Although welcomed by conservatives seeking a remedy for violent crime, the three-strikes policy is controversial because a person convicted of a minor felony can receive a life sentence. In two well-known California cases, defendants received life sentences for (a) stealing a slice of pizza and (b) stealing some chocolate chip cookies.[36] The pizza thief, Jerry Dewayne Williams, later had his sentence reduced to "only" six years.

Three-strikes laws have undeniable political appeal to legislators being pressured by their constituents to "do something about crime." But even if such laws

EVIDENCE-based justice

DO THREE-STRIKES LAWS DETER?

In 1994, Washington became the first state to enact a three-strikes law. Other states quickly followed suit. Among the many versions of three-strikes laws, California's is the most punitive. It provides that a person who has two prior convictions for serious felonies and is convicted of *any* third felony can be sent to prison for the rest of his or her life. California's law has been rather controversial, in part because of legal challenges raised by offenders who ended up going to prison for a long time after committing relatively minor third felonies (see the accompanying discussion of *Lockyer v. Andrade* and *Ewing v. California*). Because of the controversial nature of three-strikes laws, researchers have been drawn to them. They have been particularly interested in the general deterrent effects of such laws. Do offenders refrain from committing third felonies for fear of being sentenced to prison for the rest of their lives? Clearly, three-strikes laws have a *specific* deterrent effect because a repeat offender who is in prison cannot harm the community, but do three-strikes laws also discourage would-be offenders from breaking the law? Researchers have focused heavily on California's law because of its harsh nature, but nationwide studies have been published, as well.

It is certainly plausible that three-strikes laws have a general deterrent effect. The very phrase "three strikes" is catchy and easy to remember. Unfortunately, though, precious little research supports any kind of deterrent effect. Joanna Shepherd, an economist, published a 2002 study wherein she found that California's three-strikes law led to significant reductions in serious crime, but her findings have been largely drowned out by a number of more recent studies that have detected little if any deterrent effect. John Worrall replicated Shepherd's approach and found no evidence that three strikes deters. Interestingly, two teams of researchers have found that three-strikes laws may actually *increase* crime, particularly homicide, as offenders who face possible life terms go to lethal lengths (that is, they kill their pursuers) to resist apprehension. We cannot definitively state that three-strikes laws do nothing to deter crime, but we can certainly conclude that the jury is still out.

Sources: Joanna M. Shepherd, "Fear of the First Strike: The Full Deterrent Effect of California's Two- and Three-Strikes Legislation," *Journal of Legal Studies* 31 (2002): 159–201; John L. Worrall, "The Effect of Three-Strikes Legislation on Serious Crime in California," *Journal of Criminal Justice* 32 (2004): 283–296; Thomas B. Marvell and Carlisle E. Moody, "The Lethal Effects of Three-Strikes Laws," *Journal of Legal Studies* 30 (2001): 89–106; Tomislav Kovandzic, John J. Sloan III, and Lynne M. Vieraitis, "Unintended Consequences of Politically Popular Sentencing Policy: The Homicide-Promoting Effects of Three Strikes in U.S. Cities (1980–1999)," *Criminology and Public Policy* 1 (2002): 399–424.

are possibly effective against crime (see the accompanying Evidence-Based Justice feature), any effort to deter criminal behavior through tough laws is not without costs. Criminologist Marc Mauer, a leading opponent of the three-strikes law, finds that the approach may satisfy the public's hunger for retribution but makes little practical sense. First, many "three-time losers" are on the brink of aging out of crime; locking them up for life should have little effect on the crime rate. In addition, current sentences for chronic violent offenders are already severe, yet their punishment seems to have had little effect in reducing national violence rates. The efficacy of a three-strikes policy also suffers because criminals typically underestimate their risk of apprehension, while overestimating the rewards of crime. Given their inflated view of the benefits of crime, coupled with a seeming disregard of the risks of apprehension and punishment, it is unlikely a three-strikes policy can have a measurable effect on the crime rate.

Even if such a policy could reduce the number of career offenders on the street, the drain in economic resources that might have gone for education and social welfare ensures that a new generation of young criminals will fill the offending shoes of their incarcerated brethren. Mauer also suggests that a three-strikes policy severely stresses an already overburdened prison system, driving up costs, and, presumably, reducing resources available to house other inmates.

Mauer warns too that African Americans face an increased risk of being sentenced under three-strikes statutes, expanding the racial disparity in sentencing. More ominous is the fact that police officers may be put at risk because two-time offenders would violently resist arrest, knowing that they face a life sentence.

LEGAL CONTROLS Is it fair to give someone a life sentence for a petty crime merely because she or he has prior convictions? On March 6, 2003, the Supreme Court in *Lockyer v. Andrade* upheld the three-strikes sentence of Leandro Andrade, a man sentenced to prison in California for 50 years for stealing $153 worth of videotapes.[37] It also upheld the conviction of Gary Ewing, who appealed his 25-year sentence for stealing a set of golf clubs.[38] In both cases the Court ruled that the challenged sentences were not so grossly disproportionate as to violate the Eighth Amendment's prohibition against cruel and unusual punishment. In her majority decision, Justice Sandra Day O'Connor added that any criticism of the law "is appropriately directed at the legislature" and is not a judicial matter. Four judges dissented in the case, arguing that the Court's test for sentence disproportionality had been met. Writing in the *Andrade* case, Justice David Souter said, "If Andrade's sentence is not grossly disproportionate, the principle has no meaning."

Truth in Sentencing

truth in sentencing
A sentencing scheme requiring that offenders serve at least 85 percent of their original sentence before being eligible for parole or other forms of early release.

As you may recall, even though criminal sentences are getting shorter, people are spending more of their sentence behind bars. One reason is a get-tough measure designed to fight a rising crime rate: **truth in sentencing**. These laws require offenders to serve a substantial portion of their prison sentence behind bars.[39] Parole eligibility and good-time credits are restricted or eliminated. The movement was encouraged by the Violent Offender Incarceration and Truth-in-Sentencing Incentive Grants Program, part of the federal government's 1994 crime act, which offered funds to help the states pay the costs involved with creating longer sentences. To qualify for federal funds, states must require persons convicted of a violent felony crime to serve not less than 85 percent of their prison sentence. The provision is already having an effect: Violent offenders released from prison in 1996 served slightly more than half of their prison sentence, or 45 months. Under truth-in-sentencing laws, violent inmates entering prison today will serve an average of 88 months behind bars. Today, more than half the states and the District of Columbia meet the federal Truth-in-Sentencing Incentive Grants Program eligibility criteria, and another 13 have adopted some form of truth-in-sentencing program.

How People Are Sentenced

L07 Discuss how people are sentenced today.

The federal government conducts surveys on sentencing practices in state and federal courts.[40] The most recent survey found that more than 1.1 million adults are convicted of felonies in a single year. What happens after conviction? About 70 percent of all felons convicted in state courts are sentenced to a period of confinement—41 percent to state prisons and 28 percent to local jails.[41] The rest are sentenced to straight probation with no jail or prison time to serve.

The average felony sentence is approximately five years, but most offenders are likely to serve only half of that sentence before release.[42] Besides being sentenced to incarceration (in prison or jail), about one-third of all sentenced felons are put on probation or expected to pay a fine, pay victim restitution, receive treatment, perform community service, or comply with some other additional penalty. As Table 11.1 shows, violent felons who are given a prison sentence average about eight years, while property offenders are typically sentenced to about four years. If they receive a jail sentence, their period of confinement is considerably less.

TABLE 11.1 Lengths of Felony Sentences Imposed by State Courts

| Most Serious Conviction Offense | AVERAGE MAXIMUM SENTENCE LENGTH (IN MONTHS) FOR FELONS SENTENCED TO: | | | |
| | Incarceration | | | Probation |
	Total	Prison	Jail	
All offenses	38	57	6	38
Violent offenses	71	96	7	44
Property offenses	30	47	6	38
Drug offenses	31	50	5	37
Weapon offenses	32	48	6	37
Other offenses	24	41	5	36

Source: Sean Rosenmerkel, Matthew Durose, and Donald Farole Jr., *Felony Sentences in State Courts, 2006—Statistical Tables* (Washington, DC: Bureau of Justice Statistics, 2009), Table 1.3, http://bjs.ojp.usdoj.gov/content/pub/pdf/fssc06st.pdf (accessed July 2014).

What Factors Affect Sentencing?

What factors influence judges when they decide on criminal sentences? State sentencing codes usually include various factors that can legitimately influence the length of prison sentences. These factors include:

- The severity of the offense
- The offender's prior criminal record
- Whether the offender used violence
- Whether the offender used weapons
- Whether the crime was committed for money

Research does in fact show a strong correlation between these legal variables and the type and length of sentence meted out. Judges sentence more severely in cases involving the most serious criminal charges, such as terrorism, while being more lenient in low-severity cases.[43] As Figure 11.3 shows, people with prior convictions are much more likely to receive prison time than those convicted of similar offenses without a prior record.

Besides these legally appropriate factors, sentencing experts suspect that judges are also influenced by the defendant's age, race, gender, and income. Consideration of such variables would be a direct violation of constitutional due process and equal protection, as well as of federal statutes, such as the Civil Rights Act. Limiting judicial bias is one reason why states have adopted determinate and mandatory sentencing statutes. Do extralegal factors actually influence judges when they make sentencing decisions?

SOCIAL CLASS Evidence supports an association between social class and sentencing outcomes: Members of the lower class may expect to get longer prison sentences than more affluent defendants. One reason is that defendants who are poor may be unable to obtain quality legal representation or to make bail, factors that influence sentencing.[44] Not all research efforts have found a consistent relationship between social class and sentence length. The relationship may be more robust for some crime patterns than for others. Nonetheless, the consensus is that affluent defendants are more likely than the indigent to receive lenient sentences.[45]

GENDER Does a defendant's gender influence how he or she is sentenced? Some theorists believe that women benefit from sentence disparity because the criminal justice system is dominated by men who have a paternalistic, or protective, attitude toward women; this claim is referred to as the **chivalry hypothesis**.

chivalry hypothesis
The view that the low rates of crime and delinquency among females reflect the leniency with which female offenders are treated.

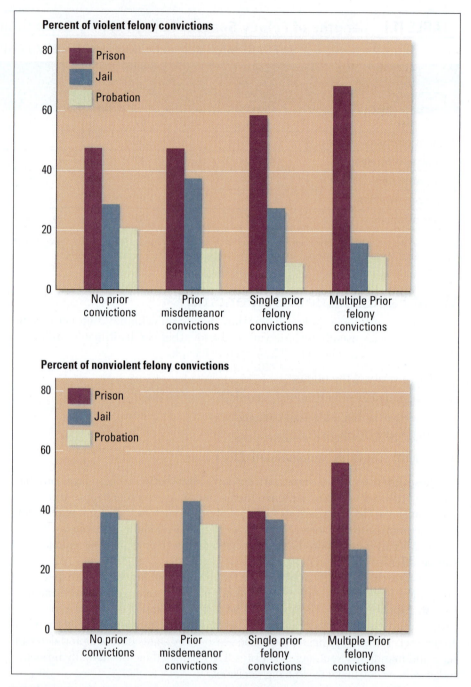

FIGURE 11.3   Type of Sentence received for a felony conviction in the 75 largest countries, by prior conviction record, 2009

Source: Brian A. Reaves, *Felony Defendants in Large Urban Counties, 2009* (Washington, DC: Bureau of Justice Statistics, 2013), p. 20.

Others argue that female criminals can be the victim of bias because their behavior violates what men believe is "proper" female behavior.[46]

Most research indicates that women receive more favorable outcomes the further they go in the criminal justice system. They are more likely to receive preferential treatment from a judge at sentencing than they are from the police officer making the arrest or the prosecutor seeking the indictment.[47] Favoritism crosses both racial and ethnic lines, benefiting African American, white, and Hispanic women.[48] Gender bias may be present because judges perceive women as better risks than men. Women have been granted more lenient pretrial release conditions and lower bail amounts than men; women are also more likely to spend less time in pretrial detention.[49] Ironically, mandatory and structured sentences, designed originally to limit bias and discretion, have resulted in harsher sentences for women. Because these methods are "gender neutral," they reverse any advantage women may have had in sentencing decisions. Some women who are peripherally involved in drug trafficking through association with boyfriends and husbands have received very long sentences.[50]

AGE Another extralegal factor that may play a role in sentencing is age. It should be expected that older people will be punished more harshly than younger ones because they have had a greater opportunity to accumulate a criminal record and most state laws increase penalties for multiple offenders. Of course, this creates the dilemma whereby an older offender, because of crimes he might have committed years ago, is punished more severely than a younger offender who is more dangerous or is committing more crimes in the present.[51]

This association is not necessarily linear. On the one hand, some judges may actually be more lenient with older defendants and more punitive toward younger ones.[52] Although sentencing leniency may result from judges' perception that the elderly pose little risk to society, such practices are a violation of the civil rights of younger defendants.[53] On the other hand, some judges may also wish to protect the youngest defendants, sparing them the pains of a prison experience.[54]

VICTIM CHARACTERISTICS Victim characteristics may also influence sentencing. Victims may be asked or allowed to make a **victim impact statement** before the sentencing judge, giving them the opportunity to tell of their experiences and describe their ordeal. In a murder case, the surviving family can recount the effect the crime has had on their lives and well-being.[55] The effect of victim and witness statements on sentencing has been the topic of some debate. See the accompanying Victim Experience box for more on victim impact statements.

Sentences may be reduced when victims have "negative" personal characteristics or qualities. For example, people convicted of raping prostitutes or substance abusers receive much shorter sentences than those who assault women without these characteristics.[56]

Sentences may also be tailored to the needs of offenders, especially when they have severe psychological deficits. In making their decision, judges may rely

victim impact statement
A postconviction statement by the victim of crime or the victim's family that may be used to guide sentencing decisions.

AP Images/*Press of Atlantic City/Danny Drake*

Martin Caballero's family (from left, stepson William Cruz, daughter Jessica Caballero, stepdaughter Nancy Cruz, stepson Christian Martinez, and wife Libia Martinez) make a victim impact statement before Judge Michael Donio during sentencing of Craig Arno for the murder of Martin Caballero in Superior Court, Mays Landing, New Jersey.

the VICTIM experience

VICTIM IMPACT STATEMENTS

BACKGROUND "She put her arms around me and told me how much she loved me. ... I remember thinking I was on top of the world." Recalling the last time he saw his wife alive, Kent Gibbons offered these heartfelt words into testimony during the penalty phase of the capital murder trial of Jason Michael Balcom, who was convicted of killing Gibbons's wife, Malinda Gibbons. "I kissed her, and I walked out the door," he told a jury. When he returned home that night, he found her on her back, bound and gagged, with a stab wound in her chest. He recalled her being cold to the touch. "I tried to wake her up, (but) she wouldn't wake up." Malinda's sister also offered a victim impact statement, telling the jury, "I cannot go to her grave ... because it is a reminder of the awful evil that put her there." And Malinda's brother said, "It is irreconcilable to learn how she died. ... to imagine her last moments was excruciating for us." Victim statements such as these are offered into evidence on a routine basis in all manner of criminal trials across the United States. But should they be?

THE BIG PICTURE In a 1982 White House Rose Garden ceremony, President Ronald Reagan announced the creation of the President's Task Force on Victims of Crime. Since that time, a powerful victims' rights movement has emerged. And among the most influential of victims' rights is the victim impact statement. All 50 states now allow some form of victim impact information at sentencing, whether by way of oral testimony or a written statement.

The nature of a victim impact statement varies from state to state and is usually spelled out in applicable statutes. The most commonly utilized method is to allow the victim (and/or co-victims, such as surviving family members) to write a letter to the sentencing judge. In crafting their letters, victims are often asked to answer a number of questions. Here is a list of possible questions, this one from Spokane County, Washington:

- How has your life changed since the crime occurred?
- How has the crime affected you emotionally or psychologically?
- How has the crime affected you financially?
- Is this crime a culmination of other crimes or violence committed by the same person?
- What fears or hopes do you have?

- What do you want to happen to the defendant (jail or prison time, treatment, etc.)?
- In your experience, do you think this defendant can be rehabilitated?
- How do you think it will affect you, your family, or the community when the defendant is released?

The vast majority of victims who offer victim impact testimony report that doing so is important, but there is concern in some circles that allowing victims to offer input at the sentencing phase could introduce an element of vengeance into the criminal justice process. What does the research tell us? Myers and colleagues found that victim impact evidence had no effect on the sentencing outcome. In contrast, Paternoster and Deise found that victim impact evidence *is* associated with the sentencing outcome. Hypothetical jurors were more likely to recommend a death sentence when they formulated favorable opinions toward the victim and victim's family. Remaining evidence is mixed, meaning it is far from clear whether victim impact statements are helpful or harmful. At the least, victim impact statements are cathartic for those who prepare and present them.

CLASSROOM EXERCISE Select 6 or 12 jurors from the class. Divide the remaining students into groups of three. Each three-member group should consist of a prosecutor, a defense attorney, and a victim. Conduct a series of hypothetical sentencing hearings, such that the jury hears victim impact evidence in some cases and not others. Alter the hypothetical crime scenarios as needed based on the size of the class, but ensure that for each, two hearings are held: one with victim impact evidence, another without. Record the sentencing outcomes and discuss possible discrepancies based on the presence/absence of victim impact evidence.

Sources: Larry Welborn, "Relatives of Woman Slain in 1988 Offer Victim-Impact Statements," *Orange County Register*, March 14, 2012, Local, p. B; Spokane County, Victim/Witness Services, *Victim Impact Statements*, http://www .spokanecounty.org/prosecuting/victimwitness/ (accessed July 2014); National Center for Victims of Crime, *Victim Impact Statements*, http://www.victimsofcrime .org (accessed July 2014); Brian Myers, Draven Godwin, Rachel Latter, and Scott Winstanley, "Victim Impact Statements and Mock Juror Sentencing: The Impact of Dehumanizing Language on a Death Qualified Sample," *American Journal of Forensic Psychology* 22 (2004): 39–55; Ray Paternoster and Jerome Deise, "A Heavy Thumb on the Scale: The Effect of Victim Impact Evidence on Capital Decision Making," *Criminology* 49 (2011): 129–161.

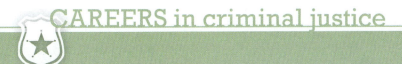

CAREERS in criminal justice

FORENSIC PSYCHOLOGIST

DUTIES AND CHARACTERISTICS OF THE JOB

Forensic psychologists apply the knowledge and scientific methods that are characteristic of the field of psychology in legal settings. They evaluate the mental health of parolees, run inmate mental health programs, and provide counseling to victims. In the court system, forensic psychologists consult with attorneys to assess individuals' mental health to determine what bearing, if any, their mental state has on the trial. They may help in crafting sentences based on the clinical needs of the criminal defendant. They consult with law enforcement at all levels in order to apprehend criminals. They might create a psychological model of a suspect to predict her behavior.

JOB OUTLOOK

The employment outlook for forensic psychologists is good. Because recognition of the importance of psychological factors in behavior and functioning is increasing, the need for forensic psychologists should expand.

SALARY

Like that of other psychologists, a forensic psychologist's mean annual salary is approximately $70,000. The majority of these psychologists make between $54,100 and $115,720 a year. Some will earn less than $40,000, and others will earn as much as or more than $150,000 a year.

OPPORTUNITIES

The number of educational institutions that offer graduate programs in forensic science is relatively small, so entry into a program is competitive.

QUALIFICATIONS

The primary qualifier for a position as a forensic psychologist is educational.

EDUCATION AND TRAINING

A forensic psychologist will have to gain entrance into one of a select number of master's or doctorate programs. A master's degree will prepare future forensic psychologists for entry-level work in places such as police departments, prisons and jails, and mental health centers. The two most advanced programs lead to a Ph.D. in psychology and a Psy.D. in forensic psychology, respectively. Some states require certification. A doctoral program prepares students primarily for administrative or management positions at law enforcement and health organizations and enables them to provide services such as mediation and research for organizations. Psy.D. training prepares students for an applied focus in jobs, such as providing mental health treatment and being an expert court witness.

Sources: The British Psychological Society, Forensic Psychology, http://www .bps.org.uk/networks-and-communities/member-networks/division-forensic- psychology (accessed July 2014); Bureau of Labor Statistics, *Occupational Outlook Handbook*, "Psychologists," http://www.bls.gov/ooh/Life-Physical-and- Social-Science/Psychologists.htm (accessed July 2014).

on the opinion of a forensic psychologist, who may be asked to clinically evaluate the defendant before sentencing. The Careers in Criminal Justice feature discusses forensic psychologists.

RACE No issue concerning personal factors in sentencing is more important than the suspicion that race influences sentencing outcomes. Racial disparity in sentencing has been suspected because a disproportionate number of African American inmates are in state prisons and on death row. Minorities seem to receive longer sentences than Caucasians, especially those who are indigent or unemployed.[57] Young black men are more likely to be imprisoned for drug offenses, a practice (says sentencing expert Michael Tonry) that places the entire cohort of young African American males in jeopardy.[58] Because this issue is so important, it is the focus of the accompanying Analyzing Criminal Justice Issues feature.

analyzing criminal justice ISSUES

DOES RACE MATTER?

There are more minorities in prison per capita than whites, a condition that suggests to some the existence of a racial bias in sentencing. The problem of race-based disparity is disturbing because of the impact the justice system has on the minority community. As sociologist Bruce Western points out, by the time they reach their mid-thirties, 60 percent of black high school dropouts are either prisoners or ex-cons. This, Western warns, has resulted in "a collective experience for young black men that is wholly different from the rest of American society." Is Western's analysis correct? Does race still matter in the sentencing process?

A number of studies (far too many to list here) do find that race bias still exists in the judicial process. In one recent study of federal sentencing, Jill Doerner and Stephen Demuth found, like many before them, that Hispanics and blacks receive harsher sentences on the whole than white defendants. Shawn Bushway and Anne Morrison Piehl studied sentencing outcomes in Maryland and found that, on average, African Americans receive 20 percent longer sentences than whites, even when age, gender, and recommended sentence length are held constant. So the nagging issue of racial disparity in sentencing still haunts the justice process. In a review of over 70 published studies, Ojmarrh Mitchell found that, indeed, African Americans are sentenced more harshly than similarly situated white offenders.

Although evidence of unequal treatment exists, research has failed to show a definitive pattern of racial *discrimination*. Although some research does indicate that a defendant's race has a direct impact on sentencing outcomes, other efforts show that the influence of race on sentencing is less clear, and, as John Wooldredge has found, in some contexts minority group members actually get lesser sentences than whites. It is possible, the counterargument goes, that the disproportionate number of minority group members in prison is not a function of racial bias by judges but, rather, reflects actual racial and ethnic differences in the crime rate: minority group members go to prison more often simply because they commit more crime.

Why does the critical issue of racial disparity remain so murky? One reason is that it may involve multiple factors that lie outside judicial sentencing practices:

● African Americans are more likely to be detained before trial than whites.

● Prosecutors are less likely to divert minorities from the legal system than they are whites.

● Minorities have less money for bail and private attorneys.

Capital Punishment

The most severe sentence used in the United States is capital punishment, or execution. More than 14,500 confirmed executions have been carried out in America under civil authority, starting with the execution of Captain George Kendall in 1608; today there are more than 3,000 people on death row, and about 40 are executed each year (see Figure 11.4). Most of these executions have been for murder and rape. However, federal, state, and military laws have imposed the death penalty for other crimes, including robbery, kidnapping, treason (offenses against the federal government), espionage, and desertion from military service.

In recent years, the Supreme Court has limited the death penalty to first-degree murder, and even then it is available only when aggravating circumstances, such as murder for profit or murder using extreme cruelty, are present.[59] The federal government still has provisions for imposing the death penalty for espionage by a member of the armed forces, treason, and killing during a criminal conspiracy, such as drug trafficking. Some states have laws permitting capital punishment for such crimes as aircraft piracy, ransom kidnapping, and the aggravated rape of a child, but it remains to be seen whether the courts will allow criminals to be executed today for any crime less serious than aggravated first-degree murder. The most recent death penalty data are included in Exhibit 11.1.

- Minorities live in poor communities, and people living in poor areas get harsher sentences, regardless of their race.

- African Americans receive longer sentences for drug crimes than whites because (a) they are more likely to be arrested for crack possession and sales, and (b) crack dealing is more severely punished by state and federal laws than other drug crimes.

Other factors may also obscure the associations. For example, ample research indicates that it is the victim's race, rather than the offender's, that structures sentencing outcomes. Minority defendants are sanctioned more severely if their victim is white than if their target is a fellow minority group member; minorities who kill whites are more likely to get the death penalty than are those who kill other minorities.

In sum, even though the true association between race and sentencing remains to be established, there is little question that issues of ethnicity and race help shape the contours of justice. Whatever the cause, the effects can be devastating. As Bruce Western warns, marginalizing and incarcerating so many African American men has destabilized whole communities. And doing prison time, Western warns, can turn minor offenders into hardened criminals, which removes any chance of rehabilitation and later opportunities. The prison boom, Western writes, "may be a self-defeating strategy for crime control."

CRITICAL THINKING

1. Because of the lingering problem of racial and class bias in the sentencing process, one primary goal of the criminal justice system has been to reduce disparity by creating new forms of criminal sentences that limit judicial discretion and are aimed at uniformity and fairness. Can such measures as sentencing guidelines and mandatory sentences reduce race-based disparity?

2. What is the difference between unequal treatment and racial discrimination? Which term better characterizes sentencing in the United States?

Sources: Bruce Western, *Punishment and Inequality in America* (New York: Russell Sage Foundation, 2006); Jill K. Doerner and Stephen Demuth, "Independent and Joint Effects of Race/Ethnicity, Gender, and Age on Sentencing Outcomes in U.S. Federal Courts," *Justice Quarterly* 27 (2010): 1–27; Shawn Bushway and Anne Morrison Piehl, "Judging Judicial Discretion: Legal Factors and Racial Discrimination in Sentencing," *Law and Society Review* 35 (2001): 733–765; Ojmarrh Mitchell, "Meta-Analysis of Race and Sentencing Research: Explaining the Inconsistencies," *Journal of Quantitative Criminology* 21 (2005): 439–466; John Wooldredge, "Neighborhood Effects on Felony Sentencing," *Journal of Research in Crime and Delinquency* 44 (2007): 238–263.

FIGURE 11.4   **Number of persons executed in the United States, 1930–2011**

Source: Tracy L. Snell, *Capital Punishment, 2012* (Washington, DC: Bureau of Justice Statistics, 2014), p. 1.

Defense lawyer Kevin Spellacy checks the reaction of Denny Obermiller to hearing a sentence of death pronounced by a three-judge panel in his sentencing. Obermiller pleaded guilty to multiple counts of aggravated murder, kidnapping, rape, and other crimes.

Thomas Ondrey/*The Plain Dealer/Landov*

EXHIBIT 11.1   Death Penalty Facts and Trends

- In 2013, 39 inmates were executed, which was four fewer than in 2012.

- Of the 39 executions carried out in the United States in 2013, there were 16 in Texas, 7 in Florida, 6 in Oklahoma, 3 in Ohio, 2 each in Arizona and Missouri, and one each in Alabama, Georgia, and Virginia.

- Of the 39 persons executed in 2013, 23 were white, 13 were black, and 3 were Latino.

- Of the 39 executed persons, all but one was male.

- Kimberly McCarthy was the only female executed in 2013 (Texas).

- All but one of the executions carried out in 2013 were by lethal injection. Robert Gleason was executed by electrocution in Virginia.

- Thirty-two states and the federal government retain the death penalty as a form of punishment, although some have not used it in decades.

- The states that currently can impose the death penalty are Alabama, Arizona, Arkansas, California, Colorado, Delaware, Florida, Georgia, Idaho, Indiana, Kansas, Kentucky, Louisiana, Mississippi, Missouri, Montana, Nebraska, Nevada, New Hampshire, North Carolina, Ohio, Oklahoma, Oregon, Pennsylvania, South Carolina, South Dakota, Tennessee, Texas, Utah, Virginia, Washington, and Wyoming.

- The states that currently cannot impose the death penalty are Alaska, Connecticut, Hawaii, Illinois, Iowa, Maine, Maryland, Massachusetts, Michigan, Minnesota, New Jersey, New Mexico, New York, North Dakota, Rhode Island, Vermont, West Virginia, and Wisconsin (plus the District of Columbia).

- In 2007, New Jersey was the first U.S. state to abolish capital punishment by law since the death penalty was reintroduced in the United States in 1972. In April 2012, Connecticut voted to abolish the death penalty. Maryland is the most recent state to abolish the death penalty.

- Thirty states, plus the District of Columbia, have not executed anyone in over five years.

- At year-end 2013, 3,108 persons were held under a sentence of death.

- The youngest person executed in 2011 was 30 years old. The oldest was 66.

Source: Death Penalty Information Center, http://deathpenaltyinfo.org/views-executions (accessed July 2014); Tracy L. Snell, *Capital Punishment, 2012* (Washington, DC: Bureau of Justice Statistics, 2014), p. 1. http://www.bjs.gov/content/pub/pdf/cp11st.pdf (accessed July 2014).

Despite its continued use and public acceptance, there seems to be growing unease with administration of the death penalty, and the recent use of scientific evidence based on DNA has resulted in numerous exonerations of death row inmates. On January 11, 2003, Illinois Governor George Ryan announced his decision to commute all Illinois death sentences—a gesture that spared the lives of 163 men and 4 women who have served a collective 2,000 years for the murders of more than 250 people. In the case of *People v. Stephen LaValle* (2004), a New York appellate court declared the state's capital punishment law unconstitutional, placing a moratorium on its use for the near term.[60] And in 2007, as we have noted, New Jersey became the first state since 1976 to abolish the death penalty by law. Other states have since followed suit, with Maryland being the most recent as of this writing.

No issue in the criminal justice system is more controversial or emotional than implementation of the death penalty.[61] Opponents and proponents have formulated a number of powerful arguments in support of their positions; these arguments are reviewed in the following sections.

L08 Describe the nature of capital punishment in the United States and abroad.

Arguments for the Death Penalty

Supporters advance a number of arguments for retaining the death penalty in the United States.

INCAPACITATION Supporters argue that death is the "ultimate incapacitation" and the only one that can ensure that convicted killers can never be pardoned, be paroled, or escape. Most states that do not have capital punishment provide the sentence of "life in prison without the chance of parole." However, 48 states (a) give their chief executive the right to grant clemency and commute a life sentence and (b) may give "lifers" eligibility for various furlough and release programs.

Death penalty advocates believe that the potential for recidivism is a serious enough threat to require that murderers be denied further access to the public.[62] About 8 percent of prisoners under a sentence of death have prior homicide convictions; if they had been executed for their first offense, their victims would still be alive.[63]

DETERRENCE Proponents of capital punishment argue that executions serve as a strong deterrent for serious crimes. Although capital punishment would probably not deter the few mentally unstable criminals, it could have an effect on the cold, calculating murderer, such as the hired killer or someone who kills for profit. The fear of death may also convince felons not to risk using handguns during robberies.

Proponents argue that the deterrent effect of an execution can produce a substantial decline in the murder rate.[64] They argue, for example, that homicide rates increased dramatically in the 1960s and 1970s when executions were halted by the courts and death penalty laws were subsequently abolished. It is not a coincidence that murder rates have dropped since the death penalty was reinstated; murder rates would actually be much higher if capital punishment were not being used.[65] The death penalty scares would-be criminals, and not surprisingly, homicide rates drop after a well-publicized execution.[66]

Some research supports these claims. Economists Hashem Dezhbakhsh, Paul H. Rubin, and Joanna M. Shepherd performed an advanced statistical analysis on county-level homicide data in order to calculate the effect of each execution on the number of homicides that would otherwise have occurred.[67] Using a variety of models (such as the long-term effect of an execution), they found that each execution leads to an average of 18 fewer murders. In another study, Shepherd found that capital punishment may have differing influence depending on where and how it is used.[68] The death penalty may influence each state's murder rate

L09 Articulate the arguments for and against capital punishment.

differently, and lumping all state data together masks the deterrent effect of the death penalty. She found that the use of capital punishment deterred murder in states that conducted more executions than the norm. In contrast, in states that conducted relatively few executions (one or two per year), the average execution either increased the murder rate or had no effect. Shepherd concludes that only if a state routinely uses executions does the deterrent effect take place; only then do potential criminals become convinced that the state is serious about the use of capital punishment. Land and his colleagues analyzed data from Texas and found that homicides decrease in the short term following an execution.[69]

MORALLY CORRECT This argument contends that the death penalty is morally correct: it is mentioned in the Bible and other religious works. Although the U.S. Constitution forbids "cruel and unusual punishments," this prohibition does not include the death penalty because capital punishment was widely used at the time the Constitution was drafted. The "original intent" of the founding fathers was to allow the states to use the death penalty; capital punishment may be cruel, but it is not unusual.

The death penalty is morally correct because it provides the greatest justice for the victim and helps alleviate the psychic pain of the victim's family and friends. The death penalty makes a moral statement: there is behavior that is so unacceptable to a community of human beings that one who engages in such behavior forfeits his right to live.[70]

PROPORTIONAL TO THE CRIME Putting dangerous criminals to death also conforms to the requirement that the punishment must be proportional to the seriousness of the crime. Since we use a system of escalating punishments, it follows that the most serious punishment should be used to sanction the most serious crime. Before the brutality of the death penalty is considered, the cruelty with which the victim was treated must not be forgotten.

REFLECTS PUBLIC OPINION The death penalty is justified because it represents the will of the people. A majority of the general public believe that criminals who kill innocent victims should forfeit their own lives. Public opinion polls show that nearly two-thirds of Americans favor the use of the death penalty for people convicted of murder.[71] Public approval rests on the belief that the death penalty is an important instrument of social control, can deter crime, and is less costly than maintaining a murderer in prison for life.[72] Research by Alexis Durham and his associates found that almost everyone (95 percent) would give criminals the death penalty under some circumstances, and the most heinous crimes are those for which the public is most likely to approve capital punishment.[73]

UNLIKELY CHANCE OF ERROR The many legal controls and appeals currently in use make it almost impossible for an innocent person to be executed or for the death penalty to be used in a racist or capricious manner. Although some unfortunate mistakes have been made in the past, the current system makes it virtually impossible to execute an innocent person. Federal courts closely scrutinize all death penalty cases and rule for the defendant in an estimated 60 to 70 percent of the appeals. Such judicial care should ensure that only those who are both truly guilty and deserving of death are executed.

FACT CHECK ☑

YOUR OPINION: Do you favor the death penalty for people convicted of murder?

PUBLIC OPINION:

YES, IN FAVOR: 60%

NO, OPPOSE: 35%

REALITY: While nearly two-thirds of Americans favor the death penalty (in 2013, the year this poll was taken), that percentage has been mostly trending downward for the past 20 years. Based on data going back to the 1950s, public support for capital punishment was at its highest level in 1994. There is also a problem with the poll question posed above: it is overly simplistic. If we were to list specific facts of a heinous mass murder committed by a repeat offender, support would likely increase (see "Weak Public Support" section where we discuss opposition to the death penalty). If we were to ask whether the death penalty *deters* murder, as some polls have, it is clear that the majority of respondents do not think it does. And if we broke responses down by political affiliations or religious preferences, opinions differ wildly.

DISCUSSION: Why does public support for capital punishment remain as high as it is?

Sources: *Sourcebook of Criminal Justice Statistics*, http://www.albany.edu/sourcebook/pdf/t2512013.pdf and http://www.albany.edu/sourcebook/pdf/t2582011.pdf (sites accessed July 2014).

In sum, those who favor the death penalty find it to be a traditional punishment for serious crimes and one that can help prevent criminality, is in keeping with the traditional moral values of fairness and equity, and is highly favored by the public.

Arguments Against the Death Penalty

These arguments for the death penalty are countered as follows by those who support its abolition.

POSSIBILITY OF ERROR Critics of the death penalty believe capital punishment has no place in a mature democratic society.[74] They point to the finality of the act and to the real possibility that innocent persons can be executed. Examples of people wrongfully convicted of murder abound. According to a classic study by Michael Radelet and Hugo Bedeau, there were 350 wrongful murder convictions between 1900 and the time of their study. Twenty-three of those led to executions. They further estimated that about three death sentences were returned every two years in cases where the defendant was falsely accused. More than half the errors stemmed from perjured testimony, false identifications, coerced confessions, and suppression of evidence. In addition to the 23 who were executed, 128 of the falsely convicted served more than 6 years in prison, 39 served more than 16 years in confinement, and 8 died while serving their sentence.[75]

An important congressional report cited 48 cases in which people who served time on death row were released because of new evidence proving their innocence; one Maryland man served nine years on death row before DNA testing proved that he could not have committed the crime.[76] These findings show that even with the best intentions, there is grave risk that an innocent person can be executed.[77] Most recently, a study published in the prestigious *Proceedings of the National Academy of Sciences* estimated that one in 25 death row inmates is innocent.[78] The accompanying Analyzing Criminal Justice Issues feature addresses wrongful convictions in more depth.

Because of the chances of error, a number of states have placed a moratorium on executions until the issue of errors in the process can be adequately addressed.[79] Because these errors may occur, some commentators have called for a new evidentiary standard of "absolute certainty" to replace "beyond a reasonable doubt" in death penalty cases. Others argue that such a standard would end guilty verdicts because at least one juror would always have some uncertainty.[80]

NICHOLAS KAMM/Getty Images

A great deal of research shows that the death penalty has little effect on crime and is therefore not a deterrent to murder. The lack of a clear-cut deterrent effect has encouraged abolitionists to campaign against capital punishment: if it does not stop crime, why have it? Here, an opponent of the death penalty attends the 15th Annual Fast and Vigil to Abolish the Death Penalty in front of the Supreme Court in Washington. Organized by the Abolition Action Committee (ABA) and the National Coalition to Abolish the Death Penalty (NCADP), the event commemorates the historic 1972 Supreme Court ruling that suspended the death penalty in the United States. Four years later, however, the Court ruled that executions could resume.

analyzing criminal justice ISSUES

REDUCING WRONGFUL CONVICTIONS

Researchers have estimated that on the order of 2,000 innocent defendants go to prison every year. Thanks to the advent of DNA evidence, some 300 wrongfully convicted individuals have been exonerated in recent years, but the wrongful conviction problem persists. This raises several questions. Why are these cases coming to light? How often are innocent people imprisoned? Has an innocent person been executed in the last 40 years? Why do wrongful convictions occur? What can be done to reduce justice system errors?

In the early 1990s, only two organizations existed to take on cases of prisoners claiming to be factually innocent. Today, more than 50 innocence projects exist. Collectively, as an Innocence Network, they screen claims of innocence, work to exonerate the factually innocent, promote policies to reduce errors of justice, and provide support for exonerees.

According to the Innocence Project, more than 300 DNA exonerees have been released after being convicted of crimes they did not commit. Almost all of these exonerations were for the crimes of murder and rape. Experts and criminal justice officials estimate that at least one-half of 1 percent of all types of felony convictions are "wrong-person convictions." This would mean that of the 1.1 million convictions each year, at least 5,500 people suffer the humiliation of being wrongly convicted, and 3,800 of them the anguish of being jailed or imprisoned for a crime they did not commit. Recent research by Samuel Gross and his colleagues estimates that one in 25 death row inmates is innocent.

The pressures to ensure convictions in homicide cases may lead to a higher rate of wrongful convictions in murder cases. There have been no official exonerations of an innocent person executed since 1973, but intensive investigations provide strong evidence that at least some people have been executed for murders they did not commit.

WHY DO ERRORS OCCUR?

There are several reasons why the criminal justice system produces a steady stream of such serious errors. As many as 25 percent of all eyewitness identifications may be wrong; many of these errors are caused by suggestive police lineups. Once a person is misidentified, police may develop "tunnel vision"—an unshakeable belief that the suspect is the real criminal. Tunnel vision can lead police to become overly aggressive during interrogations, causing innocent persons to confess in order to escape the enormous psychological strain of high-pressure interrogation. This is a special problem with suspects who are more easily manipulated, such as teenagers and mentally challenged suspects. Police often rely on informants, especially jailhouse snitches claiming that a suspect confessed. These snitches may be pathological liars willing to say anything to get a break in their cases.

Police are also not required to include exculpatory evidence—evidence that favors innocence—in their investigative reports. Even if they do, many prosecutors fail to turn over exculpatory evidence to defense lawyers, although required to do so by law. Overworked or incompetent defense attorneys often fail to provide a competent defense. Judges and appellate courts tend to favor the prosecution and, in a large proportion of cases, simply overlook serious errors. In a number of cases, junk science, substandard forensic laboratories, or fraudulent forensic scientists have presented juries with completely erroneous conclusions.

UNFAIR USE OF DISCRETION Critics also frown on the tremendous discretion used in seeking the death penalty and on the arbitrary manner in which it is imposed. Of the approximately 10,000 persons convicted each year on homicide charges, only 250 to 300 are sentenced to death, while an equal number receive a sentence of probation or community supervision only. It is true that many convicted murderers do not commit first-degree murder and therefore are ineligible for execution, but it is also likely that many serious criminals who could have received the death penalty are not sentenced to death because of prosecutorial discretion. Some escape death by cooperating or giving testimony against their

REFORM EFFORTS

In the last few years, a number of reform efforts have begun to percolate through several cities and states in response to the crisis of convicting the innocent. In 2006, North Carolina became the first state to establish an Innocence Inquiry Commission to review and investigate prisoners' claims that they were wrongly convicted. Several states and a large number of police departments have started videotaping the entire interrogation of suspects, not just the confession. This reform is well liked by police, because confessions by guilty suspects provide strong proof at trial, and the videotape can be used to confirm that they used proper procedures.

A number of lineup reforms are shown by psychological experiments to reduce eyewitness errors. The most important include "double-blind" lineup administration, where the officer running the lineup does not know the identity of the suspect. Other procedures to ensure lineup accuracy include carefully documenting the identification, telling eyewitnesses that the perpetrator may or may not be included in the lineup, and picking "fillers" from witnesses' verbal descriptions and not the likeness of the suspect (who might be innocent). Somewhat more controversial is the recommendation to replace the traditional side-by-side live or photographic simultaneous lineups with a one-at-a-time, or sequential, lineup.

In addition to these and many other suggested reforms, there has been a call for all states to provide monetary compensation and psychological and other support for the wrongly convicted, many of whom suffer serious psychological damage from their ordeals. The conviction of a factually innocent person creates multiple victims: the wrongly convicted person who does time for another person's crime; the original crime victims, who later learn that instead of providing closure, the criminal justice system compounded their woes; and those people later victimized by the real criminal who was not caught in the first place. Knowledge about wrongful convictions should be viewed as an important topic in criminal justice and an opportunity to create a more professional criminal justice system.

CRITICAL THINKING

1. Describe how the conviction of an innocent person actually creates multiple victims, and see whether you can cite other people or institutions that are damaged by a wrongful conviction.

2. Apply what you know about criminal justice to create an innovative approach that might help reduce wrongful convictions. What role, if any, does technology play in your plan to reduce wrongful convictions?

Sources: Marvin Zalman, "Qualitatively Estimating the Incidence of Wrongful Convictions," *Criminal Law Bulletin* 48 (2012): 221–279; the Innocence Project, http://www.innocenceproject.org; the Innocence Network, http://www.innocencenetwork.org; Samuel R. Gross, Barbara O'Brien, and Edward H. Kennedy, "Rate of False Conviction of Criminal Defendants Who Are Sentenced to Death," *Proceedings of the National Academy of Sciences*, published online before print, doi: 10.1073; D. Michael Risinger, "Innocents Convicted: An Empirically Justified Factual Wrongful Conviction Rate," *Journal of Criminal Law and Criminology* 97 (2007): 761–806; Barry Scheck, Peter Neufeld, and Jim Dwyer, *Actual Innocence: When Justice Goes Wrong and How to Make It Right* (New York: Penguin/New American Library, 2003); the Justice Project, "Eyewitness Identification: A Policy Review," http://www.psychology.iastate.edu/~glwells/The_Justice%20Project_Eyewitness_Identification_%20A_Policy_Review.pdf; Samuel R. Gross, Kristen Jacoby, Daniel J. Matheson, Nicholas Montgomery, and Sujata Patil, "Exonerations in the United States, 1989 through 2003," *Journal of Criminal Law and Criminology* 95 (2005): 523–560 (all sites accessed July 2014).

partners in the crime. A person who commits a particularly heinous crime and knows full well that he will receive the death penalty if convicted may be the one most likely to plea bargain to avoid capital punishment. Is it fair to spare the life of a dangerous killer who cooperates with the prosecutor, while executing another who does not?

Abolitionists also argue that juries use inappropriate discretion when they make capital punishment recommendations. The ongoing Capital Jury Project has been interviewing members of juries involved in making death penalty decisions and finds that many are motivated by ignorance and error.

Web App 11.3

For more information about capital punishment, visit http://www.deathpenaltyinfo.org/.

Those who abhor the use of discretion in capital cases also point to instances where offenders who killed on the spur of the moment are executed, while truly vicious criminals who grievously injure victims during murder attempts are spared the death penalty. Some particularly heinous crimes are not punished with death simply because a physician's skill saved the victim. Some notable cases come to mind. Lawrence Singleton used an axe to cut off the arms of a woman he raped, yet he served only eight years in prison because the victim's life was saved by prompt medical care (after being released from prison, Singleton killed a female companion in 1997). In another case, "David," a boy severely burned in a murder attempt, lives in fear because his assailant—his father, Charles Rothenberg—was paroled from prison after serving a short sentence.[81] Although these horrific crimes received national attention and the intent to kill the victim was present, the death penalty could not be applied because of the availability of effective medical treatment. Areas that have superior medical resources actually have lower murder rates than less well-equipped areas; for example, ambulance response time can reduce the death rate by expeditiously transporting victims to an appropriate treatment center.[82] It makes little sense to punish someone for an impulsive murder while sparing the life of those who intentionally maim and torture victims who happen by chance to live because of prompt medical care.

MISPLACED VENGEANCE Although critics acknowledge that the general public approves of the death penalty, they maintain that prevailing attitudes reflect a primitive desire for revenge and not just desert. Public acceptance of capital punishment has been compared to the approval of human sacrifices practiced by the Aztecs in Mexico 500 years ago.[83] It is ironic that many death penalty advocates also oppose abortion on the grounds that it is the taking of human life.[84] The desire to be vengeful and punitive outweighs their concern about taking life.

At least 30 states now have a sentence of life in prison without parole, and this can more than make up for an execution. Being locked up in a hellish prison without any chance of release (barring a rare executive reprieve) may be a worse punishment than a painless death by lethal injection. If vengeance is the goal, life without parole may eliminate the need for capital punishment.

WEAK PUBLIC SUPPORT Some politicians endorse the death penalty in the mistaken belief that the public favors such harsh punishment for criminal offenders.[85] But approval ratings have been in decline for the past decade.[86] When surveys give respondents a choice of punishments, such as life without parole, support for the death penalty declines to the 50 percent level. Well-publicized incidents of innocent people being sentenced to death have helped erode support for capital punishment.[87] So even though a majority of the public still support the death penalty in principle, a substantial proportion lack confidence in its use and believe that executions should be halted until the system can be made foolproof.[88]

Public opinion in favor of the death penalty is not solid and may be influenced by such factors as the personal characteristics of the offender and the circumstances of the offense.[89] People who generally support the death penalty may not want to see it used with juveniles, the mentally challenged, or the mentally ill.[90] And even if a majority support capital punishment, their motives must be closely examined: is it possible that support for the death penalty is a function of racist attitudes and the belief that capital punishment helps control and hold back the minority population?[91]

LITTLE DETERRENT EFFECT Those opposed to the death penalty also find little merit in the argument that capital punishment deters crime.[92] They charge that there is little hard evidence that the threat of a death sentence can convince potential murderers to forgo their criminal activity. Three methods are typically used to determine whether capital punishment reduced the murder rate:

■ *Immediate-impact studies*, which calculate the effect a well-publicized execution has on the short-term murder rate

■ *Time-series analysis*, which compares long-term trends in murder and capital punishment rates

■ *Contiguous-state analysis*, which compares murder rates in states that have the death penalty with a similar state that has abolished capital punishment

Using these three methods over a 60-year period, most researchers have failed to show any deterrent effect of capital punishment.[93] These studies show that murder rates do not seem to rise when a state abolishes capital punishment any more than they decrease when the death penalty is adopted. The murder rate is also quite similar both in states that use the death penalty and neighboring states that have abolished capital punishment. Finally, little evidence shows that executions can lower the murder rate. One test of the deterrent effect of the death penalty in Texas found no association between the frequency of execution during the years 1984 to 1997 and murder rates.[94] International studies show that homicide rates in countries that routinely employ the death penalty are no lower than rates in countries that rarely if ever use capital punishment.[95]

Why doesn't the death penalty deter murder? According to abolitionists, most murders involve people who knew each other, very often friends and family members. Because murderers are often under the influence of alcohol or drugs or are suffering severe psychological turmoil, no penalty is likely to be a deterrent. Another problem is that the death penalty is rarely applied outside of certain states, notably Texas and Virginia. This makes it exceedingly difficult to detect a deterrent effect.[96]

NO HOPE OF REHABILITATION The death sentence rules out any hope of offender rehabilitation. There is evidence that convicted killers often make good parole risks; convicted murderers are often model inmates and, once released, commit fewer crimes than other parolees. It is possible that the general public, including people who sit on juries, overestimate the dangerousness of people who commit murder. In reality, those people who are given a life sentence for capital murder have a *less than 1 percent* (0.2%) chance of committing another homicide over a 40-year term; the risk of their committing an assault is about 16 percent.[97]

RACE, GENDER, AND OTHER BIAS Capital punishment may be tarnished by gender, racial, ethnic, and other biases. More people are sentenced to death, and the death penalty is used more often, in nations with a large minority population. This is referred to as the "minority group–threat hypothesis" (in other words, use of extreme punishment is related to the regulation of groups that are racially, culturally, or ethnically different).[98]

■ There is evidence that homicides with male offenders and female victims are more likely to result in a death sentence than homicides involving female offenders and male victims.[99]

■ Homicides involving strangers are more likely to result in a death sentence than homicides involving nonstrangers or acquaintances.

■ Prosecutors are more likely to recommend the death sentence for people who kill white victims than they are in any other racial combination of victim and criminal.[100] Prosecutors are less likely to seek the death penalty if the victim is a minority group member.[101] Killing a white female is more likely to result in the death penalty than any other combination of race/gender.[102]

Since the death penalty was first instituted in the United States, disproportionate numbers of minorities have been executed. Charges of racial bias are supported by the disproportionate numbers of African Americans who have received the death sentence, who are currently on death row, and who have been executed (54 percent of all executions). Racism was particularly blatant when the death penalty was invoked in rape cases: of those receiving the death penalty for rape, 90 percent in the South and 63 percent in the North and West were African American.[103] Today, about 40 percent of the inmates on death row are African American, a number disproportionate to the minority representation in the population. When a black criminal kills a white victim, the likelihood of the death penalty being invoked is far greater than when a white kills a black victim.[104] In contrast, since 1976 only two white criminals have been executed for murdering a black victim, the most recent being Kermit Smith, who was executed on January 24, 1995, in North Carolina for the kidnapping, rape, and murder of a 20-year-old college cheerleader.[105] It is not surprising, considering these patterns, that support for the death penalty in the minority community is significantly lower than among European Americans.[106]

CAUSES MORE CRIME THAN IT DETERS Some critics fear that the introduction of capital punishment will encourage criminals to escalate their violent behavior, consequently putting police officers at risk. A suspect who kills someone during a botched robbery may be inclined to "fire away" upon encountering police rather than to surrender peacefully; the killer faces the death penalty already, so what does he have to lose? Geoffrey Rapp studied the effect of capital punishment on the killings of police and found that, all other things being equal, the greater the number of new inmates on death row, the greater the number of police officers killed by citizens.[107] Rapp concluded that what the death penalty seems to do is create an extremely dangerous environment for law enforcement officers because it does not deter criminals and may lull officers into a false sense of security, leading them to believe that the death penalty will deter violence directed against them and causing them to let their guard down.

IT IS BRUTAL Abolitionists believe that executions are unnecessarily cruel and inhuman and come at a high moral and social cost. Even death by lethal injection, considered relatively painless by advocates, has been challenged because it may cause extreme pain and can take much longer to cause death than was originally believed.[108] Our society does not punish criminals by subjecting them to the same acts they themselves committed. Rapists are not sexually assaulted, and arsonists do not have their houses burned down. Why, then, should murderers be killed?

Robert Johnson has described the execution process as a form of torture in which the condemned are first tormented psychologically by being made to feel powerless and alone while on death row; suicide is a constant problem among those on death row.[109] The execution itself is a barbaric affair, he believes. In addition, the executioners suffer from delayed stress reactions, including anxiety and a dehumanized personal identity.

The brutality of the death penalty may actually produce more violence than it prevents—the so-called **brutalization effect**.[110] Executions may increase murder rates because they raise the general violence level in society and because violence-prone people actually identify with the executioner, not with the target of the death penalty. When someone gets in a conflict with such violence-prone individuals or challenges their authority, these individuals may execute them in the same manner the state executes people who violate its rules.[111] There is evidence that the brutalization effect does influence murder rates: homicides of strangers increase after an execution.[112] People may be more inclined to settle conflicts with violence after a state executes a criminal—"If they can do it, why can't I?"[113]

brutalization effect
The belief that capital punishment creates an atmosphere of brutality that enhances, rather than reduces, the level of violence in society. The death penalty reinforces the view that violence is an appropriate response to provocation.

Because of its brutality, many enlightened countries around the globe have long since abandoned the death penalty, and 40 percent of the countries with a death penalty have active abolitionist movements.[114] It is ironic that citizens of countries that have eliminated the death penalty sometimes find themselves on death row in the United States.

IT IS EXPENSIVE Some people complain that they do not want to support "some killer in prison for 30 years." Abolitionists counter that legal appeals drive the cost of executions far higher than the cost of years of incarceration. If the money spent on the judicial process were invested, the interest would more than pay for the lifetime upkeep of death row inmates. Because of numerous appeals, the median time between conviction by a jury, sentencing by a judge, and execution averages 14 years in California; the state spends more than $5 million per year on death row appeals.[115]

MORALLY WRONG The death penalty is brutal and demeaning. Even if the general public voices approval of the death penalty, abolitionists argue, "social vengeance by death is a primitive way of revenge which stands in the way of moral progress."[116] And although early religious leaders accepted the death penalty, today others, such as the Catholic Church, condemn the practice.[117] In his book *The Contradictions of American Capital Punishment*, Franklin Zimring links America's obsession with the death penalty—unique among Westernized nations—with its vigilante tradition, in which people on the frontier took justice into their own hands, assuming that their targets were always guilty as charged.[118] The death penalty was widely practiced against slaves, and at one time, mass executions were a brutal and common practice to stifle any thought of escapes and/or revolts.[119]

While the debate continues, there seems to be little question that the public's support for the death penalty has weakened, and, concomitantly, the number of death sentences being handed down is in sharp decline.[120] Whether these developments are harbingers of the demise of capital punishment remains to be seen.

Legal Issues in Capital Punishment

The constitutionality of the death penalty has been a major concern to both the nation's courts and its social scientists. In 1972, the U.S. Supreme Court decided, in *Furman v. Georgia*,[121] that the discretionary imposition of the death penalty was cruel and unusual punishment under the Eighth and Fourteenth Amendments of the U.S. Constitution. The Supreme Court did not completely rule out the use of capital punishment as a penalty; rather, it objected to the arbitrary and capricious manner in which it was imposed. After *Furman*, many states changed statutes that had allowed jury discretion in imposing the death penalty. Then, in July 1976, the Supreme Court ruled on the constitutionality of five state death penalty statutes. In the first case, *Gregg v. Georgia*,[122] the Court found valid the Georgia statute holding that a finding by the jury of at least one "aggravating circumstance" out of ten is required in pronouncing the death penalty in murder cases. In the *Gregg* case, the jury imposed the death penalty after finding beyond a reasonable doubt two aggravating circumstances: (1) the offender was engaged in the commission of two other capital felonies, and (2) the offender committed the offense of murder for the purpose of receiving money and other financial gains (an automobile).[123] The *Gregg* case signaled the return of capital punishment as a sentencing option.

Although the Court has generally supported the death penalty, it has also placed some limitations on its use. Rulings have promoted procedural fairness in the capital sentencing process. In *Ring v. Arizona*, the Court found that juries, not judges, must make the critical findings that send convicted killers to death row. The Court reasoned that the Sixth Amendment's right to a jury trial would be "senselessly

 **LO10** Discuss the legality of the death penalty.

diminished" if it did not allow jurors to decide whether a person deserves the death penalty.[124] The Court has also limited who may be eligible for death:

- The Court has limited the crimes for which the death penalty can be employed by ruling that it is not permissible to punish rapists with death.[125] Only people who commit intentional or felony murder may be executed.

- People who are mentally ill may not be executed.[126] In a 2002 case, *Atkins v. Virginia*, the Court ruled that execution of mentally retarded criminals is "cruel and unusual punishment" prohibited by the Eighth Amendment.[127]

- In *Roper v. Simmons* (2005), the Court set 18 years as the minimum age of defendants who could be sentenced to death.[128] The Court said that executing young teens violates "the evolving standards of decency that mark the progress of a maturing society" and that American society regards juveniles as less responsible than adult criminals. Although 19 states had allowed the execution of juvenile murderers prior to *Simmons*, only Texas, Virginia, and Oklahoma have executed any in the past decade.

- In *Kennedy v. Louisiana* (2008), the Court barred capital punishment for child rapists—unless the rape resulted in (or was intended to result in) the death of the child.[129]

In an important 2008 case, *Baze v. Rees*, the Supreme Court settled the issue of whether lethal injection was cruel and unusual punishment.[130] Two death row inmates, Ralph Baze and Thomas C. Bowling, had argued that the combination of drugs used to execute prisoners in Kentucky, and in at least 29 other states with the same procedure, carried an "unnecessary risk" of inflicting cruel and unusual punishment, in violation of the Eighth Amendment. The inmates did not challenge the death penalty itself. Chief Justice John Roberts, writing a lead opinion, said the mere fact that there may be a safer alternative to Kentucky's protocol doesn't mean that the current regimen is unconstitutional. The inmates had argued that a single drug could be administered to the condemned, similar to the process used to euthanize animals, to reduce the risk of agonizing pain. However, the Court ruled that capital punishment is constitutional, and so there must be a means for its implementation.

The accompanying "Evolution of *Furman v. Georgia*" feature highlights the key death penalty decisions since 1972. Note that in the wake of the *Gregg* decision, the Supreme Court has become more and more restrictive with respect to application of the death penalty.[131]

The Evolution of *Furman v. Georgia*

***Furman v. Georgia* (1972)** The death penalty (in three Georgia cases) amounts to cruel and unusual punishment in violation of the Eighth Amendment. *Furman* led to a de facto moratorium on capital punishment.[132]

***Gregg v. Georgia* (1976)** The punishment of death for the crime of murder does not violate the Eighth Amendment under all circumstances.[133]

***Woodson v. North Carolina* (1976)** Mandatory death penalty laws (those that do not take into account aggravating and mitigating circumstances) violate the Eighth Amendment and are thus unconstitutional.[134]

***Coker v. Georgia* (1977)** Rapists cannot be sentenced to death.[135]

***Lockett v. Ohio* (1978)** The defendant must be allowed to present all mitigating evidence pertaining to his or her "character, record, and circumstances of the crime."[136]

***Enmund v. Florida* (1982)** It is a violation of the Eighth Amendment to impose the death penalty on a person who commits a felony that results in murder without considering the person's level of intent.[137]

***Glass v. Louisiana* (1985)** Death by electrocution is not cruel and unusual punishment.[138]

(*continued*)

***Cabana v. Bullock* (1986)** The death penalty cannot be imposed on an accomplice unless it is proved that the accomplice killed, attempted to kill, or intended to kill.[139]

***Ford v. Wainwright* (1986)** It is a violation of the Eighth Amendment to execute a person who is insane (or was insane at the time of the crime).[140]

***Atkins v. Virginia* (2002)** The execution of a mentally retarded individual violates the Eighth Amendment.[141]

***Ring v. Arizona* (2002)** It is a violation of the Sixth Amendment's jury trial provision to allow a judge, rather than a jury, to find aggravating circumstances necessary for imposition of the death penalty.[142]

***Roper v. Simmons* (2005)** It is a violation of the Eighth Amendment to sentence to death a defendant who committed his or her capital crime under the age of 18.[143]

***Deck v. Missouri* (2005)** It is unconstitutional to force the defendant to wear visible shackles during the sentencing phase of a capital trial.[144]

***Oregon v. Guzek* (2006)** Death penalty defendants may not present new evidence during the sentencing phase of the criminal process.[145]

***Baze v. Rees* (2008)** A three-drug lethal injection procedure does not violate the Eighth Amendment.[146]

***Kennedy v. Louisiana* (2008)** A child rapist cannot be sentenced to death if the crime did not result in (or was not intended to result in) the child's death.[147]

Significant Cases in Punishment and Sentencing

Case	Issue	Decision
Apprendi v. New Jersey (2000)	Sentencing guidelines	Any factor other than a prior conviction that increases the penalty for the crime beyond the statutory minimum must be submitted to a jury and proved beyond a reasonable doubt.
Blakely v. Washington (2004)	Sentencing guidelines	Washington's sentencing guidelines are unconstitutional because they permit a judge, not a jury, to consider aggravating factors that would enhance the sentence.
Ewing v. California (2003)	Three strikes	A sentence of 25 years to life resulting from California's three-strikes law does not violate the Eighth Amendment's prohibition against cruel and unusual punishment.
Furman v. Georgia (1972)	Death penalty	The death penalty as applied in three Georgia cases is unconstitutional. For review of additional death penalty cases, see the "Evolution of *Furman v. Georgia*" feature in this chapter.
Graham v. Florida (2010)	Juvenile sentencing	Juvenile offenders cannot be sentenced to life in prison for nonhomicide offenses.
Gregg v. Georgia (1976)	Death penalty	The death penalty does not constitute cruel and unusual punishment in all circumstances. For review of additional death penalty cases, see the "Evolution of *Furman v. Georgia*" feature in this chapter.
Harmelin v. Michigan (1991)	Mandatory sentencing	A statutorily mandated sentence that does not take into account mitigating circumstances does not violate the Eighth Amendment's cruel and unusual punishment clause.
Kimbrough v. United States (2007)	Sentencing guidelines, cocaine	The federal cocaine sentencing guidelines are advisory.

(continued)

Significant Cases in Punishment and Sentencing (*continued*)

Case	Issue	Decision
Lockyer v. Andrade (2003)	Three strikes	There is no *habeas corpus* relief from a sentence imposed under California's three-strikes law.
Payne v. Tennessee (1991)	Victim impact statements	The Eighth Amendment is not violated if a capital sentencing jury hears a victim impact statement from surviving family members.
Ring v. Arizona (2002)	Death penalty	Juries, not judges, must make the critical findings (aggravating circumstances) that send killers to death row. For review of additional death penalty cases, see the "Evolution of *Furman v. Georgia*" feature in this chapter.
Rita v. United States (2007)	Sentencing guidelines	Any sentence that falls within the federal sentencing guidelines is presumptively reasonable.
United States v. Booker (2005)	Sentencing guidelines	The federal sentencing guidelines are advisory, not mandatory.
United States v. Comstock (2010)	Civil commitment	It is constitutionally permissible to use civil commitment to further detain sexually dangerous offenders beyond their date of scheduled release.

ETHICAL CHALLENGES in Criminal Justice

A WRITING ASSIGNMENT

Hank was charged with capital murder in the stabbing deaths of his former girlfriend, Emily, and two of her children, Sarah, age 10, and Jim, age 3. In announcing the charge, the district attorney held a press conference with Emily's parents, other family members, and Emily's only surviving child, who had been staying at his grandparents' house the night of the murders. She described the crime scene as "a house of horror, the most heinous she had ever seen in her 25 years as a prosecutor." The DA also refused to accept Hank's guilty plea in exchange for a sentence of life in prison. And in her opening statements at trial, the DA portrayed Hank as a depraved monster, calling him "evil incarnate." Finally, during her closing statements at trial, the DA asked the jury to avenge Emily: "You can hear Emily calling from her grave, 'Avenge me and my children,'" she said with all the dramatic flair of an Oscar-winning actress.

Write an essay on the ethics of the district attorney's behavior in this scenario. In doing so, answer the following questions: Was the press conference warranted? Did it have any bearing on the fairness of the trial? What about the opening statements? Were they unnecessarily inflammatory? Why or why not? Did the DA perform her ethical duty to seek justice? In addition to representing the government, should prosecutors act as "champions of the people?" Does it matter that the district attorney is an elected official? To what extent could facing reelection sway a district attorney's behavior in a situation such as this?

Summary

LO1 **Outline the historical development of punishment.**

- Historically, people who violated the law were considered morally corrupt and in need of strong discipline.
- In early Greece and Rome, the most common state-administered punishment was banishment or exile.
- During the Middle Ages, people found guilty of crime faced a wide range of punishments, including physical torture, branding, whipping, and (for most felony offenses) death. The main emphasis of criminal law and punishment was on maintaining public order.
- The development of the common law in the eleventh century brought some standardization to penal practices.
- By the end of the sixteenth century, many offenders were made to do hard labor for their crimes.
- In England, transporting convicts to the colonies became popular.
- By 1820, long periods of incarceration in walled institutions called reformatories or penitentiaries began to replace physical punishment in England and the United States.

LO2 **List the major goals of contemporary sentencing.**

- The objectives of criminal sentencing today can be grouped into six distinct areas: general deterrence, incapacitation, specific deterrence, retribution/just desert, rehabilitation, and equity/restitution.

LO3 **Distinguish among general and specific deterrence, incapacitation, and retribution.**

- According to the concept of general deterrence, people will be too afraid to break the law if they believe that they will be caught and punished severely.
- The purpose of specific deterrence, another goal of punishment, is to convince offenders that the pains of punishment are greater than the potential benefits of crime.
- Incapacitation is intended to keep criminals from repeating their criminal acts while they are under state control.
- According to the retributive goal of sentencing, the essential purpose of the criminal process is to punish offenders—fairly and justly—in a manner that is proportionate to the gravity of their crimes.

LO4 **Compare rehabilitation with just desert.**

- Rehabilitation, or treatment, is built on the view that the justice system is obligated to *help* criminals, not just to punish them for their misdeeds.
- According to just desert, punishment should be no more or less than the offender's actions warrant.

LO5 **Explain how sentences are imposed.**

- In some instances, when an accused is convicted of two or more charges, the judge must decide whether to impose consecutive (back-to-back) or concurrent (overlapping) sentences.
- When judges impose an incarceration sentence, they know and take into account the fact that the amount of time spent in prison is reduced by the implementation of "time off for good behavior."

LO6 **Classify the various types of sentencing structures.**

- Indeterminate sentences are tailored to fit individual needs. Convicted offenders are typically given a "light" minimum sentence that must be served and a lengthy maximum sentence that is the outer boundary of the time that can be served.
- Determinate sentences offer a fixed term of years, the maximum set in law by the legislature, to be served by the offender sentenced to prison for a particular crime.
- Sentencing guidelines have been implemented to provide judges with a recommended sentence based on the seriousness of a crime and the background of an offender.
- Some states have passed mandatory sentence legislation prohibiting people convicted of certain offenses, such as violent crimes and drug trafficking, from being placed on probation; they must serve at least some time in prison.
- Three-strikes (and you're out) laws provide lengthy terms for any person convicted of three felony offenses, even if the third crime is relatively trivial.
- Truth-in-sentencing laws require offenders to serve a substantial portion of their prison sentence behind bars.

LO7

Discuss how people are sentenced today.

- About 70 percent of all felons convicted in state courts are sentenced to a period of confinement—41 percent to state prisons and 28 percent to local jails. The remaining third are sentenced to straight probation with no jail or prison time to serve.

- State sentencing codes usually include various factors that can legitimately influence the length of prison sentences, including the severity of the offense, the offender's prior criminal record, whether the offender used violence, whether the offender used weapons, and whether the crime was committed for money.

- Evidence supports an association between social class and sentencing outcomes: members of the lower class may expect to get longer prison sentences than more affluent defendants.

- Most research indicates that women receive more favorable outcomes the further they go in the criminal justice system.

- Older people will be punished more harshly than younger ones because they have had a greater opportunity to accumulate a criminal record and most state laws increase penalties for multiple offenders.

- Minorities seem to receive longer sentences than Caucasians, especially those who are indigent or unemployed.

LO8

Describe the nature of capital punishment in the United States and abroad.

- The most severe sentence used in the United States is capital punishment, or execution.

- The United States is not alone in using the death penalty, but over half the countries in the world have now abolished the death penalty in law or practice.

- Despite its continued use and public acceptance, there seems to be growing unease with the administration of the death penalty, and the recent use of scientific evidence based on DNA has resulted in numerous exonerations of death row inmates.

LO9

Articulate the arguments for and against capital punishment.

- Supporters argue that death is the "ultimate incapacitation" and the only one that can ensure that convicted killers can never be pardoned, be paroled, or escape.

- Proponents of capital punishment argue that executions serve as a strong deterrent for serious crimes.

- Putting dangerous criminals to death also conforms to the requirement that the punishment be proportional to the seriousness of the crime.

- The death penalty is justified because it represents the will of the people.

- The many legal controls and appeals currently in use make it almost impossible for an innocent person to be executed or for the death penalty to be used in a racist or capricious manner.

- Critics of the death penalty believe capital punishment has no place in a mature democratic society.

- Because of the chances of error, a number of states have placed a moratorium on executions until the issue of errors in the process can be adequately addressed.

- The pressures to ensure convictions in homicide cases may lead to a higher rate of wrongful convictions in murder cases.

- Critics frown on the tremendous discretion used in seeking the death penalty and on the arbitrary manner in which it is imposed.

- Politicians favor the death penalty in the mistaken belief that the public favors such harsh punishment for criminal offenders.

- Capital punishment may be tarnished by gender, racial, ethnic, and other biases.

- Abolitionists believe that executions are unnecessarily cruel and inhuman and come at a high moral and social cost.

- The constitutionality of the death penalty has been a major concern to both the nation's courts and its social scientists.

LO10

Discuss the legality of the death penalty.

- In *Gregg v. Georgia*, the Court found valid the Georgia statute holding that a finding by the jury of at least one "aggravating circumstance" out of ten is required in pronouncing the death penalty in murder cases.

- The Court has limited the crimes for which the death penalty can be employed by ruling that it is not permissible to punish rapists with death.

- People who are mentally ill may not be executed.

- In *Roper v. Simmons* (2005), the Court set a limit of 18 years as the age of defendants who could be sentenced to death.

Key Terms

Critical Thinking Questions

1. Discuss the sentencing dispositions in your jurisdiction. What are the pros and cons of each?
2. Compare the various types of incarceration sentences. What are the similarities and differences?
3. What are the arguments for and against three-strikes laws? Who is more persuasive, the supporters or the critics?
4. Summarize the arguments for and against capital punishment. Who is more persuasive, the supporters or the critics?
5. Why does sentencing disparity exist? Are there programs that can reduce disparity in sentencing? If so, what are they? Should all people who commit the same crime receive the same sentence? Explain.

Notes

1. New York Times, "Justice Criticizes Lengthy Sentences," http://www.nytimes.com/2003/08/10/us/justice-criticizes-lengthy-sentences.html (accessed July 2014).
2. Connie de la Vega, Amanda Solter, Soo-Ryun Kwon, and Dana Marie Isaac, *Cruel and Unusual: U.S. Sentencing Practices in a Global Context* (San Francisco: University of San Francisco School of Law, 2012).
3. Among the most helpful sources for this section were Benedict Alper, *Prisons Inside-Out* (Cambridge, MA: Ballinger, 1974); Gustave de Beaumont and Alexis de Tocqueville, *On the Penitentiary System in the United States and Its Applications in France* (Carbondale: Southern Illinois University Press, 1964, originally published in 1833); Orlando Lewis, *The Development of American Prisons and Prison Customs, 1776–1845* (Montclair, NJ: Patterson-Smith, 1967); Leonard Orland, ed., *Justice, Punishment, and Treatment* (New York: Free Press, 1973); J. Goebel, *Felony and Misdemeanor* (Philadelphia: University of Pennsylvania Press, 1976); Georg Rusche and Otto Kircheimer, *Punishment and Social Structure* (New York: Russell & Russell, 1939); Samuel Walker, *Popular Justice* (New York: Oxford University Press, 1980); Graeme R. Newman, *The Punishment Response* (Philadelphia: Lippincott, 1978); David Rothman, *Conscience and Convenience* (Boston: Little, Brown, 1980); George Ives, *A History of Penal Methods* (Montclair, NJ: Patterson-Smith, 1970); Robert Hughes, *The Fatal Shore* (New York: Knopf, 1986); Leon Radzinowicz, *A History of English Criminal Law*, vol. 1 (London: Stevens, 1943), p. 5.
4. *Crime and Punishment in America, 1999*, Report 229 (Washington, DC: National Center for Policy Analysis, 1999).
5. Matthew R. Durose, Donald Farole Jr., and Sean P. Rosenmerkel, *Felony Sentences in State Courts, 2006–Statistical Tables* (Washington, DC: Bureau of Justice Statistics, 2009).
6. Ibid.
7. E. Ann Carson, *Prisoners in 2012* (Washington, DC: Bureau of Justice Statistics, 2013).
8. Tomislav Kovandzic and Lynne Vieraitis, "The Effect of County-Level Prison Population Growth on Crime Rates," *Criminology and Public Policy* 5 (2006): 213–244.

9. Lynne Vieraitis, Tomislav Kovandzic, and Thomas Marvell, "The Criminogenic Effects of Imprisonment: Evidence from State Panel Data, 1974–2002," *Criminology and Public Policy* 6 (2007): 589–622.
10. Raymond Liedka, Anne Morrison Piehl, and Bert Useem, "The Crime-Control Effect of Incarceration: Does Scale Matter?" *Criminology and Public Policy* 5 (2006): 245–276.
11. Ibid.
12. Positive results were achieved by Lawrence Sherman and Richard Berk, "The Specific Deterrent Effects of Arrest for Domestic Assault," *American Sociological Review* 49 (1984): 261–272; negative by Christopher Maxwell, Joel Garner, and Jeffrey Fagan, *The Effects of Arrest in Intimate Partner Violence: New Evidence from the Spouse Assault Replication Program* (Washington, DC: National Institute of Justice, 2001); Robert Davis, Barbara Smith, and Laura Nickles, "The Deterrent Effect of Prosecuting Domestic Violence Misdemeanors," *Crime and Delinquency* 44 (1998): 434–442.
13. Matthew R. Durose, Alexia D. Cooper, and Howard N. Snyder, *Recidivism of Prisoners Released in 30 States in 2005: Patterns from 2005 to 2010* (Washington, DC: Bureau of Justice Statistics, 2014).
14. Christina Dejong, "Survival Analysis and Specific Deterrence," *Criminology* 35 (2006): 561–576; Raymond Paternoster and Alex Piquero, "Reconceptualizing Deterrence: An Empirical Test of Personal and Vicarious Experiences," *Journal of Research in Crime and Delinquency* 32 (1995): 251–258.
15. David Lovell, L. Clark Johnson, and Kevin Cain, "Recidivism of Supermax Prisoners in Washington State," *Crime and Delinquency* 53 (2007): 633–656.
16. Greg Pogarsky and Alex R. Piquero, "Can Punishment Encourage Offending? Investigating the 'Resetting' Effect," *Journal of Research in Crime and Delinquency* 40 (2003): 92–117.
17. Faith Lutze, "The Influence of Shock Incarceration Program on Inmate Adjustment and Attitudinal Change," *Journal of Criminal Justice* 29 (2001): 255–266.
18. Charles Logan, *Criminal Justice Performance Measures for Prisons* (Washington, DC: Bureau of Justice Statistics, 1993), p. 3.

19. Alexis Durham, "The Justice Model in Historical Context: Early Law, the Emergence of Science, and the Rise of Incarceration," *Journal of Criminal Justice* 16 (1988): 331–346.

20. Andrew von Hirsch, *Doing Justice: The Choice of Punishments* (New York: Hill and Wang, 1976).

21. Shawn Bushway, "The Impact of an Arrest on the Job Stability of Young White American Men," *Journal of Research in Crime and Delinquency* 35 (1998): 454–479.

22. Lawrence W. Sherman, David P. Farrington, Doris Layton MacKenzie, Brandon Walsh, Denise Gottfredson, John Eck, Shawn Bushway, and Peter Reuter, *Evidence-Based Crime Prevention* (London: Routledge and Kegan Paul, 2002); see also Arnulf Kolstad, "Imprisonment as Rehabilitation: Offenders' Assessment of Why It Does Not Work," *Journal of Criminal Justice* 24 (1996): 323–335.

23. Francis Cullen, John Paul Wright, Shayna Brown, Melissa Moon, and Brandon Applegate, "Public Support for Early Intervention Programs: Implications for a Progressive Policy Agenda," *Crime and Delinquency* 44 (1998): 187–204; Richard McCorkle, "Research Note: Punish and Rehabilitate? Public Attitudes Toward Six Common Crimes," *Crime and Delinquency* 39 (1993): 240–252; D. A. Andrews, Ivan Zinger, Robert Hoge, James Bonta, Paul Gendreau, and Francis Cullen, "Does Correctional Treatment Work? A Clinically Relevant and Psychologically Informed Meta-Analysis," *Criminology* 28 (1990): 369–404.

24. Gordon Bazemore and Curt Taylor Griffiths, "Conferences, Circles, Boards, and Mediations: The 'New Wave' of Community Justice Decision Making," *Federal Probation* 61 (1997): 25–37.

25. Paula Ditton and Doris James Wilson, *Truth in Sentencing in State Prisons* (Washington, DC: Bureau of Justice Statistics, 1999).

26. Jo Dixon, "The Organizational Context of Criminal Sentencing," *American Journal of Sociology* 100 (1995): 1157–1198.

27. Michael Tonry, *The Fragmentation of Sentencing and Corrections in America* (Washington, DC: National Institute of Justice, 1999).

28. *Apprendi v. New Jersey*, 530 U.S. 466 (2000).

29. *Blakely v. Washington*, 124 S.Ct. 2531 (2004).

30. *United States v. Booker*, 543 U.S. 220 (2005).

31. News Release, "U.S. Sentencing Commission Votes Unanimously to Apply Amendment Retroactively for Crack Cocaine Offenses, Effective Date for Retroactivity Set for March 3, 2008," http://www.ussc.gov/Legislative_and_Public_Affairs/Newsroom/Press_Releases/20110630_Press_Release.pdf (accessed July 2014).

32. *Kimbrough v. United States*, 552 U.S. 85 (2007).

33. *Rita v. United States*, 551 U.S. 338 (2007).

34. United States Sentencing Commission, *Demographic Differences in Federal Sentencing Practices: An Update of the* Booker *Report's Multivariate Regression Analysis* (Washington, DC: U.S. Sentencing Commission), http://www.albany.edu/scj/documents/USSC_Multivariate_Regression_Analysis_Report_001.pdf (accessed July 2014), p. 2.

35. *Harmelin v. Michigan*, 501 U.S. 957 (1991).

36. "Man Who Stole Slice of Pizza Sentenced to 25 Years to Life in California," *New York Times*, March 5, 1995; "Cookie Burglar Gets at Least 25 Years," http://www.cnn.com/US/Newsbriefs/9510/10-27/ (accessed July 2014).

37. *Lockyer v. Andrade*, 538 U.S. 63 (2003).

38. *Ewing v. California*, 538 U.S. 11 (2003).

39. Ditton and Wilson, *Truth in Sentencing in State Prisons*.

40. Rosenmerkel, Durose, and Farole Jr., *Felony Sentences in State Courts, 2006—Statistical Tables*.

41. Ibid.

42. Ibid., Table 1.3.

43. Brent Smith and Kelly Damphouse, "Terrorism, Politics, and Punishment: A Test of Structural-Contextual Theory and the Liberation Hypothesis," *Criminology* 36 (1998): 67–92.

44. For a general look at the factors that affect sentencing, see Susan Welch, Cassia Spohn, and John Gruhl, "Convicting and Sentencing Differences Among Black, Hispanic, and White Males in Six Localities," *Justice Quarterly* 2 (1985): 67–80.

45. Stewart D'Alessio and Lisa Stolzenberg, "Socioeconomic Status and the Sentencing of the Traditional Offender," *Journal of Criminal Justice* 21 (1993): 61–77.

46. Cecilia Saulters-Tubbs, "Prosecutorial and Judicial Treatment of Female Offenders," *Federal Probation* 57 (1993): 37–41.

47. See, generally, Janet Johnston, Thomas Kennedy, and I. Gayle Shuman, "Gender Differences in the Sentencing of Felony Offenders," *Federal Probation* 49 (1987): 49–56; Cassia Spohn and Susan Welch, "The Effect of Prior Record in Sentencing Research: An Examination of the Assumption That Any Measure Is Adequate," *Justice Quarterly* 4 (1987): 286–302; David Willison, "The Effects of Counsel on the Severity of Criminal Sentences: A Statistical Assessment," *Justice System Journal* 9 (1984): 87–101.

48. Cassia Spohn, Miriam DeLone, and Jeffrey Spears, "Race/Ethnicity, Gender, and Sentence Severity in Dade County, Florida: An Examination of the Decision to Withhold Adjudication," *Journal of Crime and Justice* 21 (1998): 111–132.

49. Ellen Hochstedler Steury and Nancy Frank, "Gender Bias and Pretrial Release: More Pieces of the Puzzle," *Journal of Criminal Justice* 18 (1990): 417–432.

50. Shimica Gaskins, "Women of Circumstance—The Effects of Mandatory Minimum Sentencing on Women Minimally Involved in Drug Crimes," *American Criminal Law Review* 41 (2004): 1533–1563.

51. Shawn Bushway and Anne Morrison Piehl, "The Inextricable Link Between Age and Criminal History in Sentencing," *Crime and Delinquency* 53 (2007): 156–183.

52. Dean Champion, "Elderly Felons and Sentencing Severity: Interregional Variations in Leniency and Sentencing Trends," *Criminal Justice Review* 12 (1987): 7–15.

53. Darrell Steffensmeier, John Kramer, and Jeffery Ulmer, "Age Differences in Sentencing," *Justice Quarterly* 12 (1995): 583–601.

54. Darrell Steffensmeier, Jeffery Ulmer, and John Kramer, "The Interaction of Race, Gender, and Age in Criminal Sentencing: The Punishment Cost of Being Young, Black, and Male," *Criminology* 36 (1998): 763–798.

55. *Payne v. Tennessee*, 501 U.S. 808 (1991).

56. Rodney Kingsworth, Randall MacIntosh, and Jennifer Wentworth, "Sexual Assault: The Role of Prior Relationship and Victim Characteristics in Case Processing," *Justice Quarterly* 16 (1999): 276–302.

57. Tracy Nobiling, Cassia Spohn, and Miriam DeLone, "A Tale of Two Counties: Unemployment and Sentence Severity," *Justice Quarterly* 15 (1998): 459–486.

58. Michael Tonry, *Malign Neglect: Race, Crime, and Punishment in America* (New York: Oxford University Press, 1995), pp. 105–109.

59. *Coker v. Georgia*, 433 U.S. 584 (1977).

60. *People v. Stephen LaValle*, Sup.C. #71 (2004).

61. For more on this issue, read Hugo Adam Bedeau and Paul Cassell, *Debating the Death Penalty: Should America Have Capital Punishment? The Experts on Both Sides Make Their Best Case* (London: Oxford University Press, 2003).

62. Stephen Markman and Paul Cassell, "Protecting the Innocent: A Response to the Bedeau-Radelet Study," *Stanford Law Review* 41 (1988): 121–170.

63. Tracy L. Snell, *Capital Punishment, 2011—Statistical Tables* (Washington, DC: Bureau of Justice Statistics), http://www.bjs.gov/content/pub/pdf/cp11st.pdf (accessed July 2014).

64. Stephen Layson, "United States Time-Series Homicide Regressions with Adaptive Expectations," *Bulletin of the New York Academy of Medicine* 62 (1986): 589–619.

65. James Galliher and John Galliher, "A 'Commonsense' Theory of Deterrence and the 'Ideology' of Science: The New York State Death Penalty Debate," *Journal of Criminal Law and Criminology* 92 (2002): 307.

66. Steven Stack, "The Effect of Well-Publicized Executions on Homicide in California," *Journal of Crime and Justice* 21 (1998): 1–12.

67. Hashem Dezhbakhsh, Paul H. Rubin, and Joanna M. Shepherd, "Does Capital Punishment Have a Deterrent Effect? New Evidence from Postmoratorium Panel Data," *American Law and Economics Review* 5 (2003): 344–376.

68. Joanna Shepherd, "Deterrence versus Brutalization: Capital Punishment's Differing Impacts Among States," *Michigan Law Review* 104 (2005): 203–253.

69. Kenneth C. Land, Raymond H. C. Teske Jr., and Hui Zheng, "The Short Term Effects of Executions on Homicides: Deterrence, Displacement, or Both?" *Criminology* 47 (2009): 1009–1043.

70. David Friedrichs, "Comment—Humanism and the Death Penalty: An Alternative Perspective," *Justice Quarterly* 6 (1989): 197–209.

71. Sourcebook of Criminal Justice Statistics, *Attitudes Toward the Death Penalty for Persons Convicted of Murder*, http://www .albany.edu/sourcebook/pdf/t2512011.pdf (accessed July 2014).

72. For an analysis of the formation of public opinion on the death penalty, see Kimberly Cook, "Public Support for the Death Penalty: A Cultural Analysis," paper presented at the annual meeting of the American Society of Criminology, San Francisco, November 1991.

73. Alexis Durham, H. Preston Elrod, and Patrick Kinkade, "Public Support to the Death Penalty: Beyond Gallup," *Justice Quarterly* 13 (1996): 705–736.

74. See, generally, Hugo Bedeau, *Death Is Different: Studies in the Morality, Law, and Politics of Capital Punishment* (Boston: Northeastern University Press, 1987); Keith Otterbein, *The Ultimate Coercive Sanction* (New Haven, CN: HRAF Press, 1986).

75. Michael Radelet and Hugo Bedeau, "Miscarriages of Justice in Potentially Capital Cases," *Stanford Law Review* 40 (1987): 121–181.

76. House Subcommittee on Civil and Constitutional Rights, *Innocence and the Death Penalty: Assessing the Danger of Mistaken Executions* (Washington, DC: Government Printing Office, 1993).

77. David Stewart, "Dealing with Death," *American Bar Association Journal* 80 (1994): 53.

78. Samuel R. Gross, Barbara O'Brien, and Edward H. Kennedy, "Rate of False Conviction of Criminal Defendants Who Are Sentenced to Death," *Proceedings of the National Academy of Sciences*, published online before print, doi: 10.1073.

79. "The Innocence Protection Act," editorial, *America* 187 (2002): 2–3.

80. Erik Lillquist, "Absolute Certainty and the Death Penalty," *American Criminal Law Review* 42 (2005): 45–92.

81. "A Victim's Progress," *Newsweek*, June 12, 1989, p. 5.

82. William Doerner, "The Impact of Medical Resources on Criminally Induced Lethality: A Further Examination," *Criminology* 26 (1988): 171–177.

83. Elizabeth Purdom and J. Anthony Paredes, "Capital Punishment and Human Sacrifice," in *Facing the Death Penalty: Essays on Cruel and Unusual Punishment*, ed. Michael Radelet (Philadelphia: Temple University Press, 1989), pp. 152–153.

84. Kimberly Cook, "A Passion to Punish: Abortion Opponents Who Favor the Death Penalty," *Justice Quarterly* 15 (1998): 329–346.

85. John Whitehead, Michael Blankenship, and John Paul Wright, "Elite versus Citizen Attitudes on Capital Punishment: Incongruity Between the Public and Policy Makers," *Journal of Criminal Justice* 27 (1999): 249–258.

86. Julian Roberts, "Capital Punishment, Innocence, and Public Opinion," *Criminology and Public Policy* 4 (2005): 1–3.

87. James Unnever and Francis Cullen, "Executing the Innocent and Support for Capital Punishment: Implications for Public Policy," *Criminology and Public Policy* 4 (2005): 3–37.

88. Scott Vollum, Dennis Longmire, and Jacqueline Buffington-Vollum, "Confidence in the Death Penalty and Support for Its Use: Exploring the Value-Expressive Dimension of Death Penalty Attitudes," *Justice Quarterly* 21 (2004): 521–546.

89. Gennaro Vito and Thomas Keil, "Elements of Support for Capital Punishment: An Examination of Changing Attitudes," *Journal of Crime and Justice* 21 (1998): 17–25.

90. Denise Paquette Boots, Kathleen Heide, and John Cochran, "Death Penalty Support for Special Offender Populations of Legally Convicted Murderers: Juveniles, the Mentally Retarded, and the Mentally Incompetent," *Behavioral Sciences and the Law* 22 (2004): 223–238.

91. James Unnever and Francis Cullen, "The Racial Divide in Support for the Death Penalty: Does White Racism Matter?" *Social Forces* 85 (2007): 1281–1301.

92. John Donohue and Justin Wolfers, "Uses and Abuses of Empirical Evidence in the Death Penalty Debate," *Stanford Law Review* 58 (2005): 791–845.

93. Walter C. Reckless, "Use of the Death Penalty," *Crime and Delinquency* 15 (1969): 43; Thorsten Sellin, "Effect of Repeal and Reintroduction of the Death Penalty on Homicide Rates," in *The Death Penalty*, ed. Thorsten Sellin (Philadelphia: American Law Institute, 1959); Robert H. Dann, "The Deterrent Effect of Capital Punishment," *Friends Social Service Series* 29 (1935): 1; William Bailey and Ruth Peterson, "Murder and Capital Punishment: A Monthly Time-Series Analysis of Execution Publicity," *American Sociological Review* 54 (1989): 722–743; David Phillips, "The Deterrent Effect of Capital Punishment," *American Journal of Sociology* 86 (1980): 139–148; Sam McFarland, "Is Capital Punishment a Short-Term Deterrent to Homicide? A Study of the Effects of Four Recent American Executions," *Journal of Criminal Law and Criminology* 74 (1984): 1014–1032; Richard Lempert, "The Effect of Executions on Homicides: A New Look in an Old Light," *Crime and Delinquency* 29 (1983): 88–115.

94. Jon Sorensen, Robert Wrinkle, Victoria Brewer, and James Marquart, "Capital Punishment and Deterrence: Examining the Effect of Executions on Murder in Texas," *Crime and Delinquency* 45 (1999): 481–493.

95. Keith Harries and Derral Cheatwood, *The Geography of Execution: The Capital Punishment Quagmire in America* (Lanham, MD: Rowman and Littlefield, 1997).

96. Land, Teske, and Zheng, "The Short Term Effects of Executions on Homicides: Deterrence, Displacement, or Both?" 1012–1013.

97. Jonathan R. Sorensen and Rocky L. Pilgrim, "An Actuarial Risk of Assessment of Violence Posed by Murder Defendants," *Journal of Criminal Law and Criminology* 90 (2000): 1251–1271.

98. Rick Ruddell and Martin Urbina, "Minority Threat and Punishment: A Cross-National Analysis," *Justice Quarterly* 21 (2004): 903–931.

99. Marian Williams and Jefferson Holcomb, "Racial Disparity and Death Sentences in Ohio," *Journal of Criminal Justice* 29 (2001): 207–218.

100. Jon Sorensen and Donald Wallace, "Prosecutorial Discretion in Seeking Death: An Analysis of Racial Disparity in the Pretrial Stages of Case Processing in a Midwestern County," *Justice Quarterly* 16 (1999): 559–578.

101. Catherine Lee, "Hispanics and the Death Penalty: Discriminatory Charging Practices in San Joaquin County, California," *Journal of Criminal Justice* 35 (2007): 17–27.

102. Jefferson Holcomb, Marian Williams, and Stephen Demuth, "White Female Victims and Death Penalty Disparity Research," *Justice Quarterly* 21 (2004): 877–902.

103. Lawrence Greenfield and David Hinners, *Capital Punishment, 1984* (Washington, DC: Bureau of Justice Statistics, 1985).

104. Gennaro Vito and Thomas Keil, "Capital Sentencing in Kentucky: An Analysis of the Factors Influencing Decision Making in the Post-Gregg Period," *Journal of Criminal Law and Criminology* 79 (1988): 483–508.

105. David Brown, "Man Is Executed in Carolina: Second of a White Who Killed a Black," *Boston Globe*, January 25, 1995, p. 3.

106. James Unnever and Francis Cullen, "Reassessing the Racial Divide in Support for Capital Punishment: The Continuing Significance of Race," *Journal of Research in Crime and Delinquency* 44 (2007): 124–158.

107. Geoffrey Rapp, "The Economics of Shootouts: Does the Passage of Capital Punishment Laws Protect or Endanger Police Officers?" *Albany Law Review* 65 (2002): 1051–1084.

108. *Hill v. McDonough*, 547 U.S. 573 (2006).

109. Robert Johnson, *Death Work: A Study of the Modern Execution Process* (Pacific Grove, CA: Brooks/Cole, 1990).

110. William Bailey, "Disaggregation in Deterrence and Death Penalty Research: The Case of Murder in Chicago," *Journal of Criminal Law and Criminology* 74 (1986): 827–859.

111. Gennaro Vito, Pat Koester, and Deborah Wilson, "Return of the Dead: An Update on the Status of Furman-Commuted Death Row Inmates," in *The Death Penalty in America: Current Research*, ed. Robert Bohm (Cincinnati: Anderson, 1991), pp. 89–100; Gennaro Vito, Deborah Wilson, and Edward Latessa, "Comparison of the Dead: Attributes and Outcomes of Furman-Commuted Death Row Inmates in Kentucky and Ohio," in *The Death Penalty in America: Current Research*, ed. Bohm, pp. 101–112.

112. John Cochran, Mitchell Chamlin, and Mark Seth, "Deterrence or Brutalization? An Impact Assessment of Oklahoma's Return to Capital Punishment," *Criminology* 32 (1994): 107–134.

113. William Bailey, "Deterrence, Brutalization, and the Death Penalty: Another Examination of Oklahoma's Return to Capital Punishment," *Justice Quarterly* 36 (1998): 711–734.

114. Joseph Schumacher, "An International Look at the Death Penalty," *International Journal of Comparative and Applied Criminal Justice* 14 (1990): 307–315.

115. Don Terry, "California Prepares for Faster Execution Pace," *New York Times*, October 17, 1998, p. A7.

116. See, for example, Ernest Van Den Haag, *Punishing Criminals: Concerning a Very Old and Painful Question* (New York: Basic Books, 1975), pp. 209–211; Walter Berns, "Defending the Death Penalty," *Crime and Delinquency* 26 (1980): 503–511.

117. Thoroddur Bjarnason and Michael Welch, "Father Knows Best: Parishes, Priests, and American Catholic Parishioners' Attitudes Toward Capital Punishment," *Journal for the Scientific Study of Religion* 43 (2004): 103–118.

118. Franklin Zimring, *The Contradictions of American Capital Punishment* (London: Oxford University Press, 2003).

119. Vance McLaughlin and Paul Blackman, "Mass Legal Executions in Georgia," *Georgia Historical Quarterly* 88 (2004): 66–84.

120. Austin Sarat, "Innocence, Error, and the 'New Abolitionism': A Commentary," *Criminology and Public Policy* 4 (2005): 45–53.

121. *Furman v. Georgia*, 408 U.S. 238 (1972).

122. *Gregg v. Georgia*, 428 U.S. 153 (1976).

123. Ibid.

124. *Ford v. Wainwright*, 477 U.S. 399 (1986).

125. *Atkins v. Virginia*, 536 U.S. 304 (2002).

126. *Ring v. Arizona*, 536 U.S. 584 (2002).

127. *Roper v. Simmons*, 543 U.S. 551 (2005).

128. *Deck v. Missouri*, 544 U.S. 622 (2005).

129. *Oregon v. Guzek*, 546 U.S. 517 (2006).

130. *Baze v. Rees*, 553 U.S. 35 (2008).

131. *Kennedy v. Louisiana*, 128 S.Ct. 2641 (2008).

132. *Ring v. Arizona*, 536 U.S. 584 (2002).

133. *Coker v. Georgia*, 430 U.S. 349 (1977).

134. *Ford v. Wainwright*, 477 U.S. 399 (1986).

135. *Atkins v. Virginia*, 536 U.S. 304 (2002).

136. *Roper v. Simmons*, 543 U.S. 551 (2005).

137. *Kennedy v. Louisiana*, 128 S.Ct. 2641 (2008).

138. *Baze v. Rees*, 553 U.S. 35 (2008).

139. See also Adam S. Goldstone, "The Death Penalty: How America's Highest Court Is Narrowing Its Application," *Criminal Law Brief* 4 (2009): 23–39.

140. *Furman v. Georgia*, 408 U.S. 238 (1972).

141. *Gregg v. Georgia*, 428 U.S. 153 (1976).

142. *Woodson v. North Carolina*, 428 U.S. 280 (1976).

143. *Coker v. Georgia*, 430 U.S. 349 (1977).

144. *Lockett v. Ohio*, 438 U.S. 586 (1978).

145. *Enmund v. Florida*, 458 U.S. 782 (1982).

146. *Glass v. Louisiana*, 471 U.S. 1080 (1985).

147. *Cabana v. Bullock*, 474 U.S. 376 (1986).

CORRECTIONS

CORRECTIONS IS A SIGNIFICANT PART of the criminal justice system, employing more than half a million people and costing taxpayers close to $70 billion per year. Though challenging, correctional work can also be rewarding. Many correctional employees work in community corrections and attempt to help their clients turn their lives around without need for a term in a secure prison facility. Take, for instance, the career of Ann Beranis, who first became interested in the justice system while a student of clinical psychology. After receiving a master's degree, she decided to work as a probation officer. Ann finds the job both challenging and rewarding. She believes that most people she meets do not understand that community corrections is not about punishing offenders but about helping them change their thinking and behavior. She says, "Most of a probation officer's time is spent diagnosing the cause of an individual's antisocial behavior and then devising strategies for behavior change. It is challenging when clients are resistant to change. But while difficult, accurate assessments can be made and techniques applied to increase the client's motivation." Ann finds that probation officers must learn to tap into community resources, such as employment opportunities, and create strong partnerships with service providers. Her greatest reward on the job is seeing clients leave probation with confidence in themselves and hope for the future. "It is also rewarding," she says, "knowing that [my] hard work helps crime victims and protects the community from further victimization."

Just as working in community corrections is a challenge, so is working in secure correctional facilities. Rachel Anita Jung, executive development program manager in the Arizona Department of Corrections, always knew she would be in a helping/public service profession. She channeled her basic curiosity about human behavior into a career in corrections, which has included stints as a jail screener, a case manager for a treatment and referral program for substance abusers, and an adult probation officer. Most recently, Rachel has managed executive development for the corrections staff. She relishes the opportunity to develop in-service programming that not only influences leadership practices but also affects the way staff interact with inmates throughout the entire state system. ◼

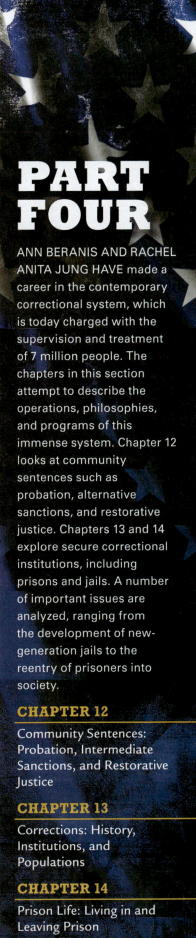

PART FOUR

ANN BERANIS AND RACHEL ANITA JUNG HAVE made a career in the contemporary correctional system, which is today charged with the supervision and treatment of 7 million people. The chapters in this section attempt to describe the operations, philosophies, and programs of this immense system. Chapter 12 looks at community sentences such as probation, alternative sanctions, and restorative justice. Chapters 13 and 14 explore secure correctional institutions, including prisons and jails. A number of important issues are analyzed, ranging from the development of new-generation jails to the reentry of prisoners into society.

Community Sentences: Probation, Intermediate Sanctions, and Restorative Justice

Learning Objectives

 LO1 Describe the concept of community sentencing.

 LO2 Discuss the history of community sentences.

 LO3 Characterize the different types of probation sentences.

 LO4 Summarize the rules of probation.

 LO5 Discuss the organization and administration of probation services.

 LO6 Define and discuss the term *risk classification*.

 LO7 Interpret the legal issues of probation.

 LO8 Discuss the effectiveness of probation.

 LO9 Explain what is meant by intermediate sanctions.

 LO10 Explain the concept of restorative justice and discuss its merits.

Chapter Outline

The Concept of Probation
The History of Community Sentencing
Contemporary Probation Services
Conditions of Probation
Analyzing Criminal Justice Issues: Can Criminals be Reformed?
Awarding Probation
Administration of Probation Services
Duties of Probation Officers
Criminal Justice and Technology: Monitoring Probationers with Technology
Evidence-Based Justice: Treating Probationers with Cognitive Behavioral Therapy
Legal Rights of Probationers
Careers in Criminal Justice: Probation Officer
How Successful Is Probation?
What Causes Probation Success and Failure?
The Future of Probation
Evidence-Based Justice: Hawaii HOPE

Other Alternatives to Imprisonment
Advantages of Intermediate Sanctions
Fines
Forfeiture
Restitution
Shock Probation and Split Sentencing
Intensive Probation Supervision
House Arrest/Electronic Monitoring
Residential Community Corrections

Restorative Justice
Global Criminal Justice: Restoration in Australia and New Zealand
The Concept of Restoration
Restoration Programs
Restoration in Practice
Court-Based Programs

Chad Johnson, AKA Chad Ochocinco, was one of the most feared receivers in the NFL. Despite his fame, Johnson endured marital problems and was arrested on August 11, 2012, after head-butting his wife, Evelyn Lozada, during an argument in the driveway of their home in Miami. Johnson agreed to plead guilty to a misdemeanor domestic assault charge in exchange for a lenient sentence, helping him avoid jail time: one year of probation, complete batterers' intervention counseling, and pay restitution for medical costs. In 2013, he was arrested for violating his probation conditions and spent some time in jail.[1]

Johnson joins a long list of celebrities and athletes who have been placed on parole:

- On August 23, 2007, Lindsay Lohan pleaded guilty to misdemeanor cocaine use and driving under the influence and was sentenced to one day's imprisonment and 10 days' community service, and ordered to pay fines, complete an alcohol education program, and spend three years on probation. In 2010, she violated her probation order by failing to attend substance abuse classes and was jailed for 90 days (though she served only 23 behind bars). In 2011,

Lohan spent 35 days on house arrest for another breach in her probation: she was accused of taking a necklace from a local jewelry store. She has faced continued legal troubles ever since.

- After he pleaded guilty in January 2011 to sexual misconduct and patronizing an underage prostitute, former New York Giants great Lawrence Taylor was sentenced to six years on probation. The former all-star linebacker was also required to register as a sex offender.[2]

- In 2011, movie star Mel Gibson was sentenced to three years' probation and ordered to undergo a year of counseling after pleading no contest to a charge of simple misdemeanor battery for attacking his girlfriend Oksana Grigorieva during a heated argument in January 2010.[3]

- In 2009, Chris Brown was sentenced to five years of probation and 180 days of community service after a plea bargain in his felony assault case for beating his girlfriend Rihanna.[4] In 2014, he was charged with assaulting a fan outside the W Hotel in Washington, DC. Brown rejected a plea deal and the case went to trial as of this writing.[5]

■ In 2013, singer Kanye West attempted to wrestle a camera from the hands of a paparazzi member who tried to take pictures of him at while he was passing through the Los Angeles International Airport. West was sentenced to two years' probation as part of a misdemeanor battery conviction. He was also ordered to complete anger management classes, perform 250 hours of community service, and pay restitution to the victim.[6]

Are these people being given special treatment, being able to avoid a prison sentence and placed on probation simply because they are celebs? Does this special treatment conflict with the core values of the American justice system that all people are "equal before the law"? Would the average person be sent to prison for domestic violence, possessing drugs, threatening someone with a gun, or having sex with an underage prostitute? Hardly: probation and other approaches to community sentencing are the most commonly used means of correction today and are not just reserved for the rich and famous; millions of people are on probation for these and similar crimes, some for violent felonies. ■

Community sentencing, including probation, is the most common form of correctional treatment because it makes no sense to lock up nondangerous, repentant offenders in an overcrowded and dangerous correctional system, which can damage them and lock them into a life of crime. It may be both more effective and less costly to have them remain in the community under the supervision of a trained court officer, where they can receive treatment that will help them turn their lives around. Rehabilitation would be aided immensely if those who commit crime could be made to understand the problems their actions cause their family, friends, and community. Other reasons for the attractiveness of community sentences include:

■ They are less costly than a sentence to jail or prison.

■ They help the offender maintain family and community ties.

■ They can be structured to maximize security and maintain public safety.

■ They can be scaled in severity to correspond to the seriousness of the crime.

■ They can feature restoration and reintegration rather than punishment and ostracism.

■ They give convicted offenders a "second chance" that can enable them to resume a more productive lifestyle.[7]

In a tight economic environment, cost-effective programming such as probation makes economic sense. It is not surprising that a growing number of convicted offenders are being offered community sentences ranging from traditional probation to house arrest and placement in community correctional centers, simply because this approach makes both economic and practical sense. For example, when Christopher Krebs and his associates carefully compared treatment outcomes of large groups of drug-involved offenders in Florida they found that community-based drug treatment reduced the chances for a subsequent felony arrest by 22 percent. In comparison, prison- or jail-based treatment, which cost three times as much as community-based treatment, did not have similar success; inmates showed no particular improvement after attending an institutional drug treatment program.[8] Clearly community-based programs can be both practical and cost effective.

L01 Describe the concept of community sentencing.

This chapter reviews these criminal sanctions. It begins by discussing the role of traditional probation as a community-based correctional practice and a brief history of community sentencing. Then it focuses on so-called alternative or intermediate sanctions, such as intensive supervision, house arrest, and electronic monitoring. Finally, the chapter turns to a discussion of the concept of restorative justice and programs based on its principles.

The Concept of Probation

Probation is a criminal sentence that suspends or delays a correctional term in a prison or jail in return for a period of community supervision during which the probationer must abide by certain conditions set forth by the court, under the supervision of a probation officer.

The philosophy of probation today rests on the assumption that the typical offender is not a dangerous criminal or a "menace to society," but someone who has made a mistake and has the ability and potential to reform. When such offenders are institutionalized instead of being granted community release, the prison community becomes their new reference point, they are forced to interact with hardened criminals, and they develop an "ex-con" label that interferes with successful adjustments to society—all conditions that both impede their successful rehabilitation and increase the likelihood of recidivism. It is widely assumed that the opportunity to avoid stigma and negative labels can be critical to rehabilitation. Offenders who are able to avoid official criminal labels are significantly less likely to recidivate than those branded with official criminal labels.[9] Following this logic, it is evident that the stigma of a prison sentence would have far more devastating effects than a community sentence.

The History of Community Sentencing

How did this idea of community supervision and control begin? The roots of probation can be traced back to the traditions of the English common law. During the Middle Ages, judges who wished to spare deserving offenders from commonly used punishments such as torture, mutilation, and death used their power to grant clemency and stays of execution. The common-law practice of **judicial reprieve** allowed judges to suspend punishment so that convicted offenders could seek a pardon, gather new evidence, or demonstrate that they had reformed their behavior. Similarly, the practice of **recognizance** enabled convicted offenders to remain free if they agreed to enter into a debt obligation with the state. The debt would have to be paid only if the offender was caught engaging in further criminal behavior. Sometimes sureties were required—these were people who made themselves responsible for the behavior of an offender after he was released.

JOHN AUGUSTUS Early U.S. courts continued the practice of indefinitely suspending sentences of criminals who seemed deserving of a second chance, but it was John Augustus of Boston who is usually credited with originating the modern probation concept.[10] As a private citizen, Augustus began in 1841 to supervise offenders released to his custody by a Boston judge. Over an 18-year period, Augustus supervised close to 2,000 probationers and helped them get jobs and establish themselves in the community. Augustus had an amazingly high success rate, and few of his charges became involved in crime again.

In 1878, Augustus's work inspired the Massachusetts legislature to pass a law authorizing the appointment of a paid probation officer for the city of Boston. In 1880, probation was extended to other jurisdictions in Massachusetts, and by 1898 the probation movement had spread to the superior (felony) courts.[11] The Massachusetts experience was copied by Missouri (1887) and Vermont (1898), and soon after by most other states. In 1925, the federal government established a probation system for the U.S. district courts. The probation concept soon became the most widely used correctional mechanism in the United States.[12]

Contemporary Probation Services

Considering its benefits, it's not surprising that the probation population has undergone continual growth. About 4 million people are currently on probation.[13] This translates into approximately one in 61 U.S. adult residents. More

probation
A sentence entailing the conditional release of a convicted offender into the community under the supervision of the court (in the form of a probation officer), subject to certain conditions for a specified time.

judicial reprieve
The common-law practice that allowed judges to suspend punishment so that convicted offenders could seek a pardon, gather new evidence, or demonstrate that they had reformed their behavior.

recognizance
The medieval practice of allowing convicted offenders to go unpunished if they agreed to refrain from any further criminal behavior.

 LO2 Discuss the history of community sentences.

 Web App 12.1

For more information about John Augustus and the history of probation, visit http://www.nyc.gov/html/prob/html/about/history.shtml.

LO3 Characterize the different types of probation sentences.

LO4 Summarize the rules of probation.

Web App 12.2

For a list of typical probation conditions, see http://www.law.cornell.edu/uscode/text/18/3563.

than 2 million people are still being placed on probation annually, and a slightly larger number exit their probation sentence. Without probation, the correctional system would rapidly become even more overcrowded, overly expensive, and unmanageable.

Conditions of Probation

Most probation orders involve a contract between the court and the offender in which a prison or jail term is suspended and the probationer promises to obey a set of **probation rules**, or conditions, mandated by the court. If the rules are violated (technical violation), or if the probationer commits a subsequent criminal offense (legal violation), then probation may be revoked. **Revocation** means that the community sentence is terminated and the original sentence of incarceration is enforced. If an offender on probation commits a second offense that is more serious than the first, he or she may also be indicted, tried, and sentenced on the second offense. However, probation may be revoked simply because the conditions of probation have not been met; it is not necessary for the offender to commit another crime. This outcome is quite serious because it is estimated that almost 10 percent of all offenders who exit probation supervision are incarcerated in state or local facilities due to rule violations, helping to overcrowd correctional facilities and increase costs.[14]

Some conditions (such as "do not leave the jurisdiction") are standard and are applied in every probation case, but the sentencing judge usually has broad discretion to set specific conditions on a case-by-case basis. Sometimes an individual probationer is given specific rules related to his or her particular circumstances, such as a requirement to obtain counseling or attend AA meetings.[15] Conditions cannot be capricious or cruel conditions, of course, such as requiring an offender to make restitution out of proportion to the seriousness of the criminal act.[16] Judges may, however, legally impose restrictions tailored to fit the probationer's individual needs and/or to protect society from additional harm. Do these conditions work? Can criminals really be reformed? How long does it take the typical criminal to reoffend? The accompanying Analyzing Criminal Justice Issues box touches on this subject.

PROBATION CONDITIONS IN THE INTERNET AGE Because the personal computer and the Internet are commonplace, probation orders now account for Internet use, including entry into chat rooms, visits to adult entertainment websites, purchasing of drugs via the Web, and so on. One area of concern is that the Internet has made it easier for sex offenders to search for pornography sites—or their next victim. As a result, probationers may be ordered either to avoid certain sites or to allow probation officers to monitor what they are viewing. Probation authorities have worked with social networking sites to identify and remove registered sex offenders and have asked the sites to turn over the identities of registered sex offenders who may be using the service.[17] This approach is not without controversy. Court rulings say Internet use is so broadly ingrained in today's society that restricting access would be like barring individuals from all telephone use because they used the telephone to commit fraud.[18]

Awarding Probation

Probationary sentences may be granted by state and federal district courts and state superior (felony) courts. Probation is not restricted to petty or first-time criminals. Most people convicted of felonies do receive some form of incarceration, in either prison or jail, but about 30 percent of felons are sentenced to probation.[19]

analyzing criminal justice ISSUES

CAN CRIMINALS BE REFORMED?

Is there a point where offenders no longer pose a threat to society? This is an important issue since more than 80 percent of U.S. employers perform criminal background checks on prospective employees and those that do may not want to hire ex-offenders. It is often difficult for ex-offenders to overcome this financial handicap, thereby increasing their chances of recidivism.

This situation prompted researchers Alfred Blumstein and Kiminori Nakamura to ask the question: is it possible to determine when it is no longer necessary for an employer to be concerned about a criminal offense in a prospective employee's past, for example, if the crime was committed two decades earlier? Of course, all employers and all employment opportunities are different. Those serving vulnerable populations like children and the elderly would be particularly sensitive to a prior record involving violence or sexual misconduct, while a bank hiring a teller would be particularly sensitive to embezzlement. When employers decide to hire an ex-offender they may go on their gut feeling, rejecting someone who would make a good employee or hiring someone who is still a risk.

To help improve the accuracy of these decisions, Blumstein and Nakamura studied the criminal history records of 88,000 individuals arrested in 1980 in order to estimate a point in time when they were at no greater risk of committing another crime than other individuals of the same age.

First they determined whether people in the sample had committed any other crime(s) during the ensuing 25 years or if they had stayed clean. Then they compared those data against two populations:

- People in the general population who were the same age
- People of the same age who had never been arrested

Their analysis calculated a "hazard rate," which is the probability, over time, that someone who has stayed clean will be arrested. For a person who has been arrested in the past, the hazard rate declines the longer he or she stays clean. Using this type of analysis, Blumstein and Nakamura found the hazard rate declined to the same arrest rate for the general population of same aged individuals at age 26, or about eight years after their robbery arrest. After that point, the probability that individuals would commit another crime was less than the probability of other 26-year-olds in the general population. The hazard rates of people who committed burglary at age 18 declined to the same as the general population in about four years post-arrest at age 22. For aggravated assault, the hazard rates of the study group and the general population of same-aged individuals also occurred four years postarrest or at age 22. The younger a person was at their first brush with the law, the longer they were a hazard for committing further crime. The longer the ex-offender stayed clean, the less likely they were to commit another crime. These data show that, over time, ex-offenders are no more likely to offend than other members of the general population.

CRITICAL THINKING

How would you deal with this problem? An employer refuses to hire ex-offenders even though they have not reoffended for more than a decade. After all, he argues, there are plenty of people without jobs who have never committed a crime. As an advocate for the rights of ex-offenders, what would you say to help him change his mind?

Source: Alfred Blumstein and Kiminori Nakamura, "'Redemption' in an Era of Widespread Criminal Background Checks," National Institute of Justice, *NIJ Journal* 263 (2009), http://www.nij.gov/journals/263/redemption.htm (accessed July 2014).

In some states, juries may recommend probation if the case meets certain legally regulated criteria (for example, if it falls within a certain class of offenses as determined by statute). Even in those jurisdictions that allow juries to recommend probation, judges have the final say in the matter and may grant probation at their discretion. In nonjury trials, probation is granted solely by judicial mandate. Some states have attempted to shape judicial discretion by creating guidelines for granting probation.

L05 Discuss the organization and administration of probation services.

---

suspended sentence
A prison term that is delayed while the defendant undergoes a period of community treatment. If the treatment is successful, the prison sentence is terminated.

intake
The process in which a probation officer settles cases at the initial appearance before the onset of formal criminal proceedings.

More than half of all cases involve a direct sentence to probation without a prison term being suspended or delayed. In about 20 percent of sentences, judges formulate a prison sentence and then suspend it if the offender agrees to obey the rules of probation while living in the community (a **suspended sentence**). Some offenders (about 10 percent) receive some form of split sentence in which they must first serve a jail term before being released on probation; in about 10 percent of cases, the imposition of the sentence is suspended and the case continued, without a finding, until further notice.

The term of a probationary sentence may simply extend to the limit of the suspended prison term, but in most cases the judge will devise a specific probationary period. For misdemeanors, probation usually extends for the entire period of the jail sentence, whereas felonies are more likely to warrant probationary periods that are actually shorter than the suspended prison sentences. The typical probation sentence for felons in urban counties is about 35 months for violent offenses, 32 months for property offenses, and 31 months for drug crimes.[20]

Administration of Probation Services

The United States has approximately 2,000 adult probation agencies. More than half are associated with a state-level agency. In the rest of the states, probation is primarily a local responsibility; probation departments in these jurisdictions are housed within the local court and controlled by judicial authorities. About 30 states combine probation and parole supervision into a single agency. A number of states have also permitted the private sector to administer probation supervision.

One of the most persuasive arguments for local administration is that citizens and agencies of the community more readily support programs that are open to their participation and are responsive to local needs and problems. Locally controlled departments tend to be smaller and more flexible, able to adjust more quickly to change, and less encumbered by bureaucratic rigidity.

Although these arguments are persuasive, some policy makers believe that:

■ A state-administered probation system can set standards of service, thereby ensuring uniformity of procedures, policies, and services.

■ A larger agency can make more effective use of funds and personnel.

■ Greater efficiency in the disposition of resources is possible when all probation officers are state employees.

Regardless of the administrative setup, probation department staff usually engage in the following activities:

■ Supervise or monitor cases to ensure that the rules of probation are followed

■ Create effective treatment plans

■ Conduct sentencing investigations to help judges formulate a proper and effective sentence

■ In some cases conduct an **intake** hearing in which victims, complainants, and defendants are contacted and interviewed in order to determine whether criminal charges should be filed or whether cases can be handled informally

How probation officers carry out these tasks may be a function of their self-image and professional orientation. Some POs view themselves as "social workers" and maintain a treatment orientation; their goal is to help offenders adjust in the community. Others are "law enforcers" who are more concerned with supervision, control, and public safety.[21] Ironically, younger officers appear to be more control- and safety-oriented than older officers, who are more likely to embrace the rehabilitation ideal. As these older officers retire, probation may adopt a more conservative focus.[22]

Duties of Probation Officers

Staff officers in probation departments are usually charged with five primary tasks: investigation, intake, diagnosis, treatment supervision, and risk classification.

INVESTIGATION In the investigative stage, the supervising probation officer accumulates important information on the background and activities of the offender being considered for probation. This **presentence investigation** serves as the basis for sentencing and controls whether the convicted defendant will be granted community release or sentenced to secure confinement. In the event that the offender is placed on probation, the investigation becomes useful as a tool to shape treatment and supervision efforts.

presentence investigation
An investigation performed by a probation officer attached to a trial court after the conviction of a defendant.

The style and content of presentence investigations may vary among jurisdictions and also among individual POs within the same jurisdiction. Some departments require voluminous reports covering every aspect of the defendant's life; other departments, which may be rule oriented, require that officers stick to the basic facts, such as the defendant's age, race, sex, and previous offense record. Each department also has its own standards for presentence investigations.

At the conclusion of most presentence investigations, a recommendation is made to the presiding judge that reflects the department's sentencing posture on the case. Among the most critical factors that contribute to a recommendation of community treatment are the probationer's demeanor, amenability to treatment, and willingness to abide by both legal and probationary rules.[23] Under normal circumstances, the department's recommendation is accepted by the judge when they hand down the actual sentence.

INTAKE Probation officers who conduct intake interviews may be looking to settle the case without the necessity of a court hearing. The probation officer works with all parties involved in the case—offender, victim, police officer, and so on—to design an equitable resolution. If the intake process is successful, the probation officer may settle the case without further court action, recommend restitution or other compensation, or recommend unofficial or informal probation. If an equitable solution cannot be found, the case is filed for a court hearing.

DIAGNOSIS In order to select appropriate treatment modes, probation officers—using their training in counseling, social work, or psychology—analyze the probationer's character, attitudes, and behavior. Many probationers have personal and social problems that might help explain their involvement in antisocial activities. Many have substance abuse problems—rates of drug abuse and dependence among probationers are two to three times as high as rates in the general population—and treating drug use remains a persistent challenge. Similarly, rates of any mental illness, serious mental illness, serious psychological distress, and depression are two to three times higher among probationers than the general population. Probationers are more likely than members of the general population to have received some mental health services and are also more likely to report an unmet need for mental health services.[24] Consequently, the goal of diagnosis is to develop a personality profile that may be helpful in treating the offender.

criminal justice and TECHNOLOGY

MONITORING PROBATIONERS WITH TECHNOLOGY

Technology is now being used to improve the effectiveness and efficiency of probation supervision. A number of new methods are being tried.

ELECTRONIC REPORTING

To improve efficiency, probation departments are allowing clients to report in without appearing personally. New York City is employing a kiosk system that allows low-risk offenders to report in electronically, using hand biometrics as identification, instead of meeting with the officer assigned. This innovation helps probation officers focus their attention on the high-risk offenders, automates the offender reporting process, and also permits real-time information exchange. Designed for flexibility and portability, the kiosk system can be used as a stand-alone system or as part of a larger case management system. Similar kiosk systems are now used in several large probation agencies nationwide.

SLEEP PATTERN ANALYSIS

Sleep pattern analysis technology, already used by some jurisdictions, can provide preliminary indications of substance abuse and help community corrections officials determine whether more testing is warranted. Sleep disruption due to substance abuse can occur in several ways, including altering the sequence and duration of various stages of sleep, total sleep time, and the amount of time needed to fall asleep. The technology consists of a small device, secured to an offender's wrist with a tamper-evident band, that measures sleep quality by recording gross motor activity. Analysis of the data collected may indicate sleep disorders, which could be caused by substance abuse. The device passively collects and records body movement information, and when the offender reports to the probation office or drug court, data can be downloaded and analyzed in a matter of minutes. If data analysis indicates possible substance abuse, the offender

An effective diagnosis integrates all that has been learned about the individual, organized in such a way as to provide a means for the establishment of future treatment goals. The emergence of standardized diagnostic tools and tests has diminished the probationer officer's individual role in diagnosis. To some commentators, this is problematic because it removes the human element from diagnosis and treatment.[25]

TREATMENT SUPERVISION   After the diagnosis has been completed, the probation staff is asked to carry out the treatment supervision, a program of therapy designed to help the client deal with the problems that resulted in her or his antisocial behavior. In years past, the probation staff had primary responsibility for supervision and treatment, but today's large caseloads limit opportunities for hands-on treatment; most probation treatment efforts rely on community resources.

A probation officer who discovers that a client has a drinking problem may place the client in a detoxification program. A spousal abuser may be required to enroll in an anger management or drug treatment program, to make a personal apology to the victim, or to have no contact with his or her ex-spouse.[26] In the case of juvenile delinquency, a probation officer may work with teachers and other school officials to help a young offender stay in school. The need for treatment is critical, and the vast size of probation caseloads, especially the large numbers of narcotics abusers, can be a formidable challenge to community-based substance abuse programs.[27]

Exhibit 12.1 discusses a few recent probation-based treatment approaches. The Criminal Justice and Technology feature describes how probation officers are using technology to monitor offender activities. The notion of treating probationers with cognitive behavioral therapy is discussed in the accompanying Evidence-Based Justice box.

can be required to immediately provide a urine specimen for further testing.

INFRARED SPECTROSCOPY

This technology seeks to modify a glucose-monitoring device into an alcohol-testing product. The device uses a light source, an optical detector, and spectrometers to conduct chemical analysis of tissue and measure alcohol levels. Results, available within just one minute, have accuracy comparable to that of Breathalyzers and blood tests. The technology uses infrared spectroscopy to make a nonintrusive examination of a subject's inner forearm; the device also could be modified to examine other parts of the body. The analysis process incorporates a biometric component that identifies an individual's unique tissue structure and tissue chemistry, thus ensuring accurate identification of the person being tested.

GPS MONITORING

Managing offenders within the community requires knowing what inmates are doing at all times. A number of corrections agencies around the country now utilize GPS-based monitoring systems that use GIS (geographic information system) to analyze patterns of movement of offenders. Some of these programs are designed to let probation officers better assess offenders' locations, identify patterns that lead to problem behavior as it unfolds, and improve corrections-based GPS monitoring systems. Knowing an offender's movement patterns also helps assess treatment issues and make decisions about early intervention.

CRITICAL THINKING

Would you place limits on the electronic monitoring of probationers? On the one hand, some of these methods seem awfully intrusive. On the other hand, should community safety be sacrificed in order to maintain an individual's dignity and privacy? After all, probationers have been convicted of a crime, sometimes even of a felony offense.

Sources: National Institute of Justice, *Evaluating a Location-Based Offender Monitoring System, 2012*, http://www.nij.gov/nij/topics/corrections/community/monitoring-technologies/location-based-monitoring.htm (accessed July 2014); National Law Enforcement and Corrections Technology Center, "The Greening of Probation," *Tech Beat* (Fall 2009), http://www.justnet.org/pdf/The%20Greening%20of%20Probation.pdf (accessed July 2014).

EXHIBIT 12.1 Innovative Probation Treatment Methods

The *Risk-Need-Responsivity (RNR)* program is being used in a number of jurisdictions, including Maine, Illinois, and Oregon, to classify each probationer and match them to the right treatment program; higher-risk offenders receive the most services. Cognitive behavioral and "social learning" techniques—ranging from anger management training to sessions devoted to reducing negative and antisocial attitudes—are emphasized. RNR programs rely on peers and family members to reinforce their messages. Several research efforts have found that they can cut the recidivism of high-risk offenders by as much as 20 percent.

The *Good Lives Model (GLM)* is being used for sex offender treatment programs. The GLM is a strengths-based approach to offender rehabilitation, premised on the idea that the capabilities and strengths of probationers must be built up in order to reduce their risk of reoffending. According to the GLM, offending represents a desire to succeed that manifests itself in harmful and antisocial behavior, due to a range of deficits and weaknesses within the offender and his environment. Essentially, these deficits prevent the offender from securing his desired ends in prosocial and sustainable ways, thus requiring that he resort to inappropriate and damaging means—that is, offending behavior. Rather than threaten punishment, GLM focuses on developing strengths. Intervention is viewed as an activity that should add to an individual's repertoire of personal functioning, rather than an activity that simply removes a problem or is devoted to managing problems, as if a lifetime of restricting one's activity is the only way to avoid offending.

Sources: Joan Petersilia, "Beyond the Prison Bubble," *NIJ Journal* 268 (October 2011), http://www.nij.gov/nij/journals/268/prison-bubble.htm (accessed July 2014); the Good Lives Model, http://www.goodlivesmodel.com (sites accessed April 28, 2014).

EVIDENCE-based justice

TREATING PROBATIONERS WITH COGNITIVE BEHAVIORAL THERAPY

Cognitive behavioral therapy (CBT) is a correctional treatment approach that focuses on patterns of thinking and the beliefs, attitudes, and values that underlie thinking. The therapy assumes that most people can become conscious of their own thoughts and behaviors and then make positive changes. A person's thoughts are often the result of experience, and behavior is often influenced and prompted by these thoughts. In addition, thoughts may sometimes become distorted and fail to reflect reality accurately.

When a probationer is placed in a CBT program, the goal is to restructure distorted thinking and perception, which in turn changes a person's behavior for the better. Characteristics of distorted thinking may include immature or developmentally arrested thoughts; poor problem solving and decision making; an inability to consider the effects of one's behavior; a hampered ability to reason and accept blame for wrongdoing; or an inability to manage feelings of anger. These distorted thinking patterns can lead to making poor decisions and engaging in antisocial behavior to solve problems.

Recently Patrick Clark reviewed the existing literature on cognitive behavior to assess its effectiveness. He found that, unlike other approaches, CBT places responsibility in the hands of clients while supplying them with the tools to solve their problems, focusing on the present rather than the past. People taking part in CBT learn specific skills that can be used to solve the problems they confront all the time as well as skills they can use to achieve legitimate goals and objectives. CBT first concentrates on developing skills to recognize distorted or unrealistic thinking when it happens, and then on changing that thinking or belief to mollify or eliminate problematic behavior.

PROGRAM EFFECTIVENESS

CBT is one of the few treatment approaches that have been broadly validated with research. Unlike other traditional and popular therapies, CBT has been the subject of more than 400 clinical trials involving a broad range of conditions and populations. For example, Sesha Kethineni and Jeremy Braithwaite found excellent results when they evaluated a CBT program used with juvenile probationers. CBT has shown to be reliably effective with a wide variety of personal problems and behaviors, including substance abuse, antisocial and aggressive behavior, and mood disorders, all of which have been linked to criminality.

Evidence of the treatment's effectiveness has been produced by Mark Lipsey, who examined the effectiveness of various approaches to intervention with offenders. His review analyzed the results of 548 studies from 1958 to 2002 that assessed intervention policies, practices, and programs. Lipsey found that interventions based on punishment and deterrence actually increased recidivism. On the other hand, therapeutic approaches based on counseling, skill building, and multiple services had the greatest impact in reducing further problem behavior. In a recent review of correctional treatment, Lipsey, along with Nana Landenberger, found that CBT significantly reduced recidivism. The greatest effects were found among more serious offenders, perhaps because CBT's enabling, self-help approach increases program participation and is therefore most effective with clients who shun or resist other approaches. The therapy is also more effective in reducing further criminal behavior when clients simultaneously receive other support, such as supervision, employment, education and training, and other mental health counseling.

CRITICAL THINKING

If changing or altering disruptive thinking patterns is key to changing behavior, does that mean that crime is more of an individual problem than a result of poverty, social inequality, and disorganization? Is the logical conclusion, then, that if crime is more common in poor neighborhoods and communities, affluent people have better cognitive skills than the poor?

Sources: Sesha Kethineni and Jeremy Braithwaite, "The Effects of a Cognitive-Behavioral Program for At-Risk Youth: Changes in Attitudes, Social Skills, Family, and Community and Peer Relationships," *Victims and Offenders* 6 (2011): 93–116; Patrick Clark, "Preventing Future Crime with Cognitive Behavioral Therapy," *National Institute of Justice Journal* 265 (2010), http://www.ojp.usdoj.gov/nij/journals/265/therapy.htm (accessed July 2014); Martin Lipsey, "The Primary Factors that Characterize Effective Interventions with Juvenile Offenders: A Meta-analytic Overview," *Victims and Offenders* 4 (2009): 124–147; Nana Landenberger and Martin Lipsey, "The Positive Effects of Cognitive-Behavioral Programs for Offenders: A Meta-analysis of Factors Associated with Effective Treatment," *Journal of Experimental Criminology* 1 (2005): 451–476.

RISK CLASSIFICATION As part of clients' entry into probation, an assessment is made about the risk level they pose to the community and themselves. Based on this assessment, offenders are assigned to specific supervision levels, where a variety of tools and techniques will be applied in an attempt to manage the risk they pose to the community and to themselves. Because more than 4 million people must now be managed, experts argue that risk assessment is the single most important decision being made by probation officers today.[28]

Probationers typically receive a **risk classification** that assigns them to a level and type of supervision on the basis of their particular needs and the risks they present to the community. Some clients may receive frequent (intensive) supervision in which they are contacted by their supervising probation officer almost every day, whereas other, minor offenders are assigned to minimum monitoring. A number of risk assessment classification approaches are used, but most employ such objective measures as the offender's age, employment status, drug abuse history, prior felony convictions, and number of address changes in the year before sentencing. Some departments are using standardized tests to predict failure and assign treatment. One of the most widely advertised systems is the Level of Service Inventory–Revised (LSI-R), which was first developed in Canada and has been adopted by a number of U.S. correctional agencies. The LSI-R consists of 54 items that are believed to be related to future criminal behavior.[29]

Evaluations of risk assessment instruments show that when they are used properly, they can be highly valid and effective.[30] However, there is room for further improvement. Simpler, easier-to-score measurement devices should be created. And because some communities present greater risks than others, the neighborhood where probationers reside must be considered in their individual risk classification.[31] Finally, the validity of measurement devices must be improved. Can they really predict dangerousness and future crime? Or are they merely indicators of the probability that the client will succeed on probation?[32]

The Careers in Criminal Justice feature describes the duties and qualifications of a probation officer.

Legal Rights of Probationers

What are the legal rights of probationers? How has the U.S. Supreme Court set limits on the probation process? A number of important legal issues surround probation, one set involving the civil rights of probationers and another involving the rights of probationers during the revocation process.

CIVIL RIGHTS The Court has ruled that probationers have a unique status and therefore are entitled to fewer constitutional protections than other citizens.

■ *Minnesota v. Murphy* (1984). In *Murphy*, the Supreme Court ruled that the probation officer–client relationship is not confidential, as physician–patient and attorney–client relationships are. If a probationer admits to committing a crime to his or her probation supervisor, that information can be passed on to the police or district attorney. Furthermore, the *Murphy* decision held that a probation officer could even use trickery or psychological pressure to get information and turn it over to the police.[33]

 L06 Define and discuss the term *risk classification*.

risk classification
An assessment of the risk level probationers pose to the community and themselves.

 Web App 12.3
For more information about the LSI-R, visit http://www.mhs.com/LSIR.

L07 Interpret the legal issues of probation.

A probation officer interviews one of his clients. Assessing the probationer's risk of recidivism is an important part of this process. Sometimes probation departments maintain specific units that perform risk assessments; other times this responsibility falls on probation officers themselves.

Joel Gordon/Joel Gordon Photography

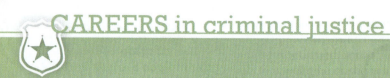

CAREERS in criminal justice

PROBATION OFFICER

DUTIES AND CHARACTERISTICS OF THE JOB

There are about 100,000 probation officers and other community corrections personnel. They work with criminal offenders, some of whom may be dangerous. While supervising offenders, they may interact with others, such as family members and friends of their clients, who may be upset or difficult to work with. Workers may be assigned to fieldwork in high-crime areas or in institutions where there is a risk of violence or communicable disease. The number of cases a probation officer has depends on both the counseling needs of offenders and the risks they pose to society. Although stress makes these jobs difficult at times, the work also can be rewarding. Many probation officers gain personal satisfaction from counseling members of their community and helping them become productive citizens.

JOB OUTLOOK

Jobs for probation officers are more plentiful in urban areas. There are also more jobs in states that have many men and women on probation.

SALARY

Median annual wages of probation officers and correctional treatment specialists is now about $48,000. Higher wages tend to be found in urban areas.

OPPORTUNITIES

Employment of probation officers and correctional treatment specialists is expected to grow by 18 percent by 2020, about as fast as average for all occupations. Continued growth in the demand for probation and parole services will lead to new openings for officers. Openings will result from the need to replace workers who leave the occupation permanently—including the large number expected to retire over the next several years.

QUALIFICATIONS

Prospective probation officers must be in good physical condition and be emotionally stable. Most agencies require applicants to be at least 21 years old and, for federal employment, not older than 37. Those convicted of felonies may not be eligible for employment in these occupations. Probation officers need strong writing skills because of the large number of reports they must prepare. Familiarity with computers is often required. Job candidates also should be knowledgeable about laws and regulations pertaining to corrections.

EDUCATION AND TRAINING

Educational requirements for probation officers vary by state, but a bachelor's degree in social work or criminal justice is usually required. Some states require probation officers to have one year of work experience in a related field or one year of graduate study in criminal justice, social work, or psychology. Most probation officers must complete a training program and work as trainees for about six months. Candidates who successfully complete the training period obtain a permanent position. Some states require applicants to take a certification test during or after training. Applicants usually must also pass written, oral, psychological, and physical examinations.

Source: Bureau of Labor Statistics, *Occupational Outlook Handbook, 2010–11 Edition*, "Probation Officers and Correctional Treatment Specialists," http://www.bls.gov/ooh/Community-and-Social-Service/Probation-officers-and-correctional-treatment-specialists.htm (accessed July 2014).

■ *Griffin v. Wisconsin* (1987). In *Griffin*, the Supreme Court held that a probationer's home may be searched without a warrant on the grounds that probation departments "have in mind the welfare of the probationer" and must "respond quickly to evidence of misconduct."[34]

■ *United States v. Knights* (2001). In *Knights*, the Supreme Court upheld the legality of a warrantless search of a probationer's home for the purposes of gathering criminal evidence. The Court ruled that the home of a probationer who is suspected of a crime can be searched without a warrant if (a) the search is based on reasonable suspicion that he had committed another crime while on probation and (b) a condition of his previous probation was that he would submit to searches. The Court reasoned that the government's interest in preventing crime, combined with *Knights's* diminished expectation of privacy, required only a *reasonable suspicion* to make the search legal, rather than a violation of the probationer's Fourth Amendment right to privacy.[35]

REVOCATION RIGHTS During the course of a probationary term, a violation of the rules or terms of probation or the committing of a new crime can result in probation being revoked, at which time the offender may be placed in an institution. Revocation is not often an easy decision, because it conflicts with the treatment philosophy of many probation departments.

When revocation is chosen, the offender is notified, and a formal hearing is scheduled. If the charges against the probationer are upheld, the offender can then be placed in an institution to serve the remainder of the sentence. Most departments will not revoke probation unless the offender commits another crime or seriously violates the rules of probation.

Because placing a person on probation implies that probation will continue unless the probationer commits some major violation, the defendant has been given certain procedural due process rights at this stage of the criminal process. In some significant decisions, the U.S. Supreme Court provided procedural safeguards to apply at proceedings to revoke probation (and parole):

- *Mempa v. Rhay* (1967). In *Mempa*, the Court unanimously held that a probationer was constitutionally entitled to counsel in a revocation-of-probation proceeding where the imposition of sentence had been suspended.[36]

- *Morrissey v. Brewer* (1972). In *Morrissey*, the Supreme Court required an informal inquiry to determine whether there was probable cause to believe the arrested parolee had violated the conditions of parole, as well as a formal revocation hearing with minimum due process requirements. Because the revocations of probation and parole are similar, the standards in the *Morrissey* case affected the probation process as well.[37]

- *Gagnon v. Scarpelli* (1973). In *Gagnon*, the Supreme Court held that both probationers and parolees have a constitutionally limited right to counsel in revocation proceedings.[38] This means that during a probation revocation hearing, the defendant must be given counsel if it is required for an effective defense. A judge may deny counsel under some circumstances, such as when probation will be continued despite the violation.

- *Beardon v. Georgia* (1983). In *Beardon*, the U.S. Supreme Court ruled that a judge cannot revoke a defendant's probation for failure to pay a fine and make restitution, unless the probation is somehow responsible for the failure or the alternative forms of punishment are inadequate to meet the state's interest in punishment and deterrence. *Beardon* involved a Georgia defendant who was unable to pay his restitution because he lost his job and could not find another. The trial court revoked probation, and the defendant was sent to prison. On appeal, the Supreme Court ruled that if a state determines a fine or restitution to be appropriate and an adequate penalty for the crime, it may not thereafter imprison a defendant solely because he or she lacks the resources to pay, because this would be a violation of a probationer's right to equal protection.[39]

- *United States v. Granderson* (1994). In *Granderson*, the Supreme Court helped clarify what can happen to a probationer whose community sentence is revoked. Granderson was eligible for a 6-month prison sentence but instead was given 60 months of probation. When he tested positive for drugs, his probation was revoked. The statute he was sentenced under required that he serve one-third of his original sentence in prison. When the trial court sentenced him to 20 months, he appealed. Was his original sentence 6 months or 60 months? The Supreme Court found that it would be unfair to force a probationer to serve more time in prison than he would have served if originally incarcerated and ruled that the proper term should have been one-third of the 6 months, or 2 months.[40]

How Successful Is Probation?

National data indicate that almost 65 percent of probationers successfully complete their probationary sentence, whereas about 30 percent are either incarcerated, violate probation rules, abscond, or are otherwise considered unsatisfactory. Most revocations occur for technical violations during the first three months of the probation sentence.[41]

Among those receiving probation are convicted felons, including rapists and murderers. How do these more dangerous criminals fare in their community sentence? In a now classic study, Joan Petersilia and her colleagues at the RAND Corporation, a private think tank, traced 1,672 men convicted of felonies who had been granted probation in Los Angeles and Alameda Counties in California.[42] Petersilia found that 1,087 (65 percent) were rearrested; of those rearrested, 853 (51 percent) were convicted; and of those convicted, 568 (34 percent) were sentenced to jail or prison. Of the probationers who had new charges filed against them, 75 percent were charged with burglary, theft, robbery, and other predatory crimes; 18 percent were convicted of serious violent crimes. Although the felony probation failure rate that Petersilia found seems disturbingly high, her findings still support the continued use of probation because people with similar criminal backgrounds who are sentenced to incarceration are more likely to recidivate than the community treatment group.[43]

 **L08** Discuss the effectiveness of probation.

What Causes Probation Success and Failure?

What does it take to succeed on probation and what causes people to fail? Stability helps: probationers who are married with children, have lived in the area for two or more years, and are adequately employed are the most likely to be successful on probation.[44] Conviction offense also matters. People with long histories of substance abuse do not fare well; surprisingly, people convicted on sexual offenses seem to do quite well on probation.[45] Among female probationers, those who have stable marriages, are better educated, and are employed full-time or part-time are more likely to complete probation orders.[46]

Not all probation sentences are successful, and many probationers recidivate. Probationers bring with them a lot of emotional baggage that may reduce their chances of successful rehabilitation. Many are felons who have long histories of offending; more than 75 percent of all probationers have had prior convictions. Others suffer from a variety of social and psychological disabilities. Surveys indicate that almost 20 percent suffer from mental illness.[47] The increase in the use of probation for felony offenders means that caseloads now include significant numbers of serious sex offenders, a group that demands a great deal of attention.[48] Ironically, many failures are linked to probationers' avoiding required treatment programs originally created to help them stay out of trouble and succeed on probation.[49]

Whether mentally ill or mentally sound, probationers are likely to have grown up in households in which family members were incarcerated, so they have lived part of their lives in foster homes or state institutions. Many had parents or guardians who abused drugs; they also suffered high rates of physical and sexual abuse. They are now unemployed or underemployed, and almost half are substance abusers. Considering their harsh and abusive backgrounds and their current economic distress and psychological stresses and strains, it is not surprising that many find it difficult to comply with the rules of probation and forgo criminal activity. As for individual characteristics, young males who are unemployed or who have a very low income, a prior criminal record, and a history of instability are most likely to be rearrested.[50]

The Future of Probation

Some critics are worried that probation is now undergoing a shift from traditional casework methods that featured diagnosis and treatment to an emphasis on risk assessment and control.[51] To improve the effectiveness of probation even more (what Petersilia calls "reforming, reinvesting, and restructuring"), several steps appear to be necessary.[52] More financial resources must be provided to implement quality programming for appropriate probation target groups. The credibility of probation with the public and the judiciary must be improved. Support is needed from a public that views the probation sanction as sufficiently punitive to make up for the harm of criminal behavior and from a judiciary that is convinced offenders should be held accountable for their behavior. A number of initiatives are now ongoing or being suggested that may help shape the future of probation:

■ *Making probationers pay.* At least 25 states now impose some form of fee on probationers to defray the cost of community corrections. Massachusetts initiated **day fees**, which are based on the probationer's wages (the usual fee is between one and three days' wages each month).[53] Texas requires judges to impose supervision fees unless the offender is truly unable to pay; fees make up more than half the probation department's annual budget.[54]

■ *Enhanced community engagement.* The New York City Department of Probation recently launched a series of Neighborhood Opportunity Networks (NeONs). Probation staff in the target areas work with and in neighborhood-based organizations, allowing them and the probationers they supervise to more thoroughly integrate with educators, employers, and service providers. The primary goal of the program is to improve probationers' "attachment" to the communities in which they reside.[55]

■ *Area needs.* Some experts suggest that probation caseloads be organized around area rather than client needs. Research shows that probationers' residences are concentrated in certain locations. In the future, probation officers may be assigned cases on the basis of where they live in order to develop a working knowledge of community issues and develop expertise on how to best serve their clients' interests and needs.[56]

day fees
A program requiring probationers to pay in part for the costs of their treatment.

SPECIALIZED PROBATION Some probation departments are experimenting with focused or specialized probation. Teams of probation officers take on clients convicted of one specific type of crime, such as drug offenses or domestic violence, rather than treating a mixed bag of offenders. Focusing on specialized caseloads enables probation officers to develop specific treatment and control skills. This approach may have utility: a recent examination of specialized supervision of domestic violence probation found that clients, especially lower-risk abusers, were significantly less likely to be rearrested for domestic violence and nondomestic violence crimes than were those supervised in the traditional mixed caseloads.[57]

PRIVATIZATION Probation services have been privatized in some jurisdictions for more than 30 years, and the practice is now being used in least 10 states, including Colorado and Missouri. The Private Probation Services company (established in 2003) specializes in providing offender supervision; it serves the courts and communities of northwest Missouri. For a fee, Private Probation Services performs many typical probation activities:

■ Probation supervision

■ Bond supervision

■ Electronic monitoring (house arrest)

EVIDENCE-based justice

HAWAII HOPE

Hawaii's HOPE (Honest Opportunity Probation with Enforcement) program is designed to keep people on probation by threatening them at a formal "warning" hearing with "swift and certain" punishment, rather than severe sanctions, for violating terms of probation. The program is geared to drug-involved offenders. Before HOPE, probationers in Hawaii typically received notice of drug tests as much as a month ahead of time. Under HOPE, probationers are given a color code at the warning hearing. Every morning, they must call a hotline to hear which color has been selected for that day. If it is their color, they must appear at the probation office before 2 P.M. for a drug test. If a HOPE probationer fails to appear for the drug test, a bench warrant is issued and served immediately. A probationer who fails the random drug test is immediately arrested and within 72 hours is brought before a judge. If the probationer is found to have violated the terms of probation, he or she is immediately sentenced to a short jail stay. Typically, the term is several days, servable on the weekend if the

probationer is employed; sentences increase for successive violations.

HOPE differs from other programs by:

- Focusing on reducing drug use and missed appointments rather than on drug treatment and imposing drug treatment on every participant.

- Mandating drug treatment for probationers only if they continue to test positive for drug use, or if they request a treatment referral. A HOPE probationer who has a third or fourth missed or "dirty" drug test may be mandated into residential treatment as an alternative to probation revocation.

- Requiring probationers to appear before a judge only when a violation is detected—in this respect, HOPE requires less treatment and court resources than drug courts.

- Having probationers who are employed serve any jail time, at least initially, on a weekend so they do not jeopardize their employment.

- Secure continuous remote alcohol monitoring (SCRAM)
- Ignition interlock
- On-site urinalysis testing
- Alcohol Breathalyzer testing
- Timely and informative reports to the court[58]

Privatization can help alleviate the burden of providing effective probation services. By utilizing private probation for low-risk offenders, state probation departments can commit more resources to high-risk offenders. However, some reviews suggest that existing statutory guidelines are currently insufficient to monitor and control the operations of private probation supervision agencies and that greater state oversight is needed to maintain quality.[59]

SWIFT AND SURE PUNISHMENT   The threat of swift and sure punishment that is somewhat less than a full revocation of probation may help reduce rule violations. Hawaii has been experimenting with a system that provides immediate punishment for any probationers found in violation of their court orders. Probationers are warned during a court hearing that if they violate the conditions of probation, they will be immediately arrested, will appear in court within hours, and will have the terms of their supervision modified to include a short stay in jail. The jail terms imposed are usually only a few days, but sentence length

Because only a small fraction of HOPE probationers receive mandated treatment, the program can afford to use intensive long-term residential treatment, rather than relying primarily on outpatient drug-free counseling as do most diversion programs and drug courts. Careful evidence-based evaluations of the HOPE program found:

- It is more cost-efficient because it covers a large number of clients while delivering intensive treatment to those who prove to need it.

- It puts a smaller strain on treatment capacity by avoiding the situation in which clients for whom treatment is mandated crowd out clients who voluntarily seek treatment.

- Because the treatment mandate follows repeated failures, it helps break through denial; an offender who has spent three brief spells in jail for dirty drug tests may find it hard to keep telling himself that he is in control of his drug use.

One study of the program, in which randomly selected samples of general-population probationers were compared to a similar group of HOPE probationers, found that after one year the HOPE probationers were:

- Fifty-five percent less likely to be arrested for a new crime

- Seventy-two percent less likely to use drugs

- Sixty-one percent less likely to skip appointments with their supervisory officer

- Fifty-three percent less likely to have their probation revoked

As a result, HOPE probationers served or were sentenced to 48 percent fewer days, on average, than the control group of traditional probationers. Probationers assigned to HOPE had large reductions in positive drug tests and missed appointments, and were significantly less likely to be arrested during follow-up at 3 months, 6 months, and 12 months. They averaged approximately the same number of days in jail for probation violations, serving more but shorter terms. They spent about one-third as many days in prison on revocations or new convictions.

Source: National Institute of Justice, "'Swift and Certain' Sanctions in Probation Are Highly Effective: Evaluation of the HOPE Program," http://www.nij.gov/topics/corrections/community/drug-offenders/hawaii-hope.htm (accessed July 2014); http://hopehawaii.net/ (accessed July 2014).

increases for successive violations. The program appears to be highly successful in reducing violations.[60] The Evidence-Based Justice feature discusses this highly regarded program in more detail.

Probation is unquestionably undergoing dramatic changes. In many jurisdictions, traditional probation is being supplemented by intermediate sanctions, which are penalties that fall between traditional community supervision and confinement in jail or prison. These new correctional services are discussed in the following section.

Other Alternatives to Imprisonment

Probation is not the only alternative to imprisonment. An offender's sentence may include the requirement that he or she pay a fine or provide restitution. A convicted criminal may also have his or her property taken away in a process known as forfeiture. There is also a growing trend to add sanctions to traditional probation sentences. These programs can be viewed as "probation plus," since they add restrictive penalties and conditions to traditional community service orders, which emphasized treatment and rehabilitation more than control and restraint.[61] Some of these so-called **intermediate sanctions** include programs that are administered by probation departments: intensive probation supervision, house arrest, electronic monitoring, restitution orders, shock probation or split sentences, and residential community corrections.[62]

 LO9 Explain what is meant by intermediate sanctions.

intermediate sanctions
The group of punishments falling between probation and prison ("probation plus"). Community-based sanctions, including house arrest and intensive supervision, serve as alternatives to incarceration.

Intermediate sanctions are often used when those convictions do not pose a danger to society. Here, former KB Home chief executive Bruce Karatz, his wife, philanthropist Lilly Tartikoff, and his attorney, John Keker, leave U.S. District Court after Karatz's conviction on four criminal charges following an investigation into alleged stock manipulation in Los Angeles. Karatz was sentenced to five years of probation and eight months of home detention with electronic monitoring for a stockoption backdating scam.

Jason Redmond/Reuters/Landov

Advantages of Intermediate Sanctions

Although there is concern that intermediate sanctions will "widen the net" of justice and involve probationers in new, more intrusive and extensive programs, probation plus sentences also provide a number of benefits not offered in either traditional probation or incarceration sentences:

■ *Cost benefits.* Though somewhat more costly than traditional probation, intermediate sanctions are far less expensive to run than prisons or jails. If those offenders who are given alternative sanctions would otherwise have been incarcerated, the extra cost would have been significant. In addition, offenders given intermediate sanctions generate income, pay taxes, reimburse victims, perform community service, and generate other cost savings that would be nonexistent had they been incarcerated. They also reduce the need for costly future prison and jail construction.

■ *Equitable community sentences.* Intermediate sanctions help meet the need for developing community sentences that are fair, equitable, and proportional.[63] It seems unfair to treat both a rapist and a shoplifter with the same type of probationary sentence, considering the differences in their crimes. As Figure 12.1 illustrates, intermediate sanctions can form the successive steps of a meaningful "ladder" of scaled punishments outside of prison, thereby restoring fairness and equity to nonincarceration sentences.[64] Forgers may be ordered to make restitution to their victims, and rapists can be placed in a community facility and receive counseling at a local clinic. This feature of intermediate sanctions allows judges to fit the punishment to the crime without resorting to a prison sentence.

■ *Increased control.* Intermediate sanctions can be designed to increase control over probationers whose serious or repeat crimes make a straight probation sentence inappropriate, yet for whom a prison sentence would be unduly harsh and counterproductive.[65] Some forms, such as electronic monitoring, provide increased surveillance for probationers who might otherwise continue to commit crimes while in the community. Self-report surveys suggest that about half of probationers commit at least one offense while they are on probation and that about a third report committing more than four offenses during this same time.[66] Intermediate sanctions may help reduce this hidden recidivism.

■ *Reduced overcrowding.* Intermediate sanctions can reduce the number of convicted criminals who might otherwise be given an incarceration sentence but who either pose a low risk of recidivism or are of little threat to society (such as nonviolent property offenders). For example, overcrowding in jails can be reduced by providing alternatives to incarceration for misdemeanants and cutting the number of pretrial detainees, who currently make up about half of the inmate population.[67] Some forms of bail require conditions such as supervision by court officers and periods of home confinement (conditional bail).

■ *Use with different classes of offenders.* Intermediate sanctions can potentially be used as halfway-back strategies for probation and parole violators. Probationers who violate the conditions of their community release could be placed under increasingly intensive supervision before actual incarceration was required. Parolees who pose the greatest risk of recidivism might receive conditions that require close monitoring or home confinement. Parole violators could be returned to a community correctional center rather than a walled institution.

In sum, rather than being a net-widening measure, intermediate sanctions can act as a "net-repairing" strategy.[68] The various types of intermediate sanctions currently in use are more thoroughly discussed in the following sections.

Fines

Monetary payments, or **fines**, can be imposed on offenders as punishment for their criminal acts. Fines are a direct offshoot of the early common-law practice of requiring that compensation be paid to the victim and the state (wergild) for criminal acts. Fines are still commonly used in Europe, where they are often the sole penalty, even in cases involving chronic offenders who commit fairly serious crimes.

In the United States, fines are most commonly used in cases involving misdemeanors and lesser offenses. Fines are also frequently used in felony cases where the offender benefited financially. Fines may be used as a sole sanction but are typically combined with other punishments such as probation. Judges commonly supplement fines with other monetary sanctions (such as court costs, public defender fees, probation and treatment fees, and victim restitution) to increase the force of the financial punishment. However, there is evidence that many offenders fail to pay fines and that courts are negligent in their efforts to collect unpaid fees.[69]

In most jurisdictions, little guidance is given to the sentencing judge who directs the imposition of the fine. Judges often have inadequate information on the offender's ability to pay, and this results in defaults and contempt charges. Because the standard sanction for nonpayment is incarceration, many offenders held in local jails are confined for nonpayment of criminal fines. Even though the U.S. Supreme Court in *Tate v. Short* (1971) recognized that incarcerating a person who is financially unable to pay a fine discriminates against the poor, many judges continue to incarcerate offenders for noncompliance with financial orders.[70]

DAY FINES Because judges rely so heavily on offense seriousness to fix the level of fines, financial penalties may have a negative impact on success rates. The more serious the offense and the higher the fine, the greater the chances that the

FIGURE 12.1 Punishment Ladder

fine
Levying a money payment on offenders to compensate society for their misdeeds.

day fine

A fine geared to the average daily income of the convicted offender in an effort to bring equity to the sentencing process.

offender will fail to pay the fine and risk probation revocation. To overcome this sort of problem, justice systems in European nations such as Finland and Sweden have employed the concept of **day fines** geared to an offender's net daily income. In an effort to make them equitable and fairly distributed, fines are based on the severity of the crime, weighted by a daily-income value taken from a chart similar to an income tax table; the number of the offender's dependents is also taken into account. The day fine concept means that the severity of punishment is geared to the offender's ability to pay.[71]

Forfeiture

forfeiture

The seizure of personal property by the state as a civil or criminal penalty.

Criminal (*in personam*) and civil (*in rem*) **forfeiture** are also available as a means of targeting crime. Both seek to take the "profit" out of crime. They involve the seizure of goods and instrumentalities related to the commission or outcome of a criminal act. The difference is that criminal forfeiture proceedings target criminal defendants and can only follow a criminal conviction. In contrast, civil forfeiture proceedings target property used in a crime and do not require that formal criminal proceedings be initiated against a person or that the person be proved guilty of a crime.[72] Federal law provides that after arresting drug traffickers, the government may seize the boats they used to import the narcotics, the cars they used to carry the drugs overland, the warehouses in which the drugs were stored, and the homes paid for with the drug profits; upon their conviction, the drug dealers permanently lose ownership of these "instrumentalities" of crime.

Forfeiture is not a new sanction. During the Middle Ages, "forfeiture of estate" was a mandatory result of most felony convictions. The Crown could seize all of a felon's real and personal property. Forfeiture derived from the common-law concept of "corruption of blood" or "attaint," which prohibited a felon's family from inheriting or receiving his property or estate. The common law mandated that descendants could not inherit property from a relative who might have acquired the property illegally: "[T]he Corruption of Blood stops the Course of Regular Descent, as to Estates, over which the Criminal could have no Power, because he never enjoyed them."[73]

Forfeiture was reintroduced into U.S. law with passage of the Racketeer Influenced and Corrupt Organization (RICO) Act and the Continuing Criminal Enterprises Act, both of which allow the seizure of any property derived from illegal enterprises or conspiracies. Although these acts were designed to apply to ongoing criminal conspiracies, such as drug or pornography rings, they are now being applied to a far-ranging series of criminal acts, including white-collar crimes. Hundreds of state and federal statutes use forfeiture of property as a punishment.

Restitution

restitution

A condition of probation in which the offender repays society or the victim of crime for the trouble the offender caused.

monetary restitution

A sanction requiring that convicted offenders compensate crime victims by reimbursing them for out-of-pocket losses caused by the crime. Losses can include property damage, lost wages, and medical costs.

community service restitution

An alternative sanction that requires an offender to work in the community at such tasks as cleaning public parks or working with disabled children in lieu of an incarceration sentence.

Another popular alternative to incarceration is **restitution**, which can take the form of requiring offenders to either pay back the victims of crime (**monetary restitution**) or serve the community to compensate for their criminal acts (**community service restitution**).[74] Restitution programs offer offenders a chance to avoid a jail or prison sentence or a lengthier probation period. The programs may help them develop a sense of allegiance to society, better work habits, and some degree of gratitude for being given a second chance. Restitution serves many other purposes, including giving the community something of value without asking it to foot the bill for an incarceration stay and helping victims regain lost property and income.

If a defendant is sentenced to pay monetary restitution as part of her probation order, a determination of victim loss is made and a plan for paying fair compensation developed. To avoid the situation in which a wealthy offender can fill a restitution order by merely writing a check, judges will sometimes order that compensation be paid out of income derived from a low-paid social service or public works job.

Community service orders usually require duty in a public nursing home, shelter, hospital, drug treatment unit, or public works program; some young vandals may find that they must clean up the damage they caused to the school or the park. Judges and probation officers have embraced the concept of restitution because it appears to benefit the victim, the offender, the criminal justice system, and society.[75]

Does restitution work? Most reviews rate it as a qualified success. An evaluation of community service in Texas found that nearly three-fourths of offenders with community service orders met their obligations and completed community service work.[76] The Texas experience is not atypical; most restitution clients successfully complete their orders and have no subsequent contact with the justice system.[77]

Shock Probation and Split Sentencing

Shock probation and split sentences are intermediate sanctions designed to allow judges to grant offenders community release only after they have sampled prison life. These sanctions are based on the premise that if offenders are given a taste of incarceration sufficient to shock them into law-abiding behavior, they will be reluctant to violate the rules of probation or commit another crime.

In a number of states and in the U.S. Criminal Code, a jail term can actually be a condition of probation; this practice is known as **split sentencing**. About 10 percent of probationers are now given split sentences. The **shock probation** approach involves resentencing an offender to probation after a short prison stay. The shock comes because the offender originally received a long maximum sentence but is then eligible for release to community supervision at the discretion of the judge (usually within 90 days of incarceration).

Some states have linked the short prison stay with a boot camp experience referred to as *shock incarceration*, in which young inmates undergo a brief but intense period of military-like training and hard labor designed to impress them with the rigors of prison life.[78] (Boot camp programs are discussed in greater detail in Chapter 13.) Shock probation and split sentencing have been praised as ways to limit prison time, reintegrate the client quickly into the community, maintain family ties, and reduce prison populations and the costs of corrections.[79] An initial jail sentence probably makes offenders more receptive to the conditions of probation, because it amply illustrates the problems they will face if probation is violated.

But split sentences and shock probation programs have been criticized by those who believe that even a brief period of incarceration can interfere with the purpose of probation, which is to provide the offender with nonstigmatizing, community-based treatment. Even a short-term commitment subjects probationers to the destructive effects of institutionalization, disrupts their life in the community, and stigmatizes them for having been in jail.

> **split sentence**
> A practice that requires convicted criminals to spend a portion of their sentence behind bars and the remainder in the community.
>
> **shock probation**
> A sentence in which offenders serve a short prison term before they begin probation, to impress them with the pains of imprisonment.

Restitution is sometimes used as a part of sentence to compensate the injured parties. Here, in a Los Angeles Criminal Court, former student midwife Katharine McCall, right, listens as she is sentenced to three years of probation for practicing medicine without a license after she delivered a baby without supervision. McCall was ordered to complete 280 hours of community service and pay $10,000 in restitution.

AP Images/Damian Dovarganes

intensive probation supervision (IPS)
A type of intermediate sanction involving small probation caseloads and strict monitoring on a daily or weekly basis.

Intensive Probation Supervision

Intensive probation supervision (IPS) programs, also referred to as intensive supervision programs, have been implemented in some form in about 40 states and today include about 100,000 clients. IPS, another form of intermediate sanctions, involves small caseloads of 15 to 40 clients who are kept under close watch by probation officers. IPS programs typically have three primary goals:

■ *Decarceration.* Without intensive supervision, clients would normally be sent to already overcrowded prisons or jails.

■ *Control.* High-risk offenders can be maintained in the community under much closer security than traditional probation efforts can provide.

■ *Reintegration.* Offenders can maintain community ties and be reoriented toward a more productive life, while avoiding the pains of imprisonment.

IS IPS EFFECTIVE? There are indications that the failure rate in IPS caseloads is high, in some cases approaching 50 percent; IPS clients have a higher rearrest rate than other probationers.[80]

Joan Petersilia found that despite their good intentions, most of the ISP dollars wound up being used to fund more drug testing, parole agent contacts, and electronic monitoring rather than enhanced social services. The main result was that offenders who violated court conditions by using drugs, for example, were identified more quickly and sent into custody. Within a decade, ISPs went from being a correctional panacea to a failed social experiment. Most of the programs were dismantled by the late 1990s. But as Petersilia points out, the RAND study found that in places where efforts were actually implemented according to the original design, they were rather effective. Offenders who participated in drug or alcohol treatment, community service, and employment programs had recidivism rates 10 to 20 percent below those of nonparticipating offenders.[81]

House Arrest/Electronic Monitoring

House arrest is a form of intermediate sanction that requires that the convicted offender spend a designated amount of time per week in his or her own home—such as from 6 P.M. Friday until 8 A.M. Monday. House arrest initiatives can vary in administration, client services, and goals. Some are administered by probation departments, while others are simply judicial sentences monitored by surveillance officers. Some check clients 20 or more times a month, while others do only a few curfew checks. Some impose 24-hour confinement, while others allow offenders to attend work or school.

For house arrest to work, sentencing authorities must be assured that arrestees are actually at home during their assigned times. Random calls and visits are one way to check on compliance with house arrest orders. Another is to use **electronic monitoring (EM)** devices to manage offender obedience to home confinement orders, a practice that has been popular for more than two decades.[82]

Electronically monitored offenders wear devices that send signals to a control office; the devices are worn around their ankle, wrist, or neck. Two basic types of systems are used: active and passive. Active systems constantly monitor offenders by continuously sending a signal to the central office. If offenders leave their home at an unauthorized time, the signal is broken, and the "failure" is recorded. In some cases, the control officer is automatically notified electronically through a beeper. In contrast, passive systems usually involve random phone calls generated by computers to which the offenders must respond within a particular time (such as 30 seconds). EM can also be used at the front end of the system with bailees and at the back end with parolees. A number of states, including

electronic monitoring (EM)
Requiring convicted offenders to wear a monitoring device as part of their community sentence. Typically part of a house arrest order, this enables the probation department to ensure that offenders are complying with court-ordered limitations on their freedom.

Web App 12.4

For more information about the Massachusetts Probation Service's GPS tracking program, visit http://www.mass.gov/courts/docs/probation/elmofactsheet.pdf.

Massachusetts, routinely use GPS systems with certain classes of probationers (such as sex offenders) to monitor their whereabouts and ensure that they obey their probation orders (such as staying at least 1,000 yards away from a school).

Electronic monitoring supporters claim EM has the benefits of relatively low cost and high security, while helping offenders avoid the pains of imprisonment in overcrowded, dangerous state facilities. Electronic monitoring is capital-intensive rather than labor-intensive. Because offenders are monitored by computers, an initial investment in hardware rules out the need to hire many more supervisory officers to handle large numbers of clients.

Evaluations of the ability of EM programs to reduce recidivism have yielded mixed results. Some evaluations indicate that offenders monitored via EM misunderstand its purpose and are just as likely to recidivate as those released without such supervision.[83] Other evaluations have achieved much better results. In one extensive effort, Kathy Padgett and her associates evaluated data on more than 75,000 offenders placed on home confinement in Florida and found that EM significantly reduced the likelihood of technical violations, reoffending, and absconding. Probationers placed on home confinement with EM had been previously involved in significantly more serious crimes than those placed on home confinement without EM, indicating that the procedure is being used with the appropriate offender population—that is, the most serious probation population.[84] Thus the EM program produced little "net widening." However, some critics argue that the evidence that EM can lower recidivism rates is thin and that it may not work well as a stand-alone program. Instead, EM can improve public safety when it is combined with some other treatment modality, such as social interventions and counseling.[85]

FACT CHECK ✓

YOUR OPINION: Does electronic monitoring deter crime?

PUBLIC OPINION: Strongly agree: 3.4%

STRONGLY AGREE:	3.4%
AGREE:	37.5%
DISAGREE:	48.3%
STRONGLY DISAGREE:	10.7%

REALITY: Electronic monitoring has its share of critics. It is cheaper than prison, but few evaluations give it glowing reviews. Old school electronic monitoring devices only alerted authorities when the offender was where he or she should not be. Now GPS monitoring permits tracking offenders wherever they go, but even GPS monitoring is not perfect. In one recent case, two parolees who were wearing GPS trackers allegedly raped and killed two women.

DISCUSSION: What are the strengths and limitations of electronic monitoring? What about GPS monitoring.

Sources: Brian K. Payne, Matthew DeMichele, and Nonso Okafo, "Attitudes About Electronic Monitoring: Minority and Majority Racial Group Differences," *Journal of Criminal Justice* 37 (2009): 155–162; Associated Press, "Sex Offender Serial Killers Wore GPS Trackers When Raping, Killing at Least 4 Women," http://www.nydailynews.com/news/crime/sex-offender-serial-killers-wore-gps-trackers-raping-killing-4-women-police-article-1.1756415 (accessed July 2014).

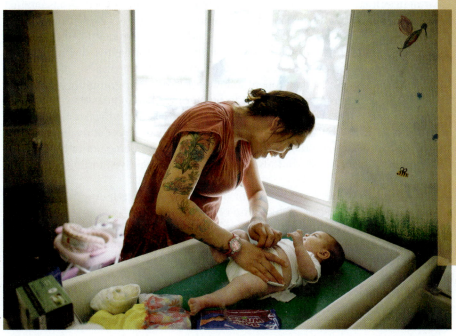

Vanessa Moreno, 24, changes the diapers of her 2-month-old baby Makayla at Prototypes residential treatment program in Pomona, California. Prototypes is part of the Second Chance Women's Re-entry Court program, one of the first in the United States to focus on women. It offers a cost-saving alternative to prison for women who plead guilty to nonviolent crimes and volunteer for treatment. Of the 297 women who have been through the program since 2007, 100 have graduated, and only 35 have been returned to state prison.

LucyNicholson/Reuters/Landov

Residential Community Corrections

residential community corrections (RCC)

A nonsecure facility, located in the community, that houses probationers who need a more secure environment. Typically, residents are free during the day to go to work, school, or treatment, and return in the evening for counseling sessions and meals.

The most secure intermediate sanction is a sentence to a **residential community corrections (RCC)** facility. Such facilities house offenders at night but allow them the freedom to work, attend school, and/or participate in community-based treatment activities and programs during the day.

Traditionally, the role of residential community corrections was to reintegrate soon-to-be-paroled prison inmates into the community. Inmates spent the last few months of their sentence in the halfway house, finding suitable employment, building up cash reserves, obtaining an apartment, and acquiring a job-related wardrobe.

The traditional concept of community corrections has expanded, and it is now a direct-sentencing option for judges who believe particular offenders need a correctional alternative halfway between traditional probation and a stay in prison. Placement in an RCC center can be used as a condition of probation for offenders who need a nonsecure community facility that provides a more structured treatment environment than traditional probation. One example is California's Substance Abuse and Crime Prevention Act (SACPA), which allows adults convicted of nonviolent drug-possession offenses to participate in community-based drug treatment programs. Evaluations of the program found that SACPA clients were likely to be rearrested for drug crimes, undercutting the effectiveness of the treatment initiative.[86] One reason for the failure may have been that the sudden influx of offenders overwhelmed the treatment resources of an already strained community treatment system; many clients were simply "undertreated."

day reporting centers (DRCs)

Nonresidential community-based treatment programs.

DAY REPORTING CENTERS A number of states have set up a system of **day reporting centers (DRCs)** to oversee intermediate sanctions and treatment placements. These provide a single location to which a variety of clients can report for supervision and treatment. In Georgia, Delaware, Utah, Massachusetts, and other jurisdictions, DRCs serve nonresidential clients using RCC facilities. They can be used as a step up in security for probationers who have failed in the community and as a step down in security for jail or prison inmates. For example, 13 DRCs are now operating throughout Georgia, providing intensive substance abuse treatment for up to 100 offenders sentenced by the courts and also supervising probationers who have not responded to more traditional supervision and treatment efforts. Failure at a DRC results in revocation proceedings against the offender. Although the cost is greater than that of field probation, a DRC placement can be made at only a fraction of the cost of a residential alternative.[87] The program includes substance abuse counseling, cognitive restructuring, adult basic education, employment enhancement, intensive supervision, and community service. An aftercare component follows the on-site programming. Offenders assigned to the program are required to be employed as soon as they have completed the initial orientation, assessment, diagnostics, and programming. There is evidence that the DRC concept may work: results of a recent evaluation conducted in Pennsylvania indicate that day reporting sentencing not only saved the county incarceration costs, but also yielded a lower recidivism rate to a statistically significant degree.[88]

Evaluations show that DRCs can be successful at reducing recidivism.[89] DRCs seem to work better with certain types of offenders, such as those who are older and more experienced, than with others, such as younger offenders.[90] DRC participants with alcohol problems, criminal companions, and poor living situations are also more likely to fail. In contrast, those who receive counseling seem to do better.[91]

Concept Summary 12.1 summarizes the leading alternatives to imprisonment besides probation.

CONCEPT SUMMARY 12.1
Alternatives to Imprisonment

Sanction	Goal	Problems
Fines	Monetary sanction	Overburdens the poor
Forfeiture	Monetary sanction, equity	Can be overreaching
Restitution	Pay back victim	Does not reduce recidivism

Intermediate Sanctions

Shock incarceration and split sentence	"Taste of bars" as a deterrent	Can cause labeling and stigma
Intensive probation	Small caseloads, more supervision	High failure rate
House arrest	Avoids jail	Lacks treatment possibility
Electronic monitoring	Supervision by computer	Technology-dependent, no treatment
Residential community	Less secure than prison	Expensive, high failure rate

Restorative Justice

One of the goals of contemporary sentencing is to "restore" offenders into society. This goal has particular relevance today because many crime experts believe that, ironically, rather than reducing crime and recidivism, policies based on "getting tough on crime," even intermediate sanctions, can cause crime rates to fluctuate higher and offenders to commit more crime. Punishment may not work because it both carries hard-to-erase stigma and destroys the offender's dignity and peace of mind. When traditional community-based correctional models such as probation are supplemented by the new alternative/intermediate sanctions, the effect is to add a punitive aspect that can further hinder rehabilitation efforts. Instead, **restorative justice** advocates suggest a policy based on restoring harmony to the damage caused by crime and creating a system of justice that includes all the parties harmed by the criminal act: the victim, the offender, the community, and society.[92]

Restorative justice models jibe with the thoughts of Australian justice expert John Braithwaite, who argues that crime control today involves shaming and stigmatizing offenders. This helps set them apart from normative society and undermines their potential for change. He calls instead for a policy of "reintegrative shaming." Here disapproval is limited to the offender's evil deeds; it is not directed at the offender himself. Law violators must be made to realize that even though their actions have caused harm, they are still valuable people—people who can be reaccepted by society. A critical element of reintegrative shaming occurs when the offenders themselves begin to understand and recognize their wrongdoing and shame. To be reintegrative, shaming must be brief and controlled and must be promptly followed by ceremonies of forgiveness, apology, and repentance.[93] Braithwaite's work is at the core of the restorative justice movement. The Global Criminal Justice feature discusses restorative justice in New Zealand and Australia.

restorative justice
A view of criminal justice that focuses on crime as an act against the community rather than the state. Justice should involve all parties affected by crime—victims, criminals, law enforcement, and the community.

LO10 Explain the concept of restorative justice and discuss its merits.

Web App 12.5

For information about restorative justice, visit http://www.restorativejustice.org/.

GLOBAL criminal justice

RESTORATION IN AUSTRALIA AND NEW ZEALAND

Australia and New Zealand have been leaders in adopting restoration programs. One innovative effort in New Zealand, Family Group Conferences, is based in part on native Maori practices and aims to give families a greater say in the resolution of both child protection and juvenile justice matters. The Children, Young Persons and Their Families Act in 1989 made conferencing the primary decision-making process within the child protection system. If official action is to be taken after an investigation, a conference is convened, and support is made available if family members lack the financial resources to travel. Conferences are arranged and facilitated in New Zealand by specialist care and protection coordinators, who are employed directly by Child, Youth and Family, the child protection agency in New Zealand. Coordinators work with the family to bring together the conference. This usually includes the child/young person, his or her advocate and/or legal representative, the parents, extended family members, any other support person the family wishes, and the referring care and protection worker. These people are all entitled by law to attend the conference. Other professionals who are not involved in the decision making may be invited to provide information. The purpose of the conference is for the family to hear the child protection concerns, to decide whether the child is in need of care and protection, and to make plans that can address these concerns.

Conferences occur in three stages. In the first stage, child protection workers and other professionals share information with the family. The second stage involves the family having time on their own to deliberate and agree on possible solutions. In the final phase of the conference, the aim is to arrive at agreement on (1) whether the child is in need of care and protection, and (2) a plan that will address these concerns. This may involve negotiation among the family, care and protection workers, and other agencies about the services and supports that can be provided. For a conference agreement to go into effect, it is necessary that all participants agree. Recent estimates suggest that more than 50,000 conferences have been convened during the past 20 years, a number that reflects the central role that conferences play in New Zealand's child protection system.

CONFERENCING IN AUSTRALIA

Conferencing was introduced into the Australian criminal justice systems in the early 1990s by police in the city of Wagga Wagga, New South Wales. Other police experimented with the idea, and police-run conferences were established in the Australian Capital Territory (ACT) and were tried on a pilot basis in Western Australia, the Northern Territory, Queensland, and Tasmania. Since then, other applications of the conferencing idea have been launched in schools and workplaces in New South Wales and Queensland, and these continue to operate.

Conferencing is not offered when offenders wish to contest their guilt. Those who do not are referred to the conference, which normally lasts one to two hours and is attended by the victims and their supporters, the offenders and their supporters, and other relevant parties. The conference coordinator focuses the discussion on condemning the act without condemning the character of the actor. Offenders are asked to explain what happened, how they have felt about the crime, and what they think should be done. The victims and others are asked to describe the physical, financial, and emotional consequences of the crime. This discussion may lead the offenders, their families, and their friends to experience the shame of the act, prompting an apology to the victim. A plan of action is developed and signed by key participants. The plan may include the offender paying compensation to the victim, doing work for the victim or the community, or any other undertaking the participants may agree upon. It is the responsibility of the conference participants to determine the outcomes that are most appropriate for these particular victims and these particular offenders.

CRITICAL THINKING

1. Would a method that works in New Zealand and/or Australia also have utility in the United States, with its more heterogeneous population, greater social problems, and more violent crime?

2. How can this essentially humanistic approach be sold to the general public, who now support more punitive sanctions? Would it be feasible to claim that using restorative justice with nonviolent offenders frees resources for dealing with the relatively few dangerous people in the criminal population?

Sources: Australian Institute of Criminology, "Restorative Justice," http://www.aic.gov.au/criminal_justice_system/rjustice.aspx (accessed July 2014); Nathan Harris, "Family Group Conferencing in Australia 15 Years On," Australian Institute of Family Studies, http://www.aifs.gov.au/nch/pubs/issues/issues27/issues27.html (accessed July 2014).

The Concept of Restoration

According to the restorative view, even though crimes can seem quite different, ranging from a violent assault to a white-collar fraud scheme, they all share one common trait: they inflict harm on the community in which they occur. And yet, the traditional justice system has done little to involve the community in the justice process and has not adequately involved the victim in the justice process.[94] What has developed is a system of coercive punishments administered by bureaucrats that is inherently harmful to offenders and reduces the likelihood that they will ever again be productive members of society.[95] This system relies on punishment, stigma, and disgrace. What is needed instead is a justice policy that repairs the harm caused by crime and comprises all parties that have suffered from that harm, including the victim, the community, and the offender.

An important aspect of achieving these goals is that offenders accept accountability for their actions and responsibility for the harm their actions caused. Only then can they be restored as productive members of their community. Restoration involves turning the justice system into a "healing" process rather than a distributor of retribution and revenge.

Most people involved in offender–victim relationships actually know one another or were related in some way before the criminal incident took place. Instead of treating one of the involved parties as a victim deserving sympathy and the other as a criminal deserving punishment, it is more productive to address the issues that produced the conflict between these people. Rather than take sides and choose whom to isolate and punish, society should try to reconcile the parties involved in conflict. The effectiveness of justice ultimately depends on the stake a person has in the community (or a particular social group). If a person does not value her membership in the group, she will be unlikely to accept responsibility, show remorse, or repair the injuries caused by her actions.

Restoration Programs

Restoration programs try to include all the parties involved in a criminal act: the victim, the offender, and the community. Although processes differ in structure and style, they generally include the following:

■ Recognition by offenders that they have caused injury to personal and social relations, and a determination and acceptance of responsibility (ideally accompanied by a statement of remorse)

AP Images/*Daily Star,* Kari Wheeler

A Florida Parishes Juvenile Detention Center detainee works in the center's garden in Goodbee, Louisiana. Detainees contribute time and effort for the benefit of the community, harvesting the produce and donating it to a local food pantry. Juvenile detainees are learning restorative justice with programs such as these that teach new skills and encourage them to share the benefits of what they have learned with the larger community.

- A commitment to both material reparation (such as monetary restitution) and symbolic reparation (such as an apology)
- A determination of community support and assistance for both victim and offender

The intended result of the process is to repair injuries suffered by the victim and the community, while ensuring reintegration of the offender.

Negotiation, mediation, consensus building, and peacemaking have been part of the dispute resolution process in European and Asian communities for centuries.[96] Native American and Canadian First Nations people have long used (in sentencing circles, sentencing panels, and elders panels) the type of community participation in the adjudication process that restorative justice advocates are now embracing.[97]

In some Native American communities, people accused of breaking the law meet with community members, victims (if any), village elders, and agents of the justice system in a **sentencing circle**. All members of the circle express their feelings about the act that was committed and raise questions or concerns. The accused can express regret about his or her actions and a desire to change the harmful behavior. People may suggest ways in which the offender can make things up to the community and to those who were harmed. A treatment program such as Alcoholics Anonymous may be suggested, if appropriate.

sentencing circles
A type of sentencing in which victims, family members, community members, and the offender participate in an effort to devise fair and reasonable sanctions that are ultimately aimed at reintegrating the offender into the community.

Restoration in Practice

Restorative justice policies and practices are now being adapted around the world. Legislation in 19 states includes reference to the use of victim–offender mediation. There are now thousands of victim–offender mediation programs worldwide.[98] Restorative justice is being embraced on many levels in the justice system.

SCHOOLS Some schools have employed restorative justice practices to avoid more punitive measures such as expulsion in dealing with students involved in drug and alcohol abuse.[99] Schools in Minnesota, Colorado, and elsewhere are now trying to involve students in "relational rehabilitation" programs, which strive to improve offenders' relationships with key figures in the community who may have been harmed by their actions.[100] Restorative justice programs have also been suggested to control and maintain school yard bullying, a growing national concern.[101] Some programs work on creating a cooperative context so that future conflicts can be managed constructively, and relevant parties are taught to adopt civic values to settle conflicts and help create positive relationships.[102]

POLICE Restorative justice has also been implemented when crime is first encountered by police. The new community policing models can be viewed as an attempt to bring restorative concepts into law enforcement. Restorative justice relies on criminal justice policy makers listening to and responding to the needs of those who will be affected by their actions, and community policing relies on policies established with input and exchanges between officers and citizens.[103] The technique is also being used by police around the world. In England, police are using a format called restorative cautioning. After an arrest is made, police in England and Wales traditionally had four procedures they could follow: (1) take no further action, (2) give an informal warning, (3) administer a formal police caution, or (4) decide to prosecute by sending the case to the Crown Prosecution Service. English police forces now use restorative cautioning, a program that employs a trained police facilitator with a script to encourage an offender to take responsibility for repairing the harm caused by the offense. Sometimes the victim is present, in which case the meeting is called a restorative conference; usually, however, the victim is not present. Traditional cautioning, on the other hand, lasts only a few minutes, requires no special training, and focuses on the officer explaining the possible consequences of future offending.

Court-Based Programs

■ A woman who stole from a patient in a nursing home where she works was sentenced to making potpourri-filled vases for a senior center.

■ A man convicted of driving with a suspended license agrees to carve a cane for an elderly person.

■ An artist convicted of driving under the influence had to paint a painting for an organization whose lawn she drove over.

These are some examples of restorative sentences crafted by Vermont's ground-breaking reparative probation system, which involves defendants with community volunteers—and in some cases victims—to craft their sentences instead of taking them from a judge.[104]

Sentencing options are not the only restorative-based concept now being used by the nation's court system. Some restorative programs divert offenders from the formal court process. They encourage reconciliation between offenders and victims via victim advocacy, mediation programs, or sentencing circles, in which crime victims and their families are brought together with offenders and their families in an effort to formulate a sanction that addresses the needs of each party. Victims are given a chance to voice their stories, and offenders can help compensate them financially or provide some service (such as repairing damaged property).[105] Again, the goal is to enable offenders to appreciate the damage they have caused, make amends, and be reintegrated into society.

ETHICAL CHALLENGES in Criminal Justice

A WRITING ASSIGNMENT

You are an appellate court judge. Before you is the case of Justin Starman, the first-round draft choice of the local NFL team, who was arrested for reckless driving at 2 A.M. Starman, who has had a long history of battles with the law, was already under a probation order forbidding any misbehavior and imposing an 11 P.M. curfew. The sentencing judge sentenced Starman to 45 days in county jail, reminding him that he had been warned against any further violations and it had been made clear that violating the conditions of probation would not be tolerated. The day he arrived in jail, however, the county sheriff signed orders allowing him to serve 40 days of home confinement and electronic monitoring. Starman would be allowed to attend training camp so he would not miss the season. When the news media got hold of the story, there was a public outcry, the home confinement order was withdrawn, and Starman was ordered to report to jail.

Starman's lawyers have filed an emergency appeal, asking you, the appellate court judge, to grant him relief and suggesting (a) that the original sentence was overly harsh and (b) the withdrawal of the house arrest order solely because of media attention was a violation of his due process rights. Write an essay on how you would deal with the case. In your paper, address whether you think Starman should be jailed for his behavior or believe, along with the sheriff, that more appropriate, alternative sanctions are available. In formulating your answer, you may want to refer to the sections on alternative sanctions. You may also want to address these issues: Would it be fair to give a celebrity a lenient sentence so they can attend football camp while indigent people go to jail for much the same crime? How would the public be served by putting Starman in jail and jeopardizing his career?

Summary

L01 **Describe the concept of community sentencing.**

- Many of those convicted in criminal courts can be reintegrated into the community and, if given the proper treatment, are unlikely to recidivate.
- There is now a great variety of community sentences, ranging from traditional probation to house arrest and placement in community correctional centers.
- Community sentences can be structured to maximize security and maintain public safety.

L02 **Discuss the history of community sentences.**

- The roots of community sentencing can be traced to the traditions of the English common law. During the Middle Ages, judges who wanted to spare deserving offenders from the pains of (sometimes horrific) punishment granted clemency and stays of execution.
- The common-law practice of judicial reprieve allowed judges to suspend punishment so that convicted offenders could seek a pardon, gather new evidence, or demonstrate that they had reformed their behavior.
- John Augustus of Boston is usually credited with originating the modern probation concept.

L03 **Characterize the different types of probation sentences.**

- Most probation orders involve a contract between the court and the offender in which a prison or jail term is suspended and the probationer promises to obey a set of probation rules or conditions mandated by the court.
- Offenders who are on probation have been convicted of a crime, but instead of being incarcerated, they are returned to the community for a period during which they must abide by certain conditions set forth by the court under the supervision of a probation officer.
- Probationary sentences may be granted by state and federal district courts and state superior (felony) courts.

L04 **Summarize the rules of probation.**

- When granting probation, the court sets down certain conditions or rules of behavior that the probationer is bound to obey.
- Rules can set curfews, prohibit behaviors such as drinking or owning a gun, and/or mandate that the probationer hold a job and not leave the jurisdiction without permission.
- Probation may be revoked if clients fail to comply with rules or disobey reasonable requests to meet their treatment obligations.

L05 **Discuss the organization and administration of probation services.**

- In some states, there is a statewide probation service, but each court jurisdiction controls its local department. Other states maintain a strong statewide authority with centralized control and administration.
- Staff officers in probation departments are usually charged with five primary tasks: investigation, intake, diagnosis, treatment supervision, and risk classification.

L06 **Define and discuss the term *risk classification*.**

- As part of clients' entry into probation, an assessment is made about the risk level they pose to the community and themselves.
- On the basis of this assessment, offenders are assigned to a specific supervision level.

L07 **Interpret the legal issues of probation.**

- The U.S. Supreme Court has ruled that probationers have a unique status and therefore are entitled to fewer constitutional protections than other citizens.
- During the course of a probationary term, violating the rules or terms of probation or committing a new crime can result in probation being revoked.
- In some significant decisions, the Supreme Court has provided procedural safeguards to apply at proceedings convened to consider revoking probation.

Discuss the effectiveness of probation.

- Probation is cost effective. Incarcerating an inmate typically costs over $25,000 per year, whereas probation costs about $2,000 per year.
- National data indicates that almost 60 percent of probationers successfully complete their probationary sentence, while more than 40 percent are rearrested, violate probation rules, or abscond.
- Although the failure rate seems disturbingly high, even the most serious criminals who receive probation are less likely to recidivate than those who are sent to prison for committing similar crimes.

Explain what is meant by intermediate sanctions.

- Alternatives to imprisonment include fines, forfeiture, restitution, and intermediate sanctions.
- Intermediate sanctions include shock incarceration, split sentencing, intensive probation supervision, house arrest, electronic monitoring, and residential community corrections.
- Intermediate sanctions have the potential to save money; although they are more expensive than traditional probation, they are far less costly than incarceration.

Interpret the concept of restorative justice and discuss its merits.

- Restorative justice advocates suggest a policy based on restoring the damage caused by crime and creating a system of justice that includes all the parties harmed by the criminal act: the victim, the offender, the community, and society.
- Restorative justice advocates believe what is needed is a justice policy that repairs the harm caused by crime and includes all parties that have suffered from that harm.
- Restorative justice programs stress healing and redemption rather than punishment and deterrence.

Key Terms

probation, 467
judicial reprieve, 467
recognizance, 467
probation rules, 468
revocation, 468
suspended sentence, 470
intake, 470
presentence investigation, 471
risk classification, 475

day fees, 479
intermediate sanctions, 481
fine, 483
day fine, 484
forfeiture, 484
restitution, 484
monetary restitution, 484
community service restitution, 484
split sentence, 485

shock probation, 485
intensive probation supervision (IPS), 486
electronic monitoring (EM), 486
residential community corrections (RCC), 488
day reporting center (DRC), 488
restorative justice, 489
sentencing circles, 492

Critical Thinking Questions

1. What is the purpose of probation? Identify some conditions of probation, and discuss the responsibilities of the probation officer.
2. Discuss the procedures involved in probation revocation. What are the rights of the probationer? Is probation a privilege or a right? Explain.
3. Should a convicted criminal make restitution to the victim? Why or why not? When is restitution inappropriate?
4. Should offenders be fined on the basis of the severity of what they did or according to their ability to pay? Is it fair to base day fines on wages? Why or why not? Should offenders be punished more severely because they are financially successful? Explain.
5. Does house arrest involve a violation of personal freedom? Does wearing an ankle bracelet smack of "Big Brother"? Would you want the government monitoring your daily activities? Could this be expanded, for example, to monitoring the whereabouts of AIDS patients? Explain.
6. Do you agree that criminals can be restored through community interaction? Considering the fact that recidivism rates are so high, are traditional sanctions a waste of time and restorative ones the wave of the future?

Notes

1. ESPN.com, "Chad Johnson's Jail Term Ends Early," http://espn .go.com/nfl/story/_/id/9395324/chad-johnson-leaving-jail- apologizing-judge (accessed July 2014).

2. UPI.Com, "Lawrence Taylor Gets Probation in Sex Case," http:// www.upi.com/Sports_News/2011/03/22/Lawrence-Taylor-gets- probation-in-sex-case/UPI-92091300814565/ (accessed July 2014).

3. Starpulse.com, "Mel Gibson Gets Probation, Must Undergo Counseling," http://www.starpulse.com/news/index .php/2011/03/11/mel_gibson_gets_probation_must_undergo (accessed July 2014).

4. Ken Lee, "Chris Brown Avoids Jail Time in Rihanna Assault," http://www.people.com/people/article/0,20286732,00.html (accessed July 2014).

5. Associated Press, "Chris Brown Faces Assault Trial After Plea Deal Collapses," http://www.people.com/article/chris-brown- rejects-plea-deal-faces-assault-trial (accessed July 2014).

6. Alan Duke, "Kanye West Gets Probation in Paparazzi Attack," CNN, March 17, 2014, http://www.cnn.com/2014/03/17/showbiz/ kanye-west-plea-deal/ (accessed July 2014).

7. Brandon Applegate, Hayden Smith, Alicia Sitren, and Nicolette Fariello Springer, "From the Inside: The Meaning of Probation to Probationers," *Criminal Justice Review* 34 (2009): 80–95.

8. Christopher Krebs, Kevin Strom, Willem Koetse, and Pamela Lattimore, "The Impact of Residential and Nonresidential Drug Treatment on Recidivism Among Drug-Involved Probationers: A Survival Analysis," *Crime and Delinquency* 55 (2009): 442–471.

9. Ted Chiricos, Kelle Barrick, William Bales, and Stephanie Bontrager, "The Labeling of Convicted Felons and Its Consequences for Recidivism," *Criminology* 45 (2007): 547–581.

10. For a history of probation, see Edward Sieh, "From Augustus to the Progressives: A Study of Probation's Formative Years," *Federal Probation* 57 (1993): 67–72.

11. Ibid.

12. David Rothman, *Conscience and Convenience* (Boston: Little, Brown, 1980), pp. 82–117.

13. Laura M. Maruschak and Thomas P. Bonczar, *Probation and Parole in the United States, 2012* (Washington, DC: Bureau of Justice Statistics, 2013).

14. Alison Lawrence, *Probation and Parole Violations: State Responses* (Washington, DC: National Conference of State Legislatures, 2008), p. 1.

15. Heather Barklage, Dane Miller, and Gene Bonham, "Probation Conditions versus Probation Officer Directives: Where the Twain Shall Meet," *Federal Probation* 70 (2006).

16. Karl Hanson and Suzanne Wallace-Carpretta, "Predictors of Criminal Recidivism Among Male Batterers," *Psychology, Crime and Law* 10 (2004): 413–427.

17. *Higdon v. United States*, 627 F.2d 893 (1980); Elinor Mills, "Conn. AG to MySpace: Turn over Sex Offender Data," *Digital Media*, January 23, 2009, http://www.cnet.com/news/conn-ag-to- myspace-turn-over-sex-offender-data/ (accessed July 2014).

18. *John Doe and Steve Morris v. Prosecutor, Marion County, Indiana*, Case No. 1:08-cv-0436-DFH-TAB (2008), http://media .courierpress.com/media/static/federal_court_ruling.pdf (accessed July 2014).

19. Sean Rosenmerkel, Matthew Durose, and Donald Farole, Jr., *Felony Sentences in State Courts, 2006* (Washington, DC: Bureau of Justice Statistics, 2009).

20. Brian A. Reaves, *Felony Defendants in Large Urban Counties, 2009* (Washington, DC: Bureau of Justice Statistics, 2013).

21. Craig Schwalbe, "Toward an Integrated Theory of Probation," *Criminal Justice and Behavior* 39 (2012): 185–201.

22. Geoff Ward and Aaron Kupchik, "What Drives Juvenile Probation Officers? Relating Organizational Contexts, Status Characteristics, and Personal Convictions to Treatment and Punishment Orientations," *Crime and Delinquency* 56 (2010): 35–69.

23. Jeffrey Lin, Joel Miller, and Mayumi Fukushima, "Juvenile Probation Officers' Dispositional Recommendations: Predictive Factors and Their Alignment with Predictors of Recidivism," *Journal of Crime and Justice* 31 (2008): 1–34.

24. Thomas E. Feucht and Joseph Gfroerer, "Mental and Substance Use Disorders Among Adult Men on Probation or Parole: Some Success Against a Persistent Challenge," Substance Abuse and Mental Health Services Administration Department of Health and Human Services, 2011, http://oas.samhsa.gov/2k11/NIJ_ Data_Review/MentalDisorders.htm (accessed July 2014).

25. Diana Wendy Fitzgibbon, "Deconstructing Probation: Risk and Developments in Practice," *Journal of Social Work Practice* 22 (2008): 85–101.

26. Hanson and Wallace-Carpretta, "Predictors of Criminal Recidivism Among Male Batterers."

27. David Duffee and Bonnie Carlson, "Competing Value Premises for the Provision of Drug Treatment to Probationers," *Crime and Delinquency* 42 (1996): 574–592.

28. James Byrne, "Introduction: Why Assessment 'Matters' in an Evidence-Based Community Corrections System," *Federal Probation* 70 (2006), http://www.uscourts.gov/uscourts/ FederalCourts/PPS/Fedprob/2006-09/intro.html (accessed July 2014).

29. James Austin, "How Much Risk Can We Take? The Misuse of Risk Assessment in Corrections," *Federal Probation* 70 (2006), http://www.uscourts.gov/uscourts/FederalCourts/PPS/ Fedprob/2006-09/risk.html (accessed July 2014).

30. Carolin Kröner, Cornelis Stadtland, Matthias Eidt, and Norbert Nedopil, "The Validity of the Violence Risk Appraisal Guide (VRAG) in Predicting Criminal Recidivism," *Criminal Behaviour and Mental Health* 17 (2007): 89–100.

31. James Byrne and April Pattavina, "Assessing the Role of Clinical and Actuarial Risk Assessment in an Evidence-Based Community Corrections System: Issues to Consider," *Federal Probation* 70 (2006), http://www.uscourts.gov/uscourts/FederalCourts/PPS/ Fedprob/2006-09/issues.html (accessed July 2014).

32. Kathleen Auerhahn, "Conceptual and Methodological Issues in the Prediction of Dangerous Behavior," *Criminology and Public Policy* 5 (2006): 771–778.

33. *Minnesota v. Murphy*, 465 U.S. 420 (1984).

34. *Griffin v. Wisconsin*, 483 U.S. 868 (1987).

35. *United States v. Knights*, 534 U.S. 112 (2001).

36. *Mempa v. Rhay*, 389 U.S. 128 (1967).

37. *Morrissey v. Brewer*, 408 U.S. 471 (1972).

38. *Gagnon v. Scarpelli*, 411 U.S. 778 (1973).

39. *Beardon v. Georgia*, 461 U.S. 660 (1983).

40. *United States v. Granderson*, 511 U.S. 39 (1994).

41. M. Kevin Gray, Monique Fields, and Sheila Royo Maxwell, "Examining Probation Violations: Who, What, and When," *Crime and Delinquency* 47 (2001): 537–557.

42. Joan Petersilia, Susan Turner, James Kahan, and Joyce Peterson, *Granting Felons Probation: Public Risks and Alternatives* (Santa Monica, CA: RAND, 1985).

43. Cassia Spohn and David Holleran, "The Effect of Imprisonment on Recidivism Rates of Felony Offenders: A Focus on Drug Offenders," *Criminology* 40 (2002): 329–358.

44. Kathryn Morgan, "Factors Influencing Probation Outcome: A Review of the Literature," *Federal Probation* 57 (1993): 23–29.

45. Michelle Meloy, "The Sex Offender Next Door: An Analysis of Recidivism, Risk Factors, and Deterrence of Sex Offenders on Probation," *Criminal Justice Policy Review* 16 (2005): 211–236.

46. Kathryn Morgan, "Factors Associated with Probation Outcome," *Journal of Criminal Justice* 22 (1994): 341–353.

47. Paula M. Ditton, *Mental Health and Treatment of Inmates and Probationers* (Washington, DC: Bureau of Justice Statistics, 1999).

48. Naomi Freeman, "Predictors of Rearrest for Rapists and Child Molesters on Probation," *Criminal Justice and Behavior* 34 (2007): 752–768.

49. Nancy Rodriguez and Vincent Webb, "Probation Violations, Revocations, and Imprisonment: The Decisions of Probation Officers, Prosecutors, and Judges Pre- and Post-Mandatory Drug Treatment," *Criminal Justice Policy Review* 18 (2007): 3–30.

50. Morgan, "Factors Associated with Probation Outcome."

51. Fitzgibbon, "Deconstructing Probation."

52. Joan Petersilia, "Probation in the United States," in *Crime and Justice: A Review of Research*, v. 21, ed. Michael Tonry (Chicago: University of Chicago Press, 1997), p. 185.

53. "Law in Massachusetts Requires Probationers to Pay 'Day Fees,'" *Criminal Justice Newsletter*, September 15, 1988, p. 1.

54. Peter Finn and Dale Parent, *Making the Offender Foot the Bill: A Texas Program* (Washington, DC: National Institute of Justice, 1992).

55. Association of Prosecuting Attorneys, "Innovations in New York City Probation Practices," http://www.apainc.org/html/NYC%20Probation%20Guide.pdf (accessed July 2014).

56. Todd R. Clear, "Places Not Cases: Rethinking the Probation Focus," *Howard Journal of Criminal Justice* 44 (2005): 172–184.

57. Andrew Klein and Ann Crowe, "Findings from an Outcome Examination of Rhode Island's Specialized Domestic Violence Probation Supervision Program," *Violence Against Women* 14 (2008): 226–246.

58. Private Probation Services, http://www.privateprobationservices.com (accessed July 2014).

59. Christine Schloss and Leanne Alarid, "Standards in the Privatization of Probation Services: A Statutory Analysis," *Criminal Justice Review* 32 (2007): 233–245.

60. "HOPE in Hawaii: Swift and Sure Changes in Probation" (government monograph), National Institute of Justice, 2008, http://www.ncjrs.gov/pdffiles1/nij/222758.pdf (accessed July 2014).

61. Todd Clear and Patricia Hardyman, "The New Intensive Supervision Movement," *Crime and Delinquency* 36 (1990): 42–60.

62. For a thorough review of these programs, see James Byrne, Arthur Lurigio, and Joan Petersilia, eds., *Smart Sentencing: The Emergence of Intermediate Sanctions* (Newbury Park, CA: Sage, 1993). Hereinafter cited as *Smart Sentencing*.

63. Norval Morris and Michael Tonry, *Between Prison and Probation: Intermediate Punishments in a Rational Sentencing System* (New York: Oxford University Press, 1990).

64. Michael Tonry and Richard Will, *Intermediate Sanctions* (Washington, DC: National Institute of Justice, 1990).

65. Ibid., p. 8.

66. Stephen Farrall, "Officially Recorded Convictions for Probationers: The Relationship with Self-Report and Supervisory Observations," *Legal and Criminological Psychology* 10 (2005): 121–132.

67. Michael Maxfield and Terry Baumer, "Home Detention with Electronic Monitoring: Comparing Pretrial and Postconviction Programs," *Crime and Delinquency* 36 (1990): 521–556.

68. Robert Homant and Mark DeMercurio, "Intermediate Sanctions in Probation Officers' Sentencing Recommendations: Consistency, Net Widening, and Net Repairing," *Prison Journal* 89 (2009): 426–439.

69. George Cole, "Monetary Sanctions: The Problem of Compliance," in *Smart Sentencing*, pp. 51–64.

70. *Tate v. Short*, 401 U.S. 395 (1971).

71. Lina Eriksson and Robert Goodin, "The Measuring Rod of Time: The Example of Swedish Day-Fines," *Journal of Applied Philosophy* 24 (2007): 125–136.

72. John L. Worrall, "Addicted to the Drug War: The Role of Civil Asset Forfeiture as a Budgetary Necessity in Contemporary Law Enforcement," *Journal of Criminal Justice* 29 (2001): 171–187.

73. C. Yorke, *Some Consideration on the Law of Forfeiture for High Treason*, 2nd ed. (1746), p. 26; cited in David Fried, "Rationalizing Criminal Forfeiture," *Journal of Criminal Law and Criminology* 79 (1988): 328–436.

74. For a general review, see Burt Galaway and Joe Hudson, *Criminal Justice, Restitution, and Reconciliation* (New York: Criminal Justice Press, 1990).

75. Frederick Allen and Harvey Treger, "Community Service Orders in Federal Probation: Perceptions of Probationers and Host Agencies," *Federal Probation* 54 (1990): 8–14.

76. Gail Caputo, "Community Service in Texas: Results of a Probation Survey," *Corrections Compendium* 30 (2005): 8–12.

77. Sudipto Roy, "Two Types of Juvenile Restitution Programs in Two Midwestern Counties: A Comparative Study," *Federal Probation* 57 (1993): 48–53.

78. Joan Petersilia, *The Influence of Criminal Justice Research* (Santa Monica, CA: RAND, 1987).

79. Ibid.

80. Joan Petersilia and Susan Turner, "Evaluating Intensive Supervision Probation/Parole: Results of a Nationwide Experiment," National Institute of Justice, Research in Brief (Washington, DC: National Institute of Justice, 1993).

81. Joan Petersilia, "Beyond the Prison Bubble," *NIJ Journal* 268 (2011), http://www.nij.gov/nij/journals/268/prison-bubble.htm (accessed July 2014).

82. Robert N. Altman, Robert E. Murray, and Evey B. Wooten, "Home Confinement: A '90s Approach to Community Supervision," *Federal Probation* 61 (1997): 30–32.

83. Brian K. Pane and Randy R. Gainey, "The Electronic Monitoring of Offenders Released from Jail or Prison: Safety, Control, and Comparisons to the Incarceration Experience," *Prison Journal* 84 (2004): 413–435; Mary Finn and Suzanne Muirhead-Steves, "The Effectiveness of Electronic Monitoring with Male Parolees," *Justice Quarterly* 19 (2002): 293–313.

84. Kathy Padgett, William Bales, and Thomas Blomberg, "Under Surveillance: An Empirical Test of the Effectiveness and Consequences of Electronic Monitoring," *Criminology and Public Policy* 5 (2006): 61–91.

85. William Burrell and Robert Gable, "From B. F. Skinner to Spiderman to Martha Stewart: The Past, Present and Future of Electronic Monitoring of Offenders," *Journal of Offender Rehabilitation* 46 (2008): 101–118.

86. David Farabee, Yih-Ing Hser, Douglas Anglin, and David Huang, "Recidivism Among an Early Cohort of California's Proposition 36 Offenders," *Criminology and Public Policy* 3 (2004): 563–583.

87. Georgia Department of Corrections, Day Reporting Centers, http://www.dcor.state.ga.us/Divisions/Corrections/ProbationSupervision/DayReporting.html (accessed July 2014).

88. David Champion, Patrick Harvey, and Youngyol Yim Schanz, "Day Reporting Center and Recidivism: Comparing Offender Groups in a Western Pennsylvania County Study," *Journal of Offender Rehabilitation* 50 (2011): 433–446.

89. Michael Ostermann, "An Analysis of New Jersey's Day Reporting Center and Halfway Back Programs: Embracing the Rehabilitative Ideal Through Evidence-Based Practices," *Journal of Offender Rehabilitation* 48 (2009): 139–153.

90. Dae-Young Kim, Hee-Jong Joo, and William McCarty "Risk Assessment and Classification of Day Reporting Center Clients: An Actuarial Approach," *Criminal Justice and Behavior* 35 (2008): 792–812.

91. Amy Craddock, "Day Reporting Center Completion: Comparison of Individual and Multilevel Models," *Crime and Delinquency* 55 (2009): 105–133; Sudipto Roy and Shannon Barton, "Convicted Drunk Drivers in Electronic Monitoring Home Detention and Day Reporting Centers," *Federal Probation* 70 (2006), http://www.uscourts.gov/uscourts/FederalCourts/PPS/Fedprob/2006-06/drunkdrivers.html (accessed July 2014).

92. Kathleen Daly and Russ Immarigeon, "The Past, Present, and Future of Restorative Justice: Some Critical Reflections," *Contemporary Justice Review* 1 (1998): 21–45.

93. John Braithwaite, *Crime, Shame, and Reintegration* (Melbourne, Australia: Cambridge University Press, 1989).

94. Clare McGlynn, Nicole Westmarland, and Nikki Godden, "'Just Wanted Him to Hear Me': Sexual Violence and the Possibilities of Restorative Justice," *Journal of Law and Society* 39 (2012): 213–240.

95. Anne-Marie McAlinden, "'Transforming Justice': Challenges for Restorative Justice in an Era of Punishment-based Corrections," *Contemporary Justice Review* 14 (2011): 383–406.

96. Kay Pranis, "Peacemaking Circles: Restorative Justice in Practice Allows Victims and Offenders to Begin Repairing the Harm," *Corrections Today* 59 (1997): 74.

97. Carol LaPrairie, "The 'New' Justice: Some Implications for Aboriginal Communities," *Canadian Journal of Criminology* 40 (1998): 61–79.

98. Victim–Offender Reconciliation Program, Information and Resource Center, http://www.vorp.com (accessed July 2014).

99. Brenda Morrison and Dorothy Vaandering, "Restorative Justice: Pedagogy, Praxis, and Discipline," *Journal of School Violence* 11 (2012): 138–155.

100. David R. Karp and Beau Breslin, "Restorative Justice in School Communities," *Youth and Society* 33 (2001): 249–272.

101. Eliza Ahmed and Valerie Braithwaite, "Learning to Manage Shame in School Bullying: Lessons for Restorative Justice Interventions," *Critical Criminology* 20 (2012): 79–97.

102. David Johnson and Roger Johnson, "Restorative Justice in the Classroom: Necessary Roles of Cooperative Context, Constructive Conflict, and Civic Values," *Negotiation and Conflict Management Research* 5 (2012): 4–28.

103. Paul Jesilow and Deborah Parsons, "Community Policing as Peacemaking," *Policing and Society* 10 (2000): 163–183.

104. Vermont Department of Corrections, *Novel Sentencing Program Really Works*, http://doc.vermont.gov/justice/restorative-justice/novel_sentencing_program_article.pdf (accessed July 2014).

105. Gordon Bazemore and Curt Taylor Griffiths, "Conferences, Circles, Boards, and Mediations: The 'New Wave' of Community Justice Decision Making," *Federal Probation* 61 (1997): 25–37.

CHAPTER 13

Corrections: History, Institutions, and Populations

Learning Objectives

L01 Identify the various components of the correctional institution system.

L02 Discuss some of the most significant problems facing the correctional system.

L03 Articulate how the first penal institutions developed in England.

L04 Explain how William Penn and the Quakers revolutionized corrections in Pennsylvania.

L05 Compare the early New York and Pennsylvania prison models.

L06 Discuss the development of penal reform.

L07 Explain the purposes of jails and understand the characteristic makeup of jail populations.

L08 Define the term *new-generation jail*.

L09 Classify the different types of federal and state penal institutions.

L010 Discuss prison population trends.

Chapter Outline

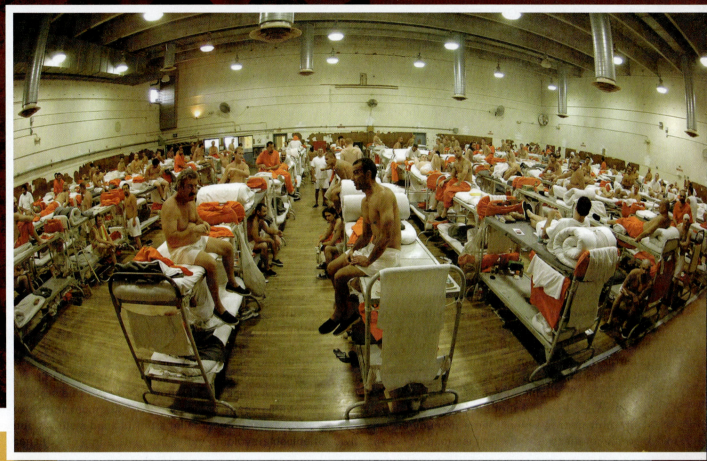

California's prisons are designed to house approximately 80,000 inmates, but at one point the state's prison population was almost double that. So crowded were the state's prisons that two federal class action lawsuits were filed in which inmates challenged the conditions of their confinement. In 2009, a three-judge panel sided with the inmates and ordered California to reduce its prison population to 137.5 percent of design capacity.[1] In 2011, the U.S. Supreme Court affirmed the decision, holding that "[t]he court-mandated population limit is necessary to remedy the violation of prisoners' constitutional rights."[2]

Shortly thereafter, California began an elaborate and controversial process of "realignment" in which responsibility for housing and supervising a large number of "non-serious, non-violent, and non-sex registrant," so-called "non-non-non" offenders, was shifted from the state to California's 58 counties. In addition, most inmates released from state prison would be subject to county-level probation supervision rather than state parole supervision. Finally, parolees who violate their probation terms would not be sent back to state prison, but rather required to serve out any custodial punishment in a county jail.

California's governor said this after signing the changes into law:

> California's correctional system has to change, and this bill is a bold move in the right direction. For too long, the State's prison system has been a revolving door for lower-level offenders and parole violators who are released within months—often before they are even transferred out of a reception center. Cycling these offenders through state prisons wastes money, aggravates crowded conditions, thwarts rehabilitation, and impedes local law enforcement supervision.[3]

What are the effects of realignment? The California Department of Corrections and Rehabilitation tracked 58,746 inmates who were released from prison in the first year after realignment and concluded "there is very little difference between the one-year arrest and conviction rates of offenders released pre- and post-realignment."[4] At the same time, realignment has placed a strain on county probation departments, which are tasked with supervising more and more offenders. And although counties received funding to assist in this process, there is concern that the state has not established uniform standards to ensure consistency across counties.[5] ■

California's prison realignment initiative is emblematic of a problem running throughout America's prison: overcrowding. What should be done about overcrowding? What sentencing options are ideal? Should courts be tough on offenders and sentence them to long prison terms? Should parolees be sent back to prison for technical violations? If so, who should supervise them? What, if anything, besides the "warehousing" of offenders could be done to minimize recidivism? How should such programs be funded? There are no easy answers to these questions, and there is still great debate over the true role of corrections, whether at the state *or* county level.

Some corrections officials maintain that **jails** and **prisons** should be used to help treat and rehabilitate convicted offenders in "therapeutic communities."[6] In contrast, others believe secure facilities should be designed to deter would-be criminals and keep those convicted of crime apart from society.[7] Under this latter model, prison success is measured by such factors as physical security, length of incapacitation, a lower crime rate, and the fear of criminal sanctions.

On the surface, the get-tough approach appears to be effective: After all, the crime rate has declined in the United States as the number of people under lock and key has risen.[8] The United States has nearly one-quarter of the world's prisoners, but only 5 percent of its population.[9] Yet there is still uncertainty over whether the use of secure confinements is responsible for the crime rate drop in America. Police effectiveness and improving social conditions may be more important factors in lowering crime rates than the current prison boom.[10] And even if imprisonment has led to crime reductions, America's prisons and jails can only accommodate so many people, as the California experience has made abundantly clear!

While the effects of America's high incarceration rate are still being debated, there is no question that the nation's vast secure corrections system, with branches in the federal, state, and county levels of government, has not met its stated goals. Although the majority of inmates yearn for freedom, one of the great tragedies of our time is that correctional institutions do not seem to correct: the majority of former inmates offend again soon after reentering society. This means that each year hundreds of thousands of former inmates return to prison because they have failed to resist the temptation to commit further crimes after returning to the community.

There is no question that the contemporary correctional system has become quite complex and now contains a variety of institutions designed to house and correct different classes of offenders. Felons are housed in high-security prisons while misdemeanants are housed in county jails, which are sometimes called reformatories or houses of correction. Juvenile offenders have their own institutions, called schools, camps, ranches, or homes. There are also prison farms for adult offenders, and there are community correctional centers, such as halfway houses, for inmates who are about to return to society.

In this chapter, we explore the correctional system, beginning with the history and nature of correctional institutions. Then in Chapter 14 we examine institutional life in some detail.

The History of Correctional Institutions

The original legal punishments were typically banishment or slavery, restitution, corporal punishment, and execution. The concept of incarcerating convicted offenders for long periods of time as a punishment for their misdeeds did not become the norm in corrections until the nineteenth century.[11]

Although the use of incarceration as a routine punishment began much later, some early European institutions were created specifically to detain and control criminal offenders. Penal institutions were constructed in England during the

---

jail

A correctional facility designed to hold pretrial detainees and misdemeanants serving their criminal sentence.

prison

A correctional facility designed to hold convicted felons while they serve their criminal sentence.

 LO1 Identify the various components of the correctional institution system.

 LO2 Discuss some of the most significant problems facing the correctional system.

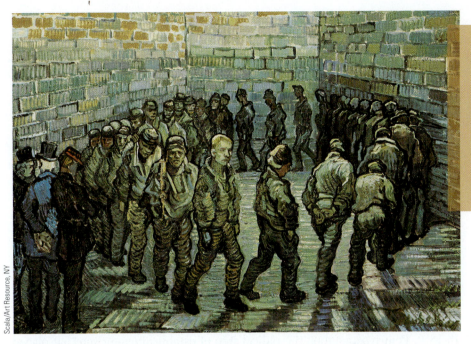

Scala/Art Resource, NY

Even though he himself was voluntarily committed to the asylum shown here, Vincent van Gogh captured the despair of the nineteenth-century penal institution in this detail from an 1890 painting sometimes titled *Prisoners Exercising*. The face of the prisoner near the center of the picture looking at the viewer is van Gogh's.

tenth century to hold pretrial detainees and those waiting for their sentence to be carried out.[12] During the twelfth century, King Henry II constructed a series of county jails to hold thieves and vagrants prior to the disposition of their sentence. In 1557, the workhouse in Bridewell was built to hold people convicted of relatively minor offenses who would work to pay their debt to society. Those who had committed more serious offenses were held there pending execution.

The first penal institutions were foul places devoid of proper care, food, or medical treatment. Jail conditions were deplorable because jailers ran them for personal gain. The fewer services provided, the greater their profit. Early jails were catchall institutions that held not only criminal offenders awaiting trial but also vagabonds, debtors, the mentally ill, and assorted others. The jailer, usually a shire reeve (sheriff)—an official appointed by the king or a noble landholder as chief law enforcement official of a county—ran the jail under a fee system, whereby inmates were required to pay for their own food and services. Those who could not pay were fed scraps until they starved to death.[13]

From 1776 to 1785, a growing inmate population that could no longer be transported to North America forced the English to house prisoners on **hulks**, abandoned ships anchored in harbors. The hulks became infamous for their degrading conditions and brutal punishments but were not abandoned until 1858.[14]

The Origin of Corrections in the United States

Although Europe had jails and a variety of other penal facilities, correctional reform was first instituted in the United States. The first American jail was built in James City in the Virginia colony in the early seventeenth century. However, the modern American correctional system had its origin in Pennsylvania under the leadership of William Penn.

At the end of the seventeenth century, Penn revised Pennsylvania's criminal code to forbid torture and the capricious use of mutilation and physical punishment. Penn ordered that a new type of institution be built to replace the widely used public forms of punishment—stocks, pillories, gallows, and branding irons. Each county was instructed to build a house of corrections similar to today's jails. Penn's reforms remained in effect until his death in 1718, when the criminal penal code was changed back to open public punishment and harsh brutality.

L03 Articulate how the first penal institutions developed in England.

hulk
Mothballed ship used to house prisoners in eighteenth-century England.

L04 Explain how William Penn and the Quakers revolutionized corrections in Pennsylvania.

Creating a Correctional System

The origin of the modern correctional system is usually traced to eighteenth-century developments in Pennsylvania. In 1776, post-revolutionary Pennsylvania again adopted William Penn's code, and in 1787, a group of Quakers led by Benjamin Rush formed the Philadelphia Society for Alleviating the Miseries of Public Prisons. The aim of the society was to bring some degree of humane and orderly treatment to the growing penal system. The Quakers' influence on the legislature resulted in limiting the use of the death penalty to cases involving treason, murder, rape, and arson. Their next step was to reform the institutional system so that the prison could serve as a suitable alternative to physical punishment.

Under pressure from the Quakers, the Pennsylvania legislature in 1790 called for renovation of the prison system. The eventual result was the creation of a separate wing of Philadelphia's **Walnut Street Jail** to house convicted felons (except those sentenced to death). Prisoners were placed in solitary cells, where they remained in isolation and did not have the right to work.[15] Quarters that contained the solitary or separate cells were called **penitentiary houses**, as was already the custom in England. Similar institutions were erected in New York (Newgate in 1791) and New Jersey (Trenton in 1798).

The Pennsylvania System

In 1818, Pennsylvania took the radical step of establishing a prison that placed each inmate in a single cell for the duration of his sentence. Classifications were abolished because each cell was intended as a miniature prison that would prevent inmates from associating with one another. In 1827, the Western State Penitentiary was built in Allegheny County. It took the form of a semicircle, with the cells positioned along its circumference. Built back to back, some cells faced the boundary wall and others faced the internal area of the circle. Inmates were kept at hard labor in solitary confinement, being allowed out for about an hour a day for exercise. The Western Penitentiary solitary system soon failed, because the small cells lacked adequate air and light, making solitary work impossible. The entire building had to be demolished in the 1830s and rebuilt in 1882 with larger individual cells. Known as Riverside, it survives and is still in use.

Two years later, in 1829, the Eastern State Penitentiary was built outside Philadelphia. Eastern State abandoned the use of corporal punishment and ill treatment of inmates that were common during that period. This new-style penitentiary was intended not merely to punish but also to move the criminal toward spiritual reflection and change. The method was a Quaker-inspired system of isolation from other prisoners, with labor. The early system was strict: inmates were hooded whenever they were outside their cells. But the proponents of the system believed strongly that if induced in silence to ponder their behavior and the ugliness of their crimes, criminals would become genuinely penitent. The building's design was quite radical: seven cell blocks radiated from a central surveillance rotunda. Each prisoner had a private cell, centrally heated, with running water, a flush toilet (conveniences not available to the president in the White House at the time), and a skylight. Adjacent to the cell was a private outdoor exercise yard surrounded by a 10-foot wall. Each inmate was given a Bible to read and honest work (including shoemaking and weaving), thought to lead to penitence.[16] Women were held in the prison until 1923 when a separate facility was built in Muncy, Pennsylvania.

Supporters of the **Pennsylvania system** believed that the penitentiary was truly a place to do penance. By removing sinners from society and allowing them a period of isolation in which to consider the evils of crime, the Pennsylvania system reflected the influence of religion and religious philosophy on corrections. Its supporters believed that solitary confinement with in-cell labor would make work so attractive that, upon release, the inmate would be well suited to resume a productive existence in society.

Walnut Street Jail
The birthplace of the modern prison system and of the Pennsylvania system of solitary confinement.

penitentiary houses
A correctional institution for those convicted of major crimes.

L05 Compare the early New York and Pennsylvania prison models.

Pennsylvania system
A prison system, developed in Pennsylvania during the nineteenth century, based on total isolation and individual penitence.

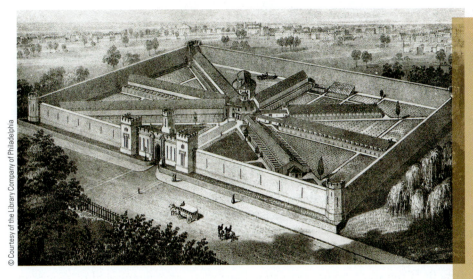

© Courtesy of the Library Company of Philadelphia

Eastern State Penitentiary, built in 1829, was at the time the largest and most expensive public structure in the country. Designed by John Haviland, it consisted of an octagonal center connected by corridors to seven radiating single-story cell blocks. Each cell had hot water heating, a water tap, toilet, and an individual exercise yard the same width as the cell. There were rectangular openings in the cell wall through which food and work materials could be passed to the prisoner, as well as peepholes for guards to observe prisoners without being seen. Each cell contained a skylight so that the inmate could look to the heavens.

The Auburn System

In 1816, New York built a new prison at Auburn, hoping to alleviate some of the overcrowding at Newgate. The Auburn Prison design became known as the **tier system** because cells were built vertically on five floors of the structure. It was also referred to as the **congregate system** because most prisoners ate and worked in groups.

The philosophy of the **Auburn system** was crime prevention through fear of punishment and silent confinement. The worst felons were to be cut off from all contact with other prisoners, and although they were treated and fed relatively well, they had no hope of pardon to relieve their solitude or isolation.

Hard work and silence became the foundation of the Auburn system wherever it was adopted. Silence was the key to prison discipline. It prohibited the formulation of escape plans, it prevented plots and riots, and it allowed prisoners to contemplate their infractions.

Many fiery debates occurred between advocates of the Pennsylvania system and adherents of the Auburn system. The Auburn system eventually prevailed and spread throughout the United States (however, Eastern State Penitentiary remained in use until 1971). Many of its features are still used today. Its innovations included congregate working conditions, the use of solitary confinement to punish unruly inmates, military regimentation, and discipline. In Auburn-like institutions, prisoners were marched from place to place. Their time was regulated by bells telling them when to wake up, sleep, and work. The system was so like the military that many of its early administrators were recruited from the armed services. See Concept Summary 13.1 for a comparison of the two systems.[17]

tier system
A type of prison in which cells are located along corridors in multiple layers or levels.

congregate system
A prison system, originated in New York, in which inmates worked and ate together during the day and then slept in solitary cells at night.

Auburn system
A prison system, developed in New York during the nineteenth century, based on congregate (group) work during the day and separation at night.

CONCEPT SUMMARY 13.1
Early Correctional Systems

Prison	Structure	Living Conditions	Activities	Discipline
Auburn system	Tiered cells	Congregate	Group work	Silence, harsh punishment
Pennsylvania system	Single cells set in semicircle	Isolated	In-cell work, Bible study	Silence, harsh punishment

contract system

A prison industry system, widely employed until after the Civil War, in which officials sold the labor of prison inmates to private businesses, for use either inside or outside the prison.

convict-lease system

A contract system in which a private business leased prisoners from the state for a fixed annual fee and assumed full responsibility for their supervision and control.

public account system

A prison industry system, popular after the Civil War, in which employment was directed by the state and the products of the prisoners' labor were sold for the benefit of the state.

L06   Discuss the development of penal reform.

Creating Prison Industry

Prison industry developed and became the predominant theme around which institutions were organized. Some prisons used the **contract system**, in which officials sold the labor of inmates to private businesses. Sometimes the contractor supervised the inmates inside the prison itself. Under the **convict-lease system**, the state leased its prisoners to a business for a fixed annual fee and gave up supervision and control. Finally, some institutions had prisoners produce goods for the prison's own use.[18]

The development of prison industry quickly led to the abuse of inmates, who were forced to work for almost no wages, and to profiteering by dishonest administrators and business owners. During the Civil War era, prisons were major manufacturers of clothes, shoes, boots, furniture, and the like. Beginning in the 1870s, opposition by trade unions sparked restrictions on interstate commerce in prison goods. After the Civil War, a number of states abandoned the contract system and introduced the **public account system**, under which employment was directed by the state and the products of the prisoners' labor were sold for the benefit of the state. Some correctional jurisdictions compensated prisoners for their labor but deducted funds for room, board, clothing, and the costs of trial; remaining funds were sent to the inmates' families and dependents. For inmates who had no family and/or dependents, their earnings accumulated and were paid to them upon their release.

Prison Reform Efforts

The National Congress of Penitentiary and Reformatory Discipline, held in Cincinnati in 1870, heralded a new era of prison reform. Organized by penologists Enoch Wines and Theodore Dwight, the congress provided a forum for corrections experts from around the nation to call for better treatment, education, and training of inmates. Overseas, another penal reform was being developed in which inmates could earn early release and serve out their sentence in the community; this innovation was called parole and is discussed below.

One of the most famous people to attend the congress, Zebulon Brockway, warden of the Elmira Reformatory in New York, advocated individualized treatment, the indeterminate sentence, and parole. The reformatory program initiated by Brockway included elementary education for illiterates, designated library hours, lectures by faculty members of the local Elmira College, and a group of vocational training shops. From 1888 to 1920, Elmira administrators used military-like training to discipline the inmates and organize the institution. The military organization could be seen in every aspect of the institution: schooling, manual training, sports, supervision of inmates, and even parole decisions.[19] The cost to the state of the institution's operations was to be held to a minimum.

Although Brockway proclaimed Elmira to be an ideal reformatory, his achievements were limited. The greatest significance of his contribution was the injection of a degree of humanitarianism into the industrial prisons of that day.[20] Many institutions were constructed across the nation and labeled reformatories based on the Elmira model, but most of them continued to be industrially oriented.[21]

The Granger Collection, New York

Prison in the late nineteenth century was a brutal place. This line engraving from 1869 shows an inmate undergoing water torture in New York's Sing Sing Prison.

Prisons in the Twentieth Century

The early twentieth century was a time of contrasts in the U.S. prison system.[22] At one extreme were those who advocated reform, such as the Mutual Welfare League, led by Thomas Mott Osborne. Prison reform groups proposed better treatment for inmates, an end to harsh corporal punishment, the creation of meaningful prison industries, and educational programs. Reformers argued that prisoners should not be isolated from society and that the best elements of society—education, religion, meaningful work, and self-governance—should be brought to the prison. Osborne went so far as to spend a week in New York's notorious Sing Sing Prison to learn firsthand about its conditions.

In time, some of the more rigid prison rules gave way to liberal reform. By the mid-1930s, few prisons required inmates to wear the red-and-white-striped convict suit; nondescript gray uniforms were substituted. The code of silence ended, as did the lockstep shuffle. Prisoners were allowed "the freedom of the yard" to mingle and exercise an hour or two each day.[23] Movies and radio appeared in the 1930s. Visiting policies and mail privileges were liberalized.

A more important trend was the development of specialized prisons designed to treat particular types of offenders. In New York, for example, the prisons at Clinton and Auburn were viewed as industrial facilities for hard-core inmates, Great Meadow was an agricultural center for nondangerous offenders, and Dannemora was a facility for the criminally insane. In California, San Quentin housed inmates whom correctional authorities considered salvageable, and Folsom was reserved for hard-core offenders.[24]

Prison industry also evolved. Opposition by organized labor helped put an end to the convict-lease system and forced inmate labor. By 1900, a number of states had restricted the sale of prisoner-made goods on the open market. The worldwide Great Depression, which began in 1929, prompted industry and union leaders to further pressure state legislators to reduce competition from prison industries. A series of ever more restrictive federal legislative initiatives led to the Sumners-Ashurst Act (1940), which made it a federal offense to transport interstate commerce goods made in prison for private use, regardless of the laws of the state receiving the goods.[25] The restrictions imposed by the federal government helped to severely curtail prison industry for 40 years. Private entrepreneurs

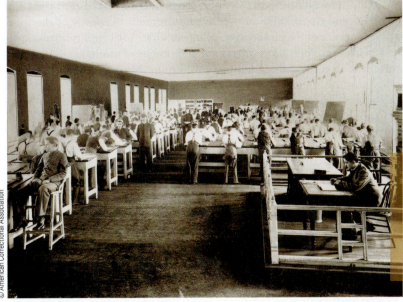

© American Correctional Association

Elmira Reformatory, training course in drafting, 1909. Inmates stand at drafting tables as guards watch and a supervisor sits at a fenced-off desk at the front of the hall. Elmira was one of the first penal institutions to employ education and training programs.

shunned prison investments because they were no longer profitable. The result was inmate idleness and make-work jobs.[26]

Despite some changes and reforms, the prison in the mid-twentieth century remained a destructive total institution. Although some aspects of inmate life improved, severe discipline, harsh rules, and solitary confinement were the way of life in prison.

The Development of Parole

While the prison is an American invention, parole was a concept that developed overseas and was later brought to the United States.[27] The term "parole" itself comes from the French for "promise," referring to the practice of releasing captured enemy soldiers if they promised (or gave their word) not to fight again, with the threat that they would be executed if recaptured.

In the early seventeenth century, English judges began to spare the lives of offenders by banishing them to the newly formed overseas colonies. In 1617, the Privy Counsel of the British Parliament standardized this practice by passing an order granting reprieves and stays of execution to convicts willing to be transported to the colonies. Such *transportation* was viewed as an answer to labor shortages caused by war, disease, and the opening of new commercial markets.

By 1665, transportation orders were modified to include specific conditions of employment and to provide for reconsideration of punishment if the conditions were not met—for example, if the person returned to England before the expiration of the sentence. In 1717, the British Parliament passed legislation creating the concept of *property in service*, which transferred control of prisoners to a contractor or shipmaster until the expiration of their sentences. When the prisoners arrived in the colonies, their services could be resold to the highest bidder. After sale, an offender's status changed from convict to indentured servant.

Transportation quickly became the most common sentence for theft offenders. In the American colonies, property in service had to be abandoned after the revolution. Thereafter, Australia, which had been claimed as a British colony in 1770, became the destination for most transported felons. From 1815 to 1850, large numbers of inmates were shipped to Australia to serve as indentured servants working for plantation owners, in mines, or on sheep stations.

In England, opposition to penal servitude and the deprivations associated with transportation produced such organizations as the Society for the Improvement of Prison Discipline. This group asked the famous reformer Alexander Maconochie to investigate conditions in Australia. Maconochie condemned transportation and eventually helped end the practice. Later, when appointed director of the infamous Australian prison on Norfolk Island, Maconochie instituted reforms, such as classification and rehabilitation programs, that became models for the treatment of convicted offenders. Recalled from Australia, Maconochie returned to England, where his efforts led to the English Penal Servitude Act of 1853, which all but ended transportation and substituted imprisonment as a punishment.

Part of this act made it possible to grant a *ticket-of-leave* to those who had served a sufficient portion of their prison sentence. This form of conditional release permitted former prisoners to be at large in specified areas. The conditions of their release were written on a license that the former inmates were required to carry with them at all times. Conditions usually included sobriety, lawful behavior, and hard work. Many releasees violated these provisions, prompting criticism of the system. Eventually, prisoner aid society members helped supervise and care for releasees.

In Ireland, Sir Walter Crofton, a disciple of Maconochie's reforms, liberalized Irish prisons. He instituted a mark system in which inmates could earn their ticket-of-leave by accumulating credits for good conduct and hard work in prison. Crofton also instituted a system in which private volunteers or police agents could monitor ticket-of-leave offenders in the community. Crofton's work is considered an early form of parole.

The concept of parole spread to the United States. As early as 1822, volunteers from the Philadelphia-based Society for Alleviating the Miseries of Public Prisons began to help offenders once they were released from prison. In 1851, the society appointed two agents to work with inmates discharged from Pennsylvania penal institutions. Massachusetts appointed an agent in 1845 to help released inmates obtain jobs, clothing, and transportation.

In the 1870s, using a carefully weighted screening procedure, Zebulon Brockway selected rehabilitated offenders from Elmira Reformatory for early release under the supervision of citizen volunteers known as *guardians*. The guardians met with the parolees at least once a month and submitted written reports on their progress. The parole concept spread rapidly. Ohio created the first parole agency in 1884. By 1901, as many as 20 states had created some type of parole agency. By 1927, only three states (Florida, Mississippi, and Virginia) had not established some sort of parole release. Parole had become institutionalized as the primary method of release for prison inmates, and half of all inmates released in the United States were paroled.

Contemporary Correctional Institutions

The modern era has been a period of change and turmoil in the nation's correctional system. Three trends stand out. First, between 1960 and 1980, came the prisoners' rights movement. After many years of indifference (the so-called hands-off doctrine), state and federal courts ruled in case after case that institutionalized inmates had rights to freedom of religion and speech, medical care, procedural due process, and proper living conditions. Inmates won rights unheard of in the nineteenth and early twentieth centuries. Since 1980, however, an increasingly conservative judiciary has curtailed the growth of inmate rights.

Second, violence within the correctional system became a national concern. Well-publicized riots at New York's Attica Prison and the New Mexico State Penitentiary drew attention to the potential for death and destruction that lurks in every prison. Prison rapes and killings have become commonplace. The locus of control in many prisons has shifted from the correctional staff to violent inmate gangs. In reaction, some administrators have tried to improve conditions and provide innovative programs that give inmates a voice in running the institution. Another reaction has been to tighten discipline and build new super-maximum-security prisons to control the most dangerous offenders. Prison overcrowding has made attempts to improve conditions extremely difficult.

Third, the view that traditional correctional rehabilitation efforts have failed has prompted many penologists to reconsider the purpose of incarcerating criminals. Between 1960 and 1980, it was common for correctional administrators to cling to the **medical model**, which viewed inmates as sick people who were suffering from some social malady that prevented them from adjusting to society. It was assumed that correctional treatment could help cure them and enable them to live productive lives once they returned to the community.

Since the 1980s, as the nation moved toward a more conservative political outlook, prisons came to be viewed as places for control, incapacitation, and punishment, rather than as sites for rehabilitation and reform. What has developed is a dual correctional policy: keep as many nonviolent offenders out of the correctional system as possible by means of community-based programs; incarcerate dangerous, violent offenders for long periods of time.[28] These efforts have been compromised by a growing get-tough stance in judicial and legislative sentencing policy, accented by mandatory minimum sentences for gun crimes and drug trafficking.

The following sections review the most prominent types of correctional facilities in operation today.

medical model
A view of corrections holding that convicted offenders are victims of their environment who need care and treatment to transform them into valuable members of society.

CAREERS in criminal justice

CORRECTIONS COUNSELOR

DUTIES AND CHARACTERISTICS OF THE JOB

The responsibility of corrections counselors is to review the situation of individual offenders and determine the most effective method of rehabilitation. They create, enact, manage, and sometimes evaluate programs designed to improve the psychosocial functions of offenders. Corrections counselors also provide counseling and educational sessions, survey the needs of offenders, and prepare reports for court. Counselors may choose a field of specialization, such as substance abuse or juvenile rehabilitation. They most often work in an office setting. Counseling can be a stressful job, given the population being served, the often serious nature of inmate problems, and the pressure for immediate results.

JOB OUTLOOK

The employment of counselors is expected to grow at a faster than average rate in the near future. The expansion of the prison system means that opportunities for employment as a corrections counselor are good.

SALARY

The median annual salary for correctional officers is $39,000 and for correctional treatment specialists about $48,000; the highest 10 percent recently earned more than $80,000 per year. Higher wages tend to be found in urban areas, and those with graduate-level education are also more likely to have higher salaries and greater opportunities for advancement.

OPPORTUNITIES

Thanks to high rates of turnover within the field, prospects for employment are very good. A corrections counselor with the proper education and training has the potential to find employment readily and to be promoted to administrative and supervisory positions.

Jails

The nation's 3,200[29] jails are institutional facilities with five primary purposes:

- They detain accused offenders who cannot make or are not eligible for bail prior to trial.
- They hold convicted offenders awaiting sentence.
- They serve as the principal institution of secure confinement for offenders convicted of misdemeanors.
- They hold probationers and parolees picked up for violations and waiting for a hearing.
- They house felons when state prisons are overcrowded.

In addition to county jails, about 15,000 local jurisdictions maintain short-term police or municipal lockups that house offenders for no more than 48 hours before a bail hearing can be held; thereafter, detainees are kept in the county jail. In some jurisdictions, such as Massachusetts, a house of corrections holds convicted misdemeanants, and a county jail holds pretrial detainees.

 **Web App 13.1**

For more information about jails, visit http://www.americanjail.org/.

 L07 Explain the purposes of jails and understand the characteristic makeup of jail populations.

Jail Populations and Trends

The jail incarceration rate is now about 240 jail inmates per 100,000 U.S. residents, and about 730,000 jail inmates are behind bars at any one time.[30] Today about nine out of every ten jail inmates are adult males, and although whites make up more than 45 percent of the jail population, minority overrepresentation is still a significant problem: African Americans represent almost

In addition, many openings will be created by the need to replace large numbers of these workers expected to retire in the coming years. For these reasons, job opportunities should be excellent for those who qualify.

QUALIFICATIONS

Qualifications for higher-paid positions are more demanding. A corrections counselor's education and work experience should familiarize him or her with the criminal justice system and prepare him or her for determining how to reduce a client's chances of recidivism, as well as how to deal with unwilling clients. The ability to speak more than one language is also an advantage. Personality characteristics and skills such as the desire to help others and the ability to communicate well are important. Because of the settings and populations counselors work with, a counselor will need to pass a background check and gain security clearance of the appropriate level. Some states also require certification before a corrections counselor can work in that state.

EDUCATION AND TRAINING

Corrections counselors should have a bachelor's degree in a field such as social work, criminal justice, or psychology. Additional education at the master's level in these fields may be necessary to advance or to get certain positions. For some positions, clinical training can take the place of experience. Specialized skills such as expertise working with drug addiction or violent offenders can also lead to a higher-paying position. In addition to educational requirements, many entry-level jobs require some previous work experience, such as substance abuse counseling or corrections casework.

Source: Bureau of Labor Statistics, United States Department of Labor, *Correctional Treatment Specialists Occupational Outlook Handbook*, http://www .bls.gov/ooh/Community-and-Social-Service/Probation-officers-and- correctional-treatment-specialists.htm (accessed July 2014).

---

40 percent and Hispanics an additional 16 percent of all inmates; minority overrepresentation in the jail inmate population has remained stable for the past decade.

At one time many thousands of minor children were held in jails as runaways, truants, and so on. The number of juveniles held in adult jails has been in decline since 2000, a result of ongoing federal government initiatives to remove juveniles from adult facilities.[31] Nonetheless, about 5,400 minors are still being held in adult jails each day (down from a high of 7,600 in 2000). Some are runaways who are being detained in an adult jail because no juvenile facility is available, while others are being held simply because the local jurisdiction has not accepted the federal mandates.

FEMALE JAIL INMATES About 13 percent of jail inmates are women.[32] However, even though men make up 87 percent of the jail population, during the past two decades the percentage of adult females in jail increased at a faster pace than that of males. Female jail inmates face many challenges. Most come from significantly disadvantaged backgrounds. Many have experienced abuse and severe economic disadvantage, have high rates of lifetime trauma exposure, and suffer from current mental disorders and drug/alcohol problems.[33]

Given this background, it is often difficult for female inmates to make a successful reentry into society. Employment seems to be a key issue. Those who have worked recently before their incarceration are most likely to have other survival skills and assets. They are more likely to have a high school education, to have a skill, and to have a driver's license with access to a car.[34]

One problem faced by female inmates is forced separation from their children and families. A number of institutions have created programs to remedy this loss. Here, Harris County, Texas, inmate Gwendolyn Jackson and her son Jarell, 8, share a laugh together during a Christmas event for 15 female inmates in the Harris County Sheriff's Office Reentry Services Program. The inmates had presents donated by Navidad en el Barrio to give their children. The women are minimum risk inmates who have had good relationships with their children. The female inmates are also working with Reentry Services in setting goals for a successful transition back into the community in efforts to reduce recidivism. Children accompanied by adults can visit inmates on routine visitation days but without physical contact.

Jail Conditions

Jails are usually a low-priority item in the criminal justice system. Because they are often administered on a county level, jail services have not been sufficiently regulated nor has a unified national policy been developed to mandate what constitutes adequate jail conditions. Consequently, jails in some counties are physically deteriorated, holding dangerous and troubled people, many of whom suffer from emotional problems that remain untreated.[35]

Many inmates have been victims of prior physical and sexual abuse—more than 10 percent of male inmates and nearly 50 percent of female inmates. About two-thirds of all jail inmates report having a mental health problem, including more than 15 percent who display psychotic symptoms. That means more than 100,000 people in jail today are suffering from severe psychosis, and more than 400,000 have some form of mental disorder.[36] It is not surprising that some counties report that inmate suicides are their biggest concern.[37] Although the jail suicide rate has declined significantly, the percentage of jail inmates who take their own lives is higher than that of the general population.

Being warehoused in local jails does little to alleviate social and individual problems. For example, national surveys show that about 1.6 percent of inmates (12,100 nationwide) reported a coercive sexual incident involving another inmate, and 2.0 percent (15,200) reported an incident involving staff.[38] The survey also revealed that:

■ Inmate-on-inmate victimization occurred most often in the victim's cell (56 percent); staff-on-inmate victimization occurred in a closet, office, or other locked room (47 percent).[39]

■ An estimated 5.1 percent of female inmates, compared to 2.9 percent of male inmates, said they had experienced one or more incidents of sexual victimization.[40]

Jails are considered the revolving door of the justice system. Millions of people enter jail each year and millions are released, only to be rearrested and incarcerated again soon after returning to their communities.

New-Generation Jails

 Define the term *new-generation jail.*

To relieve overcrowding and improve effectiveness, a jail-building boom has been under way. Many of the new jails are using modern designs to improve effectiveness; these are referred to as *new-generation jails.*[41] Traditional jails are constructed on what is referred to as the linear/intermittent surveillance model. Jails designed this way are rectangular, with corridors leading to either single- or multiple-occupancy cells arranged at right angles to the corridor. Correctional officers must patrol to see into cells or housing areas, and when they are in a position to observe one cell, they cannot observe others; unobserved inmates are essentially unsupervised.

In contrast, new-generation jails allow for continuous observation of residents. There are two types: direct-supervision and indirect-supervision jails. Direct-supervision jails contain a cluster of cells surrounding a living area or "pod," which contains tables, chairs, and televisions. A correctional officer is stationed within the pod. The officer has visual observation of inmates and maintains the ability to relate to them on a personal level. Placing the officer in the pod increases the officer's awareness of the behaviors and needs of the inmates. This results in a safer environment for both staff and inmates. Because interaction between inmates is constantly and closely monitored, dissension can be quickly detected before it escalates. During the day, inmates stay in the open area (dayroom) and typically are not permitted to go into their rooms except with permission of the officer in charge.

The officer controls door locks to cells from the control panel. In case of trouble or if the officer leaves the station for an extended period of time, command of this panel can be switched to a panel at a remote location, known as central control. The officer usually wears a device that permits immediate communication with central control in case of trouble, and the area is also covered by a video camera monitored by an officer in the central control room.

Indirect-supervision jails use similar construction; however, the correctional officer's station is located inside a secure room. Microphones and speakers inside the living unit permit the officer to hear and communicate with inmates. Research shows that these kinds of institutions may help reduce postrelease offending in some situations.[42] However, some critics suggest new-generation jails have failed to live up to their promise because they lack important components, such as a normalized living environment, in their facilities.[43]

Prisons

There are about 1,800[44] secure public and private adult correctional facilities housing more than 1.5 million[45] state and federal prisoners. Usually, prisons are organized or classified on three levels—maximum, medium, and minimum security—and each has distinct characteristics.

Maximum-Security Prisons

Housing the most notorious criminals, and the subject of numerous films and stories, **maximum-security prisons** are probably the incarceration institutions most familiar to the public. Famous "max prisons" have included Sing Sing, Joliet, Attica, Walpole, and the most fearsome prison of all, the now-closed federal facility on Alcatraz Island known as the Rock.

A typical maximum-security facility is fortress-like, surrounded by stone walls with guard towers at strategic places. These walls may be 25 feet high, and sometimes inner and outer walls divide the prison into courtyards. Barbed wire or electrified fences are used to discourage escapes. High security, armed guards, and stone walls give the inmate the sense that the facility is impregnable and reassure the citizens outside that convicts will be completely incapacitated. Because they fear that violence may flare up at any moment, prison administrators have been quick to adopt the latest high-tech security measures. Today, prison administrators rely on technology to help them maintain security, a topic covered in the Criminal Justice and Technology feature.

Inmates live in interior, metal-barred cells that contain their own plumbing and sanitary facilities and are locked securely by either key or electronic device. Cells are organized in sections called blocks, and in large prisons a number of cell blocks make up a wing. During the day, the inmates engage in closely controlled activities: meals, workshops, education, and so on. Rule violators may be confined to their cells, and working and other shared recreational activities are viewed as privileges.

The byword of the maximum-security prison is "security." Correctional workers are made aware that each inmate may be a dangerous criminal or violent, and that as a result, the utmost security must be maintained. These

maximum-security prison
A correctional institution that houses dangerous felons and maintains strict security measures, high walls, and limited contact with the outside world.

criminal justice and TECHNOLOGY

INCREASING SECURITY/REDUCING ESCAPES

Technical experts have identified numerous areas of correctional management that can be aided by information technology (IT), including reception and commitment, sentence and time accounting, classification, caseload management, security, discipline, housing/bed management, medical, grievances, programs, scheduling, investigations/gang management, property, deposits into inmates' bank accounts, visitation, release and discharge, and community supervision. Because there are so many areas in which IT can be applied within correctional establishments, prison administrators have begun to take advantage of the potential offered by these technologies. How has IT been applied within prison walls? Following are a few examples of efforts that have been made to improve institutional security and reduce the chance of escapes.

GROUND-PENETRATING RADAR

Ground-penetrating radar (GPR) can locate tunnels that inmates use to escape. GPR works almost like an old-fashioned Geiger counter, but instead of detecting radiation, the system detects changes in ground composition, including voids such as those created by a tunnel.

HEARTBEAT MONITORING

Now it is possible to prevent escapes by monitoring inmates' heartbeats! The Advanced Vehicle Interrogation and Notification (AVIAN) System detects the presence of persons who try to escape by hiding in vehicles. Using data from seismic sensors that are placed on the vehicle, AVIAN reads the shock wave generated by the beating heart, which couples to any surface or object with which the body is in contact. It collects and analyzes the data almost immediately using advanced signal-processing algorithms to detect a person hiding in a vehicle, such as a large truck. The system works by accounting for all the frequencies of movement in the vehicle, such as the expansion and contraction of an engine or rain hitting the roof.

NONLETHAL ELECTRIFIED FENCES

Nonlethal electrified containment fences stop inmates from trying to escape by climbing prison security fences. If an inmate tries to climb or cut through the perimeter fence, he or she will receive a nonlethal jolt of electricity, which causes temporary immobilization. At the same time, the system alerts prison staff that an escape attempt has occurred and identifies its location.

L09 Classify the different types of federal and state penal institutions.

super-maximum-security prison

A form of a maximum-security prison, which uses high-level security measures to incapacitate the nation's most dangerous criminals. Most inmates are in lockdown 23 hours per day.

Web App 13.2

Read more about the supermax prison in Florence, Colorado, here: http://www.bop.gov/locations/institutions/flm/.

prisons are designed to eliminate hidden corners where people can congregate, and passages are constructed so that they can be easily blocked off to quell disturbances.

Super-Maximum-Security Prisons

Some states have constructed **super-maximum-security prisons** (supermax prisons) to house the most predatory criminals. These high-security institutions can be independent correctional centers or locked wings of existing prisons.[46] Some supermax prisons lock inmates in their cells 22 to 24 hours a day, never allowing them out unless they are shackled.[47] The supermax model is based on the assumption that prison disorder is primarily the result of a handful of disruptive, violent inmates and that if these few can be strictly controlled, the violence level in the entire correctional system can be reduced.

The 484-bed facility in Florence, Colorado, has the most sophisticated security measures in the United States, including 168 video cameras and 1,400 electronically controlled gates. Inside the cells, all furniture is unmovable; the desk, bed, and TV stand are made of cement. All potential weapons, including soap dishes, toilet seats, and toilet handles, have been removed. The cement walls are 5,000-pound quality, and steel bars crisscross every eight inches inside the walls. Cells are angled so that inmates can see neither each other nor the

TRANSMITTER WRISTBANDS

These wristbands broadcast a unique serial number via radio frequency every two seconds so that antennas throughout the prison can pick up the signals and pass the data via a local area network to a central monitoring station PC. The wristbands can sound an alert when a prisoner gets close to the perimeter fence or when an inmate doesn't return from a furlough on time; they can even tag gang members and notify guards when rivals come in contact with each other.

UNDER-VEHICLE SURVEILLANCE SYSTEM

An under-vehicle surveillance system uses a drive-over camera that records a video image of the license plate and the underside of any vehicle entering or leaving the secure perimeter of the prison. This system enables prison staff to check each vehicle for possible escape attempts and keeps a digital recording of every vehicle that enters or exits the prison.

RADIO FREQUENCY IDENTIFICATION (RFID) TECHNOLOGY

Corrections officials use radio frequency identification (RFID) technology to monitor and track jail inmates. RFID uses small transponders called tags to track movements. RFID tags can be attached to or incorporated into a variety of objects, such as wristbands. Each tag has an integrated circuit and a tiny antenna to handle radio signals and can be used with a network of sensors—called RFID readers—to track movements. For example, a few correctional institutions have used the systems to provide information on prisoners' movements and to alert staff if there is an unusual concentration of people in a certain area. Movement information can be stored in computers and could prove useful in investigations to determine who was present in a certain part of a building at a particular time.

CRITICAL THINKING

1. **Some elements of information technology intrude on the privacy of inmates. Should the need for security outweigh an inmate's right to privacy?**

2. **Should probationers and parolees be monitored with modern technology? Do they deserve more privacy than incarcerated inmates?**

Sources: Philip Bulman, "Using Technology to Make Prisons and Jails Safer," *NIJ Journal* 262 (March 2009), http://nij.gov/journals/262/pages/corrections-technology.aspx (accessed July 2014); John Ward, "Jump-Starting Projects to Automate Correctional Processes," *Corrections Today* 68 (2006): 82–83; Debbie Mahaffey, "Security and Technology: The Human Side," *Corrections Today* 66 (2004): 8; Frank Lu and Laurence Wolfe, "Automated Record Tracking (SMART) Application," *Corrections Today* 66 (2004): 78–81.

outside. This cuts down on communication and denies inmates a sense of location, to prevent escapes.

ARE THEY EFFECTIVE? Supermax prisons have received mixed reviews. Although they can achieve correctional benefits by enhancing security and quality of life, they also deprive inmates of basic human rights and eliminate any opportunity for rehabilitation.[48] Civil rights watchdog groups charge that these supermax prisons violate the United Nations standards for the treatment of inmates. They are typically located in rural areas, which makes staffing difficult in the professional areas of dentistry, medicine, and counseling. Senior officers prefer not to work in these institutions, so the most difficult inmates are often in the hands of the least experienced correctional officers. Although conditions vary from state to state, many supermax prisons subject inmates to nearly complete isolation and deprivation of sensory stimuli.[49]

PSYCHOLOGICAL DAMAGE? There is also the fear that the long hours of isolation inmates experience in a supermax environment may be associated with mental illness and psychological disturbances. Again, the evidence is mixed. Some research efforts show that supermax inmates seem to have a more difficult time readjusting upon release. A stay in a supermax prison inhibits reintegration into other prisons, communities, and families.[50] Some correctional experts such as Leena Kurki and Norval Morris believe that supermax prisons are likely to have extremely harmful effects, especially on those who suffer from preexisting mental illness and those with subnormal intelligence.[51] In contrast, a recent study using 14 tests to measure psychological states such as anxiety, depression, and psychosis in a sample of inmates housed in supermax-like conditions showed initial *improvements* in psychological well-being. The testing showed that 20 percent of the study sample improved and 7 percent worsened during the study period.[52]

Medium-Security Prisons

medium-security prison
A less secure institution that houses nonviolent offenders and provides more opportunities for contact with the outside world.

Although **medium-security prisons** are similar in appearance to maximum-security prisons, the security is not so tight or the atmosphere so tense. Medium-security prisons are also surrounded by walls, but there may be fewer guard towers or other security precautions; visitations with personal contact may be allowed. Although most prisoners are housed in cells, individual honor rooms in medium-security prisons are used to reward those who make exemplary rehabilitation efforts. Finally, medium-security prisons promote greater treatment efforts, and the relaxed atmosphere allows freedom of movement for rehabilitation workers and other therapeutic personnel.

Minimum-Security Prisons

minimum-security prison
The least secure correctional institution, which houses white-collar and nonviolent offenders, maintains few security measures, and has liberal furlough and visitation policies.

Operating without armed guards or perimeter walls, **minimum-security prisons** usually house the most trustworthy and least violent offenders; white-collar criminals may be their most common occupants. Inmates are allowed a great deal of personal freedom. Instead of being marched to activities by guards, they are summoned by bells or loudspeaker announcements, and they assemble on their own. Work furloughs and educational releases are encouraged, and vocational training is of the highest level. Dress codes are lax, and inmates are allowed to grow beards or mustaches or demonstrate other individual characteristics.

Minimum-security facilities may have dormitories or small private rooms for inmates. Prisoners are allowed to own personal possessions that might be deemed dangerous in a maximum-security prison, such as radios. Minimum-security prisons have been criticized for being like "country clubs"; at one time some federal facilities even had tennis courts and pools (they are derisively called "Club Fed"). Yet they remain prisons, and the isolation and loneliness of prison life deeply affect the inmates.

Alternative Correctional Institutions

In addition to prisons and jails, a number of other correctional institutions are operating within the United States. Some have been in use for quite a while, whereas others have been developed more recently as part of innovative or experimental programs.

Prison Farms and Camps

Prison farms and camps are used to detain offenders. These types of facilities are found primarily in the South and the West and have been in operation since the nineteenth century. Today, numerous farms, forest camps, road camps, and similar facilities (vocational training centers, ranches, and so on) exist in the nation. Prisoners on farms produce dairy products, grain, and vegetable crops that are used in the state correctional system and other governmental facilities, such as hospitals and schools. Forestry camp inmates maintain state parks, fight forest fires, and do reforestation work. Ranches, primarily a western phenomenon, employ inmates in cattle raising and horse breeding, among other activities. Road gangs repair roads and state highways.

Inmate Damion Sanders looks for eggs in one of the inmate work farm's chicken houses in Ocala, Florida. The inmate work farm and citrus groves supply the jail with fresh fruit, vegetables, eggs, and some meat, at a much lower cost than purchasing it.

Alan Youngblood/Ocala Star-Banner/Landov

Shock Incarceration in Boot Camps

Another correctional innovation that gained popularity in the 1980s and 1990s, **boot camp** involves youthful, first-time offenders in military discipline and physical training. The concept is that short periods (90 to 180 days) of high-intensity exercise and work will "shock" the inmate into going straight. Tough physical training is designed to promote responsibility and improve decision-making skills, build self-confidence, and teach socialization skills. Inmates are treated with rough intensity by drillmasters who may call them names and punish the entire group for the failure of one member.[53]

Some programs also include educational and training components, counseling sessions, and treatment for special-needs populations, whereas others devote little or no time to therapeutic activities. Some receive program participants directly from court sentencing, whereas others choose potential candidates from the general inmate population. Some allow voluntary participation and others voluntary termination.[54]

Some experts viewed the boot camp as a low-cost correctional panacea, and a number of states, including Georgia, South Carolina, and New York, made extensive use of **shock incarceration** facilities. However, empirical research (the majority of it contributed by Doris Layton MacKenzie, a criminologist who has been involved in many evaluations of boot camp) yielded disappointing results.[55] Because of these sketchy results, the future of the boot camp approach is clouded at best and many state programs have been canceled; in 2005, the federal government decided to close its boot camp program.[56]

Community Correctional Facilities

One goal of correctional treatment is to help reintegrate the offender into society. Placing offenders in a prison makes them more likely to adopt an inmate lifestyle than to reassimilate conventional social norms. As a result, the **community treatment** concept began to take off in the 1960s. State and federal correctional systems created community-based correctional models as an alternative to closed institutions. Many are **halfway houses** to which inmates are transferred just before their release into the community. These facilities are designed to bridge the gap between institutional living and the community. However, commitment

boot camp
A short-term, militaristic correction facility in which inmates undergo intensive physical conditioning and discipline.

shock incarceration
A short-term correctional program based on a boot camp approach that makes use of a military-like regime of high-intensity physical training.

community treatment
The attempt by correctional agencies to maintain convicted offenders in the community rather than in a secure facility; it includes probation, parole, and residential programs.

halfway house
A community-based correctional facility that houses inmates before their outright release so that they can become gradually acclimated to conventional society.

AP Images/*The Maryland Gazette*, Andy Carruthers

Inside the Ordnance Road Correctional Center in Glen Burnie, Maryland, 19-year-old inmate Kenneth Lee puts sheets on his plastic covered mattress. He serves his prison sentence one weekend at a time, living in a dormitory-style room housing a dozen men. Alternative correctional institutions have sprung up around the nation as a response to overcrowding and high recidivism rates.

to a community correctional center may also be used as an intermediate sanction and sole mode of treatment. An offender may be assigned to a community treatment center operated by the state department of corrections or to probation. Alternatively, the corrections department can contract with a private community center. Community corrections programs often offer specialized treatment or focus on specific groups of offenders, helping residents use the experience to cushion the shock of reentering society. This practice is common in the treatment of drug abusers and other nonviolent offenders whose special needs can be met in a self-contained community setting that specializes in specific types of treatment.

Private Prisons

On January 6, 1986, the U.S. Corrections Corporation opened the first private state prison in Marion, Kentucky—a 300-bed minimum-security facility for inmates who are within three years of parole. Today, about 415 correctional facilities are being run by private firms as business enterprises housing almost 140,000 inmates. In all, about 16 percent of federal prisoners and nearly 9 percent of state prisoners are housed in private facilities.[57] Private prisons play an important correctional role in the United States, Australia, and the United Kingdom.[58]

One industry leader, Corrections Corporation of America (CCA), houses more than 80,000 inmates in more than 60 facilities, 44 of which are company-owned, with a total bed capacity of more than 90,000.[59] CCA currently partners with all three federal corrections agencies (the Federal Bureau of Prisons, the U.S. Marshals Service, and Immigration and Customs Enforcement), nearly half of all states, and more than a dozen local municipalities.[60]

A competitor, the GEO Group, employs 18,000 people and is responsible for the management and/or ownership of about 100 correctional, detention, and residential treatment facilities in Australia, New Zealand, and South Africa as well as in the United States.[61] GEO correctional facilities house around 70,000 inmates. GEO runs the Arizona State Prison at Florence West, an institution specifically designed for return-to-custody (RTC) inmates and those convicted of driving under the influence (DUI). The GEO Group offers employment skills, parenting classes, substance abuse education and counseling, nutrition/diet education, GED classes, case management, individual and group counseling, stress management, facility work programs, job placement, and prison works/prison labor.[62]

In the abstract, a private correctional enterprise may be an attractive alternative to a costly correctional system, but so far there is little sound evidence that they are cheaper to run and/or produce better results.[63] Private and state institutions seem to cost about the same to operate and produce the same results in terms of security issues and recidivism.[64] While the jury is still out on their effectiveness, some state governments still view private prisons as a low-cost

Web App 13.3

For more information about the Corrections Corporation of America (CCA), visit http://cca.com/.

alternative to costly state-run correctional systems whose employees are entitled to lucrative state pension plans and retirement benefits. In 2012, New Hampshire became the first state to solicit bids to turn their entire correctional system over to private enterprise.[65]

LO10 Discuss prison population trends.

Inmate Populations

The backgrounds and characteristics of inmates reflect arrest data and are similar to those of the jail population: disproportionately young, male, minority, and poor.[66] Compared to the estimated numbers of black, white, and Hispanic males in the U.S. resident population, black males were six times as likely, and Hispanic males twice as likely, as white males to be held in custody. Women still make up less than 10 percent of the total prison population.

Many inmates suffer from multiple social problems. Inmates are undereducated, are underemployed, and come from abusive homes. A disproportionate number have experienced homelessness (living on the street or in a homeless shelter) and associated social problems, including mental illness, substance abuse, and unemployment.[67] Only about one-third of current inmates have a high school diploma, compared with more than 80 percent of the general population.[68] It is not surprising, then, that surveys show that inmates suffer from serious psychological and emotional problems, including psychosis and major depression.[69] These problems have helped keep recidivism rates high, and correctional officials have been searching for answers to this ongoing problem.

Population Trends

There are now indications that after decades of growth the prison population may be "maxing out." The crime rate drop coupled with alternatives to incarceration have cut and/or stabilized the prison population. Convicted criminals are receiving shorter prison sentences than five years ago. In addition, some distinguished crime policy experts have suggested that incarceration is not an effective crime control method. Instead it would be more cost effective to shift from a reliance on punishment-based policies to the more effective use of police to make the risks of crime clearer and the consequences of criminal activity more certain.[70] This is especially true in the case of elderly inmates, who can be very expensive to supervise yet low risk in many cases. The accompanying Analyzing Criminal Justice Issues box touches on this subject further.

As a result of these trends and policy shifts, the growth in the prison population has finally stabilized. With virtually every state facing huge deficits, many have begun cutting prison budgets and closing institutions, especially prison camps and minimum-security prisons, to help balance the budget. In 2011, at least 13 states either closed prisons or are considering doing so. Michigan has led the nation in closing 21 facilities, including prison camps, as a result of parole and sentencing reforms. Overall, the state has reduced capacity by over 12,000 beds for a cost savings of $339 million. New Jersey and Kansas are other states that have also closed prisons in recent years; Maryland further reduced prison capacity when it closed the Maryland House of Corrections in 2007 and transferred 850 prisoners to other prisons.[71] California's

Web App 13.4

For data on U.S. prisoner population counts, see http://www.bjs.gov/index .cfm?ty=tp&tid=131.

YOUR OPINION: What is your preferred punishment for a first-time offender convicted of drug possession? Incarceration? Home confinement? A fine? Probation? Something else?

PUBLIC OPINION:

INCARCERATION:	20.7%
HOME CONFINEMENT:	16.3%
FINE:	28.2%
SUPERVISION:	36.4%
OTHER:	4.1%

NOTE: Percentages do not sum to 100% because poll respondents could make more than one choice.

REALITY: People's perceptions of appropriate punishment vary, of course, by the type of offense. Had we used assault instead of drug possession, prison would have been the favored punishment almost 40 percent of the time. The same is true for the *amount* of drugs our hypothetical individual had in his/her possession; had the individual been convicted of possession a huge quantity of illegal drugs, people would support harsher punishment, and the courts would likely impose a harsh sentence. Where does reality lie? One study found that 23 percent of first-time offenders convicted of a nonviolent felony received a prison sentence, which is not out of line with the opinions expressed here. However, nonviolent felonies can include much more than drug offenses (e.g., burglary), and misdemeanor convictions would carry either jail or probation terms, so public opinion is probably harsher than actual punishment.

DISCUSSION: What explains discrepancies between survey respondents' perceptions of the ideal punishment versus the reality of punishment?

Source: Brian A. Reaves, *Felony Defendants in Large Urban Counties, 2009* (Washington, DC: Bureau of Justice Statistics, 2013), p. 26.

analyzing criminal justice ISSUES

ELDERLY INMATES

The population of elderly prisoners in the United States has increased by more than 1,400 percent since 1981. Three decades ago, American prisons housed fewer than 9,000 prisoners age 55 and older; today, that number stands at 125,000. By 2040, the elderly prisoner population may top 400,000.

The aging of the prison population has come about from longer sentences resulting from the get-tough-on-crime measures that impose truth-in-sentencing, mandatory sentences, and three-strikes laws, and an increasing number of older people convicted of sex crimes and murder.

There are different adjustment rates for elderly prisoners. The longer the amount of time remaining to be served, the harder it usually is for the elderly person to deal with confinement. Background factors, such as level of education and marital status, can also affect the adjustment of the elderly. Some inmates, especially those imprisoned early in life, are more institutionally dependent than others. Some have higher morale and are more involved in programs and prison life than others. There is the problem that in many prisons there is little programming or specialized treatment geared for elderly inmates.

The elderly prisoner is vulnerable to victimization and requires special attention when it comes to medical treatment, housing, nutrition, and institutional activities. The care of the elderly is extremely expensive. For example, the average cost of housing an inmate over 60 is $70,000 a year, which is about three times the average cost for other prisoners. Inmates over 50 are also more likely to have health and mental health problems than noninstitutionalized Americans because they often come from poor backgrounds, have a greater likelihood of drug and alcohol abuse, and have more restricted access to health care.

realignment initiative, discussed at the outset of this chapter, is also consistent with this belt-tightening approach.

Budget cutbacks may halt the expansion of prison construction and cause the housing of ever more prisoners in already crowded prison facilities. Some

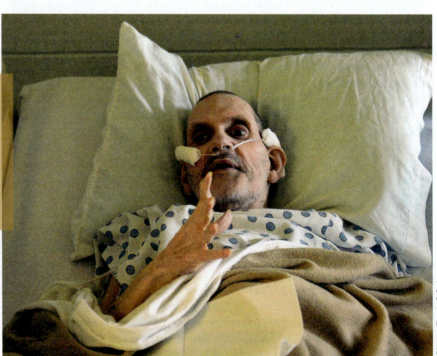

Patrick O'Hara, a patient in the Kentucky State Reformatory's medical unit, speaks with staff members. It costs the state $3.3 million a year to care for 50 elderly inmates who can't take care of themselves, a burden the state would like to shift to the federal government.

AP Images/Timothy D. Easley

Some elderly prisoners find prison physically difficult to manage. One study of 120 female prisoners aged 55 or older in a California prison found that 69 percent of the women reported that at least one prison activity of daily living was very difficult to perform. These women also had higher rates of hypertension, asthma or other lung disease, and arthritis. In another study, Lauren Glaze and Doris James found that nearly 40 percent of state inmates 55 and older have a recent history of mental health problems or disorders.

CRITICAL THINKING

Older prisoners need more orderly conditions, safety precautions, emotional feedback, and familial support than younger prisoners. They are particularly uncomfortable in crowded conditions, tend to prefer small groups, and want time alone. Should they be housed in traditional prisons, no matter what they have done in the past? Would community-based institutions be a more suitable alternative?

Sources: American Civil Liberties Uniton, *At America's Expense: The Mass Incarceration of the Elderly*, https://www.aclu.org/criminal-law-reform/americas-expense-mass-incarceration-elderly (accessed July 2014); "Elderly Inmates Swell Prisons, Driving Up Health Care Costs," *Nation*, http://www.usatoday.com/news/nation/2004-02-28-elderly-inmates_x.htm (accessed July 2014); Anthony A. Sterns and Greta Lax, "The Growing Wave of Older Prisoners: A National Survey of Older Prisoner Health, Mental Health and Programming," *Corrections Today* 70 (2008): 70–76; B. A. Williams, M. F. Stern, J. Mellow, M. Safer, and R. B. Greifinger, "Aging in Correctional Custody: Setting a Policy Agenda for Older Prisoner Health Care," *American of Journal Public Health* 102 (2012): 1475–1481; Lauren E. Glaze and Doris J. James, *Mental Health Problems of Prison and Jail Inmates* (Washington, DC: Bureau of Justice Statistics, 2006); Rebecca S. Allen, Laura Lee Phillips, Lucinda Lee Roff, Ronald Cavanaugh, and Laura Day, "Religiousness/Spirituality and Mental Health Among Older Male Inmates," *Gerontologist* 46 (2008): 692–697; Steven J. Caverley, "Older Mentally Ill Inmates: A Descriptive Study," *Journal of Correctional Health Care* 12 (2006): 1–7.

rural communities that welcomed prison construction as a means of juicing up the economy and creating jobs may now be regretting their decision. Although prison construction may produce a short-term gain, in the long run it may actually impede economic development and retard job growth.[72] In the final analysis, change in the correctional population may depend on the faith that judges and legislators place in incarceration as a crime control policy. As long as policy makers believe that incarcerating predatory criminals can bring down crime rates, the likelihood of a significant decrease in the institutional population seems remote. If there is little evidence that this costly system does lower crime rates, then less costly and equally effective alternatives may be sought.

ETHICAL CHALLENGES in Criminal Justice

A WRITING ASSIGNMENT

The governor of your state is running for reelection and wants to build a supermax prison to show her willingness to crack down on crime. She also wants to increase the use of mandatory sentences for drug and violent offenders and to put the worst ones in the supermax prison. She has asked you, as a criminal justice expert, to write a paper outlining the pros and cons (no pun intended) of this correctional policy and to come with a plan. Even if supermax prisons do work, are there ethical considerations that cloud their effectiveness? In your essay, touch upon these issues—for example, should youthful offenders or nonviolent criminals be held in a supermax prison? What other ethical questions need to be answered before such a facility is built?

Summary

LO1

Identify the various components of the correctional institution system.

- The contemporary correctional system has branches in the federal, state, and county levels of government.

- Felons may be placed in state or federal penitentiaries (prisons), which are usually isolated, high-security structures. Misdemeanants are housed in county jails, sometimes called reformatories or houses of correction.

- Other types of correctional institutions include ranches and farms for adult offenders and community correctional settings, such as halfway houses, for inmates who are about to return to society.

LO2

Discuss some of the most significant problems facing the correctional system.

- Many former inmates recidivate soon after reentering society.

- Correctional overcrowding is still a problem and the United States has a far higher incarceration rate than other industrial societies.

- Some administrators believe inmates are being coddled and suggest a no-frills approach.

LO3

Articulate how the first penal institutions developed in England.

- Penal institutions were constructed in England during the tenth century to hold pretrial detainees and those waiting for their sentence to be carried out.

- During the twelfth century, county jails were built to hold thieves and vagrants.

- In 1557, the workhouse in Bridewell was built to hold people convicted of relatively minor offenses and those awaiting execution.

- From 1776 to 1785, a growing inmate population forced the English to house prisoners on hulks—abandoned ships anchored in harbors.

LO4

Explain how William Penn and the Quakers revolutionized corrections in Pennsylvania.

- The "modern" American correctional system had its origins in Pennsylvania under the leadership of William Penn.

- Philadelphia's Walnut Street Jail was used to house convicted felons, except those sentenced to death. The Quakers' political influence resulted in limiting the use of the death penalty to cases involving treason, murder, rape, and arson.

- They called for reform of the institutional system so that incarceration could serve as a suitable alternative to physical punishment.

LO5

Compare the early New York and Pennsylvania prison models.

- In 1816, Auburn Prison design was referred to as the congregate system since most prisoners ate and worked in groups.

- Pennsylvania established a prison that placed each inmate in a single cell for the duration of his sentence. Each cell was intended as a miniature prison that would prevent the inmates from contaminating one another.

LO6

Discuss the development of penal reform.

- The National Congress of Penitentiary and Reformatory Discipline, held in Cincinnati in 1870, heralded a new era of prison reform.

- Prison reform groups proposed better treatment for inmates, an end to harsh corporal punishment, the creation of meaningful prison industries, and educational programs.

- Another important trend was the development of specialized prisons designed to treat particular types of offenders.

LO7

Explain the purposes of jails and understand the characteristic makeup of jail populations.

- Jails are used to detain accused offenders who cannot make or are not eligible for bail prior to trial; they hold convicted offenders awaiting sentence; they serve as the principal institution of secure confinement for offenders convicted of misdemeanors.

- Almost nine out of every ten jail inmates are adult males, but the number of adult females in jail has been increasing faster than the number of males.

- Characteristics of jail inmates tend to reflect arrest data: men, the poor, and racial and ethnic minorities are overrepresented.

LO8 **Define the term *new-generation jail*.**

- New-generation jails allow for continuous observation of residents.
- Correctional officers have closer contact with inmates.
- Research shows that such jails may help reduce postrelease offending and recidivism.

LO9 **Classify the different types of federal and state penal institutions.**

- Maximum-security prisons, which house the most notorious criminals, are fortress-like, surrounded by stone walls with guard towers at strategic places.
- Medium-security prisons are similar in appearance to maximum-security prisons, but security is not quite so tight, and the atmosphere is less tense.
- Operating without armed guards or perimeter walls, minimum-security prisons usually house the most trustworthy and least violent offenders.

LO10 **Discuss prison population trends.**

- The vast correctional system, with more than 1,800 institutions, now contains about 1.6 million prison inmates.
- The inmate population has finally begun to stabilize after years of rapid expansion.
- One reason may be changing correctional policies that feature use of community treatment.

Key Terms

jail, 502
prison, 502
hulk, 503
Walnut Street Jail, 504
penitentiary house, 504
Pennsylvania system, 504
tier system, 505
congregate system, 505

Auburn system, 505
contract system, 506
convict-lease system, 506
public account system, 506
medical model, 509
maximum-security prison, 513
super-maximum-security prison, 514
medium-security prison, 516

minimum-security prison, 516
boot camp, 517
shock incarceration, 517
community treatment, 517
halfway house, 517

Critical Thinking Questions

1. Would you want a community correctional center to be built in your neighborhood? Why or why not?
2. Should pretrial detainees and convicted offenders be kept in the same institution? Explain.
3. Trace the history of corrections and compare changes in correctional policy to social change. Is there a correlation?
4. Should private companies be allowed to run correctional institutions? Why or why not?
5. What are the drawbacks of shock incarceration?

Notes

1. The judges' decision is available here: http://cdn.ca9.uscourts .gov/datastore/general/2009/08/04/Opinion%20&%20Order%20 FINAL.pdf (accessed July 2014).
2. *Brown v. Plata*, 563 U.S. ___ (2011)
3. AB 109 Signing Message, http://gov.ca.gov/docs/AB_109_Signing_ Message.pdf (accessed July 2014).
4. California Department of Corrections and Rehabilitation, *Realignment Report: An Examination of Offenders Released from State Prison in the First Year of Public Safety Realignment* (Sacramento: California Department of Corrections and Rehabilitation, 2013), p. i.

5. Magnus Lofstrom, Joan Petersilia, and Steven Raphael, *Evaluating the Effects of California's Corrections Realignment on Public Safety* (San Francisco: Public Policy Institute of California, 2012), http://www.ppic.org/content/pubs/report/R_812MLR.pdf (accessed July 2014).
6. Francis Cullen, "The Twelve People Who Saved Rehabilitation: How the Science of Criminology Made a Difference," *Criminology* 43 (2005): 1–42.
7. See David Fogel, *We Are the Living Proof*, 2nd ed. (Cincinnati: Anderson, 1978); Andrew von Hirsch, *Doing Justice: The Choice of Punishments* (New York: Hill and Wang, 1976); R. G. Singer,

Just Deserts—Sentencing Based on Equality and Desert (Cambridge, MA: Ballinger, 1979). The most widely cited source on the failure of rehabilitation is Robert Martinson; see Douglas Lipton, Robert Martinson, and Judith Wilks, *The Effectiveness of Correctional Treatment: A Survey of Treatment Evaluation Studies* (New York: Praeger, 1975).

8. Thomas Stucky, Karen Heimer, and Joseph Lang, "Partisan Politics, Electoral Competition, and Imprisonment: An Analysis of States over Time," *Criminology* 43 (2005): 211–247.

9. National Academy of Science, "U.S. Should Significantly Reduce Rate of Incarceration; Unprecedented Rise in Prison Population 'Not Serving the Country Well,' Says New Report," http://www8 .nationalacademies.org/onpinews/newsitem.aspx?RecordID=18613 (accessed July 2014).

10. Paul Schupp and Craig Rivera, "Identifying Imprisonment Patterns and Their Relation to Crime Among New York Counties 1990–2000," *Criminal Justice Policy Review* 21 (2010): 50–75.

11. Among the most helpful sources in developing this section were Mark Colvin, *Penitentiaries, Reformatories, and Chain Gangs* (New York: St. Martin's, 1997); David Duffee, *Corrections: Practice and Policy* (New York: Random House, 1989); Harry Allen and Clifford Simonsen, *Correction in America*, 5th ed. (New York: Macmillan, 1989); Benedict Alper, *Prisons Inside-Out* (Cambridge, MA: Ballinger, 1974); Harry Elmer Barnes, *The Story of Punishment*, 2nd ed. (Montclair, NJ: Patterson-Smith, 1972); Gustave de Beaumont and Alexis de Tocqueville, *On the Penitentiary System in the United States and Its Applications in France* (Carbondale: Southern Illinois University Press, 1964); Orlando Lewis, *The Development of American Prisons and Prison Customs, 1776–1845* (Montclair, NJ: Patterson-Smith, 1967); Leonard Orland, ed., *Justice, Punishment, and Treatment* (New York: Free Press, 1973); J. Goebel, *Felony and Misdemeanor* (Philadelphia: University of Pennsylvania Press, 1976); Georg Rusche and Otto Kircheimer, *Punishment and Social Structure* (New York: Russell and Russell, 1939); Samuel Walker, *Popular Justice* (New York: Oxford University Press, 1980); Graeme Newman, *The Punishment Response* (Philadelphia: J. B. Lippincott, 1978); David Rothman, *Conscience and Convenience* (Boston: Little, Brown, 1980).

12. F. Pollock and F. Maitland, *History of English Law* (London: Cambridge University Press, 1952).

13. Margaret Wilson, *The Crime of Punishment, Life and Letters Series*, no. 64 (London: Jonathan Cape, 1934), p. 186.

14. John Howard, *The State of Prisons*, 4th ed. (1792; reprint, Montclair, NJ: Patterson-Smith, 1973).

15. Lewis, *The Development of American Prisons and Prison Customs*, p. 17.

16. Pennsylvania Correctional Industries, "The Pioneer in United States Prison Labor," http://www.pci.state.pa.us/portal/server.pt/ community/history_of_pci/17812 (accessed July 2014).

17. Walker, *Popular Justice*, p. 70.

18. Ibid., p. 71.

19. Beverly Smith, "Military Training at New York's Elmira Reformatory, 1880–1920," *Federal Probation* 52 (1988): 33–41.

20. Ibid.

21. See Z. R. Brockway, "The Ideal of a True Prison System for a State," in *Transactions of the National Congress on Penitentiary and Reformatory Discipline* (reprint, Washington, DC: American Correctional Association, 1970), pp. 38–65.

22. This section leans heavily on Rothman, *Conscience and Convenience*.

23. Ibid., p. 23.

24. Ibid., p. 133.

25. 18 U.S.C. 1761.

26. Barbara Auerbach, George Sexton, Franklin Farrow, and Robert Lawson, *Work in American Prisons: The Private Sector Gets Involved* (Washington, DC: National Institute of Justice, 1988), p. 72.

27. This section relies heavily on William Parker, *Parole: Origins, Development, Current Practices, and Statutes* (College Park, MD: American Correctional Association, 1972); Samuel Walker, *Popular Justice* (New York: Oxford University Press, 1980).

28. See, generally, Jameson Doig, *Criminal Corrections: Ideals and Realities* (Lexington, MA: Lexington Books, 1983).

29. James Stephan and Georgette Walsh, *Census of Jail Facilities, 2006* (Washington, DC: Bureau of Justice Statistics, 2011).

30. Todd S. Minton, *Jail Inmates at Midyear 2012* (Washington, DC: Bureau of Justice Statistics, 2013).

31. Ibid.

32. Ibid.

33. Bonnie Green, Jeanne Miranda, Anahita Daroowalla, and Juned Siddique, "Trauma Exposure, Mental Health Functioning, and Program Needs of Women in Jail," *Crime and Delinquency* 51 (2005): 133–151.

34. Sonia Alemagno and Jill Dickie, "Employment Issues of Women in Jail," *Journal of Employment Counseling* 42 (2005): 67–74.

35. Kevin Krause, "Inspectors Fault Medical Care at Dallas County Jail," WFAA.com, August 15, 2009, http://www.wfaa.com/news/ local/64542207.html (accessed July 2014).

36. Doris James and Lauren Glaze, *Mental Health Problems of Prison and Jail Inmates* (Washington, DC: Bureau of Justice Statistics, 2006).

37. NBC5.com, Chicago, "Suicides Top List of Lake County Jail's Problems, Federal Report: Inmates Killing Themselves at Alarming Rate," May 20, 2007.

38. Allen Beck and Paige Harrison, *Sexual Victimization in Local Jails Reported by Inmates, 2007* (Washington, DC: Bureau of Justice Statistics, 2008).

39. Ibid.

40. Ibid.

41. Brandon Applegate, Ray Surette, and Bernard McCarthy, "Detention and Desistance from Crime: Evaluating the Influence of a New Generation of Jail on Recidivism," *Journal of Criminal Justice* 27 (1999): 539–548.

42. James Williams, Daniel Rodeheaver, and Denise Huggins, "A Comparative Evaluation of a New Generation Jail," *American Journal of Criminal Justice* 23 (1999): 223–246.

43. Christine Tartaro, "Watered Down: Partial Implementation of the New Generation Jail Philosophy," *Prison Journal* 86 (2006): 284–300.

44. James J. Stephan, *Census of State and Federal Correctional Facilities, 2005* (Washington, DC: Bureau of Justice Statistics, 2008).

45. Lauren E. Glaze and Erinn J. Herberman, *Correctional Populations in the United States, 2012* (Washington, DC: Bureau of Justice Statistics, 2013).

46. Human Rights Watch, *Prison Conditions in the United States*, http://www.hrw.org/wr2k2/prisons.html (accessed July 2014).

47. "Suit Alleges Violations in California's 'Super-Max' Prison," *Criminal Justice Newsletter*, September 1, 1993, p. 2.

48. Jody Sundt, Thomas Castellano, and Chad Briggs, "The Sociopolitical Context of Prison Violence and Its Control: A Case Study of Supermax and Its Effect in Illinois," *Prison Journal* 88 (2008): 94–122.

49. Daniel Mears and Jamie Watson, "Towards a Fair and Balanced Assessment of Supermax Prisons," *Justice Quarterly* 23 (2006): 232–270.

50. Daniel Mears, "An Assessment of Supermax Prisons Using an Evaluation Research Framework," *Prison Journal* 88 (2008): 43–68; Daniel Mears and Jennifer Castro, "Wardens' Views on the

Wisdom of Supermax Prisons," *Crime and Delinquency* 52 (2006): 398–431; Mears and Watson, "Towards a Fair and Balanced Assessment of Supermax Prisons."

51. Leena Kurki and Norval Morris, "The Purpose, Practices, and Problems of Supermax Prisons," in *Crime and Justice: An Annual Edition*, ed. Michael Tonry (Chicago: University of Chicago Press, 2001), pp. 385–422.

52. Philip Bulman, Marie Garcia, and Jolene Hernon, "Study Raises Questions About Psychological Effects of Solitary Confinement" *National Institute of Justice*, http://www.nij.gov/nij/journals/269/solitary-confinement.htm (accessed July 2014).

53. James Anderson, Laronistine Dyson, and Jerald Burns, *Boot Camps: An Intermediate Sanction* (Lanham, MD: University Press of America, 1999), pp. 1–17.

54. Ibid., pp. 328–329.

55. Doris Layton MacKenzie and James Shaw, "The Impact of Shock Incarceration on Technical Violations and New Criminal Activities," *Justice Quarterly* 10 (1993): 463–487.

56. Vanessa St. Gerard, "Federal Prisons to Eliminate Boot Camps," *Corrections Today* 67 (2005): 13–16.

57. E. Ann Carson and Daniela Golinelli, *Prisoners in 2012: Trends in Admissions and Releases, 1991–2012* (Washington, DC: Bureau of Justice Statistics, 2013).

58. Richard Harding, "Private Prisons," in *Crime and Justice: An Annual Edition*, ed. Michael Tonry (Chicago: University of Chicago Press, 2001), pp. 265–347.

59. For details, see http://cca.com/locations (accessed July 2014).

60. Corrections Corporation of America, http://cca.com/about-cca (accessed July 2014).

61. The GEO Group, Inc., *2012 Annual Report*, http://www.geogroup.com/documents/GEO_2012_Annual_Report.pdf (accessed July 2014).

62. The GEO Group, Inc., http://www.geogroup.com/ (accessed July 2014).

63. William Bales, Laura Bedard, Susan Quinn, David Ensley, and Glen Holley, "Recidivism of Public and Private State Prison Inmates in Florida," *Criminology and Public Policy* 4 (2005): 57–82; Lonn Lanza-Kaduce, Karen Parker, and Charles Thomas, "A Comparative Recidivism Analysis of Releases from Private and Public Prisons," *Crime and Delinquency* 45 (1999): 28–47.

64. Gerry Gaes, "Cost, Performance Studies Look at Prison Privatization," *NIJ Journal* 259 (2008), http://www.nij.gov/journals/259/pages/prison-privatization.aspx (accessed July 2014).

65. Bob Sanders "Proposal Under Review Would Put All New Hampshire Prisoners in Private, For-Profit Facilities—The First State to Do So," *New Hampshire Business Review* April 6, 2012, http://www.nhbr.com/April-6-2012/Proposal-under-review-would-put-all-New-Hampshire-prisoners-in-private-for-profit-facilities-the-first-state-to-do-so/ (accessed July 2014).

66. For details, see Carson and Golinelli, *Prisoners in 2012: Trends in Admissions and Releases, 1991–2012.*

67. Greg Greenberg and Robert Rosenheck, "Homelessness in the State and Federal Prison Population," *Criminal Behaviour and Mental Health* 18 (2008): 88–103.

68. Caroline Wolf Harlow, *Education and Correctional Populations* (Washington, DC: Bureau of Justice Statistics, 2003).

69. Seena Fazel and John Danesh, "Serious Mental Disorder in 23,000 Prisoners: A Systematic Review of Sixty-Two Surveys," *Lancet* 359 (2002): 545–561.

70. Steven N. Durlauf and Daniel S. Nagin, "'Imprisonment and Crime: Can Both Be Reduced," *Criminology and Public Policy* 10 (2011), pp. 13–54.

71. The Sentencing Project, "On the Chopping Block: State Prison Closings," 2011 report, Washington, DC, p. 1.

72. Gregory Hooks, Clayton Mosher, Shaun Genter, Thomas Rotolo, and Linda Lobao, "Revisiting the Impact of Prison Building on Job Growth: Education, Incarceration, and County-Level Employment, 1976–2004," *Social Science Quarterly* 91 (2010): 228–244.

CHAPTER 14

Prison Life: Living in and Leaving Prison

Learning Objectives

 LO1 Discuss the problems of the adult correctional system.

 LO2 Explain the term *total institution*.

 LO3 Explain the "prisonization" process and the development of the inmate social code.

 LO4 Compare the lives and cultures of male and female inmates.

 LO5 Discuss the causes of prison violence

 LO6 Discuss the different forms of correctional treatment.

 LO7 Describe the world of correctional officers.

 LO8 Explain what is meant by prisoners' rights, and discuss some key privileges that have been granted to inmates.

 LO9 Describe the problems of prisoner reentry.

Chapter Outline

Scott Howard, a 39-year-old federal prisoner, went to Washington to testify before a congressional committee about his experiences behind bars. During the three years he'd spent in Colorado state prisons he was repeatedly raped, assaulted, and extorted by members of a large, notorious gang. The gang was the 211 Crew, a white supremacist group whose leaders pressured him for money and demanded that he help them in an ambitious $300,000 fraud scheme; their threats soon turned into physical attacks, then sexual assaults. Howard was forced to perform oral sex on gang members and raped repeatedly.

Having been housed in other facilities, Howard thought he knew how to keep out of trouble. He'd seen plenty of intimidation and gang-related fights at other lockups, but nothing like the atmosphere in Colorado's Fremont Prison where he had been assigned. Prisoners sporting black eyes in the lunch line were a common sight. Members of the 211 Crew commanded their own set of tables in the dining hall, known as the Four Corners, and charged weaker white inmates tribute for the privilege of living in one of "their" units. Howard spent well over a year trying to get protection by writing to officials, he told the committee. "My efforts to report were mostly fruitless—and often put me at greater risk," he said. "Because I am openly gay, officials blamed me for the attacks. They said as a homosexual I should expect to be targeted by one gang or another."

On his last day as a Colorado prisoner before going to federal prison, Howard was put in a cell with one of the gang leaders and sexually assaulted. He eventually settled a civil rights lawsuit against several corrections officials for $165,000.[1]

Is it ethical and fair to house a vulnerable inmate such as Scott Howard in the general prison population? Then again, should someone get special housing based on their sexual orientation? If so, should there be a separate wing for gay inmates? Following this logic, should prisons be racially or ethnically segregated? Or segregated in some other way so was to improve security and promote inmate safety? ■

L01 Discuss the problems of the adult correctional system.

Scott Howard's travails are not unique. The prison experience can be harsh and demeaning. And America relies heavily on incarceration. While the inmate population has been in recent decline, there are still about 1.6 million people in prison in the United States.[2] As a result of this policy of mass incarceration, the nation has undergone a prison building boom: there were 568 state prisons in 1979, 957 in 1990, and there are more than 1,700 as of the most recent prison census.[3] These facilities take a variety of forms, including prisons, prison hospitals, prison farms, and boot camps; centers for reception, classification, or alcohol and drug treatment; and work release centers.[4] Not all prisons are brand new: 25 were built before 1875, 79 between 1875 and 1924, and 141 between 1925 and 1949. In fact, some of the first prisons ever constructed, such as the Concord Reformatory in Massachusetts, are still in operation.

Although most prisons are classified as medium-security, more than half of all inmates are held in large maximum-security institutions. Despite the continuous outcry by penologists against the use of fortress-like prisons, institutions holding 1,000 or more inmates still predominate.

Many of these institutions are also operating above stated capacity. Recreation and workshop space has been turned into dormitories housing 30 or more inmates in a single room. And, rather than rehabilitating their residents, penal institutions seem to exacerbate their criminal tendencies. It is popular to describe the typical prison as a "school for crime" in which young offenders are taught by older cons to become sophisticated criminals.

This chapter presents a brief review of some of the most important issues confronting the nation's troubled correctional system, including inmate life, treatment strategies, inmate legal rights, and release from prison.

total institution
A regimented, dehumanizing institution, such as a prison, in which like-situated people are kept in social isolation, cut off from the world at large.

no-frills policy
A correctional policy that stipulates that prisons are intended to punish, not coddle, inmates. This usually means a strict regimen of work and discipline and reduced opportunities for recreation and education.

L02 Explain the term *total institution*.

Men Imprisoned

Prisons in the United States are what is known as **total institutions**. Inmates locked within their walls are segregated from the outside world, kept under constant scrutiny and surveillance, and forced to obey strict official rules to avoid facing formal sanctions. Their personal possessions are taken from them, and they must conform to institutional dress and personal appearance norms. Many human functions are strictly curtailed; heterosexual sex, friendships, family relationships, education, and participation in groups become privileges of the past. Some institutions employ a "**no-frills policy**," which means that inmates receive the bare minimum of food, services, and medical care required by law. The purpose: convince them that prison is no place to be, and they'd better not return.

Living in Prison

Inmates quickly learn what the term "total institution" really means. When they arrive at prison, they are stripped, searched, shorn, and assigned living quarters. Before they get there, though, their first experience occurs in a classification or reception center, where they are given a series of psychological and other tests and evaluated on the basis of their personality, background, offense history, and treatment needs. Based on the classification they are given, they will be assigned to a permanent facility. Hard-core, repeat, and violent offenders go to the maximum-security unit. Offenders with learning disabilities may be assigned to an institution that specializes in educational services. Mentally disordered offenders will be held in a facility that can provide psychiatric care. Some states have instituted rigorous classification instruments designed to maximize the effectiveness of placements, thereby cutting down on the cost of incarceration. If classification can be conducted in an efficient and effective manner, nondangerous offenders will not needlessly be kept in expensive, high-security facilities.[5]

All previous concepts of personal privacy and dignity are soon forgotten. Inmate turned author James A. Paluch Jr. calls prison cells "cold coffin[s] … leaving a chilling effect on anyone forced to live inside them." Serving a life term without hope of parole, Paluch views prison life as one of constant manipulation and deceit both by guards and by other inmates. Trusting anyone can bring personal hardship and victimization.[6] Personal losses include the deprivation of liberty, goods and services, heterosexual relationships, autonomy, and security.[7] Newcomers may be subject to verbal and physical attack and threats from older cons, with little chance of legal redress. Even if new inmates are not abused, the staff may be quick to warn them about the danger of violence and sexual coercion they now face. The threats are not lost on them: scared or naïve inmates often refuse to participate in social activities, such as watching television in a day room or playing cards.[8]

Overcrowded prisons are filled with young, aggressive men who are responsible for the majority of inmate-on-inmate assaults.[9] Although criminal law applies to inmates, just as to any other citizen, it is rarely enforced within prison walls.[10] Therefore, part of living in prison involves learning to protect oneself and developing survival instincts. Frightened inmates remain in close proximity to their cells or to the sleeping area in dorms. Victims of physical and/or sexual violence may not use shower facilities out of fear of further such attacks.[11]

Inmates in large, inaccessible prisons may find themselves physically cut off from families, friends, and associates. Visitors may find it difficult to travel great distances to see them; mail is censored and sometimes destroyed. And while incarcerated, inmates are forced to associate with a peer group who bring with them a disproportionate share of mental and physical problems. Various communicable diseases are commonly found, such as hepatitis C virus, HIV, and syphilis. Not surprisingly, inmate health is significantly worse than that of the general population.[12]

Web App 14.1

For more information about life in prison, and even the ability to communicate with a prisoner, visit http://www.inmate.com/.

Lucy Nicholson/Reuters/Landov

Living in prison is a total experience. Personal privacy and freedom are quickly stripped away in today's overcrowded institutions. Here, an inmate sits in a cage at the California Institution for Men state prison in Chino, California. Cages are used for prisoners waiting for medical appointments, counseling, or permanent cells. The Supreme Court has ordered California to release more than 30,000 inmates or take other steps to ease overcrowding in its prisons to prevent "needless suffering and death." California's 33 adult prisons were designed to hold about 80,000 inmates but contained about 145,000 before the court order.

Adjusting to Prison

Inmates go through a variety of attitude and behavior changes, or cycles, as their sentence unfolds. During the early part of their prison stay, inmates may become easily depressed as they consider the long duration of the sentence and the loneliness and dangers of prison life. They must learn the ins and outs of survival in the institution: Which persons can be befriended, and which are best avoided? Who will grant favors and for what repayment? To avoid victimization, inmates must learn to adopt a defensive lifestyle.[13] They must discover areas of safety and danger. Sex offenders in particular often find it difficult to adjust to prison, and some try to create new identities and secure niches that enable them to survive in the prison's general population. Ironically, these new identities and protective niches are jeopardized when they enter a sex offender treatment program that, although designed to help them, gives them away to the other inmates.[14]

Some learn how to fight back to prove they are not people who can be bullied. People who viewed violence as an acceptable method of settling disputes before entering prison are the ones most likely to use violence while they are inmates.[15] Research shows that inmates who have a history of prearrest drug use and have been incarcerated for violent crimes are the ones most likely to get involved in assaults and drug/alcohol offenses while they are incarcerated.[16] Rule violations may be more common among inmates who, having lived in a subculture of violence on the outside, bring their beliefs regarding crime and violence into the prison environment. Survival in prison may depend on one's ability to identify troubled inmates and avoid contact.

Whereas some kill their attackers and get even longer sentences, others join cliques and gangs that provide protection and the ability to acquire power within the institution. Gangs are powerful in the larger prison systems, especially in California. Some inmates seek transfers to a different cell block or prison, ask for protective custody, or simply remain in their cells all the time.

Inmates may find that some prisoners have formed cliques, or groups, based on ethnic backgrounds or personal interests; they are also likely to encounter Mafia-like or racial terror groups that must be dealt with. Inmates may find that power in the prison is shared by correctional officers and inmate gangs; the only way to avoid being beaten and raped may be to learn how to beat and rape. If they are weak and unable to defend themselves, new inmates may find that they are considered "punks"; if they ask a guard for help, they are labeled "snitches." Those most likely to be targets of sexual assaults may spend their sentence in protective custody, sacrificing the "freedom of the yard" and rehabilitation services for personal protection.[17]

COPING IN PRISON Despite all these hardships, many inmates learn to adapt to the prison routine. Each prisoner has his own method of coping. He may stay alone, become friends with another inmate, join a group, or seek the advice of treatment personnel. Inmates soon learn that their lifestyle and activities can contribute to their being victimized by more aggressive inmates. The more time they spend in closely guarded activities, the less likely they are to become the victims of violence. The more they isolate themselves from others who might protect them, the greater their vulnerability to attack. The more visitors they receive, the more likely they are to be attacked by fellow inmates jealous of their relationships with the outside world.[18]

Of course, not all inmates learn to cope. Some inmates repeatedly violate institutional rules. Predicting who will become an institutional troublemaker is difficult, but rule-breaking behavior has been associated with being a younger inmate with a low IQ, with having had numerous juvenile convictions, with being a repeat offender, and with having victimized a stranger. Inmates who have limited intelligence and little self-control may not be able to form adaptive coping mechanisms and manage the stress of being in prison.[19]

The Inmate Social Code

For many years, criminal justice experts maintained that inmates formed their own world with a unique set of norms and rules known as the **inmate subculture**.[20] A significant aspect of the inmate subculture was a unique **inmate social code**—unwritten guidelines that expressed the values, attitudes, and type of behavior that older inmates demanded of young ones. Passed on from one generation of inmates to another, the inmate social code represented the values of interpersonal relations in the prison.

National attention was first drawn to the inmate social code and subculture by Donald Clemmer's classic book *The Prison Community*, in which he presented a detailed sociological study of life in a maximum-security prison.[21] Clemmer was able to identify a unique language, or argot, that prisoners use. He found that prisoners tend to group themselves into cliques on the basis of such personal criteria as sexual preference, political beliefs, and offense history. He found complex sexual relationships in prison and concluded that many heterosexual men will turn to homosexual relationships when faced with long sentences and the loneliness of prison life.

Clemmer's most important contribution may have been his identification of what he called the **prisonization** process. This he defined as the inmate's assimilation into the existing prison culture through acceptance of its language, sexual code, and norms of behavior. Those who become the most "prisonized" will be the least likely to reform on the outside.

Using Clemmer's work as a jumping-off point, a number of prominent sociologists have set out to explore more fully the various roles in the prison community. The most important principles of the dominant inmate culture are listed in Exhibit 14.1.

Although some inmates violate the code and exploit their peers, the "right guy" is someone who uses the inmate social code as his personal behavior guide. He is always loyal to his fellow prisoners, keeps his promises, is dependable and trustworthy, and never interferes with inmates who are conniving against the

inmate subculture
The loosely defined culture that pervades prisons and has its own norms, rules, and language.

inmate social code
An unwritten code of behavior, passed from older inmates to younger ones, that serves as a guideline for appropriate inmate behavior within the correctional institution.

 L03 Explain the "prisonization" process and the development of the inmate social code.

prisonization
Assimilation into the separate culture of the prison. This loosely defined culture that pervades prisons has its own norms, rules, and language. The traditional prison culture is now being replaced by a violent gang culture.

EXHIBIT 14.1 Elements of the Inmate Social Code

- *Don't interfere with inmates' interests.* Within this area of the code are maxims concerning serving the least amount of time in the greatest possible comfort. For example, inmates are warned never to betray another inmate to authorities; in other words, grievances must be handled personally. Other aspects of the non-interference doctrine include "Don't be nosy," "Don't have a loose lip," "Keep off the other inmates' backs," and "Don't put another inmate on the spot."

- *Don't lose your head.* Inmates are also cautioned to refrain from arguing, quarreling, or engaging in other emotional displays with fellow inmates. The novice may hear such warnings as "Play it cool," and "Do your own time."

- *Don't exploit inmates.* Prisoners are warned not to take advantage of one another—"Don't steal from cons," "Don't welsh on a debt," and "Be right."

- *Be tough and don't lose your dignity.* Although the second rule forbids conflict, once it starts an inmate must be prepared to deal with it effectively and thoroughly. Maxims include "Don't cop out," "Don't weaken," and "Be tough; be a man."

- *Don't be a sucker.* Inmates are cautioned not to make fools of themselves and support the guards or prison administration over the interest of the inmates—"Be sharp."

Source: Gresham Sykes, *The Society of Captives* (Princeton, NJ: Princeton University Press, 1958).

officials.[22] The right guy does not go around looking for a fight, but he never runs away from one; he acts like a man. In contrast, the exploiter is shunned by his peers. Rapists, for example, are unwelcome in mainstream inmate society; they have few companions, and their social life rests precariously on the margin of inmate society.[23]

The effects of prisonization may be long-term and destructive. Many inmates become hostile to the legal system, learning to use violence as a means of solving problems and to value criminal peers.[24] For some this change may be permanent; for others it is temporary, and they may revert to their "normal" life after release.

The New Inmate Culture

The importation of outside values into the inmate culture has had a dramatic effect on prison life. Although the "old" inmate subculture may have been harmful because its norms and values insulated the inmate from change efforts, it also helped maintain order in the institution and prevented violence among the inmates. People who violated the code and victimized others were sanctioned by their peers. An understanding developed between guards and inmate leaders: the guards would let the inmates have things their own way, and the inmates would not let things get out of hand and draw the attention of the administration.

The old system may be dying or already dead in most institutions. The change seems to have been precipitated by the black power movement in the 1960s and 1970s. Black inmates were no longer content to play a subservient role and challenged the power of established white inmates. As the black power movement gained prominence, racial tension in prisons created divisions that severely altered the inmate subculture. Older, respected inmates could no longer cross racial lines to mediate disputes. Predatory inmates could victimize others without fear of retaliation. Consequently, more inmates than ever are now assigned to protective custody for their own safety.

In the new culture, African American and Latino inmates are much more cohesively organized than whites.[25] Their groups sometimes form out of religious or political affiliations, such as the Black Muslims; out of efforts to combat discrimination in prison, such as the Latino group La Nuestra Familia; or from street gangs, such as the Vice Lords or Gangster Disciples in the Illinois prison system and the Crips in California. Where white inmates have successfully organized, it is in the form of a neo-Nazi group called the Aryan Brotherhood. Racially homogeneous gangs are so cohesive and powerful that they are able to supplant the original inmate code with one of their own.

Women Imprisoned

Before 1960, few women were in prison. Women's prisons were relatively rare and were usually an outgrowth of male institutions. Only four institutions for women were built between 1930 and 1950; in comparison, 34 women's prisons were constructed during the 1980s as crime rates soared.

At the turn of the twentieth century, female inmates were viewed as morally depraved people who flouted conventional rules of female behavior. The treatment of white and African American women differed significantly. In some states, white women were placed in female-only reformatories designed to improve their deportment; black women were placed in male prisons, where they were put on chain gangs and were subject to beatings.[26]

Female Institutions

State jurisdictions have been responding to the influx of female offenders into the correctional system by expanding the facilities for housing and treating them. Women's prisons tend to be smaller than those housing male inmates. Although

Web App 14.2

For more information about the Women's Prison Association, visit http://www.wpaonline.org/.

some female institutions are strictly penal, with steel bars, concrete floors, and other security measures, the majority are nonsecure institutions similar to college dormitories and group homes in the community. Women's facilities, especially those in the community, commonly offer inmates a great deal of autonomy and allow them to make decisions affecting their daily lives.

However, like men's prisons, women's prisons suffer from a lack of adequate training, health, treatment, and educational facilities. Psychological counseling often takes the form of group sessions conducted by laypeople, such as correctional officers. Most trained psychologists and psychiatrists restrict themselves to such activities as conducting intake classifications and court-ordered examinations and prescribing mood-controlling medication.

Female Inmates

Like their male counterparts, female inmates are disproportionately more likely to be young (most are under age 30), minority group members, unmarried, undereducated, and either unemployed or underemployed.[27] The typical woman behind bars is a poor, unskilled woman of color with small children who has health problems, has a history of abuse, and is incarcerated for low-level drug or property offenses.[28]

 LO4 Compare the lives and cultures of male and female inmates.

Incarcerated women also have had a troubled family life. Significant numbers were at-risk children, products of broken homes and the welfare system; over half have received welfare at some time during their adult lives. Many claim to have been physically or sexually abused at some point in their lives. This pattern continued in adult life: many female inmates were victims of domestic violence. It is not surprising that many display psychological problems.[29]

It is now estimated that 4 percent of women in state prisons and 3 percent of women in federal prisons were pregnant at the time of admittance; about 6 percent of women in local jails were pregnant at the time of admittance. Despite this trend, there is no national policy that dictates what happens to children born to mothers who are under correctional supervision. The overwhelming majority of children born to incarcerated mothers are separated from their mothers immediately after birth and placed with relatives or into foster care. In a handful of states, women have other options: prison nurseries and community-based residential parenting programs.

A national study sponsored by the Women's Prison Association found that the number of prison-based nursery programs is growing, but such programs are still rare. Though every state has seen a dramatic rise in its women's prison population over the past three decades, only nine states have prison nursery programs in operation or under development.[30]

A significant number of female inmates report having substance abuse problems. About three-fourths have used drugs at some time in their lives, and almost half were involved with addictive drugs, such as cocaine, heroin, or PCP. The incarceration of so many women who are low criminal risks, yet face a high risk of exposure to HIV (human immunodeficiency virus, which causes AIDS) and other health issues because of their prior history of drug abuse, presents a significant problem. Up to one-third report that before their arrest, they had traded sex for money or drugs.[31] Such risky behavior significantly increases the likelihood of their carrying the AIDS virus or other sexually transmitted diseases.

The picture that emerges of the female inmate is troubling. After a lifetime of emotional turmoil, physical and sexual abuse, and drug use, it seems improbable that overcrowded, underfunded correctional institutions can forge a dramatic turnaround in the behavior of at-risk female inmates. Many have lost custody of their children, a trauma that is more likely to afflict those who are already substance abusers and suffer from depression.[32] It is not surprising that these conditions also produce high suicide rates in the female prison population.[33]

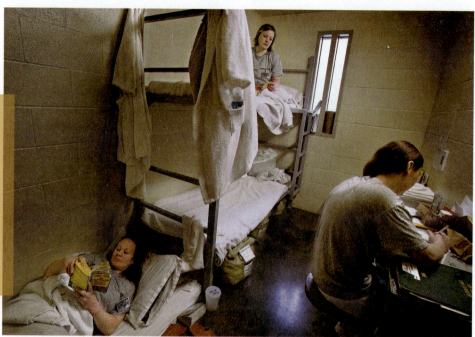

Lucy Rumel, lower left, found little comfort and a fitful night's sleep on the floor at the Washington Corrections Center for Women's reception and diagnostic center in Purdy, Washington. Women's prisons, like all male prisons, face their share of crowding, forcing inmates into sometimes uncomfortable living arrangements.

Adapting to the Female Institution

Daily life in women's prisons differs somewhat from that in male institutions. For one thing, unlike male inmates, women usually do not present an immediate physical danger to staff and fellow inmates. Relatively few engage in violent behavior, and incidents of inmate-initiated sexual aggression, so common in male institutions, are rare in women's prisons.[34] Few female inmates experience the violent atmosphere common in male institutions or suffer the same racial and ethnic conflict and divisiveness.[35] Although female inmates may experience less discomfort than males, that does not mean their experience is a bed of roses. Many still experience fear and are forced to undergo a process of socialization fraught with danger and volatile situations.[36] However, female inmates seem to receive more social support from both internal sources (e.g., inmate peers, correctional staff) and external sources (e.g., families, peers), a factor that may help lessen the pains of prison life, help them adjust, and improve the social climate within female institutions.[37]

The rigid, anti-authority inmate social code found in many male institutions does not exist in female institutions.[38] Confinement for women, however, may produce severe anxiety and anger because of separation from families and loved ones and the inability to function in normal female roles. Unlike men, who direct their anger outward, female prisoners may turn to more self-destructive acts to cope with their problems. Female inmates are more likely than males to harm their own bodies and attempt suicide. For example, one common practice among female inmates is self-mutilation, or "carving." This ranges from simple scratches to carving the name of their boyfriend on their body or even complex statements or sentences ("To mother, with hate").[39]

Another form of adaptation to prison used by women is the **make-believe family**. This group contains masculine and feminine figures acting as fathers and mothers; some even act as children and take on the role of brother or sister. Formalized marriages and divorces may be conducted. Sometimes one inmate plays multiple roles, so that a "sister" in one family may "marry" and become the "wife" of another inmate. It is estimated that about half of all female inmates are members of make-believe families.[40]

make-believe families
In female prisons, substitute family groups with a faux father, mother, and siblings.

Many incarcerated women are mothers, and keeping them in contact with their children is considered important for their rehabilitation. Alicia Stenzel stands with her child at the fence of the Indiana Women's Prison (IWP), where she is currently incarcerated. Her child's visit is made possible by the Family Preservation Program. The program has expanded to include the Wee Ones Nursery, which enables eligible offenders who deliver while incarcerated at IWP to reside with their infant at the facility for up to 18 months or until the mother's earliest possible release date, whichever is sooner.

Why do make-believe families exist? Experts suggest that they provide the warm, stable relationships that are otherwise unobtainable in the prison environment. Some prison officials find make-believe families disruptive, but their attitudes may stem from preconceived notions rather than from any real harm caused by such pairings.[41]

Prison Violence

Conflict, violence, and brutality are sad but ever-present facts of institutional life for both male and female inmates. Violence can involve individual conflict: inmate versus inmate, inmate versus staff, staff versus inmate. Violence can be sexual in nature, involving rape and coercion. Violence can also involve collective prison riots; several hundred have occurred since the first one in 1774.[42]

Discuss the causes of prison violence.

Individual Violence

Each year in U.S. prisons, about 50 to 70 inmates are killed and some 200 suicides are recorded.[43] Many more suffer nonlethal attacks, including sexual assault. What are the causes of prison violence? The motives for individual violence vary widely. They include sexual dominance and coercion, the aggressor's desire to shake down the victim for money and personal favors, racial conflict, and the need to establish power within the institution. Although there is no single cause of individual prison violence, a number of explanations have been suggested[44]:

■ *History of prior violence.* Younger inmates, especially those with histories of violence, are the ones most likely to be aggressive behind bars. Some are former gang members, who routinely used force to get their own way on the outside and who quickly join inmate gangs.[45] In many instances, street gangs maintain prison branches that unite the inmate with their former violence-prone peers. Having this connection supports and protects gang members while they are in prison, and it assists in supporting gang members' families and associates outside the wall.[46]

Shaul Schwarz/Edit/Getty Images

■ *Psychological malady.* Many inmates suffer from personality disorders. Recent research shows that among institutionalized offenders, psychopathy is the strongest predictor of violent recidivism and indifferent response to treatment.[47] In the crowded, dehumanizing world of the prison, it is not surprising that people suffering extreme psychological distress may resort to violence to dominate others.[48]

■ *Prison conditions.* The prison experience itself causes people to become violent. Inhuman conditions, including overcrowding, depersonalization, and the threat of sexual assault, are violence-producing conditions. Even in the most humane prisons, life is a constant put-down, and prison conditions are a threat to the inmates' sense of self-worth; violence may be a not-unexpected consequence of these conditions.[49] Just as prison conditions may produce violence, effective prison administration may reduce it. Consistent and firm disciplinary actions may help disruptive inmates realize that repeated violent incidents are punished by long-term stays in segregation and other negative consequences.[50]

■ *Lack of dispute resolution mechanisms.* Many prisons lack effective mechanisms for handling inmate grievances against either prison officials or other inmates fairly and equitably. Prisoners who complain about other inmates are viewed as "rats" or "snitches" and may be marked for death by their enemies. Similarly, inmates' complaints or lawsuits filed against the prison administration may result in the inmate being placed in solitary confinement—"the hole."

■ *Basic survival.* Inmates resort to violence in order to survive. The lack of physical security, inadequate mechanisms for resolving complaints, and the code of silence promote individual violence by inmates who might otherwise be much less dangerous.

Collective Violence

Collective violence also is an ever-present danger in the prison community, and prison riots have become routine. The most famous of these outbreaks include the infamous Attica riot in 1971, which claimed 39 lives, and the New Mexico State Penitentiary riot of February 1980, in which the death toll was 33. The 1980 New Mexico State Penitentiary riot drew national attention to the problem of prison overcrowding and the conflict it produced. The prison was designed for 800 prisoners but actually held 1,135; overcrowding, squalor, poor food, and lack of medical treatment were chronic conditions. The state government had been called on to improve guard training, upgrade physical plant quality, and relieve the overcrowding, but it was reluctant to spend the necessary money. Even though conditions have improved in most facilities, prison rioting still remains a threat. For example, on March 28, 2008, a riot at the federal penitentiary in Three Rivers, Texas, left one prisoner dead and 22 others injured. Intelligence sources said they believe the riot began when tensions over prison leadership developed between Mexican American inmates who consider themselves Chicanos and inmates who have closer ties to Mexico.[51]

The suggested causes of collective prison violence include:

■ *Inmate-balance theory.* Riots and other forms of collective violence occur when prison officials make an abrupt effort to take control of the prison and limit freedoms. Crackdowns occur when officials perceive that inmate leaders have too much power and take measures to control their illicit privileges, such as gambling or stealing food.[52]

■ *Administrative-control theory.* Collective violence is caused by prison mismanagement, lack of strong security, and inadequate control by prison officials. Poor management may inhibit conflict management and set the stage for violence. Repressive administrations give inmates the feeling that nothing will ever change, that they have nothing to lose, and that violence is the only means for change.

■ *Prison overcrowding theory.* As the prison population continues to climb, unmatched by expanded capacity, prison violence may increase. Overcrowding caused by the rapid increases in the prison population has also been linked to increases in both inmate substance abuse and prison violence.[53]

To reduce violence and monitor inmates more closely, correctional authorities are relying on developing forms of technology. The accompanying Criminal Justice and Technology feature describes some of these efforts.

Sexual Violence

Who are the targets of prison sexual violence? Young males may be raped and kept as sexual slaves by older, more aggressive inmates. When these "slave holders" are released, they may sell their "prison wives" to other inmates.[55] Some inmates demand that regular sexual payments be made to them in exchange for protection from even more violent inmates who threaten rape and beatings.[56] The weaker inmates who agree to such arrangements in return for protection are called "punks" and occupy the bottom of the inmate sexual hierarchy. Straight inmates are more likely to respect "true" homosexuals, because they were gay before entering prison and are therefore "true to themselves," whereas punks are despised because they are weak: they did not want to have sex with other men but were too weak to resist or not brave enough to stand up to sexual predators. Even "queens" (inmates who look and act as women) get more respect than punks, because they chose their lifestyle and did not have it forced upon them by others.[57]

HOW COMMON IS PRISON RAPE? Even though media exposés typically suggest that prison rape is an everyday occurrence, it is actually very difficult to get an accurate reading of the true incidence of prison rape. Some research efforts indicate that rape is very rare, whereas others find that nearly half of all inmates experience some form of sexual coercion.[58]

What explains the difficulty in getting an accurate count? Many inmates refuse to report rape and others may misunderstand what constitutes a "rape"; that is, they don't consider verbal coercion a form of sexual assault. Reasons for non-reporting include embarrassment and the belief that nothing can be done. Other reasons include:

■ Inmates fear that if they report sexual assault they will be harassed by other inmates.

■ Inmates do not want to report rape because they fear retaliation from their attacker.

■ Inmates may believe that sexual assault is a personal matter and nobody else's business.

■ Victims may want to stay in the general population and fear that reporting victimization may result in their being placed in segregation.[59]

The Bureau of Justice Statistics tried to avoid these problems by surveying inmates after they were released from prison, thereby removing the threat of coercion that occurs while they are still behind bars. This post-prison survey found that almost 1 in every 10 former state or local prisoners in America reported being sexually victimized at least once by an inmate or staff member in prison. The National Former Prisoners Survey found evidence that prison

criminal justice and TECHNOLOGY

MONITORING PEOPLE AND PLACES IN PRISON

There have been ongoing efforts to monitor both places and people in prison. Employing technology to improve monitoring effectiveness would elevate safety levels while saving costs.

MONITORING PLACES

Florida's Correctional Operational Trend Analysis System (COTAS) was developed to identify potential trouble spots within prisons.[54] The system consolidates historical and current data and uses a predictive scoring system to alert staff to areas of brewing concern, such as potential for riots or inmate work strikes. Knowing ahead of time where trouble might arise lets managers assign extra staff or take other actions that can prevent violence and other problems. The user interface allows managers to interact with the system's pictures, symbols, and charts and make proactive decisions that will minimize or prevent criminal activity in the facility.

MONITORING PEOPLE

Another approach is to monitor people to head off potential trouble. For example, an automated suicide warning system is being developed as a cost-effective, noninvasive approach to behavior monitoring. This radar-based automated suicide watch system can measure an inmate's heart rate, breathing rate, and body motions without being attached to the individual. The system consists of:

- Personal health status sensors that can be enclosed in a box on the ceiling to remotely and noninvasively monitor inmates' pulse and breathing
- Network connections to remote monitors
- Software designed to interpret motion data and create a decision tree for when to notify officers

A wall-mounted range controlled radar (RCR) system—originally designed for home security motion detectors—measures subtle motions on the body's surface caused

rape is a greater problem than previously thought: about 8 percent of former prison inmates said they were sexually victimized. Just about the same number of former inmates were victimized by staff members as by other inmates. Any sexual contact between staff and inmate is of course considered nonconsensual and illegal. About half who reported sexual involvement with a prison staff member said they were offered favors or privileges in exchange, while a third said they were verbally coerced. Gay and bisexual men seemed to be by far the most frequently targeted in prison: 39 percent of gay men and 34 percent of bisexual men reported being sexually victimized by another inmate, while only 3.5 percent of heterosexual men reported incidents. This relationship did not hold for lesbian and heterosexual women, who were victimized by other inmates at the same rate. However, the rate of inmate-on-inmate sexual victimization was at least three times higher for females (13.7 percent) than males (4.2 percent).[60]

WHAT FACTORS LEAD TO SEXUAL VICTIMIZATION? Studies show that institutions with the highest sexual coercion rates had several things in common, including barrack-style housing, large prison populations, and lenient security.[61] In these institutions, sexual harassment leads to fights, social isolation, fear, anxiety, and crisis. When James Austin studied sexual violence in the Texas prison system, he made the following discoveries:

■ *White inmates are attacked more than any other race.* Nearly 60 percent of the 43 "sustained" incidents—those proved to be true by an investigation—involved a white victim.

by heart and lung activity. Alarms are activated when the system detects suspicious changes.

When implemented, the automated suicide watch system will provide benefits including:

- *Less obtrusive, less prone to destruction.* A key feature of the device is that it is less obtrusive. Inmates are prone to tamper with or destroy monitoring devices but a device that does not require physical contact with the prisoner could make tampering or destruction less likely.

- *Detect disguised suicide attempts.* Correctional officers mistake cleverly disguised suicide attempts as normal behavior. An automated system could safeguard against human error.

- *Provide continuous monitoring.* An inmate under traditional suicide watch typically is checked on by corrections staff every fifteen minutes. Even with this intense effort by corrections facilities, inmates still have ample time to commit or attempt suicide. Monitoring technology can provide continuous surveillance to supplement the visual inspections and alert officers quickly to any attempt.

- *Fewer people needed to staff suicide watch.* By installing these devices, prisons may be able to reduce the number of officers needed to monitor prisoners, freeing staff for other corrections tasks.

- *Watch more prisoners at risk.* An automated system could be installed to monitor inmates who are at high risk, such as those on suicide watch or new prisoners awaiting trial.

CRITICAL THINKING

1. Should prison inmates have some privacy rights? Do all these new technological advances reduce inmate independence and hamper their adjustment? Or does the need for prison security outweigh individual rights of inmates?

Sources: National Institute of Justice, "Predicting Trouble Spots Within Prisons," http://www.nij.gov/topics/corrections/institutional/monitoring-inmates/Pages/predicting-trouble.aspx (accessed July 2014); National Institute of Justice, "Suicide Watch Technologies Could Improve Monitoring, Reduce Staff Time," http://www.nij.gov/topics/corrections/institutional/monitoring-inmates/Pages/suicide-watch.aspx (accessed July 2014).

- *Victims are generally younger than their assailants.* The average age of victims in "sustained" cases was three years younger than the average age of the assailants.

- *Mentally ill or intellectually impaired inmates are more likely to be victimized.* Although only 12 percent of the allegations involved a mentally ill or intellectually impaired prisoner, this percentage is 8 times the proportion of mentally ill inmates in the general prisoner population (1.6 percent).

- *Cellblocks with solid cell fronts may contribute to sexual assault.* Solid cell fronts, while permitting privacy for the inmates and reducing noise within the unit, also provide the degree of privacy that permits sexual assaults to occur. Unlike older prison designs, in which the cell fronts consist of bars, solid doors limit visual observation by staff and soundproof the cells enough so that staff have difficulty hearing what is going on in individual cells.[62]

SEXUAL VIOLENCE IN WOMEN'S PRISONS There are numerous reports of female prisoners being sexually abused and exploited by male correctional workers who either use brute force or psychological coercion to gain sexual control over inmates. Staff-on-inmate sexual misconduct covers a wide range of behaviors, from lewd remarks to voyeurism, to assault and rape. Few if any of these incidents are reported, and perpetrators rarely go to trial. Institutional workers cover for each other, and women who file complaints are offered little protection from vengeful guards.[63] Because this situation persists, more than 40 states and the District of Columbia have been forced to pass laws criminalizing some types of staff sexual misconduct in prisons.[64] However, not all sexual liaisons in women's prisons are unwanted, and when Rebecca Trammell conducted interviews with former female inmates, she learned that some inmates fight over correctional officers as the only men in their lives.[65]

Correctional Rehabilitation

Almost every prison facility uses some mode of treatment to help in inmate rehabilitation. This may come in the form of individual or group therapy programs, drug counseling, anger management, and/or educational or vocational training. Some inmates are in significant need of services, and it is often difficult to match inmates with the correct treatment assistance.[66] This section presents a selected number of therapeutic methods that have been used nationally in correctional settings and identifies some of their salient features.

L06 Discuss the different forms of correctional treatment.

Individual and Group Counseling

Prison inmates typically suffer from a variety of cognitive and psychosocial deficits, such as poor emotional control, social skills, and interpersonal problem solving. Modern counseling programs help inmates to control emotions (e.g., understanding why they feel the way they do, dealing with nervousness or anxiety, solving their problems creatively); to communicate with others (e.g., understanding what people tell them, communicating clearly when they write); to deal with legal concerns (e.g., keeping out of legal trouble, avoiding breaking laws); to manage general life issues (e.g., finding a job, dealing with difficult coworkers, being a good parent); and to develop and maintain social relationships (e.g., having good relations with others, making others happy, making others proud).[67] Some counseling programs use traditional techniques such as group therapy, whereas others employ nontraditional artistic and spiritual activities, such as visual and performance arts, meditation, and yoga.[68]

One popular approach has been to aim counseling efforts at inmates whose anger and lack of self-control have been linked to violent criminal behavior both in the institution and upon release in the community. As a result, **anger management** programs have been developed to help inmates cope with their violent behavioral urges and tendencies. One survey of group psychotherapy services in correctional facilities indicated that anger therapy may be the type of group therapy most frequently offered within prison settings today.[69] Anger management is often combined with other group techniques as part of drug treatment and sex offender treatment programs. Anger management or violence programs have also been implemented in other countries; for example, violence management programs are widely used in Australia.[70]

anger management
Programs designed to help people who have become dependent on anger as a primary means of expressing themselves and those who inappropriately use anger or the threat of violence to get their way.

Anger management programs often rely on cognitive-behavioral therapy (CBT), a technique used to help restructure distorted thinking and perception. A recent evaluation of CBT programs provides valuable insight into their effectiveness and is the subject of the accompanying Evidence-Based Justice feature.

There is evidence that programs using counseling and other therapies to affect inmate change can be effective. A meta-analysis examining 68 studies covering a variety of treatment programs and their impact on inmate misconduct conducted by Sheila French and Paul Gendreau found that behavioral programs were generally effective and helped reduce inmate conduct while behind bars and reduced recidivism after release.[71]

Faith-Based Programs

Research has shown that inmates involved in religious programs and education do better following release than those in comparison groups, but differences quickly erode.[72] Nonetheless, under the George W. Bush administration, religion-oriented

EVIDENCE-based justice

TREATING INMATES WITH COGNITIVE-BEHAVIORAL THERAPY

Cognitive-behavioral therapy (CBT) is a correctional treatment approach that focuses on patterns of thinking and the beliefs, attitudes, and values that underlie thinking. The therapy assumes that most people can become conscious of their own thoughts and behaviors and then make positive changes. A person's thoughts are often the result of experience, and behavior is often influenced and prompted by these thoughts. In addition, thoughts may sometimes become distorted and fail to reflect reality accurately.

When used in a correctional setting, the goal of CBT is to restructure distorted thinking and perception, which in turn changes a person's behavior for the better. Characteristics of distorted thinking may include immature or developmentally arrested thoughts; poor problem solving and decision making; an inability to consider the effects of one's behavior; a hampered ability to reason and accept blame for wrongdoing; or an inability to manage feelings of anger. These distorted thinking patterns can lead to making poor decisions and engaging in antisocial behavior to solve problems. People taking part in CBT learn specific skills that can be used to solve the problems they confront all the time as well as skills they can use to achieve legitimate goals and objectives. CBT first concentrates on developing skills to recognize distorted or unrealistic thinking when it happens, and then on changing that thinking or belief to mollify or eliminate problematic behavior.

IS IT EFFECTIVE?

Social scientists Mark Lipsey, Nana Landenberger, and Sandra Wilson conducted a national study of cognitive-behavioral therapy programs in the prison setting and found them highly successful. Using sophisticated research techniques, they found that the programs that worked best had three components:

- The inclusion of anger control and interpersonal problem solving in the treatment program's intended effects.

- High-quality implementation. This means there were a low proportion of treatment dropouts, close monitoring of the quality and fidelity of the treatment implementation, and adequate training for the providers.

- Use with high-risk offenders.

That last element is surprising. Cognitive-behavioral therapy seems to be more effective with more dangerous, hard-core offenders than with less dangerous subjects. The best results occur when higher-risk offenders receive more intensive services that target criminogenic characteristics, such as criminal thinking patterns, using cognitive-behavioral and social learning approaches.

Sources: Sesha Kethineni and Jeremy Braithwaite, "The Effects of a Cognitive-Behavioral Program for At-Risk Youth: Changes in Attitudes, Social Skills, Family, and Community and Peer Relationships," *Victims and Offenders* 6 (2011): 93–116; Patrick Clark, "Preventing Future Crime with Cognitive Behavioral Therapy," *National Institute of Justice Journal* 265 (2010), http://www.nij.gov/journals/265/pages/therapy.aspx (accessed July 2014); Mark Lipsey, Nana Landenberger, and Sandra Wilson, "Effects of Cognitive-Behavioral Programs for Criminal Offenders," *Campbell Systematic Reviews* (2007): 6, http://www.campbellcollaboration.org/lib/download/143/ (accessed July 2014).

rehabilitation efforts flourished.[73] In 2003, then-governor Jeb Bush dedicated the first faith-based prison in the United States, a 750-bed medium-security facility for males in Lawtey, Florida. Governor Bush claimed that the only way to achieve the rehabilitation of criminals and to reduce recidivism is to "lead them to God."[74] In 2004, Florida converted what was then the all-male Hillsborough Correctional Institution into the nation's first faith-based correctional facility for women. At least five states—Texas, Kansas, Minnesota, Florida, and Iowa—have opened new prison facilities in which the central philosophy involves religious teaching. The privately run Corrections Corporation of America (CCA) announced its interest in developing faith-based correctional facilities in partnership with Basic-Life Principles, a Chicago-based prison ministry group, to develop faith-based programming that would eventually be extended to all 64 CCA jails, detention centers, and prisons throughout the United States. Missouri and Florida also opened facilities for youthful offenders founded on faith-based principles.[75]

Imam, chaplain, and prison outreach coordinator Fareed M. Rashid leads an Islamic prayer in a prison. He also gives sermons and offers kufis, prayer rugs, literature, and other religious items and assistance to the inmates. What are the strengths and weaknesses of in-prison faith-based programming?

Joel Gordon/Joel Gordon Photography

While these programs are based on faith or spiritual principles, the study of religious texts or materials, and participation in religious services or rituals are not viewed as their central focus. Instead, faith-based programs are more often involved in secular activities such as helping clients gain skills or training, building support networks, and creating supportive relationships between staff, volunteers, and clients.[76]

Drug Treatment Programs

Most prisons have programs designed to help inmates suffering from alcohol and substance abuse; the most recent data suggest that about 30 percent of all inmates are provided with some form of services.[77] Some institutions use 12-step meetings, group and/or individual counseling, and recovery training to try to provide a psychological climate conducive to change. Another approach is multisystemic treatment that relies on a combination of services, including psychological treatment, medical care, vocational training, educational enhancement, family therapy, and so on. Another approach is to provide abusers with the long-term administration of a medication that either replaces the illicit drug or blocks its actions. Pharmacological treatment may include the following medications, among others:

- Methadone, a narcotic analgesic that is an effective substitute for heroin, morphine, codeine, and other opiate derivatives
- Naltrexone, an opioid antagonist that blocks the effects of opioids, such as heroin, thereby discouraging their use[78]

Because substance abuse is so prevalent among correctional clients, some correctional facilities have been reformulated into treatment-dispensing total institutions referred to as "therapeutic communities" (TC) in order to best serve their clientele.[79] TC uses a psychosocial, experiential learning process that relies on positive peer pressure within a highly structured social environment. The community itself, including staff and program participants, becomes the primary method of change. All work together as members of a "family" in order to create a culture where community members confront each other's negative behavior and attitudes and establish an open, trusting, and safe environment.[80]

Despite such positive indications, treating substance-abusing offenders has proven difficult. Even such highly touted programs such as cognitive behavioral therapy and the therapeutic community approach have yielded mixed results: some evaluations have found clients in these programs are just as likely to recidivate as those in the general population.[81] Finding the proper mix of programming to be effective with the drug-involved inmate remains an elusive goal.

Treating the AIDS-Infected Inmate

The AIDS-infected inmate has been the subject of great concern. Two groups of people at high risk of contracting HIV are intravenous drug users who share needles and males who engage in same-sex relations, two lifestyles common in prison. Because drug use is common and syringes scarce, many high-risk inmates share drug paraphernalia, increasing the danger of HIV transmission.[82] Although the numbers are on the decline, there are about 21,000 HIV-infected inmates in state and federal prisons.[83]

Correctional administrators have found it difficult to arrive at effective policies to confront AIDS. Even though all state and federal jurisdictions do some AIDS testing, only some states and the Federal Bureau of Prisons conduct mass screenings of all inmates. Most states test inmates only if there are significant indications that they are HIV-positive.

Most correctional systems are now training staff about AIDS. But educational programs for inmates are often inadequate, because administrators are reluctant to give them information on the proper cleaning of drug paraphernalia and safe sex (since both drug use and sexual relations are forbidden in prison).

Educational and Vocational Programs

Besides treatment programs stressing personal growth through individual analysis or group process, inmate rehabilitation is also pursued through vocational and educational training. Although these two kinds of training sometimes differ in style and content, they can also overlap when, for example, education involves practical job-related study.

The first prison treatment programs were in fact educational. A prison school was opened at the Walnut Street Jail in 1784. Elementary courses were offered in New York's prison system in 1801 and in Pennsylvania's in 1844. An actual school system was established in Detroit's House of Corrections in 1870, and the Elmira Reformatory opened a vocational trade school in 1876. Today, most institutions provide some type of educational program. At some prisons, inmates can obtain a high school diploma or a General Educational Development (GED) certificate through equivalency exams. Other institutions provide an actual classroom education, in programs usually staffed by certified teachers employed full-time at the prison or by part-time teachers who also teach full-time at nearby public schools.

The number of hours devoted to educational programs and the quality and intensity of these efforts vary greatly. Some are full-time programs employing highly qualified and concerned educators, whereas others are part-time programs without any real goals or objectives. Although worthwhile attempts are being made, prison educational programs often suffer from inadequate funding and administration. The picture is not totally bleak, however. In some institutions, programs have been designed to circumvent the difficulties inherent in the prison structure. They encourage volunteers from the community and local schools to tutor willing and motivated inmates. Some prison administrators have arranged flexible schedules for inmate students and actively encourage their participation in these programs. In several states, statewide school districts serving prisons have been created. Forming such districts can make better-qualified staff available and provide the materials and resources necessary for meaningful educational programs.

Most research indicates that participation in correctional education and vocational programs have benefits both in and out of prison. Karen Lahm found that inmates who take part in GED, high school, vocational, and/or college programs report much fewer rule violations while incarcerated than those who ignore educational opportunities.[84] Participation in prison-based education produces higher postrelease earnings and employment rates, especially for minority inmates.[85] A meta-analysis by Steve Aos and his associates found that vocational programs in prison reduce reoffending by more than 12 percent, and participation in basic adult education programs yields a reduction in recidivism of more than 5 percent.[86]

Every state correctional system also has some job-related services for inmates. Some have elaborate training programs inside the institution, whereas others have instituted prerelease and postrelease employment services. Inmates who hope to obtain parole need to participate in prison industry. Documenting a history of stable employment in prison is essential if parole agents are to convince prospective employers that the ex-offender is a good risk, and postrelease employment is usually required for parole eligibility.[87]

A few of the more important work-related services are discussed in the following sections.

VOCATIONAL TRAINING   Most institutions provide vocational training programs. On the federal level, the Federal Prison Industries, more commonly known as UNICOR, teach inmates to produce goods and services. About 25 percent of federal prisoners work in 100 or so factories within federal prisons.[88] The minimum UNICOR wage is 23 cents an hour, and the maximum wage is $1.15. UNICOR sales average about $800 million a year, and they turn a profit of $120 million a year—making UNICOR the most profitable line of business in the United States.[89]

Despite the promising aspects of such programs, they have also been seriously criticized. Upon their release, inmates often have trouble finding skill-related, high-paying jobs. Equipment in prisons is often secondhand, obsolete, and hard to come by. Some programs are thinly disguised excuses for prison upkeep and maintenance, and unions and other groups resent the intrusion of prison labor into their markets.

WORK RELEASE   To supplement programs stressing rehabilitation via in-house job training or education, more than 40 states have attempted to implement **work release** or **furlough** programs. These allow deserving inmates to leave the institution and hold regular jobs in the community.

Inmates enrolled in work release may live at the institution at night while working in the community during the day. However, security problems (for instance, contraband may be brought in), combined with the fact that prisons are often located in remote areas, often make this arrangement difficult. More typical is the extended work release, where prisoners are allowed to remain in the community for significant periods of time. To help inmates adjust, some states operate community-based prerelease centers where inmates live while working. Some inmates may work at their previous jobs, whereas others seek new employment.

Like other programs, work release has its good and bad points. On the one hand, inmates are sometimes reluctantly received in the community and find that certain areas of employment are closed to them. Citizens are often concerned about prisoners "stealing" jobs or working for lower than normal wages; consequently, such practices are prohibited by Public Law 89-176, which controls the federal work release program.

On the other hand, inmates gain many benefits from work release, including the ability to hone work skills, maintain community ties, and make an easier

work release
A prison treatment program that allows inmates to be released during the day to work in the community, returning to prison at night.

furlough
A correctional policy that allows inmates to leave the institution for vocational or educational training, for employment, or to maintain family ties.

transition from prison to the outside world. For those who have learned a skill in the institution, work release offers an excellent opportunity to test a new occupation. For others, the job may be a training situation in which new skills are acquired. A number of states have reported that few work release inmates abscond while in the community.

PRIVATE PRISON ENTERPRISE Opposition from organized labor ended the profitability of commercial prison industries, but a number of interesting efforts have been made to vary the type and productivity of prison labor. The federal government helped put private industry into prisons when it approved the Free Venture Program in 1976. Seven states, including Connecticut, South Carolina, and Minnesota, were given grants to implement private industries inside prison walls. This successful program led to the Percy Amendment (1979), federal legislation that allowed prison-made goods to be sold across state lines if the projects complied with strict rules, such as making sure unions were consulted and preventing manufacturers from undercutting the existing wage structure.[90] The new law authorized a number of prison industry enhancement pilot projects. These were certified as meeting the Percy Amendment operating rules and were therefore free to ship goods out of state; by 1987, 15 projects had been certified.

Today, private prison industries use a number of models. One approach, the state-use model, makes the correctional system a supplier of goods and services that serves state-run institutions. The California Prison Industry Authority (PIA) is an inmate work program that provides work assignments for thousands of inmates and operates 70 service, manufacturing, and agricultural industries in 23 prisons. These industries produce a variety of goods and services, including flags, printing services, signs, binders, eyewear, gloves, office furniture, clothing, and cell equipment. PIA products and services are available to government entities, including federal, state, and local government agencies.[91]

In another approach, the free-enterprise model, private companies set up manufacturing units on prison grounds or purchase goods made by inmates in shops owned and operated by the corrections department. In the corporate model, a semi-independent business is created on prison grounds; its profits go to the state government and inmate laborers.

POSTRELEASE PROGRAMS A final element of job-related programming involves helping inmates to obtain jobs before they are released and to keep them once they are on the outside. A number of correctional departments have set up employment services designed to ease the transition between institution and community. Employment program staffs assess inmates' backgrounds to determine their abilities, interests, goals, and capabilities. They also help inmates create job plans essential to receiving early release (parole) and successfully reintegrating into the community. Some programs maintain community correctional placements in sheltered environments that help inmates bridge the gap between institutions and the outside world. Services include job placement, skill development, family counseling, and legal and medical assistance.

Can Rehabilitation Work?

In oft-cited research, Robert Martinson and his associates (1975) found that a majority of treatment programs were failures, giving birth to the generalization that "nothing works" in prison rehabilitation.[92] In the decades since Martinson's work was published, there has been considerable debate about the effectiveness of correctional treatment.[93] Correctional treatment proponents have dismissed the "nothing works" philosophy as exaggerated and, using sophisticated data analysis techniques, have found evidence that correctional rehabilitation can be effective.[94] When Paul Gendreau and Robert R. Ross reviewed the

Web App 14.3

For more information about prison enterprise, visit http://www.ct.gov/doc/cwp/view.asp?Q=521088.

published work on correctional rehabilitation programs, they found that many intervention programs reported success.[95] According to Gendreau and Ross, there is now "convincing evidence that some treatment programs, when they are applied with integrity by competent practitioners in appropriate target populations, can be effective in preventing crime or reducing recidivism."[96] More recently, Mark Lipsey and Francis Cullen's comprehensive review of the studies of correctional rehabilitation found consistently positive effects on reducing recidivism.[97]

REHABILITATION DOES WORK   Despite challenges to the efficacy of rehabilitation, many experts still believe in the rehabilitative ideal.[98] They view it as not only humanistic but also cost-effective: even though treatment programs may be expensive, if they reduce crime, the savings in suffering and loss will more than offset their costs.[99] And some reviews have found evidence that the right mix of behavioral adjustment programs can produce large reductions in misconduct within the institution that may carry over into reductions in recidivism in the community.[100]

Evaluations of education, vocation, and work programs indicate that they may be able to lower recidivism rates and increase postrelease employment.[101] Inmates who have completed higher levels of education find it easier to gain employment upon release and consequently are less likely to recidivate over long periods.[102] The programs that have produced positive results both in the community and inside correctional institutions:

■ Teach interpersonal skills

■ Provide individual counseling

■ Make use of behavior modification techniques

■ Use cognitive-behavioral therapy

■ Stress improving moral reasoning

■ Combine in-prison therapeutic communities with follow-up community treatment[103]

It is also possible that a combination of efforts rather than a singular approach can have beneficial results; an example might be combining institutional treatment with postrelease aftercare.[104] Thus, even though not all programs are successful for all inmates, many treatment programs are effective, and some participants, especially younger clients, have a better chance of success on the outside than those who forgo treatment.[105]

Guarding the Institution

Control of a prison is a complex task. On the one hand, a tough, high-security environment may meet the goals of punishment and control but fail to reinforce positive behavior changes. On the other hand, too liberal an administrative stance can lower staff morale and place inmates in charge of the institution. For many years, prison guards were viewed as ruthless people who enjoyed their power over inmates, fought rehabilitation efforts, were racist, and had a "lock psychosis" developed over their years of counting, numbering, and checking on inmates. This view has changed in recent years. Correctional officers are now viewed as public servants who are seeking the security and financial rewards of a civil service position.[106] Most are in favor of rehabilitation efforts and do not hold any particular animosity toward the inmates. The correctional officer has been characterized as both a "people worker" who must be prepared to deal with the problems of inmates on a personal level and a member of a complex bureaucracy who must be able to cope with its demands.

LO7   Describe the world of correctional officers.

Corrections officers play a number of roles in the institution. They supervise cell houses, dining areas, shops, and other facilities, as well as perching on the walls, armed with rifles, to oversee the yard and prevent escapes. Corrections officers also sit on disciplinary boards and escort inmates to hospitals and court appearances.

The greatest problem that correctional officers face is the duality of their role: maintainers of order and security and advocates of treatment and rehabilitation. Added to this basic dilemma is the changing inmate role. In earlier times, corrections officers could count on inmate leaders to help them maintain order, but now they are confronted by a racially charged atmosphere in which violence is a way of life. Today, correctional work in some institutions can be filled with danger, tension, boredom, and little evidence that efforts to help inmates lead to success. Research indicates that correctional work is extremely high risk.[107] And unlike police officers, correctional officers apparently do not form a close-knit subculture with unique values and a sense of intergroup loyalty. Correctional officers experience alienation and isolation from inmates, from the administration, and from each other. Interestingly, this sense of alienation seems greatest in younger officers; evidence exists that later in their careers, officers enjoy a revival of interest in their work and take great pride in providing human services to inmates.[108] It is not surprising that correctional officers experience significant stress related to such job factors as lack of safety, inadequate career opportunities, and work overload.[109] Eric Lambert and his associates found that the stress of the prison experience can lead to emotional exhaustion, a powerful dimension of job burnout that, if left unchecked, is associated with high levels of turnover and absenteeism and with general job dissatisfaction.[110]

However, correctional officers who have high levels of job satisfaction, good relations with their coworkers, and high levels of social support seem to be better able to deal with the stress of the correctional setting.[111] Mike Vuolo and Candace Kruttschnitt found that correctional officers can have a sizable impact on prisoners' ability to adjust to prison life. Correctional staff members who conduct themselves professionally and gain the respect and cooperation of the inmates are able to have a very positive influence on these inmates' later readjustment to society. In contrast, those who fail miserably on both counts may be contributing the nation's high recidivism rates.[112] For more on a career as a correctional officer, read the Careers in Criminal Justice feature.

Female Correctional Officers

The issue of female correctional officers in male institutions comes up repeatedly. Research finds that they differ little from their male colleagues in their behavior or their use of aggressive tactics.[113]

The employment of women as guards in close contact with male inmates has raised many questions of privacy and safety and spawned a number of legal cases. In one important case, *Dothard v. Rawlinson* (1977), the U.S. Supreme Court upheld Alabama's refusal to hire female correctional officers on the grounds that it would put them in significant danger from the male inmates.[114] Despite such setbacks, women now work side by side with male guards in almost every state, performing the same duties. Research indicates that discipline has not suffered because of the inclusion of women in the guard force. Sexual assaults have been rare, and more negative attitudes have been expressed by the female guards' male peers than by inmates. Most commentators believe that the presence of female guards can have an important beneficial effect on the self-image of inmates and improve the guard–inmate working relationship.

Ironically, female correctional officers may find that an assignment to a male institution can boost their career. Recent restrictions on male staff in women's prisons, in the wake of well-publicized sex scandals, have forced administrators to assign women officers to the dormitory areas, the least desirable areas in which to work. Women officers are not similarly restricted in male-only facilities.[115]

CAREERS in criminal justice

CORRECTIONAL OFFICER

DUTIES AND CHARACTERISTICS

In maximum-security and most medium-security cell houses, the correctional officer is required to do the following: (a) open and close the steel-barred door that allows entrance and exit to cell houses, (b) conduct an inmate count several times a day, (c) distribute medicine, mail, and laundry, (d) supervise maintenance activities, and (e) answer the telephone.

The inmates' daily showers must also be supervised. If violations of rules occur, the cell house guard must write disciplinary tickets. During the day shift, the majority of correctional officers are assigned to work areas, such as the metal factory, the furniture factory, the yard, the canteen, or some other prison industry. Officers primarily enforce regulations through communication skills and moral authority and attempt to avoid conflict at all costs. Most officers attend to their duties unarmed, but a few officers hold positions in lookout towers, armed with high-powered rifles. In addition to the custodial duties they perform in more secure facilities, correctional officers in federal institutions and some minimum-security state facilities are also responsible for providing rehabilitative services.

JOB OUTLOOK

With the continued construction of federal, state, and private prisons, there are jobs available for those who are interested in becoming correctional officers. With so many existing prisons in small towns and in isolated areas, applicants may need to be willing to relocate for these positions.

SALARY

Recently, median annual wages of correctional officers and jailers were about $39,000; the highest-paid 10 percent earned more than $66,000.

 L08 Explain what is meant by prisoners' rights, and discuss some key privileges that have been granted to inmates.

hands-off doctrine

The legal practice of allowing prison administrators a free hand in running the institution, even if correctional practices violate inmates' constitutional rights; this practice ended with the onset of the prisoners' rights movement in the 1960s.

Prisoners' Rights

Before the early 1960s, it was accepted that upon conviction, an individual forfeited all rights not expressly granted by statutory law or correctional policy; in other words, inmates were civilly dead. The U.S. Supreme Court held that convicted offenders should expect to be penalized for their misdeeds and that part of their punishment was the loss of freedoms that ordinary citizens take for granted.

One reason why inmates lacked rights was that state and federal courts were reluctant to intervene in the administration of prisons unless the circumstances of a case clearly indicated a serious breach of the Eighth Amendment protection against cruel and unusual punishment. This judicial policy is referred to as the **hands-off doctrine**. The courts used three basic justifications for their neglect of prison conditions:

1. Correctional administration was a technical matter best left to experts rather than to courts ill equipped to make appropriate evaluations.
2. Society as a whole was apathetic to what went on in prisons, and most individuals preferred not to associate with or know about the offenders.
3. Prisoners' complaints involved privileges rather than rights. Prisoners were considered to have fewer constitutional rights than other members of society.[116]

As the 1960s drew to a close, the hands-off doctrine was eroded. Federal district courts began seriously considering prisoners' claims about conditions in the various state and federal institutions and used their power to intervene on behalf

OPPORTUNITIES

Job opportunities for correctional officers are expected to be excellent. The need to replace correctional officers who transfer to other occupations, retire, or leave the labor force, coupled with rising employment demand, will generate thousands of job openings each year. Employment for correctional officers is expected to grow 16 percent between 2006 and 2016, faster than the average for all occupations. Some employment opportunities also will arise in the private sector, as public authorities contract with private companies to provide and staff corrections facilities. Both state and federal corrections agencies are increasingly using private prisons.

QUALIFICATIONS

Most correctional officer positions require that the applicant have a high school education or its equivalent, be at least 18 or 21 years of age, be a U.S. citizen, and have no felony convictions. A potential corrections officer must also be in excellent health and must meet formal standards for physical fitness, eyesight, and hearing. Drug testing and background checks of applicants are usually done.

EDUCATION AND TRAINING

A high school diploma or graduation equivalency degree is required. Some state and local corrections agencies require some college credits, but law enforcement or military experience may be substituted to fulfill this requirement. In the Federal Bureau of Prisons and many state facilities, the salaries offered for new officers are sufficient to attract a large applicant pool. As a result, most of those selected have college educations or at least degrees from two-year institutions. Federal, state, and some local departments of corrections provide training for correctional officers. Some states have regional training academies that are available to local agencies. State and local correctional agencies also provide on-the-job training, including training on legal restrictions and interpersonal relations. Officer trainees typically receive several weeks or months of training in an actual job setting under the supervision of an experienced officer. However, on-the-job training varies widely from agency to agency.

Source: Bureau of Labor Statistics, U.S. Department of Labor, "Correctional Officers," *Occupational Outlook Handbook*, http://www.bls.gov/ooh/protective-service/correctional-officers.htm (accessed July 2014).

---

of the inmates. In some ways, this concern reflected the spirit of the times, which saw the onset of the civil rights movement, and subsequently was paralleled in such areas as student rights, public welfare, mental institutions, juvenile court systems, and military justice.

Beginning in the late 1960s, such activist groups as the NAACP Legal Defense Fund and the American Civil Liberties Union's National Prison Project began to search for appropriate legal vehicles to bring prisoners' complaints before state and federal courts. The most widely used device was the federal Civil Rights Act, 42 U.S.C. 1983:

> Every person who, under color of any statute, ordinance, regulation, custom, or usage of any State or Territory[,] subjects, or causes to be subjected, any citizen of the United States or other person within the jurisdiction thereof to the deprivation of any rights, privileges, or immunities secured by the Constitution and laws shall be liable to the party injured in an action at law, suit in equity, or other proper proceeding for redress.

The legal argument went that, as U.S. citizens, prison inmates could sue state officials if their civil rights were violated—for example, if they were the victims of racial or religious discrimination.

The U.S. Supreme Court first recognized the right of prisoners to sue for civil rights violations in cases involving religious freedom brought by the Black Muslims. This well-organized group had been frustrated by prison administrators who feared its growing power and wanted to limit its recruitment activities. In the 1964 case of *Cooper v. Pate*, however, the Supreme Court ruled that inmates who were being denied the right to practice their religion were entitled to legal

Web App 14.4

For more information about prisoner rights, visit https://www.aclu.org/prisoners-rights.

redress under 42 U.S.C. 1983.[117] Although *Cooper* applied to the narrow issue of religious freedom, it opened the door to providing other rights for inmates.

The subsequent prisoners' rights crusade, stretching from 1964 to 1980, paralleled the civil rights and women's movements. Battle lines were drawn between prison officials, who hoped to maintain their power and resented interference by the courts, and inmate groups and their sympathizers, who used state and federal courts as a forum for demanding better living conditions for prisoners and recognition of their personal rights. Each decision handed down by the courts was viewed as a victory for one side or the other.

To slow down prison litigation, which had been clogging the federal courts, Congress passed the Prison Litigation Reform Act in 1996.[118] The most important provision of this act requires prisoners to exhaust *all* internal administrative grievance procedures before they can file a civil rights case in federal court. It also bars litigation if a prisoner has not suffered a physical injury in addition to a violation of his or her constitutional rights. There is a limit on the number of times an appeal can be filed, and if a judge decides that an appeal is frivolous, is malicious, or does not state a proper claim, that appeal counts as a "strike." After getting three strikes, an inmate who wants to file another lawsuit must pay the entire court filing fee up-front.

The U.S. Supreme Court has upheld the provisions of the act in two cases—one dealing with a request for monetary relief and the other dealing with allegations of excessive use of force. In *Booth v. Churner* (2001) and *Porter v. Nussle* (2002), the Court ruled that it is constitutional to require that an inmate go through all administrative processes before a case can be brought to the courts.[119] In 2012, the Supreme Court in *Minneci v. Pollard* further restricted inmates' rights when in a vote of 8–1 it limited possible avenues for inmates in a private prison to state courts if they sought damages while incarcerated; access to federal courts for redress was denied.[120] Civil rights groups believe that these cases have a chilling effect on inmate litigation.[121]

While the prisoners' movement may have slowed, it has not ended. Below, some of the most important substantive and procedural rights of inmates are discussed.

Substantive Rights

Through a slow process of legal review, the courts have granted inmates a number of **substantive rights** that have significantly influenced the entire correctional system. The most important of these rights are discussed in the following sections.

ACCESS TO COURTS, LEGAL SERVICES, AND MATERIALS Without the ability to seek judicial review of conditions that cause discomfort or violate constitutional rights, the inmate must depend solely on the slow and often insensitive administrative mechanism of relief within the prison system. Therefore, the right of easy access to the courts gives inmates hope that their rights will be protected during incarceration. Courts have held that inmates are entitled to have legal materials available and to be provided with assistance in drawing up and filing complaints. Inmates who help others, so-called **jailhouse lawyers**, cannot be interfered with or harassed by prison administrators.

FREEDOM OF THE PRESS AND OF EXPRESSION Correctional administrators traditionally placed severe limitations on prisoners' speech and expression. For example, they read and censored inmate mail and restricted inmates' reading material. With the lifting of the hands-off doctrine, courts have consistently ruled that only when a compelling state interest exists can prisoners' First Amendment rights be modified. Correctional authorities must justify the limiting of free speech by showing that granting it would threaten institutional security.

substantive rights
Civil rights that include the right of inmates to receive mail and medical benefits and to practice their religion.

jailhouse lawyer
An inmate trained in law, or otherwise educated, who helps other inmates prepare legal briefs and appeals.

In a 2001 case, *Shaw v. Murphy*, the Supreme Court ruled that inmates do not have an absolute right to correspond with other inmates, even if it concerns legal advice. If prison administrators believe such correspondence undermines prison security, the First Amendment rights of inmates can be curtailed.[122]

FREEDOM OF RELIGION Freedom of religion is a fundamental right guaranteed by the First Amendment. In general, the courts have ruled that inmates have the right to assemble and pray in the religion of their choice, but that religious symbols and practices that interfere with institutional security can be restricted. Administrators can draw the line if religious needs become cumbersome or impossible to carry out for reason of cost or security. Granting special privileges can also be denied on the grounds that they will cause other groups to make similar demands. Although the Court recognized the right to practice religion, the most important case on this issue limited absolute religious freedom and placed the security of an institution above the right to attend religious services. In *O'Lone v. Estate of Shabazz*, Muslim inmates in a minimum-security classification requested permission to attend services held in another portion of the prison.[123] They argued that these services were essential to the practice of their religion. The request was denied on the basis of security. The Supreme Court upheld the denial, holding that "[w]hen a prison regulation impinges on inmates' constitutional rights, the regulation is valid if it is reasonably related to legitimate penological interests."[124] To determine whether there was such a relationship, the trial court should consider:

- Whether there is a logical connection between the restriction and the governmental interests invoked to justify it
- The availability of alternative means to exercise the restricted right
- The impact that accommodation of the right might have on other inmates, on prison personnel, and on allocation of prison resources generally
- Whether there are "obvious, easy alternatives" to the policy that could be adopted at a minimal cost

In an important 2005 case, *Cutter v. Wilkinson*, the Court ruled that the Religious Land Use and Institutionalized Persons Act of 2000, which was intended to protect the rights of prisoners, is not an unconstitutional government promotion of religion.[125] Writing for the majority, Justice Ruth Bader Ginsburg stated, "It confers no privileged status on any particular religious sect, and singles out no bona fide faith for disadvantageous treatment." *Cutter* allows inmates to practice their own religion unless their practices clearly undermine prison security and safety.

MEDICAL RIGHTS In early prisons, inmates' right to medical treatment was restricted through the "exceptional circumstances doctrine." Using this policy, the courts would hear only those cases in which the circumstances totally disregarded human dignity, while denying hearings to less serious cases. The cases that were allowed access to the courts usually represented a situation of total denial of medical care.

To gain their medical rights, prisoners have resorted to class action suits (suits brought on behalf of all individuals affected by similar circumstances—in this case, poor medical attention). In one of the more significant cases to date, *Newman v. Alabama* (1972), the entire Alabama prison system's medical facilities were declared inadequate.[126] The U.S. District Court for the Middle District of Alabama cited the following factors as contributing to inadequate care: insufficient physician and nurse resources, reliance on untrained inmates for paramedical work, intentional failure in treating the sick and injured, and failure to conform to proper medical standards. The *Newman* case forced corrections departments to upgrade prison medical facilities.

It was not until 1976, in *Estelle v. Gamble*, that the U.S. Supreme Court clearly mandated an inmate's right to have medical care.[127] Gamble had hurt his back in a Texas prison and filed suit because he contested the type of treatment he had received and questioned the lack of interest that prison guards had shown in his case. The Supreme Court said, "Deliberate indifference to serious medical needs of prisoners constitutes the 'unnecessary and wanton infliction of pain' proscribed by the Eighth Amendment."[128] Gamble was allowed to collect monetary damages for his injuries. Consequently, correctional administrators must consider access, quality, and cost of health care as part of the prison regime.[129]

cruel and unusual punishment

Physical punishment or punishment that far exceeds that given to people under similar circumstances and is therefore banned by the Eighth Amendment. The death penalty has so far not been considered cruel and unusual if it is administered in a fair and nondiscriminatory fashion.

CRUEL AND UNUSUAL PUNISHMENT The concept of **cruel and unusual punishment** is founded in the Eighth Amendment of the Constitution. The term itself has not been specifically defined by the Supreme Court, but the Court has held that treatment constitutes cruel and unusual punishment when it does the following:

■ Degrades the dignity of human beings [130]

■ Is more severe than (disproportionate to) the offense for which it has been given [131]

■ Shocks the general conscience and is fundamentally unfair [132]

■ Is deliberately indifferent to a person's safety and well-being [133]

■ Punishes people because of their status, such as race, religion, and mental state [134]

■ Is in flagrant disregard of due process of law, such as punishment that is capriciously applied [135]

State and federal courts have placed strict limits on disciplinary methods that may be considered inhumane. Corporal punishment all but ended after the practice was condemned in *Jackson v. Bishop* (1968).[136] Although the solitary confinement of disruptive inmates continues, its prolonged use under barbaric conditions has been held to be in violation of the Eighth Amendment. Courts have found that inmates placed in solitary have the right to adequate personal hygiene, exercise, mattresses, ventilation, and rules specifying how they can earn their release.

PHYSICAL ABUSE There are two critical contexts in which physical abuse occurs in prisons: inmate-on-inmate abuse and guard-on-inmate abuse. The courts have generally been unwilling to impose liability on prison officials for failing to protect prisoners from physical abuse and sexual assault by other inmates. However, the courts have ruled that prison officials are liable for damages if they display indifference to attacks on inmates occurring inside the prison.

The most important case in this area is *Farmer v. Brennan*.[137] In *Farmer*, a biological male who had undergone sex change treatment was transferred to a male high-security prison and placed in the general population. Within two weeks, he was beaten and raped by another prisoner. He sued for damages, alleging that his transfer violated the Eighth Amendment. The Court held that prisoners, in the presence of other prisoners, some of whom are very dangerous, have no real means to protect themselves. Prison officials cannot close their eyes to the inevitable and are liable for their care and protection. The test of liability is "deliberate indifference," which is the conscious or reckless disregard of the consequences of one's acts or omissions. If prison officials were aware in advance of a serious risk to an inmate's safety, they are liable for injuries suffered, even though they did not know with absolute certainty that the inmate would be harmed. Prison officials may be liable if they had knowledge of the risk of harm but failed to take reasonable steps for its prevention. Thus, the Court stated that in these circumstances, a prison official cannot escape liability by arguing that "he merely refused to verify underlying factors that he strongly suspected to be true, or declined to confirm inferences of risk that he strongly suspect[ed] to exist."[138]

In *Hudson v. McMillian* (1992), a Louisiana prison inmate testified that he had suffered minor bruises, facial swelling, loosened teeth, and a cracked dental plate after receiving a beating by two prison guards. A supervisor on duty watched the beating but merely told the officers "not to have too much fun." The magistrate hearing the case ruled that the staff had violated the Eighth Amendment's prohibition on cruel and unusual punishments, and Hudson was awarded damages. The case was appealed to the Supreme Court, which ruled that as long as force is used in a good-faith effort to maintain control, there is no liability. It is only in instances when prisoners can provide evidence that correctional officers acted maliciously that liability is held.[139]

In a 2002 case, *Hope v. Pelzer*, the Supreme Court ruled that correctional officials who knowingly violate the Eighth Amendment rights of inmates can be held liable for damages.[140] Larry Hope, an Alabama prison inmate, was twice handcuffed to a hitching post for disruptive conduct while he was working outside the prison on a chain gang. He was handcuffed above shoulder height, and when he tried moving his arms to improve circulation, the handcuffs cut into his wrists, causing pain and discomfort. He spent seven hours on the hitching post, during which he was given one or two water breaks but no bathroom breaks, and a guard taunted him about his thirst. Hope filed a suit against three guards, charging them with violating his civil rights. The guards argued that they were entitled to **qualified immunity** from lawsuits, a legal doctrine that protects government officials from liability from civil damages if their conduct did not violate clearly established statutory or constitutional rights of which a reasonable person would have been aware.

The Supreme Court ruled that Hope's allegations established an Eighth Amendment violation. It ruled that among the "'unnecessary and wanton' inflictions of pain [constituting cruel and unusual punishment forbidden by the amendment] are those that are 'totally without penological justification.'" In the context of prison conditions, this determination is made by ascertaining whether an official acted with "deliberate indifference" to the inmate's health or safety, a state of mind that can be inferred from the fact that the risk of harm is obvious. The Court reasoned that any safety concerns had long since ended by the time Hope was handcuffed to the hitching post, because he had already been subdued, handcuffed, placed in leg irons, and transported back to prison. The *Hope* case shows that correctional officials can be successfully sued if their behavior violates an inmate's constitutional rights and if they or any reasonable person should have surmised that the behavior was in violation of accepted practices.

qualified immunity
A legal doctrine that shields government officials from liability if their conduct did not violate clearly established civil rights that a reasonable person would have known about.

RACIAL SEGREGATION On August 8, 2009, a riot in the California prison at Chino left hundreds injured, buildings burnt, and property destroyed.[141] The disturbance was sparked by racial tensions between Latino and black inmates, and it later generated a great deal of controversy over the issue of racial segregation in prison. Should prisons be segregated to prevent violence among gangs such as the Aryan Brotherhood, the Mexican Mafia, and the Black Guerrilla Family? Or, as in other institutions, are inmates entitled to equal treatment under the law such that any form of segregation is considered inherently unconstitutional?

In a 2005 case, *Johnson v. California*, the Supreme Court ruled that the segregation of prison inmates on the basis of race, in their cells or anywhere on prison grounds, is an inappropriate form of racial classification.[142] However, it left it open for lower courts to decide, using a standard of *strict scrutiny*, when segregation is inappropriate and unconstitutional. *Johnson* focused on the policy of segregating inmates upon their arrival at a prison. However, the Court's ruling seemed to suggest that if racial segregation were allowed for incoming inmates,

Racial conflict is an ever-present danger in the nation's prison system. Consequently, in some institutions inmates prefer segregated housing units. Here, inmates Tim Heffernan, left, and Daniel Mabson talk while sitting on their adjacent bunks at the Sierra Conservation Center in Jamestown, California. Despite efforts by California prison officials to end institutionalized, government-mandated racial segregation, powerful race-based gangs violently oppose desegregation in prison housing units. Blacks, whites, and Hispanics are willing to sleep side by side in bunk beds spaced an arm's length apart, but they would brawl or risk longer sentences rather than accept an inmate of another race in a bed above or below them in the same bunk bed stack.

AP Images/Rich Pedroncelli

there was a danger that it might also be imposed "in the dining halls, yards, and general housing areas...." Segregation should be allowed, the judges reasoned, only when a prison administrator could prove that it served a compelling interest to promote prison safety. The Court recognized that "prisons are dangerous places, and the special circumstances they present may justify racial classifications in some contexts." Because the Chino riot occurred after California began to integrate prison entry centers, it is possible that future efforts to racially integrate prisons will be frustrated. State courts, even when using a "strict scrutiny" standard, may conclude that racial integration, in some instances, is just too dangerous.

OVERALL PRISON CONDITIONS Prisoners have long had the right to the minimal conditions necessary for human survival, such as the food, clothing, shelter, and medical care necessary to sustain human life. A number of attempts have been made to articulate reasonable standards of prison care and to make sure they are applied. Courts have held that although people are sent to prison for punishment, it does not mean that prison should be a punishing experience.[143] As explained earlier, in the 1994 case of *Farmer v. Brennan*, the court ruled that prison officials are legally liable if, knowing that an inmate faces a serious risk of harm, they disregard that risk by failing to take measures to avoid or reduce it. Furthermore, prison officials should be able to infer the risk from the evidence at hand; it is not necessary for them to have been warned or told.[144]

Overcrowding

Although inmates retain the right to reasonable care, if there is a legitimate purpose for the use of governmental restrictions, they may be considered constitutional. Thus, it might be possible to restrict reading material, allow strip searches, and prohibit inmates from receiving packages from the outside if the restrictions are legitimate security measures. If overcrowded conditions require it, inmates may be double-bunked in cells designed for a single inmate.[145]

While double-bunking is allowed, if conditions get too overcrowded the courts may consider it a violation of the Eighth Amendment's ban on cruel and unusual punishment. In 2011, the Supreme Court did just that, ordering the state of California to reduce its prison population by more than 30,000 inmates (we touched on this in the Chapter 13 opening story). In his majority opinion, Justice Anthony M. Kennedy described a prison system that failed to deliver minimal care to prisoners with serious medical and mental health problems and produced "needless suffering and death."

Justice Kennedy described "telephone-booth-sized cages without toilets" used to house suicidal inmates. He noted that suicide rates in the state's prisons are 80 percent higher than the average for inmates nationwide: "an inmate in one of California's prisons needlessly dies every six or seven days due to constitutional deficiencies.... A prison that deprives prisoners of basic sustenance, including adequate medical care, is incompatible with the concept of human dignity and has no place in civilized society."[146] State officials were given two years to comply with the order.

Leaving Prison

At the expiration of their prison term, most inmates return to society and try to resume their lives. As Figure 14.1 shows, around 500,000 inmates are either released on **parole** or complete their term of parole each year. The total parole population each year is around 850,000.[147]

About 35 percent of inmates who enter parole supervision go before a parole board, a group of correctional officials who determine whether an inmate is eligible for and/or worthy of early release.[148] The board is a duly constituted body of men and women who review inmate cases and determine whether offenders have reached a rehabilitative level sufficient to deal with the outside world. The board also dictates what specific parole rules parolees must obey.

In states where determinate-sentencing statutes have eliminated discretionary parole, offenders are released after having served their determinate sentence, minus time off for good behavior and any other credits by which the term of

L09 Describe the problems of prisoner reentry.

parole
The early release of a prisoner from imprisonment subject to conditions set by correctional authorities.

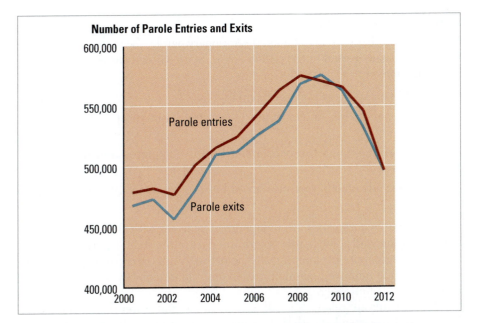

FIGURE 14.1 Estimated parole entries and exits, 2000–2012

Source: Laura M. Maruschak and Thomas P. Bonczar, *Probation and Parole in the United States, 2012* (Washington, DC: Bureau of Justice Statistics, 2013, p. 8).

incarceration can be reduced. Their release may involve supervision in the community, and rule violations can result in return to prison for the balance of their unexpired sentence. In these jurisdictions, the amount of time a person must remain in prison is a predetermined percentage of the inmate's sentence, assuming that there are no infractions or escape attempts.

With mandatory parole release, the inmate is released when the unserved portion of the maximum prison term equals the inmate's earned good time (less time served in jail awaiting trial). In some states, sentences can be reduced by more than half with a combination of statutory and earned good time. If the conditions of their release are violated, mandatory releasees can have their good time revoked and be returned to the institution to serve the remainder of their unexpired term. More than half of all parolees are now released in this fashion. The remaining inmates are released for a variety of reasons, including expiration of their term, commutation of their sentence, and court orders to relieve overcrowding in prisons.

Depending on the jurisdiction, inmates must serve a certain portion of their sentences before becoming eligible for parole. The conditions of parole may require the individual to report regularly to a parole officer, to refrain from criminal conduct, to maintain and support his or her family, to avoid contact with other convicted criminals, to abstain from using alcohol and drugs, to remain within the jurisdiction, and so on. Violations of the conditions of parole may result in revocation, in which case the individual will be returned to prison. The concept behind parole is to allow the release of the offender to community supervision, where rehabilitation and readjustment can be facilitated.

In a few instances, inmates are released after their sentences have been commuted by a board of pardons or directly by a governor or even the president. About 15 percent of prison inmates are released after serving their entire maximum sentence, without any time excused or forgiven. Regardless of the method of their release, former inmates face the formidable task of readjusting to society. This means regaining legal rights they may have lost on their conviction, reestablishing community and family ties, and finding employment. After being in prison, these goals are often difficult to achieve.

The Parole Board

In those states that have maintained discretionary parole, the authority to release inmates is usually vested in the parole board. State parole boards have four primary functions:

- To select and place prisoners on parole
- To aid, supervise, and provide continuing control of parolees in the community
- To determine when the parole function is completed and to discharge parolees
- To determine whether parole should be revoked if violations of conditions occur

Most parole authorities are independent agencies with their own staff and administration, and a few parole boards are part of the state department of corrections. Arguments for keeping the board within a corrections department usually include improved communication and the availability of more intimate knowledge about offenders.

Most boards are relatively small, usually numbering fewer than 10 members. This limited size, coupled with their large caseloads and the varied activities they are expected to perform, can prevent board members from becoming as well acquainted with the individual inmates as might be desired.

Parole Hearings

The actual (discretionary) parole decision is made at a parole-granting hearing. At this hearing the full board or a selected subcommittee reviews information, may meet with the offender, and then decides whether the parole applicant has a reasonable probability of succeeding outside of prison. Each parole board has its own way of reviewing cases. In some, the full board meets with the applicant; in others, only a few members do that. In a number of jurisdictions, a single board member can conduct a personal investigation and submit the findings to the full board for a decision. Whether in an individual or group format, face-to-face meetings can be beneficial, because the panel can get feedback from inmates to more thoroughly evaluate parole readiness. Parole board officials, many of whom have had varied professional training and experience, can use these meetings to assess an inmate's sincerity and readiness for release.[149]

When parole is discretionary, most parole boards look at the inmate's crime, institutional record, and willingness to accept responsibility before making the release decision. Some jurisdictions rely on standardized tests that predict whether a potential parolee will recidivate upon release.[150] Letters may be solicited from the inmate's friends and family members. In some jurisdictions, victims may appear and make statements about the losses they suffered. By speaking directly to the applicant, the board can also promote and emphasize the specific types of behavior and behavior changes it expects to see if the inmate is to eventually qualify for or effectively serve parole. Inmates who maintain their innocence may find that denying responsibility for their crimes places their release date in jeopardy. The requirement that they admit guilt or culpability is especially vexing for those inmates who actually are innocent and who actively refuse to accept their institutional label of "convicted criminal."[151]

The inmate's specific rights at a parole-granting hearing also vary from jurisdiction to jurisdiction. In about half of the parole-granting jurisdictions, inmates are permitted counsel or are allowed to present witnesses on their behalf; other jurisdictions do not permit these privileges. Because the federal courts have declared that the parole applicant is not entitled to any form of legal representation, the inmate may have to pay for legal services when this privilege is allowed. In almost all discretionary parole-granting jurisdictions, the reasons for the parole decision must be given in writing, and in about half of the jurisdictions, a verbatim record of the hearing is made.

Is There a Legal Right to Parole?

What happens if the parole authority denies early release, but the inmate believes he is deserving of parole? Perhaps he has witnessed other inmates receiving parole who have similar institutional records. Can he question the parole board's decision via the courts? The Supreme Court answered this question in 2011 when it ruled in the consolidated cases of *Swarthout v. Cooke* and *Cate v. Clay* that due process requirements are satisfied when a prisoner has an opportunity to be heard and is provided a statement of the reasons why parole is denied; there is in essence no absolute or legal right to receiving parole. The first case, *Swarthout v. Cooke*, involved Damon Cooke, who was incarcerated in California for attempted first-degree murder. In 2002, the California Board of Prison Terms rejected his parole request. California law provides that if the board denies parole, the prisoner can seek judicial review. Subsequently the California Superior Court, the California Court of Appeal, and the California Supreme Court all denied Cooke's petitions, prompting him to seek federal assistance. Similarly, *Cate v. Clay* began with the 1978 conviction of Elijah Clay for first-degree murder. In 2003, the board found Clay suitable for parole, but the governor reviewed the case and found him unsuitable. After going through the state process, Clay filed a claim in federal court, and the district court concluded that the governor's reliance on the nature of Clay's original offense rather than his prison behavior violated his right to due process. The Ninth Circuit affirmed, concluding that the governor's decision was unreasonable.

The Supreme Court reversed both decisions, holding that while the due process clause requires fair procedures in parole hearing, both Cooke and Clay received adequate process because they were allowed an opportunity to be heard and were provided a statement of the reasons why parole was denied. However, the courts do not have the right to step in and conclude the parole board (and governor's) decisions were faulty. If the process is fair, then the inmate must live with the outcome.[152]

The Parolee in the Community

Once released into the community, a parolee is given a standard set of rules and conditions that must be obeyed. The offender who violates these rules may have parole revoked and be sent back to the institution to serve the remainder of the sentence. Once in the community, the parolee is supervised by a trained staff of parole officers who help the offender search for employment and monitor the parolee's behavior and activities to ensure that the conditions of parole are met.

Parole is generally viewed as a privilege granted to deserving inmates on the basis of their good behavior while in prison. Parole has two conflicting sides, however. On one hand, the paroled offender is allowed to serve part of the sentence in the community, an obvious benefit for the deserving offender. On the other hand, because parole is a privilege and not a right, the parolee is viewed as a potentially dangerous criminal who must be carefully watched and supervised. The conflict between the treatment and enforcement aspects of parole has not been reconciled by the criminal justice system, and the parole process still contains elements of both.

To overcome these roadblocks to success, the parole officer may have to play a much greater role than the probation officer in directing and supervising clients' lives. In some instances, parole programs have become active in creating new postrelease treatment-oriented programs designed to increase the chances of parole success. For example, the Kansas Parole Department has adopted a restorative justice approach and is now having parolees work in community service settings upon their release. Jobs may include work at soup kitchens, homeless shelters, and halfway houses. Reports indicate that the program is quite successful.[153] In other instances, parole agencies have implemented law enforcement–oriented services that work with local police agencies to identify and apprehend parolees who may have been involved in criminal activity. The California Department of Corrections has established the Special Service Unit, which (among its other tasks) acts as a liaison to help local police agencies solve major crimes when inmates or state parolees are the known or suspected offenders.[154]

INTENSIVE SUPERVISION PAROLE To aid supervision, some jurisdictions are implementing systems that classify offenders on the basis of their supervision needs. Typically, a point or guideline system (sometimes called a salient factor score) based on prior record and prison adjustment divides parolees into three groups: (1) those who require intensive surveillance, (2) those who require social services instead of surveillance, and (3) those who require limited supervision.

In some jurisdictions, parolees in need of closer surveillance are placed on **intensive supervision parole (ISP)**. These programs use limited caseload sizes, treatment facilities, the matching of parolee and supervisor by personality, and

intensive supervision parole (ISP)
A form of parole characterized by smaller caseloads and closer surveillance; it may include frequent drug testing and, in some cases, electronic monitoring.

shock parole (which involves immediate short-term incarceration for parole violators to impress them with the seriousness of a violation). ISP clients are required to attend more office and home visits than routine parolees. ISP may also require frequent drug testing, a term in a community correctional center, and electronic monitoring in the home.

Evaluations of ISP programs have yielded mixed results. Some show that ISP may actually produce a higher violation rate than traditional parole supervision, because limiting caseload size enables parole officers to supervise their clients more closely and spot infractions more easily.[155] Some recent research shows that under some conditions, a properly run ISP program can significantly reduce recidivism upon release. The key factors may be parole officer orientation (a balance between social service and law enforcement seems to work best) and a supportive organizational environment in which the program is being run.[156]

The Effectiveness of Parole

Despite all efforts to treat, correct, and rehabilitate incarcerated offenders, a majority still return to prison shortly after their release. A recent study found that more than two-thirds of released state prisoners are rearrested within three years.[157] Nearly 80 percent are rearrested within five years. These statistics are discouraging to say the least. Other key findings from the study include:

■ Within five years of release, 82.1 percent of property offenders were arrested for a new crime, compared to 76.9 percent of drug offenders, 73.6 percent of public order offenders, and 71.3 percent of violent offenders.

■ More than a third (36.8 percent) of all prisoners who were arrested within five years of release were arrested within the first six months after release, with more than half (56.7 percent) arrested by the end of the first year.

■ A sixth (16.1 percent) of released prisoners were responsible for almost half (48.4 percent) of the nearly 1.2 million arrests that occurred in the five-year follow-up period.

■ Within five years of release, 84.1 percent of inmates who were age 24 or younger at release were arrested, compared to 78.6 percent of inmates ages 25 to 39 and 69.2 percent of those age 40 or older.[158]

Why Do People Fail on Parole?

Persons released from prison face a multitude of difficulties. They remain largely uneducated, unskilled, and usually without solid family support systems. Then add to this the burden of a prison record, which can make securing employment more than a little difficult.

It may come as no surprise that those who violate parole are typically younger, less well educated inmates who have histories of criminal activity and drug dependence and who live in deteriorated, crime-ridden communities. These social problems reduce the likelihood of post-prison success for both male and female offenders.[159]

A report by the influential Pew Foundation found that not all states had the same parole failure rates. The more successful ones made important correctional decisions—such as the types of offenders sentenced to prison, how inmates are selected for release, how long they are under supervision. Which strategies were the most successful? States that made extensive use of probation for petty offenders had relatively higher inmate recidivism rates, since only the most hard-core inmates were actually sent to prison. Parole was more successful in states that employed programs that target motivated offenders to stay crime- and drug-free through a combination of swift and certain sanctions for prison violations and rewards for obeying correctional rules.[160]

The Problem of Reentry

Why has the phenomenon of parole failure remained so stubborn and hard to control? Why is it so difficult to reenter society?

PRISON EXPERIENCE One reason may be the very nature of the prison experience itself. The psychological and economic problems that lead offenders to recidivism are rarely addressed by a stay in prison. Despite rehabilitation efforts, the typical ex-convict is still the same undereducated, unemployed, substance-abusing, lower-socioeconomic-status male he was when arrested. Being separated from friends and family, not sharing in conventional society, associating with dangerous people, and adapting to a volatile lifestyle probably have done little to improve the offender's personality or behavior. It seems naïve to think that incarceration alone can help someone overcome these lifelong disabilities. By their very nature, prisons seek to impose and maintain order and conformity rather than to help inmates develop skills such as independence and critical thinking—factors that may be essential once the inmate is forced to cope outside the prison walls.[161]

SUPERVISION ON THE OUTSIDE Many inmates are not assigned to supervision caseloads once they are back in the community. About 200,000 released inmates go unsupervised each year, three-quarters because they were released after completing their maximum sentence and are therefore not required to be supervised. A number of research efforts indicate that supervision can be valuable. When Michael Ostermann looked at the records of those released from prison in New Jersey he found that after three years, those released with parole supervision were generally less involved in new crimes when compared with those who were released unconditionally.[162] Another study of offenders who violated their conditions of release while under supervision in Ohio found that community-based sanctions (e.g., a short stay in a halfway house) that were administered in a certain, severe, and swift manner were effective in reducing parole violators' odds of recidivism and time to recidivism.[163]

Of course, inmates who "max out" or otherwise go unsupervised may be the more serious offenders whose survival in the community would be lower even if they were supervised. If these differences are controlled, the effect of supervision is neutralized.[164] So the actual effect of supervision after release is still open to debate.[165]

Regardless of how they are released, the risks the flood of newly released inmates present to the community include increases in child abuse, family violence, the spread of infectious diseases, homelessness, and community disorganization. Many have no way to cope and wind up in homeless shelters.[166] These problems take a heavy toll on communities and also limit reentry success.

PERSONAL DEFICITS It is also possible that reentry problems are related to the releasee's own lifelong personal deficits. Most research efforts indicate that recidivates are young men and women who have managed to accumulate a long history of drug abuse and criminal behavior in a short time.[167] They may have an antisocial personality, and childhood experiences with family dysfunction; many have suffered from a lifetime of substance abuse or dependence disorder.[168] More than three-fourths of the inmates leaving prison report drug and/or alcohol abuse in the year following their release. Inmates with mental illness are also increasingly being imprisoned—and then released.

Once the parolee is on the outside, these problems do not easily subside. Some ex-inmates may feel compelled to prove that the prison experience has not changed them: Taking drugs or being sexually aggressive may show friends that they have not lost their "heart."[169] It is not surprising that releasees who maintain criminal peer associations, carry weapons, abuse alcohol, and harbor aggressive

EVIDENCE-based justice

WHO MAKES IT ON THE OUTSIDE?

In a recent study, sociologists Stephen Bahr, Lish Harris, James Fisher, and Anita Harker Armstrong sought to identify what differentiates successful parolees from those who fail on parole. Their goal was to achieve a better understanding of the reentry process in order to enable professionals, friends, and family members to help former inmates adjust to life outside of prison and successfully complete their parole.

To achieve their research objective, they followed 51 parolees during the three years that followed their release from parole. They found that at the end of the three-year period, 55 percent (28) of the parolees had successfully completed their parole and were formally discharged; 25 percent (13) remained on parole; 20 percent (10) were back in prison.

What differentiated the successes from the failures? One big reason for parole failure, as might be expected, is continued trouble with the law. Successes committed fewer crimes and were arrested less than failures: the mean number of arrests for those who successfully completed parole was 0.28—only 5 of the 28 successful parolees had been arrested. By contrast, those who returned to prison had been arrested at least twice within the three years after release.

Another factor that shaped parole outcome was participation in a prison-based treatment program. Those who succeeded on parole were more likely to have taken a substance abuse class while in prison, an experience that helped some parolees succeed in their attempt to stay off drugs after release and change their identity. The class may have provided the skills, motivation, and support useful in learning to remain substance free.

A number of other economic, personal and social factors contributed to successful reentry into society. Those who worked at least 40 hours a week were more likely to have completed parole successfully. Work may be important in establishing routines that reduce opportunities and time for associations with deviant peers. Full-time work may also help parolees establish a conventional identity.

Nurturing family ties and friendship networks were also important for parole success. Conventional family and friendship networks insulated the successful parolees from the influence of friends who used drugs. Those without social supports drifted back into crime because they were less connected and more alone.

CRITICAL THINKING

Success on parole is a multifaceted construct, involving support from family and friends as well as institutional support from employees and the correctional system. Given these factors, how would you structure parole to enhance effective reentry?

Source: Stephen J. Bahr, Lish Harris, James K. Fisher, and Anita Harker Armstrong, "Successful Reentry: What Differentiates Successful and Unsuccessful Parolees?" *International Journal of Offender Therapy and Comparative Criminology* 54 (2010): 667–692.

---

feelings are the most likely to fail upon reentry.[170] In contrast, parolees who have had a good employment record in the past and who maintain jobs after their release are the most likely to avoid recidivating.[171] The accompanying Evidence-Based Justice box looks at the characteristics of the successful parolee.

ECONOMIC DEFICITS Former inmates soon find that imprisonment reduces their income and employment opportunities.[172] By law, ex-convicts are denied the right to work in certain occupations. And even if a criminal record does not automatically prohibit employment, many employers are reluctant to hire people who have served time. Why would someone hire an ex-con when other applicants are available? Many find that it is difficult to get jobs because potential employers are unconvinced that reform is possible or doubt that former inmates have the "people skills" that will enable them to succeed in the workplace. Some business owners are concerned about customers' reactions if they know that an employee is an ex-inmate.[173] If ex-offenders lie about their prison experience and are later found out, they can be dismissed for misrepresentation.

The stress of economic deprivation, in turn, can lead to family breakup and to less involvement with their children.[174]

EMPLOYMENT HELPS Research shows that former inmates who gain and keep meaningful employment are more likely to succeed on parole than those who are unemployed or underemployed.[175] Parolees who had a good employment record before their incarceration and who are able to find jobs after their release are the ones most likely to avoid recidivating.[176] A four-state survey conducted by Paul Hirschfield and Alex Piquero found that although some people regard ex-offenders as dangerous and dishonest, many reject these stereotypes, and a majority say they would be willing to work and associate with people who had been incarcerated recently. Employers may view ex-offenders with caution, but workers may be more comfortable working alongside ex-offenders than their more conservative supervisors realize. One reason, the survey showed, was that the less faith people have in the fairness of the justice system, the more likely they are to espouse notions of redeemability and compassion toward ex-offenders. Even people who believe in harsh punishment may be willing to work alongside people who have paid their debt to society. If more people were acquainted with ex-offenders, more would be willing to hire them and give them the economic opportunity to succeed.[177]

MARRIAGE AND FAMILY DEFICITS Inmates with strong social support and close family ties have a better chance of making it on the outside.[178] But prison can take its toll on social relationships, and being a former inmate can devastate family economic and social functioning. Poor inmates and their families may be no longer welcome in subsidized public housing complexes. This is a consequence of the U.S. Department of Housing and Urban Development's "one strike and you're out" policy, whereby all members of the household are evicted if one member is involved in crime.[179] Without government subsidies, former inmates' families may not have the economic means to find affordable housing. The Pew Foundation found that family income averaged over the years a father is incarcerated is 22 percent lower than family income was the year before a father is incarcerated. Even in the year after the father is released, family income remains 15 percent lower than it was the year before incarceration.[180]

Kids are hurt educationally, socially, and financially if a parent is a former inmate. The Pew Foundation found that children with fathers who have been incarcerated are significantly more likely than other children to be expelled or suspended from school (23 percent compared with 4 percent). Children of incarcerated and released parents may suffer confusion, sadness, and social stigma, and these feelings often result in difficulties in school, low self-esteem, aggressive behavior, and general emotional dysfunction. One reason is that mothers released from prison have difficulty finding services such as housing, employment, and child care, and this causes stress for them and their children.

Another problem is that if the parents are negative role models, children fail to develop positive attitudes about work and responsibility. Children of incarcerated parents are five times more likely to serve time in prison than children whose parents are not incarcerated.

A prison experience also harms the life chances of unmarried single inmates: incarceration significantly reduces the chances of marriage for all men. Since marriage has proved to be a significant neutralizer of future criminality, the suppression effect on marriage that a prison sentence inflicts may help explain high recidivism rates.[181] And even if they do marry, former inmates may be restricted in their choice of mates. Their circumstances may force them to choose partners with equally checkered backgrounds, a circumstance that may enhance rather than depress the likelihood of future criminality.

COMMUNITY DEFICITS Community characteristics can also influence the way parole violations are handled. Parolees returning to communities with high unemployment rates, a factor considered by parole board members to be an unstable environment, are more likely to have their parole revoked.[182] Similarly, parolees living in areas with concentrated disadvantages and social disorder, where bars are plentiful and liquor stores abundant, also suffer higher rates of recidivism. Clearly the neighborhood plays a significant role in parole success.

Communities that can provide social and mental health services also influence parole success. For example, many former inmates need mental and psychological services that some communities simply cannot provide. Even when public mental health services are available, many mentally ill individuals fail to use them because they fear institutionalization, deny they are mentally ill, or distrust the mental health system. The situation will become more serious as more and more parolees are released into the same disorganized communities where deteriorated conditions may have motivated their original crimes. Having mental health services nearby seems to have a significant effect on parole board decision making.[183] The further parolees live from social service providers, the more likely they will be returned to prison.

The Risks of Reentry

As criminologist Joan Petersilia warns, many of those being released have not received adequate treatment and are ill prepared for life in conventional society.[184] Returning offenders struggle to adapt to life outside of prison and those that can't adapt wind up on the streets or in homeless shelters. One study of shelters in New York City found that 23 percent of the occupants had been released from New York prisons and jails in the past two years.[185]

Petersilia argues that most leave prison with no savings, no immediate entitlement to unemployment benefits, and few employment prospects. A year after release, as many as 60 percent of former inmates are not employed in the regular labor market, and employers are increasingly reluctant to hire ex-offenders. Ex-offenders are commonly barred from working in the fields in which most jobs are being created, such as childcare, education, security, nursing, and home health care. More jobs are also now unionized, and many unions exclude ex-offenders.

Being barred from work opportunities produces chronic unemployment, a status closely related to drug and alcohol abuse. Losing a job can lead to substance abuse, which in turn is related to child and family violence.

THE SPECIAL PROBLEMS OF FEMALE INMATES Women released from prison face special challenges, and nearly half are either reconvicted or reincarcerated soon after parole release. Which women have the most trouble making it on the outside? As might be expected, those who are drug dependent, live in disorganized areas, and lack close personal relationships are the ones most likely to fail on parole.

Having a history of drug abuse is particularly harmful. According to recent research conducted by Beth Huebner and her associates, substance abuse makes it very difficult to readjust.[186] It compromises returning women's employment opportunities, relationships with children, and social support. The impact of drug abuse is felt most acutely by minority women who must balance the demands of substance abuse treatment, employment, and family responsibilities, all the while living in disorganized areas with little access to services or social support. Drug convictions may close doors to both social service providers and employers, who have little interest in helping or employing abusers.

Recent welfare reform acts deny government benefits to people convicted of drug offenses and/or their families, a policy that has a significant impact on African American and Hispanic mothers, who are disproportionately represented in the welfare system. And although being a mother seems to be a deterrent to recidivism, women in prison who are substance abusers and are marginally employed may face loss of parental rights upon release, further undermining their chances of successful reintegration.

THE EFFECT ON COMMUNITIES Parole expert Richard Seiter notes that when there were only a few hundred thousand prisoners, and a few thousand releasees per year, the issues surrounding the release of offenders did not overwhelm communities.[187] Families could house ex-inmates, job-search organizations could find them jobs, and community social service agencies could respond to their individual needs for mental health or substance abuse treatment. Today, the sheer number of reentering inmates has taxed the communities to which they are returning. Charis Kubrin and Eric Stewart have found that communities that already face the greatest social and economic disadvantages are those where the highest recidivism rates occur.[188] Obviously, the influx of returning inmates can magnify their problems.

Research shows that high rates of prison admissions produce high crime rates. Clearly, the national policy of relying on prison as a deterrent to crime may produce results that policy makers had not expected or wanted.

IMPROVING CHANCES ON REENTRY Can something be done to ease reentry? Now that the scope of the problem has been recognized, both the federal and state governments have devoted energy to improving reentry success. On April 9, 2008, the Second Chance Act was signed into law. This federal legislation authorized various grants to government agencies and nonprofit groups to provide a variety of services, including employment assistance, housing, substance abuse treatment, and family programming, that can help to reduce reoffending and violations of probation and parole.

At the federal level, a number of initiatives have been taken to help prepare inmates for reentry. The emphasis on release preparation intensifies at least 18 months prior to the end of the prison stay when inmates enter the Release Preparation Program, which includes classes in areas such as résumé writing, job search, and job retention. The program also includes presentations by members of community-based organizations that help ex-inmates find jobs and training opportunities after release. The Federal Bureau of Prisons then places appropriate inmates in halfway houses prior to release to help them adjust to life in the community and find employment. Some inmates become eligible for a release gratuity, clothing, or money for transportation to their release destination. The Inmate Transition Branch also provides additional prerelease employment assistance. Many institutions hold mock job fairs to give inmates an opportunity to practice job interview skills and to acquaint community recruiters with the skills available among inmates being released. Qualified inmates may apply for jobs with companies that have posted job openings. This branch also helps inmates prepare release folders that include a résumé; education certificates, diplomas, and transcripts; and other significant documents needed for a successful job interview.

There have also been a number of initiatives on the state level[189]:

■ *Offender notification forums.* As part of its Project Safe Neighborhood (PSN) initiative, the city of Chicago launched an offender notification forum. In designated neighborhoods, individuals recently assigned to parole or probation who had a history of gun violence and gang participation attended a forum hosted by the PSN team. In these forums, the individual met with representatives from state and local law enforcement agencies, community representatives, and service providers. The meetings focused on the consequences of gun crimes and the choices individuals can make based on alternatives that are available, including job training, education programs, drug treatment, temporary shelter, and counseling. An evaluation of the PSN initiative indicates that the forums have been "remarkably effective in reducing neighborhood crime rates."[190]

■ *Reentry courts.* The concept of a reentry court, first proposed nearly a decade ago, is taking hold in state and federal systems. By placing a judge (or magistrate) in the role of reentry manager, these courts, inspired by the successes of drug courts and other problem-solving courts, create a different relationship between returning prison inmates and the criminal justice system. They provide for coordinated services in ways that are not possible in traditional parole systems.

■ *Community-based interventions.* Recognizing that some communities are experiencing high rates of incarceration and reentry, these projects approach reentry as a community phenomenon. They create coalitions of community organizations to interact with every person returning home from prison. The NYC Justice Corps provides transitional employment for young adults returning home from prison and jail in two New York City neighborhoods most impacted by incarceration and reentry. In each location, a local organization brings together young people and their community to identify community improvement projects that NYC Justice Corps members can execute while developing valuable skills that help ready them for the labor market.

LEGAL RESTRICTIONS Ex-inmates may also find that going straight is an economic impossibility. Research shows that former inmates who gain and keep meaningful employment are more likely to succeed on parole than those who are unemployed or underemployed.[191] One reason why ex-inmates find it so difficult to make it on the outside is the legal restrictions they are forced to endure (see the accompanying Analyzing Criminal Justice Issues box for one rather telling story). These may include prohibitions on certain kinds of employment, limits on obtaining licenses, serving on juries, holding public office, voting and restrictions on their freedom of movement. Some states consider a felony conviction grounds for divorce and termination of parental rights.[192]

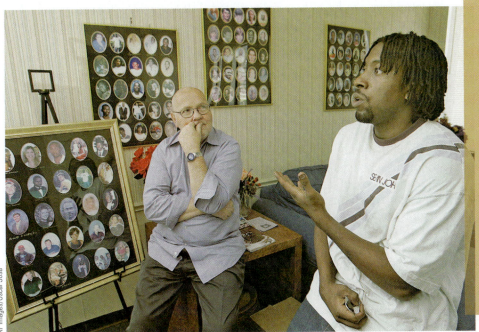

AP Images/Oscar Sosa

Many inmates fail on parole, and making good is often a challenge. One way to ease reentry is through restoration programs. Here, Glen Mitchell (left), founder of Compassionate Families, and Ellis Curry talk in Mitchell's Jacksonville, Florida, office, where photos of murder victims hang on the wall. Mitchell's 14-year-old son Jeff was shot and killed by Curry and three other young men 13 years ago. But Mitchell harbors no ill feelings toward Curry, because he has expressed remorse for causing Jeff Mitchell's death. Curry is now out of prison and is making joint appearances with Mitchell, spreading the message that violence is not the answer.

analyzing criminal justice ISSUES

CRIMINAL RECORDS AND REENTRY SUCCESS

I am writing this letter ... out of desperation and to tell you a little about the struggles of re-entering society as a convicted felon. I have worked hard to turn my life around. I have remained clean for nearly eight years, I am succeeding in college, and I continue to share my story in schools, treatment facilities, and correctional institutions, yet I have nothing to show for it.... I have had numerous interviews and sent out more than 200 résumés for jobs for which I am more than qualified. I have had denial after denial because of my felony. I do understand that you are not responsible for the choices that have brought me to this point. Furthermore, I recognize that if I was not abiding by the law, if I was not clean, and if I was not focusing my efforts toward a successful future, I would have no claim to make.

So writes Jay, a man convicted of involuntary vehicular manslaughter and sentenced to 38 months in state prison nine years before. He is not alone: a criminal label can haunt people for the rest of their life, well beyond their offending years and despite the fact that they have stayed "clean" for quite some time.

Many people with records suffer stigma that prevents them from getting jobs. A recent study shows that nearly one-third of American adults have been arrested by age 23. This record will keep many people from obtaining employment, even if they have paid their dues, are qualified for the job, and are unlikely to reoffend.

Criminal records run the gamut from one-time arrests where charges are dropped to lengthy, serious, and violent criminal histories. Many people who have been arrested—and, therefore, technically have a criminal record that shows up on a background check—were never convicted of a crime. This is true not only among those charged with minor crimes, but also for many individuals arrested for serious offenses.

The impact of having a criminal record is most often felt among African Americans, who may already experience racial discrimination in the labor market and are more likely than whites to have a

In general, states have placed greater restrictions on former felons, part of the get-tough movement. However, courts have considered individual requests by convicted felons to have their rights restored. It is common for courts to look at such issues as how recently the criminal offense took place and its relationship to the right in question before deciding whether to restore it.

A number of experts and national commissions have condemned the loss of rights of convicted offenders as a significant cause of recidivism. Consequently, courts have generally moved to eliminate the most restrictive elements of post-conviction restrictions.[193]

In the final analysis, successful reentry may rely on a willingness to accept personal deficits and to change. When justice expert Shadd Maruna interviewed a group of serious criminals to understand how they were able to reform their lives, he found that going straight was a long process, not an instantaneous event.[194] Those who do well after prison have undergone a long-term cognitive change in which they begin to see themselves as a new person or adopt a new outlook on life. They begin to try to understand their past and develop insights into why they behaved the way they did and why and how things went wrong. Those who leave a life of crime begin to feel a sense of fulfillment in engaging in productive behaviors, and in so doing, they become agents of their own change. They start feeling in control of their future and have a newfound purpose in life. Instead of running from the past, they view their prior history as a learning experience, finding a silver lining on an otherwise dark horizon.

criminal record. Research shows that a criminal record reduces the likelihood of a job callback or offer by approximately 50 percent. This criminal record "penalty" is substantially greater for African Americans than for white applicants. Latinos suffer similar penalties in the employment market.

In addition to these significant and often overlapping challenges, an extra set of punishments, or "collateral consequences," is imposed on individuals as a direct result of their criminal convictions. These legal restrictions create barriers to jobs, housing, benefits, and voting. More than 80 percent of the statutes that place restrictions on people convicted of crime operate as denial of employment opportunities. Although some of these consequences serve important public safety purposes, others may be antiquated and create unnecessary barriers to legitimate work opportunities. A commonly cited example is that in some states formerly incarcerated people who were trained as barbers cannot hold those jobs after release because state laws prohibit felons from practicing the trade, presumably because their access to sharp objects makes them a threat to the public.

Regardless of the legal restrictions, the majority of employers indicate they would "probably" or "definitely" not be willing to hire an applicant with a criminal record. A recent report by the National Employment Law Project found frequent use of blanket "no-hire" policies among major corporations. Employers do not want to hire individuals who might commit future crimes and who may be a risk to their employees' and customers' safety. The assumption, of course, is that a prior record signals higher odds that the individual will commit more crimes in the future.

CRITICAL THINKING

What can be done to reduce the effect of labels and stigma placed on people who have paid their debt? Should records be expunged within a certain time frame if a person does not reoffend? Or should knowledge of a prior criminal record be available since an employer has a right to know about the background of people they are considering hiring?

Source: Amy Solomon, "In Search of a Job: Criminal Records as Barriers to Employment," *NIJ Journal* 270 (2012), http://www.nij.gov/journals/270/pages/criminal-records.aspx (accessed July 2014).

Significant Cases in Corrections

Case	Issue	Decision
Bell v. Wolfish (1979)	Cruel and unusual punishment	Although people are sent to prison for punishment, it does not mean that prison should be a punishing experience.
Cooper v. Pate (1964)	Freedom of religion	Inmates who are being denied the right to practice their religion are entitled to legal redress.
Cutter v. Wilkinson (2005)	Freedom of religion	Inmates may practice their own religion unless their practices clearly undermine prison security and safety.
Estelle v. Gamble (1976)	Medical care	Inmates have a right to have medical care. Access to quality health care is part of the prison regime.
Farmer v. Brennan (1994)	Inmate safety	If prison officials were aware of a serious risk to an inmate's safety, but failed to take reasonable steps for its prevention, they are liable for injuries suffered.

(continued)

Significant Cases in Corrections (*continued*)

Case	Issue	Decision
Hope v. Pelzer (2002)	Cruel and unusual punishment	Correctional officials who knowingly violate the Eighth Amendment rights of inmates can be held liable for damages if their actions are "totally without penological justification."
Hudson v. McMillian (1992)	Use of force	As long as force is used in a good-faith effort to maintain control, there is no liability. To be liable, correctional officers must act maliciously.
Jackson v. Bishop (1968)	Physical punishment	The use of corporal punishment is forbidden in prison.
Johnson v. California (2005)	Racial segregation	The segregation of prison inmates based on race, in their cells or anywhere on prison grounds, is an inappropriate form of racial classification.
Newman v. Alabama (1972)	Medical care	An entire state prison system's medical facilities are inadequate if they provide insufficient physician and nurse resources, rely on untrained inmates for paramedical work, intentionally fail to treat the sick and injured, and fail to conform to proper medical standards.
O'Lone v. Estate of Shabazz (1987)	Prison regulations	A prison regulation is valid if it is reasonably related to legitimate penological interests.
Rhodes v. Chapman (1981)	Prison care and conditions	If there is a legitimate purpose for the use of governmental restrictions, they may be considered constitutional.
Shaw v. Murphy (2001)	Correspondence	Inmates do not have an absolute right to correspond with other inmates, even if it concerns legal advice.

ETHICAL CHALLENGES in Criminal Justice

A WRITING ASSIGNMENT

Some prison administrators and politicians believe that prisoners are being coddled and have too many privileges. They want to adopt a no-frills policy designed to convince inmates never to repeat their criminal acts. Prisons, they believe, are places of confinement and nothing more. Write an essay that challenges their ethics. Is it moral to lock people up without (a) providing them proper living conditions and (b) attempting to aid their rehabilitation? If you prefer to support aspects of the no-frills policy and consider it moral and proper, you may do so, but be sure to explain the basis of your feelings.

Summary

L01 **Discuss the problems of the adult correctional system.**

- A significant number of facilities are old and in ill repair.
- More than half of all inmates are held in large, maximum-security institutions that lack proper treatment facilities.
- Institutions are overcrowded, and meaningful treatment efforts are often a matter of wishful thinking.

L02 **Explain the term *total institution*.**

- Prisons in the United States are referred to as total institutions.
- Inmates locked within their walls are segregated from the outside world, kept under constant surveillance, and forced to obey strict official rules to avoid facing formal sanctions.

L03 **Explain the "prisonization" process and the development of the inmate social code.**

- Inmates go through a variety of attitude and behavior changes, or cycles, as their sentence unfolds.
- Inmates form their own world, known as the inmate subculture, which has a unique set of norms and rules.
- The traditional inmate culture has given way to one dominated by race- and ethnicity-based gangs.

L04 **Compare the lives and cultures of male and female inmates.**

- Unlike male inmates, women usually do not present an immediate physical danger to staff and fellow inmates.
- Make-believe family groups in women's prisons consist of masculine and feminine figures acting as fathers and mothers.
- Female correctional institutions do not get the same level of support as male facilities, and as a result, educational and vocational programs are deficient.

L05 **Discuss the causes of prison violence.**

- Conflict, violence, and brutality are sad but ever-present facts of institutional life.
- Violence can involve individual conflict: inmate versus inmate, inmate versus staff, or staff versus inmate.

- Prison violence has been linked to overcrowding, lack of effective dispute resolution mechanisms, individual inmate history of violence, and poor prison conditions.

L06 **Discuss the different forms of correctional treatment.**

- Counseling programs help inmates to control emotions, communicate with others, deal with legal concerns, manage general life issues, and develop and maintain social relationships.
- Most prisons have programs designed to help inmates suffering from alcohol and substance abuse.
- The AIDS-infected inmate has been the subject of great concern.
- Inmate rehabilitation is also pursued through vocational and educational training.

L07 **Describe the world of correctional officers.**

- For many years, prison guards were viewed as ruthless people who enjoyed and exploited their power over inmates. Correctional officers are now viewed more as dedicated public servants.
- There are few gender differences in the behavior of correctional officers.

L08 **Explain what is meant by prisoners' rights, and discuss some key privileges that have been granted to inmates.**

- Before the early 1960s, it was accepted that upon conviction, an individual forfeited all legal rights.
- As the 1960s drew to a close, inmates began to be granted legal rights.
- Today inmates have the right to medical care, freedom from cruel and unusual punishment, the right to an attorney, and the right to practice their religion.

L09 **Describe the problems of prisoner reentry.**

- Despite all efforts to treat, correct, and rehabilitate incarcerated offenders, more than half return to prison shortly after their release.
- Recidivism may be a by-product of the disruptive effect a prison experience has on personal relationships.
- Parole failure has been linked to being barred from work opportunities.

Key Terms

Critical Thinking Questions

1. Considering the dangers that men face during their prison stay, should nonviolent inmates be placed in separate institutions to protect them from harm?

2. Should women be allowed to work as guards in male prisons? What about male guards in female prisons? Why or why not?

3. Should prison inmates be allowed a free college education while noncriminals must pay tuition?

Why or why not? Do you believe in less parole eligibility for prisoners?

4. Define parole, including its purposes and objectives. How does it differ from probation?

5. What is the role of the parole board?

6. Should a former prisoner have all the civil rights afforded the average citizen? Explain.

7. Should people be further penalized after they have paid their debt to society? Why or why not?

Notes

1. Alan Prendergast, "Raped and Extorted by a Prison Gang, Scott Howard Was Called a 'Drama Queen' by Corrections Officials," *Denver Westword News*, http://www.westword.com/2011-02-03/news/211-crew-rapes-extorts-scott-howard-colorado-prison/ (accessed July 2014).

2. E. Ann Carson and Daniela Golinelli, *Prisoners in 2012: Trends in Admissions and Releases, 1991–2012* (Washington, DC: Bureau of Justice Statistics, 2013).

3. James J. Stephan, *Census of State and Federal Correctional Facilities, 2005* (Washington, DC: Bureau of Justice Statistics, 2008).

4. Ibid.

5. Richard Berk, Heather Ladd, Heidi Graziano, and Jong-Ho Baek, "A Randomized Experiment Testing Inmate Classification Systems," *Criminology and Public Policy* 2 (2003): 215–242.

6. James A. Paluch Jr., *A Life for a Life, Life Imprisonment (America's Other Death Penalty)* (Los Angeles: Roxbury Press, 2004), p. 4.

7. Gresham Sykes, *The Society of Captives* (Princeton, NJ: Princeton University Press, 1958).

8. Mark Fleisher and Jessie Krienert, "The Culture of Prison Sexual Violence," final report submitted to the National Institute of Justice, November 2006, http://www.ncjrs.gov/pdffiles1/nij/grants/216515.pdf (accessed July 2014).

9. Karen Lahm, "Inmate-on-Inmate Assault: A Multilevel Examination of Prison Violence," *Criminal Justice and Behavior* 35 (2008): 120–137.

10. David Eichenthal and James Jacobs, "Enforcing the Criminal Law in State Prisons," *Justice Quarterly* 8 (1991): 283–303.

11. Fleisher and Krienert, "The Culture of Prison Sexual Violence."

12. Manop Kanato, "Drug Use and Health Among Prison Inmates," *Current Opinion in Psychiatry* 21 (2008): 252–254.

13. John Wooldredge, "Inmate Lifestyles and Opportunities for Victimization," *Journal of Research in Crime and Delinquency* 35 (1998): 480–502.

14. Charles Schwaebe, "Learning to Pass: Sex Offenders' Strategies for Establishing a Viable Identity in the Prison General Population," *International Journal of Offender Therapy and Comparative Criminology* 49 (2005): 614–625.

15. Mark Kellar and Hsiao-Ming Wang, "Inmate Assaults in Texas County Jails," *Prison Journal* 85 (2005): 515–534.

16. Benjamin Steiner and John Wooldredge, "Inmate versus Environmental Effects on Prison Rule Violations," *Criminal Justice and Behavior* 35 (2008): 438–456.

17. Robert Johnson, *Hard Time: Understanding and Reforming the Prison* (Monterey, CA: Brooks/Cole, 1987), p. 115.

18. Wooldredge, "Inmate Lifestyles and Opportunities for Victimization."

19. Leonore Simon, "Prison Behavior and Victim-Offender Relationships Among Violent Offenders," paper presented at the annual meeting of the American Society of Criminology, San Francisco, November 1991.

20. John Irwin, "Adaptation to Being Corrected: Corrections from the Convict's Perspective," in *Handbook of Criminology*, ed. Daniel Glazer (Chicago: Rand McNally, 1974), pp. 971–993.

21. Donald Clemmer, *The Prison Community* (New York: Holt, Rinehart & Winston, 1958).

22. Gresham Sykes and Sheldon Messinger, "The Inmate Social Code," in *The Sociology of Punishment and Corrections*, ed. Norman Johnston, Leonard Savitz, and Marvin Wolfgang (New York: Wiley, 1970), pp. 401–408.

23. Fleisher and Krienert, "The Culture of Prison Sexual Violence."

24. Ibid.

25. James B. Jacobs, ed., *New Perspectives on Prisons and Imprisonment* (Ithaca, NY: Cornell University Press, 1983); Jacobs, "Street Gangs Behind Bars," *Social Problems* 21 (1974): 395–409; Jacobs, "Race Relations and the Prison Subculture," in *Crime and Justice*, vol. 1, ed. Norval Morris and Michael Tonry (Chicago: University of Chicago Press, 1979), pp. 1–28.

26. Nicole Hahn Rafter, *Partial Justice* (New Brunswick, NJ: Transaction Books, 1990), pp. 181–182.

27. Vernetta Young and Rebecca Reviere, *Women Behind Bars: Gender and Race in U.S. Prisons* (Boulder, CO: Lynne Rienner Publishers, 2006).

28. Amanda Noblet, "Women in Prison: A Review of the Current Female Prison System: Future Directions and Alternatives," *Internet Journal of Criminology* 2008, http://www.internet-journalofcriminology.com (accessed July 2014).

29. Seena Fazel and John Danesh, "Serious Mental Disorder in 23,000 Prisoners: A Systematic Review of 62 Surveys," *Lancet* 359 (2002): 545–561.

30. Chandra Kring Villanueva, Sara From, and Georgia Lerner, *Mothers, Infants and Imprisonment, A National Look at Prison Nurseries and Community-Based Alternatives* (New York: Women's Prison Association, 2009).

31. Gary Michael McClelland, Linda Teplin, Karen Abram, and Naomi Jacobs, "HIV and AIDS Risk Behaviors Among Female Jail Detainees: Implications for Public Health Policy," *American Journal of Public Health* 92 (2002): 818–826.

32. Christine Grella and Lisa Greenwell, "Correlates of Parental Status and Attitudes Toward Parenting Among Substance-Abusing Women Offenders," *Prison Journal* 86 (2006): 89–113.

33. Lauren Sharkey, "Does Overcrowding in Prisons Exacerbate the Risk of Suicide Among Women Prisoners?" *Howard Journal of Criminal Justice* 49 (2010): 111–124.

34. Candace Kruttschnitt and Sharon Krmpotich, "Aggressive Behavior Among Female Inmates: An Exploratory Study," *Justice Quarterly* 7 (1990): 370–389.

35. Candace Kruttschnitt, Rosemary Gartner, and Amy Miller, "Doing Her Own Time? Women's Responses to Prison in the Context of the Old and New Penology," *Criminology* 38 (2000): 681–718.

36. Mark Pogrebin and Mary Dodge, "Women's Accounts of Their Prison Experiences: A Retrospective View of Their Subjective Realities," *Journal of Criminal Justice* 29 (2001): 531–541.

37. Shanhe Jiang and L. Thomas Winfree Jr., "Social Support, Gender, and Inmate Adjustment to Prison Life," *Prison Journal* 86 (2006): 32–55.

38. Edna Erez, "The Myth of the New Female Offender: Some Evidence from Attitudes Toward Law and Justice," *Journal of Criminal Justice* 16 (1988): 499–509.

39. Robert Ross and Hugh McKay, *Self-Mutilation* (Lexington, MA: Lexington Books, 1979).

40. Alice Propper, *Prison Homosexuality* (Lexington, MA: Lexington Books, 1981).

41. Denise Huggins, Loretta Capeheart, and Elizabeth Newman, "Deviants or Scapegoats: An Examination of Pseudofamily Groups and Dyads in Two Texas Prisons," *Prison Journal* 86 (2006): 114–139.

42. David Duffee, *Corrections, Practice and Policy* (New York: Random House, 1989), p. 305.

43. Margaret E. Noonan, *Mortality in Local Jails and State Prisons, 2000–2011* (Washington, DC: Bureau of Justice Statistics, 2013), p. 19, Table 14.

44. Randy Martin and Sherwood Zimmerman, "A Typology of the Causes of Prison Riots and an Analytical Extension to the 1986 West Virginia Riot," *Justice Quarterly* 7 (1990): 711–737.

45. David Allender and Frank Marcell, "Career Criminals, Security Threat Groups, and Prison Gangs," *FBI Law Enforcement Bulletin* 72 (2003): 8–12.

46. Terri Compton and Mike Meacham, "Prison Gangs: Descriptions and Selected Intervention," *Forensic Examiner* 14 (2005): 26–31.

47. Grant Harris, Tracey Skilling, and Marnie Rice, "The Construct of Psychopathy," in *Crime and Justice: An Annual Edition*, ed. Michael Tonry (Chicago: University of Chicago Press, 2001), pp. 197–265.

48. For a series of papers on the position, see A. Cohen, G. Cole, and R. Baily, eds., *Prison Violence* (Lexington, MA: Lexington Books, 1976).

49. Scott Camp and Gerald Gaes, "Criminogenic Effects of the Prison Environment on Inmate Behavior: Some Experimental Evidence," *Crime and Delinquency* 51 (2005): 425–442.

50. Hans Toch, "Cumulative Default: The Cost of Disruptive Prison Careers," *Criminal Justice and Behavior* 35 (2008): 943–955.

51. *San Antonio Express News*, March 28, 2008.

52. Bert Useem and Michael Resig, "Collective Action in Prisons: Protests, Disturbances, and Riots," *Criminology* 37 (1999): 735–760.

53. Wayne Gillespie, "A Multilevel Model of Drug Abuse Inside Prison," *Prison Journal* 85 (2005): 223–246.

54. Florida Department of Corrections, *Correctional Operations Trend Analysis System (COTAS) System Summary* (Washington, DC: National Institute of Justice, 2014), https://www.ncjrs.gov/pdffiles1/nij/grants/247030.pdf (accessed July 2014).

55. Wilbert Rideau and Ron Wikberg, *Life Sentences: Rage and Survival Behind Bars* (New York: Times Books, 1992), pp. 78–80.

56. Christopher Hensley, Mary Koscheski, and Richard Tewksbury, "Examining the Characteristics of Male Sexual Assault Targets in a Southern Maximum-Security Prison," *Journal of Interpersonal Violence* 20 (2005): 667–679.

57. Mark Fleisher and Jessie Krienert, *The Myth of Prison Rape: Sexual Culture in American Prisons* (Lanham, MD: Rowman & Littlefield, 2009).

58. Tonisha Jones and Travis Pratt, "The Prevalence of Sexual Violence in Prison," *International Journal of Offender Therapy and Comparative Criminology* 52 (2008): 280–295.

59. Kristine Levan Miller, "The Darkest Figure of Crime: Perceptions of Reasons for Male Inmates to Not Report Sexual Assault," *Justice Quarterly* (2009): 1–21.

60. Allen Beck and Candace Johnson, *Sexual Victimization Reported by Former State Prisoners, 2008* (Washington, DC: Bureau of Justice Statistics, 2012), http://www.bjs.gov/content/pub/ascii/svrfsp08.txt (accessed July 2014).

61. Thomas Noll, "Sexual Violence in Prison," *International Journal of Offender Therapy and Comparative Criminology* 52 (2008): 251–252.

62. James Austin, Tony Fabelo, Angela Gunter, and Ken McGinnis, *Sexual Violence in the Texas Prison System*, final report submitted to the National Institute of Justice, September 2006, https://www.ncjrs.gov/pdffiles1/nij/grants/215774.pdf (accessed July 2014)

63. Meda Chesney-Lind, "Vengeful Equity: Sentencing Women to Prison," in *The Female Offender: Girls, Women, and Crime*, ed. Medea Chesney-Lind and Lisa J. Pasko (Thousand Oaks, CA: Sage, 1997).

64. General Accounting Office, *Women in Prison: Sexual Misconduct by Correctional Staff* (Washington, DC: U.S. Government Printing Office, 1999).

65. Rebecca Trammell, "Relational Violence in Women's Prison: How Women Describe Interpersonal Violence and Gender," *Women and Criminal Justice* 19 (2009): 267–285.

66. Alyssa Whitby Chamberlain, "Offender Rehabilitation: Examining Changes in Inmate Treatment Characteristics, Program Participation, and Institutional Behavior," *Justice Quarterly* 29 (2012).

67. Dianna Newbern, Donald Dansereau, and Urvashi Pitre, "Positive Effects on Life Skills Motivation and Self-Efficacy: Node-Link Maps in a Modified Therapeutic Community," *American Journal of Drug and Alcohol Abuse* 25 (1999): 407–410.

68. Rose Parkes and Charlotte Bilby, "The Courage to Create: The Role of Artistic and Spiritual Activities in Prisons," *Howard Journal of Criminal Justice* 49 (2010): 97–110.

69. Steven D. Vannoy and William T. Hoyt, "Evaluation of an Anger Therapy Intervention for Incarcerated Adult Males," *Journal of Offender Rehabilitation* 39 (2004): 40.

70. University of South Australia, School of Psychology, http://www .unisa.edu.au/education-arts-and-social-sciences/psychology-social-work-and-social-policy/ (accessed July 2014).

71. Sheila French and Paul Gendreau, "Reducing Prison Misconducts: What Works!" *Criminal Justice and Behavior* 33 (2006): 185–218.

72. Byron R. Johnson, "Religious Programming, Institutional Adjustment and Recidivism Among Former Inmates in Prison Fellowship Programs," *Justice Quarterly* 21 (2004): 329–354.

73. Charles McDaniel, Derek Davis, and Sabrina Neff, "Charitable Choice and Prison Ministries: Constitutional and Institutional Challenges to Rehabilitating the American Penal System," *Criminal Justice Policy Review* 16 (2005): 164–189.

74. Lawrence T. Jablecki, "A Critique of Faith-Based Prison Programs," *Humanist* 65 (2005): 11–16.

75. Ibid.

76. Janeen Buck Willison, Diana Brazzell, and KiDeuk Kim, *Faith-Based Corrections and Reentry Programs: Advancing a Conceptual Framework for Research and Evaluation* (Washington, DC: Urban Institute, 2010), http://www.ncjrs.gov/ pdffiles1/nij/grants/234058.pdf (accessed July 2014).

77. Philip R. Magaletta, Pamela M. Diamond, Beth M. Weinman, Ashley Burnell, and Carl G. Leukefeld, "Preentry Substance Abuse Services: The Heterogeneity of Offender Experiences," *Crime and Delinquency*, first published online April 28, 2010.

78. Kate Dolan, James Shearer, Bethany White, Zhou Jialun, John Kaldor, and Alex Wodak, "Four-Year Follow-up of Imprisoned Male Heroin Users and Methadone Treatment: Mortality, Re-incarceration and Hepatitis C Infection," *Addiction* 100 (2005): 820–828.

79. James Inciardi, Steven Martin, and Clifford Butzin, "Five-Year Outcomes of Therapeutic Community Treatment of Drug-Involved Offenders After Release from Prison," *Crime and Delinquency* 50 (2004): 88–107; Clayton Mosher and Dretha Phillips, "The Dynamics of a Prison-Based Therapeutic Community for Women Offenders: Retention, Completion, and Outcomes," *Prison Journal* 86 (2006): 6–31.

80. Wayne Welsh, "A Multisite Evaluation of Prison-Based Therapeutic Community Drug Treatment," *Criminal Justice and Behavior* 34 (2007): 1481–1498.

81. Sheldon X. Zhang, Robert E. L. Roberts, and Kathryn E. McCollister, "Therapeutic Community in a California Prison: Treatment Outcomes After 5 Years," *Crime and Delinquency* 57 (2011): 82–101; J. Mitchell Miller and Holly Ventura Miller, "Considering the Effectiveness of Drug Treatment Behind Bars: Findings from the South Carolina RSAT Evaluation," *Justice Quarterly* 28 (2011): 70–86.

82. Daniel Werb, Thomas Kerr, Will Small, Kathy Li, Julio Montaner, and Evan Wood, "HIV Risks Associated with Incarceration Among Injection Drug Users: Implications for Prison-Based Public Health Strategies," *Journal of Public Health* 30 (2008): 126–132; Will Small, S. Kain, Nancy Laliberte, Martin Schechter, Michael O'Shaughnessy, and Patricia Spittal, "Incarceration, Addiction and Harm Reduction: Inmates Experience Injecting Drugs in Prison," *Substance Use and Misuse* 40 (2005): 831–843.

83. Laura M. Maruschak, *HIV in Prisons, 2001–2010* (Washington, DC: Bureau of Justice Statistics, 2012).

84. Karen Lahm, "Educational Participation and Inmate Misconduct," *Journal of Offender Rehabilitation* 48 (2009): 37–52.

85. Rosa Minhyo Cho and John H. Tyler, "Does Prison-Based Adult Basic Education Improve Postrelease Outcomes for Male Prisoners in Florida?" *Crime and Delinquency*, published online November 30, 2010.

86. Steve Aos, Marna Miller, and Elizabeth Drake, *Evidence-Based Public Policy Options to Reduce Future Prison Construction, Criminal Justice Costs, and Crime Rates* (Olympia: Washington State Institute for Public Policy, 2006), http://www.wsipp.wa.gov/ rptfiles/06-10-1201.pdf (accessed July 2014).

87. Howard Skolnik and John Slansky, "A First Step in Helping Inmates Get Good Jobs After Release," *Corrections Today* 53 (1991): 92.

88. Federal Bureau of Prisons, UNICOR, http://www.bop.gov/ inmates/custody_and_care/unicor.jsp (accessed July 2014).

89. Federal Bureau of Prisons, "Doing Business wih UNICOR," http://www.unicor.gov/fpi_contracting/ (accessed July 2014).

90. Public Law 96-157, Sec. 827, codified as 18 U.S.C., Sec. 1761(c).

91. California Prison Industry Authority, http://pia.ca.gov/ (accessed July 2014).

92. Douglas Lipton, Robert Martinson, and Judith Wilks, *The Effectiveness of Correctional Treatment: A Survey of Treatment Evaluation Studies* (New York: Praeger, 1975).

93. James Wilson and Robert Davis, "Good Intentions Meet Hard Realities: An Evaluation of the Project Greenlight Reentry Program," *Criminology and Public Policy* 5 (2006): 303–338.

94. Paula Smith, Paul Gendreau, and Kristin Swartz, "Validating the Principles of Effective Intervention: A Systematic Review of the Contributions of Meta-Analysis in the Field of Corrections," *Victims and Offenders* 4 (2009): 148–169.

95. Paul Gendreau and Robert Ross, "Effective Correctional Treatment: Bibliotherapy for Cynics," *Crime and Delinquency* 27 (1979): 463–489.

96. Robert R. Ross and Paul Gendreau, eds., *Effective Correctional Treatment* (Toronto: Butterworth, 1980), p. viii; Paul Gendreau and Robert R. Ross, "Revivification or Rehabilitative Evidence," *Justice Quarterly* 4 (1987): 349–407.

97. Mark W. Lipsey and Francis T. Cullen, "The Effectiveness of Correctional Rehabilitation: A Review of Systematic Reviews," *Annual Review of Law and Social Science* 3 (2007): 297–320.

98. Francis Cullen and Karen Gilbert, *Reaffirming Rehabilitation* (Cincinnati: Anderson Publications, 1982).

99. Michael Caldwell, Michael Vitacco, and Gregory Van Rybroek, "Are Violent Delinquents Worth Treating? A Cost–Benefit Analysis," *Journal of Research in Crime and Delinquency* 43 (2006): 148–168.

100. French and Gendreau, "Reducing Prison Misconducts: What Works!"

101. David Wilson, Catherine Gallagher, and Doris MacKenzie, "A Meta-Analysis of Corrections-Based Education, Vocation, and Work Programs for Adult Offenders," *Journal of Research in Crime and Delinquency* 37 (2000): 347–368.

102. Mary Ellen Batiuk, Paul Moke, and Pamela Wilcox Rountree, "Crime and Rehabilitation: Correctional Education as an Agent of Change—A Research Note," *Justice Quarterly* 14 (1997): 167–180.

103. David Wilson, Leana Bouffard, and Doris MacKenzie, "A Quantitative Review of Structured, Group-Oriented, Cognitive-Behavioral Programs for Offenders," *Criminal Justice and Behavior* 32 (2005): 172–204; Mark Lipsey and David Wilson, "Effective Intervention for Serious Juvenile Offenders: A Synthesis of Research," in *Serious and Violent Juvenile Offenders: Risk Factors and Successful Interventions*, ed. Rolf Loeber and David Farrington (Thousand Oaks, CA: Sage, 1998).

104. Megan Kurlychek and Cynthia Kempinen, "Beyond Boot Camp: The Impact of Aftercare on Offender Reentry," *Criminology and Public Policy* 5 (2006): 363–388.

105. David Farrington and Brandon Welsh, "Randomized Experiments in Criminology: What Have We Learned in the Last Two Decades?" *Journal of Experimental Criminology* 1 (2005): 9–38.

106. Lucien X. Lombardo, *Guards Imprisoned* (New York: Elsevier, 1981); James Jacobs and Norma Crotty, "The Guard's World," in *New Perspectives on Prisons and Imprisonment*, ed. James Jacobs (Ithaca, NY: Cornell University Press, 1983), pp. 133–141.

107. Claire Mayhew and Duncan Chappell, "An Overview of Occupational Violence," *Australian Nursing Journal* 9 (2002): 34–35.

108. John Klofas and Hans Toch, "The Guard Subculture Myth," *Journal of Research in Crime and Delinquency* 19 (1982): 238–254.

109. Ruth Triplett and Janet Mullings, "Work-Related Stress and Coping Among Correctional Officers: Implications from the Organizational Literature," *Journal of Criminal Justice* 24 (1996): 291–308.

110. Eric Lambert, Nancy Hogan, and Irshad Altheimer, "An Exploratory Examination of the Consequences of Burnout in Terms of Life Satisfaction, Turnover Intent, and Absenteeism Among Private Correctional Staff," *Prison Journal* 90 (2010): 94–114.

111. Stephen Owen, "Occupational Stress Among Correctional Supervisors," *Prison Journal* 86 (2006): 164–181; Eugene Paoline, Eric Lambert, and Nancy Hogan, "A Calm and Happy Keeper of the Keys: The Impact of ACA Views, Relations with Coworkers, and Policy Views on the Job Stress and Job Satisfaction of Jail Staff," *Prison Journal* 86 (2006): 182–205.

112. Mike Vuolo and Candace Kruttschnitt, "Prisoners' Adjustment, Correctional Officers, and Context: The Foreground and Background of Punishment in Late Modernity," *Law and Society Review* 42 (2008): 307–335.

113. Richard Tewksbury and Sue Caner Collins, "Aggression Levels Among Correctional Officers: Reassessing Sex Differences," *Prison Journal* 86 (2006): 327–343.

114. *Dothard v. Rawlinson*, 433 U.S. 321 (1977).

115. Dana Britton, *At Work in the Iron Cage: The Prison as Gendered Organization* (New York: New York University Press, 2003), Ch. 6.

116. National Advisory Commission on Criminal Justice Standards and Goals, *Corrections* (Washington, DC: U.S. Government Printing Office, 1973), p. 18.

117. *Cooper v. Pate*, 378 U.S. 546 (1964).

118. Prison Litigation Reform Act P.L. 104-134, 110 Stat. 1321 (2006); 42 U.S.C. § 1997e (1994 ed. & Supp. II).

119. *Booth v. Churner*, U.S. 731 (2001); *Porter v. Nussle*, 534 U.S. 516 (2002).

120. *Minneci et al. v. Pollard et al.*, 10-1104 (2011).

121. ACLU, "Know Your Rights: The Prison Litigation Reform Act (PLRA)," http://www.aclu.org/images/asset_upload_file79_25805.pdf (accessed July 2014).

122. *Shaw v. Murphy*, 532 U.S. 223 (2001).

123. *O'Lone v. Estate of Shabazz*, 482 U.S. 342 (1987).

124. Ibid., p. 349.

125. *Cutter v. Wilkinson*, 544 U.S. 709 (2005).

126. *Newman v. Alabama*, 349 F>Supp. 278 (M.D. Ala. 1972).

127. *Estelle v. Gamble*, 429 U.S. 97 (1976).

128. Ibid.

129. Lester Wright, "Health Care in Prison Thirty Years After *Estelle v. Gamble*," *Journal of Correctional Health Care* 14 (2008): 31–35.

130. *Trop v. Dulles*, 356 U.S. 86 (1958); see also *Furman v. Georgia*, 408 U.S. 238 (1972).

131. *Weems v. United States*, 217 U.S. 349 (1910).

132. *Lee v. Tahash*, 352 F.2d 970 (1965).

133. *Estelle v. Gamble*, 429 U.S. 97 (1976).

134. *Robinson v. California*, 370 U.S. 660 (1962).

135. *Gregg v. Georgia*, 428 U.S. 153 (1976).

136. *Jackson v. Bishop*, 404 F.2d 571 (1968).

137. *Farmer v. Brennan*, 511 U.S. 825 (1994).

138. Ibid., at 843 n. 8.

139. *Hudson v. McMillian*, U.S. 1 (1992).

140. *Hope v. Pelzer et al.*, 536 U.S. 730 (2002).

141. *L.A. Times*, "Report Predicted Violence at Chino Prison Dorm Hit by Race Riots," August 10, 2009, http://latimesblogs.latimes.com/lanow/2009/08/report-warned-of-violence-at-chino-prison-baracks-hit-by-race-riots.html (accessed July 2014).

142. *Johnson v. California*, 543 U.S. 499 (2005).

143. *Bell v. Wolfish*, 99 S.Ct. 1873-1974 (1979); see "*Bell v. Wolfish*: The Rights of Pretrial Detainees," *New England Journal of Prison Law* 6 (1979): 134.

144. *Farmer v. Brennan*, 511 U.S. 825 (1994).

145. *Rhodes v. Chapman*, 452 U.S. 337 (1981); for further analysis of *Rhodes*, see Randall Pooler, "Prison Overcrowding and the Eighth Amendment: The Rhodes Not Taken," *New England Journal on Criminal and Civil Confinement* 8 (1983): 1–28.

146. *Brown v. Plata*, 563 U.S. ____ (2011).

147. Laura M. Maruschak and Thomas P. Bonczar, *Probation and Parole in the United States, 2012* (Washington, DC: Bureau of Justice Statistics, 2013).

148. Ibid.

149. Sandra Crockett Mack and Khalil Osiris, "Successful Reentry, One Case at a Time," *Corrections Today* 69 (2007): 50–55.

150. Carolin Kröner, Cornelis Stadtland, Matthias Eidt, and Norbert Nedopil, "The Validity of the Violence Risk Appraisal Guide (VRAG) in Predicting Criminal Recidivism," *Criminal Behaviour and Mental Health* 17 (2007): 89–100.

151. Kathryn Campbell and Myriam Denov, "The Burden of Innocence: Coping with a Wrongful Imprisonment," *Canadian Journal of Criminology and Criminal Justice* 46 (2004): 139–164.

152. *Swarthout v. Cooke* and *Cate v. Clay* 562 U. S. ____ (2011).

153. Gregg Etter and Judy Hammond, "Community Service Work as Part of Offender Rehabilitation," *Corrections Today* 63 (2001): 114–117.

154. Brian Parry, "Special Service Unit: Dedicated to Investigating and Apprehending Violent Offenders," *Corrections Today* 63 (2001): 120.

155. Thomas Hanlon, David N. Nurco, Richard W. Bateman, and Kevin E. O'Grady, "The Response of Drug Abuser Parolees to a Combination of Treatment and Intensive Supervision," *Prison Journal* 78 (1998): 31–44; Susan Turner and Joan Petersilia, "Focusing on High-Risk Parolees: An Experiment to Reduce Commitments to the Texas Department of Corrections," *Journal of Research in Crime and Delinquency* 29 (1992): 34–61.

156. Mario Paparozzi and Paul Gendreau, "An Intensive Supervision Program that Worked: Service Delivery, Professional Orientation, and Organizational Supportiveness," *Prison Journal* 85 (2005): 445–466.

157. Matthew R. Durose, Alexia D. Cooper, and Howard N. Snyder, *Recidivism of Prisoners Released in 30 States in 2005: Patterns from 2005 to 2010* (Washington, DC: Bureau of Justice Statistics, 2014).

158. Ibid., p. 1

159. Beth Huebner, Christina DeJong, and Jennifer Cobbina, "Women Coming Home: Long-Term Patterns of Recidivism," *Justice Quarterly* 27 (2010): 225–254.

160. Pew Center on the States, *State of Recidivism: The Revolving Door of America's Prisons* (Washington, DC: The Pew Charitable Trusts, April 2011), http://www.pewtrusts.org/uploadedFiles/wwwpewtrustsorg/Reports/sentencing_and_corrections/State_Recidivism_Revolving_Door_America_Prisons%20.pdf (accessed July 2014).

161. Stephen Duguid, *Can Prisons Work? The Prisoner as Object and Subject in Modern Corrections* (Toronto: University of Toronto Press, 2000).

162. Michael Ostermann, "How Do Former Inmates Perform in the Community? A Survival Analysis of Rearrests, Reconvictions, and Technical Parole Violations," *Crime and Delinquency*, published online February 18, 2011.

163. Benjamin Steiner, Matthew D. Makarios, Lawrence F. Travis III, and Benjamin Meade, "Examining the Effects of Community-Based Sanctions on Offender Recidivism" *Justice Quarterly* 29 (2012): 229–257.

164. Micheal Ostermann, "Parole? Nope, Not for Me: Voluntarily Maxing Out of Prison," *Crime and Delinquency* 57 (2011): 686–708.

165. Megan Kurlychek, Andrew Wheeler, Leigh Tinik, and Cynthia Kempinen, "How Long After? A Natural Experiment Assessing the Impact of the Length of Aftercare Service Delivery on Recidivism" *Crime and Delinquency* 57 (2011): 778–800.

166. Stephen Metraux and Dennis Culhane, "Recent Incarceration History Among a Sheltered Homeless Population," *Crime and Delinquency* 52 (2006): 504–517.

167. Beth Huebner and Mark Berg, "Examining the Sources of Variation in Risk for Recidivism," *Justice Quarterly* 28 (2011): 146–173; Huebner, DeJong, and Cobbina, "Women Coming Home: Long-Term Patterns of Recidivism."

168. Catherine Hamilton, Louise Falshaw, and Kevin D. Browne, "The Link Between Recurrent Maltreatment and Offending Behavior," *International Journal of Offender Therapy and Comparative Criminology* 46 (2002): 75–95.

169. J. E. Ryan, "Who Gets Revoked? A Comparison of Intensive Supervision Successes and Failures in Vermont," *Crime and Delinquency* 43 (1997): 104–118.

170. Brent Benda, "Gender Differences in Life-Course Theory of Recidivism: A Survival Analysis," *International Journal of Offender Therapy and Comparative Criminology* 49 (2005): 325–342.

171. Hanlon, Nurco, Bateman, and O'Grady, "The Response of Drug Abuser Parolees to a Combination of Treatment and Intensive Supervision," 108.

172. Jeffrey Fagan and Richard Freeman, "Crime and Work," in *Crime and Justice: A Review of Research*, vol. 25, ed. Michael Tonry (Chicago: University of Chicago Press, 1999), pp. 211–229.

173. Rachelle Giguere and Lauren Dundes, "Help Wanted: A Survey of Employer Concerns About Hiring Ex-Convicts," *Criminal Justice Policy Review* 13 (2002): 396–408.

174. John Hagan and Ronit Dinovitzer, "Collateral Consequences of Imprisonment for Children, Communities, and Prisoners," in *Crime and Justice: A Review of Research*, vol. 26, ed. Michael Tonry and Joan Petersilia (Chicago: University of Chicago Press, 1999), pp. 89–107.

175. Thomas Hanlon, David Nurco, Richard Bateman, and Kevin O'Grady, "The Response of Drug Abuser Parolees to a Combination of Treatment and Intensive Supervision," *Prison Journal* 78 (1998): 31–44.

176. Hanlon, Nurco, Bateman, and O'Grady, "The Response of Drug Abuser Parolees to a Combination of Treatment and Intensive Supervision."

177. Paul Hirschfield and Alex Piquero, "Normalization and Legitimation: Modeling Stigmatizing Attitudes Toward Ex-Offenders," *Criminology* 48 (2010): 27–55.

178. Mark Berg and Beth Huebner, "Reentry and the Ties that Bind: An Examination of Social Ties, Employment, and Recidivism," *Justice Quarterly* 28 (2011): 382–410; Andy Hochstetler, Matt DeLisi, and Travis C. Pratt, "Social Support and Feelings of Hostility Among Released Inmates," *Crime and Delinquency* 56 (2010): 588–607.

179. National Drug Strategy Network, "HUD Announces 'One Strike' Rules for Public Housing Tenants," May 1996, http://www.ndsn .org/may96/onestrik.html (accessed July 2014).

180. The Pew Charitable Trusts, *Collateral Costs: Incarceration's Effect on Economic Mobility* (Washington, DC: The Pew Charitable Trusts, 2010), http://www.pewtrusts.org/en/research-and-analysis/reports/0001/01/01/collateral-costs (accessed July 2014).

181. Beth Huebner, "Racial and Ethnic Differences in the Likelihood of Marriage: The Effect of Incarceration," *Justice Quarterly* 24 (2007): 156–183.

182. Ryken Grattet, Joan Petersilia, and Jeffrey Lin, *Parole Violations and Revocations in California* (Washington, DC: National Institute of Justice, 2008).

183. John Hipp, Joan Petersilia, and Susan Turner, "Parolee Recidivism in California: The Effect of Neighborhood Context and Social Service Agency Characteristics," *Criminology* 48 (2010): 947–979.

184. Joan Petersilia, *When Prisoners Come Home: Parole and Prisoner Reentry* (New York: Oxford University Press, 2003); Petersilia, "Hard Time Ex-Offenders Returning Home After Prison," *Corrections Today* 67 (2005): 66–72; Petersilia, "When Prisoners Return to Communities."

185. Stephen Metraux and Dennis Culhane, "Recent Incarceration History Among a Sheltered Homeless Population," *Crime and Delinquency* 52 (2006): 504–517.

186. Huebner, DeJong, and Cobbina, "Women Coming Home: Long-Term Patterns of Recidivism."

187. Richard Seiter, "Prisoner Reentry and the Role of Parole Officers," *Federal Probation* 66 (2002): 50–54.

188. Charis Kubrin and Eric Stewart, "Predicting Who Reoffends: The Neglected Role of Neighborhood Context in Recidivism Studies," *Criminology* 44 (2006): 165–197.

189. This section relies on Jeremy Travis, Anna Crayton, and Debbie Mukamal, "A New Era in Inmate Reentry," *Corrections Today* 71 (2009): 38–41.

190. Project Safe Neighborhoods, https://www.bja.gov/programdetails .aspx?program_id=74 (accessed July 2014).

191. Hanlon, Nurco, Bateman, and O'Grady, "The Response of Drug Abuser Parolees to a Combination of Treatment and Intensive Supervision."

192. Kathleen Olivares, Velmer Burton, and Francis Cullen, "The Collateral Consequences of a Felony Conviction: A National Study of State Legal Codes Ten Years Later," *Federal Probation* 60 (1996): 10–17.

193. See, for example, *Bush v. Reid*, 516 P.2d 1215 (Alaska, 1973); *Thompson v. Bond*, 421 F.Supp. 878 (W.D. Mo., 1976); *Delorne v. Pierce Freightlines Co.*, 353 F.Supp. 258 (D. Or., 1973); and *Beyer v. Werner*, 299 F.Supp. 967 (E.D. N.Y., 1969).

194. Shadd Maruna, *Making Good: How Ex-Convicts Reform and Rebuild Their Lives* (Washington, DC: American Psychological Association, 2000).

CONTEMPORARY CHALLENGES IN CRIMINAL JUSTICE

WHEN ASKED WHAT CRIMES SCARE them, most people express fear over murders, rapes, assaults, and other "traditional" crimes that make newspaper headlines and are featured on the evening news. It is not often that someone worries about being killed by a child in a mass shooting at a public school, being caught in the crossfire of rival camps in an international criminal syndicate, or being the victim of a terrorist attack. These problems, heinous as they are, are uncommon, relatively isolated, and therefore not on most people's minds as they go about their daily lives. But such problems are of great interest to criminal justice practitioners, because they are among those who serve on the front lines of the battle to keep us free and safe from dangers of this kind.

Juvenile crime is one of those harms that does not necessarily benefit from the traditional approach of locking up offenders and throwing away the keys. Sometimes a more delicate approach is needed, especially in the case of kids who have not yet chosen a life of crime. Kevin Kellems, a juvenile probation officer in Calhoun County, Michigan, says that "the goal of the juvenile system is treatment. The law requires that treatment be attempted in the home and community if possible." Kevin's job is challenging because much of his time is spent "working with a population of young people and their families, which are often highly chaotic and dysfunctional."

Terrorism, too, is a difficult problem that has only recently become a priority for the criminal justice system. The September 11, 2001, terrorist attacks caused a dramatic change in the priorities of the federal government. The Department of Homeland Security was created, and the priorities of several law enforcement agencies were changed to emphasize the prevention of terrorist attacks. Mark O., a special agent with the Department of Homeland Security, is one of many people who was moved by the 9/11 attacks and decided to do something to help protect his country. He became a special agent with Immigration and Customs Enforcement (ICE), conducting criminal investigations into suspected, alleged, and known violations of federal law. He states, "Investigations require patience, and answers aren't always clear-cut, so an investigator must maintain a high level of alertness, flexibility, and focus." ▪

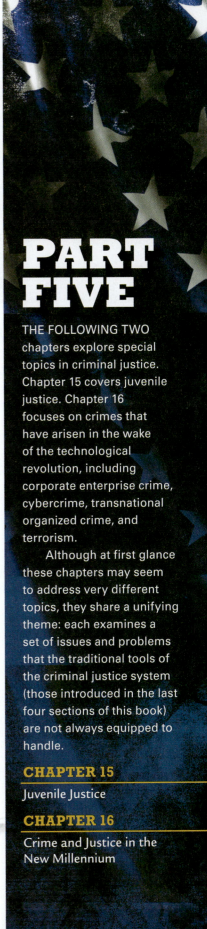

PART FIVE

THE FOLLOWING TWO chapters explore special topics in criminal justice. Chapter 15 covers juvenile justice. Chapter 16 focuses on crimes that have arisen in the wake of the technological revolution, including corporate enterprise crime, cybercrime, transnational organized crime, and terrorism.

Although at first glance these chapters may seem to address very different topics, they share a unifying theme: each examines a set of issues and problems that the traditional tools of the criminal justice system (those introduced in the last four sections of this book) are not always equipped to handle.

CHAPTER 15

Juvenile Justice

CHAPTER 16

Crime and Justice in the New Millennium

CHAPTER 15

Juvenile Justice

Learning Objectives

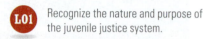
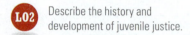

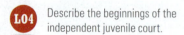

LO1 Recognize the nature and purpose of the juvenile justice system.

LO2 Describe the history and development of juvenile justice.

LO3 Discuss the child savers and their vision of juvenile justice.

LO4 Describe the beginnings of the independent juvenile court.

LO5 State the changes in juvenile justice that began in the 1960s and continue today.

LO6 Discuss police processing of juvenile offenders.

LO7 Discuss the detention of juveniles.

LO8 Recite the problems and legal issues surrounding the waiver decision.

LO9 Describe the juvenile trial and sentencing process.

LO10 Explain the efforts to treat troubled kids in the juvenile justice system.

Chapter Outline

The History of Juvenile Justice
Care of Children in Early America
The Child-Saving Movement
The Reform Movement Spreads
Establishment of the Juvenile Court
The Victim Experience: Victim #1
Juvenile Justice Today

Police Processing of the Juvenile Offender
Helping Juvenile Offenders
Use of Discretion
Analyzing Criminal Justice Issues:
    Minority Overrepresentation in
    Juvenile Justice
Legal Rights of Juveniles in Custody
Police Investigation in the School
    Setting

The Juvenile Court Process
The Intake Process
The Detention Process
Bail

Plea Bargaining
Waiver of Jurisdiction
Should Youths Be Transferred to
    Adult Court?
Evidence-Based Justice: Is Waiver
    Effective?
Adjudication
Disposition and Treatment
Juvenile Sentencing Reform

The Juvenile Correctional Process
Probation
Intensive Supervision
Institutionalization
Deinstitutionalization
Aftercare
Preventing Delinquency
Careers in Criminal Justice:
    Social Worker

The Future of Juvenile Justice

It was a case that shook the Commonwealth of Massachusetts to its core. On January 19, 2007, 16-year-old John Odgren followed James Alenson, a young boy he had never met, into the bathroom at Lincoln-Sudbury Regional High School, drew out a long knife, and stabbed him to death. Because he was 16 at the time, Massachusetts law required that Odgren be charged as an adult, and he was tried on a charge of first-degree murder before a jury in Middlesex Superior Court. Odgren's attorney, Jonathan Shapiro, defended him by suggesting that he was delusional and psychotic at the time of the murder: "Why did a geeky, uncoordinated, awkward 16-year-old who had never been in any trouble with the law suddenly and without provocation ferociously stab to death a 15-year-old classmate who he did not even know?" Shapiro said. "The illnesses that John Odgren suffers from made him lose touch with reality."

According to the defense, Odgren had attention deficit hyperactivity disorder, depression, anxiety, and possibly bipolar disorder and also suffered from Asperger syndrome, a form of autism whose symptoms include significant difficulties in social interaction, repetitive patterns of behavior and interests, physical clumsiness, and atypical use of language. Odgren was reportedly obsessed with the number 19, and the fact that he committed his crime on the 19th day of the month was not viewed as a coincidence. The prosecution did not deny that Odgren had a history of mental illness but maintained that his condition was not serious enough to be considered legal insanity; he was not delusional and knew that his actions were a crime. The jury heard that Odgren had a history of secretly bringing knives to school and enjoying violent novels, as if he were carefully planning "the perfect murder."

After two weeks of testimony, the jurors rejected the defense argument that Odgren was criminally insane when he randomly selected Alenson as his target. The jury also rejected the option of the lesser offense of second-degree murder, which would have made Odgren eligible for parole after 15 years. Under state law, Odgren's first-degree murder conviction was automatically reviewed and upheld by the State Supreme Judicial Court.[1] ◼

The Odgren case is representative of the difficult choices that agents of the juvenile justice system are continually asked to make: How should troubled children be treated? What can be done to treat dangerous young offenders? Should youthful law violators be given special treatment because of their age, or should they be treated in a similar fashion to an adult committing the same crime? As we shall see, the Supreme Court has prohibited life sentences for juvenile offenders unless the sentencing judge considers their age. Is it fair to place a troubled youth such as John Odgren in prison for the rest of his life without the possibility of parole? (More on this later.) Should his age and chance for rehabilitation prohibit the government from giving him life in prison even if he committed a murder? But what about the victim, in this case James Alenson? Doesn't he deserve justice also? He did nothing to prompt his attacker. Why should his death go unpunished? And if Odgren's attack was the product of a mental defect, is the juvenile justice system really equipped to help him, and if not, how can we ever be sure that he is "cured"?

Independent of (yet interrelated with) the adult criminal justice system, the juvenile justice system is primarily responsible for dealing with juvenile and youth crime, as well as with incorrigible and truant children and runaways. Conceived at the turn of the twentieth century, the juvenile justice system was originally viewed as a quasi–social welfare agency that was to act as a surrogate parent in the interests of the child; this is referred to as the ***parens patriae*** philosophy. Many people who work in the system still adhere to the original social welfare principles of the juvenile justice system. In contrast, those who take a crime control orientation suggest that the juvenile justice system's *parens patriae* philosophy is outdated. They question whether the system really is designed to handle youths who commit serious violent acts, such as John Odgren, whose acts were brutal but certainly not unique. They point to nationally publicized incidents of juvenile violence, such as the shooting at Sandy Hook Elementary in Newtown, Connecticut, as indicators that serious juvenile offenders are out there and that something must be done to protect society from their depraved and violent acts. In the Odgren case, this meant trying him as an adult and giving him a life sentence. Violent young criminals, they suggest, should be punished and disciplined rather than treated and rehabilitated.

It remains to be seen whether the juvenile justice system will continue on its path toward deterrence, punishment, and control or return to its former role as a treatment-dispensing agency. This chapter reviews the history of juvenile justice and discusses the justice system's processing of youthful offenders.

The History of Juvenile Justice

The modern practice of legally separating adult and juvenile offenders can be traced to two developments in English custom and law: poor laws and chancery courts. Both were designed to allow the state to take control of the lives of needy, but not necessarily criminal, children.[2] They set the precedent for later American developments.

As early as 1535, the English passed statutes known as **poor laws**, which in part mandated the appointment of overseers who placed destitute or neglected children with families who then trained them in agricultural, trade, or domestic services; this practice was referred to as indenture. The Elizabethan poor laws of 1601 created a system of church wardens and overseers who, with the consent of justices of the peace, identified vagrant, delinquent, and neglected children and took measures to put them to work. Often this meant placing them in poorhouses or workhouses or, more commonly, apprenticing them until their adulthood. The indenture, or involuntary apprentice, system set the precedent, which continues today, of allowing the government to take control of youths who have committed no illegal acts but are deemed unable to care for themselves.

 LO1 Recognize the nature and purpose of the juvenile justice system.

parens patriae
Latin term meaning "father of his country." According to this legal philosophy, the government is the true guardian of the needy and infirm, including dependent children. It refers to the power of the state to act on behalf of a child and provide care and protection equivalent to that of a parent.

 LO2 Describe the history and development of juvenile justice.

poor laws
Sixteenth-century English laws under which vagrants and abandoned and neglected children were bound to masters as indentured servants.

In contrast, **chancery courts** protected the property rights and welfare of more affluent minor children who could not care for themselves—children whose position and property were of direct concern to the monarch. They dealt with issues of guardianship and the use and control of property. Chancery courts operated under the *parens patriae* philosophy, which held that children were under the protective control of the state and that its rulers were justified in intervening in their lives.[3] In the famous English case *Wellesley v. Wellesley*, a duke's children were taken from him in the name of *parens patriae* because of his scandalous behavior.[4]

The concept of *parens patriae* came to represent the primacy of the state and its power to act in "the best interests of the child." In the twentieth century, the idea that the state was legally obligated to protect the immature, the incompetent, the neglected, and the delinquent became a major influence on the development of the U.S. juvenile justice system.

Care of Children in Early America

The forced apprenticeship system and the poor laws were brought from England to colonial America. Poor laws were passed in Virginia in 1646 and in Connecticut and Massachusetts in 1678, and they continued in force until the early nineteenth century. They mandated care for wayward and destitute children. However, those youths who committed serious criminal offenses were tried in the same courts as adults.

To accommodate dependent youths, local jurisdictions developed almshouses, poorhouses, and workhouses. Crowded and unhealthy, these accepted the poor, the insane, the diseased, and vagrant and destitute children. Middle-class civic leaders, who referred to themselves as **child savers**, began to develop organizations and groups to help alleviate the burdens of the poor and immigrants by sponsoring shelter care for youths, educational and social activities, and the development of settlement houses. In retrospect, their main focus seems to have been on extending government control over a whole range of youthful activities that previously had been left to private or family control, including idleness, drinking, vagrancy, and delinquency.[5]

The Child-Saving Movement

The child savers were responsible for creating a number of programs for indigent youths, including the New York House of Refuge, which began operations in 1825.[6] Its creation was effected by prominent Quakers and influential political leaders, such as Cadwallader Colden and Stephen Allen. In 1816, they formed the Society for the Prevention of Pauperism, which was devoted to protecting indigent youths who were at risk of leading a life of crime by taking them off the streets and reforming them in a family-like environment.[7]

The first House of Refuge constructed in New York City was the product of their reform efforts. Although the program was privately managed, the state legislature began providing funds partly through a head tax on arriving transatlantic passengers and seamen, plus the proceeds from license fees for New York City's taverns, theaters, and circuses. These revenue sources were deemed appropriate, given that supporters blamed immigration, intemperance, and commercial entertainment for juvenile crime.

The reformatory opened on January 1, 1825, with only six boys and three girls. However, within the first decade of its operation, 1,678 youths were admitted. Most kids were

chancery courts
Early English courts established to protect the property rights and welfare of the minor children of affluent families.

child savers
Civic leaders who focused their attention on the misdeeds of poor children to control their behavior.

 L03 Discuss the child savers and their vision of juvenile justice.

The Granger Collection, New York

This nineteenth-century photo shows indigent boys sleeping on the front door landing of an abandoned tenement building in New York City. The child savers were concerned that if left alone, children such as these would enter a life of crime. Critics, however, accused the child savers of class and race discrimination and thought they sought to maintain control over the political system.

sent to the reformatory because of vagrancy and petty crimes and were sentenced or committed indefinitely until they reached adulthood. Originally, the institution accepted inmates from across the state, but when a Western House of Refuge was opened in Rochester, New York, in 1849, residents of the original reformatory came only from the eastern quarters.

In the reformatory, a large part of the adolescent's daily schedule was devoted to supervised labor, which was regarded as beneficial to education and discipline. Inmate labor also supported operating expenses for the reformatory. Male inmates worked in shops that produced brushes, cane chairs, brass nails, and shoes. Female inmates sewed uniforms, did laundry, and carried out other domestic work. A badge system was used to segregate inmates according to their behavior. Although students acquired a rudimentary education, greater emphasis was placed on evangelical religious instruction; non-Protestant clergy were excluded. The reformatory had the authority to commit inmates to indenture agreements with private employers. Most males became farm workers; most females became domestic laborers.

The Reform Movement Spreads

When the House of Refuge opened, the majority of children admitted were status offenders placed there because of vagrancy or neglect. Children were put in the institution by court order, sometimes over parents' objections. Their length of stay depended on need, age, and skill. Critics complained that the institution was run like a prison, with strict discipline and absolute separation of the sexes. Such a harsh program drove many children to run away, and the House of Refuge was forced to take a more lenient approach. Despite criticism, the concept enjoyed expanding popularity. In 1826, the Boston City Council founded the House of Reformation for juvenile offenders.[8] The courts committed children found guilty of criminal violations, or found to be beyond the control of their parents, to these schools. Because the child savers considered parents of delinquent children to be as guilty as convicted offenders, they sought to have the reform schools assume control over the children. Refuge managers believed they were preventing poverty and crime by separating destitute and delinquent children from their parents and placing them in an institution.[9]

The child savers also influenced state and local governments to create independent correctional institutions to house minors. The first of these reform schools opened in Westboro, Massachusetts, in 1848 and in Rochester, New York, in 1849. Other states soon followed suit—Ohio in 1850 and Maine, Michigan, and Rhode Island in 1860. Children lived in congregate conditions and spent their days working at institutional jobs, learning a trade when possible, and receiving some basic education. They were racially and sexually segregated, discipline was harsh and often involved whipping and isolation, and the physical care was of poor quality.

In 1853, New York philanthropist Charles Loring Brace helped develop the **Children's Aid Society** as an alternative for dealing with neglected and delinquent youths. Brace proposed rescuing wayward youths from the harsh environment of the city and providing them with temporary shelter and care. He then sought to place them in private homes in rural communities where they could engage in farming and agricultural work outside the harsh influence of the city. Although some placements proved successful, others resulted in the exploitation of children in a strange environment with few avenues of escape.

Establishment of the Juvenile Court

As the nation expanded, it became evident that private charities and public organizations were not caring adequately for the growing number of troubled youths. The child savers lobbied for an independent, state-supported **juvenile court**, and their efforts prompted the development of the first comprehensive juvenile court

Children's Aid Society
A group created by Charles Loring Brace to place indigent city children with farm families.

juvenile court
A court that has original jurisdiction over persons defined by statute as legal minors and alleged to be involved in juvenile delinquency or status offenses. In some jurisdictions, these are family courts that also deal with custody and neglect issues.

in Illinois in 1899. The Illinois Juvenile Court Act set up an independent court to handle criminal law violations by children under 16 years of age, as well as to care for neglected, dependent, and wayward youths. The act also created a probation department to monitor youths in the community and to direct juvenile court judges to place serious offenders in secure schools for boys and industrial schools for girls. The ostensible purpose of the act was to separate juveniles from adult offenders and provide a legal framework in which juveniles could get adequate care and custody. By 1925, most states had developed juvenile courts. Enactment of the Juvenile Court Act of 1899 was a major event in the history of the juvenile justice movement in the United States.

Although the creation of the first independent juvenile courts was originally seen as liberal reform, modern scholars commonly view them as a symbol of class conflict: members of the upper classes used the courts to control and punish lower-class youths if they did not conform to social expectations.[10] Thus, according to this revisionist approach, the reformers applied the concept of *parens patriae* for their own purposes, which included the perpetuation of middle- and upper-class values, control over the political system, and the maintenance of a child labor system that exploited lower-class workers with marginal skills.

L04 Describe the beginnings of the independent juvenile court.

The juvenile court movement quickly spread across the United States. In its early form it provided youths with quasi-legal, quasi-therapeutic, personalized justice. The main concern was the "best interests of the child," not strict adherence to legal doctrine, constitutional rights, or due process of law. The court was paternalistic, not adversarial. For example, attorneys were not required. Hearsay evidence, inadmissible in criminal trials, was commonly employed in the adjudication of juvenile offenders. Children were encouraged to admit their guilt in open court in violation of their Fifth Amendment rights. Verdicts were based on a "preponderance of the evidence" instead of "beyond a reasonable doubt." Juvenile courts functioned as quasi–social service agencies.

REFORM SCHOOLS Youngsters who were found delinquent in juvenile court could spend years in a state training school. Though priding themselves on not being punitive, these early reform schools were generally aimed at punishment and were based on the concept of reform through hard work and discipline. In the second half of the nineteenth century, the emphasis shifted from massive industrial schools to the cottage system. Juvenile offenders were housed in a series of small cabins, each one holding 20 to 40 children, run by "cottage parents" who attempted to create a home-like atmosphere. The first cottage system was established in Massachusetts, the second in Ohio. The system was generally applauded as a great improvement over the industrial training schools. It represented a general movement away from punishment and toward rehabilitation by attending to the needs of the individual and by implementing complex programs of diagnosis and treatment.[11] In the 1950s, the influence of such therapists as Karen Horney and Carl Rogers promoted the introduction of psychological treatment in juvenile corrections. Group counseling techniques became standard procedure in most juvenile institutions.

JUVENILE JUSTICE 1960–1980 In the 1960s and 1970s, the U.S. Supreme Court radically altered the juvenile justice system when it issued a series of decisions that established the right of juveniles to due process of law.[12] The Court ruled that juveniles had the same rights as adults in important areas of trial process, including the right to confront witnesses, notice of charges, and the right to counsel. That brought procedural due process to the juvenile justice system. Also during this period, Congress passed the Juvenile Justice and Delinquency Prevention Act of 1974 (the JJDP Act), which established the federal Office of Juvenile Justice and Delinquency Prevention (OJJDP).[13] This legislation was enacted to identify the needs of youths and to fund programs in the juvenile justice system. Some of

the VICTIM experience

VICTIM #1

BACKGROUND In 2012, Jerry Sandusky, longtime assistant football coach at Penn State, was accused of molesting a score of young boys, many of whom he met at Second Mile, a foundation the former coach created for needy children. One of these boys, known as Victim #1, stayed at Jerry Sandusky's house more than 100 times where he was repeatedly sexually abused. Testifying at Sandusky's trial, he told the court, "At first he would kiss me on the forehead goodnight. Then it was kissing me on the cheek, then rubbing my back and cracking my back." Sandusky's hands would later move to "rub underneath my shorts," he said. The alleged abuse further escalated when Sandusky "put his mouth on my privates."

"I spaced," the alleged victim said. "I didn't know what to do." Later, the former coach allegedly told him,

"It's your turn." The alleged victim added, "He made me put my mouth on his privates." Victim #1 is one of 10 boys who were sexually abused by Sandusky over a span of 15 years.

THE BIG PICTURE According to the latest data, cases like Victim #1 are sadly not unique: about 60,000 verified cases of child abuse are reported each year. But this may be only the tip of the iceberg since many children are too young to report abuse and others too frightened or bewildered to seek help.

The problem is severe because adolescent victims of sexual abuse later suffer significant psychological deficits, including acute stress disorders, depression, eating disorders, nightmares, anxiety, suicidal ideation,

---

status offender

A noncriminal youth who falls under the jurisdiction of the juvenile court by reason of having engaged in behavior prohibited to minors, such as being truant from school, running away from home, or being habitually disobedient and ungovernable.

State the changes in juvenile justice that began in the 1960s and continue today.

the most important provisions of the act were to insulate juveniles from contact with more dangerous and/or older offenders. In practice, this meant that juveniles who were being held by the state for noncriminal actions such as cutting school or running away from home (referred to as **status offenders**) could not be detained in the same institutions with delinquent youths who had committed actual crimes. The *deinstitutionalization of status offenders and nonoffenders* provision of the JJDP Act mandated that juveniles not charged with conduct that would be crimes for adults "shall not be placed in secure detention facilities or secure correctional facilities." In addition, delinquents were expected to be removed from facilities housing adults and, failing that, were protected from having any sight or sound contact with adult inmates who were in custody because they were awaiting trial on criminal charges or had been convicted of a crime. The "sight and sound" provision requires that juvenile and adult inmates not be able to see each other and that no conversation between them be possible.

JUVENILE JUSTICE 1980–2000 During the last two decades of the twentieth century, public concern over juvenile crime helped reshape the philosophy of the juvenile justice system. The media picked up on stories of violent juvenile gangs, school shootings, and juvenile predators. Media frenzy helped fuel legislative change. States began to pass laws that made it easier to exclude from juvenile court jurisdiction juveniles who commit serious crimes such as violent acts or drug trafficking. Some states gave prosecutors greater discretion to prosecute cases directly in criminal court rather than in juvenile court, and other states passed laws making it easier to transfer juvenile offenders to the criminal justice system, where they could be treated as adults. Many states increased the length and severity of sentences allowed for juvenile offenders. There was also an effort to make juvenile proceedings more open, an effort that included making juvenile records and court proceedings, which had historically been kept confidential, more easily accessible to the public. The victims' rights movement invaded the juvenile court, and the victims of juvenile crime were now being heard during and other psychological problems. Many run away to escape their environment, which puts them at risk for juvenile arrest and involvement with the justice system. This stress does not end in childhood. Children who are sexually abused are more likely to suffer low self-esteem and be more suicidal as adults. They are also placed at greater risk to be abused as adults than those who escaped childhood victimization. The re-abused carry higher risks for psychological and physical problems, ranging from sexual promiscuity to increased HIV infection rates.

CLASSROOM EXERCISE In 1974, Congress passed the Child Abuse Prevention and Treatment Act (CAPTA), which provides funds to states to bolster their services for maltreated children and their parents. The act provides federal funding to states in support of prevention, investigation, and treatment. It also provides grants to public agencies and nonprofit organizations for demonstration programs. The Child Abuse Prevention and Treatment Act has been the impetus for states to improve the legal frameworks of their child protection systems. Investigate how the state in which you reside has conformed with CAPTA and create a model of its child protective services.

Sources: CNN, "Alleged Sandusky Victim Details Abuse," http://www.cnn.com/2012/06/12/justice/pennsylvania-sandusky-trial/ (accessed July 2014); Department of Health and Human Services, *Child Maltreatment, 2012*, http://www.acf.hhs.gov/programs/cb/resource/child-maltreatment-2012 (accessed July 2014); Catherine Grus, "Child Abuse: Correlations with Hostile Attributions," *Journal of Developmental and Behavioral Pediatrics* 24 (2006): 296–298; Michael Miner, Jill Klotz Flitter, and Beatrice Robinson, "Association of Sexual Revictimization with Sexuality and Psychological Function," *Journal of Interpersonal Violence* 21 (2006): 503–524.

court proceedings. In sum, as a reaction to a rising tide of juvenile crime, the juvenile justice system was modified to look and act more like the adult system.[14] One notorious instance of juvenile victimization is covered in the Victim Experience feature. The various stages in juvenile justice history are set out in Concept Summary 15.1.

CONCEPT SUMMARY 15.1

Shifting Philosophies of Juvenile Justice

- Before 1899: Juveniles treated similarly to adult offenders. Little distinction by age was made between youth and adults who committed criminal acts.

- 1899–1950s: Children treated differently, beginning with the Illinois Juvenile Court Act of 1899. By 1925, juvenile court acts established in virtually every state. *Parens patriae* philosophy dominates.

- 1950–1970: Recognition by experts that the rehabilitation model and the protective nature of *parens patriae* had failed to prevent delinquency.

- 1970–1980: Introduction of constitutional due process into the juvenile justice system. Experimentation with diversion and concern about stigma and labeling. Juvenile Justice and Delinquency Prevention Act of 1974 enacted.

- 1980–2000: Rising juvenile crime rates coupled with the perceived failure of rehabilitation to control delinquency led to a shift to a crime control and punishment philosophy similar to that of the adult criminal justice system. Focus on expanding the crime control capabilities of the juvenile justice system so that it resembles the adult system.

- 2000–today: Balanced approach. Attempt to provide treatment to needy youth and get tough with dangerous repeat offenders. Restorative justice.

Juvenile Justice Today

Today, the juvenile justice system has jurisdiction over two distinct categories of offenders: delinquents and status offenders.[15] The term **juvenile delinquency** refers to children who fall under a jurisdictional age limit, which varies from state to state, and who commit an act in violation of the penal code. Status offenders, in contrast, commit acts forbidden to minors, which include truancy and being a habitually disobedient and ungovernable child. They are commonly characterized in state statutes as persons or children in need of supervision (PINS or CHINS). Most states distinguish such behavior from delinquent conduct to reduce the effect of any stigma on children, although in most jurisdictions status offenders can be placed on probation, much as delinquent offenders can. In most instances, however, they cannot be placed in secure facilities that hold delinquent offenders. In addition, juvenile courts generally have jurisdiction over situations involving conduct directed at (rather than committed by) juveniles, such as parental neglect, deprivation, abandonment, and abuse.

> **juvenile delinquency**
> Participation in illegal behavior by a minor who falls under a statutory age limit.

The states have also set different maximum ages below which children fall under the jurisdiction of the juvenile court. Many states include all children under 18 years of age, others set the limit at 17, and a few at 16.

Some states exclude certain classes of offenders or offenses from the juvenile justice system. Those youths who commit serious violent offenses such as rape or murder may be automatically excluded from the juvenile justice system and treated as adults on the premise that they stand little chance of rehabilitation within the confines of the juvenile system. Juvenile court judges may also waive—transfer to the adult justice system—repeat offenders whom they deem untreatable by the juvenile authorities.

NEW JUVENILE COURT STRUCTURES A number of states have created family courts, which include a broad range of family- and child-related issues within their jurisdictions. They are designed to provide more individualized, client-focused treatment than traditional juvenile courts and to bring a holistic approach to helping kids and their families rather than focusing on punishing and/or controlling delinquency.[16]

In order to relieve overcrowding and provide an alternative to traditional forms of juvenile courts, jurisdictions across the country are experimenting with teen courts, also called youth courts. These differ from other juvenile justice programs because young people rather than adults determine the disposition in a case. Cases handled in these courts typically involve young juveniles (ages 10 to 15) with no prior arrest records who are being charged with minor law violations, such as shoplifting, vandalism, and disorderly conduct. Usually, young offenders are asked to volunteer to have their case heard in a teen court instead of the more formal court of the traditional juvenile justice system. The teen court movement is one of the fastest growing delinquency intervention programs in the country, with more than 1,050 of these courts in operation in 49 states and the District of Columbia, serving an estimated 110,000 to 125,000 young offenders each year; another 100,000 youths benefit from their participation as volunteers. A number of evaluations of teen courts have been conducted and results have been mixed: some have found they have a positive effect on future behavior, while others show little or no benefit.[17]

> **drug courts**
> Courts whose focus is providing treatment for youths accused of drug-related acts.

There are also more than 450 juvenile **drug courts** (with more in the planning process) operating in 49 states and the District of Columbia, Guam, and Northern Mariana Islands.[18] These special courts have jurisdiction over cases involving substance abuse and trafficking in which a minor is involved. Although juvenile drug courts operate under a number of different frameworks, the aim is to place nonviolent first offenders into intensive treatment programs rather than in a custodial institution.[19]

EXHIBIT 15.1 Similarities and Differences Between Juvenile and Adult Justice Systems

Similarities	Differences
Discretion used by police officers, judges, and correctional personnel	The primary purpose of juvenile procedures is protection and treatment; with adults, the aim is to punish the guilty.
Right to receive *Miranda* warning	Jurisdiction is determined by age in the juvenile system, by the nature of the offense in the adult system.
Protection from prejudicial lineups or other identification procedures	Juveniles can be apprehended for acts that would not be criminal if committed by an adult (status offenses).
Procedural safeguards when making an admission of guilt	Juvenile proceedings are not considered criminal; adult proceedings are criminal matters.
Advocacy roles of prosecutors and defense attorneys	Juvenile court proceedings are generally informal and private; adult court proceedings are more formal and are open to the public.
Right to counsel at most key stages of the court process	Courts cannot release to the press identifying information about a juvenile.
Availability of pretrial motions	Parents are highly involved in the juvenile process but not in the adult process.
Plea negotiation/plea bargaining	The standard of arrest is more stringent for adults than for juveniles.
Right to a hearing and an appeal	Juveniles are released into parental custody; adults are generally given bail.
Standard of proof beyond a reasonable doubt	Juveniles have no constitutional right to a jury trial in school without probable cause or a warrant.
Pretrial detention possible	A juvenile's record is generally sealed when the age of majority is reached; an adult's record is permanent.
Detention without bail if considered dangerous	A juvenile court cannot sentence juveniles to county jails or state prisons.
Probation as a sentencing option	The U.S. Supreme Court has declared that the Eighth Amendment prohibits the death penalty for juveniles under age 18.
Community treatment as a sentencing option	Juveniles waived to adult court cannot get a life sentence without possibility of parole.

The juvenile justice system has evolved into a parallel yet independent system of justice with its own terminology and rules of procedure. Exhibit 15.1 describes the basic similarities and differences between the juvenile and adult justice systems. Exhibit 15.2 points out how the language used in the juvenile court differs from that used in the adult system.

EXHIBIT 15.2 Comparison of Terms Used in Adult and Juvenile Justice Systems

	Juvenile Terms	Adult Terms
The person and the act	Delinquent child	Criminal
	Delinquent act	Crime
Preadjudicatory stage	Take into custody	Arrest
	Petition	Indictment

(*continued*)

EXHIBIT 15.2   (continued)

	Juvenile Terms	Adult Terms
	Agree to a finding	Plead guilty
	Deny the petition	Plead not guilty
	Adjustment	Plea bargain
	Detention facility; child-care shelter	Jail
Adjudicatory stage	Substitution	Reduction of charges
	Adjudicatory or fact-finding hearing	Trial
	Adjudication	Sentencing hearing
Postadjudicatory stage	Dispositional hearing	Sentence
	Disposition	Incarceration
	Commitment	Prison
	Youth development center; treatment center; training school	
	Residential child-care facility	Halfway house
	Aftercare	Parole

Today, the juvenile justice system is responsible for processing and treating almost 1.4 million cases of delinquency annually.[20] Each state's system is unique, so it is difficult to give a precise accounting of the justice process. Keeping this in mind, the following sections offer a general description of some key processes and decision points in juvenile justice. Figure 15.1 shows a model of the juvenile justice process.

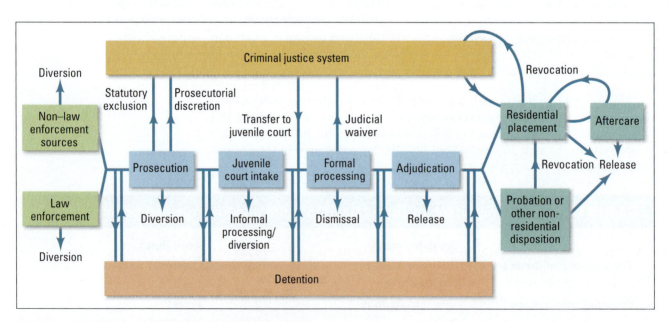

FIGURE 15.1   Chart of Juvenile Justice Case Flow

Source: Office of Juvenile Justice and Delinquency Prevention, http://ojjdp.ncjrs.gov/ojstatbb/structure_process/case.html.

Police Processing of the Juvenile Offender

According to the Uniform Crime Reports, police officers arrest about 1.3 million juveniles each year, including about 270,000 under age 15.[21] Most large police departments have detectives who handle only juvenile delinquency cases and focus their attention on the problems of youth. In addition to conducting their own investigations, they typically take control of cases after an arrest is made by a uniformed officer.

Most states do not have specific statutory provisions distinguishing the arrest process for children from that for adults. Some jurisdictions, however, give broad arrest powers to the police in juvenile cases by authorizing the officer to make an arrest whenever he or she believes the child's behavior falls within the jurisdiction of the juvenile court. Consequently, police may arrest youths for behavior considered legal for adults, including running away, curfew violations, and being in possession of alcohol.

Helping Juvenile Offenders

In addition to their role as law enforcers, police departments also engage in delinquency prevention efforts. Helping kids before they get in trouble fits nicely with community policing models that stress intervention rather than enforcement. For example, the Gang Resistance Education and Training (G.R.E.A.T.) program was developed among a number of Arizona police departments in an effort to reduce adolescent involvement in criminal behavior. Today the program is in school curricula in all 50 states and the District of Columbia, and evaluations have found it to be successful.[22]

Use of Discretion

When a juvenile is found to have engaged in delinquent or incorrigible behavior, police agencies are charged with deciding whether to release or to detain the child and refer him or her to juvenile court. Because of the state's interest in the child, the police generally have more discretion in the investigatory and arrest stages of the juvenile process than they do when dealing with adult offenders. This discretionary decision—to release or to detain—is based not only on the nature of the offense but also on police attitudes and the child's social and personal conditions at the time of the arrest:

- The type and seriousness of the child's offense
- The ability of the parents to be of assistance in disciplining the child
- The child's past contacts with police
- The degree of cooperation obtained from the child and parents and their demeanor, attitude, and personal characteristics
- Whether the child denies the allegations in the petition and insists on a court hearing[23]

Whereas police officers' actions in cases involving adults are usually controlled by the law and their own judgment or discretion, cases involving a juvenile demand that the officer consider the "best interests of the child" and how the officer's actions will influence the child's future well-being.[24] It was long believed that young people were significantly more likely to be arrested than adults, and a disrespectful demeanor on the part of juveniles increased the likelihood of their arrest.[25] However, some recent research indicates that police are more willing to arrest juveniles if they perceive the youths are in need of services and not

L06 Discuss police processing of juvenile offenders.

Web App 15.1

For more information about Gang Resistance Education and Training (G.R.E.A.T.), visit http://www.great-online.org/.

analyzing criminal justice ISSUES

MINORITY OVERREPRESENTATION IN JUVENILE JUSTICE

It has long been charged that police are more likely to act formally with African American suspects and to use their discretion to benefit European Americans. Many studies have found that African Americans are disproportionately stopped by police and that race is the primary reason for this practice. African American youths are arrested at a rate disproportionate to their representation in the population.

One reason for this phenomenon is that minority and lower-class neighborhoods experience much greater police scrutiny than white, middle-class areas, and their residents face a greater chance of arrest. For example, a significant body of literature shows that police are more likely to "hassle" or arrest African American males in poor neighborhoods. It is therefore not surprising that, as Harvard criminologist Robert Sampson has found, teenage residents of neighborhoods with low socioeconomic status (SES) have a significantly greater chance of acquiring police records than youths living in higher-SES areas, regardless of the actual crime rates in these areas. Sampson's research indicates that even though police officers may not discriminate on an individual level, departmental policy that focuses on lower-class areas may result in class and racial bias in the police processing of delinquent youth.

Once arrested, minority youths face other problems as they are processed through the system. Those accused of delinquent acts are less likely than European American youths to be diverted from the court system into informal sanctions and are more likely to receive sentences involving incarceration. Today, more than six in ten juveniles in custody belong to racial or ethnic minorities. In some states, the ratio of minority custody to white custody is four or more to one. Minority youths are also waived to the adult justice system at a

rate that is greater than their representation in the population. About 40 percent of all waived youths are African Americans, even though they represent less than a third of the juvenile court population.

Racial disparity in juvenile disposition is an ongoing problem that demands immediate public scrutiny. In response, many jurisdictions have initiated studies of racial disproportion in their juvenile justice systems, along with responding to federal requirements to reduce disproportionate minority confinement (DMC), as contained in the Juvenile Justice and Delinquency Prevention Act of 2002. The most recent federal government report on state compliance to reduce DMC demonstrates that some progress has been made but that many challenges remain, including the basic need to identify factors that contribute to DMC (at least 18 states have yet to initiate this process), incomplete and inconsistent data systems, and the need for ongoing evaluation of focused interventions and system-wide efforts to reduce DMC.

The disproportionate minority representation in juvenile correctional facilities is a very serious matter, but it also reflects the racial disparity that occurs at every stage of the juvenile justice process. A disproportionate number of minority youths suffer arrest, detention, waivers, and so on. It is not surprising then that they also face disparity in the probability of incarceration.

The National Council on Crime and Delinquency report *Treatment of Youth of Color in the Justice System* describes how minority youths receive differential treatment at every stage of the justice process. Among the findings from the council's report are these:

● Although African American youths make up 16 percent of the adolescent population in the United States, they constitute 38 percent of the almost 100,000 youths confined in local detention

if they are disrespectful. Two-thirds (66 percent) of all juvenile arrests are now being referred to juvenile court for treatment and supervision; most of the rest are handled informally at the station or sent to social services. Police today may be more cautious with juveniles and more willing to refer them to juvenile court services than in the past.

One of the more troubling issues of discretion is whether race plays a role in decision making and, if it does, how that affects the entire system of juvenile justice. This is the topic of the Analyzing Criminal Justice Issues feature.

and state correctional systems. They are overrepresented in all offense categories.

- Youths of color make up the majority of young people held in both public and private facilities.

- Youths of color, especially Latino youths, are a much larger proportion of the young in public facilities than in private facilities, which tend to be less harsh environments.

- Although they represent just 34 percent of the U.S. population, youths of color are 62 percent of young people in detention, 66 percent of those committed to public facilities, and 55 percent of those committed to private facilities.

- Nationwide, youths of color are represented in the detained population at 3.1 times the rate of white youths, are committed to public facilities at 2.9 times the rate of white youths, and are committed to private institutions at 2.0 times the rate of white youths.

- Overall, custody rates are four times greater for African American youths than for white youths. Custody rates for Latino and Native American youths are 1.8 and 2.6 times the custody rate for white youths, respectively.

The council report concludes with this statement:

Even though "Equal Justice Under the Law" is the foundation of our legal system, and is carved on the front of the U.S. Supreme Court building, the juvenile justice system is anything but equal for all. Throughout the system, youths of color—especially African American youths—receive different and harsher treatment. This is true even when white youths and youths of color are charged with similar offenses. This report documents a juvenile justice system that is "separate and unequal." It is time for a nationwide effort to identify the causes of this differential treatment of youths of color and to mount a concerted campaign to provide a fair and equal justice system for juveniles in this country.

To try to alleviate this problem, since 1988 the Juvenile Justice and Delinquency Prevention Act has required that in order to receive funding, states must monitor whether the proportion of juvenile minorities in confinement exceeds their proportion in the general population.

CRITICAL THINKING

Achieving the goal of proportional representation has been elusive in actual practice. A number of strategies have been attempted, ranging from cultural competency training to providing increasing community-based detention alternatives. What would you suggest be done to reduce minority overrepresentation in the juvenile justice system?

Sources: Public Law 93-415, 42 USC 5601 et seq.; Emily Cabaniss, James Frabutt, Mary Kendrick, and Margaret Arbuckle, "Reducing Disproportionate Minority Contact in the Juvenile Justice System: Promising Practices," *Aggression and Violent Behavior* 12 (2007): 393–401; Mark Soler and Lisa M. Garry, *Reducing Disproportionate Minority Contact: Preparation at the Local Level* (Washington, DC: Office of Juvenile Justice and Delinquency Prevention, 2009), http://www.ncjrs.gov/pdffiles1/ojjdp/218861.pdf (accessed July 2014); Charles Puzzanchera and Sean Addie, *Delinquency Cases Waived to Criminal Court, 2010* (Washington, DC: Bureau of Justice Statistics, 2014), http://www.ojjdp.gov/pubs/243042.pdf (accessed July 2014); John F. Chapman, Rani A. Desai, Paul R. Falzer, and Randy Borum, "Violence Risk and Race in a Sample of Youth in Juvenile Detention: The Potential to Reduce Disproportionate Minority Confinement," *Youth Violence and Juvenile Justice* 4 (2006): 170–184; Robert Sampson, "Effects of Socioeconomic Context on Official Reaction to Juvenile Delinquency," *American Sociological Review* 51 (1986): 876–885.

Legal Rights of Juveniles in Custody

Once a juvenile has been taken into custody, the child has the same Fourth Amendment right as an adult to be free from unreasonable searches and seizures. Children in police custody can be detained prior to trial, interrogated, and placed in lineups. However, because of their youth and inexperience, children are generally afforded more protections than adults. Police must be careful that the juvenile suspect understands his constitutional rights and, if there is some question, must provide access to a parent or guardian to protect the child's legal interests.

In the past, police often questioned juveniles in the absence of their parents or an attorney. Any incriminatory statements or confessions made by juveniles could be placed in evidence at their trials. That is no longer permissible, and children have the same (or more) *Miranda* rights as adults, which was confirmed in the case of *Fare v. Michael C.* (1979).[26]

In 2011, the Supreme Court, in *J.D.B. v. North Carolina*, ruled that age does matter and that greater care must be taken by the police when questioning children in their custody.[27] J.D.B. was a 13-year-old special education student when the police showed up at his school to question him about a string of neighborhood burglaries. He was escorted to a school conference room where he was interrogated in the presence of school officials. J.D.B.'s parents were not contacted, and he was not given any warnings about his right to remain silent or to have access to a lawyer. J.D.B. confessed to the crimes, but later sought to have his confession suppressed on the basis that he was never read his *Miranda* rights. The state countered that his confession should stand because he was not in police custody when he incriminated himself. The question at law was whether a youth such as J.D.B. could fully comprehend whether he was in custody or free to leave. Writing for the majority, Justice Sonia Sotomayor said, "It is beyond dispute that children will often feel bound to submit to police questioning when an adult in the same circumstances would feel free to leave. Seeing no reason for police officers or courts to blind themselves to that commonsense reality, we hold that a child's age properly informs the *Miranda* custody analysis." As a result of these decisions, police will interrogate a juvenile without an adult present only if they believe that the youth is unquestionably mature and experienced enough to understand his or her legal rights.

Legal expert Barry Feld finds that police interrogation tactics with juveniles are quite similar to their questioning of adults. Once juveniles waive their *Miranda* rights, police used the same strategies and tactics to question them, including the use of false statements and evidence. Juveniles responded to those tactics, cooperated or resisted, and provided incriminating evidence at about the same rate as did adults. Feld's conclusion: the law treats juveniles just like adults, and police question them just as they do older suspects. Although the questioning was somewhat more benign than Feld had expected, the danger of false confessions and convictions still exists.[28]

Police Investigation in the School Setting

Because a great deal of juvenile crime occurs on school grounds, police departments have been stationing officers within schools. These police officers are generally referred to as school resource officers (SROs). The increased presence of law enforcement officers within schools raises the question of the legal rights of students in the educational environment. The issue of student privacy relates not only to police but also to school officials, who often assume quasi-police powers over children. Both police officers and school officials may wish to search students to determine whether they are in possession of contraband, such as drugs or weapons; to search their lockers and desks; and to interrogate them about illegal activities.

In *New Jersey v. T.L.O.* (1985), the U.S. Supreme Court held that a school official had the authority to search a student's purse even though no warrant had been issued and no probable cause existed that a crime had been committed, only a suspicion that T.L.O. had violated school rules.[29] This case involved an assistant principal's search of the purse of a 14-year-old female student who had been observed smoking a cigarette in a school lavatory. The assistant principal found cigarette-rolling papers when a pack of cigarettes was removed from the purse. A further search revealed marijuana and several items indicating marijuana selling. As a result, T.L.O. was adjudicated as a delinquent. The Supreme Court held that the Fourth Amendment protections against unreasonable searches and

Web App 15.2

For information about a police juvenile division, visit http://www.lapdonline.org/juvenile_division.

Thomas Barwick/The Image Bank/Getty Images

Students do not lose their rights at the schoolhouse door. However, they do not have the same protections as adults in society. For example, they can be searched without a warrant if they violate school rules, even if their behavior does not amount to a crime. And although they have the right to limited, passive free speech, such as wearing a peace symbol, they can be suspended if school officials believe that their behavior constitutes a security risk. For example, writing an article in the school newspaper explaining how to smoke marijuana might not be allowed.

seizures apply to students but that the need to maintain an orderly educational environment modified the usual Fourth Amendment requirements of warrants and probable cause. The Court relaxed the usual probable cause standard and found the search to be reasonable. It declared that the school's right to maintain discipline on school grounds allowed it to search students and their possessions as a safety precaution. The Court, which had guarded the warrant requirement and its exceptions in the past, now permits warrantless searches in school, based on the lesser standard of "reasonable suspicion." This landmark decision did not deal with other thorny issues, however, such as the search and seizure of contraband from a student's locker or desk.

SEARCHING FOR DRUGS Faced with crime by students in public schools, particularly illicit drug use, school administrators have gone to extreme measures to enforce drug-control statutes and administrative rules. Some urban schools routinely employ Breathalyzers, drug-sniffing dogs, hidden video cameras, and routine searches of students' pockets, purses, lockers, and cars. In general, courts consider such searches permissible when they are not overly offensive and when reasonable grounds are found to suspect that the student has violated the law. School administrators are walking a tightrope between a student's constitutional right to privacy and school safety. The Supreme Court has allowed school authorities to conduct random drug tests on the grounds that these are less intrusive than a search of a student's body.

In the 1995 case *Vernonia School District 47J v. Acton*, the Court allowed the testing of student athletes who were going off campus to engage in events.[30] Underlying this decision is the recognition that drug use is a serious threat to public safety that interferes with the right of children to receive a decent and safe education. Although drug tests are intrusive, maintaining school safety was viewed as outweighing the attendant minor inconvenience and loss of personal privacy. In a subsequent case, *Board of Education of Independent School District No. 92 of Pottawatomie County et al. v. Earls et al.*, the Court extended the right to test for drugs without probable cause to all students as long as the drug-testing policies were "reasonable." In this instance, the need for applying swift

Officer Lucero Cardenas searches a United South High School classroom with a drug dog, in Laredo, Texas. What constitutional questions are raised when officers use drug dogs to search students' belongings?

AP Images/ERIC GAY

Web App 15.3

For more information about juveniles and the law, go to http://www.law.cornell.edu/wex/juvenile_justice.

and informal disciplinary procedures to maintain order in a public school outweighs the right to personal privacy. Because the school's responsibility for children cannot be disregarded, it would not be unreasonable to search students for evidence of drug usage even if no single student was suspected of abusing drugs.

The Court also ruled that, within this context, students have a limited expectation of privacy. In their complaint, the students argued that children participating in nonathletic extracurricular activities have a stronger expectation of privacy than athletes who regularly undergo physicals as part of their participation in sports. The Court disagreed, maintaining that students who participate in competitive extracurricular activities voluntarily subject themselves to many of the same intrusions on their privacy as do athletes.[31]

LIMITING DRUG SEARCHES How far can school officials go in their efforts to preserve a safe school environment? The Court clarified this issue in *Safford Unified School District v. Redding*, a 2009 case that drew national headlines. Savana Redding was a 13-year-old eighth-grade honors student at Safford Middle School, located about 125 miles from Tucson, Arizona, when on October 3, 2003, she was taken out of class by the school's vice principal. It seems that one of Redding's classmates had been caught possessing four prescription-strength ibuprofen pills (400 mg, the strength of two Advils), and when asked where she got the pills, she blamed Redding, who had no history of disciplinary issues or drug abuse. Although Redding claimed that she had no knowledge of the pills, she was subjected to a strip search by the school nurse and another female employee, because the school has a zero-tolerance policy for all over-the-counter medication (which students could not possess without prior written permission). During the search, Redding was forced to strip to her underwear and her bra, and her underpants were pulled away from her body.[32] On June 25, 2009, the Supreme Court held that Redding's Fourth Amendment rights were indeed violated by the search. With Justice David Souter writing for the majority, the Court agreed that search measures used by school officials to root out contraband must be "reasonably related to the objectives of the search and not excessively intrusive in light of the age and sex of the student and the nature of the infraction."

The Juvenile Court Process

Most children come into the justice system as a result of contact with a police officer. When a juvenile commits a serious crime, the police are empowered to make an arrest. Less serious offenses may also require police action, but in these instances, instead of being arrested, the child may be warned or a referral may be made to a social service program. After the police have determined that a case warrants further attention, they bind it over to the prosecutor's office, which then is responsible for channeling the case through the juvenile court. In addition, cases may be petitioned to the court from other than law enforcement sources, such as when educational authorities ask the court to intervene in cases of truancy or parents directly petition the court asking that their child be considered a status offender. The juvenile court plays a major role in controlling juvenile behavior and delivering social services to children in need.

The Intake Process

After police processing, the juvenile offender is usually remanded to the local juvenile court's intake division. At this juncture, court intake officers or probation personnel review and initially screen the child and the family to determine whether the child needs to be handled formally or the case can be settled without the necessity of costly and intrusive official intervention. Their report helps the prosecutor decide whether to handle the case informally or bind it over for trial. The intake stage represents an opportunity to place a child in informal programs both within the court and in the community. The intake process also is critically important because more than half of the referrals to the juvenile courts never go beyond this stage.

The Detention Process

After a juvenile is formally taken into custody, either as a delinquent or as a status offender, the prosecutor usually decides whether to release the child to the parent or guardian or to detain the child in a secure shelter pending trial.

Detention has always been a controversial area of juvenile justice. Far too many children have been routinely placed in detention while awaiting court appearances. Status offenders and delinquents have been held in the same facility, and in many parts of the country, adult county jails were used to detain juvenile offenders. The Juvenile Justice Act of 1974 emphasized reducing the number of children placed in inappropriate detention facilities. Even though the act was largely successful, the practice continues.

Despite such measures, hundreds of thousands of youths, most of whom are already living under difficult circumstances, are placed in pretrial detention each year. Many have suffered long histories of abuse and mental health problems.[33] The detention decision may reflect a child's personal characteristics and the quality of his or her home life, rather than any dangerousness or flight risk.[34] Detention is widely misapplied, according to the report by the Justice Policy Institute, a Washington, D.C.–based group, because detention facilities are meant to temporarily house those youths who are likely to reoffend before their trial or who are unlikely to appear for their court date, but many of the youths in this country's more than 750 detention centers do not meet these criteria. Seventy percent of youths in detention are held for nonviolent charges. More than two-thirds are charged with property offenses, public-order offenses, technical probation violations, or status offenses (such as running away or breaking curfew).[35]

LEGAL ISSUES Most state statutes ordinarily require a hearing on the appropriateness of detention if the initial decision is to keep the child in custody. At this hearing, the child has a right to counsel and may be given other procedural due process safeguards, notably the privilege against self-incrimination and the right to confront and cross-examine witnesses. Most state juvenile court acts provide criteria to support a decision to detain the child. These include (a) the need to protect the child, (b) whether the child presents a serious danger to the public, and (c) the likelihood that the juvenile will return to court for adjudication. Whereas in adult cases most offenders are released if they can afford bail, juveniles may be detained for a variety of reasons, including their own protection. Normally, the finding of the judge that the child should be detained must be supported by factual evidence. In the 1984 case of *Schall v. Martin*, the U.S. Supreme Court upheld the right of the states to detain a child before trial to protect his welfare and the public safety.[36]

REFORMING DETENTION There has been an ongoing effort to reform detention. The most important reform has been the successful effort to remove status offenders from lockups containing delinquents. After decades of effort, nearly all states have passed laws requiring that status offenders be placed in

Web App 15.4

For more information about the juvenile justice process, including more details related to Figure 15.1, see http://www.ojjdp.gov/ojstatbb/structure_process/case.html.

L07 Discuss the detention of juveniles.

detention
The temporary care of a child alleged to be a delinquent or status offender who requires secure custody, pending court disposition.

nonsecure shelters, rather than in secure detention facilities, thereby reducing their contact with more dangerous delinquent youths.

Another serious problem is the detention of youths in adult jails. This practice is common in rural areas where there are relatively few separate facilities for young offenders.[37] The OJJDP has given millions of dollars in aid to encourage the removal of juveniles from adult lockups. These grants have helped jurisdictions develop intake screening procedures, specific release or detention criteria, and alternative residential and nonresidential programs for juveniles awaiting trial. By 1980, amendments to the act mandating the absolute removal of juveniles from jails had been adopted. Despite such efforts, many states are not complying with the removal provisions and still detain juveniles in adult jails. Adding to their numbers are youths who commit nonserious acts—such as runaways—but are apprehended in rural areas where there are no juvenile facilities. There are also states that define the age limit for delinquency as 16 or 17 and therefore treat minors of that age as legal adults. Because jail stays are of short duration, it is likely that hundreds of thousands of minors are held in adult jails each year.

Whatever the actual number jailed today, placing young offenders in adult jails continues to be a significant problem in the juvenile justice system. Juveniles detained in adult jails often live in squalid conditions and are subject to physical and sexual abuse. The practice is widely condemned, but eliminating the confinement of juveniles in adult institutions remains a difficult task.

Bail

If a child is not detained, the question of bail arises. Federal courts have not found it necessary to rule on the issue of a juvenile's constitutional right to bail because liberal statutory release provisions act as appropriate alternatives. Although only a few state statutes allow release on money bail, many others have juvenile code provisions that emphasize the release of the child to the parents as an acceptable substitute. A constitutional right to bail that on its face seems to benefit a child may have unforeseen results. The imposition of money bail might create a serious economic strain on the child's family, while conflicting with the protective and social concerns of the juvenile court. Considerations of economic liabilities and other procedural inequities have influenced the majority of courts confronting this question to hold that juveniles do not have a right to bail.

Plea Bargaining

Before trial, prosecutors in the juvenile courts may attempt to negotiate a settlement to the case. For example, if the offender admits to the facts of the petition, he may be offered placement in a special community-based treatment program in lieu of a term in a secure state facility. Or a status offense petition may be substituted for one of delinquency so that the adolescent can avoid being housed in a state training school and, instead, be placed in a more treatment-oriented facility.

If a bargain can be reached, the child will be asked to admit in open court that he did in fact commit the act of which he stands accused. State juvenile courts tend to minimize the stigma associated with the use of adult criminal standards by using other terminology, such as "agree to a finding" or "accept the petition" rather than "admit guilt." When the child makes an admission, juvenile courts require the following procedural safeguards: The child must know of the right to a trial, the plea or admission must be made voluntarily, and the child must understand the charges and the consequences of the plea.

Waiver of Jurisdiction

Before development of the first modern juvenile court in Illinois in 1899, juveniles were tried for violations of the law in adult criminal courts. The consequences were devastating; many children were treated as criminal offenders and sentenced to adult prisons. Although the subsequent passage of state legislation creating juvenile courts eliminated this problem, the juvenile justice system did recognize that certain forms of conduct require that children be tried as adults. Today, most American jurisdictions provide by statute for **waiver**, or transfer, of juvenile offenders to the criminal courts. Waiver is also widely used in juvenile courts in Europe and Great Britain.[38] The number of judicially waived cases hit a historic peak in 1994—when about 13,100 cases were waived—and has fallen 42 percent since that year.[39] One reason for the decline has been the reduction in violent crimes by juveniles; another reason is the creation of new laws giving adult courts original jurisdiction for serious crimes, bypassing the juvenile court, and making waiver a moot issue.

The major forms of waiver administration are described below[40]:

- *Direct file waiver.* The prosecutor has the discretion of filing charges for certain legislatively designated offenses in either juvenile or criminal court. About 15 states have this provision.

- *Excluded offense waiver.* State laws exclude from juvenile court jurisdiction certain offenses that are either very minor, such as traffic or fishing violations, or very serious, such as murder. About 30 states now have such laws for certain crimes.

- *Judicial waiver.* After a formal **transfer hearing** at which both prosecutor and defense attorney present evidence, a juvenile court judge may decide to waive jurisdiction and transfer the case to criminal court. Most commonly considered are the child's age and the nature of the offense alleged in the petition.

- *Reverse waiver.* State laws mandate that certain offenses be tried in adult court. Once the case is heard in the adult court, the trial judge may decide that the offender would be better served by the juvenile court and order a reverse waiver. About 25 states have this provision for certain circumstances.

- *Blended sentencing laws.* These either provide juvenile courts with criminal sentencing options (juvenile blended sentencing) or allow criminal courts to impose juvenile dispositions (criminal blended sentencing).

Some jurisdictions require that children be over a certain age (typically 14) before they can be waived. Others mandate that the youth be charged with a felony before being tried as an adult, whereas others permit waiver of jurisdiction to the criminal court regardless of the seriousness of the offense when a child is a chronic offender. In 31 states, once a juvenile is tried in adult court, she is no longer eligible for juvenile justice on any subsequent offense (this provision and waiver in general will be discussed again in this chapter).

LEGAL CONTROLS Because of the nature of the waiver decision and its effect on the child in terms of status and disposition, the Supreme Court has imposed procedural protections for juveniles in the waiver process. In *Kent v. United States* (1966), the Court held that the waiver proceeding is a critically important stage in the juvenile justice process and that juveniles must be afforded minimum requirements of due process of law at such proceedings, including the right to legal counsel.[41] Then, in *Breed v. Jones* (1975), the Court held that the prosecution of juveniles as adults in the California Superior Court violated the double jeopardy clause of the Fifth Amendment if they had previously been tried on the same charge in juvenile court.[42] The Court concluded that jeopardy attaches when the juvenile court begins to hear evidence at the adjudicatory hearing; thus the waiver hearing must take place before any adjudication.

waiver (juvenile)
A practice in which the juvenile court waives its jurisdiction over a juvenile and transfers the case to adult criminal court for trial. In some states, a waiver hearing is held to determine jurisdiction; in others, juveniles may be automatically waived if they are accused of committing a serious crime such as murder.

transfer hearing
The hearing in which a judge decides whether to waive a juvenile to the criminal court. Waiver decisions are based on such criteria as the child's age, his or her prior offense history, and the nature of the offense.

 LO8 Recite the problems and legal issues surrounding the waiver decision.

THE EFFECT OF WAIVER Although waiver has its advocates, many experts question its utility, arguing that it does more harm than good. Although some youths transferred to adult court never spend a day in prison, thousands do, and many of them become enmeshed in the daily life of an adult correctional facility. They miss out on being housed in juvenile facilities that are smaller, have much lower inmate-to-staff ratios, and place greater emphasis on treatment, counseling, education, and mentoring of inmates. Some adult facilities do provide easy access to education and treatment, but young inmates still lose out on developing the more supportive, mentoring-focused style of staff–inmate interactions that a juvenile facility provides.[43]

Instead, those forced to serve time in adult prisons are exposed to experienced criminals in what are essentially "schools for crime." In addition, children may be targets of adult predators if they are confined to adult institutions. About 7,500 young people are held in adult facilities in the United States on any given day, and the yearly rate may be several times higher, resulting in the jailing of tens of thousands of young people.[44] The risks they face include:

■ *Sexual assault.* When youths are placed with adults in adult jails, they are at risk of physical and sexual assault. More than 20 percent of all substantiated victims of inmate-on-inmate sexual violence were under 18 years old, even though youths make up less than 1 percent of the total jail population.

■ *Suicide.* Youths have the highest suicide rates of all inmates in jails. They are 36 times more likely to commit suicide in an adult jail than in a juvenile detention facility, and youths in an adult jail are 19 times more likely to commit suicide than youths in the general population.

■ *Damage to communities and public safety.* New evidence shows that placing youths in the adult criminal justice system increases their likelihood of reoffending. Children who are prosecuted in adult court are more likely to be rearrested more often and more quickly for serious offenses.

AP Images/Jeff Scheid

Turner Bronson, 15, makes an initial appearance in Clark County Justice Court in Las Vegas, Nevada. He was tried as an adult on a murder charge in the shooting death of his brother, 18-year-old Clayton. Is there a specific age at which juveniles should be considered adults for purposes of criminal prosecution?

Should Youths Be Transferred to Adult Court?

Most juvenile justice experts oppose waiver, because it clashes with the rehabilitative ideal. First, there are distinct racial and gender differences in processing that makes waiver suspect: transferred juveniles are more likely than their adult counterparts to be male (96 percent versus 84 percent) and black (55 percent versus 45 percent).[45]

Another problem is that there are tremendous differences in waiver policies between legal jurisdictions. For example, one three-state comparison that looked at waiver in Florida, Arizona, and California found that over the period from 2003 through 2008, Florida transferred youth at about twice the rate of Arizona and about eight times the rate of California. One reason is Florida's expansive prosecutorial discretion law, which permits prosecutors to opt for criminal handling of (among others) all 16- and 17-year-olds accused of felonies.[46]

Basing waiver decisions on type and seriousness of offense rather than on the rehabilitative needs of the child has advanced the *criminalization* of the juvenile court and interfered with its traditional mission of treatment and rehabilitation.[47] And despite this sacrifice, there is little evidence that strict waiver policies can lower crime rates.[48] What is accomplished by treating juveniles like adults? Studies of the impact of the recent waiver statutes have yielded several interesting—and conflicting—results. Research by Benjamin Steiner and Emily Wright on the effect of direct waiver laws found that they have little effect on juvenile violent crime rates in the states that have adopted them into law.[49] Other studies have found that juveniles waived to adult court receive harsher punishment and may be viewed as dangerous and incapable of being rehabilitated.[50] This important issue is explored further in the accompanying Evidence-Based Justice feature.

PUNISHING JUVENILES: DEATH PENALTY AND LIFE IN PRISON

If juveniles can be waived to adult courts, then it stands to reason that they can be punished as adults. Or can they? For example, can a minor convicted of murder in an adult court receive the death penalty? You may be surprised to know that the execution of minor children has not been uncommon in our nation's history; at least 366 juvenile offenders have been executed since 1642.[51] However, on March 1, 2005, the U.S. Supreme Court, in the case of *Roper v. Simmons*, put an end to infliction of the death penalty on juveniles in the United States. At issue was the minimum age at which juveniles who were under the age of 18 when they committed their crimes could be eligible for the death penalty.[52] At the time, 16- and 17-year-olds were eligible for the death penalty; 21 states permitted the death penalty for juveniles.[53] A total of 72 juvenile offenders were on death row at the time.[54] In a 5–4 decision,

EVIDENCE-based justice

IS WAIVER EFFECTIVE?

In all the debate surrounding transfers of juvenile offenders to adult or criminal court, one of the most important issues is whether transfers are effective in reducing crime rates. Are juveniles who are transferred to and convicted in adult court less likely to recidivate than similar youths who are convicted in juvenile court? To answer this question, the Task Force on Community Preventive Services, an independent group that receives support from the U.S. Department of Health and Human Services and the Centers for Disease Control and Prevention, conducted the first comprehensive, methodologically rigorous systematic review of studies measuring the effects of transfer laws and policies on crime rates. The review identified six high-quality evaluation studies that measured the specific deterrent effect of transfers on violent crime rates. Not one of the studies found that transfers produced lower violent crime rates. In fact, four of the studies found a harmful effect; that is, juveniles transferred to adult court had higher violent rearrest rates than their counterparts who were retained in juvenile court. For these four studies, rearrest rates for the transferred juveniles were between 27 and 77 percent higher than rates for the nontransferred juveniles. The authors of the review reported that these studies found harmful effects for total crime rates as well.

On the matter of a general deterrent effect of transfers, less could be said. The task force concluded that there was insufficient evidence at present to make a determination on the effectiveness of transfer laws and policies in reducing juvenile violence generally. Based on the overall findings, the Task Force on Community Preventive Services concluded that transferring juvenile offenders to the adult system is "counterproductive for the purpose of reducing juvenile violence and enhancing public safety." The task force did not go so far as to recommend that states repeal their transfer laws and discontinue the practice of transfers altogether, possibly because of the inconsistent results found for general deterrent effects.

Source: Angela McGowan, Robert Hahn, Akiva Liberman, Alex Crosby, Mindy Fullilove, Robert Johnson, Eve Mosciki, LeShawndra Price, Susan Snyder, Farris Tuma, Jessica Lowy, Peter Briss, Stella Cory, Glenda Stone, and the Task Force on Community Preventive Services, "Effects on Violence of Laws and Policies Facilitating the Transfer of Juveniles from the Juvenile Justice System to the Adult Justice System: A Systematic Review," *American Journal of Preventive Medicine* 32(4S) (2007): 7–28.

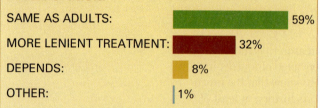

YOUR OPINION: In your view, how should juveniles between the ages of 14 and 17 who commit violent crimes be treated in the criminal justice system—should they be treated the same as adults, or should they be given more lenient treatment in a juvenile court?

PUBLIC OPINION:

SAME AS ADULTS:	59%
MORE LENIENT TREATMENT:	32%
DEPENDS:	8%
OTHER:	1%

REALITY: A majority of people clearly favor getting tough with juveniles—at least with respect to violent crime. Certainly some juveniles are capable of forming criminal intent and should be held as accountable as any adult. Yet others may not understand the consequences of their actions. Unfortunately, it is all but impossible to firmly settle on a point at which any person of a certain age should be tried as an adult for committing a violent crime. Interestingly, juvenile crime has mostly been on the decline for the past decade, so perceptions concerning treatment of juvenile offenders are driven by something else.

DISCUSSION: Why do so many people feel we should treat certain juveniles as adults? What is the appropriate age of criminal responsibility?

Sources: Sourcebook of Criminal Justice Statistics, http://www.albany.edu/sourcebook/pdf/t248.pdf (accessed July 2014); OJJDP Statistical Briefing Book, http://www.ojjdp.gov/ojstatbb/crime/JAR_Display.asp?ID=qa05201 (accessed July 2014).

the Court ruled that the juvenile death penalty was in violation of the Eighth Amendment's ban on cruel and unusual punishment. The Court held that it was cruel and unusual to execute a person who was under the age of 18 at the time of the murder; in reaching its decision, the Court relied on a significant body of sociological and scientific research that showed that juveniles lack the maturity and sense of responsibility found in adults.[55]

What about a life sentence? Experts such as Barry Feld, an opponent of life sentences for kids, have long held that the Supreme Court's reasoning in *Roper v. Simmons* should also apply to cases in which juvenile offenders are receiving life sentences without the possibility of parole.[56] Feld proposed that "states formally recognize youthfulness as a mitigating factor by applying a 'youth discount' to adult sentence lengths."[57] This issue was taken up by the Supreme Court in *Graham v. Florida*, where the Court ruled that a child's immaturity excluded them from being given a sentence of life without parole if the crime they committed did not involve murder.[58] Writing for the majority, Justice Anthony Kennedy stated: "A state need not guarantee the offender eventual release, but if it imposes the sentence of life, it must provide him or her with some realistic opportunity to obtain release before the end of that term."[59]

In a 2012 case, *Miller v. Alabama*, the Court extended the ban on mandatory life sentences for juveniles even if they have committed murder. Justice Elena Kagan wrote, "It prevents taking into account the family and home environment that surrounds him—and from which he cannot usually extricate himself—no matter how brutal or dysfunctional."[60] *Miller* does not forbid life terms for those convicted of murder under age 18, but ruled that judges must consider the defendant's youth and the nature of the crime before putting him behind bars with no hope for parole.

Adjudication

initial appearance

A juvenile's first appearance before the juvenile court judge in which the charges are reviewed and an effort is made to settle the case without a trial. If the child does not have legal counsel, an attorney is appointed.

There are usually two judicial hearings in the juvenile court process. The first, typically called an **initial appearance**, is similar to the arraignment in the adult system. The child is informed of the charges against him, attorneys are appointed, bail is reviewed, and in many instances cases are settled with an admission of the facts, followed by a community sentence. If the case cannot be settled at this initial stage, it is bound over for trial.

During the adjudicatory or trial process, which in juvenile proceedings is often called the fact-finding hearing, the court hears evidence on the allegations stated in the delinquency petition. In its early development, the juvenile court did not emphasize judicial rule making similar to that of the criminal trial process. Absent were such basic requirements as the standard of proof, rules of evidence, and similar adjudicatory formalities. Proceedings were to be nonadversarial, informal, and noncriminal. Gradually, however, the juvenile trial process became a target of criticism because judges were handing out punishments to children without affording them legal rights. This changed in 1967 when the Supreme Court's landmark *In re Gault* decision radically altered the juvenile justice system.[61] In *Gault*, the Court ruled that the concept of fundamental fairness is applicable to juvenile delinquency proceedings. The Court granted critical rights to juvenile defendants, the most important being notice of the charges, the right to counsel, the right to confront and cross-examine witnesses, the privilege against self-incrimination, and the right to a transcript of the trial record.

The *Gault* decision completely altered the juvenile trial process. Instead of dealing with children in a benign and paternalistic fashion, the courts were forced to process juvenile offenders within the framework of appropriate constitutional procedures. And though *Gault* was technically limited to the adjudicatory stage, it has spurred further legal reform throughout the juvenile system. Today, the right to counsel, the privilege against self-incrimination, the right to treatment in detention and correctional facilities, and other constitutional protections are applied at all stages of the juvenile process, from investigation through adjudication to parole. *Gault* ushered in an era of legal rights for juveniles.

Once an adjudicatory hearing has been completed, the court is normally required to enter a judgment against the child. This may take the form of declaring the child delinquent or a ward of the court or possibly even suspending judgment to avoid the stigma of a juvenile record. Following the entering of a judgment, the court can begin its determination of possible **dispositions** for the child.

Disposition and Treatment

At the dispositional hearing, the juvenile court judge imposes on the juvenile offender a sentence based on her offense, prior record, and family background. Normally, the judge has broad discretionary power to issue a range of dispositions from dismissal to institutional **commitment**. In theory, the dispositional decision is an effort by the court to serve the best interests of the child, the family, and the community. In many respects, this postadjudicative process is the most important stage in the juvenile court system, because it represents the last opportunity for the court to influence the child and control her behavior.

To ensure that only relevant and appropriate evidence is considered by the court during trial, most jurisdictions require a separate hearing to formulate an appropriate disposition. The bifurcated hearing process ensures that the adjudicatory hearing is used solely to determine the merits of the allegations, whereas the dispositional hearing determines whether the child is in need of rehabilitation.

In theory, the juvenile court seeks to provide a disposition that represents an individualized **treatment** plan for the child. This decision is normally based on the presentence investigation of the probation department, reports from social agencies, and possibly a psychiatric evaluation. The judge generally has broad discretion in dispositional matters but is limited by the provisions of the state's juvenile court act. The following are typical juvenile court dispositions:

■ Suspended judgment

■ Probation

disposition
For juvenile offenders, the equivalent of sentencing for adult offenders. The theory is that disposition is more rehabilitative than retributive. Possible dispositions: dismissing the case, releasing the youth to the custody of his or her parents, placing the offender on probation, or sending him or her to an institution or state correctional institution.

commitment
Decision of a judge who orders an adjudicated and sentenced juvenile offender to be placed in a correctional facility.

 L09 Describe the juvenile trial and sentencing process.

treatment
The rehabilitative method used to effect a change of behavior in the juvenile offender; treatment may take the form of therapy or educational or vocational programs.

AP Images/*St. Petersburg Times*/Daniel Wallace

In 1991, gang members instructed 13-year-old Ian Manuel to commit a robbery during which he shot Debbie Baigrie in the face and got a life sentence for attempted murder. Manuel's attorney told him to plead guilty in exchange for a 15-year prison sentence. Manuel accepted responsibility and pleaded guilty but was sentenced to life imprisonment without possibility of parole. His lawyer never appealed or withdrew the plea. Manuel was sent to prison, where he was so small no prison uniform fit him. He spent years in solitary confinement and repeatedly attempted suicide. When the Supreme Court in 2012 ruled that juveniles can't be given life sentences, Manuel's life sentence was vacated by the Florida courts.

- Placement in a community treatment program
- Commitment to the state agency responsible for juvenile institutional care

In addition, the court may place the child with parents or relatives, make dispositional arrangements with private youth-serving agencies, or order the child committed to a mental institution.

DISPOSITION OUTCOMES   In dispositional hearings, juvenile court judges must determine the most appropriate sanction for delinquent youths. Disposition options include commitment to an institution or another residential facility, probation, and a variety of other dispositions, such as referral to an outside agency or treatment program, community service, fines, or restitution. Very often the court imposes some combination of these sanctions. What have been the trends in juvenile disposition? The number of adjudicated delinquency cases resulting in residential placement has increased significantly during the past decade, and today about 10 percent of all cases petitioned to juvenile court get some form of residential treatment. The committed child may be sent to a state training school or a private residential treatment facility. These are usually minimum-security facilities with small populations and an emphasis on treatment and education. Some states, however, maintain facilities with populations of over 1,000 youths. Currently there are more than 70,000 youths in some form of correctional institution in the United States.[62] An additional 400,000 kids are put on probation each year.

Juvenile Sentencing Reform

Over the past decade, juvenile justice experts and the general public have become aroused about the serious juvenile crime rate in general and about violent acts committed by children in particular. As a result, some law enforcement officials and conservative legislators have demanded that the juvenile justice system take a more serious stance with dangerous juvenile offenders. Many state legislatures have responded by toughening their juvenile codes. Some jurisdictions have passed mandatory or determinate incarceration sentences for juveniles convicted of serious felonies. Not all jurisdictions have abandoned rehabilitation as a primary dispositional goal, however, and some still adhere to the philosophy that placements should be based on the least detrimental alternative. This view requires that judges employ the least intrusive measures possible to safeguard a child's growth and development.[63]

A second reform has been the concerted effort to remove status offenders from the juvenile justice system and restrict their entry into institutional programs. Because of the development of numerous diversion programs, many children involved in truancy and incorrigible behavior who ordinarily would have been sent to a closed institution are now being placed in community programs. There are far fewer status offenders in detention or institutions than ever before.

A third reform effort has been to standardize dispositions in juvenile court. As early as 1977, Washington passed one of the first determinate-sentencing laws for juvenile offenders, resulting in other states adopting similar statutes.[64] All children found to be delinquent are evaluated on a point system based on their age, prior juvenile record, and type of crime committed. Minor offenders are handled in the community. Those committing more serious offenses are placed on probation. Children who commit the most serious offenses are subject to standardized institutional penalties. As a result, juvenile offenders who commit such crimes as rape or armed robbery are being sentenced to institutionalization for two, three, and four years. This approach is different from the indeterminate sentencing under which children who have committed a serious crime might be released from institutions in less than a year if correctional authorities believe they have been rehabilitated.

The Juvenile Correctional Process

After disposition in juvenile court, delinquent offenders may be placed in some form of correctional treatment. Although many are placed in the community, almost 90,000 are now in secure facilities.

Probation

The most commonly used formal sentence for juvenile offenders is probation, and many states require that a youth must have failed on probation before being sent to an institution (unless the criminal act is quite serious). Probation involves placing the child under the supervision of the juvenile probation department for the purpose of community treatment. A juvenile may also be required to follow special rules, such as maintaining a curfew or attending substance abuse meetings. Alternative sanctions such as community service or monetary restitution may be ordered. Serious offenders can be placed in intensive supervision or under house arrest. Just as in the adult system, probation can be revoked if the juvenile violates the probation conditions, and the court may impose stricter sanctions.

Juvenile probation is an important component of the juvenile justice system. It is the most widely used method of community treatment in juvenile court. Similar in form and function to adult probation, supervising juveniles in the community combines elements of treatment and control. Some probation officers maintain a social work orientation and want to provide needy kids with an effective treatment plan, whereas others maintain a law enforcement orientation, believing that their clients are offenders who need close monitoring.[65]

Intensive Supervision

Juvenile intensive probation supervision (JIPS) involves treating offenders who would normally have been sent to a secure treatment facility as part of a very small probation caseload that receives almost daily scrutiny.[66] The primary goal of JIPS is decarceration; without intensive supervision, youngsters would normally be sent to secure juvenile facilities that are already overcrowded. The second goal is control; high-risk juvenile offenders can be maintained in the community under much closer security than traditional probation efforts can provide. A third goal is maintaining community ties and reintegration; offenders can remain in the community and complete their education while avoiding the pains of imprisonment.

Intensive probation programs get mixed reviews. Some jurisdictions find that they are more successful than traditional probation supervision and cost much less than incarceration.[67] However, some studies indicate that the failure rate is high and that younger offenders who commit petty crimes are the most likely to fail when placed in intensive supervision programs.[68] It is not surprising that intensive probation clients fail more often, because, after all, they are more serious offenders who might otherwise have been incarcerated and are now being watched and supervised more closely than probationers.

juvenile intensive probation supervision (JIPS)

A true alternative to incarceration that involves almost daily supervision of the juvenile by the probation officer assigned to the case.

Institutionalization

The most severe of the statutory dispositions available to the juvenile court involves commitment of the child to an institution. Juvenile facilities are known by many different names: detention centers, juvenile halls, shelters, reception and diagnostic centers, group homes, wilderness camps, ranches, farms, youth development centers, residential treatment centers, training or reform schools, and juvenile correctional institutions. Some facilities resemble adult prisons or jails, some resemble campuses, and others resemble houses.[69]

State statutes vary when determining the length of the child's commitment. Traditionally, many jurisdictions committed the child up to her or his majority, which usually meant until the individual reached 21 years of age. This normally deprived the child of freedom for an extensive period of time—sometimes longer than an adult sentenced for the same offense would be confined. As a result, some states have passed legislation under which children are committed for periods ranging from one to three years.

The number of youths being held in some form of incarceration has declined from over 100,000 in 2000 to about 70,000 today, a trend that reflects the ongoing decline in juvenile crime.[70] Minority youth account for about 75 percent of juveniles held in custody.[71] Females account for about 11 percent, and almost 60 percent of all youth in custody are 16 or 17 years old.[72]

Deinstitutionalization

Some experts in delinquency and juvenile law question the policy of institutionalizing juvenile offenders. Many believe that large institutions are too costly to operate and only produce more sophisticated criminals. That is why the concept of *deinstitutionalization*—removing as many youths from secure confinement as possible—was established by the Juvenile Justice and Delinquency Act of 1974. Considerable research supports the fact that warehousing juveniles without proper treatment does little to deter criminal behavior. The most effective secure corrections programs are those that provide individual services for a small number of participants.[73]

The Commonwealth of Massachusetts closed all its state training schools more than 20 years ago (subsequently, however, public pressure caused a few secure facilities to be reopened). Many other states have established small residential facilities operated by juvenile-care agencies to replace larger units.

DEINSTITUTIONALIZING STATUS OFFENDERS For several decades there has been an ongoing effort to deinstitutionalize status offenders (DSO). This means removing noncriminal youths from institutions housing delinquents in order to prevent them from interacting with violent or chronic offenders.

Since its inception, the DSO approach has been hotly debated. Some have argued that early intervention is society's best hope of forestalling future delinquent behavior and reducing victimization. Other experts maintain that legal control over status offenders is a violation of youths' rights. Still others have viewed status-offending behavior as a symptom of some larger trauma or problem that requires attention. These diverse opinions still exist today.

Since Congress passed the JJDP Act in 1974, all 50 states have complied with some aspect of the deinstitutionalization mandate. Millions of federal, state, and local dollars have been spent on the DSO movement. Programs have been created around the country to reduce the number of juveniles in secure confinement. What remains to be done, however, is to study the effect DSO has had on juveniles and the justice system.

Aftercare

LO10 Explain the efforts to treat troubled kids in the juvenile justice system.

Aftercare marks the final stage of the formal juvenile justice process. Its purpose is to help youths make the transition from residential or institutional settings back into the community. Effective aftercare programs provide adequate supervision and support services to help juvenile offenders avoid criminal activity. Examples of programs include electronic monitoring, counseling, treatment and community service referrals, education, work training, and intensive parole supervision.

Through the Serious and Violent Offender Reentry Initiative (SVORI), the federal government has invested $150 million in reentry programs for adult and juvenile offenders in all 50 states, the District of Columbia, and the Virgin Islands.[74] Promising results are beginning to emerge from this initiative as well as from other juvenile reentry programs across the country.[75] Take, for instance, the **Intensive Aftercare Program (IAP)** model developed by David Altschuler and Troy Armstrong. This program offers a continuum of intervention for serious juvenile offenders returning to the community following placement.[76] The IAP

Intensive Aftercare Program (IAP)
A balanced, highly structured, comprehensive continuum of intervention for serious and violent juvenile offenders returning to the community.

model begins by drawing attention to five basic principles, which collectively establish a set of fundamental operational goals:

1. Preparing youths for progressively increased responsibility and freedom in the community
2. Facilitating youth–community interaction and involvement
3. Working with both the offender and targeted community support systems (families, peers, schools, employers) on qualities needed for constructive interaction and the youths' successful community adjustment
4. Developing new resources and supports where needed
5. Monitoring and testing the youths and the community on their ability to deal with each other productively

These basic goals are then translated into practice, which incorporates individual case planning with a family and community perspective. The program stresses a mix of intensive surveillance and services and a balance of incentives and graduated consequences, coupled with the imposition of realistic, enforceable conditions. There is also "service brokerage," in which community resources are used and linkage with social networks is established.[77] So far, evaluations of the program indicate that it holds promise.

Preventing Delinquency

Although the juvenile justice system has been concerned with controlling delinquent behavior, there are now important efforts being made to prevent delinquency before it occurs. "Delinquency prevention" consists of intervening in young people's lives before they engage in delinquency in the first place, thus preventing delinquency from developing at all. In the past, delinquency prevention was the responsibility of treatment-oriented agencies such as day care providers, YMCA and YWCA, Boys and Girls Clubs of America, and other private and public agencies. Today, there are many community-based programs involving a combination of juvenile justice and treatment agencies. Some programs focus on the educational experience and attempt to help kids maintain their bond to society by strengthening their attachments to school. Some, such as the Job Corps and YouthBuild U.S.A., help kids prepare for the adult workforce by providing training and vocational counseling.[78] Many of these efforts are conducted

Motoya Nakamura/*The Oregonian*/Landov

Portland, Oregon, police officer Kristine Butcher congratulates a fifth-grader for his outstanding participation in the Gang Resistance Education and Training (G.R.E.A.T.) program at Alder Elementary School. The G.R.E.A.T. program is a school-based, law enforcement officer–instructed classroom curriculum. With prevention as its primary objective, the program is intended as an immunization against delinquency, youth violence, and gang membership.

CAREERS in criminal justice

SOCIAL WORKER

DUTIES AND CHARACTERISTICS OF THE JOB

Social workers aid individuals or families who are disadvantaged or facing particular challenges. Social workers pick an area of specialization within one of several larger categories. Public health social workers help individuals and families dealing with the consequences of a serious illness. Child, family, and health social workers will aid families dealing with issues of social functioning, such as child abuse or truancy. Clinical social workers help families deal with issues related to mental health and substance abuse through a rehabilitation program. Other social workers take positions where they aren't dealing with the public; instead, they teach or provide psychotherapy in private practices. There are also policy writers and advocates who attempt to find legislative solutions to social problems and lobby for funding.

Social work is a demanding profession both intellectually and emotionally. Social workers traditionally work a 40-hour office workweek, but working overtime or during evening hours to attend meetings or meet clients is not unusual.

JOB OUTLOOK

The prospects for employment as a social worker are good since jobs are expected to grow faster than average in the near future, and in many places there are more jobs than there are applicants. Because of the impending retirement of the baby boom generation, there are many job opportunities in hospices and nursing homes for social workers specializing in elder care. The employment of school and private social service agencies will also increase.

SALARY

Recent median annual earnings of child, family, and school social workers are $44,200. The lowest 10 percent earn less than $27,450, and the top 10 percent earn more than $72,980. Social workers' salaries vary according to their specialization. For example, social workers who specialize in medical and public health have an average

by social workers whose specialty is working with troubled youths. The Careers in Criminal Justice feature describes this occupation.

Comprehensive community-based delinquency prevention programs take a systematic approach or apply a comprehensive planning model to develop preventive interventions. This includes analyzing the delinquency problems that exist, identifying resources available in the community, prioritizing the delinquency problems, becoming familiar with successful programs in other communities, and tailoring them to local conditions and needs.[79] Not all comprehensive community-based prevention programs follow this model, but evidence suggests that this approach yields the greatest reductions in juvenile delinquency.[80]

The Future of Juvenile Justice

The juvenile justice system is at a crossroads: Can it provide meaningful treatment to youths in an age of budget cutting and reductions in social services? Should it maintain the *parens patriae* vision of its founders, or should it adopt a law-and-order approach to dealing with violent kids? Should the system be maintained, or should it be abolished?

Even those experts who want to retain an independent juvenile court have called for its restructuring.[81] Crime control advocates want to reduce the court's jurisdiction over juveniles charged with serious crimes and liberalize the prosecutor's ability to try them in adult courts. In *Bad Kids: Race and the Transformation of the Juvenile Court*, Barry Feld makes the controversial suggestion that the juvenile court system should be discontinued and replaced by salary of about $50,000, while those in the child/family context earn closer to $41,000.

OPPORTUNITIES

A majority of social worker positions are in urban and suburban areas; potential social workers will find more competition for a limited number of jobs in urban areas. Because there will be greater competition for these jobs in urban areas, applicants with more education and/or some specialized experience stand a better chance of getting desirable positions and career advancement. It may be considerably easier to find a job in a rural area, and educational requirements will be less stringent. Those who leave social work often successfully pursue careers in related fields, such as counseling.

QUALIFICATIONS

The ability to meet the challenging education requirements and certification are the primary qualifications necessary to become a social worker. Personal characteristics such as sensitivity, responsibility, and the ability to work independently are also very important. Potential social workers must have at least a bachelor's degree in social

work to start at entry-level positions, and additional education for higher degrees will prepare them for more advanced duties, such as clinical assessments and supervisory positions. In addition to being well educated, social workers have to meet the particular licensing requirements of the state where they are seeking employment before they can begin to work.

EDUCATION AND TRAINING

For entry-level positions, a bachelor's degree in social work (B.S.W.) or in a similar field, such as sociology, is necessary. Those who wish to advance further should earn a master's degree in social work (M.S.W.) or a doctorate (Ph.D. or D.S.W.). Those who wish to ascend to the highest-level positions in an organization employing social workers or design new social work policies or programs should pursue a Ph.D. Social workers' education is never truly complete; they must keep up on recent developments by attending conferences and reading the most recent literature.

Source: Bureau of Labor Statistics, U.S. Department of Labor, Social Worker, *Occupational Outlook Handbook*, http://www.bls.gov/ooh/Community-and-Social-Service/Social-workers.htm (accessed May 15, 2014).

an alternative method of justice.[82] During its history, various legal developments have further undermined its purpose—most notably the *In re Gault* ruling, which ultimately led to juveniles being accorded legal protections similar to those accorded to adults and to children being treated like adults in all respects. Then, in the 1980s, the sudden rise in gang membership, gun violence, and homicide committed by juveniles further eroded the juvenile court's mission and resulted in legislation creating mandatory sentences for juvenile offenders and mandatory waiver to the adult court. As a result, the focus of the court has shifted from treating the offender to dealing with the offense. In Feld's words, the juvenile court has become a "deficient second-rate criminal court." The welfare and rehabilitative purposes of the juvenile court have been subordinated to its role as law enforcement agent, so there is little purpose in retaining it in its current state.

Robert Dawson suggests that because the legal differences between the juvenile and criminal systems are narrower than they ever have been, it may be time to abolish the juvenile court.[83] The call to abolish juvenile court is substantiated by research showing that at least in some jurisdictions, the spirit of juvenile justice has shifted from a focus on individual needs to the seriousness of the crime, giving the prosecution more power to make decisions and promoting a reliance on the adversarial process at the expense of *parens patriae*.[84]

Not all experts agree that the juvenile court has become redundant. Some, such as John Kerbs, believe that the get-tough approach will force the criminal courts to apply harsher sentences and tougher treatment, and that the brunt of these draconian sentences will fall squarely on the shoulders of minority youths. Research efforts routinely show that African American adults are punished with undue severity in adult courts. Sending juvenile offenders to these venues is likely to enmesh them further in an already unfair system.[85] Peter Greenwood contends that, despite these and other limitations, the treatment programs that the modern juvenile court currently provides play a central role in society's response to the most serious delinquents.[86] He argues that juvenile courts must take on a number of specific responsibilities to ensure that these programs are indeed effective. Among these responsibilities are awareness of the most up-to-date scientific evidence on the effectiveness of court-based programs, diversion of cases that can be handled informally outside of the system, disposition of cases to appropriate programs, and quality control.[87]

Regardless of which position is correct, there has been an ongoing effort to modify the juvenile justice system in response to the public's fear of predatory juvenile offenders. As a result, states began to institute policies that increased the punitive dimensions of the juvenile court movement.[88] For example, since 1990, more than 40 states and the District of Columbia have changed their transfer statutes to make it easier to waive juveniles to adult courts.[89] Today, at least 22 states and the District of Columbia specify no minimum age beneath which a juvenile cannot be transferred to adult court.[90] Some states, such as Arizona, have initiated legislation that significantly restricts eligibility for juvenile justice processing and criminalizes acts that heretofore would have fallen under the jurisdiction of the juvenile court. Arizona excludes from the juvenile justice system 15-, 16-, and 17-year-olds charged with any felony if they had two or more prior delinquency adjudications and dispositions for offenses that would have been felonies if committed by an adult.[91] It also added the provision "once an adult, always an adult," whereby if a juvenile was previously tried and convicted in criminal court, any future offenses involving that juvenile will be tried in adult court.[92] A number of other states and the District of Columbia have also adopted the "once an adult, always an adult" provision.[93]

Those who support the juvenile justice concept believe that it is too soon to write off its rehabilitative principles. Fears of a juvenile crime wave are misplaced, and the actions of a few violent children should not obscure the needs of millions who can benefit from solicitous treatment rather than harsh punishments. Nor have the concepts of rehabilitation and change been lost on the people who actually work in the juvenile justice system. While politicians have passed laws easing the waiver of kids to the adult system, the actual number of juvenile offenders who are waived has been on the decline. The number of delinquency cases judicially waived to criminal court peaked in 1994 at 13,200 cases; since then the number of waivers has declined to about 6,000, which represents less than 0.5 percent of the delinquency caseload.[94] Although a get-tough approach may seem attractive to some, its costs generally outweigh its benefits.[95]

Significant Cases in Juvenile Justice

Case	Issue	Decision
Kent v. United States (1966)	Waiver	Ruled that a child has the right to an attorney at a waiver hearing.
In re Gault (1967)	Due process	Ruled that a minor has basic due process rights at trial.
In re Winship (1970)	Level of evidence at trial	Determined that the level of evidence for a finding of "juvenile delinquency" is proof beyond a reasonable doubt.
McKeiver v. Pennsylvania (1971)	Right to a jury trial	Held that trial by jury in a juvenile court's adjudicative stage is not a constitutional requirement.

(continued)

Breed v. Jones (1975)	Double jeopardy	Ruled that a child has the protection of the double jeopardy clause of the Fifth Amendment and cannot be tried twice for the same crime.
Fare v. Michael C. (1979)	Interrogation	Established that a child has the protection of *Miranda* and may request that a lawyer be provided to protect his or her interests.
Schall v. Martin (1984)	Preventive detention	Allowed for the placement of children in preventive detention before their adjudication.
New Jersey v. T.L.O. (1985)	Search	Determined that although the Fourth Amendment protection against unreasonable search and seizure applies to children, school officials can legally search kids who violate school rules (e.g., smoking on campus) even though there is no evidence that the student violated the law.
Vernonia School District v. Acton (1995)	Drug testing in school	Held that the Fourth Amendment's guarantee against unreasonable searches is not violated by drug testing all students who choose to participate in interscholastic athletics.
Safford Unified School District v. Redding (2009)	Search in schools	Held that a search cannot be unreasonable and overly intrusive.
Graham v. Florida (2010)	Sentencing of waived juveniles	Children waived to adult court cannot receive a life sentence without parole unless they commit murder.
Miller v. Alabama (2012)	Sentencing of juveniles	Juveniles cannot receive a mandatory life sentence without parole even if they are convicted of murder.

ETHICAL CHALLENGES in Criminal Justice

A WRITING ASSIGNMENT

You are a juvenile court judge. John has been arrested for robbery and rape. His victim, a young neighborhood girl, was seriously injured in the attack and needed extensive hospitalization; she is now in counseling. Because the charges are serious, John can be waived to the adult court and tried as an adult even though he is only 14 years old. Under existing state law, a hearing must be held to determine whether there is sufficient evidence that John cannot be successfully treated in the juvenile justice system and therefore warrants transfer to the adult system; the final decision on the matter is yours alone.

At the waiver hearing, you discover that John is the oldest of three siblings living in a single-parent home. He has had no contact with his father for more than 10 years. His psychological evaluations show hostility, anger toward females, and deep feelings of frustration. His intelligence is above average, but his behavioral and academic records are poor. John is a loner with few friends. This is his first formal involvement with the juvenile court. Previous contact was limited to an informal complaint for disorderly conduct at age 13, which was dismissed by the court's intake department. During the hearing, John verbalizes what you interpret to be superficial remorse for his offenses. The victim and her family demand justice and want to see John punished for his violent act.

Write an essay discussing whether it is legally ethical to waive someone like John to the adult court and give the reasons for your decision. As you make your decision and prepare to explain your reasoning, refer to the sections on waiver and treatment. Is it immoral to refuse to offer treatment alternatives in the juvenile justice system that may work as well as or better than anything in the adult system simply because John needs to be punished for his misdeeds? Is punishment an appropriate response to a juvenile's misbehavior? Consider the harmful consequences, such as stigma and labeling, that John may experience if he is waived. What arguments, on the other hand, can be advanced in favor of waiving John to the adult court? What will be your ruling, and why?

Summary

L01 **Recognize the nature and purpose of the juvenile justice system.**

- The juvenile justice system is primarily responsible for dealing with juvenile and youth crime, as well as with incorrigible and truant children and runaways.
- In some ways the juvenile justice system is like a quasi–social welfare agency: it acts as a surrogate parent in the interests of the child. In other ways, it operates as a social control agency: it deters delinquent behavior and punishes youthful offenders.
- Many people who work in the system believe that its sole purpose is to treat and rehabilitate young people before they enter a life of crime.

L02 **Describe the history and development of juvenile justice.**

- The modern practice of legally separating adult and juvenile offenders can be traced back to the development of Elizabethan-era poor laws and the creation of the English chancery court.
- Poor laws and chancery courts were brought from England to colonial America.
- To accommodate dependent youths, local jurisdictions developed almshouses, poorhouses, and workhouses.
- Juvenile justice was originally based on the *parens patriae* philosophy.

L03 **Discuss the child savers and their vision of juvenile justice.**

- The child savers were responsible for creating a number of programs for indigent youths, including the New York House of Refuge, which began operations in 1825.
- The child savers also influenced state and local governments to create independent correctional institutions to house minors.
- The first of these reform schools opened in Westboro, Massachusetts, in 1848 and in Rochester, New York, in 1849.
- In 1853, New York philanthropist Charles Loring Brace helped develop the Children's Aid Society, which placed neglected and delinquent youths in private homes in rural communities.

L04 **Describe the beginnings of the independent juvenile court.**

- The child savers lobbied for an independent, state-supported juvenile court. Their efforts prompted the development of the first comprehensive juvenile court in Illinois in 1899.
- The Illinois Juvenile Court Act set up an independent court to handle criminal law violations by children under 16 years of age, as well as to care for neglected, dependent, and wayward youths.
- The main concern was the "best interests of the child," not strict adherence to legal doctrine, constitutional rights, or due process of law.

L05 **State the changes in juvenile justice that began in the 1960s and continue today.**

- In the 1960s and 1970s, the U.S. Supreme Court radically altered the juvenile justice system by issuing a series of decisions that established the right of juveniles to due process of law.
- The trend has been to create family courts, which address a broad range of family- and child-related issues within their jurisdictions.

L06 **Discuss police processing of juvenile offenders.**

- Most states do not have specific statutory provisions distinguishing the arrest process for children from that for adults.
- Some jurisdictions give broad arrest powers to the police in juvenile cases by authorizing the officer to make an arrest whenever she or he believes that the child's behavior falls within the jurisdiction of the juvenile court.
- Police may arrest youths for behavior considered legal for adults, such as running away, violating curfew, and being in possession of alcohol.

L07 **Discuss the detention of juveniles.**

- After a juvenile is formally taken into custody, either as a delinquent or as a status offender, the prosecutor usually decides whether to release the child to the parent or guardian or to detain the child in a secure shelter pending trial.
- There has been an ongoing effort to reform detention. The most important reform has been the successful effort to remove status offenders from lockups containing delinquents.
- Although only a few state statutes allow release on money bail, many others have juvenile code provisions that emphasize the release of the child to the parents as an acceptable substitute.

Recite the problems and legal issues surrounding the waiver decision.

- Before trial, prosecutors in the juvenile courts may attempt to negotiate a settlement to the case.
- Today, most U.S. jurisdictions provide by statute for the waiver, or transfer, of juvenile offenders to the criminal courts.
- Waiver does not seem to influence crime or recidivism rates.

Describe the juvenile trial and sentencing process.

- There are usually two judicial hearings in the juvenile court process. The first, typically called an initial appearance, is similar to the arraignment in the adult system.
- During the adjudicatory or trial process, the court hears evidence on the allegations stated in the delinquency petition.

- At the dispositional hearing, the juvenile court judge imposes a sentence on the juvenile offender. Some jurisdictions have passed mandatory or determinate incarceration sentences for juveniles convicted of serious felonies.

 Explain the efforts to treat troubled kids in the juvenile justice system.

- Although the juvenile justice system has been concerned with controlling delinquent behavior, there are now important efforts being made to prevent delinquency before it occurs.
- Some experts question whether the juvenile justice system should exist in its present form.
- While the get-tough approach seems to have prevailed, the rehabilitative ideal of juvenile justice still exists.

Key Terms

parens patriae, 578
poor laws, 578
chancery courts, 579
child savers, 579
Children's Aid Society, 580
juvenile court, 580
status offender, 582

juvenile delinquency, 584
drug courts, 584
detention, 593
waiver (juvenile), 595
transfer hearing, 595
initial appearance, 598
disposition, 599

commitment, 599
treatment, 599
juvenile intensive probation
supervision (JIPS), 601
Intensive Aftercare Program
(IAP), 602

Critical Thinking Questions

1. Should status offenders be treated by the juvenile court? Should they be placed in confinement for such acts as running away or cutting school?
2. Should a juvenile ever be waived to adult court, with the risk that the child will be incarcerated with adult felons?

3. Do you support the death penalty for children?
4. Should juveniles be given mandatory incarceration sentences for serious crimes, as adults are?
5. Is it fair to deny juveniles a jury trial?
6. Do you think the trend toward treating juveniles like adult offenders is desirable?

Notes

1. Patricia Wen, "Odgren Sentenced to Life in Prison, No Parole Option for Teen Killer; Lawyer Brands Ruling 'Barbaric,'" Boston Globe, May 1, 2010, http://www.boston.com/news/local/massachusetts/articles/2010/05/01/odgren_sentenced_to_life_in_prison/ (accessed July 2014); Bill Ahearn, "Asperger's Syndrome on Trial? That Behavior Is Determined Has No Bearing on Personal Responsibility," Psychology Today, April 14, 2010, http://www.psychologytoday.com/blog/radical-behaviorist/201004/aspergers-syndrome-trial (accessed July 2014).
2. Material in this section depends heavily on Sanford J. Fox, "Juvenile Justice Reform: A Historical Perspective," *Stanford Law Review* 22 (1970): 1187–1205; Lawrence Stone, *The Family, Sex, and Marriage in England: 1500–1800* (New York: Harper and Row, 1977); Philippe Aries, *Century of Childhood: A Social History of Family Life* (New York: Vintage, 1962); Douglas R. Rendleman, "*Parens Patriae*: From Chancery to the Juvenile Court," *South Carolina Law Review* 23 (1971): 205–229;

Anthony Platt, "The Rise of the Child-Saving Movement: A Study in Social Policy and Correctional Reform," *Annals of the American Academy of Political and Social Science* 381 (1979): 21–38; Anthony M. Platt, *The Child Savers: The Intervention of Delinquency* (Chicago: University of Chicago Press, 1969); Robert S. Pickett, *House of Refuge: Origins of Juvenile Reform in New York State, 1815–1857* (Syracuse, NY: Syracuse University Press, 1969).
3. Douglas Besharov, *Juvenile Justice Advocacy: Practice in a Unique Court* (New York: Practicing Law Institute, 1974), p. 2. See also Jay Albanese, *Dealing with Delinquency—The Future of Juvenile Justice* (Chicago: Nelson-Hall, 1993).
4. 4 Eng.Rep. 1078 (1827).
5. Platt, *The Child Savers*, pp. 11–38.
6. See, generally, Anne Meis Knupfer, *Reform and Resistance: Gender, Delinquency, and America's First Juvenile Court* (London: Routledge, 2001).

7. This section is based on material from the New York State Archives, *The Greatest Reform School in the World: A Guide to the Records of the New York House of Refuge: A Brief History 1824–1857* (Albany, NY: 2001); Sanford J. Fox, "Juvenile Justice Reform: A Historical Perspective," *Stanford Law Review* 22 (1970): 1187.

8. Pickett, *House of Refuge*.

9. Robert Mennel, "Origins of the Juvenile Court: Changing Perspectives on the Legal Rights of Juvenile Delinquents," in *Juvenile Justice Philosophy*, ed. Frederick Faust and Paul Brantingham (St. Paul, MN: West, 1974), pp. 69–70.

10. Platt, *The Child Savers*, p. 116.

11. LaMar T. Empey, *American Delinquency: Its Meaning and Construction* (Homewood, IL: Dorsey, 1978), p. 515.

12. *Kent v. United States*, 383 U.S. 541, 86 S.Ct. 1045, 16 L.Ed.2d 84 (1966); *In re Gault*, 387 U.S. 1, 87 S.Ct. 1428, 18 L.Ed.2d 527 (1967); *In re Winship*, 397 U.S. 358, 90 S.Ct. 1068, 25 L.Ed.2d 368 (1970); *Breed v. Jones*, 421 U.S. 519, 95 S.Ct. 1779, 44 L.Ed.2d 346 (1975).

13. Public Law 93-415 (1974).

14. *2006 National Report*, pp. 96–97.

15. For a comprehensive view of juvenile law, see, generally, Joseph J. Senna and Larry J. Siegel, *Juvenile Law: Cases and Comments*, 2nd ed. (St. Paul, MN: West, 1992).

16. Erika Gebo, "Do Family Courts Administer Individualized Justice in Delinquency Cases?" *Criminal Justice Policy Review* 16 (2005): 190–210.

17. National Association of Youth Courts, "Facts and Stats," http://www.youthcourt.net (accessed July 2014); Michael Norris, Sarah Twill, and Chigon Kim, "Smells Like Teen Spirit: Evaluating a Midwestern Teen Court," *Crime and Delinquency* 57 (2011): 199–221; Denise M. Wilson, Denise C. Gottfredson, and Wendy Povitsky Stickle, "Gender Differences in Effects of Teen Courts on Delinquency: A Theory-Guided Evaluation," *Journal of Criminal Justice* 37 (2009): 21–27.

18. *Summary of Drug Court Activity by State and County: Juvenile/Family Drug Courts* (Washington, DC: Bureau of Justice Assistance Drug Court Clearinghouse at American University, July 2010).

19. Office of Juvenile Justice and Delinquency Prevention, *How OJJDP Is Serving Children, Families, and Communities: 2008 Annual Report* (Washington, DC: U.S. Department of Justice, OJJDP, 2009).

20. Charles Puzzanchera and Crystal Robson, *Delinquency Cases in Juvenile Court, 2010* (Washington, DC: Bureau of Justice Statistics, 2014).

21. Federal Bureau of Investigation, *Crime in the United States, 2012*, http://www.fbi.gov/about-us/cjis/ucr/crime-in-the-u.s/2012/crime-in-the-u.s.-2012/tables/36tabledatadecoverviewpdf (accessed July 2014).

22. Finn-Aage Esbensen, Dana Peterson, Terrance J. Taylor, and D. Wayne Osgood, "Results from a Multi-Site Evaluation of the G.R.E.A.T. Program," *Justice Quarterly* 29 (2012): 125–151.

23. Richard J. Lundman, "Routine Police Arrest Practices," *Social Problems* 22 (1974): 127–141; Robert E. Worden and Stephanie M. Myers, *Police Encounters with Juvenile Suspects* (Albany: Hindelang Criminal Justice Research Center and School of Criminal Justice, State University of New York, 2001).

24. Richard Lundman, "Demeanor or Crime? The Midwest City Police–Citizen Encounters Study," *Criminology* 32 (1994): 631–653; Robert Worden and Robin Shepard, "On the Meaning, Measurement, and Estimated Effects of Suspects' Demeanor Toward the Police," paper presented at the annual meeting of the American Society of Criminology, Miami, November 1994.

25. Robert A. Brown, Kenneth J. Novak, and James Frank, "Identifying Variation in Police Officer Behavior Between Juveniles and Adults," *Journal of Criminal Justice* 37 (2009): 200–208.

26. *Fare v. Michael C.*, 442 U.S. 707 (1979).

27. *J.D.B. v. North Carolina*, 564 U.S._ (2011).

28. Barry Feld, "Police Interrogation of Juveniles: An Empirical Study of Policy and Practice," *Journal of Criminal Law and Criminology* 97 (2006): 219–316.

29. *New Jersey v. T.L.O.*, 469 U.S. 325 (1985).

30. *Vernonia School District 47J v. Acton*, 515 U.S. 646 (1995); Bernard James and Jonathan Pyatt, "Supreme Court Extends School's Authority to Search," *National School Safety Center News Journal* 26 (1995): 29.

31. *Board of Education of Independent School District No. 92 of Pottawatomie County et al. v. Earls et al.*, 536 U.S. 822 (2002).

32. *Safford United School District No. 1 v. Redding*, 557 U.S. _ (2009).

33. Ana Abrantes, Norman Hoffmann, and Ronald Anton, "Prevalence of Co-occurring Disorders Among Juveniles Committed to Detention Centers," *International Journal of Offender Therapy and Comparative Criminology* 49 (2005): 179–194.

34. Nancy Rodriguez, "Juvenile Court Context and Detention Decisions: Reconsidering the Role of Race, Ethnicity, and Community Characteristics in Juvenile Court Processes," *Justice Quarterly* 24 (2007): 629–656.

35. Barry Holman and Jason Ziedenberg, *The Dangers of Detention: The Impact of Incarcerating Youth in Detention and Other Secure Facilities* (Washington, DC: Justice Policy Institute, 2006), http://www.justicepolicy.org/uploads/justicepolicy/documents/dangers_of_detention.pdf (accessed July 2014).

36. *Schall v. Martin*, 467 U.S. 253 (1984).

37. See Juvenile Justice and Delinquency Prevention Act of 1974, 42 U.S.C., sec. 5633.

38. Catherine Van Dijk, An Nuytiens, and Christian Eliaerts, "The Referral of Juvenile Offenders to the Adult Court in Belgium: Theory and Practice," *Howard Journal of Criminal Justice* 44 (2005): 151–166.

39. Charles Puzzanchera and Sean Addie, *Delinquency Cases Waived to Criminal Court, 2010* (Washington, DC: Bureau of Justice Statistics, 2014).

40. Patrick Griffin, Sean Addie, Benjamin Adams, and Kathy Firestine, *Trying Juveniles as Adults: An Analysis of State Transfer Laws and Reporting* (Washington, DC: Bureau of Justice Statistics, 2011).

41. *Kent v. United States*, 383 U.S. 541 (1966).

42. *Breed v. Jones*, 421 U.S. 519 (1975).

43. Aaron Kupchik, "The Correctional Experiences of Youth in Adult and Juvenile Prisons," *Justice Quarterly* 24 (2007): 247–270.

44. Campaign for Youth Justice, "Jailing Juveniles: The Dangers of Incarcerating Youth in Adult Jails in America" (2008), http://www.campaignforyouthjustice.org/Downloads/Jailing_Juveniles_Take_Action_Kit.pdf (accessed July 2014).

45. Griffin, Addie, Adams, and Firestine, *Trying Juveniles as Adults: An Analysis of State Transfer Laws and Reporting*.

46. Ibid.

47. Brandon K. Applegate, Robin King Davis, and Francis T. Cullen, "Reconsidering Child Saving: The Extent and Correlates of Public Support for Excluding Youths from Juvenile Courts," *Crime and Delinquency* 55 (2009): 51–77; Jeffrey Fagan, "Juvenile Crime and Criminal Justice: Resolving Border Disputes," *The Future of Children* 18, no. 2 (2008): 81–118.

48. See Richard E. Redding, *Juvenile Transfer Laws: An Effective Deterrent to Delinquency?* (Washington, DC: Office of Juvenile Justice and Delinquency Prevention, 2010), http://www.ncjrs.gov/pdffiles1/ojjdp/220595.pdf (accessed July 2014); Craig A. Mason, Derek A. Chapman, Chang Shau, and Julie Simons, "Impacting Re-Arrest Rates Among Youth Sentenced in Adult Court: An Epidemiology Examination of the Juvenile Sentencing Advocacy Project," *Journal of Clinical Child and Adolescent Psychology* 32 (2003): 205–214; David L. Myers, "The Recidivism of Violent Youths in Juvenile and Adult Court: A Consideration of Selection Bias," *Youth Violence and Juvenile Justice* 1 (2003): 79–101.

49. Benjamin Steiner and Emily Wright, "Assessing the Relative Effects of State Direct File Waiver Laws on Violent Juvenile Crime: Deterrence or Irrelevance?" *Journal of Criminal Law and Criminology* 96 (2006): 1451–1477.

50. Benjamin Steiner, "The Effects of Juvenile Transfer to Criminal Court on Incarceration Decisions," *Justice Quarterly* 26 (2009): 77–106; Megan Kurlychek and Brian Johnson, "The Juvenile Penalty: A Comparison of Juvenile and Young Adult Sentencing Outcomes in Criminal Court," *Criminology* 42 (2004): 485–517.

51. Victor L. Streib, *The Juvenile Death Penalty Today: Death Sentences and Executions for Juvenile Crimes, January 1, 1973–September 30, 2003* (Ada, OH: Claude W. Pettit College of Law, Ohio Northern University, October 6, 2003), p. 3.

52. *Roper v. Simmons*, 125 S.Ct. 1183 (2005).

53. Erica Goode, "Young Killer: Bad Seed or Work in Progress?" *New York Times*, November 25, 2003.

54. Adam Liptak, "Court Takes Another Step in Reshaping Capital Punishment," *New York Times*, March 2, 2005.

55. *Roper v. Simmons*, 125 S.Ct. 1183 (2005).

56. Barry C. Feld, "A Slower Form of Death: Implications of *Roper v. Simmons* for Juveniles Sentenced to Life Without Parole," *Notre Dame Journal of Law, Ethics and Public Policy* 22 (2008): 9–65.

57. Ibid., at 10.

58. Elizabeth S. Scott and Laurence Steinberg, "The Young and the Reckless," *New York Times*, November 13, 2009, http://www.nytimes.com/2009/11/14/opinion/14scott.html (accessed July 2014).

59. *Graham v. Florida*, 08-7412, May 17, 2010.

60. *Miller v. Alabama*, 567 U.S. _ (2012).

61. *In re Gault*, 387 U.S. 1 (1967).

62. Melissa Sickmund, T. J. Sladky, W. Kang, and Charles Puzzanchera, "Easy Access to the Census of Juveniles in Residential Placement" (2011), http://www.ojjdp.gov/ojstatbb/ezacjrp/ (accessed July 2014).

63. See Joseph Goldstein, Anna Freud, and Albert Solnit, *Beyond the Best Interest of the Child* (New York: Free Press, 1973).

64. See Michael Serrill, "Police Write a New Law on Juvenile Crime," *Police Magazine* (September 1979): 47; see also A. Schneider and D. Schram, *Assessment of Juvenile Justice Reform in Washington State*, vols. 1–4 (Washington, DC: Department of Justice, Institute of Policy Analysis, 1983); T. Castellano, "Justice Model in the Juvenile Justice System—Washington State's Experience," *Law and Policy* 8 (1986): 479.

65. Emily Gaarder, Nancy Rodriguez, and Marjorie Zatz, "Criers, Liars, and Manipulators: Probation Officers' Views of Girls," *Justice Quarterly* 21 (2004): 547–578.

66. See Richard G. Wiebush, "Juvenile Intensive Supervision: The Impact on Felony Offenders Diverted from Institutional Placement," *Crime and Delinquency* 39 (1993): 68–89.

67. For a review of these programs, see James Austin, Kelly Dedel Johnson, and Ronald Weitzer, *Alternatives to the Secure Detention and Confinement of Juvenile Offenders* (Washington, DC: OJJDP Bulletin, 2005), pp. 18–19.

68. James Ryan, "Who Gets Revoked? A Comparison of Intensive Supervision Successes and Failures in Vermont," *Crime and Delinquency* 43 (1997): 104–118.

69. Melissa Sickmund, *Juveniles in Residential Placement: 1997–2008* (Washington, DC: Office of Juvenile Justice and Delinquency Prevention, 2010), http://www.ncjrs.gov/pdffiles1/ojjdp/229379.pdf (accessed July 2014).

70. Sarah Hockenberry, *Juveniles in Residential Placement, 2010* (Washington, DC: Bureau of Justice Statistics, 2014).

71. Ibid., p. 12.

72. Ibid., p. 11.

73. Peter W. Greenwood and Susan Turner, "Juvenile Crime and Juvenile Justice," in *Crime and Public Policy*, ed. James Q. Wilson and Joan Petersilia (New York: Oxford University Press, 2011).

74. Pamela K. Lattimore, "Reentry, Reintegration, Rehabilitation, Recidivism, and Redemption," *The Criminologist* 31 (2006): 1, 3–6; see also Laura Winterfield, Christine Lindquist, and Susan Brumbaugh, *Sustaining Juvenile Reentry Programming after SVORI* (Washington, DC: Urban Institute, 2007).

75. Jeffrey A. Bouffard and Kathleen J. Bergseth, "The Impact of Reentry Services on Juvenile Offenders' Recidivism," *Youth Violence and Juvenile Justice* 6 (2008): 295–318; He Len Chung, Carol A. Schubert, and Edward P. Mulvey, "An Empirical Portrait of Community Reentry Among Serious Juvenile Offenders in Two Metropolitan Cities," *Criminal Justice and Behavior* 34 (2007): 1402–1426.

76. David M. Altschuler and Troy L. Armstrong, "Juvenile Corrections and Continuity of Care in a Community Context: The Evidence and Promising Directions," *Federal Probation* 66 (2002): 72–77.

77. David M. Altschuler and Troy L. Armstrong, "Intensive Aftercare for High-Risk Juveniles: A Community Care Model" (Washington, DC: Office of Juvenile Justice and Delinquency Prevention, 1994).

78. Rolf Loeber and David P. Farrington, eds., *From Juvenile Delinquency to Adult Crime: Criminal Careers, Justice Policy, and Prevention* (New York: Oxford University Press, 2012).

79. J. David Hawkins, Richard F. Catalano, and associates, *Communities That Care: Action for Drug Abuse Prevention* (San Francisco: Jossey-Bass, 1992).

80. Richard F. Catalano, Michael W. Arthur, J. David Hawkins, Lisa Berglund, and Jeffrey J. Olson, "Comprehensive Community- and School-Based Interventions to Prevent Antisocial Behavior," in *Serious and Violent Juvenile Offenders: Risk Factors and Successful Interventions*, ed. Rolf Loeber and David P. Farrington (Thousand Oaks, CA: Sage, 1998).

81. David Smith, "The Effectiveness of the Juvenile Justice System," *Criminal Justice: International Journal of Policy and Practice* 5 (2005): 181–195.

82. Barry C. Feld, *Bad Kids: Race and the Transformation of the Juvenile Court* (New York: Oxford University Press, 1999).

83. Robert O. Dawson, "The Future of Juvenile Justice: Is It Time to Abolish the System?" *Journal of Criminal Law and Criminology* 81 (1990): 136–155; see also Leonard P. Edwards, "The Future of the Juvenile Court: Promising New Directions in the Center for the Future of Children," in *The Future of Children: The Juvenile Court* (Los Altos, CA: David and Lucile Packard Foundation, Center for the Future of Children, 1996).

84. Alexes Harris, "Diverting and Abdicating Judicial Discretion: Cultural, Political, and Procedural Dynamics in California Juvenile Justice," *Law and Society Review* 41 (2007): 387–428.

85. John Johnson Kerbs, "(Un)equal Justice: Juvenile Court Abolition and African Americans," *Annals, AAPSS* 564 (1999): 109–125.

86. Peter W. Greenwood, *Changing Lives: Delinquency Prevention as Crime-Control Policy* (Chicago: University of Chicago Press, 2006), p. 183.

87. Ibid., pp. 193–194.

88. Peter J. Benekos and Alida V. Merlo, "Juvenile Justice: The Legacy of Punitive Policy," *Youth Violence and Juvenile Justice* 6 (2009): 28–46; Hunter Hurst, "Juvenile Court: As We Enter the Millennium," *Juvenile and Family Court Journal* 50 (1999): 21–27.

89. Howard N. Snyder and Melissa Sickmund, *Juvenile Offenders and Victims: 2006 National Report* (Pittsburgh: National Center for Juvenile Justice, 2006), p. 113.

90. Patrick Griffin and Melanie King, "National Overviews," in *State Juvenile Justice Profiles* (Pittsburgh: National Center for Juvenile Justice, 2008).

91. Ibid.

92. Ibid.

93. Ibid.

94. Charles Puzzanchera and Sean Addie, *Delinquency Cases Waived to Criminal Court, 2010* (Washington, DC: Bureau of Justice Statistics, 2014).

95. Simon M. Fass and Chung-Ron Pi, "Getting Tough on Juvenile Crime: An Analysis of Costs and Benefits," *Journal of Research in Crime and Delinquency* 39 (2002): 363–399.

CHAPTER 16

Crime and Justice in the New Millennium

Learning Objectives

LO1 Explain the influence of globalization on crime.

LO2 Discuss the impact of corporate enterprise crime.

LO3 Describe the various forms of cybercrime.

LO4 Discuss what is being done to thwart cybercriminals.

LO5 Define the concept of transnational crime.

LO6 Explain how law enforcement is taking on transnational criminal syndicates.

LO7 Define terrorism and describe the factors that motivate terrorists.

LO8 Discuss the various forms of contemporary terrorism.

LO9 Explain how the criminal justice system fights terrorism.

LO10 Identify trends that are likely to influence criminal justice in the future.

Chapter Outline

AP Images/Anonymous

Daniel Patrick Boyd was a charismatic figure. But the U.S. citizen used his persuasive powers to no good end—he promoted violent jihad against Americans at home and abroad. Prompted by a tip, his activities were investigated by the Raleigh-Durham (North Carolina) Joint Terrorism Task Force (JTTF), which included members of the FBI, Raleigh Police Department, Durham Police Department, Defense Criminal Investigative Service, as well as members of the prosecutorial team at the United States Attorney's Office Eastern District of North Carolina, and members of the Department of Justice in Washington, D.C.

Raised as a Christian, Boyd converted to the Muslim faith and became a local hero when at age of 19 he had traveled to Pakistan and Afghanistan to receive military training and to fight with the mujahedeen. Returning home, he recruited young people to the cause. In 2006, one of Boyd's North Carolina jihad recruits traveled to Jordan and e-mailed his mentor to ask how to get to the front lines to fight. Over the next three years, the JTTF monitored the group using a variety of investigative tools, including court-ordered wiretaps and sources who infiltrated the group.

During one conversation monitored by federal agents that took place inside the food market Boyd owned, one of the foreign-born co-conspirators bragged about his experience as a skilled sniper and graphically described how he shot a man overseas. Investigators tracked Boyd's network across the United States and six foreign countries. It became very clear that Boyd's followers wanted to fight on the front lines overseas. And if they didn't have the opportunity to do that, then they would wage jihad here at home. Investigators found that the group was buying a lot of weapons and ammunition. Boyd dug a hole in his yard to bury a cache of weapons and positioned long guns in every room of his house. He took his sons and recruits out to train with weapons and taught them military tactics.[1]

After a four-year investigation, Boyd and two of his sons, along with five other conspirators—known as the Triangle Terror Group—were arrested in 2009 and charged with providing material support to terrorists and conspiring to murder persons overseas, including U.S. military personnel. Boyd pleaded guilty and was sentenced in 2012 to 18 years in prison. ■

Just a few years ago, agents of the criminal justice system would rarely work together to bring down global criminal conspiracies or terror cells. The technological revolution has provided new tools for criminals and terrorists to misappropriate funds, damage property, sell illicit material, and/or conduct warfare, and in so doing has broadened the scope of crime and increased the demands on the justice system. It is now routine for offenders to use complex and technologically sophisticated methods to secure illegal profits and provide criminal services. Criminal conspiracies may not only be national in scope, but can also be transnational criminal enterprises that involve criminal gangs whose activities cross nations and continents. The tech revolution has also enabled law enforcement agencies to eavesdrop on conversations, monitor phone calls, and track suspects with GPS—innovations that frighten civil libertarians concerned about the expansion of governmental interference with citizens' private lives.

In some instances this new brand of crime can involve a single individual who engages in a complex criminal enterprise, such as the multibillion-dollar fraud perpetrated by financier Bernard Madoff (more on him later). It can also involve people acting in transnational organized crime syndicates that actively traffic in contraband, such as narcotics and weapons, and even humans for pornography and prostitution.

In this chapter, we review three independent, yet interrelated, emerging criminal activities that are presenting challenges for the criminal justice system: corporate enterprise crime, cybercrime, and transnational organized crime. They are linked here because, in each category, offenders twist the legal rules of commerce for criminal purposes. Though distinct and independent, these emerging types of crime often overlap. Transnational criminals may use cyberspace to perpetrate fraud and then seek legitimate enterprises to launder money, diversify their sources of income, increase their power and influence, and gain and enhance their surface respectability.[2] Transnational criminals may also borrow from corporate enterprise: they may appropriate marketing concepts from legitimate business enterprise, even though they use threats, extortion, and smuggling to distribute their "products."[3] Otherwise legitimate corporate enterprise executives may turn to international crime cartels to help them with economic problems such as breaking up a strike or dumping hazardous waste products, stifling competition (or threatening competitors), and increasing their influence.[4] Whereas some corporate executives cheat to improve their company's position in the business world, others are motivated purely by personal gain, acting more like organized criminals than indiscreet businesspeople.[5]

The latter part of this chapter delves into terrorism. Covered are definitions of terrorism, varieties of terrorism, terrorist motivations, and the like. We also examine efforts that have been taken to deal with terrorists, particularly in the courts. The law enforcement section of this text examines some approaches taken to prevent terrorism. This chapter then wraps up with a look at the future, including the problems most likely to face the criminal justice system going forward.

Globalization and Justice

The new global economy is a particularly vexing development for agents of the criminal justice system because it vastly expands the reach of criminal organizations, while at the same time creating new opportunities for criminal conspiracies. The term **globalization** refers to the process of creating transnational markets and political and legal systems; globalization has shifted the focus of crime from a local to a world perspective.

Globalization began when large companies decided to establish themselves in foreign markets by adapting their products or services to the local culture. The process took off with the fall of the Soviet Union, which opened new

globalization
The process of creating a global economy through transnational markets and political and legal systems.

European markets. The development of China into an industrial superpower encouraged foreign investors to take advantage of China's huge supply of workers. As the Internet and communication revolution unfolded, companies were able to establish instant communications with their far-flung corporate empires, a technological breakthrough that further boosted trade and foreign investments. A series of transnational corporate mergers and takeovers produced ever-larger transnational corporations.

Some experts believe globalization can improve the standard of living in third-world nations by providing jobs and training. Others, however, view it as a means by which larger, more powerful nations exploit the natural resources of third-world nations, avoid regulation, and take advantage of desperate workers. When these giant corporations set up a factory in a developing nation, claim critics, it is not to help the local population but to get around environmental laws and exploit needy workers who may be forced to labor in substandard conditions.[6]

L01 Explain the influence of globalization on crime.

It is not surprising, then, that globalization has created a fertile ground for contemporary enterprise crimes. By expanding the reach of both criminal and noncriminal organizations, globalization also increases the vulnerability of indigenous peoples with a traditional way of life.[7] With money and power to spare, criminal enterprise groups can recruit new members, bribe government officials, and even fund private armies. International organized crime has globalized its activities for the same reasons that impel legitimate multinational corporations to expand around the world: new markets bring new sources of profits. As international crime expert Louise Shelley puts it,

> Just as multinational corporations establish branches around the world to take advantage of attractive labor or raw material markets, so do illicit businesses. Furthermore, international businesses, both legitimate and illicit, also establish facilities worldwide for production, marketing, and distribution needs. Illicit enterprises are able to expand geographically to take advantage of these new economic circumstances thanks to the communications and international transportation revolution.[8]

Shelley argues that two elements of globalization encourage criminality, one technological and the other cultural. Technological advances such as efficient and widespread commercial airline traffic, improvements in telecommunications (ranging from global cell phone connectivity to the Internet), and the growth of international trade have all aided the growth in illicit transnational activities. These changes have facilitated the cross-border movement of goods and people—conditions exploited by criminals who now use Internet chat rooms to plan their activities. On a cultural level, globalization brings with it an ideology of free markets and free trade. This cultural shift means less intervention and regulation—conditions exploited by crime groups to cross unpatrolled borders and expand their activities to new regions of the world. Transnational crime groups aggressively exploit this new freedom to travel to regions where they cannot be extradited, base their operations in countries with ineffective or corrupt law enforcement, and launder their money in countries with bank secrecy or few effective controls. Globalization has allowed both individual offenders and criminal gangs to gain tremendous operational benefits and has markedly reduced the risk of apprehension and punishment.

Corporate Enterprise Crime

In the late 1930s, the distinguished criminologist Edwin Sutherland first used the phrase "white-collar crime" to describe the criminal activities of the rich and powerful: "a crime committed by a person of respectability and high social status in the course of his occupation."[9] As Sutherland saw it, white-collar crime involved conspiracies by members of the wealthy classes to use their positions in commerce and industry for personal gain without regard to the law. These unscrupulous executives crafted elaborate criminal conspiracies designed to improve market share or simply to illegally siphon off corporate profits into their own pockets.[10] Most often civil courts handled these actions because injured parties were more concerned with recovering their losses than with seeing the offenders punished criminally. As a consequence, Sutherland believed, the great majority of white-collar criminals avoided detection, and those who were caught generally avoided punishment.[11] As time has passed, the definition of white-collar crime has been expanded to include almost any type of business-related crime, from simple business fraud to international criminal conspiracies, and today it is widely referred to as **corporate enterprise crime**.

corporate enterprise crime

Illegal activities of people and organizations whose acknowledged purpose is to profit through illegitimate business enterprise.

Recent events seem to support Sutherland's original focus on widespread corporate wrongdoing, because it is the crimes of the rich and powerful that seem to be having the most significant impact on society.[12] Experts place its total monetary value in the hundreds of billions of dollars, far outstripping the cost to society of any other type of crime. The FBI is currently pursuing more than 700 corporate fraud cases, several of which involve losses to public investors that individually exceed $1 billion.[13] Bernard Madoff is not the only person to have pulled off a billion-dollar investment scheme: R. Allen Stanford, owner of Stanford Financial Group and other affiliated companies, was sentenced to a 110-year term in connection with a $7 billion Ponzi scheme.[14] In the following sections, some of the most significant illegal corporate enterprise schemes are discussed in some detail.

Fraud on Wall Street

Discuss the impact of corporate enterprise crime.

The creation of global capital markets has created unprecedented opportunities for U.S. businesses to access capital and for investors to diversify their portfolios.[15] Whether through college savings plans or retirement accounts, larger numbers of Americans are choosing to invest in the securities and commodities markets than ever before. This large-scale investment growth, however, has also led to significant growth in the amount of fraud and misconduct seen on Wall Street. Investment firms have engaged in deceptive schemes to defraud clients. Investment counselors and insurance agents have used their positions to cheat individual clients by misleading them on the quality of their investments. Financial organizations have cheated their clients by promoting risky investments as being iron-clad safe.

Perhaps the greatest of these crimes was pulled off by financier Bernard Madoff, who operated Bernard L. Madoff Investment Securities LLC. Madoff Investments became one of Wall Street's largest "specialist" trading firms, dedicated to investment management and advice. Managing billions in assets, Madoff was a member of the jet set and trusted advisor to many wealthy people, including director Steven Spielberg, as well as to sophisticated financial managers and investors. For a while, Madoff delivered the high returns he had promised, which of course attracted a constant flow of new investors. But things went south when the market crashed and people demanded their money back, only to find there was none available. It turns out that Madoff's asset management firm was a giant **Ponzi scheme**. Madoff had not invested any of the money he had taken in from investors. Instead, he had deposited it in various banks, using the interest and principal to pay off investors when they wanted to take money out of their accounts. Few did so, because they were making fantastic paper profits and kept reinvesting dividends and capital gains. Madoff actively convinced them to keep their profits in the account rather than asking for a distribution. When the market turned and people began asking for their principal, Madoff's house of cards tumbled down: more than $60 billion was missing, and authorities were left trying to figure out where it all went.

Ponzi scheme

An investment fraud that involves the payment of purported returns to existing investors from funds contributed by new investors.

Madoff's Ponzi scheme may have been the largest criminal conspiracy in history. On March 12, 2009, he pleaded guilty to an 11-count criminal complaint, charging him with violations of the antifraud provisions of the Securities Act of 1933, the Securities Exchange Act of 1934, and the Investment Advisers Act of 1940.[16] On June 29, 2009, Madoff was sentenced to 150 years in prison, a life sentence.

Madoff's attempted Ponzi scheme is not unique. There have been numerous attempts to fraudulently siphon off clients' money, some so great that they have threatened to collapse the financial markets (see Exhibit 16.1). Among these large-scale securities schemes was the prime bank fraud perpetrated by Robert Allen Stanford, but this one netted only $8 billion.[17] "Sir Robert," as he liked to be called after the Antiguan prime minister knighted him, ran a high-flying investment bank in the Caribbean nation of Antigua that offered investors high-yielding bank certificates of deposit. Sir Robert's financial activities raised

---

EXHIBIT 16.1 Wall Street Fraud Schemes

Market Manipulation

These schemes, commonly referred to as "pump and dumps," are effected by creating artificial buying pressure for a targeted security, generally a low-trading volume issuer in the over-the-counter securities market, that is largely controlled by the fraud perpetrators. This artificially increased trading volume has the effect of increasing the price of the targeted security (i.e., the pump), which is rapidly sold off into the inflated market for the security by the fraud perpetrators (i.e., the dump), resulting in illicit gains for the perpetrators and losses for innocent third-party investors. Typically, the increased trading volume is generated by inducing unwitting investors to purchase shares of the targeted security through false or deceptive sales practices and/or public information releases.

High Yield Investment Fraud

HYIF schemes may take many forms but are all characterized by offers of low-risk or no-risk investments that guarantee unusually high rates of return. Most common among this type of fraud are the following schemes:

- *Ponzi scheme.* Named after its early twentieth-century creator, Charles Ponzi, this scheme uses money collected from new "investors" (i.e., victims), rather than profits from the purported underlying business venture, to pay the high rates of return promised to earlier victims. This arrangement gives victims the impression that there is a legitimate money-making enterprise behind the perpetrator's story when, in reality, victim monies are the only source of funding.

- *Pyramid scheme.* As in Ponzi schemes, the money collected from newer victims of the fraud is paid to earlier victims to provide a veneer of legitimacy. In pyramid schemes, however, the victims themselves are induced to recruit further victims through the payment of recruitment commissions.

- *Prime bank scheme.* Victims are induced to invest in financial instruments, allegedly issued by well-known institutions, that offer risk-free opportunities for high rates of return—benefits which are allegedly the result of the perpetrator's access to a secret worldwide exchange ordinarily open only to the world's largest financial institutions.

Advance Fee Fraud

This category of fraud encompasses a broad variety of schemes designed to induce their victims into remitting up-front payments in exchange for the promise of goods, services, and/or prizes. In the securities and commodities fraud context, victims are informed that in order to participate in a promising investment opportunity, they must first pay various taxes and/or fees.

Hedge Fund Fraud

Hedge funds are private investment partnerships that have historically accepted only high-net worth clients willing to meet significant minimum investment thresholds. The industry as a whole has been largely unregulated but has become increasingly relevant to middle-class investors through their exposure to hedge fund activities via ancillary

(continued)

EXHIBIT 16.1 Wall Street Fraud Schemes (*Continued*)

investments (e.g., pension funds). The relative lack of regulatory scrutiny has made the industry vulnerable to fraud by fund managers, including overstatement/misappropriation of fund assets, overcharging for fund management fees, insider trading, market timing, and late trading.

Commodities Fraud

These schemes typically involve the deceptive or fraudulent sale of commodities investments. In such instances, false or deceptive sales practices are used to solicit victim funds for commodities transactions that either never occur or are inconsistent with the original sales pitches. Alternatively, commodities market participants may attempt to illegally manipulate the market for a commodity by such actions as fraudulently reporting price information or cornering the market to artificially increase the price of the targeted commodity.

Foreign Exchange Fraud

These schemes are characterized by the use of false or deceptive sales practices, alleging high rates of return for minimal risk, to induce victims to invest in the foreign currency exchange market. In such instances, the touted transactions never occur, are inconsistent with the original sales pitches, or are executed for the sole purpose of generating excessive trading commissions in breach of fiduciary responsibilities to the victim client. Alternatively,

individual corrupt currency traders employed by large financial institutions may attempt to manipulate foreign currency exchange prices in an effort to generate illicit trading profits for their own enrichment.

Broker Embezzlement

These schemes involve illicit and unauthorized actions by brokers to steal directly from their clients. Such schemes may be facilitated by the forging of client documents, doctoring of account statements, unauthorized trading/funds transfer activities, or other conduct in breach of the broker's fiduciary responsibilities to the victim-client.

Late-Day Trading

These schemes involve the illicit purchase and sale of securities after regular market hours. Such trading is restricted in order to prevent individuals from profiting on market-moving information released after the close of regular trading. Unscrupulous traders attempt to illegally exploit such opportunities by buying or selling securities at the market close price, secure in the knowledge that the market-moving information will generate illicit profits at the opening of trading on the following day.

Source: Federal Bureau of Investigation, *Financial Crimes Report to the Public, 2010–2011*, http://www.fbi.gov/stats-services/publications/financial-crimes-report-2010-2011 (accessed July 2014).

eyebrows among American authorities as far back as a decade ago. Like Bernard Madoff, Stanford offered investment opportunities that promised lofty returns on relatively safe certificates of deposit—returns that were often more than twice the going rate offered by mainstream banks. Unfortunately for investors, these assurances were too good to be true. Instead of the safe investments promised, Stanford used the money in very risky long-term real estate and private equity investments, which only he and another associate oversaw; Antiguan auditors neither examined the bank's portfolio nor verified its assets. Stanford withheld this information from investors and told them, instead, that their money was totally safe because it was being monitored by a team of more than 20 analysts and yearly audits by bank regulators in Antigua. Before being seized by the government, Stanford's bank had misappropriated $8.5 billion in assets belonging to 30,000 clients in 131 countries.

The Subprime Mortgage Scandal

During 2008 and 2009, the nation was rocked by another form of Wall Street fraud that threatened to destroy the financial system, undermine the real estate market, and create a 1929-style crash: the collapse of the subprime mortgage system. As a result of this financial disaster, several prominent financial institutions, including Bear Stearns and Lehman Brothers, went out of business; banks such as IndyMac Bank and Washington Mutual failed; and the federal government was forced to provide over a trillion dollars in relief to keep other companies, such as American Insurance Group (AIG) and CitiGroup, in business.

The cornerstone of the crisis was the collapse of the subprime mortgage sector. A subprime mortgage is a home loan given to borrowers who, because of inadequate income, would not ordinarily qualify for bank loans. Once the subprime loans have been issued, the vendors typically bundle them into large pools and sell them as securities, a process known as **securitization**. Because they carry risk, they typically pay a higher interest rate than normal securities, making them attractive to investors. By 2006, subprimes had grown to 20 percent of the mortgage market, up from 2 percent a decade earlier; this means that an estimated $1.3 trillion of the total $4.5 trillion in outstanding mortgage loans were subprime.

Although subprime mortgages can help first-time home buyers of limited means, they also have been the source of fraud by both borrowers and lenders. Borrowers have provided false information to the mortgage broker and/or lender in order to get loans for which they were not qualified. Those involved in mortgage lending, including mortgage brokers, lenders, appraisers, underwriters, accountants, real estate agents, settlement attorneys, land developers, investors, builders, bank account representatives, trust account representatives, investment banks, and credit rating agencies, have gotten involved in criminal fraud to maintain or increase their current standard of living. In addition to traditional industry conspirators, various organized criminal groups and gang members have become involved in mortgage fraud activity.[18]

Subprime lenders made risky loans, assuming that real estate values would always be increasing, enabling borrowers to refinance or sell their properties before going into default. However, when sales slowed down in the housing market, loan defaults increased and the securities lost value. As a result, mortgage companies experienced financial distress and bankruptcy.[19]

Desperate for funds, some subprime lenders, in order to stave off regulators, engaged in false accounting entries and fraudulently inflated their assets and revenues. Some manipulated their reported loan portfolio risks and used various accounting schemes to inflate their financial reports. And in some cases, before these subprime lenders' stocks rapidly declined in value, executives with insider information sold their equity positions and profited illegally. As a result of these practices, some subprime lenders were investigated by federal agencies for corporate fraud and insider trading. In one case, officers of Mercury Finance Company were convicted of intentionally misstating the company's financial records: they falsely reported a profit of more than $120 million instead of a loss of $30 million. Executives provided materially false financial statements to more than 20 financial institutions, enabling Mercury to obtain more than $1.5 billion in loan commitments and lines of credit. When the fraud was discovered, Mercury's stock price dropped significantly,

securitization
The process in which vendors take individual subprime loans, bundle them into large pools, and sell them as securities.

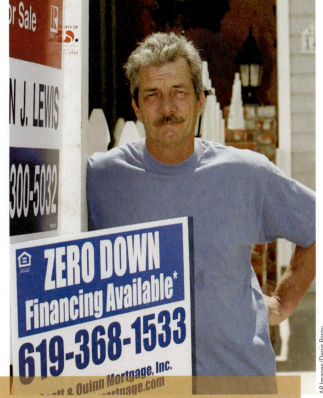

Daniel Peart stands next to a "for sale" sign in front of his home in Poway, California. Divorce led Peart to refinance his home with a subprime loan. Like many borrowers with spotty credit, he agreed to a relatively high interest rate in exchange for two years of low fixed payments. In less than a year, however, the payments jumped beyond his budget and he had to put the house up for sale.

costing shareholders nearly $2 billion in market value. A number of company officers went to prison, including former CEO John Brincat Sr., who pleaded guilty to wire fraud and making a false statement to a bank and was sentenced to 10 years imprisonment.[20]

FORECLOSURE RESCUE SCAMS   Not only has the availability of subprime mortgages presented opportunities for people to commit fraud, but it also created scams designed to prey upon people who obtained mortgages and then cannot make payments. There have been a variety of foreclosure rescue scams:

- *Phantom help.* Desperate homeowners are offered help by a supposed "expert" in avoiding foreclosures. They are then saddled with charges for things they could have done on their own, such as calling the bank. The phantom helper promises help, collects a fee, and never follows through. Soon it's too late to stop the foreclosure from taking place.

- *Bailout.* In this scam, someone offers to bail out the homeowner by taking the house off their hands with the promise that they can stay on as renters and buy the house back once things have been "fixed." The homeowner soon finds out that he or she cannot buy the house back, and the supposed rescuers get most, if not all, of the equity.

- *Bait and switch.* Scammers tell the victim that they are signing documents for a new loan that will solve their problems. In reality, they are signing forged documents that transfer ownership of the home, which the scammers quickly try to sell to a third party at a reduced rate. The victim still owes whatever remains on the mortgage but no longer has the asset.[21]

BUILDER-BAILOUT SCHEMES   The housing crisis also induced unscrupulous home builders to engage in fraud in order to unload unsold homes. Buyers have been offered an incentive of a mortgage with no down payment in order to get them to buy a house they could not normally afford. For example, say a builder wishes to sell a property for $300,000, a price that allows him to make a profit. He inflates the value of the property to $360,000 and finds buyers by offering to give them $60,000 to be used as a down payment. The buyers then go to a bank and show that they owe $300,000 on a $360,000 property; the lender funds a mortgage loan of $300,000, believing that $60,000 was paid to the builder and the borrower thus had the required 20 percent home equity. However, the lender is actually funding 100 percent of the home's value. The builder acquires $300,000 from the sale of the home and keeps any profits. If the home goes into foreclosure, the lender who provided the mortgage money finds out that there was actually no equity in the home and loses both the loan and the interest the lender would have collected over the term of the mortgage.[22]

In addition to the subprime mortgage scandal, a number of other mortgage schemes have been used by unscrupulous lenders and borrowers (see Exhibit 16.2).

Billion-Dollar Management Fraud

Sometimes executives in large corporations take advantage of their position to engage in management frauds, which typically involve falsifying financial information for their own financial benefit. Managers may create false accounting entries and false records of transactions, and they may engage in bogus trades, insider trading, kickbacks, backdating of executive stock options, and misuse or misappropriation of company property. Solidifying one's position within the company by manipulating accounts and concealing unacceptable performance from stockholders is also a form of management fraud.

EXHIBIT 16.2 Common Mortgage Fraud Schemes

- *Illegal property flipping.* Property is purchased, falsely appraised at an inflated value, and then quickly sold. The scheme also frequently involves doctored loan documentation and/or inflation of buyer income. Kickbacks to buyers, investors, property/loan brokers, appraisers, and title company employees are common, as well.

- *Silent second.* The buyer of a property borrows the down payment from the seller through the issuance of an undisclosed second mortgage. The primary lender believes the borrower has invested his own money in the down payment, when in fact the money has been borrowed. The second mortgage may not be recorded to further conceal its status from the primary lender.

- *Nominee loans/straw buyers.* The identity of the borrower is concealed through the use of a nominee who allows the borrower to use the nominee's name and credit history to apply for a loan.

- *Fictitious/stolen identity.* A fictitious/stolen identity may be used on the loan application. The applicant may be involved in an identity theft scheme. That is, someone else's name, personal identifying information, and credit history are used without that person's knowledge.

- *Inflated appraisals.* An appraiser acts in collusion with a borrower and provides the lender with a misleading appraisal report that deliberately states an inflated property value.

- *Foreclosure schemes.* The perpetrator identifies homeowners who are at risk of defaulting on loans or whose houses are already in foreclosure. Perpetrators mislead the homeowners into believing they can save their homes in exchange for a transfer of the deed and up-front fees. The perpetrator profits from these schemes by remortgaging the property or pocketing fees paid by the homeowner.

- *Equity skimming.* An investor may use a straw buyer, false income documents, and false credit reports to obtain a mortgage loan in the straw buyer's name. Subsequent to closing, the straw buyer signs the property over to the investor in a quit claim deed that relinquishes all rights to the property and provides no guaranty to title. The investor does not make any mortgage payments and rents the property until foreclosure takes place several months later.

- *Air loans.* Loans are made on property that does not exist, usually without collateral. For example, a broker might invent borrowers and properties, establish accounts for payments, and maintain custodial escrow accounts. Such a fraudulent broker may set up an office with a bank of telephones, one each for the employer, the appraiser, and the credit agency, for verification purposes.

Management fraud is not a new phenomenon, but multibillion-dollar schemes have recently rocked the nation's financial system. And management fraud has involved some of the nation's largest companies and richest people.

■ *Tyco International case.* In 2005, Tyco's chief executive officer L. Dennis Kozlowski and its chief financial officer Marc Swartz were convicted on a variety of fraud and larceny charges, including misappropriating $170 million in company funds by hiding unauthorized bonuses and secretly forgiving loans to themselves. Kozlowski and Swartz were also accused of making more than $430 million by lying about Tyco's financial condition in order to inflate the value of their stock. Kozlowski was convicted of looting the company of $150 million and sentenced to 8.33 to 25 years in prison.[23]

■ *Enron case.* Executives of this oil and gas trading firm, once one of the largest companies in the United States, engaged in a massive fraud scheme that caused the company to go bankrupt. Chairman Kenneth L. Lay was charged with conspiracy, securities fraud, wire fraud, bank fraud, and making false statements. Enron CEO Jeffrey K. Skilling and former Enron chief accounting officer Richard Causey were also charged with money laundering and conspiracy. The government claimed that executives oversaw a conspiracy to delude investors into believing that Enron was a growing company when, in fact, it was undergoing business setbacks. Why did they do it? Greed. Between 1998 and 2001, Lay received approximately $300 million from the sale of Enron stock options and restricted stock and made over $217 million in profit; he was also paid more than $19 million in salary and bonuses.[24] Lay died suddenly before he could be put on trial.

■   *WorldCom case.* In 2005, WorldCom CEO Bernie Ebbers was found guilty of falsifying the company's financial statements by more than $9 billion. One of the most important elements of the case was the more than $400 million that WorldCom lent or guaranteed to lend Ebbers at an interest rate of 2.15 percent. When the market collapsed, Ebbers was in no position to pay back the loans, and the company collapsed. On May 15, 2005, a federal jury in New York convicted Ebbers on all nine counts with which he was charged and sentenced him to 25 years in prison.[25]

Strategies to Control Corporate Crime

What efforts have been made to bring violators of the public trust to justice? Controlling corporate criminal activity typically involves two strategies designed to control organizational deviance: civil law (compliance) and criminal law (deterrence).[26]

CIVIL LAW STRATEGIES   One approach to controlling corporate crime relies on the threat of economic sanctions or civil penalties to control potential violators and gain their compliance with regulations. Compliance strategies use the threat of civil sanctions in an attempt to create a marketplace incentive to obey the law: the more a company pollutes, the more costly and unprofitable that pollution becomes; the less income you report, the greater your civil fine. Compliance strategies also avoid stigmatizing and shaming businesspeople by focusing on the act, rather than the actor.[27]

Compliance is regulated by administrative agencies set up to oversee business activity. For example, the Securities and Exchange Commission regulates Wall Street activities; the Environmental Protection Agency is assigned to oversee pollution, monitor waterways, and prevent illegal dumping of waste products; and the Food and Drug Administration regulates drugs, cosmetics, medical devices, meats, and other foods. The legislation creating these agencies usually spells out the penalties for violating regulatory standards. For example, this approach has been used to control environmental crimes by levying heavy fines based on the quantity and quality of pollution released into the environment.[28] Those who oppose compliance strategies complain that even billion-dollar fines are a drop in the bucket to corporations that routinely earn tens of billions of dollars each year.

CRIMINAL LAW STRATEGIES   These strategies rely on the threat of punishment of individual offenders to deter other would-be violators. They are deterrence strategies oriented toward apprehending violators and punishing them criminally, rather than creating conditions that induce conformity to the law. Even though law enforcement agencies and the courts have traditionally been reluctant to throw corporate executives in jail, a number of well-publicized cases, such as that of Bernard Madoff, indicate that the gloves are off and the government is willing to punish high-profile corporate criminals with long prison sentences. Because the Madoff, Enron, WorldCom, and other scandals have deprived so many people of their life savings and caused such disruption in the financial markets, both justice system personnel and the general public now consider corporate crimes as more serious offenses than common-law theft offenses and the perpetrators as deserving of severe punishment.[29] Penalties have been increasing, and long prison sentences are being routinely handed out for corporate crimes.[30]

Enforcement of Corporate Crime Laws

The detection and enforcement of large-scale corporate crime is primarily in the hands of administrative departments and agencies with investigative arms to police the areas of commerce that are their responsibility. For example, the Securities and Exchange Commission (SEC) has responsibility for overseeing the nation's capital markets; it is assigned the tasks of protecting investors, as well as maintaining fair, orderly, and efficient economic markets.

If SEC investigators detect inappropriate behavior in the financial system, they may decide to bring a case either in federal court or before an administrative law judge, depending on the type of sanction or relief that is being sought. For example, if the commission seeks to bar or remove someone from acting as a corporate officer, it must take the case to a federal district court. During the proceeding, the SEC will ask the judge to issue a court order, called an injunction, prohibiting any further acts or practices that violate the law or SEC rules. An injunction can also require that the offending company open its books for tax and accounting audits. In addition to barring or suspending the individual from serving as a corporate officer or director, the SEC can seek civil monetary penalties or the return of illegal profits (called disgorgement). A person who violates the court's order may be found in contempt and be subject to additional fines or imprisonment.

The decision to pursue criminal rather than civil violations usually is based both on the seriousness of the case and on the perpetrator's intent, actions to conceal the violation, and prior record. Any evidence of criminal activity is then sent to the Department of Justice or the FBI for investigation. Some other federal agencies, such as the Environmental Protection Agency (EPA) and the U.S. Postal Service, have their own investigative arms. Enforcement generally is reactive (generated by complaints) rather than proactive (involving ongoing investigations or the monitoring of activities). Investigations are carried out by the various federal agencies and the FBI. If criminal prosecution is called for, the case will be handled by attorneys from the criminal, tax, antitrust, and civil rights divisions of the Justice Department. If insufficient evidence is available to warrant a criminal prosecution, the case will be handled civilly or administratively by some other federal agency. For example, the Federal Trade Commission can issue a cease and desist order in antitrust or merchandising fraud cases.

Web App 16.1

For more information about the Securities and Exchange Commission (SEC), visit http://www.sec.gov/.

Cybercrime

In October 2013, law enforcement officials shut down the infamous Silk Road website, an online marketplace in which users could use what is known as a TOR ("the onion router") service to browse anonymously and securely, looking to do everything from purchase illegal drugs to hire hitmen. Silk Road was part of the so-called "deep web," or "deepnet," which consists of World Wide Web content that is not indexed by standard search engines and therefore lies beneath the "surface web." In May 2014, a 23-year-old Dutchman, Cornelis Jan "SuperTrips" Slomp, pleaded guilty to drug charges linked to his online

Pictured here is the Glen Park Library in San Francisco, where Ross William Ulbricht, the alleged mastermind behind the marketplace Silk Road, was arrested. Federal law enforcement officials shut Silk Road down in 2013, but many similar marketplaces continue to operate on the "deep web."

Nick Bilton/The New York Times/Redux

L03 Describe the various forms of cybercrime.

cybercrime

Illegal activity that uses a computer as its primary means of commission. Common forms of cybercrime include theft and destruction of information, resources, and funds.

activities. According to authorities, he was the most prolific online drug dealer on Silk Road, having amassed over $3 million in bitcoins, a form of online currency. Estimates suggest, in its prime, Silk Road had a million registered users and $1.2 billion in revenue.[31] Disturbingly, it was just one of many sites on the deep web; many illegal online marketplaces still exist and thrive to this day.

This case illustrates one of the newest challenges facing the justice system: **cybercrime**. A relatively new breed of offenses that can be singular or ongoing, cybercrime consists of basically any criminal activity that uses a computer as its primary means of commission. This new category of crimes presents a compelling challenge for the justice system and the law enforcement community because (a) it is rapidly evolving, with new schemes being created daily, (b) it is difficult to detect through traditional law enforcement channels, and (c) to control it, agents of the justice system must develop technical skills that match those of the perpetrators. It is even possible that the recent decline in crime is actually a result of cybercrime replacing traditional street crime. Instead of robbing a bank at gun point, a new group of contemporary thieves find it easier to hack into accounts and transfer funds to offshore banks. Instead of shoplifting from a bricks-and-mortar store, the contemporary cyberthief devises clever schemes to steal from etailers.

The Internet, coupled with ever more powerful computers, is now the medium of choice for providing a wide range of global services, from entertainment and communication to research and education. The cyber age has also generated an enormous amount of revenue. Worldwide IT spending was projected to pass $3.8 trillion in 2014.[32] Magnifying the importance of the Internet is the fact that many critical infrastructure functions, ranging from banking to control of shipping on the Mississippi River, are now being conducted online.[33] This vast network has now become a target for illegal activities and enterprise.

Cybertheft: Cybercrimes for Profit

cybertheft

The use of computer networks for criminal profits. Copyright infringement, identity theft, and Internet securities fraud are examples of cybertheft.

Some cybercriminals use modern technology to accumulate goods and services. **Cybertheft** schemes range from illegally copying material under copyright protection to using technology to commit traditional theft-based offenses such as larceny and fraud. Computer-based technologies enable criminals to operate in a more efficient and effective manner. Cyberthieves now have the luxury of remaining anonymous, living almost anywhere on the planet, conducting their business during the day or at night, and working alone or in a group, while at the same time reaching a much greater number of potential victims than ever before. No longer are con artists and criminal entrepreneurs limited to fleecing victims in a particular geographic locale; the whole world can be their target. And the technology revolution has opened up novel avenues of attack for cybertheft—ranging from the unlawful distribution of computer software to Internet security fraud—that heretofore were nonexistent.

Cyberthieves conspire to use cyberspace either to distribute illegal goods and services or to defraud people for quick profits. Some of the most common methods are described below.

COMPUTER FRAUD Computer fraud is not a unique offense but, rather, a common-law crime committed using contemporary technology. Consequently, many computer crimes are prosecuted under such traditional criminal statutes as those prohibiting larceny and fraud. However, not all computer crimes fall under common-law statutes because the property stolen may be intangible—that is, it may consist of electronic and/or magnetic impulses. Such crimes include:

■ *Theft of information.* The unauthorized obtaining of information from a computer (for example, "hacking"), including software that is copied for profit.

■ *The "salami slice" fraud.* The perpetrator carefully "skims" small sums from the balances of a large number of accounts in order to bypass internal controls and escape detection.

■ *"One-off kamikaze" fraud.* Similar to a "salami slice," this manipulation of accounts in the banking system occurs on a much larger and usually more complex scale.

■ *Software theft.* The comparative ease of making copies of computer software has led to a huge illegal market, depriving authors of very significant revenues.

■ *Corporate espionage.* Trade secrets are stolen by a company's competitors, which can be either domestic or foreign. The goal is to increase the rival company's (or nation's) competitive edge in the global marketplace.[34]

COPYRIGHT INFRINGEMENT For more than a decade, groups of individuals have been working together to obtain software illegally and then "crack" or "rip" its copyright protections before posting it on the Internet for other members of the group to use. Its criminal purveyors refer to this pirated material as **warez** (pronounced like "wares," as in "software").

Frequently, these new pirated copies reach the Internet days or weeks before the legitimate product is commercially available. The government has actively pursued members of the warez community, and some have been charged and convicted under the Computer Fraud and Abuse Act (CFAA), which criminalizes accessing computer systems without authorization to obtain information,[35] and the Digital Millennium Copyright Act (DMCA), which makes it a crime to circumvent the antipiracy measures built into most commercial software and also outlaws the manufacture, sale, or distribution of code-cracking devices used to illegally copy software.[36] The United States Criminal Code provides penalties for a first-time offender of incarceration for five years and a fine of $250,000.[37] Other provisions provide for the forfeiture and destruction of infringing copies and all equipment used to make those copies.[38]

INTERNET SECURITIES FRAUD Internet fraud involves using the Internet to intentionally manipulate the securities marketplace for profit. Three major types of Internet securities fraud are common today:

■ *Market manipulation.* Stock market manipulation occurs when an individual tries to control the price of stock by interfering with the natural forces of supply and demand. A modern variation on these schemes involves largely foreign-based computer criminals gaining unauthorized access and intruding into the online brokerage accounts of unsuspecting victims in the United States. These intruded victim accounts are then utilized to engage in coordinated online purchases of the targeted security to effect manipulation, while the fraud perpetrators sell their preexisting holdings in the targeted security into the inflated market.

■ *Fraudulent offerings of securities.* Some cybercriminals create websites specifically designed to sell securities fraudulently. To make the offerings look more attractive than they really are, assets may be inflated, expected returns overstated, and risks understated. In these schemes, investors are promised abnormally high profits on their investments. No investment is actually made. Early investors are paid returns with the investment money received from the later investors. The system usually collapses, and the later investors do not receive dividends and lose their initial investment.

■ *Illegal touting.* This crime occurs when individuals make securities recommendations and fail to disclose that they are being paid to disseminate their favorable opinions.

warez
Copyrighted software illegally downloaded and sold by organized groups without license to do so.

Web App 16.2

Visit the Federal Trade Commission website on identity theft at http://www.consumer.ftc.gov/features/feature-0014-identity-theft.

identity theft

Using the Internet to steal someone's identity and/or impersonate the victim in order to conduct illicit transactions, such as committing fraud using the victim's name and identity.

phishing

Also known as carding and spoofing, phishing consists of illegally acquiring personal information, such as bank passwords and credit card numbers, by masquerading as a trustworthy person or business in what appears to be an official electronic communication, such as an e-mail or an instant message. The term comes from the lures used to "fish" for financial information and passwords.

etailing fraud

Using the Internet to buy or sell merchandise illegally.

IDENTITY THEFT **Identity theft** occurs when a person uses the Internet to steal someone's identity and/or impersonate the victim to open a new credit card account or conduct some other financial transaction. It is a type of cybercrime that has grown at startling rates over the past few years.[39]

Identity theft can damage a person's good name and inflict severe losses and inconvenience by manipulating credit records or depleting bank accounts. Some identity thieves create false e-mails and/or websites that look legitimate but are designed to gain illegal access to a victim's personal information; this is known as **phishing** (and also as *carding* and *spoofing*).

Phishing e-mails and websites have become even more of a problem now that cybercriminals can easily copy brand names, the names of corporate personnel, and their insignia directly into the e-mail. The look is so authentic that victims believe the e-mail comes from the advertised company. Most phishers send out spam e-mails to a large number of recipients, knowing that some of those recipients will have accounts with the company they are impersonating. Some phishing schemes involve job offers. Once the unsuspecting victims fill out the "application," answering personal questions and including their Social Security number, the phisher has them in his grasp.[40]

ETAILING FRAUD New fraud schemes are evolving to exploit the fact that billions of dollars of goods are sold on the Internet each year. **Etailing fraud** can involve both buying and selling merchandise illegally on the Internet. Some etailing scams involve failure to deliver promised purchases or services, and others involve the substitution of cheaper or used material for higher-quality purchases.

Pornography and Prostitution

The IT revolution has revitalized the porn industry. The Internet is an ideal venue for selling and distributing adult material; the computer is an ideal device for storing and viewing it. Because of their vast numbers, it is difficult to estimate how many websites feature sexual content, including nude photos, videos, live sex acts, and webcam strip sessions, among other forms of "adult entertainment."[41] We do know that the number of pornography web pages has soared over time. Revenue from Internet porn comes from a number of sources: paid subscriptions, advertisements for other porn sites, fees for diverting web traffic to other sites, sale of sex-related products, and providing auxiliary services such as age verification.

The government has moved to control the broadcast of obscene films via satellite and other technological innovations. However, the First Amendment right to free speech makes legal control of pornography, even child porn, quite difficult. For example, to control the spread of Internet pornography, Congress passed the Communications Decency Act (CDA), which made all Internet service providers, commercial online services, bulletin board systems, and electronic mail providers criminally liable whenever their services were used to transmit material considered "obscene, lewd, lascivious, filthy, or indecent" (§ 314, 1996). However, in *Reno v. ACLU* (1997), the Supreme Court ruled that the CDA unconstitutionally restricted free speech, illustrating the difficulty law enforcement has when trying to balance the need to control obscenity with the First Amendment.[42]

FACT CHECK ☑

YOUR OPINION: How often do you worry about being a victim of identity theft—frequently, occasionally, rarely, or never?

PUBLIC OPINION:

FREQUENTLY/OCCASIONALLY:	66%
RARELY/NEVER:	34%

REALITY: According to a report by the Bureau of Justice Statistics, there were nearly 17 million victims of identity theft in 2012, the most recent year for which complete data were available as of this writing. About 7 percent of people age 16 and older were victims. These numbers include the victims of credit card theft through data breaches. While fear still outstrips reality, it is clear identity theft in all its forms is one type of crime Americans have a legitimate reason to worry about.

DISCUSSION: What can be done to rein in identity theft? Will the problem improve or continue to get worse?

Sources: Gallup, http://www.gallup.com/poll/123713/two-in-three-americans -worry-about-identity-theft.aspx; Erika Harrell and Lynn Langton, *Victims of Identity Theft, 2012* (Washington, DC: Bureau of Justice Statistics, 2013), http:// www.bjs.gov/content/pub/pdf/vit12.pdf; Blake Ellis, "Identity Fraud Hits New Victim Every Two Seconds," *CNN Money*, February 6, 2014, http://money.cnn .com/2014/02/06/pf/identity-fraud/ (sites accessed July 2014).

In 1996, Congress again attempted to control the growth of Internet porn when it passed the Child Pornography Prevention Act (CPPA). The CPPA expanded the federal prohibition on child pornography to include not only pornographic images made using actual children but also any visual depiction that is, or appears to be, of a minor engaging in sexually explicit conduct. The careful language of the act was used to ban "virtual child pornography" that appears to depict minors, whether or not minors are actually used.[43] In 2002, however, the U.S. Supreme Court struck down some sections of the CPPA as being unconstitutionally deficient, especially those that ban "virtual porn."[44] Since the Court's ruling, the act has not been enforced. The legal difficulties encountered by the CPPA illustrate the trouble society has controlling the distribution of sexually related materials and why it is today a multibillion-dollar industry.[45]

Cybervandalism: Cybercrime with Malicious Intent

Some cybercriminals may be motivated not by greed or profit but by the thirst for revenge, by the desire to inflict wanton destruction, or by other malicious intent. **Cybervandalism** includes the introduction of viruses and worms, web defacement, and denial-of-service attacks. Here are some common characteristics of cybervandals:

> **cybervandalism**
> Malicious attacks aimed at disrupting, defacing, and destroying technology.

- Some desire to exhibit their technical prowess and superiority.
- Some wish to highlight the vulnerability of computer security systems.
- Some want to spy on other people's private financial and personal information ("computer voyeurism").
- Some want to destroy computer security because they believe in open access to all systems and programs.[46]

VIRUSES AND WORMS A computer virus is one type of malicious software program (also called malware) that disrupts or destroys existing programs and networks, causing them to perform, instead, the task for which the virus was designed.[47] The virus is then spread from one computer to another when a user sends out an infected file through e-mail, a network, or portable media. Computer worms are similar to viruses, but they use computer networks or the Internet to self-replicate and "send themselves" to other users, generally via e-mail, without the aid of the operator.

TROJAN HORSES Some hackers may introduce a Trojan horse program into a computer system. The Trojan horse looks like a benign application, but it contains illicit codes that can damage the system operations. Sometimes hackers with a cruel sense of irony install a Trojan horse and claim that it is an antivirus program. When it is opened, it spreads viruses in the computer system. Trojan horses do not replicate themselves as viruses do, but they can be just as destructive.

DENIAL-OF-SERVICE ATTACK In a **denial-of-service attack**, users of an Internet service are prevented from access to that service. Cybercriminals who use this technology may attempt to extort money from the service providers (which may include banks and credit card companies) and its legitimate users in exchange for stopping the attack.[48]

> **denial-of-service attack**
> Malicious attempts to prevent access by legitimate network traffic, disrupt connections within a computer network, or disrupt service to a specific system or person.

Examples include attempts to "flood" a computer network, thereby preventing access by legitimate network traffic; attempts to disrupt connections within a computer network, thereby interrupting access to a service; attempts to prevent a particular individual from accessing a service; and attempts to disrupt service to a specific system or person.

WEB DEFACEMENT Cybervandals may target the websites of their victims. Web defacement is a type of cybervandalism that occurs when a computer hacker intrudes on another person's website by inserting or substituting codes that expose visitors to the site to misleading or provocative information.

CYBERSTALKING Traditional stalking involves repeated harassing or threatening behavior, such as following a person, appearing at a person's home or place of business, making harassing phone calls, leaving written messages or objects, or vandalizing a person's property. **Cyberstalking** is the use of the Internet, e-mail, or other electronic communications devices to stalk another person.[49] Some cyberstalkers pursue minors through online chat rooms, establish a relationship with a child, and later make contact for the purpose of engaging in criminal sexual activities. Today, Internet predators are more likely to meet, develop relationships with, and beguile at-risk adolescents and underage teenagers, rather than using coercion and violence.[50]

Cyberbullying

Experts define bullying among children as repeated negative acts committed by one or more children against another.[51] These negative acts may be physical or verbal in nature—for example, hitting or kicking, teasing or taunting—or they may involve indirect actions such as manipulating friendships or purposely excluding other children from activities. Bullying is a problem that remains to be solved, and it has now expanded from the physical environment to the virtual.

Because of the availability of cyberspace, physical distance is no longer a refuge from the frequency and depth of harm doled out by a bully to his or her victim.[52] **Cyberbullying** is willful and repeated harm inflicted through the medium of electronic text. Like their real-world counterparts, cyberbullies are malicious and cowardly aggressors who seek pleasure or profit through the mistreatment of other individuals. Although power in traditional bullying might derive from physical (stature) or social (competency or popularity) advantage, online power may simply stem from proficiency on the Net. Cyberbullies who are able to navigate the Internet and utilize technology in a way that enables them to harass others are in a position of power relative to their victims. There are four major approaches that cyberbullies employ to harass their victims:

- Bullies can send harassing e-mails or instant messages.
- They can post obscene, insulting, and slanderous messages on social networking sites.
- They can develop websites to promote and disseminate defamatory content.
- They can send harassing text messages to the victim via cell phones.[53]

Cyberwarfare

The justice system must now also be on guard against attacks of cyberwarfare that are aimed at the United States by overseas adversaries. Although the term may be difficult to define, **cyberwarfare** can be viewed as an effort by covert forces to disrupt the points where the virtual electronic reality of computers intersects the physical world.[54]

Cyberwarfare has been defined as "premeditated, politically motivated attack[s] against information, computer systems, computer programs, and data which result in violence against noncombatant targets

cyberstalking
Using the Internet, e-mail, or other electronic communications devices to stalk or harass another person.

cyberbullying
Willful and repeated harm done through the medium of electronic text.

cyberwarfare
Politically motivated attacks designed to compromise the electronic infrastructure of an enemy nation and disrupt its economy.

AP Images/Marcio Jose Sanchez

Sheila Pott, mother of Audrie Pott, reads a statement in support of Audrie's Law on Friday, March 7, 2014, in Saratoga, California. Audrie's Law is a legislative proposal aimed at deterring the bullying, cyberbullying, and sexual assault that played roles in the 15-year-old high school student's suicide.

by sub-national groups or clandestine agents."[55] Cyberwarfare may involve the use of computer network tools to shut down critical national infrastructures or to coerce or intimidate a government or civilian population.[56]

Even though they may come from a region where computer databases and the Internet are not widely used, terrorist organizations are beginning to understand the damage that cybercrime can inflict on their targets. Terrorist organizations are now adapting information technology into their arsenal, and agencies of the justice system have to be ready for a sustained attack on the nation's electronic infrastructure.

One form of attack is cyberespionage. This involves hacking into secure computer networks at the target nation's most sensitive military bases, defense contractors, and aerospace companies in order to steal important data or to assess their defenses. Infrastructure attacks can also be aimed at water treatment plants, electric plants, dams, oil refineries, and nuclear power plants. These industries all provide vital services to society by allowing people to go about their daily lives. Terrorist computer hackers could make a dam overflow or cause real property damage to oil refineries or nuclear plants by shutting down safeguards in the system designed to prevent catastrophic meltdowns.

The Extent and Costs of Cybercrime

How common are cybercrimes and how costly are they to American businesses and the general public? The Internet has become a major source of illegal profits. Criminal entrepreneurs view this vast pool as a target for cybercrime, and although an accurate accounting of cybercrime will probably never be made because so many offenses go unreported, there is little doubt that its incidence is growing rapidly.

Thousands of breaches occur each year, but most are not reported to local, state, or federal authorities. Some cybercrimes go unreported because they involve low-visibility acts that are rarely detected, such as copying computer software in violation of copyright laws.[57] Some businesses choose not to report cybercrime because they fear revealing the weaknesses in their network security systems. However, the information that is available indicates that the profit in cybercrime is enormous and continually growing.[58] Losses are now in the billions, and they continue to rise with the continuing growth of e-commerce.

Controlling Cybercrime

The proliferation of cybercrimes has created the need for new laws and enforcement processes. Because technology evolves so rapidly, enforcement presents challenges that are particularly vexing. Numerous organizations have been set up to provide training and support for law enforcement agents. In addition, new federal and state laws have been aimed at particular areas of high-tech crimes.[59] What are some of the legislative initiatives designed to limit or control cybercrime?

SOFTWARE PIRACY The government has actively pursued members of the warez community, and some have been charged and convicted under the Computer Fraud and Abuse Act (CFAA), which criminalizes accessing computer systems without authorization to obtain information.[60] The Digital Millennium Copyright Act (DMCA) makes it a crime to circumvent antipiracy measures built into most commercial software and also outlaws the manufacture, sale, or distribution of code-cracking devices used to copy software illegally.[61]

COPYRIGHT INFRINGEMENT The United States Criminal Code provides penalties for a first-time illegal copyright offender of five years of incarceration and a fine of $250,000.[62] Infringing copies and all equipment used to make those copies are also subject to forfeiture and destruction.[63]

 LO4 Discuss what is being done to thwart cybercriminals.

IDENTITY THEFT To meet this increasing threat, Congress passed the Identity Theft and Assumption Deterrence Act of 1998 (the Identity Theft Act) to make it a federal crime to knowingly transfer or use, without lawful authority, a means of identification of another person with the intent to commit, or to aid or abet, any activity that constitutes a violation of federal law, or that constitutes a felony under any applicable state or local law.[64] Violations of the act are investigated by federal investigative agencies such as the U.S. Secret Service, the FBI, and the U.S. Postal Inspection Service.

In 2004, the Identity Theft Penalty Enhancement Act was signed into law. The act increases existing penalties for the crime of identity theft, establishes aggravated identity theft as a criminal offense, and establishes mandatory penalties for aggravated identity theft. According to this law, anyone who knowingly "transfers, possesses, or uses, without lawful authority" someone else's identification will be sentenced to an extra prison term of two years with no possibility of parole. Individuals committing identity fraud while engaged in crimes associated with terrorism—such as aircraft destruction, arson, airport violence, or kidnapping top government officials—will receive a mandatory sentence enhancement of five years.

INTERNET PORNOGRAPHY As noted previously, it is difficult to detect and control Internet pornography. Opponents of any controls warn that they may violate the right of free speech. Congress has struggled to create legislation that will restrict objectionable use without violating First Amendment freedoms. For example, the Child Online Protection Act (H.R. 3783) banned web postings of material deemed "harmful to minors," but the law failed to survive a number of legal challenges.[65] In contrast, the Children's Online Privacy Protection Act, passed in 1998, has survived challenge. However, its focus is more on protecting children's personal information and limiting website marketing to young kids.

COMPUTER CRIMES Congress has treated computer-related crimes as distinct federal offenses since passage of the Counterfeit Access Device and Computer Fraud and Abuse Law in 1984.[66] The 1984 act protected classified United States defense and foreign relations information, financial institution and consumer reporting agency files, and access to computers operated for the government. The act was supplemented in 1996 by the National Information Infrastructure Protection Act (NIIPA), which significantly broadens the scope of the law.

Enforcing Laws Against Cybercrime

How has the justice system responded to cybercrime? Most of the efforts are being made at the federal level. One approach is to create working groups that coordinate the activities of numerous federal agencies involved in investigating cybercrime.[67] Another is to team federal agencies with state and local partners. An example is the New York/New Jersey Electronic Crimes Task Force (NYECTF), a partnership between the Secret Service and a host of other public safety agencies and private corporations.[68] Since 1995, the New York task force has charged more than 1,000 individuals with causing electronic crime losses exceeding $1.0 billion. It has trained more than 60,000 law enforcement personnel, prosecutors, and private industry representatives in cybercrime prevention. Its success has prompted other large jurisdictions to set up similar task forces.

OTHER SPECIALIZED ENFORCEMENT AGENCIES Specialized enforcement agencies are being created to fight cybercrime. The Internet Crime Complaint Center (IC3), based in Fairmont, West Virginia, is run by the FBI and the National White Collar Crime Center. It analyzes fraud-related complaints for patterns, develops additional information on particular cases, and sends investigative packages to law enforcement authorities in the jurisdiction that seem likely to have the greatest investigative interest in the matter. In 2013, the IC3 received more than 260,000 consumer complaints with an estimated loss of almost $800 million, a 48 percent increase over the previous year.[69]

Law enforcement has made remarkable strides in dealing with the crime of identity theft. Nonetheless, the problem is serious and may expand despite efforts to control it.

Transnational Organized Crime

Another major threat involves **transnational organized crime**—ongoing international criminal enterprise groups whose goal is personal economic gain through illegitimate means. Though sophisticated in the use of technology for communication and recruitment, these criminal groups also use systematic violence and corruption to achieve their ends. They are involved in money laundering; human smuggling; cybercrime; and the trafficking of humans, drugs, weapons, endangered species, body parts, or nuclear material.[70] There is also a troubling overseas trade in prostitution, in which men from wealthy countries frequent semi-regulated areas in needy nations such as Thailand in order to procure young girls forced or sold into prostitution—a phenomenon known as *sex tourism*. In addition to sex tours, there has also been a soaring demand for pornography, strip clubs, lap dancing, escorts, and telephone sex in developing countries.[71] Transnational sex trafficking, exporting women for the purpose of prostitution, is the subject of the accompanying Global Criminal Justice feature.

transnational organized crime
Use of illegal tactics to gain profit in the global marketplace, typically involving the cross-border sale and distribution of illegal commodities.

 L05 Define the concept of transnational crime.

GLOBAL criminal justice

TRANSNATIONAL SEX TRAFFICKING

Every year, hundreds of thousands of women and children—primarily from Southeast Asia and Eastern Europe—are lured by the promise of good jobs and then end up in the sex trade in industrialized countries. Data are unreliable, but estimates of the number of people trafficked internationally each year range between 600,000 and one million men, women, and children. Japan has more than 10,000 commercial sex establishments, and 150,000 to 200,000 foreign girls are trafficked into the country each year. It is believed that traffickers import up to 50,000 women and children every year into the United States, despite legal prohibitions and enforcement efforts. According to a 2012 report by the United Nations, the most common form of human trafficking (58 percent) is sexual exploitation, and the victims are predominantly women and girls; about 20 percent of the victims are children.

The UN report found that the majority of sex traffickers are women. Many were in the sex trade themselves and were encouraged by their recruiter/trafficker to return home and recruit other women, often under the scrutiny of people working for the trafficker to make sure they don't try to escape.

Because it is a global enterprise, there is a great deal of cooperation in trafficking; thus in Eastern Europe a single gang may include Russians, Moldavians, Egyptians, and Syrians. Cooperation makes it possible to traffic sex slaves not only to neighboring countries but all around the globe. The UN found that victims from East Asia were detected in more than 20 countries in regions throughout the world, including Europe, the Americas, the Middle East, Central Asia, and Africa.

CONTRIBUTING FACTORS

Human trafficking is facilitated by social problems and disorder, such as disruptions in the global economy, war, and social unrest. Economic crisis hits young girls especially hard. Female victims are often poor and aspire to a better life. They may be forced, coerced, deceived, and psychologically manipulated into industrial or agricultural work, marriage, domestic servitude, organ donation, or sexual exploitation. Some traffickers exploit victims' frustration with low salaries in their home countries, and others take advantage of a crisis in the victim's family that requires her to make money abroad. The traffickers then promise to take the victim abroad and find some traditionally female service sector job, such as waitress, salesperson, domestic worker, or au pair/babysitter.

Victims often come from poorer countries, but the market for labor and sex is found in wealthier countries or in countries that, even though they themselves are economically poor, cater to the demands of citizens from wealthy countries, of corporations, or of tourists.

COMBATING TRAFFICKING

Recently, the United States made stopping the trafficking of women a top priority. In 1998, the "Memorandum on Steps to Combat Violence against Women and the Trafficking of Women and Girls" directed the secretary of state, the attorney general, and the president's Interagency Council on Women to expand their work against violence against women to include efforts to stop the trafficking of women.

In the former Soviet Union, prevention education projects are aimed at potential victims of trafficking, and nongovernmental organizations have established hotlines for victims or women seeking information about the risks of accepting job offers abroad.

The UN report found that the number of convictions for human trafficking is increasing, especially in a handful of countries. Nonetheless, most countries' conviction rates rarely exceed 1.5 per 100,000 people, which is even below the level normally recorded for rare crimes such as kidnapping. According to the 2012 report, conviction rates are exceptionally low, on par with conviction rates for homicide in Iceland (0.3 convicted per 100,000 people) and kidnappings in Norway (0.14). Clearly, the problem remains.

CRITICAL THINKING

1. If put in charge, what would you do to slow or end the international sex trade? Before you answer, remember the saying that prostitution is the oldest profession, which implies that curbing it may prove quite difficult.

2. Should men who hire prostitutes be punished very severely in order to deter them from getting involved in the exploitation of these vulnerable young women?

Sources: Mark Lusk and Faith Lucas, "The Challenge of Human Trafficking and Contemporary Slavery," *Journal of Comparative Social Welfare* 25 (2009): 49–57; United Nations Office on Drugs and Crime, "Global Reports on Trafficking in Persons," http://www.unodc.org/documents/data-and-analysis/glotip/Trafficking_in_Persons_2012_web.pdf (accessed July 2014); Shannon Devine, "Poverty Fuels Trafficking to Japan," *Herizons* 20 (2007): 18–22; Linda Williams and Jennifer Ngo, "Human Trafficking," in *Encyclopedia of Interpersonal Violence*, ed. Claire Renzetti and Jeffrey Edelson (Thousand Oaks, CA: Sage, 2007).

Transnational Crime Groups

Transnational crime networks may locate themselves in nations whose governments are too weak to present effective opposition. If they believe that the government may be interfering with their illegal activities that bring them immense profits, such as drug trafficking, they will carry out a terror campaign, killing police officials and using bribery, violence, or terror to achieve their goals. The political turmoil of the twenty-first century, coupled with advances in telecommunications and computer technology, has had the unintended effect of providing avenues for the rapid expansion of transnational organized crime.[72]

There are a variety of transnational gangs whose membership is spread across the globe. Chinese groups are heavily involved in human trafficking—bringing large numbers of Chinese migrants to North America and essentially enslaving them. Eastern gangs trace their origin to countries spanning the Baltics, the Balkans, Central/Eastern Europe, Russia, the Caucasus, and Central Asia. Though ethnically homogenous, they work with other ethnic groups when

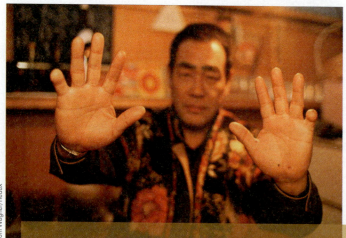

Tom Wagner/Redux

A member of the Yakuza, the Japanese mafia, shows the marks of his trade. He claims his pinkies were cut off because of violations of the organization's conduct code.

perpetrating crimes. Trading in illegal arms, narcotics, pornography, and prostitution, they operate a multibillion-dollar transnational crime cartel. Organized groups prey upon women in the poorest areas of Europe—Romania, the Ukraine, and Bosnia—and sell them into virtual sexual slavery. Many of these women are transported as prostitutes around the world, and some find themselves in the United States. Among the best known of the Asian transnational crime groups are:

■ *Yakuza*. Japanese criminal group. It is often involved in multinational criminal activities, including human trafficking, gambling, prostitution, and undermining licit businesses.

■ *Fuk Ching*. Chinese organized crime group in the United States. It has been involved in smuggling, street violence, and human trafficking.

■ *Triads*. Underground criminal societies based in Hong Kong. They control secret markets and bus routes and are often involved in money laundering and drug trafficking.

■ *Heijin*. Taiwanese gangsters who are often executives in large corporations. They are often involved in white-collar crimes, such as illegal stock trading and bribery, and they sometimes run for public office.

■ *Jao Pho*. Organized crime group in Thailand. It is often involved in illegal political and business activity.

■ *Red Wa*. Gangsters from Thailand. They are involved in manufacturing and trafficking methamphetamine.[73]

Two other powerful transnational crime groups, the Russian mob and Mexican drug trafficking cartels, are discussed in the following sections.

RUSSIAN TRANSNATIONAL CRIME GROUPS Since the collapse of the Soviet Union in 1991, criminal organizations in Russia and other former Soviet republics, such as Ukraine, have engaged in a variety of crimes: drugs and arms trafficking, stolen automobiles, trafficking in women and children, and money laundering.[74] No area of the world seems immune to this menace, especially not the United States. America is the land of opportunity for unloading criminal goods and laundering dirty money.

Russian organized crime is not based primarily on ethnic or family structures. Instead, it is based on economic necessity that was inflicted by the oppressive Soviet regime. A professional criminal class developed in Soviet prisons during the Stalinist period that began in 1924—the era of the gulag. These criminals adopted behaviors, rules, values, and sanctions that bound them together in what was called the thieves' world, led by the elite *vory v zakone*, criminals who lived according to the "thieves' law." This thieves' world, and particularly the *vory*, created and maintained the bonds and climate of trust necessary for carrying out organized crime.

The following are some specific characteristics of Russian organized crime in the post-Soviet era:

■ Russian criminals make extensive use of the state governmental apparatus to protect and promote their criminal activities. For example, most businesses in Russia—legal, quasi-legal, and illegal—must operate with the protection of a *krysha* (roof). This protection is often provided by police or security officials employed outside their official capacities for this purpose. In other cases, officials are silent partners in criminal enterprises that they, in turn, protect.

■ The criminalization of the privatization process has resulted in the massive use of state funds for criminal gain. Valuable properties are purchased through insider deals for much less than their true value and then resold for lucrative profits.

■ Criminals have been able to directly influence the state's domestic and foreign policies to promote the interests of organized crime, either by attaining public office themselves or by buying public officials.

The organized crime threat to Russia's national security is becoming a global threat. Russian organized crime operates both on its own and in cooperation with foreign groups. The latter cooperation often comes in the form of joint money-laundering ventures. Russian criminals have become involved in killings for hire in Central and Western Europe, Israel, Canada, and the United States.

In the United States, with the exception of extortion and money laundering, Russians have had little involvement in some of the more traditional types of organized crime, such as drug trafficking, gambling, and loan sharking. However, thousands of Russian immigrants are believed to be involved in criminal activity, primarily in Russian enclaves in New York City.[75] Russian criminal groups are extensively engaged in a broad array of frauds and scams, including health care fraud, insurance scams, stock frauds, antiquities swindles, forgery, and fuel tax evasion schemes. Russians are believed to be the main purveyors of credit card fraud in the United States. Legitimate businesses, such as the movie business and the textile industry, have become targets of criminals from the former Soviet Union, and they are often used for money laundering and extortion.

MEXICAN DRUG CARTELS Mexican drug cartels have become large-scale suppliers of narcotics, marijuana, and methamphetamines to the United States, and Mexico has become a drug-producing and transit country. In addition, an estimated 90 percent of cocaine entering the United States travels through Mexico. Mexican drug gangs routinely use violence, and the battle for control of the border regions continues to get more and more violent.

Although Mexican drug cartels, or drug-trafficking organizations, have existed for quite some time, they have grown more powerful since Colombia was able to crack down on the Cali and Medellín cartels in the 1990s. Mexican drug cartels now dominate the whole-sale illicit drug market in the United States. As a result, Mexican cartels are the leading wholesale launderers of drug money from the United States. Mexican and Colombian trafficking organizations annually smuggle an estimated $25 billion in drug proceeds into Mexico for laundering.

There are numerous drug cartels operating in Mexico, among them the Gulf, Tijuana, Sinaloa, Juárez, Millennium, Oaxaca, Colima, and Los Zetas cartels. Some are dominant in local regions, whereas the major gangs are present throughout Mexico. In recent years, new cartels have formed and others have become allies, in a constantly shifting landscape of drug activity. For example, Los Zetas was once the military wing of the Gulf Cartel. It has since branched out on its own and is, by several accounts, the most violent, technologically advanced, and sophisticated criminal syndicate in

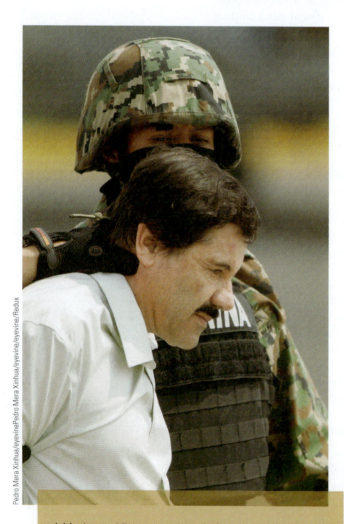

Pedro Mera Xinhua/eyevinePedro Mera Xinhua/eyevine/eyevine/Redux

A Mexican soldier escorts Joaquin Guzman Loera (a.k.a. "El Chapo Guzman"), leader of the Sinaloa cartel, who was captured in 2014. His arrest was heralded as the biggest blow to illicit drug trade since Columbian drug lord Pablo Escobar was killed in 1993.

Mexico. It is also the largest cartel, at least in terms of its presence throughout Mexico. Several Los Zetas members once worked in the Mexican Army's elite forces before deserting and joining up with the cartels. (See Figure 16.1 for a map of the cartels' approximate areas of influence.)

Controlling Transnational Crime

Efforts to combat transnational organized crime are typically organized by federal agencies. One approach is to form international working groups to collect intelligence, share information, and plot unified strategies among member nations. The FBI, for example, belongs to several international working groups aimed at targeting transnational gangs in various parts of the world. In response to Eurasian organized crime, the FBI is involved in the following groups and activities:

- *Eurasian Organized Crime Working Group.* Established in 1994, this group meets to discuss and jointly address the transnational aspects of Eurasian organized crime that affect member countries and the international community in general. The member countries are Canada, Great Britain, Germany, France, Italy, Japan, the United States, and Russia.

- *Central European Working Group.* This group is part of a project that brings together the FBI and Central European law enforcement agencies to discuss cooperative investigative matters covering the broad spectrum of Eurasian organized crime. A principal concern is the growing presence of Russian and other Eurasian organized criminals in Central Europe and the United States.

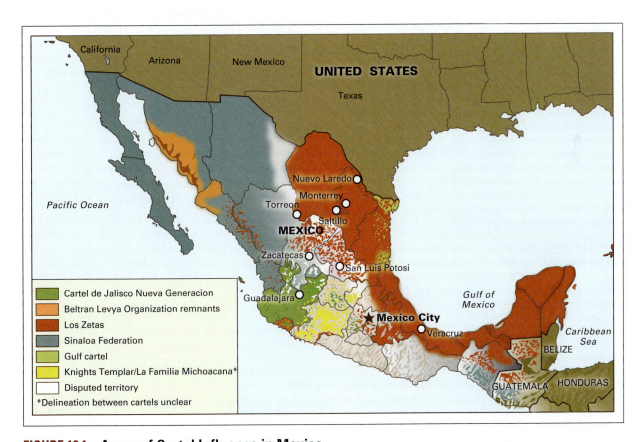

FIGURE 16.1 **Areas of Cartel Influence in Mexico**

Source: Stratfor Global Intelligence, *Areas of Cartel Influence in Mexico 2013*, http://www.stratfor.com/image/areas-cartel-influence-mexico-2013 (accessed May 19, 2014).

The initiative works on practical interaction between the participating agencies to establish lines of communication and working relationships, to develop strategies and tactics to address transnational organized crime matters that affect the region, and to identify potential common targets.

■ *Southeast European Cooperative Initiative.* This is an international organization established to coordinate police and customs regional actions for preventing and combating cross-border crime. It is headquartered in Bucharest, Romania, and has 12 fully participating member countries. The United States has been one of 14 countries with observer status since 1998. The initiative's center serves as a clearinghouse for information and intelligence sharing, allowing the quick exchange of information in a professional and trustworthy environment. The initiative also supports specialized task forces for countering cross-border crime such as the trafficking of people, drugs, and cars; smuggling; financial crimes; terrorism; and other serious cross-border crimes.

In addition, U.S. law enforcement agencies have cooperated in cross-border operations to eradicate gang activity. For example, in 2009, Homeland Security Investigations (HSI), the largest investigative agency in the Department of Homeland Security, launched Operation Pacific Rim. Agents from U.S. Immigration and Customs Enforcement (ICE), working in cooperation with Mexican authorities and the Columbian National Police, took down what some described as a "super cartel," a criminal organization so large that it was likened to a Fortune 500 company. The crooks were so successful smuggling drugs into the United States that after the bust it took authorities a month just to count the money seized. Cash was being smuggled back into Central America in fertilizer bags stored in large shipping containers. The Bogota-based operation was said to have supplied over 40 percent of the Colombian cocaine in the United States, which amounted to some 900 tons over a period of several years.[76]

LAWS TARGETING ORGANIZED CRIME Congress has passed a number of laws that have made it easier for agencies to bring transnational gangs to justice. One of the first measures aimed directly at organized crime was the Interstate and Foreign Travel or Transportation in Aid of Racketeering Enterprises Act (Travel Act).[77] The Travel Act prohibits travel in interstate commerce, or use of interstate facilities, with the intent to promote, manage, establish, carry on, or facilitate an unlawful activity; it also prohibits the actual or attempted engagement in these activities. In 1970, Congress passed the Organized Crime Control Act. Title IX of the act, probably its most effective measure, is the **Racketeer Influenced and Corrupt Organization Act (RICO)**.[78] RICO did not create new categories of crimes but rather new categories of offenses in racketeering activity, which it defined as involvement in two or more acts prohibited by 24 existing federal and 8 state statutes. The offenses listed in RICO include state-defined crimes, such as murder, kidnapping, gambling, arson, robbery, bribery, extortion, and narcotics violations; and federally defined crimes, such as bribery, counterfeiting, transmission of gambling information, prostitution, and mail fraud. RICO is designed to limit patterns of organized criminal activity by prohibiting involvement in acts intended to:

■ Derive income from racketeering or the unlawful collection of debts and use or investment of such income

■ Acquire through racketeering an interest in or control over any enterprise engaged in interstate or foreign commerce

■ Conduct business through a pattern of racketeering

■ Conspire to use racketeering as a means of making income, collecting loans, or conducting business

LO6 Explain how law enforcement is taking on transnational criminal syndicates.

Web App 16.3

Watch the full *60 Minutes* story about ICE's takedown of the Columbian "super cartel" here: http://www.cbsnews.com/videos/taking-down-colombias-super-cartel/.

Racketeer Influenced and Corrupt Organization Act (RICO)

Federal legislation that enables prosecutors to bring additional criminal or civil charges against people engaged in two or more acts prohibited by 24 existing federal and 8 state laws. RICO features monetary penalties that allow the government to confiscate all profits derived from criminal activities. Originally intended to be used against organized criminals, RICO has also been used against white-collar criminals.

CAREERS in criminal justice

DRUG ENFORCEMENT AGENT

DUTIES AND CHARACTERISTICS OF THE JOB

Drug Enforcement Administration (DEA) agents enforce the controlled substances laws and regulations of the United States of America. They bring to justice organizations—including those with ties to terrorism—and their principal members, who are involved in the growing, manufacture, or distribution of controlled substances. They also work to dismantle drug-trafficking organizations, to prosecute drug traffickers, and to destroy the financial infrastructure of these organizations.

JOB OUTLOOK

Law enforcement career opportunities are expected to grow modestly in the coming years, about as fast as the average for all occupations. Population growth is the main source of increased demand for police services. Competition for jobs in federal law enforcement agencies is significant. Bilingual applicants with a bachelor's degree and several years of law enforcement or military experience, especially investigative experience, have the best opportunities in federal agencies.

SALARY

DEA special agents are generally hired at the GS-7 or GS-9 level, depending on education and experience. The salary includes federal law enforcement officer base pay, plus a locality payment that depends on the duty station. Upon successful graduation from the DEA Training Academy, 25 percent availability pay is added to base and locality pay. After graduation, the starting salaries are approximately $50,000 for a GS-7 and $55,500 for a GS-9. After four years of service special agents are eligible to progress to the

GS-13 level and can earn approximately $92,600 or more per year.

QUALIFICATIONS

In order to become a DEA special agent, a candidate must successfully complete all phases of a rigorous, in-depth hiring process. This process may take up to 12 months or longer and includes the following phases:

- Written assessment and panel interview
- Urinalysis drug test
- Medical examination
- Physical task test
- Polygraph examination
- Psychological assessment
- Full-field background investigation
- Final hiring decision

EDUCATION AND TRAINING

The best-qualified candidates possess a bachelor's or master's degree with a GPA of 2.95 or higher. Special consideration is given to candidates with degrees in criminal justice/police science or related disciplines; finance, accounting, or economics; foreign languages (with fluency verified) in Spanish, Russian, Hebrew, Arabic, dialects of Nigerian languages, Chinese, and/or Japanese; computer science/information systems; and telecommunications/electrical/mechanical engineering.

Sources: U.S. Drug Enforcement Administration, *DEA Special Agents*, http://www.justice.gov/dea/careers/agent/ (accessed July 2014); U.S. Office of Personnel Management, http://www.opm.gov/policy-data-oversight/pay-leave/salaries-wages/#url=2014 (accessed July 2014).

An individual convicted under RICO is subject to 20 years in prison and a $25,000 fine. Additionally, the accused must forfeit to the U.S. government any interest in a business in violation of RICO. These penalties are much more potent than simple conviction and imprisonment.

Terrorism

Although terrorism is sometimes viewed as a contemporary phenomenon, terrorism and terrorists have been around for quite some time. The first terrorist activities were committed by members of minority religious groups who engaged in violence to (a) gain the right to practice their own form of religion, (b) establish the supremacy of their own religion over others, or (c) meet the requirements of the bloodthirsty gods they worshipped.[79] In some instances, a conquered people used force and violence to maintain their right to worship in their own faith. Zealots—Hebrew warrior groups active during the Roman occupation of Palestine during the first century CE—carried out attacks in broad daylight in order to send the message that the Roman authorities and those Jews who collaborated with them would not be safe.

The term *terrorist* first appeared at the time of the French Revolution, when Edmund Burke, a noted British political philosopher, referred to the violence he observed in Paris as the "reign of terror."[80] Terror was also associated with the unrest in Russia that led to the 1917 Bolshevik takeover. In May 1881, a terror group killed Tsar Alexander II. After the revolution, Bolshevik leaders Vladimir Lenin and Leon Trotsky made terror an instrument of state policy. Terror has also been identified with the civil war in Ireland and the Irish Republican Army, which is considered to be the model for most contemporary terrorist organizations.[81]

Defining Terrorism

Because of its complexity, an all-encompassing definition of terrorism is difficult to formulate. According to the U.S. State Department, the term **terrorism** means premeditated, politically motivated violence that is perpetrated against noncombatant targets by subnational groups or clandestine agents and is usually intended to influence an audience. The term *international terrorism* means terrorism involving citizens or the territory of more than one country.[82] Terrorism can be distinguished from conventional warfare, because it requires secrecy and clandestine operations to exert social control over large populations.[83]

To be considered terrorism, an act must be aimed at a goal that sets it apart from a common-law crime committed for greed or egotism.[84] It is erroneous to equate terrorism with political goals, because not all terrorist actions are aimed at political change. Some terrorists may try to bring about what they consider to be economic or social reform—for example, by attacking women wearing fur coats or sabotaging property during a labor dispute. "Terrorist" is also often used interchangeably with "guerilla," "insurgent," and "revolutionary," although each is really an independent concept. (See Exhibit 16.3.)

L07 Define terrorism and describe the factors that motivate terrorists.

terrorism
Premeditated, politically motivated violence perpetrated by subnational groups or clandestine agents against noncombatant targets, usually intended to influence an audience.

EXHIBIT 16.3   Terrorist, Guerrilla, Insurgent, Revolutionary

Terrorist

A terrorist uses criminal and violent acts to influence an audience beyond the immediate target. According to Alex Schmid and Albert Jongman, "Terrorism is an anxiety-inspiring method of repeated violent action, employed by (semi-)clandestine individual, group or state actors, for idiosyncratic, criminal or political reasons, whereby—in contrast to assassination—the direct targets of violence are not the main targets." These authors also note that "[t]he immediate human victims of violence are generally chosen randomly (targets of opportunity) or selectively (representative or symbolic targets) from a target population, and serve as message generators." Finally, "[t]hreat- and violence-based communication processes between terrorist (organization), (imperiled) victims, and main targets are used to manipulate the main target (audience[s]), turning it into a target of terror, a target of demands, or a target of attention, depending on whether intimidation, coercion, or propaganda is primarily sought."

Guerilla

Guerillas (from the Spanish term meaning "little war") are irregular military bands located in rural areas who attack military, police, and government targets. Guerilla warfare employs mobile and surprise tactics, traps, and ambushes to defeat a more powerful foe. Typically, guerillas try to draw their enemy into their terrain so that hit-and-run tactics and ambushes can be used to neutralize the enemy's superior power. Although the objective of some guerillas is to overthrow the existing

(continued)

government or carve out an independent territory, others may fight alongside government troops as they participate in conventional warfare. During World War II, partisan guerilla groups fought the Nazi occupiers in Russia, Poland, and other occupied nations. The goal of such operations is to increase the cost of maintaining an occupation or to exceed the limits of what the invading army may wish to bear or is capable of enduring.

Insurgent

An insurgency is a political movement with a specific aim. Insurgents confront the existing government for control of all or a portion of its territory, or they may force political concessions in sharing political power. Whereas terrorists are inherently violent, insurgents do not necessarily need to use terror or violence to meet their aims; they may employ nonviolent methods or political tactics instead. They may set up food distribution centers and schools in areas where they gain control in order to provide the population with needed services, while contrasting their benevolent rule with the government's incompetence and corruption.

Insurgents, unlike terrorists, require the support of a significant portion of the population. They may also seek external support from other nations to bring pressure on the government.

Revolutionary

A revolutionary, from the Latin *revolutio* ("a turn-around"), is generally seen as fighting a civil war between nationalists and a sovereign power that holds control of the land, or between the existing government and local groups over issues of ideology and power. Historically, the American Revolution may be considered an example of a struggle between nationalistic groups and an imperialistic overseas government. Some revolutions rely on armed force, but others can be nonviolent, depending on large urban protests and threats (an example is the Iranian Revolution of 1979).

Sources: Alex P. Schmid and Albert J. Jongman, *Political Terrorism: A New Guide to Actors, Authors, Concepts, Databases, Theories, and Literature* (Amsterdam: Transaction Books, 1988), p. 28; Andrew Silke, "Holy Warriors: Exploring the Psychological Processes of Jihadi Radicalization," *European Journal of Criminology* 5 (2008): 99–123.

Who Is the Terrorist?

Before terrorism can be effectively fought, controlled, and eradicated, it is important for agents of the justice system to understand something about the kind of people who become terrorists, what motivates their behavior, and how their ideas are formed. Unfortunately, this is not an easy task. Terrorism researchers have generally concluded that there is no single personality trait or behavior pattern that distinguishes the majority of terrorists or sets them apart so they can be easily identified and apprehended. Some seem truly disturbed, but many others have not suffered long-term mental illness or displayed sociopathic traits and/or tendencies; if that were so, bizarre or violent behavior in their early childhood would be a giveaway.[85] Thus there have been a number of competing visions of why terrorists engage in criminal activities such as bombings, shootings, and kidnappings to achieve a political end. Four stand out.

PSYCHOLOGICAL VIEW Not all terrorists suffer from psychological deficits, but enough do so that the typical terrorist can be described as an emotionally disturbed individual who acts out his or her psychoses within the confines of violent groups. According to this view, terrorist violence is not so much a political instrument as an end in

YOUR OPINION: How often do you worry about being a victim of terrorism—frequently, occasionally, rarely, or never?

PUBLIC OPINION:

FREQUENTLY/OCCASIONALLY: 35%

RARELY/NEVER: 65%

REALITY: Terrorist attacks are exceptionally rare in the United States, but when they do occur, they engender widespread fear and affect people's perceptions in irrational ways. According to a study by the National Consortium for the Study of Terrorism and Responses to Terrorism, terrorist attacks in the U.S. have been on the decline since the 1970s, and your odds of dying in a terrorist attack are about 1 in 20 million.

DISCUSSION: Why does one in three people worry frequently or occasionally about the terrorist threat? What, if anything, could be done to alter those perceptions?

Sources: Gallup, http://www.gallup.com/poll/123713/two-in-three-americans-worry-about-identity-theft.aspx (accessed July 2014); Gary LaFree, Laura Dugan, and Erin Miller, *Integrated United States Security Database (IUSSD): Terrorism Data on the United States Homeland, 1970 to 2011*, Final Report to the Resilient Systems Division, DHS Science and Technology Directorate, U.S. Department of Homeland Security (College Park, MD: START, 2012); Brad Plumer, "Eight Facts About Terrorism in the United States," *Washington Post*, April 16, 2013, http://www.washingtonpost.com/blogs/wonkblog/wp/2013/04/16/eight-facts-about-terrorism-in-the-united-states/ (accessed July 2014).

itself; it is the result of compulsion or psychopathology. Terrorists do what they do because of a wide variety of emotional problems, including but not limited to self-destructive urges and disturbed emotions combined with problems with authority.[86]

SOCIALIZATION VIEW Terrorists have been raised to hate their opponents, and they learn at an early age that they have been victimized by some oppressor.[87] Often, this socialization occurred in dysfunctional families from which the father was absent or, if present, was a distant and cold figure.[88] Terrorists report that they were estranged from their fathers, whom they viewed as economically, socially, or politically weak and ineffective. Because of this family estrangement, the budding terrorist may have been swayed to join a group or cult by a charismatic leader who served as an alternative father figure. In this sense, terror groups, like urban street gangs, provide a substitute family that can nurture a heretofore emotionally underprivileged youth.

IDEOLOGICAL VIEW Terrorists hold extreme ideological beliefs that prompt their behavior. At first they have heightened perceptions of oppressive conditions, believing that they are being victimized by some group or government. Once these potential terrorists recognize that such conditions can be changed by an active reform effort that has not yet been made, they conclude that they must resort to violence to encourage change. The violence need not be aimed at a specific goal. Rather, terror tactics must help set in motion a series of events that enlist others in the cause and lead to long-term change. "Successful" terrorists believe that their "self-sacrifice" outweighs the guilt they incur by harming innocent people. Terrorism, therefore, requires violence without guilt; the cause justifies the violence.

ALIENATION VIEW Terrorist operatives are not poor or lacking in education. And yet lack of economic opportunity and recessionary economies are positively correlated with terrorism.[89] Terrorists may be motivated by feelings of alienation and by being deprived of the tools to compete in a post-technological society.[90] Some terrorists appear alienated from modern society, and some feel that a suicide mission would cleanse them of the corruption of the modern world.

LO8 Discuss the various forms of contemporary terrorism.

Armed police officers search for gunmen and help people escape at Westgate mall in Nairobi, Kenya. A group of armed men attacked the upscale shopping mall, killing at least 67 people and wounding more than 175.

The Contemporary Terrorist

Terrorism encompasses many different behaviors and goals. It can be directed toward a foreign occupying power, a local politician, or even a corporation that produces something terrorists find objectionable. Some of the more common forms of terrorism are briefly described here and summarized in Concept Summary 16.1.

REVOLUTIONARY TERRORISM Revolutionary terrorists use violence to frighten those in power and their supporters; their goal is to replace the existing government with a regime that holds political or religious views acceptable to them. Terrorist actions such as kidnapping, assassination, and bombing are designed to elicit repressive responses from governments trying to defend themselves. These responses help revolutionaries to expose, through the skilled use of media coverage, the government's inhumane nature. The terrorists hope that the original reason for the government's harsh response will be forgotten as people who are not philosophically involved witness the effect of its counterterrorist activities.

POLITICAL TERRORISM Political terrorism is directed at people or groups with whom the terrorists live in close connection but who (a) oppose the terrorists' political ideology or (b) are defined by the terrorists as outsiders who must be either exiled or destroyed. Political terrorists want the government to be more sensitive to their views and see things their way. In the United States, right-wing terrorists are organized around such themes as white supremacy, pro-life militancy, militant tax resistance, and religious revisionism. On the left, domestic political terror groups are involved in violent actions to protect the environment and support animal rights (known as eco-terrorism).

NATIONALIST TERRORISM Nationalist terrorism promotes the interests of a minority ethnic or religious group that believes it has been persecuted under majority rule and wishes to carve out its own independent homeland. In Spain, the Basque Fatherland and Liberty (Euzkadi Ta Askatasuna, or ETA) is devoted to establishing a Basque homeland; in the Middle East, Hamas and Hezbollah fight for the destruction of Israel and the establishment of a Palestinian state.

RETRIBUTIVE TERRORISM Rather than fighting for a homeland, retributive terrorists fight for a cause.[91] Their enemies are not local groups whom they oppose or have conflict with but, rather, people anywhere whose ideology and/or religion they find objectionable. Rather than having a unified central command, they are organized in far-flung nets. Not located in any particular nation or area, they have no identifiable address. They are capable of attacking anyone at any time with great destructive force. They may use technology to attack their targets' economic infrastructure—such as through the Internet—and actually profit from the resulting economic chaos by buying or selling securities in advance of their own attack. Because they do not hope to regain a homeland or a political voice, they are willing to engage in suicide missions to achieve their goals.

STATE-SPONSORED TERRORISM State-sponsored terrorism occurs when a repressive government regime forces its citizens into obedience, oppresses minorities, and stifles political dissent. Death squads and the use of government troops to destroy political opposition parties are often associated with political terrorism. According to the U.S. Department of State, there were four state sponsors of terrorism at the time of this writing: Cuba, Iran, Sudan, and Syria.[92]

CULT TERRORISM Some cults may be classified as terror groups because their leaders demand that followers prove their loyalty through violence or intimidation.[93] These destructive cults are willing to have members commit violence, including murder. Members typically follow a charismatic leader who may be viewed as having god-like powers or even as the reincarnation of an important religious figure. The leader and his or her lieutenants commonly enforce loyalty by severe discipline and by physically preventing members from leaving the group. They may go through doomsday drills and maintain a siege mentality, fearing attacks from the government. It is not uncommon for such destructive groups to begin stockpiling weapons and building defensive barricades.[94]

CRIMINAL TERRORISM Sometimes terrorist groups become involved in common-law crimes such as drug dealing and kidnapping, or even selling nuclear materials. Their illegal activities may on occasion become so profitable that they replace the group's original focus. In some cases there has been close cooperation between organized criminal groups and guerillas. In other instances the relationship is more superficial. For example, the Revolutionary Armed Forces of Colombia (FARC) imposes a tax on Colombian drug producers, but evidence

Web App 16.4

For more information about state-sponsored terror, visit http://www.state.gov/j/ct/list/c14151.htm.

CONCEPT SUMMARY 16.1
The Variety of Terror Groups

■ *Revolutionary terrorism.* Groups that use violence to frighten those in power and their supporters in order to replace the existing government with a regime that holds acceptable political or religious views.

■ *Political terrorism.* Terrorism directed at people or groups who oppose the terrorists' political ideology or who are defined by the terrorists as outsiders who must be destroyed.

■ *Eco-terrorism.* Political terror groups involved in violent actions to protect the environment.

■ *Nationalist terrorism.* Groups whose actions promote the interests of a minority ethnic or religious group that has been persecuted under majority rule and/or wishes to carve out its own independent homeland.

■ *Retributive terrorism.* Groups that use violence as a method of influence, persuasion, or intimidation in order to achieve a particular aim or objective.

■ *State-sponsored terrorism.* Terrorism carried out by a repressive government regime in order to force its citizens into obedience, oppress minorities, and stifle political dissent.

■ *Cult terrorism.* Cults whose leaders demand that followers prove their loyalty through violence or intimidation.

■ *Criminal terrorism.* Groups that become involved in common-law crimes such as drug dealing and kidnapping, or even selling nuclear materials.

indicates that the group cooperates with Colombia's top drug barons in running the trade. In some instances, the line becomes blurred between being a terrorist organization with political support and vast resources and being an organized criminal group engaged in illicit activities for profit. What appears to be a politically motivated action, such as the kidnapping of a government official for ransom, may turn out to be merely a for-profit crime.[95]

Now that this new breed of terrorist has made his mark upon the world, how has the criminal justice system responded to the threat? What has been done in the United States to create homeland security?

Terrorism in the Courts

Numerous laws have been passed in an effort to catch terrorists and prevent acts of terrorism, among them the well-known USA Patriot Act. Law enforcement officials at all levels of government have also engaged in sophisticated, multi-faceted initiatives to combat the terrorism threat. We have already introduced such efforts at various points throughout the book. However, we have not yet discussed the important role of the courts in fighting terrorism. Indeed, federal trial courts have prosecuted, convicted, and sentenced a number of would-be and successful terrorists. The U.S. Supreme Court, too, has been rather vocal of late with respect to the treatment of terror suspects both here and abroad. Federal courts are usually the venue of choice because most anti-terrorism laws are federal (or because federal statutes provide for harsher penalties).

 **L09** Explain how the criminal justice system fights terrorism.

TYPES OF CASES Terrorism cases generally fall into two categories, each involving violations of federal law:

■   Category I cases involve violations of federal statutes that are directly related to international terrorism and that are utilized regularly in international terrorism matters. These statutes prohibit, for example, terrorist acts abroad against United States nationals, the use of weapons of mass destruction, conspiracy to murder persons overseas, providing material support to terrorists or foreign terrorist organizations, receiving military-style training from foreign terrorist organizations, and bombings of public places or government facilities.

■ Category II cases include defendants charged with violating a variety of other statutes where the investigation involved an identified link to international terrorism. These Category II cases include offenses such as those involving fraud, immigration, firearms, drugs, false statements, perjury, and obstruction of justice, as well as general conspiracy charges.[96]

TERROR CONVICTIONS In May 2014, former British cleric Mostafa Kamel Mostafa was convicted for his part in orchestrating the 1998 kidnappings of 16 American, British, and Australian tourists in Yemen.[97] Four hostages were killed in the kidnapping. Also in May 2014, Abu Hamza al-Masri, a radical Islamist cleric who was known for his hate-filled sermons, was convicted following a five-week trial of providing material support to terrorist organizations.[98] His conviction followed that of Sulaiman Abu Ghaith, the son-in-law of Osama bin Laden, in March. Abu Ghaith was convicted for his work as a chief spokesman for al-Qaeda in the days following the 9/11 terror attacks. Other notable terrorism prosecutions in recent years include the following[99]:

Attorney Stanley Cohen speaks to reporters after his client Sulaiman Abu Ghaith was convicted of conspiring to kill Americans. Cohen said that Abu Ghaith, the most senior advisor to Osama bin Laden to be tried in an American civilian court since the 9/11 attacks, was "at ease" with the verdict and expected to appeal.

Bryan R. Smith/The New York Time/Redux

■ *Attempted bombing of Federal Reserve Bank in New York.* In 2013, Quazi Mohammad Rezwanul Ahsan Nafis, 22, was sentenced to 30 years in prison for attempting to detonate a 1,000-pound bomb at the New York Federal Reserve Bank in lower Manhattan.

■ *Cleveland bridge plot.* In 2012, three men, Douglas Wright, Brandon Baxter, and Connor Stevens, all in their 20s, were arrested for conspiring to blow up a bridge near Cleveland, Ohio. The men purchased military-grade explosives and attached them to the bridge before authorities intervened. All three were sentenced to lengthy prison terms.

■ *Dallas skyscraper bombing attempt.* In 2009, Hosam Maher Husein Smadi took possession of a truck (supplied to him by an undercover agent) containing a supposed bomb that he planned to detonate underneath the Fountain Place high-rise building in Dallas. He parked the truck in a garage under the building, activated a timer that he thought would detonate the device, and then walked away and joined his partner, the undercover agent. Smadi pleaded guilty to the offense in May 2010.

■ *Mohammed Jabarah (Southern District of New York).* In January 2008, Jabarah was sentenced to life in prison after pleading guilty to terrorism charges stemming from his participation in a plot to bomb U.S. embassies in Singapore and the Philippines. Jabarah trained in al-Qaeda camps in Afghanistan and spent time with Osama bin Laden, to whom he swore an oath of allegiance.

■ *Jose Padilla and co-defendants (Southern District of Florida).* In August 2007, a federal jury convicted Padilla, Adham Hassoun, and Kifah Jayyousi of conspiracy to murder, kidnap, and maim individuals in a foreign country, conspiracy to provide material support, and providing material support to terrorists. Padilla was sentenced to more than 17 years in prison.

■ *Zacarias Moussaoui (Eastern District of Virginia).* In May 2006, Moussaoui was sentenced to six consecutive life terms after pleading guilty in April 2005 to various terrorism violations and admitting that he conspired with al-Qaeda to hijack and crash planes into prominent U.S. buildings as part of the 9/11 attacks.

■ *Ahmed Omar Abu Ali (Eastern District of Virginia).* In November 2005, Ali was convicted on all counts of an indictment charging him with, among other violations, providing material support to al-Qaeda, conspiracy to assassinate the U.S. president, conspiracy to commit air piracy, and conspiracy to destroy aircraft. Ali was sentenced to 30 years in prison.[100]

These are just a few of the hundreds of terrorism prosecutions that have taken place in the United States since the 1980s. There was a notable spike in prosecutions right after 9/11, but prosecutions continue to this day. In the years since 9/11, there have been more than 1,000 prosecutions of suspected terrorists in the United States.[101] This number continues to grow.

A report by the organization Human Rights First concluded that the U.S. criminal justice system is well equipped to handle a broad variety of criminal cases arising from terrorist incidents.[102] The report's authors also claim, however, that "the criminal justice system, by itself, is not 'the answer' to the problem of international terrorism."[103] The criminal justice system, including the courts, is but one piece of a larger puzzle, they argue: "Given the magnitude and complexity of the international terrorism threat, it is plain that the government must employ a multifaceted approach involving the use of military, intelligence, diplomatic, economic, and law enforcement resources in order to address the threat of international terrorism."[104]

THE SUPREME COURT AND TERRORISM During times of national emergency, the government has sometimes taken drastic measures to curtail the rights of its enemies. For example, during the Civil War, Lamdin Milligan, a civilian and sympathizer with the South, was tried and convicted before a military tribunal (a military court that limits the rights a person would otherwise enjoy in a civilian court) for conspiring to free Confederate prisoners from jail. He challenged his conviction, arguing that since the civilian courts were still functioning, he should have been tried in one of them. In *Ex parte Milligan*,[105] the Supreme Court agreed. Since then, and especially during times of war, the Court has decided a number of landmark cases. In the wake of 9/11, it has handed down decisions in several important cases.

Shortly after the 9/11 attacks, Congress authorized President George W. Bush to use "all necessary and appropriate force" against those responsible for the attacks in New York and Washington, D.C. Yaser Hamdi, an American citizen who had left the United States in his youth, was captured in Afghanistan and detained by military forces at Guantanamo Bay, Cuba, for supposedly aiding the Taliban. He was later moved to a military prison in Norfolk, Virginia, where he filed a writ of *habeas corpus*, arguing that, as a U.S. citizen, he was entitled to challenge the constitutionality of his confinement in federal court. In *Hamdi v. Rumsfeld* (2004),[106] the Supreme Court agreed with his argument, holding in a 6–3 decision that the due process clause of the Fifth Amendment requires that U.S. citizens be given the opportunity to challenge their confinement in this way. The Court also decided, in *Rasul v. Bush* (2004), that the federal courts have jurisdiction to hear *habeas corpus* petitions from foreign nationals captured outside the United States.[107]

One year later, the Supreme Court heard a case involving Salim Hamdan, a Yemeni and a former driver for Osama bin Laden. He was captured by Afghan warlords and turned over to U.S. forces in 2001. He was transferred to Guantanamo Bay in 2002 and in 2003 was slated to be tried for various conspiracy offenses before a military tribunal. He filed a *habeas corpus* petition in the U.S. District Court for the Western District of Washington, basically claiming that he could not legally be tried by a military tribunal. In a 5–3 decision, the Supreme Court agreed.[108] It held that the military commission at issue violated the Uniform Code of Military Justice and the four Geneva Conventions signed in 1949. Charges against him were subsequently dropped, but Hamdan was later deemed an "unlawful enemy combatant," tried once again before a military tribunal, and convicted. He was sentenced to five and a half years in prison, given credit for time served, and sent back to Yemen. He was not named a combatant before going into his first trial, which is one reason why the first military tribunal was illegal.

Shortly after Hamdan's case was decided, Congress passed the Military Commissions Act of 2006, which stripped the federal courts of jurisdiction to hear *habeas corpus* petitions from detainees who have been designated "enemy combatants." But in a 5–4 decision, the Supreme Court held that prisoners (even foreign nationals held at Guantanamo Bay) have the right to *habeas corpus* under the U.S. Constitution and that their arguments can be heard in the federal courts.[109] In effect, the Court held that the Military Commissions Act of 2006 was an unconstitutional suspension of the right to *habeas corpus*. In October 2009, President Obama signed into law the Military Commissions Act of 2009, which attempted to improve on—and address some of the deficiencies of—the earlier legislation. For example, the new law does not permit a U.S. citizen to be tried by a military commission.[110]

It is not particularly easy to understand all the nuances of the Supreme Court's terrorism cases, especially those decided in the wake of 9/11. This is partly because antiterrorism legislation continues to evolve. That said, there is an underlying theme in all of the cases we just considered: detainees, enemy combatants, terror suspects, and the like enjoy greater protection now than they did in the past. Indeed, all but a few of them enjoy the same rights as anyone else, whether or not they are U.S. citizens.

The Future of Criminal Justice

What will criminal justice be like a decade from now? Two decades from now? A whole generation from now? How will crime itself evolve? What about offenders? The answers are anyone's guess. History tells us as much. In the mid-1990s, for example, several prominent criminologists predicted a surge in serious crime,[111] particularly among juveniles, but the last decade of the twentieth century saw some of the largest crime drops in history, underscoring the difficulty of predicting the future. Even so, inaccurate predictions have not stopped the experts from planning for the future.

Predicting the Future

Several organizations are involved in long-range planning and forecasting. One example is the Society of Police Futurists International (PFI). Its Futures Working Group has come up with a number of predictions about crime and the nature of criminal justice over the next decade.[112] The National Institute of Corrections' "Forward Thinking" project works to identify forces that will shape America's correctional landscape going forward.[113] The National Center for State Courts has also focused attention on future trends likely to shape adjudication in America.[114] Even the National Institute of Justice has begun preparing for the

LO10 Identify trends that are likely to influence criminal justice in the future.

Web App 16.5

For more information about the Society of Police Futurists International, visit http://www.policefuturists.org/.

future, calling on the experts to speculate about what lies in store.[115] They have come up with a number of shifts, trends, and changes that criminal justice will need to be prepared for. A few of the more notable ones follow.

DEMOGRAPHIC SHIFTS The population is aging. Over the next several decades, the proportion of males aged 15 to 19 in the population will shrink. The over-65 population will grow markedly from around 43 million to over 90 million (see Figure 16.2). This will have interesting implications for crime and criminal justice, because young people are typically the most crime-prone group. What will the impact be? According to Bryan Vila, "there will be more people to be either victims or solutions."[116] On the one hand, if there are more elderly people, there is a chance that more of them will become crime victims. On the other hand, the criminal justice system could draw on the volunteer services of retired people to report crime and guide children.

TECHNOLOGICAL ADVANCES Technological advances continue at a feverish pace. Surveillance technologies, biometric tools, and DNA analysis, to name just a few, will continue to evolve and improve. Increasingly sophisticated and integrated databases will improve law enforcement's crime fighting capability. The criminal element will improve its technological capabilities, as well, forcing criminal justice to try to keep pace.

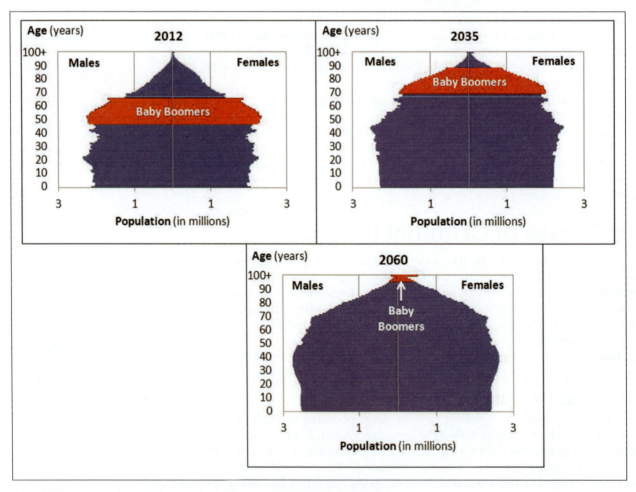

FIGURE 16.2   Population by Age and Sex: 2012, 2035 and 2060

Source: United States Census Bureau, *Population by Age and Sex: 2012, 2035, and 2060*, http://www.census.gov/newsroom/releases/img/babyboomers_pyramid.jpg (accessed May 19, 2014).

INCREASED DIVERSITY The number of foreign-born Americans continues to grow. This diversity, though advantageous in many ways, will exert pressures on criminal justice. Chris Stone points to the example of South Africa, noting that its court system now recognizes 11 distinct languages: "Often, the only two people in the courtroom speaking the same language are the victim and defendant—with the judge, prosecutor, and defense lawyer relying on interpreters."[117] Even the racial and ethnic composition of the American population will change markedly. See Figure 16.3 for Census Bureau projections through 2060. According to the Census Bureau, the Hispanic population will nearly double by 2060.

A FOCUS ON WHAT WORKS Evidence-Based Justice features appear throughout this book. This focus on *what works and what doesn't* will continue to gain steam as taxpayers increase their efforts to hold the government accountable for spending. The days of throwing money at the crime problem, with little attention to what solutions are best, are surely numbered. The popular Campbell Collaboration reflects this thinking. This organization's goal is to improve decision making in a number of realms, including criminal justice.[118] A new U.S. government website, CrimeSolutions.gov, provides a similar service.

Web App 16.6

For more information about what works and doesn't work in crime control and prevention, visit https://www.crimesolutions.gov/.

DOING MORE WITH LESS America's record debt is forcing cutbacks in government services. The same is true of state and local governments. This will pressure criminal justice agencies to do more with less—and again to focus their resources on tried and true successes. Innovative strategies will be necessary, and officials will need to rely increasingly on "civilianization" and related strategies that help to cut costs. Service sharing between municipalities will become more

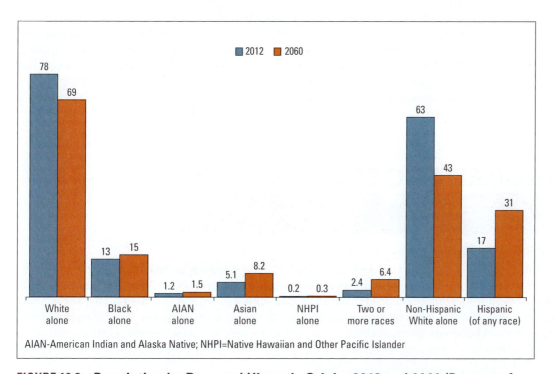

AIAN-American Indian and Alaska Native; NHPI=Native Hawaiian and Other Pacific Islander

FIGURE 16.3 **Population by Race and Hispanic Origin: 2012 and 2060 (Percent of total Population)**

Source: United States Census Bureau, *Population by Race and Hispanic Origin: 2012 and 2060*, http://www.census.gov/newsroom/releases/img/racehispanic_graph.jpg (accessed May 19, 2014).

attractive as a means of maintaining a healthy "bottom line." Privatization initiatives will continue to gain steam, as well, on the theory that the private sector may be more cost-effective and efficient than the public sector in certain criminal justice operations (such as providing security and running prisons).

GLOBALIZATION One of the most significant trends in the future will be globalization. Boundaries will continue to be challenged, and international criminal syndicates will continue to pose threats. Emerging industrial nations will continue to vie for scarce resources. We have seen gas creep above $4.00 per gallon in certain parts of the country. What if gas prices rise above that? What if they go to, say, $8.00 a gallon? What implications will this hold for police patrols?

GREEN CRIME BP's massive oil spill in the Gulf of Mexico is still being cleaned up, and untold damage to wildlife, ecosystems, and the local economy remains. But oil spills are just part of the problem. Critical criminologists and environmental activists have long called attention to a variety of environmental threats that they feel should be deemed criminal: "... green crimes involve a wide range of actions and outcomes that harm the environment and that stem from corporate behaviors such as decisions about what is produced and how it is produced."[119] Global warming, overdevelopment, population growth, and other changes will continue to bring these issues front and center, but so-called "green-collar" offenders are still not punished as harshly on the whole as their traditional criminal counterparts.[120]

ILLEGAL IMMIGRATION Continued immigration is certain to impact crime and criminal justice, though it is less certain what these effects will be. According to some sources, the economic downturn of 2008 led to reductions in illegal immigration, but criminal justice officials are still busy.[121] And as the economy rebounds, the problem could rear its head again. Look no further than Arizona, where lawmakers required police, "when practicable," to detain people they suspected were in the country illegally and to demand proof of citizenship.[122] Shortly after the law was enacted, a federal judge issued an injunction blocking enforcement of the so-called "Papers, please" provision. Then, on June 25, 2012, the U.S. Supreme Court declared key provisions of the law unconstitutional, but left intact a provision that permits police to arrest and hold anyone they believe has committed a crime and who is in the country illegally, such that the arrestee's immigration status can be confirmed with federal officials.[123]

ETHICAL CHALLENGES in Criminal Justice

A WRITING ASSIGNMENT

A tracking device has been developed that can be implanted in every new computer to constantly monitor every web page visited on the Internet. This device can record every transaction and all activity, and it automatically sends the data to government computers programmed to look for suspicious Web activity. This surveillance device enables the government to keep tabs on what people are doing, what they buy, what they download, and so on. Once a person becomes a suspect in a crime, she or he can be easily monitored from a distance, without the person's knowledge and with no danger to any government agent. Suspects cannot hide or escape detection.

Write an essay discussing the pros and cons of employing this device. You might want to refer to the sections on cybercrime, including etailing fraud and copyright infringement. If you approve of the device, what questions might you want answered before it becomes standard equipment on home computers?

Summary

L01 Explain the influence of globalization on crime.

- Globalization has shifted the focus of crime from a local to a world perspective. With money and power to spare, criminal enterprise groups can recruit new members, bribe government officials, and even fund private armies.

- Technological advances ranging from global cell phone connectivity to the Internet, along with the growth of international trade, have contributed to the growth in illicit transnational criminal activities.

- Globalization brings with it an ideology of free markets and free trade that means less intervention and regulation, conditions that crime groups exploit to cross unpatrolled borders and expand their activities to new regions of the world.

L02 Discuss the impact of corporate enterprise crime.

- The crimes of the rich and powerful have the most significant impact on society. Experts place their total monetary value in the hundreds of billions of dollars, far outstripping the expense of any other type of crime.

- Large-scale investment growth has led to significant increases in the amount of fraud and misconduct on Wall Street. Investment firms have engaged in deceptive securities sales that have cost investors billions.

L03 Describe the various forms of cybercrime.

- Cybercrime typically involves the theft and/or destruction of information, resources, or funds via computers, computer networks, and the Internet.

- Cybertheft is the use of computer networks for criminal profits. Copyright infringement, identity theft, and Internet securities fraud are examples of cybertheft.

- Cybervandalism, or technological destruction, involves malicious attacks aimed at disrupting, defacing, and destroying technology.

- Other types of cybercrime include, but are not limited to, computer fraud, certain types of pornography, denial-of-service attacks, etailing fraud, and cyberbullying.

L04 Discuss what is being done to thwart cybercriminals.

- Numerous organizations have been set up to provide training and support for law enforcement agents. In addition, new federal and state laws have been enacted to help discourage particular types of high-tech crimes.

- In the future, technological prowess may make it possible to identify cybercriminals and bring them to justice before they can carry out their attacks.

L05 Define the concept of transnational crime.

- Transnational organized crime involves ongoing international criminal enterprise groups whose purpose is personal economic gain through illegitimate means.

- Transnational gangs are involved in money laundering, human smuggling, cybercrime, and trafficking of humans, drugs, weapons, endangered species, body parts, or nuclear material.

- There is also a troubling cross-border trade in prostitution. Transnational gangs export women from third-world nations for the purposes of prostitution. Some may be kidnapped or forced into prostitution against their will through violence and threats.

L06 Explain how law enforcement is taking on transnational criminal syndicates.

- Efforts to combat transnational organized crime are typically in the hands of federal agencies. One approach is for them to form international working groups to collect intelligence, share information, and plot unified strategies among member nations.

- U.S. law enforcement agencies have cooperated in cross-border operations to combat gang activity.

- Congress has passed a number of laws that have made it easier for agencies to bring transnational gangs to justice. These include the Interstate and Foreign Travel or Transportation in Aid of Racketeering Enterprises Act (the Travel Act) and the Racketeer Influenced and Corrupt Organization Act (RICO).

LO7 **Define terrorism and describe the factors that motivate terrorists.**

- Terrorism involves the illegal use of force against innocent people to achieve a political objective.

- Confronting terrorism is critical because of the lethal tactics now being used—bombings, killing hostages, chemical warfare, and spreading toxic biological agents.

- Not all terrorists suffer from psychological deficits, but enough do so that the typical terrorist can be described as an emotionally disturbed individual who acts out his or her psychoses within the confines of violent groups.

- Terrorists have been raised to hate their opponents, and they learn at an early age that they have been victimized by some oppressor.

- Terrorists hold extreme ideological beliefs that prompt their behavior.

- Terrorists may be motivated by feelings of alienation and failure to possess the tools they need to compete in a post-technological society.

LO8 **Discuss the various forms of contemporary terrorism.**

- Revolutionary terrorists use violence to frighten those in power and their supporters in an effort to replace the existing government with a regime that holds acceptable political or religious views.

- Political terrorism is directed at people or groups with whom the terrorists live in close connection but who (a) oppose the terrorists' political ideology or (b) are defined as outsiders by the terrorists.

- Nationalist terrorism promotes the interests of a minority ethnic or religious group that

believes it has been persecuted under majority rule and wishes to carve out its own independent homeland.

- Rather than fighting for a homeland, retributive terrorists fight for a cause.

- State-sponsored terrorism occurs when a repressive government regime forces its citizens into obedience, oppresses minorities, and stifles political dissent.

- Some cults may be classified as terror groups because their leaders demand that followers prove their loyalty through violence or intimidation.

LO9 **Explain how the criminal justice system fights terrorism.**

- A number of laws have been enacted to fight terrorism, and law enforcement agencies seek to prevent terrorist attacks through a variety of means.

- The numbers of terrorism prosecutions and convictions have increased steadily since 9/11.

- Since 9/11, the U.S. Supreme Court has decided several important cases involving the treatment of terror suspects.

- The Court's decisions have given terrorism suspects increased opportunities to challenge the legality of their confinement.

LO10 **Identify trends that are likely to influence criminal justice in the future.**

- The criminal justice system will need to be braced for demographic shifts (particularly an older population), technological advances, increased diversity, a focus on what works (evidence-based justice), continued cutbacks in funding, globalization, green crime, and illegal immigration.

Key Terms

globalization, 614
corporate enterprise crime, 616
Ponzi scheme, 616
securitization, 619
cybercrime, 624
cybertheft, 624
warez, 625

identity theft, 626
phishing, 626
etailing fraud, 626
cybervandalism, 627
denial-of-service attack, 627
cyberstalking, 628
cyberbullying, 628

cyberwarfare, 628
transnational organized crime, 631
Racketeer Influenced and
    Corrupt Organization Act
    (RICO), 636
terrorism, 638

Critical Thinking Questions

1. Should people who illegally download movies or music be prosecuted for theft?
2. How can Internet pornography be controlled, considering that a great deal of adult content is available on foreign websites?
3. Given the threat of transnational drug trafficking, should drugs be legalized and controlled by the government?
4. Should the Internet be more closely monitored and controlled to reduce the threat of cyberwarfare?
5. Is there any point in placing economic sanctions on billion-dollar corporations? Should corporate executives be put in prison? What is the purpose of incarcerating someone like 72-year-old Bernard Madoff? Is he a threat to society?
6. What American groups might be the breeding ground of terrorist activity in the United States?

Notes

1. Federal Bureau of Investigation, *Homegrown Violent Extremism: Dismantling the Triangle Terror Group*, http://www.fbi.gov/news/stories/2012/december/dismantling-the-triangle-terror-group/dismantling-the-triangle-terror-group (accessed July 2014).
2. Nikos Passas and David Nelken, "The Thin Line Between Legitimate and Criminal Enterprises: Subsidy Frauds in the European Community," *Crime, Law, and Social Change* 19 (1993): 223–243.
3. Mark Haller, "Illegal Enterprise: A Theoretical and Historical Interpretation," *Criminology* 28 (1990): 207–235.
4. For a thorough review, see David Friedrichs, *Trusted Criminals* (Belmont, CA: Wadsworth, 1996).
5. Kitty Calavita and Henry Pontell, "Savings and Loan Fraud as Organized Crime: Toward a Conceptual Typology of Corporate Illegality," *Criminology* 31 (1993): 519–548.
6. Andrew Nikiforuk, *Pandemonium: How Globalization and Trade Are Putting the World at Risk* (Queensland, NZ: University of Queensland Press, 2007).
7. David Friedrichs and Jessica Friedrichs, "The World Bank and Crimes of Globalization: A Case Study," *Social Justice* 29 (2002): 13–36.
8. Louise Shelley, "The Globalization of Crime and Terrorism," State Department's Bureau of International Information Programs (IIP), 2006, http://cuwhist.files.wordpress.com/2009/12/the-globalization-of-crime-and-terrorism.pdf (accessed July 2014).
9. Edwin Sutherland, *White-Collar Crime: The Uncut Version* (New Haven, CT: Yale University Press, 1983).
10. Ronald Kramer and Raymond Michalowski, "State-Corporate Crime," paper presented at the annual meeting of the American Society of Criminology, Baltimore, November 1990.
11. Edwin Sutherland, "White-Collar Criminality," *American Sociological Review* 5 (1940): 2–10.
12. Natalie Taylor, "Under-Reporting of Crime Against Small Business: Attitudes Towards Police and Reporting Practices," *Policing and Society* 13 (2003): 79–90.
13. Federal Bureau of Investigation, *Financial Crimes Report to the Public*, http://www.fbi.gov/stats-services/publications/financial-crimes-report-2010-2011 (accessed July 2014).
14. FBI, "Ponzi Scheme Indictments: Five Charged in $7 Billion Ploy," June 19, 2009, http://www.fbi.gov/page2/june09/stanford_061909.html (accessed July 2014).
15. Federal Bureau of Investigation, *Financial Crimes Report to the Public*.
16. Securities and Exchange Commission, "SEC Charges Bernard L. Madoff for Multi-Billion Dollar Ponzi Scheme," December 11, 2008, http://www.sec.gov/news/press/2008/2008-293.htm (accessed July 2014).
17. CliffordKrauss, Phillip L. Zweig, and Julie Creswell, "Texas Firm Accused of $8 Billion Fraud," *New York Times*, February 18, 2009, http://www.nytimes.com/2009/02/18/business/18stanford.html (accessed July 2014).
18. Federal Bureau of Investigation, *2010 Mortgage Fraud Report*, http://www.fbi.gov/stats-services/publications/mortgage-fraud-2010 (accessed July 2014).
19. Federal Bureau of Investigation, *Financial Crimes Report to the Public*.
20. Ibid.
21. Fraudguides, "Mortgage Foreclosure Rescue Scams," http://www.fraudguides.com/mortgage-foreclosure-rescue-scam.asp (accessed July 2014).
22. FBI, *2010 Mortgage Fraud Report*.
23. MSNBC, "Ex-Tyco Executives Get Up to 25 Years in Prison," September 20, 2005, http://www.msnbc.msn.com/id/9399803/ (accessed July 2014).
24. Kurt Eichenwald, "Ex-Andersen Partner Pleads Guilty in Record-Shredding," *New York Times*, April 12, 2002, p. C1; John A. Byrne, "At Enron, the Environment Was Ripe for Abuse," *Business Week*, February 25, 2002, p. 12; Peter Behr and Carrie Johnson, "Govt. Expands Charges Against Enron Execs," *Washington Post*, May 1, 2003, p. 1.
25. Krysten Crawford, CNN, "Ex-WorldCom CEO Ebbers Guilty," March 15, 2006, http://money.cnn.com/2005/03/15/news/newsmakers/ebbers/ (accessed July 2014); MSNBC, "Ebbers Sentenced to 25 Years in Prison," July 13, 2005, http://www.msnbc.msn.com/id/8474930/ns/business/t/ebbers-sentenced-years-prison/ (accessed July 2014); Lynne W. Jeter, *Disconnected: Deceit and Betrayal at WorldCom* (New York: Wiley, 2003).
26. This section relies heavily on Albert Reiss Jr., "Selecting Strategies of Social Control over Organizational Life," in *Enforcing Regulation*, ed. Keith Hawkins and John M. Thomas (Boston: Kluwer Publications, 1984), pp. 25–37.
27. Michael Benson, "Emotions and Adjudication: Status Degradation Among White-Collar Criminals," *Justice Quarterly* 7 (1990): 515–528; John Braithwaite, *Crime, Shame, and Reintegration* (Sydney: Cambridge University Press, 1989).
28. John Braithwaite, "The Limits of Economism in Controlling Harmful Corporate Conduct," *Law and Society Review* 16 (1981–1982): 481–504.
29. Sean Rosenmerkel, "Wrongfulness and Harmfulness as Components of Seriousness of White-Collar Offenses," *Journal of Contemporary Criminal Justice* 17 (2001): 308–328.
30. Jonathan Lechter, Daniel Posner, and George Morris, "Antitrust Violations," *American Criminal Law Review* 39 (2002): 225–273.

31. Donna Leinwand, "How the FBI Brought Down Cyber-Underworld Site Silk Road," *USA Today*, May 15, 2014, http://www.usatoday.com/story/news/nation/2013/10/21/fbi-cracks-silk-road/2984921/ (accessed July 2014).

32. "Gartner Says Worldwide IT Spending on Pace to Grow 3.2 Percent in 2014," http://www.gartner.com/newsroom/id/2698017 (accessed July 2014).

33. Giles Trendle, "An E-jihad Against Government?" *EGOV Monitor*, September 2002.

34. Vogon International, http://www.vogon-investigation.com (accessed July 2014).

35. The Computer Fraud and Abuse Act (CFAA), 18 U.S.C. §1030 (1998).

36. The Digital Millennium Copyright Act, Public Law 105-304 (1998).

37. Title 18, United States Code, section 2319.

38. Title 17, United States Code, section 506.

39. Erika Harrell and Lynn Langton, *Victims of Identity Theft, 2012* (Washington, DC: Bureau of Justice Statistics, 2013), http://www.bjs.gov/content/pub/pdf/vit12.pdf (accessed July 2014).

40. Identity Theft Resource Center (ITRC), http://www.idtheftcenter.org (accessed July 2014).

41. Andreas Philaretou, "Sexuality and the Internet," *Journal of Sex Research* 42 (2005): 180–181.

42. *Reno v. ACLU*, No. 96-511.

43. ACLU, news release, "*ACLU v. Reno*, Round 2: Broad Coalition Files Challenge to New Federal Net Censorship Law," October 22, 1998.

44. *Ashcroft, Attorney General, et al. v. Free Speech Coalition, et al.* 535 U.S. 234 (2002).

45. Anthony Flint, "Skin Trade Spreading Across U.S.," *Boston Sunday Globe*, December 1, 1996, A1.

46. Anne Branscomb, "Rogue Computer Programs and Computer Rogues: Tailoring Punishment to Fit the Crime," *Rutgers Computer and Technology Law Journal* 16 (1990): 24–26.

47. Heather Jacobson and Rebecca Green, "Computer Crimes," *American Criminal Law Review* 39 (2002): 272–326.

48. CERT® Coordination Center, "Denial of Service Attacks," http://www.cert.org/historical/tech_tips/denial_of_service.cfm (accessed July 2014).

49. United States Department of Justice, *Cyberstalking: A New Challenge for Law Enforcement and Industry: A Report from the Attorney General to the Vice President* (Washington, DC: U.S. Department of Justice, 1999).

50. Janis Wolak, David Finkelhor, Kimberly Mitchell, and Michele Ybarra, "Online Predators and Their Victims: Myths, Realities, and Implications for Prevention and Treatment," *American Psychologist* 63 (2008): 111–128.

51. Jane Ireland and Rachel Monaghan, "Behaviours Indicative of Bullying Among Young and Juvenile Male Offenders: A Study of Perpetrator and Victim Characteristics," *Aggressive Behavior* 32 (2006): 172–180.

52. This section relies heavily on Justin Patchin and Sameer Hinduja, "Bullies Move Beyond the Schoolyard: A Preliminary Look at Cyberbullying," *Youth Violence and Juvenile Justice* 4 (2006): 148–169.

53. Ibid.

54. Barry C. Collin, "The Future of CyberTerrorism: Where the Physical and Virtual Worlds Converge," Institute for Security and Intelligence, 2004, http://www.egov.ufsc.br/portal/sites/default/files/anexos/29436-29454-1-PB.html (accessed July 2014).

55. Mark Pollitt, "Cyberterrorism—Fact or Fancy?" *Computer Fraud and Security* 2 (1998): 8–10.

56. James Lewis, "Assessing the Risks of Cyberterrorism, Cyber War, and Other Cyber Threats," report submitted to the Center for Strategic and International Studies, Washington, DC, 2002, p. 1.

57. Clyde Wilson, "Software Piracy: Uncovering Mutiny on the Cyberseas," *Trial* 32 (1996): 24–31.

58. Deloitte, 2010 TMT Global Security Study http://www.deloitte.com/view/en_HU/hu/industries/tmt/015ddf7ed9b49210VgnVCM100000ba42f00aRCRD.htm (accessed July 2014).

59. Heather Jacobson and Rebecca Green, "Computer Crime," *American Criminal Law Review* 39 (2002): 273–326; Identity Theft and Assumption Act of 1998 (18 U.S.C. S 1028(a)(7)); Bruce Swartz, Deputy Assistant General, Criminal Division, Justice Department, Internet Fraud Testimony Before the House Energy and Commerce Committee, May 23, 2001; Comprehensive Crime Control Act of 1984, PL 98-473, 2101-03, 98 Stat. 1837, 2190 (1984), adding 18 U.S.C. 1030 (1984); Counterfeit Active Device and Computer Fraud and Abuse Act Amended by PL 99-474, 100 Stat. 1213 (1986) Codified at 18 U.S.C. 1030 (Supp. V 1987); Computer Abuse Amendments Act 18 U.S.C. section 1030 (1994); Copyright Infringement Act 17 U.S.C. section 506(a) 1994; Electronic Communications Privacy Act of 198618 U.S.C. 2510–2520 (1988 and Supp. II 1990).

60. The Computer Fraud and Abuse Act (CFAA) 18 U.S.C. section 1030 (1998).

61. The Digital Millennium Copyright Act, Public Law 105-304 (1998).

62. Title 18, United States Code, section 2319.

63. Title 17, United States Code, section 506.

64. Identity Theft and Assumption Deterrence Act, as amended by Public Law 105-318, 112 Stat. 3007 (October 30, 1998).

65. ACLU, "*ACLU v. Reno*, Round 2."

66. PL 98-473, Title H, Chapter XXI, [sections] 2102(a), 98 Stat. 1837, 2190 (1984).

67. See U.S. Department of Justice, "Interagency Working Groups," http://www.justice.gov/criminal/fraud/working-grps/ (accessed July 2014).

68. See U.S. Secret Service, "New York/New Jersey Electronic Crimes Task Force," http://www.secretservice.gov/ectf_newyork.shtml (accessed July 2014).

69. Federal Bureau of Investigation, Internet Crime Complaint Center, *2013 Internet Crime Report* (Washington, DC: Federal Bureau of Investigation, 2013), http://www.ic3.gov/media/annualreport/2013_IC3Report.pdf (accessed July 2014).

70. National Institute of Justice, "Transnational Organized Crime," http://www.nij.gov/topics/crime/organized-crime/ (accessed July 2014).

71. Elizabeth Bernstein, "The Meaning of the Purchase: Desire, Demand, and the Commerce of Sex," *Ethnography* 2 (2001): 389–420.

72. National Institute of Justice, *Major Transnational Organized Crime Groups*, http://www.nij.gov/topics/crime/organized-crime/Pages/major-groups.aspx (accessed July 2014).

73. Ibid.

74. Louise I. Shelley, "Crime and Corruption: Enduring Problems of Post-Soviet Development," *Demokratizatsiya* 11 (2003): 110–114; James O. Finckenauer and Yuri A. Voronin, *The Threat of Russian Organized Crime* (Washington, DC: National Institute of Justice, 2001).

75. Omar Bartos, "Growth of Russian Organized Crime Poses Serious Threat," *CJ International* 11 (1995): 8–9.

76. Immigration and Customs Enforcement, "ICE Takes Down Billion-Dollar Columbian Drug Trafficking Organization," http://www.ice.gov/news/releases/1006/100618eldorado.htm (accessed July 2014).

77. 18 U.S.C. 1952 (1976).

78. Public Law 91-452, Title IX, 84 Stat. 922 (1970) (codified at 18 U.S.C. 1961–68, 1976).

79. Walter Laqueur, *The New Terrorism: Fanaticism and the Arms of Mass Destruction Terrorism and History* (New York: Oxford University Press, 1999).

80. Edmund Burke, *Reflections on the Revolution in France, 1790* (New York: Penguin Classics; reprint edition 1982).

81. Lindsay Clutterbuck, "The Progenitors of Terrorism: Russian Revolutionaries or Extreme Irish Republicans?" *Terrorism and Political Violence* 16 (2004): 154–181.

82. Title 22 of the United States Code section 2656f (d) (1999).

83. Jack Gibbs, "Conceptualization of Terrorism," *American Sociological Review* 54 (1989): 329–340, at 330.

84. Ibid.

85. Stephen J. Morgan, *The Mind of a Terrorist Fundamentalist: The Psychology of Terror Cults* (Awe-Struck E-Books, 2001); Martha Crenshaw, "The Psychology of Terrorism: An Agenda for the 21st Century," *Political Psychology* 21 (2000): 405–420.

86. Andrew Silke, "Courage in Dark Places: Reflections on Terrorist Psychology," *Social Research* 71 (2004): 177–198.

87. Jerrold Post, "When Hatred Is Bred in the Bone: Psycho-Cultural Foundations of Contemporary Terrorism," *Political Psychology* 25 (2005): 615–637.

88. This section leans heavily on Anthony Stahelski, "Terrorists Are Made, Not Born: Creating Terrorists Using Social Psychological Conditioning," *Journal of Homeland Security*, March 2004.

89. Ethan Bueno de Mesquita, "The Quality of Terror," *American Journal of Political Science* 49 (2005): 515–530.

90. Haruki Murakami, *Underground* (New York: Vintage Books, 2001).

91. Sanjeev Gupta, Benedict Clements, Rina Bhattacharya, and Shamit Chakravarti, "Fiscal Consequences of Armed Conflict and Terrorism in Low- and Middle-Income Countries," *European Journal of Political Economy* 20 (2004): 403–421; Andrew Chen and Thomas Siems, "Effects of Terrorism on Global Capital Markets," *European Journal of Political Economy* 20 (2004): 349–356.

92. U.S. Department of State, *State Sponsors of Terrorism*, http://www.state.gov/j/ct/list/c14151.htm (accessed July 2014).

93. Lawrence Miller, "The Terrorist Mind: A Psychological and Political Analysis, Part II," *International Journal of Offender Therapy and Comparative Criminology* 50 (2006): 255–268.

94. Ibid.

95. Chris Dishman, "Terrorism, Crime, and Transformation," *Studies in Conflict and Terrorism* 24 (2001): 43–56.

96. U.S. Justice Department, *Introduction to National Security Division Statistics on Unsealed International Terrorism and Terrorism-Related Convictions*, http://www.fas.org/irp/agency/doj/doj032610-stats.pdf (accessed July 2014).

97. Benjamin Weiser, "Cleric Convicted of All Terrorism Charges," *New York Times*, May 19, 2014, http://www.nytimes.com/2014/05/20/nyregion/british-cleric-is-convicted-in-terror-trial.html (accessed July 2014).

98. Karen McVeigh, "Abu Hamza Found Guilty of 11 Terrorism Charges," *The Guardian*, May 19, 2014, http://www.theguardian.com/world/2014/may/19/abu-hamza-found-guilty-terrorism-charges (accessed July 2014).

99. A more thorough list, from which the following examples are drawn, is available here: http://www.fbi.gov/about-us/investigate/terrorism/terrorism_cases (accessed July 2014).

100. U.S. Justice Department, "Fact Sheet: Justice Department Counter-Terrorism Efforts Since 9/11," http://www.justice.gov/opa/pr/2008/September/08-nsd-807.html (accessed July 2014).

101. Center of Law and Security, New York School of Law, *Terrorist Trial Report Card: September 11, 2001–September 11, 2011*, http://www.lawandsecurity.org/Portals/0/Documents/TTRC%20Ten%20Year%20Issue.pdf (accessed July 2014), p. 7.

102. Richard B. Zabel and James J. Benjamin Jr., *In Pursuit of Justice: Prosecuting Terrorism Cases in the Federal Courts* (Washington, DC: Human Rights First, 2008).

103. Ibid., p. 2.

104. Ibid.

105. *Ex Parte Milligan*, 71 U.S. 2 (1866).

106. *Hamdi v. Rumsfeld*, 542 U.S. 507 (2004).

107. *Rasul v. Bush*, 542 U.S. 466 (2004).

108. *Hamdan v. Rumsfeld*, 548 U.S. 557 (2006).

109. *Boumediene v. Bush*, 553 U.S. 723 (2008).

110. See Section 948c of the Military Commissions Act of 2009, http://www.defense.gov/news/2009%20MCA%20Pub%20%20Law%20111-84.pdf (accessed July 2014).

111. See, for example, James Alan Fox, *Trends in Juvenile Justice: A Report to the United States Attorney General on Current and Future Rates of Juvenile Offending* (Washington, DC: Bureau of Justice Statistics, 2006); James Q. Wilson, "Crime and Public Policy," in *Crime*, ed. James Q. Wilson and Joan Petersilia (San Francisco: ICS Press, 1995), p. 507.

112. Joseph A. Schafer, ed., *Policing 2020: Exploring the Future of Crime, Communities and Policing* (Carbondale, IL: Police Futurists International, 2007).

113. National Institute of Corrections, *Forward Thinking*, http://nicic.gov/forwardthinking (accessed July 2014).

114. T. Peters, N. Kauder, C. Campbell, and C. Flango, *Future Trends in State Courts 2005* (Williamsburg, VA: National Center for State Courts, 2005).

115. Nancy M. Ritter, "Preparing for the Future: Criminal Justice in 2040," *National Institute of Justice Journal* 255 (2006), http://www.nij.gov/journals/255/pages/2040.aspx (accessed July 2014).

116. Ibid.

117. Ibid.

118. The Campbell Collaboration, http://www.campbellcollaboration.org (accessed July 2014).

119. Michael J. Lynch and Paul Stretesky, "Green Criminology in the United States," pp. 248–269 in *Issues in Green Criminology*, Piers Beirne and Nigel South, ed. (Portland, OR: Willan, 2008), p. 249.

120. Michael M. O'Hear, "Sentencing the Green-Collar Offender: Punishment, Culpability, and Environmental Crime," *Journal of Criminal Law and Criminology* 95 (2004): 133–276.

121. Nathan Thornburgh, "Recession May Be Driving Off Illegals," *Time*, June 4, 2008, http://content.time.com/time/nation/article/0,8599,1811660,00.html (accessed July 2014).

122. Randal C. Archibold, "Arizona's Effort to Bolster Local Immigration Authority Divides Law Enforcement," *New York Times*, April 21, 2010, http://www.nytimes.com/2010/04/22/us/22immig.html (accessed July 2014).

123. *Arizona v. United States*, 567 U.S. ___ (2012).

The Constitution of the United States

Preamble

We the People of the United States, in Order to form a more perfect Union, establish Justice, insure domestic Tranquility, provide for the common defence, promote the general Welfare, and secure the Blessings of Liberty to ourselves and our Posterity, do ordain and establish this Constitution for the United States of America.

Article I

SECTION 1 All legislative Powers herein granted shall be vested in a Congress of the United States, which shall consist of a Senate and House of Representatives.

SECTION 2 The House of Representatives shall be composed of Members chosen every second Year by the People of the several States, and the Electors in each State shall have the Qualifications requisite for Electors of the most numerous Branch of the State Legislature.

No Person shall be a Representative who shall not have attained to the Age of twenty five Years, and been seven Years a Citizen of the United States, and who shall not, when elected, be an Inhabitant of that State in which he shall be chosen.

Representatives and direct Taxes shall be apportioned among the several States which may be included within this Union, according to their respective Numbers, which shall be determined by adding to the whole Number of free Persons, including those bound to Service for a Term of Years, and excluding Indians not taxed, three fifths of all other Persons. The actual Enumeration shall be made within three Years after the first Meeting of the Congress of the United States, and within every subsequent Term of ten Years, in such Manner as they shall by Law direct. The Number of Representatives shall not exceed one for every thirty Thousand, but each State shall have at Least one Representative; and until such enumeration shall be made, the State of New Hampshire shall be entitled to choose three, Massachusetts eight, Rhode Island and Providence Plantations one, Connecticut five, New York six, New Jersey four, Pennsylvania eight, Delaware one, Maryland six, Virginia ten, North Carolina five, South Carolina five, and Georgia three.

When vacancies happen in the Representation from any State, the Executive Authority thereof shall issue Writs of Election to fill such Vacancies.

The House of Representatives shall choose their Speaker and other Officers; and shall have the sole Power of Impeachment.

SECTION 3 The Senate of the United States shall be composed of two Senators from each State, chosen by the Legislature thereof, for six Years; and each Senator shall have one Vote.

Immediately after they shall be assembled in Consequence of the first Election, they shall be divided as equally as may be into three Classes. The Seats of the Senators of the first Class shall be vacated at the Expiration of the second Year, of the second Class at the Expiration of the fourth Year, and of the third Class at the Expiration of the sixth Year, so that one third may be chosen every second Year; and if Vacancies happen by Resignation, or otherwise, during the Recess of the Legislature of any State, the Executive thereof may make temporary Appointments until the next Meeting of the Legislature, which shall then fill such Vacancies.

No Person shall be a Senator who shall not have attained to the Age of thirty Years, and been nine Years a Citizen of the United States, and who shall not, when elected, be an Inhabitant of that State for which he shall be chosen.

The Vice-President of the United States shall be President of the Senate, but shall have no Vote, unless they be equally divided.

The Senate shall choose their other Officers, and also a President pro tempore, in the Absence of the Vice-President, or when he shall exercise the Office of President of the United States.

The Senate shall have the sole Power to try all Impeachments. When sitting for that Purpose, they shall be on Oath or Affirmation. When the President of the United States is tried the Chief Justice shall preside: And no Person shall be convicted without the Concurrence of two thirds of the Members present.

Judgment in Cases of Impeachment shall not extend further than to removal from Office, and disqualification to hold and enjoy any Office of honor, Trust or Profit under the United States: but the Party convicted shall nevertheless be liable and subject to Indictment, Trial, Judgment, and Punishment, according to Law.

SECTION 4 The Times, Places and Manner of holding Elections for Senators and Representatives, shall be prescribed in each State by the Legislature thereof; but the Congress may at any time by Law make or alter such Regulations, except as to the Places of choosing Senators.

The Congress shall assemble at least once in every Year, and such Meeting shall be on the first Monday in December, unless they shall by Law appoint a different Day.

SECTION 5 Each House shall be the Judge of the Elections, Returns and Qualifications of its own Members, and a Majority of each shall constitute a Quorum to do Business; but a smaller Number may adjourn from day to day, and may be authorized to compel the Attendance of absent Members, in such Manner, and under such Penalties as each House may provide.

Each House may determine the Rules of its Proceedings, punish its Members for disorderly Behaviour, and, with the Concurrence of two thirds, expel a Member.

Each House shall keep a Journal of its Proceedings, and from time to time publish the same, excepting such Parts as may in their Judgment require Secrecy; and the Yeas and Nays of the Members of either House on any question shall, at the Desire of one fifth of those Present, be entered on the Journal.

Neither House, during the Session of Congress, shall, without the Consent of the other, adjourn for more than three days, nor to any other Place than that in which the two Houses shall be sitting.

SECTION 6 The Senators and Representatives shall receive a Compensation for their Services, to be ascertained by Law, and paid out of the Treasury of the United States. They shall in all Cases, except Treason, Felony and Breach of the Peace, be privileged from Arrest during their Attendance at the Session of their respective Houses, and in going to and returning from the same; and for any Speech or Debate in either House, they shall not be questioned in any other Place.

No Senator or Representative shall, during the Time for which he was elected, be appointed to any civil Office under the Authority of the United States, which shall have been created, or the Emoluments whereof shall have been increased during such time; and no Person holding any Office under the United States, shall be a Member of either House during his Continuance in Office.

SECTION 7 All Bills for raising Revenue shall originate in the House of Representatives; but the Senate may propose or concur with Amendments as on other Bills.

Every Bill which shall have passed the House of Representatives and the Senate, shall, before it become a Law, be presented to the President of the United States; If he approve he shall sign it, but if not he shall return it, with his Objections to that House in which it shall have originated, who shall enter the Objections at large on their Journal, and proceed to reconsider it. If after such Reconsideration two thirds of that House shall agree to pass the Bill, it shall be sent, together with the Objections, to the other House, by which it shall likewise be reconsidered, and if approved by two thirds of that House, it shall become a Law. But in all such Cases the Votes of both Houses shall be determined by Yeas and Nays, and the Names of the Persons voting for and against the Bill shall be entered on the Journal of each House respectively. If any Bill shall not be returned by the President within ten Days (Sundays excepted) after it shall have been presented to him, the Same shall be a Law, in like Manner as if he had signed it, unless the Congress by their Adjournment prevent its Return, in which Case it shall not be a Law.

Every Order, Resolution, or Vote to which the Concurrence of the Senate and House of Representatives may be necessary (except on a question of Adjournment) shall be presented to the President of the United States; and before the Same shall take Effect, shall be approved by him, or being disapproved by him, shall be repassed by two thirds of the Senate and House of Representatives, according to the Rules and Limitations prescribed in the Case of a Bill.

SECTION 8 The Congress shall have Power To lay and collect Taxes, Duties, Imposts and Excises, to pay the Debts and provide for the common Defence and general Welfare of the United States; but all Duties, Imposts and Excises shall be uniform throughout the United States;

To borrow Money on the credit of the United States;

To regulate Commerce with foreign Nations, and among the several States, and with the Indian Tribes;

To establish an uniform Rule of Naturalization, and uniform Laws on the subject of Bankruptcies throughout the United States;

To coin Money, regulate the Value thereof, and of foreign Coin, and fix the Standard of Weights and Measures;

To provide for the Punishment of counterfeiting the Securities and current Coin of the United States;

To establish Post Offices and post Roads;

To promote the Progress of Science and useful Arts, by securing for limited Times to Authors and Inventors the exclusive Right to their respective Writings and Discoveries;

To constitute Tribunals inferior to the supreme Court;

To define and punish Piracies and Felonies committed on the high Seas, and Offences against the Law of Nations;

To declare War, grant Letters of Marque and Reprisal, and make Rules concerning Captures on Land and Water;

To raise and support Armies, but no Appropriation of Money to that Use shall be for a longer Term than two Years;

To provide and maintain a Navy;

To make Rules for the Government and Regulation of the land and naval Forces;

To provide for calling forth the Militia to execute the Laws of the Union, suppress Insurrections and repel Invasions;

To provide for organizing, arming, and disciplining, the Militia, and for governing such Part of them as may be employed in the Service of the United States, reserving to the States respectively, the Appointment of the Officers, and the Authority of training the Militia according to the discipline prescribed by Congress;

To exercise exclusive Legislation in all Cases whatsoever, over such District (not exceeding ten Miles square) as may, by Cession of particular States, and the Acceptance of Congress, become the Seat of the Government of the United States, and to exercise like Authority over all Places purchased by the Consent of the Legislature of the State in which the Same shall be, for the Erection of Forts, Magazines, Arsenals, dock-Yards, and other needful Buildings;—And

To make all Laws which shall be necessary and proper for carrying into Execution the foregoing Powers, and all other Powers vested by this Constitution in the Government of the United States, or in any Department or Officer thereof.

SECTION 9 The Migration or Importation of such Persons as any of the States now existing shall think proper to admit, shall not be prohibited by the Congress prior to the Year one thousand eight hundred and eight, but a Tax or duty may be imposed on such Importation, not exceeding ten dollars for each Person.

The privilege of the Writ of Habeas Corpus shall not be suspended, unless when in Cases of Rebellion or Invasion the public Safety may require it.

No Bill of Attainder or ex post facto Law shall be passed.

No Capitation, or other direct, Tax shall be laid, unless in Proportion to the Census or Enumeration herein before directed to be taken.

No Tax or Duty shall be laid on Articles exported from any State.

No Preference shall be given by any Regulation of Commerce or Revenue to the Ports of one State over those of another: nor shall Vessels bound to, or from, one State be obliged to enter, clear, or pay Duties in another.

No Money shall be drawn from the Treasury, but in Consequence of Appropriations made by Law; and

a regular Statement and Account of the Receipts and Expenditures of all public Money shall be published from time to time.

No Title of Nobility shall be granted by the United States: And no Person holding any Office of Profit or Trust under them, shall, without the Consent of the Congress, accept of any present, Emolument, Office, or Title, of any kind whatever, from any King, Prince, or foreign State.

SECTION 10 No State shall enter into any Treaty, Alliance, or Confederation; grant Letters of Marque and Reprisal; coin Money; emit Bills of Credit; make any Thing but gold and silver Coin a Tender in Payment of Debts; pass any Bill of Attainder, ex post facto Law, or Law impairing the Obligation of Contracts, or grant any Title of Nobility.

No State shall, without the Consent of the Congress, lay any Imposts or Duties on Imports or Exports, except what may be absolutely necessary for executing its inspection Laws: and the net Produce of all Duties and Imposts, laid by any State on Imports or Exports, shall be for the Use of the Treasury of the United States; and all such Laws shall be subject to the Revision and Control of the Congress.

No State shall, without the Consent of Congress, lay any Duty of Tonnage, keep Troops, or Ships of War in time of Peace, enter into any Agreement or Compact with another State, or with a foreign Power, or engage in War, unless actually invaded, or in such imminent Danger as will not admit of delay.

Article II

SECTION 1 The executive Power shall be vested in a President of the United States of America. He shall hold his Office during the Term of four Years, and, together with the Vice-President, chosen for the same Term, be elected, as follows:

Each State shall appoint, in such Manner as the Legislature thereof may direct, a Number of Electors, equal to the whole Number of Senators and Representatives to which the State may be entitled in the Congress; but no Senator or Representative, or Person holding an Office of Trust or Profit under the United States, shall be appointed an Elector.

The Electors shall meet in their respective States, and vote by Ballot for two Persons, of whom one at least shall not be an Inhabitant of the same State with themselves. And they shall make a List of all the Persons voted for, and of the Number of Votes for each; which List they shall sign and certify, and transmit sealed to the Seat of Government of the United States, directed to the President of the Senate. The President of the Senate shall, in the Presence of the Senate and House of Representatives, open all the Certificates, and the Votes shall then be counted. The Person having the greatest Number of Votes shall be the President, if such Number be a Majority of the whole Number of Electors appointed; and if there be more than one who have such Majority, and have an equal Number of Votes, then the House of Representatives shall immediately choose by Ballot one of them for President; and if no Person have a Majority, then from the five highest on the List the said House shall in like Manner choose the President. But in choosing the President, the Votes shall be taken by States, the Representation from each State having one Vote; A quorum for this Purpose shall consist of a Member or Members from two thirds of the States, and a Majority of all the States shall be necessary to a Choice. In every Case, after the Choice of the President, the Person having the greatest Number of Votes of the Electors shall be the Vice-President. But if there should remain two or more who have equal Votes, the Senate shall choose from them by Ballot the Vice-President.

The Congress may determine the Time of choosing the Electors, and the Day on which they shall give their Votes; which Day shall be the same throughout the United States.

No Person except a natural born Citizen, or a Citizen of the United States, at the time of the Adoption of this Constitution, shall be eligible to the Office of President; neither shall any Person be eligible to that Office who shall not have attained to the Age of thirty five Years, and been fourteen Years a Resident within the United States.

In Case of the Removal of the President from Office, or of his Death, Resignation, or Inability to discharge the Powers and Duties of the said Office, the same shall devolve on the Vice-President, and the Congress may by Law provide for the Case of Removal, Death, Resignation or Inability, both of the President and Vice-President declaring what Officer shall then act as President, and such Officer shall act accordingly, until the Disability be removed, or a President shall be elected.

The President shall, at stated Times, receive for his Services, a Compensation, which shall neither be increased nor diminished during the Period for which he shall have been elected, and he shall not receive within that Period any other Emolument from the United States, or any of them.

Before he enter on the Execution of his Office, he shall take the following Oath or Affirmation: "I do solemnly swear (or affirm) that I will faithfully execute the Office of President of the United States, and will to the best of my Ability, preserve, protect and defend the Constitution of the United States."

SECTION 2 The President shall be Commander in Chief of the Army and Navy of the United States, and of the Militia of the several States, when called into the actual Service of the United States; he may require the Opinion, in writing, of the principal Officer in each of the executive Departments, upon any Subject relating to the Duties of their respective Offices, and he shall have Power to grant Reprieves and Pardons for Offenses against the United States, except in Cases of Impeachment.

He shall have Power, by and with the Advice and Consent of the Senate, to make Treaties, provided two thirds of the Senators present concur; and he shall nominate, and by and with the Advice and Consent of the Senate, shall appoint Ambassadors, other public Ministers and Consuls, Judges of the supreme Court, and all other Officers of the United States, whose Appointments are not herein otherwise provided for, and which shall be established by Law; but the Congress may by Law vest the Appointment of such inferior Officers, as they think proper, in the President alone, in the Courts of Law, or in the Heads of Departments.

The President shall have Power to fill up all Vacancies that may happen during the Recess of the Senate, by granting Commissions which shall expire at the End of their next Session.

SECTION 3 He shall from time to time give to the Congress Information of the State of the Union, and recommend to their Consideration such Measures as he shall judge necessary and expedient; he may, on extraordinary Occasions, convene both Houses, or either of them, and in Case of Disagreement between them, with Respect to the Time of Adjournment, he may adjourn them to such Time as he shall think proper; he shall receive Ambassadors and other public Ministers; he shall take Care that the Laws be faithfully executed, and shall Commission all the Officers of the United States.

SECTION 4 The President, Vice-President and all civil Officers of the United States, shall be removed from Office on Impeachment for, and Conviction of, Treason, Bribery, or other high Crimes and Misdemeanors.

Article III

SECTION 1 The judicial Power of the United States, shall be vested in one supreme Court, and in such inferior Courts as the Congress may from time to time ordain and establish. The Judges, both of the supreme and inferior Courts, shall hold their Offices during good Behaviour, and shall, at stated Times, receive for their Services a Compensation which shall not be diminished during their Continuance in Office.

SECTION 2 The judicial Power shall extend to all Cases, in Law and Equity, arising under this

Constitution, the Laws of the United States, and Treaties made, or which shall be made, under their Authority;—to all Cases affecting Ambassadors, other public Ministers and Consuls;—to all Cases of admiralty and maritime Jurisdiction;—to Controversies to which the United States shall be a Party;—to Controversies between two or more States;—between a State and Citizens of another State;—between Citizens of different States;—between Citizens of the same State claiming Lands under Grants of different States, and between a State, or the Citizens thereof, and foreign States, Citizens or Subjects.

In all Cases affecting Ambassadors, other public Ministers and Consuls, and those in which a State shall be Party, the supreme Court shall have original Jurisdiction. In all the other Cases before mentioned, the supreme Court shall have appellate Jurisdiction, both as to Law and Fact, with such Exceptions, and under such Regulations as the Congress shall make.

The Trial of all Crimes, except in Cases of Impeachment, shall be by Jury; and such Trial shall be held in the State where the said Crimes shall have been committed; but when not committed within any State, the Trial shall be at such Place or Places as the Congress may by Law have directed.

SECTION 3 Treason against the United States shall consist only in levying War against them, or in adhering to their Enemies, giving them Aid and Comfort. No Person shall be convicted of Treason unless on the Testimony of two Witnesses to the same overt Act, or on Confession in open Court.

The Congress shall have Power to declare the Punishment of Treason, but no Attainder of Treason shall work Corruption of Blood, or Forfeiture except during the Life of the Person attainted.

Article IV

SECTION 1 Full Faith and Credit shall be given in each State to the public Acts, Records, and judicial Proceedings of every other State. And the Congress may by general Laws prescribe the Manner in which such Acts, Records and Proceedings shall be proved, and the Effect thereof.

SECTION 2 The Citizens of each State shall be entitled to all Privileges and Immunities of Citizens in the several States.

A Person charged in any State with Treason, Felony, or other Crime, who shall flee from Justice, and be found in another State, shall on Demand of the executive Authority of the State from which he fled, be delivered up, to be removed to the State having Jurisdiction of the Crime.

No Person held to Service or Labour in one State, under the Laws thereof, escaping into another, shall, in Consequence of any Law or Regulation therein, be discharged from such Service or Labour, but shall be delivered up on Claim of the Party to whom such Service or Labour may be due.

SECTION 3 New States may be admitted by the Congress into this Union; but no new State shall be formed or erected within the Jurisdiction of any other State; nor any State be formed by the Junction of two or more States, or Parts of States, without the Consent of the Legislatures of the States concerned as well as of the Congress.

The Congress shall have Power to dispose of and make all needful Rules and Regulations respecting the Territory or other Property belonging to the United States; and nothing in this Constitution shall be so construed as to Prejudice any Claims of the United States, or of any particular State.

SECTION 4 The United States shall guarantee to every State in this Union a Republican Form of Government, and shall protect each of them against Invasion; and on Application of the Legislature, or of the Executive (when the Legislature cannot be convened) against domestic Violence.

Article V

The Congress, whenever two thirds of both Houses shall deem it necessary, shall propose Amendments to this Constitution, or, on the Application of the Legislatures of two thirds of the several States, shall call a Convention for proposing Amendments, which, in either Case, shall be valid to all Intents and Purposes, as Part of this Constitution, when ratified by the Legislatures of three fourths of the several States, or by Conventions in three fourths thereof, as the one or the other Mode of Ratification may be proposed by the Congress; Provided that no Amendment which may be made prior to the Year One thousand eight hundred and eight shall in any Manner affect the first and fourth Clauses in the Ninth SECTION of the first Article; and that no State, without its Consent, shall be deprived of its equal Suffrage in the Senate.

Article VI

All Debts contracted and Engagements entered into, before the Adoption of this Constitution, shall be as valid against the United States under this Constitution, as under the Confederation.

This Constitution, and the Laws of the United States which shall be made in Pursuance thereof; and all Treaties made, or which shall be made, under the Authority of the United States, shall be the supreme Law of the Land; and the Judges in every State shall be bound thereby, any Thing in the Constitution or Laws of any State to the Contrary notwithstanding.

The Senators and Representatives before mentioned, and the Members of the several State Legislatures, and all executive and judicial Officers, both of the United States and of the several States, shall be bound by Oath or Affirmation, to support this Constitution; but no religious Test shall ever be required as a Qualification to any Office or public Trust under the United States.

Article VII

The Ratification of the Conventions of nine States shall be sufficient for the Establishment of this Constitution between the States so ratifying the Same.

Done in Convention by the Unanimous Consent of the States present the Seventeenth Day of September in the Year of our Lord one thousand seven hundred and Eighty seven and of the Independence of the United States of America the Twelfth IN WITNESS whereof We have hereunto subscribed our Names,

Amendment 1 [1791]

Congress shall make no law respecting an establishment of religion, or prohibiting the free exercise thereof; or abridging the freedom of speech, or of the press; or the right of the people peaceably to assemble, and to petition the Government for a redress of grievances.

Amendment 2 [1791]

A well regulated Militia, being necessary to the security of a free State, the right of the people to keep and bear Arms, shall not be infringed.

Amendment 3 [1791]

No Soldier shall, in time of peace be quartered in any house, without the consent of the Owner, nor in time of war, but in a manner to be prescribed by law.

Amendment 4 [1791]

The right of the people to be secure in their persons, houses, papers, and effects, against unreasonable searches and seizures, shall not be violated, and no Warrants shall issue, but upon probable cause, supported by Oath or affirmation, and particularly describing the place to be searched, and the persons or things to be seized.

Amendment 5 [1791]

No person shall be held to answer for a capital, or otherwise infamous crime, unless on a presentment or indictment of a Grand Jury, except in cases arising in the land or naval forces, or in the Militia, when in actual service in time of War or public danger; nor shall any person be subject for the same offence to be twice put in jeopardy of life or limb; nor shall be compelled in any criminal case to be a witness against himself, nor be deprived of life, liberty, or property, without due process of law; nor shall private property be taken for public use, without just compensation.

Amendment 6 [1791]

In all criminal prosecutions, the accused shall enjoy the right to a speedy and public trial, by an impartial jury of the State and district wherein the crime shall have been committed, which district shall have been previously ascertained by law, and to be informed of the nature and cause of the accusation; to be confronted with the witnesses against him; to have compulsory process for obtaining witnesses in his favor, and to have the Assistance of Counsel for his defence.

Amendment 7 [1791]

In Suits at common law, where the value in controversy shall exceed twenty dollars, the right of trial by jury shall be preserved, and no fact tried by a jury, shall be otherwise re-examined in any Court of the United States, than according to the rules of the common law.

Amendment 8 [1791]

Excessive bail shall not be required, nor excessive fines imposed, nor cruel and unusual punishments inflicted.

Amendment 9 [1791]

The enumeration in the Constitution, of certain rights, shall not be construed to deny or disparage others retained by the people.

Amendment 10 [1791]

The powers not delegated to the United States by the Constitution, nor prohibited by it to the States, are reserved to the States respectively, or to the people.

Amendment 11 [Jan. 8, 1798]

The Judicial power of the United States shall not be construed to extend to any suit in law or equity, commenced or prosecuted against one of the United States by Citizens of another State, or by Citizens or Subjects of any Foreign State.

Amendment 12 [Sept. 25, 1804]

The Electors shall meet in their respective states, and vote by ballot for President and Vice-President, one of whom, at least, shall not be an inhabitant of the same state with themselves; they shall name in their ballots the person voted for as President, and in distinct ballots the person voted for as Vice-President, and they shall make distinct lists of all persons voted for as President, and of all persons voted for as Vice-President, and of the number of votes for each, which list they shall sign and certify, and transmit sealed to the seat of the government of the United States, directed to the President of the Senate;—The President of the Senate shall, in the presence of the Senate and House of Representatives, open all the certificates and the votes shall then be counted;—The person having the greatest number of votes for President, shall be the President, if such number be a majority of the whole number of Electors appointed; and if no person have such majority, then from the persons having the highest numbers not exceeding three on the list of those voted for as President, the House of Representatives shall choose immediately, by ballot, the President. But in choosing the President, the votes shall be taken by states, the representation from each state having one vote; a quorum for this purpose shall consist of a member or members from two-thirds of the states, and a majority of all the states shall be necessary to a choice. And if the House of Representatives shall not choose a President whenever the right of choice shall devolve upon them, before the fourth day of March next following, then the Vice-President shall act as President, as in the case of the death or other constitutional disability of the President.—The person having the greatest number of votes as Vice-President, shall be the Vice-President, if such number be a majority of the whole number of Electors appointed, and if no person have a majority, then from the two highest numbers on the list, the Senate shall choose the Vice-President; a quorum for the purpose shall consist of two-thirds of the whole number of Senators, and a majority of the whole number shall be necessary to a choice. But no person constitutionally ineligible to the office of President shall be eligible to that of Vice-President of the United States.

Amendment 13 [Dec. 18, 1865]

SECTION 1 Neither slavery nor involuntary servitude, except as a punishment for crime whereof the party shall have been duly convicted, shall exist within the United States, or any place subject to their jurisdiction.

SECTION 2 Congress shall have power to enforce this article by appropriate legislation.

Amendment 14 [July 28, 1868]

SECTION 1 All persons born or naturalized in the United States, and subject to the jurisdiction thereof, are citizens of the United States and of the State wherein they reside. No State shall make or enforce any law which shall abridge the privileges or immunities of citizens of the United States; nor shall any State deprive any person of life, liberty, or property, without due process of law; nor deny to any person within its jurisdiction the equal protection of the laws.

SECTION 2 Representatives shall be apportioned among the several States according to their respective numbers, counting the whole number of persons in each State, excluding Indians not taxed. But when the right to vote at any election for the choice of electors for President and Vice-President of the United States, Representatives in Congress, the Executive and Judicial officers of a State, or the members of the Legislature thereof, is denied to any of the male inhabitants of such State, being twenty-one years of age, and citizens of the United States, or in any way abridged, except for participation in rebellion, or other crime, the basis of representation therein shall be reduced in the proportion which the number of such male citizens shall bear to the whole number of male citizens twenty-one years of age in such State.

SECTION 3 No person shall be a Senator or Representative in Congress, or elector of President and Vice-President, or hold any office, civil or military, under the United States, or under any State, who, having previously taken an oath, as a member of Congress, or as an officer of the United States, or as a member of any State legislature, or as an executive or judicial officer of any State, to support the Constitution of the United States, shall have engaged in insurrection or rebellion against the same, or given aid or comfort to the enemies thereof. But Congress may by a vote of two-thirds of each House, remove such disability.

SECTION 4 The validity of the public debt of the United States, authorized by law, including debts incurred for payment of pensions and bounties for services in suppressing insurrection or rebellion, shall not be questioned. But neither the United States nor any State shall assume or pay any debt or obligation incurred in aid of insurrection or rebellion against the United States, or any claim for the loss or emancipation of any slave; but all such debts, obligations and claims shall be held illegal and void.

SECTION 5 The Congress shall have power to enforce, by appropriate legislation, the provisions of this article.

Amendment 15 [March 30, 1870]

SECTION 1 The right of citizens of the United States to vote shall not be denied or abridged by the United States or by any State on account of race, color, or previous condition of servitude.

SECTION 2 The Congress shall have power to enforce this article by appropriate legislation.

Amendment 16 [Feb. 25, 1913]

The Congress shall have power to lay and collect taxes on incomes, from whatever source derived, without apportionment among the several States, and without regard to any census or enumeration.

Amendment 17 [May 31, 1913]

SECTION 1 The Senate of the United States shall be composed of two Senators from each State, elected by the people thereof, for six years; and each Senator shall have one vote. The electors in each State shall have the qualifications requisite for electors of the most numerous branch of the State legislatures.

SECTION 2 When vacancies happen in the representation of any State in the Senate, the executive authority of such State shall issue writs of election to fill such vacancies: Provided, that the legislature of any State may empower the executive thereof to make temporary appointments until the people fill the vacancies by election as the legislature may direct.

SECTION 3 This amendment shall not be so construed as to affect the election or term of any Senator chosen before it becomes valid as part of the Constitution.

Amendment 18 [Jan. 29, 1919; repealed Dec. 5, 1933]

SECTION 1 After one year from the ratification of this article the manufacture, sale, or transportation of intoxicating liquors within, the importation thereof into, or the exportation thereof from the United States and all territory subject to the jurisdiction thereof for beverage purposes is hereby prohibited.

SECTION 2 Congress and the several States shall have concurrent power to enforce this article by appropriate legislation.

SECTION 3 This article shall be inoperative unless it shall have been ratified as an amendment to the Constitution by the legislatures of the several States, as provided in the Constitution, within seven years from the date of the submission hereof to the States by the Congress.

Amendment 19 [Aug. 26, 1920]

SECTION 1 The right of citizens of the United States to vote shall not be denied or abridged by the United States or by any State on account of sex.

SECTION 2 Congress shall have power to enforce this article by appropriate legislation.

Amendment 20 [Feb. 6, 1933]

SECTION 1 The terms of the President and Vice-President shall end at noon on the 20th day of January, and the terms of Senators and Representatives at noon on the third day of January, of the years in which such terms would have ended if this article had not been ratified; and the terms of their successors shall then begin.

SECTION 2 The Congress shall assemble at least once in every year, and such meeting shall begin at noon on the third day of January, unless they shall by law appoint a different day.

SECTION 3 If, at the time fixed for the beginning of the term of the President, the President elect shall have died, the Vice-President elect shall become President. If a President shall not have been chosen before the time fixed for the beginning of his term, or if the President elect shall have failed to qualify, then the Vice-President elect shall act as President until a President shall have qualified; and the Congress may by law provide for the case wherein neither a President elect nor a Vice-President elect shall have qualified, declaring who shall then act as President, or the manner in which one who is to act shall be selected, and such person shall act accordingly until a President or Vice-President shall have qualified.

SECTION 4 The Congress may by law provide for the case of the death of any of the persons from whom the House of Representatives may choose a President whenever the right of choice shall have devolved upon them, and for the case of the death of any of the persons from whom the Senate may choose a Vice-President whenever the right of choice shall have devolved upon them.

SECTION 5 Sections 1 and 2 shall take effect on the 15th day of October following the ratification of this article.

SECTION 6 This article shall be inoperative unless it shall have been ratified as an amendment to the Constitution by the legislatures of three-fourths of the several States within seven years from the date of its submission.

Amendment 21 [Dec. 5, 1933]

SECTION 1 The eighteenth article of amendment to the Constitution of the United States is hereby repealed.

SECTION 2 The transportation or importation into any State, Territory, or possession of the United States for delivery or use therein of intoxicating liquors, in violation of the laws thereof, is hereby prohibited.

SECTION 3 This article shall be inoperative unless it shall have been ratified as an amendment to the Constitution by conventions in the several States, as provided in the Constitution, within seven years from the date of the submission hereof to the States by the Congress.

Amendment 22 [March 1, 1951]

SECTION 1 No person shall be elected to the office of the President more than twice, and no person who has held the office of President, or acted as President, for more than two years of a term to which some other person was elected President shall be elected to the office of the President more than once. But this Article shall not apply to any person holding the office of President when this Article was proposed by the Congress, and shall not prevent any person who may be holding the office of President, or acting as President, during the term within which this Article becomes operative from holding the office of President or acting as President during the remainder of such term.

SECTION 2 This article shall be inoperative unless it shall have been ratified as an amendment to the Constitution by the legislatures of three-fourths of the several States within seven years from the date of its submission to the States by the Congress.

Amendment 23 [April 3, 1961]

SECTION 1 The District constituting the seat of Government of the United States shall appoint in such manner as the Congress may direct:

A number of electors of President and Vice-President equal to the whole number of Senators and Representatives in Congress to which the District would be entitled if it were a State, but in no event

more than the least populous State; they shall be in addition to those appointed by the States, but they shall be considered, for the purposes of the election of President and Vice-President, to be electors appointed by a State; and they shall meet in the District and perform such duties as provided by the twelfth article of amendment.

SECTION 2 The Congress shall have power to enforce this article by appropriate legislation.

Amendment 24 [Feb. 4, 1964]

SECTION 1 The right of citizens of the United States to vote in any primary or other election for President or Vice-President, for electors for President or Vice-President, or for Senator or Representative in Congress, shall not be denied or abridged by the United States or any State by reason of failure to pay any poll tax or other tax.

SECTION 2 The Congress shall have power to enforce this article by appropriate legislation.

Amendment 25 [Feb. 10, 1967]

SECTION 1 In case of the removal of the President from office or his death or resignation, the Vice-President shall become President.

SECTION 2 Whenever there is a vacancy in the office of the Vice-President, the President shall nominate a Vice-President who shall take the office upon confirmation by a majority vote of both houses of Congress.

SECTION 3 Whenever the President transmits to the President pro tempore of the Senate and the Speaker of the House of Representatives his written declaration that he is unable to discharge the powers and duties of his office, and until he transmits to them a written declaration to the contrary, such powers and duties shall be discharged by the Vice-President as Acting President.

SECTION 4 Whenever the Vice-President and a majority of either the principal officers of the executive departments, or of such other body as Congress may by law provide, transmit to the President pro tempore of the Senate and the Speaker of the House of Representatives their written declaration that the President is unable to discharge the powers and duties of his office, the Vice-President shall immediately assume the powers and duties of the office as Acting President.

Thereafter, when the President transmits to the President pro tempore of the Senate and the Speaker of the House of Representatives his written declaration that no inability exists, he shall resume the powers and duties of his office unless the Vice-President and a majority of either the principal officers of the executive department, or of such other body as Congress may by law provide, transmit within four days to the President pro tempore of the Senate and the Speaker of the House of Representatives their written declaration that the President is unable to discharge the powers and duties of his office. Thereupon Congress shall decide the issue, assembling within forty-eight hours for that purpose if not in session. If the Congress, within twenty-one days after receipt of the latter written declaration, or, if Congress is not in session, within twenty-one days after Congress is required to assemble, determines by two-thirds vote of both Houses that the President is unable to discharge the powers and duties of his office, the Vice-President shall continue to discharge the same as Acting President; otherwise, the President shall resume the powers and duties of his office.

Amendment 26 [June 30, 1971]

SECTION 1 The right of citizens of the United States, who are eighteen years of age or older, to vote shall not be denied or abridged by the United States or any state on account of age.

SECTION 2 The Congress shall have power to enforce this article by appropriate legislation.

Amendment 27 [May 7, 1992]

No law, varying the compensation for the services of Senators and Representatives, shall take effect until an election of Representatives shall have intervened.

GLOSSARY

accountability system A system that makes police supervisors responsible for the behavior of the officers in their command.

actus reus An illegal act, or failure to act when legally required.

adjudication The determination of guilt or innocence—a judgment concerning criminal charges.

adolescent-limited offenders Kids who get into minor scrapes as youths but whose misbehavior ends when they enter adulthood.

alternative dispute resolution A means of settling disputes outside the courtroom.

anger management Programs designed to help people who have become dependent on anger as a primary means of expressing themselves and those who inappropriately use anger or the threat of violence to get their way.

anomie The absence or weakness of rules, norms, or guidelines on what is socially or morally acceptable.

antisocial personality A personality characterized by a lack of warmth and feeling, inappropriate behavioral responses, and an inability to learn from experience (also called sociopath or psychopath).

appeal A request for an appellate court to examine a lower court's decision in order to determine whether proper procedures were followed.

appellate court A court to which appeals are made on points of law resulting from the judgment of a lower court; the appellate court may be asked to evaluate the impact of new evidence but more typically decides whether the state or federal constitution was improperly interpreted during a case.

arbitration A process of dispute resolution in which a neutral third party (arbitrator) renders a decision after a hearing at which both parties agree to be heard.

arraignment Initial trial court appearance, at which the accused is read the charges, advised of his or her rights, and asked to enter a plea.

arrest Occurs when a police officer takes a person into custody or deprives a person of freedom for having allegedly committed a criminal offense.

arrest warrant An order, issued by a judge, directing officers to arrest a particular individual.

assigned counsel A private attorney appointed by the court to represent a criminal defendant who cannot afford to pay for a lawyer.

attorney general The chief legal officer and prosecutor of each state and of the United States.

Auburn system A prison system, developed in New York during the nineteenth century, based on congregate (group) work during the day and separation at night.

avertable recidivist A person whose crime would have been prevented if he or she had not been given discretionary release and instead had been kept behind bars.

bail The monetary amount required for pretrial release, normally set by a judge at the initial appearance. The purpose of bail is to ensure the return of the accused at subsequent proceedings.

beats Designated police patrol areas.

bench trial The trial of a criminal matter by a judge only. The accused waives any constitutional right to a jury trial.

biometrics Automated methods of recognizing a person based on a physiological or behavioral characteristic.

blue curtain The secretive, insulated police culture that isolates officers from the rest of society.

booking The administrative record of an arrest, listing the offender's name, address, physical description, date of birth, employer, time of arrest, offense, and name of arresting officer; it also includes photographing and fingerprinting of the offender.

boot camp A short-term, militaristic correction facility in which inmates undergo intensive physical conditioning and discipline.

broken windows model The role of the police as maintainers of community order and safety.

brutalization effect The belief that capital punishment creates an atmosphere of brutality that enhances, rather than reduces, the level of violence in society. The death penalty reinforces the view that violence is an appropriate response to provocation.

bus sweep Police investigation technique in which officers board a bus or train without suspicion of illegal activity and question passengers, asking for identification and seeking permission to search their baggage.

career criminals Persistent repeat offenders who organize their lifestyle around criminality.

challenge for cause Dismissal of a prospective juror by either the prosecution or the defense because he or she is biased, because he or she has prior knowledge about a case, or for other reasons that demonstrate the individual's inability to render a fair and impartial judgment.

chancery courts Early English courts established to protect the property rights and welfare of the minor children of affluent families.

Children's Aid Society A group created by Charles Loring Brace to place indigent city children with farm families.

child savers Civic leaders who focused their attention on the misdeeds of poor children to control their behavior.

chivalry hypothesis The view that the low rates of crime and delinquency among females reflect the leniency with which female offenders are treated.

chronic offenders As defined by Marvin Wolfgang, Robert Figlio, and Thorsten Sellin, delinquents arrested five or more times before the age of 18, who commit a disproportionate amount of all criminal offenses.

civil law All law that is not criminal, including tort, contract, personal property, maritime, and commercial law.

cleared An offense is cleared by arrest or solved when at least one person is arrested or charged with the commission of the offense and is turned over to the court for prosecution

collective efficacy A condition of mutual trust and cooperation that develops in neighborhoods that have a high level of formal and informal social control.

commitment Decision of a judge who orders an adjudicated and sentenced juvenile offender to be placed in a correctional facility.

community-oriented policing Programs designed to bring police and public closer together and create a more cooperative environment between them.

community policing A law enforcement program that seeks to integrate officers into the local community to reduce crime and gain good community relations. It typically involves personalized service and decentralized policing, citizen empowerment, and an effort to reduce community fear of crime, disorder, and decay.

community prosecution A prosecutorial philosophy that emphasizes community support and cooperation with other agencies in preventing crime, as well as a less centralized and more proactive role for local prosecutors.

community service restitution An alternative sanction that requires an offender to work in the community at such tasks as cleaning public parks or working with disabled children in lieu of an incarceration sentence.

community treatment The attempt by correctional agencies to maintain convicted offenders in the community rather than in a secure facility; it includes probation, parole, and residential programs.

complaint A sworn written statement addressed to a court or judge by the police, prosecutor, or individual alleging that an individual has committed an offense and requesting indictment and prosecution.

compulsory process Compelling the production of a witness or evidence via a subpoena

concurrent sentences Prison sentences for two or more criminal acts, served simultaneously and run together.

conflict view of crime The view that criminal law is created and enforced by those who hold political and economic power and is a tool used by the ruling class to control dissatisfied have-not members of society.

confrontation clause The constitutional right of a criminal defendant to see and cross-examine all the witnesses against him or her.

congregate system A prison system, originated in New York, in which inmates worked and ate together during the day and then slept in solitary cells at night.

consecutive sentences Prison sentences for two or more criminal acts, served one after the other.

consensus view of crime The view that the great majority of citizens agree that certain behaviors must be outlawed or controlled, and that criminal law is designed to protect citizens from social harm.

constable In early English towns, an appointed peacekeeper who organized citizens for protection and supervised the night watch.

contract system (labor) A prison industry system, widely employed until after the Civil War, in which officials sold the labor of prison inmates to private businesses, for use either inside or outside the prison.

contract system (legal services) Provision of legal services to indigent defendants by private attorneys under contract to the state or county.

convict-lease system A contract system in which a private business leased prisoners from the state for a fixed annual fee and assumed full responsibility for their supervision and control.

corporate crime Crime committed by a corporation, or by individuals who control the corporation or other business entity, for such purposes as illegally increasing market share, avoiding taxes, or thwarting competition.

corporate enterprise crime Illegal activities of people and organizations whose acknowledged purpose is to profit through illegitimate business enterprise.

corruption Exercising legitimate discretion for improper reasons or using illegal means to achieve approved goals.

court of general jurisdiction A state or federal court that has jurisdiction over felony offenses—serious crimes that carry a penalty of incarceration in a state or federal prison for one year or more.

court of last resort A court that handles the final appeal on a matter—in the federal system, the U.S. Supreme Court.

court of limited jurisdiction A court that has jurisdiction over misdemeanors and conducts preliminary investigations of felony charges.

courtroom work group A term used to imply that all parties in the justice process work together in a cooperative effort to settle cases efficiently rather than to engage in a true adversarial procedure.

crime A violation of social rules of conduct, interpreted and expressed by a written criminal code, created by people holding social and political power. Its content may be influenced by prevailing public sentiments, historically developed moral beliefs, and the need to protect public safety.

crime control perspective A model of criminal justice that emphasizes the control of dangerous offenders and the protection of society through harsh punishment as a deterrent to crime.

criminal justice system The system of law enforcement, adjudication, and correction that is directly involved in the apprehension, prosecution, and control of those charged with criminal offenses.

criminal law The body of rules that define crimes, set out their punishments, and mandate the procedures for carrying out the criminal justice process.

criminal negligence Liability that can occur when a person's careless and inattentive actions cause harm.

criminal propensity A natural inclination toward criminality, present at birth or soon after.

criminologists Social scientists who use the scientific method to study the nature, extent, cause, and control of criminal behavior.

critical criminology The view that crime results because the rich and powerful impose their own moral standards and economic interests on the rest of society.

cross-examination The questioning of a prosecution witness by the defense, or of a defense witness by the prosecution.

cruel and unusual punishment
Physical punishment or punishment that far exceeds that given to people under similar circumstances and is therefore banned by the Eighth Amendment. The death penalty has so far not been considered cruel and unusual if it is administered in a fair and nondiscriminatory fashion.

culture of poverty The view that people in the lower class of society form a separate culture with its own values and norms that are in conflict with those of conventional society.

curtilage Grounds or fields attached to a house.

cyberbullying Willful and repeated harm done through the medium of electronic text.

cybercrime Illegal activity that uses a computer as its primary means of commission. Common forms of cybercrime include theft and destruction of information, resources, and funds.

cyberstalking Using the Internet, e-mail, or other electronic communications devices to stalk or harass another person.

cybertheft The use of computer networks for criminal profits. Copyright infringement, identity theft, and Internet securities fraud are examples of cybertheft.

cybervandalism Malicious attacks aimed at disrupting, defacing, and destroying technology.

cyberwarfare Politically motivated attacks designed to compromise the electronic infrastructure of an enemy nation and disrupt its economy.

cynicism The belief that most people's actions are motivated solely by personal needs and selfishness.

data mining Using sophisticated computer software to conduct analysis of behavior patterns in an effort to identify crime patterns and link them to suspects.

day fees A program requiring probationers to pay in part for the costs of their treatment.

day fine A fine geared to the average daily income of the convicted offender in an effort to bring equity to the sentencing process.

day reporting center (DRC) A nonresidential community-based treatment program.

deadly force The intentional use of a firearm or other instrument, resulting in a high probability of death.

decriminalization Reducing the penalty for a criminal act without legalizing it.

defense attorney Legal counsel for the defendant in a criminal case, representing the accused person from arrest to final appeal.

deinstitutionalization The policy of removing from secure confinement as many first offenders of minor, nonviolent crimes as possible and treating them in the community.

demeanor The way a person outwardly manifests his or her personality.

denial-of-service attack Malicious attempts to prevent access by legitimate network traffic, disrupt connections within a computer network, or disrupt service to a specific system or person.

detention The temporary care of a child alleged to be a delinquent or status offender who requires secure custody, pending court disposition.

determinate sentence A fixed term of incarceration, such as three years' imprisonment. Determinate sentences are felt by many to be too restrictive for rehabilitative purposes; the advantage is that offenders know how much time they have to serve—that is, when they will be released.

deterrent effect The assumed ability of the threat of criminal sanctions to discourage crime before it occurs.

developmental theories A view of crime holding that as people travel through the life course, their experiences along the way influence their behavior patterns. Behavior changes at each stage of the human experience.

differential association theory The view that criminal acts are related to a person's exposure to antisocial attitudes and values.

directed verdict A judge's order directing a jury to acquit a defendant because the state has not proved the elements of the crime or otherwise has not established guilt according to law.

direct examination The initial questioning of one's own (prosecution or defense) witness during a trial.

discretion The use of personal decision making and choice in carrying out operations in the criminal justice system.

displacement An effect that occurs when criminals move from an area targeted for increased police presence to another that is less well protected.

disposition For juvenile offenders, the equivalent of sentencing for adult offenders. The theory is that disposition is more rehabilitative than retributive. Possible dispositions: dismissing the case, releasing the youth to the custody of his or her parents, placing the offender on probation, or sending him or her to an institution or state correctional institution.

district attorney The county prosecutor who is charged with bringing offenders to justice and enforcing the criminal laws of the state.

diversion The use of an alternative to trial, such as referral to treatment or employment programs.

DNA profiling The identification of criminal suspects by matching DNA samples taken from their person with specimens found at the crime scene.

double marginality According to Nicholas Alex, the social burden that African American police officers carry by being both minority group members and law enforcement officers.

drug courts Courts whose focus is providing treatment for youths accused of drug-related acts.

due process perspective A perspective on criminal justice that emphasizes individual rights and constitutional safeguards against arbitrary or unfair judicial or administrative proceedings.

early onset The beginning of antisocial behavior during early adolescence, after which criminal behavior is more likely to persist throughout the life span.

electronic monitoring (EM) Requiring convicted offenders to wear a monitoring device as part of their community sentence. Typically part of a house arrest order, this enables the probation department to ensure that offenders are complying with court-ordered limitations on their freedom.

equal justice perspective A perspective on criminal justice based on the idea that all people should receive the same treatment under the law and should be evaluated on the basis of their current behavior, not on what they have done in the past.

equity The action or practice of awarding each person his or her just due. Sanctions based on equity seek to compensate individual victims and the general society for their losses due to crime.

etailing fraud Using the Internet to buy or sell merchandise illegally.

evidence-based justice Determining through the use of the scientific method whether criminal justice programs actually reduce crime rates and offender recidivism.

excited delirium An overdose of adrenaline that can occur in heated confrontations with the police.

exclusionary rule The principle that prohibits using illegally obtained evidence in a trial.

exculpatory evidence All information that is material and favorable to the accused defendant because it casts doubt on the defendant's guilt or on the evidence the government intends to use at trial.

excuse defense A defense in which a person states that his or her mental state was so impaired that he or she lacked the capacity to form sufficient intent to be held criminally responsible.

exigent circumstances Emergency or urgent circumstances.

***ex post facto* law** A law that makes an act criminal after it was committed or retroactively increases the penalty for a crime; such laws are forbidden by the U.S. Constitution.

expressive violence Violent behavior motivated by rage, anger, or frustration.

Federal Bureau of Investigation (FBI) The arm of the Justice Department that investigates violations of federal law, gathers crime statistics, runs a comprehensive crime laboratory, and helps train local law enforcement officers.

fine Levying a money payment on offenders to compensate society for their misdeeds.

First Amendment The amendment to the U.S. Constitution that guarantees freedom of speech, religion, press, and assembly, and the right of the people to petition the government for redress of grievances.

foot patrol Police patrol that takes officers out of cars and puts them on a walking beat to strengthen ties with the community.

forfeiture The seizure of personal property by the state as a civil or criminal penalty.

fruit of the poisonous tree Secondary evidence obtained from a search that violates the exclusionary rule.

furlough A correctional policy that allows inmates to leave the institution for vocational or educational training, for employment, or to maintain family ties.

fusion center A mechanism to exchange information and intelligence, maximize resources, streamline operations, and improve the ability to fight crime and terrorism by analyzing data from a variety of sources.

general deterrence A crime control policy that depends on the fear of criminal penalties. General deterrence measures, such as long prison sentences for violent crimes, are aimed at convincing the potential law violator that the pains associated with the crime outweigh the benefits.

globalization The process of creating a global economy through transnational markets and political and legal systems.

good faith exception The principle that evidence may be used in a criminal trial even though the search warrant used to obtain it was technically faulty, as long as the police acted in good faith when they sought the warrant from a judge.

grand jury A group of citizens chosen to hear charges against persons accused of crime and to determine whether there is sufficient evidence to bring those persons to trial.

grass eater A term used to describe a police officer who accepts payoffs when everyday duties place him or her in a position to be solicited by the public.

halfway house A community-based correctional facility that houses inmates before their outright release so that they can become gradually acclimated to conventional society.

hands-off doctrine The legal practice of allowing prison administrators a free hand in running the institution, even if correctional practices violate inmates' constitutional rights; this practice ended with the onset of the prisoners' rights movement in the 1960s.

hate crimes (bias crimes) Criminal acts directed toward a particular person or members of a group because they share a discernible racial, ethnic, religious, or gender characteristic.

hearsay evidence Testimony that is not firsthand but, rather, relates information told by a second party.

hot pursuit A legal doctrine that allows police to perform a warrantless search of premises where they suspect a crime has been committed when delay would endanger their lives or the lives of others and lead to the escape of the alleged perpetrator.

hot spots of crime The relatively few locations—bars, malls, the bus depot, hotels, and certain apartment buildings—from which a significant portion of police calls typically originate in metropolitan areas.

hue and cry In medieval England, a call for mutual aid against trouble or danger.

hulk Mothballed ship used to house prisoners in eighteenth-century England.

hundred In medieval England, a group of 100 families responsible for maintaining order and trying minor offenses.

identity theft Using the Internet to steal someone's identity and/or impersonate the victim in order to conduct illicit transactions, such as committing fraud using the victim's name and identity.

impact munitions Less-lethal weapons that are used to stun or otherwise incapacitate uncooperative suspects so they can be subdued. Examples include rubber bullets and beanbag projectiles.

incapacitation The policy of keeping dangerous criminals in confinement to eliminate the risk of their repeating their offense in society.

indeterminate sentence A term of incarceration with a stated minimum and maximum length, such as a sentence to prison for a period of from 3 to 10 years. The prisoner is eligible for parole after the minimum sentence has been served. Based on the belief that sentences should fit the criminal, indeterminate sentences allow individualized sentences and provide for sentencing flexibility. Judges can set a high minimum to override the purpose of the indeterminate sentence.

indictment A written accusation returned by a grand jury, charging an individual with a specified crime after determination of probable cause.

indigent defendant A defendant who lacks the funds to hire a private attorney and is therefore entitled to free counsel.

inevitable discovery rule The principle that evidence can be used in court even though the information that led to its discovery was obtained in violation of the *Miranda* rule if a judge finds it would have been discovered anyway by other means or sources.

information A formal charging document, similar to an indictment, based on probable cause as determined at a preliminary hearing.

initial appearance A juvenile's first appearance before the juvenile court judge in which the charges are reviewed and an effort is made to settle the case without a trial. If the child does not have legal counsel, an attorney is appointed.

inmate social code An unwritten code of behavior, passed from older inmates to younger ones, that serves as a guideline for appropriate inmate behavior within the correctional institution.

inmate subculture The loosely defined culture that pervades prisons and has its own norms, rules, and language.

in-presence requirement The principle that in order to make an arrest in a misdemeanor, the arresting officer must have personally witnessed the crime being committed.

instrumental violence Violent behavior that results from criminal activity designed to improve the financial status of the culprit, such as shooting someone during a bank robbery.

intake The process in which a probation officer settles cases at the initial appearance before the onset of formal criminal proceedings.

intelligence-led policing (ILP) The collection and analysis of information to generate an "intelligence end product" designed to inform police decision making at both the tactical and the strategic level.

Intensive Aftercare Program (IAP) A balanced, highly structured, comprehensive continuum of intervention for serious and violent juvenile offenders returning to the community.

intensive probation supervision (IPS) A type of intermediate sanction involving small probation caseloads and strict monitoring on a daily or weekly basis.

intensive supervision parole (ISP) A form of parole characterized by smaller caseloads and closer surveillance; it may include frequent drug testing and, in some cases, electronic monitoring.

interactionist view of crime The view that criminal law reflects the preferences and opinions of people who hold social power in the society and use their influence to impose their own values and moral code on the rest of the population.

intermediate sanctions The group of punishments falling between probation and prison ("probation plus"). Community-based sanctions, including house arrest and intensive supervision, serve as alternatives to incarceration.

internal affairs The police unit that investigates allegations of police misconduct.

jail A correctional facility designed to hold pretrial detainees and misdemeanants serving their criminal sentence.

jailhouse lawyer An inmate trained in law, or otherwise educated, who helps other inmates prepare legal briefs and appeals.

judge The senior officer in a court of law, who is authorized to hear and decide cases.

judicial reprieve The common-law practice that allowed judges to suspend punishment so that convicted offenders could seek a pardon, gather new evidence, or demonstrate that they had reformed their behavior.

jury nullification A jury's refusal to render a verdict according to the law and fact regardless of the evidence presented.

just desert The philosophy of justice asserting that those who violate the rights of others deserve to be punished. The severity of punishment should be commensurate with the seriousness of the crime.

justice of the peace Official appointed to act as the judicial officer in a county.

justification A defense for a criminal act claiming that the criminal act was reasonable or necessary under the circumstances.

juvenile court A court that has original jurisdiction over persons defined by statute as legal minors and alleged to be involved in juvenile delinquency or status offenses. In some jurisdictions, these are family courts that also deal with custody and neglect issues.

juvenile delinquency Participation in illegal behavior by a minor who falls under a statutory age limit.

juvenile intensive probation supervision (JIPS) A true alternative to incarceration that involves almost daily supervision of the juvenile by the probation officer assigned to the case.

Knapp Commission A public body that conducted an investigation into police corruption in New York City in the early 1970s and uncovered a widespread network of payoffs and bribes.

latent trait theories The view that human behavior is controlled by a master trait, present at birth or soon after, that influences and directs behavior.

Law Enforcement Assistance Administration (LEAA) Federal agency that provided technical assistance and hundreds of millions of dollars in aid to state and local justice agencies between 1969 and 1982.

liberal feminist theory An ideology holding that women suffer oppression, discrimination, and disadvantage as a result of their sex and calling for gender equality in pay, opportunity, child care, and education.

life course theories The view that criminality is a dynamic process influenced by people's perceptions and experiences throughout their lives, which may change their behavior for the better or the worse.

life-course persisters Delinquents who begin their offending career at a very early age and continue to offend well into adulthood.

lineup Placing a suspect in a group for the purpose of being viewed and identified by a witness.

low-visibility decision making Decision making by police officers that is not subject to administrative review—for example, a decision not to arrest someone or not to stop a speeding vehicle.

make-believe families In female prisons, substitute family groups with a faux father, mother, and siblings.

mala in se In common law, offenses that are by their own nature evil, immoral, and wrong; such offenses include murder, theft, and arson.

mandatory sentence A statutory requirement that a certain penalty shall be set and carried out in all cases upon conviction for a specified offense or series of offenses.

mass murderer Type of multiple killer who kills many victims in a single violent outburst.

maximum-security prison A correctional institution that houses dangerous felons and maintains strict security measures, high walls, and limited contact with the outside world.

meat eater A term used to describe a police officer who actively solicits bribes and vigorously engages in corrupt practices.

mediation An informal dispute resolution process in which a neutral third party (mediator) helps disputing parties reach an agreement.

medical model A view of corrections holding that convicted offenders are victims of their environment who need care and treatment to transform them into valuable members of society.

medium-security prison A less secure institution that houses nonviolent offenders and provides more opportunities for contact with the outside world.

mens rea A guilty mind: the intent to commit a criminal act.

Metropolitan Police Act Sir Robert Peel's legislation that established the first organized police force in London.

minimum-security prison The least secure correctional institution, which houses white-collar and nonviolent offenders, maintains few security measures, and has liberal furlough and visitation policies.

***Miranda* warning** The requirement that when a person is custodially interrogated, police inform the individual of the right to remain silent, the consequences of failing to remain silent, and the constitutional right to counsel.

Missouri Plan A method of judicial selection that combines a judicial nominating commission, executive appointment, and nonpartisan confirmation elections.

Mollen Commission An investigative unit set up to inquire into police corruption in New York City in the 1990s.

monetary restitution A sanction requiring that convicted offenders compensate crime victims by reimbursing them for out-of-pocket losses caused by the crime. Losses can include property damage, lost wages, and medical costs.

moral entrepreneurs People who wage campaigns to control behaviors they view as immoral or wrong.

National Crime Victimization Survey (NCVS) The ongoing victimization study conducted jointly by the Justice Department and the U.S. Census Bureau that surveys victims about their experiences with law violation.

National Criminal Intelligence Sharing Plan (NCISP) A formal intelligence-sharing initiative that identifies the security and intelligence-sharing needs recognized in the wake of the 9/11 terrorist attacks.

National Incident-Based Reporting System (NIBRS) A form of crime data collection created by the FBI requiring local police agencies to provide at least a brief account of each incident and arrest within 22 crime patterns, including the incident, victim, and offender information.

National Law Enforcement Officers Memorial The nation's monument to police officers who have died in the line of duty.

neurotransmitters Chemical substances that carry impulses from one nerve cell to another. Neurotransmitters are found in the space (synapse) that separates the transmitting neuron's terminal (axon) from the receiving neuron's terminal (dendrite).

no bill The action by a grand jury when it votes not to indict an accused suspect.

no-frills policy A correctional policy that stipulates that prisons are intended to punish, not coddle, inmates. This usually means a strict regimen of work and discipline and reduced opportunities for recreation and education.

nolle prosequi The decision by a prosecutor to drop a case after a complaint has been made because of, for example, insufficient evidence, witness reluctance to testify, police error, or office policy.

nolo contendere A plea of "no contest"—the defendant submits to sentencing without any formal admission of guilt that could be used against him or her in a subsequent civil suit.

nondeadly force Force that is unlikely to cause death or significant bodily harm.

nonintervention perspective A perspective on criminal justice that favors the least intrusive treatment possible: decarceration, diversion, and decriminalization.

obitiatry Helping people take their own lives: assisted suicide.

open field Any unoccupied or undeveloped real property outside the curtilage of a home.

oppositional defiant disorder (ODD) A psychological condition whose symptoms include rebellious and aggressive behavior toward authority figures that seriously interferes with proper life functioning.

order maintenance (peacekeeping) Maintaining order and authority without the need for formal arrest ("handling the situation")—keeping things under control by means of threats, persuasion, and understanding.

overload hypothesis The theory that police workload influences discretion so that as workload increases, less time and attention can be devoted to new cases, especially petty crimes.

parens patriae Latin term meaning "father of his country." According to this legal philosophy, the government is the true guardian of the needy and infirm, including dependent children. It refers to the power of the state to act on behalf of a child and provide care and protection equivalent to that of a parent.

parental efficacy Parents who are able to be supportive and who can therefore effectively control their children in a nonthreatening fashion.

parole The early release of a prisoner from imprisonment subject to conditions set by correctional authorities.

Part II crimes All other crimes reported to the FBI; these are less serious crimes and misdemeanors, excluding traffic violations.

particularity The requirement that a search warrant state precisely where the search is to take place and what items are to be seized.

penitentiary A state or federal correctional institution for incarceration of felony offenders for terms of one year or more.

Pennsylvania system A prison system, developed in Pennsylvania during the nineteenth century, based on total isolation and individual penitence.

peremptory challenge Dismissal of a prospective juror by either the prosecution or the defense for unexplained, discretionary reasons.

phishing Also known as carding and spoofing, phishing consists of illegally acquiring personal information, such as bank passwords and credit card numbers, by masquerading as a trustworthy person or business in what appears to be an official electronic communication, such as an e-mail or an instant message. The term comes from the lures used to "fish" for financial information and passwords.

plain view doctrine The principle that evidence in plain view of police officers may be seized without a search warrant.

plea negotiations/plea bargaining Discussions between defense counsel and prosecution in which the accused agrees to plead guilty in exchange for certain considerations, such as reduced charges or a lenient sentence.

police brutality Actions such as using abusive language, making threats, using force or coercion unnecessarily, prodding with nightsticks, and stopping and searching people to harass them.

police productivity The amount of order maintenance, crime control, and other law enforcement activities provided by individual police officers and concomitantly by police departments as a whole.

police styles The working personalities adopted by police officers that can range from being a social worker in blue to being a hard-charging crime fighter.

Ponzi scheme An investment fraud that involves the payment of purported returns to existing investors from funds contributed by new investors.

poor laws Sixteenth-century English laws under which vagrants and abandoned and neglected children were bound to masters as indentured servants.

preliminary hearing Hearing before a magistrate to determine whether the government has sufficient evidence to show probable cause that the defendant committed the crime.

preponderance of the evidence The level of proof in civil cases; more than half the evidence supports the allegations of one side.

presentence investigation An investigation performed by a probation officer attached to a trial court after the conviction of a defendant.

presentment The report of a grand jury investigation, which usually includes a recommendation of indictment.

pretrial detainees People who either are denied bail or cannot afford to post bail before trial and are kept in secure confinement.

pretrial procedures Legal and administrative actions that take place after arrest and before trial, including grand jury indictments, preliminary hearings, bail, and plea negotiation.

preventive detention The statutory authorization to deny bail to a particular individual who is considered dangerous or a flight risk.

prison A correctional facility designed to hold convicted felons while they serve their criminal sentence.

prisonization Assimilation into the separate culture of the prison. This loosely defined culture that pervades prisons has its own norms, rules, and language. The traditional prison culture is now being replaced by a violent gang culture.

private policing Crime prevention, detection, and the apprehension of criminals carried out by private organizations or individuals for commercial purposes.

proactive policing An aggressive law enforcement style in which patrol officers take the initiative against crime instead of waiting for criminal acts to occur. For example, they stop motor vehicles to issue citations and aggressively arrest and detain suspicious persons.

probable cause The evidentiary criterion necessary to sustain an arrest or the issuance of an arrest or search warrant: a set of facts, information, circumstances, or conditions that would lead a reasonable person to believe that an offense was committed and that the accused committed that offense.

probable cause hearing If a person is subjected to a warrantless arrest, a hearing is held to determine whether probable cause exists that he committed the crime.

probation A sentence entailing the conditional release of a convicted offender into the community under the supervision of the court (in the form of a probation officer), subject to certain conditions for a specified time.

probation rules Conditions or restrictions mandated by the court that must be obeyed by a probationer.

problem-oriented policing (POP) A style of police management that stresses proactive problem solving instead of reactive crime fighting.

pro bono The practice by private attorneys of taking the cases of indigent offenders without fee as a service to the profession and the community.

procedural criminal laws The methods that must be followed in obtaining warrants, investigating offenses, effecting lawful arrests, conducting trials, introducing evidence, sentencing convicted offenders, and reviewing cases by appellate courts.

procedural justice A concern with making decisions that are arrived at through procedures viewed as fair.

proof beyond a reasonable doubt The standard of proof needed to convict in a criminal case. The evidence offered in court does not have to amount to absolute certainty, but it should leave no reasonable doubt that the defendant committed the alleged crime

prosecutor An appointed or elected member of the practicing bar who is responsible for bringing the state's case against the accused.

prosecutorial discretion The prosecutor's authority to decide whether to bring a case to trial or to dismiss it outright.

public account system A prison industry system, popular after the Civil War, in which employment was directed by the state and the products of the prisoners' labor were sold for the benefit of the state.

public defender An attorney employed by the government to represent criminal defendants who cannot afford to pay for a lawyer.

public law The branch of law that deals with the state or government agencies and controls their administrative relationships with individuals, corporations, or other branches of government.

public order crimes Behaviors that are illegal because they run counter to existing moral standards. Obscenity and prostitution are considered public order crimes.

public safety doctrine The principle that a suspect can be questioned in the field without a *Miranda* warning if the information the police seek is needed to protect public safety.

public safety or strict liability crime A criminal violation—usually one that endangers the public welfare—that is defined by the act itself, irrespective of intent.

qualified immunity A legal doctrine that shields government officials from liability if their conduct did not violate clearly established civil rights that a reasonable person would have known about.

racial animus model The view that white America has developed a mental image of the typical offender as a young, inner-city black male who offends with little remorse.

racial threat hypothesis The view that young minority males are subject to greater police control—for example, formal arrest—when their numbers increase within the population.

Racketeer Influenced and Corrupt Organization Act (RICO) Federal legislation that enables prosecutors to bring additional criminal or civil charges against people engaged in two or more acts prohibited by 24 existing federal and 8 state laws. RICO features monetary penalties that allow the government to confiscate all profits derived from criminal activities. Originally intended to be used against organized criminals, RICO has also been used against white-collar criminals.

recognizance The medieval practice of allowing convicted offenders to go unpunished if they agreed to refrain from any further criminal behavior.

recoupment Process by which the state later recovers some or all of the cost of providing free legal counsel to an indigent defendant.

rehabilitation perspective A perspective on criminal justice that sees crime as an expression of frustration and anger created by social inequality that can be controlled by giving people the means to improve their lifestyles through conventional endeavors.

release on recognizance (ROR) A pretrial release in which a defendant with ties to the community is not required to post bail but promises to appear at all subsequent proceedings.

residential community corrections (RCC) A nonsecure facility, located in the community, that houses probationers who need a more secure environment. Typically, residents are free during the day to go to work, school, or treatment, and return in the evening for counseling sessions and meals.

restitution A condition of probation in which the offender repays society or the victim of crime for the trouble the offender caused.

restorative justice A view of criminal justice that focuses on crime as an act against the community rather than the state. Justice should involve all parties affected by crime—victims, criminals, law enforcement, and the community.

revocation An administrative act performed by a parole authority that removes a person from parole, or a judicial order by a court removing a person from parole or probation, in response to a violation on the part of the parolee or probationer.

risk classification An assessment of the risk level probationers pose to the community and themselves.

routine activities theory The view that crime is a product of three everyday factors: motivated offenders, suitable targets, and a lack of capable guardians.

rule of four The convention that four justices must agree to hear a case before a writ of certiorari is granted.

search A government actor's infringement on a person's reasonable expectation of privacy.

search incident to a lawful arrest An exception to the search warrant rule, limited to the immediate surrounding area.

search warrant An order, issued by a judge, directing officers to conduct a search of specified premises for specified objects.

securitization The process in which vendors take individual subprime loans, bundle them into large pools, and sell them as securities.

self-report survey A research approach that questions large groups of subjects, such as high school students, about their own participation in delinquent or criminal acts.

sentencing circles A type of sentencing in which victims, family members, community members, and the offender participate in an effort to devise fair and reasonable sanctions that are ultimately aimed at reintegrating the offender into the community.

sentencing guidelines A set of standards that defines parameters for trial judges to follow in their sentencing decisions.

serial killer Type of multiple killer who kills over a long period of time but typically assumes a "normal" identity between murders.

sheriff The chief law enforcement officer in a county.

shire reeve In early England, the chief law enforcement official in a county, forerunner of today's sheriff.

shock incarceration A short-term correctional program based on a boot camp approach that makes use of a military-like regime of high-intensity physical training.

shock probation A sentence in which offenders serve a short prison term before they begin probation, to impress them with the pains of imprisonment.

social capital Positive relations with individuals and institutions that foster self-worth and inhibit crime.

social control A society's ability to control individual behavior in order to serve the best interests and welfare of the society as a whole.

social control theory The view that most people do not violate the law because of their social bonds to family, peer group, school, and other institutions. If these bonds are weakened or absent, individuals are much more likely to commit crime.

social learning theory The view that human behavior is learned through observation of human social interactions, either directly from those in close proximity or indirectly from the media.

social reaction (labeling) theory The view that society produces criminals by stigmatizing certain individuals as deviants, a label that they come to accept as a personal identity.

social structure   The stratifications, classes, institutions, and groups that characterize a society.

specialized court   A court that has primary jurisdiction over specific types of offenses and that operates differently than a traditional criminal court, such as with a concern over outcomes and extensive judicial monitoring.

specific deterrence   A crime control policy suggesting that punishment should be severe enough to convince convicted offenders never to repeat their criminal activity.

split sentence   A practice that requires convicted criminals to spend a portion of their sentence behind bars and the remainder in the community.

spree killer   Type of multiple killer who spreads the murderous outburst over a few days or weeks.

stalking   The willful, malicious, and repeated following, harassing, or contacting of another person. Such behavior becomes a criminal act when it causes the victim to feel fear for his or her safety or the safety of others.

stare decisis   To stand by decided cases: the legal principle by which the decision or holding in an earlier case becomes the standard by which subsequent similar cases are judged.

state dependence   A process in which criminal behavior becomes embedded because antisocial behavior erodes social ties that encourage conformity and creates incentives to commit crime.

state-organized crime   Criminal acts committed by state officials in pursuit of their jobs as government representatives.

status offender   A noncriminal youth who falls under the jurisdiction of the juvenile court by reason of having engaged in behavior prohibited to minors, such as being truant from school, running away from home, or being habitually disobedient and ungovernable.

sting operation   Organized groups of detectives who deceive criminals into openly committing illegal acts or conspiring to engage in criminal activity.

stop and frisk   The situation in which police officers who are suspicious of an individual run their hands lightly over the suspect's outer garments to determine whether the person is carrying a concealed weapon; also called a threshold inquiry or pat-down.

strain   The emotional turmoil and conflict caused when people believe that they cannot achieve their desires and goals through legitimate means.

strategic intelligence   Information about the changing nature of certain problems and threats for the purpose of developing response strategies and reallocating resources.

subpoena   A court order requiring a witness to appear in court at a specified time and place.

substantive criminal law   A body of specific rules that declare what conduct is criminal and prescribe the punishment to be imposed for such conduct.

substantive rights   Civil rights that include the right of inmates to receive mail and medical benefits and to practice their religion.

super-maximum-security prison   A form of a maximum-security prison, which uses high-level security measures to incapacitate the nation's most dangerous criminals. Most inmates are in lockdown 23 hours per day.

suspended sentence   A prison term that is delayed while the defendant undergoes a period of community treatment. If the treatment is successful, the prison sentence is terminated.

tactical intelligence   Gaining or developing information related to threats of terrorism or crime and using this information to apprehend offenders, harden targets, and use strategies that will eliminate or mitigate the threat.

Taser   A nonlethal conducted energy device that administers a shock to an uncooperative suspect by way of an electrified dart.

terrorism   Premeditated, politically motivated violence perpetrated by subnational groups or clandestine agents against noncombatant targets, usually intended to influence an audience.

thermal imager   A device that detects radiation in the infrared range of the electromagnetic spectrum, used in law enforcement to detect variations in temperature (warm images stand out against cool backgrounds).

three-strikes laws   Sentencing codes that require that an offender receive a life sentence after conviction for a third felony. Some states allow parole after a lengthy prison stay—for example, 25 years.

tier system   A type of prison in which cells are located along corridors in multiple layers or levels.

time-in-rank system   The promotion system in which a police officer can advance in rank only after spending a prescribed amount of time in the preceding rank.

torts   The law of personal injuries.

total institution   A regimented, dehumanizing institution, such as a prison, in which like-situated people are kept in social isolation, cut off from the world at large.

transfer hearing   The hearing in which a judge decides whether to waive a juvenile to the criminal court. Waiver decisions are based on such criteria as the child's age, his or her prior offense history, and the nature of the offense.

transnational organized crime   Use of illegal tactics to gain profit in the global marketplace, typically involving the cross-border sale and distribution of illegal commodities.

treatment   The rehabilitative method used to effect a change of behavior in the juvenile offender; treatment may take the form of therapy or educational or vocational programs.

true bill of indictment   A written statement charging a defendant with the commission of a crime, drawn up by a prosecuting attorney and considered by a grand jury. If the grand jury finds sufficient evidence to support the indictment, it will issue a true bill of indictment.

truth-in-sentencing laws   Laws requiring convicted felons to spend a significant portion of their sentence behind bars.

tything (tithing)   In medieval England, a collective group of 10 families that pledged to help one another and provide mutual aid.

U.S. attorneys   The nation's principal (federal) litigators, appointed by the president. Assistant United States attorneys are tasked with, among other duties, prosecuting criminal defendants in federal court.

U.S. court of appeals   An appellate court in the federal court system.

U.S. district court A trial court in the federal court system.

U.S. Supreme Court The highest appellate court in the United States.

venire The group called for jury duty from which jury panels are selected.

verdict The finding of a jury or a judge on questions of fact at a trial.

vice squads Police units assigned to enforce morality-based laws, such as those addressing prostitution, gambling, and pornography.

victim impact statement A postconviction statement by the victim of crime or the victim's family that may be used to guide sentencing decisions.

victim precipitation The role of the victim in provoking or encouraging criminal behavior.

vigilantes In the Old West, members of a vigilance committee or posse called upon to capture cattle thieves or other felons.

voir dire The process in which a potential jury panel is questioned by the prosecution and the defense in order to select jurors who are unbiased and objective.

waiver (juvenile) A practice in which the juvenile court waives its jurisdiction over a juvenile and transfers the case to adult criminal court for trial. In some states, a waiver hearing is held to determine jurisdiction; in others, juveniles may be automatically waived if they are accused of committing a serious crime such as murder.

Walnut Street Jail The birthplace of the modern prison system and of the Pennsylvania system of solitary confinement

warez Copyrighted software illegally downloaded and sold by organized groups without license to do so.

watch system In medieval England, groups of men who organized in church parishes to guard at night against disturbances and breaches of the peace under the direction of the local constable.

white-collar crime White-collar crimes involve the violation of rules that control business enterprise. They include employee pilferage, bribery, commodities law violations, mail fraud, computer fraud, environmental law violations, embezzlement, Internet scams, extortion, forgery, insurance fraud, price fixing, and environmental pollution.

Wickersham Commission Formally known as the National Commission on Law Observance and Enforcement, a commission created in 1929 by President Herbert Hoover to study the U.S. criminal justice system, including the police.

work release A prison treatment program that allows inmates to be released during the day to work in the community, returning to prison at night.

writ of certiorari An order of a superior court requesting that a record of an inferior court (or administrative body) be brought forward for review or inspection.

writ of *habeas corpus* A judicial order requesting that a person who detains another person produce the body of the prisoner and give reasons for his or her capture and detention. *Habeas corpus* is a legal device used to request that a judicial body review the reasons for a person's confinement and the conditions of confinement. *Habeas corpus* is known as "the great writ."

NAME INDEX

In this index *p* indicates photograph.

SUBJECT INDEX

In this index *f* indicates figures, *p* indicates photograph, *t* indicates table.

CASE INDEX

In this index *f* indicates figures, *p* indicates photograph, *t* indicates table.